"The Theology of Work project is providing desperately needed resources to pastors and the entire church on what the Bible has to say about our work. I hope that every pastor will preach regularly on how the gospel changes the way we work and sometimes the work that we do. And I hope that every Christian will see the ways their work connects to God's work!"

Tim Keller, Senior Pastor
Redeemer Presbyterian Church, New York City
author of *Every Good Endeavor:*
Connecting Your Work to God's Work

"From the very beginning, God designed us to work. We each have gifts and callings intended to reflect his glory and to bring us fulfillment, even as we serve others. While there are various resources addressing this subject, this unique commentary offers a comprehensive survey of an important biblical theme. With its added online availability, it is an invaluable resource for pastors and business professionals alike."

Ravi Zacharias, author and speaker

"Did you ever wonder what your work has to do with your faith? The short answer is everything, and now you can read all about it in this *Theology of Work Bible Commentary*, now in print for the first time. Heartily recommended."

Eric Metaxas, *New York Times* **best-selling author of**
Bonhoeffer: Pastor, Martyr, Prophet, Spy

"When it comes to biblical preaching and teaching, the church today has an elephant-in-the-room problem. We spend the least amount of time addressing the very thing that people spend their waking hours doing the most: work and career. The result is that people assume, perhaps unconsciously, that the Bible doesn't address their actual lived experience. But it does, and between these pages you will find the resources to help you connect the dots between faith and work."

Gregory Alan Thornbury, PhD
President, The King's College, New York City

"The Bible encourages us to 'follow hard' after the Lord (Psalm 63:8). Now, a new resource helps us daily on that quest, especially in our work. Crafted by experts who love God's Word, the Theology of Work team's robust scholarship, timely insights, and wisdom are a gift for the ages."

John D. Beckett, Chairman
The Beckett Companies, North Ridgeville, Ohio
author of *Loving Monday* **and** *Mastering Monday*

"Recapturing the power of vocation in daily work is completely dependent on understanding how Scripture speaks into our labors. The *Theology of Work Bible Commentary* is an invaluable resource for pastors who want to connect themselves and their churches to the Lord's creative callings on our everyday lives."

Daniel M. Harrell, PhD, Senior Minister
Colonial Church, Edina, Minnesota

"The *Theology of Work Bible Commentary* states its thesis quite succinctly in its introduction to the Gospel of Matthew, 'The workplace consequences of living in God's kingdom are profound.' As a layman, I am always on the lookout for Bible research tools that illumine God's word in a way that offers practical guidance for my life and work. This commentary fits the bill. Look no further than the excellent treatment of Matthew 6:19–34 to see an example of guidance on the ways in which our treasure profoundly transforms us. I highly recommend this resource to my fellow laypersons."

Scott Griffin, Founder and Chief Architect
Pro Bono Publico, Seattle, Washington

"The Bible is full of business lessons and leadership principles that are often missed. The *Theology of Work Bible Commentary* provides valuable insights and a provocative, yet practical guide to incorporating those lessons into our everyday lives, as well as simple tips and tools to follow. The *Theology of Work Bible Commentary* is simply incredible!"

Gloria S. Nelund, Chair and CEO, TriLinc Global
Former CEO, Deutsche Bank North America
Private Wealth Management, Manhattan Beach, California

"The *Theology of Work Bible Commentary* is an excellent and vital addition to a growing interest surrounding the integration of calling, vocation, and mission. Whether you are a business owner, barista, mechanic, policymaker, or aid worker, The *Theology of Work Bible Commentary* is a tool you will want to have as you navigate your role as a leader—regardless of your position—in the work God has given you."

Travis Vaughn, Director of Cultural Renewal
Perimeter Church, Johns Creek, Georgia

"This commentary provides a unique resource for the person who wants to better understand God's purpose for work and how our work, whatever it may be, can be a ministry for the kingdom of God as we learn to integrate the claims of our faith with the demands of our work."

C. William Pollard, Chairman Emeritus
The ServiceMaster Company, Wheaton, Illinois

"The *Theology of Work Bible Commentary* is a long-awaited and welcome resource for pastors and serious Christians seeking to make Jesus the Lord of their work lives. It is the product of a diverse team including 'in the trenches' business leaders alongside first rate biblical scholars. As valuable as the insights and comments of the authors themselves is the constant, implicit challenge to readers to listen carefully for themselves to what God might be saying about work on every page of Scripture."

David W. Gill, PhD, Mockler-Phillips Professor of
Workplace Theology & Business Ethics
Director, Mockler Center for Faith & Ethics in the Workplace
Gordon-Conwell Theological Seminary
South Hamilton, Massachusetts

"As a longtime advocate for a theology of work, I have urged people to see the Bible as a guidebook for our working lives. Reading these marvelous commentaries, however, has given me inspiring new insights into how rich a guidebook God's Word really is!"

Richard J. Mouw
President Emeritus and Professor of Faith and Public Life
Fuller Theological Seminary, Pasadena, California

"I struggled for the first decade of my business career, mostly alone and in the middle of the night, to find meaning in my work and gradually came to see that I was looking at work all wrong. I was trying to derive meaning *from* my work, instead of bringing meaning *to* my work. The *Theology of Work Bible Commentary* skillfully articulates God's perspective—the source of our work's ultimate meaning. This book is the helpful guide I never had, and I hope that as you read it your work life will come alive!"

Barry Rowan
Executive Vice President and Chief Financial Officer
Cool Planet Energy Systems, Greenwood Village, Colorado

"This commentary is a revolutionary document! It does what no other commentary has done, which is to turn us around and to see what the Bible actually says about work. Human enterprise is the main thing we do with our waking hours. It is about time we saw that the Word of God gives meaning, purpose, perspective, and practical guidelines for daily work. It is hard not to be enthusiastic about something that is just plain wonderful and transformative. This commentary can turn the church inside out as the people of God serve God full time from Monday to Friday."

R. Paul Stevens
Professor Emeritus, Marketplace Theology
Regent College, Vancouver, BC

"My calling is to form Christian leaders for their callings, so I am always looking for resources that help followers of Jesus truly hear God's voice the real world. The *Theology of Work Bible Commentary* is the right tool for the job. Bringing together serious biblical scholarship with keen pastoral perspective and the insights of a wise mentor, this commentary helps us read the scriptures with a Monday-through-Friday lens. Work, calling, career, relationships, family, friendships, and all that shapes our ability to hear and heed the voice of God in a world where we struggle to slow down even for Sundays. I'll be recommending this commentary to seminarians, pastors and 'fellow-workers' all."

Tod Bolsinger, PhD
Vice President for Vocation and Formation
Assistant Professor of Practical Theology
Fuller Theological Seminary, Pasadena, California

"An elucidating exploration of an issue that is relevant to all believers, this is a wonderful resource for anyone who wants Scripture to inform their life at work. This tremendous commentary has my wholehearted recommendation."

D. Michael Lindsay, President
Gordon College, Wenham, Massachusetts

"In this unique commentary, the Gospels and Acts are discussed through the lens of work—how why we work informs how we work, the example of Jesus Christ as a worker, and God's principles applied to the workplace. A great guide for clergy and laity alike; either a surface or detailed examination point out the Bible's relevance for everyday life, including work. This commentary is a gift to the Church."

Bob Doll, Chief Equity Strategist
Nuveen Asset Management, New York City

"An easily readable book that will give you much to think about, on every conceivable topic related to the world of work. Even if you end up disagreeing with some of the positions taken or views shared, overall this book will enlighten you on your way to work, and in your day at work."

Prabhu Guptara, Distinguished Professor of
Global Business, Management and Public Policy
William Carey University, India
Member of the Board, Institute of Management
University of St. Gallen, Switzerland
Chairman, Relational Thinking Network

"The *Theology of Work Bible Commentary* is an exceptional resource for not only Christians in the marketplace, but for everyone who works, period. The design and layout are brilliant! It's easy to access material by subject and topic. I'm impressed by the contributors and know others will feel inspired and encouraged by their collective wisdom, too."

Nancy Matheson Burns, Chief Executive Officer
Dole & Bailey Inc., Woburn, Massachusetts

"Some suggest that modern industrial society made work a pervasive concern of modern humankind. But in the creation accounts God is presented as a worker who labors six days and takes a 'breather' on the seventh day, and is represented as a potter in his making of man and as a temple builder in his making of woman. Moreover, humankind's first obligation in the Bible after being fruitful is to 'work' the Garden of Eden. Indeed, the subject of work pervades the Bible. There are many popular books on the doctrine of work and a few on the theology of work. But this *Theology of Work Bible Commentary* is the first to investigate the biblical text book by book in order to glean insights into work from God's perspective. Unfortunately, work pervades much of the Christian's life apart from God and rules it. But this book helps Christian workers to relate their labor to God and thereby make their work holy and meaningful."

Bruce Waltke, Professor Emeritus of Biblical Studies
Regent College, Vancouver, Canada

"This series is a magnificent contribution to one of the most neglected themes in Christian ethics. Avoiding the easy anachronism of finding a few proof-texts that might apply to modern work, the authors let the distinctive voices and broader themes of Scripture illuminate our working life. The conversation about faith and work is deeper and richer thanks to the Theology of Work Project."

Andy Crouch, Executive Editor, *Christianity Today*
author of *Culture Making* and *Playing God*

"This commentary was written exactly for those of us who aim to integrate our faith and work on a daily basis, and is an excellent reminder that God hasn't called the world to go to church, but has called the Church to go to the world (and there is no place we do that more than at our place of work!). Having served for more than thirty-five years in global leadership roles in both the for-profit and, now, the nonprofit sectors, I only wish I had had access to the insights shared in the *Theology of Work Bible Commentary* many years ago."

Bonnie Wurzbacher, Chief Resource Development Officer
World Vision International, London
Sr. Vice President, Global Customer Leadership
The Coca-Cola Company (retired)

GENESIS THROUGH REVELATION

THEOLOGY OF WORK BIBLE COMMENTARY

GENESIS THROUGH REVELATION

THEOLOGY OF WORK PROJECT

HENDRICKSON
PUBLISHERS

Table of Contents

Job and Work

Psalms and Work

Proverbs and Work

Abbreviations

Old Testament

Gen.	Genesis	Eccl.	Ecclesiastes
Exod.	Exodus	Song	Song of Songs
Lev.	Leviticus	Isa.	Isaiah
Num.	Numbers	Jer.	Jeremiah
Deut.	Deuteronomy	Lam.	Lamentations
Josh.	Joshua	Ezek.	Ezekiel
Judg.	Judges	Dan.	Daniel
Ruth	Ruth	Hos.	Hosea
1 Sam.	1 Samuel	Joel	Joel
2 Sam.	2 Samuel	Amos	Amos
1 Kgs.	1 Kings	Obad.	Obadiah
2 Kgs.	2 Kings	Jonah	Jonah
1 Chr.	1 Chronicles	Mic.	Micah
2 Chr.	2 Chronicles	Nah.	Nahum
Ezra	Ezra	Hab.	Habakkuk
Neh.	Nehemiah	Zeph.	Zephaniah
Est.	Esther	Hag.	Haggai
Job	Job	Zech.	Zechariah
Ps(s).	Psalm(s)	Mal.	Malachi
Prov.	Proverbs		

New Testament

Matt.	Matthew	Acts	Acts
Mark	Mark	Rom.	Romans
Luke	Luke	1 Cor.	1 Corinthians
John	John	2 Cor.	2 Corinthians

Gal.	Galatians	Heb.	Hebrews
Eph.	Ephesians	James	James
Phil.	Philippians	1 Pet.	1 Peter
Col.	Colossians	2 Pet.	2 Peter
1 Thess.	1 Thessalonians	1 John	1 John
2 Thess.	2 Thessalonians	2 John	2 John
1 Tim.	1 Timothy	3 John	3 John
2 Tim.	2 Timothy	Jude	Jude
Titus	Titus	Rev.	Revelation
Philem.	Philemon		

Any commentary references not in this particular volume can be found at the Theology of Work website (www.theologyofwork.org), along with video interviews and sidebars on people in the work world.

Foreword

The *Theology of Work Bible Commentary* is unique in that it explores what the entire Bible says about work. It represents more than five years of research by 140 contributors from sixteen countries, guided by an international steering committee of twenty scholars, pastors, and Christians from a variety of workplaces. We are thankful to God for this opportunity to present it to you in this volume.

Why does anyone need a theology of work? When we talk about a "theology," it can sound as stuffy as a tomb. Theology is often considered the domain of scholars who are wrestling with questions that no one ever asks, or solving problems that have never really arisen. When we talk about theology, however, we are really talking about what we know or do not know about God. Everyone does theology. Atheists who say they don't believe in God are already dealing with theology. Wars are fought over theology by people who are convinced that they are doing God's will. Agree with them or not, everyone everywhere does theology. People in the workplace who may never attend church are dealing with theology in some way every day. Ultimately, the questions we ask about God are not merely religious, they are life altering. In fact, what you believe about God may be the most important thing you ever think about. That's theology!

When it comes to work, theology is seldom practiced out loud. During my early years as president at Denver Seminary, I hosted a morning Bible study for business people. After class, over breakfast, we discussed the myriad dilemmas these workers and leaders faced in the workplace. Again and again, I heard, "You're the first pastoral person to actively address how my faith relates to my work." It was then that I realized there was a great divide between the leadership of the church and the everyday lives of the people they are called to equip.

At its heart, the perceived distance between God and everyday work is a theological issue. Most Christians believe that God cares about how we relate to others, how we relate to him, and whether we cheat, steal, lie, or break the Ten Commandments. However, it would surprise a lot of us to learn that our work matters to God. God cares what we do for a living, how we do it, and how we use our resources. As it turns out, the Bible has much to say about work. In fact, work is a major topic in the Bible, beginning with the surprising statement in Genesis 2:15 that God created people to work—not as a punishment, but as a pleasure and a way of relating to God himself.

The Scriptures provide principles that both give *meaning* to work and tell us *how* to work. Unfortunately, there is not a book in the Bible called First and Second Executive or Letter to the Christian Plumbers. Instead, what the Bible teaches about God's view of work is embedded in the Scriptures. Only a few of the biblical writers speak directly about the work that people do. They simply assume it. For instance, one of the Ten Commandments declares, "Remember the sabbath day and keep it holy" (Exod. 20:8), as if the only day God cared about was the Sabbath. But the command also says, "Six days you shall labor and do all your work" (Exod. 20:9). So the command deals not only with a special day when we can rest, but with the other days of the week designed for work.

The *Theology of Work Bible Commentary* goes through the Bible book by book to bring to the surface what we might not have seen about work at first blush. For example, consider the last book of the Bible, Revelation. It is possible to be so caught up in the visions in Revelation and questions about when they will occur, that we do not see that the Scripture also tells us about work now and in the future. You might be surprised that the Song of Solomon, a love poem, has quite a bit to say about workers and work. This book attempts through a study of the Scriptures to answer the question, "Does the work we do matter to God?"

This commentary deals with the theology of *work*. In that sense, it is limited. And in another sense, it is very broad. It is limited to work, but work is as diverse as are the people in the world. One question that may come to mind is, "What is work?" The answer to that question seems obvious. Work is what we do to make a living. Saying that, however, implies that people work for forty or fifty hours a week in order to live for the other hours of the week. There is more to work than that. A farmer, for example, doesn't "work to make a living." Plowing a field, planting a crop, bringing in a harvest is really his life. Or when we say that people "work to make a living," we imply that they work to receive a salary or a wage. But what about volunteers who travel to another country at their own expense to help people who have suffered in an earthquake or a flood? What about the person who raises children, cooks meals, and takes care of the family home? Certainly these people work, and work hard, but do not receive a salary. What, then, do we mean when we talk about their "work"?

Others might insist that the opposite of work is play. These are the folks who say, "TGIF: Thank God, it's Friday and the weekend is coming!" The recreation we enjoy on the weekend stands in contrast to the labor we put in during the week. But what about the professional basketball or tennis player? Do they work? How does their "work" differ from recreation?

If you own a business, what responsibility do you have to the people who work for you and to the people who buy your products or services? If you're an employee, does God care about the products you make or the way your company advertises them? Is what you talk about when you're having coffee with co-workers important to God? Does God have anything to do with the work that consumes a major part of your life?

If you're a pastor reading this material on a theology of work, do you find yourself thinking about a woman in the eighth row, three seats from the end, who works in financial services, or the man behind her who is a nurse? Or a couple on the other side of the sanctuary who has recently invested everything they have to open a restaurant? Do you think about yourself as a pastor? Do you work? Perhaps you are tempted to respond, "Of course I do, but it's really not the same thing. I have a special calling from God." That leads to another question: What do you mean by a "call"? Is it reserved for missionaries, teachers at a Bible college or a seminary, or translators of the Bible? How about the executive, the vice president of an insurance company, or the bus driver who attends your church? Do they have a call from God? Does God call men and women in business, government, or nonprofit organizations to their positions? Can you imagine God "calling" a pastor to go back into the world of work? Is that whole way of thinking true to the Bible?

So you see, there is a flood of questions about the simple concept of work. In fact, we are barraged by questions about work that have to be answered. This commentary will not answer these sticky issues by providing a set of rules, but it will give you direction in coming to your own conclusions. After all, the Scriptures resemble a compass rather than a road map. But when you're on the journey, a compass can be very helpful. The *Theology of Work Bible Commentary* helps us plumb the depths of God's word, so that we can hear and respond to Jesus' voice in the calling of our everyday work.

Haddon W. Robinson
President
Theology of Work Project

Harold John Ockenga Distinguished Professor of Preaching
Gordon-Conwell Theological Seminary
Hamilton, Massachusetts, USA

Introduction to the Theology of Work

Work is not only a human calling, but also a divine one. "In the beginninig God created the heavens and the earth." God worked to create us and created us to work. "The LORD God took the man and put him in the garden of Eden to till it and keep it" (Gen. 2:15). God also created work to be good, even if it's hard to see in a fallen world. To this day, God calls us to work to support ourselves and to serve others (Eph. 4:28).

Work can accomplish many of God's purposes for our lives—the basic necessities of food and shelter, as well as a sense of fulfillment and joy. Our work can create ways to help people thrive; it can discover the depths of God's creation; and it can bring us into wonderful relationships with co-workers and those who benefit from our work (customers, clients, patients, and so forth).

Yet many people face drudgery, boredom, or exploitation at work. We have bad bosses, hostile relationships, and unfriendly work environments. Our work seems useless, unappreciated, faulty, frustrating. We don't get paid enough. We get stuck in dead-end jobs or laid off or fired. We fail. Our skills become obsolete. It's a struggle just to make ends meet. But how can this be if God created work to be good—and what can we do about it? God's answers for these questions must be somewhere in the Bible, but where?

The Theology of Work Project's mission has been to study what the Bible says about work and to develop resources to apply the Christian faith to our work. It turns out that every book of the Bible gives practical, relevant guidance that can help us do our jobs better, improve our relationships at work, support ourselves, serve others more effectively, and find meaning and value in our work. The Bible shows us how to live all of life—including work—in Christ. Only in Jesus can we and our work be transformed to become the blessing it was always meant to be.

To put it another way, if we are not following Christ during the 100,000 hours of our lives that we spend at work, are we really following Christ? Our lives are more than just one day a week at church. The fact is that God cares about our life *every day of the week*. But how do we become equipped to follow Jesus at work? In the same ways we become equipped for every aspect of life in Christ—listening to sermons, modeling our lives on others' examples, praying for God's guidance, and most of all by studying the Bible and putting it into practice.

This Theology of Work series contains a variety of books to help you apply the Scriptures and Christian faith to your work. This book is one volume in the multivolume *Theology of Work Bible Commentary*, examining what the Gospels and the book of Acts say about work. These commentaries are intended to assist those with theological training or interest to conduct in-depth research into passages or books of Scripture.

Pastors will find these volumes helpful as they consider the Bible's perspective on work when teaching on particular passages or topics. Professors may use the commentary to help prepare classes or as a textbook for students. Laypeople may find practical help for workplace decisions (the topical index could be helpful in this regard), or they may read it as part of their personal or group Bible study. Other books in the Theology of Work series include Bible studies adapted from the *Theology of Work Commentary* and additional materials to help apply the Christian faith to daily work.

Christians today recognize God's calling to us in and through our work—for ourselves and for those whom we serve. May God use this book to help you follow Christ in every sphere of life and work.

Will Messenger, Executive Editor
Theology of Work Project

Genesis 1–11 and Work

Introduction to Genesis 1–11

The book of Genesis is the foundation for the theology of work. Any discussion of work in biblical perspective eventually finds itself grounded on passages in this book. Genesis is incomparably significant for the theology of work because it tells the story of God's work of creation, the first work of all and the prototype for all work that follows. God is not dreaming an illusion but creating a reality. The created universe that God brings into existence then provides the material of human work—space, time, matter, and energy. Within the created universe, God is present in relationship with his creatures and especially with people. Laboring in God's image, we work *in* creation, *on* creation, *with* creation and—if we work as God's intends—*for* creation.

In Genesis we see God at work, and we learn how God intends us to work. We both obey and disobey God in our work, and we discover that God is at work in both our obedience and disobedience. The other sixty-five books of the Bible each have their own unique contributions to add to the theology of work. Yet they all spring from the source found here, in Genesis, the first book of the Bible.

God Creates the World (Genesis 1:1–2:3)

The first thing the Bible tells us is that God is a creator. "In the beginning God created the heavens and the earth" (Gen. 1:1, NRSV alternate reading). God speaks and things come into being that were not there before, beginning with the universe itself. Creation is solely an act of God. It is not an accident, a mistake, or the product of an inferior deity, but the self-expression of God.

God Works to Create the World (Genesis 1:1–25)

God Brings the Material World into Being (Genesis 1:2)

Genesis continues by emphasizing the materiality of the world. "The earth was a formless void and darkness covered the face of the deep, while a wind from God swept over the face of the waters" (Gen. 1:2). The nascent creation, though still "formless," has the material dimensions of space ("the deep") and matter ("waters"), and God is fully engaged with this materiality ("a wind from God swept over the face of the waters"). Later, in chapter 2, we even see God working the dirt of his creation. "The LORD God formed man from the dust of the ground" (Gen. 2:7). Throughout chapters 1 and 2, we see God engrossed in the physicality of his creation.

Any theology of work must begin with a theology of creation. Do we regard the material world, the stuff we work with, as God's first-rate stuff, imbued with lasting value? Or do we dismiss it as a temporary job site, a testing ground, a sinking ship from which we must escape to get to God's true location in an immaterial "heaven." Genesis argues against any notion that the material world is any less important to God than the spiritual world. Or putting it more precisely, in Genesis there is no sharp distinction between the material and the spiritual. The *ruah* of God in Genesis 1:2 is simultaneously "breath," "wind," and "spirit" (see footnote b in the NRSV or compare NRSV, NASB, NIV, and KJV).

"The heavens and the earth" (Gen. 1:1; 2:1) are not two separate realms, but a Hebrew figure of speech meaning "the universe"[1] in the same way that the English phrase "kith and kin" means "relatives."

Most significantly, the Bible ends where it begins—on earth. Humanity does not depart the earth to join God in heaven. Instead, God perfects his kingdom on earth and calls into being "the holy city, the new Jerusalem, coming down out of heaven from God" (Rev. 21:2). God's dwelling with humanity is here, in the renewed creation. "See, the home of God is among mortals" (Rev. 21:3). This is why Jesus told his disciples to pray in the words, "Your kingdom come. Your will be done, on earth as it is in heaven" (Matt. 6:10). During the time between Genesis 2 and

---

[1] Gordon J. Wenham, *Genesis 1–15*, vol. 1, *Word Biblical Commentary* (Dallas: Word, 1998), 15.

Revelation 21, the earth is corrupted, broken, out of kilter, and filled with people and forces that work against God's purposes. (More on this in Genesis 3 and following.) Not everything in the world goes according to God's design. But the world is still God's creation, which he calls "good." (For more on the new heaven and new earth, see "Revelation 17–22" in *Revelation and Work*.)

Many Christians, who work mostly with material objects, say it seems that their work matters less to the church—and even to God—than work centering on people, ideas, or religion. A sermon praising good work is more likely to use the example of a missionary, social worker, or teacher than a miner, auto mechanic, or chemist. Fellow Christians are more likely to recognize a call to become a minister or doctor than a call to become an inventory manager or sculptor. But does this have any biblical basis? Leaving aside the fact that working with people *is* working with material objects, it is wise to remember that God gave people the tasks both of working with people (Gen. 2:18) and working with things (Gen. 2:15). God seems to take the creation very seriously indeed.

God's Creation Takes Work (Genesis 1:3–25; 2:7)

Creating a world is work. In Genesis 1 the power of God's work is undeniable. God speaks worlds into existence, and step by step we see the primordial example of the right use of power. Note the order of creation. The first three of God's creative acts separate the formless chaos into realms of heavens (or sky), water, and land. On day one, God creates light and separates it from darkness, forming day and night (Gen. 1:3–5). On day two, he separates the waters and creates the sky (Gen. 1:6–8). On the first part of day three, he separates dry land from the sea (Gen. 1:9–10). All are essential to the survival of what follows. Next, God begins filling the realms he has created. On the remainder of day three, he creates plant life (Gen. 1:11–13). On day four he creates the sun, moon, and stars (Gen. 1:14–19) in the sky. The terms "greater light" and "lesser light" are used rather than the names "sun" and "moon," thus discouraging the worship of these created objects and reminding us that we are still in danger of worshiping the creation instead of the Creator. The lights are beautiful in themselves and also essential for plant life, with its need for sunshine, nighttime, and seasons. On day five, God fills the water and sky with fish and birds that could not have survived without the plant life created earlier (Gen. 1:20–23). Finally, on day six, he creates the animals (Gen. 1:24–25) and—the apex of creation—humanity to populate the land (Gen. 1:26–31).[2]

In chapter 1, God accomplishes all his work by speaking. "God said . . ." and everything happened. This lets us know that God's power is more than sufficient to create and maintain the creation. We need not worry that God is running out of gas or that the creation is in a precarious state of existence. God's creation is robust, its existence secure. God does not need help from anyone or anything to create or maintain the world. No battle with the forces of chaos threatens to undo the creation. Later, when God chooses to share creative responsibility with human beings, we know that this is God's choice, not a necessity. Whatever people may do to mar the creation or render the earth unfit for life's fullness, God has infinitely greater power to redeem and restore.

The display of God's infinite power in the text does *not* mean that God's creation is not work, any more than writing a computer program or acting in a play is not work. If the transcendent majesty of God's work in Genesis 1 nonetheless tempts us to think it is not actually work, Genesis 2 leaves us no doubt. God works immanently with his hands to sculpt human bodies (Gen. 2:7, 21), dig a garden (Gen. 2:8), plant an orchard (Gen. 2:9), and—a bit later—tailor "garments of skin" (Gen. 3:21). These are only the beginnings of God's physical work in a Bible full of divine labor.[3]

Creation Is of God, but Is Not Identical with God (Genesis 1:11)

God is the source of everything in creation. Yet creation is not identical with God. God gives his creation what Colin Gunton calls *Selbständig-*

---

[2] For a helpful discussion of the interpretation of the "Days" of creation, see Bruce K. Waltke, *Genesis: A Commentary* (Grand Rapids: Zondervan, 2001), 74–78.

[3] For a long list of the many kinds of work God does in the Bible, see R. Paul Stevens, *The Other Six Days* (Grand Rapids: Wm. B. Eerdmans, 2000), 18–123; and Robert Banks, *God the Worker: Journeys into the Mind, Heart, and Imagination of God* (Eugene, OR: Wipf & Stock, 2008).

keit or a "proper independence." This is not the absolute independence imagined by the atheists or Deists, but rather the meaningful existence of the creation as distinct from God himself. This is best captured in the description of God's creation of the plants. "God said, 'Let the earth put forth vegetation: plants yielding seed, and fruit trees of every kind on earth that bear fruit with the seed in it.' And it was so" (Gen. 1:11). God creates everything, but he also literally sows the seed for the perpetuation of creation through the ages. The creation is forever dependent on God—"In him we live and move and have our being" (Acts 17:28)—yet it remains distinct. This gives our work a beauty and value above the value of a ticking clock or a prancing puppet. Our work has its source in God, yet it also has its own weight and dignity.

God Sees that His Work Is Good (Genesis 1:4, 10, 12, 18, 21, 25, 31)

Against any dualistic notion that heaven is good while earth is bad, Genesis declares on each day of creation that "God saw that it was good" (Gen. 1:4, 10, 12, 18, 21, 25). On the sixth day, with the creation of humanity, God saw that it was "very good" (Gen. 1:31). People—the agents through whom sin is soon to enter God's creation—are nonetheless "very good." There is simply no support in Genesis for the notion, which somehow entered Christian imagination, that the world is irredeemably evil and the only salvation is an escape into an immaterial spiritual world, much less for the notion that while we are on earth we should spend our time in "spiritual" tasks rather than "material" ones. There is no divorce of the spiritual from the material in God's good world.

God Works Relationally (Genesis 1:26a)

Even before God creates people, he speaks in the plural, "Let *us* make humankind in our image" (Gen. 1:26; emphasis added). While scholars differ on whether "us" refers to a divine assembly of angelic beings or to a unique plurality-in-unity of God, either view implies that God is inherently relational.[4] It is difficult to be sure exactly what the ancient Israelites would have understood the plural to mean here. For our purposes it seems best to follow the traditional Christian interpretation

---

[4] Waltke, 64–65.

that it refers to the Trinity. In any case, we know from the New Testament that God is indeed in relationship with himself—and with his creation—in a Trinity of love. In John's Gospel we learn that the Son—"the Word [who] became flesh" (John 1:14)—is present and active in creation from the beginning.

> In the beginning was the Word, and the Word was with God and the Word was God. He was in the beginning with God. All things came into being through him, and without him not one thing came into being. What has come into being in him was life, and the life was the light of all people. (John 1:1–4)

Thus Christians acknowledge our Trinitarian God, the unique Three-Persons-in-One-Being, God the Father, God the Son, and God the Holy Spirit, all personally active in creation.

God Limits His Work (Genesis 2:1–3)

At the end of six days, God's creation of the world is finished. This doesn't mean that God ceases working, for as Jesus said, "My Father is still working, and I also am working" (John 5:17). Nor does it mean that the creation is complete, for, as we will see, God leaves plenty of work for people to do to bring the creation further along. But chaos had been turned into an inhabitable environment, now supporting plants, fish, birds, animals, and human beings.

> God saw everything that he had made, and indeed, it was very good. And there was evening and there was morning, the sixth day. Thus the heavens and the earth were finished, and all their multitude. And on the seventh day God finished the *work* that he had done, and he rested on the seventh day from all the work that he had done. (Gen. 1:31–2:2; emphasis added)

God crowns his six days of work with a day of rest. While creating humanity was the climax of God's creative work, resting on the seventh day was the climax of God's creative week. Why does God rest? The majesty of God's creation by word alone in chapter 1 makes it clear that God is not tired. He doesn't *need* to rest. But he chooses to limit his creation in time as well as in space. The universe is not infinite. It has a beginning, attested by Genesis, which science has learned how to observe in light of the big bang theory. Whether it has an end in time is not unambiguously clear, in either the Bible or science, but God gives time a limit *within* the world as we know it. As long as time is running, God blesses six days for work and one for rest. This is a limit that God himself observes, and it later becomes his command to people as well (Exod. 20:8–11).

God Creates and Equips People to Work (Genesis 1:26–2:25)

People are Created in God's Image (Genesis 1:26, 27; 5:1)

Having told the story of God's work of creation, Genesis moves on to tell the story of human work. Everything is grounded on God's creation of people in his own image.

> God said, "Let us make humankind in our image, according to our likeness." (Gen. 1:26)

> So God created humankind in his image, in the image of God he created them; male and female he created them. (Gen. 1:27)

> When God created humankind, he made them in the likeness of God. (Gen. 5:1)

All creation displays God's design, power, and goodness, but only human beings are said to be made in God's image. A full theology of the image of God is beyond our scope here, so let us simply note that something about us is uniquely like him. It would be ridiculous to believe that we are *exactly* like God. We can't create worlds out of pure chaos, and we shouldn't try to do everything God does. "Beloved, never avenge yourselves, but leave room for the wrath of God; for it is written, 'Vengeance is mine, I will repay, says the Lord'" (Rom. 12:19). But the chief thing we know about God, so far in the narrative, is that God is a creator who works in the material world, who works in relationship, and whose work observes limits. We have the ability to do the same.

The rest of Genesis 1 and 2 develops human work in five specific categories: dominion, relationships, fruitfulness/growth, provision, and limits. The development occurs in two cycles, one in Genesis 1:26–2:4 and the other in Genesis 2:4–25. The order of the categories is not exactly in the same order both times, but all the categories are present in both cycles. The first cycle develops what it means to *work* in God's image. The second cycle describes how God *equips* Adam and Eve for their work as they begin life in the Garden of Eden.

The language in the first cycle is more abstract and therefore well suited for developing principles of human labor. The language in the second cycle is earthier, speaking of God forming things out of dirt and other elements, and is well suited for practical instruction for Adam and Eve in their particular work in the garden. This shift of language—with similar shifts throughout the first four books of the Bible—has attracted uncounted volumes of research, hypothesis, debate, and even division among scholars. Any general purpose commentary will provide a wealth of details. Most of these debates, however, have little impact on what the book of Genesis contributes to understanding work, workers, and workplaces, and we will not attempt to take a position on them here. What is relevant to our discussion is that chapter 2 repeats five themes developed earlier—in the order of dominion, provision, fruitfulness/growth, limits, and relationships—by describing how God equips people to fulfill the work we are created to do in his image. In order to make it easier to follow these themes, we will explore Genesis 1:26–2:25 category by category, rather than verse by verse.

Dominion (Genesis 1:26; 2:5)

To Work in God's Image Is to Exercise Dominion (Genesis 1:26)

A consequence we see in Genesis of being created in God's image is that we are to "have dominion over the fish of the sea, and over the birds of the air, and over the cattle, and over all the wild animals of the earth, and over every creeping thing that creeps upon the earth" (Gen. 1:26). As Ian Hart puts it, "Exercising royal dominion over the earth as God's representative is the basic purpose for which God created man. . . . Man is appointed king over creation, responsible to God the ultimate king, and as such expected to manage and develop and care for creation, this task to include actual physical work."[5] Our work in God's image begins with faithfully representing God.

As we exercise dominion over the created world, we do it knowing that we mirror God. We are not the originals but the images, and our duty is to use the original—God—as our pattern, not ourselves. Our work is meant to serve God's purposes more than our own, which prevents us from domineering all that God has put under our control.

Think about the implications of this in our workplaces. How would God go about doing our job? What values would God bring to it? What products would God make? Which people would God serve? What organizations would God build? What standards would God use? In what ways, as image-bearers of God, should our work display the God we represent? When we finish a job, are the results such that we can say, "Thank you, God, for using me to accomplish this?"

God Equips People for the Work of Dominion (Genesis 2:5)

The cycle begins again with dominion, although it may not be immediately recognizable as such. "No plant of the field was yet in the earth and no herb of the field had yet sprung up—for the LORD God had not caused it to rain upon the earth, and *there was no one to till the ground*" (Gen. 2:5; emphasis added). The key phrase is "there was no one to till the ground." God chose not to bring his creation to a close until he created people to work with (or under) him. Meredith Kline puts it this way, "God's making the world was like a king's planting a farm or park or orchard, into which God put humanity to 'serve' the ground and to 'serve' and 'look after' the estate."[6]

Thus the work of exercising dominion begins with tilling the ground. From this we see that God's use of the words *subdue*[7] and *dominion* in

---

[5] Ian Hart, "Genesis 1:1–2:3 as a Prologue to the Book of Genesis," *TynBul* 46, no. 2 (1995): 322.

[6] Meredith G. Kline, *Kingdom Prologue: Genesis Foundations for a Covenantal Worldview* (Eugene, OR: Wipf & Stock, 2006), 69.

[7] "Subdue" (*kavash*) applies to cultivation (farming), domestication (shepherding), even mining, "making use of all the economic and cultural potential

chapter 1 do not give us permission to run roughshod over any part of his creation. Quite the opposite. We are to act as if we ourselves had the same relationship of love with his creatures that God does. Subduing the earth includes harnessing its various resources as well as protecting them. Dominion over all living creatures is not a license to abuse them, but a contract from God to care for them. We are to serve the best interests of all whose lives touch ours; our employers, our customers, our colleagues or fellow workers, or those who work for us or who we meet even casually. That does not mean that we will allow people to run over us, but it does mean that we will not allow our self-interest, our self-esteem, or our self-aggrandizement to give us a license to run over others. The later unfolding story in Genesis focuses attention on precisely that temptation and its consequences.

Today we have become especially aware of how the pursuit of human self-interest threatens the natural environment. We were meant to tend and care for the garden (Gen. 2:15). Creation is meant for our use, but not *only* for our use. Remembering that the air, water, land, plants, and animals are good (Gen. 1:4–31) reminds us that we are meant to sustain and preserve the environment. Our work can either preserve or destroy the clean air, water, and land, the biodiversity, the ecosystems, and biomes, and even the climate with which God has blessed his creation. Dominion is not the authority to work *against* God's creation, but the ability to work *for* it.

Relationships (Genesis 1:27; 2:18, 21–25)

To Work in God's Image Is to Work in Relationship with Others (Genesis 1:27)

A consequence we see in Genesis of being created in God's image is that we work in relationship with God and one another. We have already seen that God is inherently relational (Gen. 1:26), so as images of a relational God, we are inherently relational. The second part of Genesis 1:27 makes the point again, for it speaks of us not individually but in

---

associated with the concept of 'land,' " according to Robert B. Chisholm Jr., *From Exegesis to Exposition: A Practical Guide to Using Biblical Hebrew* (Grand Rapids: Baker, 1998), 46.

twos, "Male and female he created them." We are in relationship with our creator and with our fellow creatures. These relationships are not left as philosophical abstractions in Genesis. We see God talking and working with Adam in naming the animals (Gen. 2:19). We see God visiting Adam and Eve "in the garden at the time of the evening breeze" (Gen. 3:8).

How does this reality impact us in our places of work? Above all, we are called to love the people we work with, among, and for. The God of relationship is the God of love (1 John 4:7). One could merely say that "God loves," but Scripture goes deeper to the very core of God's *being* as Love, a love flowing back and forth among the Father, the Son (John 17:24), and the Holy Spirit. This love also flows out of God's being to us, doing nothing that is not in our best interest (*agape* love in contrast to human loves situated in our emotions).

Francis Schaeffer explores further the idea that because we are made in God's image and because God is personal, we can have a personal relationship with God. He notes that this makes genuine love possible, stating that machines can't love. As a result, we have a responsibility to care consciously for all that God has put in our care. Being a relational creature carries moral responsibility.[8]

God Equips People to Work in Relationship with Others (Genesis 2:18, 21–25)

Because we are made in the image of a relational God, we are inherently relational ourselves. We are made for relationships with God himself and also with other people. God says, "It is not good that the man should be alone; I will make him a helper as his partner" (Gen. 2:18). All of his creative acts had been called "good" or "very good," and this is the first time that God pronounces something "not good." So God makes a woman out of the flesh and bone of Adam himself. When Eve arrives, Adam is filled with joy. "This at last is bone of my bones and flesh of my flesh" (Gen. 2:23). (After this one instance, all new people will continue to come out of the flesh of other human beings, but born by women rather than men.) Adam and Eve embark on a relationship so close that "they become one flesh" (Gen. 1:24). Although this may sound

---

[8] Francis A. Schaeffer, *Genesis in Space and Time* (Downers Grove, IL: InterVarsity Press, 1972), 47–48.

like a purely erotic or family matter, it is also a working relationship. Eve is created as Adam's "helper" and "partner" who will join him in working the Garden of Eden. The word *helper* indicates that, like Adam, she will be tending the garden. To be a helper means to work. Someone who is not working is not helping. To be a partner means to work *with* someone, in relationship.

When God calls Eve a "helper," he is not saying she will be Adam's inferior or that her work will be less important, less creative, less *anything*, than his. The word translated as "helper" here (Hebrew *ezer*) is a word used elsewhere in the Old Testament to refer to God himself. "God is my helper [*ezer*]" (Ps. 54:4). "LORD, be my helper [*ezer*]" (Ps. 30:10). Clearly, an *ezer* is not a subordinate. Moreover, Genesis 2:18 describes Eve not only as a "helper" but also as a "partner." The English word most often used today for someone who is both a helper and a partner is "co-worker." This is indeed the sense already given in Genesis 1:27, "male and female he created them," which makes no distinction of priority or dominance. Domination of women by men—or vice versa—is not in accordance with God's good creation. It is a tragic consequence of the Fall (Gen. 3:16).

Relationships are not incidental to work; they are essential. Work serves as a place of deep and meaningful relationships, under the proper conditions at least. Jesus described our relationship with himself as a kind of work, "Take my yoke upon you, and learn from me; for I am gentle and humble in heart, and you will find rest for your souls" (Matt. 11:29). A yoke is what makes it possible for two oxen to work together. In Christ, people may truly work together as God intended when he made Eve and Adam as co-workers. While our minds and bodies work in relationship with other people and God, our souls "find rest." When we don't work with others towards a common goal, we become spiritually restless. For more on yoking, see the section on 2 Corinthians 6:14–18 in the *Theology of Work Bible Commentary*.

A crucial aspect of relationship modeled by God himself is delegation of authority. God delegated the naming of the animals to Adam, and the transfer of authority was genuine. "Whatever the man called every living creature, that was its name" (Gen. 2:19). In delegation, as in any other form of relationship, we give up some measure of our power and independence and take the risk of letting others' work affect us. Much of the past fifty years of development in the fields of leadership and management has come in the form of delegating authority, empowering workers, and fostering teamwork. The foundation of this kind of development has been in Genesis all along, though Christians have not always noticed it.

Many people form their closest relationships when some kind of work—whether paid or not—provides a common purpose and goal. In turn, working relationships make it possible to create the vast, complex array of goods and services beyond the capacity of any individual to produce. Without relationships at work, there are no automobiles, no computers, no postal services, no legislatures, no stores, no schools, no hunting for game larger than one person can bring down. And without the intimate relationship between a man and a woman, there are no future people to do the work God gives. Our work and our community are thoroughly intertwined gifts from God. Together they provide the means for us to be fruitful and multiply in every sense of the words.

Fruitfulness/Growth (Genesis 1:28; 2:15, 19–20)

To Work in God's Image Is to Bear Fruit and Multiply (Genesis 1:28)

Since we are created in God's image, we are to be fruitful, or creative. This is often called the "creation mandate" or "cultural mandate." God brought into being a flawless creation, an ideal platform, and then created humanity to continue the creation project. "God blessed them, and God said to them, 'Be fruitful and multiply, and fill the earth'" (Gen. 1:28a). God could have created everything imaginable and filled the earth himself. But he chose to create humanity to work alongside him to actualize the universe's potential, to participate in God's own work. It is remarkable that God trusts us to carry out this amazing task of building on the good earth he has given us. Through our work God brings forth food and drink, products and services, knowledge and beauty, organizations and communities, growth and health, and praise and glory to himself.

A word about beauty is in order. God's work is not only productive, but it is also a "delight to the eyes" (Gen. 3:6). This is not surprising, since people, being in the image of God, are inherently beautiful. Like any other good, beauty can become an idol, but Christians have often been too worried about the dangers of beauty and too unappreciative of beauty's value in God's eyes. Inherently, beauty is not a waste of resources, or a distraction from more important work, or a flower doomed to fade away at the end of the age. Beauty is a work in the image of God, and the kingdom of God is filled with beauty "like a very rare jewel" (Rev. 21:11). Christian communities do well at appreciating the beauty of music with words about Jesus. Perhaps we could do better at valuing all kinds of true beauty.

A good question to ask ourselves is whether we *are* working more productively and beautifully. History is full of examples of people whose Christian faith resulted in amazing accomplishments. If our work feels fruitless next to theirs, the answer lies not in self-judgment, but in hope, prayer, and growth in the company of the people of God. No matter what barriers we face—from within or without—by the power of God we can do more good than we could ever imagine.

God Equips People to Bear Fruit and Multiply (Genesis 2:15, 19–20)

"The Lord God took the man and put him in the Garden of Eden to till it and keep it" (Gen. 2:15). These two words in Hebrew, *avad* ("work" or "till") and *shamar* ("keep"), are also used for the worship of God and keeping his commandments, respectively.[9] Work done according to God's purpose has an unmistakable holiness.

Adam and Eve are given two specific kinds of work in Genesis 2:15–20, gardening (a kind of physical work) and giving names to the animals (a kind of cultural/scientific/intellectual work). Both are creative enterprises that give specific activities to people created in the image of the Creator. By growing things and developing culture, we are indeed fruitful. We bring forth the resources needed to support a growing population and to increase the productivity of creation. We develop the means to fill, yet not overfill, the earth. We need not imagine that gardening and naming animals are the *only* tasks suitable for human beings. Rather the human task is to extend the creative work of God in a multitude of ways limited only by God's gifts of imagination and skill, and the limits God sets. Work is forever rooted in God's design for human life. It is an

---

[9] R. Laird Harris, Gleason L. Archer, Jr., and Bruce K. Waltke, eds., *Theological Wordbook of the Old Testament* (Chicago: Moody Press, 1999), 639, 939.

avenue to contribute to the common good and as a means of providing for ourselves, our families, and those we can bless with our generosity.

An important (though sometimes overlooked) aspect of God at work in creation is the vast imagination that could create everything from exotic sea life to elephants and rhinoceroses. While theologians have created varying lists of those characteristics of God that have been given to us that bear the divine image, imagination is surely a gift from God we see at work all around us in our workspaces as well as in our homes.

Much of the work we do uses our imagination in some way. We tighten bolts on an assembly line truck and we imagine that truck out on the open road. We open a document on our laptop and imagine the story we're about to write. Mozart imagined a sonata and Beethoven imagined a symphony. Picasso imagined *Guernica* before picking up his brushes to work on that painting. Tesla and Edison imagined harnessing electricity, and today we have light in the darkness and myriad appliances, electronics, and equipment. Someone somewhere imagined virtually everything surrounding us. Most of the jobs people hold exist because someone could imagine a job-creating product or process in the workplace.

Yet imagination takes work to realize, and after imagination comes the work of bringing the product into being. Actually, in practice the imagination and the realization often occur in intertwined processes. Picasso said of his *Guernica*, "A painting is not thought out and settled in advance. While it is being done, it changes as one's thoughts change. And when it's finished, it goes on changing, according to the state of mind of whoever is looking at it."[10] The work of bringing imagination into reality brings its own inescapable creativity.

Provision (Genesis 1:29–30; 2:8–14)

To Work in God's Image Is to Receive God's Provision (Genesis 1:29–30)

Since we are created in God's image, God provides for our needs. This is one of the ways in which those made in God's image are not God himself. God has no needs, or if he does he has the power to meet them all on his own. We don't. Therefore:

---

[10] While this quote is widely repeated, its source is elusive. Whether or not it is genuine, it expresses a reality well known to artists of all kinds.

God said, "See, I have given you every plant yielding seed that is upon the face of all the earth, and every tree with seed in its fruit; you shall have them for food. And to every beast of the earth, and to every bird of the air, and to everything that creeps on the earth, everything that has the breath of life, I have given every green plant for food." And it was so. (Gen. 1:29–30)

On the one hand, acknowledging God's provision warns us not to fall into hubris. Without him, our work is nothing. We cannot bring ourselves to life. We cannot even provide for our own maintenance. We need God's continuing provision of air, water, earth, sunshine, and the miraculous growth of living things for food for our bodies and minds. On the other hand, acknowledging God's provision gives us confidence in our work. We do not have to depend on our own ability or on the vagaries of circumstance to meet our need. God's power makes our work fruitful.

God Equips People with Provision for Their Needs (Genesis 2:8–14)

The second cycle of the creation account shows us something of *how* God provides for our needs. He prepares the earth to be productive when we apply our work to it. "The LORD God planted a garden in Eden, in the east; and there he put the man whom he had formed" (Gen. 2:8). Though we till, God is the original planter. In addition to food, God has created the earth with resources to support everything we need to be fruitful and multiply. He gives us a multitude of rivers providing water, ores yielding stone and metal materials, and precursors to the means of economic exchange (Gen. 2:10–14). "There is gold, and the gold of that land is good" (Gen. 2:11–12). Even when we synthesize new elements and molecules or when we reshuffle DNA among organisms or create artificial cells, we are working with the matter and energy that God brought into being for us.

Limits (Genesis 2:3; 2:17)

To Work in God's Image Is to Be Blessed by the Limits God Sets (Genesis 2:3)

Since we are created in God's image, we are to obey limits in our work. "God blessed the seventh day and hallowed it, because on it God rested from all the work that he had done in creation" (Gen. 2:3). Did

God rest because he was exhausted, or did he rest to offer us image-bearers a model cycle of work and rest? The fourth of the Ten Commandments tells us that God's rest is meant as an example for us to follow.

> Remember the sabbath day, and keep it holy. Six days you shall labor and do all your work. But the seventh day is a sabbath to the LORD your God; you shall not do any work—you, your son or your daughter, your male or female slave, your livestock, or the alien resident in your towns. For in six days the LORD made heaven and earth, the sea, and all that is in them, but rested the seventh day; therefore the Lord blessed the sabbath day and consecrated it. (Exod. 20:8–11)

While religious people over the centuries tended to pile up regulations defining what constituted keeping the Sabbath, Jesus said clearly that God made the Sabbath for us—for our benefit (Mark 2:27). What are we to learn from this?

When, like God, we stop our work on whatever is our seventh day, we acknowledge that our life is not defined only by work or productivity. Walter Brueggemann put it this way, "Sabbath provides a visible testimony that God is at the center of life—that human production and consumption take place in a world ordered, blessed, and restrained by the God of all creation."[11] In a sense, we renounce some part of our autonomy, embracing our dependence on God our Creator. Otherwise, we live with the illusion that life is completely under human control. Part of making Sabbath a regular part of our work life acknowledges that God is ultimately at the center of life. (Further discussions of Sabbath, rest, and work can be found in the sections on "Mark 1:21–45," "Mark 2:23–3:6," "Luke 6:1–11," and "Luke 13:10–17" in the *Theology of Work Bible Commentary*.)

God Equips People to Work within Limits (Genesis 2:17)

Having blessed human beings by his own example of observing workdays and Sabbaths, God equips Adam and Eve with specific instructions about the limits of their work. In the midst of the Garden of Eden, God plants two trees, the tree of life and the tree of the knowledge of good

---

[11] Walter Brueggemann, "Sabbath," in *Reverberations of Faith: A Theological Handbook of Old Testament Themes* (Louisville: Westminster John Knox Press, 2002), 180.

and evil (Gen. 2:9). The latter tree is off limits. God tells Adam, "You may freely eat of every tree of the garden; but of the tree of the knowledge of good and evil you shall not eat, for in the day that you eat of it you shall die" (Gen. 2:16–17).

Theologians have speculated at length about why God would put a tree in the Garden of Eden that he didn't want the inhabitants to use. Various hypotheses are found in the general commentaries, and we need not settle on an answer here. For our purposes, it is enough to observe that not everything that *can* be done *should* be done. Human imagination and skill can work with the resources of God's creation in ways inimical to God's intents, purposes, and commands. If we want to work *with* God, rather than *against* him, we must choose to observe the limits God sets, rather than realizing everything possible in creation.

Francis Schaeffer has pointed out that God didn't give Adam and Eve a choice between a good tree and an evil tree, but a choice whether or not to acquire the knowledge of evil. (They already knew good, of course.) In making that tree, God opened up the possibility of evil, but in doing so God validated choice. All love is bound up in choice; without choice the word *love* is meaningless.[12] Could Adam and Eve love and trust God sufficiently to obey his command about the tree? God expects that those in relationship with him will be capable of respecting the limits that bring about good in creation.

In today's places of work, some limits continue to bless us when we observe them. Human creativity, for example, arises as much from limits as from opportunities. Architects find inspiration from the limits of time, money, space, materials, and purpose imposed by the client. Painters find creative expression by accepting the limits of the media with which they choose to work, beginning with the limitations of representing three-dimensional space on a two-dimensional canvas. Writers find brilliance when they face page and word limits.

All good work respects God's limits. There are limits to the earth's capacity for resource extraction, pollution, habitat modification, and the use of plants and animals for food, clothing, and other purposes. The human body has great yet limited strength, endurance, and capacity to

---

[12] Schaeffer, 71–72.

work. There are limits to healthy eating and exercise. There are limits by which we distinguish beauty from vulgarity, criticism from abuse, profit from greed, friendship from exploitation, service from slavery, liberty from irresponsibility, and authority from dictatorship. In practice it may be hard to know exactly where the line is, and it must be admitted that Christians have often erred on the side of conformity, legalism, prejudice, and a stifling dreariness, especially when proclaiming what other people should or should not do. Nonetheless, the art of living as God's image-bearers requires learning to discern where blessings are to be found in observing the limits set by God and that are evident in his creation.

The Work of the "Creation Mandate" (Genesis 1:28, 2:15)

In describing God's creation of humanity in his image (Gen. 1:1–2:3) and equipping humanity to live according to that image (Gen. 2:4–25), we have explored God's creation of people to exercise dominion, to be fruitful and multiply, to receive God's provision, to work in relationships, and to observe the limits of creation. We noted that these have often been called the "creation mandate" or "cultural mandate," with Genesis 1:28 and 2:15 standing out in particular:

> God blessed them, and God said to them, "Be fruitful and multiply, and fill the earth and subdue it; and have dominion over the fish of the sea and over the birds of the air and over every living thing that moves upon the earth." (Gen. 1:28)

> The Lord God took the man and put him in the garden of Eden to till it and keep it. (Gen. 2:15)

The use of this terminology is not essential, but the idea it stands for seems clear in Genesis 1 and 2. From the beginning God intended and created human beings to be his junior partners in the work of bringing his creation to fulfillment. It is not in our nature to be satisfied with things as they are, to receive provision for our needs without working, to endure idleness for long, to toil in a system of uncreative regimentation, or to work in social isolation. To recap, we are created to work as sub-creators in relationship with other people and with God, depending on God's provision to make our work fruitful and respecting the limits given in his Word and evident in his creation.

People Fall into Sin in Work (Genesis 3:1–24)

Until this point, we have been discussing work in its ideal form, under the perfect conditions of the Garden of Eden. But then we come to Genesis 3:1–6.

> Now the serpent was more crafty than any other wild animal that the LORD God had made. He said to the woman, "Did God say, 'You shall not eat from any tree in the garden'?" The woman said to the serpent, "We may eat of the fruit of the trees in the garden; but God said, 'You shall not eat of the fruit of the tree that is in the middle of the garden, nor shall you touch it, or you shall die.'" But the serpent said to the woman, "You will not die; for God knows that when you eat of it your eyes will be opened, and *you will be like God*, knowing good and evil." So when the woman saw that the tree was good for food, and that it was a delight to the eyes, and that the tree was to be desired to make one wise, she took of its fruit and ate; and she also gave some to her husband, who was with her, and he ate. (emphasis added)

The serpent represents anti-god, the adversary of God. Bruce Waltke notes that God's adversary is malevolent and wiser than human beings. He's shrewd as he draws attention to Adam and Eve's vulnerability even as he distorts God's command. He maneuvers Eve into what looks like a sincere theological discussion, but distorts it by emphasizing God's prohibition instead of his provision of the rest of the fruit trees in the garden. In essence, he wants God's word to sound harsh and restrictive.

The serpent's plan succeeds, and first Eve, then Adam, eats the fruit of the forbidden tree. They break the limits God had set for them, in a vain attempt to become "like God" in some way beyond what they already had as God's image-bearers (Gen. 3:5). Already knowing from experience the goodness of God's creation, they choose to become "wise" in the ways of evil (Gen. 3:4–6). Eve's and Adam's decisions to eat the fruit are choices to favor their own pragmatic, aesthetic, and sensual tastes over God's word. "Good" is no longer rooted in what God says enhances life but in what people think is desirable to elevate life. In short, they turn what is good into evil.[13]

By choosing to disobey God, they break the relationships inherent in their own being. First, their relationship together—"bone of my bones and flesh of my flesh," as it had previously been (Gen. 2:23)—is riven apart as they hide from each other under the cover of fig leaves (Gen. 3:7). Next to go is their relationship with God, as they no longer talk with him in the evening breeze, but hide themselves from his presence (Gen. 3:8). Adam further breaks the relationship between himself and Eve by blaming her for his decision to eat the fruit, and getting in a dig at God at the same time. "The woman whom you gave to be with me, she gave me fruit from the tree, and I ate" (Gen. 3:12). Eve likewise breaks humanity's relationship with the creatures of the earth by blaming the serpent for her own decision (Gen. 3:13).

Adam's and Eve's decisions that day had disastrous results that stretch all the way to the modern workplace. God speaks judgment against their sin and declares consequences that result in difficult toil. The serpent will have to crawl on its belly all its days (Gen. 3:14). The woman will face hard labor in delivering children, and also feel conflict over her desire for the man (Gen. 3:16). The man will have to toil to wrest a living from the soil, and it will produce "thorns and thistles" at the expense of the desired grain (Gen. 3:17–18). All in all, human beings will still do the work they were created to do, and God will still provide for their needs (Gen. 3:17–19). But work will become more difficult, unpleasant, and liable to failure and unintended consequences.

It is important to note that when work became toil, it was not the beginning of work. Some people see the curse as the origin of work, but Adam and Eve had already worked the garden. Work is not inherently a curse, but the curse affects work. In fact, work becomes more important as a result of the Fall, not less, because more work is required now to yield the necessary results. Furthermore, the source materials from which Adam and Eve sprang in God's freedom and pleasure now become sources of subjugation. Adam, made from dirt, will now struggle to till the soil until his body returns to dirt at his death (Gen. 3:19); Eve, made

---

[13] Waltke, 90–91.

from a rib in Adam's side, will now be subject to Adam's domination, rather than taking her place beside him (Gen. 3:16). Domination of one person over another in marriage and work was not part of God's original plan, but sinful people made it a new way of relating when they broke the relationships that God had given them (Gen. 3:12, 13).

Two forms of evil confront us daily. The first is natural evil, the physical conditions on earth that are hostile to the life God intends for us. Floods and droughts, earthquakes, tsunamis, excessive heat and cold, disease, vermin, and the like cause harm that was absent from the garden. The second is moral evil, when people act with wills that are hostile to God's intentions. By acting in evil ways, we mar the creation and distance ourselves from God, and we mar the relationships we have with other people.

We live in a fallen, broken world and we cannot expect life without toil. We were made for work, but in this life that work is stained by all that was broken that day in the Garden of Eden. This too is often the result of failing to respect the limits God sets for our relationships, whether personal, corporate, or social. The Fall created alienation between people and God, among people, and between people and the earth that was to support them. Suspicion of one another replaced trust and love. In the generations that followed, alienation nourished jealousy, rage, even murder. All workplaces today reflect that alienation between workers—to greater or lesser extent—making our work even more toilsome and less productive.

People Work in a Fallen Creation (Genesis 4–8)

When God drives Adam and Eve from the Garden of Eden (Gen. 3:23–24), they bring with them their fractured relationships and toilsome work, scratching out an existence in resistant soil. Nonetheless, God continues to provide for them, even to the point of sewing clothes for them when they lack the skill themselves (Gen. 3:21). The curse has not destroyed their ability to multiply (Gen. 4:1–2), or to attain a measure of prosperity (Gen. 4:3–4).

The work of Genesis 1 and 2 continues. There is still ground to be tilled and phenomena of nature to be studied, described, and named.

Men and women must still be fruitful, must still multiply, must still govern. But now, a second layer of work must also be accomplished—the work of healing, repairing, and restoring the things that go wrong and the evils that are committed. To put it in a contemporary context, the work of farmers, scientists, midwives, parents, leaders, and everyone in creative enterprises is still needed. But so is the work of exterminators, doctors, funeral directors, corrections officers, forensic auditors, and everyone in professions that restrain evil, forestall disaster, repair damage, and restore health. In truth, everyone's work is a mixture of creation and repair, encouragement and frustration, success and failure, joy and sorrow. Roughly speaking, there is twice as much work to do now than there was in the garden. Work is not less important to God's plan, but more.

The First Murder (Genesis 4:1–25)

Genesis 4 details the first murder when Cain kills his brother Abel in a fit of angry jealousy. Both brothers bring the fruit of their work as offerings to God. Cain is a farmer, and he brings some of the fruit of the ground, with no indication in the biblical text that this is the first or the best of his produce (Gen. 4:3). Abel is a shepherd and brings the "firstlings," the best, the "fat portions" of his flock (Gen. 4:4). Although both are producing food, they are neither working nor worshiping together. Work is no longer a place of good relationships.

God looks with favor on the offering of Abel but not on that of Cain. In this first mention of anger in the Bible, God warns Cain not to give into despair, but to master his resentment and work for a better result in the future. "If you do well, will you not be accepted?" the Lord asks him (Gen. 4:7). But Cain gives way to his anger instead and kills his brother (Gen. 4:8; cf. 1 John 3:12; Jude 11). God responds to the deed in these words:

> "Listen; your brother's blood is crying out to me from the ground! And now you are cursed from the ground, which has opened its mouth to receive your brother's blood from your hand. When you till the ground, it will no longer yield to you its strength; you will be a fugitive and a wanderer on the earth." (Gen. 4:10–12)

Adam's sin did not bring God's curse upon people, but only upon the ground (Gen. 3:17). Cain's sin brings the ground's curse on Cain himself

(Gen. 4:11). He can no longer till the ground, and Cain the farmer becomes a wanderer, finally settling in the land of Nod, east of Eden, where he builds the first city mentioned in the Bible (Gen. 4:16–17). (See Gen. 10–11 for more on the topic of cities.)

The remainder of chapter 4 follows Cain's descendants for seven generations to Lamech, whose tyrannical deeds make his ancestor Cain seem tame. Lamech shows us a progressive hardening in sin. First comes polygamy (Gen. 4:19), violating God's purpose in marriage in Genesis 2:24 (cf. Matt. 19:5–6). Then, a vendetta that leads him to kill someone who had merely struck him (Gen. 4:23–24). Yet in Lamech we also see the beginnings of civilization. Division of labor—which spelled trouble between Cain and Abel—brings a specialization here that makes certain advances possible. Some of Lamech's sons create musical instruments and ply crafts using bronze and iron tools (Gen. 4:21–22). The ability to create music, to craft the instruments for playing it, and to develop technological advances in metallurgy are all within the scope of the creators we are created to be in God's image. The arts and sciences are a worthy outworking of the creation mandate, but Lamech's crowing about his vicious deeds points to the dangers that accompany technology in a depraved culture bent on violence. The first human poet after the Fall celebrates human pride and abuse of power. Yet the harp and the flute can be redeemed and used in the praise of God (1 Sam. 16:23), as can the metallurgy that went into the construction of the Hebrew tabernacle (Exod. 35:4–19, 30–35).

As people multiply, they diverge. Through Seth, Adam had hope of a godly seed, which includes Enoch and Noah. But in time there arises a group of people who stray far from God's ways.

> When people began to multiply on the face of the ground, and daughters were born to them, the sons of God saw that they were fair, and they took wives for themselves of all that they chose. . . . The Nephilim [giants, heroes, fierce warriors—the meaning is unclear] were on the earth in those days—and also afterward—when the sons of God went in to the daughters of humans, who bore children to them. These were the heroes that were of old, warriors of renown. The LORD saw that the wickedness of humankind was great in the earth, and that every inclination of the thoughts of their hearts was only evil continually. (Gen. 6:1–5)

What could the godly line of Seth—narrowed eventually to only Noah and his family—do against a culture so depraved that God would eventually decide to destroy it utterly?

A major workplace issue for many Christians today is how to observe the principles that we believe reflect God's will and purposes for us as his image-bearers or representatives. How can we do this in cases where our work puts us under pressure toward dishonesty, disloyalty, low-quality workmanship, unlivable wages and working conditions, exploitation of vulnerable co-workers, customers, suppliers, or the community at large? We know from Seth's example—and many others in Scripture—that there is room in the world for people to work according to God's design and mandate.

When others may fall into fear, uncertainty, and doubt, or succumb to unbounded desire for power, wealth, or human recognition, God's people can remain steadfast in ethical, purposeful, compassionate work because we trust God to bring us through the hardships that may prove too much to master without God's grace. When people are abused or harmed by greed, injustice, hatred, or neglect, we can stand up for them, work justice, and heal hurts and divisions because we have access to Christ's redeeming power. Christians, of all people, can afford to push back against the sin we meet at our places of work, whether it arises from others' actions or within our own hearts. God quashed the project at Babel because "nothing that they propose to do will now be impossible for them" (Gen 11:6), for people did not refer to our actual abilities but to our hubris. Yet by God's grace we actually do have the power to accomplish all God has in store for us in Christ, who declares that "nothing will be impossible for you" (Matt. 17:20) and "nothing will be impossible with God" (Luke 1:37).

Do we actually work as if we believe in God's power? Or do we fritter away God's promises by simply trying to get by without causing any fuss?

God Says "Enough!" and Creates a New World (Genesis 6:9–8:19)

Some situations may be redeemable. Others may be beyond redemption. In Genesis 6:6–8, we hear God's lament about the state of the pre-flood world and culture, and his decision to start over:

> The LORD was sorry that he had made humankind on the earth, and it grieved him to his heart. So the LORD said, "I will blot out from the earth the human beings I have created—people together with animals and creeping things and birds of the air, for I am sorry that I have made them." But Noah found favor in the sight of the LORD.

From Adam to us, God looks for persons who can stand against the culture of sin when needed. Adam failed the test but sired the line of Noah, "a righteous man, blameless in his generation; Noah walked with God" (Gen. 6:9). Noah is the first person whose work is primarily redemptive. Unlike others, who are busy wringing a living from the ground, Noah is called to save humanity and nature from destruction. In him we see the progenitor of priests, prophets, and apostles, who are called to the work of reconciliation with God, and those who care for the environment, who are called to the work of redeeming nature. To greater or lesser degrees, all workers since Noah are called to the work of redemption and reconciliation.

But what a building project the ark is! Against the jeers of neighbors, Noah and his sons must fell thousands of cypress trees, then hand plane them into planks enough to build a floating zoo. This three-deck vessel needs the capacity to carry the various species of animals and to store the food and water required for an indefinite period. Despite the hardship, the text assures us that "Noah did this; he did all that God commanded him" (Gen. 6:13–22).

In the business world, entrepreneurs are used to taking risks, working against conventional wisdom in order to come up with new products or processes. A long-term view is required, rather than attention to short-term results. Noah faces what must at times have seemed to be an impossible task, and some biblical scholars suggest that the actual building of the ark took a hundred years. It also takes faith, tenacity, and careful planning in the face of skeptics and critics. Perhaps we should add project management to the list of Noah's pioneering developments. Today innovators, entrepreneurs, and those who challenge the prevailing opinions and systems in our places of work still need a source of inner strength and conviction. The answer is not to talk ourselves into taking foolish risks, of course, but to turn to prayer and the counsel of those wise in God when we are confronted with opposition and discouragement. Perhaps we need a flowering of Christians gifted and trained for the work of encouraging and helping refine the creativity of innovators in business, science, academia, arts, government, and the other spheres of work.

The story of the flood, found in Genesis 7:1–8:19, is well known. For more than half a year Noah, his family, and all of the animals bounce around inside the ark as the floods rage, swirling the ark in water covering the mountaintops. When at last the flood subsides, the ground is dry and new vegetation is springing up. The occupants of the ark once again step on dry land. The text echoes Genesis 1, emphasizing the continuity of creation. God blows a "wind" over "the deep" and "the waters" recede (Gen. 8:1–3). Yet it is, in a sense, a new world, reshaped by the force of the flood. God was giving human culture a new opportunity to start from scratch and get it right. For Christians, this foreshadows the new heaven and new earth in Revelation 21–22, when human life and work are brought to perfection *within* the cosmos healed from the effects of the Fall, as we discussed in "God brings the material world into being" (Gen. 1:1–2).

What may be less apparent is that this, humanity's first large-scale engineering work, is an environmental project. Despite—or perhaps as a result of—humanity's broken relationship with the serpent and all creatures (Gen. 3:15), God assigns a human being the task of saving the animals and trusts him to do it faithfully. People have not been released from God's call to "have dominion over the fish of the sea and over the birds of the air and over every living thing that moves upon the earth" (Gen. 1:28). God is always at work to restore what was lost in the Fall, and he uses fallen-but-being-restored humanity as his chief instrument.

God Works to Keep His Promise (Genesis 9–11)

God's Covenant with Noah (Genesis 9:1–19)

Once again on dry land with this new beginning, Noah's first act is to build an altar to the Lord (Gen. 8:20). Here he offers sacrifices that please God, who resolves never again to destroy humanity "as long as the earth endures, seedtime and harvest, cold and heat, summer and winter, day and night, shall not cease" (Gen. 8:22). God binds himself to a covenant with Noah and his descendants, promising never to destroy the earth by flood (Gen. 9:8–17). God gives the rainbow as a sign of his promise. Although the earth has radically changed again, God's purposes for work remain the same. He repeats his blessing and promises that Noah and his sons will "be fruitful and multiply, and fill the earth" (Gen. 9:1). He affirms his promise of provision of food through their work (Gen. 9:3). In return he sets requirements for justice among humans and for the protection of all creatures (Gen. 9:4–6).

The Hebrew word translated "rainbow" actually omits the sense of "rain." It refers simply to a bow—a battle and hunting tool. Waltke notes that in ancient Near East mythologies, stars in the shape of a bow were associated with the anger or hostility of the god, but that "here the warrior's bow is hung up, pointed away from the earth."[14] Meredith Kline observes that "the symbol of divine bellicosity and hostility has been transformed into a token of reconciliation between God and man."[15] The relaxed bow stretches from earth to heaven, from horizon to horizon. An instrument of war has become a symbol of peace through God's covenant with Noah.

Noah's Fall (Genesis 9:20–29)

After his heroic work on behalf of humanity, Noah falls into a troubling domestic incident. It begins—as so many domestic and workplace tragedies do—with substance abuse, in this case alcohol. (Add alcoholic beverage production to the list of Noah's innovations; Gen. 9:20.) After becoming drunk, Noah passes out naked in his tent. His son Ham bursts in and sees him in this state, but his other sons—alerted by Ham—circumspectly enter the tent backwards and cover up their father without looking upon him in the raw. Exactly what is so shameful or immoral about this situation is hard for most modern readers to understand, but he and his sons clearly understand it to be a family disaster. When Noah regains consciousness and finds out, his response permanently destroys the family's tranquility. Noah curses Ham's descendants via Canaan and

---

[14] Waltke, 146.
[15] Kline, 152.

makes them slaves to the other two sons' branches. This sets the stage for thousands of years of enmity, war, and atrocity among Noah's family.

Noah may be the first person of great stature to come crashing down into disgrace, but he was not the last. Something about greatness seems to make people vulnerable to moral failure—especially, it seems, in our personal and family lives. In an instant, all of us could name a dozen examples on the world stage. The phenomenon is common enough to spawn proverbs, whether biblical—"Pride goes before destruction, and a haughty spirit before a fall" (Prov. 16:18)—or colloquial—"The bigger they come, the harder they fall."

Noah is undoubtedly one of the great figures of the Bible (Heb. 11:7), so our best response is not to judge Noah but to ask God's grace for ourselves. If we find ourselves seeking greatness, it's better to seek humility first. If we have become great, it's best to beg God for the grace to escape Noah's fate. If we have fallen, similarly to Noah, let us confess swiftly and ask those around us to prevent us from turning a fall into a disaster through our self-justifying responses.

Noah's Descendants and the Tower of Babel (Genesis 10:1–11:32)

In what is called the Table of Nations, Genesis 10 traces first the descendants of Japheth (Gen. 10:2–5), then the descendants of Ham (Gen. 10:6–20), and finally the descendants of Shem (Gen. 10:21–31). Among them, Ham's grandson Nimrod stands out for his significance to the theology of work. Nimrod founds an empire of naked aggression based in Babylon. He is a tyrant, a mighty hunter to be feared, and most significantly a builder of cities (Gen. 10:8–12).

With Nimrod, the tyrannical city-builder, fresh in our memory, we come to the building of the tower of Babel (Gen. 11:1–9). Babel, like many cities in the ancient Near East is designed as a walled enclosure of a great temple or ziggurat, a mud-brick stair tower designed to reach to the realm of the gods. With such a tower, people could ascend to the gods, and the gods could descend to earth. Although God does not condemn this drive to reach the heavens, we see in it the self-aggrandizing ambition and escalating sin of pride that drives these people to begin building such a mighty tower. "Let us build ourselves a city, and a tower with its top in the heavens, and let us make a name for ourselves; otherwise we shall be scattered abroad upon the face of the whole earth" (Gen. 11:4). What did they want? Fame. What did they fear? Being scattered without the security of numbers. The tower they envisioned building seemed huge to them, but the Genesis narrator smiles while telling us that it was so puny that God "came down to see the city and the tower" (Gen. 11:5). How different from the city of peace, order, and virtue that are God's purposes for the world.[16]

God's objection to the tower is that it will give people the expectation that "nothing that they propose to do will now be impossible for them" (Gen. 11:6). Like Adam and Eve before them, they intend to use the creative power they possess as image-bearers of God to act against God's purposes. In this case, they plan to do the opposite of what God commanded in the cultural mandate. Instead of filling the earth, they intend to concentrate themselves here in one location. Instead of exploring the fullness of the name God gave them—*adam*, "humankind" (Gen. 5:2)—they decide to make a name for themselves. God sees that their arrogance and ambition are out of bounds and says, "Let us go down and confuse their language there, so that they will not understand one another's speech" (Gen. 11:7). Then "the Lord scattered them abroad from there over the face of all the earth, and they left off building the city. Therefore it was called Babel, because there the Lord confused the language of all the earth; and from there the Lord scattered them abroad over the face of all the earth" (Gen. 11:8–9).

These people were originally of one blood, all descended from Noah through his three sons. But after God destroyed the Tower of Babel, the descendants of these sons migrated to different parts of the Middle East: Japheth's descendants moved west into Anatolia (Turkey) and Greece; Ham's descendants went south into Arabia and Egypt; and Shem's descendants remained in the east in what we know today as Iraq. From these three genealogies in Genesis 10, we discover where the tribal and national divisions of the ancient Near East developed.

We might be tempted to conclude from this study that cities are inherently bad, but this is not so. God gave Israel their capital city of

---

[16] Augustine, *City of God*, Book XIX.

Jerusalem, and the ultimate abode of God's people is God's holy city coming down from heaven (Rev. 21:2). The concept of "city" is not evil, but the pride that we may come to attach to cities is what displeases God (Gen. 19:12–14). We sin when we look to civic triumph and culture, in place of God, as our source of meaning and direction. Bruce Waltke concludes his analysis of Genesis 11 in these words:

> Society apart from God is totally unstable. On the one hand, people earnestly seek existential meaning and security in their collective unity. On the other hand, they have an insatiable appetite to consume what others possess. . . . At the heart of the city of man is love for self and hatred for God. The city reveals that the human spirit will not stop at anything short of usurping God's throne in heaven.[17]

While it might appear that God's scattering of the peoples is a punishment, in fact it is also a means of redemption. From the beginning, God intended people to disperse across the world. "Be fruitful and multiply, and fill the earth" (Gen. 1:28). By scattering people after the fall of the tower, God put people back on the path of filling the earth, ultimately resulting in the beautiful array of peoples and cultures that populate it today. If people had completed the tower under a singularity of malicious intent and social tyranny, with the result that "nothing that they propose to do will now be impossible for them" (Gen. 11:6), we can only imagine the horrors they would have worked in their pride and strength of sin. The scale of evil worked by humanity in the twentieth and twenty-first centuries gives a mere glimpse of what people might do if all things were possible without dependence on God. As Dostoevsky put it, "Without God and the future life, it means everything is permitted."[18] Sometimes God will not give us our way because his mercy toward us is too great.

What can we learn from the incident of the Tower of Babel for our work today? The specific offense the builders committed was disobeying God's command to spread out and fill the earth. They centralized not only their geographical dwellings, but also their culture, language, and

---

[17] Waltke, 182–183.

[18] Fyodor Dostoevsky, *The Brothers Karamazov*, trans. Richard Pevear and Larissa Volokhonsky (San Francisco: North Point Press, 1990), 589.

institutions. In their ambition to do one great thing ("make a name for ourselves" [Gen. 11:4]), they stifled the breadth of endeavor that ought to come with the varieties of gifts, services, activities, and functions with which God endows people (1 Cor. 12:4–11). Although God wants people to work together for the common good (Gen. 2:18; 1 Cor. 12:7), he has not created us to accomplish it through centralization and accumulation of power. He warned the people of Israel against the dangers of concentrating power in a king (1 Sam. 8:10–18). God has prepared for us a divine king, Christ our Lord, and under him there is no place for great concentration of power in human individuals, institutions, or governments.

So, then, we could expect Christian leaders and institutions to be careful to disperse authority and to favor coordination, common goals and values, and democratic decision-making instead of concentration of power. But in many cases Christians have sought something different, the same kind of concentration of power that tyrants and authoritarians seek, though with more benevolent goals. In this mode, Christian legislators seek just as much control over the populace, though with the object of enforcing piety or morality. In this mode, Christian businesspeople seek as much oligopoly as others, though for the purpose of enhancing quality, customer service, or ethical behavior. In this mode, Christian educators seek as little freedom of thought as authoritarian educators do, though with the intent of enforcing moral expression, kindness, and sound doctrine.

As laudable as all these goals are, the events of the Tower of Babel suggest they are often dangerously misguided (God's later warning to Israel about the dangers of having a king echo this suggestion; see 1 Sam. 8:10–18). In a world where even those in Christ still struggle with sin, God's idea of good dominion (by humans) seems to be to disperse people, power, authority, and capabilities, rather than concentrating it in one person, institution, party, or movement. Of course, some situations demand decisive exercise of power by one person or a small group. A pilot would be foolish to take a passenger vote about which runway to land on. But could it be that more often than we realize, when we are in positions of power, God is calling us to disperse, delegate, authorize, and train others, rather than exercising it all ourselves? Doing so is messy, inefficient, hard to measure, risky, and anxiety-inducing. But it may be exactly what God calls Christian leaders to do in many situations.

Conclusions from Genesis 1–11

In the opening chapters of the Bible, God creates the world and brings us forth to join him in further creativity. He creates us in his image to exercise dominion, to be fruitful and multiply, to receive his provision, to work in relationship with him and with other people, and to observe the limits of his creation. He equips us with resources, abilities, and communities to fulfill these tasks, and gives us the pattern of working toward them six days out of seven. He gives us the freedom to do these things out of love for him and his creation, which also gives us the freedom to *not* do the things for which he created us. To our lasting injury, the first human beings chose to violate God's mandate, and people have continued to choose disobedience—to a greater or lesser degree—to the present day. As a result, our work has become less productive, more toilsome, and less satisfying, and our relationships and work are diminished and at times even destructive.

Nonetheless, God continues to call us to work, equipping us and providing for our needs. And many people have the opportunity to do good, creative, fulfilling work that provides for their needs and contributes to a thriving community. The Fall has made the work that began in the Garden of Eden more necessary, not less. Although Christians have sometimes misunderstood this, God did not respond to the Fall by withdrawing from the material world and confining his interests to the spiritual, nor is it possible to divorce the material and the spiritual anyway. Work, including the relationships that pervade it and the limits that bless it, remains God's gift to us, even if it is severely marred by the conditions of existence after the Fall.

At the same time, God is always at work to redeem his creation from the effects of the Fall. Genesis 4–11 begins the story of how God's power is working to order and reorder the world and its inhabitants. God is sovereign over the created world and over every living creature, human and otherwise. He continues to tend to his own image in humanity. But he does not tolerate human efforts to "be like God" (Gen. 3:5) in order either to acquire excessive power or to substitute self-sufficiency for relationship with God. Those, like Noah, who receive work as a gift from God and do their best to work according to his direction, find blessing and fruitfulness in their work. Those like the builders of the tower of Babel, who try to grasp power and success on their own terms, find violence and frustration, especially when their work turns toward harming others. Like all the characters in these chapters of Genesis, we face the choice of whether to work with God or in opposition to him. How the story of God's work to redeem his creation will turn out is not told in the book of Genesis, but we know that it ultimately leads to the restoration of creation—including the work of God's creatures—as God has intended from the beginning.

Genesis 12–50 and Work

Introduction to Genesis 12–50 and Work

Genesis chapters 12 through 50 tell about the life and work of Abraham, Sarah, and their descendants. God called Abraham, Sarah, and their family to leave their homeland for the new country that God would show them. Along the way, God promised to make them into a great nation: "In you all the families of the earth shall be blessed" (Gen. 12:3). As Abraham's spiritual descendants, blessed by this great family and brought to faith through their descendant Jesus Christ, we are called to follow in the footsteps of the faith of the father and mother of all who truly believe (Rom. 4:11; Gal. 3:7, 29).

The story of Abraham and Sarah's family is perfused with work. Their work encompasses nearly every facet of the work of seminomadic peoples in the ancient Near East. At every point, they face crucial questions about *how* to live and work in faithful observance of God's covenant. They struggle to make a living, endure social upheaval, raise children in safety, and remain faithful to God in the midst of a broken world, much as we do today. They find that God is faithful to his promise to bless them in all circumstances, although they themselves prove faithless again and again.

But the purpose of God's covenant is not merely to bless Abraham's family in a hostile world. Instead, he intends to bless the whole world through these people. This task is beyond the abilities of Abraham's family, who fall again and again into pride, self-centeredness, foolhardiness, anger, and every other malady to which fallen people are apt. We recognize ourselves in them in this aspect too. Yet by God's grace, they retain a core of faithfulness to the covenant, and God works through the work of these people, beset with faults, to bring unimaginable blessings to the world. Like theirs, our work also brings blessings to those around us because in our work we participate in God's work in the world.

When seen from beginning to end, it is clear that Genesis is a literary whole, yet it falls into two distinct parts. The first part (Gen. 1–11) deals with God's creation of the universe, then traces the development of humanity from the original couple in the Garden of Eden to the three sons of Noah and their families who spread out into the world. This section closes on a low note when people from the whole world gather in unity to construct a city to make a name for themselves and instead experience defeat, confusion, and scattering as judgment from God. The second part (Gen. 12–50) opens with the Lord's call to the particular man, Abraham.[1] God called him to leave his homeland and family to set out for a new life and land, which he did. The rest of the book follows the life of this man and the next three generations who begin to experience the fulfillment of the divine promises made to their father Abraham.

Abraham (Genesis 12:1–25:11)

Abraham's Faithfulness Contrasted with the Faithlessness of Babel (Genesis 12:1–3)

God called Abraham into a covenant of faithful service, as is told at the beginning of Genesis 12. By leaving the territory of his faithless extended family and following God's call, Abraham distinguished himself sharply from his distant relatives who stayed in Mesopotamia and attempted to build the Tower of Babel, as was told at the close of Genesis 11. The comparison between Abraham's immediate family in chapter 12 and Noah's other descendants in chapter 11 highlights five contrasts.

First, Abraham puts his trust in God's guidance, rather than on human device. In contrast, the tower builders believed that by their own skill and ingenuity, they could devise a tower "with its top in the heavens" (Gen. 11:4), and in so doing achieve significance and security in a way that usurped God's authority.[2]

---

[1] God's changing of Abram's name to Abraham (17:5) is important in the book of Genesis, but not particularly relevant to the topic of work. We will refer to him throughout by his familiar name, Abraham, and likewise, for Sarai/Sarah.

[2] Bruce K. Waltke, *Genesis: A Commentary* (Grand Rapids: Zondervan, 2001), 182–83.

Second, the builders sought to make a name for themselves (Gen. 11:4), but Abraham trusted God's promise that *he* would make Abraham's name great (Gen. 12:2). The difference was not the desire to achieve greatness, per se, but the desire to pursue fame on one's own terms. God did indeed make Abraham famous, not for his own sake but in order that "all the families of the earth shall be blessed" (Gen. 12:3). The builders sought fame for their own sake, yet they remain anonymous to this day.

Third, Abraham was willing to go wherever God led him, while the builders attempted to huddle together in their accustomed space. They created their project out of fear that they would be scattered across the earth (Gen. 11:4). In doing so, they rejected God's purpose for humanity to "fill the earth" (Gen. 1:28). They seem to have feared that spreading out in an apparently hostile world would be too difficult for them. They were creative and technologically innovative (Gen. 11:3), but they were unwilling to fully embrace God's purpose for them to "be fruitful and multiply" (Gen. 1:28). Their fear of engaging the fullness of creation coincided with their decision to substitute human ingenuity for God's guidance and grace. When we cease to aspire for more than we can attain on our own, our aspirations become insignificant.

By contrast, God made Abraham into the original entrepreneur, always moving on to fresh endeavors in new locations. God called him away from the city of Haran toward the land of Canaan where Abraham would never settle into a fixed address. He was known as a "wandering Aramean" (Deut. 26:5). This lifestyle was inherently more God-centered in that Abraham would have to depend on God's word and leadership in order to find his significance, security, and success. As Hebrews 11:8 puts it, he had to "set out, not knowing where he was going." In the world of work, believers must perceive the contrast in these two fundamental orientations. All work entails planning and building. Ungodly work stems from the desire to depend on no one but ourselves, and it restricts itself narrowly to benefit only ourselves and the few who may be close to us. Godly work is willing to depend on God's guidance and authority, and it desires to grow widely as a blessing to all the world.

Fourth, Abraham was willing to let God lead him into new relationships. While the tower builders sought to close themselves off in a guarded fortress, Abraham trusted God's promise that his family would grow into a great nation (Gen. 12:2; 15:5). Though they lived among strangers in the land of Canaan (Gen. 17:8), they had good relationships with those they came in contact with (Gen. 21:22–34; 23:1–12). This is the gift of community. Another key theme thus emerges for the theology of work: God's design is for people to work in healthy networks of relationship.

Finally, Abraham was blessed with the patience to take a long-term view. God's promises were to be realized in the time of Abraham's offspring, not in the time of Abraham himself. The Apostle Paul interpreted the "offspring" to be Jesus (Gal. 3:19), meaning that the payoff date was more than a thousand years in the future. In fact, the promise to Abraham will not be fulfilled completely until the return of Christ (Matt. 24:30–31). Its progress cannot be adequately measured by quarterly reports! The tower builders, in comparison, took no thought for how their project would affect future generations, and God criticized them explicitly for this lapse (Gen. 11:6).

In sum, God promised Abraham fame, fruitfulness, and good relationships, by which meant he and his family would bless the whole world, and in due course be blessed themselves beyond imagining (Gen. 22:17). Unlike others, Abraham realized that an attempt to grasp such things on his own power would be futile, or worse. Instead, he trusted God and depended every day on God's guidance and provision (Gen. 22:8–14). Although these promises were not fully realized by the end of Genesis, they initiated the covenant between God and the people of God through which the redemption of the world will come to completion in the day of Christ (Phil. 1:10).

God promised a new land to Abraham's family. Making use of land requires many kinds of work, so a gift of land reiterates that work is an essential sphere of God's concern. Working the land would require occupational skills of shepherding, tent-making, military protection, and the production of a wide array of goods and services. Moreover, Abraham's descendants would become a populous nation whose members would be as innumerable as the stars in the sky. This would require the work of developing personal relationships, parenting, politics, diplomacy and administration, education, the healing arts, and other social occupations. To bring such blessings to all the earth, God called Abraham and his descendants to "walk before me, and be blameless" (Gen. 17:1). This required the work of worship, atonement, discipleship, and other religious occupations. Joseph's work was to create a solution responding to the impact of the famine, and sometimes our work is to heal brokenness. All these types of work, and the workers who engage in them, come under God's authority, guidance, and provision.

The Pastoral Lifestyle of Abraham and His Family (Genesis 12:4–7)

When Abraham left his home in Haran and set out for the land of Canaan, his family was probably already quite large by modern standards. We know that his wife Sarah and his nephew Lot came with him, but so did an unspecified number of people and possessions (Gen. 12:5). Soon Abraham would become very wealthy, having acquired servants and livestock as well as silver and gold (Gen. 12:16; 13:2). He received people and animals from Pharaoh during his stay in Egypt, and the precious metals would have been the result of commercial transactions, indicating the Lord as the ultimate one to bestow blessing.[3] Evidence that both Abraham and Lot had become successful lies in the quarreling that broke out between the herders for each family over the inability of the land to support so many grazing animals. Eventually, the two had to part company in order to support their business activities (Gen. 13:11).

Anthropological studies of this period and region suggest the families in these narratives practiced a mix of seminomadic pastoralism and herdsman husbandry (Gen. 13:5–12; 21:25–34; 26:17–33; 29:1–10; 37:12–17).[4] These families needed seasonal mobility and thus lived in tents of leather, felt, and wool. They owned property that could be borne by donkeys or, if one was wealthy enough, also camels. Finding the balance between the optimal availability of usable pasture land and water required good judgment and intimate knowledge of weather and geography. The wetter months of October through March afforded grazing on the lower plains, while in the warmer and drier months of April through September the shepherds would take their flocks to higher

---

[3] Waltke, 216.

[4] Victor H. Matthews, "Nomadism, Pastoralism" in *Eerdmans Dictionary of the Bible*, eds. David Noel Freedman, Allen C. Myers, and Astrid B. Beck (Grand Rapids: Wm. B. Eerdmans, 2000), 972.

elevations for greener vegetation and flowing springs.[5] Because a family could not be entirely supported through shepherding, it was necessary to practice local agriculture and trade with those living in more settled communities.[6]

Pastoral nomads cared for sheep and goats to obtain milk and meat (Gen. 18:7–8; 27:9; 31:38), wool, and other goods made from animal products such as leather. Donkeys carried loads (Gen. 42:26), and camels were especially suited for long-range travel (Gen. 24:10, 64; 31:17). The skills required to maintain these herds would have involved grazing and watering, birthing, treating the sick and injured, protecting animals from predators and thieves, as well as locating strays.

Fluctuations in weather and the size of growth in the population of the flocks and herds would have affected the economy of the region. Weaker groups of shepherds could easily become displaced or assimilated at the expense of those who needed more territory for their expanding holdings.[7] Profit from shepherding was not stored as accumulated savings or investments on behalf of the owners and managers, but shared throughout the family. By the same token, the effects of hardship due to famine conditions would have been felt by all. While individuals certainly had their own responsibilities and were accountable for their actions, the communal nature of the family business generally stands apart from our contemporary culture of personal achievement and the expectation to show ever-increasing profits. Social responsibility would have been a daily concern, not an option.

In this way of life, shared values were essential for survival. Mutual dependence among the members of a family or tribe and awareness of their common ancestry would have resulted in great solidarity, as well as vengeful hostility toward anyone who would disrupt it (Gen. 34:25–31).[8]

---

[5] John H. Walton, Victor H. Matthews, and Mark W. Chavalas, *The IVP Bible Background Commentary: Old Testament* (Downers Grove, IL: IVP Academic, 2000), 44.

[6] Matthews, "Nomadism, Pastoralism," 971.

[7] T. C. Mitchell, "Nomads," in *New Bible Dictionary*, 3rd ed., eds. I. Howard Marshall, A. R. Millard, J. I. Packer, and D. J. Wiseman (Downers Grove, IL: InterVarsity Press, 1996), 828–31.

[8] Mitchell, 829.

Leaders had to know how to tap the wisdom of the group in order to make sound decisions about where to travel, how long to stay, and how to divide the herds.[9] They must have had ways of communicating with shepherds who took the flocks away at some distance (Gen. 37:12–14). Conflict-resolution skills were necessary to settle inevitable disputes over grazing land and water rights to wells and springs (Gen. 26:19–22). The high mobility of life in the country and one's vulnerability to marauders made hospitality much more than a courtesy. It was generally considered a requirement of decent people to offer refreshment, food, and lodging.[10]

The patriarchal narratives repeatedly mention the great wealth of Abraham, Isaac, and Jacob (Gen. 13:2; 26:13; 31:1). Shepherding and animal husbandry were honorable fields of work and could be lucrative, and Abraham's family became very wealthy. For example, to soften the attitude of his offended brother Esau prior to their meeting after a long time, Jacob was able to select from his property a gift of at least 550 animals: 200 female goats with 20 males, 200 ewes with 20 rams, 30 female camels with their calves, 40 cows with 10 bulls, and 20 female donkeys with 10 males (Gen. 32:13–15). It is therefore fitting that at the end of his life when Jacob conferred blessings on his sons, he testified that the God of his fathers had been "my shepherd all my life to this day" (Gen. 48:15). Although many passages in the Bible warn that wealth is often inimical to faithfulness (e.g., Jer. 17:11, Hab. 2:5, Matt. 6:24), Abraham's experience shows that God's faithfulness can be expressed in prosperity as well. As we shall see, this is by no means a promise that God's people should expect prosperity on a continuous basis.

Abraham's Journey Begins with Disaster in Egypt (Genesis 12:8–13:2)

The initial results of Abraham's journeys were not promising. There was fierce competition for the land (Gen. 12:6), and Abraham spent a long time trying to find a niche to occupy (Gen. 12:8–9). Eventually,

---

[9] Matthews, "Nomadism, Pastoralism," 972.

[10] Julian Pitt-Rivers, "The Stranger, the Guest, and the Hostile Host: Introduction to the Study of the Laws of Hospitality," in *Contributions to Mediterranean Sociology*, ed. John G. Peristiany (Paris: Mouton, 1968), 13–30.

deteriorating economic conditions forced him to pull out entirely and take his family to Egypt, hundreds of miles away from the land of God's promise (Gen. 12:10).

As an economic migrant to Egypt, Abraham's vulnerable position made him fearful. He feared that the Egyptians might murder him to obtain his beautiful wife, Sarah. To prevent this, Abraham told Sarah to claim that she was his sister rather than his wife. As Abraham anticipated, one of the Egyptians—Pharaoh, in fact—did desire Sarah and she "was taken into Pharaoh's house" (Gen 12:15). As a result, "the Lord afflicted Pharaoh and his house with great plagues" (Gen. 12:17). When Pharaoh found out the reason—that he had taken another man's wife—he returned Sarah to Abraham and immediately ordered them both to depart his country (Gen. 12:18–19). Nevertheless, Pharaoh enriched them with sheep and cattle, male and female donkeys, male and female servants as well as camels (Gen. 12:16), and silver and gold (Gen. 13:2), a further indication that Abraham's wealth (Gen. 13:2) was due to royal gifts.[11]

This incident dramatically indicates both the moral quandaries posed by great disparities in wealth and poverty and the dangers of losing faith in the face of such problems. Abraham and Sarah were fleeing starvation. It may be hard to imagine being so desperately poor or afraid that a family would subject its female members to sexual liaisons in order to survive economically, but even today millions face this choice. Pharaoh berates Abraham for taking this course of action, yet God's response to a later, similar incident (Gen. 20:7, 17) shows more of compassion than judgment.

On the other hand, Abraham had received God's direct promise, "I will make of you a great nation" (Gen. 12:2). Did his faith in God to make good on his promises fail so quickly? Did survival really require him to lie and allow his wife to become a concubine, or would God have provided another way? Abraham's fears seem to have made him forget his trust in God's faithfulness. Similarly, people in difficult situations often convince themselves that they have no choice but to do something they regard as wrong. However, unpleasant choices, no matter our feelings about them, are not the same as having no choice at all.

---

[11] Waltke, 216.

Abraham and Lot Parted (Genesis 13:3–18)

When Abraham and his family reentered Canaan and came to the region around Bethel, the friction that erupted between the herders of Abraham and those of his nephew Lot posed Abraham with a choice regarding the scarcity of land. A division had to be made, and Abraham took the risk of offering Lot first choice of the real estate. The central ridge of land in Canaan is rocky and does support much vegetation for grazing. Lot's eye fell to the east and the plain around the Jordan River, which he regarded as "like the garden of the LORD," so he chose this better portion for himself (Gen. 13:10). Abraham's trust in God released him from the anxiety of looking out for himself. No matter how Abraham and Lot would prosper in the future, the fact that Abraham let Lot make the choice displayed generosity and established trust between him and Lot.

Generosity is a positive trait in both personal and business relationships. Perhaps nothing establishes trust and good relationships as solidly as generosity. Colleagues, customers, suppliers, even adversaries, respond strongly to generosity and remember it for a long time. When Zacchaeus the tax collector welcomed Jesus into his home and promised to give half of his possessions to the poor and to repay fourfold those he had cheated, Jesus called him a "son of Abraham" for his generosity and fruit of repentance (Luke 19:9). Zacchaeus was responding, of course, to the relational generosity of Jesus, who had unexpectedly, and uncharacteristically for the people of that time, opened his heart to a detested tax collector.

Abraham and Sarah's Hospitality (Genesis 18:1–15)

The story of Abraham and Sarah's generous hospitality to three visitors who came to them by the oaks of Mamre is told in Genesis 18. Seminomadic life in the country would often bring people from different families into contact with one another, and the character of Canaan as a natural land bridge between Asia and Africa made it a popular trade route. In the absence of a formal industry of hospitality, people living in cities and encampments had a social obligation to welcome strangers. From Old Testament descriptions and other Ancient Near Eastern texts, Matthews derived seven codes of conduct defining what counts for good hospitality that maintains the honor of persons, their households, and communities by receiving and offering protection to strangers.[12] Around a settlement was a zone in which the individuals and the town were obliged to show hospitality.

1. In this zone, the villagers were responsible to offer hospitality to strangers.

2. The stranger must be transformed from being a potential threat to becoming an ally by the offer of hospitality.

3. Only the male head of household or a male citizen of a town or village may offer the invitation of hospitality.

4. The invitation may include a time span statement for the period of hospitality, but this can then be extended, if agreeable to both parties, on the renewed invitation of the host.

5. The stranger has the right of refusal, but this could be considered an affront to the honor of the host and could be a cause for immediate hostilities or conflict.

6. Once the invitation is accepted, the roles of the host and the guest are set by the rules of custom. The guest must not ask for anything. The host provides the best he has available, despite what may be modestly offered in the initial offer of hospitality. The guest is expected to reciprocate immediately with news, predictions of good fortune, or expressions of gratitude for what he has been given, and praise of the host's generosity and honor. The host must not ask personal questions of the guest. These matters can only be volunteered by the guest.

7. The guest remains under the protection of the host until the guest has left the zone of obligation of the host.

---

[12] Abstracted from Victor H. Matthews, "Hospitality and Hostility in Judges 4," *Biblical Theology Bulletin* 21, no. 1 (1991): 13–15.

This episode provides the background for the New Testament command, "Do not neglect to show hospitality to strangers, for by doing that some have entertained angels without knowing it" (Heb. 13:2).

Hospitality and generosity are often underappreciated in Christian circles. Yet the Bible pictures the kingdom of heaven as a generous, even extravagant, banquet (Isa. 25:6–9; Matt. 22:2–4). Hospitality fosters good relationships, and Abraham and Sarah's hospitality provides an early biblical insight to the way relationships and sharing a meal go hand in hand. These strangers reaped a deeper understanding of each other by sharing a meal and an extended encounter. This remains true today. When people break bread together, or enjoy recreation or entertainment, they often grow to understand and appreciate each other better. Better working relationships and more effective communication are often fruits of hospitality.

In Abraham and Sarah's time, hospitality was almost always offered in the host's home. Today, this is not always possible, or even desirable, and the hospitality industry has come into being to facilitate and offer hospitality in a wide variety of ways. If you want to offer hospitality and your home is too small or your cooking skills too limited, you might take someone to a restaurant or hotel and enjoy camaraderie and deepening relationships there. Hospitality workers would assist you in offering hospitality. Moreover, hospitality workers have in their own right the opportunity to refresh people, create good relationships, provide shelter, and serve others much as Jesus did when he made wine (John 2:1–11) and washed feet (John 13:3–11). The hospitality industry accounts for 9 percent of the world gross domestic product and employs 98 million people,[13] including many of the less-skilled and immigrant workers who represent a rapidly growing portion of the Christian church. Even more engage in unpaid hospitality, offering it to others as an act of love, friendship, compassion, and social engagement. The example of Abraham and Sarah shows that this work can be profoundly important as a service to God and humanity. How could we do more to encourage each other to be generous in hospitality, no matter what our professions are?

---

[13] World Travel and Tourism Council, *Travel and Tourism Economic Impact 2012, World* (London: 2012), 1.

Abraham's Dispute with Abimelech (Genesis 20:1–16; 21:22–34)

When Abraham and Sarah entered the country of King Abimelech, Abimelech inadvertently violated the rules of hospitality, and as restitution awarded Abraham free grazing rights to whatever land he wanted (Gen. 20:1–16). Subsequently, a dispute erupted over a certain well of water that Abraham had originally dug but Abimelech's servants later seized (Gen. 21:25). Seemingly unaware of the situation, when Abimelech heard of the complaint he entered into a sworn agreement initiated by Abraham, a treaty that publicly acknowledged Abraham's right to the well and therefore his continued business activity in the region (Gen. 21:27–31).

Elsewhere we have seen Abraham give up what was rightfully his to keep (Gen. 14:22–24). Yet here, Abraham doggedly protects what is his. The narrator does not imply that Abraham is again wavering in faith, for the account concludes with worship (Gen. 21:33). Rather, he is a model of a wise and hard-working person who conducts his business openly and makes fair use of appropriate legal protections. In the business of shepherding, access to water was essential. Abraham could not have continued to provide for his animals, workers, and family without it. The fact of Abraham's protection of water rights is therefore important, as well as the means by which he secured those rights.

Like Abraham, people in every kind of work have to discern when to act generously to benefit others, and when to protect resources and rights for the benefit of themselves or their organizations. There is no set of rules and regulations that can lead us to a mechanical answer. In all situations, we are stewards of God's resources, though it may not always be clear whether God's purposes are better served by giving away resources or by protecting them. But Abraham's example highlights an aspect that is easy to forget. The decision is not only a matter of who is in the right, but also of how the decision will affect our relationships with those around us. In the earlier case of dividing the land with Lot, Abraham's willing surrender of first choice to Lot laid the ground work for a good long-term working relationship. In the present case of his demanding access to the well according to his treaty rights, Abraham ensured the resources needed to keep his enterprise functioning. In addition, it seems that Abraham's forcefulness actually improved relationships between himself and Abimelech. Remember that the dispute between them arose because Abraham *didn't* assert his position when first encountering Abimelech (Gen. 20).

A Burial Plot for Sarah (Genesis 23:1–20)

When Sarah died, Abraham engaged in an exemplary negotiation to buy a burial plot for her. He conducted the negotiations openly and honestly in the presence of witnesses, taking due care for the needs of both himself and the seller (Gen. 23:10–13, 16, 18). The property in question is clearly identified (Gen. 23:9), and Abraham's intended use as a burial site is mentioned several times (Gen. 23:4, 6, 9, 11, 13, 15, 20). The dialogue of the negotiation is exceptionally clear, socially proper, and transparent. It takes place at the gate of the city where business was done in public. Abraham initiates the request for a real-estate transaction. The local Hittites freely offer a choice tomb. Abraham demurs, asking them to contact a certain owner of a field with a cave appropriate for a burial site so that he could buy it for the "full price." Ephron, the owner, overheard the request and offered the field as a gift. Because this would not have resulted in Abraham having permanent claim, he politely offered to pay market value for it. Contrary to the staged bargaining that was typical of business transactions (Prov. 20:14), Abraham immediately agreed to Ephron's price and paid it "according to the weights current among the merchants" (Gen. 23:16). This expression meant that the deal conformed to the standard for silver used in real-estate sales.[14] Abraham could have been so wealthy that he did not need to bargain, and/or he could have been wishing to buy a measure of good will along with the land. Additionally, he could have wished to forestall any questioning of the sale and of his right to the land. In the end, he received the title deed to the property with its cave and trees (Gen. 23:17–20). It was the important burial site of Sarah and later Abraham himself, as well as that of Isaac and Rebekah, and Jacob and Leah.

In this matter, Abraham's actions modeled core values of integrity, transparency, and business acumen. He honored his wife by mourning

---

[14] Walton, Matthews, and Chavalas, 55.

and properly caring for her remains. He understood his status in the land and treated its long-term residents with respect. He transacted business openly and honestly, doing so in front of witnesses. He communicated clearly. He was sensitive to the negotiating process and politely avoided accepting the land as a gift. He swiftly paid the agreed amount. He used the site only for the purpose he stated during the negotiations. He thus maintained good relationships with everyone involved.

Isaac (Genesis 21:1–35:29)

Isaac was the son of a great father and the father of a great son, but he himself left a mixed record. In contrast to the sustained prominence that Genesis gives to Abraham, the life of Isaac is split apart and told as attachments to the stories of Abraham and Jacob. The characterization of Isaac's life falls into two parts: one decidedly positive and one negative. Lessons regarding work may be derived from each.

On the positive side, Isaac's life was a gift from God. Abraham and Sarah treasured him and passed on their faith and values, and God reiterated Abrahamic promises to him. Isaac's faith and obedience when Abraham bound him as a sacrifice is exemplary, for he must have truly believed what his father had told him: "God himself will provide the lamb for a burnt offering, my son" (Gen. 22:8). Throughout most of his life, Isaac followed in Abraham's footsteps. Expressing the same faith, Isaac prayed for his childless wife (Gen. 25:21). Just as Abraham gave an honorable burial to Sarah, together Isaac and Ishmael buried their father (Gen. 25:9). Isaac became such a successful farmer and shepherd that the local population envied him and asked him to move away (Gen. 26:12–16). He reopened the wells that had been dug during the time of his father, which again became subjects of disputes with the people of Gerar concerning water rights (Gen. 26:17–21). Like Abraham, Isaac entered into a sworn agreement with Abimelech about treating one another fairly (Gen. 26:26–31). The writer of Hebrews noted that by faith Isaac lived in tents and blessed both Jacob and Esau (Heb. 11:8–10, 20). In short, Isaac had inherited a large family business and considerable wealth. Like his father, he did not hoard it, but fulfilled the role that God had chosen for him to pass on the blessing that would extend to all nations.

In these positive events, Isaac was a responsible son who learned how to lead the family and to manage its business in a way that honored the example of his capable and godly father. Abraham's diligence in preparing a successor and instituting long-lasting values brought blessing to his enterprise once again. When Isaac was a hundred years old, it became his turn to designate his successor by passing on the family blessing. Although he would live another eighty years, this bestowal of the blessing was the last meaningful thing about Isaac recorded in the book of Genesis. Regrettably, he nearly failed in this task. Somehow he remained oblivious to God's revelation to his wife that, contrary to normal custom, the younger son, Jacob, was to become head of the family instead of the older (Gen. 25:23). It took a clever ploy by Rebecca and Jacob to put Isaac back on track to fulfill God's purposes.

Maintaining the family business meant that the fundamental structure of the family had to be intact. It was the father's job to secure this. Foreign to most of us today, two related customs were prominent in Isaac's family, the birthright (Gen. 25:31) and the blessing (Gen. 27:4). The birthright conferred the right to inherit a larger share of the father's estate both in terms of goods and land. Though sometimes the birthright was transferred, it was typically reserved for the firstborn son. The specific laws concerning it varied, but it seems to have been a stable feature of Ancient Near Eastern culture. The blessing was the corresponding invocation of prosperity from God and succession of leadership in the household. Esau wrongly believed that he could surrender the birthright yet still get the blessing (Heb. 12:16–17). Jacob recognized that they were inseparable. With both in his possession, Jacob would assume the right to carry on the heritage of the family economically, socially, and in terms of its faith as well. Central to the unfolding plot of Genesis, the blessing entailed not only receiving the covenantal promises that God had made to Abraham but also mediating them to the next generation.

Isaac's failure to recognize that Jacob should receive the birthright and the blessing arose from Isaac putting his personal comfort above the needs of the family organization. He preferred Esau because he loved the wild game that Esau the hunter got for him. Although Esau did not value the birthright as much as a single meal—meaning that he was neither fit for nor interested in the position of leading the enterprise—Isaac wanted Esau to have it. The private circumstances under which Isaac gave the blessing suggests that he knew such an act would invite criticism. The only positive aspect of this episode is that Isaac's faith led him to recognize that the divine blessing he had mistakenly given to Jacob was irrevocable. Generously, this is what the writer of Hebrews remembered him for. "By faith Isaac invoked blessings for the future on Jacob and Esau" (Heb. 11:20). God had chosen Isaac to perpetuate this blessing and tenaciously worked his will through him, despite Isaac's ill-informed intentions.

Isaac's example reminds us that immersing ourselves in our private perspective too deeply can lead us into serious errors of judgment. Each of us is tempted by personal comforts, prejudices, and private interests to lose sight of the wider importance of our work. Our weakness may be for accolades, financial security, conflict avoidance, inappropriate relationships, short-term rewards, or other personal benefits that may be at odds with doing our work to fulfill God's purposes. There are both individual and systemic factors involved. On the individual level, Isaac's bias toward Esau is repeated today when those in power choose to promote people based on bias, whether recognized or not. On the systemic level, there are still many organizations that enable leaders to hire, fire, and promote people at their own whim, rather than developing successors and subordinates in a long-term, coordinated, accountable process. Whether the abuses are individual or systemic, merely resolving to do better or to change organizational processes is not an effective solution. Instead, both individuals and organizations need to be transformed by God's grace to put the truly important ahead of the personally beneficial.

Jacob (Genesis 25:19–49:33)

The names Abraham, Isaac, and Jacob appear often as a group, because they all received covenantal promises from God and shared the same faith. But Jacob was far different from his grandfather Abraham. Ever wily, Jacob lived much of his life according to his craftiness and ingenious wit. No stranger to conflict, Jacob was driven by a passion to get what he wanted for himself. This struggle was hard work indeed and eventually led him to the signature point of his existence, a wrestling match with a mysterious man in whom Jacob saw God face to face (Gen. 32:24, 30). Out of his weakness, Jacob called out in faith for God's blessing and was transformed by grace.

Jacob's occupational life as a shepherd is of interest to the theology of work. It takes on added significance, however, when set in the larger context of his life that moves in broad stokes from alienation to reconciliation. We have seen with Abraham that the work he did was an inseparable part of his sense of purpose stemming from his relationship with God. The same is true of Jacob, and the lesson holds for us as well.

Jacob's Unethical Procurement of Esau's Birthright and Blessing (Genesis 25:19–34; 26:34–28:9)

Although it was God's plan for Jacob to succeed Isaac (Gen. 25:23), Rebekah and Jacob's use of deception and theft to obtain it put the family in serious jeopardy. Their unethical treatment of husband and brother in order to secure their future at the expense of trusting God resulted in a deep and long-lived alienation in the family enterprise.

God's covenantal blessings were gifts to be received, not grasped. They carried the responsibility that they be used for others, not hoarded. This was lost on Jacob. Though Jacob had faith (unlike his brother Esau), he depended on his own abilities to secure the rights he valued. Jacob exploited hungry Esau into selling him the birthright (Gen. 25:29–34). It is good that Jacob valued the birthright, but deeply faithless for him to secure it for himself, especially in the manner he did so. Following the advice of his mother Rebekah (who also pursued right ends by wrong means), Jacob deceived his father. His life as a fugitive from the family testifies to the odious nature of his behavior.

Jacob began a long period of genuine belief in God's covenantal promises, yet he fails to live in confidence of what God will do for him. Mature, godly people who have learned to let their faith transform their choices (and not the other way around) are in a position to serve out of their strength. Courageous and astute decisions that result in success may be rightly praised for their sheer effectiveness. But when profit comes at the expense of exploiting and deceiving others, something is wrong. Beyond the fact that unethical methods are wrong in themselves, they also may reveal the fundamental fears of those who employ them. Jacob's relentless drive to gain benefits for himself reveals how his fears made him resistant to God's transforming grace. To the extent we come to believe in God's promises, we will be less inclined toward manipulating circumstances to benefit ourselves; we always need to be aware of how readily we can fool even ourselves about the purity of our motives.

Jacob Gains His Fortune (Genesis 30–31)

In escaping from Esau, Jacob ended up at the family farm of Laban, his mother's brother. Jacob worked for Laban for twenty-one frustrating years, during which Laban broke a string of promises to him. Despite this, Jacob succeeded in marrying two of Laban's daughters and starting a family. Jacob wanted to return home, but Laban convinced him to stay on and work for him with the promise that he could "name [his own] wages" (Gen. 30:28). Clearly Jacob had been a good worker, and Laban had been blessed through his association with Jacob.

During this time Jacob had learned the trade of breeding animals, and he used this skill to get back at Laban. Through his breeding techniques, he was able to gain a great deal of wealth at Laban's expense. It got to the point that Laban's sons were complaining that "Jacob has taken all that was our father's; he has gained all this wealth from what belonged to our father" (Gen. 31:1–2). Jacob noticed that Laban's attitude toward him was not what it had been. Yet Jacob claimed the gain as a gift from God, saying, "If the God of my father, the God of Abraham and the Fear of Isaac, had not been on my side, surely now you would have sent me away empty-handed" (Gen. 31:42).

Jacob felt that he had been dealt with poorly by Laban. His response, through his schemes, was to make yet another enemy, similar to the way he had exploited Esau. This is a repeated pattern in Jacob's life. It seems that anything was fair game, and although he ostensibly gave God the credit, it is clear that he did these things as a schemer. We don't see much integration of his faith with his work at this point, and it is interesting that when Hebrews recognizes Jacob as a man of faith, it mentions only his actions at the end of his life (Heb. 11:21).

Jacob's Transformation and Reconciliation with Esau (Genesis 32–33)

After increasing tension with his father-in-law and a business separation in which both men acted less than admirably, Jacob left Laban. Having obtained his position by Laban's dirty trick years ago, Jacob now saw an opportunity to legitimize his position by coming to an agreement with his estranged brother Esau. But he expected the negotiations to be tense. Wracked with fear that Esau would come to the meeting with his four hundred armed men, Jacob split his family and animals into two groups to help ensure some measure of survival. He prayed for protection and sent an enormous gift of animals on ahead of him to pacify Esau before the encounter. But the night before he arrived at the meeting point, the trickster Jacob was visited by a shadowy figure out to play a surprise on *him*. God himself attacked him in the form of a strongman, against whom Jacob was forced to wrestle all night. God, it turns out, is not only the God of worship and religion, but the God of work and family enterprises, and he is not above turning the tables on a slippery operator like Jacob. He pressed his advantage to the point of permanently injuring Jacob's hip, yet Jacob in his weakness said that he would not give up until his attacker had blessed him.

This became the turning point of Jacob's life. He had known years of struggling with people, yet all along Jacob had also been struggling in his relationship with God. Here at last, he met God and received his blessing amid the struggle. Jacob received a new name, Israel, and even renamed the location to honor the fact that there he had seen God face to face (Gen. 32:30). The once-ominous meeting with Esau followed in the morning and contradicted Jacob's fearful expectation in the most delightful way imaginable. Esau ran to Jacob and embraced him. Esau graciously tried to refuse Jacob's gifts, though Jacob insisted he take them. A transformed Jacob said to Esau, "Truly to see your face is like seeing the face of God" (Gen. 33:10).

The ambiguous identity of Jacob's wrestling opponent is a deliberate feature of the story. It highlights the inseparable elements of Jacob's struggling with both God and man. Jacob models for us a truth at the core of our faith: our relationships with God and people are linked. Our reconciliation with God makes possible our reconciliation with others. Likewise, in that human reconciliation, we come to see and know God better. The work of reconciliation applies to families, friends, churches, companies, even people groups and nations. Christ alone can be our peace, but we are his ambassadors for it. Springing from God's initial promise to Abraham, this is a blessing that ought to touch the whole world.

Joseph (Genesis 37:2–50:26)

Recall that God accompanied his call to Abraham with core promises (Gen. 12:2–3). First, God would multiply his descendants into a great nation. Second, God would bless him. Third, God would make Abraham's name great, meaning that Abraham would be worthy of his renown. Fourth, Abraham would be a blessing. This last item pertains to the future generations of Abraham's family and beyond them, to all the families of the earth. God would bless those who blessed Abraham and curse those who cursed him. The book of Genesis traces the partial fulfillment of these promises through the chosen lines of Abraham's descendants, Isaac, Jacob, and Jacob's sons. Among them all, it is in Joseph that God most directly fulfills his promise to bless the nations through the people of Abraham. Indeed, people from "all the world" were sustained by the food system that Joseph managed (Gen. 41:57). Joseph understood this mission and articulated the purpose of his life in line with God's intention: "the saving of many lives" (Gen. 50:20 New International Version).

Joseph Rejected and Sold into Slavery by His Brothers (Genesis 37:2–36)

From a young age, Joseph believed God had destined him for greatness. In dreams, God assured Joseph that he would rise to a position of leadership over his parents and brothers (Gen. 37:5–11). From Joseph's point of view, these dreams were evidence of divine blessing, rather than his own ambition. From his brothers' point of view, however, the dreams were further manifestations of the unfair privilege that Joseph enjoyed as the favorite son of their father, Jacob (Gen. 37:3–4). Being sure that we are in the right does not absolve us from empathizing with others who may not share that same view. Good leaders strive to foster cooperation rather than envy. Joseph's failure to recognize this put him at severe odds with his brothers. After initially plotting murder against him, his brothers settled for selling him to a caravan of traders bearing goods through Canaan to Egypt. The merchants, in turn, sold Joseph to Potiphar, "the captain of the guard" who was "an officer of Pharaoh" in Egypt (Gen. 37:36; 39:1).

The Schemes of Potiphar's Wife and Joseph's Imprisonment (Genesis 39:1–20)

Joseph's stint in Potiphar's employ gave him a wide range of fiduciary responsibilities. At first, Joseph was merely "in" his master's house. We don't know in what capacity he served, but when Potiphar recognized Joseph's general competence, he promoted him to be his personal steward and "put him in charge of all that he had" (Gen. 39:4).

After a time, Potiphar's wife took a sexual interest in Joseph (Gen. 39:7). Joseph's refusal of the wife's advances was articulate and reasonable. He reminded her of the broad trust that Potiphar had placed in him and described the relationship she sought in the moral/religious terms "wickedness" and "sin" (Gen. 39:9). He was sensitive to both the social and theological dimensions. Furthermore, he offered his verbal resistance repeatedly, and he even avoided being in her presence. When physically assaulted, Joseph made the choice to flee half-naked rather than to submit.

The sexual harassment by this woman took place in a power relationship that disadvantaged Joseph. Although she believed that she had the right and power to use Joseph in this way, her words and contact were clearly unwelcome to him. Joseph's work required him to be at home where she was, yet he could not call the matter to Potiphar's attention without interfering in their marital relationship. Even after his escape and arrest on false charges, Joseph seems to have had no legal recourse.

The facets of this episode touch closely on the issues of sexual harassment in the workplace today. People have different standards of what counts for inappropriate speech and physical contact, but the whims of those in power are what often count in practice. Workers are often expected to report incidences of potential harassment to their superiors, but often are reluctant to do so because they know the risk of obfuscation and retaliation. To compound this, even when harassment can be documented, workers may suffer for having come forward. Joseph's godliness did not rescue him from false accusation and imprisonment. If we find ourselves in a parallel situation, our godliness is no guarantee that we will escape unscathed. But Joseph did leave an instructive testimony to Potiphar's wife and possibly others in the household. Knowing that we belong to the Lord and that he defends the weak will certainly help us to face difficult situations without giving up. This story is a realistic recognition that standing up to sexual harassment in the workplace may have devastating consequences. Yet it is also a story of hope that by God's grace, good may eventually prevail in the situation. Joseph also provides a model for us, that even when we are falsely accused and wrongly treated, we carry on with the work God has given us, allowing God to make it right in the end.

Joseph's Interpretation of Dreams in Prison (Genesis 39:20–40:23)

Joseph's service in prison was marked by the Lord's presence, the jailer's favor, and Joseph's promotion to leadership (Gen. 39:21–23). In prison, Joseph met two of Pharaoh's officials who were incarcerated, the chief cupbearer and the chief baker. Many Egyptian texts mention the role of cupbearers, who not only tasted wine for quality and to detect poison but also who enjoyed proximity to those with political power. They often became confidants who were valued for their counsel (see Neh. 2:1–4).[15] Like chief cupbearers, chief bakers were also trusted officials

---

[15] Kenneth A. Kitchen, "Cupbearer," in *New Bible Dictionary*, 3rd ed., eds. I. Howard Marshall, A. R. Millard, J. I. Packer, and D. J. Wiseman (Downers Grove, IL: InterVarsity Press, 1996), 248.

who had open access to the highest persons in the government and who may have performed duties that extended beyond the preparation of food.[16] In prison, Joseph did the work of interpreting dreams for these politically connected individuals.

Interpreting dreams in the ancient world was a sophisticated profession involving technical "dream books" that listed elements of dreams and their meanings. Records of the veracity of past dreams and their interpretations provided empirical evidence to support the interpreter's predictions.[17] Joseph, however, was not schooled in this tradition and credited God with providing the interpretations that eventually proved true (Gen. 40:8). In this case, the cupbearer was restored to his former post, where he promptly forgot about Joseph.

The dynamics present in this story are still present today. We may invest in the success of another who rises beyond our reach, only to be discarded when our usefulness has been spent. Does this mean that our work has been for nothing and that we would have been better off to focus on our own position and promotion? What's more, Joseph had no way of independently verifying the stories of the two officials in prison. "The one who first states a case seems right, until the other comes and cross-examines" (Prov. 18:17). After sentencing, however, any prisoner can assert his or her own innocence.

We may have doubts about how our investment in others may eventually benefit us or our organizations. We may wonder about the character and motives of the people we help. We may disapprove of what they do afterward and how that might reflect on us. These matters can be varied and complex. They call for prayer and discernment, but must they paralyze us? The Apostle Paul wrote, "Whenever we have an opportunity, let us work for the good of all" (Gal. 6:10). If we start with a commitment to work for God above all others, then it is easier to move ahead, believing that "in all things God works for the good of those who love him, who have been called according to his purpose" (Rom. 8:28 NIV).

---

[16] Roland K. Harrison, "Baker," in *The International Standard Bible Encyclopedia*, ed. Geoffrey W. Bromiley (Grand Rapids: Eerdmans, 1979), 1:404.

[17] John H. Walton, *Genesis*, NIV Application Commentary (Grand Rapids: Zondervan, 2001), 672–73.

Joseph's Promotion by Pharaoh (Genesis 41:1–45)

Two more years passed until Joseph gained an opportunity for release from his misery in prison. Pharaoh had begun to have disturbing dreams, and the chief cupbearer remembered the skill of the young Hebrew in prison. Pharaoh's dreams about cows and stalks of grain befuddled his most skilled counselors. Joseph testified to God's ability to provide interpretations and his own role as merely the mediator of this revelation (Gen. 41:16). Before Pharaoh, Joseph did not use the covenant name of God exclusive to his own people. Instead, he consistently referred to God with the more general term *elohim*. In so doing, Joseph avoided making any unnecessary offense, a point supported by the fact that Pharaoh credited God with revealing to Joseph the meaning of Pharaoh's dreams (Gen. 41:39). In the workplace, sometimes believers can give God credit for their success in a shallow manner that ends up putting people off. Joseph's way of doing it impressed Pharaoh, showing that publicly giving God credit can be done in a believable way.

God's presence with Joseph was so obvious that Pharaoh promoted Joseph to second-in-command of Egypt, especially to take charge of preparations for the coming famine (Gen. 41:37–45). God's word to Abraham was bearing fruit: "I will bless those who bless you . . . and in you all the families of the earth shall be blessed" (Gen. 12:3). Like Joseph, when we confess our own inability to meet the challenges we face and find appropriate ways to attribute success to God, we forge a powerful defense against the pride that often accompanies public acclaim.

Joseph's promotion brought him significant accoutrements of leadership: a royal signet ring and gold chain, fine clothing appropriate to his high office, official transportation, a new Egyptian name, and an Egyptian wife from an upper class family (Gen. 41:41–45). If ever there was a lure to leave his Hebrew heritage behind, this was it. God helps us deal with failure and defeat, yet we may need his help even more when dealing with success. The text presents several indications of how Joseph handled his promotion in a godly way. Part of this had to do with Joseph's preparation before his promotion.

Back in his father's home, the dreams of leadership that God gave him convinced Joseph that he had a divinely ordained purpose and destiny that he never forgot. His personal nature was basically trusting of people. He seems to have held no grudge against his jealous brothers or the forgetful cupbearer. Before Pharaoh promoted him, Joseph knew that the Lord was with him and he had tangible evidence to prove it. Repeatedly giving God credit was not only the right thing to do, but it also reminded Joseph himself that his skills were from the Lord. Joseph was courteous and humble, showing a desire to do whatever he could to help Pharaoh and the Egyptian people. Even when the Egyptians were bereft of currency and livestock, Joseph earned the trust of the Egyptian people and of Pharaoh himself (Gen. 41:55). Throughout the rest of his life as an administrator, Joseph consistently devoted himself to effective management for the good of others.

Joseph's story to this point reminds us that in our broken world, God's response to our prayers doesn't necessarily come quickly. Joseph was seventeen years old when his brothers sold him into slavery (Gen. 37:2). His final release from captivity came when he was thirty (Gen. 41:46), thirteen long years later.

Joseph's Successful Management of the Food Crisis (Genesis 41:46–57; 47:13–26)

Joseph Creates a Long-term Agricultural Policy and Infrastructure (Genesis 41:46–57)

Joseph immediately went about the work to which Pharaoh had appointed him. His primary interest was in getting the job done for others, rather than taking personal advantage of his new position at the head of the royal court. He maintained his faith in God, giving his children names that credited God with healing his emotional pain and making him fruitful (Gen. 41:51–52). He recognized that his wisdom and discernment were gifts from God, but nevertheless that he still had much to learn about the land of Egypt, its agricultural industry in particular. As the senior administrator, Joseph's work touched on nearly every practical area of the nation's life. His office would have required that he learn much about legislation, communication, negotiation, transportation, safe and efficient methods of food storage, building, economic strategizing and forecasting, record-keeping, payroll, the handling of transactions both by means of currency and through bartering, human resources, and the acquisition of real estate. His extraordinary abilities with respect to God and people did not operate in separate domains. The genius of Joseph's success lay in the effective integration of his divine gifts and acquired competencies. For Joseph, all of this was godly work.

Pharaoh had already characterized Joseph as "discerning and wise" (Gen. 41:39), and these characteristics enabled Joseph to do the work of strategic planning and administration. The Hebrew words for *wise* and *wisdom* (*hakham* and *hokhmah*) denote a high level of mental perceptivity, but also are used of a wide range of practical skills including craftsmanship of wood, precious stones, and metal (Exod. 31:3–5; 35:31–33), tailoring (Exod. 28:3; 35:26, 35), as well as administration (Deut. 34:9; 2 Chr. 1:10) and legal justice (1 Kgs. 3:28). These skills are found among unbelievers as well, but the wise in the Bible enjoy the special blessing of God who intends Israel to display God's ways to the nations (Deut. 4:6).

As his first act, "Joseph . . . went through all the land of Egypt" (Gen. 41:46) on an inspection tour. He would have to become familiar with the people who managed agriculture, the locations and conditions of the fields, the crops, the roads, and means of transportation. It is inconceivable that Joseph could have accomplished all of this on a personal level. He would have had to establish and oversee the training of what amounted to a Department of Agriculture and Revenue. During the seven years of abundant harvest, Joseph had the grain stored in cities (Gen. 41:48–49). During the seven lean years that followed, Joseph dispensed grain to the Egyptians and other people who were affected by the widespread famine. To create and administer all this, while surviving the political intrigue of an absolute monarchy, required exceptional talent.

Joseph Relieves the Poverty of Egypt's People (Genesis 47:13–26)

After the people ran out of money, Joseph allowed them to barter their livestock for food. This plan lasted for one year during which Joseph collected horses, sheep, goats, cattle, and donkeys (Gen. 47:15–17). He would have had to determine the value of these animals and establish an equitable system for exchange. When food is scarce, people are especially concerned for the survival of themselves and their loved ones. Providing access to points of food distribution and treating people even-handedly become acutely important administrative matters.

When all of the livestock had been traded, people willingly sold themselves into slavery to Pharaoh and sold him the ownership of their lands as well (Gen. 47:18–21). From the perspective of leadership, this must have been awful to witness. Joseph, however, allowed the people to sell their land and to enter into servitude, but he did not take advantage of them in their powerlessness. Joseph would have had to see that these properties were valued correctly in exchange for seed for planting (Gen. 47:23). He enacted an enduring law that people return 20 percent of the harvest to Pharaoh. This entailed creating a system to monitor and enforce the people's compliance with the law and establishing a department dedicated to managing the revenue. In all of this, Joseph exempted the priestly families from selling their land because Pharaoh supplied them with a fixed allotment of food to meet their needs adequately (Gen. 47:22, 26). Handling this special population would have entailed having a smaller, distinct system of distribution that was tailored for them.

Poverty and its consequences are economic realities. Our first duty is to help eliminate them, but we cannot expect complete success until God's kingdom is fulfilled. Believers may not have the power to eliminate the circumstances that require people to make hard choices, but we can find ways to support people as they—or perhaps we ourselves—cope. Choosing the lesser of two evils may be necessary work and can be emotionally devastating. In our work, we may experience tension arising from feeling empathy for the needy, yet bearing responsibility to do what is good for the people and organizations we work for. Joseph experienced God's guidance in these difficult tasks, and we also have received God's promise that "I will never leave you or forsake you" (Heb. 13:5).

Happily, by applying his God-given skill and wisdom, Joseph successfully brought Egypt through the agricultural catastrophe. When the seven years of good harvests came, Joseph developed a stockpiling system to store the grain for use during the coming drought. When the seven years of drought arrived, "Joseph opened the storehouses" and provided enough food to bring the nation through the famine. His wise strategy and effective implementation of the plan even allowed Egypt to supply grain to the rest of the world during the famine (Gen. 41:57). In this case, God's fulfillment of his promise that Abraham's descendants would be a blessing to the world occurred not only for the benefit of foreign nations, but even through the industry of a foreign nation, Egypt.

In fact, God's blessing for the people of Israel came only after and through his blessing of foreigners. God did not raise up an Israelite in the land of Israel to provide for Israel's relief during the famine. Instead God enabled Joseph, working in and through the Egyptian government, to provide for the needs of the people of Israel (Gen. 47:11–12). Nonetheless, we shouldn't idealize Joseph. As an official in a sometimes repressive society, he became part of its power structure, and he personally imposed slavery on uncounted numbers of people (Gen. 47:21).

Applications from Joseph's Management Experience (Genesis 41:46–57; 47:13–26)

Genesis's interest in Joseph's management of the food crisis lies more in its effect on the family of Israel than in developing principles for effective management. Nonetheless, to the degree that Joseph's extraordinary leadership can serve as an example for leaders today, we can derive some practical applications from his work:

1. Become as familiar as possible with the state of affairs as they exist at the beginning of your service.

2. Pray for discernment regarding the future so that you can make wise plans.

3. Commit yourself to God first and then expect him to direct and establish your plans.

4. Gratefully and appropriately acknowledge the gifts God has given you.

5. Even though others recognize God's presence in your life and the special talents you have, do not broadcast these in a self-serving effort to gain respect.

6. Educate yourself about how to do your job and carry it out with excellence.

7. Seek the practical good for others, knowing that God has placed you where you are to be a blessing.

8. Be fair in all of your dealings, especially when the circumstances are grim and deeply problematical.

9. Although your exemplary service may propel you to prominence, remember your founding mission as God's servant. Your life does not consist in what you gain for yourself.

10. Value the godliness of the myriad types of honorable work that society needs.

11. Generously extend the fruit of your labor as widely as possible to those who truly need it, regardless of what you think of them as individuals.

12. Accept the fact that God may bring you into a particular field of work under extremely challenging conditions. This does not mean that something has gone terribly wrong or that you are out of God's will.

13. Have courage that God will fit you for the task.

14. Accept the fact that sometimes people must choose what they regard as the better of two unpleasant yet unavoidable situations.

15. Believe that what you do will not only benefit those whom you see and meet, but also that your work has the potential to touch lives for many generations to come. God is able to accomplish abundantly far more than we can ask or imagine (Eph. 3:20).

Joseph's Dealings with His Brothers (Genesis 42–43)

In the midst of the crisis in Egypt, Joseph's brothers arrived from Canaan, seeking to buy food, as the famine severely affected their land also. They did not recognize Joseph, and he did not reveal himself to them. He dealt with his brothers largely through the language of commerce.

The word *silver* (*kesef*) appears twenty times in chapters 42 through 45 and the word for *grain* (*shever*) nineteen. Trading in this commodity provided the framework on which the intricate personal dynamics hung.

Joseph's behavior in this situation became quite shrewd. First, he concealed his identity from his brothers, which—while not necessarily rising to the level of open deceit (Hebrew *mirmah*, as with Jacob in Gen. 27:35)—certainly was less than forthright. Second, he spoke harshly to his brothers with accusations he knew were unfounded (Gen. 42:7, 9, 14, 16; 44:3–5). In short, Joseph took advantage of his power to deal with a group he knew could be untrustworthy because of their earlier treatment of him.[19] His motive was to discern the present character of the people he was dealing with. He had suffered greatly at their hands over twenty years prior, and had every reason to distrust their words, actions, and commitment to the family.

Joseph's methods verged on deception. He withheld critical information and manipulated events in various ways. Joseph acted in the role of a detective conducting a tough interrogation. He could not proceed with full transparency and expect to get reliable information from them. The biblical concept for this tactic is shrewdness. Shrewdness may be exercised for good or for ill. On the one hand the serpent was "the shrewdest of all the wild animals" (Gen. 3:1 New Living Translation), and employed shrewd methods for disastrously evil purposes. (The NLT's consistent use of "shrewd" makes it clear that the same Hebrew word is being translated. The NRSV uses "crafty" here.) The Hebrew word for shrewdness (*ormah* and cognates) is also translated as "good judgment," "prudence," and "clever" (Prov. 12:23; 13:16; 14:8; 22:3; 27:12), indicating it may take foresight and skill to make godly work possible in difficult contexts. Jesus himself counseled his disciples to be "as shrewd as snakes and harmless as doves" (Matt. 10:16 NLT). The Bible often commends shrewdness in the pursuit of noble purposes (Prov. 1:4; 8:5, 12).

Joseph's shrewdness had the intended effect of testing his brothers' integrity, and they returned the silver Joseph had secretly packed in the baggage (Gen. 43:20–21). When he tested them further by treating the youngest, Benjamin, more generously than the others, they proved they

---

[19] Waltke, 545.

had learned not to fall into animosity among themselves the way they had done when they sold Joseph into slavery.

It would be superficial to read into Joseph's actions the claim that thinking you are on God's side is always a justification for deceit. But Joseph's long career of service and suffering in God's service gave him a deeper understanding of the situation than his brothers had. Seemingly, the promise that God would make them into a large nation hung in the balance. Joseph knew that it was not in his human power to save them, but he took advantage of his God-given authority and wisdom to serve and help. Two important factors differentiate Joseph in making the decision to use means that otherwise would not be commendable. First, he gained nothing from these machinations for himself. He had received a blessing from God, and his actions were solely in the service of *becoming* a blessing to others. He could have exploited his brothers' desperate predicament and spitefully exacted a greater sum of silver, knowing they would have given anything to survive. Instead, he used knowledge to save them. Second, his actions were necessary if he was to be able to offer the blessings. If he had dealt with his brothers more openly, he could not have tested their trustworthiness in the matter.

Judah's Transformation to a Man of God (Genesis 44:1–45:15)

In the final episode of Joseph's testing of his brothers, Joseph framed Benjamin for an imaginary crime and claimed Benjamin as a slave in recompense. When he demanded that the brothers return home to Isaac without Benjamin (Gen. 44:17), Judah emerged as the group's spokesman. What gave him the standing to take on this role? He had broken faith with his family by marrying a Canaanite (Gen. 38:2), had raised such wicked sons that the Lord put two of them to death (Gen. 38:7, 10), had treated his daughter-in-law as a prostitute (Gen. 38:24), and had hatched the plan to sell his own brother as a slave (Gen. 37:27). But the story Judah told Joseph showed a changed man. He exhibited unexpected compassion in telling of the family's heart-wrenching experience of starvation, of his father's undying love for Benjamin, and of Judah's own promise to his father that he would bring Benjamin back home, lest Jacob literally die from grief. Then, in an ultimate expression of compassion, Judah offered to substitute *himself* in place of Benjamin! He proposed that he be retained in Egypt for the rest of his life as the governor's slave if only the governor would let Benjamin go home to his father (Gen. 44:33–34).

Seeing the change in Judah, Joseph was able to bless them as God intended. He disclosed to them the full truth: "I am Joseph" (Gen. 45:3). It appears that Joseph finally saw that his brothers could be trusted. In our own dealings with those who would exploit and deceive us, we must tread carefully, to be as wise as serpents and as innocent as doves, as Jesus instructed the disciples (Matt. 10:16). As one writer put it, "Trust requires trustworthiness." All of the planning Joseph had done in his discussions with his brothers reached this culmination, allowing him to enter into a right relationship with them. He calmed his terrified brothers by pointing to the work of God who was responsible for placing Joseph in charge of all Egypt (Gen. 45:8). Waltke spells out the importance of the interaction between Joseph and his brothers:

> This scene exposes the anatomy of reconciliation. It is about loyalty to a family member in need, even when he or she looks guilty; giving glory to God by owning up to sin and its consequences; overlooking favoritism; offering up oneself to save another; demonstrating true love by concrete acts of sacrifice that create a context of trust; discarding control and the power of knowledge in favor of intimacy; embracing deep compassion, tender feelings, sensitivity, and forgiveness; and talking to one another. A dysfunctional family that allows these virtues to embrace it will become a light to the world.[20]

God is more than able to bring his blessings to the world through deeply flawed people. But we must be willing to continually repent of the evil we do and turn to God for transformation, even if we are never perfectly purged of our errors, weaknesses, and sins in this life.

Contrary to the values of the societies around Israel, the willingness of leaders to offer themselves in sacrifice for the sins of others was intended to be a signature trait of leadership among the people of God. Moses would show it when Israel sinned regarding the golden calf. He prayed, "Alas, this people has sinned a great sin; they have made for

---

[20] Waltke, 565–66.

themselves gods of gold. But now, if you will only forgive their sin—but if not, blot me out of the book that you have written" (Exod. 32:31–32). David would show it when he saw the angel of the Lord striking down the people. He prayed, "What have they done? Let your hand, I pray, be against me and against my father's house" (2 Sam. 24:17). Jesus, the Lion of the tribe of Judah, would show it when he said, "For this reason the Father loves me, because I lay down my life in order to take it up again. No one takes it from me, but I lay it down of my own accord" (John 10:17–18).

Jacob's Family's Move to Egypt (Genesis 45:16–47:12)

Joseph and Pharaoh lavishly gave Joseph's brothers "the best of all the land of Egypt" (Gen. 45:20) and supplied them for their return to Canaan and transportation of the family. This apparently happy ending, however, has a dark side. God had promised Abraham and his descendants the land of *Canaan*, not Egypt. Long after Joseph passed from the scene, Egypt's relationship with Israel turned from hospitality to hostility. Seen this way, how does Joseph's benevolence to the family fit with his role as mediator of God's blessing to all families of the earth (Gen. 12:3)? Joseph was a man of insight who planned for the future, and he did bring about the portion of God's blessing assigned to him. But God did not reveal to him the future rise of a "new king . . . who did not know Joseph" (Exod. 1:8). Each generation needs to remain faithful to God and receive God's blessings in their own time. Regrettably, Joseph's descendants forgot God's promises and drifted into faithlessness. Yet God did not forget his promise to Abraham, Isaac, Jacob, and their descendants. Among their descendants God would raise up new men and women to impart God's promised blessings.

God Meant All for Good (Genesis 50:15–21)

The penitent words of the brothers led Joseph to one of the finest theological points of his life and, indeed, much of Genesis. He told them not to be afraid, for he would not retaliate for their mistreatment of him. "Even though you intended to do harm to me," he told them, "God intended it for good, in order to preserve a numerous people, as he is doing today. So have no fear; I myself will provide for you and your little ones" (Gen. 50:20–21). Joseph's reference to "numerous people" echoes God's covenantal promise to bless "all families of the earth" (Gen. 12:3). From our vantage point today, we can see that God sent far more blessing than Joseph could have ever asked or imagined (see Eph. 3:20).

God's work in and through Joseph had real, practical, serious value—to preserve lives. If we ever have the impression that God wants us in the workplace only so we can tell others about him, or if we get the impression that the only part of our work that matters to God is building relationships, Joseph's work says otherwise. The things we make and do in our work are themselves crucial to God and to other people. Sometimes this is true because our work is a piece of a bigger whole, and we lose sight of the result of the work. Joseph took a larger perspective on his work, and he was not discouraged by its inevitable ups and downs.

This is not to say that relationships at work aren't also of the highest importance. Perhaps Christians have the special gift of offering forgiveness to people in our workplaces. Joseph's reassurance to his brothers is a model of forgiveness. Following the instruction of his father, Joseph forgave his brothers and thus verbally released them from guilt. But his forgiveness—like all true forgiveness—was not just verbal. Joseph used the extensive resources of Egypt, which God had placed under his control, to support them materially so that they could prosper. He acknowledged that judgment was not his role. "Am I in the place of God?" (Gen. 50:19). He did not usurp God's role as judge but helped his brothers to connect with God who had saved them.

The relationship Joseph had with his brothers was both familial and economic. There is no clearly defined boundary between these areas; forgiveness is appropriate to both. We may be tempted to think that our most cherished religious values are primarily meant to function in identifiably religious spheres, such as the local church. Of course, much of our work life does take place in the public realm, and we must respect the fact that others do not share our Christian faith. But the neat division of life into separate compartments labeled "sacred" and "secular" is something foreign to the worldview of Scripture. It is not sectarian, then, to affirm that forgiveness is a sound workplace practice.

There will always be plenty of hurt and pain in life. No company or organization is immune from that. It would be naive to assume generally that nobody deliberately means to cause harm by what they say or do. Just as Joseph acknowledged that people *did* intend to harm him, we can do likewise. But in the same sentence lives the larger truth about God's intention for good. Recalling that point when we feel hurt both helps us to bear the pain and to identify with Christ.

Joseph saw himself as an agent of God who was instrumental in effecting the work of God with his people. He knew the harm that people were capable of and accepted that sometimes people are their own worst enemies. He knew the family stories of faith mixed with doubt, of faithful service mingled with self-preservation, of both truth and deceit. He also knew of the promises God made to Abraham, of God's commitment to bless this family, and of God's wisdom in working with his people as he refined them through the fires of life. He did not paint over their sins; rather, he absorbed them into his awareness of God's grand work. Our awareness of the inevitable, providential successfulness of God's promises makes our labor worthwhile, no matter the cost to us.

Of the many lessons about work in the book of Genesis, this one in particular endures and even explains redemption itself—the crucifixion of the Lord of glory (1 Cor. 2:8–10). Our places of work provide contexts in which our values and character are brought to light as we make decisions that affect ourselves and those around us. In his wise power, God is capable of working with our faithfulness, mending our weakness, and forging our failures to accomplish what he himself has prepared for us who love him.

Conclusions from Genesis 12–50

Genesis 12–50 tells the story of the first three generations of the family through whom God chose to bring his blessings to the whole world. Having no particular power, position, wealth, fame, ability, or moral superiority of their own, they accepted his call to trust him to provide for them and fulfill the great vision he had for them. Although God proved faithful in every way, their own faithfulness was often fitful, timid, foolish, and precarious. They proved to be as dysfunctional as any family, yet they maintained, or at least kept returning to, the seed of faith he placed in them. Functioning in a broken world, surrounded by hostile people and powers, by faith they "invoked blessings for the future" (Heb. 11:20) and lived according to God's promises. "Therefore God is not ashamed to be called their God; indeed, he has prepared a city for them" (Heb. 11:16), the same city in which we also work as followers of "Jesus the Messiah, the son of David, the son of Abraham" (Matt. 1:1).

Exodus and Work

The theology of work does not begin with our understanding of what God wants us to do or even how to do it. It begins with the God who has revealed himself to us as Creator and Redeemer, and who shows us how to follow him by being formed in his character. We do what God wants us to do by becoming more like God. Through reading Exodus, we hear God describe his own character, and we see this particular God actively forming his people. As his people, Christians cannot settle for doing our work according to godly principles unless we apprehend these truths as uniquely rooted in *this certain* God, who does *this particular kind* of redemptive work, through the *unique* person of his Son, by the power of *his* Holy Spirit. In essence, we learn that God's character is revealed in his work, and his work shapes our work. Following God in our work is thus a major topic in Exodus, even though work is not the primary point of the book.

We find much in Exodus that speaks to everyday work. But these instructions and rules take place in a work context that existed over three thousand years ago. Time has not stood still, and our workplaces have changed. Some passages, such as "You shall not murder" (Exod. 20:13), seem to fit today's context much as they did in Moses' time. Others, such as "If someone's ox hurts the ox of another, so that it dies, then they shall sell the live ox and divide the price of it" (Exod. 21:35), seem less directly applicable to most modern workplaces. How can we honor, obey, and apply God's word in Exodus without falling into the traps of legalism or misapplication?

To answer these questions, we start with the understanding that this book is a narrative. Just as it helped Israel to locate itself in God's story, it helps us to find out how we fit into the fuller expression of the narrative that is our Bible today. The purpose and shape of God's work not only frames our identity as his people, but it also directs the work God has called us to do.

Introduction to Exodus

The book of Exodus opens and closes with Israel at work. At the onset, the Israelites are at work for the Egyptians. By the book's end, they have finished the work of building the tabernacle according to the Lord's instructions (Exod. 40:33). God did not deliver Israel *from* work. He set Israel free *for* work. God released them from oppressive work under the ungodly king of Egypt and led them to a new kind of work under his gracious and holy kingship. Although the book's title in Christian Bibles, "Exodus," means "the way out,"[1] the forward-leaning orientation of Exodus could legitimately lead us to conclude that the book is really about the way *in*, for it recounts Israel's entrance to the Mosaic covenant that will frame their existence, not only in the wilderness wanderings around the Sinai Peninsula but also in their settled life in the Promised Land. The book conveys how Israel ought to understand their God, and how this nation should work and worship in their new land. On all counts, Israel must be mindful of how their life under God would be distinct from and better than life for those who followed the gods of Canaan. Even today, *what* we do in work flows from *why* we do it and for *whom* we are ultimately working. We usually don't have to look very far in society to find examples of harsh and oppressive work. Certainly, God wants us to find better ways to conduct our business and to treat others. But the way *into* that new way of acting depends on seeing ourselves as recipients of God's salvation, knowing what God's work is, and training ourselves to follow his words.

The book of Exodus begins about four hundred years after the point where Genesis ends. In Genesis, Egypt had been a hospitable place where God providentially elevated Joseph so that he could save the lives of Abraham's descendants (Gen. 50:20). This accords well with God's promises to make Abraham into a great nation, to bless him and make him a blessing to others, to make his name great, and to bless all families of the earth through him (Gen. 12:2–3). In the book of Exodus, however, Egypt was an oppressive place where Israel's growth raised the

---

[1] In Hebrew, the title is simply *shemot*, the word for "names of," which appears in the first sentence.

specter of death. The Egyptians hardly saw Israel as a divine blessing, though they did not want to let go of their slave labor. In the end, Israel's deliverance at the Red Sea cost Pharaoh and his people many lives. In light of God's promises to Abraham's chosen family and God's intentions to bless the nations, the people of God in the book of Exodus are very much in transition. The magnitude of Israel's numbers indicated God's favor, yet the next generation of male children faced immediate extinction (Exod. 1:15–16). The nation as a whole was still not in the land God had promised to them.

The entire Pentateuch echoes this theme of partial fulfillment. God's promises to Abraham of descendants, favored relationship with God, and a land in which to live all express God's intentions, yet they are all in some state of jeopardy throughout the narrative.[2] Among the five books of the Pentateuch, Exodus in particular takes up the element of relationship with God, both in terms of God's deliverance of his people from Egypt and the establishment of his covenant with them at Sinai.[3] This is especially significant for how we read the book for insights about our work today. We value the shape and content of this book as we remember that our relationship with God through Jesus Christ flows from what we see here, and it orients all of our life and work around God's intentions.

To capture Israel's character as a nation in transition, we outline the book and assess its contribution to the theology of work according to the geographical stages of its journey beginning in Egypt, then at the Red Sea and on the way to Sinai, and finally at Sinai itself.

Israel in Egypt (Exodus 1:1–13:16)

Israel's mistreatment by the Egyptians provides the background and impetus for their redemption. Pharaoh did not allow them to follow Moses into the wilderness to worship the Lord and thus denied a measure of their religious freedom. But their oppression as workers in the Egyptian economic system is what really gets our attention. God

---

[2] David J. A. Clines, *Theme of the Pentateuch*, 2nd ed. (London: T&T Clark, 1997), 29.

[3] Clines, 47.

hears the cry of his people and does something about it. But we must remember that the people of Israel do not groan because of work in general,
but because of the harshness of their work. In response, God does not
deliver them into a life of total rest, but a release from oppressive work.

The Harshness of the Israelites' Slave Labor in Egypt (Exodus 1:8–14)

The work that the Egyptians forced on the Israelites was evil in motive and cruel in nature. The opening scene presents the land as filled
with Israelites who had been fruitful and multiplied. This echoes God's
creational intent (Gen. 1:28; 9:1) as well as his promise to Abraham and
his chosen descendants (Gen. 17:6; 35:11; 47:27). As a nation, they were
destined to bless the world. Under a previous administration, the Israelites had royal permission to live in the land and to work it. But here
the new king of Egypt sensed in their numbers a threat to his national
security and thus decided to deal "shrewdly" with them (Exod. 1:10).
We are not told whether or not the Israelites were a genuine threat. The
emphasis falls on Pharaoh's destructive fear that led him first to de-
grade their working environment and then to use infanticide to curb the
growth of their population.

Work may be physically and mentally taxing, but that does not make
it wrong. What made the situation in Egypt unbearable was not only the
slavery but also its extreme harshness. The Egyptian masters worked
the Israelites "ruthlessly" (*befarekh*, Exod. 1:13, 14) and made their lives
"bitter" (*marar*, Exod. 1:14) with "hard" (*qasheh*, in the sense of "cruel,"
Exod. 1:14; 6:9) service. As a result, Israel languished in "misery" and
"suffering" (Exod. 3:7) and a "broken spirit" (Exod. 6:9). Work, one of
the chief purposes and joys of human existence (Gen. 1:27–31; 2:15), was
turned into a misery by the harshness of oppression.

The Work of Midwifery and Mothering (Exodus 1:15–2:10)

In the midst of harsh treatment, the Israelites remained faithful to
God's command to be fruitful and multiply (Gen. 1:28). That entailed
bearing children, which in turn depended on the work of midwives.

In addition to its presence in the Bible, the work of midwifery is well-attested in ancient Mesopotamia and Egypt. Midwives assisted women in childbearing, cut the infant's umbilical cord, washed the baby, and presented the child to the mother and father.

The midwives in this narrative possess a fear of God that led them to disobey the royal order to kill all of the male children born to the Hebrew women (Exod. 1:15–17). Generally speaking, the "fear of the Lord" (and related expressions) in the Bible refer to a healthy and obedient relationship with the covenant-making God of Israel (Hebrew, *YHWH*). Their "fear of God" was stronger than any fear that Pharaoh of Egypt could put them under. In addition, perhaps their courage arose from their work. Would those who shepherd new life into birth every day come to value life so highly that murder would become unthinkable, even if commanded by a king?

Moses' mother, Jochebed (Exod. 6:20), was another woman who faced a seemingly impossible choice and forged a creative solution. One can hardly imagine her relief at secretly and successfully bearing a male child, followed by her pain at having to place him into the river, and to do so in a way that would actually *save* his life. The parallels to Noah's ark—the Hebrew word for "basket" is used only one other place in the Bible, namely for Noah's "ark"—let us know that God was acting not only to save one baby boy, or even one nation, but also to redeem the whole creation through Moses and Israel. Parallel to his reward to the midwives, God showed kindness to Moses' mother. She recovered her son and nursed him until he was old enough to be adopted as the son of Pharaoh's daughter. The godly work of bearing and raising children is well-known to be complex, demanding, and praiseworthy (Prov. 31:10–31). In Exodus, we read nothing of the inner struggles experienced by Jochebed, the unsung heroine. From a narrative point of view, Moses' life is the main issue. But the Bible later commended both Jochebed and Amram, Moses' father, for how they put their faith into action (Heb. 11:23).

Too often the work of bearing and raising children is overlooked. Mothers, especially, often get the message that childrearing is not as important or praiseworthy as other work. Yet when Exodus tells the story of how to follow God, the first thing it has to tell us is the incomparable importance of bearing, raising, protecting, and helping children.

The first act of courage, in this book filled with courageous deeds, is the courage of a mother, her family, and her midwives in saving her child.

God's Call to Moses (Exodus 2:11–3:22)

Although Moses was a Hebrew, he was raised in Egypt's royal family as the grandson of Pharaoh. His revulsion to injustice erupted into a lethal attack on an Egyptian man he found beating a Hebrew worker. This act came to Pharaoh's attention, so Moses fled for safety and became a shepherd in Midian, a region several hundred miles east of Egypt on the other side of the Sinai Peninsula. We do not know exactly how long he lived there, but during that time he married and had a son. In addition, two important things happened. The king in Egypt died, and the Lord heard the cry of his oppressed people and remembered his covenant with Abraham, Isaac, and Jacob (Exod. 2:23–25). This act of remembering did not mean that God had forgotten about his people. It signaled that he was about to act on their behalf.[4] For that, he would call Moses.

God's call to Moses came while Moses was at work. The account of how this happened comprises six elements that form a pattern evident in the lives of other leaders and prophets in the Bible. It is therefore instructive for us to examine this call narrative and to consider its implications for us today, especially in the context of our work.

First, God *confronted* Moses and arrested his attention at the scene of the burning bush (Exod. 3:2–5). A brushfire in the semi-desert is nothing exceptional, but Moses was intrigued by the nature of this particular one. Moses heard his name called and responded, "Here I am" (Exod. 3:4). This is a statement of availability, not location. Second, the Lord *introduced* himself as the God of the patriarchs and communicated his intent to rescue his people from Egypt and to bring them into the land he had promised to Abraham (Exod. 3:6–9). Third, God *commissioned* Moses to go to Pharaoh to bring God's people out of Egypt (Exod. 3:10). Fourth, Moses *objected* (Exod. 3:11). Although he had just heard a powerful revelation of who was speaking to him in this moment, his immediate concern was, "Who am I?" In response to this, God *reassured*

---

[4] Brevard S. Childs, *Memory and Tradition in Israel* (London: SCM Press, 1962).

Moses with a promise of God's own presence (Exod. 3:12a). Finally, God spoke of a *confirming sign* (Exod. 3:12b).

These same elements are present in a number of other call narratives in Scripture—for example in the callings of Gideon, Isaiah, Jeremiah, Ezekiel, and some of Jesus' disciples. This is not a rigid formula, for many other call narratives in Scripture follow a different pattern. But it does suggest that God's call often comes via an extended series of encounters that guide a person in God's way over time.

	The Judge Gideon	The Prophet Isaiah	The Prophet Jeremiah	The Prophet Ezekiel	Jesus' Disciples in Matthew
Confrontation	6:11b–12a	6:1–2	1:4	1:1–28a	28:16–17
Introduction	6:12b–13	6:3–7	1:5a	1:28b–2:2	28:18
Commission	6:14	6:8–10	1:5b	2:3–5	28:19–20a
Objection	6:15	6:11a	1:6	2:6, 8	—
Reassurance	6:16	6:11b–13	1:7–8	2:6–7	28:20b
Confirming Sign	6:17–21	—	1:9–10	2:9–3:2	Possibly the book of Acts

Notice that these callings are *not* primarily to priestly or religious work in a congregation. Gideon was a military leader; Isaiah, Jeremiah, and Ezekiel social critics; and Jesus a king (although not in the traditional sense). In many churches today, the term "call" is limited to religious occupations, but this is not so in Scripture, and certainly not in Exodus. Moses himself was not a priest or religious leader (those were Aaron's and Miriam's roles), but a shepherd, statesman, and governor. The

Lord's question to Moses "What is that in your hand?" (Exod. 4:2) re-purposes Moses' ordinary tool of sheep-keeping for uses he would never have imagined possible (Exod. 4:3–5).

God's Work of Redemption for Israel (Exodus 5:1–6:28)

In the book of Exodus, God is the essential worker. The nature and intent of that divine work set the agenda for Moses' work and through him, the work of God's people. God's initial call to Moses included an explanation of God's work. This drove Moses to speak in the name of the Lord to Pharaoh saying, "Let my people go" (Exod. 5:1). Pharaoh's rebuttal was not merely verbal; he oppressed the Israelites more harshly than before. By the end of this episode, even the Israelites themselves had turned against Moses (Exod. 5:20–21). It is at this crucial point that in response to Moses' questioning God about the entire enterprise, God clarified the design of his work. What we read here in Exodus 6:2–8 pertains not only to the immediate context of Israel's oppression in Egypt. It frames an agenda that embraces all of God's work in the Bible.[5] It is important for all Christians to be clear about the scope of God's work, because it helps us to understand what it means to pray for God's kingdom to come and for his will to be done on earth as it is in heaven (Matt. 6:10). The fulfillment of these intentions is God's business. To accomplish them, he will involve the full range of his people, not merely those who do "religious" work. Coming to a clearer understanding of God's work equips us to consider better not only the nature of our work but the manner in which God intends for us to do it.

In order to better appreciate this key text, we will make some brief observations about it and then suggest how it is relevant to the theology of work. After an initially assuring response to Moses' accusatory question about God's mission (Exod. 5:22–6:1), God frames his more extended response with the words "I am the LORD" at the beginning and the end (Exod. 6:2, 8). This key phrase demarcates the paragraph and gives the content especially high priority. English readers must be care-

---

[5] Elmer Martens, *God's Design: A Focus on Old Testament Theology*, 3rd ed. (Grand Rapids: Baker, 1994). This section follows Martens's analysis of the four-part outline of God's design.

ful to note that this phrase does not communicate *what* God is in terms of a title. It reveals God's own name and therefore speaks to *who* he is.[6] He is the covenant-making, promise-keeping God who appeared to the patriarchs. The work God is about to do for his people is therefore grounded in the intentions that God has expressed to them. Namely, these are to multiply Abraham's descendants, to make his name great, and to bless him so that through Abraham, God would bless all the families of the earth (Gen. 12:2–3).

God's work then appears in four parts. These four redemptive purposes of God reappear in various ways throughout the Old Testament and even give shape to the pinnacle of God's redemptive work in Jesus Christ. First is the work of *deliverance*. "I will free you from the burdens of the Egyptians and deliver you from slavery to them. I will redeem you with an outstretched arm and with mighty acts of judgment" (Exod. 6:6). Inherent in this work of liberation is the frank truth that the world is a place of manifold oppression. Sometimes we use the word *salvation* to describe this activity of God, but we must be careful to avoid understanding it either in terms of rescue from earth to heaven (and certainly not from matter to spirit) or as merely forgiveness of sin. The God of Israel delivered his people by stepping into their world and effecting a change "on the ground," so to speak. Exodus not only shows God's deliverance of Israel from Pharaoh in Egypt, but it also sets the stage for the messianic king, Jesus, to *deliver* his people from their sins and conquer the devil, the ultimate evil tyrant (Matt. 1:21; 12:28).

Second, the Lord will form a *godly community*. "I will take you as my people, and I will be your God" (Exod. 6:7a). God did not deliver his people so they could live however they pleased, nor did he deliver them as isolated individuals. He intended to create a qualitatively different kind of community in which his people would live with him and one another in covenantal faithfulness. Every nation in ancient times had their "gods," but Israel's identity as God's people entailed a lifestyle of obedience to all of God's decrees, commands, and laws (Deut. 26:17–18).

---

[6] English Bibles employ the convention of using the word "Lᴏʀᴅ" (in small capital letters as distinct from "Lord") to represent the Hebrew name of God, YHWH.

As these values and actions would saturate their dealings with God and each other (and even those outside the covenant), Israel would increasingly demonstrate what it genuinely means to be God's people. Again, this forms the background for Jesus who would build his "church," not as a physical structure of brick or stone, but as a new *community* with disciples from all nations (Matt. 16:18; 28:19).

Third, the Lord will create an ongoing *relationship* between himself and his people. "You shall know that I am the LORD your God, who has freed you from the burdens of the Egyptians" (Exod. 6:7b). All of the other statements of God's purpose begin with the word *I* except this one. Here, the focus is on *you*. God intends *his people* to have a certain experience of their relationship with God who graciously rescued them. To us, knowledge seems practically equivalent to information. The biblical concept of knowledge embraces this notion, but it also includes interpersonal experience of knowing others. To say that God did not make himself "known" as "LORD" to Abraham does not mean that Abraham was unaware of the divine name "*YHWH*" (Gen. 13:4; 21:33). It means that Abraham and family had not yet personally experienced the significance of this name as descriptive of their promise-keeping God who would fight on behalf of his people to deliver them from slavery on a national scale.[7] Ultimately, this is taken up by Jesus, whose name "Emmanuel" means God "with us" in *relationship* (Matt. 1:23).

Fourth, God intends for his people to experience the *good life*. "I will bring you into the land that I swore to give to Abraham, Isaac, and Jacob; I will give it to you for a possession" (Exod. 6:8). God promised to give Abraham the land of Canaan, but it is not accurate to simply equate this "land" with our concept of a "region." It is a land of promise and provision. The regular and positive description of it as "flowing with milk and honey" (Exod. 3:8) highlights its symbolic nature as a place in which to live with

---

[7]The literature in Old Testament theology on this point is immense both in scope and depth of analysis. This is understandable, given the pivotal importance of God's self-revelation. Providing even a summary of the issues and approaches to this matter exceeds the scope of this article. For an able discussion of what is at stake and a fuller understanding of the position taken in this article, see Bruce K. Waltke and Charles Yu, *An Old Testament Theology: An Exegetical, Canonical, and Thematic Approach* (Grand Rapids: Zondervan, 2007), 359–69.

God and God's people in ideal conditions, something we understand as the "abundant life."[8] Here again we see that God's work of salvation is a setting to right of his entire creation—physical environment, people, culture, economics, everything. This is also the mission of Jesus as he initiates the kingdom of God coming to earth, where the meek inherit the earth (the land) and experience eternal life (Matt. 5:5; John 17:3).[9] This comes to completion in the New Jerusalem of Revelation 21 and 22. Exodus thus sets the path for the entirety of the Bible that follows.

Consider how our work today may express these four redemptive purposes. First, God's will is to *deliver* people from oppression and the harmful conditions of life. Some of that work rescues people from physical dangers; other work focuses on the alleviation of psychological and emotional trauma. The work of healing touches people one by one; those who forge political solutions to our needs can bless whole societies and classes of people. Workers in law enforcement and in the judicial system should aim to restrain and punish those who do evil, to protect people, and to care for victims. Given the pervasive extent of oppression in the world, there will always be manifold opportunities and means to work for deliverance.

The second and third purposes (*community* and *relationship*) are closely related to each other. Godly work that promotes peace and true harmony in heaven will enhance mercy and justice on earth. This is the gist of Paul's address to the Corinthians: through Christ, God has reconciled us to himself and thus given us the message and ministry of reconciliation (2 Cor. 5:16–20). Christians have experienced this reconciliation and therefore have motive and means to do this kind of work. The work of evangelism and spiritual development honors one dimension of the area; the work of peace and justice honors the interpersonal dimension. In essence, the two are inseparable and those who work in these fields do well to remember the holistic nature of what God is doing. Jesus taught that because we *are* the light of the world, we should let our light shine before others (Matt. 5:14–16).

Building community and relationships can be the *object* of our job, as in the case of community organizers, youth workers, social directors, event

---

[8] Martens, 10.

[9] For more on the land in the New Testament, see Waltke and Yu, 558–87.

planners, social media workers, parents and family members, and many others. But they can also be *elements* of our job, whatever our occupation. When we welcome and assist new workers, ask and listen as others talk about matters of significance, take the trouble to meet someone in person, send a note of encouragement, share a memorable photo, bring good food to share, include someone in a conversation, or myriad other acts of cama-raderie, we are fulfilling these two purposes of work, day by day.

Finally, godly work promotes the *good life*. God led his people *out* of Egypt in order to bring them *in* to the Promised Land where they could settle, live, and develop. Yet, what Israel experienced there was far less than God's ideal. Likewise, what Christians experience in the world is not ideal either. The promise of entering God's rest is still open (Heb. 4:1). We still wait for a new heaven and a new earth. But many of the laws of the covenant that God gave through Moses have to do with ethical treatment of one another. It is vital, then, that God's blessing be worked out in the way we live and work with one another. Seen from the negative side, how can we reasonably expect all families of the earth to experience God's blessing through us (the people of Abraham through faith in Christ), if we ourselves ignore God's instructions about how to live and do our work? As Christopher Wright has noted, "The people of God in both testaments are called to be a light to the nations. But there can be no light to the nations that is not shining already in transformed lives of a holy people."[10] It thus becomes clear that the kind of "good life" in view here has nothing to do with unbridled selfish prosperity or conspicuous consumption, for it embraces the wide spectrum of life as God intends it to be: full of love, justice, and mercy.

Moses and Aaron Announce God's Judgment to Pharaoh (Exodus 7:1–12:51)

God began the first step—deliverance—by sending Moses and Aaron to tell Pharaoh "to let the Israelites go out of his land" (Exod. 7:2). For this task, God made use of Aaron's natural skill in public speaking (Exod. 4:14; 7:1). He also equipped Aaron with skill surpassing that of the high

---

[10] Christopher J. H. Wright, *The Mission of God: Unlocking the Bible's Grand Narrative* (Downers Grove, IL: IVP Academic, 2006), 358.

officials of Egypt (Exod. 7:10–12). This reminds us that God's mission requires both word and action.

Pharaoh refused to listen to God's demand, through Moses, to release Israel from slavery. In turn, Moses announced God's judgment to Pharaoh through an increasingly severe series of ecological disasters (Exod. 7:17–10:29). These disasters caused personal misery. More significantly, they drastically impaired the productive capacity of Egypt's land and people. Disease caused livestock to die (Exod. 9:6). Crops failed and forests were ruined (Exod. 9:25). Pests invaded multiple ecosystems (Exod. 8:6, 24; 10:13–15). In Exodus, ecological disaster is the retribution of God against the tyranny and oppression of Pharaoh. In the modern world, political and economic oppression is a major factor in environmental degradation and ecological disaster. We would be fools to think we can assume Moses' authority and declare God's judgment in any of these. But we can see that when economics, politics, culture, and society are in need of redemption, so is the environment.

Each of these warnings-in-action convinced Pharaoh to release Israel, but as each passed, he reneged. Finally, God brought on the disaster of slaying every firstborn son among the people and animals of the Egyptians (Exod. 12:29–30). The appalling effect of slavery is to "harden" the heart against compassion, justice, and even self-preservation, as Pharaoh soon discovered (Exod. 11:10). Pharaoh then accepted God's demand to let Israel go free. The departing Israelites "plundered" the Egyptians' jewelry, silver, gold, and clothing (Exod. 12:35–36). This reversed the effects of slavery, which was the legalized plunder of exploited workers. When God liberates people, he restores their right to labor for fruits they themselves can enjoy (Isa. 65:21–22). Work, and the conditions under which it is performed, is a matter of the highest concern to God.

Israel at the Red Sea and on the Way to Sinai (Exodus 13:17–18:27)

The foundational expression of God's work came to dramatic fruition when God decisively led his people through the Red Sea, releasing them from Egypt's tyrannical hold. The God who had separated the waters of chaos and created dry land, the God who had brought Noah's family through the deluge to dry land, "divided" the waters of the Red Sea and led Israel across on "dry ground" (Exod. 14:21–22). Israel's journey from Egypt to Sinai is thus the continuation of the story of God's creation and redemption. Moses, Aaron, and others work hard, yet God is the real worker.

The Work of Justice among the People of Israel (Exodus 18:1–27)

While on the journey from Egypt to Sinai, Moses reconnected with his father-in-law Jethro. This former outsider to the Israelites offered much-needed counsel to Moses concerning justice in the community. God's work of redemption *for* his people was expanded into the work of justice *among* his people. Israel had already experienced unjust treatment at the hand of the Egyptian taskmasters. Out on their own, they rightly sought for *God's* answers to their own disputes. Walter Brueggemann has observed that biblical faith is not just about telling the story of what God has done. It is also "about the hard, sustained work of nurturing and practicing the daily passion of healing and restoring, and the daily rejection of dishonest gain."[11]

One of the first things we learned earlier about Moses was his desire to mediate between those embroiled in a dispute. Initially, when Moses tried to intervene, he was rebuked with the words, "Who made you a ruler and a judge over us?" (Exod. 2:14). In the current episode, we see just the opposite. Moses is in such demand as the ruler-judge that a multitude of people in need of his decisions gathered around him "from morning until evening" (Exod. 18:14; see also Deut. 1:9–18). Moses' work apparently has two aspects. First, he rendered legal decisions for people in dispute. Second, he taught God's statutes and instructions for those seeking moral and religious guidance.[12] Jethro observed that Moses was the sole agent in this noble work, but deemed the entire process to be unsustainable. "What you are doing is not good" (Exod. 18:17). Further-

---

[11] Walter Brueggemann, "The Book of Exodus," in vol. 1, *The New Interpreter's Bible: Genesis to Leviticus* (Nashville: Abingdon Press, 1994), 829.

[12] Umberto Moshe David Cassuto, *A Commentary on the Book of Exodus* (Skokie, IL: Varda Books, 2005), 219.

more, it was detrimental to Moses and unsatisfying for the people he was trying to help. Jethro's solution was to let Moses continue doing what he was uniquely qualified to do as God's representative: intercede with God for the people, instruct them, and decide the difficult cases. All of the other cases were to be delegated to subordinate judges who would serve in a four-tiered system of judicial administration.

The qualification of these judges is the key to the wisdom of the plan, for they were not selected according to the tribal divisions of the people or their religious maturity. They must meet four qualifications (Exod. 18:21). First, they must be capable. The Hebrew expression "men of *hayil*" connotes ability, leadership, management, resourcefulness, and due respect.[13] Second, they must "fear God." Third, they must be "trust-worthy." Because truth is an abstract concept as well as a way of acting, these people must have a public track record of truthful character as well as conduct. Finally, they must be haters of unjust gain. They must know how and why corruption occurs, despise the practice of bribery and all kinds of subversion, and actively guard the judicial process from these infections.

Delegation is essential to the work of leadership. Though Moses was *uniquely* gifted as a prophet, statesman, and judge, he was not *infinitely* gifted. Anyone who imagines that only he or she is capable of doing God's work well has forgotten what it means to be human. Therefore, the gift of leadership is ultimately the gift of giving away power ap-propriately. The leader, like Moses, must discern the qualities needed, train those who are to receive authority, and develop means to hold them accountable. The leader also needs to be held accountable. Jethro performed this task in Moses' case, and the passage is remarkably frank in showing how even the greatest of all the Old Testament prophets had to be confronted by someone with the power to hold him accountable. Wise, decisive, compassionate leadership is a gift from God that every human community needs. Yet Exodus shows us that it is not so much a matter of a gifted leader assuming authority over people, as it is God's

---

[13] For more on the word *hayil*, see Bruce Waltke and Alice Matthews, *Proverbs and Work*, Proverbs 31:10–31, beginning with the section "The Valiant Woman" at www.theologyofwork.org.

process for a community to develop structures of leadership in which gifted people can succeed. Delegation is the only way to increase the capacity of an institution or community, as well as the way to develop future leaders.

The fact that Moses accepted this counsel so quickly and thoroughly may be evidence of how personally desperate he was. But on a wider scale, we also can see that Moses (the Hebrew and heir of the Abrahamic promises) was completely open to God's wisdom mediated to him through a Midianite priest. This observation may encourage Christians to receive and respect input from a wide range of traditions and religions, notably in matters of work. Doing so is not necessarily a mark of disloyalty to Christ, nor does it expose a lack of confidence in our own faith. It is not an improper concession to religious pluralism. On the contrary, it may even be a poor witness to produce biblical quotes of wisdom too frequently, for in so doing, outsiders may perceive us as narrow and possibly insecure. Christians do well to be discerning about the specifics of the counsel we adopt, whether it comes from within or without. But in the final analysis, we are confident that "all truth is God's truth."[14]

Israel at Mount Sinai (Exodus 19:1–40:38)

At Mount Sinai, Moses received the Ten Commandments from the Lord. As the *NIV Study Bible* puts it, "The Ten Commandments are the central stipulations of God's covenant with Israel made at Sinai. It is almost impossible to exaggerate their effect on subsequent history. They constitute the basis of the moral principles found throughout the Western world and summarize what the one true God expects of his people in terms of faith, worship and conduct."[15] As we will see, the role of the Israelite law for Christians is the subject of a great deal of controversy. For these reasons, we will be attentive to what the text of Exodus actually says, for this is what we hold in common. At the same time, we hope to

---

[14] Arthur Holmes, *All Truth is God's Truth* (Downers Grove, IL: InterVarsity Press, 1983).

[15] Kenneth Barker, ed., *The NIV Study Bible* (Grand Rapids: Zondervan, 1999), 269.

be aware and respectful of the variety of ways that Christians may wish to draw lessons from this part of the Bible.

The Meaning of Law in Exodus (Exodus 19:1–24:18)

We begin by recognizing that Exodus is an integral part of the whole of Scripture, not a stand-alone legal statue. Christopher Wright has written:

> The common opinion that the Bible is a moral code book for Christians falls far short, of course, of the full reality of what the Bible is and does. The Bible is essentially the story of God, the earth and humanity; it is the story of what has gone wrong, what God has done to put it right, and what the future holds under the sovereign plan of God. Nevertheless, within that grand narrative, moral teaching does have a vital place. The Bible's story is the story of the mission of God. The Bible's demand is for the appropriate response from human beings. God's mission calls for and includes human response. And our mission certainly includes the ethical dimension of that response.[16]

The English word *law* is a traditional yet inaccurate rendering of the key Hebrew word *Torah*. Because this term is so central to the entire discussion at hand, it will help us to clarify how this Hebrew word actually works in the Bible. The word *Torah* appears once in Genesis in the sense of instructions from God that Abraham followed. It can refer to instructions from one human to another (Ps. 78:1). But as something from God, the word *Torah* throughout the Pentateuch and the rest of the Old Testament designates a standard of conduct for God's people pertaining to ceremonial matters of formal worship, as well as statutes for civil and social conduct.[17] The biblical notion of Torah conveys the sense of "divinely authoritative instruction." This concept is far from our modern ideas of law as a body of codes crafted and enacted by legislators or "natural" laws.

---

[16] Wright, 357–58.

[17] Peter Enns, "Law of God," in *New International Dictionary of Old Testament Theology and Exegesis*, ed. Willem A. VanGemeren (Grand Rapids: Zondervan, 1997), 4:893. The word also refers to a body of literature in that the historical core of the book of Deuteronomy is called "the Book of the Law" (Deuteronomy 31:26). Traditionally, the entire Pentateuch is called "the Torah."

To highlight the rich and instructive nature of law in Exodus, we shall sometimes refer to it as Torah with no attempt at translation.

In Exodus, it is clear that Torah in the sense of a set of specific instructions is part of the covenant and not the other way around. In other words, the covenant as a whole describes the relationship that God has established between himself and his people by virtue of his act of deliverance on their behalf (Exod. 20:2). As the people's covenantal king, God then specifies how he desires Israel to worship and behave. Israel's pledge to obey is a *response* to God's gift of the covenant (Exod. 24:7). This is significant for our understanding of the theology of work. The way we discern God's will for our behavior at work and the way we put that into practice in the workplace are enveloped by the relationship that God has established with us. In Christian terms, we love God because he first loved us and we demonstrate that love in how we treat others (1 John 4:19–21). The categorical nature of God's command for us to love our neighbors means that God intends for us to apply it everywhere, regardless of whether we find ourselves in a church, café, home, civic venue, or place of work.

The Role of the Law for Christians (Exodus 20:1–24:18)

It can be a challenge for a Christian to draw a point from a verse in the book of Exodus or especially Leviticus, and then suggest how that lesson should be applied today. Anyone who tries this should be prepared for the comeback, "Sure, but the Bible also permits slavery and says we can't eat bacon or shrimp! Plus, I don't think God really cares if my clothes are a cotton-polyester blend" (Exod. 21:2–11; Lev. 11:7, 12; and 19:19, respectively). Since this happens even within Christian circles, we should not be surprised to find difficulties when applying the Bible to the subject of work in the public sphere. How are we to know what applies today and what doesn't? How do we avoid the charge of inconsistency in our handling of the Bible? More importantly, how do we let God's word truly transform us in every area of life? The diversity of laws in Exodus and the Pentateuch presents one type of challenge. Another comes from the variety of ways that Christians understand and apply Torah and the Old Testament in relationship to Christ and the New Testament. Still, the issue of Torah in Christianity is crucial and must be addressed in order for us to glean anything about what this part of the Bible says concerning our work. The following brief treatment aims to be helpful without being overly narrow.

The New Testament's relationship to the law is complex. It includes both Jesus' saying that "Not one letter, not one stroke of a letter, will pass from the law" (Matt. 5:18), and Paul's statement that "we are discharged from the law . . . not under the old written code but in the new life of the Spirit" (Rom. 7:6). These are not two opposing statements, but two ways of saying a common reality—that the Torah continues to reveal God's gift of justice, wisdom, and inner transformation to those he has brought to new life in Christ. God gave the Torah as an expression of his holy nature and as a consequence of his great deliverance. Reading the Torah makes us aware of our inherent sinfulness and of our need for a remedy in order for us to live at peace with God and one another. God expects his people to obey his instructions by applying them to real issues of life both great and small. The specific nature of some laws does not mean God is an unrealistic perfectionist. These laws help us to understand that no issue we face is too small or insignificant for God. Even so, the Torah is not just about outward behavior, for it addresses matters of the heart such as coveting (Exod. 20:17). Later, Jesus would condemn not just murder and adultery, but the roots of anger and lust as well (Matt. 5:22, 28).

However, obeying the Torah by applying it to the real issues of life today does not equate to repeating the actions that Israel performed thousands of years ago. Already in the Old Testament we see hints that some parts of the law were not intended to be permanent. The tabernacle certainly was not a permanent structure and even the temple was demolished at the hands of Israel's enemies (2 Kgs. 25:9). Yet Jesus spoke of his own sacrificial death and resurrection when he said he would raise the destroyed "temple" in three days (John 2:19). In some important sense, he embodied all that the temple, its priesthood, and its activities stood for. Jesus' declaration about food—that it is not what goes into people that makes them unclean—meant that the specific food laws of the Mosaic Covenant were no longer in force (Mark 7:19).[18] Moreover, in

---

[18] Tim Keller, "Keller on Rules of the Bible: Do Christians Apply them Inconsistently?" The Gospel Coalition, http://thegospelcoalition.org/blogs/tgc/2012/07/09/making-sense-of-scriptures-inconsistency/.

the New Testament the people of God live in various countries and cultures around the world where they have no legal authority to apply the sanctions of the Torah. The apostles considered such issues and, under the Holy Spirit's guidance, decided that the particulars of the Jewish law did not in general apply to Gentile Christians (Acts 15:28–29).

When asked about which commandments were most important, Jesus' answer was not controversial in light of the theology of his time. "Love the Lord your God with all your heart, and with all your soul, and with all your mind, and with all your strength" and "Love your neighbor as yourself" (Mark 12:30–31).[19]

Much in the New Testament confirms the Torah, not only in its negative commands against adultery, murder, theft, and coveting, but also in its positive command to love one another (Rom. 13:8–10; Gal. 5:14). According to Timothy Keller, "The coming of Christ changed how we worship, but not how we live."[20] This is not surprising, given that in the new covenant, God said he would put his law within his people and write it on their hearts (Jer. 31:33; Luke 22:20). Israel's faithfulness to the laws of Mosaic Covenant depended on their determination to obey them. In the end, only Jesus could accomplish this. On the other hand, new covenant believers do not work that way. According to Paul, "We serve in the new way of the Spirit" (Rom. 7:6 NIV).

For our purposes in considering the theology of work, the previous explanation suggests several points that may help us to understand and apply the laws in Exodus that relate to the workplace. The specific laws dealing with proper treatment of workers, animals, and property express abiding values of God's own nature. They are to be taken seriously but not slavishly. On the one hand, items in the Ten Commandments are worded in general terms and may be applied freely in varied contexts. On the other hand, particular laws about servants, livestock, and personal injuries exemplify applications in the specific historical and social context of ancient Israel, especially in areas that were controversial at the time. These laws are illustrative of right behavior but do not exhaust

---

[19] James Tabor and Randall Buth, *Living Biblical Hebrew for Everyone* (Pasadena, CA: Internet Language Corp., 2003).

[20] Keller, "Rules of the Bible."

every possible application. Christians honor God and his law not only by regulating our behavior, but also by allowing the Holy Spirit to transform our attitudes, motives, and desires (Rom. 12:1–2). To do anything less would amount to sidestepping the work and will of our Lord and Savior. Christians should always seek how love may guide our policies and behaviors.

Instructions about Work (Exodus 20:1–17 and 21:1–23:9)

Israel's "Book of the Covenant" (Exod. 24:7) included the Ten Commandments, also known as the Decalogue (literally, the "words," Exod. 20:1–17), and the ordinances of Exodus 21:1–23:19. The Ten Commandments are worded as general commands either to do or not do something. The ordinances are a collection of case laws, applying the values of the Decalogue in specific situations using an "if . . . then" format. These laws fit the social and economic world of ancient Israel. They are not an exhaustive legal code, but they function as exemplars, serving to curb the worst excesses and setting legal precedent for handling difficult cases.[21]

The Ten Commandments (Exodus 20:1–17)

The Ten Commandments are the supreme expression of God's will in the Old Testament and merit our close attention. They are to be thought of not as the ten most important commands among hundreds of others, but as a digest of the entire Torah. The foundation of all the Torah rests in the Ten Commandments, and somewhere within them we should be able to find *all* the law. Jesus expressed the essential unity of the Ten Commandments with the rest of the law when he summarized the law in the famous words, " 'You shall love the Lord your God with all your heart, and with all your soul, and with all your mind.' This is the greatest and first commandment. And a second is like it: 'You shall love your neighbor as yourself.' On these two commandments hang all the law and the prophets" (Matt. 22:37–40). *All* the law, as well as the prophets, is indicated whenever the Ten Commandments are expressed.

---

[21] Gordon J. Wenham, *Exploring the Old Testament, A Guide to the Pentateuch*, vol. 1 (Downers Grove, IL: IVP Academic, 2008), 71.

The essential unity of the Ten Commandments with the rest of the law, and their continuity with the New Testament, invites us to apply them to today's work broadly in light of the rest of the Scripture. That is, when applying the Ten Commandments, we will take into account related passages of Scripture in both the Old and New Testaments.

"You Shall Have No Other Gods before Me" (Exodus 20:3)

The first commandment reminds us that everything in the Torah flows from the love we have for God, which in turn is a response to the love he has for us. This love was demonstrated by God's deliverance of Israel "out of the house of slavery" in Egypt (Exod. 20:2). Nothing else in life should concern us more than our desire to love and be loved by God. If we *do* have some other concern stronger to us than our love for God, it is not so much that we are breaking God's rules, but that we are not really in relationship with God. The other concern—be it money, power, security, recognition, sex, or anything else—has become our god. This god will have its own commandments at odds with God's, and we will inevitably violate the Torah as we comply with this god's requirements. Observing the Ten Commandments is only conceivable for those who start by having no other god than God.

In the realm of work, this means that we are not to let work or its requirements and fruits displace God as our most important concern in life. "Never allow anyone or anything to threaten God's central place in your life," as David Gill puts it.[22] Because many people work primarily to make money, an inordinate desire for money is probably the most common work-related danger to the first commandment. Jesus warned of exactly this danger. "No one can serve two masters. . . . You cannot serve God and wealth" (Matt. 6:24). But almost anything related to work can become twisted in our desires to the point that it interferes with our love for God. How many careers come to a tragic end because the *means* to accomplish things for the love of God—such as political power, financial sustainability, commitment to the job, status among peers, or

---

[22] David W. Gill, *Doing Right: Practicing Ethical Principles* (Downers Grove, IL: IVP Books, 2004), 83. Gill's book contains an extended exegesis and application of the Ten Commandments in the modern world, which merits careful attention.

superior performance—become ends in themselves? When, for example, recognition on the job becomes more important than character on the job, is it not a sign that reputation is displacing the love of God as the ultimate concern?

A practical touchstone is to ask whether our love of God is shown by the way we treat people on the job. "Those who say, 'I love God,' and hate their brothers or sisters, are liars; for those who do not love a brother or sister whom they have seen, cannot love God whom they have not seen. The commandment we have from him is this: those who love God must love their brothers and sisters also" (1 John 4:20–21). If we put our individual concerns ahead of our concern for the people we work with, for, and among, then we have made our individual concerns our god. In particular, if we treat other people as things to be manipulated, obstacles to overcome, instruments to obtain what we want, or simply neutral objects in our field of view, then we demonstrate that we do not love God with all our heart, soul, and mind.

In this context, we can begin to list some work-related actions that have a high potential to interfere with our love for God. Doing work that violates our conscience. Working in an organization where we have to harm others to succeed. Working such long hours that we have little time to pray, worship, rest, and otherwise deepen our relationship with God. Working among people who demoralize us or seduce us away from our love for God. Working where alcohol, drug abuse, violence, sexual harassment, corruption, disrespect, racism, or other inhumane treatment mar the image of God in us and the people we encounter in our work. If we can find ways to avoid these dangers at work—even if it means finding a new job—it would be wise to do so. If that is not possible, we can at least be aware that we need help and support to maintain our love of God in the face of our work.

"You Shall Not Make for Yourself an Idol" (Exodus 20:4)

The second commandment raises the issue of idolatry. Idols are gods of our own creation, gods that have nothing to them that did not originate with us, gods that we feel we control. In ancient times, idolatry often took the form of worshiping physical objects. But the issue is really one of trust and devotion. On what do we ultimately pin our hope of well-being and success? Anything that is not capable of fulfilling our hope—that is, anything other than God—is an idol, whether or not it is a physical object. The story of a family forging an idol with the intent to manipulate God, and the disastrous personal, social, and economic consequences that follow, are memorably told in Judges 17–21.

In the world of work, it is common to speak of money, fame, and power as potential idols, and rightly so. They are not idolatrous, per se, and in fact may be necessary for us to accomplish our roles in God's creative and redemptive work in the world. Yet when we imagine that we have ultimate control over them, or that by achieving them our safety and prosperity will be secured, we have begun to fall into idolatry. The same may occur with virtually every other element of success, including preparation, hard work, creativity, risk, wealth and other resources, and favorable circumstances. As workers, we have to recognize how important these are. As God's people, we must recognize when we begin to idolize them. By God's grace, we can overcome the temptation to worship these good things in their own right. The development of genuinely godly wisdom and skill for any task is "*so that* your trust may be in the Lord" (Prov. 22:19; emphasis added).

The distinctive element of idolatry is the human-made nature of the idol. At work, a danger of idolatry arises when we mistake our power, knowledge, and opinions for reality. When we stop holding ourselves accountable to the standards we set for other, cease listening to others' ideas, or seek to crush those who disagree with us, are we not beginning to make idols of ourselves?

"You Shall Not Make Wrongful Use of the Name of the LORD Your God" (Exodus 20:7)

The third commandment literally prohibits God's people from making "wrongful use" of the name of God. This need not be restricted to the name "YHWH" (Exod. 3:15), but includes "God," "Jesus," "Christ," and so forth. But what is wrongful use? It includes, of course, disrespectful use in cursing, slandering, and blaspheming. But more significantly it includes falsely attributing human designs to God. This prohibits us from claiming God's authority for our own actions and decisions. Regrettably, some Christians seem to believe that following God at work consists primarily of speaking for God on the basis of their individual understanding, rather than working respectfully with others or taking responsibility for their actions. "It is God's will that . . ." or "God is punishing you for . . ." are very dangerous things to say, and almost never valid when spoken by an individual without the discernment of the community of faith (1 Thess. 5:20–21). In this light, perhaps the traditional Jewish reticence to utter even the English translation "God"—let alone the divine name itself—demonstrates a wisdom Christians often lack. If we were a little more careful about bandying the word "God" about, perhaps we would be more judicious in claiming to know God's will, especially as it applies to other people.

The third commandment also reminds us that respecting human names is important to God. The Good Shepherd "calls his own sheep by name" (John 10:3) while warning us that if you call another person "you fool," then "you will be liable to the hell of fire" (Matt. 5:22). Keeping this in mind, we shouldn't make wrongful use of other people's names or call them by disrespectful epithets. We use people's names wrongfully when we use them to curse, humiliate, oppress, exclude, and defraud. We use people's names well when we use them to encourage, thank, create solidarity, and welcome. Simply to learn and say someone's name is a blessing, especially if he or she is often treated as nameless, invisible, or insignificant. Do you know the name of the person who empties your trash can, answers your customer service call, or drives your bus? If these examples do not concern the very name of the Lord, they do concern the name of those made in his image.

"Remember the Sabbath Day and Keep It Holy. Six Days You Shall Labor" (Exodus 20:8–11)

The issue of the Sabbath is complex, not only in the book of Exodus and the Old Testament, but also in Christian theology and practice. The first part of the command calls for ceasing labor one day in seven. The other references in Exodus to the Sabbath are in chapter 16 (about gathering manna), Exodus 23:10–12 (the seventh year and the goal of weekly rest), Exodus 31:12–17 (penalty for violation), Exodus 34:21 and Exodus 35:1–3. In the context of the ancient world, the Sabbath was unique to Israel. On the one hand, this was an incomparable gift to the people of Israel. No other ancient people had the privilege of resting one day in seven. On the other hand, it required an extraordinary trust in God's provision. Six days of work had to be enough to plant crops, gather the harvest, carry water, spin cloth, and draw sustenance from creation. While Israel rested one day every week, the encircling nations continued to forge swords, feather arrows, and train soldiers. Israel had to trust God not to let a day of rest lead to economic and military catastrophe.

We face the same issue of trust in God's provision today. If we heed God's commandment to observe God's own cycle of work and rest, will we be able to compete in the modern economy? Does it take seven days of work to hold a job (or two or three jobs), clean the house, prepare the meals, mow the lawn, wash the car, pay the bills, finish the school work, and shop for the clothes, or can we trust God to provide for us even if we take a day off during the course of every week? Can we take time to worship God, to pray and to gather with others for study and encourage-ment, and, if we do, will it make us more or less productive overall? The fourth commandment does not explain how God will make it all work out for us. It simply tells us to rest one day every seven.

Christians have translated the day of rest to the Lord's Day (Sunday, the day of Christ's resurrection), but the essence of the Sabbath is not choosing one particular day of the week over another (Rom. 14:5–6). The polarity that actually undergirds the Sabbath is *work* and *rest*. Both work and rest are included in the fourth commandment. The six days of work are as much a part of the commandment as the one day of rest. Although many Christians are in danger of allowing work to squeeze the time set aside for rest, others are in danger of the opposite, of shirking work and trying to live a life of leisure and dissipation. This is even worse than neglecting the Sabbath, for "whoever does not provide for relatives, and especially for family members, has denied the faith and is worse than an unbeliever" (1 Tim. 5:8). What we need is a proper rhythm of work and rest, which together are good for us, our family, workers, and guests. The rhythm may or may not include twenty-four continuous hours of rest falling on Sunday (or Saturday). The proportions may change due to temporary necessities (the modern equivalent of pulling an ox out of the well on the Sabbath, see Luke 14:5) or the changing needs of the seasons of life.

If overwork is our main danger, we need to find a way to honor the fourth commandment without instituting a false, new legalism pitting the spiritual (worship on Sunday worship) against the secular (work on Monday through Saturday). If avoiding work is our danger, we need to learn how to find joy and meaning in working as a service to God and our neighbors (Eph. 4:28).

"Honor Your Father and Your Mother" (Exodus 20:12)

There are many ways to honor—or dishonor—your father and mother. In Jesus' day, the Pharisees wanted to restrict this to speaking well of them. But Jesus pointed out that obeying this commandment requires working to provide for your parents (Mark 7:9–13). We honor people by working for their good.

For many people, good relationships with parents are one of the joys of life. Loving service to them is a delight, and obeying this commandment is easy. But we are put to the test by this commandment when we find it burdensome to work on behalf of our parents. We may have been ill-treated or neglected by them. They may be controlling and meddlesome. Being around them may undermine our sense of self, our commitment to our spouses (including our responsibilities under the third commandment), even our relationship with God. Even if we have good relationships with our parents, there may come a time when caring for them is a major burden simply because of the time and work it takes. If aging or dementia begins to rob them of their memory, capabilities, and good nature, caring for them can become a deep sorrow.

Yet the fifth commandment comes with a promise, "that your days may be long in the land that the Lord your God is giving you" (Gen. 20:12). Somehow, honoring our father and mother in such practical ways has the practical benefit of giving us longer (perhaps in the sense of more fulfilling) life in God's kingdom. We are not told how this will occur, but we are told to expect it, and to do that we must trust God (see the first commandment).

Because this is a command to work for the benefit of parents, it is inherently a workplace command. The place of work may be where we earn money to support them, or it may be in the place where we assist them in the tasks of daily life. Both are work. When we take a job because it allows us to live near them, or send money to them, or make use of the values and gifts they developed in us, or accomplish things they taught us are important, we are honoring them. When we *limit* our careers so that we can be present with them, clean and cook for them, bathe and embrace them, take them to the places they love, or diminish their fears, we are honoring them.

We must also recognize that in many cultures, the work people do is dictated by the choices of their parents and needs of their families rather than their own decisions and preferences. At times this gives rise to serious conflict for Christians who find the demands of the first commandment (to follow God's call) and fifth commandment competing with each other. They find themselves forced to make hard choices that parents don't understand. Even Jesus experienced such parental misunderstanding when Mary and Joseph could not understand why he remained behind in the temple while his family departed Jerusalem (Luke 2:49).

In our workplaces, we can help other people fulfill the fifth commandment, as well as obeying it ourselves. We can remember that employees, customers, co-workers, bosses, suppliers, and others also have families, and then can adjust our expectations to support them in honoring their families. When others share or complain about their struggles with parents, we can listen to them compassionately, support them practically (for example, by offering to take a shift so they can be with their parents), perhaps offer a godly perspective for them to consider, or simply reflect the grace of Christ to those who feel they are failing in their parent-child relationships.

"You Shall Not Murder" (Exodus 20:13)

Sadly, the sixth commandment has an all-too-practical application in the modern workplace, where 10 percent of all job-related fatalities (in the United States) are homicides.[23] However, admonishing readers of this article, "Don't murder anyone at work," isn't likely to change this statistic much.

---

[23] "Fact Sheet: Workplace Shootings 2010," United States Department of Labor, *Bureau of Labor Statistics*, http://www.bls.gov/iif/oshwc/cfoi/osar0014.htm.

But murder isn't the only form of workplace violence, just the most extreme. Jesus said that even anger is a violation of the sixth commandment (Matt. 5:21–22). As Paul noted, we may not be able to prevent the feeling of anger, but we can learn how to cope with it. "Be angry but do not sin; do not let the sun go down on your anger" (Eph. 4:26). The most significant implication of the sixth commandment for work then may be, "If you get angry at work, get help in anger management." Many employers, churches, state and local governments, and nonprofit organizations offer classes and counseling in anger management, and availing yourself of these may be a highly effective way of obeying the sixth commandment.

Murder is intentional killing, but the case law that stems from the sixth commandment shows that we also have the duty to prevent unintended deaths. A particularly graphic case is when an ox (a work animal) gores a man or woman to death (Exod. 21:28–29). If the event was predictable, the ox's owner is to be treated as a murderer. In other words, owners/managers are responsible for ensuring workplace safety within reason. This principle is well established in law in most countries, and workplace safety is the subject of significant government policing, industry self-regulation, and organizational policy and practice. Yet workplaces of all kinds continue to require or allow workers to work in needlessly unsafe conditions. Christians who have any role in setting the conditions of work, supervising workers, or modeling workplace practices are reminded by the sixth commandment that safe working conditions are among their highest responsibilities in the world of work.

"You Shall Not Commit Adultery" (Exodus 20:14)

The workplace is one of the most common settings for adultery, not necessarily because adultery occurs in the workplace itself, but because it arises from the conditions of work and relationships with co-workers. The first application to the workplace, then, is literal. Married people should not have sex with people other than their spouses at, in, or because of their work. Obviously this rules out sex professions such as prostitution, pornography, and sex surrogacy, at least in most cases. But any kind of work that erodes the bonds of marriage infringes the seventh commandment. There are many ways this can occur. Work that encourages strong emotional bonds among co-workers without adequately supporting their commitments to their spouses, as can happen in hospitals, entrepreneurial ventures, academic institutions and churches, among other places. Working conditions that bring people into close physical contact for extended periods or that fail to encourage reasonable limits to off-hour encounters, as could happen on extended field assignments. Work that subjects people to sexual harassment and pressure to have sex with those holding power over them. Work that inflates people's egos or exposes them to adulation, as could occur with celebrities, star athletes, business titans, high-ranking government officials, and the super-rich. Work that demands so much time away (physically, mentally, or emotionally) that it frays the bonds between spouses. All of these may pose dangers that Christians would do well to recognize and avoid, ameliorate, or guard against. Yet the seriousness of the seventh commandment arises not so much because adultery is illicit sex, as because it breaks a covenant ordained by God. God created husband and wife to become "one flesh" (Gen. 2:24), and Jesus' commentary on the seventh commandment highlights God's role in the marriage covenant. "What God has joined together, let no one separate" (Matt. 19:6). To commit adultery, therefore, is not only to have sex with someone you shouldn't, but also to break a covenant with the Lord God. In fact, the Old Testament frequently uses the word *adultery*, and the imagery surrounding it, to refer not to sexual sin but to idolatry. The prophets often refer to Israel's faithlessness to its covenant to worship God alone as "adultery" or "whoring," as in Isaiah 57:3, Jeremiah 3:8, Ezekiel 16:38, and Hosea 2:2, among many others. Therefore, any breaking of faith with the God of Israel is figuratively adultery, whether it involves illicit sex or not. This use of the term "adultery" unites the first, second, and seventh commandments, and reminds us that the Ten Commandments are expressions of a single covenant with God, rather than some kind of top-ten list of rules.

Therefore, work that requires or leads us into idolatry or worshipping other gods is to be avoided. It's hard to imagine how a Christian could work as a tarot reader, a maker of idolatrous art or music, or a publisher of blasphemous books. Christian actors may find it difficult to perform profane, irreligious, or spiritually demoralizing roles. Everything we do in life, including work, tends in some degree either to enhance or diminish our relationship with God; over a lifetime, the constant stress of work that diminishes us spiritually may prove devastating. It's a factor we would do well to include in our career decisions, to the degree we have choices.

The distinctive aspect of covenants violated by adultery is that they are covenants with God. But isn't every promise or agreement made by a Christian implicitly a covenant with God? Paul exhorts us, "Whatever you do, in word or deed, do everything in the name of the Lord Jesus" (Col. 3:17). Contracts, promises and agreements are surely things we do in word or deed, or both. If we do them all in the name of the Lord Jesus, it cannot be that some promises must be honored because they are covenants with God, while others may be broken because they are merely human. We are to honor all our agreements, and to avoid inducing others to break theirs. Whether this is contained in Exodus 20:14 itself, or expounded in the Old and New Testament teachings that arise from it, "Keep your promises, and help others keep theirs" may serve as a fine derivation of the seventh commandment in the world of work.

"You Shall Not Steal" (Exodus 20:15)

The eighth commandment is another that takes work as its primary subject. Stealing is a violation of proper work because it dispossesses the victim of the fruits of his or her labor. It is also a violation of the commandment to labor six days a week, since in most cases stealing is intended as a shortcut around honest labor, which shows again the interrelation of the Ten Commandments. So we may take it as the word of God that we are not to steal from those we work for, with, or among.

Stealing occurs in many forms besides robbing someone. Any time we acquire something of value from its rightful owner without consent, we are engaging in theft. Misappropriating resources or funds for personal use is stealing. Using deception to make sales, gain market share, or raise prices is stealing because the deception means that whatever the buyer consents to is not the actual situation. (See the section on "Puffery/ Exaggeration" in *Truth & Deception* at www.theologyofwork.org for more on this topic.) Likewise, profiting by taking advantage of people's fears, vulnerabilities, powerlessness, or desperation is a form of stealing because their consent is not truly voluntary. Violating patents, copyrights, and other intellectual property laws is stealing because it deprives owners of the ability to profit from their creation under the terms of civil law.

Regrettably, many jobs seem to include an element of taking advantage of others' ignorance or lack of alternatives to force them into transactions they otherwise wouldn't agree to. Companies, governments, individuals, unions, and other players may use their power to coerce others into unfair wages, prices, financial terms, working conditions, hours, or other factors. Although we may not rob banks, steal from our employers, or shoplift, we may very likely be participating in unfair or unethical practices that deprive others of what rights should be theirs. It can be difficult, even career-limiting, to resist engaging in these practices, but we are called to do so nonetheless.

"You Shall Not Bear False Witness against Your Neighbor" (Exodus 20:16)

The ninth commandment honors the right to one's own reputation.[24] It finds pointed application in legal proceedings where what people say depicts reality and determines the course of lives. Judicial decisions and other legal processes wield great power. Manipulating them undercuts the ethical fabric of society and thus constitutes a very serious offense. Walter Brueggemann says this commandment recognizes "that community life is not possible unless there is an arena in which there is public confidence that social reality will be reliably described and reported."[25]

Although stated in courtroom language, the ninth commandment also applies to a broad range of situations that touch practically every aspect of life. We should never say or do anything that misrepresents someone else. Brueggemann again provides insight:

> Politicians seek to destroy one another in negative campaigning; gossip columnists feed off calumny; and in Christian living rooms, reputations are tarnished or destroyed over cups of coffee served in fine china with dessert. These de facto courtrooms are conducted without due process of law. Accusations are made; hearsay allowed; slander, perjury, and libelous comments uttered without objection. No evidence, no defense. As Christians, we must refuse to participate in or to tolerate any conversa-

---

[24] Brueggemann, 431.
[25] Brueggemann, 848.

tion in which a person is being defamed or accused without the person being there to defend himself. It is wrong to pass along hearsay in any form, even as prayer requests or pastoral concerns. More than merely not participating, it is up to Christians to stop rumors and those who spread them in their tracks.[26]

This further suggests that workplace gossip is a serious offense. Some of it pertains to personal, off-site matters, which is evil enough. But what about cases when an employee tarnishes the reputation of a co-worker? Can truth ever truly be spoken when those being talked about are not there to speak for themselves? And what about assessments of performance? What safeguards ought to be in place to ensure that reports are fair and accurate? On a large scale, the business of marketing and advertisement operates in the public space among organizations and individuals. In the interest of presenting one's own products and services in the best possible light, to what extent may one point out the flaws and weaknesses of the competition, without incorporating their perspective? Is it possible that the rights of "your neighbor" could include the rights of other companies? The scope of our global economy suggests this command may have very wide application indeed. In a world where perception often counts for reality, the rhetoric of effective persuasion may or may not have much, if anything, to do with genuine truth. The divine origin of this command reminds us that people may not be able to detect when our representation of others is accurate or not, but God cannot be fooled. It's good to do the right thing when nobody is watching. With this command, we understand that we must *say* the right thing when *anybody* is listening. (See *Truth & Deception* at www.theologyofwork.org for a much fuller discussion of this topic, including whether the prohibition of "false witness against your neighbor" includes all forms of lying and deception.)

"You Shall Not Covet . . . Anything That Belongs to Your Neighbor" (Exodus 20:17)

Envy and acquisitiveness can arise anywhere in life, including at work where status, pay, and power are routine factors in our relation-

---

[26] Brueggemann, 432.

ships with people we spend a lot of time with. We may have many good reasons to desire achievement, advancement, or reward at work. But envy isn't one of them. Nor is working obsessively out of envy for the social standing it may enable.

In particular, we face temptation at work to falsely inflate our accomplishments at the expense of others. The antidote is simple, although hard to do at times. Make it a consistent practice to recognize the accomplishments of others and give them all the credit they deserve. If we can learn to rejoice in—or at least acknowledge—others' successes, then we cut off the lifeblood of envy and covetousness at work. Even better, if we can learn how to work so that our success goes hand-in-hand with others' success, covetousness is replaced by collaboration and envy by unity.

Leith Anderson, former pastor of Wooddale Church in Eden Prairie, Minnesota, says, "As the senior pastor, it's as if I have an unlimited supply of coins in my pocket. Whenever I give credit to a staff member for a good idea, praise a volunteer's work, or thank someone, it's like I'm slipping a coin from my pocket into theirs. That's my job as the leader, to slip coins from my pocket to others' pockets, to build up the appreciation other people have for them."[27]

Case Laws in the Book of the Covenant (Exodus 21:1–23:33)

A collection of case laws follows, flowing from the Ten Commandments. Instead of developing detailed principles, it gives examples of how to apply God's law to the kinds of cases that commonly arose in the conduct of daily life. As cases, they are all embedded in the situations faced by the people of Israel. Indeed, throughout the Pentateuch (the Torah), it can be difficult to sift out the specific laws from the surrounding narrative and exhortation. Four sections of the case law are particularly applicable to work today.

Slavery or Indentured Servitude (Exodus 21:1–11)

Although God liberated the Hebrews from slavery in Egypt, slavery is not universally prohibited in the Bible. Slavery was permissible in

---

[27] Reported by William Messenger from a conversation with Leith Anderson on October 20, 2004, in Charlotte, North Carolina.

certain situations, so long as slaves were regarded as full members of the community (Gen. 17:12), received the same rest periods and holidays as non-slaves (Exod. 23:12; Deut. 5:14–15; 12:12), and were treated humanely (Exod. 21:7, 26–27). Most importantly, slavery was not intended as a permanent condition, but a voluntary, temporary refuge for people suffering what would otherwise be desperate poverty. "When you buy a male Hebrew slave, he shall serve six years, but in the seventh he shall go out a free person, without debt" (Exod. 21:2). Cruelty on the part of the owner resulted in immediate freedom for the slave (Exod. 21:26–27). This made Hebrew slavery more like a kind of long-term labor contract among individuals, and less like the kind of permanent racial/class/ethnic exploitation that has characterized slavery in modern times.

Also in contrast to slavery in the United States, which generally forbade marriage among slaves, the regulations in Exodus aim to preserve families intact. "If he comes in single, he shall go out single; if he comes in married, then his wife shall go out with him" (Exod. 21:3). The general equality between slave owners and slaves is highlighted by the regulations about female slaves in Exodus 21:7–11. The only purpose contemplated for buying a female slave was so that she could become the wife of either the buyer or the buyer's son (Exod. 21:8–9). She became the social equal (as wife) of the slaveholder, and the purchase functioned much like the giving of a dowry. Indeed, she is even called a "wife" by the regulation (Exod. 21:10). Moreover, if the buyer failed to treat the female slave with all the rights due an ordinary wife, he was required to set her free. "She shall go out without debt, without payment of money" (Exod. 21:11). Despite these regulations, it appears that in some cases, girls or women were bought as wives for a male slave, rather than for the slave owner or a son, which resulted in a very problematic situation (Exod. 21:4).

By no means does this suggest that slavery was an idyllic situation. Slaves were, for the duration of their enslavement, property. Whatever the regulations, in practice there was probably little protection against maltreatment, and abuses undoubtedly occurred. The safeguards for foreign-born slaves were not as stringent as for Hebrews (Lev. 25:44–46). As in much of the Bible, God's word in Exodus did not demand a new form of social and economic organization, but instructed God's people how to live with justice and compassion in their present circumstances.

In any case, before we become too smug, we should take a look at the
working conditions that prevail among poor people in every corner of the
world, including the developed nations. Ceaseless labor for those working two or three jobs to support families, abuse and arbitrary exercise
of power by those in power, and misappropriation of the fruits of labor
by illicit business operators, corrupt officials, and politically connected
bosses. Millions work today without so much as the regulations provided
by the Law of Moses. If it was God's will to protect Israel from exploitation even in slavery, what does God expect followers of Christ to do for
those who suffer the same oppression, and worse, today?

Commercial Restitution (Exodus 21:18–22:15)

The casuistic laws spelled out penalties for offenses, including many
relating directly to commerce, especially in the case of liability for loss or
injury. The so-called *lex talionis*, which also appears in Leviticus 24:17–
21 and Deuteronomy 19:16–21, is central to the concept of retribution.[28]
Literally, the law says to pay with a life for a life that is taken, as well as
an eye for an eye, tooth for tooth, hand for hand, foot for foot, burn for
burn, wound for wound, and stripe for stripe (Exod. 21:23–25). The list
is notably specific. When Israel's judges did their work, are we really to
believe they applied punishments in this way? Would a plaintiff who was
burned due to someone's negligence really be satisfied to see the offender
literally burned to the same degree? Interestingly, in this very part of
Exodus, we do not see the *lex talionis* being applied in this manner. Instead, a man who seriously injures another in a fight must pay for the
victim's lost time and cover his medical expenses (Exod. 21:18–19). The
text does not go on to say he must sit still for a public and comparable
beating by his former victim. It appears that the *lex talionis* did not determine the standard penalty for major offenses, but that it set an upper
ceiling for damages that could be claimed. Gordon Wenham notes, "In
Old Testament times there were no police or public prosecution services,
so all prosecution and punishment had to be carried out by the injured
party and his family. Thus it would be quite possible for injured parties

---

[28] Brueggemann, 433. The principle is also present in the Code of Hammu-
rabi (about 1850–1750 BC), though that code does not prioritize human life as
highly as the Torah does.

not to insist on their full rights under the *lex talionis*, but negotiate a lower settlement or even forgive the offender altogether."[29] This law may be perceived by some today as savage, but Alec Motyer observed, "When English law hanged a person for stealing a sheep, it was not because the principle of 'an eye for an eye' was being practiced but because it had been forgotten."[30]

This issue of interpreting the *lex talionis* illustrates that there may be a difference between doing what the Bible literally says and applying what the Bible instructs. Obtaining a biblical solution to our problems will not always be a straightforward matter. Christians must use maturity and discernment, especially in light of Jesus' teaching to forego the *lex talionis* by not resisting an evildoer (Matt 5:38–42). Was he speaking of a personal ethic, or did he expect his followers to apply this principle in business? Does it work better for small offenses than it does for big ones? Those who do evil create victims whom we are bound to defend and protect (Prov. 31:9).

The specific instructions about restitution and penalties for thievery accomplished two aims. First, they made the thief responsible for returning the original owner to his original state or fully compensating him for his loss. Second, they punished and educated the thief by causing him to experience the full pain that he had caused for the victim. These aims can form a Christian basis for the work of civil and criminal law today. Current judicial work operates according to specific statutes and guidelines set by the state. But even so, judges have a measure of freedom to set sentences and penalties. For disputes that are settled out of court, attorneys negotiate to help their clients reach a conclusive agreement. In recent times, a perspective called "restorative justice" has emerged with an emphasis on punishment that restores the victim's original condition and, to the extent possible, restores the perpetrator as a productive member of society. A full description and assessment of such approaches is beyond our scope here, but we want to note that Scripture has much to offer contemporary systems of justice in this regard.

---

[29] Wenham, 73.

[30] J. A. Motyer, *The Message of Exodus: The Days of Our Pilgrimage* (Downers Grove, IL: IVP Academic, 2005), 240.

In business, leaders sometimes must mediate between workers who have serious work-related issues with one another. Deciding the right and fair thing affects not only the ones embroiled in the dispute, it also can affect the whole atmosphere of the organization and even serve to set precedent for how workers may expect to fare in the future. The immediate stakes may be very high. On top of this, when Christians must make these kinds of decisions, onlookers draw conclusions about us as people, as well as the legitimacy of the faith we claim to live by. Clearly, we cannot anticipate every situation (and neither does the book of Exodus). But we do know that God expects us to apply his instructions, and we can be confident that asking God how to love our neighbors as ourselves is the best place to start.

Productive Opportunities for the Poor (Exodus 22:21–27 & 23:10–11)

God's intent to provide opportunities for the poor is seen in the regulations benefiting aliens, widows, and orphans (Exod. 22:21–22). What these three groups had in common was that they did not possess land on which to support themselves. Often this made left them poor, so that aliens, widows, and orphans are the main subjects whenever "the poor" are mentioned in the Old Testament. In Deuteronomy, God's concern for this triad of vulnerable people called for Israel to provide them with justice (Deut. 10:18; 27:19) and access to food (Deut. 24:19–22). Case law on this matter is also developed in Isaiah 1:17, 23; 10:1–2; Jeremiah 5:28, 7:5–7; 22:3; Ezekiel 22:6–7; Zechariah 7:8–10; and Malachi 3:5.

One of the most important of these regulations is the practice of allowing the poor to harvest, or "glean," the leftover grain active fields and to harvest all volunteer crops in fields lying fallow. The practice of gleaning was not a handout, but an opportunity for the poor to support themselves. Landowners were required to leave each field, vineyard, and orchard fallow one year in every seven, and the poor were allowed to harvest anything that might grow there (Exod. 23:10–11). Even in active fields, owners were to leave some of the grain in the field for the poor to harvest, rather than exhaustively stripping the field bare (Lev. 19:9–10). For example, an olive grove or a vineyard was to be harvested only once each season (Deut. 24:20). After that, the poor were entitled to gather what was left over, perhaps what was of lesser quality or slower to ripen. This practice was not only an expression of kindness, but it was also a matter of justice. The book of Ruth revolves around gleaning to enchanting effect (see "Ruth 2:17–23" in *Ruth and Work* at www.theologyofowork.org).

Today, there are many ways that growers, food producers, and distributors share with the poor. Many of them donate the day's leftover but wholesome food to pantries and shelters. Others work to made food more affordable by increasing their own efficiency. But most people, in developed nations at least, no longer engage in agriculture for a living, and opportunities for the poor are needed in other sectors of society. There is nothing to glean on the floor of a stock exchange, assembly plant, or programming lab. But the principle of providing productive work for vulnerable workers is still relevant. Corporations can productively employ people with mental and physical disabilities, with or without government assistance. With training and support, people from disadvantaged backgrounds, prisoners returning to society, and others who have difficulty finding conventional employment can become productive workers and earn a living.

Other economically vulnerable people may have to depend on contributions of money instead of receiving opportunities to work. Here again the modern situation is too complex for us to proclaim a simplistic application of the biblical law. But the values underlying the law may offer a significant contribution to the design and execution of systems of public welfare, personal charity, and corporate social responsibility. Many Christians have significant roles in hiring workers or designing employment policies. Exodus reminds us that employing vulnerable workers is an essential part of what it means for a people to live under God's covenant. Together with Israel of old, Christians have also experienced God's redemption, though not necessarily in identical terms. But our basic gratitude for God's grace is certainly a powerful motive for finding creative ways to serve the needy around us.

Lending and Collateral (Exodus 22:25–27)

Another set of case laws regulated money and collateral (Exod. 22:25–27). Two situations are in view. The first pertains to a needy member of God's people who requires a financial loan. This loan shall not be made according to the usual standards of money-lending. It shall be given without "interest." The Hebrew word *neshekh* (which in some contexts means a "bite") has garnered a great deal of academic attention. Did *neshek* refer to *excessive* and therefore unfair interest charged, on top of the reasonable amount of interest required to keep the practice of money-lending financially viable? Or did it refer to *any* interest? The text does not have enough detail to settle this conclusively, but the latter view seems more likely, because in the Old Testament *neshek* always pertains to lending to those who are in miserable and vulnerable circumstances, for whom paying any interest at all would be an excessive burden.[31] Placing the poor into a never-ending cycle of financial indebtedness will stir Israel's compassionate God to action. Whether or not this law was good for business is not in view here. Walter Brueggemann notes, "The law does not argue about the economic viability of such a practice. It simply requires the need for care in concrete ways, and it expects the community to work out the practical details."[32] The other situation envisages a man who puts up his only coat as collateral for a loan. It should be returned to him at night so that he can sleep without endangering his health (Exod. 22:26–27). Does this mean that the creditor should visit him in the morning to collect the coat for the day and to keep doing so until the loan is repaid? In the context of such obvious destitution, a godly creditor could avoid the near absurdity of this cycle by simply not expecting the borrower to put up any collateral at all. These regulations may have less application to today's banking system in general than to today's systems of protection and assistance for the poor. For example, microfinance in less developed countries was developed with interest rates and collateral policies tailored to meet the needs of poor people who otherwise have no access to credit. The goal—at least in the earliest years beginning in the 1970s—was not to maximize profit for the lenders, but to provide sustainable lending institutions to help the poor escape poverty. Even so, microfinance struggles with balancing the lend-

---

[31] Robin Wakely, "#5967 NSHK," in *New International Dictionary of Old Testament Theology and Exegesis*, ed. Willem A. VanGemeren (Grand Rapids: Zondervan, 1997), 3:185–89.

[32] Brueggemann, 868.

ers' need for a sustainable return and default rates with the borrowers' need for affordable interest rates and nonrestrictive collateral terms.[33]

The presence of specific regulations following the Ten Command-ments means that God wants his people to honor him by putting his instructions into actual practice to serve real needs. Emotional concern without deliberate action doesn't give the poor the kind of help they need. As the Apostle James put it, "Faith without works is also dead" (James 2:26). Studying the specific applications of these laws in an-cient Israel helps us to think about the particular ways we can act today. But we remember that even then, these laws were illustrations. Terence Fretheim thus concludes, "There is an open-endedness to the application of the law. The text invites the hearer/reader to extend this passage out into every sphere of life where injustice might be encountered. In other words, *one is invited by the law to go beyond the law*."[34]

A careful reading reveals three reasons why God's people should keep these laws and apply them to fresh situations.[35] First, the Israelites themselves were oppressed as foreigners in Egypt (Exod. 22:21; 23:9). Rehearsing this history not only keeps God's redemption in view, but memory becomes a motivation to treat others as we would like to be treated (Matt. 7:12). Second, God hears the cry of the oppressed and acts on it, especially when we won't (Exod. 22:22–24). Third, we are to be his holy people (Exod. 22:31; Lev. 19:2).

The Tabernacle (Exodus 25:1–40:38)

The work of building the tabernacle may seem to lie outside the scope of the Theology of Work Project because of its liturgical focus. We should note, however, that the book of Exodus does not so easily separate Israel's life in the categories of sacred and secular that we are so accustomed to. Even if we delineate between Israel's liturgical and extra-liturgical activities, nothing in Exodus suggests that one is more

[33] Rob Moll, "Christian Microfinance Stays on a Mission," *Christianity Today*, http://www.christianitytoday.com/ct/2011/may/stayingonmission.html.

[34] Terence E. Fretheim, *Exodus: Interpretation: A Bible Commentary for Teaching and Preaching* (Louisville: Westminster John Knox Press, 1991), 248.

[35] Motyer, 241.

important than the other. Furthermore, what actually happened at the tabernacle cannot be equated fairly with "church work" today. Certainly, its construction has no close parallel in the construction of church buildings. The chapters in Exodus dealing with the tabernacle are all about the *establishment* of a unique institution. Although the work of the tabernacle would go on from year to year and be subsumed by the temple, each of these buildings was by design central and solitary. They were not exemplars to be reproduced wherever Israelites would settle down to live. In fact, the construction and operation of local shrines throughout the land proved to be a huge detriment to Israel's national spiritual health. Finally, the purpose of the tabernacle was not to give Israel an authorized place to worship. It was about the presence of God in their midst. This is clear from the outset in God's words, "Have them make me a sanctuary, so that I may dwell among them" (Exod. 25:8). Christians today understand that God dwelt among us in the person of his Son (John 1:14). Through his work, the entire community of believers has become God's temple in which God's Spirit lives (1 Cor. 3:16). In light of these observations, we will take up two claims that relate to work. First, God is an architect. Second, God equips his people to do his work.

The large section in Exodus about the tabernacle is organized according to God's command (Exod. 25:1–31:11) and Israel's response (Exod. 35:4–40:33). But God did more than tell Israel what he wanted from them. He provided the actual design for it. This is clear from his words to Moses, "In accordance with all that I show you concerning the pattern of the tabernacle and the pattern of all its furniture, so you shall make it" (Exod. 25:9).[36] The Hebrew word for "pattern" (*tavnit*) here pertains to the building and the items associated with it. Architects today use blueprints to direct construction, but it may have been that some kind of archetypal model was in view.[37] Temples were often seen as earthy

---

[36] The translation here slightly modifies the New Revised Standard Version to show how the key word *pattern* appears twice.

[37] Victor Hurowitz, "The Priestly Account of Building the Tabernacle," *Journal of the American Oriental Society* 105 (1985): 22. The word *tavnit* describes the three-dimensional shape of idols (Deut. 4:16–18; Ps. 106:20; Isa. 44:13), a replica of an altar (Josh. 22:28; 2 Kgs. 16:10), and the form of hands (Ezek. 8:3, 10; 10:8).

replicas of celestial sanctuaries (Isa. 6:1–8). By the Spirit, King David received such a pattern for the temple and gave it to his son Solomon, who sponsored the temple's construction (1 Chr. 28:11–12, 19). From the descriptions that follow, it is clear that God's architectural design is exquisite and artful. The principle that God's design precedes God's building is true of Israel's sanctuaries, as well as the New Testament worldwide community of Christians (1 Cor. 3:5–18). The future New Jerusalem is a city only God could design (Rev. 21:10–27). God's work as architect does give dignity to that particular career. But in a general sense, the people of God may engage in their work (whatever it is) with the awareness that God has a design for it too. As we will see next, there are many details to work out within the contours of God's plan, but the Holy Spirit helps with even that.

The accounts of Bezalel, Oholiab, and all of the skilled workers on the tabernacle are full of work-related terms (Exod. 31:1–11; 35:30–36:5). Bezalel and Oholiab are important not only for their work on the tabernacle, but also as role models for Solomon and Huram-abi who built the temple.[38] The comprehensive set of crafts included metalwork in gold, silver, and bronze as well as stonework and woodwork. The fabrication of garments would have required getting wool, spinning it, dyeing it, weaving it, designing clothes, manufacturing and tailoring them, and the work of embroidery. The craftsmen even prepared anointing oil and fragrant incense. What unites all of these practices is God filling the workers with his Spirit. The Hebrew word for "ability" and "skill" in these texts (*hokhmah*) is usually translated as "wisdom," which causes us to think about the use of words and decision-making. Here, it describes work that is clearly hands-on yet spiritual in the fullest theological sense (Exod. 28:3; 31:3, 6; 35:26, 31, 35; 36:1–2).

The wide range of construction activities in this passage illustrates, but does not exhaust, what building in the ancient Near East entailed. Since God inspired them, we can safely assume he desired them and blessed them. But do we really need texts like these to assure us that God approves of these kinds of work? What about related skills that are

---

[38] Raymond B. Dillard, *2 Chronicles*, vol. 15, *Word Biblical Commentary* (Dallas: Word, 1998), 4–5.

not mentioned? Somewhat facetiously, had the tabernacle needed an air-conditioning system, we assume God would have given plans for a good one. Robert Banks wisely recommends, "In the biblical writings, we should not interpret comparisons with the [modern] process of construction in too narrow or job-specific a fashion. Occasionally this may be justified, but generally not."[39] The point here is not that God cares more about certain types of labor than others. The Bible does not have to name every noble profession for us to see it as a godly thing to do. Just as people were not made for the Sabbath but the Sabbath for people (Mark 2:27), building and cities are made for people too. The law that ancient houses be built with a protective parapet around the flat roof (Deut. 22:8) illustrates God's concern for responsible construction that truly serves and protects people. The point about the Spirit-gifting of the tabernacle-workers is that God cared about *this particular* project for *these particular* purposes. Based on that truth, perhaps the enduring lesson for us in our work today is that whatever God's work is, he does not leave his great work in our unskilled hands. The ways in which he equips us for his work may be as varied as are those many tasks. In divine faithfulness, the spiritual gifts God gives to us will strengthen us in doing God's work to the very end (1 Cor. 1:4–9). He provides us with every blessing in abundance so that we may share abundantly in every good work (2 Cor. 9:8).

Conclusions from Exodus

In Exodus, we see God bring his people out of oppressive labor into the glorious freedom of the children of God. It is not a freedom from working, but a freedom to love and serve the Lord through work in every aspect of life. God provides guidance for life and labor that will glorify him and bless Israel. And he provides a place for his presence to bless all they do.

---

[39] Robert Banks, *God the Worker: Journeys into the Mind, Heart, and Imagination of God* (Eugene, OR: Wipf & Stock, 2008), 349.

Leviticus and Work

Introduction—Does Leviticus Have Anything to Tell Us about Our Work?

Leviticus is a great source for people seeking guidance about their work. It is filled with direct, practical instructions, even though the action takes place in a workplace different from what most of us experience today. Moreover, Leviticus is one of the central places where God reveals himself and his aims for our life and work. The book is at the physical center of the Pentateuch, the third of the five books of Moses that form the narrative and theological foundation of the Old Testament. The second book, Exodus, tells what God took his people *out of*. Leviticus tells what God leads his people *into*,[1] a life full of the God's own presence. In Leviticus, work is one of the most important arenas where God is present with Israel, and God is still present with his people in our work today.

Leviticus is also central to Jesus' teaching and the rest of the New Testament. The Great Commandment that Jesus taught (Mark 12:28–31) comes directly from Leviticus 19:18: "You shall love your neighbor as yourself." The "Year of Jubilee" in Leviticus 25 lies at the center of Jesus' mission statement: "The Spirit of the Lord is upon me, because he has anointed me to . . . proclaim the year of the Lord's favor [the Jubilee]" (Luke 4:18–19). When Jesus said that "not one letter, not one stroke" of the law would pass away (Matt. 5:18), many of those letters and strokes are found in Leviticus. Jesus offered a new take on the law—that the way to fulfill the law is not found in complying with regulations, but in cooperating with the purposes for which God created the law. We are to fulfill the law in a "more excellent way" (1 Cor. 12:31) that surpasses,

---

[1]Nine times the book of Leviticus refers to the Lord having brought Israel out of Egypt, often as a motive for Israel's future obedience (11:45; 19:36; 22:33; 23:43; 25:38, 42, 55; 26:13, 45).

not ignores, the letter of the law. If we wish to fulfill the Spirit of the law, as Jesus did, then we must begin by learning what the law actually says. Much of it is found in Leviticus, and much of it applies to work.

Because Leviticus is central to Jesus' teaching about work, as followers of Jesus we are right to go to the book for guidance about God's will for our work. Of course, we must keep in mind that the codes in Leviticus must be understood and applied to the different economic and social situations today. Current society does not stand in a close parallel to ancient Israel, either in terms of our societal structure or our covenant relationship. Most workers today, for example, have little need to know what to do with an ox or sheep that has been torn apart by wild animals (Lev. 7:24). The Levitical priesthood to whom much of the book is addressed—priests performing animal sacrifice to the God of Israel—no longer exists. Moreover, in Christ we understand the law to be an instrument of God's grace in a way different from how ancient Israel did. So we cannot simply quote Leviticus as if nothing has changed in the world. We cannot read a verse and proclaim "Thus says the Lord" as a judgment against those we disagree with. Instead, we have to understand the meaning, purposes, and mind of God revealed in Leviticus, and then ask God's wisdom to apply Leviticus today. Only so will our lives reflect his holiness, honor his intentions, and enact the rule of his heavenly kingdom on earth.

The Foundational Concept of Holiness in Leviticus

The book of Leviticus is grounded in the truth that God is holy. The word *qodesh* occurs over a hundred times in the Hebrew text of Leviticus. To say that God is holy means that he is completely separate from all evil or defect. Or to put it in another way, God is completely and perfectly good. The Lord is worthy of total allegiance, exclusive worship, and loving obedience.

Israel's identity arises because by God's actions they *are* holy, yet also because the Lord expects Israel to *act* holy in practical ways. Israel is called to be holy because the Lord himself is holy (Lev. 11:44–45; 19:2; 20:7; 21:8). The seemingly disparate laws of Leviticus that deal with the ritual, ethical, commercial, and penal aspects of life all rest on this core notion of holiness.

Alexander Hill, then, is following Leviticus's central principle when he grounds his discussion of Christian business ethics on God's holiness, justice, and love. "A business act is ethical if it reflects God's holy-just-loving character."[2] Hill claims that Christians in business reflect divine holiness when they have zeal for God who is their ultimate priority, and who then behave with purity, accountability, and humility. These, rather than trying to reproduce the commercial code designed for an agrarian society, are what it means to put Leviticus into practice today. This does not mean ignoring the specifics of the law, but discerning how God is guiding us to fulfill it in today's context.

Holiness in Leviticus is not separation for separation's sake, but for the sake of a thriving community of the people of God and the reconciliation of each person to God. Holiness is not only about individuals' behavior following regulations, but about how what each person does affects the whole people of God in their life together and their work as agents of God's kingdom. In this light, Jesus' call for his people to be "salt" and "light" to outsiders (Matt. 5:13–16) makes complete sense. To be holy is to go beyond the law to love your neighbor, to love even your enemy, and to "be perfect, therefore, as your heavenly Father is perfect" (Matt. 5:48, echoing Lev. 19:2).

In short, ancient Israel did not obey Leviticus as a peculiar set of regulations, but as an expression of God's presence in their midst. This is as relevant to God's people today as it was then. In Leviticus, God is taking a collection of nomadic tribes and shaping their culture as a people. Likewise today, when God's people enter their places of work, through them God is shaping the cultures of their work units, organizations, and communities. God's call to be holy, even as he is holy, is a call to shape our cultures for the good.

Israel's Sacrificial System (Leviticus 1–10)

The book of Leviticus opens with regulations for Israel's sacrificial system, conveyed from two perspectives. The first perspective is that

---

[2] Alexander Hill, *Just Business: Christian Ethics for the Marketplace*, 2nd ed. (Downers Grove, IL: IVP Academic, 2008), 15.

of the laypersons who bring the sacrifice and participate in its offering (chapters 1–5). The second perspective is that of the priests who officiate (chapters 6–7). After this, we learn how the priests were ordained and began their ministry at the tabernacle (chapters 8–9), followed by further regulations for the priests in light of how God put the priests Nadab and Abihu to death for violating God's command about their ritual responsibilities (chapter 10). We should not assume that this material is empty liturgy irrelevant to the world of modern work. Instead, we must look through the way the people of Israel coped with their problems in order to explore how we, as people in Christ, may cope with ours—including the challenges we face in business and work.

The Dwelling of God in the Community (Leviticus 1–10)

The purpose of sacrifice was not merely to remedy occasional lapses of purity. The Hebrew verb for "offering" a sacrifice means literally to "bring (it) near." Bringing a sacrifice near to the sanctuary brought the worshipper near to God. The worshipper's individual degree of misbehavior was not the main issue. The pollution caused by impurity is the consequence of the entire community, comprised of the relative few who have committed either brazen or inadvertent sins *together with* the silent majority that has allowed the wicked to flourish in their midst. The people as a whole bear collective responsibility for corrupting society and thus giving God legitimate reason to depart his sanctuary, an event tantamount to destruction of the nation.[3] Drawing near to God is still the aim of those who call Jesus "Immanuel" ("God with us"). The dwelling of God with his people is a serious matter indeed.

Christians in their workplaces should look beyond finding godly tips for finding whatever the world defines as "success." Being aware that God is holy and that he desires to dwell at the center of our lives changes our orientation from success to holiness, whatever work God has called us to do. This does not mean doing religious activities at work, but doing all our work as God would have us do it. Work is not primarily a way to enjoy the fruit of our labor, but a way to experience God's presence. Just

---

[3] Jacob Milgrom, *Leviticus: A Book of Ritual and Ethics, A Continental Commentary* (Minneapolis: Fortress Press, 2004), 15.

as Israel's sacrifices were a "pleasing odor" to the Lord (Lev. 1:9 and sixteen other instances), Paul called Christians to "lead lives worthy of the Lord, fully pleasing to him" (Col. 1:10), "for we are the aroma of Christ to God" (2 Cor. 2:15).

What might result if we walked through our workplaces and asked the fundamental question, "How could this be a place for God's holy presence?" Does our workplace encourage people to express the best of what God has given them? Is it a place characterized by the fair treatment of all? Does it protect workers from harm? Does it produce goods and services that help the community to thrive more fully?

The Whole People of God at Work (Leviticus 1–10)

Leviticus brings together the perspectives of two groups who were often at odds against each other—the priests and the people. Its purpose is to bring the whole people of God together, without regard to distinctions of status. In today's workplace, how are Christians to handle offenses between people regardless of their wealth or position in the company? Do we tolerate abuses of power when the result seems expedient to our careers? Do we participate in judging co-workers by gossip and innuendo, or do we insist on airing grievances through unbiased systems? Do we pay attention to the harm that bullying and favoritism do at work? Do we promote a positive culture, foster diversity, and build a healthy organization? Do we enable open and trustworthy communication, minimize backdoor politicking, and strive for top performance? Do we create an atmosphere where ideas are surfaced and explored, and the best ones put into action? Do we focus on sustainable growth?

Israel's sacrificial system addressed not only the religious needs of the people, but their psychological and emotional ones as well, thus embracing the whole person and the whole community. Christians understand that businesses have aims that are not usually religious in nature. Yet we also know that people are not equivalent to what they do or produce. This does not reduce our commitment to work at being productive, but it reminds us that because God has embraced us with his forgiveness, we have even more reason than others to be considerate, fair, and gracious to all (Luke 7:47; Eph. 4:32; Col. 3:13).

The Workplace Significance of the Guilt Offering (Leviticus 6:1–7)

Each offering in Israel's sacrificial system has its place, but there is a special feature of the guilt offering (also known as the reparation offering) that makes it particularly relevant to the world of work. The guilt offering of Leviticus is the seed of the biblical doctrine of repentance.[4] (Numbers 5:5–10 is directly parallel.) According to Leviticus, God required offerings whenever a person deceived another with regard to a deposit or a pledge, committed robbery or fraud, lied about lost property that had been found, or swore falsely about a matter (Lev. 6:2–3). It was not a fine imposed by a court of law, but a reparation offered by perpetrators who got away with the offense, but who then felt guilty later when they came to "realize" their guilt (Lev. 6:4–5). Repentance by the sinner, not prosecution by the authorities, is the basis of the guilt offering.

Often such sins would have been committed in the context of commerce or other work. The guilt offering calls for the remorseful sinner to return what was wrongfully taken plus 20 percent (Lev. 6:4–5). Only after settling the matter on a human level may the sinner receive forgiveness from God by presenting an animal to the priest for sacrifice (Lev. 6:6–7).

The guilt offering uniquely emphasizes several principles about healing personal relationships that have been damaged by financial abuse.

1. Mere apology is not enough to right the wrong, and neither is full restoration for what was taken. In addition, something akin to today's concept of punitive damages was added. But with guilt offerings—unlike court-ordered punitive damages—offenders willingly take on a share of the harm themselves, thereby sharing in the distress they caused the victim.

2. Doing all that is required to right a wrong against another person is not only fair for the offended, but it is also good for the offender. The guilt offering recognizes the torment that seizes the conscience of those who become aware of their crime and its damaging effects. It then provides a way for the guilty to deal more fully with the

---

[4] Jacob Milgrom, *Leviticus 1–16* (New Haven: Yale University Press, 1998), 345.

matter, bringing a measure of closure and peace. This offering expresses God's mercy in that the pain and hurt is neutralized so as not to fester and erupt into violence or more serious offenses. It also extinguishes the need for the victim (or the victim's family) to take matters into their own hands to exact restitution.

3. Nothing in Jesus' atoning work on the cross releases the people of God today from the need for making restitution. Jesus taught his disciples, "So when you are offering your gift at the altar, if you remember that your brother or sister has something against you, leave your gift there before the altar and go; first be reconciled to your brother or sister, and then come and offer your gift" (Matt. 5:23–24). Loving our neighbors as ourselves lies at the heart of the law's requirements (Lev. 19:18 as quoted in Rom. 13:9), and making restitution is an essential expression of any genuine kind of love. Jesus granted salvation to the rich tax collector Zacchaeus who offered more restitution than the law required, lifting him up as an example of those who truly understood forgiveness (Luke 19:1–10).

4. Jesus' words in Matthew 5:23–24 also teach us that settling matters with people is a necessary prerequisite for making things right with God. Forgiveness from God is a stage of redemption that goes beyond, but does not replace, restitution.

The guilt offering is a potent reminder that God does not exercise his right of forgiveness at the expense of people harmed by our misdeeds. He does not offer us psychological release from our guilt as a cheap substitute for making right the damage and hurt we have caused.

The Unclean and the Clean (Leviticus 11–16)

At the heart of it, Leviticus 11:45 explains the thematic logic of this entire section. "I am the LORD who brought you up from the land of Egypt, to be your God; you shall be holy, for I am holy" (Lev. 11:45). God calls Israel to mirror his holiness in every aspect of life. Leviticus 11–16 deals with the classification of "clean" and "unclean" food (chapter 11) and rites of cleansing (chapters 12–15). It closes with the procedure for celebrating the Day of Atonement to cleanse the people and God's sanctuary (chapter 16).

Christians also recognize that every aspect of our lives is meant to be a response to God's holy presence among us. But the subjects and scope of the laws in Leviticus tend to baffle us today. Are there enduring ethical principles to be found in these particular regulations? For example, it's hard to understand the rationale for why God permitted Israel to eat some animals and not others. Why is there such concern for particular skin diseases (which we cannot even identify today with certainty) and not other, more serious diseases? Of all the ills facing society, is the issue of mold really all that important? Narrowing our focus to matters of work, should we expect these texts to tell us anything we can apply to the food industry, medicine, or environmental contamination of homes and workspaces? As noted before, we will find answers not by asking whether to obey regulations made for a different situation, but by looking for how the passages guide us to serve the welfare of the community.

The Permissibility of Eating Particular Animals (Leviticus 11)

There are several plausible theories about the rules governing animals for human consumption in Leviticus 11. Each cites supporting evidence, yet none enjoys a general consensus. Sorting them out is beyond our scope here, but Jacob Milgrom offers a perspective directly related to the workplace.[5] He notes three dominant elements: God severely limited Israel's choice of animal food, gave them specific rules for slaughter, and prohibited them from eating blood that represents life and therefore belongs to God alone. In light of these, Milgrom concludes that Israel's dietary system was a method of controlling the human instinct to kill. In short, "Though they may satisfy their appetite for food, they must curb their hunger for power. Because life is inviolable it may not be tampered with indiscriminately."[6] If God chooses to get involved in the details of

---

[5] Milgrom, *Leviticus*, 704–42.
[6] Milgrom, *Leviticus 1–16*, 105.

which animals may be killed and how it is to be done, how could we miss the point that the killing of humans is even more restricted and subject to God's scrutiny? This view suggests more applicability to the present day. For example, if every agricultural, animal, and food service facility practiced daily accountability to God for the treatment and condition of its animals, wouldn't it be all the more attentive to the safety and working conditions of its people?

In spite of the extensive details in Leviticus that initiate the ongoing discussion of food in the Bible, it would be inappropriate for any Christian to try to dictate what all believers must do and avoid doing regarding the provision, preparation, and consumption of food. Nonetheless, whatever we eat or don't eat, Derek Tidball rightly reminds Christians of the centrality of holiness. Whatever one's stance on these complex issues, it cannot be divorced from the Christian's commitment to holiness. Holiness calls upon us even to eat and drink "for the glory of God."[7] The same applies to the work of producing, preparing, and consuming food and drink.

Dealing with Skin Diseases and Mold Infections (Leviticus 13–14)

In contrast to the dietary laws, the laws about diseases and environmental contamination *do* seem to be primarily concerned with health. Health is a critical issue today as well, and even if the book of Leviticus were not in the Bible, it would still be a noble and godly concern. But it would be unwise to assume that Leviticus provides instructions for coping with contagious diseases and environmental contamination that we can directly apply today. At our distance of thousands of years from that time period, it is difficult even to be certain exactly what diseases the passages refer to. The enduring message of Leviticus is that the Lord is the God of life and that he guides, honors, and ennobles all those who bring healing to people and the environment. If the particular rules of Leviticus do not dictate the way we perform the work of healing and environmental protection, then certainly this greater point does.

---

[7] Derek Tidball, *The Message of Leviticus* (Downers Grove, IL: InterVarsity Press, 1996), 15.

Holiness (Leviticus 17–27)

Some of the instructions in the holiness code seem relevant only in Israel's ancient world, while others seem timeless. On the one hand, Leviticus tells men not to mar the edges of their beards (Lev. 19:27), but on the other hand, judges must not render unfair judgments in court but show justice to all (Lev. 19:15). How do we know which ones apply directly today? Mary Douglas helpfully explains how a clear understanding of holiness as moral *order* both grounds these instructions in God and makes sense of their variety.

> Developing the idea of holiness as order, not confusion, upholds rectitude and straight-dealing as holy, and contradiction and double-dealing as against holiness. Theft, lying, false witness, cheating in weights and measures, all kinds of dissembling such as speaking ill of the deaf (and presumably smiling to their faces), hating your brother in your heart (while presumably speaking kindly to him), these are clearly contradictions between what seems and what is.[8]

Some aspects of what leads to good order (e.g., the trimming of beards) may be important in one context but not in another. Others are essential in all situations. We can sort them out by asking what contributes to good order in our particular contexts. Here we shall explore passages that touch directly on matters of work and economics.

Gleaning (Leviticus 19:9–10)

Although ancient methods of harvesting were not as efficient as today, Leviticus 19:9–10 instructs Israelites to make them even *less* so. First, they were to leave the margins of their grain fields unharvested. The width of this margin appears to be up to the owner to decide. Second, they were not to pick up whatever produce fell to the ground. This would apply when a harvester grasped a bundle of stalks and cut them with the sickle, as well as when grapes fell from a cluster just cut from the vine. Third, they were to harvest their vineyards just once, presumably taking

---

[8] Mary Douglas, *Purity and Danger: An Analysis of the Concepts of Pollution and Taboo* (London: Routledge, 1966), 53–54.

only the ripe grapes so as to leave the later ripening ones for their poor and the immigrants living among them.[9] These two categories of people—the poor and resident foreigners—were unified by their lack of owning land and thus were dependent on their own manual labor for food. Laws benefiting the poor were common in the ancient Near East, but only the regulations of Israel extended this treatment to the resident foreigner. This was yet another way that God's people were to be distinct from the surrounding nations. Other texts specify the widow and the orphan as members of this category. (Other biblical references to gleaning include Exod. 22:21–27; Deut. 24:19–21; Judg. 8:2; Ruth 2:17–23; Job 24:6; Isa. 17:5–6; 24:13; Jer. 6:9, 49:9; Obad. 1:5; Mic. 7:1.)

We might classify gleaning as an expression of compassion or justice, but according to Leviticus, allowing others to glean on our property is the fruit of holiness. We do it because God says, "I am the LORD your God" (Lev. 19:10). This highlights the distinction between charity and gleaning. In charity, people voluntarily give to others who are in need. This is a good and noble thing to do, but it is not what Leviticus is talking about. Gleaning is a process in which landowners have an *obligation* to provide poor and marginalized people access to the means of production (in Leviticus, the land) and to work it *themselves*. Unlike charity, it does not depend on the generosity of landowners. In this sense, it was much more like a tax than a charitable contribution. Also unlike charity, it was not given to the poor as a transfer payment. Through gleaning, the poor earned their living the same way as the landowners did, by working the fields with their own labors. It was simply a command that everyone had a right to access the means of provision created by God.

In contemporary societies, it may not be easy to discern how to apply the principles of gleaning. In many countries, land reform is certainly needed so that land is securely available to farmers, rather than being controlled by capricious government officials or landowners who obtained it corruptly. In more industrialized and knowledge-based economies, land is not the chief factor of production. Access to education, capital, product and job markets, transport systems, and nondiscriminatory laws and regulations may be what poor people need to be productive.

---

[9] Milgrom, *Leviticus 1–16*, 225.

As Christians may not be more capable than anyone else of determining precisely what solutions will be most effective, solutions need to come from across society. Certainly Leviticus does not contain a system ready-made for today's economies. But the gleaning system in Leviticus does place an obligation on the owners of productive assets to ensure that marginalized people have the opportunity to work for a living. No individual owner can provide opportunities for every unemployed or underemployed worker, of course, no more than any one farmer in ancient Israel could provide gleanings for the entire district. But owners are called to be the point people in providing opportunities for work. Perhaps Christians in general are also called to appreciate the service that business owners do in their role as job creators in their communities.

(For more on gleaning in the Bible, see "Exodus 22:21–27" in *Exodus and Work* above and "Ruth 2:17–23" in *Ruth and Work* at www.theologyofwork.org.)

Behaving Honestly (Leviticus 19:11–12)

The commands in Leviticus against stealing, dealing falsely, lying, and violating God's name by swearing to false oaths all find more familiar expression among the Ten Commandments of Exodus 20. (For more on honesty, see "Truth-telling in the Bible" and "There May Be Exceptions to Truth-telling in the Workplace," in the article *Truth & Deception* at www.theologyofwork.org.) Unique to Leviticus, however, is the Hebrew wording behind "you shall not lie *to one another*" (Lev. 19:11; emphasis added). Literally, it says that "a person shall not lie to his *amit*," meaning "companion," "friend," or "neighbor." This surely includes fellow members of Israel's community; but based on Leviticus 24:19 in the context of Leviticus 24:17–22, it also seems to take in the resident alien. Israel's ethics and morality were to be distinctly better than the nations around them, even to the point of treating immigrants from other nations the same way they treated native-born citizens.

In any case, the point here is the relational aspect of telling the truth versus lying. A lie is not only a misstatement of cold fact, but it is also a betrayal of a companion, friend, or neighbor. What we say to each other must truly flow out of God's holiness in us, not merely out of a technical analysis of avoiding blatant lies. When U.S. president Bill Clinton said, "I did not have sexual relations with that woman," he may have had some tortuous logic in mind under which the statement was not technically a lie. But his fellow citizens rightly felt that he had broken trust with them, and he later recognized and accepted this assessment. He had violated the duty not to lie *to another*.

In many workplaces, there is a need to promote either the positive or negative aspects of a product, service, person, organization, or situation. Christians need not refuse to communicate vigorously to make a point. But they must not communicate in such a way that what they convey *to another* is false. If technically true words add up to a false impression in the mind of *another*, then the duty to tell the truth is broken. As a practical matter, whenever a discussion of truthfulness descends into a technical debate about wording, it's wise to ask ourselves if the debate is about whether to lie *to another* in this sense.

Treating Workers Fairly (Leviticus 19:13)

"You shall not defraud your neighbor; you shall not steal; and you shall not keep for yourself the wages of a laborer until morning" (Lev. 19:13). Day laborers were generally poorer people who lacked land to farm themselves. They were especially dependent on immediate payment for their work, and thus needed to be paid at the close of each day (cf. Deut. 24:14–15). In our world, a comparable situation occurs when employers have the power to dictate terms and conditions of labor that take advantage of workers' vulnerabilities. This occurs, for example, when employees are pressed to contribute to their bosses' favored political candidates or expected to continue working after clocking out. These practices are illegal in most places, but unfortunately remain common.

A more controversial state of affairs concerns day laborers who lack documentation for legal employment. This situation occurs around the world, applying to refugees, internally displaced persons, rural citizens lacking urban residency permits, illegal immigrants, children under the age of legal employment, and others. Such people often work in agriculture, landscaping, piecework manufacturing, food service, and small projects, in addition to illegal occupations. Because both employers and employees are working outside the law, such workers seldom receive the protections of employment agreements and government regulations. Employers may take advantage of their situation by paying them less per hour than legal workers, by denying benefits, and by providing poor or dangerous working conditions. They may be subject to abuse and sexual harassment. In many cases, they are completely at the mercy of the employer. Is it legitimate for employers to treat them this way? Surely not.

But what if people in such situations offer themselves for substandard employment apparently willingly? In many places, undocumented workers are available outside garden and building supply stores, at agricultural markets, and other gathering places. Is it right to employ them? If so, is it the employers' responsibility to provide the things legal workers get by rights, such as the minimum wage, health benefits, retirement plans, sick pay, and termination benefits? Must Christians be strict about the legality of such employment, or should we be flexible on the grounds that legislation has not yet caught up with reality? Thoughtful Christians will inevitably differ in their conclusions about this, and so it is difficult to justify a "one size fits all" solution. However a Christian processes these issues, Leviticus reminds us that holiness (and not practical expediency) must be at the core of our thinking. And holiness in labor matters arises out of a concern for the needs of the most vulnerable workers.

Rights of People with Disabilities (Leviticus 19:14)

"You shall not revile the deaf or put a stumbling block before the blind; you shall fear your God: I am the LORD" (Lev. 19:14). These commands paint a vivid picture of cruel treatment of people with disabilities. A deaf person could not hear such a curse, nor could a blind person see the block. For these reasons, Leviticus 19:14 reminds Israelites to "fear your God" who hears and sees how *everyone* is treated in the workplace. For example, workers with disabilities do not necessarily need the same office furniture and equipment as those without disabilities. But they *do* need to be offered the opportunity for employment to the full extent of their productivity, like everyone else. In many cases, what people with disabilities most need is not to be *prevented* from working in jobs they are capable of doing. Again, the command in Leviticus is not that the people of God ought to be charitable to others, but that the holiness of God gives all people created in his image the *right* to appropriate opportunities for work.

Doing Justice (Leviticus 19:15–16)

"You shall not render an unjust judgment; you shall not be partial to the poor or defer to the great: with justice you shall judge your neighbor. You shall not go around as a slanderer among your people, and you shall not profit by the blood of your neighbor: I am the LORD." (Lev. 19:15–16)

This short section upholds the familiar biblical value of justice and then broadens considerably. The first verse begins with an application for judges, but ends with an application for everyone. Do not judge court cases with partiality, and don't judge your neighbor unfairly. The wording of the Hebrew highlights the temptation to judge the external appearance of a person or issue. Woodenly rendered, Leviticus 19:15 says, "Do not do injustice in judgment. Do not lift up the face of the poor one and do not honor the face of the great one. With rightness you shall judge your neighbor." Judges must look through their preconceptions (the "face" they perceive) in order to understand the issue impartially. The same is true of our social relationships at work, school, and civic life. In every context, some people are privileged and others oppressed because of social biases of every kind. Imagine the difference Christians could make if we simply waited to make judgments until knowing people and situations in depth. What if we took the time to know the annoying person on our team before complaining behind his or her back? What if we dared to spend time with people outside our comfort zone at school, university, or civic life? What if we sought out newspaper, TV, and media that offer a different perspective from what we are comfortable with? Would digging below the surface give us greater wisdom to do our work well and justly?

The latter part of Leviticus 19:16 reminds us that social bias is no light matter. Literally, the Hebrew says, "Do not stand by the blood of your neighbor." In the language of the courtroom in the previous verse, biased testimony ("slander") endangers the life ("blood") of the accused.

In that case, not only would it be wrong to speak biased words, but it would be wrong even to stand idly by without volunteering to testify on behalf of the falsely accused.

Leaders in workplaces must often act in the role of an arbiter. Workers may witness an injustice in the workplace and legitimately question whether or not it is appropriate to get involved. Leviticus claims that proactively standing in favor of the mistreated is an essential element of belonging to God's holy people.

On a larger level, Leviticus brings its theological vision of holiness to bear on the whole community. The health of the community and the economy we share is at stake. Hans Küng points out the necessary interrelationship of business, politics, and religion:

> It should not be forgotten that economic thought and actions, too, are not value-free or value-neutral. . . . Just as the social and ecological responsibility of business cannot simply be foisted onto politicians, so moral and ethical responsibility cannot simply be foisted onto religion. . . . No, ethical action should not be just a private addition to marketing plans, sales strategies, ecological bookkeeping and social balance-sheets, but should form the natural framework for human social action.[10]

Every kind of workplace—home, business, government, academia, medicine, agriculture, and all the rest—have a distinctive role to play. Yet all of them are called to be holy. In Leviticus 19:15–16, holiness begins by seeing others with a depth of insight that gets beneath face value.

Loving Your Neighbor as Yourself (Leviticus 19:17–18)

The most famous verse in Leviticus may be the command, "Love your neighbor as yourself" (Lev. 19:18). This imperative is so sweeping that both Jesus and the rabbis regarded it as one of the two "great" commandments, the other being "Hear, O Israel: the LORD our God, the LORD is one" (Mark 12:29–31; cf. Deut. 6:4). In quoting Leviticus 19:18, the Apostle Paul wrote that "love is the fulfilling of the law" (Rom. 13:10).

---

[10] Hans Küng, *Global Responsibility: In Search of a New World Ethic* (New York: Continuum, 1993), 32–33, quoted in Roy Gane, *The NIV Application Commentary: Leviticus, Numbers* (Grand Rapids: Zondervan, 2004), 352.

Working for Others as Much as for Ourselves

The crux of the command lies in the words "as yourself." At least to some degree, most of us work to provide for ourselves. There is a strong element of self-interest in working. We know that if we don't work, we won't eat. Scripture commends this motivation (2 Thess. 3:10), yet the "as yourself" aspect of Leviticus 19:18 suggests that we should be equally motivated to serve others through our work. This is a high call—to work as much to serve others as to meet our own needs. If we had to work twice as long to accomplish it—say one shift a day for ourselves and another shift for our neighbor—it would be nearly impossible.

Providentially, it is possible to love ourselves and our neighbors through the same work, at least to the degree that our work provides something of value to customers, citizens, students, family members, and other consumers. A teacher receives a salary that pays the bills, and at the same time imbues students with knowledge and skills that will be equally valuable to them. A hotel housekeeper receives wages while providing guests with a clean and healthy room. In most jobs, we would not stay employed for long if we don't provide a value to others at least equal to what we draw in pay. But what if we find ourselves in a situation where we can skew the benefits in favor of ourselves? Some people may have enough power to command salaries and bonuses in excess of the value they truly provide. The politically connected or corrupt may be able to wring large rewards for themselves in the form of contracts, subsidies, bonuses, and make-work jobs, while providing little of value for others. Nearly all of us have moments when we can shirk our duties yet still get paid.

Thinking more broadly, if we have a wide range of choices in our work, how much of a role does serving others make in our job decisions, compared to making the most for ourselves? Almost every kind of work can serve others and please God. But that does not mean that every job or work opportunity is of equal service to others. We love ourselves when we make work choices that bring us high pay, prestige, security, comfort, and easy work. We love others when we choose work that provides needed goods and services, opportunities for marginalized people, protection for God's creation, justice and democracy, truth, peace, and beauty. Leviticus 19:18 suggests that the latter should be as important to us as the former.

Be Nice?

Instead of striving to meet this high calling, it is easy to relax our understanding of "love your neighbor as yourself" into something banal like "be nice." But being nice is often nothing more than a facade and an excuse for disengaging from the people around us. Leviticus 19:17 commands us to do the opposite. "Reprove your neighbor, or you will incur guilt yourself" (Lev. 19:17). These two commands—both to love and to reprove your neighbor—seem like unlikely fellows, but they are brought together in the proverb, "Better is open rebuke than hidden love" (Prov. 27:5).

Regrettably, too often the lesson we absorb at church is always to be nice. If this becomes our rule in the workplace, it can have disastrous personal and professional effects. Niceness can lull Christians into allowing bullies and predators to abuse and manipulate them and to do the same to others. Niceness can lead Christian managers to gloss over workers' shortcomings in performance reviews, depriving them of a reason to sharpen their skills and keep their jobs in the long run. Niceness may lead anyone into holding onto resentment, bearing a grudge, or seeking revenge. Leviticus tells us that loving people sometimes means making an honest rebuke. This is not a license for insensitivity. When we rebuke, we need to do so with humility—we may also need to be rebuked in the situation—and compassion.

Who Is My Neighbor? (Leviticus 19:33–34)

Leviticus teaches that Israelites must not "oppress" resident foreigners (Lev. 19:33). (The same Hebrew verb appears in Lev. 25:17, "You shall not cheat one another.") The command continues, "The alien who resides with you shall be to you as the citizen among you; you shall love the alien as yourself, for you were aliens in the land of Egypt: I am the LORD your God" (Lev. 19:34). This verse is a particularly strong example of the unbreakable connection in Leviticus between the moral force of the law ("love the alien as yourself") and the very being of God, "I am the LORD your God." You do not oppress foreigners because you belong to a God who is holy.

Resident aliens, along with widows and the poor (see Lev. 19:9–10 above), typify outsiders lacking power. In today's workplaces, power differentials arise not only from nationality and gender differences, but also from a variety of other factors. Whatever the cause, most workplaces develop a hierarchy of power that is well known to everyone, regardless of whether it is openly acknowledged. From Leviticus 19:33–34, we may conclude that Christians should treat other people fairly in business as an expression of genuine worship of God.

Trading Fairly (Leviticus 19:35–36)

This passage prohibits cheating in business by falsely measuring length, weight, or quality, and is made more specific by reference to scales and stones, the standard equipment of trade. The various measurements mentioned indicate that this rule would apply across a wide spectrum, from tracts of land to the smallest measure of dry and wet goods. The Hebrew word *tsedeq* (NRSV "honest") that appears four times in Leviticus 19:36 denotes character that is right in terms of having integrity and being blameless. All weights and measures should be accurate. In short, buyers should get what they have paid for.

Sellers possess a vast array of means to deliver less than what buyers think they are getting. These are not limited to falsified measurements of weight, area, and volume. Exaggerated claims, misleading statistics, irrelevant comparisons, promises that can't be kept, "vaporware," and hidden terms and conditions are merely the tip of the iceberg. (For applications in various workplaces, see "Truth-telling in the Workplace" at www.theologyofwork.org.)

A woman who works for a large credit card issuer tells a disturbing story along these lines.

> Our business is providing credit cards to poor people with bad credit histories. Although we charge high interest rates, our customers' default rate is so high that we can't make a profit simply by charging interest. We have to find a way to generate fees. One challenge is that most of our customers are afraid of debt, so they pay their monthly balance on time. No fees for us that way. So we have a trick for catching them off-guard. For the first six months, we send them a bill on the 15th of the month, due the 15th of the following month. They learn the pattern and diligently send us the payment on the 14th every month. On the seventh month, we send their bill on the 12th, due on the 12th of the next month. They don't notice the

change, and they send us the payment on the 14th as usual. Now we've got them. We charge them a \$30 service charge for the late payment. Also, because they are delinquent, we can raise their interest rate. Next month they are already in arrears and they're in a cycle that generates fees for us month after month.[11]

It is hard to see how any trade or business that depends on deceiving or misleading people to make a profit could be a fit line of work for those who are called to follow a holy God.

The Sabbath Year and the Year of Jubilee (Leviticus 25)

Leviticus 25 ordains a sabbath year, one in every seven (Lev. 25:1–7), and a jubilee year, one in every fifty (Lev. 25:8–17), to sanctify Israel's internal economy. In the sabbath year, each field was to lie fallow, which appears to be a sound agricultural practice. The year of jubilee was much more radical. Every fiftieth year, all leased or mortgaged lands were to be returned to their original owners, and all slaves and bonded laborers were to be freed (Lev. 25:10). This naturally posed difficulties in banking and land transactions, and special provisions were designed to ameliorate them (Lev. 25:15–16), which we will explore in a moment. The underlying intent is the same as seen in the law of gleaning (Lev. 19:9–10), to ensure that everyone had access to the means of production, whether the family farm or simply the fruits of their own labor.

There is no clear evidence that Israel ever actually observed the jubilee year or the antislavery provisions associated with it (e.g., Lev. 25:25–28, 39–41). Regardless, the sheer detail of Leviticus 25 strongly suggests that we treat the laws as something that Israel potentially could have implemented. Rather than see the jubilee year as a utopian literary fiction, it seems better to believe that Israel neglected it not because it was unfeasible, but because the wealthy were unwilling to accept the social and economic implications that would have been costly and disruptive to them.

---

[11]Name withheld by request, as told to TOW Project editor William Messenger at a meeting of the Fordham Consortium at Seattle Pacific University, August 5, 2011.

Protection for the Destitute

After Israel conquered Canaan, the land was assigned to Israel's clans and families as described in Numbers 26 and Joshua 15–22. This land was never to be sold in perpetuity for it belonged to the Lord, not the people (Lev. 25:23–24).[12] The effect of the jubilee was to prevent any family from becoming permanently landless through sale, mortgage, or permanent lease of its assigned land. In essence, any sale of land was really a term lease that could last no longer than the next year of jubilee (Lev. 25:15). This provided a means for the destitute to raise money (by leasing the land) without depriving the family's future generations of the means of production. The rules of Leviticus 25 are not easy to figure out, and Milgrom makes good sense of them as he defines three progressive stages of destitution.[13]

1. The first stage is depicted in Leviticus 25:25–28. A person could simply become poor. The presumed scenario is that of a farmer who borrowed money to buy seed but did not harvest enough to repay the loan. He therefore must sell some of the land to a buyer in order to cover the debt and buy seed for the next planting. If there was a person who belonged to the farmer's clan who wished to act as a "redeemer," he could pay the buyer according to the number of remaining annual crops until the jubilee year when it reverted to the farmer. Until that time, the land belonged to the redeemer, who allowed the farmer to work it.

2. The second stage was more serious (Lev. 25:35–38). Assuming that the land was not redeemed and the farmer again fell into debt from which he could not recover, he would forfeit all of his land to the creditor. In this case, the creditor must lend the farmer the funds necessary to continue working as a tenant farmer on his own land, but must not charge him interest. The farmer would amortize this loan with the profit made from the crops, perhaps

---

[12] Christopher J. H. Wright, *The Mission of God: Unlocking the Bible's Grand Narrative* (Downers Grove, IL: IVP Academic, 2006), 296.

[13] Bruce K. Waltke and Charles Yu, *An Old Testament Theology: An Exegetical, Canonical, and Thematic Approach* (Grand Rapids: Zondervan, 2007), 528.

eliminating the debt. If so, the farmer would regain his land. If the loan was not fully repaid before the jubilee, then at that time the land would revert back to the farmer or his heirs.

3. The third stage was more serious still (Lev. 25:39–43). Assuming that the farmer in the previous stage could neither pay on the loan or even support himself and his family, he would become temporarily bound to the household of the creditor. As a bound laborer he would work for wages, which were entirely for reduction of the debt. At the year of jubilee, he would regain his land and his freedom (Lev. 25:41). Throughout these years, the creditor must not work him as a slave, sell him as a slave, or rule over him harshly (Lev. 25:42–43). The creditor must "fear God" by accepting the fact that all of God's people are God's slaves (NRSV "servants") whom he graciously brought out from Egypt. No one else can own them because God already does.

The point of these rules is that Israelites were never to become slaves to other Israelites. It was conceivable, though, that impoverished Israelites might sell themselves as slaves to wealthy resident aliens living in the land (Lev. 25:47–55). Even if this happened, the sale must not be permanent. People who sold themselves must retain the right to buy themselves out of slavery if they prospered. If not, a near relative could intervene as a "redeemer" who would pay the foreigner according to the number of years left until the jubilee when the impoverished Israelites were to be released. During that time, they were not to be treated harshly but be regarded as hired workers.

What Does the Year of Jubilee Mean for Today?

The year of jubilee operated within the context of Israel's kinship system for the protection of the clan's inalienable right to work their ancestral land, which they understood to be owned by God and to be enjoyed by them as a benefit of their relationship with him. These social and economic conditions no longer exist, and from a biblical point of view, God no longer administers redemption through a single political state. We must therefore view the jubilee from our current vantage point.

A wide variety of perspectives exists about the proper application, if any, of the jubilee to today's societies. To take one example that engages seriously with contemporary realities, Christopher Wright has written extensively on the Christian appropriation of Old Testament laws.[14] He identifies principles implicit in these ancient laws in order to grasp their ethical implications for today. His treatment of the jubilee year thus considers three basic angles: the theological, the social, and the economic.[15]

Theologically, the jubilee affirms that the Lord is not only the God who owns Israel's land; he is sovereign over all time and nature. His act of redeeming his people from Egypt committed him to provide for them on every level because they were his own. Therefore, Israel's observance of the Sabbath day and year and the year of jubilee was a function of obedience and trust. In practical terms, the jubilee year embodies the trust all Israelites could have that God would provide for their immediate needs and for the future of their families. At the same time, it calls on the rich to trust that treating creditors compassionately will still yield an adequate return.

Looking at the *social* angle, the smallest unit of Israel's kinship structure was the household that would have included three to four generations. The jubilee provided a socioeconomic solution to keep the family whole even in the face of economic calamity. Family debt was a reality in ancient times as it is today, and its effects include a frightening list of social ills. The jubilee sought to check these negative social consequences by limiting their duration so that future generations would not have to bear the burden of their distant ancestors.[16]

The *economic* angle reveals the two principles that we can apply today. First, God desires just distribution of the earth's resources. According to God's plan, the land of Canaan was assigned equitably among the people. The jubilee was not about redistribution but restoration. According to

---

[14] Milgrom, *Leviticus*, 299–303.

[15] Christopher J. H. Wright, *Old Testament Ethics for the People of God* (Downers Grove, IL: InterVarsity Press, 2004), chapter 9.

[16] The following discussion of these three angles is indebted to Wright's exposition in *Mission of God*, 296–300. Chapter 5, "Economics and the Poor," in *Old Testament Ethics* is also helpful and relevant, but ranges far beyond the jubilee concerns of Leviticus 25.

Wright, "The jubilee thus stands as a critique not only of massive private accumulation of land and related wealth but also of large-scale forms of collectivism or nationalization that destroy any meaningful sense of personal or family ownership."[17] Second, family units must have the opportunity and resources to provide for themselves.

In most modern societies, people cannot be sold into slavery to pay debts. Bankruptcy laws provide relief to those burdened with unpayable debts, and descendants are not liable for ancestors' debts. The basic property needed for survival may be protected from seizure. Nonetheless, Leviticus 25 seems to offer a broader foundation than contemporary bankruptcy laws. It is founded not on merely protecting personal liberty and a bit of property for destitute people, but on ensuring that everyone has access to the means of making a living and escaping multigenerational poverty. As the gleaning laws in Leviticus show, the solution is neither handouts nor mass appropriation of property, but social values and structures that give every person an opportunity to work productively. Have modern societies actually surpassed ancient Israel in this regard? What about the millions of people enslaved or in bonded labor today in situation where anti-slavery laws are not adequately enforced? What would it take for Christians to be capable of offering real solutions?

Conclusions from Leviticus

The single most important conclusion we can draw from Leviticus is that our call as God's people is to reflect God's holiness in our work. This calls us to separate ourselves from the actions of any around us who oppose God's ways. When we reflect God's holiness, we find ourselves in God's presence, whether at work, home, church, or society. We reflect God's holiness not by hanging up Scripture verses, reciting prayers, wearing crosses, or even by being nice. We do it by loving our co-workers, customers, students, investors, competitors, rivals, and everyone we encounter as much as we love ourselves. In practical terms, this means doing as much good for others through our work as we do for ourselves.

---

[17] Wright, *Mission of God*, 296–97.

This enlivens our motivation, our diligence, our exercise of power, our skill development, and perhaps even our choice of work. It also means working for the benefit of the entire community and working in harmony with the rest of society, so far as it depends on us. And it means working to change the structures and systems of society to reflect God's holiness as the one who delivered Israel from slavery and oppression. When we do this, we find by God's grace that his words are fulfilled: "I will place my dwelling in your midst, and I shall not abhor you. And I will walk among you, and will be your God, and you shall be my people" (Lev. 26:11–12).

Numbers and Work

Introduction to Numbers

The book of Numbers contributes significantly to our understanding and practice of work. It shows us God's people, Israel, struggling to work in accordance with God's purposes in challenging times. In their struggles, they experience conflicts about identity, authority, and leadership as they work their way across the wilderness toward God's Promised Land. Most of the insight we can gain for our work comes by example, where we see what pleases God and what does not, rather than by a series of commands.

The book is called "Numbers" in English because it records a series of censuses that Moses took of the tribes of Israel. Censuses were taken to quantify the human and natural resources available for the economic and governmental affairs, including military service (Num. 1:2–3; 26:2–4), religious duties (Num. 4:2–3, 22–23), taxation (Num. 3:40–48), and agriculture (Num. 26:53–54). Effective resource allocation depends on good data. But these censuses serve as a framework for a narrative that goes beyond merely reporting the numbers. In the narratives, the statistics are often misused leading to dissent, rebellion, and social unrest. Quantitative reasoning itself is not the problem—God himself orders censuses (Num. 1:1–2). But when numerical analysis is used as a pretext for deviating from the word of the Lord, disaster follows (Num. 14:20–25). A distant echo of this manipulation of numbers as a substitute for genuine moral reasoning can be heard in today's accounting scandals and financial crises.

Numbers takes place in that wilderness region that is neither Egypt nor the Promised Land. The Hebrew title of the book, *bemidbar,* is shorthand for the phrase "in the wilderness of Sinai" (Num. 1:1), which describes the main action in the book—Israel's journey through the wilderness. The nation progresses from Sinai toward the Promised Land, concluding with Israel in the region east of the Jordan River. They came to be in this location because God's "mighty hand" (Exod. 6:1) had liberated them from slavery in Egypt, the story told in the book of Exodus. Getting the people out of slavery was one matter; getting the slavery out of the people would prove to be quite another. In short, the book of Numbers is about life with God during the journey to the destination of his promises, a journey we as God's people are still undertaking. From Israel's experience in the wilderness, we find resources for challenges in our life and work today, and we can draw encouragement from God's ever-present help.

God Numbers and Orders the Nation of Israel (Numbers 1:1–2:34)

Prior to the Exodus, Israel had never been a nation. Israel began as the family of Abraham and Sarah and their descendants, prospered as a clan under Joseph's leadership, but fell into bondage as an ethnic minority in Egypt. The Israelite population in Egypt grew to become nation-sized (Exod. 12:37) but, as an enslaved people, they were permitted no national institutions or organizations. They had departed Egypt as a barely organized refugee mob (Exod. 12:34–39) who now had to be organized into a functioning nation.

God directs Moses to enumerate the population (the first census, Num. 1:1–3) and create a provisional government headed by tribal leaders (Num. 1:4–16). Under God's further direction, Moses appoints a religious order, the Levites, and equips them with resources to build the tabernacle of the covenant (Num. 1:48–54). He lays out camp housing for all the people, then regiments the men of fighting age into military echelons, and appoints commanders and officers (Num. 2:1–9). He creates a bureaucracy, delegates authority to qualified leaders, and institutes a civil judiciary and court of appeal (this is told in Exodus 18:1–27, rather than in Numbers). Before Israel can come into possession of the Promised Land (Gen. 28:15) and fulfill its mission to bless all the nations (Gen. 18:18), the nation had to be ordered effectively.

Moses' activities of organization, leadership, governance, and resource development are closely paralleled in virtually every sector of society today—business, government, military, education, religion, nonprofits, neighborhood associations, even families. In this sense, Moses is the godfather of all managers, accountants, statisticians, economists, military officers, governors, judges, police, headmasters, community organizers, and myriad others. The detailed attention Numbers gives to organizing workers, training leaders, creating civic institutions, developing logistical capabilities, structuring defenses, and developing accounting systems suggests that God still guides and empowers the ordering, governing, resourcing, and maintaining of social structures today.

The Levites and the Work of God (Numbers 3–8)

Numbers 3 through 8 focuses on the work of the priests and Levites. (The Levites are the tribe whose men serve as priests—to a large degree the terms are interchangeable in Numbers.) They have the essential role of mediating God's redemption to all the people (Num. 3:40–51). Like other workers, they are enumerated and organized into work units, although they are exempted from military service (Num. 4:2–3; 22–23). It may seem that their work is singled out as higher than the work of others, as it "concerns the most holy things" (Num. 4:4). It's true that the uniquely detailed attention given to the tent of meeting and its utensils seems to elevate the priests' role above those of the rest of the people. But the text actually portrays how intricately their work is related to the work of *all* Israelites. The Levites assist *all* people in bringing their life and work into line with God's law and purposes. Moreover, the work performed by the Levites in the tent is quite similar to the work of most Israelites—breaking, moving and setting up camp, kindling fire, washing linens, butchering animals, and processing grain. The emphasis, then, is on the integration of the Levites' work with everyone else's. Numbers pays careful attention to the priests' work of mediating God's presence, not because religious work is the most important occupation, but because *God* is the center point of *every* occupation.

Offering God the Products of Human Labor (Numbers 4 and 7)

The Lord gives detailed instructions for setting up the tent of meeting, the location of his presence with Israel. The tent of meeting requires materials produced by a wide variety of workers—fine leather, blue cloth, crimson cloth, curtains, poles and frames, plates, dishes, bowls, flagons, lamp stands, snuffers, trays, oil and vessels to hold it, a golden altar, fire pans, forks, shovels, basins, and fragrant incense (Num. 4:5–15). (For a similar description, see "The Tabernacle" in Exodus 31:1–12 above.) In the course of worship, the people bring into it further products of human labor, such as offerings of drink (Num. 4:7, et al.), grain (4:16, et al.), oil (7:13, et al.), lambs and sheep (6:12, et al.), goats (7:16, et al.), and precious metals (7:25, et al.). Virtually every occupation—indeed nearly every person—in Israel is needed to make it possible to worship God in the tent of meeting.

The Levites fed their families largely with a portion of the sacrifices. These were allotted to the Levites because, unlike the other tribes, they were not given land to farm (Num. 18:18–32). The Levites did not receive sacrifices because *they* were holy men, but because by presiding at sacrifices, they brought *everyone* into a holy relation with God. The people, not the Levites, were the prime beneficiaries of the sacrifices. In fact, the sacrificial system itself was a component in Israel's food supply system. Aside from some portions burned on the altar and the Levites' allotment mentioned above, the main parts of the grain and animal offerings were designated for consumption by those who brought them.[1] Everyone in Israel was thus fed in part by the system. Overall, the sacrificial system did not serve to isolate a few holy things from the rest of human production, but to mediate God's presence in the entire life and work of the nation.

Likewise today, the products and services of all God's people are expressions of God's power at work in human beings, or at least they

---

[1] David P. Wright, "The Disposal of Impurity: Elimination Rites in the Bible and in Hittite and Mesopotamian Literature," *Society of Biblical Literature Dissertation Studies* 101 (1987): 34–36.

should be. The New Testament develops this theme from the Old Testament explicitly. "You are a chosen race, a royal priesthood, a holy nation, God's own people, in order that you may proclaim the mighty acts of him who called you out of darkness into his marvelous light" (1 Pet. 2:9). All the work we do is priestly work when it proclaims God's goodness. The items we produce—leather and cloth, dishes and plates, construction materials, lesson plans, financial forecasts, and all the rest—are priestly items. The work we do—washing clothes, growing crops, raising children, and every other form of legitimate work—is priestly service to God. All of us are meant to ask, "How does my work reflect the goodness of God, make him visible to those who do not recognize him and serve his purposes in the world?" All believers, not just clergy, are descendants of the priests and Levites in Numbers, doing God's work every day.

Confession and Restitution (Numbers 5:5–10)

An essential role of the people of God is bringing reconciliation and justice to scenes of conflict and abuse. Although the people of Israel bound themselves to obey God's commandments, they routinely fell short, as we do today. Often this took the form of mistreating other people. "When a man or a woman wrongs another, breaking faith with the LORD, that person incurs guilt" (Num. 5:6). Through the work of the Levites, God provides a means of repentance, restitution, and reconciliation in the aftermath of such wrongs. An essential element is that the guilty party not only repays the loss he or she caused, but also adds 20 percent (Num. 5:7), presumably as a way of suffering loss in sympathy with the victim. (This passage is parallel with the guilt offering described in Leviticus; see "The Workplace Significance of the Guilt Offering" in *Leviticus and Work* above.)

The New Testament gives a vivid example of this principle at work. When the tax collector Zacchaeus comes to salvation in Christ, he offers to pay back four times the amount he overcharged his fellow citizens. A more modern example—though not explicitly grounded in the Bible—is the growing practice of hospitals admitting mistakes, apologizing, and offering immediate financial restitution and assistance to patients and families involved.[2] But you don't have to be a tax collector or a medical worker to make mistakes. All of us have ample opportunities to confess our mistakes and offer to make up for them, and more. It is in the workplace where much of this challenge takes place. Yet do we actually do it, or do we try to cover up our shortcomings and minimize our responsibility?

Aaron's Blessing for the People (Numbers 6:22–27)

One of the chief roles of the Levites is invoking God's blessing. God ordains these words for the priestly blessing:

> The LORD bless you and keep you;
> the LORD make his face to shine upon you, and be gracious to you;
> the LORD lift up his countenance upon you, and give you peace.
>   (Num. 6:24–26)

God blesses people in countless ways—spiritual, mental, emotional, and material. But the focus here is on blessing people with words. Our good words become the moment of God's grace in the lives of people. "So they shall put my name on the Israelites, and I will bless them," God promises (Num. 6:27).

The words we use in our places of work have the power either to bless or curse, to build up others or to tear them down. Our choice of words often has more power than we realize. The blessings in Numbers 6:24–26 declare that God will "keep" you, be "gracious" to you and give you "peace." At work our words can "keep" another person—that is, reassure, protect, and support. "If you need help, come to me. I won't hold it against you." Our words can be full of grace, making the situation better than it otherwise would be. We can accept responsibility for a shared error, for example, rather than shifting the blame by minimizing our

---

[2] Steve S. Kraman and Ginny Hamm, "Risk Management: Extreme Honesty May Be the Best Policy," *Annals of Internal Medicine* 131 (Dec. 1999): 963–67. Further coverage is found in Pauline Chen, "When Doctors Admit Their Mistakes," *New York Times*, Aug. 19, 2010.

role. Our words can bring peace by restoring relationships that have been broken. "I realize that things have gone wrong between us, but I want to find a way to have a good relationship again," for example. Of course, there are times we have to object, critique, correct, and perhaps punish others at work. Even so, we can choose whether to criticize the faulty action or whether to damn the whole person. Conversely, when others do well, we can choose to praise instead of keeping silent, despite the slight risk to our reputation or cool reserve.

Retirement from Regular Service (Numbers 8:23–26)

Numbers contains the only passage in the Bible that specifies an age limit for work. The Levites entered their service as young men who would be strong enough to erect and transport the tabernacle with all of its sacred elements. The censuses of Numbers 4 did not include names of any Levites over the age of fifty, and Numbers 8:25 specifies that at age fifty Levites must retire from their duties. In addition to the heavy lifting of the tabernacle, Levites' job also included inspecting skin diseases closely (Lev. 13). In a time before reading glasses, virtually no one over the age of fifty would be able to see anything at close range. The point is not that fifty is a universal retirement age, but that a time comes when an aging body performs with less effectiveness at work. The process varies highly among individuals and occupations. Moses was eighty when he began his duties as Israel's leader (Exod. 7:7).

Retirement, however, was not the end of the Levites work. The purpose was not to remove productive workers from service, but to redirect their service in a more mature direction, given the conditions of their occupation. After retirement they could still "assist their brothers in the tent of meeting in carrying out their duties" (Num. 8:26). Sometimes, some faculties—judgment, wisdom, and insight, perhaps—may actually improve with increasing age. By "assisting their brothers," older Levites transitioned to different ways of serving their communities. Modern notions of retirement that consist of ceasing work and devoting time exclusively to leisure are not found in the Bible.

Like the Levites, we should not seek a total cessation of meaningful work in old age. We may want or need to relinquish our positions, but our abilities and wisdom are still valuable. We may continue to serve others in our occupations by leadership in trade associations, civic organizations, boards of directors, and licensing bodies. We may consult, train, teach, or coach. We may finally have the time to serve to our fullest in church, clubs, elective office, or service organizations. We may be able to invest more time with our families, or if it is too late for that, in the lives of other children and young people. Often our most valuable new service is coaching and encouraging (blessing) younger workers (see Num. 6:24–27).

Given these possibilities, old age can be one of the most satisfying periods in a person's life. Sadly, retirement sidelines many people just at the moment when their gifts, resources, time, experience, networks, influence, and wisdom may be most beneficial. Some choose to pursue only leisure and entertainment or simply give up on life. Others find that age-related regulations and social marginalization prevent them from working as fully as they desire. There is too little material in Scripture to derive a specific theology of retirement. But as we age, each of us can prepare for retirement with as much, or more, care as we have prepared for work. When young, we can respect and learn from more experienced colleagues. At every age, we can work toward retirement policies and practices that are fairer and more productive for both younger and older workers.

The Challenge to Moses' Authority (Numbers 12)

In Numbers 12, Moses' brother and sister, Aaron and Miriam, try to launch a revolt against his authority. They appear to have a reasonable complaint. Moses teaches that Israelites are not to marry foreigners (Deut. 7:3), yet he himself has a foreign wife (Num. 12:1). If this complaint had been their true concern, they could have brought it to Moses or to the council of elders he had recently formed (Num. 11:16–17) for resolution. Instead, they agitate to put themselves in Moses' place as leaders of the nation. In reality, their complaint was merely a pretext to launch a general rebellion with the aim of elevating themselves to positions of ultimate power.

God punishes them severely on Moses' behalf. He reminds them he has chosen Moses as his representative to Israel, speaking "face to face" with Moses, and entrusts him with "all my house" (Num. 12:7–8). "Why then were you not afraid to speak against my servant Moses?" he demands (Num. 12:8). When he hears no answer, Numbers tells us that "the anger of the LORD was kindled against them" (Num. 12:9). His punishment falls first on Miriam who becomes leprous to the point of death, and Aaron begs Moses to forgive them (Num. 12:10–12). The authority of God's chosen leader must be respected, for to rebel against such a leader is to rebel against God himself.

When We Have Grievances against Those in Authority

God was uniquely present in Moses' leadership. "Never since then has there arisen a prophet in Israel like Moses, whom the LORD knew face to face" (Deut. 34:10). Today's leaders do not manifest God's authority face to face as Moses did. Yet God commands us to respect the authority of all leaders, "for there is no authority except from God" (Rom. 13:1–3). This does not mean that leaders must never be questioned, held accountable, or even replaced. It does mean that whenever we have a grievance against those in legitimate authority—as Moses was—our duty is to discern the ways in which their leadership is a manifestation of God's authority. We are to respect them for whatever portion of God's authority they truly bear, even as we seek to correct, limit, or even remove them from power.

A telling detail in the story is that Aaron and Miriam's purpose was to thrust themselves into positions of power. A thirst for power can never be a legitimate motivation for rebelling against authority. If we have a grievance against our boss, our first hope should be to resolve the grievance with him or her. If the boss's abuse of power or incompetence prevents this, our next aim would be to have him or her replaced by someone of integrity and ability. But if our purpose is to magnify our own power, then our aim is untrue, and we have even lost the standing to perceive whether the boss is acting legitimately or not. Our own cravings have made us incapable of discerning God's authority in the situation.

When Others Oppose Our Authority

Although Moses was both powerful and in the right, he responds to the leadership challenge with gentleness and humility. "The man Moses was very humble, more so than anyone else on the face of the earth" (Num. 12:3). He remains with Aaron and Miriam throughout the episode, even when they begin to receive their deserved punishment. He intervenes with God to restore Miriam's health, and succeeds in reducing her punishment from death to seven days banishment from camp (Num. 12:13–15). He retains them in the senior leadership of the nation.

If we are in positions of authority, we are likely to face opposition as Moses did. Assuming that we, like Moses, have come to authority legitimately, we may be offended by opposition and even recognize it as an offense against God's purpose for us. We may well be in the right if we attempt to defend our position and defeat those who are attacking it. Yet, like Moses, we must care first for the people over whom God has placed us in authority, including those who are opposing us. They may have legitimate grievances against us, or they may be aspiring to tyranny. We may succeed in resisting them, or we may lose. We may or may or not continue in the organization, and they also may or may not continue. We may find common ground, or we may find it impossible to restore good working relationships with our opponents. Nonetheless, in every situation we have a duty of humility, meaning that we act for the good of those God has entrusted to us, even at the expense of our comfort, power, prestige, and self-image. We will know we are fulfilling this duty when we find ourselves advocating for those who oppose us, as Moses did with Miriam.

When Leadership Leads to Unpopularity
(Numbers 13 and 14)

Another challenge to Moses' authority arises in Numbers 13 and 14. The Lord tells Moses to send spies into the land of Canaan to prepare for the conquest. Both military and economic intelligence are to be collected, and spies are named from every tribe (Num. 13:18–20). This means the spies' report could be used not only to plan the conquest, but also to begin discussions about allocating territory among the Israelite tribes. The spies' report confirms that the land is very good, that "it flows with milk and honey" (Num. 13:27). However, the spies also report that "the people who live in the land are strong, and the towns are fortified and very large" (Num. 13:28). Moses and his lieutenant, Caleb, use the intelligence to plan the attack, but the spies become fearful and declare that the land cannot be conquered (Num. 13:30–32). Following the spies' lead, the people of Israel rebel against the Lord's plan and resolve to find a new leader to take them back to slavery in Egypt. Only Aaron, Caleb, and a young man named Joshua remain with him.

But Moses stands fast, despite the plan's unpopularity. The people are on the verge of replacing him, yet he sticks to what the Lord has revealed to him as right. He and Aaron plead with the people to cease their rebellion, but to no avail. Finally, the Lord chastises Israel for its lack of faith and declares he will strike them with a deadly pestilence (Num. 14:5–12). By abandoning the plan, they thrust themselves into an even worse situation—imminent, utter destruction. Only Moses, steadfast in his original purpose, knows how to avert disaster. He appeals to the Lord to forgive the people, as he has done before. (We have seen in Numbers 12 how Moses is always ready to put his peoples' welfare first, even at his own expense.) The Lord relents, but declares there are inescapable consequences for the people. None of those who joined the rebellion will be allowed to enter the Promised Land (Num. 14:20–23).

Moses' actions demonstrate that leaders are chosen for the purpose of decisive commitment, not for blowing in the wind of popularity. Leadership can be a lonely duty, and if we are in positions of leadership, we may be severely tempted to acquiesce to popular opinion. It is true that good leaders do listen to others' opinions. But when a leader knows the best course of action, and has tested that knowledge to the best of his or her ability, the leader has a responsibility to do what is best, not what is most popular.

In Moses' situation, there was no doubt about the right course of action. The Lord commanded Moses to occupy the Promised Land. As we have seen, Moses himself remained humble in demeanor, but he did not waver in direction. He did not, in fact, succeed in carrying out the Lord's command. If people will not follow, the leader cannot accomplish the mission alone. In this case, the consequence for the people was the disaster of an entire generation missing out on the land God had chosen for them. At least Moses himself did not contribute to the disaster by changing his plan in response to their opinions.

The modern era is filled with examples of leaders who *did* give in to popular opinion. British Prime Minister Neville Chamberlain's capitulation to Hitler's demands in Munich in 1938 comes readily to mind. In contrast, Abraham Lincoln became one of America's greatest presidents by steadfastly refusing to give in to popular opinion to end the American Civil War by accepting the nation's division. Although he had the humility to acknowledge the possibility that he might be wrong ("as God gives us to see the right"), he also had the fortitude to do what he knew was right despite enormous pressure to give in. The book *Leadership on the Line* by Ronald Heifetz and Martin Linsky[3] explores the challenge of remaining open to others' opinions while maintaining steadfast leadership in times of challenge. (For more on this episode, see "Israel Refuses to Enter the Promised Land" in Deuteronomy 1:19–45 above.)

Offering God Our Firstfruits
(Numbers 15:20–21; 18:12–18)

Building on the sacrificial system described in Numbers 4 and 7, two passages in Numbers 15 and 18 describe the offering of the *first* produce of labor and the land to God. In addition to the offerings described earlier, the Israelites are to offer to God "the first fruits of all that is in their land" (Num. 18:13). Because God is the sovereign in possession of all things, the *entire* produce of the land and people actually belong to God already. When the people bring the firstfruits to the altar, they acknowledge God's ownership of everything, not merely what is left over after they meet their own needs. By bringing the firstfruits *before* making use of the rest of the increase themselves, they express respect for God's sovereignty, as well as the urgent hope that God will bless the continuing productivity of their labor and resources.[4]

---

[3] Martin Linsky and Ronald A. Heifetz, *Leadership on the Line: Staying Alive Through the Dangers of Leading* (Boston: Harvard Business Press, 2002).

[4] Richard O. Rigsby, "First Fruits," in *The Anchor Yale Bible Dictionary*, ed. David Noel Freedman (New York: Doubleday, 1992), 797.

The offerings and sacrifices in Israel's sacrificial system are different from the gifts and offerings we make today to God's work, but the concept of giving our firstfruits to God is still applicable. By giving first to God, we acknowledge God to be the owner of everything we have. Therefore, we give him our first and best. In this way, offering our firstfruits becomes a blessing for us as it was for ancient Israel.

Reminders of the Covenant (Numbers 15:37–41)

A short passage in Numbers 15 commands the Israelites to make fringes or tassels on the corners of their garments, with a blue cord at each corner, "so that, when you see it, you will remember all the commandments of the LORD and do them." In work, as elsewhere, there is always the temptation to "follow the lust of your own heart and your own eyes" (Num. 15:39). In fact, the more diligently you pay attention to your work (your "eyes"), the greater the chance that things in your workplace that are not of the Lord will influence you (your "heart"). The answer is not to stop paying attention at work or to take it less seriously. Instead, it could be a good thing to plant reminders that will remind you of God and his way. It may not be tassels, but it could be a Bible that will come across your eyesight, an alarm reminding you to pray momentarily from time to time, or a symbol worn or carried in a place that will catch your attention. The purpose is not to show off for others, but to draw "your own heart" back to God. Although this is a small thing, it can have a significant effect. By doing so, "you shall remember and do all my commandments, and you shall be holy to your God" (Num. 15:40).

Moses' Unfaithfulness at Meribah (Numbers 20:2–13)

Moses' moment of greatest failure came when the people of Israel resumed complaining, this time about food and water (Num. 20:1–5). Moses and Aaron decided to bring the complaint to the Lord, who commanded them to take their staff, and in the people's presence command a rock to yield water enough for the people and their livestock (Num. 20:6–8). Moses did as the Lord instructed but added two flourishes of his own. First he rebuked the people, saying, "Listen, you rebels, shall we bring water for you out of this rock?" Then he struck the rock twice with his staff. Water poured out in abundance (Num. 20:9–11), but the Lord was extremely displeased with Moses and Aaron.

God's punishment was harsh. "Because you did not trust in me, to show my holiness before the eyes of the Israelites, therefore you shall not bring this assembly into the land that I have given them" (Num. 20:12). Moses and Aaron, like all the people who rebelled against God's plan earlier (Num. 14:22–23), will not be permitted to enter the Promised Land.

Scholarly arguments about the exact action Moses was punished for may be found in any of the general commentaries, but the text of Numbers 20:12 names the underlying offense directly, "You did not trust in me." Moses' leadership faltered in the crucial moment when he stopped trusting God and started acting on his own impulses.

Honoring God in leadership—as all Christian leaders in every sphere must attempt to do—is a terrifying responsibility. Whether we lead a business, a classroom, a relief organization, a household, or any other organization, we must be careful not to mistake our authority for God's. What can we do to keep ourselves in obedience to God? Meeting regularly with an accountability (or "peer") group, praying daily about the tasks of leadership, keeping a weekly Sabbath to rest in God's presence, and seeking others' perspective on God's guidance are methods some leaders employ. Even so, the task of leading firmly while remaining wholly dependent on God is beyond human capability. If the most humble man on the face of the earth (Num. 12:3) could fail in this way, so can we. By God's grace, even failures as great as Moses' at Meribah, with disastrous consequences in this life, do not separate us from the ultimate fulfillment of God's promises. Moses did not enter the Promised Land, yet the New Testament declares him "faithful in all God's house" and reminds us of the confidence that all in God's house have in the fulfillment of our redemption in Christ (Heb. 3:2–6).

When God Speaks through Unexpected Sources (Numbers 22–24)

In Numbers 22 and 23, the protagonist is not Moses but Balaam, a man residing near the path Israel was slowly taking toward the Promised Land. Although he was not an Israelite, he was a priest or prophet of the Lord. The king of Moab recognized God's power in Balaam's words, saying, "I know that whomever you bless is blessed, and whomever you curse is cursed." Fearing the strength of the Israelites, the king of Moab sent emissaries asking Balaam to come to Moab and curse the Israelites to rid him of the perceived threat (Num. 22:1–6).

God informs Balaam that he has chosen Israel as a blessed nation and commands Balaam neither to go to Moab nor to curse Israel (Num. 22:12). However, after multiple embassies from the king of Moab, Balaam agrees to go to Moab. His hosts try to bribe him to curse Israel, but Balaam warns them that he will do only what the Lord commands (Num. 22:18). God seems to agree with this plan, but as Balaam rides his donkey toward Moab, an angel of the Lord blocks his way three times. The angel is invisible to Balaam, but the donkey sees the angel and turns aside each time. Balaam becomes infuriated at the donkey and begins to beat the animal with his staff. "Then the Lord opened the mouth of the donkey, and it said to Balaam, 'What have I done to you, that you have struck me these three times?' " (Num. 22:28). Balaam converses with the donkey and comes to realize that the animal has perceived the Lord's guidance far more clearly than Balaam has. Balaam's eyes are opened; he sees the angel and receives God's further instructions about dealing with the king of Moab. "Go with the men; but speak only what I tell you," the Lord reminds him (Num. 22:35). Over the course of chapters 23 and 24, the king of Moab continues to entreat Balaam to curse Israel, but each time Balaam replies that the Lord declares Israel blessed. Eventually he succeeds in dissuading the king from attacking Israel (Num. 24:12–25), thus sparing Moab from immediate destruction by the hand of the Lord.

Balaam is similar to Moses because he manages to follow the Lord's guidance despite personal failings at times. Like Moses he plays a significant role in fulfilling God's plan to bring Israel to the Promised Land. But Balaam is also very unlike Moses and most of the other heroes of the

Hebrew Bible. He is not an Israelite himself. And his primary accomplishment is to save Moab, not Israel, from destruction. For both of these reasons, the Israelites would be quite surprised to read that God spoke to Balaam as clearly and directly as to Israel's own prophets and priests. Even more surprising—both to Israel and to Balaam himself—is that God's guidance at the crucial moment came to him through the mouth of an animal, a lowly donkey. In two surprising ways, we see that God's guidance comes not from the sources most favored by people, but from the sources God chooses himself. If God chooses to speak through the words of a potential enemy or even a beast of the field, we should pay attention.

The passage does not tell us that the best source of God's guidance is necessarily foreign prophets or donkeys, but it does give us some insight about listening for God's voice. It is easy for us to listen for God's voice only from sources we know. This often means listening only to those people who think like we do, belong to our social circles, or speak and act like us. This may mean we never pay attention to others who would take a different position from us. It becomes easy to believe that God is telling us exactly what we already thought. Leaders often reinforce this by surrounding themselves with a narrow band of like-minded deputies and advisors. Perhaps we are more like Balaam than we would like to believe. But by God's grace, could we somehow learn to listen to what God might be saying to us, even through people we don't trust or sources we don't agree with?

Land Ownership and Property Rights (Numbers 26–27; 36:1–12)

As time passes and demographics change, another new census is needed (Num. 26:1–4). A crucial purpose of this census is to begin developing socioeconomic structures for the new nation. Economic production and governmental organization is to be organized around tribes, with their subunits of clans and household. The land is to be divided among the clans in proportion to their population (Num. 26:52–56), and the assignment is to be made randomly. The result is that each household (extended family) receives a plot of land sufficient to support itself.

Unlike in Egypt—and later, the Roman Empire and medieval Europe—
land is not to be owned by a class of nobles and worked by a dispossessed
class of commoners or slaves. Instead, each family owns its own means
of agricultural production. Crucially, the land can never be permanently
lost to the family though debt, taxation, or even voluntary sale. (See Lev.
25 for the legal protections to keep families from losing their land.) Even
if one generation of a family fails at farming and falls into debt, the next
generation has access to the land needed to make a living.

The census is enumerated according to male heads of tribes and clans,
whose heads of households each receive an allotment. But in cases where
women are the heads of households (for example, if their fathers die before receiving their allotment), the women are allowed to own land and
pass it on to their descendants (Num. 27:8). This could complicate the
ordering of Israel, however, because a woman might marry a man from
another tribe. This would transfer the woman's land from her father's
tribe to her husband's, weakening the social structure. In order to prevent
this, the Lord decrees that although women may "marry whom they think
best" (Num. 36:6), "no inheritance shall be transferred from one tribe to
another" (Num. 36:9). This decree holds the rights of all people—women
included—to own property and marry as they choose in balance with the
need to preserve social structures. Tribes have to respect the rights of
their members. Heads of household have to respect the needs of society.

In much of today's economy, owning land is not the chief means
to make a living, and social structures are not ordered around tribes
and clans. Therefore, the specific regulations in Numbers and Leviticus
do not apply directly today. Conditions today require different specific
solutions. Wise, just, and fairly enforced laws respecting property and
economic structures, individual rights, and the common good are essential in every society. According to the United Nations Development
Programme, "The advancement of the rule of law at the national and
international levels is essential for sustained and inclusive economic
growth, sustainable development, the eradication of poverty and hunger
and the full realization of all human rights and fundamental freedoms."[5]

---

[5] United Nations Development Programme, *Issue Brief: Rule of Law and
Development* (New York: United Nations, 2013), 3.

Christians have much to contribute to the good governance of society, not only through the law but also through prayer and transformation of life. And increasingly, Christians are discovering that by working together, we can provide effective opportunities for marginalized people to gain permanent access to the resources needed to thrive economically. One example is Agros International, which is guided by a Christian "moral compass" to help poor, rural families in Latin America acquire and successfully cultivate land.[6]

Succession Planning (Numbers 27:12–23)

Building a sustainable organization—in this case, the nation of Israel—requires orderly transitions of authority. Without continuity, people become confused and fearful, work structures fall apart, and workers become ineffective, "like sheep without a shepherd" (Num. 27:17). Preparing a successor takes time. Poor leaders may be afraid to equip someone capable of succeeding them, but great leaders like Moses begin developing successors long before they expect to leave office. The Bible doesn't tell us what process Moses uses to identify and prepare Joshua, except that he prays for God's guidance (Num. 27:16). Numbers does tell us that he makes sure to publicly recognize and support Joshua and to follow the recognized procedure to confirm his authority (Num. 27:17–21).

Succession planning is the responsibility of both the current executive (like Moses) and those who exercise complementary authority (like Eleazar and the leaders of the congregation), as we see in Numbers 27:21. Institutions, whether as big as a nation or as small as a work group, need effective processes for training and succession.

Daily Offering for the People (Numbers 28 and 29)

Although people make individual and family offerings at appointed times, there is also a sacrifice on behalf of the entire nation every day

---

[6]Agros International, http://www.agros.org/ag/how-we-work/frequently-asked-questions.

(Num. 28:1–8). There are additional offerings on the Sabbath (Num. 28:9–10), new moons (Num. 28:11–15), Passover (Num. 28:16–25), and the Festivals of Weeks (Num. 28:26–31), Trumpets (Num. 29:1–6), the Atonement (Num. 29:7–10), and Booths (Num. 29:12–40). Through these communal offerings, the people receive the benefits of the Lord's presence and favor even when they are not personally at worship.[7]

The Israelite sacrifice system is no longer in operation, and it is impossible to apply it directly to life and work today. But the importance of sacrificing, offering, and worshiping for the benefit of others remains (Rom. 12:1–6). Some believers—notably, certain orders of monks and nuns—spend most of their day praying for those who cannot or do not worship or pray for themselves. In our work, it would not be right to neglect our duties to pray. But in the times we do pray, we can pray for the people we work among, especially if we know no one else is praying for them. We are, after all, called to bring blessings to the world around us (Num. 6:22–27). We can certainly emulate Numbers 28:1–8 by praying on a daily basis. Praying every day, or multiple times throughout the day, seems to keep us closest to God's presence. Faith is not only for the Sabbath.

Honoring Commitments (Numbers 30)

Chapter 30 of Numbers gives an elaborate system for determining the validity of promises, oaths, and vows. The basic position, however, is simple: Do what you say you will do.

> When a man makes a vow to the Lord, or swears an oath to bind himself by a pledge, he shall not break his word; he shall do according to all that proceeds out of his mouth. (Num. 30:2)

Elaborations are given to handle exceptions to the rule when someone makes a promise that exceeds their authority. (The regulations in the text deal with situations where certain women are subject to the authority of particular men.) Although the exceptions are valid—you can't enforce the

---

[7] Phillip J. Budd, *Numbers*, vol. 5, *Word Biblical Commentary* (Dallas: Word, 1998), 319.

promise of a person who lacks the authority to make it in the first place—when Jesus commented on this passage, he proposed a much simpler rule of thumb: Don't make promises you can't or won't keep (Matt. 5:33–37).

Work-related commitments tempt us to pile up elaborations, qualifications, exceptions, and justifications for not doing what we promise. No doubt many of them are reasonable, such as *force majeure* clauses in contracts, which excuse a party from fulfilling its obligations if prevented by court orders, natural disasters, and the like. It doesn't stop at honoring the letter of the contract. Many agreements are made with a handshake. Sometimes there are loopholes. Can we learn to honor the intent of the agreement and not just the letter of the law? Trust is the ingredient that makes workplaces work, and trust is impossible if we promise more than we can deliver, or deliver less than we promise. This is not only a fact of life, but a command of the Lord.

Civic Planning for Levitical Towns (Numbers 35:1–5)

Unlike the rest of the tribes, the Levites were to live in towns scattered throughout the Promised Land where they could teach the people the law and apply it in local courts. Numbers 35:2–5 details the amount of pasture land each town should have. Measuring from the edge of town, the area for pasture was to extend outward a thousand cubits (about 1,500 feet) in each direction, east, south, west, and north.

Jacob Milgrom has shown that this geographical layout was a realistic exercise in town planning.[8] The diagram shows a town with pastureland extending beyond the town diameter in each direction. As the town diameter grows and absorbs the closest pasture, additional pasture land is added so that the pasture remains 1,000 cubits beyond the town limits in each direction. (In the diagram the shaded areas remain the same size as they move outward, but the cross-hatched areas get wider as the town center gets wider.)

---

[8] Jacob Milgrom, "Excursus 74: The Levitical Town: An Exercise in Realistic Planning," *JPS Torah Commentary: Numbers* (The Jewish Publication Society, 1990), 502–4.

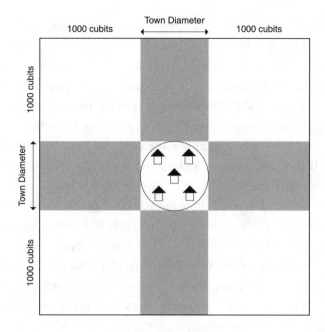

You shall measure, outside the town, for the east side two thousand cubits, for the south side two thousand cubits, for the west side two thousand cubits, and for the north side two thousand cubits, with the town in the middle. (Num. 35:5)

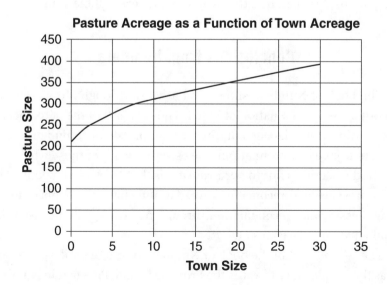

Mathematically, as the town grows, so does the area of its pasture land, but at a lower rate than the area of the inhabited town center. That means the population is growing faster than agricultural area. For this to continue, agricultural productivity per square meter must increase. Each herder must supply food to more people, freeing more of the population for industrial and service jobs. This is exactly what is required for economic and cultural development. To be sure, the town planning doesn't *cause* productivity to increase, but it creates a social-economic structure adapted for rising productivity. It is a remarkably sophisticated example of civic policy creating conditions for sustainable economic growth.

This passage in Numbers 35:5 illustrates again the detailed attention God pays to enabling human work that sustains people and creates economic well-being. If God troubles to instruct Moses on civic planning, based on semi-geometrical growth of pastureland, doesn't it suggest that God's people today should vigorously pursue all the professions, crafts, arts, academics, and other disciplines that sustain and prosper communities and nations? Perhaps churches and Christians could do more to encourage and celebrate its members' excellence in all fields of endeavor. Perhaps Christian workers could do more to become excellent at our work as a way of serving our Lord. Is there any reason to believe that excellent city planning, economics, childcare, or customer service bring less glory to God than heartfelt worship, prayer, or Bible study?

Conclusions from Numbers

The book of Numbers shows God at work through Moses to order and organize the new nation of Israel. The first part of the book focuses on worship, which depends on the work of priests in conjunction with laborers from every occupation. The essential work of those who represent God's people is not to perform rituals, but to bless all people with God's presence and reconciling love. All of us have the opportunity to bring blessing and reconciliation through our work, whether we think of ourselves as priests or not.

The second part of the book of Numbers traces the ordering of society as the people move towards the Promised Land. Passages in Numbers can help us gain a godly perspective on contemporary work issues such as offering the fruit of our labor to God, conflict resolution, retirement, leadership, property rights, economic productivity, succession planning, social relationships, honoring our commitments, and civic planning.

Leaders in Numbers—especially Moses—provide examples of what it means both to follow God's guidance and to fail in doing so. Leaders have to be open to wisdom from other people and from surprising sources. Yet they need to remain firm in following God's guidance as best as they can understand it. They must be bold enough to confront kings, yet humble enough to learn from the beasts of the field. No one in the book of Numbers succeeds completely in the task, but God remains faithful to his people in their successes and in their failings. Our mistakes have real—but not eternal—negative consequences, and we look for a hope beyond ourselves for the fulfillment of God's love for us. We see God's Spirit guiding Moses and hear God's promise to give the leaders who come after Moses a portion of God's Spirit too. By this, we ourselves can be encouraged in seeking God's guidance for the opportunities and challenges in our work. Whatever we do, we can be confident of God's presence with us as we work, for he tells us, "I the LORD dwell among the Israelites" (Num. 35:34) in whose steps we tread.

Deuteronomy and Work

Introduction to Deuteronomy

Work is a major subject of the book of Deuteronomy and prominent topics include the following:

- *The meaning and value of work.* God's command to work for the benefit of others, the blessings of work for the individual and the community, the consequences of failure and the dangers of success, and the responsibility that comes from representing God to others.

- *Relationships at work.* The importance of good relationships, the development of dignity and respect for others, and the requirement not to harm others or speak unjustly of them in our work.

- *Leadership.* The wise exercise of leadership and authority, succession planning and training, and the responsibility of leaders to work for the benefit of the people they lead.

- *Economic justice.* Respect for property, worker's rights, and courts of law, productive use of resources, lending and borrowing, and honesty in commercial agreements and fair trade

- *Work and rest.* The requirement to work, the importance of rest, and the invitation to trust God to provide for us whether at work or at rest.

Despite the centuries of change in commerce and vocation, Deuteronomy can help us better understand how to live in response to God's love and serve others through our work.

The book's dramatic, unified presentation makes it especially memorable. Jesus quoted from Deuteronomy at length. In fact, his first Scripture quotations were three passages from Deuteronomy (Matt. 4:4, 7, 10). The New Testament refers to Deuteronomy more than fifty times, a number exceeded only by Psalms and Isaiah.[1] And Deuteronomy contains the first formulation of the Great Commandment, "You shall love the LORD your God with all your heart, and with all your soul, and with all your might" (Deut. 6:4–5).

Underlying all the themes in Deuteronomy is Israel's covenant with the one true God. Everything in the book flows from the keystone of the covenant, "I am the LORD your God . . . you shall have no other gods before me" (Deut. 5:6–7). When people worship the Lord alone, good governance, productive work, ethical commerce, civic good, and fair treatment for all will generally result. When people put other motivations, values, and concerns ahead of God, work and life come to grief.

Deuteronomy covers the same material as the other books of the law—Exodus, Leviticus, and Numbers—but heightens the attention paid to work, most notably in the Ten Commandments. It seems as if in retelling the events and teachings of the other books, Moses feels a need to emphasize the importance of work in the life of God's people. Perhaps in some sense this foreshadows the growing attention that Christians are giving work in the present day. Looking at Scripture with fresh eyes, we discover that work is more important to God than we realized before, and that God's word gives more direction to our work than we thought.

Rebellion and Complacency (Deuteronomy 1:1–4:43)

Deuteronomy begins with a speech by Moses recounting the major events in Israel's recent history. Moses draws lessons from these events and exhorts Israel to respond to God's faithfulness by obeying him in trust (Deut. 4:40). Two sections—about violating trust in God by rebellion and complacency, respectively—are particularly important to the theology of work.

---

[1] Bruce K. Waltke and Charles Yu, *An Old Testament Theology: An Exegetical, Canonical, and Thematic Approach* (Grand Rapids: Zondervan, 2007), 479–80.

Israel Refuses to Enter the Promised Land (Deuteronomy 1:19–45)

In the wilderness, the people's fear leads to a failure to trust God. As a result they rebel against God's plan for them to enter the land he promised to Abraham, Isaac, and Jacob (Deut. 1:7–8). God had brought Israel out of slavery in Egypt, given the law at Mt. Horeb (Sinai), and brought the people swiftly to the borders of the promised land (Deut. 1:19–20). Moses then announces it is time to enter the land, but the people are fearful of the Amorites who occupy the borders. They convince Moses to send a scouting expedition as a matter of prudent planning. The scouts return with a good report of the land. At this point the people's true concern is revealed—they are afraid. "The people are stronger and taller than we; the cities are large and fortified up to heaven," they tell Moses, adding that "our hearts melt" (Deut. 1:28). The people do not trust God to fulfill his promises, so they refuse to follow his commands.

God's response is severe. "Not one of these—not one of this evil generation—shall see the good land that I swore to give to your ancestors" (Deut. 1:35). Entering Canaan had been delayed for the children and lost forever for the parents. Even Moses is barred from entering the land because he demonstrated a lack of trust in God himself, perhaps by agreeing to send scouts. Soon after, the people realize that they have condemned themselves to a lifetime of eking out an existence in the desert instead of enjoying the "good land" (Deut. 1:25) God had prepared for them. Belatedly, they make their own plans to attack the Amorites. But God declares, "Do not go up and do not fight, for I am not in the midst of you; otherwise you will be defeated by your enemies" (Deut. 1:42). A lack of trust in God's promises leads Israel to miss the blessings he had in store for them.

When we know what is right, but are tempted to violate it, trust in God is all we have to keep us in God's ways. This is not a matter of moral fiber. If even Moses failed to trust God completely, can we really imagine that we will succeed? Instead, it is a matter of God's grace. We can pray for God's Spirit to strengthen us when we stand for what is right, and we can ask for God's forgiveness when we fall. Like Moses and the people of Israel, failure to trust God can have serious consequences in life, but our failure is ultimately redeemed by God's grace. (For more on this episode, see "When Leadership Leads to Unpopularity" in Numbers 13–14 above.)

When Success Leads to Complacency (Deuteronomy 4:25–40)

In the wilderness, Israel's abandon of trust in God arises not only from fear, but also from success. At this point in his first speech, Moses is describing the prosperity that awaits the new generation about to enter the Promised Land. Moses points out that success is likely to breed a spiritual complacency far more dangerous than failure. "When you have had children and children's children, and become complacent in the land, if you act corruptly by making an idol in the form of anything . . . you will soon utterly perish from the land" (Deut. 4:25–26). We will come to idolatry, per se, in Deuteronomy 5:8, but the point here is the spiritual danger caused by complacency. In the wake of success, people cease fearing God and begin to believe success is a birthright. Instead of gratitude, we forge a sense of entitlement. The success for which we strive is not wrong, but it is a moral danger. The truth is that the success we achieve is mixed from a pinch of skill and hard work, combined with a heaping of fortunate circumstances and the common grace of God. We cannot actually provide for our own wants, desires, and security. Success is not permanent. It does not truly satisfy. A dramatic illustration of this truth is found in the life of King Uzziah in 2 Chronicles. "He was marvelously helped [by God] until he became strong. But when he had become strong he grew proud, to his destruction" (2 Chr. 26:15–16). Only in God can we find true security and satisfaction (Ps. 17:15).

It may be surprising that the result of complacency is not atheism but idolatry. Moses foresees that if the people abandon the Lord, they will not become spiritual free agents. They will bind themselves to "objects of wood and stone that neither see, nor hear, nor eat, nor smell" (Deut. 4:28). Perhaps in Moses' day the idea of religionless existence did not occur to anyone. But in our day it does. A growing tide of secularism attempts to throw off what it sees—sometimes quite correctly—as shackles of domination by corrupt religious institutions, belief, and practices. But does this result in a true freedom, or is the worship of God necessarily replaced by the worship of human-made fabrications?

Although this question sounds abstract, it has tangible effects on work and workplaces. For example, prior to the last half of the twentieth century, questions about business ethics were generally settled by reference to the Scriptures. This practice was far from perfect, but it did give serious standing to those on the losing side of power struggles related to work. The most dramatic case was probably the religiously based opposition to slavery in England and the United States of America, which ultimately succeeded in abolishing both the slave trade and slavery itself. In secularized institutions, there is no moral authority to which one can appeal. Instead, ethical decisions must be based on law and "ethical custom," as Milton Friedman put it.[2] Law and ethical custom being human constructs, business ethics becomes reduced to rule by the powerful and the popular. No one wants a workplace dominated by religious elite, but does a fully secularized workplace simply open the door for a different kind of exploitation? It is certainly possible for believers to bring the blessings of God's faithfulness to their workplaces without trying to reimpose special privileges for themselves.

All this is not to say that success must necessarily lead to complacency. If we can remember that God's grace, God's word, and God's guidance are at the root of whatever success we have, then we can be grateful, not complacent. The success we experience could then honor God and bring us joy. The caution is simply that over the course of history success seems to be spiritually more dangerous than adversity. Moses further warns Israel about the dangers of prosperity in Deuteronomy 8:11–20.

God's Law and Its Applications
(Deuteronomy 4:44–30:20)

Deuteronomy continues with a second speech containing the main body of the book. This section centers on God's covenant with Israel, especially the law, or principles and rules by which Israel should live. After a narrative introduction (Deut. 4:44–49), the speech itself consists of three parts. In the first part, Moses expounds the Ten Commandments (Deut. 5:1–11:33). In the second part, he describes in detail the "statutes and ordinances" that Israel is to follow (Deut. 12:1–26:19). In the third part, Moses describes the blessings Israel will experience if they keep

---

[2] Milton Friedman, "The Social Responsibility of Business Is to Increase Its Profits," *New York Times*, September 13, 1970.

the covenant, and the curses that will destroy them if they do not (Deut. 27:1–28:68). The second speech thus has the pattern of first giving the larger, governing principles (Deut. 5:1–11:32), then the specific rules (Deut. 12:1–26:19), and then the consequences for obedience or disobedience (Deut. 27:1–28:68).

The Ten Commandments (Deuteronomy 5:6–21)

The Ten Commandments are great contributors to the theology of work. They describe the essential requirements of Israel's covenant with God and are the core principles that govern the nation and the work of its people. Moses' exposition begins with the most memorable statement of the book, "Hear, O Israel: The LORD is our God, the LORD alone. You shall love the LORD your God with all your heart, and with all your soul, and with all your might" (Deut. 6:4–5). As Jesus pointed out centuries later, this is the greatest commandment of the entire Bible. Then Jesus added a quotation from Leviticus 19:18, "And a second is like it: 'You shall love your neighbor as yourself'" (Matt. 22:37–40). Although the "second" greatest commandment is not stated explicitly in Deuteronomy, we will see that the Ten Commandments do indeed point us to love of both God and neighbor.

The passage is virtually identical to Exodus 20:1–17—grammatical variations aside—except for some differences in the fourth (keeping the Sabbath), fifth (honoring mother and father), and tenth (coveting) commandments. Intriguingly, the variations in these commandments specifically address work. We will repeat the commentary from *Exodus and Work* here, with additions exploring the variations between the Exodus and Deuteronomy accounts.

"You Shall Have No Other Gods before Me" (Deuteronomy 5:7; Exodus 20:3)

The first commandment reminds us that everything in the Torah flows from the love we have for God, which is a response to the love he has for us. This love was demonstrated by God's deliverance of Israel "out of the house of slavery" in Egypt (Deut. 5:6). Nothing else in life should concern us more than our desire to love and be loved by God. If we *do* have some other concern stronger to us than our love for God, it is not so much that we are breaking God's rules, but that we are not really in relationship with God. The other concern—be it money, power, security, recognition, sex, or anything else—has become our god. This false god will have its own commandments at odds with God's, and we will inevitably violate the Torah as we comply with this god's requirements. Observing the Ten Commandments is conceivable only for those who start by worshipping no other god than the Lord.

In the realm of work, this means that we are not to let work or its requirements and fruits displace God as our most important concern in life. "Never allow anyone or anything to threaten God's central place in your life," as David Gill puts it.[3]

Because many people work primarily to make money, an inordinate desire for money is probably the most common work-related danger to the first commandment. Jesus warned of exactly this danger: "No one can serve two masters. . . . You cannot serve God and wealth" (Matt. 6:24). But almost anything related to work can become twisted in our desires to the point that it interferes with our love for God. How many careers come to a tragic end because the *means* to accomplish things for the love of God—such as political power, financial sustainability, commitment to the job, status among peers, or superior performance—become ends in themselves? When, for example, recognition on the job becomes more important than character on the job, is this not a sign that reputation is displacing the love of God as the ultimate concern?

"You Shall Not Make for Yourself an Idol" (Deuteronomy 5:8; Exodus 20:4)

The second commandment raises the issue of idolatry. Idols are gods of our own creation, gods that we feel will give us what we want. In ancient times, idolatry often took the form of worshiping physical objects. But the issue is really one of trust and devotion. On what do we ultimately pin our hope of well-being and success? Anything that is not capable of fulfilling our hope—that is, anything other than God—is an idol, whether or not it is a physical object. The story of a family forging

---

[3] David W. Gill, *Doing Right: Practicing Ethical Principles* (Downers Grove, IL: IVP Books, 2004), 83. Gill's book contains an extended exegesis and application of the Ten Commandments in the modern world.

an idol with the intent to manipulate God, and the disastrous personal, social and economic consequences that follow, are memorably told in Judges 17–21.

In the world of work, it is common to speak of money, fame, and power as potential idols, and rightly so. They are not idols, per se, and in fact may be necessary for us to accomplish our roles in God's creative and redemptive work in the world. Yet when we imagine that by achieving them our safety and prosperity will be secured, we have begun to fall into idolatry. Idolatry begins when we place our trust and hope in these things more than in God. The same may occur with virtually every other element of success, including preparation, hard work, creativity, risk, wealth and other resources, and even luck. Are we able to recognize when we begin to idolize these things? By God's grace, we can overcome the temptation to worship them in God's place.

"You Shall Not Make Wrongful Use of the Name of the LORD Your God" (Deuteronomy 5:11; Exodus 20:7)

The third commandment literally prohibits God's people from making "wrongful use" of the name of God. This need not be restricted to the name "YHWH" (Deut. 5:11), but includes "God," "Jesus," "Christ," and so forth. But what is wrongful use? It includes, of course, disrespectful use in cursing, slandering, and blaspheming. But more significantly, it includes falsely attributing human designs to God. This prohibits us from claiming God's authority for our own actions and decisions. Regrettably, some Christians seem to believe that following God at work consists primarily of speaking for God on the basis of their individual understanding, rather than working respectfully with others or taking responsibility for their actions. "It is God's will that . . . ," or "God is punishing you for . . . ," are dangerous things to say, and almost never valid when spoken by an individual without the discernment of the community of faith (1 Thess. 5:20–21). In this light, perhaps the traditional Jewish reticence to utter even the English translation "God"—let alone the divine name itself—demonstrates a wisdom Christians often lack. If we were a little more careful about bandying the word *God* about, perhaps we would be more judicious in claiming to know God's will, especially as it applies to other people.

The third commandment also reminds us that respecting human names is important to God. The Good Shepherd "calls his own sheep by name" (John 10:3), while warning us that if you call another person "you fool," then "you will be liable to the hell of fire" (Matt. 5:22). Keeping this in mind, we shouldn't make wrongful use of other people's names or call them by disrespectful epithets. We use people's names wrongfully when we use them to curse, humiliate, oppress, exclude, and defraud. We use people's names well when we use them to encourage, thank, create solidarity, and welcome. Simply to learn and say someone's name is a blessing, especially if he or she is often treated as nameless, invisible, or insignificant. Do you know the name of the person who empties your trash can, answers your customer service call, or drives your bus? People's names are not the very name of the Lord, but they are the names of those made in his image.

"Observe the Sabbath Day and Keep It Holy" (Deuteronomy 5:12; Exodus 20:8–11)

The issue of the Sabbath is complex, not only in the books of Deuteronomy and Exodus and the Old Testament, but also in Christian theology and practice. The precise applicability of the fourth commandment, keeping the Sabbath, to Gentile believers has been a matter of debate since New Testament times (Rom. 14:5–6). Nonetheless, the general principle of the Sabbath applies directly to the matter of work.

The Sabbath and the Work We Do

The first part of the fourth commandment calls for ceasing labor one day in seven. On the one hand, this was an incomparable gift to the people of Israel. No other ancient people had the privilege of resting one day in seven. On the other hand, it required an extraordinary trust in God's provision. Six days of work had to be enough to plant crops, gather the harvest, carry water, spin cloth, and draw sustenance from creation. While Israel rested one day every week, the encircling nations continued to forge swords, feather arrows, and train soldiers. Israel had to trust God not to let a day of rest lead to economic and military catastrophe.

We face the same issue of trust in God's provision today. If we heed God's commandment to observe God's own cycle of work and rest, will we be able to compete in the modern economy? Does it take seven days of work to hold a job (or two or three jobs), clean the house, prepare the meals, mow the lawn, wash the car, pay the bills, finish the school work, and shop for the clothes, or can we trust God to provide for us even if we take a day off during the course of every week? Can we take time to worship God, to pray, and to gather with others for study and encouragement, and if we do, will it make us more or less productive overall? The fourth commandment does not explain how God will make it all work out for us. It simply tells us to rest one day every seven.

Christians have translated the day of rest to the Lord's Day (Sunday, the day of Christ's resurrection), but the essence of the Sabbath is not choosing one particular day of the week over another (Rom. 14:5–6). The polarity that actually undergirds the Sabbath is *work* and *rest*. Both work and rest are included in the fourth commandment: "Six days you shall labor and do all your work" (Deut. 5:13). The six days of work are as much a part of the commandment as the one day of rest. Although many Christians are in danger of allowing work to squeeze the time set aside for rest, others are in danger of the opposite—of shirking work and trying to live a life of leisure and dissipation. This is even worse than neglecting the Sabbath, for "whoever does not provide for relatives, and especially for family members, has denied the faith and is worse than an unbeliever" (1 Tim. 5:8). What we need are times and places for both work and rest, which together are good for us, our family, workers, and guests. This may or may not include twenty-four continuous hours of rest falling on Sunday (or Saturday). The proportions may change due to temporary necessities or the changing needs of the seasons of life.

If overwork is our main danger, then we need to find a way to honor the fourth commandment without instituting a false, new legalism pitting the spiritual (worship on Sunday) against the secular (work on Monday through Saturday). If avoiding work is our danger, we need to learn how to find joy and meaning in working as a service to God and our neighbors (Eph. 4:28).

The Sabbath and the Work People Do for Us

Of the few variations between the two versions of the Ten Commandments, the majority occur as additions to the fourth commandment in

Deuteronomy. First, the list of those you cannot force to work on the Sabbath is expanded to include "your ox or your donkey, or any of your livestock" (Deut. 5:14a). Second, a reason is given why you cannot force slaves to work on the Sabbath: "So that your male and female slave may rest as well as you. Remember that you were a slave in the land of Egypt" (Deut. 5:14b–15a). Finally, a reminder is added that your ability to rest securely in the midst of military and economic competition from other nations is a gift from God, who protects Israel "with a mighty hand and an outstretched arm" (Deut. 5:15b).

An important distinction between the two texts on this commandment is their grounding in creation and redemption, respectively. In Exodus, the Sabbath is rooted in the six days of creation followed by a day of rest (Gen. 1:3–2:3). Deuteronomy adds the element of God's redemption. "The LORD your God brought you out from there with a mighty hand and an outstretched arm; therefore the LORD your God commanded you to keep the sabbath day" (Deut. 5:15). Bringing the two together, we see that the foundations for keeping the Sabbath are both the way God made us and the way he redeems us.

These additions highlight God's concern for those who work under the authority of others. Not only must you rest, those who work for you—slaves, other Israelites, even animals—must be given rest. When you "remember that you were a slave in the land of Egypt," it reminds you not to take your own rest as a special privilege, but to bring rest to others just as the Lord brought it to you. It does not matter what religion they follow or what they may choose to do with the time. They are workers, and God directs us to provide rest for those who work. We may be accustomed to thinking about keeping the Sabbath in order to rest ourselves, but how much thought do we give to resting those who work to serve us? Many people work at hours that interfere with their relationships, sleep rhythms, and social opportunities in order to make life more convenient for others.

The so-called "blue laws" that once protected people—or prevented people, depending on your point of view—from working at all hours have disappeared from most developed countries. Undoubtedly this has opened many new opportunities for workers and the people they serve. But is this always something we should participate in? When we shop late at night, golf on Sunday morning, or watch sporting events that continue past midnight, do we consider how it may affect those working at these times? Perhaps our actions help create a work opportunity that wouldn't otherwise exist. On the other hand, perhaps we simply require someone to work at a miserable time who otherwise would have worked at a convenient hour.

The fast-food restaurant chain Chick-fil-A is well known for being closed on Sundays. It is often assumed this is because of founder Truett Cathy's particular interpretation of the fourth commandment. But according to the company's website, "His decision was as much practical as spiritual. He believes that all franchised Chick-fil-A Operators and Restaurant employees should have an opportunity to rest, spend time with family and friends, and worship if they choose to do so." Of course, reading the Fourth Commandment as a way to care for the people who work for you *is* a particular interpretation, just not a sectarian or legalistic one. The issue is complex, and there is no one-size-fits-all answer. But we do have choices as consumers and (in some cases) as employers that affect the hours and conditions of other people's rest and work.

"Honor Your Father and Your Mother" (Deuteronomy 5:16; Exodus 20:12)

The fifth commandment says that we must respect the most basic authority among human beings, that of parents for children. To put it another way, parenting children is among the most important kinds of work there are in the world, and it both deserves and requires the greatest respect. There are many ways to honor—or dishonor—your father and mother. In Jesus' day, the Pharisees wanted to restrict this to speaking well of them. But Jesus pointed out that obeying this commandment requires working to provide for your parents (Mark 7:9–13). We honor people by working for their good.

For many people, good relationships with parents are one of the joys of life. Loving service to them is a delight and obeying this commandment is easy. But we are put to the test by this commandment when we find it burdensome to work on behalf of our parents. We may have been ill-treated or neglected by them. They may be controlling and meddlesome. Being around them may undermine our sense of self, our commitment to our spouses (including our responsibilities under the third commandment), even our relationship with God. Even if we have good relationships with our parents, there may come a time when caring for them is a major burden simply because of the time and work it takes. If aging or dementia begins to rob them of their memory, capabilities, and good nature, caring for them can become a deep sorrow.

Yet the fifth commandment comes with a promise: "that your days may be long and that it may go well with you in the land that the LORD your God is giving you" (Deut. 5:16). Through proper honor of parents, children learn proper respect in every other kind of relationship, including those in their future workplaces. Obeying this command enables us to live long and do well because developing proper relationships of respect and authority is essential to individual success and social order.

Because this is a command to work for the benefit of parents, it is inherently a workplace command. The place of work may be where we earn money to support them, or it may be in the place where we assist them in the tasks of daily life. Both are work. When we take a job because it allows us to live near them, or send money to them, or make use of the values and gifts they developed in us, or accomplish things they taught us are important, we are honoring them. When we *limit* our careers so that we can be present with them, clean and cook for them, bathe and embrace them, take them to the places they love, or diminish their fears, we are honoring them.

Parents therefore have the duty to be worthy of trust, respect, and obedience. Raising children is a form of work, and no workplace requires higher standards of trustworthiness, compassion, justice, and fairness. As the Apostle Paul put it, "Fathers, do not provoke your children to anger, but bring them up in the discipline and instruction of the Lord" (Eph. 6:4). Only by God's grace could anyone hope to serve adequately as a parent, another indication that worship of God and obedience to his ways underlies all of Deuteronomy.

In our workplaces, we can help other people fulfill the fifth commandment, as well as obey it ourselves. We can remember that employees, customers, co-workers, bosses, suppliers, and others also have families, and then adjust our expectations to support them in honoring their families. When others share or complain about their struggles with parents, we can listen to them compassionately, support them practically (say, by offering to take a shift so they can be with their parents), or perhaps offer a godly perspective for them to consider. For example, if a career-focused colleague reveals a family crisis, we have a chance both to pray for the family and to suggest that the colleague think about re-balancing time between career and family.

"You Shall Not Murder" (Deuteronomy 5:17; Exodus 20:13)

Sadly, the sixth commandment has an all-too-practical application in the modern workplace, where 10 percent of all job-related fatalities (in the United States) are homicides.[4] However, admonishing readers of this article, "Don't murder anyone at work," isn't likely to change this statistic much.

But murder isn't the only form of workplace violence, just the most extreme. A more practical course arises when we remember that Jesus said even anger is a violation of the sixth commandment (Matt. 5:21–22). As Paul noted, we may not be able to prevent the feeling of anger, but we can learn how to cope with our anger. "Be angry but do not sin; do not let the sun go down on your anger" (Eph. 4:26). The most signifi-cant implication of the sixth commandment for work then may be, "If you get angry at work, get help in anger management." Many employ-ers, churches, state and local governments, and nonprofit organizations offer classes and counseling in anger management. Availing yourself of these may be a highly effective way of obeying the sixth commandment.

Murder is the intentional killing of a person, but the case law that stems from the sixth commandment shows that we also have the duty to prevent unintended deaths. A particularly graphic case is when an ox (a work animal) gores a man or woman to death (Exod. 21:28–29). If the event was predictable, the ox's owner is to be treated as a murderer. In other words, owners/managers are responsible for ensuring work-place safety within reason. This principle is well established law in most countries, and workplace safety is the subject of significant government policing, industry self-regulation, and organizational policy and practice. Yet workplaces of all kinds continue to require or allow workers to work in needlessly unsafe conditions. Christians who have any role in set-ting the conditions of work, supervising workers, or modeling workplace

---

[4]"Fact Sheet: Workplace Shootings 2010," United States Department of Labor, *Bureau of Labor Statistics*, http://www.bls.gov/iif/oshwc/cfoi/osar0014.htm.

practices are reminded by the sixth commandment that safe working conditions are among their highest responsibilities in the world of work.

"You Shall Not Commit Adultery" (Exodus 20:14; Deuteronomy 5:18)

The workplace is one of the most common settings for adultery, not necessarily because adultery occurs in the workplace itself, but because it arises from the conditions of work and relationships with co-workers. The first application to the workplace, then, is literal. Married people should not have sex with people other than their spouses at, in, or because of their work. Some professions such as prostitution and pornography almost always violate this commandment, as they almost always require sex between people married to others. But any kind of work that erodes the bonds of marriage infringes the seventh commandment. There are many ways this can occur. Work may encourage strong emotional bonds among co-workers without adequately supporting their commitments to their spouses, as can happen in hospitals, entrepreneurial ventures, academic institutions and churches, among other places. Working conditions may bring people into close physical contact for extended periods or fail to encourage reasonable limits to off-hour encounters, as could happen on extended field assignments. Work may subject people to sexual harassment and pressure to have sex with those holding power over them. Work may inflate people's egos or expose them to adulation, as could occur with celebrities, star athletes, business titans, high-ranking government officials, and the super-rich. Work may demand so much time away—physically, mentally, or emotionally—that it frays the bond between spouses. All of these may pose dangers that Christians would do well to recognize and avoid, ameliorate, or guard against

"You Shall Not Steal" (Exodus 20:15; Deuteronomy 5:19)

The eighth commandment is another that takes work as its primary subject. Stealing is a violation of proper work because it dispossesses the victim of the fruits of his or her labor. It is also a violation of the commandment to labor six days a week, since in most cases stealing is intended as a shortcut around honest labor, which shows again the interrelation of the Ten Commandments. So we may take it as the word of God that we are not to steal from those we work for, with, or among.

The very idea that there is such a thing as "stealing" implies the existence of property and property rights. There are only three ways to acquire things—by making them ourselves, by the voluntary exchange of goods and services with others (trade or gifts), or by confiscation. Stealing is the most blatant form of confiscation, when someone grabs what belongs to another and runs away. But confiscation also occurs on a larger, more sophisticated scale, as when a corporation defrauds customers or a government imposes ruinous taxation on its citizens. Such institutions lack respect for property rights. This is not the place to explore what constitutes fair versus monopolistic commerce or legitimate versus excessive taxation. But the eighth commandment tells us that no society can thrive when property rights are violated with impunity by individuals, criminal gangs, businesses, or governments.

In practical terms, this means that stealing occurs in many forms besides robbing someone. Any time we acquire something of value from its rightful owner without consent, we are engaging in theft. Misappropriating resources or funds for personal use is stealing. Using deception to make sales, gain market share, or raise prices is stealing because the deception means that whatever the buyer consents to is not the actual situation. (See the section on "Puffery/Exaggeration" in *Truth & Deception* at www.theologyofwork.org for more on this topic.) Likewise, profiting by taking advantage of people's fears, vulnerabilities, powerlessness, or desperation is a form of stealing because their consent is not truly voluntary. Violating patents, copyrights, and other intellectual property laws is stealing because it deprives the owner of the ability to profit from their creation under the terms of civil law.

Respect for the property and rights of others means that we don't take what is theirs or meddle in their affairs. But it does not mean that we look out only for ourselves. Deuteronomy 22:1 states, "You shall not watch your neighbor's ox or sheep straying away and ignore them; you shall take them back to their owner." Saying "It's none of my business" is no excuse for callousness.

Regrettably, many jobs seem to include an element of taking advantage of others' ignorance or lack of alternatives to force them into transactions they otherwise wouldn't agree to. Companies, governments, individuals, unions, and other players may use their power to coerce others into unfair wages, prices, contract terms, working conditions, hours, or other factors. Although we may not rob banks, steal from our employers, or shoplift, we may very likely be participating in unfair or unethical practices that deprive others of what rights should be theirs. It can be difficult, even career limiting, to resist engaging in these practices, but we are called to do so nonetheless.

"You Shall Not Bear False Witness against Your Neighbor" (Exodus 20:16; Deuteronomy 5:20)

The ninth commandment honors the right to one's own reputation.[5] It finds pointed application in legal proceedings where what people say depicts reality and determines the course of lives. Judicial decisions and other legal processes wield great power. Manipulating them undercuts the ethical fabric of society and thus constitutes a serious offense. Walter Brueggemann says this commandment recognizes "that community life is not possible unless there is an arena in which there is public confidence that social reality will be reliably described and reported."[6]

Although stated in courtroom language, the ninth commandment also applies to a broad range of situations that touch practically every aspect of life. We should never say or do anything that misrepresents someone else. Brueggemann again provides insight:

Politicians seek to destroy one another in negative campaigning; gossip columnists feed off calumny; and in Christian living rooms, reputations are tarnished or destroyed over cups of coffee served in fine china with dessert. These de facto courtrooms are conducted without due process of law. Accusations are made; hearsay allowed; slander, perjury, and libelous comments uttered without objection. No evidence, no defense. As Christians, we must refuse to participate in or to tolerate any conversation in which a person is being defamed or accused without the person being there to defend himself. It is wrong to pass along hearsay in any form, even as prayer requests or pastoral concerns. More than merely not participating, it is up to Christians to stop rumors and those who spread them in their tracks.[7]

---

[5] Walter Brueggemann, "The Book of Exodus," in vol. 1, *The New Interpreter's Bible: Genesis to Leviticus* (Nashville: Abingdon Press, 1994), 431.

[6] Brueggemann, 848.

[7] Brueggemann, 432.

This further suggests that workplace gossip is a serious offense. Some of it pertains to personal, off-site matters, which is evil enough. But what about cases when an employee tarnishes the reputation of a co-worker? Can truth ever truly be spoken when the person being talked about is not there to speak for him or herself? And what about assessments of performance? What safeguards ought to be in place to ensure that reports are fair and accurate? On a large scale, the business of marketing and advertisement operates in the public space among organizations and individuals. In the interest of presenting one's own products and services in the best possible light, to what extent may one point out the flaws and weaknesses of the competition without incorporating their perspective? Is it possible that the rights of "your neighbor" could include the rights of other companies? The scope of our global economy suggests this command may have wide application indeed.

The commandment specifically prohibits speaking falsely about another person, but it brings up the question of whether we must tell the truth in every kind of situation. Is issuing false or misleading financial statements a violation of the ninth commandment? How about exaggerated advertising claims, even if they do not falsely disparage competitors? What about assurances from management that mislead employees about impending layoffs? In a world where perception often counts for reality, the rhetoric of persuasion may care little for truth. But the divine origin of the ninth commandment reminds us that God cannot be fooled. At the same time, we recognize that deception is sometimes practiced, accepted, and even approved in the Scriptures. A complete theology of truth and deception draws on texts including, but not limited to, the ninth commandment. (See *Truth & Deception* at www.theologyofwork.org for a much fuller discussion of this topic, including whether the prohibition of "false witness against your neighbor" includes all forms of lying and deception.)

"You Shall Not Covet . . . Anything That Belongs to Your Neighbor" (Exodus 20:17; Deuteronomy 5:21)

The tenth commandment prohibits coveting "anything that belongs to your neighbor" (Deut. 5:21). It is not wrong to notice the things that belong to our neighbors, nor even to desire to obtain such things for ourselves legitimately. Coveting happens when someone sees the prosperity, achievements, or talents of another, and then *resents* it, or wants to *take it,* or wants to *punish* the successful person. It is the harm to another person, "your neighbor"—not the desire to have something—that is prohibited.

We can either take inspiration from the success of others or we can covet. The first attitude provokes hard work and prudence. The second attitude causes laziness, generates excuses for failure, and provokes acts of confiscation. We will never succeed if we convince ourselves that life is a zero-sum game and that we are somehow harmed when other people do well. We will never do great things if, instead of working hard, we fantasize that other people's achievements are our own. Here again, the ultimate grounding of this commandment is the command to worship God alone. If God is the focus of our worship, desire for him displaces all unholy, covetous desire for anything else, including that which belongs to our neighbors. As the Apostle Paul put it, "I have learned to be content with whatever I have" (Phil. 4:11).

Deuteronomy adds the words "or field" to Exodus's list of your neighbor's things you are not to covet. As in the other additions to the Ten Commandments' in Deuteronomy, this one draws attention to the workplace. Fields are workplaces, and to covet a field is to covet the productive resources another person has.

Envy and acquisitiveness are indeed especially dangerous at work where status, pay, and power are routine factors in our relationships with people we spend a lot of time with. We may have many good reasons to desire achievement, advancement, or reward at work. But envy isn't one of them. Nor is working obsessively out of envy for the social standing it may enable.

In particular, we face temptation at work to falsely inflate our accomplishments at the expense of others. The antidote is simple, although hard to do at times. Make it a consistent practice to recognize the accomplishments of others and give them all the credit they deserve. If we can learn to rejoice in—or at least acknowledge—others' successes, we cut off the lifeblood of envy and covetousness at work. Even better, if we can learn how to work so that our success goes hand in hand with others' success, covetousness is replaced by collaboration and envy by unity.

Leith Anderson, former pastor of Wooddale Church in Eden Prairie, Minnesota, says, "As the senior pastor, it's as if I have an unlimited supply of coins in my pocket. Whenever I give credit to a staff member for a good idea, praise a volunteer's work, or thank someone, it's like I'm slipping a coin from my pocket into theirs. That's my job as the leader, to slip coins from my pocket to others' pockets, to build up the appreciation other people have for them."[8]

Statues and Ordinances (Deuteronomy 4:44–28:68)

In the second part of his second speech, Moses describes in detail the "statutes and ordinances" that God charges Israel to obey (Deut. 6:1). These rules deal with a wide array of matters, including war, slavery, tithes, religious festivals, sacrifices, kosher food, prophecy, the monarchy, and the central sanctuary. This material contains several passages that speak directly to the theology of work. We will explore them in their biblical order.

The Blessings of Obeying God's Covenant (Deuteronomy 7:12–15; 28:2–12)

In case the commandments, statutes, and ordinances in God's covenant might come to seem like nothing but a burden to Israel, Moses reminds us that their primary purpose is to bless us.

> If you heed these ordinances, by diligently observing them, the LORD your God will maintain with you the covenant loyalty that he swore to your ancestors; he will love you, bless you, and multiply you; he will bless the fruit of your womb and the fruit of your ground, your grain and your wine and your oil, the increase of your cattle and the issue of your flock, in the land that he swore to your ancestors to give you. (Deut. 7:12–13)

> If you obey the LORD your God: Blessed shall you be in the city, and blessed shall you be in the field. Blessed shall be the fruit of your womb, the fruit of your ground, and the fruit of your livestock, both the increase of your cattle and the issue of your flock. Blessed shall be your basket and your kneading bowl. Blessed shall you be when you come in, and blessed shall you be when you go out. . . . The LORD will make you abound in prosperity, in the fruit

---

[8] Reported by William Messenger from a conversation with Leith Anderson on October 20, 2004 in Charlotte, North Carolina.

of your womb, in the fruit of your livestock, and in the fruit of your ground
in the land that the LORD swore to your ancestors to give you. The LORD will
open for you his rich storehouse, the heavens, to give the rain of your land
in its season and to bless all your undertakings. (Deut. 28:2–7; 11–12)

Obeying the covenant is meant to be a source of blessing, prosperity,
joy, and health for God's people. As Paul says, "The law is holy, and the
commandment is holy and just and good" (Rom. 7:12), and "Love is the
fulfilling of the law" (Rom. 13:10).

This is not to be confused with the so-called "Prosperity Gospel,"
which incorrectly claims that God inevitably brings wealth and health
to individuals who gain his favor. It does mean that if *God's people* lived
according to his covenant, the world would be a better place for *everyone*.
Of course, the Christian witness is that we are *not* capable of fulfilling the
law through any power we possess. That is why there is a new covenant
in Christ, in which God's grace is made available to us through Christ's
death and resurrection, rather than being limited by our own obedience.
By living in Christ, we find that we *are* able to love and serve God, and
that we *do* after all receive the blessings described by Moses, in part in the
present day, and in full when Christ brings God's kingdom to fulfillment.

In any case, obedience to God's covenant is the overarching theme
running through the book of Deuteronomy. In addition to these three extended passages, the theme is sounded on many brief occasions throughout the book, and Moses returns to it in his final speech at the end of his
life in chapters 29 and 30.

The Dangers of Prosperity (Deuteronomy 8:11–20)

In contrast to joyful obedience to God is the arrogance that often
accompanies prosperity. This is similar to the danger of complacency
that Moses warns about in Deuteronomy 4:25–40, but with a focus on
active pride rather than passive entitlement.

When you have eaten your fill and have built fine houses and live in them,
and when your herds and flocks have multiplied, and your silver and
gold is multiplied, and all that you have is multiplied, then do not exalt
yourself, forgetting the LORD your God, who brought you out of the land of
Egypt, out of the house of slavery. (Deut. 8:12–14)

When, after many years of sweat equity, a person sees a business, career, research project, child raising, or other work become a success, he or she will have a justifiable sense of pride. But we can allow joyful pride to slip into arrogance. Deuteronomy 8:17–18 reminds us, "Do not say to yourself, 'My power and the might of my own hand have gotten me this wealth.' But remember the LORD your God, for it is he who gives you power to get wealth, so that he may confirm his covenant that he swore to your ancestors, as he is doing today." As part of his covenant with his people, God gives us the ability to engage in economic production. We need to remember, however, that it *is* a gift of God. When we attribute our success entirely to our abilities and effort, we forget that God gave us those abilities as well as life itself. We are not self-created. The illusion of self-sufficiency makes us hard-hearted. As always, the proper worship and awareness of dependence on God provides the antidote (Deut. 8:18).

Generosity (Deuteronomy 15:7–11)

The topic of generosity arises in Deuteronomy 15:7–8. "If there is among you anyone in need . . . do not be hard-hearted or tight-fisted toward your needy neighbor. You should rather open your hand." Generosity and compassion are of the essence of the covenant. "Give liberally and be ungrudging when you do so, for on this account the LORD your God will bless you in all your work" (Deut. 15:10). Our work becomes fully blessed only when it blesses others. As Paul put it, "Love is the fulfilling of the law" (Rom. 13:10).

For most of us, the money earned by work gives us the means to be generous. Do we actually use it generously? Moreover, are there ways we can be generous in our work itself? The passage speaks of generosity specifically as an aspect of work ("all your work"). If a co-worker needs help developing a skill or capability, or an honest word of recommendation from us, or patience dealing with his or her shortcomings, would these be opportunities for generosity? These kinds of generosity may cost us time and money, or they may require us to reconsider our self-image, examine our complicity, and question our motives. If we could become ungrudging in making these sacrifices, would we open a new door for God's blessing through our work?

Slavery (Deuteronomy 15:12–18)

A troubling topic in Deuteronomy is slavery. The allowance of slavery in the Old Testament generates a great deal of debate, and we cannot resolve all the issues here. We should not, however, equate Israelite slavery with slavery in the modern era, including slavery in the United States. The latter involved kidnapping West Africans from their homeland for sale as slaves, followed by the perpetual enslavement of their descendants. The Old Testament condemns this kind of practice (Amos 1:6), and makes it punishable by death (Deut. 24:7; Exodus 21:16). Israelites became slaves to one another not through kidnapping or unfortunate birth, but because of debt or poverty (Deut. 15:12, NRSV footnote a). Slavery was preferable to starvation, and people might sell themselves into slavery to pay off a debt and at least have a home. But the slavery was not to be lifelong. "If a member of your community, whether a Hebrew man or a Hebrew woman, is sold to you and works for you six years, in the seventh year you shall set that person free" (Deut. 15:12). Upon release, former slaves were to receive a share of the wealth their work had created. "When you send a male slave out from you a free person, you shall not send him out empty-handed. Provide liberally out of your flock, your threshing floor, and your wine press, thus giving to him some of the bounty with which the Lord your God has blessed you" (Deut. 15:13–14).

In some parts of the world people are still sold (usually by parents) into debt bondage—a form of work that is slavery in all but name. Others may be lured into sex trafficking from which escape is difficult or impossible. Christians in some places are taking the lead in rooting out such practices, but much more could be done. Imagine the difference it would make if many more churches and individual Christians made this a high priority for mission and social action.

In more developed countries, desperate workers are not sold into involuntary labor but take whatever jobs they may be able to find. If Deuteronomy contains protections even for slaves, don't these protections also apply to workers? Deuteronomy requires that masters must abide by contract terms and labor regulations including the fixed release date, the provision of food and shelter, and the responsibility for working conditions. Work hours must be reasonably limited, including a weekly day off (Deut. 5:14). Most significantly, masters are to regard slaves as equals in God's eyes, remembering that *all* God's people are rescued slaves. "Remember that you were a slave in the land of Egypt, and the LORD your God redeemed you; for this reason I lay this command upon you today" (Deut. 15:15).

Modern employers might abuse desperate workers in ways similar to the ways ancient masters abused slaves. Do workers *lose* these protections merely because they are not actually slaves? If not, then employers have a duty at least not to treat workers worse than slaves. Vulnerable workers today may face demands to work extra hours without pay, to turn over tips to managers, to work in dangerous or toxic conditions, to pay petty bribes in order to get shifts, to suffer sexual harassment or degrading treatment, to receive inferior benefits, or to endure illegal discrimination and other forms of mistreatment. Even well-off workers may find themselves unfairly denied a reasonable share of the fruits of their labor.

To modern readers, the Bible's acceptance of temporary slavery seems difficult to accept—even though we recognize that ancient slavery was not the same as sixteenth- through nineteenth-century slavery—and we can be thankful that slavery is at least technically illegal everywhere today. But rather than regarding the Bible's teaching about slavery as obsolete, we would do well to work to abolish modern forms of involuntary servitude, and to follow and promote the Bible's protections for economically disadvantaged members of society.

Bribery and Corruption (Deuteronomy 16:18–20)

The effectiveness of property rights and workers' protections often depends on law enforcement and judicial systems. Moses' charge to judges and officials is especially important when it comes to work. "You must not distort justice; you must not show partiality; and you must not accept bribes, for a bribe blinds the eyes of the wise and subverts the cause of those who are in the right" (Deut. 16:19). Without impartial justice, it would be impossible to "live and occupy the land that the LORD your God is giving you" (Deut. 16:20).

Modern workplaces and societies are no less susceptible to bribery, corruption, and bias than ancient Israel was. According to the United Nations, the greatest impediment to economic growth in less developed countries is lapses in the impartial rule of law.[9] In places where corruption is endemic, it may be impossible to make a living, travel across town, or abide in peace without paying bribes. This statute seems to recognize that in general those who have the power to demand bribes are more at fault than those who acquiesce in paying them, for the prohibition is against accepting bribes, not against paying them. Even so, whatever Christians can do to reduce corruption—whether on the giving or the receiving end—is a contribution to the "just decisions" (Deut. 16:18) that are sacred to the Lord. (For a more in-depth exploration of economic applications of the rule of law, see "Land Ownership and Property Rights" in Numbers 26–27; 36:1–12 above.)

Obeying Decisions of Courts of Law (Deuteronomy 17:8–13)

Moses sets up a system of trial courts and courts of appeal that are surprisingly similar to the structure of modern courts of law. He commands the people to obey their decisions. "You must carry out fully the law that they interpret for you or the ruling that they announce to you; do not turn aside from the decision that they announce to you, either to the right or to the left" (Deut. 17:11).

Workplaces today are governed by laws, regulations, and customs with procedures, courts, and appeal processes to interpret and apply them appropriately. We are to obey these legal structures, as Paul also affirmed (Rom. 13:1). In some countries, laws and regulations are routinely ignored by those in power or circumvented by bribery, corruption, or violence. In other countries, businesses and other workplace institutions seldom intentionally break the law, but may try to contravene it through nuisance lawsuits, political favors, or lobbying that opposes the common good. But Christians are called to respect the rule of law, to obey it, uphold it, and seek to strengthen it. This is not to say that civil disobedience never has a place. Some laws are unjust and must be broken if change is not feasible. But these instances are rare and always involve personal sacrifice in pursuit of the common good. Subverting the law for self-interested purposes, by contrast, is not justifiable.

---

[9] United Nations Development Programme, *Issue Brief: Rule of Law and Development* (New York: United Nations, 2013), 3.

Using Governmental Authority Justly (Deuteronomy 17:14–20)

Just as people and institutions must not contravene legitimate authority, people in positions of power must not use their authority illegitimately. Moses specifically deals with the case of a king.

> He must not acquire many horses for himself . . . and he must not acquire many wives . . . also silver and gold he must not acquire in great quantity for himself. When he has taken the throne of his kingdom, he shall have a copy of this law written for him. . . . It shall remain with him and he shall read it . . . diligently observing all the words of this law and these statutes. (Deut. 17:16–19)

In this text we see two restrictions on the use of authority—those in authority are not above the law but must obey and uphold it, and those in authority must not abuse their power by enriching themselves.

Today, people in authority may try to put themselves above the law, as for example when police and court workers "fix" traffic tickets for themselves and their friends, or when high-ranking public servants or business employees do not obey the expense policies others are subject to. Similarly, officials may use their power to enrich themselves receiving bribes, zoning, and licensing exemptions, access to privileged information, or personal use of public or private property. Sometimes special perks are granted to those in power as a matter of policy or law, but this does not really eliminate the offense. Moses' command to kings is not to make sure to get legal authorization for their excesses, but to avoid the excesses altogether. When those in power use their authority not simply to gain special privileges but to create monopolies for their cronies, to appropriate vast lands and assets, and to jail, torture, or kill opponents, the stakes become deadly. There is no difference in kind between petty abuses of power and totalitarian oppression, merely in degree.

Employing Assets for the Common Good (Deuteronomy 23:1–24:13)

Deuteronomy requires owners of productive assets to employ them to benefit the community, and it does so in a clear-headed way. For example, landowners are to allow neighbors to use their land to help meet their immediate needs. "If you go into your neighbor's vineyard, you may eat your fill of grapes, as many as you wish, but you shall not put any in a container. If you go into your neighbor's standing grain, you may pluck the ears with your hand, but you shall not put a sickle to your neighbor's standing grain" (Deut. 23:24–25). This was the law that allowed Jesus' disciples to pluck grain from local fields as they went on their way (Matt. 12:1). Gleaners were responsible for harvesting food for themselves, and landowners were responsible for giving them access to do so. (See "Gleaning" in Leviticus 19:9–10 above for more on this practice.)

Likewise, those who lend capital must not demand terms that put the borrower's health or livelihood in jeopardy (Deut. 23:19–20; 24:6, 10–13). In some cases, they must even be willing to lend when a loss is likely, simply because the neighbor's need is so great (Deut. 15:7–9). (See "Lending and Collateral" in Exodus 22:25–27 above for more detail.)

God requires us to be open with our resources to those in need, while also exercising good stewardship of the resources he entrusts to us. On the one hand everything we have belongs to God, and his command is that we use what is his for the good of the community (Deut. 15:7). On the other hand, Deuteronomy does not treat a person's field as common property. Outsiders could not cart off as much as they pleased. The requirement for contribution to the public good is set within a system of private ownership as the primary means of production. The balance between private and public ownership, and the suitability of various economic systems for today's societies, is a matter of debate to which the Bible can contribute principles and values but cannot prescribe regulations.

Economic Justice (Deuteronomy 24:14–15; 25:19; 27:17–25)

Differences of class and wealth can create opportunities for injustice. Justice requires treating workers fairly. We read in Deuteronomy 24:14, "You shall not withhold the wages of poor and needy laborers, whether other Israelites or aliens who reside in your land in one of your towns." Neither the poor nor the aliens had the standing in the community to challenge wealthy landowners in the courts, and thus they were vulnerable to such abuse. James 5:4 contains a similar message. Employers must regard their obligations to their lowest employees as sacred and binding.

Justice also requires treating customers fairly. "You shall not have in your bag two kinds of weights, large and small" (Deut. 25:13). The weights in question are used for measuring grain or other commodities in a sale. For the seller, it would be advantageous to weigh the grain against a weight that was lighter than advertised. The buyer would profit from using a falsely heavy weight. But Deuteronomy demands that a person always use the same weight, whether buying or selling. Protection against fraud is not limited to sales made to customers, but to all kinds of dealings with all the people around us.

> Cursed be anyone who moves a neighbor's boundary marker. (Deut. 27:17)

> Cursed be anyone who misleads a blind person on the road. (Deut. 27:18)

> Cursed be anyone who deprives the alien, the orphan, and the widow of justice. (Deut. 27:19)

> Cursed be anyone who takes a bribe to shed innocent blood. (Deut. 27:25)

In principle, these rules prohibit every kind of fraud. As a modern analogy, a company might knowingly sell a defective product while oblivious to the moral implication. Customers might abuse store policies on returning used merchandise. Companies might issue financial statements in violation of generally accepted accounting principles. Workers might conduct personal business or ignore their work during paid time. Not only are these practices unjust, they violate the commitment to worship God alone, "for you to be a people holy to the LORD your God" (Deut. 26:19).

Moses' Final Appeal for Obedience to God (Deuteronomy 29:1–30:20)

Moses concludes with a third speech, a final appeal for obedience to God's covenant, which will result in human thriving. It reinforces his earlier exhortations in Deuteronomy 7:12–15 and 28:2–12. Deuteronomy 30:15 summarizes it well: "See, I have set before you today life and prosperity, death and adversity." Obedience to God leads to blessing and life, while disobedience leads to curses and death. In this context, "obedience to God" meant keeping the Sinai covenant and was thus an obligation that related solely to Israel. Yet obedience to God, leading to blessing, is a timeless principle not limited to ancient Israel, and it applies to work and life today. If we love God and do as he commands, we find it the best plan for our life and in work. This does not mean that following Christ never involves hardship and want (Christians may be persecuted, ostracized, or imprisoned). It does mean that those who live with genuine piety and integrity will do well not just because they have good character but also because they are under God's blessing. Even in evil times, when obedience to God may lead to persecution, the sweet fruit of God's blessing is better than the sour residue of complicity in evil. In the big picture, we are always better off in God's ways than in any other.

The End of Moses' Work (Deuteronomy 31:1–34:12)

Succession Planning (Deuteronomy 31:1–32:47)

After the speeches, Joshua succeeds Moses as leader of Israel. "Moses summoned Joshua and said to him in the sight of all Israel: 'Be strong and bold, for you are the one who will go with this people into the land'" (Deut. 31:7). Moses conducts the transition publicly for two reasons. First, Joshua has to acknowledge before the whole nation that he has accepted the duties laid upon him. Second, the whole nation has to acknowledge that Joshua is Moses' sole, legitimate successor. After this, Moses steps aside in the most complete possible way—he dies. Any organization, be it a nation, a school, a church, or a business, will be in confusion if the matter of legitimate succession is unclear or unresolved.

Notice that Joshua is not a capricious, last-minute choice. Under the Lord's direction, Moses has long been preparing Joshua to succeed him. As early as Deuteronomy 1:38, the Lord refers to Joshua as Moses' "assistant." Moses had noticed Joshua's military capability not long after the departure from Egypt, and over time delegated leadership of the army to him (Deut. 31:3). Moses observed that Joshua was able to see things from God's perspective and was willing to risk his own safety to stand up

for what was right (Num. 14:5–10). Moses had trained Joshua in state-
craft in the incident with the kings of the Amorites (Deut. 3:21). Praying
to God on Joshua's behalf was an important element of Moses' training
regimen (Deut. 3:28). By the time Joshua takes over from Moses, he is
fully prepared for leadership, and the people are fully prepared to follow
him (Deut. 34:9).

Moses also sings his final song (Deut. 32:1–43), a prophetic text
warning that Israel will not obey the covenant, will suffer terribly, but will
finally experience redemption by a mighty act of God. Finally, Moses exhorts the people one last time to take the law seriously (Deut. 32:46–47).

Moses' Last Acts (Deuteronomy 32:48–34:12)

Moses' final act before departing Israel and this world is to bless
the nation tribe by tribe in the song of Deuteronomy 33:1–29. This
song is analogous to Jacob's blessing of the tribes just before his death
(Gen. 49:1–27). This is apt since Jacob was the biological father of the
twelve tribes, but Moses is the spiritual father of the nation. Also, in
this song Moses departs Israel with words of blessing and not with
words of chiding and exhortation. "Then Moses, the servant of the Lord,
died" (Deut. 34:5). The text honors Moses with a title both humble and
exalted, "the servant of the Lord." He had not been perfect, and Israel
under his leadership had not been perfect, but he had been great. Even
so, he was not irreplaceable. Israel would continue, and the leaders who
came after him would have their own successes and failures. When the
people of any institution consider their leader irreplaceable, they are
already in crisis. When a leader considers himself irreplaceable, it is a
calamity for all.

Conclusions from Deuteronomy

In retelling the events of Israel's early history and God's giving of
the law, Deuteronomy vividly portrays the importance of work to the
fulfillment of God's covenant with his people. The overarching themes
of the book are the need to trust God, to obey his commandments, and
to turn to him for help. To abandon any of these pursuits is to fall into

idolatry, the worship of false gods of our own making. Although these themes may initially sound abstract or philosophical, they are enacted in concrete, practical ways in daily work and life. When we trust God, we give him thanks for the good things he gives us the ability to produce. We recognize our limitations and turn to God for guidance. We treat others with respect. We observe a rhythm of work and rest that refreshes both ourselves and the people who work for our benefit. We exercise authority, obey authority diligently with an accurate sense of justice, and we exercise authority wisely for the common good. We limit ourselves to work that serves, rather than harms, others and that builds up, rather than destroys, families and communities. We make generous use of the resources God puts at our disposal, and we do not confiscate resources belonging to others. We are honest in our dealings with others. We train ourselves to be joyful in the work God gives us and not to envy other people.

Each day gives us opportunities to be thankful and generous in our work, to make our workplaces fairer, freer, and more rewarding for those we work among, and to work for the common good. In our own way, each of us has the opportunity—whether great or small—to transform ourselves, our families, our communities, and the nations of the world to eradicate idolatrous practices such as slavery and exploitation of workers, corruption and injustice, and indifference to the lack of resources suffered by the poor.

But if Deuteronomy were nothing but a long list of do's and don'ts for our work, the burden on us would be intolerable. Who could possibly fulfill the law, even if only in the sphere of work? By God's grace, Deuteronomy is not at its heart a list of rules and regulations but an invitation to a relationship with God. "Seek the LORD your God, and you will find him if you search after him with all your heart and soul" (Deut. 4:29). "For you are a people holy to the LORD your God; the LORD your God has chosen you out of all the peoples on earth to be his people, his treasured possession" (Deut. 7:6). If we find that our work falls short of the picture painted by Deuteronomy, let our response be not a grim resolve to try harder, but a refreshing acceptance of God's invitation to a closer relationship with him. A living relationship with God is our only hope for the power to live according to his word. This, of course, is the gospel

Jesus preached, and it was rooted deeply in the book of Deuteronomy. As Jesus put it, "My yoke is easy, and my burden is light" (Matt. 11:30). It is not an impossible list of demands, but an invitation to draw close to God. In this he echoes Moses: "O Israel, what does the LORD your God require of you? Only to fear the LORD your God, to walk in all his ways, to love him, to serve the LORD your God with all your heart and with all your soul" (Deut. 10:12).

Joshua & Judges and Work

Introduction to Joshua and Judges

Joshua and Judges tell the story of ancient Israel's occupation of the land God promised to Abraham, Isaac, and Jacob (Gen. 15:18–21; 28:13) and the formation of a tribal confederacy there. The books' overall theme is that when God's people abide by his commandments and his guidance, their work prospers and they experience peace and joy. But when they follow their own inclinations and set themselves up as the ultimate authority, then poverty, strife, and every kind of evil bring grief and suffering.

Conquering, settling, and governing a territory was the work of God's designated leaders, prophets, armies, and all the people of ancient Israel. While there is every reason to expect these books to contribute to our understanding of work from a biblical perspective, it takes some effort on our part to uncover how the work we see in Joshua and Judges applies to the circumstances of our contemporary workplaces. (Note that we are not considering the modern nation-state of Israel and its neighbors, which is a topic beyond the scope of our inquiry.)

But if we look carefully, we find that insights for today's issues do arise from the incidents in the text, including leadership development and management, the relative roles of hard work and God's guidance in attaining our objectives, conflict over resources, the tension between driving for success and serving others, God's guidance in our work, and the ever-present peril of making an idol of our work. The events in Joshua and Judges give us models—both good and bad—for resolving workplace conflicts, motivating workers, meeting the challenges of elective office, and planning for new leaders to succeed those who retire or depart. The characters we meet in the books illustrate the remarkable value of women's leadership, the economic effects of war, and the complicity of the powerful in the abuse of the vulnerable at work.

The primary storyline of both Joshua and Judges is that while God's chosen people are repeatedly rebellious against God, turning to serve other gods and forgetting God's covenant with them, God is always ready to respond to their crises and deliver them. Only when they cease to desire God's blessings do they fall into misery and social devastation. This is a remarkably contemporary message as well. We often find ourselves drifting away from God as we decide how to handle the many opportunities and challenges that arise in our work. We discover that we have elevated other concerns above receiving his love and loving and serving him through our work. The message of Joshua and Judges is that God is ready, now and here, for us to return to him and receive his blessings in our life and work.

We will organize our treatment of the books around four major themes, which roughly correspond to the flow of the narrative: conquest, coordination, covenant, and chaos.[1]

Conquest (Joshua 1–12)

The book of Joshua begins with the reiteration to Joshua of the promise of land and divine presence.

> "My servant Moses is dead. Now proceed to cross the Jordan, you and all this people, into the land that I am giving to them, to the Israelites. Every place that the sole of your foot will tread upon I have given to you, as I promised to Moses. From the wilderness and the Lebanon as far as the great river, the river Euphrates, all the land of the Hittites, to the Great Sea in the west shall be your territory. No one shall be able to stand against you all the days of your life. As I was with Moses, so I will be with you; I will not fail you or forsake you." (Josh. 1:2–5)

Joshua, the land, and God's presence are all worthy of note, as we will explore in the following sections.

---

[1] For a helpful overview of the key themes of Joshua, see David M. Howard Jr., *Joshua*, vol. 5, The New American Commentary (Nashville: Broadman & Holman, 1998), 56–64.

Joshua (Joshua 1)

Joshua is Moses' successor as leader of Israel. While he is not a king, he does in some ways foreshadow the kings who will rule over Israel in subsequent centuries. He leads the nation into battle, he executes judgment when necessary, and he attempts to hold the people to the terms of the covenant God made with the Israelites at Mount Sinai.

To use modern terms, we could call the transition from Moses to Joshua an example of good succession planning. Moses, as led by God, appointed in Joshua a leader who matches Moses' own character of faithfulness to God. He is described as a man of valor and learning, strong and courageous (Josh. 1:6–7), and well informed about and obedient to God's law (Josh. 1:8–9). More importantly, he is a spiritual man. Ultimately, the foundation of Joshua's leadership is not his own strength, nor even Moses' tutelage, but God's guidance and power. God promises him, "The LORD your God is with you wherever you go" (Josh. 1:9). (More about Joshua's preparation to succeed Moses can be found at "Succession Planning" in Numbers 27:12–23, and "The End of Moses' Work" in Deuteronomy 31:1–34:12 in the *Theology of Work Bible Commentary*.)

As an example to today's leaders, Joshua's most notable characteristic may be his willingness to keep growing in virtue throughout his life. Unlike Samson, who seems stuck in infantile willfulness, Joshua transitions from a hotheaded young man (Num. 14:6–10) to a military commander (Josh. 6:1–21) to a national chief executive (Josh. 20) and eventually to a prophetic visionary (Josh. 24). He is more than willing to subject himself to a long period of training under Moses and to learn from those more experienced than himself (Num. 27:18–23; Deut. 3:28). He is not afraid to give orders in times of action, yet he continues to share leadership among a team including the priest Eleazar and the elders of the twelve tribes (e.g., Josh. 19:51). He never seems to refuse an opportunity to grow in character or to benefit from the wisdom of others.

The Land (Joshua 2–12)

Throughout both Joshua and Judges, the land is of such central importance that it is virtually a character itself: "And the land had rest"

(Judg. 3:11, 30, etc.). The major action of the book of Joshua is Israel's conquest of the land God had promised their ancestors (Josh. 2:24, following 1:6). The land is the central stage upon which God's drama with Israel is played out, and it rests at the core of God's promises to the nation. The Law of Moses itself is inextricably bound to the land. Many of the law's chief provisions make sense only for Israel in the land, and the chief punishment under the covenant consists of expulsion from the land.

> I will devastate the land, so that your enemies who come to settle in it shall be appalled at it. And you I will scatter among the nations, and I will unsheathe the sword against you; your land shall be a desolation, and your cities a waste. (Lev. 26:32–33)

The land—the earth, the ground under our feet—is where our existence takes place. God's promise to his people is not a disembodied abstraction, but a concrete place where his will is done and his presence is found. The place we are at any moment is the place we encounter God and the only place we have to go about his work. Creation can be a place where either evil or good dwells. Our task is to work good in the actual creation and culture where we work. Joshua was given the task of making the land of Canaan holy by adhering to God's covenant there. We are given the task of making our workplaces holy by also working according to God's covenant.

Working the Land (Joshua 5)

The land was, of course, bountiful by the standards of the ancient Near East. But the blessings of the land went beyond the favorable climate, abundant water, and other natural benefits provided by the hand of the Creator. Israel would also inherit a well-developed infrastructure from the Canaanites. "I gave you a land on which you had not labored, and towns that you had not built, and you live in them; you eat the fruit of vineyards and olive yards that you did not plant" (Josh. 24:13; cf. Deut. 6:10–11). Even the signature description of the land as "flowing with milk and honey" (Josh. 5:6; cf. Exod. 3:8) assumes some degree of livestock management and beekeeping.

There is thus an inextricable link between land and labor. Our ability to produce does not arise solely from our ability or diligence, but also from the resources available to us. Conversely, the land does not work itself. By the sweat of our faces, we must produce bread (Gen. 3:19). This point is made quite precisely in Joshua 5:11–12. "On the day after the Passover, on that very day, they ate the produce of the land, unleavened cakes and parched grain. The manna ceased on the day they ate the produce of the land, and the Israelites no longer had manna; they ate the crops of the land of Canaan that year."

Israel survived on the divine gift of manna throughout their wilderness wanderings, but God had no intention of making this a permanent solution to the problem of provision. The land was to be worked. Sufficient resources and fruitful labor were integral elements of the Promised Land. The point may seem obvious, but it is worth making nonetheless. While God may provide miraculously at times for our physical needs, the norm is for us to subsist on the fruit of our labors.

Conquering the Land (Joshua 6–12)

The fact that the Israelites' productive economy was founded on dispossessing the Canaanites from the land does, however, raise uncomfortable questions. Did (or does) God endorse conquest as a means for a nation to acquire land? Does God tolerate ethnic war? Was ancient Israel more deserving of the land than the Canaanites were? A full theological analysis of the conquest is beyond the scope of this article.[2] While we cannot hope to answer the myriad issues that spring up, there are at least a few things to keep in mind:

1. God chooses to come to his people in the rough-and-tumble of the actual ancient Near East, where the forces arrayed against Israel are vast and violent.

2. The work of military conquest is certainly the most prominent work in the book of Joshua, but it is not presented as a model for

---

[2] For more on the conquest, see C. S. Cowles, Eugene H. Merrill, Daniel L. Gard, and Tremper Longman III, *Show Them No Mercy: 4 Views on God and Canaanite Genocide* (Grand Rapids: Zondervan, 2003).

any work that follows it. We find aspects of work or leadership in Joshua and Judges that are applicable today, but the dispossession of people from land is not one of them.

3. The command to dispossess the Canaanites (Josh. 1:1–5) is a *highly specific* one to ancient Israel and is not indicative of the general disposition of God's commands to the Israelites or any other people group.

4. The eradication of the Canaanites stems from their notoriously wicked ways. The Canaanites were known to practice child sacrifice, divination, sorcery, and necromancy, which God could not tolerate in the midst of the people he had chosen to be a blessing to the world (Deut. 18:10–12). The land was to be stripped of idolatry so that the world might have the opportunity to see the nature of the one true God, creator of heaven and earth.[3]

5. Repentant Canaanites like Rahab (Josh. 2:1–21; 6:22–26) are spared—and indeed the putative wholesale destruction of the Canaanites is never fully realized (see below).

6. Ancient Israel would in turn practice much of the same wickedness as the Canaanites, giving a firm answer of "no" to the question of whether Israel was more deserving of the land. Like the Canaanites, the Israelites would also suffer displacement from the land through conquest by others, which the Bible likewise attributes to the hand of God. Israel is also subject to God's judgment (see Amos 3:1–2 for example).

7. The full Christian ethic of power is not to be found in the book of Joshua, but in the life, death, and resurrection of Jesus, who embodies all of God's word. The Bible's definitive model for the use of power is not that God conquers nations for his people, but that the Son of God lays down his life for all who come to him

---

[3] See J. Gordon McConville and Stephen N. Williams, *Joshua,* Two Horizons Old Testament Commentary (Grand Rapids: Eerdmans, 2010), 113–4.

(Mark 10:42–45; John 10:11–18). The biblical ethic of power is ultimately founded on humility and sacrifice.

Remembering God's Presence in the Land (Joshua 4:1–9)

The ultimate blessing for the people in the land is that God will be with them. The people celebrate this blessing by passing in front of the ark of the Lord—the abode of his presence—and dropping memorial stones in the Jordan riverbed. Israel's prosperity and security in the land are to come from the hand of God. Israel's work is always derived from the prior work of God on their behalf. Whenever they become disconnected from the presence of God, the trajectory of their labor turns downward. Witness the somber note sounded in Judges 2:10: "Moreover, that whole generation was gathered to their ancestors, and another generation grew up after them, who did not know the Lord or the work that he had done for Israel." The subsequent problems of Israel stem from their failure to acknowledge God's work on their behalf.

We also could ask ourselves whether we are paying attention to God's work on our behalf. The question here is not whether we are working well for God, but whether we can see him at work for us. At work, most of us find a tension between advancing ourselves and serving others, or between "a very I-centered system of self-interest" and "the welfare of the other side," as Laura Nash puts it in her excellent exploration of this dynamic.[4] Could it be that we are trying too hard to look out for number one because we are afraid no one else cares about us?

What if we made it a practice to keep track of the things God does on our behalf? Many of us keep mementos of our successes at work—awards, plaques, photos, commendations, certificates, and the like. What if every time our eyes passed over them we thought, "God has been with me every day here," rather than "I've got what it takes"? Would that free us to care more generously for others, yet still feel more taken care of ourselves? A simple way to start would be to mentally note or even jot down each unexpected good thing that happens during the day, whether it happens to you or to someone else through you. Each of these could become a

---

[4] Laura Nash, *Believers in Business* (Nashville: Thomas Nelson, 1994), 96.

kind of memorial stone to God, like the stones the Israelites placed in the waters of Jordan to remember how God brought them into the Promised Land. According to the text, this was a powerful reminder to them "and they are there to this day" (Josh. 4:1–9).

Coordination (Joshua 13–22)

The length of text devoted to land allotment in Joshua 13 to 22 reflects the essential role of the land in shaping Israel's identity, although it can make eyelid-drooping reading if we don't look at the big picture of the action. These chapters detail the work of setting boundaries, assigning cities and towns, and creating procedures to resolve conflicts—the work of organizing and cultivating a society for human flourishing and glorifying God. Joshua takes scrupulous measures to ensure the distribution was done fairly (Josh. 14:1–2). Such passages remind us that productive labor depends in large measure on cooperation and fair play, meaning *organization* and *justice*. The Israelites need to know what belongs to whom, so that they can then organize their communities in a peaceful and productive manner. It takes work (in this case, quite a bit of work) to address the realities of geographical and social organization.

These realities are brought home with special force in Joshua 22, when the Transjordan tribes are accused of separatism after they erect an altar in their territory. As it turns out, the installation of the memorial altar is a shrewd move on the part of those tribes, which serves to maintain their standing within Israel.

> "If it was in rebellion or in breach of faith toward the Lord, do not spare us today for building an altar to turn away from following the Lord; or if we did so to offer burnt offerings or grain offerings or offerings of well-being on it, may the Lord himself take vengeance. No! We did it from fear that in time to come your children might say to our children, 'What have you to do with the Lord, the God of Israel? For the Lord has made the Jordan a boundary between us and you, you Reubenites and Gadites; you have no portion in the Lord.' So your children might make our children cease to worship the Lord. Therefore we said, 'Let us now build an altar, not for burnt offering, nor for sacrifice, but to be a witness between us and you, and between the generations after us, that we do perform the service of

the Lord in his presence with our burnt offerings and sacrifices and offerings of well-being; so that your children may never say to our children in time to come, 'You have no portion in the LORD.'" (Josh. 22:22–27)

We see from all the detail that allotting the land fairly, creating governance structures, resolving conflicts, and maintaining a united mission was a complex process. Joshua was in overall charge, but all the people had roles to play, and even the tussles and crafty positioning were necessary to keep a coalition of imperfect individuals working in harmony. This could give us an appreciation for the practice and science of management today. Building an international supply chain, for example, requires aligning incentives, communicating specifications, sharing ideas, resolving competing-yet-cooperative interests, increasing your own profitability without driving other elements into losses, attracting and motivating skilled contributors, and overcoming unforeseeable obstacles, similarly to what Israel's leaders had to do. The same is true in universities, government agencies, banks, agricultural cooperatives, media companies, and virtually every kind of workplace. Society also depends on those who research and teach management methods and who shape corporate and government policy accordingly.

If God guided Joshua and the other leaders and people of Israel, can we expect him to guide today's managers? We have the resources of Scripture, prayer, worship, group studies, and the counsel of other Christians. How, exactly, can each of us weave these into our own ways of receiving guidance from God about the administration, management, and leadership we exercise?

Although possession of the land and governance of the people were of first importance to the Israelites, the later chapters in this section show us that neither the conquest of the land nor the organization of the nation was fully completed. In chapter after chapter, we hear the troubling refrain, "but they did not drive out" the various Canaanite tribes in their territories (Josh. 15:63; 16:10; 17:12–13). The Lord had commanded Israel to drive out the Canaanites in order to establish a new order not degraded by the previous occupants' abominable practices. The Canaanites' continued presence became a major cause of Israel's later faithlessness to God's covenant, although this did not occur during the period covered by the book of Joshua.

Covenant (Joshua 23–24)

The renewal of God's covenant with Israel concludes the book of Joshua. The high point occurs in the very last chapter, when Joshua inspires the people with a rousing challenge to their commitment to serve God alone. His speech is a model of communication. First he recounts God's amazing acts on Israel's behalf in Egypt, the wilderness, and the Promised Land. Why then, Joshua asks, are they still carrying idols and false gods with them? Using what we today might call reverse psychology, he challenges them: "If you are unwilling to serve the LORD, choose this day whom you will serve" (Josh. 24:15). This gets their attention. "Far be it from us that we should forsake the LORD to serve other gods" (Josh. 24:16). But Joshua challenges them further. "You cannot serve the LORD," he tells them, "for he is a holy God" (Josh. 24:19). "If you forsake the LORD and serve foreign gods, then he will turn and do you harm, and consume you, after having done you good" (Josh. 24:20). This brings them to a point of decision and they resolve, "No, we will serve the LORD!" (Josh. 24:21). Let's put it in writing, Joshua says, and he has the people sign and witness their commitment (Josh. 24:25–27). In more recent times, John Wesley published a covenant renewal service that is widely used today, and many churches have developed their own approaches to renewing the covenant.[5]

When people seem to be wavering in their commitment, leaders can be tempted to minimize the task at hand or mislead people into thinking things will be easier than they actually are. Perhaps there are times when this technique can gain compliance for a while. But as Ronald Heifetz argues in *Leadership without Easy Answers*,[6] misleading followers rapidly diminishes a leader's authority. This is not only because followers eventually discover the deception, but because it prevents them from contributing to solving the group's challenges. Unless the leader knows the solution to every challenge—an extremely unlikely possibility—solutions

---

[5] John Wesley, *Covenant Renewal Service*, 2nd ed. (London: 1781). The text, along with modern adaptations, may be found at http://wesley.nnu.edu/john -wesley/covenant-service-directions-for-renewing-our-covenant-with-god/.

[6] Ronald A. Heifetz, *Leadership without Easy Answers* (Cambridge, MA: Harvard University Press, 1994).

will have to come from the creativity and commitment of group members. But if the leader has misled the people about the nature of the challenges, the people cannot contribute to finding a solution. This all but guarantees that the leader will fail. Instead, leaders who are honest with their followers about the difficulty of the challenges have an opportunity to involve their people in creating solutions. Joshua, through his relationship with God, provides an excellent model for leaders seeking to build commitment toward a difficult course of action through honesty and transparency, rather than secrecy and false hope.

Chaos (Judges 1–21)

After the death of Joshua, Israel has no permanent national leadership position. Instead, as threats arise—a military attack, for example— men and women are raised to leadership for the duration of each crisis. The English term "judges" does not really capture the role these men and women play. (The Hebrew word *shopet,* usually translated "judge," means an arbitrator of conflicts, military commander, and governor of a territory.[7]) The judges do settle disputes, but they also take responsibility for military and political affairs in the face of hostile surrounding peoples. While we will maintain the traditional designation of judges, the epithet "deliverers" is a more accurate description of these leaders.

In the book of Judges, we find an altogether more dismal view of Israel's leaders than in the book of Joshua. Bit by bit, the succession of judges diminishes in quality until finally leading Israel into utter chaos. The book concludes with stories of rape, murder, and civil war, with the appropriately grim coda, "In those days there was no king in Israel; all the people did what was right in their own eyes" (Judg. 21:25). Doing right in their own eyes does not refer to virtuous people acting ethically on their own accord, but to the unfettered pursuit of looking out for number one, as we might put it today. It means the failure to obey God's command, through Joshua, that "this book of the law shall not depart from your mouth; you shall meditate on it day and night, so that you may

---

[7]Temba L. J. Mafico, "Judge, Judging," in *The Anchor Bible Dictionary*, ed. David Noel Freedman (New York: Doubleday, 1992), 1105.

be careful to act in accordance with all that is written in it" (Josh. 1:8). The command is to do what is right in God's eyes, not what seems good in our own biased and self-serving vision. The judges failed to lead the Israelites in observing God's law, and thereby failed both to administer justice and to govern people.[8]

Failing the Driving (Out) Test (Judges 1–2)

Judges 1–2 picks up where Joshua 13–22 left off, with the failure of Israel to drive out the Canaanite peoples from the land. "When Israel grew strong, they put the Canaanites to forced labor, but did not utterly drive them out" (Josh. 17:13). There is a certain irony in the newly liberated Israelites becoming slave owners at the first opportunity. But the chief reason Israel was supposed to drive out the Canaanites was to prevent their idolatry from infecting Israel. Like the snake in the garden, the idolatry of the Canaanites would test the Israelites' loyalty to God and his covenant. Israel fared no better than Adam or Eve did. Failing to remove the temptation of the Canaanites, they soon began "serving" the Canaanite gods, Baal and Astarte (Judg. 2:11–13; 10:6; etc.). (The NRSV translates the Hebrew as "worshiping," but virtually every other English translation more accurately reads "serving.") This is not merely a question of occasionally bowing before an image or uttering a prayer to a foreign god. Instead, Israel's life *and their labor* were spent in futile service to idols, as Israel came to believe that their success in labor depended on assuaging the local Canaanite deities.[9]

Most of our work today is dedicated to serving someone or something other than the God of Israel. Businesses serve customers and shareholders. Governments serve citizens. Schools serve students. Unlike worshipping the Canaanite gods, serving these objects is not evil in itself. In fact, serving other people is one of the ways we serve God. But if serving customers, shareholders, citizens, students, and the like becomes *more* important to us than serving God, or if it becomes simply

---

[8] Daniel I. Block, *Judges, Ruth,* vol. 6, The New American Commentary (Nashville: Broadman & Holman, 1999), 83–4.

[9] John Gray, *Joshua, Judges, and Ruth,* The New Century Bible Commentary (London: Nelson, 1967), 256.

a means of enlarging ourselves, we are following the ancient Israelites into worshipping false gods. Tim Keller observes that idols are not an obsolete relic of ancient religiosity, but a sophisticated, though false, spirituality we encounter every day.

What is an idol? It is anything more important to you than God, anything that absorbs your heart and imagination more than God, anything you seek to give you what only God can give. A counterfeit god is anything so central and essential to your life that, should you lose it, your life would feel hardly worth living. An idol has such a controlling position in your heart that you can spend on it most of your passion and energy, your emotional and financial resources, without a second thought. It can be family and children, career and making money, achievement and critical acclaim, or saving "face" and social standing. It can be a romantic relationship, peer approval, competence and skill, secure and comfortable circumstances, your beauty or your brains, a great political or social cause, your morality and virtue, or even success in the Christian ministry.[10]

For example, elected officials rightly desire to serve the public. In order to do that, they must continue to have a public to serve, that is, to stay in office and keep winning elections. If serving the public becomes their *ultimate* goal, then anything necessary to win an election becomes justifiable, including pandering, deception, intimidation, false accusations, and even vote-rigging. An unlimited desire to serve the public—combined with an unshakable belief that he was the only person who could lead them effectively—seems to be exactly what motivated United States President Richard Nixon in the 1972 election. It seems that an unlimited desire to serve the public is what caused him to pursue winning the election at all costs, including spying on the Democratic National Committee at the Watergate Hotel. This in turn led to his impeachment, loss of office, and disgrace. Serving an idol always ends in disaster.

People in every occupation—even the family occupations of spouse, parent, and child—face the temptation to elevate some intermediate

---

[10] Timothy Keller, *Counterfeit Gods: The Empty Promises of Money, Sex, and Power, and the Only Hope That Matters* (New York: Dutton Adult, 2009), xvii–xviii.

good above serving God. When serving any good becomes an ultimate goal, rather than an expression of service to God, idolatry creeps in. For more on the dangers of idolizing work, see the sections on the first and second commandments in "Exodus and Work" ("You Shall Have No Other Gods Before Me," Exod. 20:3; "You Shall Not Make for Yourself an Idol," Exod. 20:4), and "Deuteronomy and Work" ("You Shall Have No Other Gods Before Me," Deut. 5:7; "You Shall Not Make for Yourself an Idol," Deut. 5:8) in the *Theology of Work Bible Commentary*.

The Judges (Judges 3–16)

Deborah (Judges 4–5)

The best of the judges is Deborah. The people recognize her wisdom and come to her for counsel and conflict resolution (Judg. 4:5). The military hierarchy recognizes her as supreme commander and in fact will only go to war on her personal command (Judg. 4:8). Her governance is so good that "the land had rest for forty years" (Judg. 5:31), a rare occurrence at any point in Israel's history.

Some today may find it surprising that a woman who was neither the widow nor the daughter of a male ruler could arise as the national chief of a pre-modern people. But the book of Judges regards her as equal—in her own right—to the greatest leaders of Israel. Alone among the judges, she is called a prophet or prophetess (Judg. 4:4), indicating how closely she resembles Moses and Joshua, to whom God also spoke directly. Neither the women, including the undercover agent Jael, nor the men, including the commanding general Barak, exhibit any concern about having a female leader. Deborah's service as a prophetess-judge of Israel suggests that God does not regard women's political, judicial, or military leadership as problematic. It is also evident that her husband Lappidoth and her immediate family had no trouble structuring the work of the household so that she had time to "sit under the palm of Deborah" to fulfill her duties when "the Israelites came up to her for judgment" (Judg. 4:5).

Today in some societies, many sectors of work, and certain organizations, women's leadership has become as uncontroversial as Deborah's was. But in many other contemporary cultures, sectors, and organizations, women are not accepted as leaders or are subject to constraints not imposed on men. Could reflecting on Deborah's leadership of ancient Israel help Christians today clarify our understanding of God's intent in these situations? Could we serve our organizations and societies by helping demolish improper obstacles to women's leadership? Would we personally benefit from seeking women as bosses, mentors, and role models in our work?

The Economic Effects of War (Judges 6:1–11)

After Deborah, the quality of the judges begins to decline. Judges 6:1–11 illustrates what was likely a common feature of Israelite life at this time—economic hardship stemming from war.

> The Israelites did what was evil in the sight of the LORD, and the LORD gave them into the hand of Midian seven years. The hand of Midian prevailed over Israel; and because of Midian the Israelites provided for themselves hiding places in the mountains, caves and strongholds. For whenever the Israelites put in seed, the Midianites and the Amalekites and the people of the east would come up against them. They would encamp against them and destroy the produce of the land, as far as the neighborhood of Gaza, and leave no sustenance in Israel, and no sheep or ox or donkey. For they and their livestock would come up, and they would even bring their tents, as thick as locusts; neither they nor their camels could be counted; so they wasted the land as they came in. Thus Israel was greatly impoverished because of Midian; and the Israelites cried out to the LORD for help.

The effects of war on work are felt throughout many parts of the world today. In addition to the damage done by direct strikes against economic targets, the instability brought about by armed conflict can devastate people's livelihood. Farmers in war-torn areas are reluctant to plant crops when they are likely to be dislocated before the harvest comes. Investors judge war-torn countries to be a poor risk and are unlikely to funnel resources to improving infrastructure. With little hope of economic development, people may be drawn into armed factions fighting over whatever resources may be left to exploit. So the dismal cycle of war and destitution continues. Peace precedes plenty.

Israel's economic situation was so precarious under the Midianites that we find the future judge Gideon "beating out wheat in the wine press, to hide it from the Midianites" (Judg. 6:11). Daniel Block shows the rationale for his behavior.

> In the absence of modern technology, grain was threshed by first beat-ing the heads of the cut stalks with a flail, discarding the straw, and then tossing the mixture of chaff and grain in the air, allowing the wind to blow away the chaff while the heavier kernels of grain fell to the floor. In the present critical circumstances this obviously would have been unwise. Threshing activity on the hilltops would only have aroused the attention of the marauding Midianites. Therefore Gideon resorts to beating the grain in a sheltered vat used for pressing grapes. Generally wine presses involved two excavated depressions in the rock, one above the other. The grapes would be gathered and trampled in the upper, while a conduit would drain the juices to the lower.[11]

Today, Christians and non-Christians alike overwhelmingly agree that it is immoral to conduct business in ways that perpetuate armed conflict. The international ban on "conflict diamonds" is a current ex-ample.[12] Are Christians taking a lead in such endeavors? Are we the ones who track down whether the businesses, governments, universities, and other institutions in which we work are unwittingly participating in vio-lence? Do we take the risk to raise such questions when our superiors might prefer to ignore the situation? Or do we, like Gideon, hide behind the excuse of just doing our jobs?

Gideon's Ambivalent Leadership (Judges 6:12–8:35)

Gideon is a prime example of the paradoxical character of Israel's judges and the ambivalent lessons they offer for leadership in the work-place and elsewhere. Gideon's name literally means "hacker,"[13] and it

---

[11] Block, *Judges, Ruth*, 258–59.

[12] "Conflict Diamonds," Amnesty International, http://www.amnestyusa.org/our-work/issues/business-and-human-rights/oil-gas-and-mining-industries/conflict-diamonds.

[13] Robert G. Boling, "Gideon (Person)," in *The Anchor Bible Dictionary*, ed. David Noel Freedman (New York: Doubleday, 1992), 1013.

seems to point in a positive direction when he hacks up his father's idols in Judges 6:25–7. (The fact that he does this at night, out of fear, is a disturbing detail.)[14] Despite the fact that God has promised to be with him, however, Gideon is forever seeking signs, most notably in the incident of the fleece in Judges 6:36–40. God does condescend to assure Gideon in this instance, but it is hardly an example for others to follow as many modern Christians argue in relation to guidance and specifically vocational guidance. It is instead a sign of the wavering commitment that will come to ultimately collapse into idolatry at the end of the story.[15] See *Decision-Making by the Book*[16] and *Decision Making and the Will of God*[17] for in-depth analysis of Gideon's discernment methods.

The high point of the tale is, of course, Gideon's astonishing triumph over the Midianites (Judg. 7). Less well known are his subsequent failures of leadership (Judg. 8). The inhabitants of Succoth and Penuel refuse to help his men after the battle, and his brutal destruction of those cities might strike some as disproportionate to the offense. Gideon is again living up to his name, but now he is hacking down anyone who crosses him.[18] Despite his protestations that he does not want to be king, he becomes a despot in all but name (Judg. 8:22–26). Even more troubling is his subsequent fall into idolatry. The ephod he makes becomes a "snare" for his people, and "all Israel prostituted themselves to it there" (Judg. 8:27). How the mighty are fallen!

A lesson for us today may be finding gratitude for the gifts of great people without idolizing them. Like Gideon, a general today may lead us to victory in war, yet prove a tyrant in peace. A genius may bring us

---

[14] D. I. Block and J. Clinton McCann, *Judges,* Interpretation (Louisville: Westminster John Knox Press, 1989), 61.

[15] See, for example, McCann's comment on the fleece incident (66): "In short, Gideon is beginning to look at least a little ridiculous. Instead of growing more faithful, he seems to be growing more faithless and more fearful."

[16] Haddon W. Robinson, *Decision-Making by the Book: How to Choose Wisely in an Age of Options* (Wheaton, IL: Victor Books, 1991).

[17] Garry Friesen and J. Robin Maxson, *Decision Making and the Will of God: A Biblical Alternative to the Traditional View* (Portland, OR: Multnomah Books, 2004).

[18] Cf. Block, *Judges, Ruth,* 287: "Gideon, the fearful young man, has become a brutal aggressor."

sublime insight in music or film, yet lead us astray in parenting or politics. A business leader may rescue a business in crisis, only to destroy it in times of ease. We may even find the same discontinuities within ourselves. Perhaps we rise in the ranks at work while sinking into discord at home, or vice versa. Maybe we prove capable as individual performers but fail as managers. Most likely of all, perhaps, we accomplish much good when, unsure of ourselves, we depend on God but wreak havoc when success leads us to self-reliance.[19] Like the judges, we are people of contradiction and frailty. Our only hope, or else despair, is the forgiveness and transformation made possible for us in Christ.

The Judges' Failure of Leadership (Judges 9–16)

Gideon's failures are intensified in the judges who follow. Gideon's son Abimelech unites the people around him, but only by killing his seventy brothers standing in his way (Judg. 9). Jephthah starts as a brigand, goes on to deliver the people from the Ammonites, but destroys his own family and future with a dreadful vow that leads to the death of his daughter (Judg. 11). The most famous of the judges, Samson, wreaks havoc among the Philistines, but infamously succumbs to the seductions of the pagan Delilah to his own ruin (Judg. 13–16).

What are we to make of all this for our work in today's world? First of all, the stories of the judges affirm the truth that God works through broken people. This is surely true, for a number of the judges—Gideon, Barak, Samson, and Jephthah—are praised in the New Testament, along with Rahab (Heb. 11:31–34). The book of Judges does not hesitate to point out that the Spirit of God empowered them to bring about mighty acts of deliverance in the face of overwhelming odds (Judg. 3:10; 6:34; 11:29; 13:25; 14:6–9; 15:14). Furthermore they were more than instruments in God's hand. They responded positively toward God's call to deliver Israel, and through them God delivered his people again and again.

Yet the overall tenor of Judges does not encourage us to make these men into role models. The burden of the book is that Israel is a mess,

---

[19]Tomas Chamorro-Premuzic, "Less-Confident People Are More Successful," *Harvard Business Review*, July 6, 2012, http://blogs.hbr.org/2012/07/less-confident-people-are-more-su/.

awash in compromise, and its leaders are a disappointment in their disobedience of God's covenant. A more appropriate lesson to draw might be that success—*even God-given success*—is not necessarily a pronouncement of God's favor. When our efforts in the workplace are blessed, especially in the face of adverse circumstances, it is tempting to reason, "Well, God obviously has his hand in this, so he must be rewarding me for being a good person." But the history of the judges shows that God works when he wishes, and how he wishes, and through whom he wishes. He acts according to his plans, not according to our merit or lack thereof. We cannot take credit as if we deserved the blessings of success. Likewise, we cannot judge those whom we deem less deserving of God's favor, as Paul reminds us in Romans 2:1.

Israel Falls Apart (Judges 17–21)

The Prosperity Gospel Unmasked in Early Form (Judges 17)

If the central section of Judges offers us flawed heroes caught in a depressing cycle of oppression and deliverance, the final chapters portray a fallen people seemingly beyond the hope of redemption. Judges 17 opens with almost a parody of idolatry. A man named Micah has lots of money, his mother uses the money to make an idol, and Micah hires a freelancing Levite as his personal priest. It is not surprising that Micah's tawdry homegrown cult features an equally abysmal theology. "Micah said, 'Now I know that the Lord will prosper me, because the Levite has become my priest'" (Judg. 17:13). In other words, by getting a religious authority to bless his idolatrous enterprise, Micah believes that he can co-opt God into churning out the goods he craves. Human creativity is wasted here in the worst possible way, in the manufacture of make-believe gods as a cover for greed and arrogance.

The impulse to turn God into a prosperity machine has never died away. A notorious form of it today is the so-called prosperity gospel or gospel of success, which claims that those who profess faith in Christ will necessarily be rewarded with wealth, health, and happiness. With respect to work, this leads some to neglect their work and descend into licentiousness while waiting for God to shower them with riches. It leads others—who expect God to deliver prosperity *though* their work—to neglect family and community, to abuse co-workers, and to do business unethically, certain that God's favor exempts them from ordinary morality.

Human Depravity and the Complicity of Religious Authorities Unveiled (Judges 18–21)

The final episode in Judges is the most appalling event in Israel's long slide into depravity, idolatry, and anarchy. Some men from the tribe of Dan make off with Micah's whole religious enterprise, including the Levite and the idol (Judg. 18:1–31). The Levite takes a concubine from a distant village (Bethlehem, as it happens), but after a domestic quarrel, she returns to her father's house. The Levite goes to Bethlehem to retrieve her. After a five-day drinking binge with her father, the Levite with his concubine and servant foolishly begin the journey back home not long before sunset. They find themselves alone at night in the town square of a village in the tribe of Benjamin. No one will take them in until at last one old man offers the hospitality of a place to stay the night.

That night the men of the city surround the house and demand that the old man bring out the stranger so they can rape him (Judg. 19:22). The old man tries to protect the stranger, but his idea of protecting visitors is stomach-turning, to put it mildly. In order to spare the Levite, the man offers his young daughter and the Levite's concubine for the men to rape instead. The Levite himself casts the concubine out the door, in perhaps the earliest recorded instance of religious authorities' complicity in sexual abuse. Then "they wantonly raped her, and abused her all through the night until the morning" (Judg. 19:25). The Levite subsequently dismembers her body and disperses the parts to the tribes of Israel, who almost exterminate the tribe of Benjamin in reprisal (Judg. 20–21). The Canaanization of the Israelites is complete.[20]

The concluding line of the book sums up things succinctly. "In those days there was no king in Israel; all the people did what was right in their own eyes" (Judg. 21:25). In case it's not obvious, this means that without leadership into the Lord's ways, the people followed their own

---

[20] Note that Block makes the Canaanization of the people the central theme of his commentary on Judges. See Block, *Judges, Ruth*.

evil devices and desires, not that people's inherent moral compasses led them to do right without needing supervision.

In our spheres of work today, threats against the powerless—including abuse of women and foreigners—remain shockingly common. Individually, we have to choose whether to stand with those who face injustice—undoubtedly at risk to ourselves—or lie low until the damage is past.

Organizationally and societally, we have to decide whether to work for systems and structures that restrain the evils of human behavior, or whether to stand aside while people do what is right in their own eyes. Even our passivity can contribute to abuses in our places of work, especially if we are not in positions of authority. But anytime others perceive you as having power—because you are older, have worked there longer, are better dressed, are seen often talking with the boss, belong to a privileged ethnic or language group, have more education, or are better at expressing yourself—and you fail to stick up for those being abused, you are contributing to the system of abuse. For example, if people tend to come to you for help, then that means you have a significant amount of perceived power. If then you stand idly by when a derogatory joke is told or a new employee is bullied, you are adding your weight to the victim's burden, and you are helping pave the way for the next abuse.

Reading the horrible events in the last chapters of Judges may make us grateful that we do not live in those days. But if we are truly aware, we can see that simply going to work is as freighted with moral significance as was the work of any leader or person in ancient Israel.

Conclusions from Joshua and Judges

Our journey through Joshua and Judges has been a sobering one. We began with the inspiring example of Joshua, in whom were combined skill, wisdom, and godly virtue. The Lord himself guided the people of Israel into the land of promise, and they promised to follow him all their lives. God granted them a society unencumbered by tyranny, with a fresh start free of corruption, domination, and institutionalized injustice. At the point of need he raised up leaders, exemplified by Joshua and

Deborah—wise, courageous, and universally acclaimed—who delivered the people from every successive threat.

We saw Israel's early leaders and people constructing the structures they needed for peace and prosperity in the land. They allocated resources fairly and productively. They pursued a unifying mission while maintaining a diverse and flexible culture. They distributed power while at the same time maintaining mutual accountability and learning how to resolve conflicts productively and creatively. They prospered and had peace.

But soon after, we saw Israel degenerate from a well-governed, smartly organized, secure, covenant people into a violent and fractious mob. Every aspect of their lives, including their work, became corrupted by their abandonment of God's precepts and presence. God gave them a bountiful land primed for productive labor, but they forgot his work on their behalf and squandered their resources on idols. They opened themselves up to war and consequent economic deprivation, and in short order they began to fully embrace the evils of the surrounding peoples. In the end, they became their own worst enemy.

The chief lesson for us, then, is the same one with which John ended his first letter centuries later: "Little children, keep yourselves from idols" (1 John 5:21). When we work in faithfulness to God, obeying his covenant and seeking his guidance, our work brings unimaginable good for ourselves and our societies. But when we break covenant with the God who works on our behalf, and when we begin to practice the injustices that we so easily learn from the culture around us, we find that our labors are as empty as the idols we've fallen into serving.

Ruth and Work

Introduction to the Book of Ruth

The book of Ruth tells the extraordinary story of God's faithfulness to Israel in the life and work of three ordinary people—Naomi, Ruth, and Boaz. As they work through both economic hardship and prosperity, we see the hand of God at work most clearly in their productive agricultural labor, generous management of resources for the good of all, respectful treatment of co-workers, ingenuity in the face of necessity, and the conception and raising of children. Throughout everything God's faithfulness to them creates opportunities for fruitful work, and their faithfulness to God brings the blessing of provision and security to one another and the people around them.

The events in the book of Ruth take place at the time of the festival of the barley harvest (Ruth 1:22; 2:17, 23; 3:2, 15, 17), when the connection between God's blessing and human labor was celebrated. Two passages from the Torah give the background of the festival:

> You shall observe the festival of harvest, of the first *fruits of your labor*, of what you sow in the field. (Exod. 23:16; emphasis added)

> You shall keep the festival of weeks for the LORD your God, contributing a freewill offering in proportion to the *blessing that you have received from the LORD* your God. Rejoice before the LORD your God—you and your sons and your daughters, your male and female slaves, the Levites resident in your towns, as well as the *strangers, the orphans, and the widows* who are among you—at the place that the LORD your God will choose as a dwelling for his name. *Remember that you were a slave in Egypt*, and diligently observe these statutes. (Deut. 16:10–12; emphasis added)

Together these passages establish a theological foundation for the events in the book of Ruth.

1. God's blessing is the source of human productivity ("blessing that you have received from the LORD").

2. God bestows his blessing of productivity through human labor ("fruits of your labor").

3. God calls people to provide opportunities for poor and vulnerable people ("the strangers, the orphans, and the widows") to work productively ("remember that you were a slave in Egypt," an allusion to God's liberation of his people from slavery in Egypt, and his provision for them in the wilderness and the land of Canaan).

In sum, the productivity of human labor is an extension of God's work in the world, and God's blessing on human labor is inextricably linked to God's command to provide generously for those without the means to provide for themselves. These principles underlie the book of Ruth. But the book is a narrative, not a theological treatise, and the story is compelling.

Tragedy Strikes the Family of Ruth and Naomi (Ruth 1:1–22)

The story begins with a famine "in the days when the judges ruled" (Ruth 1:1). This was a time when the people of Israel had abandoned God's ways and fallen into idolatry, horrific social conditions, and a disastrous civil war, as told in the chapters of Judges immediately preceding the book of Ruth in Christian Bibles. (The books occur in different order in Hebrew Bibles.) As a whole, the nation certainly had not been following the precepts of the Torah with respect to work or anything else. Because of this, the nation was losing God's blessings, as Naomi, among others, recognized (Ruth 1:13, 20–21). As a result, the socioeconomic fabric of society was falling apart and a famine gripped the land.

Responding to the famine, Elimelech, his wife Naomi, and their two sons moved to Moab—a move of desperation given the long enmity between Israel and Moab—where they thought the prospects for productive work were greater. We do not know whether they were successful in finding work, but the sons both found wives in Moab. But within ten years, they experienced both social and economic tragedy—the death of all the men left Naomi and her two daughters-in-law without husbands (Ruth 1:3–5). The three widows then had to support themselves without the legal and economic rights accorded to men in their society. In short, they had no husbands, no clear title to land, and no resources with which to make a living. "Call me *Mara* [bitter], for the Almighty has dealt bitterly with me," Naomi lamented, reflecting the harshness of their situation (Ruth 1:20).

Along with aliens and the fatherless, widows received a great deal of attention in the law of Israel.[1] Because they had lost the protection and support of their husbands, they were easy targets for economic and social abuse and exploitation. Many resorted to prostitution simply to survive, a situation all too common for vulnerable women in our day as well. Naomi had not only become a widow, but was also an alien in Moab. Yet, if she returned to Bethlehem with her daughters-in-law, the younger women would be widows and aliens in Israel.[2] Perhaps in response to the vulnerability they faced no matter where they might live, Naomi urged them to return to their maternal homes, and prayed that the God of Israel would grant each of them security within the household of a (Moabite) husband (Ruth 1:8–9). Yet one of the daughters-in-law, Ruth, could not bear to be separated from Naomi, no matter the hardship. Her words to Naomi sing the depth of her love and loyalty:

> "Do not press me to leave you or to turn back from following you! Where you go, I will go; where you lodge, I will lodge; your people shall be my people, and your God my God. Where you die, I will die—there will I be buried." (Ruth 1:16–17)

Life can be hard, and these women faced its worst.

---

[1] Deut. 10:18; 14:29; 16:11, 14; 24:19–22; 26:12–13; 27:19.

[2] On the difficulties of being a Moabite in an Israelite world, see Daniel I. Block, *Judges, Ruth,* vol. 6, The New American Commentary (Nashville: Broadman & Holman, 2002), 627.

God's Blessing Is the Source of Human Productivity (Ruth 2:1–4)

The Scriptures portray God as the divine Worker who provides a paradigm for human work. The Bible opens with a picture of God at work—speaking, creating, forming, building. Throughout the Hebrew Bible, not only does God appear as the subject of many "work" verbs, but people often refer to him metaphorically as "Worker." In the Exodus version of the Decalogue, the Sabbath command bases the 6 + 1 day pattern of work in Israel on the divine pattern (Exod. 20:9–11).

But in God, hardship is not hopelessness. Although the people of Israel had forsaken their covenant with him and experienced social and economic breakdown as a result, God remained faithful to his people. Long ago God had promised Abraham, "I will make you exceedingly fruitful; and I will make nations of you, and kings shall come from you" (Gen. 17:6). The Lord made good his promise by restoring Israel's agricultural productivity (Ruth 1:6), despite his people's unfaithfulness. When Naomi heard of it, she determined to return home to Bethlehem to try to find food. Ruth, true to her word, went with her, intending to find work to support both herself and Naomi. As the story unfolds, God's blessings pour out on the two of them—and ultimately on all humanity—through Ruth's work and its results.

God's Faithfulness to Us Underlies All Productivity

Although we encounter no obvious miraculous interventions in the book of Ruth, the hand of God is by no means absent. On the contrary, God is at work at every moment, especially through the actions of faithful people in the book. Throughout the Hebrew Bible, God not only engages in many kinds of work himself,[3] but he also commands the people of

---

[3] God creates (Gen. 1:1), builds (1 Sam. 2:35; 2 Sam. 7:27), makes (Gen. 2:4), forms (Gen. 2:7–8), and fashions "works of his hands" (Ps. 8:6). He is depicted as a creator (Gen. 1–2; Job 10:3–12; Ps. 139:13–16), builder, architect (Prov. 8:27–31), musician/composer (Deut. 31:19), metalworker (Isa. 1:24–26), tailor (Job 29:14; Isa. 40:22), potter (Isa. 31:9), farmer (Hos. 10:11), shepherd (Ps. 23; Ezek. 34), tentmaker/camper (Job 9:8), temple designer and builder (Exod. 25; 35; 1 Chr. 28:11–19), and scribe/writer (Exod. 24:12; 31:18; 34:28; etc.).

Israel to work according to the divine pattern (Exod. 20:9–11). That is, God works directly and God works through people.

The main characters acknowledge God as the foundation for their work by the way they bless each other and through their repeated declarations of faith.[4] Some of these expressions are praise for actions God has already taken (he has not withheld his kindness, Ruth 2:20; he provided a kinsman redeemer, Ruth 4:14). Others are pleas for divine blessing (Ruth 2:4, 19; 3:10), or presence (Ruth 2:4), or kindness (Ruth 1:8). A third group involves more specific requests for divine action. May God grant rest (Ruth 1:9). May God make Ruth an equal of Rachel and Leah (Ruth 4:11–12). The blessing in Ruth 2:12 is particularly significant: "May the LORD reward you for your deeds, and may you have a full reward from the LORD, the God of Israel, under whose wings you have come for refuge!" All of these blessings express the assurance that God is at work to provide for his people.

Ruth desired to receive God's blessing of productivity, whether from God himself (Ruth 2:12) or through a human being "in whose sight I might find favor" (Ruth 2:2). Despite being a Moabite, she was wiser than many in Israel when it came to recognizing the Lord's hand in her work.

For the action of the story, one of the most important blessings from God is that he had blessed Boaz with a productive farm (Ruth 2:3). Boaz was fully aware of God's role in his labor, as shown in his repeated invoking of the Lord's blessing (Ruth 2:4; 3:10).

God Uses Apparently Chance Events to Empower People's Work

One of the ways God fulfills his promise of fruitfulness is his mastery of the world's circumstances. The odd construction of "her chance chanced upon" (rendered, "as it happened" by the NRSV) in Ruth 2:3 is deliberate. In colloquial English, we would say, "As her luck would have it." But the statement is ironic. The narrator intentionally uses an expression that forces the reader to sit up and ask how it could be that Ruth "happened" to land in the field of a man who was not only gracious (Ruth 2:2) but also a kinsman (Ruth 2:1). As the story unfolds, we see that Ruth's arrival at Boaz's field was evidence of God's providential

---

[4] Ruth 1:8–9; 2:4, 12, 19 (without naming the Lord), 20; 3:10; 4:11–12, 14–15.

hand. The same can be said for the appearance of the next of kin just as Boaz sat down at the gate in Ruth 4:1–2.

What a dreary world it would be if we had to go to work every day expecting nothing except what we ourselves have the power to accomplish. We must depend on the work of others, the unexpected opportunity, the burst of creativity, the unforeseen blessing. Surely one of the most comforting blessings of following Christ is his promise that when we go to work, he goes to work alongside us and shoulders the load with us. "Take my yoke upon you . . . for my yoke is easy, and my burden is light" (Matt. 11:29–30). Ruth did not have the words of Jesus, but she lived in faith that under God's wings she would find all she needed (Ruth 2:12).

Human Productivity Is an Outgrowth of Our Faithfulness to God

God's faithfulness to Israel was mirrored in Ruth's faithfulness to Naomi. Ruth had promised, "Where you go I will go; where you lodge, I will lodge; your people shall be my people, and your God my God" (Ruth 1:16). Ruth's promise was not a plea to stay on as a passive consumer in what remained of Elimelech's household, but a commitment to provide for her mother-in-law as much as she was able. Although not an Israelite herself, she seems to have been living according to the law of Israel, as embodied in the fifth commandment, "Honor your mother and father." The restoration of productive work for her and her family began with her commitment to working in faithfulness to God's law.

God Bestows His Blessing of Productivity through Human Labor (Ruth 2:5–7)

Although God's faithfulness underlies human productivity, people have to do the actual work. This was God's intent from the beginning (Gen. 1:28; 2:5, 15). Ruth was eager to work hard to support herself and Naomi. "Let me go to the field," she implored, and when she was given a chance to work, her co-workers reported that "she has been on her feet from early this morning until now, without resting even for a moment" (Ruth 2:7). Her work was exceptionally productive. When she came home after her first day at work and beat out the barley from the stalks, her harvest yielded a full ephah of grain (Ruth 2:17). This amounted to approximately five gallons of barley.[5] Both God and Boaz commended (and rewarded) her for her faith and industry (Ruth 2:12, 17–23; 3:15–18).

To a greater or lesser degree, we are all vulnerable to circumstances that might make it difficult or impossible to earn a living. Natural disaster, layoff, redundancy, prejudice, injury, illness, bankruptcy, unfair treatment, legal restrictions, language barriers, lack of relevant training or experience, age, sex, economic mismanagement by government or industry, geographic barriers, getting fired, the need to take care of family members, and a host of other factors can prevent us from working to support ourselves and the people who depend on us. Nonetheless, God expects us to work as fully as we are able (Exod. 20:9).

Even if we cannot find a job that meets our needs, we need to work to the highest degree we can. Ruth did not have a steady job with regular hours and a paycheck. She was anxious about whether her station in life would be enough to find "favor" (Ruth 2:13) in the workplace, and she could not necessarily expect to earn enough to feed her family. She went to work anyway. Many of the conditions we face today in unemployment and underemployment are deeply discouraging. If the lack of high-skilled jobs leaves us only what seem like menial opportunities, if discrimination prevents us from getting the job we are qualified for, if circumstances prevent us from getting the education we need for a good job, if conditions make work seem hopeless, Ruth's example is that we are called to work nonetheless. Our work might not even earn any income at first, be it volunteering to help others, caring for family members, getting education or training, or caring for our homes.

The saving grace is that God is the power behind our work. We do not depend on our own ability or the circumstances around us to provide for our needs. Instead, we work faithfully as we are able, knowing that God's faithfulness to his promise of fruitfulness is what gives us confidence

---

[5] Jack B. Scott, "82 הָפִיא," in *Theological Wordbook of the Old Testament*, ed. R. Laird Harris, Gleason L. Archer Jr., and Bruce K. Waltke (Chicago: Moody Press, 1999), 38.

that our work is worthwhile, even in the most adverse situations. We are seldom able to see in advance how God can make use of our work to fulfill his promises, but God's power extends far beyond what we can see.

Receiving God's Blessing of Productivity Means Respecting Co-workers (Ruth 2:8–16)

As Ruth 2:1 relates, Boaz was "a prominent rich man." Whatever connotations that might have today, in Boaz's case it meant he was one of the best bosses in the Bible. His leadership style began with respect. When he came out to the field where his men were working, he greeted them with a blessing ("The Lord be with you"), and they responded in kind ("The Lord bless you," Ruth 2:4). Boaz's workplace was remarkable at many levels. He owned and managed an enterprise that depended on a hired workforce. He controlled the work environment of others. In contrast to many work environments where supervisors and owners treat their workers with disdain and workers have no respect for their bosses, Boaz had fostered a relationship of trust and mutual respect.

Boaz put his respect for his workers into practice by providing them with water as they worked (Ruth 2:9), by eating with them, and most of all by sharing his food with the person regarded as the lowest among them (Ruth 2:14). Later we learn that at harvest time, Boaz the landowner winnowed with his harvesters and slept with them out in the field (Ruth 3:2–4, 14).

Boaz demonstrated a high view of every human being as an image of God (Gen. 1:27; Prov. 14:31; 17:5) by the sensitive way he treated the alien woman in his workplace. When he spotted her among the workers, he asked gently, "To whom does this woman belong?" (Ruth 2:5), assuming she was attached to or dependent upon some man—either as wife or daughter—perhaps some landowner in the area. When he heard that she was a Moabite woman who had returned from Moab with Naomi (Ruth 2:6), and heard of her plea for permission to glean behind his harvesters (Ruth 2:7), shockingly, the first words he said were, "Listen carefully my daughter" (Ruth 2:8). Sharing his food with a foreign woman (Ruth 2:14) was a more significant act than it might appear. Respectable, landowning men were not accustomed to conversing with foreign women,[6] as Ruth herself points out (Ruth 2:10). A man with more concern for social appearances and business opportunities, and less compassion for someone in need, might have sent a female Moabite intruder off his land at once. But Boaz was more than willing to stand up for the vulnerable worker, whatever the reaction of others might be.

Indeed, with this account we may have encountered the world's earliest recorded anti-sexual harassment policy in the workplace. Perhaps he was aware that many farm owners and workers were abusive men,[7] and perhaps this is why he informed Ruth that he had told his men not to touch her (Ruth 2:9). Naomi's comment, "It is better, my daughter, that you go out with his young women, otherwise you might be bothered in another field" (Ruth 2:22), certainly shows that she feared for the safety of her daughter-in-law. The terms of Boaz's policy are clear:

1. The male workers were not to "bother" this woman. Normally the word *naga* means "to touch," but here it functions more generally as "to strike, harass, take advantage of, mistreat."[8] Boaz recognizes that the implication of being touched is determined by how the person being touched perceives it.

2. Ruth was to have equal access to water (Ruth 2:9) and to the lunch table (Ruth 2:14). At meal time, Boaz invited Ruth to come sit with him and his workers and to dip her morsel of bread in his sauce (Ruth 2:14). Then he himself served her until she was more than satisfied. The choice of the verb *nagash*, "to come near, approach," suggests that as a stranger Ruth had deliberately and appropriately (according to custom) kept her distance. Boaz's sexual harassment policy is not simply restrictive—prohibiting certain actions—but it is positive in its intent, meaning that the response of the one in danger of harassment is the gauge of what others

---

[6] Frederic W. Bush, *Ruth, Esther*, vol. 9, *Word Biblical Commentary* (Dallas: Word, 1998), 129.

[7] Daniel I. Block, "Unspeakable Crimes: The Abuse of Women in the Book of Judges," *The Southern Baptist Theological Journal* 2 (1998): 46–55.

[8] Block, *Judges, Ruth*, 659–60.

may do. Boaz looked to whether Ruth felt safe as the measure of whether he was offering the protection she needed. He demonstrated by example how he expected vulnerable female workers to be respected.

3. Boaz's regular employees were not to reproach (Ruth 2:15) or rebuke (Ruth 2:16) her. Along with the word *bother* in 2:9, these expressions demonstrate that harassment comes in many forms: physical, emotional, and verbal abuse. In fact, with his effusive pronouncement of blessing upon Ruth (Ruth 2:12), Boaz represents a dramatically affirming model.

4. The regular employees were to make Ruth's work environment as secure as possible and to go out of their way to assist her in achieving her work tasks (Ruth 2:15–16). In the workplace, prevention of harassment goes beyond creating a safe environment. It also entails elimination of barriers to productivity, advancement, and their attendant rewards. Boaz could have made Ruth safe by keeping her at a great distance from the male workers. But this would have denied her access to water and food, and might have caused loss of grain due to wind or animals before she could gather the sheaves. Boaz made sure that the safeguards he created enabled her to be fully productive.

Boaz's workers seemed to catch his generous spirit. When their boss greeted them with a blessing, they blessed him in return (Ruth 2:4). When Boaz asked about the identity of the woman who had appeared at his field, the supervisor of the workforce acknowledged that Ruth was a Moabite, but exhibited a gracious tone (Ruth 2:6–7). The fact that Ruth brought an entire ephah of grain home to Naomi testifies to the workers' positive response to Boaz's charge to treat Ruth well. Not only had they obviously cut a lot of grain for her, but they had also accepted this Moabite woman as a co-worker for the duration of the harvest (Ruth 2:21–23).

The positive effects of Boaz's leadership extended beyond the workplace. When Naomi saw the results of Ruth's efforts, she blessed the employer who had given her work and praised God for his kindness and generosity (Ruth 2:20). Later, it becomes obvious that Boaz's high reputation in the community brought social harmony and glory to God (Ruth 4:11–12). All leaders—indeed all workers—shape the culture in which they work. Although we may think we are constrained by our culture to conform to unfair, meaningless, or unproductive ways of working, in reality the way we work profoundly influences others. Boaz, a man of means in the midst of a corrupt and faithless society (Ruth 1:1, where "when the judges ruled" is shorthand for a corrupt society), succeeded in creating an honest, successful business. The harvest supervisor shaped egalitarian practices in a society rife with misogyny and racism (Judg. 19–21). In the face of great loss and hardship, Ruth and Naomi created a loving family. When we feel pressure to conform to a bad environment at work, the promise of God's faithfulness can overcome all the doubts we take on board from the cultural and social dysfunction around us.

God Calls People to Provide Opportunities for the Poor to Work Productively (Ruth 2:17–23)

The most important way God overcomes the barriers to our fruitfulness is through the actions of other people. In the book of Ruth, we see this both in God's law in society and in his guidance of individuals.

God's Law Calls People of Means to Provide Economic Opportunities for the Poor (Ruth 2:17–23)

The action of the book of Ruth centers on gleaning, which was one of the most important elements of the law for the protection of poor and vulnerable people. The requirements are laid out in Leviticus, Deuteronomy, and Exodus:

> When you reap the harvest of your land, you shall not reap to the very edges of your field, or gather the gleanings of your harvest. You shall not strip your vineyard bare, or gather the fallen grapes of your vineyard; you shall leave them for the poor and the alien: I am the LORD your God. (Lev. 19:9–10, repeated partly in Lev. 23:22; see Leviticus 19:9–10 in "Leviticus and Work" in the *Theology of Work Bible Commentary*.)

> When you reap your harvest in your field and forget a sheaf in the field,
> you shall not go back to get it; it shall be left for the alien, the orphan, and
> the widow, so that the LORD your God may bless you in all your undertak-
> ings. When you beat your olive trees, do not strip what is left; it shall be
> for the alien, the orphan, and the widow. When you gather the grapes
> of your vineyard, do not glean what is left; it shall be for the alien, the
> orphan, and the widow. Remember that you were a slave in the land of
> Egypt; therefore I am commanding you to do this. (Deut. 24:19–22)

> For six years you shall sow your land and gather in its yield; but the sev-
> enth year you shall let it rest and lie fallow, so that the poor of your people
> may eat; and what they leave the wild animals may eat. You shall do the
> same with your vineyard, and with your olive orchard.
> (Exod. 23:10–11; see Exodus 22:21–27 and 23:10–11 in "Exodus and
> Work" in the *Theology of Work Bible Commentary*.)

The basis of the law is the intention that all people are to have access to the means of production necessary to support themselves and
their families. In general, every family (except among the priestly tribe
of Levites, who were supported by tithes and offerings) was to have a
perpetual allotment of land that could never be alienated (Num. 27:5–11;
36:5–10; Deut. 19:14; 27:17; Lev. 25). Thus everyone in Israel would have
the means to grow food. But foreigners, widows, and orphans typically
would not inherit land, so they were vulnerable to poverty and abuse.
The gleaning law gave them the opportunity to provide for themselves by
harvesting the edges of the field, the grain and produce that were unripe
or missed during the initial harvest, and whatever sprang up in the fields
that lay fallow any given year. Access to gleaning was to be provided free
of charge by every landowner.

These passages suggest three grounds for the gleaning laws. Generosity toward the poor (1) was a prerequisite to God blessing the work
of peoples' hands (Deut. 24:19), (2) was to be driven by the memory
of Israel's experience under cruel and abusive slave masters in Egypt
(Deut. 24:22a), and (3) is a matter of obedience to the will of God (Deut.
24:22b). We see all three of these motivations in Boaz's actions: (1) he
blessed Ruth, (2) he remembered God's graciousness to Israel, and
(3) he commended her for placing herself in God's hands (Ruth 2:12).

Although it is an open question how fully the land and harvest laws were enforced in ancient Israel, Boaz kept them in exemplary fashion.

The gleaning laws provided a remarkable support network for poor and marginalized people, at least to the extent the laws were actually practiced. We have already seen that God's intention is for people to receive his fruitfulness by working. Gleaning did exactly this. It provided an opportunity for productive work for those who otherwise would have to depend on begging, slavery, prostitution, or other forms of degradation. Gleaners maintained the skills, self-respect, physical conditioning, and work habits that would make them productive in ordinary farming, should the opportunity of marriage, adoption, or return to their country of origin arise. Landowners provided opportunities but did not gain an opportunity for exploitation. There was no forced labor. The benefit was available locally, everywhere in the nation, without the need for a cumbersome and corruption-prone bureaucracy. It did, however, depend on the character formation of every landowner to fulfill the gleaning law, and we should not romanticize the circumstances poor people faced in ancient Israel.

In the case of Boaz, Ruth, and Naomi, the gleaning laws worked as intended. If it weren't for the possibility of gleaning, Boaz would have faced two alternatives once he became aware of Ruth and Naomi's poverty. He could let them starve, or he could have had ready-made food (bread) delivered to their house. The former is unacceptable, but the latter, while it may have alleviated their hunger, would have made them ever more dependent on Boaz. Because of the opportunity of gleaning, however, Ruth not only could work for the harvest, but she would also be able to use the grain to make bread through her own labors. The process preserved her dignity, made use of her skills and abilities, freed her and Naomi from long-term dependency, and made them less vulnerable to exploitation.

In today's social, political, and theological debates about poverty and private and public responses to it, these aspects of gleaning are well worth keeping in mind and debating vigorously. Christians disagree with each other about questions such as individual vs. social responsibilities, private vs. public means, and income distribution. Careful reflection on the book of Ruth is unlikely to resolve these disagreements, but perhaps it can highlight shared aims and common ground. Modern society may not be well suited to gleaning in the literal, agricultural sense, but are there aspects that can be incorporated into ways societies care for poor and vulnerable people today? In particular, how can we provide opportunities for people to gain access to the means of productive work rather than being smothered by dependency or exploitation?

God Leads Individuals to Provide Economic Opportunities for the Poor and Vulnerable (Ruth 2:17–23)

Boaz was inspired to go significantly beyond what the law required in providing for the poor and vulnerable. The gleaning laws merely required landowners to leave some produce in the fields for foreigners, orphans, and widows to glean. This generally meant the poor and vulnerable had difficult, dangerous, uncomfortable work, such as harvesting grain at the weedy edges of fields or high up in olive trees. The produce they obtained this way was usually of inferior quality, such as grapes and olives that had fallen to the ground or had not fully ripened. But Boaz tells his workers to be actively generous. They were to remove first-quality grain from the stalks they had cut, and leave them lying on top of the stubble so Ruth needed only to pick them up. Boaz's concern was not to minimally fulfill a regulation, but to genuinely provide for Ruth and her family.

Furthermore, he insisted that she glean in his fields (keeping what she harvested for herself and Naomi, of course) and attach herself to his workers. He not only gave her access to his fields, but he effectively made her one of his hired hands, even to the point of making sure she received a pro-rata share of the harvest (Ruth 2:16).

In a world in which every nation, every society, has under- and unemployed people in need of opportunities for work, how can Christians emulate Boaz? How can we encourage people to apply their God-given skills and talents to creating goods and services that employ people productively? How can we shape the character formation of people who own and manage society's resources so that they eagerly and creatively provide opportunities for the poor and marginalized?

How, indeed, do these questions apply to us? Is each of us a person of means, even if we are not rich like Boaz? Do middle-class people have the means and the responsibility to provide opportunities for poor people? How about poor people themselves? What might God be leading each of us to do to bring his blessing of fruitfulness to other workers and would-be workers?

God's Blessing Is Redoubled When People Work according to His Ways (Ruth 3:1–4:18)

In the episode of Ruth gleaning in Boaz's field, Boaz demonstrates compassion and generosity, while engaging in a remarkable example of ethnic reconciliation. This raises the questions, why was Boaz's heart so soft toward Ruth, and why would he create this environment where anyone, even an alien Moabite woman, would feel at home? According to Boaz's own testimony, Ruth embodied nobility and faithfulness to the true God (Ruth 3:10–11). As a result, he wished her to "have a full reward from the Lord, the God of Israel, under whose wings you have come for refuge" (Ruth 2:12). Born in Moab, she had nonetheless turned to the God of Israel for salvation (Ruth 1:16). Boaz recognized God's wings over her and was eager to be the instrument of God's blessing for her. By caring for a destitute foreigner, Boaz honored the God of Israel. In the words of the Israelite proverb: "Those who oppress the poor insult their Maker, but those who are kind to the needy honor him" (Prov. 14:31; see also Prov. 17:5). The Apostle Paul expressed this theme centuries later: "Whenever we have an opportunity, let us work for the good of all, and especially for those of the family of faith" (Gal. 6:10).

As the story progressed, Boaz began to see Ruth as more than an industrious worker and faithful daughter-in-law to Naomi. In time he spread the wings of his garment over Ruth (Ruth 3:9)—an apt metaphor for marriage, mirroring the love and commitment represented by the wings of God. There is a work-related aspect to this love story, for there was real estate involved. Naomi still had some claim to the land that belonged to her late husband, and according to Israelite law, his next of kin had the right to acquire the land and keep it in the family by marrying Naomi. Boaz, whom Naomi mentioned was a kinsman of her husband (Ruth 2:1), was actually second in line to this right. He informed the man who was next of kin of his right, but when the man learned that claiming the land meant he must also bring the Moabite Ruth into his household, he repudiated the right (Ruth 4:1–6).

In contrast, Boaz was pleased to be chosen by God to show favor to this woman, despite her being considered racially, economically, and socially inferior (Ruth 4:1–12). He exercised his right to redeem the property, not by wedding the elderly Naomi in a marriage of convenience, but with Naomi's permission by marrying Ruth in a match of love and respect. By marrying this Moabite woman, he fulfilled in his own way a bit of God's promise to Abraham that "by your offspring shall all the nations of the earth gain blessing" (Gen. 22:18). He also gained yet more property, which we may assume he managed as productively and generously as the property he already owned, foreshadowing Christ's words that "to those who have, more will be given" (Mark 4:25). As we will soon learn, it is entirely apt that Boaz served as a forerunner to Jesus. Along the way, the events of the story reveal still more about how God is at work in the world for good.

God Works through Human Boldness (Ruth 3:1–18)

In instigating the courtship between Boaz and Ruth, necessity once again led Naomi to move beyond the bounds of convention. She sent Ruth to Boaz's threshing floor in the middle of the night to "uncover his feet and lie down" (Ruth 3:4). Regardless of the meaning of "feet" in Ruth 3:4, 7, 8, 14—which may be a sexual euphemism[9]—the scheme Naomi concocted was suspicious from the standpoint of custom and morality, and it was fraught with danger. Ruth's preparations and the choice of location for the encounter suggested the actions of a prostitute. Under normal circumstances, if a self-respecting and morally noble man like Boaz, sleeping at the threshing floor, should wake up in the middle of the night and discover a woman beside him he would surely send her off, protesting that he had nothing to do with women like her. Ruth's request that Boaz marry her was similarly bold from the perspective of custom: a foreigner propositioning an Israelite; a woman propositioning a man;

---

[9] Block, *Judges, Ruth*, 683–88.

a young person propositioning an older person; a destitute field worker propositioning a rich landowner. But instead of taking offense at Ruth's forwardness, Boaz blessed her, praised her for her commitment to the well-being of her family, called her "my daughter," reassured her by telling her not to fear, promised to do whatever she asked, and pronounced her a noble woman (Ruth 3:10–13). This extraordinary reaction is best attributed to the inspiration of God filling his heart.

God Works through Legal Processes (Ruth 4:1–12)

Boaz accepted Ruth's request to marry her if her next of kin relinquished his right to do so. He wasted no time arranging for the legal resolution of the issue (Ruth 4:1–12). By now the reader knows that nothing in this book happens by chance, and when on the following day the next of kin happens to pass by the gate where Boaz had sat down, this too is attributable to the hand of God. If Ruth had been present for the legal proceedings in the gate, her heart would have sunk as the man with first rights announced he would claim Elimelech's land. However, when Boaz reminded him that Ruth goes with the land, and he consequently changed his mind, her hope would have risen. What accounted for his change of mind? He said that he had just remembered a contravening legal obligation: "I cannot redeem it for myself without damaging my own inheritance" (Ruth 4:6). The excuse was garbled and feeble, yet it was enough for Boaz, whose speech of acceptance of the verdict is a model of clarity and logic. The case could easily have gone the other way, but it appears that the outcome was guided by God from the beginning.

God Works through the Fruitfulness of Childbearing (Ruth 4:13–18)

In Ruth 4:13, we encounter only the second instance in the book (in addition to Ruth 1:6) where an event is expressly attributed to the hand of God. "When they [Ruth and Boaz] came together, the LORD made her conceive, and she bore a son." While the Hebrew term for conception/pregnancy (*herayon*) occurs elsewhere only in Genesis 3:16 and Hosea

9:11, the particular idiom "to grant/give conception" occurs only here. We should interpret this statement against the backdrop of Ruth's apparently childless ten-year marriage with Mahlon (Ruth 1:4). After Ruth's faithfulness in coming to Israel with Naomi, after Boaz's faithfulness in providing for Ruth to glean his fields, and his faithfulness in serving as her kinsman-redeemer, after the faithful prayer of the witnesses in the gate (Ruth 4:11–12), and apparently as soon as Ruth and Boaz consummated the marriage, God conceived in Ruth a child. All human effort, even sexual intercourse, depends on God for the achievement of intended or desired goals (Ruth 4:13–15; cf. 1:4).

The birth of any child is a gift from God, but there was a bigger story in the birth of Ruth and Boaz's son, Obed. He would become the grandfather of David, Israel's greatest king (Ruth 4:22), and ultimately the ancestor of Jesus the Messiah (Matt. 1:5, 16–17). In this way the foreigner Ruth became a blessing to Israel and to everyone who follows Jesus to this day.

Conclusions from Ruth

The book of Ruth presents a powerful story of God at work, directing events from all sides to take care of his people, and more importantly to accomplish his purposes. Faithfulness—both God's faithfulness to people and people's faithfulness to God—is enacted through work and its resulting fruitfulness. The characters in the book work diligently, justly, generously, ingeniously, in accordance with God's law and inspiration. They recognize the image of God in human beings, and they work together in harmony and compassion.

From the events in the book of Ruth, we can conclude that Christians today must recognize not only the dignity, but also the value of work. Work brings glory to God. It brings benefits to others. It serves the world in which we live. As Christians today we may be accustomed to recognizing God's hand most clearly in the work of pastors, missionaries, and evangelists, but theirs is not the only legitimate work in the kingdom of God. The book of Ruth reminds us that ordinary work such as agriculture is a faith-filled calling, whether it is performed by wealthy landowners or poverty-stricken foreigners. Feeding our families is holy work, and anyone who has the means to help others feed their families becomes a blessing from God. Every legitimate occupation is God's work. Through us God makes, designs, organizes, beautifies, helps, leads, cultivates, cares, heals, empowers, informs, decorates, teaches, and loves. We are the wings of God.

Our work honors God when we treat co-workers with honor and dignity, whether we have the power to shape others' working conditions or whether we put ourselves at risk by standing up for others. We live out our covenant with God when we work for the good of our fellow human beings—especially the socially and economically marginalized. We honor God when we seek others' interests and do everything in our power to humanize their work and advance their well-being.

Samuel, Kings, Chronicles and Work

Introduction to Samuel, Kings, and Chronicles

The books of 1 & 2 Samuel, 1 & 2 Kings, and 1 & 2 Chronicles take a deep interest in work. Their predominant interest is in the work of kings, including political, military, economic, and religious aspects. Governing, in the form of "having dominion," is one of the tasks God gave human beings at the very beginning (Gen. 1:28), and leadership, or governance, issues take center stage in 1 & 2 Samuel, 1 & 2 Kings, and 1 & 2 Chronicles. How should the Israelites be governed, by whom, and for what purposes? When organizations are governed well, people thrive. When good governance is violated, everyone suffers.

But kings are not the only people we see at work in these books. First of all, the work of kings affects the work of many others—such as soldiers, builders, craftspeople, and priests—and the books of Samuel, Kings, and Chronicles pay attention to how the kings' work affects these other workers. Second, kings themselves have work other than ruling, of which parenting is of particular interest in these books. Finally, as histories of Israel, these books take an interest in the people as a whole, and in many cases this means recounting the work of people not connected to the work of kingship.

Following the lead of the books themselves, we will pay greatest attention to the leadership and governance tasks of the kings of Israel, while also exploring the many other kinds of workers depicted. Included among these are soldiers and commanders, judges and civic leaders (often called "elders"), parents, shepherds, farmers, cooks and bakers, perfumers, vineyard keepers, musicians and artists, inventors, entrepreneurs, diplomats (both formal and informal), protesters or activists, political advisers, artisans and craftspeople, architects, supervisors, stonemasons, bricklayers, metal workers, carpenters, armorers, well-keepers, oil dealers, healers, slave girls, messengers, lumberjacks, and accountants. Prophets and priests are also included, although in keeping with the Theology of Work Project's focus on nonreligious work, we will limit ourselves to their role in work outside the religious sphere. They actually play a significant role in political, military, and economic affairs, as we shall see.

Virtually every kind of worker today either is represented in the books of Samuel, Kings, and Chronicles, or can find practical applications to their work in them. Generally speaking, we will discover how good governance and leadership apply to our work, rather than finding instructions about how to do our particular jobs—unless governance or leadership *is* our job.

The Historical Background of Samuel, Kings, and Chronicles

The overarching interest of the books is the work of the king as Israel becomes a monarchy. They begin at a time when the twelve tribes of Israel had long been violating the rules, ethical principles, goals, and virtues of leadership that God laid out for them, which can be found in the books of Genesis through Deuteronomy. After almost two hundred years of increasingly bad governance by a succession of "judges" (temporary leaders), Israel is in shambles. Samuel, Kings, and Chronicles narrate God's intervention in Israel's governance as his people move from a failing tribal confederation to a promising monarchy, which declines into failure as succeeding generations of kings abandon God and his ways. Regrettably, the story ends with destruction of Israel as a nation, never to be restored during the biblical period.

This may not seem like a promising backdrop for a study of governance, but God's guidance is always in evidence in the narrative, whether people choose to follow it or not. Reading the story thousands of years later, we can learn both from their success and their failures.

The books' fundamental theological position is that if the king is faithful to God, then the nation thrives economically, socially, and militarily. If the king is faithless, then national catastrophe ensues. So the history of God's people is told primarily through the actions of top governmental leaders, to use modern terms. Yet governance is needed in every sort of community or institution, whether political, civic, business, nonprofit, academic, or anything else. The lessons of the books apply to governance in all sectors of society today. These books offer a rich study of leadership, demonstrating how the livelihood of many depends on what leaders do and say.

Scholars believe that, originally, each pair of books (1 & 2 Samuel, 1 & 2 Kings, and 1 & 2 Chronicles) was a single entity split between two scrolls. The scrolls of Samuel and Kings form an integrated political history of the Israelite monarchies. Chronicles tells the same history as Kings, but with a focus on the priestly or worship aspects of Hebrew history. We will follow the narrative as in three acts: (1) From Tribal Confederation to Monarchy, (2) Monarchy's Golden Age, and (3) From Failed Monarchies to Exile.

From Tribal Confederation to Monarchy (1 Samuel)

The first book of Samuel marks the transition of Israel from a fractious coalition of tribes to a monarchy with a central government in Jerusalem. The story begins with the birth and calling of the prophet Samuel and continues with the call to kingship and the reigns of Saul and David. This is the story of state formation, the centralization of power and worship, and the establishment of a new political, military, and social order.

The Perils of Inherited Authority (1 Samuel 1–3)

From the closing words of the book of Judges and the opening chapters of 1 Samuel we know that the Israelites are both leaderless and disconnected from God. The closest thing they have to a national leader is the priest Eli, who with his sons runs the shrine at Shiloh. The Israelites' political, military, and economic prosperity depends on their faithfulness to God. So the people bring their offerings and sacrifices to God at the shrine, but the priests make a mockery of interaction with God. "Now the sons of Eli were scoundrels . . . for they treated the offerings of the Lord with contempt" (1 Sam. 2:12, 17). They are untrustworthy as human leaders, and they do not honor God in their hearts. Worshipers find that those who should direct them toward an experience of worship are instead stealing from them.

Somewhat ominously for a nation about to become a monarchy, the first thing we observe is that inherited authority is inherently dangerous for two reasons. The first is that there is no guarantee that descendants of even the greatest leader will be competent and faithful. The second is that being born to power is often a corrupting influence itself, resulting all too often either in complaisance or—as the case of Eli's sons— entitlement. The work of the priest is a sacred charge from God, but Eli's sons see it as a personal possession (1 Sam. 2:12–17). Growing up in an atmosphere somewhat analogous to a family business, they expect from a young age to inherit their father's privileges. Because this "family business" is God's own shrine—giving the family a claim to divine authority over the populace—Eli's sons' malfeasance is all the more injurious.

Family businesses and political dynasties in today's world have parallels to Eli's situation. The founder of the business or polity may have brought great good into the world, but if the heirs view it as a means for personal gain, then those whom they are meant to serve suffer harm. Everyone wins when founders and their successors are faithful to the original, good purpose. The world is a better place, the business and community thrive, and the family is well provisioned. But when the original purpose is neglected or corrupted, the business or community suffers, and the organization and the family are in jeopardy.

The sad history of inherited power in governments, churches, businesses, and other organizations warns us that those who expect to receive power as a right often sense no need to develop the skill, self-discipline, and attitude of service needed to be good leaders. This reality perplexed the Teacher of Ecclesiastes. "I hated all my toil in which I had toiled under the sun, seeing that I must leave it to those who come after me—and who knows whether they will be wise or foolish? Yet they will be master of all for which I toiled and used my wisdom under the sun" (Eccl. 2:18–19). What was true for him is true for us today. Families that gain wealth and power from the success of an entrepreneur in one generation often lose these gains by the third generation and also suffer devastating family quarrels and personal misfortunes.[1] This is not to say that inherited power or wealth always leads to poor outcomes, but that inheritance is a dangerous policy for governance. Families, organizations, or governments that do pass authority via inheritance will do well to develop a multiplicity of means to counteract the perils that inheritance entails. There are consultancies and organizations that specialize in supporting families and businesses in inheritance situations.

If not his scoundrel sons, who would succeed Eli as priest? First Samuel 3:1–4:1 and 7:3, 17 reveal God's plan to raise up young Samuel to succeed Eli. Samuel receives one of the few audible calls from God recorded in the Bible, but notice that this is *not* a call to a type of work or ministry. (Samuel had been serving in the house of the Lord since he was two or three years old, and the choice of occupation had been made by his mother. See 1 Sam. 1:20–28 and 2:18–21.) Nonetheless it is a call to a task, namely, to tell Eli that God has decided to punish him and his sons, who are soon to be removed as God's priests. After fulfilling this calling, Samuel continues to serve under Eli until he is recognized as a prophet in his own right (1 Sam. 4:1) and succeeds Eli after Eli's death (1 Sam. 4:18). Samuel becomes the leader of God's people, not because of self-serving ambition or a sense of entitlement, but because God had given him a vision (1 Sam. 3:10–14) and the gifts and skills to lead people to carry out that vision (1 Sam. 3:19–4:1). (See *Vocation Overview* for more on the topic of calling to work at www.theologyofwork.org.)

The Perils of Treating God Like a Good Luck Charm (1 Samuel 4)

It's not clear whether the corruption of the leader, Eli, causes the corruption of the people or vice versa, but chapters 4 through 6 depict the disaster that befalls those who are poorly governed. Israel has been engaged in a centuries-long struggle against the neighboring country of the Philistines. A new attack is made by the Philistines, which routs the Israelites, resulting in 4,000 casualties (1 Sam. 4:1–3). The Israelites recognize the defeat as a sign of God's disfavor. But instead of examining

---

[1] "Lost Inheritance," Missy Sullivan, *Wall Street Journal Money*, March 8, 2012, http://online.wsj.com/news/articles/SB10001424127887324662404578 334663271139552.

their fault, repenting, and coming to the Lord for guidance, they try to manipulate God into serving their purposes. They fetch the ark of the covenant of God and charge into battle against the Philistines, assuming that the ark will make them invincible. Eli's sons lend an aura of authority to the plan. But the Philistines slaughter Israel in the battle, killing 30,000 Israelite soldiers, capturing the ark, slaying Eli's sons, and causing Eli's own death (1 Sam. 4:4–19).

Eli's sons, alongside the leaders of the army, made the mistake of thinking that because they bore the name of God's people and possessed the symbols of God's presence they were in command of God's power. Perhaps those in charge believed they could actually control God's power by carrying around the ark. Or maybe they had deceived themselves into thinking that because they were God's people, whatever they wanted for themselves would be what God wanted for them. In any case, they discovered that God's presence is not a warrant to project God's power, but an invitation to receive God's guidance. Ironically, the ark contained the greatest means of God's guidance—the Ten Commandments (Deut. 10:5)—but Eli's sons did not bother to seek any kind of guidance from God before attacking the Philistines.

Can it be that we often fall into the same bad habit in our work? When we are faced with opposition or difficulty in our work, do we seek God's guidance in prayer or do we just throw up a quick prayer assuming that God will do whatever we want God to do? Do we consider the possible courses of action in the light of Scripture, or do we just keep a Bible on our desk? Do we examine our motivations and assess our actions with openness to transformation by God, or do we simply decorate ourselves with Christian symbols? If our work seems unfulfilling or our careers are not progressing as we hope, is it possible that we are using God as a good luck charm, rather than following him as the master of our work?

The Opportunities That Arise from Working Faithfully (1 Samuel 5–7)

The Philistines fare no better with the ark than the Israelites did, and it becomes dangerous property for both sides until it is retired from military use. Then Samuel calls Israel to recommit themselves to the Lord himself (1 Sam. 5:1–7:3). The people heed his call and turn back to worshipping the Lord, and Samuel's career expands rapidly. His role as priest soon grows to "judge" (meaning a military governor), and he leads the successful defense against the Philistines (1 Sam. 7:4–13). His role soon encompasses holding court for legal matters (1 Sam. 7:16). Behind all his tasks lies his calling to be "a trustworthy prophet of the Lord" (1 Sam. 3:20).

Skilled, dependable workers who are true to God's ways often find their work overflowing their job descriptions. In the face of ever-expanding responsibilities, Samuel's response is not "That's not my job." Instead, he sees the crucial needs in front of him, recognizes that he has the capacity to meet them, and steps in to resolve them. As he does so, God increases his authority and effectiveness to match his willingness.

One lesson we might take from this is to respond to God with a willingness to serve as Samuel did. Do you see opportunities in front of you at work that, strictly speaking, don't fit your job description? Do your supervisors or colleagues seem to expect you to take further responsibility in areas that aren't formally part of your job? These are often chances for growth, development, and advancement (unless your supervisors do *not* appreciate your taking on additional responsibility). What would it take for you to step forward into these opportunities? Similarly, you may see needs around you that you could help meet if you had the trust and courage to respond. What would it take to develop your trust in God and to receive the courage needed to follow his leading?

The final account of Samuel's governance (1 Sam. 7:15–17) says that he went on a circuit of the cities of Israel year by year, governing and administering justice. The chapter closes with, "And [he] built there an altar to the Lord." His civic and military services to Israel were founded on his lifelong faithfulness and worship of the Lord.

When Children Disappoint (1 Samuel 8:1–3)

As Samuel ages, he repeats Eli's error and appoints his own sons to succeed him. Like Eli's sons, they turn out to be greedy and corrupt (1 Sam. 8:1–3). Disappointing sons of great leaders is a recurrent theme in Samuel and Kings. (The tragedy of David's son Absalom occupies the bulk of 2 Samuel chapters 13–19, to which we will return. See

"David's Dysfunctional Handling of Family Conflict Leads to Civil War" in 2 Samuel 13–19.) It reminds us that the work of parenting is as challenging as every other occupation, but far more emotionally intense. No solution is given in the text, but we can observe that Eli, Samuel, and David seem to have given their troubled children many privileges but little paternal involvement. Yet we also know that even the most dedicated parents may face the heartbreak of wayward children. Rather than laying blame or stereotyping causes, let us simply note that parenting children is an occupation requiring as much prayer, skill, community support, good fortune, and love as any other, if not more. Ultimately, to be a parent—whether our children bring delight, disappointment, or some of both—is to depend on God's grace and mercy and to hope for God's redemption beyond what we see during our lifetimes. Perhaps our deepest comfort is to remember that God also experienced a parent's heartbreak for his condemned Son, yet he overcame all through the power of love.

The Israelites Ask for a King (1 Samuel 8:4–22)

Seeing the unsuitability of Samuel's sons, the Israelites ask him to "appoint for us, then, a king to govern us, like other nations." This request displeases Samuel (1 Sam. 8:4–6). Samuel warns the people that kings lay heavy burdens on a nation.

> "These will be the ways of the king who will reign over you: he will take your sons and appoint them to his chariots and to be his horsemen to run before his chariots; and he will appoint for himself commanders of thousands and commanders of fifties, and some to plow his ground and to reap his harvest, and make his implements of war and the equipment of his chariots. He will take your daughters to be perfumers and cooks and bakers. He will take the best of your fields and vineyards and olive orchards and give them to his courtiers." (1 Sam. 8:11–14)

In fact, the kings would be so rapacious that eventually the people would cry out to God to save them from the kings (1 Sam. 8:18).

God agrees that asking for a king is a bad idea because it amounts to a rejection of God himself as king. Nonetheless, the Lord decides to allow the people to choose their form of government, and he tells Samuel, "Listen to the voice of the people in all that they say to you; for they have not rejected you, but they have rejected me from being king over them" (1 Sam. 8:7). As biblical scholar John Goldingay notes, "God starts with his people where they are; if they cannot cope with his highest way, he carves out a lower one. When they do not respond to the spirit of Yahweh or when all sorts of spirits lead them into anarchy, he provides . . . the institutional safeguard of earthly rulers." Sometimes God permits institutions that are not part of his eternal purpose, and the monarchy of Israel is one of the most glaring examples.

Both God and Samuel showed great humility, resilience, and grace in allowing Israel to make choices and mistakes, learning from the consequences. There are many institutional and workplace situations where leadership must adjust to people's poor choices, yet at the same time try to provide opportunities for growth and grace. Samuel's warning to Israel could easily serve as a warning today to nations, businesses, churches, schools, and other organizations. In our fallen world, people abuse power, and we have to adjust while at the same time doing what we can to change things. Our aspiration is to love God and treat other people as God commands in the law given to Moses, which God's people have had an extremely hard time doing in every age.

The Task of Choosing a King (1 Samuel 9–16)

Saul Chosen as Israel's First King

God's first choice to be king was Saul (c. 1050–1010 BC), someone who looked the part—he literally stood "head and shoulders above everyone else" (1 Sam. 9:2). Furthermore, he won military victories, the main reason for having a king in the first place (1 Sam. 11:1–11). In the beginning, he served faithfully (1 Sam. 11:13–14), but he quickly became disobedient to God (1 Sam. 13:8–15) and arrogant with his people (1 Sam. 14:24–30). Both Samuel and God became exasperated with him and began to look for his replacement (1 Sam. 16:1). But before we measure Saul's actions against twenty-first-century leadership expectations, we should note that Saul simply did what kings did in the ancient Near

East. The people got what they asked for (and what Samuel had warned against)—a militaristic, charismatic, self-aggrandizing tyrant.

How are we to evaluate Israel's first king? Did God make a mistake in leading Samuel to anoint young Saul as king? Or was the choice of Saul an object lesson to the Israelites not to be seduced by outward appearances, handsome on the outside but hollow on the inside? In asking for a king, the Israelites showed their lack of faith in God. The king they received ultimately demonstrated that same lack of faith in God. Saul's primary task as king was to assure security for the Israelites from attack by the neighboring Philistines and other nations. But when faced with Goliath, Saul's fear overcame his faith and he proved unequal to his role (1 Sam. 17:11). Throughout his reign Saul similarly doubted God, seeking counsel in the wrong places, and finally dying by suicide as the enemy routed his army (1 Sam. 31:4).

David Chosen to Succeed Saul

As Samuel searches for Saul's replacement, he nearly makes the mistake of judging by appearances a second time (1 Sam. 16:6–7). The boy David seems inconsequential to Samuel, but with God's help, Samuel finally recognizes in David God's choice for Israel's king. On the surface David does not project the image of gravitas that people expect in a leader (1 Sam. 16:6–11). A little later in the story, the Philistine giant Goliath is similarly dismissive (1 Sam. 17:42). David is a nontraditional candidate for reasons beyond his youth. He is a last son in a society based on primacy of the firstborn. Moreover, he is ethnically mixed, not of pure Israelite descent, because one of his great-grandmothers was Ruth (Ruth 4:21–22), an immigrant from the kingdom of Moab (Ruth 1:1–4). Though David has several strikes against him, God sees great promise in him.

As we think about leadership selection today, it is valuable to remember God's word to Samuel: "The Lord does not see as mortals see: they look on the outward appearance, but the Lord looks on the heart" (1 Sam. 16:7). In God's upside-down kingdom, the last or the overlooked may end up being the best choice. The best leader may be the one nobody is looking for. It can be tempting to jump at the initially impressive candidate, the one who oozes charisma, the person that other people seem to want to follow. But high self-confidence actually leads to lower performance,

according to a 2012 *Harvard Business Review* article.[2] Charisma is not
what God values. Character is. What would it take to learn to see a person's character through God's eyes?

It is significant that David is out doing his job as shepherd, consci-
entiously caring for his father's sheep, when Samuel finds him. Faithful
performance in the job at hand is good preparation for a bigger job, as in
David's case (1 Sam. 17:34–37; see also Luke 16:10; 19:17). Samuel soon
discovers that David is the strong, confident, and competent leader the
people craved, who would "go out before us and fight our battles" (1 Sam.
8:20). Throughout his career David keeps in mind that he is serving at
God's pleasure to care for God's people (2 Sam. 6:21). God calls him "a
man after my heart" (Acts 13:22).

David's Rise to Power (1 Samuel 17–30)

Unlike Saul who had begun his reign soon after Samuel anointed him
(1 Sam. 11:1), David has a long and difficult apprenticeship before he is
acclaimed as king at Hebron. His first public success comes in slaying
the giant Goliath, who is threatening Israel's military security. As the
army returns home, a throng of women begin singing, "Saul has killed
his thousands and David his ten thousands" (1 Sam. 18:7). This enrages
Saul (1 Sam. 18:8). Rather than recognizing how both he and the nation
can benefit from David's capabilities, he regards David as a threat. He decides to eliminate David at the earliest opportunity (1 Sam. 18:9–13). Thus
begins a rivalry that eventually forces David to flee for his life, eluding Saul
while leading a band of brigands in the wildernesses of Judah for ten years.

When given opportunities to assassinate King Saul, David refuses,
knowing that the throne is not his to take. It is God's to give. As the
Psalms express it, "It is God who executes judgment, putting down one
and lifting up another" (Ps. 75:7). David respects the authority God has
given Saul even when Saul acts in dishonorable ways. This seems like
a lesson for those today who work for difficult bosses or are waiting to
be acknowledged for their leadership. Even if we sense we are called by

---

[2] Tomas Chamorro-Premuzic, "Less-Confident People Are More Successful," *Harvard Business Review*, July 6, 2012, http://blogs.hbr.org/2012/07/
less-confident-people-are-more-su/.

God to a particular task or position, this does not authorize us to grasp power by contravening the existing authorities. If everyone who thought God wanted them to be the boss tried to hasten the process by seizing power on their own, every succession of authority would bring little more than chaos. God is patient, and we are also to be patient, as David was.

Can we trust God to give us the authority we need, in his time, to do the work he wants us to do? In the workplace, having more authority is valuable for getting necessary work done. Grasping at that authority prematurely by undercutting a boss or by pushing a colleague out of the way does not build trust with colleagues or demonstrate trust in God. At times it can be frustrating when it seems it's taking too long for the needed authority to come your way, but true authority cannot be grasped, only granted. David was willing to wait until God placed that authority in his hands.

Abigail Defuses a Crisis between David and Nabal (1 Samuel 25)

As David's power grows, he comes into conflict with a rich landowner named Nabal. As it happens, David's band of rebels against Saul's rule has been encamped in Nabal's area for some time. David's men have treated Nabal's shepherds kindly, protecting them from harm or at the very least not stealing anything themselves (1 Sam. 25:15–16). David figures this means Nabal owes him something, and he sends a delegation to ask Nabal to donate some lambs for a feast for David's army. Perhaps realizing the weakness of his claim, David instructs his delegation to be extra polite to Nabal.

Nabal will have nothing of it. Not only he does he refuse to give David anything for the feast, he insults David publicly, denies knowing David, and impugns David's integrity as a rebel against Saul (1 Sam. 25:10). Nabal's own servants describe their master as "so ill-natured that no one can speak to him." David immediately sets out with four hundred armed men to slay Nabal and kill every male in his household.

Suddenly, David is about to commit mass murder, while Nabal cares more about his pride than about his workers and family. These two arrogant men are unable to resolve an argument about sheep without spilling the blood of hundreds of innocent people. Thank God that Nabal's wisehearted wife Abigail steps into the fray. She quickly prepares a feast for

David and his men, then rides out to meet David with an apology that sets a new standard for courtesy in the Old Testament (1 Sam. 25:26–31). Yet wrapped in the courteous words are some hard truths David needs to hear. He is on the verge of shedding blood without cause, bringing on himself a guilt he could never escape. David is moved by her words and abandons his plan to kill Nabal and all his men and boys. He even thanks Abigail for diverting him from his reckless plan.

> "Blessed be your good sense, and blessed be you, who have kept me today from bloodguilt and from avenging myself by my own hand! For as surely as the LORD the God of Israel lives, who has restrained me from hurting you, unless you had hurried and come to meet me, truly by morning there would not have been left to Nabal so much as one male."
> (1 Sam. 25:33–34)

This incident shows that people need to hold their leaders accountable, although doing so may come at the cost of great personal risk. You don't have to have authority status to be called to exercise influence. But you do need courage, which fortunately is something you can receive from God at any time.

Abigail's intervention also demonstrates that showing respect, even while making a pointed criticism, provides a model for challenging authority. Nabal turned a petty argument into a life-threatening situation by wrapping a minor dispute in a personal insult. Abigail resolves a life-threatening crisis by dressing a major rebuke in respectful dialogue.

In what ways may God be calling you to exercise influence to hold people in positions of higher authority accountable? How can you cultivate a godly attitude of respect along with an unwavering commitment to telling the truth? What courage do you need from God to actually do it?

The Golden Age of the Monarchy (2 Samuel 1–24; 1 Kings 1–11; 1 Chronicles 21–25)

After Saul's death, David is anointed king over the southern tribe of Judah, but not until much blood has been shed is David finally anointed king over all Israel (2 Sam. 5:1–10). When David comes into his own, he invests his talent in developing others. Contrary to Saul's fears of a rival, David surrounds himself with a company whose exploits rival his own (2 Sam. 23:8–39; 1 Chr. 11:10–47). He honors them (1 Chr. 11:19), encourages their fame, and promotes them (1 Chr. 11:25). God uses David's willingness to sponsor and encourage people to build David's own success and to bless the people of his realm.

At last, the loose confederacy of Israelite tribes has come together as a nation. For eighty years, under the rule first of David (c. 1010–970 BC) and then of his son Solomon (c. 970–931 BC), Israel experiences a golden age of prosperity and renown among all the nations of the ancient Near East. But amid their successes, these two rulers also violate God's covenant. While this does only limited damage in their own times, it sets a pattern for those who come after them to turn away from the Lord and abandon his covenant.

David's Successes and Failures as King (2 Samuel 1–24)

The Bible regards David as the model king of Israel, and the books of Samuel, Kings, and Chronicles describe his many successes. Yet even David, "a man after [God's] own heart" (1 Sam. 13:14), abuses his power and acts faithlessly at times. He tends to succeed when he does not take himself too seriously, but gets into serious trouble when power goes to his head—for example, when he takes a census in violation of God's command (2 Sam. 24:10–17), or when he sexually exploits Bathsheba and orders the assassination of her husband, Uriah (2 Sam. 11:2–17). Yet despite David's failings, God fulfills his covenant with David and treats him with mercy.

David's Dysfunctional Handling of Family Conflict Leads to Civil War (2 Samuel 13–19)

Most people feel uncomfortable in situations of conflict, so we tend to avoid facing conflict, whether at home or at work. But conflicts are a lot like illnesses. Minor ones may clear up even if we ignore them, but major ones will work their way deeper and more catastrophically into our systems if we do not treat them. This is true for David's family. David allows conflict among some of his sons to plunge his family into tragedy. His oldest son, Amnon, rapes and then shames his half-sister,

Tamar (2 Sam. 13:1–19). Tamar's full-brother, Absalom, hates Amnon for that crime, but does not speak to him about it. David knows of the matter but decides to ignore the situation (2 Sam. 13:21). (For more on children who disappoint their parents, see "When Children Disappoint" in 1 Samuel 8:1–3.)

For two years everything seems fine, but unresolved conflict of this magnitude never fades away. When Amnon and Absalom take a trip into the country together, Absalom plies his half-brother with wine, and then has his servants murder him (2 Sam. 13:28–29). The conflict draws in more of David's family, the nobles, and the army, until the entire nation is engulfed in civil war. The destruction brought about by avoiding the conflict is many times worse than the unpleasantness that might have resulted from dealing with the issues when they first arose.

Harvard professors Ronald Heifetz and Marty Linsky describe how leaders must "orchestrate conflict," face conflict squarely, rather than seeking to ignore, avoid, or suppress it. Otherwise, it will boil up on its own—usually at the worst time and in the most disruptive way—to thwart their goals and endanger their organizations.[3] Likewise, Jim Collins gives the example of Alan Iverson, who was CEO of Nucor Steel at a time when there were deep divisions about whether the company should diversify into scrap steel recycling. Iverson brought the divisions into the open by allowing everyone to speak their opinion, protecting them from reprisal from others who might disagree. The "raging debates" that ensued were uncomfortable for everyone. "People yelled. They waved their arms around and pounded on tables. Faces would get red and veins bulged out." But acknowledging the conflict and working through it openly prevented it from going underground and exploding later. Moreover, bringing out a variety of facts and opinions led to better decisions by the group. "Colleagues would march into Iverson's office and yell and scream at each other, but then emerge with a conclusion. . . . The company's strategy 'evolved through many agonizing arguments and fights.' "[4] Conflict well-orchestrated can actually be a source of creativity.

---

[3] Ronald A. Heifetz and Martin Linsky, *Leadership on the Line: Staying Alive through the Dangers of Leading* (Boston: Harvard Business Review Press, 2002), 101–22.

[4] Jim Collins, *Good to Great* (New York: Harper Business, 2001), 76.

David's Disobedience to God Causes a National Pestilence (1 Chronicles 21:1–17)

David also suffers another failure that, to us in the twenty-first century, may seem strange—he takes a census of the people of Israel. Although this seems like a prudent thing to do, the biblical text tells us that Satan incited David to do this, against the advice of David's general Joab. Furthermore, "God was displeased with this thing, and he struck Israel" (1 Chr. 21:7).

David acknowledges his sin in taking a census against God's will. He's given three choices, each of which would harm many in the kingdom: (1) three years of famine, (2) three months of devastation by the sword of his enemies, or (3) three days of a pestilence on the land. David chooses the third option, and seventy thousand people die as an angel of death passes through the land. At this David cries out to God, "Was it not I who gave the command to count the people? It is I who have sinned and done very wickedly. But these sheep, what have they done? Let your hand, I pray, O Lord my God, be against me and against my father's house; but do not let your people be plagued!" (1 Chr. 21:17).

Like David, we probably find it hard to understand why God would punish 70,000 other people for David's sin. The text does not give an answer. We can observe, however, that the transgressions of leaders inevitably harm their people. If business leaders make poor product development decisions, then people in their organization will lose their jobs when revenues plunge. If a restaurant manager doesn't enforce sanitation rules, then diners will get sick. If a teacher gives good grades for poor work, then students will fail or fall behind at the next level of education. Those who accept positions of leadership cannot evade responsibility for the effects of their actions on others.

David's Patronage of the Musical Arts (1 Chronicles 25)

First Chronicles adds a detail not found in 2 Samuel and 1 Kings. David creates a corps of musicians "to make music at the house of the Lord."

> They were all under the direction of their father for the music in the house of the LORD with cymbals, harps, and lyres for the service of the house of

God. Asaph, Jeduthun, and Heman were under the order of the king. They and their kindred, who were trained in singing to the LORD, all of whom were skillful, numbered two hundred eighty-eight. (1 Chr. 25:6–7)

Maintaining an ensemble the size of two modern symphony orchestras would be a major undertaking in an emerging nation in the tenth-century BC. David does not regard it as a luxury, however, but as a necessity. In fact, he orders it in his role as commander-in-chief of the army, with the consent of the other commanders (1 Chr. 25:1).

Many militaries today maintain bands and choruses, but few other kinds of workplaces do, unless they themselves *are* musical organizations. Yet there is something about music and the other arts that is essential to work of all kinds. God's creation—the source of human economic activity—is not only productive, it is beautiful (e.g., Gen. 3:6; Ps. 96:6; Ezek. 31:7–9), and God loves beautiful handiwork (e.g., Isa. 60:13). What is the place of beauty in your work? Would you or your organization, or the people who make use of your work, benefit if your work created more beauty? What does it even mean for work in your occupation to be beautiful?

Assessing David's Reign (1 Kings)

How are we to evaluate David and his reign? It is noteworthy that while Solomon gained more wealth, land, and renown than his father David, it is David whom the books of Kings and Chronicles acclaimed as Israel's greatest king, the model against which all other kings were measured.

We may gain hope for ourselves from God's response to the positives and negatives we see in David's life and actions. We are impressed by his fundamental piety even as we blanch at his political manipulation, lust, and violence. When we see a similar ambivalence in our own hearts and actions, we take comfort and hope in the God who forgives all our sins. The Lord's presence with David gives us hope that even in the face of our faithlessness God stays with us as the relentless Hound of Heaven.

Like Saul, David combined greatness and faithfulness with sin and error. We may wonder, then, why God preserved David's reign but not Saul's. Partly, it may be because David's heart remained true to God

(1 Kgs. 11:4; 15:3), however errant his deeds. The same is never said of Saul. Or it may be simply because the best way for God to carry out his purposes for his people was to put David on the throne and keep him there. When God calls us to a task or position, it is not necessarily us he is thinking about. He may choose us because of the effect we will have on other people. For example, God gave Cyrus of Persia victory over Babylon, not to reward or benefit Cyrus but to free Israel from captivity (2 Chr. 36:22–23).

Preparing for a Successor to Israel's Throne (1 Kings 1; 1 Chronicles 22)

Because David had shed so much blood as king, God determined not to allow him to build a house for the Lord. Instead, David's son, Solomon, was given that task (1 Chr. 22:7–10). So David accepted that his final task was to train Solomon for the job of king (1 Chr. 22:1–16) and to surround him with a capable team (1 Chr. 22:17–19). David provided the vast stores of materials for the construction of God's temple in Jerusalem, saying, "My son Solomon is young and inexperienced, and the house that is to be built for the Lord must be exceedingly magnificent" (1 Chr. 22:5). He publicly passed authority to Solomon and made sure that the leaders of Israel acknowledged Solomon as the new king and were prepared to help him succeed.

David recognized that leadership is a responsibility that outlasts one's own career. In most cases, your work will continue after you have moved on (whether by promotion, retirement, or taking a different job). You have a duty to create the conditions your successor needs to be successful. In David's preparation for Solomon, we see three elements of succession planning.

First, you need to provide the resources your successor needs to complete the tasks you leave unfinished. If you have been at least moderately successful, you will have learned how to gather the resources needed in your position. Often this depends on relationships that your successor will not immediately inherit. For example, success may depend on assistance from people who do not work in your department, but who have been willing to help you in your work. You need to make sure your successor knows who these people are, and you need to get their commitment to continue helping after you are gone. David arranged for "all kinds of artisans" with whom he had developed relationships to work for Solomon after he was gone (1 Chr. 22:15).

Second, you need to impart your knowledge and relationships to the person who succeeds you. In many situations this will come by bringing your successor to work alongside you long before you depart. For a short time before his death, David included Solomon in the leadership structures and rituals of the kingdom, although it appears he could have done a much better job of this if he'd started earlier (1 Kgs. 1:28–40). In other cases, you may not have any role in designating your successor, and you may not have any overlap with that person. In that case, you'll need to pass on information in writing and through those who will remain in the organization. What can you do to prepare the work and your successor to thrive, for God's glory, after you've gone?

Third, you need to transfer power decisively to the person who takes over the position. Whether you choose your own successor, or others make that decision without your input, you still have a choice to publicly acknowledge the transition and definitively pass on the authority you previously had. Your words and actions will confer either a blessing or a curse on your successor. A recent example is the manipulation that Vladimir Putin engaged in to maintain power after term limitations prevented him from seeking a third consecutive term as president of Russia. He arranged for some of the presidential power to be transferred to the prime minister, and then used his influence to get a former subordinate elected president, who appointed Putin as prime minister immediately afterwards.[5] After one term as prime minister, Putin easily stepped in as president again, at the invitation of the incumbent, who stepped aside.[6] As a result, concentration of power in Putin's hands has continued unabated for decades, just what term limits are intended to prevent, quite possibly to the detriment of Russia and its neighbors. In contrast, David

---

[5] C. J. Chivers, "Putin Is Approved as Prime Minister," *New York Times*, May 9, 2008, http://www.nytimes.com/2008/05/09/world/europe/09russia .html?_r=0.

[6] "Russia's Putin set to return as president in 2012," *BBC News Europe*, September 24, 2011, http://www.bbc.com/news/world-europe-15045816.

arranged for Solomon to be publicly anointed as king, transferred the symbols of monarchy to him, and presented him publicly as the new king while David himself was still living (1 Kgs. 1:32–35, 39–40).

Solomon Succeeds David as King (1 Kings 1–11)

Upon succeeding David as king, Solomon faces the vastness of his duties (1 Kgs. 3:5–15). He is acutely aware that he is inadequate to the task (1 Chr. 22:5) and that the work with which he is entrusted is immense. In addition to the temple project, he has a large, complex nation under his care, "a great people, so numerous they cannot be numbered or counted" (1 Kgs. 3:8). Even as he gains experience on the job, he realizes it is so complex that he'll never be able to figure out the right course of action in every circumstance. Needing divine help, he asks God, "Give your servant therefore an understanding mind to govern your people, able to discern between good and evil, for who can govern this, your great people?" (1 Kgs. 3:9). God answers his prayer and gives him "very great wisdom, discernment and breadth of understanding as vast as the sand on the seashore" (1 Kgs. 4:29).

Solomon Builds the Temple of the Lord (1 Kings 5–8)

Solomon's first major task is to build the temple of the Lord. To achieve this architectural feat, Solomon employs professionals from all corners of his kingdom. Three chapters (1 Kgs. 5–7) are devoted to describing the work of building the temple, of which we have space for only a small selection:

> Solomon also had seventy thousand laborers and eighty thousand stonecutters in the hill country, besides Solomon's three thousand three hundred supervisors who were over the work, having charge of the people who did the work. At the king's command, they quarried out great, costly stones in order to lay the foundation of the house with dressed stones. (1 Kgs. 5:15–17)

> He cast two pillars of bronze. Eighteen cubits was the height of the one, and a cord of twelve cubits would encircle it; the second pillar was the same. He also made two capitals of molten bronze, to set on the tops of the pillars; the height of the one capital was five cubits, and the height of

the other capital was five cubits. There were nets of checker work with wreaths of chain work for the capitals on the tops of the pillars; seven for the one capital, and seven for the other capital. (1 Kgs. 7:15–17)

So Solomon made all the vessels that were in the house of the Lord: the golden altar, the golden table for the bread of the Presence, the lampstands of pure gold, five on the south side and five on the north, in front of the inner sanctuary; the flowers, the lamps, and the tongs, of gold; the cups, snuffers, basins, dishes for incense, and firepans, of pure gold; the sockets for the doors of the innermost part of the house, the most holy place, and for the doors of the nave of the temple, of gold. Thus all the work that King Solomon did on the house of the Lord was finished. Solomon brought in the things that his father David had dedicated, the silver, the gold, and the vessels, and stored them in the treasuries of the house of the Lord. (1 Kgs. 7:48–51)

Solomon involves numerous people to help build and sustain his kingdom. From accomplished professionals to forced laborers, the people of the kingdom contribute their knowledge and skills to help build the temple. Whether or not it is Solomon's intention, employing so many people from all walks of life ensures that the vast majority of citizens hold personal investment in the political, religious, social, and economic well-being of the kingdom.

Solomon Centralizes the Rule of the Kingdom (1 Kings 9–11)

The massive national effort needed to construct the temple leaves Solomon the ruler of a powerful kingdom. During his reign, Israel reaches the peak of its military and economic might, and the kingdom covers more territory than at any other time in Israel's history. He completes the centralization of the nation's government, economic organization, and worship.

To assemble a large enough labor force, King Solomon conscripts workers out of all Israel, which numbers thirty thousand men (1 Kgs. 5:13–14). Solomon seems to have paid Israelites who were conscripted (1 Kgs. 9:22) in accordance with Leviticus 25:44–46, which forbids making slaves of Israelites. But resident aliens are simply enslaved (1 Kgs. 9:20–21). In addition, a multitude of workers are brought in from surrounding nations. Whatever their source, a wide variety of highly skilled professionals comes together, including the best artisans practicing at the time. The books of Samuel, Kings, and Chronicles—primarily interested in the work of kingship—say little about these workers except as they relate to the temple. But they are visible in the background, making all of society possible. But in obtaining their labor by force, Solomon builds the edifices of his kingdom through means that undermine its legitimacy and stability. We can see that trouble is brewing.

Solomon sees that as the central government expands, it will need food for an increasingly large work force. Soldiers need rations (1 Kgs. 5:9–11), alongside the workers on all of Solomon's building projects. The growing bureaucracy also needs to be fed. So the king organizes the nation into twelve sectors and appoints a deputy as overseer of each sector. Each deputy is charged with providing all required food rations for one month each year. As a result, the nation's daughters are conscripted into labor as "cooks and bakers" (1 Sam. 8:13). Israel becomes like other kingdoms with forced labor, heavy taxation, and a central elite wielding power over the rest of the country.

As Samuel had foretold, kings bring a greatly expanded military (1 Sam. 8:11–12). Militarization comes into full flower during Solomon's reign as the military becomes an essential component of the kingdom's stability. Soldiers of every rank from foot soldiers to generals all need weapons including javelins, spears, lances, bows and arrows, swords, daggers, knives, and slingshots. They need protective gear including shields, helmets, and body armor. To manage such a large scale army, a nationalized military organization must be maintained. In contrast to his father, Solomon is called "a man of peace," but the peace is ensured by the presence of a well-organized and well-provisioned military force.

We see in Solomon's story how society depends on the work of myriad people, coupled with structures and systems to organize large scale production and distribution. The human capacity to organize work is evidence of our creation in the image of a God who brings order out of chaos on a worldwide scale (Gen. 1). How fitting that the Bible portrays this ability through the construction of God's meeting place with humanity. It takes God-given ability to organize work on a scale large enough to build God's house. Few of us would care to return to Solomon's *methods* of organization—conscription, forced labor, and militarization—so we can be thankful that God leads us to fairer, more effective methods today. Perhaps what we take away from this episode is that God is intensely interested in the art of coordinating human work and creativity to accomplish God's purposes in the world.

Assessing Solomon's Golden Age (1 Kings)

Samuel's prophecy about the dangers of a king is fulfilled in Solomon's time.

> "These will be the ways of the king who will reign over you: he will take your sons . . . he will take your daughters . . . he will take the best of your fields and vineyards and olive orchards . . . he will take one-tenth of your grain and vineyards . . . he will take your male and female slaves, and the best of your cattle and donkeys . . . he will take one-tenth of your flocks, and you shall be his slaves. And in that day you will cry out because of your king, whom you have chosen for yourselves; but the LORD will not answer you in that day." (1 Sam. 8:11–18)

On the surface, Solomon's administration and building campaigns appear to have been very successful. The people are happy to make the required sacrifices in order to build the temple (1 Kgs. 8:65–66), a place where all can go to receive God's justice (1 Kgs. 8:12–21), forgiveness (1 Kgs. 8:33–36), healing (1 Kgs. 8:37–40), and mercy (1 Kgs. 8:46–53).

But after the temple is completed, Solomon builds a palace of the same scale and magnificence as the temple (1 Kgs. 9:1, 10). As he becomes accustomed to power and wealth, he becomes self-serving, arrogant, and unfaithful. He appropriates a large portion of the nation's productive capacity for his personal benefit. His already impressive throne of ivory is overlaid with gold (2 Chr. 9:17). He entertains lavishly (1 Kgs. 10:5). He reneges on agreements with allies (1 Kgs. 9:12), and he keeps a consort of "seven hundred princesses and three hundred concubines" (1 Kgs. 11:3). This last is his ultimate undoing, for "he loved many foreign women" (1 Kgs. 11:1) with the result that "when Solomon was old, his wives turned away his heart after other gods; and his heart was not true to the Lord his God" (1 Kgs. 11:4). He builds shrines to Astarte, Milcom, Chemosh and Molech (1 Kgs. 11:7). Given the covenant requirement that the faithfulness of the king to the Lord would be the key to the prosperity of the nation, Israel would soon descend rapidly from its peak. God, it seems, cares deeply whether we do our work for his purposes or against them. Amazing feats are possible when we work according to God's plans, but our work rapidly disintegrates when we don't.

From Failed Monarchies to Exile
(1 Kings 11–2 Kings 25; 2 Chronicles 10–36)

Solomon is only the third king of Israel, but already the kingdom has reached its high point. Over the next four hundred years, one bad king after another leads the nation into decline, disintegration, and defeat.

Solomon's Mighty Nation Divided in Two (1 Kings 11:26–12:19)

After Solomon's death it soon becomes clear that unrest had been brewing beneath the veneer of equitable and effective management. Following the great king's death, Jeroboam (earlier the head of forced laborers) and "all the assembly of Israel" approach the king's son and successor, Rehoboam (c. 931–914 BC), to ask him to "lighten the hard service of your father and his heavy yoke" (1 Kgs. 12:3–16; 2 Chr. 10:4). They are ready to pledge loyalty to the new king in return for a reduction in forced labor and high taxes.[7] But for forty years Rehoboam has known only luxurious palace living, staffed and provisioned by the Israelite people. His sense of entitlement is too strong to allow for compromise. Rather than easing the undue burden placed on the people by his father, Rehoboam chooses to make their yoke even greater.

Further fulfilling Samuel's prediction (1 Sam. 8:18), a rebellion ensues and the monarchy becomes divided forever. As much as the people of Israel had been willing to perform their fair share of labor to support the state, the emergence of unrealistic and unreasonable expectations results in revolt and division. The ten northern tribes secede, anointing Jeroboam (c. 931–910 BC) as their king. Although he had been a leader in the delegation seeking tax relief from Rehoboam, his dynasty proves no better for its people.

---

[7]Warren W. Wiersbe, *Joshua–Esther*, The Bible Exposition Commentary: Old Testament (Colorado Springs: Victor, 2004), 446.

The Northern Kingdom's March toward Exile (1 Kings 12:25–2 Kings 17:18)

For two centuries (910–722 BC) the northern kingdom of Israel is ruled by kings who do great evil in the sight of the Lord. These centuries are marked by constant war, treason, and murder, culminating in a catastrophic defeat by the nation of Assyria. To destroy all sense of national identity, Assyrian conquerors carry off the population, dispersing them in different parts of their empire and bringing in foreigners to populate the conquered land (2 Kgs. 17:5–24). As discussed under "David's Disobedience to God Causes a National Pestilence (1 Chr. 21:1–17)," the failings of leaders often have devastating effects on their people.

Obadiah Saves a Hundred People by Working within a Corrupt System (1 Kings 18:1–4)

At least two episodes during this period deserve our attention. The first, Obadiah's saving of a hundred prophets, may be of help to those facing the decision whether to quit a job in an organization that has become unethical, a decision that many face in the world of work.

Obadiah is the chief of staff in King Ahab's palace. (Ahab is infamous even today as the most wicked of Israel's kings.) Ahab's queen, Jezebel, orders the prophets of the Lord to be killed. As a high official in Ahab's court, Obadiah has advance word of the operation, as well as the means to circumvent it. He hides a hundred prophets in two caves and provides them bread and water until the crisis abates. They are saved only because someone "who revered the Lord greatly" (1 Kgs. 18:3) is in a position of authority to protect them. A similar situation occurs in the book of Esther, told in much greater detail. See "Working within a Fallen System (Esther)" below in "Ezra, Nehemiah, Esther and Work."

It is demoralizing to work in a corrupt or evil organization. How much easier it might be to quit and find someplace holier to work. Often, quitting is the only way to avoid doing evil ourselves. But no workplace on earth is purely good, and we will face ethical dilemmas wherever we work. Moreover, the more corrupt the workplace, the more it needs godly people. If there is any way to remain in place without adding to the evil ourselves, it may be that God wants us to stay. Our responsibility to do what we can to help others seems to be more important to God than our desire to think of ourselves as morally pure.

During World War II a group of officers opposed to Hitler remained in the *Abwher* (military intelligence) because it gave them a platform both for protecting Jews and for attempting to remove Hitler. Their plans failed and most were executed, including theologian Dietrich Bonhoeffer. When explaining why he remained in Hitler's army, he said, "The ultimate question for a responsible man to ask is not how he is to extricate himself heroically from the affair, but how the coming generation is to live."[8] If the way to accomplish the most good required remaining inside the German war machine, then Bonhoeffer believed it was his Christian duty to stay. Our responsibility to do what we can to help others seems to be more important to God than our desire to think of ourselves as morally pure.

Ahab and Jezebel Murder Naboth to Get His Property (1 Kings 21)

King Ahab abuses his power further when he begins to covet the vineyard of his neighbor, Naboth. Ahab offers a fair price for the vineyard, but Naboth regards the land as an ancestral inheritance and says he has no interest in selling at any price. Ahab dejectedly accepts this appropriate limitation of his power, but his wife Jezebel spurs him to tyranny. "Do you now govern Israel?" she taunts (1 Kgs. 21:7). If the king has no appetite for abuse of power, the queen does. She pays two scoundrels to bring a false charge of blasphemy and treason against Naboth, and he is quickly sentenced to death and stoned by the elders of the city. We are left to wonder why the elders acted so quickly, without even conducting a proper trial. Were they complicit with the king? Were they under his control and afraid of standing up to him? In any case, with Naboth out of the way, Ahab takes possession of the vineyard for himself.

Abuse of power, including land grabs as blatant as Ahab's, continue today, as a glance at nearly any daily newspaper will confirm. And as in Ahab's time, abuse of power requires the complicity of others who would rather tolerate injustice, even murder, than risk their own safety for the sake of their neighbors. Only Elijah, the man of God, dares to oppose

---

[8] Dietrich Bonhoeffer, *Letters and Papers from Prison* (New York: Touchstone, 1997), 7.

Ahab (1 Kgs. 21:17–24). Although his protests can do nothing to help Naboth, Elijah's opposition does curb Ahab's abuse of power, and no further abuses are recorded in Kings prior to Ahab's death. More often than we might expect, principled opposition by a small group or even a single individual can restrain the abuse of power. Otherwise, why would leaders go to so much trouble to hide their misdeeds? What do you estimate is the likelihood that you will become aware of at least one misuse of power in your working life? How are you preparing yourself to respond if you do?

The Prophet Elisha's Attention to Ordinary Work (2 Kings 2–6)

As the northern kings slide deeper into apostasy and tyranny, God raises up prophets to oppose them more forcefully than ever. Prophets were figures of immense, God-given power coming out of nowhere to speak God's truth in the halls of human power. Elijah and Elisha are by far the most prominent prophets in the books of Kings and Chronicles, and of the two, Elisha is especially notable for the attention he pays to the work of ordinary Israelites. Elisha is called to stand against Israel's rebellious kings throughout a long career (2 Kgs. 2:13–13:20). His actions show that he regards the people's economic life to be as important as the kingdom's dynastic struggles, and he tries to protect the people from the disasters brought on by the kings.

Elisha's Restoration of a City's Irrigation System (2 Kings 2:19–22)

Elisha's first major act is to cleanse the polluted well of the city of Jericho. The chief concern in the passage is agricultural productivity. Without a wholesome well, "the land is unfruitful." By restoring access to clean water, Elisha makes it possible for the people of the city to resume the God-given mission of humanity to be fruitful, multiply, and produce food (Gen. 1:28–30).

Elisha's Restoration of a Household's Financial Solvency (2 Kings 4:1–7)

After one of the prophets in Elisha's circle dies, his family falls into debt. The fate of a destitute family in ancient Israel was typically to sell some or all of its members into slavery, where at least they would be fed (see "Slavery or Indentured Servitude," Exodus 21:1–11, in "Exodus and

Work" in the *Theology of Work Bible Commentary*). On the verge of selling her two children as slaves, the prophet's widow begs Elisha for help (2 Kgs. 4:1). Elisha comes up with a plan for the family to become economically productive and support themselves. He asks the widow what she has to work with. "Nothing," she says, "except a jar of oil" (2 Kgs. 4:2). Apparently this is enough capital for Elisha to begin with. He tells her to borrow empty jars from all her neighbors and fill them with oil from her jar. She is able to fill every jar with oil before her own jar runs out, and the profit from selling the oil is enough to pay the family's debts (2 Kgs. 4:7). In essence, Elisha creates an entrepreneurial community within which the woman is able to start a small business. This is exactly what some of the most effective poverty-fighting methods do today, whether via microfinance, credit societies, agricultural cooperatives, or small-business supplier programs on the part of large companies and governments.

Elisha's actions on behalf of this family reflect God's love and concern for those in need. How can our work increase the opportunity for people in poverty to work their way toward prosperity? In what ways do we individually and collectively undermine the productive capacity of poor people and economies, and what can we do, with God's help, to reform?

Elisha's Restoration of a Military Commander's Health (2 Kings 5:1–14)

When Elisha cures the leprosy of Naaman, a commander in the army of Israel's enemy, Syria, it has important effects in the sphere of work. "It is no little thing that a sick person is made well, especially a leper," as Jacques Ellul notes in his insightful essay on this passage,[9] because the healing restores the ability to work. In this case the healing restores Naaman to his work of governance, advising his king on dealings with the king of Israel.

Interestingly, this healing of a foreigner also leads to the restoration of ethical culture in Elisha's own organization. Naaman offers to reward Elisha handsomely for the healing. But Elisha will accept nothing for what he regards as simply doing the Lord's will. However, one of Elisha's retinue, named Gehazi, sees an opportunity for a little extra remunera-

---

[9] Jacques Ellul, *The Politics of God & the Politics of Man* (Grand Rapids: Eerdmans, 1972), 35.

tion. Gehazi chases after Naaman and says that Elisha has changed his mind—he will accept a significant payment after all. After receiving the payment, Gehazi hides his ill-gotten gain and then lies to Elisha to cover it up. Elisha responds by announcing that Gehazi will be struck with the very leprosy that had left Naaman. Apparently, Elisha recognizes that tolerating corruption in his organization will rapidly undermine all the good that a lifetime of service to God has done.

Naaman's own actions demonstrate another point in this story. Naaman has a problem—leprosy. He needs to be healed. But his preformed notion of what the solution should look like—apparently, some kind of dramatic encounter with a prophet—leads him to refuse the true solution of bathing in the Jordan River when it is offered to him. When he heard this simple remedy delivered by Elisha's messenger, rather than Elisha himself, "Naaman went away angry." Neither the solution nor the source seems grand enough for Naaman to pay attention to.

In today's world, this twofold problem is often repeated. First, a senior leader misses the solution proposed by a lower level employee because they are unwilling to consider insight from someone they regard as unqualified. Jim Collins in his book *Good to Great* identifies the first sign of what he calls a "level five" leader as humility, a willingness to listen to many sources.[10] Second, the solution is not accepted because it does not match the leader's imagined approach. Thank God that many leaders today, like Naaman, have subordinates willing to take the risk of talking sense to them. Not only are humble bosses needed in organizations, but courageous subordinates also. Intriguingly, the person who puts the whole episode into motion is the lowest-status person of all, a foreign girl Naaman had captured in a raid and given to his wife as a slave (2 Kgs. 5:3). This is a wonderful reminder of how arrogance and wrong expectations can block insight, but God's wisdom keeps trying to break through anyway.

Elisha's Restoration of a Lumberjack's Ax (2 Kings 6:1–7)

Cutting wood along the bank of the Jordan River, one of Elisha's fellow prophets loses an iron axhead into the river. He had borrowed

---

[10] Collins, 22–25.

the ax from a lumberjack. The price of such a substantial piece of iron in the Bronze Age would have meant financial ruin for the owner, and the prophet who borrowed it is distraught. Elisha takes the economic loss as a matter of immediate, personal concern and causes the iron to float on top of the water, where it can be retrieved and returned to its owner. Once again, Elisha intervenes to enable someone to work for a living.

The gift of a prophet is to discern God's aims in daily life and to work and act accordingly. God calls the prophets to restore God's good creation, in the midst of a fallen world, in ways that point to God's power and glory. The theological aspect of a prophet's work—calling people to worship the true God—is inevitably accompanied by a practical aspect, restoring the good workings of the created order. The New Testament tells us that some Christians are called to be prophets as well (1 Cor. 12:28; Eph. 4:11). Elisha is not only a historical figure who demonstrates God's concern for his people's work, but he is also a model for Christians today.

The Southern Kingdom's March toward Exile (1 Kings 11:41–2 Kings 25:26; 2 Chronicles 10–36)

Following in the footsteps of the northern kingdom, the southern kingdom's rulers soon begin to decline into idolatry and evil. Under Rehoboam's rule the people "built for themselves high places, pillars, and sacred poles on every high hill and under every green tree; there were also male temple prostitutes in the land. They committed all the abominations of the nations" (1 Kgs. 14:23–24). Rehoboam's successors oscillated between faithfulness and doing evil in God's sight. For a while, Judah had enough good kings to stave off disaster, but in the final years the kingdom fell to the same state that the northern kingdom had. The nation was conquered, and the kings and elites were captured and deported by the Babylonians (2 Kgs. 24–25). The faithlessness of the kings whom the people had demanded, against God's advice hundreds of years earlier, culminates in a financial meltdown, destruction of the labor force, famine, and the mass murder or deportation of much of the population. The predicted disaster lasts seventy years until King Cyrus of Persia authorizes the return of some of the Jews to rebuild Jerusalem's temple and walls (2 Chr. 36:22–23).

Financial Accountability in the Temple (2 Kings 12:1–12)

One example of the degeneration of the kingdom ironically serves to bring to light a model of good financial practice. Like virtually all of the kingdom's leaders, the priests had become corrupt. Instead of using worshippers' donations to maintain the temple, they pilfered the money and divided it among themselves. Under the direction of Jehoash, one of the few kings who "did what was right in the sight of the LORD" (2 Kgs. 12:2), the priests devise an effective accounting system. A locked chest with a small hole in the top is installed in the temple to receive the donations. When it becomes full, the high priest and the king's secretary open the chest together, count the money, and contract with carpenters, builders, masons, and stonecutters to make repairs. This ensures that the money is used for its proper purpose.

The same system is still in use today, for example when the cash deposited in automatic teller machines is counted. The principle that even trusted individuals must be subject to verification and accountability is the foundation of good management. Whenever a person in power—especially the power of handling finances—tries to avoid verification, the organization is in danger. Because Kings includes this episode, we know that God values the work of bank tellers, accountants, auditors, bank regulators, armored car drivers, computer security workers, and others who protect the integrity of finance. It also urges all kinds of leaders to take the lead in setting a personal example of public accountability by inviting others to verify their work.

Arrogance and the End of the Kingdoms (2 Chronicles 26)

How could king after king fall so easily into evil? The story of Uzziah may give us some insight. He ascends to the throne at age sixteen and at first "he did what was right in the sight of the LORD" (2 Chr. 26:4). His young age proves to be an advantage, as he recognizes his need for God's guidance. "He set himself to seek God in the days of Zechariah, who instructed him in the fear of God; and as long as he sought the LORD, God made him prosper" (2 Chr. 26:5).

Interestingly, much of the success the Lord gives Uzziah is related to ordinary work. "He built towers in the wilderness and hewed out many cisterns, for he had large herds, both in the Shephelah and in the plain, and he had farmers and vinedressers in the hills and in the fertile lands, for he loved the soil" (2 Chr. 26:10). "In Jerusalem he set up machines, invented by skilled workers" (2 Chr. 26:15).

"He was marvelously helped," the Scripture tells us, "until he became strong" (2 Chr. 26:15). Then his strength becomes his undoing because he begins to serve himself instead of the Lord. "When he had become strong he grew proud, to his destruction. For he was false to the LORD his God" (2 Chr. 26:16). He attempts to usurp the religious authority of the priests, leading to a palace revolt that costs him the throne and leaves him an outcast the rest of his life.

Uzziah's tale is sobering for people in leadership positions today. The character that leads to success—especially our reliance on God—is easily eroded by the powers and privileges that success brings. How many business, military, and political leaders have come to believe they are invincible and so lose the humility, discipline, and attitude of service needed to remain successful? How many of us at any level of success have paid more attention to ourselves and less to God as our power increases even modestly? Uzziah even had the benefit of subordinates who would oppose him when he did wrong, although he ignored them (2 Chr. 26:18). What, or who, do you have to keep you from drifting into pride and away from God should your success increase?

Conclusions from Samuel, Kings, and Chronicles

Governance and leadership issues touch all of life. When nations and organizations are governed well, people have an opportunity to thrive. When leaders fail to act for the good of their organizations and communities, disaster follows. The success or failure of the kings of Israel and Judah in turn depended on their adherence to God's covenant and laws. With the partial exceptions of David, Solomon, and a few others, the kings chose to worship false gods, which led them to follow unethical principles and enrich themselves at the expense of their people. Their faithlessness led to the eventual destruction of both Israel and Judah.

But the fault does not lie only with the kings. The people brought the woes of tyranny upon themselves when they demanded that the prophet Samuel appoint a king for them. Not trusting God to protect them, they were willing to submit themselves to rule by an autocrat. "Every nation gets the government it deserves," observed Joseph de Maistre.[11] The corrupting influence of power is an ever-present danger, yet nations and organizations must be governed. The ancient Israelites chose strong government at the cost of corruption and tyranny, a temptation very much alive today. Other peoples have refused to make any of the sacrifices—paying taxes, obeying laws, giving up tribal and personal militias—required to establish a functional government and paid the price in anarchy, chaos, and economic self-strangulation. Sadly, this continues to the present day in various countries. An exquisite balance is needed to produce good governance, a balance almost beyond human capability. If there is one major lesson we can draw from Samuel, Kings, and Chronicles, it is that only by committing ourselves to God's grace and guidance, his covenant and commands, can a people find the ethical virtues needed for good, long-lasting government.

This lesson applies not only to nations, but also to businesses, schools, nongovernmental organizations, families, and every other kind of workplace. Good governance and leadership are essential for people to succeed and thrive economically, relationally, personally, and spiritually. Samuel, Kings, and Chronicles explore various aspects of leadership and governance among an array of workers of all kinds. Specifics include the perils of inherited authority and wealth, the dangers of treating God like a good luck charm in our work, the opportunities that arise for faithful workers, the joys and heartbreaks of parenting, godly criteria for choosing leaders, the need for humility and collaboration in leadership, the essential role of innovation and creativity, and the necessity of succession planning and leadership development.

The books pay much attention to handling conflict, showing both the destructive career of suppressed conflict and the creative potential

---

[11] Joseph-Marie de Maistre, letter 76, *Lettres et Opuscules* (27 August 1811), quoted in Edward Latham, *Famous Sayings and Their Authors* (London: Swan Sonnenschein, 1906), 181.

of open and respectful disagreement. They show the need for diplomats and reconcilers, both formal and informal, and the essential role of subordinates with the courage to speak the truth—respectfully—to those in power, despite the risk to themselves. In these books populated with flawed authority figures, the few unambiguously good leaders include Abigail, whose good conflict resolution skills saved David's integrity and the lives of her family members and the unnamed slave girl of Naaman's wife, whose boldness in the service of the very person who enslaved her (Naaman) brought peace between warring nations.

The most prominent unambiguously good leader in the books is Elisha, the prophet of God. Of all the prophets he pays the most attention to leadership in daily life, work, and economic matters. He restores a city's water system, capitalizes entrepreneurial economic communities, reconciles nations through medical missions (at the instigation of the slave girl mentioned above), creates an ethical culture in his own organization, and enhances the livelihoods of widows, working men, commanders, and farmers. Bringing God's word to humanity results in good governance, economic development, and agricultural productivity.

Regrettably, when it comes to the kings themselves there are far more examples of poor leadership and governance than good. In addition to handling conflict poorly, as described above, the kings conscript labor, break apart families, promote an elite class of civil servants and military officers at the expense of the common people, lay unbearable taxes on the people to support their lavish lifestyles, assassinate those who stand in their way, confiscate property arbitrarily, subvert religious institutions, and eventually lead their kingdoms into subjugation and exile. Surprisingly, the cause of these ills is not failure and weakness on the part of the kings, but success and strength. They twist the success and strength that God gives them into arrogance and tyranny, with the result that they abandon God and violate his covenant and commands. The dark heart of disastrous leadership is the worship of false gods in place of the true God. When we see poor leadership today—in others or in ourselves—a good first question might be, "What false gods are being worshipped in this situation?"

Just as light shines more brightly in the darkness, the failures of the kings highlight some episodes of good leadership. Music and the arts flower under David's rule. The construction of the temple in Solomon's time is a marvel of architecture, construction, craftwork, and economic organization. The priests in Jehoash's time develop a system of financial accountability still in use today. Obadiah models the good that faithful people can accomplish within corrupt systems and evil situations.

Obadiah is a much better model for us today than David, Solomon, or any of the kings. The kings' overarching concern was, "How can I acquire and maintain power?" Obadiah's was, "How can I serve people as God wishes in the situation where I find myself?" Both are questions of leadership. One focuses on the goods needed for power, the other on the power needed for good. Let us pray that God will call his people to positions of power, and that he will bring each of us the power needed to fulfill our callings. But before and after we utter such prayers, let us begin and end with, "Your will be done."

Ezra, Nehemiah, Esther and Work

Introduction to Ezra, Nehemiah, and Esther

Most Christians don't find their workplaces very supportive of their faith. Generally, there is limited scope for explicitly Christian witness and action. In a pluralistic society, some such limits may be appropriate, but they can make the workplace feel like alien territory to Christians. Moreover, workers may feel pressure to violate the ethical requirements of biblical standards, either explicitly or implicitly. The books of Ezra, Nehemiah, and Esther depict what it is like for God's people to work in unwelcoming workplaces. They show God's people working in jobs ranging from construction to politics to entertainment, always in the midst of environments openly hostile to God's values and plans. Yet along the way they receive surprising help from nonbelievers in the highest positions of civic power. God's power seems to crop up for his people's good in surprising places, yet they face extremely challenging situations and decisions, upon which they don't always agree.

Ezra had to ponder whether to trust an unbelieving ruler to protect the Jewish people as they returned to Jerusalem and began rebuilding the temple. He had to find financial support within the corrupt economic system of the Persian Empire, while remaining true to God's laws about economic integrity. Nehemiah had to rebuild the walls of Jerusalem, which required him both to trust God and to be pragmatic. He had to lead people whose motivation ranged from altruism to greed, and get them to overcome their divergent self-interests to work toward a common purpose. Esther had to survive the oppression of women and the deadly intrigue within the Persian royal court, yet remain ready to risk everything to save her people from genocide. Our titles and institutions have changed since their days, but in many ways our workplaces today have much in common, for better or worse, with the places where Ezra, Nehemiah, and Esther labored. The real life situations, challenges, and

choices found in these biblical books help us develop a theology of work
that matters in how we live each day.

Ezra and Nehemiah

In 587 BC, the Babylonians, under the rule of King Nebuchadnezzar, conquered Jerusalem. They killed the leaders of Judah, plundered
the temple before burning it to the ground, destroyed much of the city,
including its walls, and took the cream of Jerusalem's crop of citizens
to Babylon. There, these Jews lived for decades in exile, always hoping
for God's deliverance and the restoration of Israel. Their hopes were
heightened in 539 BC when Persia, led by King Cyrus, overthrew Babylon. Shortly thereafter, Cyrus issued a decree inviting the Jews in his
kingdom to return to Jerusalem and rebuild the temple and, therefore,
their life as God's people (Ezra 1:1–4).

The books of Ezra and Nehemiah, originally two parts of a single
work,[1] narrate crucial aspects of this rebuilding story, beginning with
the edict of Cyrus in 539 BC. Their purpose, however, is not simply to
describe what happened long ago out of antiquarian curiosity. Rather,
Ezra and Nehemiah use historical events to illustrate the theme of restoration. These books show how God once restored his people and how
people played a central role in this work of renewal. The books of Ezra
and Nehemiah were written by an unknown author, probably in the
fourth century BC,[2] to encourage the Jewish people to live faithfully
even under foreign rule, so that they might be participants in God's
present and future work of restoration.

Ezra and Nehemiah are highly theological books, but they do not directly address the theology of *work*. They do not include legal imperatives
or prophetic visions having to do with our daily labors. The narratives of
Ezra and Nehemiah do describe arduous work, however, implicitly placing work in a theological framework. Thus we'll find beneath the surface
of these books rich soil from which a theology of work might sprout. In

---

[1] H. G. M. Williamson, *Ezra, Nehemiah*, vol. 16, *Word Biblical Commentary*
(Waco, TX: Word Books, 1985), xxi.

[2] "Ezra-Nehemiah, Books of" in *The Anchor Bible Dictionary*, ed. David Noel
Freedman (New York: Doubleday, 1992).

particular, Ezra and Nehemiah were called to restore God's kingdom (Israel), in the midst of a partially hostile, partially supportive environment. Today's workplaces are also partially hostile and partially supportive of the work of God. This encourages us to understand how our work may contribute to implanting God's kingdom in today's world.

Esther

The book of Esther tells the story of one curious episode during the era depicted in Ezra and Nehemiah. It focuses not on the restoration of Jerusalem, but rather on events happening in Persia when Ahasuerus (better known to us by his Greek name, Xerxes) was king (485–465 BC). The narrative of Esther accounts for the origins of the Jewish festival of Purim. The unidentified author of this book wrote, in part, to explain and encourage celebration of this national holiday (see Est. 9:20–28).[3] His broader concern was to examine how Jews could survive and even thrive as exiles in a pagan and often hostile land.[4]

In contrast to Ezra and Nehemiah, Esther is not explicitly theological at all. In fact, God is never mentioned. Yet no faithful reader could fail to see the hand of God behind the events of the book. This invites the reader to ponder how God may be at work in the world unnoticed by those without eyes to see.

Restoration of the Temple (Ezra 1:1–6:22)

The book of Ezra begins with a decree from King Cyrus of Persia allowing the Jews to return to Jerusalem to rebuild the temple that had been destroyed by the Babylonians in 587 BC (Ezra 1:2–4). The introduction to this decree specifies when it was proclaimed: "In the first year of King Cyrus" (539–538 BC, shortly after the Persian defeat of Babylon). It also introduces us to one of the principal themes of Ezra-Nehemiah: the relationship between God's work and human work. Cyrus made his

---

[3] Frederic W. Bush, *Ruth–Esther*, vol. 9, *Word Biblical Commentary* (Nashville: Thomas Nelson, 1996), 326–35.

[4] Mark D. Roberts, *Ezra, Nehemiah, Esther*, vol. 11, The Preacher's Commentary (Nashville: Thomas Nelson, 2002), 315–18.

proclamation "that the word of the Lord by the mouth of Jeremiah might be accomplished," and because "the Lord stirred up the spirit of King Cyrus" (Ezra 1:1). Cyrus was doing his work as king, seeking his personal and institutional ends. Yet this was a result of God's work within him, advancing God's own purposes. We sense in the first verse of Ezra that God is in control yet choosing to work through human beings, even Gentile kings, to accomplish his will.

Workplace Christians today also live in trust that God is active through the decisions and actions of non-Christian people and institutions. Cyrus was God's chosen instrument, whether or not Cyrus himself recognized that. Similarly, the actions of our bosses, co-workers, customers and suppliers, rivals, regulators, or a myriad of other actors may be furthering the work of God's kingdom unrecognized by either us or them. That should prevent us from both despair and arrogance. If Christian people and values seem absent from your workplace, don't despair—God is still at work. On the other hand, if you are tempted to see yourself or your organization as a paragon of Christian virtue, beware! God may be accomplishing more than you realize through those with less visible connection to him. Certainly, God's work through Cyrus—who remained wealthy, powerful, and unbelieving, even while many of God's people were only slowly recovering from the poverty of exile—should warn us not to expect wealth and power as a necessary reward for our faithful work. God is using all things to work toward his kingdom, not necessarily toward our personal success.

God's work continued as many Jews took advantage of Cyrus's decree. "Every one whose spirit God had stirred" prepared to return to Jerusalem (Ezra 1:5). When they arrived in Jerusalem, their first job was to build the altar and offer sacrifices on it (Ezra 3:1–3). This epitomizes the chief sort of work chronicled in Ezra and Nehemiah. It was closely associated with the sacrificial practices of Old Testament Judaism, which took place in the temple. The work described in these books reflected and supported the centrality of the temple and its offerings in the life of God's people. Worship and work stride hand and hand through the pages of Ezra and Nehemiah.

Given the focus in Ezra upon the rebuilding of the temple, people's jobs are mentioned when they are relevant to this effort. Thus the list of people returning to Jerusalem specifically itemizes "the priests, the Levites . . . and the singers, the gatekeepers, and the temple servants" (Ezra 2:70). The text identifies "masons and carpenters" because they were necessary for the building project (Ezra 3:7). People whose skills did not equip them for working directly on the temple contributed to the task through the fruit of their work in the form of "freewill offerings" (Ezra 2:68). Thus, in a sense, the rebuilding of the temple was the work of all the people as they contributed in one way or another.

The book of Ezra identifies political leaders in addition to Cyrus because of their impact, positive or negative, on the construction effort. For example, Zerubbabel is mentioned as a leader of the people. He was the governor of the territory who oversaw the rebuilding of the temple (Hag. 1:1). Ezra mentions "Rehum the royal deputy and Shimshai the scribe," officials who wrote a letter opposing the temple's reconstruction (Ezra 4:8–10). Other kings and officials show up according to their relevance to the rebuilding project.

The temple is what the project was about, but it would be a mistake to think that God blesses craftsmanship and material work only when it is devoted to a religious purpose. Ezra's vision was to restore the whole city of Jerusalem (Ezra 4:13), not just the temple. We will discuss this point further when we come to Nehemiah, who actually undertook the work beyond the temple.

Ezra describes several efforts to squelch the construction (Ezra 4:1–23). These were successful for a while, stopping the temple project for about two decades (Ezra 4:24). Finally, God encouraged the Jews through the prophecies of Haggai and Zechariah to resume and complete the job (Ezra 5:1). Moreover, Darius, king of Persia, financially underwrote the building effort in the hope that the Lord might bless him and his sons (Ezra 6:8–10). Thus the temple was finally completed, thanks to the fact that God had "turned the heart of the king of Assyria to them" so that "he aided [the Jews] in the work on the house of God" (Ezra 6:22).

As this verse makes clear, the Jews actually did the work of rebuilding the temple. Yet their labors were successful because of help from two pagan kings, one who inaugurated the project and the other who paid for its completion. Behind these human efforts loomed the overarching work of God, who moved in the hearts of the kings and encouraged his people through the prophets. As we have seen, God is at work far beyond what meets the eye of his people.

Restoration of Covenant Life, Phase One: The Work of Ezra (Ezra 7:1–10:44)

Ironically, Ezra himself does not appear in the book bearing his name until chapter 7. This learned man, a priest and teacher of the law, came to Jerusalem with the blessing of the Persian king Artaxerxes over fifty years after the rebuilding of the temple. His assignment was to present offerings in the temple on behalf of the king and to establish the law of God in Judah, both by teaching and by appointing law-abiding leaders (Ezra 7:25–26).

Ezra did not explain the king's favor in terms of good luck. Rather, he credited God with putting "such a thing as this into the heart of the king" to send Ezra to Jerusalem (Ezra 7:27). Ezra "took courage" and acted on the king's order because, as he said, "the hand of the Lord my God was upon me" (Ezra 7:28). This language of God's hand being upon someone is a favorite of Ezra, where it appears six times out of eight times in the whole Bible (Ezra 7:6, 9, 28; 8:18, 22, 31). God was at work in and through Ezra, which explains his success in his endeavors.

Ezra's confidence in God's help was tested when it came time for his entourage to journey from Babylon to Jerusalem. "I was ashamed," Ezra explained, "to ask the king for a band of soldiers and cavalry to protect us against the enemy on our way; since we had told the king, 'The hand of our God is gracious to all who seek him, but his power and his wrath are against all who forsake him'" (Ezra 8:22). For Ezra, to depend on a royal escort implied a failure to trust in God's protection. So he and his retinue fasted and prayed rather than seek practical assistance from the king (Ezra 8:23). Note: Ezra was not following any particular Old Testament law in choosing not to receive royal protection. Rather, this decision reflected his personal convictions about what it meant to trust God in the real challenges of leadership. One might say that Ezra was an "idealistic believer" in this situation, because he was willing to stake his life on the idea of God's protection, rather than to ensure protection with human help. As we'll see later, Ezra's position was not the only one deemed reasonable by godly leaders in the books of Ezra and Nehemiah.

Ezra's strategy proved to be successful. "The hand of our God was upon us," he observed, "and he delivered us from the hand of the enemy and from ambushes along the way" (Ezra 8:31). We do not know, however, if members of Ezra's party carried weapons or used them for protection. The text seems to suggest that Ezra and company completed their journey without a threatening incident. Once again, the book of Ezra shows that human efforts are successful when God is at work in them.

The last two chapters of Ezra focus on the problem of Jews intermarrying with Gentiles. The issue of work does not emerge here, except in the example of Ezra, who exercises his leadership in faithfulness to the law with prayerful decisiveness.

Restoration of the Wall of Jerusalem (Nehemiah 1:1–7:73)

The first chapter of the book of Nehemiah introduces him as a resident of Susa, the capital of the Persian Empire. When Nehemiah heard that the walls of Jerusalem were still broken down more than a half-century after the completion of the rebuilding of the temple, he "sat down and wept," fasting and praying before God (Neh. 1:4). Implicitly, he was formulating a plan to remedy the situation in Jerusalem.

Bridging the Sacred-Secular Divide (Nehemiah 1:1–1:10)

The connection between the temple and the wall is significant for the theology of work. The temple might seem to have been a religious institution, while the walls were a secular one. But God led Nehemiah to work on the walls, no less than he led Ezra to work on the temple. Both the sacred and the secular were necessary to fulfill God's plan to restore the nation of Israel. If the walls were unfinished, the temple was unfinished too. The work was of a single piece. The reason for this is easy to understand. Without a wall, no city in the ancient Near East was safe from bandits, gangs, and wild animals, even though the empire might be at peace. The more economically and culturally developed a city was, the greater the value of things in the city and the greater the need for the wall. The temple, with its rich decorations, would have been particularly at risk. Practically speaking, without a wall there could be no city, and without a city there could be no temple.

Conversely, the city and its wall depended on the temple as the source of God's provision for law, government, security, and prosperity. Even on strictly military terms, the temple and the wall were mutually dependent. The wall was an integral part of the city's protection, yet so was the temple wherein dwelt the Lord (Ezra 1:3) who brought to nothing the violent plans of the city's enemies (Neh. 4:15). It was likewise with government and justice. The gates of the wall were where lawsuits are tried (Deut. 21:19, Isa. 29:21), while at the same time the Lord from his temple "execute[d] justice for the orphan and the widow" (Deut. 10:18). No temple meant no presence of God, and no presence of God meant no military strength, no justice, no civilization, and no need for walls. The temple and the walls were united in a society founded on God's "covenant and steadfast love" (Neh. 1:5). This at least is the ideal toward which Nehemiah fasted, prayed, and worked.

Does Trusting God Mean Turning to Prayer, Taking "Practical" Action, or Both? (Nehemiah 1:11–4:23)

The last line of Nehemiah 1 identifies him as "cupbearer to the king" (Neh. 1:11). This means that he not only had immediate access to the king as the one who tested and served his beverages, but he was also a trusted advisor and high-ranking Persian official.[5] He would use his professional experience and position to great advantage as he embarked upon the work of rebuilding the wall of Jerusalem.

When the king granted him permission to oversee the rebuilding project, Nehemiah asked for letters to the governors through whose territory he would pass on his trip to Jerusalem (Neh. 2:7). In Nehemiah's view, the king granted this request "for the gracious hand of my God was upon me" (Neh. 2:8). Apparently, Nehemiah did not believe that trust-

---

[5]"Nehemiah (person)" in *The Anchor Bible Dictionary*, ed. David Noel Freedman (New York: Doubleday, 1992).

ing God meant he should not seek the king's protection for his journey. Moreover, he was pleased to have "officers of the army and cavalry" escort him safely to Jerusalem (Neh. 2:9).

The text of Nehemiah does not suggest there was anything wrong with Nehemiah's decision to seek and accept the king's protection. In fact, it claims that God's blessing accounted for this bit of royal assistance. It is striking to note how different Nehemiah's approach to this issue was from Ezra's. Whereas Ezra believed that trusting God meant he should not ask for royal protection, Nehemiah saw the offer of such protection as evidence of God's gracious hand of blessing. This disagreement demonstrates how easy it is for godly people to come to different conclusions about what it means to trust God in their work. Perhaps each was simply doing what he was most familiar with. Ezra was a priest, familiar with the habitation of the Lord's presence. Nehemiah was a cupbearer to the king, familiar with the exercise of royal power. Both Ezra and Nehemiah were seeking to be faithful in their labors. Both were godly, prayerful leaders, but they understood trusting God for protection differently. For Ezra, it meant journeying without the king's guard. For Nehemiah, it meant accepting the offer of royal help as evidence of God's own blessing.

We find signs in several places that Nehemiah was what we could call a "pragmatic believer." In Nehemiah 2, for example, Nehemiah secretly surveyed the rubble of the former wall before even announcing his plans to the residents of Jerusalem (Neh. 2:11–17). Apparently, he wanted to know the size and scope of the work he was taking on before he publicly committed to doing it. Yet, after explaining the purpose of his coming to Jerusalem and pointing to God's gracious hand upon him, when some local officials mocked and accused him, Nehemiah answered, "The God of heaven is the one who will give us success" (Neh. 2:20). God would give this success, in part, through Nehemiah's clever and well-informed leadership. The fact that success came from the Lord did not mean Nehemiah could sit back and relax. Quite to the contrary, Nehemiah was about to commence an arduous and demanding task.

His leadership involved delegation of parts of the wall-building project to a wide variety of people including "the high priest, Eliashib, [and] his fellow-priests" (Neh. 3:1); "the Tekoites," minus their nobles who didn't want to submit to the supervisors (Neh. 3:5); "Uzziel the son of Harhaiah, one of the goldsmiths" and "Hananiah, one of the perfumers" (Neh. 3:8); "Shallum . . . ruler of half the district of Jerusalem, [and] his daughters" (Neh. 3:12); and many others. Nehemiah was able to inspire collegiality and to organize the project effectively.

But then, just as in the story in Ezra of the rebuilding of the temple, opposition arose. Leaders of local peoples attempted to hinder the Jewish effort through ridicule, but "the people had a mind to work" (Neh. 4:6). When their words did not stop the wall from being rebuilt, the local leaders "all plotted together to come and fight against Jerusalem and to cause confusion in it" (Neh. 4:8).

So what did Nehemiah lead his people to do? Pray and trust God? Or arm themselves for battle? Predictably, the pragmatic believer led them to do both: "We prayed to our God, and set a guard as a protection against them day and night" (Neh. 4:9). In fact, when threats against the wall-builders mounted, Nehemiah also stationed guards at key positions. He encouraged his people not to lose heart because of their opponents: "Do not be afraid of them. Remember the Lord, who is great and terrible, and fight for your kin, your sons, your daughters, your wives, and your homes" (Neh. 4:14). Because of their faith, the people were to fight. Then, not long thereafter, Nehemiah added a further word of encouragement, "Our God will fight for us!" (Neh. 4:20). Yet this was not an invitation to the Jews to put down their weapons and focus on building, trusting in supernatural protection alone. Rather, God would fight for his people by assisting them in battle. He would be at work in and through his people as they worked.

We Christians sometimes seem to act as if there were a rigid wall between actively pursuing our own agenda and passively waiting for God to act. We are aware that this is a false duality, which is why, for example, orthodox/historic Christian theology rejects the Christian Science premise that medical treatments are acts of unfaithfulness to God. Yet there are moments when we are tempted to become passive while waiting for God to act. If you are unemployed, yes, God wants you to have a job. To get the job God wants you to have, you have to write a résumé, conduct a search, apply for positions, interview, and get rejected dozens of times before finding that job, just as everyone else has to do. If you are a parent, yes, God wants you to have enjoyment in raising your children. But you will still have to set and enforce limits, be available at times when it's inconvenient, discuss difficult topics with them, cry and suffer with them through bumps, broken bones, and broken hearts, do homework with them, ask their forgiveness when you are wrong, and offer them forgiveness when they fail. Nehemiah and company's arduous work warns us that trusting God does not equate with sitting on our hands, waiting for magical solutions for our difficulties.

Connecting Lending Practices to the Fear of the Lord (Nehemiah 5:1–5:19)

Nehemiah's wall-building project was threatened not just from the outside, but also from the inside. Certain wealthy Jewish nobles and officials were taking advantage of economically difficult times to line their own pockets (Neh. 5). They were loaning money to fellow Jews, expecting interest to be paid on the loans, even though this was prohibited in the Jewish law (for example, Exod. 22:25).[6] When the debtors couldn't repay the loans, they lost their land and were even forced to sell their children into slavery (Neh. 5:5). Nehemiah responded by demanding that the wealthy stop charging interest on loans and give back whatever they had taken from their debtors.

In contrast to the selfishness of those who had been taking advantage of their fellow Jews, Nehemiah did not use his leadership position to enhance his personal fortune. "Because of the fear of God," he even refused to tax the people to pay for his personal expenses, unlike his predecessors (Neh. 5:14–16). Instead, he generously invited many to eat at his table, paying from for this expense from his personal savings without taxing the people (Neh. 5:17–18).

In a sense, the nobles and officials were guilty of the same kind of dualism we have just discussed. In their case, they were not waiting passively for God to solve their problems. Instead, they were actively pursuing their own gain as if economic life had nothing to do with God. But

---

[6] The question of whether the Bible prohibits lending money at interest has a long and contentious history in Christian theology. See the Theology of Work topical article, "Does the Bible Prohibit Charging Interest?" under "Finance" at www.theologyofwork.org.

Nehemiah tells them that their economic lives are of utmost importance to God, because God cares about all of society, not just its religious aspects: "Should you not walk in the fear of our God, to prevent the taunts of the nations our enemies" [to whom the nobles had forced the sale of Jewish debtors as slaves]?" (Neh. 5:9). Nehemiah connects an economic issue (usury) with the fear of God.

The issues of Nehemiah 5, though emerging from a legal and cultural setting distant from our own, challenge us to consider how much we should profit personally from our position and privilege, even from our work. Should we put our money in banks that make loans with interest, or invest our money in funds that include companies with questionable practices? Should we take advantage of special perks made available to us in our workplace, even if these they come at considerable cost to others? Nehemiah's specific commands (don't charge interest, don't foreclose on collateral, don't force the sale of people into slavery) may apply differently in our time, but underlying his commands is a prayer that still applies: "Remember for my good, O my God, all that I have done for this people" (Neh. 5:19). As it was to Nehemiah, God's call to today's workers is to do everything we can for the people around us. In practice, that means we each owe God the duty of caring for the cloud of persons who depend on our work: employers, co-workers, customers, family, and many others. Nehemiah may not tell us exactly how to handle today's workplace situations, but he tells us how to orient our minds as we decide. Put people first.

Nehemiah Gives Credit to God (Nehemiah 6:1–7:73)

The external and internal problems facing Nehemiah did not halt work on the wall, which was completed in only fifty-two days (Neh. 6:15). The enemies of Judah "were afraid and fell greatly in their own esteem; for they perceived that this work had been accomplished with the help of our God" (Neh. 6:16). Even though Nehemiah had exercised his considerable leadership to inspire and organize the builders, and even though they had worked tirelessly, and even though Nehemiah's wisdom enabled him to fend off attacks and distractions, nevertheless he saw all of this as work done with God's help. God worked through him and his people, using their gifts and labor to accomplish God's own purposes.

Restoration of Covenant Life, Phase Two: Ezra and Nehemiah Together (Nehemiah 8:1–13:31)

After the wall surrounding Jerusalem was completed, the Israelites gathered in Jerusalem in order to renew their covenant with God. Ezra reappeared at this point in order to read the law to the people (Neh. 8:2–5). As they heard the law, they wept (Neh. 8:9). Yet Nehemiah rebuked them for their sorrow, adding, "Go your way, eat the fat and drink sweet wine and send portions to him for whom nothing is prepared; for this day is holy to our LORD" (Neh. 8:10). However central work might be to serving God, so is celebration. On holy days, people are to enjoy the fruits of their labors as well as to share them with those who lack such delights.

Yet, as Nehemiah 9 demonstrates, there was also a time for godly sorrow as the people confessed their sins to God (Neh. 9:2). Their confession came in the context of an extensive recital of all the things God had done, beginning with creation itself (Neh. 9:6) and continuing through the crucial events of the Old Testament. The failure of Israel to be faithful to the Lord explained, among other things, why God's chosen people were "slaves" to foreign kings and why those kings enjoyed the fruits of Israelite labors (Neh. 9:36–37).

Among the promises made by the people as they renewed their covenant with the Lord was a commitment to honor the Sabbath (Neh. 10:31). In particular, they promised not to do business on the Sabbath with "the peoples of the land" who worked on this day. The Israelites also promised to fulfill their responsibility to support the temple and its workers (Neh. 10:31–39). They would do so by giving to the temple and its staff a percentage of the fruit of their own work. Now, as then, the commitment to give a percentage of our income to support the "service of the house of our God" (Ezra 10:32) is both a necessary means of financing the work of worship and a reminder that everything we have comes from God's hand.

After completing his task of building the wall in Jerusalem and overseeing the restoration of society there, Nehemiah returned to serve King Artaxerxes (Neh. 13:6). Later, he came back to Jerusalem, where he discovered that some of the reforms he had initiated were thriving, while others had been neglected. For example, he observed some people working on the Sabbath (Neh. 13:15). Jewish officials had been letting

Gentile traders bring their goods into Jerusalem for sale on the day of rest (Neh. 13:16). So Nehemiah rebuked those who had failed to honor the Sabbath (Neh. 13:17–18). Moreover, in his typically pragmatic approach, he closed the city gates before the Sabbath began, keeping them shut until the day of rest had passed. He also stationed some of his servants at the gates so that they might tell potential sellers to leave (Neh. 13:19).

The question of whether and/or how Christians ought to keep the Sabbath cannot be answered from Nehemiah. A much broader theological conversation is necessary.[7] Nevertheless, this book reminds us of the centrality of Sabbath-keeping to God's first covenant people and the threat posed by economic interaction with those who do not honor the Sabbath. In our own context, it was certainly easier for Christians to keep the Sabbath when the malls were closed on the Lord's Day. However, our contemporary culture of round-the-clock commerce puts us in Nehemiah's situation, in which a conscious—and potentially costly—decision about Sabbath-keeping is required.

Working within a Fallen System (Esther 1–10)

The book of Esther begins with King Ahasuerus (known to history outside the Bible as Xerxes) throwing a lavish party to display his glory (Est. 1:1–8). Having consumed ample amounts of wine, Ahasuerus commanded his servants to bring Queen Vashti before him in order that he might show her off to the other partygoers (Est. 1:10–11). But Vashti, sensing the indignity of the request, refused (Est. 1:12). Her refusal disturbed the men in attendance, who feared that her example would encourage other women in the kingdom to stand up to their husbands (Est. 1:13–18). Thus Vashti was "fired," if you will, and a process was begun to find Ahasuerus a new queen (Est. 1:21–2:4). To be sure, this episode depicts a family matter. But every royal family is also a political workplace. So Vashti's situation is also a workplace issue, in which the boss seeks to exploit a woman because of her gender and then terminates her when she fails to live up to his fantasies.

---

[7] See topic articles under "Rest and Work" at www.theologyofwork.org.

The king sought to replace Vashti, and a young Jewish woman named Esther ended up in the harem being extensively prepared to be tried out by the king for one night (Est. 2:8–14). From our point of view, she was caught in an oppressive, sexist system and was soon to lose her virginity at the hands of a selfish tyrant. But she was not a passive victim. She played the system to her own advantage, sleeping with the king, keeping silent about the oppression of Vashti, and deceiving the king about her ethnicity (Est. 2:20).

Because of Esther's exceeding beauty, she won the king's favor and was crowned as the new queen (Est. 2:17). Esther's willingness to join a royal harem and become the wife of a pagan king is even more striking, given the emphasis in both Ezra and Nehemiah on the wrongness of intermarriage between Jews and Gentiles (Ezra 9:1–4; Neh. 13:23–27). After reading Ezra's grief-filled prayer of confession following his learning that some Jews had married Gentiles (Ezra 9:13–15), we can only wonder what he might have thought about Esther's marriage to Ahasuerus.

The contrast between Ezra and Nehemiah's faithful adherence to Jewish law and Esther's religious and moral compromises could not be more starkly drawn. Esther was willing to do whatever it took to get ahead. She was eager to take advantage of another woman's misfortune and more than willing to submit herself to exploitation. Moral compromise—whether or not to Esther's extent—is familiar to almost all workplace Christians. Who has never taken morally dubious action in the course of their work? Who has never kept silent when the mistreatment of another has redounded to our own advantage—failing to stand up when the boss hides his or her own incompetence by firing a subordinate, or watching the dirtiest, most dangerous job fall once again to the ethnic outsider? Who has never shaded the truth to gain what we wanted—implying greater responsibility than we really had for a past success or pretending to know more than we really do in class or on the job?

Esther entered the palace with its access to high power and influence. She did not seem interested in whether God had any plan or purpose for her there. In fact, God is not even mentioned in the book of Esther. But that doesn't mean that God had no plan or purpose for her in Ahasuerus's court. As it happens, her cousin Mordecai was more scrupulous in keeping Jewish law, which after some time put him in conflict with Ahasuerus's highest official, Haman (Est. 3:1–6). Haman responded by plotting to kill not only Mordecai but the whole Jewish people (Est. 3:7–15). Mordecai learned of the plot and sent word of the plot to Esther. Although her entire people were about to be destroyed, she seemed unmoved.

Esther's excuse was that getting involved could jeopardize her position and even her life (Est. 4:11). Already she seemed to be losing the king's interest, having not been called into his presence for the past thirty days. It is inconceivable that the king was sleeping alone, which means that some other woman or women had been "called to come in to the king" (Est. 4:11). To intervene on behalf of her people would be too risky. Mordecai responded with two arguments. First, her life was at risk, whether or not she intervened. "Do not think that in the king's palace you will escape any more than all the other Jews" (Est. 4:13). And second, "Who knows? Perhaps you have come to royal dignity for just such a time as this" (Est. 4:14). Together, these arguments led to a remarkable about-face by Esther. "I will go to the king, though it is against the law; and if I perish, I perish" (Est. 4:16). The social climber interested in no one's good but her own suddenly offered to risk her neck for the good of others.

Notice that Mordecai's two arguments appealed to different instincts. The first argument appealed to self-preservation. You, Esther, are a Jew, and if all the Jews are ordered killed, you will be found out and slain eventually. The second argument appealed to destiny, with its hint of divine service. If you wonder, Esther, why you of all young women ended up the king's wife, perhaps it is because there is a larger purpose to your life. The first argument seems base, while the second seems noble. Which argument produced the change in Esther?

Perhaps both of Mordecai's arguments were steps toward Esther's change of heart. The first step was identification. At long last, Esther identified with her people. In this sense, she took the same step Jesus was to take at his birth, identification of himself with humanity. And perhaps this step, selfishly taken as it may have been in Esther's case, is what opened her heart to God's purposes.

The second step was service. Identifying now with her people's mortal peril, Esther took on the service of intervening with the king. She risked her position, her possessions, and her life. Her high position became a means of service, instead of self-service. Despite her initially faithless and unobservant history, God used Esther, no less than he used the morally exemplary Ezra and Nehemiah. Esther's service corresponds to today's workplace in several ways:[8]

1. Many people, Christian or not, make ethical compromises in their quest for career success. Because we all stand in Esther's shoes, we all have the opportunity—and responsibility—to let God use us anyway, despite our history of moral failure. Did you cut corners to get your job? Nonetheless, God will use you to call an end to the deceptive practices in your workplace. Have you made improper use of corporate assets? God may still use you to clean up the falsified records in your department. Past hypocrisy is no excuse for failing to heed what God needs from you now. Prior misuse of your God-given abilities is no reason to believe you cannot employ them for God's good purposes today. Esther is the model for all of us who have fallen short of the glory of God. You cannot say, "If you knew how many ethical shortcomings I made to get here. I can't be of any use to God now."

2. God makes use of the actual circumstances of our lives. Esther's position gave her unique opportunities to serve God. Mordecai's position gave him different opportunities. We should embrace the particular opportunities we have. Rather than saying, "I would do something great for God, if only I had the opportunity," we should say, "Perhaps I have come into this position for just such a time as this."

3. Our positions are spiritually dangerous. We may come to equate our value and our very existence with our positions. The higher our positions, the greater the danger. Esther ceased to see herself as a young Jewish woman, and only as the queen of Persia.

---

[8] Ideas in this section are drawn from Tim Keller's sermon "If I Perish, I Perish," which he delivered at Redeemer Presbyterian Church in New York City on April 22, 2007. It can be downloaded in MP3 and compact disk formats, 42.17, at sermons.redeemer.com/store/.

To do likewise makes us slaves to factors beyond our control. If becoming CEO, getting tenure, or keeping a good job becomes so important that we cut off the rest of ourselves, then we have lost ourselves already.

4. Serving God requires risking our positions. If you use your position to serve God, you might lose your position and your future prospects. This is doubly frightening if you have become self-identified with your job or career. Yet the truth is our positions are also at risk if we don't serve God. Esther's case is extreme. She knew she might be killed if she risked her position by intervening, and she would be killed if she didn't intervene. Are our positions really any more secure than Esther's? It is not foolish to risk what you cannot keep in order to gain what you cannot lose, as the missionary Jim Elliot famously pointed out. Work done in God's service can never truly be lost.

For Esther and the Jews, the story has a happy ending. Esther risked approaching the king unbidden, yet she received his favor (Est. 5:1–2). She employed a clever scheme to butter him up over the course of two banquets (Est. 5:4–8; 7:1–5) and to manipulate Haman into exposing his own hypocrisy in seeking to have the Jews annihilated (Est. 7:6–10). The king revoked the judgment against the Jews (Est. 8:11–14) and rewarded Mordecai and Esther with riches, honor, and power (Est. 8:1–2; 10:1–3). They in turn improved the lot of Jews throughout the Persian Empire (Est. 10:3). Haman and the enemies of the Jews were slaughtered (Est. 7:9–10; 9:1–17), and the dates of the Jews' deliverance—Adar 14 and 15—became marked thereafter as the festival of Purim (Est. 9:17–23).

God's Hidden Hand and Human Response

As noted earlier, God is not mentioned in the book of Esther. Yet it is a book of the Bible. Commentators therefore look for the veiled presence of God in Esther and generally point to the crucial verse: "Who knows? Perhaps you have come to royal dignity for such a time as this" (Est. 4:14). The implication is that she has come to her position not by luck or fate, or by her own wiles, but by the will of an unseen actor. We can see the divine handwriting on the wall here. Esther has come to her royal position because the "good hand of God was upon [her]," as Ezra and Nehemiah might have said (Ezra 8:18; Neh. 2:18).

This challenges us to ponder how God might be at work in ways we don't recognize. When a secular company eliminates bias in promotions and pay scales, is God at work there? When a Christian is able to end deceptive record-keeping practices, does she have to announce that she did so because she's a Christian? If Christians have a chance to join with Jews and Muslims to make a case for reasonable religious accommodations in a corporation, should they see it as a work of God? If you can do good by taking a job in a compromised political administration, could God be calling you to accept the offer? If you teach in a school that pushes you to the limits of your conscience, should you seek to leave, or should you redouble your commitment to staying?

Conclusions from Ezra, Nehemiah, and Esther

The books of Ezra, Nehemiah, and Esther have several common features. All three are relatively short narratives about events happening during the reign of the Persian Empire. All three involve Persian kings and other government officials. All three focus on the activities of Jews who were seeking to thrive in an environment that is, in many ways, hostile to their exercise of faith in God. All three books bear witness to the fact that a Persian king could be helpful to the Jews in their effort to survive and thrive. All three feature key leaders whose actions are held up as models for imitation. And all three books show people at work, thus providing an opportunity for us to reflect upon how these books impact our understanding of work and its relationship to God.

Yet all three books represent a wide difference in opinion about crucial matters. This is true even of Ezra and Nehemiah, which were originally two parts of one book. In Ezra, trusting God requires that God's people travel through dangerous territory without a royal escort. In Nehemiah, the offer of a royal escort is taken as evidence of God's blessing. Ezra represents what might be called "idealistic faith," while

Nehemiah practices "pragmatic faith." In Esther, God's hand is hidden, revealed primarily in Esther's shrewd use of her wits and position in the service of her people. We could call hers a "clever faith."

Nevertheless, Ezra and Nehemiah uphold a similar vision of God's work in the world. God is involved in the lives of all people, not only his chosen ones. God moves in the hearts of pagan kings, leading them to support God's purposes. The Lord inspires his people to devote their work to him, using a wide variety of strong leaders and prophetic voices to fulfill his purposes. In Ezra, God uses a faithful priest to rebuild his temple. In Nehemiah, God uses a faithful layperson to rebuild the walls of his capital. In Esther, God uses a deeply compromised, initially unobservant Jew to save the Jewish people from genocide. From the perspective of all three books, God is at work throughout the world, making use of the work of all kinds of people.

Job and Work

Introduction to Job

The book of Job explores the relationship between prosperity, adversity, and faith in God. Do we have faith that God is the source of all good things? Then what does it mean if the good things disappear from our lives? Do we abandon our faith in God or in his goodness? Or do we take it as a sign that God is punishing us? How can we remain faithful to God in times of suffering? What hope can we have for the future?

These questions arise in every sphere of life. But they have a special connection to work because one of the main reasons we work is to achieve some level of prosperity. We work—among many other reasons—to get a roof over our heads, put food on our tables, and provide good things for ourselves and the people we love. Adversity may threaten whatever prosperity we have found, and faith is difficult to maintain in times of economic adversity. The chief character in the book of Job begins in prosperity and experiences nearly unimaginable adversity, including the loss of his livelihood and wealth. Over the course of the book, his faith is severely tested as he experiences both dazzling success and crushing defeat in his work and life.

We will explore the book's many applications to work. Is economic success a sign of our abilities or of God's blessing? What does job loss or failure tell us about God's assessment of our work? How can faith in God help us handle failures and losses? How do stresses in the workplace affect our family's lives and our health? What can believers do to support one another in workplace adversities? How can we handle feelings of anger at God if he allows us to suffer unjust treatment at work? We will delve into Job's practical treatise on relationships between superiors and subordinates, founded on the equal respect due each person created by the one and only God. Finally, we will consider the remarkable contribution Job makes to the economic rights of women.

Background and Outline

The author of Job is anonymous. Job does not seem to be an Israelite, because he is said to be from the land of Uz (Job 1:1), which most scholars suggest was to the southeast of ancient Israel. Because he is cited in the book of Ezekiel (Ezek. 14:14, 20), it seems best to date his story no later than Ezekiel's life (sixth century BC). His story, in any case, is timeless.

The book contains a wide variety of literary genres (narrative, poetry, visions, dialogue, and others) woven together into a literary masterpiece. The most commonly accepted outline identifies two cycles of lament, dialogue, and revelation, sandwiched between a prologue and an epilogue:

Job 1–2	Prologue—Job's Prosperity Lost
Job 3	Job's First Lament
Job 4–23	Job's Friends Blame Job for the Calamity
Job 28	Wisdom Revealed
Job 29–31	Job's Second Lament
Job 32–37	Dialogue with Elihu
Job 38–42:9	God Appears
Job 42:7–17	Epilogue—Job's Prosperity Restored

Theology and Themes

Most familiar to Bible readers as the righteous man who suffered unjustly, Job exemplifies the person who questions why good people suffer. Job's faith in God is put to the extreme test, and the story intimates that Job's commitment to God wanes. As we will see, Job's woes begin at work, and the book gives us valuable insights into how a follower of God may faithfully function within the ups and downs of work life.

Prologue (Job 1–2)

Job's Prosperity Acknowledged as God's Blessing (Job 1:1–12)

At the beginning of the book of Job we are introduced to an exceptionally prosperous farmer/rancher named Job. He is described as "the greatest [man] among all the people of the East" (Job 1:3). Like the patriarchs Abraham, Isaac, and Jacob, his wealth is measured by his many thousand head of livestock, numerous servants, and large family. His seven sons and three daughters (Job 1:2) are both a personal joy to him and an important foundation of his wealth. In agricultural societies, children supply the most reliable part of the labor needed in a household. They are the best hope for a comfortable retirement. This was the only pension plan available in the ancient Near East, as it still is in many parts of the world today.

Job regards his success to be the result of God's blessing. We are told that God has "blessed the work of his hands, and his possessions have increased in the land" (Job 1:10). Job's recognition that he owes everything to God's blessing is highlighted by an unusual detail. He worries that his children might inadvertently offend God. Although Job takes care to remain "blameless and upright" (Job 1:1), he worries that his children may not be so fastidious. What if one of them, addled by too much drink during their frequent days-long feasts, should sin by cursing God (Job 1:4–5)? Therefore, after every feast, to forestall any offense to God, "Job would send and sanctify them, and he would rise early in the morning and offer burnt offerings according to the number of them all" (Job 1:5).

God recognizes Job's faithfulness. He remarks to his Satan (a Hebrew word meaning simply "accuser"), "Have you considered my servant Job? There is no one like him on the earth, a blameless and upright man who fears God and turns away from evil" (Job 1:8). The accuser spots an opening for mischief and replies, "Does Job fear God for nothing?" (Job 1:9). That is, does Job love God only because God has blessed him so richly? Are Job's praise and his burnt offerings "according to the number of them all" (Job 1:5) just a calculated scheme to keep the goods flowing? Or to use a modern image, is Job's faithfulness nothing more than a coin fed into the vending machine of God's blessing?

We could apply this question to ourselves. Do we relate to God primarily so that he will bless us with the stuff we want? Or worse yet, so that he won't jinx the success we seem to be achieving on our own? In good times, this may not be a burning issue. We believe in God. We acknowledge him—at least theoretically—as the source of all good things. At the same time, we work diligently, so God's goodness and our work go hand in hand. When times are good, and we do in fact prosper, it is natural to thank God and praise him for it.

God Allows Satan to Destroy Job's Prosperity (Job 1:13–22)

The problem of pain comes when times are hard. When we are passed over for promotion or lose a job, when we become chronically ill, when we lose people we love, what then? We face the question, "If God was blessing me during the good times, is he punishing me now?" This is a hugely important question.

If God is punishing us, then we need to change our ways so he will stop. But if our difficulties are not a punishment from God, then changing our ways would be foolish. It might even oppose what God wants us to do.

Imagine the case of a teacher who gets laid off during a school budget cut and thinks, "This is God's punishment because I didn't become a missionary." Taking her layoff as a sign, she enrolls in seminary and borrows money to pay for it. Three years later, she graduates and begins trying to raise support for her mission. If indeed God caused the layoff to punish her for not becoming a missionary, she has ceased the offense. She should be in good shape.

But what if her layoff was not a punishment from God? What if God actually has no intention for her to become a missionary? While in seminary, she may miss an opportunity to serve God as a teacher. Worse yet, what happens if she fails to raise support as a missionary? She will have no job and tens of thousands of dollars of debt. Will she then feel abandoned by God if her mission plan doesn't work out? Might she even lose her faith or become bitter toward God? If so, she would not be the first. Yet it would all be because she mistakenly assumed that her layoff was a sign of God's punishment. The question of whether adversity is a sign of God's disfavor is no light matter.

The accuser—Satan—hopes to set just such a trap for Job. Satan says to God that if he removes the blessings he has so richly bestowed on Job, "He will curse you to your face" (Job 1:11; 2:5). If Satan can get Job to believe he is being punished by God, Job may be caught in either of two snares. He may abandon his righteous habits in the mistaken assumption that they are offensive to God. Or, better yet from the accuser's point of view, he will become bitter at God for his undeserved punishment and abandon God altogether. Either way, it will be a curse in the face of God.

God allows Satan to proceed. We are not told why. One harrowing day, nearly everything Job treasures is stolen and the people he loves— including all his children—are murdered, or killed in violent storms (Job 1:13–16). But Job neither assumes God is punishing him nor becomes bitter over God's treatment. Instead he worships God (Job 1:20). At his lowest moment, Job blesses God's authority over all the circumstances of life, good or bad. "The Lord gave, and the Lord has taken away; blessed be the name of the Lord" (Job 1:21).

Job's finely balanced attitude is remarkable. He rightly understands his previous prosperity as a blessing from God. He does not imagine he ever *deserved* God's blessing, even though he recognizes he was righteous (implicit in Job 1:1, 5 and stated explicitly in Job 6:24–30, et al.). Because he knows he didn't deserve his former blessings, he knows he does not necessarily deserve his current sufferings.

He does not take his condition to be a measurement of God's favor. Consequently, he doesn't pretend to know why God blessed him with prosperity at one time and not at another.

The book of Job is a rebuke to the "prosperity gospel," which claims that those in right relationship with God are always blessed with prosperity. This is simply not true, and Job is Exhibit Number One. Yet Job is also a rebuke to the "poverty gospel," which claims the opposite—that a right relationship with God implies a life of poverty. The idea that believers should *intentionally* emulate Job's loss is too farfetched to appear even on the fringe of discussion in Job. God might call us to give up everything, if doing so were necessary under the circumstances to serve or follow him. But the book of Job makes no suggestion that God inherently desires anyone to live in poverty. Job's original prosperity was a genuine blessing of God, and his extreme poverty is a genuine calamity.

Job can remain faithful under adversity because he understands prosperity accurately. Because he has experienced prosperity as a blessing from God, he is prepared to suffer adversity without jumping to conclusions. He knows what he doesn't know—namely, why God blesses us with prosperity or allows us to suffer adversity. And he knows what he does know—namely, that God is faithful even while God allows us to experience great pain and suffering. As a result, "In all this Job did not sin or charge God with wrong-doing" (Job 1:22).

God Allows Satan to Destroy Job's Health (Job 2:1–11)

Job is able to endure overwhelming loss without compromising his "integrity" or blamelessness[1] (Job 2:3). But Satan does not give up. Perhaps Job merely hasn't faced *enough* pain and suffering. Satan now accuses him of serving God only because he still has his health (Job 2:4). So God allows the accuser to afflict Job with every matter of loathsome sores "from the sole of his foot to the crown of his head" (Job 2:7). This is especially galling to Job's wife, and she asks him, "Do you still persist in your integrity? Curse God, and die" (Job 2:9). She accepts that Job is blameless in God's eyes, but unlike him, doesn't see the point in being blameless if it doesn't bring God's blessings. Job responds with one of the classic verses of Scripture, "Shall we receive the good from the hand of God, and not receive the bad?" (Job 2:10).

Once again we find Job ascribing every circumstance of life to God. Meanwhile, Job is unaware of the heavenly activity that is behind his situation. He cannot see the inner workings of heaven, and it is only the integrity of his faith that prevents him from cursing God. How about us? Do we recognize that, like Job, we do not understand the mysteries of heaven that shape our prosperity and adversity? Do we prepare for adversity by practicing faithfulness and thanksgiving during good times? Job's unwavering habit of prayer and sacrifice may have seemed quaint or even obsessive when we encountered it in Job 1:5. But now we can see that a lifetime of faithful practices forged his capacity to remain faithful

---

[1]The Hebrew word *tam,* translated as "integrity," has the same root as *tummah,* translated in the same verse as "blameless."

in extreme circumstances. Faith in God may come in an instant. Integrity is formed over a lifetime.

Job's adversity arises in his workplace, with the loss of his means of income. It spreads to his family and eventually attacks his health. This pattern is familiar to us. We can easily become so identified with our work that workplace setbacks spread to our family and personal lives. Workplace failures threaten our self-identity and even our integrity. This, plus the practical strain of losing income and security, may severely disrupt family relationships. Though death on the job is rare in most occupations, work-related stresses may lead to long-term deterioration of physical and mental health and family issues. We may be unable to find peace, rest, or even a good night's sleep (Job 3:26). In the midst of such stress, Job maintains his integrity. It might be tempting to draw a moral such as, "Don't get so wrapped up in your work that its problems affect your family or your health." But that wouldn't do justice to the depth of Job's story. Job problems *did* affect his family and his health, in addition to his work. Job's wisdom is not about how to minimize adversity by maintaining wise boundaries, but about what it looks like to maintain faithfulness through the worst circumstances of life.

Job's Friends Arrive to Comfort Him (Job 2:11–13)

With Satan having done his worst, Job could really use some support. Job's three friends enter the story and are depicted as sensitive, pious, and sympathetic men. They go so far as to sit with Job for seven days and nights (Job 2:13). They are wise enough—at this point—not to say anything. Comfort comes from the friends' presence in adversity, not from anything they might say to make things better. Nothing they can say *could* make things better.

Job's First Lament (Job 3)

There is nothing left for Job but to lament. He refuses to incriminate himself falsely, and he refuses to blame or abandon God. But he does not hesitate to express his anguish in the strongest terms. "Let the day perish

in which I was born, and the night that said, 'A man-child is conceived'"
(Job 3:3). "Why did I not die at birth, come forth from the womb and
expire?" (Job 3:11). "Or why was I not buried like a stillborn child, like
an infant that never sees the light?" (Job 3:16). "Why is light given to one
who cannot see the way, whom God has fenced in?" (Job 3:23). Notice
that Job's lament is almost entirely in the form of questions. The cause
of his suffering is a mystery. Indeed, it may be the greatest mystery of
faith. Why does God allow people he loves to suffer? Job does not know
the answer, so the most honest thing he can do is ask questions.

Job's Friends Blame Job for the Calamity (Job 4–23)

Job's Friends Accuse Him of Doing Evil (Job 4–23)

Regrettably, Job's friends are not able to endure the mystery of his
suffering, so they jump to conclusions about its source. The first of the
three, Eliphaz, acknowledges that Job has been a source of strength
to others (Job 4:3–4). But then he turns and puts the blame for Job's
suffering squarely on Job himself. "Think now," he says, "who that was
innocent ever perished? Or where were the upright cut off? As I have
seen, those who plow iniquity and sow trouble reap the same" (Job
4:7–8). Job's second friend, Bildad, says much the same. "See, God
will not reject a blameless person nor take the hand of evildoers" (Job
8:20). The third friend, Zophar, repeats the refrain. "If iniquity is in
your hand, put it far away, and do not let wickedness reside in your
tents. Surely then you will lift up your face without blemish; you will be
secure, and will not fear. . . . Your life will be brighter than the noonday"
(Job 11:14–15, 17).

Their reasoning is a syllogism. God sends calamities upon wicked
people only. You have suffered a calamity. Therefore you must be wicked.
Job himself avoids this false syllogism, but it is commonly accepted by
Christians. It is called a theology of divine retribution, and it assumes
that God blesses those who are faithful to him and punishes those who
sin. It is not entirely without biblical support. There are many cases in

which God sends calamity as a punishment, as he did at Sodom (Gen. 19:1–29). Often, our experiences do bear out this theological position. In most situations, things turn out better when we follow God's ways than when we forsake them. However, God does not *always* work that way. Jesus himself pointed out that disaster is not necessarily a sign of God's judgment (Luke 13:4). In Job's case, we know the theology of divine retribution is not true because God says that Job is a righteous man (Job 1:8; 2:3). Job's friends' devastating error is to apply a generalization to Job's situation, without knowing what they're talking about.

Anyone who has spent time with a suffering friend knows how hard it is to remain present without trying to give answers. It is excruciating to suffer silently with a friend who must rebuild life piece by piece, without any certainty about the outcome. Our instinct is to investigate what went wrong and identify a solution. Then we imagine we can help our friend eliminate the cause and get back to normal as soon as possible. Knowing the cause, we will at least know how to avoid the same fate ourselves. We would rather give a reason for the suffering—be it right, be it wrong—than to accept the mystery at the heart of suffering.

Job's friends succumb to this temptation. It would be foolish to imagine that we would never do the same. How much harm have well-intentioned Christians caused by giving pious-sounding but ignorant answers to suffering, even though we have no idea what we're talking about? "It's all for the best," "It's part of God's plan," or "God never sends people more adversity than they can handle." Such platitudes are usually false and always demeaning. How arrogant to imagine we know God's plan! How foolish to think we know the reason for anyone else's suffering. We don't even know the reason for our own suffering. It would be more truthful—and far more helpful—to admit, "I don't know why this happened to you. No one should have to go through this." If we can do this, *and then remain present*, we may become agents of God's compassion.

Job's friends can't lament with Job or even acknowledge that they lack a basis for judging him. They are hell-bent (literally, given Satan's role) on defending God by placing the blame on Job. As the friends' speeches continue, their rhetoric becomes increasingly hostile. Faced with the self-imposed choice of blaming Job or blaming God, they harden their hearts against their former friend. "There is no end to your iniquities," says Eliphaz (Job 22:5), and then he invents some iniquities to charge against Job. "You have given no water to the weary to drink, and you have withheld bread from the hungry" (Job 22:8). "You have sent widows away empty-handed, and the arms of the orphans you have crushed" (Job 22:9).

Zophar's last speech observes that wicked persons will not enjoy their riches because God will make their stomachs "vomit them up again" (Job 20:15) and that "they will give back the fruit of their toil, and will not swallow it down; from the profit from their trading they will get no fruit of their enjoyment" (Job 20:18). This is an appropriate righting of the wicked person's wrongdoing, that "they have crushed and abandoned the poor, they have seized a house that they did not build" (Job 20:19). The reader knows this does not apply to Job. Why is Zophar so eager to blame Job? Are we sometimes too eager to follow in Zophar's footsteps when our friends face failures in work and life?

The book of Job demands that we see ourselves in the faces of Job's friends. We too—presumably—know right from wrong, and have some sense of God's ways. But we do not know *all* of God's ways as they apply in all times and places. "Such knowledge is too wonderful for me; it is so high that I cannot attain it" (Ps. 139:6). God's ways are often a mystery beyond our understanding. Is it possible that we also are guilty of ignorant judgments against our friends and co-workers?

But it doesn't have to be friends who accuse us. Unlike Job, most of us are quite ready to accuse ourselves. Anyone who has tasted failure has likely pondered, "What have I done to deserve this?" It's natural and not altogether incorrect. Sometimes out of sheer laziness, bad data, or incompetence, we make poor decisions that cause us to fail at work. However, not all failures are the direct result of our own shortcomings. Many are the result of circumstances outside our control. Workplaces are complex, with many factors competing for our attention, many ambiguous situations, and many decisions whose outcomes are impossible to predict. How do we know whether we are following God's ways all the time? How could we or anyone genuinely know whether our successes and failures are due to our own actions or to factors beyond our control? How could an outsider judge the rightness of our actions without knowing the intimate details of our situations? Indeed, how could we even judge ourselves, give the limits of our own knowledge?

Job's Friends Accuse Him of Abandoning God (Job 8–22)

Eventually, Job's friends move from questioning what Job did wrong to questioning whether Job has abandoned God (Job 15:4, 20:5). Along the way the friends encourage Job to return to God. Bildad directs Job to "make supplication to the Almighty" (Job 8:5) so that Job's future will be "very great" (Job 8:7) and filled with "laughter" and "shouts of joy" (Job 8:21). Eliphaz adjures him, "If you will return to the Almighty, you will be restored" (Job 22:23). Again, in general terms, this is good advice. We frequently do turn away from God and need to be recalled to him. However, we the readers know that Job has not done anything to deserve his suffering, and the effect of his friends' attacks is to make Job begin to doubt himself. Just when he needs his friends to believe in him, they keep him from believing in himself. How can they support him when they have already made up their minds against him?

Job Pleads His Case to God (Job 5–13)

In contrast, Job has wisdom that many Christians lack. He knows to direct his emotions at God rather than at himself or those around him. He believes the source of blessings—and even adversities—is God, so he takes his complaint to the source. "But I would speak to the Almighty, and I desire to argue my case with God. . . . How many are my iniquities and my sins? Make me know my transgression and my sin. Why do you hide your face, and count me as your enemy?" (Job 13:3, 23–24). He acknowledges he doesn't understand God's ways. "He does great things and unsearchable, marvelous things without number" (Job 5:9). He knows he can never prevail in an argument against God. "If one wished to contend with him, one could not answer him once in a thousand. He is wise in heart, and mighty in strength—who has resisted him, and succeeded?" (Job 9:3–4). But he knows his anguish has to come out somewhere. "Therefore I will not restrain my mouth; I will speak in the anguish of my spirit; I will complain in the bitterness of my soul" (Job 7:11). Better to direct it at God, who can handle it easily, than against himself or those he loves who cannot.

Job's Friends Try to Protect God (Job 22–23)

We all know the demons that plague us after failure. We second-guess ourselves during sleepless nights of self-torment. It even feels like the holy thing to do—to protect God by blaming ourselves. If we second-guess ourselves like this, imagine how we second-guess our friends, though we are seldom aware of it. Job's friends show us how it's done. In their eagerness to protect God from Job's protestations, they increase their attacks on Job. Yet over the centuries, the Christian reading of Job has viewed the friends as tools of Satan, not of God. God does not need protecting. He can take care of himself. Satan would like nothing more than to prove to God that Job served God only because God blessed him so richly. An admission by Job that he has done something wrong, when in reality he has not, would be the first step toward validating the accuser's attack.

For example, Eliphaz's last speech concentrates on putting God above reproach. "Can a mortal be of use to God? Can even the wisest be of service to him?" (Job 22:2). "Is not God high in the heavens?" (Job 22:12). "Agree with God, and be at peace" (Job 22:21). "If the Almighty is your gold and your precious silver, then you will delight yourself in the Almighty, and lift up your face to God. You will pray to him and he will hear you" (Job 22:25–27).

Job, however, is not trying to blame God. He is trying to *learn from* God. Despite the horrible adversity God has permitted to afflict Job, Job believes that God can use the experience to shape his soul for the better. "When God has tested me, I shall come out like gold," Job says (Job 23:10). "For he will complete what he appoints for me, and many such things are in his mind" (Job 23:14). Paul Stevens and Alvin Ung have pointed out how many soul-shaping events occur at work.[2] The dark forces of the fallen world threaten to sap our souls there, yet God intends that our souls come out like gold, refined and molded into the particular likeness of God he has in mind for each of us. Imagine what life would be like if we could find

---

[2] R. Paul Stevens and Alvin Ung, *Taking Your Soul to Work* (Grand Rapids: Eerdmans, 2010).

spiritual growth not only when we are at church, but in all the hours we spend working. For this, we would need wise, sensitive spiritual counselors when we face trials at work. Job's friends, mired in mindlessly repeating conventional spiritual maxims, are of no help to him in this regard.

Job's Complaints Take On Special Significance for Our Work (Job 24)

Like Job, our sufferings often begin with difficulties at work. But seldom are God's people equipped—or even willing—to help one another handle workplace failures and losses. We might go to a pastor or a Christian friend for help in a family or health issue, and they might be truly helpful. But would we ask them for help with workplace problems? If we did, how much help would we be likely to get?

For example, imagine you are treated unfairly by your boss, perhaps blamed for her mistake or humiliated during a legitimate disagreement. It would not be appropriate to reveal your feelings to customers, suppliers, students, patients, or others you serve in your work. It would be harmful to complain to your co-workers, even to your friends among them. It could be a unique blessing if the Christian community were equipped to help you deal with the situation. But not every church is fully equipped to help people handle work-related difficulties. Is this an area where churches need to improve?

We have seen that Job is not afraid to take his complaints—including work-related complaints—to God. The series of complaints in Job 24:1–12 and 22–25 particularly concerns work. Job complains that God lets evil people get away with injustice in work and economic activity. People appropriate public resources for personal gain, and they steal the private property of others (Job 24:2). They exploit the weak and powerless to gain outsized profit for themselves (Job 24:3). The arrogant get their way at work, while the honest and humble are ground into the dirt (Job 24:4). The poorest have no opportunity to earn a living and are reduced to scavenging, and even stealing from the rich to feed their families (Job 24:5–8). Others work hard, but do not earn enough to enjoy the fruits of their labor. "Though hungry, they carry the sheaves; between their terraces they press out oil; they tread the wine presses, but suffer thirst" (Job 24:10–11).

Job knows that all blessing comes from God, and all adversity is allowed—if not caused—by God. Therefore, we can feel the sharp sting in Job's complaint, "From the city the dying groan, and the throat of the wounded cries for help; *yet God pays no attention to their prayer*" (Job 24:12; emphasis added). Job's friends accuse him of forsaking God, but the evidence is that the righteous are forsaken *by God*. Meanwhile, the wicked seem to lead a charmed life. "God prolongs the life of the mighty by his power; they rise up when they despair of life. He gives them security, and they are supported; his eyes are upon their ways" (Job 24:22–23). Job believes the wicked will ultimately be cut down. "They are exalted a little while, and then are gone; they wither and fade like the mallow; they are cut off like the heads of grain" (Job 24:24). But why does God let the wicked prosper at all?

There is no answer in the book of Job, and there is no answer known to humanity. Economic adversity is an all-too-real pain that many Christians face for years or even a lifetime. We may have to abandon our education when we are young due to financial hardship, and it could prevent us from ever reaching our potential in the workplace. We may be exploited by others or scapegoated to the ruin of our careers. We may be born, struggle to survive, and die under the thumb of a corrupt government that keeps its people in poverty and oppression.

These are merely a few work-related examples. In a million other ways, we may suffer serious, grievous, unfair harm that we can never understand—much less remedy—in this life. By God's grace, we hope never to become complacent in the face of injustice and suffering. Yet there are times when we cannot make things right, at least not right away. In those situations, we have only three choices: make up a plausible but false explanation about how God allowed it to happen, as Job's friends do; abandon God; or remain faithful to God without receiving an answer.

Wisdom Revealed (Job 28)

Job chooses to remain faithful to God. He understands that God's wisdom is beyond his understanding. Job 28 employs mining as an analogy for searching for wisdom. It reveals that wisdom "is not found in the land of the living" (Job 28:13), but in the mind of God. "God understands the way to it and he knows its place" (Job 28:23). This is a reminder that technical knowledge and practical skill are not enough for truly meaningful work. We also need God's spirit as we go about our tasks. We need God's guidance far beyond the realm of things we commonly think of as "spiritual." When a teacher tries to discern how a student learns, when a leader tries to communicate clearly, when a jury tries to determine a defendant's intent, when an analyst tries to assess a project's risks, they all need God's wisdom. Whatever the goal of our work is, "God understands the way to it, and he knows its place" (Job 28:23).

Yet we cannot always get in touch with God's wisdom. "It is hidden from the eyes of all living, and concealed from the birds of the air" (Job 28:21). Despite our best attempts—or sometimes because of our lackluster efforts—we may not find God's guidance for every action and decision. If so, it is better to recognize our ignorance than to put our stock in speculation or false wisdom. Sometimes humility is the best way to honor God. "Truly, the fear of the Lord, that is wisdom; and to depart from evil is understanding" (Job 28:28).

Job's Second Lament (Job 29–42)

As noted in the introduction, Job 29–42 marks a second cycle of lamentation-discourse-revelation that recapitulates the first. For example, in Job 29, Job's recollection of the good old days brings us back to his idyllic scene in chapter 1. In Job 30, Job's distress that many now reject him reminds us of his wife's distancing herself in chapter 2. Job's lament in chapters 30 and 31 are prolonged versions of his lament in chapter 3. However, each phase in the second cycle brings a new emphasis.

Job Falls into Nostalgia and Self-Justification (Job 29–30)

The new emphases in Job's second lament (Job 29–42) are nostalgia and self-justification. Job longs for "the days when God watched over me" (Job 29:2) and "when the friendship of God was upon my tent" (Job 29:4). He reminisces about when his "steps were washed with milk, and the rock poured out for me streams of oil" (Job 29:6). He remembers how well respected he was in the community, which in the language of the Old Testament is most dramatically portrayed by his "seat in the square" near the "gate of the city" (Job 29:7). Job was well received by the young and old alike (Job 29:8), and treated with unusual respect by the chiefs and nobles (Job 29:10). He was respected because he tended to the needs of the poor, fatherless, widows, blind, lame, needy, strangers, and those dying (Job 29:12–16). He was their champion against the wicked (Job 29:17).

Job's nostalgia deepens his sense of loss when he realizes that much of the respect he received in work and civic life was superficial. "Because God has loosed my bowstring and humbled me, they have cast off restraint in my presence" (Job 30:11). "And now they mock me in song" (Job 30:9). Some people experience a similar sense of loss due to retirement, career setbacks, financial loss, or any kind of perceived failure. We may question our identity and doubt our worth. Other people treat us differently when we have failed, or worse yet, they simply stay away from us. (At least Job's friends come to see him.) Former friends speak cautiously if they must be around us, lowering their voices as though hoping that no one might find them near us. Maybe they think failure is a disease that's catching, or maybe being seen near a failure will brand them as a failure. "They abhor me, they keep aloof from me," laments Job (Job 30:10).

This is not to say that all civic and workplace friendships are shallow. It is true that some people befriend us only because we are useful to them, and then they abandon us when we cease to be useful. What really stings is the loss of what seemed to be genuine friendships.

In contrast to his first lament (Job 3), Job dishes up a large portion of self-justification in this round. "My justice was like a robe and a turban" (Job 29:14). "I was a father to the needy" (Job 29:16). Job touts his impeccable sexual purity (Job 31:1, 9–10). We have known all along that Job is not being punished for any fault. He may be accurate in his self-appraisal, but the self-justification is neither necessary nor endearing. Adversity may not always bring out the best in us. Yet God remains faithful, although Job is not able to see it at the moment, "for," as he later says, "I was in terror of calamity from God" (Job 31:23).

Job's Ethical Practices Apply to the Workplace (Job 31)

In the midst of Job's second lament (Job 29–42), he unveils a significant treatise on ethical behavior, which in some ways anticipates Jesus'
Sermon on the Mount (Matt. 5–7). Although in the form of justifying
his own practices, Job gives some principles that apply to many areas
of our work lives:

1. Avoid falsehood and deceit (Job 31:5).

2. Don't let the ends justify the means, expressed as not allowing
   the heart (principles) to be lured astray by the eyes (expediency)
   (Job 31:7).

3. Practice generosity (Job 31:16–23).

4. Don't become complacent during times of prosperity (Job
   31:24–28).

5. Don't make your success depend on the failure of others (Job
   31:29).

6. Admit your mistakes (Job 31:33).

7. Don't try to get something for nothing, but pay properly for the
   resources you consume (Job 31:38–40).

Of particular interest is this passage about how he treats his
employees:

> "If I have rejected the cause of my male or female slaves, when they
> brought a complaint against me, what then shall I do when God rises up?
> When he makes inquiry, what shall I answer him? Did not he who made
> me in the womb make them? And did not one fashion us in the womb?"
> (Job 31:13–15)

A godly employer will treat employees with respect and dignity. This is
particularly evident in the way Job takes his servants' complaints seriously, especially those directed toward his own treatment of them. Job

correctly points out that those in power will have to stand before God to defend their treatment of those under them. "What then shall I do when God rises up? When he makes inquiry, what shall I answer him?" (Job 31:14). God will inquire of subordinates how their superiors treated them. Superiors would be wise to ask their subordinates the same question while it is still possible to remedy their errors. The mark of true and humble followers of God is their openness to the possibility that they are in the wrong, which is most evidenced by their willingness to field any and all legitimate complaints. Wisdom is necessary for discerning which complaints do in fact merit attention. Yet the primary goal is to cultivate an environment in which subordinates know that superiors will entertain thoughtful and rational appeals. Although Job is talking about himself and his servants, his principle applies to any situation of authority: officers and soldiers, employers and employees, parents and children (raising kids is an occupation, too), leaders and followers.

Our time has seen great struggles for equality in the workplace with respect to race, religion, nationality, sex, class, and other factors. The book of Job anticipates these struggles by thousands of years. Yet Job goes beyond merely formal equality of demographic categories. He sees the equal dignity of every person in his household. We will become like Job when we treat each person with all the dignity and respect due to a child of God, regardless of our personal feelings or the sacrifice required on our part.

Of course, this truth does not preclude Christian bosses from establishing and exacting high standards in the workplace. However, it does require that the ethos of any workplace relationship be characterized by respect and dignity, especially on the part of the powerful.

Dialogue with Elihu (Job 32–37)

At this point, a young bystander named Elihu enters the discussion. His dialogue with Job parallels the discourse between Job and his friends in chapters 4 through 27. According to Elihu, the new element is that he is inspired to speak the wisdom Job's friends lacked. "One who is perfect in knowledge is with you," he announces (Job 36:4). Elihu then denounces the friends for their inability to confute Job (Job

32:8–18). Given this boast, and remembering that the more confidently Job's friends spoke against him, the more inaccurate their accusations became, we should not expect much wisdom from Elihu. For the most part, he simply reiterates arguments made earlier. His agenda is the same as the friends—first to convince Job that he has done something to deserve this punishment, and then to encourage Job to repent in order to receive restored blessings from God (Job 36:10–11). He does introduce one new work-related principle—that it is wrong to take bribes (Job 36:18). It is a true statement, discussed more deeply elsewhere in Scripture, but wrongly applied as an accusation against Job.

God Appears (Job 38–42:9)

In the book's first cycle, Job's friends' speeches were halted by the revelation of God's wisdom. The new element in the second cycle is that Elihu's speech is interrupted by the dramatic appearance of God himself (Job 38:1). At last, God fulfills Job's desire for a face-to-face encounter. The reader has been waiting to see if Job will finally break and curse God to his face. Instead, Job holds firm but gets a further education about how far God's wisdom is beyond human knowing.

Who Can Comprehend the Wisdom of God? (Job 38:4–42:6)

God's first question to Job sets the tone of their mostly one-way conversation: "Where were you when I laid the foundation of the earth? Tell me, if you have understanding" (Job 38:4). Employing some of the most spectacular creation language in the Bible, God reveals his sole authorship of the wonders of creation. This has strong resonances with work. Our work reflects our creation in the image of God, the great Creator (Gen. 1–2). But here God dwells on work that only he is capable of doing. "Who laid its cornerstone when the morning stars sang together and all the heavenly beings shouted for joy?" (Job 38:6–7). "Who shut in the sea with doors when it burst out from the womb?" (Job 38:8). "Is it by your wisdom that the hawk soars, and spreads its wings toward the south? Is it at your command that the eagle mounts up and makes its nest on high?" (Job 39:26–27).

Curiously embedded in the midst of God's authority over the natural world is a profound insight into the human condition. God asks Job, "Who has put wisdom in the inward parts, or given understanding to the mind?"(Job 38:36). The answer, of course, is God. At once this both affirms our search for understanding and demonstrates its limits. The wisdom God puts in our inward parts makes it possible for us to yearn for an answer to the mystery of suffering. Yet our wisdom comes only from God, so we cannot outsmart God with wisdom of our own. In fact, he has implanted in us only a small fraction of his wisdom, so we will never have the capacity to comprehend all his ways. As we have seen, it may be good for our souls to voice our complaints against God. But it would be foolish to expect him to reply with, "Yes, I can see now that I was in error."

Further pursuing this unequal encounter, God issues an impossible challenge to Job: "Shall a faultfinder contend with the Almighty? Anyone who argues with God must respond" (Job 40:2). Given Job's previous recognition that "I don't know" is often the wisest answer, his humble response is not surprising. "I am of small account; what shall I answer you? I lay my hand on my mouth" (Job 40:4).

Most commentators suggest that God is giving Job a larger picture of Job's circumstances. Much like someone who stands too close to a painting and cannot appreciate the artist's perspective, Job needs to step back a few steps so that he can glimpse—if not fully understand—God's larger purposes with greater clarity.

God continues with a frontal assault on those who accuse God of wrongdoing in the administration of his creation. God repudiates Job's attempts at self-justification. "Will you even put me in the wrong? Will you condemn me that you may be justified?" (Job 40:8). Job's attempt to shift the blame hearkens back to Adam's response when God asked whether he ate from the tree of knowledge of good and evil. "The woman whom you gave to be with me, she gave me fruit from the tree, and I ate" (Gen. 3:12).

Bringing our complaints to God is a good thing if we take the books of Job, Psalms, and Habakkuk as inspired models for how to approach God in times of trouble. However, accusing God for the sake of covering our own failures is the height of hubris (Job 40:11–12). God repudiates Job for doing so. Yet even so, God does not condemn Job for voicing his complaint against God. Job's accusation against God is wrong beyond reason, but not beyond forgiveness.

Job gets the audience with God that he has been asking for. It does not answer his question about whether he deserved the suffering he experienced. Job realizes the fault is his for expecting to know the answer, not God's for failing to provide it. "I have uttered what I did not understand, things too wonderful to me, which I did not know" (Job 42:3). Perhaps it is just that he is so awed by the presence of God that he no longer needs an answer.

If we are looking for a reason for Job's suffering, we will not find it either. On the one hand, Job's ordeal has given him an even greater appreciation for God's goodness. "I know that you can do all things, and that no purpose of yours can be thwarted" (Job 42:2). Job's relationship with God seems to have deepened, and he has become wiser as a result. He appreciates more than ever that his former prosperity was not due to his own strength and power. But the difference is only a matter of degree. Was the incremental improvement worth the unutterable loss? We don't get an answer to that question from Job or from God.

God Denounces Job's Friends (Job 42:7–9)

God denounces the three friends whose arrogant proclamation of false wisdom had so tormented Job. In a satisfying and ironic twist, he declares that if Job prays on their behalf he will not punish them for their ignorant speeches in God's stead (Job 42:7–8). They, who wrongly urged Job to repent, must now depend on him to accept their repentance, and on God to fulfill Job's entreaty on their behalf. Job's act of praying on their behalf reminds us of the first chapter where Job prays for his children's protection. Job is a praying man, in season and out.

As part of our recovery from failure, we would do well to pray for those who have tormented or doubted us during our grief. Jesus later called us to pray for our enemies (Matt. 5:44; Luke 6:27–36), and this teaching is seen in both contexts as more than simply therapeutic. If we can pray for those who have persecuted us, then we can transcend the fleeting circumstances of life and begin to appreciate the picture from God's perspective.

Epilogue—Job's Prosperity Restored (Job 42:7–17)

The final section of Job contains a storybook ending in which many of Job's fortunes are restored—many but not all. He receives twice the wealth he had before (Job 42:10), plus a new brood of seven sons and three daughters (Job 42:13). But his first children are gone forever, a bad trade by any reckoning. Thus, even though we read that Job's latter life is blessed "more than his beginning" (Job 42:12), we know there must still be a bittersweet taste in his mouth. We know, following the resurrection of the Son of God, what Job could not have known—that God's final redemption comes only when Christ returns to bring his kingdom to fulfillment.

Job Leaves an Inheritance for His Daughters (Job 42:13–15)

Job does something stunning in the aftermath of his ordeal. He leaves his daughters an inheritance, along with his sons (Job 42:15). Leaving an inheritance to female children was unheard of in the ancient Near East, much as it was illegal in much of Europe right up to modern times. What could have caused Job to take this unprecedented step? Did his sorrow that he could do nothing for his deceased daughters give him the resolve to do everything he could for his living daughters? Was his grief the engine that drove him through the social barriers against women's equality in this regard? Did his suffering open his heart to others' suffering? Or were his implacable demands to know God's justice answered by a higher understanding of God's love for women and men? Although we cannot know the cause, we can see the results. If nothing else in this life, the result of our suffering may be others' liberation.

The Book Comes to an End

We leave the book of Job with observations and questions, rather than neat conclusions. Job proves faithful to God in prosperity and in adversity. This surely is a model for us. But the odious judgments made by his friends caution us against making too-certain application of any model to our own lives.

God proves faithful to Job. This is our ultimate hope and comfort. But we cannot predict how his faithfulness will be manifest in our lives until his promises are fulfilled in the new heaven and new earth. It would be folly to judge others, or even ourselves, based on the fractional evidence available to us, the paltry wisdom we are able to grasp and the minuscule perspectives we hold. To the hardest questions about the circumstances of our lives, the wisest answer may often be, "I don't know."

Psalms and Work

Introduction to Psalms

The book of Psalms is part hymnbook, part prayer book, part wisdom literature, and part anthology of poems concerning Israel and God. Its subject matter is astonishingly broad. On one hand, it proclaims praise and prayer for God Most High (Ps. 50:14), and on the other, it embraces human experience as intimate as lamenting a lost mother (Ps. 35:14). Psalms is distinctive in the Old Testament in that most of it consists of people talking to God. Elsewhere, the Old Testament is mostly God talking to people (as in the law and the prophets), or it is narrative.

Although thousands of years old, virtually all the psalms, in one way or another, mirror our own struggles and joys today. Whatever a particular psalm's subject may be, each gives voice to the emotions we feel as we grapple with life's issues. Some psalms capture our delight in God as we experience the divine presence with us through a tough situation that has had a good ending. Others express raw emotions of anger or grief in a struggle to understand why God has not acted as we thought he would when "the wicked triumph." In some, God speaks. In others, God is silent. Some find resolution, while others leave us with unanswered questions.

The psalms were not all written by one person at one time, as the variety of attributions in the superscript titles indicates. In fact, the study of the book of Psalms' authorship—as well as its dates of composition, settings, purposes, uses, and transmission—is a major field in biblical studies. The tools of form criticism and comparative literary analysis (especially comparisons to Ugaritic literature) have figured highly in Psalms scholarship.[1] We will not attempt to delve into these studies in general, but we will rely on such research as necessary to help us understand and apply the psalms to work.

---

[1] Peter C. Craigie, *Psalms 1–50*, 2nd ed., vol. 19, *Word Biblical Commentary* (Nashville: Nelson Reference & Electronic, 2004), 45–55.

Work in the Psalms

Throughout the one hundred fifty psalms, work appears regularly. Sometimes the psalms' interest in work lies in individual ethics, including integrity and obedience to God in our work, dealing with opponents, and anxiety about the apparent success of unethical people. Other psalms take an interest in the ethics of organizations—whether as small as a household, or as large as a nation. Modern themes to which these psalms apply include business ethics, handling institutional pressure, globalization, and the consequences of workplace failings and national wrongdoings. Another major work-related theme in Psalms is God's presence with us in our work. Here we find topics such as God's guidance, human creativity grounded in God (who undergirds all productivity), the importance of doing truly valuable work, and God's grace in our work. The psalms take a particular interest in the work of marriage, raising children, and caring for parents. Lying underneath all the particular topics is Psalms' proclamation of God's glory in all of creation. The wide variety of work-related themes in Psalms is no surprise.

The Five Books of Psalms

The most obvious structural feature of the Psalter is its division into five books: Book 1 (Pss. 1–41), Book 2 (Pss. 42–72), Book 3 (Pss. 73–89), Book 4 (Pss. 90–106), and Book 5 (Pss. 107–150). It is not fully known when or why these divisions were made, although many theories have been proposed. Book 1 focuses heavily on the experiences of David, and Book 2 speaks of David and the Davidic kingdom. Book 3 is grimmer, having a good deal of lamentation and complaint. It ends at Psalm 89 with the Davidic covenant in tatters and the nation in ruins. Book 4 speaks soberly of human mortality (Ps. 90), but it also speaks triumphantly of God as the great king who rules all (Pss. 93 and 95–99). Book 5 is a mixture, but it ends in celebration as the nations and all creation worship the God of Israel (see Ps. 148).

Thus we see a general movement going from the man David to the Davidic kingdom, to the end of the Davidic dynasty, to the praise of God himself as king of the earth, and finally to the triumph of the kingdom of God. This gives a narrative direction to the Psalter as a whole. But many psalms in the collection do not fit this arrangement. To a degree, the reason for the current order of the psalms remains a mystery. If there is a single, grand structure, either we don't fully understand it or it is not rigidly followed.

Interpretive Strategies for the Psalms

The unique nature of the psalms can make it difficult for us to understand them in their original context, much less to apply them to life and work today. The book of Psalms is a highly diverse collection, and this makes it hard to generalize. Should we study the psalms for instruction? Read them for history? Pray or sing them alone or with others? The Bible itself does not tell us the answer to these questions. Before we can delve into applying the psalms to work, we need to develop interpretive strategies to help us make the most of the psalms.

Our approach here will be to explore a selection of psalms chosen because they seem to say something significant about work or something significant about life that applies significantly to work. In practice, this generally means that psalms have been selected because the Theology of Work Project's contributors, steering committee, or reviewers found them particularly meaningful in their own study or experience. This is an admittedly unsystematic selection method. The resulting commentary is not meant to be exhaustive, or even necessarily *right*. Instead, it is meant as a series of examples of how Christian groups or individuals can faithfully employ the psalms as they seek to integrate their faith and their work.

Book 1 (Psalms 1–41)

Book 1 consists largely of psalms spoken by David individually, rather than by Israel as a nation. They address matters that concern David personally, and this makes them applicable to the situations we face at work on our own. Later books bring in the social and communal aspects of life and work.

Personal Integrity in Work (Psalm 1)

The two opening psalms establish themes that run through the entire Psalter. Psalm 1 describes personal integrity, indicating that this is how every reader should live. It specifically applies this to work and to our desire for success. It says of the righteous, "They are like trees planted by streams of water, which yield their fruit in its season, and their leaves do not wither. In all that they do, they prosper" (Ps. 1:3). Work done ethically tends to prosper. This is a general truth and not an infallible rule. Sometimes people suffer because of acting ethically, at work or elsewhere. But it is still true that people who fear God and have integrity will likely do well. This is both because they live wisely and because God's blessing is upon them.

Obedience to God (Psalm 2)

Psalm 2 focuses on the house of David. God has chosen this kingdom and its temple, Zion, to be the focus of the kingdom of God. Someday, Gentiles will submit to it or face God's wrath. Thus Psalms 2:11–12 says, "Serve the LORD with fear, with trembling, kiss his feet, or he will be angry, and you will perish in the way; for his wrath is quickly kindled. Happy are all who take refuge in him." Jesus fulfilled the promises to David. For us, the lesson is that we must value Christ's kingdom above all things. A good work ethic is valuable, but we cannot make prosperity our priority. We cannot serve God and money (Matt. 6:24).

Foes and Opponents (Psalms 4, 6, 7, 17)

After Psalms 1 and 2, Book 1 has many psalms in which David complains to God about his enemies. These psalms can be difficult for readers today since David sometimes sounds vengeful. But we should not miss the fact that when foes are around him, he commits the problem to God. He does not take matters into his own hands.

These psalms have application to the workplace. Frequently conflicts and rivalries will appear among people on the job, and sometimes these fights can be vicious. Occupational battles can lead to depression and loss of sleep. Psalm 4:8 is a prayer about personal enemies, which says,

"I will both lie down and sleep in peace; for you alone, O LORD, make me lie down in safety." When we commit a matter to God, we can have tranquility. When we are in the midst of such a battle, however, our prayers for help may seem futile. But God hears and responds: "Depart from me, all you workers of evil, for the LORD has heard the sound of my weeping" (Ps. 6:8). On the other hand, we must be careful to maintain our integrity when in the midst of such conflicts. It will do no good for us to call out to God if we are being mean, dishonest, or unethical on the job. "O LORD my God, if I have done this, if there is wrong in my hands, if I have repaid my ally with harm . . . then let the enemy pursue and overtake me . . . and lay my soul in the dust" (Ps. 7:3–5). Psalm 17:3 makes the same point.

Authority (Psalm 8)

Psalm 8 is an exception in Book 1, as it does not pertain specifically to David. Its concern is with *all* human authority, not only David's rule. Although God created the entire universe (Ps. 8:1–3), he chose to appoint human beings to rule over the creation (Ps. 8:5–8). This is a high calling. "You have made them a little lower than God, and crowned them with glory and honor. You have given them dominion over the works of your hands; you have put all things under their feet" (Ps. 8:5–6). When we exercise authority and leadership, we do so as God's delegates. Our rule cannot be arbitrary or self-serving, but must serve God's purposes. Chief among these are caring for the creatures of the earth (Ps. 8:7–8) and protecting the weak and vulnerable, especially children (Ps. 8:2).

If we gain authority in work, it is tempting to regard our position as a reward for our hard work or intelligence and to exploit our authority for personal gain. But Psalm 8 reminds us that authority comes not as a reward, but as an obligation. It is right that we should be accountable to superiors, boards of directors, trustees, voters, or whatever earthly forms of governance we serve under, but that alone is not sufficient. We must also be accountable to God. Political leaders, for example, have a duty to pay attention to the best environmental and economic science available when considering energy policy, whether or not it accords with current political winds. Similarly, business leaders are called to anticipate and prevent possible harm to children—whether physical, mental, cultural, or spiritual—from their products and services. This applies not only to toys, movies, television, and food, but also to retailing, transportation, telecommunications, and financial services, among others.

Business Ethics (Psalms 15, 24, 34)

The Psalter says a good deal about workplace ethics. Psalm 15:1 and 5 say, "O LORD, who may abide in your tent? Who may dwell on your holy hill? . . . [Those] who do not lend money at interest, and do not take a bribe against the innocent. Those who do these things shall never be moved." If we allow that interest is not necessarily prohibited in the contemporary context (see "Does the Bible Prohibit Charging Interest?" at www.theologyofwork.org), the application of this Psalm is that we are not to take advantage of others in the workplace. Loans that put distressed borrowers into greater debt would be an example, as would credit cards that intentionally entrap unwitting cardholders with unexpected fees and interest rate escalations. In an expanded sense, any product or service that targets vulnerable (or "innocent") people and leaves them worse off is a violation of the Psalter's ethics. Good business ethics—and its counterparts in other fields of work—requires that customers genuinely benefit from the goods and services offered to them.

Psalm 24:4–5 adds to this that God accepts "those who have clean hands and pure hearts, who do not lift up their souls to what is false, and do not swear deceitfully. They will receive blessing from the LORD, and vindication from the God of their salvation." The falsehood described here is perjury. As in the modern world, so also in the ancient world, it was difficult to be involved in business without sometimes getting ensnared in lawsuits. This passage moves us to testify honestly and not pervert justice by fraud. When others are unscrupulous, our honesty might cost in lost promotions, business transactions, elections, grades, and publications. But in the long run, such setbacks are trivial in comparison to God's blessing and vindication (Ps. 24:5).

Ethics also comes to the fore in Psalm 34:12–13: "Which of you desires life, and covets many days to enjoy good? Keep your tongue from evil, and your lips from speaking deceit." This could refer to any kind of deceit, slander, or fraud. The reference to "many days to enjoy" simply points out that if you swindle people or slander them, you are likely to create enemies. In extreme cases, this could lead to your death at their hands, but even if not, life surrounded by enemies is not enjoyable. If life is your chief desire, trustworthy friends are far more profitable than ill-gotten gain. It is possible that a life of integrity will be costly in worldly terms. In a corrupt country, a businessperson who does not give bribes or a civil servant who does not take them could be unable to make a steady income. "Many are the afflictions of the righteous," the psalm acknowledges. "But the LORD rescues them from them all," it adds (Ps. 34:19). Working with integrity may or may not result in prosperity, but integrity in God's eyes is its own reward.

Trusting God in the Face of Institutional Pressure (Psalm 20)

Psalm 20 teaches us to trust God, rather than human power such as military might. "Some take pride in chariots, and some in horses, but our pride is in the name of the LORD our God" (Ps. 20:7). Financial assets, no less than military assets, can be the basis for a false faith in human power. For that matter, we should recall that in the ancient world only the upper-class soldiers had horses and chariots. The ordinary soldiers would be drawn from the peasants and be on foot. It is a disturbing reality that even modest wealth and power often draw us away from God.

God's Presence in Our Struggles at Work (Psalm 23)

"The LORD is my shepherd" (Ps. 23:1). If we trust God, then we have the tranquility of knowing that God watches over us, like a shepherd watching over sheep. This is a reminder to see our work from God's perspective—not primarily as an instrument for our gratification, but as our part in God's mission in the world. "He leads me in the right *for his name's sake*" (Ps. 23:3; emphasis added). We work to honor him and not for our own glory—a powerful reminder we need to hear on a regular basis.

Such a godly perspective on our work generally drives us *into* our work more deeply, not away from it. In Psalm 23, we see this in the way the narrative of the psalm is driven by the details of the work of shepherding. Shepherds find water, good grazing, and paths in the wilderness. They ward off predators with sticks and staffs, and comfort the sheep with their words and their presence. Psalm 23 is first of all an accurate representation of the shepherd's work. This gives it the grounding in reality needed to be meaningful as a spiritual meditation.

While we seek to honor God in our work, this does not mean the road will be easy. We sometimes may find ourselves in the "darkest valley" (Ps. 23:4). This could come as the loss of a contract, a teaching assignment that has gone bad, or feelings of isolation and meaninglessness in our work. Or it could come as a longer-term struggle, such as a toxic office environment or inability to find a job. These are things we'd prefer to avoid, but Psalm 23 reminds us that God is near in all circumstances. "I fear no evil; for you are with me" (Ps. 23:4a). His work on our behalf is not hypothetical, but tangible and real. A shepherd has a rod and staff, and God has every instrument needed to bring us safely through the worst of life (Ps. 23:4b). God will take care of us even in a sometimes hostile world, "in the presence of my enemies" (Ps. 23:5). It is easy to remember this when things are calm, but here we are called to remember it in the midst of challenge and adversity. While we would often rather not think about this, it is through the challenges of our lives that God works out his purposes in us.

Psalm 23 concludes by reminding us of the destination of our journey with God. "I shall dwell in the house of the Lord my whole life long" (Ps 23:6b). As in Psalm 127 and elsewhere, the house or household is not only a shelter where people eat and sleep, but also the basic unit of work and economic production. Thus dwelling in the house of the Lord does not mean waiting until we die to so that we can cease working and receive our reward. Rather, it promises that the time is coming when we will find a place where our work and life can thrive. The first half of the verse tells us directly that this is a promise for our present lives as well as eternity. "Goodness and mercy shall follow me all the days of my life" (Ps. 23:6). The promise that God will be with us, bringing goodness and love in all of the circumstances of our life and work, is a deeper kind of comfort than we can ever get from hoping to avoid any adversity that could befall us.

God's Guidance in Our Work (Psalm 25)

Human life is a series of choices, and many of these involve vocation. We should develop the habit of taking all such decisions to God. Psalm

25:12 teaches, "Who are they that fear the LORD? He will teach them the way that they should choose." How does God teach us the way to choose? Psalm 25 notes several ways, beginning with, "Make me to know your ways, O LORD. . . . Lead me in your truth, and teach me" (Ps. 25:4–5). This requires reading the Bible regularly, the primary way we get to know God's ways and learn his truth. Once we know God's ways, we need to put them into practice without needing special guidance from God in most cases. "The paths of the LORD are steadfast love and faithfulness, for those who keep his covenant and decrees" (Ps. 25:10). His covenant and decrees are found, of course, in the Bible.

"Do not remember the sins of my youth or my transgressions," adds Psalm 25:7. Confessing our sins and asking God's mercy is another way we receive guidance from God. When we are honest with God—and ourselves—about our sins, it opens the door for God's guidance in our hearts. "Pardon my guilt," and "forgive all my sins," the psalmist pleads (Ps. 25:11, 18). When we are forgiven by God, it frees us to cease trying to justify ourselves, which otherwise is a powerful barrier to God's guidance. Similarly, humbleness in our dealings with God and people gets us beyond the defensiveness that blocks God's guidance. "He leads the humble in . . . his way," Psalm 25:9 informs us.

"My eyes are ever toward the LORD," continues the psalm (Ps. 25:15). We receive God's guidance when we look for evidence about the things God cares about, such as justice, faithfulness, reconciliation, peace, faith, hope, and love. (The psalm does not name these particular items—they are examples from other parts of the Bible.) "May integrity and uprightness preserve me," says Psalm 25:21. Integrity means living all of life under a coherent set of values rather than, for example, being honest and compassionate with our families but deceitful and cruel with our customers or co-workers. Thinking clearly about how to apply our highest values at work thus turns out to be a means of God's guidance, at least to the degree that our highest values are formed by Scripture and faithfulness to Christ.

Although these means of guidance may seem abstract, they can be very practical when we put them to use in workplace situations. The key is to be specific in our Bible study, confession, prayer, and moral reasoning. When we bring our actual, specific work situations to God and God's word, we may find God answering with the specific guidance we need. (For more about this, see "Discerning God's Guidance to a Particular Kind of Work" in *Vocation Overview* at www.theologyofwork.org.)

Book 2 (Psalms 42–72)

All of us suffer from feelings of insecurity, and financial ruin is high on our list of worries. In the second book of the Psalter, we see a number of texts that relate to the fears that beset people and the paths to which they turn for help. We thus learn about the true and the false grounds for hope in a world of uncertainty.

God's Presence in the Midst of Disaster (Psalm 46)

At times, disaster threatens our places of work, the work itself, or our sense of well-being. These disasters include the natural (hurricanes, tornadoes, floods, typhoons, wildfires), the economic (recessions, bankruptcy, collapse of major financial institutions), and the political (sudden change in policy, priorities, war). Psalm 46 highlights the world-spanning breadth that disaster can take, and we see this today in the global economy. Currency decisions made in London and Beijing impact the price that farmers from Indiana or Indonesia get for their crops. Political turmoil in the Middle East may affect the price of gasoline in a small town anywhere in the world, and this in turn, through a chain of events, may determine whether a local restaurant stays in business. Even if the ancient economies were not so "global," people knew full well that what happened among the nations could sooner or later change their lives. The melting of the earth implies that someday all the powers of the nations will be seen to have been as ephemeral as castles made of wax. Turmoil in the world means uncertainty for trade, government, finance, and every kind of work. No matter how great the disaster, however, God is greater still.

> God is our refuge and strength, a very present help in trouble. Therefore we will not fear, though the earth should change, though the mountains shake in the heart of the sea; though its waters roar and foam, though the mountains tremble with its tumult. (Ps. 46:1–3)

In the middle of difficult, threatening circumstances, we can approach our work and our co-workers calmly, confidently, even gladly. Our ultimate trust is in God, whose own self provides a refuge of strength and well-being when our strength runs out. Not just us individually, but our communities and the whole world come under God's grace. Global disaster is no match for God's providence. Reviewing the way God has taken care of us in previous circumstances—our own and the people of God's—assures us that God is with us "in the midst of the city" (Ps. 46:5) and everywhere on earth (Ps. 46:10). At times, we may even have the privilege of serving as one of God's means for helping other people in the midst of disaster.

Anxiety When Unscrupulous People Succeed (Psalms 49, 50, 52, 62)

Sometimes the godly have a skewed perspective on how God governs, and this causes them needless anxiety. They think that the righteous should obviously do well in life while the wicked just as obviously should fall into ruin. But things don't always follow this script. When the wicked thrive, Christians feel that the world has turned upside down and that their faith has proven vain. Psalm 49:16–17 addresses this: "Do not be afraid when some become rich, when the wealth of their houses increases. For when they die they will carry nothing away; their wealth will not go down after them." Godliness does not ensure commercial success, and impiety does not ensure failure. Those who devote their lives to making money must finally fail, for they have made a treasure of something they must lose (Luke 12:16–21). See "Concern for the Wealthy" (Luke 6:25; 12:13–21; 18:18–30) in "Luke and Work" in the *Theology of Work Bible Commentary*.

It is not merely a matter of the wicked having to face God's judgment after death. When someone who is evil but successful finally falls into ruin, people notice. They understand the connection between how that person lived and the calamity that ultimately swamped him or her. Psalm 52:7 describes such a situation: "See the one who would not take refuge in God, but trusted in abundant riches, and sought refuge in wealth!" For this reason, Psalm 62:10 tells us not to seek security by following the path of the wicked or in the acquisition of wealth: "Put no confidence in extortion, and set no vain hopes on robbery; if riches increase, do not set your heart on them." In hard times we are apt to look to those who have prospered by corrupt practices or by cronyism, and to believe that we must do the same if we are to escape poverty. But we in fact only guarantee that we will share in their disgrace before people and their condemnation before God.

On the other hand, if we do decide to make God our trust, then we must do so fully and not superficially. Psalm 50:16 declares, "But to the wicked God says: 'What right have you to recite my statutes, or take my covenant on your lips?'" It is a bad thing for someone to use fraud in order to gain wealth. It is a terrible thing to do this while feigning allegiance to God.

We would do well to ask what others see when they observe our work and the way we do it. Do we justify taking ethical shortcuts, practicing discrimination, or treating people badly by babbling about "blessing" or "God's will" or "favor"? Perhaps we should be more reluctant to ascribe our apparent successes to God's will and be more ready to say simply, "I don't deserve it."

Book 3 (Psalms 73–89)

Book 3 of Psalms contains a great deal of lamentation and complaint. Divine judgment—both positive and negative—comes to the fore in many of the psalms here. Contemplating these psalms gives us a mirror in which to explore our own faithfulness—or lack of it—as well as to express our actual feelings to the God who is able to reconcile everything to himself.

Keeping Integrity in the Midst of Corruption (Psalm 73)

Psalm 73 depicts a fourfold journey of temptation and faithfulness, playing it out in the psalmist's work.[2] In the first stage, he acknowledges

---

[2] John E. Hunter, *Finding the Living Christ in the Psalms* (Grand Rapids: Zondervan, 1972), develops this idea in the chapter "The Man Who Looked Four Ways," although we have not followed his stages exactly.

that God's favorable judgment is a source of strength. "Truly God is good to the upright, to those who are pure in heart" (Ps. 73:1). Yet quickly (stage two), he becomes tempted to forsake God's ways. "But as for me," he says, "my feet had almost stumbled and my feet had nearly slipped, for I was envious of the arrogant" (Ps. 73:2). He finds himself preoccupied with the apparent success of the wicked, which he describes in obsessive detail over the next ten verses. He notes in particular those who "speak with malice" and "threaten oppression" (Ps. 73:8). In his envy, he begins to think his own integrity had been pointless. "All in vain I have kept my heart clean" (Ps. 73:13) he says, noting that he has come to the edge of joining the wicked himself (Ps. 73:14–15).

At the last minute, however, he goes "into the sanctuary of God," meaning he begins to "perceive" the situation from God's point of view (Ps. 73:17). He sees that God will make the wicked "fall to ruin" (Ps. 73:18). This begins the third stage, in which he sees that the success of people who lack integrity is only temporary. All of them eventually "are destroyed in a moment" and become "like a dream when one awakes" (Ps. 73:19–20). He realizes that when he was thinking of joining the wicked, he had been "stupid and ignorant" (Ps. 73:22). In the fourth stage, he recommits himself to God's ways. "I am continually with you," he says, and "you guide me with your counsel" (Ps. 73:23–24).

Do we also follow this four-stage journey to some degree? We also may begin with integrity and faithfulness to God. Then we see that others seem to be getting away with deception and oppression. Sometimes we become impatient with how long God is taking to execute his judgment. While God tarries, the wicked seem to be "always at ease," and "they increase in riches," while the upright seem to be "plagued and punished" by the unfairness of life (Ps. 73:12, 14). But the timing of God's judgment is God's business, not ours. In fact, because we are not perfect ourselves, let us not be eager for God to judge the wicked.

Paying too much attention to the undeserved success of others, we become tempted to seek unfair advantages for ourselves too. It is especially tempting to succumb to this impulse at work, where it may seem like there is a different set of rules. We see arrogant people (Ps. 73:3) gain recognition and bully others into giving them an undue share of the rewards (Ps. 73:6). We see people commit fraud, yet prosper for years.

Those with power over us at work seem foolish (Ps. 73:7), yet they get promoted. Maybe we should do the same ourselves. Perhaps God doesn't really know or care how we act (Ps 73:11), at least not at work.

Like the psalmist, our remedy is to remember that working alongside God—that is, in accordance to his ways—is a delight in itself. "For me it is good to be near God" (Ps. 73:28). When we do this, we open ourselves again to God's counsel and return to his ways. For example, it may be that we can climb the ladder of success faster—at least at first—by taking credit for others' work, blaming others for our mistakes, or getting others to do our work for us. But will the promotion and the extra income be worth the feeling of hollowness and the fear of being exposed as a fraud? Will success make up for the loss of friendships and the inability to trust anyone around us? If we take care of the people around us, share credit for success, and take our share of blame for failures, then it may seem like we get off to a slower start. But won't our work be more enjoyable? And when we need support, when we need our co-workers' trust and they need ours, won't we be in a better position than the arrogant and abusive? Truly, God is good to the upright.

The Economic Consequences of National Wrongdoings (Psalms 81, 85)

Despite the attention to personal judgment we have seen in Psalm 73, in most of Book 3 it is the nation of Israel that comes under judgment. The topic of national judgment per se is relevant to this article to the extent that it establishes the context for people carrying out their work in that nation. It also suggests an important type of work Christians can engage in while representing the kingdom of God, namely, national policy making. But we can note that when a national government becomes evil, the country's economy suffers. Psalm 81 is an example, for it begins with God's judgment against the nation of Israel. "My people did not listen to my voice; Israel would not submit to me. So I gave them over to their stubborn hearts" (Ps. 81:11–12). Then it goes on to describe the economic consequences. "O that my people would listen to me. . . . I would feed you with the finest of the wheat, and with honey from the rock I would satisfy you" (Ps. 81:13, 16). Here we see how national violations of God's covenant bring about scarcity and economic hardship. Had the people been faithful to God's ways, they would have experienced prosperity. Instead they have abandoned God's ways and find themselves going hungry (Ps. 81:10).

Likewise, Psalm 85 describes the economic benefits that accrue when Israel is faithful to God's commands. The people experience peace and security, productive work, and increased prosperity (Ps. 85:10–13). Without good government, none of us can hope to prosper for long. In many places Christians are highly visible in opposing government policies we disagree with, but constructive engagement is needed too. What can you do to help establish or preserve good government in your town, region, or nation?

God's Grace in the Midst of Judgment (Psalm 86)

Although God's judgment takes the fore in Book 3 of Psalms, we also find God's grace. "Be gracious to me, O Lord," Psalm 86 implores, "for you, O Lord, are good and forgiving, abounding in steadfast love to all who call on you" (Ps. 86:2, 5). The psalm comes from someone feeling worn down by opposition from those more powerful. "I am poor and needy" (Ps. 86:1). "The insolent rise up against me; a band of ruffians seeks my life" (Ps. 86:14). "Those who hate me" are a constant threat (Ps. 86:17). "Save the child of your serving girl" (Ps. 86:16b).

The psalm does not claim righteousness but rejoices that God is "slow to anger" (Ps. 86:15). It asks only for God's grace. "Turn to me and be gracious to me" (Ps. 86:16a). "In the day of my trouble I call on you, for you will answer me" (Ps. 86:7).

At times, all of us face opposition at work. Sometimes it is directly personal and dangerous. We may be oppressed by others, or we may be at fault, or a mixture of both. We may feel unworthy in our work, unloved in our relationships, incapable of changing either our circumstances or ourselves. No matter the source of opposition to us—even if we have seen the enemy and it is us—we can ask for God's grace to save us. God's grace cuts through the ambiguity that surrounds our life and work and shows us a sign of God's favor (Ps 86:17) beyond what we deserve.

Of course, God does not save anyone—neither us nor our enemies—for the purpose of inflicting further harm. With grace must come reform. "Teach me your way, O Lord, that I may walk in your truth" (Ps. 86:11a).

Accepting God's grace means putting him ahead of ourselves. "Give me an undivided heart to revere your name. I give thanks to you, O Lord my God, with my whole heart" (Ps. 86:11–12).

With God's heart, we also become merciful, even to those who oppose us. The psalm asks that opponents "be put to shame" (Ps. 86:17) for their hatred, but that as a result they will "come and bow down before you, O Lord" (Ps. 86:9) and so also come into God's grace. Grace means mercy not only for us, but also for our opponents, to show God's power to his enemies so that his name is glorified (Ps. 86:9).

Book 4 (Psalms 90–106)

Book 4 of Psalms places the brokenness of the world—including human mortality—in the context of God's sovereignty. None of us is able to make our own life—let alone the whole world—as it should be. We suffer, and we cannot shield those we love from suffering. Yet God remains in charge, and our hope for all things to be put right rests in him.

Cultivating Character Amid the Difficulties of Work (Psalms 90, 101)

Book 4 begins with the somber Psalm 90. "You turn us back to dust . . . our years come to an end like a sigh" (Ps. 90:3, 9). This psalm focuses our attention on the difficulty and the brevity of life. "The days of our life are seventy years, or perhaps eighty, if we are strong; even then their span is only toil and trouble; they are soon gone, and we fly away" (Ps. 90:10). The brevity of life shades every aspect of our life and work. We have only so many years in which to earn enough to support our families, save something for times of hardship or old age, contribute to the common good, and do our share in God's work in the world. When young, we may be too inexperienced to obtain the kind of work we want. When old, we face declining skills and abilities and sometimes age discrimination. In between, we worry whether we are on a fast enough track to achieve our objectives. Work was meant to be a creative co-laboring with God (Gen. 2:19). But the pressure of time makes work feel like "toil and trouble."

What then are we to do? Invite God to inhabit our work, no matter how toilsome it may seem. "Let your [God's] work be manifest to your servants. . . . Prosper for us the work of our hands—O prosper the work of our hands!" (Ps. 90:16–17). This does not mean merely placing reminders of our Lord in our places of work. It means getting God into the "work of our hands." This includes our awareness of God's presence at work, our recognition of God's purpose for our work, our commitment to work according to God's principles, and our service to those around us, who after all are made in God's image (Gen. 1:27; 9:6; James 3:9).

Psalm 101:2 illustrates how we become equipped for doing God's work. "I will study the way that is blameless. When shall I attain it? I will walk with integrity of heart within my house." Cultivating good character before God and people is our first task. If we have children, one of our jobs is to help them learn the knowledge of God's ways and grow in godly character. We are doing God's work when we manage our homes well and give our children the chance to grow up strong and be prepared for the hardships of life. For the nihilist and the cynic, the cruelty of life justifies immorality and selfishness. For the believer, it is all the more reason to cultivate character.

Human Creativity with God (Psalm 104)

From the beginning, God intended human work as a form of creativity under or alongside God's own creativity (Gen. 1:26–31; 2:5, 15–18). Human work is meant to fulfill God's creative intent, bring each person into relationship with other people and with God, and glorify God. Psalm 104 gives a delightful depiction of this creative partnership. It begins with a broad canvas of the glory of God's creation (Ps. 104:1–9). This leads naturally to God's active work in sustaining the world of animals, birds, and sea creatures (Ps. 104:10–12, 14, 16–18, 20–22, 25). God provides richly for human beings as well (Ps. 104:13–15, 23; see also 1 Tim. 6:17). God's work makes possible the fruitfulness of nature and humanity. "From your lofty abode you water the mountains; the earth is satisfied with the fruit of your work" (Ps. 104:13).

The work of humans is to build further, using what God gives. We have to gather and use the plants. "You cause the grass to grow for the cattle and plants for people to cultivate" (Ps. 104:14, alternate reading from NRSV footnote f). We make the wine and bread and extract the oil from the plants God causes to grow (Ps. 104:15). God provides so richly, in part by populating his creation with people who labor six days a week. Thus, while this psalm speaks of all creatures looking to God for food, and God opening his hand to supply it (Ps. 104:27–28), people still have to work hard to process and use God's good gifts. Psalm 104 goes so far as to name some of the tools used for the work of God's world—tents, garments, beams, fire, and ships (Ps. 104:1, 2, 3, 4, 26, respectively). Intriguingly, the psalm happily ascribes use of such tools to God himself, as well as to human beings. We work *with* God, and God's ample provision comes in part through human effort.

Even so, we must remember that we are the junior partners in creation with God. In keeping with Genesis, human beings are the last creatures mentioned in Psalm 104. But in distinction from Genesis, we come on the scene here with little fanfare. We are just one more of God's creatures, going about our business alongside cattle, birds, wild goats, coneys, and lions (Ps. 104:14–23). Each has its proper activity—for humans, it is to labor until evening—but underneath every activity, it is God who provides all that is needed (Ps. 104:27–30). Psalm 104 reminds us that God has done his work supremely well. In him, our work may be done supremely well also, if only we work humbly in the strength his Spirit supplies, cultivating the beautiful world in which he has placed us by his grace.

Book 5 (Psalms 107–150)

The psalms in Book 5 have less of a common theme or setting than those in the other books. However, amid the diversity of forms and settings, work appears more directly among these psalms than in other part of the Psalter. Issues of economic creativity, business ethics, entrepreneurship, productivity, the work of raising children and managing a household, the proper use of power, and the glory of God in and through the material world all emerge in these psalms.

God Undergirds All Work and Productivity (Psalm 107)

Psalm 107 relates human economic endeavors to the world of God's creation. It is worth citing at length.

Some went down to the sea in ships, doing business on the mighty waters; they saw the deeds of the LORD, his wondrous works in the deep. For he commanded and raised the stormy wind, which lifted up the waves of the sea. They mounted up to heaven, they went down to the depths; their courage melted away in their calamity; they reeled and staggered like drunkards, and were at their wits' end. Then they cried to the LORD in their trouble, and he brought them out from their distress; he made the storm be still, and the waves of the sea were hushed. Then they were glad because they had quiet, and he brought them to their desired haven. Let them thank the LORD for his steadfast love, for his wonderful works to humankind. (Ps. 107:23–31)

Then, as now, people went to sea for fishing and trading. Their ships were fragile, and they had little warning before storms surged. Their lives and livelihood depended on the weather. Notwithstanding our technological advantages, we too depend upon a multitude of factors beyond our control in much of our work. Perhaps the most honest thing anyone can say about success at work is, "I was fortunate." As Bill Gates remarked about the amazing success of Microsoft, "I was born at the right place and time."[3] To the believer, "fortunate" is a term to describe God's constant provision for our needs. Wringing success from the uncertainties inherent in our work depends a bit on skill (a gift from God in itself), a bit on hard work, and a lot on God's providence. Whatever our "desired haven" in life and work, "let us thank the LORD for his steadfast love, for his wonderful works to humankind." Perhaps James had this psalm in mind when he said, "Instead you ought to say, 'If the Lord wishes, we will live and do this or that'" (James 4:15).

A bit later, Psalm 107 adds further insight to this.

He turns a desert into pools of water, a parched land into springs of water. And there he lets the hungry live, and they establish a town to live in; they sow fields, and plant vineyards, and get a fruitful yield. By his blessing they multiply greatly, and he does not let their cattle decrease. (Ps. 107:35–38)

---

[3] "Bill Gates Answers Most Frequently Asked Questions," http://download.microsoft.com/download/0/c/0/0c020894-1f95-408c-a571-1b5033c75bbc/billg_faq.d oc.

God creates the conditions for life to thrive on earth. He can turn a desert into a pasture, or a pasture into a desert. Agriculture, including sowing crops and managing livestock, depends on God-given growth. Where agriculture prospers, towns arise. With the emergence of towns, every kind of work appears. The urban economy provides all kinds of goods and services to a growing and diverse population. In an ancient economy, in addition to farmers and shepherds, a community would need potters, metalworkers, and scribes (to record commercial agreements and transactions, as well as laws and religious texts). The whole economy of any city, past or present, depends upon agricultural abundance, whether home grown or through trade. When the world's farmers can grow more than they need for their own subsistence, complex communities can thrive. And this comes from God, who waters the dry land (Ps. 65:9, Gen. 2:5).

Psalm 107 thus covers economic activity on both land and sea, asserting that God is over it all. God is not hostile to our work, as the psalm speaks of how he saves and provides. Our livelihood depends upon God's beneficent governance of natural forces.

Virtues for Those in Business (Psalm 112)

Psalm 112 declares God's blessings on those who do business—dealing and lending, to use the psalm's terms—according to God's commandments. "Wealth and riches are in their houses," the psalm observes, and "they are not afraid of evil tidings" (Ps. 112:3, 7). The virtues that bring such blessings include graciousness, mercy, righteousness, generosity, and justice (Ps. 112:4–5). Righteousness and justice may come as no surprise to us. People want to buy and sell from businesses that are upright and just, so these virtues can be expected, in general, to bring prosperity.

But what about graciousness, mercy, and generosity? Graciousness could mean informing a customer about a lower-cost solution that brings less profit to ourselves or our company. Mercy could mean giving a supplier another chance after they miss a delivery. Generosity could mean sharing specifications with others in the industry so they can make products that interoperate with ours—good for customers, but potentially creating competition for ourselves. Does Psalm 112 mean to say that such things lead to greater prosperity, not less? Apparently so. "They have distributed freely," the psalm says, yet they are firmer, more secure, steadier, and ultimately more successful than those who do not practice such virtues (Ps. 112:7–10). The psalm attributes this to the Lord (Ps. 112:1, 7), but it doesn't say whether this is because he intervenes on their behalf or because he has created and maintained the world in such a way that these virtues tend to bring prosperity. Perhaps he does both.

Then again, perhaps the Lord blesses the upright by giving them a different picture of prosperity. Wealth and riches are included (Ps. 112:3, as above), but the overall picture includes much more than wealth. Thriving descendants (Ps. 112:2) who remember (Ps. 112:6) and honor them (Ps. 112:9), stable relationships (Ps. 112:6), heartfelt peace (Ps. 112:7), and an ability to face the future without fear (Ps. 112:8) are equally important in God's view of prosperity. Is it possible that when we follow the Lord's commandments in business, it is not only our fortunes that are changed, but also our desires? If we could come to want for ourselves what God wants for us, wouldn't we be guaranteed to find a happiness that endures forever?

Participating in God's Work (Psalm 113)

Psalm 113 informs us "from the rising of the sun to its setting, the name of the LORD is to be praised" (Ps. 113:3). Is it suggesting we should be in the temple (or in church) all day in order to praise the Lord? Or is it suggesting that in everything we do, including our daily work, we do it in praise to the Lord? From verses 7 through 9, we clearly see it is the latter. "He raises the poor from the dust, and lifts the needy from the ash heap to make them sit with princes" (Ps. 113:7–8). Although the psalm doesn't tell us how God accomplishes this, we know—as did the psalmist—that it generally means through work. The opportunity for well-paying work brings the poor out of poverty, and generally God creates such opportunities through his people's work—those in business who create economic opportunity, those in government who ensure justice, those in education who instill the skills needed for good jobs. With its emphasis on lifting the poor and needy, Psalm 113 is calling for a whole life of practical praise to God.

Although the psalm could have named myriad kinds of work to illustrate its point, it selects only one—the work of bearing and rearing children: "He gives the barren woman a home, making her the joyous mother of children" (Ps. 113:9). Perhaps this is because childlessness in ancient Israel virtually doomed a woman (and her husband) to poverty in old age. Or perhaps it is for some other reason. Regardless, it reminds us of two important matters today. Most obviously, when mothers (and fathers) conceive, feed, clean, protect, play with, teach, coach, forgive, train, and love children, it takes work! Yet many mothers feel that no one—even the church—recognizes that what they do is as valuable as the work that others do because they get paid. Second, God's relief for adults who lack children and for children who lack adults usually comes about through the work of other people. Medical professionals may be able to restore fertility. Adoption professionals and child welfare workers bring would-be parents together with children who need parents, and they remain with families to provide training and supervision as needed. All families depend on the support of a wide community of other people, including the people of God. (For more on the work of families, see "The Work of Marriage, Raising Children, and Caring for Parents" in Psalms 127, 128, 139 below.)

Producing True Value at Work (Psalm 127)

As Psalm 107 speaks of large-scale economic activity, so Psalms 127 and 128 speak of the household, the basic unit of economic production until the time of the Industrial Revolution. Psalm 127 begins with a reminder that all good work is grounded in God.

> Unless the LORD builds the house, those who build it labor in vain. Unless the LORD guards the city, the guard keeps watch in vain. It is in vain that you rise up early and go late to rest, eating the bread of anxious toil; for he gives sleep to his beloved. (Ps. 127:1–2)

Both the "house" and the "city" refer to the same thing—the goal of providing goods and security for the residents. Ultimately, all economic activity is aimed at enabling households to thrive. The passage obviously asserts that diligent labor alone is not enough (compare Prov. 26:13–16 on laziness). Beyond the obvious point, there is a deeper meaning. Hard work can produce a large and beautiful house, but it cannot create a happy home. A zealous entrepreneur can create a successful business but cannot by work alone create a good life. Only God can make it all worthwhile.

In many economies today, work other than farming is not usually performed in households, but in larger organizations. But the message of Psalm 127 applies to today's institutionalized workplaces much as it does to ancient households. To thrive, every place of work must produce something of value. Putting in hours is not enough—the work has to result in goods or services that others need.

Believers may be able to offer something of special significance in this regard. In every workplace there is a temptation to produce items that can earn fast money but don't offer any lasting value.

Businesses can increase profits—in the short term—by cutting the quality of materials. Sales people may be able to take advantage of buyers' unfamiliarity to sell dubious products and accessories. Educational institutions can offer classes that attract students without developing lasting capabilities. And so on. The more we understand the genuine needs of the people who use our goods and services, and the more we contribute to the true value of what we produce, the more we can help our work institutions resist these temptations. Because value is ultimately grounded in God, we may have a unique ability to help our organizations recognize what is truly valuable. But our input must be given with humility and careful listening. God does not give Christians a monopoly on values or ethics.

The Work of Marriage, Raising Children, and Caring for Parents (Psalms 127, 128, 139)

The work of marriage, childbearing, and caring for parents comes to the fore again in Psalms 127, 128, and 139. (The work of childbearing is also an important element of Psalm 113, "Participating in God's Work.") "Your wife will be like a fruitful vine within your house; your children will be like olive shoots around your table" (Ps. 128:3). Husbands and wives together engage in production of the most fundamental kind—reproduction! Needless to say, the wife performs more labor in this endeavor than the husband. In the Bible, this is not a despised role—it is understood to be essential for survival and was honored in ancient Israel. Beyond the bearing of children, wives typically managed the household, including both domestic and commercial production (Prov. 31:10–31).

The Bible honors those who go down to the sea and those who shepherd sheep (traditional male occupations), as well as those who manage the household (a traditional female occupation). Today, work roles are much less divided according to sex (except for managing the family home, which still is performed mostly by women[4]), but the honor accorded to marriage and to the work of families still applies.

Like every form of work (and bearing children is work!), childbearing comes from God. "It was you [God] who formed my inward parts; you knit me together in my mother's womb" (Ps. 139:13). Likewise, as with every other form of labor, this does not mean that when tragedy strikes, it is a punishment from or abandonment by God. Rather, childbearing is a point of God's common grace to humanity throughout the world. In the womb God makes us, and he makes us for a purpose. Our birthright is to do work of value to God himself.

We return to Psalm 127 for the final element of this theme, that the work of a household includes caring for those whose age diminishes their work capacity. "Sons are indeed a heritage from the Lord, the fruit of the womb a reward" (Ps. 127:3). In the ancient world, people had no institutionalized pension plans or health insurance. As they became older, their sons provided for them. (The text speaks of "sons" because typically daughters would marry and enter the households of their husbands' families.) In effect, sons were a couple's retirement plan, and this bound the generations closely together.

It may seem stark to put the value of raising children in economic terms. Today, we might feel more comfortable speaking of the emotional rewards of raising children. Be that as it may, this verse teaches that

---

[4]Man Yee Kan, Oriel Sullivan, and Jonathan Gershuny, "Gender Convergence in Domestic Work: Discerning the Effects of Interactional and Institutional Barriers from Large-scale Data," *Sociology* 45, no. 2 (April 2011): 234–51.

adults need children as much as children need adults, and that children are a gift from God, not a burden. It also reminds us of all the investments our parents made in us—emotional, physical, intellectual, creative, economic, and many more. As we grow up and our parents come to depend on us, it is right for us to take on the work of caring for parents. There are a variety of ways this may be done.

The point is simply that God's command to honor our parents (Exod. 20:12) is not only a matter of attitude, but also of work and economic care.

The Right Use of Power (Psalm 136)

Power is essential to most work, and it must be exercised rightly. Psalm 136 lays out the proper use of power by showing four examples of how God uses power.

The first example comes in verses 5 through 9. It shows God's use of power to create the world, "who by understanding made the heavens . . . who spread out the earth upon the waters" (Ps. 136:5–6). This takes us back to Genesis 1 to the God of creation, giving our world all that we need to flourish. But note the order in which God works—first creating systems (land, water, night, day, sun, and moon) that were necessary for the survival of his later creations (plants, land animals, swimming and flying creatures). God did not create animals until there was dry land and vegetation to sustain them. When it is in our power to create tasks or systems, we use power properly when we create environments in which we and those around us not only survive but thrive. For more on God's provision in creation, see "Provision" (Genesis 1:29–30; 2:8–14) in "Genesis 1–11 and Work" in the *Theology of Work Bible Commentary*.

The second example comes in Psalm 136:10–15 when God delivers his people from slavery in Egypt. The third comes immediately afterwards, when God strikes down the Canaanite kings who oppose Israel in its journey to settle the Promised Land (Ps. 136:16–22). Together these show us that God uses power to free people from oppression and to oppose those who would keep others from the good God intends for them. When our work frees others to fulfill their destiny in God's design, we are using power rightly. When our work would re-enslave workers or oppose God's work in and through them, we are abusing power.

The fourth example comes at the end of the psalm. "It is he who remembered us in our low estate . . . and rescued us from our foes . . . who gives food to all flesh" (Ps. 136:23–25). God lovingly recognizes our weakness and supplies our needs. When we use power to do work that benefits others, we are using power as God would use it.

Finally, for the proper use of power, every verse of Psalm 136 reminds us to give thanks to God, "whose steadfast love endures forever."

God's Glory in All of Creation (Psalms 146–150)

The final five psalms each begin with the shout "Praise the LORD!" As our survey of the psalms has shown, work is intended to be a form of praise to God. These five psalms depict a variety of ways in which our work can praise the Lord. In all of them, we see that our work is grounded in God's own work. When we work as God intends, we imitate, extend, and fulfill God's work.

Psalm 146

God executes justice for the oppressed (Ps. 146:7a), and so do we when we work according to God's commandments, by God's grace. God gives food to the hungry (Ps 146:7b), and so do we. God liberates people in chains, as do legislators, lawyers, judges, and juries. God restores sight to the blind, as do ophthalmologists, opticians, and glassmakers. God lifts up those who cannot rise on their own, as do physical therapists, orderlies, elevator makers, and parents of infants (Ps. 146:8). The Lord watches over strangers, as do police and security workers, flight attendants, lifeguards, health inspectors, and peacekeepers. He takes care of orphans and widows (Ps. 146:9), as do foster parents, elder care workers, family lawyers and social service workers, financial planners, and boarding school workers. Praise the Lord! (Ps. 146:10).

Psalm 147

God gathers the outcasts (Ps. 147:2), as do chaplains and teachers in prisons, and community organizers. He heals the brokenhearted (Ps. 147:3), as do grief counselors, matchmakers, humorists, and blues singers. He counts the stars and gives them names (Ps. 147:4), as do astronomers, navigators, and storytellers. He is abundant in power (Ps. 147:5a), as are presidents, chairpersons, admirals, parents, and political prisoners-turned-statesmen. He has profound understanding (Ps. 147:5b), as do professors, poets, painters, machinists, sonar operators, and people whose autism gives them extraordinary powers of concentration on details. He lifts up the downtrodden, as do civil right activists and donors, and he breaks the power of the wicked, as do district attorneys, whistle-blowers, and all those who walk away from gossip and speak up for co-workers being treated unfairly (Ps. 147:6).

God prepares the earth for the coming weather (Ps. 147:8), as do meteorologists, climate researchers, architects and builders, and air traffic controllers. He feeds the animals (Ps. 147:9), as do ranchers and shepherds and boys and girls in rural villages. He strengthens the gates, protects the children, and preserves peace at the borders (Ps. 147:13–14a), as do engineers, soldiers, customs agents, and diplomats. He prepares the finest foods (Ps. 147:14b), as do cooks, chefs, bakers, winemakers, brewers, farmers, homemakers, and two-career householders (mostly the women), recipe bloggers, grocers, and servers. He declares his word—his statutes and ordinances (Ps. 147:19). Praise the Lord! (Ps. 147:20).

Psalm 149

The Lord takes pleasure in song, dancing, and the music of instruments (Ps. 149:2–3), as do musicians, dancers, composers, songwriters, choreographers, film scorers, music librarians, teachers, arts organization workers and donors, choir members, music therapists, students in bands, choruses, and orchestras, garage bands, yodelers, laborers who sing at their work, music producers and publishers, YouTubers, hip-hop scratchers, lyricists, audio manufacturers, piano tuners, *kalimba* makers, acousticians, music app writers, and everyone who sings in the shower. Perhaps no form of human endeavor is more universal, yet more varied, than music making, and all of it derives from God's own love of music.

The Lord takes pleasure in his people (Ps. 149:4a), as do all good leaders, family members, mental health workers, pastors, salespeople, tour guides, coaches, party planners, and everyone who serves others. If situations oppress people, or systems make it impossible for people to take wholesome pleasure in others, the Lord vanquishes the oppressors and reforms the systems (Ps. 149:4b–9a), as do social and corporate reformers, journalists, ordinary women and men who refuse to accept the status quo, organizational psychologists and human resource professionals, and—if conditions are extreme and there is no other way—armies, navies, air forces, and their commanders. When justice and good governance are restored, the music can begin again (Ps. 149:6). Praise the Lord! (Ps. 149:9b).

Psalm 148

Unlike Psalms 146, 147, and 149, Psalms 148 and 150 do not depict God at work, but skip directly to our response of praise for the work he has already done. Psalm 148 speaks of God's creation, as if the creation's very existence is praise to God. "Praise the LORD from the earth, you sea monsters and all deeps, fire and hail, snow and frost, stormy wind fulfilling his command! Mountains and all hills, fruit trees and all cedars! Wild animals and all cattle, creeping things and flying birds!" (Ps. 148:7–10). His creation makes our work fruitful, so it is fitting that we offer all the work we do as praise to him. "Young men and women alike, old and young together! Let them praise the name of the LORD" (Ps. 148:12–13). Praise the Lord! (Ps. 148:14).

Psalm 150

The final psalm returns to music as our response to God's "mighty deeds," upon which all our activity and work are founded. Praise God with trumpets, lutes, harps, tambourines, strings, pipe, cymbals—both clanging and crashing—and dance. Coming as the climax of five songs full of work, and as the ultimate end of the entire collection of psalms, it gives the impression that music is important work indeed. Not music for its own sake alone, however, but because it allows us to praise the Lord louder. We can take this both literally and metaphorically. From the literal perspective, we might hold music, dance, and the other arts in a bit higher regard than is customary in the Christian community, which is not always welcoming to music (except within narrow borders) and the arts (at all). Or at the least, we might hold *our own* music and art in a bit higher esteem. If we cannot seem to find time to express our own artistic creativity, is it possible that we are missing the value of the songs that God puts in our hearts?

Metaphorically, could Psalm 150 be inviting us to go about our work as if it were a kind of music? We could probably all do with more harmony in our relationships, a steadier rhythm of work and rest, an attention to the beauty of the work we do and the people we work among. If we could see the beauty in our work, would it help us overcome work's challenges, such as ethical temptations, boredom, bad relationships, frustration, and low productivity at times? For example, imagine you are so frustrated with your boss that you are tempted to stop doing your work well. Would it help if you could see the beauty in your work beyond your relationship with your boss? What kind of beauty does your work bring to the world? What beauty does God see in what you do? Is that enough to sustain you in difficult times or to lead you to make the changes you need to make in your work or the way you do it?

In any case, no matter how we perceive our work, God intends our work to praise him. The one hundred fifty psalms in the Bible cover every aspect of life and work from the darkest terrors to the brightest hopes. Some speak of death and despair, and others of prosperity and hope. But the final conclusion of the book of Psalms is praise.

Let everything that breathes praise the LORD!
Praise the LORD! (Ps. 150:6)

Proverbs and Work

Introduction to Proverbs

What is the difference between being smart and being wise? Wisdom goes beyond knowledge. It is more than a catalog of facts; it is a masterful understanding of life, the art of living, and an expertise in good decision-making. We can be smart yet never become wise.

Where can we turn to gain wisdom? Wisdom goes beyond knowledge but cannot be gained apart from knowledge of the proverbs.[1] The book asserts this connection: "The proverbs of Solomon son of David, king of Israel: for gaining wisdom and instruction; for understanding words of insight" (Prov. 1:1–2 TNIV).[2] But to produce wisdom, this knowledge must be mixed with the fear of the Lord. The book of Proverbs declares that "the fear of the LORD is the beginning of wisdom, and knowledge of the Holy One is insight" (Prov. 9:10). Knowledge without commitment to the Lord is as useless as cement without water to make mortar. Paradoxically, accepting the proverbs by faith into the heart produces the fear of the Lord. "My child, if you accept my words and treasure up my commandments within you . . . then you will understand the fear of the LORD and find the knowledge of God" (Prov. 2:1, 5).

True wisdom for the Christian involves the whole revelation of God, especially as known in his Son, the Lord Jesus Christ. It starts with insight into who the Lord is, what he has done, and what he desires for us and for the world we live in. As we grow in our understanding of the Lord, we learn how to cooperate with him as he sustains and redeems the

---

[1] On the inseparable connection between wisdom and knowledge, see Bruce K. Waltke, *The Book of Proverbs: Chapters 1–15* (Grand Rapids: Wm. B. Eerdmans, 2004), 76–87.

[2] The NRSV translation "learning about" distorts the Hebrew *da'at* (root, *yada*) by missing its essentially experiential nature.

world. This often makes us more fruitful, in ways that benefit ourselves and in ways that help others. It causes us to revere the Lord in the midst of our daily life and work. "The fear of the LORD is life indeed; filled with it one rests secure and suffers no harm" (Prov. 19:23).

In Proverbs, gaining wisdom also makes us good and vice versa. "The wise are cautious and turn away from evil" (Prov. 14:16). "The mouth of the righteous brings forth wisdom" (Prov. 10:31). Proverbs anticipates Jesus' admonition, "Be wise as serpents and innocent as doves" (Matt. 10:16). Wisdom comes from the Lord. "I have taught you the way of wisdom; I have led you in the paths of uprightness," the Lord declares (Prov. 4:11). In Proverbs, the mental and the moral come together, and wisdom reflects the truth that a good God is still in charge.

The book of Proverbs also warns those who neglect to grow in wisdom. Wisdom, personified throughout the book as a woman,[3] speaks. "Whoever finds me finds life and obtains favor from the LORD; but those who miss me injure themselves; all who hate me love death" (Prov. 8:35–36). Wisdom brings greater, fuller life. Lack of wisdom diminishes life and ultimately leads to death.

About the Book of Proverbs

Throughout the ancient Near East, rulers often commissioned sages to gather the accepted wisdom of their nation for the instruction of young people entering professions or government service in the royal court.[4] These wise sayings, distilled from the observation of life and the realities of human experience, became the text for future generations as they reached adulthood. The book of Proverbs, however, claims King Solomon himself as its principal author (Prov. 1:1) and claims its inspiration from the Lord. "The LORD gives wisdom; from his mouth come

---

[3] For an explanation of the feminine personification, see Waltke, 83.

[4] Richard J. Clifford, "Introduction to Wisdom Literature," in *The New Interpreter's Bible*, vol. 5 (Nashville: Abingdon Press, 1997), 3–4. For more about government service from a Christian perspective, see Robert Banks, "The Role of the Bible in Bureaucratic Decision-Making," in *Private Values and Public Policy: The Ethics of Decision-Making in Government Administration* (Sydney: Lancer Books, 1983), 35–40.

knowledge and understanding" (Prov. 2:6). The book demands faith in the Lord, not in human experience.

"Trust in the LORD with all your heart, and do not lean on your own insight" (Prov. 3:5). "Do not be wise in your own eyes; fear the LORD and turn away from evil" (Prov. 3:7). Other ancient Near Eastern manuals imply or assume a divine origin of the wisdom they teach, but Proverbs is emphatic in attributing wisdom solely and directly to the Lord.[5] The central message of the book is that true wisdom is based on our relationship to God: we cannot have true wisdom apart from a living relationship with the Lord.

Thus the proverbs in this book are more than mere common sense or good advice; they teach us not only the connection between our deeds and our destiny, but also how to create a peaceful and prosperous community under the Lord, the source of true wisdom.

At the same time, these short pithy sayings we call proverbs are generalizations about life, not atomized promises. God works through them to guide our thinking, but we must be careful not to dice the collection into a grab-bag of fortune cookie inserts. No isolated proverb can be taken as expressing the whole truth; it must be nuanced by the broader context of the whole book.[6] Only a fool would read "Train up a child in the way he should go and when he is old he will not depart from it" (Prov. 22:6 NASB) and conclude that a child is a programmed robot. The proverb teaches that parental training has its effect, but it must be nuanced by other proverbs recognizing that each person bears responsibility for his or her own conduct, such as, "The eye that mocks a father and scorns to obey a mother will be pecked out by the ravens of the valley and eaten by the vultures" (Prov. 30:17). Mastering the proverbs requires weaving a garment of wisdom from the whole collection. Gaining wisdom from the book of Proverbs takes lifelong study.

This is no trivial task. Some of the proverbs are in tension with each other, though not in outright opposition. Others are stated with an ambiguity that forces the reader to reflect on a number of possible interpretations. Close attention must be paid to whom the proverb is addressed.

---

[5] Roland Murphy, *Proverbs,* vol. 22, *Word Biblical Commentary* (Nashville: Thomas Nelson, 1998), 289.

[6] Cf. Waltke, 107–9.

The warning "Do not love sleep" (Prov. 20:13) is a proverb addressed to all of God's children (see Prov. 1:4–5), but the reassurance "Your sleep will be sweet" (Prov. 3:24) is addressed to those who do not let wisdom and understanding out of their sight (Prov. 3:21). And we must be careful not to let a proverb become a legalism. "Do not love sleep" is not a prohibition against using sleep aids, or against sleeping late on your day off, or a justification for checking your e-mail obsessively all day and night. The book of Proverbs is timeless, but the application of proverbs must fit the times, as the book of Job illustrates (see "Job and Work" above). The proverbs are touchstones in the slow development of virtue and they take a long time to understand. "Let the wise also hear and gain in learning, and the discerning acquire skill, to understand a proverb and a figure, the words of the wise and their riddles" (Prov. 1:5–6).

The book of Proverbs contains seven collections. Collection 1 (Prov. 1:1–9:18) contains extended lectures to prepare the disciple's heart for the pithy sayings in the collections that follow. Collection 2 (Prov. 10:1–22:16) are "proverbs of Solomon." Collection 3 (Prov. 22:17–24:22) covers "the words of the wise," that are probably adopted and adapted by Solomon,[7] and collection 4 (Prov. 24:23–34) extends that with additional "sayings of the wise." Collection 5 (Prov. 25:1–29:27) covers "other proverbs that the officials of King Hezekiah of Judah copied," combing through ancient records from Solomon's time. (Hezekiah reigned about three hundred years after Solomon.) Collection 6 (Prov. 30:1–33) and collection 7 (Prov. 31:1–31) are attributed to Agur and Lemuel, respectively, about whom little else is known.[8] The final result is a single work of sayings, advice, instructions, and warnings, structured as a manual for young people beginning their working lives and people of all ages, challenging them to seek the wisdom of the Lord (Prov. 1:2–7).

The proverbs most often are paired in contrasts: diligence vs. laziness, honesty vs. dishonesty, planning vs. hastily made decisions, dealing justly vs. taking advantage of the vulnerable, seeking good advice vs. arrogance, and so on. More proverbs in the book talk about our wise speech than any other subject, with the second largest number covering

---

[7] See Waltke, 23ff.
[8] See Waltke, 31–37.

work and its correlate, money. Though the book divides into the seven collections referenced above, the proverbs within these collections circle back over the same topics repeatedly. For that reason, this chapter will discuss work-related teachings by topic rather than by moving through each collection in the order in which it appears in the book.

(A table of verses, listing the places they are discussed in this chapter, may be found in the "Index by Chapter/Verse" at the end of the chapter. This is intended to aid readers in locating where in the chapter a particular verse or passage is discussed, not to encourage readers to read individual verses in isolation.)

What Does Proverbs Have to Do with Work?

The central concern of the book is the call to live life in awe of God. This call opens the book (Prov. 1:7), pervades it (Prov. 9:10), and brings it to a close (Prov. 31:30). The proverbs tell us that good work habits generally lead to prosperity, and that work habits grow out of character, and that character is formed by our awe of God. Indeed the fear of the Lord and wisdom are directly equated. "You will understand the fear of the Lord and find the knowledge of God. For the Lord gives wisdom; from his mouth come knowledge and understanding" (Prov. 2:5–6).

The proverbs, in other words, are intended to form God's (or godly) character in those who read them. This is the reason many of the proverbs ground themselves explicitly in God's character:

There are six things that the Lord hates. (Prov. 6:16)

A false balance is an abomination to the Lord. (Prov. 11:1)

The eyes of the Lord are in every place. (Prov. 15:3)

Godly character—that is, wisdom—is essential in all of life, including work. A glance over the proverbs demonstrates that the book has much to contribute to work. Many of the proverbs speak directly about the workplace activities of the ancient Near East, including agriculture, animal husbandry, textile and clothing manufacture, trade, transportation, military affairs, governance, courts of law, homemaking, raising children, education, construction, and others. Money—which is closely related to work—is also a prominent topic. In addition, many other proverbs cover topics that apply significantly to work even if they are not directly about work. They often develop virtues, such as prudence, honesty, justice, insight, and good relationships that apply in many spheres of life.

The Valiant Woman

A remarkable connection between the book of Proverbs and the world of work occurs at the end of the book. Lady Wisdom, whom we meet at the beginning of the book (Prov. 1:20–33; 8:1–9:12), reappears in street clothes in the final twenty-two verses of the book (Prov. 31:10–31) as a living, breathing woman, termed "the virtuous woman" (KJV). Some translators use "wife" instead of "woman," probably because the woman's husband and children are mentioned in the passage. (Both "wife" and "woman" are possible translations of the Hebrew *ishshah*.) Indeed, she finds fulfillment in her family and ensures that "her husband is known in the city gates, taking his seat among the elders of the land" (Prov. 31:23). But the text focuses on the woman's work as an entrepreneur with a cottage industry and its servants/workers to manage (Prov. 31:15).[9] Proverbs 31:10–31 does not merely apply to the workplace; it takes place in a workplace.

The book of Proverbs is summarized, then, in a poem praising a woman who is the wise manager of diverse enterprises ranging from weaving to wine making to trade in the market. Translators variously use the words *virtuous* (KJV), *capable* (NRSV), *excellent* (NASB), or *of noble character* (NIV) to describe this woman's character in Proverbs 31:10. But these terms fail to capture the element of strength or might present in the underlying Hebrew word *chayil*. When applied to a man, this same term is translated "strength," as in Prov. 31:3. In a great majority of its 246 appearances in the Old Testament, it applies to fighting men (for example, David's "mighty warriors," 1 Chr. 7:2). Translators tend to downplay the element of strength when the word is applied to a woman, as with Ruth, whom English translations describe as "noble" (NIV, TNIV), "virtuous"

---

[9] See Waltke, 528.

(NRSV, KJV), or "excellent" (NASB). But the word is the same, whether applied to men or women. In describing the woman of Proverbs 31:10–31, its meaning is best understood as strong or valiant, as further indicated by Proverbs 31:17, "She girds herself with strength, and makes her arms strong." Al Wolters argues on account of such martial language that the most appropriate translation is "Valiant Woman."[10] Accordingly, we will refer to the woman of Proverbs 31:10–31 as the "Valiant Woman," which captures both the strength and the virtue carried by the Hebrew *chayil*.

The concluding passage in the book of Proverbs characterizes this woman of strength as a wise worker in five sets of practices in her workplace. The high importance of this section is signaled in two ways. First, it is in the form of an acrostic poem, meaning that its lines begin with the twenty-two letters of the Hebrew alphabet in order, making it memorable. Second, it is placed as the climax and summary of the entire book. Accordingly, the five sets of practices we observe in the Valiant Woman will serve as a framework for exploring the entire book.

To some people in the ancient Near East, and even to some now, portraying a woman as a model of wise entrepreneurship would be surprising. Despite the fact that God gave the gift of work to men and women equally (Gen. 1:27–28), women's work has often been denigrated and treated with less dignity than men's. Following the example of Proverbs, we will refer to this wise worker as "she," understanding that God's wisdom is available equally to men and women. "She" functions in the book as an affirmation of the dignity of every person's work.

As always in the book of Proverbs, the way of wisdom flows out of the fear of the Lord. After all the Valiant Woman's abilities and virtues are described and honored, the source of her wisdom is revealed. "A woman who fears the LORD is to be praised" (Prov. 31:30).

The Wise Worker Is Trustworthy

The first characteristic of the way of wisdom personified in the Valiant Woman is trustworthiness. "The heart of her husband trusts in her" (Prov.

---

[10] Al Wolters, "Proverbs XXXI 10–31 as Heroic Hymn: A Form-Critical Analysis," *Vetus Testamentum* 38 (October 1988): 446–57.

31:11). Trustworthiness is the foundation of wisdom and virtue. God created people to work in concert with one another (Gen. 2:15), and without trust this is not possible. Trust requires adherence to ethical principles, beginning with faithfulness in our relationships. What are the workplace implications of being trustworthy depicted in the book of Proverbs?

The Trustworthy Worker Is Faithful to Her Fiduciary Responsibilities

The first requirement of trustworthiness is that our work brings good to those who trust us. By accepting their trust in us, we acknowledge a fiduciary responsibility to work for their good. The Valiant Woman fulfills this duty by working works not only for herself, but also for the benefit of those around her. Her work benefits her customers (Prov. 31:14), her community (Prov. 31:20), her immediate family (Prov. 31:12, 28), and her co-workers (Prov. 31:15). In the economy of the ancient Near East, these spheres of responsibility all come together in the economic entity called "the "household." As in much of the world today, most people then worked in the same place they lived. Some household members worked as cooks, cleaners, caregivers, or artisans of fabric, metal, wood, and stone in rooms in the home itself. Others worked in the fields immediately outside as farmers, shepherds, or laborers. The "household" refers to the whole complex of productive enterprises as well as to the extended family, employed workers, and perhaps slaves who worked and lived there. As the manager of a household, the Valiant Woman is much like a modern-day entrepreneur or senior executive. When she "looks well to the ways of her household" (Prov. 31:27), she is fulfilling a fiduciary duty of trust to all who depend on her enterprise.

This does not mean we cannot work for own benefit as well. The Valiant Woman's duty to her household is reciprocated by its duty to her. It is proper for her to receive a share of the household's profit for her own use. The passage instructs her children and her husband and the whole community to honor and praise her. "Her children rise up and call her happy; her husband too, and he praises her. . . . Give her a share in the fruit of her hands, and let her works praise her in the city gates" (Prov. 31:28, 31).

Our fiduciary duty requires that we must not do our employers harm in the pursuit of meeting our own needs. We may dispute with them or struggle against their treatment of us, but we may not work them harm.

For example, we may not steal from (Prov. 29:24), vandalize (Prov. 18:9), or slander (Prov. 10:18) our employers in order to air our grievances. Some applications of this are obvious. We may not charge a client for hours we didn't actually work. We may not destroy our employers' property or falsely accuse them. Reflection on this principle may lead us to deeper implications and questions. Is it legitimate to cause damage to the organization's productivity or harmony by failing to assist our internal rivals? Is access to personal benefits—trips, prizes, free merchandise, and the like—leading us to steer business to certain suppliers at the expense of our employer's best interests? The mutual duty that employees and employers owe one another is a serious matter.

The same duty applies to organizations when they have a fiduciary duty to other organizations. It is legitimate for a company to negotiate with its customers to obtain a higher price. But it is not legitimate to profit by taking secret advantage of a customer, as several investment banks were found to have done when they instructed their representatives to recommend collateralized mortgage obligations (CMOs) to customers as solid investments, while at the same time selling CMOs short in the expectation that their value would fall.[11]

The fear of the Lord is the touchstone of fiduciary responsibility. "Do not be wise in your own eyes; fear the LORD, and turn away from evil" (Prov. 3:7). All people are tempted to serve themselves at the expense of others. That is the consequence of the Fall. However, this proverb tells us that fear of the Lord—remembering his goodness to us, his providence over all things, and his justice when we harm others—helps us fulfill our duty to others.

A Trustworthy Worker Is Honest

Honesty is another essential aspect of trustworthiness. It is so important that one proverb equates truth with wisdom itself. "Buy truth, and do not sell it; buy wisdom, instruction, and understanding" (Prov. 23:23). Honesty consists both in *telling* the truth and in *doing* the truth.

---

[11] "Wall Street and the Financial Crisis: Majority and Minority Staff Report" (Washington DC: United States Senate, Permanent Subcommittee on Investigations), http://hsgac.senate.gov/public/file...isisReport.pdf.

Honest Words

Chapter 6 contains a well-known list of seven things God hates. Two of the seven are forms of dishonesty: "a lying tongue" and "a lying witness who testifies falsely" (Prov. 6:16–19). Throughout the book of Proverbs, the importance of telling the truth is a steady drumbeat.

I will speak noble things, and from my lips will come what is right; for my mouth will utter truth; wickedness is an abomination to my lips. (Prov. 8:6–7)

A truthful witness saves lives, but one who utters lies is a betrayer. (Prov. 14:25)

The getting of treasures by a lying tongue is a fleeting vapor and a snare of death. (Prov. 21:6)

A false witness will not go unpunished, and a liar will not escape. (Prov. 19:5)

Do not be a witness against your neighbor without cause, and do not deceive with your lips. (Prov. 24:28)

Lying lips conceal hatred, and whoever utters slander is a fool. When words are many, transgression is not lacking, but the prudent are restrained in speech. (Prov. 10:18–19)

Whoever speaks the truth gives honest evidence, but a false witness speaks deceitfully. Rash words are like sword thrusts, but the tongue of the wise brings healing. Truthful lips endure forever, but a lying tongue lasts only a moment. Deceit is in the mind of those who plan evil, but those who counsel peace have joy. (Prov. 12:17–20)

Lying lips are an abomination to the LORD, but those who act faithfully are his delight. (Prov. 12:22)

Like a war club, a sword, or a sharp arrow is one who bears false witness against a neighbor. (Prov. 25:18)

An enemy dissembles in speaking while harboring deceit within; when an enemy speaks graciously, do not believe it, for there are seven abominations concealed within. (Prov. 26:24–25)

Although the Bible does condone lying and deceit in exceptional circumstances (for example, Rahab the prostitute in Josh. 2:1–6, the Hebrew midwives' lies to Pharaoh in Exod. 1:15–20, and David's lie to the priest in 1 Sam. 21:1–3), Proverbs does not allow lying or deception to have a role in daily life and work. The point is not only that lying is wrong, but also that telling the truth is essential. We avoid lying, not so much because there is a rule against it, but because in our awe of God we love the truth.

Lying is destructive and leads ultimately to punishment and death.[12] We are warned not only to avoid deceit, but also to beware of the deceivers around us. We are not to allow ourselves to be taken in by their lies. Even here we recognize that we ourselves may be prone to believe the lies we hear. Like gossip (which is often a lie wrapped in a tissue of truth), we find a lie drawing us into the circle of those who are in the know, and we like that. Or we find that in our own perverseness, we want to believe the lie. But the proverbs warn us forcefully away from those who lie. A workplace where only the truth is spoken (in love, see Eph. 4:15) is utopian, yet God calls us to be among those who avoid the lying tongue.

While we might think of lying and dishonesty as individual sins, organizations can also develop a culture of dishonesty. Their business practices, their marketing, even their brand identity may be based on deception. Furthermore, people at every level of the organization are susceptible to lying. A worker cheats on a timecard. A manager pads an expense report. A mortgage officer misleads a customer about the terms of the contract. A principal improves his school's test scores by changing students' answers on the standardized tests it administers. On the other hand, some organizations develop strong cultures of honesty. A powerful way to develop a culture of honesty is for leaders to publicly acknowledge their mistakes and take responsibility for failures. This reinforces the message that telling the truth is more important than maintaining a flawless image.

About half of the proverbs about truth-telling prohibit false witness in particular, echoing the ninth commandment (Exod. 20:16). If misleading others in general is ungodly, then falsifying an account of someone else's actions is a crime that "will not go unpunished" (Prov.

---

[12] See M. Scott Peck, *People of the Lie: The Hope for Healing Human Evil*, 2nd ed. (New York: Touchstone, 1998).

19:5). A false witness is a direct assault on an innocent person. Yet it may be the most common form of lying in the workplace, second only perhaps to false deceptive advertising. Whereas false advertising is at least directed against outsiders (customers) who are likely to be wary of sales pitches and generally have other sources of information, a false witness is usually an attack on a co-worker and is likely to be accepted without skepticism within the organization. It occurs when we try to shift blame or credit by misreporting others' roles and actions. It harms not only those whose actions we misreport but the entire organization, for an organization that cannot accurately understand the reasons for its present successes and failures will not be able to make the changes needed to improve and adapt. It is like shooting someone on a submarine. Not only does it maim the victim, it also sinks the ship and drowns the whole crew.

Honest Deeds

Like words, deeds can also be either truthful or false. "The righteous hate falsehood, but the wicked *act* shamefully and disgracefully" (Prov. 13:5; emphasis added). The most prominent form of dishonest action in the proverbs is the use of false weights and measures. "Honest balances and scales are the LORD's; all the weights in the bag are his work" (Prov. 16:11). Conversely, "a false balance is an abomination to the LORD, but an accurate weight is his delight" (Prov. 11:1). "Differing weights are an abomination to the LORD, and false scales are not good" (Prov. 20:23). False weights and measures refer to defrauding a customer about the product being sold. Mislabeling a product, short-cutting the promised quality, and misrepresenting the source or origin—in addition to blatantly falsifying the quantity—are examples of this kind of dishonesty. Such practices are an abomination to God. Conversely, the simple act of giving an accurate measurement is a delight to the Lord. God actually takes pleasure when people engage in honest business practices.

There are practical reasons for acting honestly. In the short run, dishonest acts may produce a larger income, but in the long run, clients or customers will catch on and take their business elsewhere. Yet ultimately, it is the fear of God that corrals us, even when we think we could get away with dishonesty on human terms. "Diverse weights and diverse measures are both alike an abomination to the LORD" (Prov. 20:10).

Apart from false weights and measures, there are other ways of being dishonest in the workplace. One example from the Old Testament concerns land ownership, which was certified with boundary markers. A dishonest person could stealthily shift those boundary markers to enlarge his own holdings at the expense of his neighbor. The proverbs condemn dishonest acts like that. "Do not remove an ancient landmark or encroach on the fields of orphans, for their redeemer is strong; he will plead their cause against you" (Prov. 23:10–11). This proverb connects dishonesty with its consequences. Not only does dishonesty cause informational damage (such as misleading people into believing something incorrect), but it also causes material damage (such as stealing property by moving a boundary marker). The proverbs do not enumerate every kind of dishonest act that could be done in ancient Israel, much less in our world today. But they establish the principle that dishonest acts are as abhorrent to the Lord as dishonest words.

What does honesty—both in word and deed—look like in today's workplace? If we remember that honesty is an aspect of trustworthiness, then the criterion of honesty becomes "Can people trust what I say and do?" rather than "Is it technically true?" There are ways to break trust without committing outright fraud. Contracts can be altered or obfuscated to give unfair advantage to the party with the most sophisticated lawyers. Products can be described in misleading terms, as when "increases energy" on a food label means nothing except "contains calories." In the end, according to the proverbs, God will plead the cause of those so deceived and will not tolerate these practices (Prov. 23:11). In the meantime, wise—that is, godly—workers will avoid such practices.

The proverbs return again and again to the theme of honesty. "The integrity of the upright guides them, but the crookedness of the treacherous destroys them" (Prov. 11:3). "Bread gained by deceit is sweet, but afterwards the mouth will be full of gravel" (Prov. 20:17). An amusing proverb fingers another form of deception: "'Bad, Bad,' says the buyer, then goes away and boasts" (Prov. 20:14). Deliberately denigrating a product we want in order to get the price reduced, and then gloating over our "bargain," is also a form of dishonesty. In the realm of haggling between knowledgeable buyers and sellers, this practice may be more entertainment than abuse. But in its modern guise of spin-doctoring—as when a political candidate tries to convince English-speaking voters that he or she is tough on immigration, while also trying to convince Hispanic voters of the opposite—it betrays the fraudulence behind intentionally misrepresenting reality.

More broadly, Proverbs 20:14 commends honest negotiation rather than haggling by deception. Real estate developer Jack van Hartesvelt describes the difference: "Here's the way it [negotiation] typically works. If I want to get a 3 percent fee, I would tell the other side that I absolutely must have 4 percent, recognizing that they are going to have to drag me down to 3 percent to feel like they 'won.' The whole negotiation is based on a lie." He says that after many years of negotiating deals this way, he discovered that it is actually more beneficial to negotiate honestly, so that both sides can work together to find a solution of mutual benefit.

The Wise Worker Is Diligent

The Valiant Woman is diligent. Proverbs portrays her diligence in three ways: (1) hard work, (2) long-term planning, and (3) profitability. As result of her diligence in these ways, she is confident about the future.

A Diligent Worker Is Hard-Working

The Valiant Woman "works with willing hands" (Prov. 31:13), meaning that she chooses to work tirelessly in pursuit of the household's goals. "She rises while it is still night" (Prov. 31:15). "She makes linen garments and sells them" (Prov. 31:24). "With the fruit of her hands she plants a vineyard" (Prov. 31:16). It adds up to a lot of work.

In an agrarian economy, the connection between hard work and well-being is easy to see. As long as they have access to land to cultivate, hard-working farmers do much better than lazy ones. The proverbs are clear that a lazy worker will lose out in the end.

> A slack hand causes poverty, but the hand of the diligent makes rich. A child who gathers in summer is prudent, but a child who sleeps in harvest brings shame. (Prov. 10:4–5)

> I passed by the field of one who was lazy, by the vineyard of a stupid person; and see, it was all overgrown with thorns; the ground was covered

with nettles, and its stone wall was broken down. Then I saw and considered it; I looked and received instruction. A little sleep, a little slumber, a little folding of the hands to rest, and poverty will come upon you like a robber, and want, like an armed warrior. (Prov. 24:30–34)

In the ancient Near East, hard work brought prosperity, but even one week of laxity during the harvest could spell a hungry winter.

Modern economies (at least in the developed world) may mask this effect in the short term. In good times, when virtually everyone can find work, the lazy worker may have a job and appear to do nearly as well as the diligent worker. Likewise, in economic downturns (and at all times in many emerging economies), a hard-working person may have no more success than a lazy one in finding a job. And at all times, rewards for hard work may be blunted by discrimination, seniority rules, union contracts, favoritism, nepotism, golden parachutes, flawed performance metrics, ignorance by managers, and many other factors.

Does this make the proverbs about hard-working diligence obsolete? No, it does not, for two reasons. First, even in modern economies, diligence is usually rewarded over the course of a working life. When jobs are scarce, it is the diligent workers who are most likely to keep their jobs or find new ones faster. Second, the chief motivation for diligence is not personal prosperity, but the fear of the Lord, as we have seen with the other virtues in the proverbs. We are diligent because the Lord calls us to our tasks, and our awe of him motivates us to diligence in our work.

Laziness or the lack of diligence in the workplace is destructive. All who have experienced lazy coworkers can appreciate this pungent proverb: "Like vinegar to the teeth and smoke to the eyes, so are the lazy to their employers" (Prov. 10:26). We hate to be stuck on the same team with people who don't shoulder their share of the burden.

A Diligent Worker Plans for the Long Term

The Valiant Woman plans ahead. "She brings her food from far away" (Prov. 31:14), meaning that she doesn't depend on last-minute convenience purchases of questionable quality and cost. She "considers a field" (Prov. 31:16) before buying it, investigating its long-term potential. She is planning to plant this particular field as a vineyard (Prov. 31:16), and vineyards don't yield their first crop until two to three years after planting. The point is that she makes decisions based on their long-term consequences. Proverbs 21:5 tells us that "the plans of the diligent lead surely to abundance, but everyone who is hasty comes only to want."

Wise planning requires making decisions for the long term, as seen in the cycle of agricultural asset management.

> Know well the condition of your flocks, and give attention to your herds; for riches do not last forever, nor a crown for all generations. When the grass is gone, and new growth appears, and the herbage of the mountains is gathered, the lambs will provide your clothing, and the goats the price of a field; there will be enough goats' milk for your food, for the food of your household and nourishment for your servant-girls. (Prov. 27:23–27)

Like the Valiant Woman planting a vineyard, the wise herdsman thinks years ahead. So, too, the wise king or governor takes a long-term view. "With an intelligent ruler there is lasting order" (Prov. 28:2). The proverbs also turn to the ant as an example of long-term diligence.

> Go to the ant, you lazybones; consider its ways, and be wise. Without having any chief or officer or ruler, it prepares its food in summer, and gathers its sustenance in harvest. How long will you lie there, O lazybones? When will you rise from your sleep? A little sleep, a little slumber, a little folding of the hands to rest, and poverty will come upon you like a robber, and want, like an armed warrior. (Prov. 6:6–11)

Planning ahead takes many forms in workplaces. Financial planning is mentioned in Proverbs 24:27: "Prepare your work outside; get everything ready for you in the field; and after that build your house." In other words, don't start building your house until your fields are producing the necessary funds to finish your construction project. Jesus picked up on this in Luke 14:28–30:

> "Which of you, intending to build a tower, does not first sit down and estimate the cost, to see whether he has enough to complete it? Otherwise, when he has laid a foundation and is not able to finish, all who see it will begin to ridicule him, saying, 'This fellow began to build and was not able to finish.'"

There are many other forms of planning, and we can't expect the proverbs to serve as a planning manual for a modern enterprise. But we can note again the link in Proverbs between wisdom, in the form of planting, and God's character.

> The plans of the mind belong to mortals, but the answer of the tongue is from the LORD. (Prov. 16:1)

> The human mind may devise many plans, but it is the purpose of the LORD that will be established. (Prov. 19:21)

God plans for the *very* long term, and we are wise to plan ahead also. But we must remain humble about our plans. Unlike God, we do not have the power to make all our plans come to pass. "Do not boast about tomorrow, for you do not know what a day may bring" (Prov. 27:1). We plan with wisdom, speak with humility, and live in expectation that God's plans are our ultimate desire.

Attention to long-term consequences may be the most important skill we can cultivate for success. For example, psychological research has shown that the ability to delay gratification—that is, the ability to make decisions based on longer-term results—is a far better predictor of success in school than IQ is.[13] Regrettably, Christians sometimes seem to take passages such as "Do not worry about tomorrow" (Matt. 6:34) to mean "Do not plan ahead for tomorrow." The proverbs—alongside Jesus' own words—show that this is both incorrect and self-indulgent. In fact, the entire Christian life, with its expectation of Christ's return to perfect the kingdom of God, is a life of planning for the long term.

A Diligent Worker Contributes to the Profitability Value of the Enterprise

The Valiant Woman makes sure that the work of her hands is marketable. She knows what the merchants are buying (Prov. 31:24), chooses her materials with care (Prov. 31:13), and works tirelessly to assure a

---

[13] Angela L. Duckworth and Martin E. P. Seligman, "Self-Discipline Outdoes IQ in Predicting Academic Performance of Adolescents," *Psychological Science* 16, no. 12 (2005): 939–44. Similar results have been reported by Mischel and Shoda (*Science*, 1989), Rosenbaum (*Journal of Personality and Social Psychology*, 1986), and Bialer (*Journal of Personality*, 1961), among others.

quality product (Prov. 31:18b). Her reward is that "her merchandise is profitable" (Prov. 31:18a), providing the resources needed by the household and the community. The proverbs are clear that an individual worker's diligence contributes to the profitability—the increased value—of the entire undertaking. "The plans of the diligent lead surely to abundance, but everyone who is hasty comes only to want" (Prov. 21:5). The converse example is shown in the proverb, "One who is slack in work is close kin to a vandal" (Prov. 18:9). A lazy worker is no better than someone who deliberately sets out to destroy the enterprise. All of these anticipate Jesus' parable of the talents (Matt. 25:14–30).

When we keep in mind that these proverbs about profit are grounded in God's character, we see God wants us to work profitably. It is not enough to complete our assigned tasks. We must care about whether our work actually adds value to the materials, capital, and labor consumed. In the world of open economies, competition dictates that making a profit can be challenging. The undiligent—lazy, complacent, or dissolute—can quickly decline into loss, bankruptcy, and ruin. The diligent—hardworking, creative, focused—perform a godly service when they make it possible for their businesses to operate profitably.

Of course, not all people work in for-profit enterprises. In applying the Valiant Woman's profitable business dealings to the academic, governmental, military, homemaking, charitable, and other not-for-profit spheres, we must translate "profit" to "value." But before generalizing too far, let us explore the specific topic of business profit. Christians have not always recognized the importance of profit in the biblical perspective. In fact, profit is often regarded with suspicion and discussed in the rhetoric of "people vs. profits." There is a suspicion that profit comes not from taking inputs and creating something more valuable from them, but from swindling buyers, workers, or suppliers. This arises from an inadequate understanding of business and economics. A truly biblical critique of businesses would ask questions such as: "What kind of profits?" "What is the source of the profit?" "Is the profit extracted by monopoly or intimidation or deception?" and "How is the profit shared among workers, managers, owners, lenders, suppliers, customers and taxation?" It would encourage and celebrate workers and businesses that bring a wholesome profitability to their work.

Not all workers are in a position to know whether their work is profitable. Employees in a large corporation may have little idea whether their particular work contributes positively to profitability of the enterprise. Profitability, in an accounting sense, does not play a role in education, government, not-for-profit corporations, and homes. But all workers can pay attention to how their work contributes to adding value or accomplishing the mission of the organization, to whether the value they add is greater than the pay and other resources they extract. To do so is a form of service to the Lord.

The Valiant Woman's profitable management of her household draws a word of exalted praise. "She is far more precious than jewels" (Prov. 31:10). This is no sentimental metaphor. It is quite literally true. A well-run enterprise can certainly earn profits over the years far exceeding the value of jewels and other stores of wealth.

A Diligent Worker Can Smile at the Future

The Valiant Woman's diligence gives her an eagerness for the future. "Strength and dignity are her clothing, and she laughs at the time to come" (Prov. 31:25). While the proverbs are not promises of personal prosperity, in general, our diligence does lead to a better future.

> Those who till their land will have plenty of food, but those who follow worthless pursuits have no sense. (Prov. 12:11)
>
> Anyone who tills the land will have plenty of bread, but one who follows worthless pursuits will have plenty of poverty. (Prov. 28:19)
>
> The hand of the diligent will rule, while the lazy will be put to forced labor. (Prov. 12:24)

Diligence is not a guarantee against future sorrow or even disaster (see "Job and Work" above). Yet the wise person trusts God for the future, and the diligent can rest in the confidence that they have done what God asks of them for themselves, their households, and their communities.

The Wise Worker Is Shrewd

The Valiant Woman sets an example of exceptional acumen in her work. The proverbs describe this virtue as "prudent" (Prov. 19:14) or "shrewd" (Prov. 1:4). We may tend to think of shrewd people as those who take advantage of others, but in Proverbs it carries the idea of making the most of resources and circumstances. If we understand shrewdness as "clever discerning awareness and hardheaded acumen,"[14] then we see the kind of shrewd wisdom God intends for workers.

A Shrewd Worker Employs Keen Awareness and Judgment

This Valiant Woman's shrewdness is displayed in the keen awareness with which she sources her materials. "She seeks wool and flax. . . . She is like the ships of the merchant" (Prov. 31:13–14). Today's manufacturer or craftsperson can be shrewd in the selection of materials or can unwisely settle for materials that will not hold up well. Investments in research and development, market analysis, logistics, strategic partnerships, and community involvement may yield large payoffs in the future. On an individual level, good judgment is invaluable. An investment adviser who can match a client's future needs with the risks and rewards inherent in various investment vehicles is performing a godly service.

A Shrewd Worker Prepares for All Known Contingencies

The Valiant Woman "is not afraid for her household when it snows, for all her household are clothed in crimson. She makes herself coverings; her clothing is fine linen and purple" (Prov. 31:21–22). Her material preparations cover every eventuality of the coming winter weather. She prepares the variety of clothing and blankets ("coverings") her household may need, whatever the season may bring. The descriptions indicate fine or rich material ("fine linen and purple"), and the Hebrew word *sanim* translated "crimson" may be a copyist's mistake for "double" (*shenayim*), that is, layered and warm.[15]

---

[14]*Merriam-Webster's Collegiate Dictionary*, 11th ed., s.v. "shrewd."
[15]Murphy, 247. The LXX and the Vulgate adopt this reading, although the Masoretic does not.

This woman is alert to possible problems and works toward solutions before the problems arise. Consider her preparations for her husband. In the middle of her preparations of clothing and coverings, she keeps in mind her husband's role as a public figure: "Her husband is known in the city gates, taking his seat among the elders of the land" (Prov. 31:23). What would happen if it snows while her husband is in the midst of a civic affair? Not to worry, for "all her household"—including her husband—are suitably attired for any occasion.

A Shrewd Worker Seeks Good Advice

A persistent myth in some circles is that the shrewdest leaders scorn advice. Their very shrewdness consists of seeing opportunities that others are too low to glimpse. It is true that just because many people advise something, that doesn't make it wise. "No wisdom, no understanding, no counsel, can avail against the LORD" (Prov. 21:30). If an idea is bad or wrong ("against the LORD"), no chorus of yes-men can make it good or wise.

But the myth of the genius who succeeds against all advice is seldom true in reality. Creativity and excellence build on multiple points of view. Innovation takes account of the known in order to step into the unknown, and great leaders who reject conventional wisdom have usually mastered it first before moving beyond it. "Without counsel, plans go wrong, but with many advisers they succeed" (Prov. 15:22). And in Proverbs 20:18 we read, "Plans are established by taking advice; wage war by following wise guidance." The wise person uses the complementing strengths of others, even when striking into new territory.

A Shrewd Worker Improves Her Skills and Knowledge

The Valiant Woman "girds herself with strength, and makes her arms strong" (Prov. 31:17). That is, she takes steps to improve her ability to do her work. She makes her arms strong; she girds herself with strength. A shrewd person acts to improve her skill set or knowledge.

As the industrial economy in the developed world has given way to a technological economy, continual training and education have become indispensable for employers and employees. In fact, this is becoming the case in many emerging economies as well. The work you are prepared for today is not likely to be the work you will be doing ten years from now. A shrewd worker recognizes this and retrains for the next opportunity in the workplace. Likewise, it is becoming harder for employers to find workers with the skills needed for many of today's jobs. The highest-performing individuals, organizations, and societies will be those that develop effective systems for lifelong learning.

The Wise Worker Is Generous

The Valiant Woman is generous. "She opens her hands to the poor and reaches out her hands to the needy" (Prov. 31:20). We are accustomed to hearing generosity praised in the Bible, and here the Valiant Woman is praised for it. But we must not reduce her generosity to a pleasant quirk in her personality. Her generosity is part and parcel of her work, as we can see in the relationship between verses 31:19 and 31:20:

> She puts her hands [Heb. *yade*] to the distaff, and her hands [*kappe*] hold the spindle.

> She opens her hand [*kap*] to the poor, and reaches out her hands [*yade*] to the needy.

Two different Hebrew words are translated "hand" (or plural "hands") in these two verses. If we look at the original Hebrew, we see they occur in the order *yade*, *kappe* in the first verse, and in the reverse order *kap*, *yade* in the second verse (*kappe* is the plural of *kap*). This "chiastic" structure of ABBA is common in the Bible and indicates that the entire structure forms a single unit of thought. In other words, her work is inseparable from her generosity. Because she is successful in spinning, she has something to give to the poor, and conversely, her generous spirit is an essential element of her capability as an entrepreneur/executive.

In other words, Proverbs claims that generosity and fiduciary duty do not conflict. Being generous to the needy out of the household's resources does not reduce the owner's wealth, but increases it. This counterintuitive argument appears throughout Proverbs. Most people curb their generosity out of fear that if they give away too much, they will not have enough left for themselves. But the proverbs teach the exact opposite:

> Some give freely, yet grow all the richer; others withhold what is due, and only suffer want. A generous person will be enriched, and one who gives water will get water. The people curse those who hold back grain, but a blessing is on the head of those who sell it. (Prov. 11:24–26)

> Whoever is kind to the poor lends to the Lord, and will be repaid in full. (Prov. 19:17)

> Whoever gives to the poor will lack nothing, but one who turns a blind eye will get many a curse. (Prov. 28:27)

The Wise Worker Is Just

The proverbs do not stop with commending generosity, but go further to claim that caring for the poor is a matter of justice. First, the proverbs recognize that people are often poor because the rich and powerful defraud or oppress them. Or if they were already poor, they have become easy targets for further fraud and oppression. This is abhorrent to God, and he will bring judgment against those who do it.

> Those who oppress the poor insult their Maker, but those who are kind to the needy honor him. (Prov. 14:31)

> Oppressing the poor in order to enrich oneself, and giving to the rich, will lead only to loss. (Prov. 22:16)

> Do not rob the poor because they are poor, or crush the afflicted at the gate; for the Lord pleads their cause and despoils of life those who despoil them. (Prov. 22:22–23)

> Whoever sows injustice will reap calamity, and the rod of anger will fail. Those who are generous are blessed, for they share their bread with the poor. (Prov. 22:8–9)

> One who augments wealth by exorbitant interest gathers it for another who is kind to the poor. (Prov. 28:8)

The bottom line is found in Proverbs 16:8, "Better is a little with righteousness than large income with injustice."

Second, even if you have not defrauded or oppressed the poor, God's justice requires that you do what you can to set things right for them, beginning with meeting their immediate needs.

> If you close your ear to the cry of the poor, you will cry out and not be heard. (Prov. 21:13)

> Those who despise their neighbors are sinners, but happy are those who are kind to the poor. (Prov. 14:21)

> Do not withhold good from those to whom it is due, when it is in your power to do it. Do not say to your neighbor, "Go, and come again; tomorrow I will give it." (Prov. 3:27–28)

> Those who mock the poor insult their Maker; those who are glad at calamity will not go unpunished. (Prov. 17:5)

To regard helping the needy as a matter of justice, not merely generosity, is no surprise if we remember that wisdom rests on the fear of the Lord. That is, wisdom consists of living in awe of our God so that we seek to do what he desires for the world. God is just. God desires that the poor be cared for and poverty be eliminated. If we truly love God, then we will care for those whom God loves. Therefore, to relieve the poor and to work to eliminate poverty are matters of justice.

Notice that many of these proverbs assume personal contact between the rich and the poor. Generosity is not only a matter of sending a donation, but also of working and perhaps even living alongside poor people. It may mean working to break down the segregation of the poor away from the middle class and wealthy in housing, shopping, education, work, and politics. Do you come into contact with people of higher and lower socioeconomic status on a daily basis? If not, your world may be too narrow.

Corporate Social Responsibility?

We can see how generosity and justice are important for an individual worker, but do they have any application for corporations? Most of Proverbs deals with individuals, but the section on the Valiant Woman addresses her as the manager of a household business. And as we have seen, her generosity is not a hindrance to her work, but an essential element of it.

Regrettably, many businesses today seem to lack the imagination or skill needed to operate in ways that benefit shareholders while also benefiting the people around them. For example, a quick read of any newspaper's financial section will find many stories about companies attempting to defraud or oppress the poor: pressuring poor and powerless people into selling property below its full value, taking advantage of ignorance or misinformation to sell questionable products, and wringing excessive short-term profits from those who are vulnerable or who lack alternatives.

Why do such companies believe that grabbing wealth from others is the only—or best—way to make a profit? Is there any evidence that a zero-sum approach to business actually improves shareholder return? How many of these practices really lead to higher long-term profitability or power? Quite the opposite: the best businesses succeed because they find a sustainable way to produce goods and services that benefit customers and society, while providing an excellent return to employees, shareholders, and lenders. Businesses and other organizations that meet social needs have an advantage when they need community support, worker commitment, and social protection from economic, political, and competitive threats.

Government Policy?

The book of Proverbs also demands justice from institutions other than business. In particular, the realm of government receives attention in the many verses dealing with kings. The message to them is the same as that to businesses. Governments can survive long term only if they care for the poor and vulnerable and bring them justice.

> If a king judges the poor with equity, his throne will be established forever. (Prov. 29:14)

> By justice a king gives stability to the land, but one who makes heavy exactions ruins it. (Prov. 29:4)

> Take away the wicked from the presence of the king, and his throne will be established in righteousness. (Prov. 25:5)

> Righteous lips are the delight of a king, and he loves those who speak what is right. (Prov. 16:13)

> It is an abomination to kings to do evil, for the throne is established by righteousness. (Prov. 16:12)

As with all wisdom, the foundation of wise governance is the fear of the Lord. "By me kings reign, and rulers decree what is just" (Prov. 8:15). In speaking to kings, the proverbs would seem to apply primarily to political leaders and civil servants in modern society. But in democratic societies, all citizens have a role in government and public policy. Contacting our representatives and voting for candidates and ballot questions that bring justice to the poor and vulnerable are ways we enact the justice that comes from wisdom today.

Competition?

The proverbs even extend the demands of generosity and justice to competition and struggle. "If your enemies are hungry, give them bread to eat; and if they are thirsty, give them water to drink; for you will heap coals of fire on their heads, and the LORD will reward you" (Prov. 25:21–22). The Apostle Paul quotes this proverb word for word in Romans 12:20, and concludes with the challenge, "Do not be overcome by evil, but overcome evil with good" (Rom. 12:21). Moreover, "Do not rejoice when your enemies fall, and do not let your heart be glad when they stumble" (Prov. 24:17). What? Are we to be generous even toward an enemy? Paul and the authors of the proverbs are convinced that when we do so, the Lord will reward us.

Does this apply to our attitude toward our competitors, whether individually (e.g., rivals for promotion) or corporately (e.g., competitors)?

The proverbs do not discuss modern competition. But if they promote service even to an enemy, it is reasonable to infer they also promote service to competitors. This is not the same thing as collusion or oligarchy. The near-universal ascendancy of market economies is arguably due to the benefits of competition. But business, politics, and other forms of competition are at heart forms of cooperation, albeit with significant competitive aspects. Society fosters competition in order that all may thrive. The proper penalty for failure in competition is not to be crushed or driven to poverty, but to be transformed or diverted to more productive work. Companies go out of business, but their successful rivals do not become monopolies. Elections have winners and losers, but the victors do not rewrite the constitution to ban the losing party. Careers rise and fall, but the proper penalty for failure is not "You'll never work in this town again," but "What help do you need to find something better suited to your talents?" The wisest individuals and organizations learn how to engage in competition that makes the most of each player's participation and offers a soft landing for those who lose today's contest but may make a valuable contribution tomorrow.

The Wise Worker Guards the Tongue

The Valiant Woman exercises care in what she says and how she speaks. The proverbs remind us that "to watch over mouth and tongue is to keep out of trouble" (Prov. 21:23). Sometimes, tongue in cheek, they also remind us that "even fools who keep silent are considered wise; when they close their lips, they are deemed intelligent" (Prov. 17:28).

There are more proverbs about the tongue than about any other topic. (See Prov. 6:17, 24; 10:20, 31; 12:18–19; 15:2, 4; 16:1; 17:4, 20; 18:21; 21:6, 23; 25:15, 23; 26:28; 28:23; in addition to Prov. 31:26). A righteous and gentle tongue brings wisdom (Prov. 10:31), healing (Prov. 12:18), knowledge (Prov. 15:2), life (Prov. 15:4; 18:21), and the word of the Lord (Prov. 16:1). A perverse and unguarded tongue sheds innocent blood (Prov. 6:17), breaks the spirit (Prov. 15:4), encourages evil (Prov. 17:4), brings on calamity (Prov. 17:20), trouble (Prov. 21:23), and anger (Prov. 25:23), breaks bones (Prov. 25:15), works ruin (Prov. 26:28), and becomes "a snare of death" (Prov. 21:6).

Communication in some form is an integral part of nearly every job. In addition, social talk at work can improve working relationships, or damage them. What do the proverbs teach about wise use of the tongue?

The Wise Worker Avoids Gossip

Is gossip really a problem in the workplace or is it merely innocent gab? The proverbs point to its danger. "A gossip reveals secrets; therefore do not associate with a babbler" (Prov. 20:19). Gossip causes strife. "A fool's lips bring strife, and a fool's mouth invites a flogging. The mouths of fools are their ruin, and their lips a snare to themselves. The words of a whisperer are like delicious morsels; they go down into the inner parts of the body" (Prov. 18:6–8). "For lack of wood the fire goes out, and where there is no whisperer, quarreling ceases. As charcoal is to hot embers and wood to fire, so is a quarrelsome person for kindling strife" (Prov. 26:20–21). "Scoundrels concoct evil, and their speech is like a scorching fire. A perverse person spreads strife, and a whisperer separates close friends" (Prov. 16:27–28). Gossip is a violation of trust, the founding virtue of a wise person. "Whoever belittles another lacks sense, but an intelligent person remains silent. A gossip goes about telling secrets, but one who is trustworthy in spirit keeps a confidence" (Prov. 11:12–13).

Gossip casts other people in a questionable light, raising doubts about a person's integrity or a decision's validity. Gossip projects evil into someone else's motives, thus showing itself a child of the Father of Lies. Gossip takes words out of context, misrepresents the intentions of the speaker, reveals what should have been kept in confidence, and attempts to elevate the gossiper at the expense of others who are not present to speak for themselves. It is not hard to see how destructive this can be in a workplace. Whether the gossip places a question mark over a person's reputation or the worth of a project or a position taken by a superior, the shadow cast by such words causes everyone around the gossiper to be more guarded and suspicious. This cannot help but inject division among workers, whether in an office, on a factory floor, or in an executive suite. Not surprisingly, St. Paul included gossip in his list of sins that are an abomination to God (Rom. 1:29).

The Wise Worker Speaks in Kindness, Not Anger

The Valiant Woman "opens her mouth with wisdom, and the teaching of kindness is on her tongue" (Prov. 31:26). No one likes to be on the receiving end of an angry outburst, so we easily recognize the danger noted in a number of the proverbs: "A soft answer turns away wrath, but a harsh word stirs up anger" (Prov. 15:1). "Those with good sense are slow to anger, and it is to their glory to overlook an offense" (Prov. 19:11). "Those who are hot-tempered stir up strife, but those who are slow to anger calm contention" (Prov. 15:18). "One who is slow to anger is better than the mighty, and one whose temper is controlled than one who captures a city" (Prov. 16:32).

The beauty of these proverbs is that they also provide a picture of the person who can deal successfully with anger. We should be "angry" (morally indignant) against sin, but we must not allow our "anger" (wrath) to control us. "Be angry but do not sin; do not let the sun go down on your anger" (Eph. 4:26). The wise person gives a soft answer, overlooks an offense, and calms contention. The "teaching of kindness" is on the Valiant Woman's tongue. Such people are "better than the mighty." In the workplace, such people are essential when irritations increase or tempers flare.[16] As followers of Jesus Christ we can live out the fruit of God's Spirit when we control our tongue, not only by avoiding angry speech ourselves, but also by being a calming influence in a sometimes-contentious atmosphere.

The Wise Worker Blesses Others

The blessings from a wise tongue rest on the reality that "a word fitly spoken is like apples of gold in a setting of silver; like a gold ring or an ornament of gold is a wise rebuke to a listening ear" (Prov. 25:11–12). In the workplace we are often surrounded by anxious coworkers, and a good word may be just what they need. "Anxiety weighs down the human heart, but a good word cheers it up" (Prov. 12:25). We stand ready to

---

[16] For more on this topic see Ronald A. Heifetz and Martin Linsky, *Leadership on the Line: Staying Alive through the Dangers of Leading* (Boston: Harvard Business Review Press, 2002), especially chapter 5, "Orchestrate the Conflict."

give that good word because "a gentle tongue is a tree of life" (Prov. 15:4). Truly, "death and life are in the power of the tongue, and those who love it will eat its fruits" (Prov. 18:21).

In today's electronic workplace, the "tongue" isn't confined to our audible words. Gossip, lies, and angry words can travel at light speed through e-mails and social media. We are called to be discerning, to recognize that death and life truly are in the words we use with or against one another in the workplace.

The Wise Worker Is Modest

The proverbs commend modesty, both in attitude (avoid excessive pride) and in the use of money (avoid lavish spending). These virtues do not appear in the description of the Valiant Woman. But they appear so strongly elsewhere in Proverbs and apply so directly to work that we cannot do justice to the book without mentioning them.

A Modest Worker Is Not Proud

"Pride goes before destruction, and a haughty spirit before a fall. It is better to be of a lowly spirit among the poor than to divide the spoil with the proud" (Prov. 16:18–19). Verse 18 may be the most famous proverb of all. There are others.

> When pride comes, then comes disgrace; but wisdom is with the humble. (Prov. 11:2)

> Haughty eyes and a proud heart—the lamp of the wicked—are sin. (Prov. 21:4)

> A person's pride will bring humiliation, but one who is lowly in spirit will obtain honor. (Prov. 29:23)

Are these commands against self-respect? No, they are calls to live in such awe of God (the "fear of the LORD") that we see ourselves as we really are and we can be honest with ourselves about ourselves. If we fear the Lord, then we no longer have to fear our own self-image, and we can let go of trying to puff ourselves up. It is to rest in the knowledge that God will ultimately triumph over this broken world of sin and destruction. The Lord knows the path of the righteous—even in the workplace. In the end, God lifts up those who put their trust in him.

A Modest Worker Is Not Driven by the Lure of Wealth

The ancient sage Agur—the source of the next-to-last collection of sayings in the book—left us a wise prayer.

> Two things I ask of you; do not deny them to me before I die: Remove far from me falsehood and lying; give me neither poverty nor riches; feed me with the food that I need, or I shall be full, and deny you, and say, "Who is the LORD?" or I shall be poor, and steal, and profane the name of my God. (Prov. 30:7–9)

These are wise words for us in the workplace, "Give me neither poverty nor riches."

We work to earn a living, to enjoy a measure of comfort and security, to provide for our families, and to contribute something to the poor and the wider community. Is that enough, or are we driven to strive for more? Agur links that desire for more to leaving God out of our lives, to ignoring our Creator and his purposes for us. Agur also prays that he will not live in poverty but that God would provide the food he needs. This is a legitimate prayer. Jesus taught us to pray, "Give us this day our daily bread" (Matt. 6:11).

Working to provide for ourselves and our families is a good thing. But Agur's point is that if we turn our work into a quest for ever-increasing wealth—in other words, greed—we have left the path of wisdom. We may seek wealth, consciously or not, because it seems to offer concrete evidence of our success and self-worth. But the comfort of wealth is imaginary. "The wealth of the rich is their strong city; in their imagination it is like a high wall" (Prov. 18:11). "The rich is wise in self-esteem, but an intelligent poor person sees through the pose" (Prov. 28:11). In reality, wealth does not bring an end to troubles. It merely substitutes the troubles of wealth for the troubles of poverty. "Wealth is a ransom for a person's life, but the poor get no threats" (Prov. 13:8).

Wealth cannot actually make us feel more secure. "Those who trust in their riches will wither" (Prov. 11:28). We should be on guard, especially against sacrificing the richness of life to obtain the riches of money. "The miser is in a hurry to get rich and does not know that loss is sure to come" (Prov. 28:22). "Do not wear yourself out to get rich; be wise enough to desist" (Prov. 23:4). In particular, the wise care more about their honest reputations than about their bank accounts. "A good name is to be chosen rather than great riches, and favor is better than silver or gold" (Prov. 22:1).

The proverbs are not opposed to wealth itself. In fact, wealth can be a blessing. "The blessing of the LORD makes rich, and he adds no sorrow with it" (Prov. 10:22). It is the obsession for wealth that causes harm.

If nothing else, the proverbs of modesty remind us that our exploration of the book through the lens of the Valiant Woman may be a helpful guide, but it does not exhaust the contributions of the book to the theory and practice of work. All the proverbs are well worth further study beyond the glimpses seen in this chapter. We encourage those who find this chapter helpful to continue reading the proverbs to discover further meanings and applications, and to reflect on their own experience in the light of God's wisdom.

Conclusions from Proverbs

In the end, our work habits are shaped by our character, which in turn is shaped by knowledge of our Lord's revelation and our awe of him. As we come to know our Lord more intimately, our character is transformed to become like God's character. Indeed, "The fear of the LORD is the beginning of wisdom" (Prov. 9:10). Wisdom brings life to all spheres of life, including the workplace, where most of us spend the largest part of our waking hours. Wisdom leads us to trustworthy actions, diligence, wholesome shrewdness, generosity and justice for those in need, controlling what we say, and to humble living. In wisdom, we trust God to shape our destiny and take charge of our ends. "Commit your work to the LORD, and your plans will be established" (Prov. 16:3).

Index by Chapter/Verse from the Book of Proverbs

Prov. 3:24   Your sleep will be sweet.

About the Book of Proverbs, 156–59

Prov. 3:27–28   Do not withhold good from those to whom it is due, when it is in your power to do it. Do not say to your neighbor, "Go, and come again; tomorrow I will give it."

The Wise Worker Is Just, 177–81

Prov. 4:11   I have taught you the way of wisdom; I have led you in the paths of uprightness.

Introduction to Proverbs, 155–56

Prov. 6:2   . . . to preserve you from the wife of another, from the smooth tongue of the adulteress.

The Wise Worker Guards the Tongue, 181–84

Prov. 6:6–11   Go to the ant, you lazybones; consider its ways, and be wise. . . . A little sleep, a little slumber, a little folding of the hands to rest, and poverty will come upon you like a robber, and want, like an armed warrior.

The Wise Worker Is Diligent, 168–73

Prov. 6:16   There are six things that the LORD hates . . .

What Does Proverbs Have to Do with Work? 159–60

Prov. 6:16–19   There are six things that the LORD hates, seven that are an abomination to him: haughty eyes, a lying tongue, and hands that shed innocent blood, a heart that devises wicked plans, feet that hurry to run to evil, a lying witness who testifies falsely, and one who sows discord in a family.

What Does Proverbs Have to Do with Work? 159–60; The Wise Worker Is Trustworthy, 161–68

Prov. 6:17   . . . haughty eyes, a lying tongue, and hands that shed innocent blood.

The Wise Worker Guards the Tongue, 181–84

Prov. 8:6–7   I will speak noble things, and from my lips will come what is right; for my mouth will utter truth; wickedness is an abomination to my lips.

The Wise Worker Is Trustworthy, 161–68

Prov. 8:15   By me kings reign, and rulers decree what is just.

The Wise Worker Is Just, 177–81

Prov. 8:35–36   Whoever finds me finds life and obtains favor from the LORD; but those who miss me injure themselves; all who hate me love death.

Introduction to Proverbs, 155–56

Prov. 9:10   The fear of the LORD is the beginning of wisdom, and knowledge of the Holy One is insight.

Introduction to Proverbs, 155–56; What Does Proverbs Have to Do with Work? 159–60

Prov. 12:17–20   Whoever speaks the truth gives honest evidence, but a false witness speaks deceitfully. Rash words are like sword thrusts, but the tongue of the wise brings healing. Truthful lips endure forever, but a lying tongue lasts only a moment. Deceit is in the mind of those who plan evil, but those who counsel peace have joy.

The Wise Worker Is Trustworthy, 161–68

Prov. 12:18   Rash words are like sword thrusts, but the tongue of the wise brings healing.

The Wise Worker Guards the Tongue, 181–84

Prov. 12:19   Truthful lips endure forever, but a lying tongue lasts only a moment.

The Wise Worker Guards the Tongue, 181–84

Prov. 12:22   Lying lips are an abomination to the LORD, but those who act faithfully are his delight.

The Wise Worker Is Trustworthy, 161–68

Prov. 12:24   The hand of the diligent will rule, while the lazy will be put to forced labor.

The Wise Worker Is Diligent, 168–73

Prov. 12:25   Anxiety weighs down the human heart, but a good word cheers it up.

The Wise Worker Guards the Tongue, 181–84

Prov. 13:5   The righteous hate falsehood, but the wicked act shamefully and disgracefully.

The Wise Worker Is Trustworthy, 161–68

Prov. 13:8   Wealth is a ransom for a person's life, but the poor get no threats.

The Wise Worker Is Modest, 184–86

Prov. 14:16   The wise are cautious and turn away from evil.

Introduction to Proverbs, 155–56

Prov. 14:21   Those who despise their neighbors are sinners, but happy are those who are kind to the poor.

The Wise Worker Is Just, 177–81

Prov. 14:25   A truthful witness saves lives, but one who utters lies is a betrayer.

The Wise Worker Is Trustworthy, 161–68

Prov. 14:31   Those who oppress the poor insult their Maker, but those who are kind to the needy honor him.

The Wise Worker Is Just, 177–81

Prov. 15:1   A soft answer turns away wrath, but a harsh word stirs up anger.

The Wise Worker Guards the Tongue, 181–84

Prov. 15:2   The tongue of the wise dispenses knowledge, but the mouths of fools pour out folly.

The Wise Worker Guards the Tongue, 181–84

Prov. 15:3   The eyes of the LORD are in every place.

What Does Proverbs Have to Do with Work? 159–60

Prov. 15:4   A gentle tongue is a tree of life, but perverseness in it breaks the spirit.

The Wise Worker Guards the Tongue, 181–84

Prov. 15:18 Those who are hot-tempered stir up strife, but those who are slow to anger calm contention.

The Wise Worker Guards the Tongue, 181–84

Prov. 15:22 Without counsel, plans go wrong, but with many advisers they succeed.

The Wise Worker Is Shrewd, 174–76

Prov. 16:1 The plans of the mind belong to mortals, but the answer of the tongue is from the LORD.

The Wise Worker Is Diligent, 168–73; The Wise Worker Guards the Tongue, 181–84

Prov. 16:3 Commit your work to the LORD, and your plans will be established.

Conclusions from Proverbs, 186

Prov. 16:8 Better is a little with righteousness than large income with injustice.

The Wise Worker Is Just, 177–81

Prov. 16:11 Honest balances and scales are the LORD's; all the weights in the bag are his work.

The Wise Worker Is Trustworthy, 161–68

Prov. 16:12 It is an abomination to kings to do evil, for the throne is established by righteousness.

The Wise Worker Is Just, 177–81

Prov. 16:13 Righteous lips are the delight of a king, and he loves those who speak what is right.

The Wise Worker Is Just, 177–81

Prov. 16:18–19 Pride goes before destruction, and a haughty spirit before a fall. It is better to be of a lowly spirit among the poor than to divide the spoil with the proud.

The Wise Worker Is Modest, 184–86

Prov. 16:27–28 Scoundrels concoct evil, and their speech is like a scorching fire. A perverse person spreads strife, and a whisperer separates close friends.

The Wise Worker Guards the Tongue, 181–84

Prov. 16:32 One who is slow to anger is better than the mighty, and one whose temper is controlled than one who captures a city.

The Wise Worker Guards the Tongue, 181–84

Prov. 17:4 An evildoer listens to wicked lips; and a liar gives heed to a mischievous tongue.

The Wise Worker Guards the Tongue, 181–84

Prov. 17:5 Those who mock the poor insult their Maker; those who are glad at calamity will not go unpunished.

The Wise Worker Is Just, 177–81

Prov. 17:20 The crooked of mind do not prosper, and the perverse of tongue fall into calamity.

The Wise Worker Guards the Tongue, 181–84

Prov. 17:28 Even fools who keep silent are considered wise; when they close their lips, they are deemed intelligent.

The Wise Worker Guards the Tongue, 181–84

Prov. 24:17 Do not rejoice when your enemies fall, and do not let your heart be glad when they stumble.

The Wise Worker Is Just, 177–81

Prov. 24:27 Prepare your work outside; get everything ready for you in the field; and after that build your house.

The Wise Worker Is Diligent, 168–73

Prov. 24:28 Do not be a witness against your neighbor without cause, and do not deceive with your lips.

The Wise Worker Is Trustworthy, 161–68

Prov. 24:30–34 I passed by the field of one who was lazy, by the vineyard of a stupid person. . . . A little sleep, a little slumber, a little folding of the hands to rest, and poverty will come upon you like a robber, and want, like an armed warrior.

The Wise Worker Is Diligent, 168–73

Prov. 25:5 Take away the wicked from the presence of the king, and his throne will be established in righteousness.

The Wise Worker Is Just, 177–81

Prov. 25:11–12 A word fitly spoken is like apples of gold in a setting of silver; like a gold ring or an ornament of gold is a wise rebuke to a listening ear.

The Wise Worker Guards the Tongue, 181–84

Prov. 25:15 With patience a ruler may be persuaded, and a soft tongue can break bones.

The Wise Worker Guards the Tongue, 181–84

Prov. 25:18 Like a war club, a sword, or a sharp arrow is one who bears false witness against a neighbor.

The Wise Worker Is Trustworthy, 161–68

Prov. 25:21–22 If your enemies are hungry, give them bread to eat; and if they are thirsty, give them water to drink; for you will heap coals of fire on their heads, and the LORD will reward you.

The Wise Worker Is Just, 177–81

Prov. 25:23 The north wind produces rain, and a backbiting tongue, angry looks.

The Wise Worker Guards the Tongue, 181–84

Prov. 26:20–21 For lack of wood the fire goes out, and where there is no whisperer, quarreling ceases. As charcoal is to hot embers and wood to fire, so is a quarrelsome person for kindling strife.

The Wise Worker Guards the Tongue, 181–84

Prov. 26:24–25 An enemy dissembles in speaking while harboring deceit within; when an enemy speaks graciously, do not believe it, for there are seven abominations concealed within.

The Wise Worker Is Trustworthy, 161–68

Prov. 26:28 A lying tongue hates its victims, and a flattering mouth works ruin.

The Wise Worker Guards the Tongue, 181–84

Prov. 27:1 Do not boast about tomorrow, for you do not know what a day may bring.

The Wise Worker Is Diligent, 168–73

Prov. 27:23–27 Know well the condition of your flocks, and give attention to your herds; for riches do not last forever, nor a crown for all generations . . . there will be enough goats' milk for your food, for the food of your household and nourishment for your servant-girls.

The Wise Worker Is Diligent, 168–73

Prov. 28:2 With an intelligent ruler there is lasting order.

The Wise Worker Is Diligent, 168–73

Prov. 28:8 One who augments wealth by exorbitant interest gathers it for another who is kind to the poor.

The Wise Worker Is Just, 177–81

Prov. 28:11 The rich is wise in self-esteem, but an intelligent poor person sees through the pose.

The Wise Worker Is Modest, 184–86

Prov. 28:19 Anyone who tills the land will have plenty of bread, but one who follows worthless pursuits will have plenty of poverty.

The Wise Worker Is Diligent, 168–73

Prov. 28:22 The miser is in a hurry to get rich and does not know that loss is sure to come.

The Wise Worker Is Modest, 184–86

Prov. 28:23 Whoever rebukes a person will afterward find more favor than one who flatters with the tongue.

The Wise Worker Guards the Tongue, 181–84

Prov. 28:27 Whoever gives to the poor will lack nothing, but one who turns a blind eye will get many a curse.

The Wise Worker Is Generous, 176–77

Prov. 29:4 By justice a king gives stability to the land, but one who makes heavy exactions ruins it.

The Wise Worker Is Just, 177–81

Prov. 29:14 If a king judges the poor with equity, his throne will be established forever.

The Wise Worker Is Just, 177–81

Prov. 29:23 A person's pride will bring humiliation, but one who is lowly in spirit will obtain honor.

The Wise Worker Is Modest, 184–86

Prov. 29:24 To be a partner of a thief is to hate one's own life; one hears the victim's curse, but discloses nothing.

The Wise Worker Is Trustworthy, 161–68

Prov. 30:7–9   Two things I ask of you; do not deny them to me before I die: Remove far from me falsehood and lying; give me neither poverty nor riches; feed me with the food that I need, or I shall be full, and deny you, and say, "Who is the LORD?" or I shall be poor, and steal, and profane the name of my God.

The Wise Worker Is Modest, 184–86

Prov. 30:17   The eye that mocks a father and scorns to obey a mother, will be pecked out by the ravens of the valley and eaten by the vultures.

About the Book of Proverbs, 156–59

Prov. 31:3   Do not give your strength to women, your ways to those who destroy kings.

The Valiant Woman, 160–61

Prov. 31:10   A capable wife who can find? She is far more precious than jewels.

The Valiant Woman, 160–61; The Wise Worker Is Diligent, 168–73

Prov. 31:11   The heart of her husband trusts in her.

The Valiant Woman, 160–61; The Wise Worker Is Trustworthy, 161–68

Prov. 31:12, 28   She does him good, and not harm, all the days of her life. . . . Her children rise up and call her happy; her husband too, and he praises her.

The Wise Worker Is Trustworthy, 161–68

Prov. 31:13   She seeks wool and flax, and works with willing hands.

The Wise Worker Is Diligent, 168–73

Prov. 31:13–14   She seeks wool and flax and works with willing hands. She is like the ships of the merchant.

The Wise Worker Is Shrewd, 174–76

Prov. 31:14   She is like the ships of the merchant, she brings her food from far away.

The Wise Worker Is Trustworthy, 161–68; The Wise Worker Is Diligent, 168–73

Prov. 31:15   She rises while it is still night and provides food for her household and tasks for her servant-girls.

The Valiant Woman, 160–61; The Wise Worker Is Trustworthy, 161–68; The Wise Worker Is Diligent, 168–73

Prov. 31:16   She considers a field and buys it; with the fruit of her hands she plants a vineyard.

The Wise Worker Is Diligent, 168–73

Prov. 31:17   She girds herself with strength, and makes her arms strong.

The Valiant Woman, 160–61; The Wise Worker Is Shrewd, 174–76

Prov. 31:18   She perceives that her merchandise is profitable. Her lamp does not go out at night.

The Wise Worker Is Diligent, 168–73

Prov. 31:19   She puts her hands to the distaff, and her hands hold the spindle.

The Wise Worker Is Generous, 176–77

Prov. 31:20 She opens her hand to the poor, and reaches out her hands to the needy.

The Wise Worker Is Trustworthy, 161–68; The Wise Worker Is Generous, 176–77

Prov. 31:21–22 She is not afraid for her household when it snows, for all her household are clothed in crimson. She makes herself coverings; her clothing is fine linen and purple.

The Wise Worker Is Shrewd, 174–76

Prov. 31:23 Her husband is known in the city gates, taking his seat among the elders of the land.

The Valiant Woman, 160–61; The Wise Worker Is Shrewd, 174–76

Prov. 31:24 She makes linen garments and sells them; she supplies the merchant with sashes.

The Wise Worker Is Diligent, 168–73

Prov. 31:25 Strength and dignity are her clothing, and she laughs at the time to come.

The Wise Worker Is Diligent, 168–73

Prov. 31:26 She opens her mouth with wisdom, and the teaching of kindness is on her tongue.

The Wise Worker Guards the Tongue, 181–84

Prov. 31:27 She looks well to the ways of her household.

The Wise Worker Is Trustworthy, 161–68

Prov. 31:30 Charm is deceitful, and beauty is vain, but a woman who fears the LORD is to be praised.

What Does Proverbs Have to Do with Work? 159–60; The Valiant Woman, 160–61

Prov. 31:31 Give her a share in the fruit of her hands, and let her works praise her in the city gates.

The Wise Worker Is Trustworthy, 161–68

Ecclesiastes and Work

Introduction to Ecclesiastes

Ecclesiastes brilliantly captures the toil and joy, fleeting success, and unanswered questions that we all experience in our work. It is one of many Christian workers' favorite books of the Bible, and its narrator—called the Teacher in most English translations—has a lot to say about work. Much of what he teaches is succinct, practical, and smart. Anyone who has ever worked on a team can appreciate the value of a maxim such as, "Two are better than one, because they have a good reward for their toil" (Eccl. 4:9). Most of us spend the largest portion of our waking lives working, and we find affirmation when the Teacher says, "I commend enjoyment, for there is nothing better for people under the sun than to eat, and drink, and enjoy themselves, for this will go with them in their toil through the days of life that God gives them under the sun" (Eccl. 8:15).

Yet the Teacher's picture of work is also deeply troubling. "I considered all that my hands had done and the toil I had spent in doing it, and again, all was vanity and a chasing after the wind" (Eccl. 2:11). The almost-overwhelming preponderance of negative observations about work threatens to swamp the reader. The Teacher opens with "vanity of vanities" (Eccl. 1:2) and ends with "all is vanity" (Eccl. 12:8). The words and phrases he repeats most often are "vanity," "a chasing after wind," "not find out," and "can't find out." Unless there is a larger perspective to temper his observations, Ecclesiastes can be a dreary book indeed.

The task of making sense of the book as a whole is difficult. Does Ecclesiastes really portray work as vanity, or does the Teacher sift through the many vain ways of working to find a core set of meaningful ones? Or, to the contrary, are the many positive maxims and observations negated by an overall assessment of work as "a chasing after wind"? The answer depends in large part in how we approach the book.

One way to read Ecclesiastes is to take it as simply a tossed salad of observations about life, including work. Under this approach, the Teacher is primarily a realistic observer who reports the ups and downs of life as he encounters them. Each observation stands on its own as a bit of wisdom. If we draw useful advice from, say, "There is nothing better for mortals than to eat and drink, and find enjoyment in their toil" (Eccl. 2:24), we need not be too concerned that it is followed shortly by, "This also is vanity and a chasing after wind" (Eccl. 2:26).

The reader who wishes to take this approach is in good company. The majority of scholars today do not recognize an overarching argument in Ecclesiastes, and even among those who do, "there is hardly one commentator who agrees with another."[1] But there is something unsatisfying about such a piecemeal approach. We want to know the overall message of Ecclesiastes. If we are to discover that, then we must look for a structure to bring together the wide range of observations living side by side in the book.

We will follow the structure first proposed by Addison Wright in 1968, which divides the book into units of thought.[2] Wright's structure commends itself for three reasons: (1) it is based objectively on the repetition of key phrases in the text of Ecclesiastes, rather than on subjective interpretations of the content; (2) it is accepted by more scholars—admittedly still a tiny minority—than any other;[3] and (3) it brings work-related topics to the foreground. We do not have space here to reproduce Wright's arguments, but we will indicate the repetitive phrases that delineate the units of thought he proposes. In the first half of the book, the phrase "a chasing after wind" marks the end of each unit. In the second half, the phrase "not find out" (or "who can find out?") performs the same function. Wright's structure will contribute directly to our overall understanding of the book.

---

[1] Roland Murphy, *Ecclesiastes*, vol. 23a, *Word Biblical Commentary* (Dallas: Word, 2002), xxxv.

[2] Addison G. Wright, "The Riddle of the Sphinx: The Structure of the Book of Qoheleth," *Catholic Biblical Quarterly* 30 (1968): 313–34.

[3] Including J. S. M. Mulder, R. Rendtorff (partially), A. Schoors (partially), and R. Murphy. See Murphy, xxxvi- xxxviii.

There is another term, "under the sun," which cannot escape our notice as we read Ecclesiastes. It occurs twenty-nine times in the book, but nowhere else in the Bible.[4] It is reminiscent of the term "in the fallen world" derived from Genesis 3, which describes the world in which God's creation is still good, yet severely marred by ills. Why does the Teacher use this phrase so often? Does he mean to reinforce the pointlessness of work by conjuring an image of the sun circling endlessly across the sky (Eccl. 1:5) while nothing ever changes? Or does he imagine there might be a world beyond the Fall, not "under the sun," where work would not be in vain? It is a question worth keeping in mind as we read Ecclesiastes.

In contrast to human life under the sun, the Teacher gives us glimpses of God in heaven. Our toil is fleeting, but "whatever God does endures forever" (Eccl. 3:14). These glimpses begin to give us an understanding of the character of God, which perhaps will help us make sense of life. We will note what Ecclesiastes reveals about God's character as aspects arise, and then take a look at them together toward the end of the book.

In any case, Ecclesiastes makes a vital contribution to the theology of work through its honest, unvarnished look at the reality of work. Any thoughtful people engaged in their work, whether a follower of Christ or not, will connect with it. Its refreshing honesty opens the door for deep conversations about work, more so than the tidy prescriptions for doing business God's way so commonly encountered in Christian circles.

Working Under the Sun (Ecclesiastes 1:1–11)

Work is the core activity explored in Ecclesiastes. It is generally called "toil" (Heb. *amal*), which indicates the hardship of work. The topic is introduced at the beginning of the book in Ecclesiastes 1:3: "What do people gain from all the toil at which they toil under the sun?" The Teacher's assessment of toil is that it is "vanity" (Eccl. 2:1). This word,

---

[4] Murphy, 7.

hebel in Hebrew, dominates Ecclesiastes. *Hebel* actually means "breath," but from that it comes to refer to something that is insubstantial, fleeting, and of no permanent value. It is superbly suited to be the keyword for this book because a breath is by nature brief, of little discernible substance, and it quickly dissipates. Yet our survival hangs upon these brief intakes and exhalations of puffs of air. Soon, however, breathing will cease and life will end. Similarly, *hebel* describes something of fleeting value that will ultimately come to an end. In one sense, "vanity" is a misleading translation, since it appears to assert that everything is utterly worthless. But the real point of *hebel* is that something has only a fleeting value. A single breath may not have permanent value, but in its one moment it keeps us alive. In the same way, what we are and do in this transitory life has real, though temporary, significance.

Consider the work of building a ship. By God's good creation, the earth holds the raw materials we need to build ships. Human ingenuity and hard work—also created by God—can create safe, capable, even beautiful, ships. They join the fleet and transport food, resources, manufactured goods, and people to where they are needed. When a ship is launched and the bottle of champagne broken across its bow, everyone involved can celebrate the builders' accomplishment. Yet once it leaves the yard, the builders have no control over it. It may be captained by a fool who smashes it against the shoals. It may be chartered to smuggle drugs, weapons, or even slaves. Its crew may be treated harshly. It may serve nobly for many years, yet even so it will wear out and become obsolete. Its eventual fate is nearly certain to be dismantled in a shipbreaking yard, probably located in a country where worker safety and environmental protection are lax. It passes, like the puffs of wind that once powered ships, first into rusty bones, then into a mix of recycled metal and discarded waste, and finally out of human knowledge. Ships are good, but they do not last forever. As long as we live, we must work in this tension.

This brings us to the image of the sun racing around the earth, which we discussed in the introduction (Eccl. 1:5). The ceaseless activity by this great object in the sky brings the light and warmth we depend on every day, yet changes nothing as the ages go by. "There is nothing new under the sun" (Eccl. 1:9). This is an unsentimental observation, though not an eternal condemnation, about our work.

Work Is a Chasing after Wind
(Ecclesiastes 1:12–6:9)

Having declared his theme that toil is vanity in Ecclesiastes 1:1–11, the Teacher nonetheless proceeds to explore various possibilities for trying to live life well. He considers, in order, achievement, pleasure, wisdom, wealth, timing, friendship, and finding joy in God's gifts. In some of these he does find a certain value, less in the earlier explorations and more in the latter. Yet nothing seems permanent, and the characteristic conclusion in each section is that work comes to "a chasing after wind."

Achievement (Ecclesiastes 1:12–18)

First the Teacher explores achievement. He was both a king and a sage—an overachiever to use today's terms—"surpassing all who were over Jerusalem before me" (Eccl. 1:16). And what did all his achievement mean to him? Not much. "It is an unhappy business that God has given to human beings to be busy with. I saw all the deeds that are done under the sun; and see, all is vanity and a chasing after wind" (Eccl. 1:13–14). No lasting achievement even seems possible. "What is crooked cannot be made straight, and what is lacking cannot be counted" (Eccl. 1:15). Achieving his goals did not give him happiness, for it only made him realize how hollow and limited anything he could accomplish must be. In sum, he says again, "I perceived that this also is but a chasing after wind" (Eccl. 1:17).

Pleasure (Ecclesiastes 2:1–11)

Next he says to himself, "Come now, I will make a test of pleasure; enjoy yourself" (Eccl. 2:1). He acquires wealth, houses, gardens, alcohol, servants (slaves), jewelry, entertainment, and ready access to sexual pleasure. "Whatever my eyes desired I did not keep from them; I kept my heart from no pleasure" (Eccl. 2:10a).

Unlike with achievement, he finds some value in seeking pleasure. "My heart found pleasure in all my toil, and this was my reward for all my toil" (Eccl. 2:10). His supposed achievements had turned out to be nothing new, but his pleasures at least were pleasurable. It seems that work undertaken as a means to an end—in this case, pleasure—is more satisfying than work undertaken as an obsession. Without necessarily taking "many concubines" (Eccl. 2:8), today's workers might do well to take time to smell the roses, as the saying goes. If we have ceased to work toward a goal beyond work, if we can no longer enjoy the fruits of our labor, then we have become slaves of work rather than its masters.

Nonetheless, toiling merely in order to gain pleasure is ultimately unsatisfying. This sections ends with the assessment that "again, all was vanity and a chasing after wind, and there was nothing to be gained under the sun" (Eccl. 2:11).

Wisdom (Ecclesiastes 2:12–17)

Perhaps it is good to seek an object outside of work itself, but a higher objective is needed than pleasure. So the Teacher reports, "I turned to consider wisdom and madness and folly" (Eccl. 2:12). In other words, he becomes something akin to today's professor or researcher. Unlike achievement for achievement's sake, wisdom can at least be attained to some degree. "I saw that wisdom excels folly as light excels darkness" (Eccl. 2:13). But other than filling the head with exalted thoughts, it makes no real difference in life, for "the wise die just like fools" (Eccl. 1:16). Pursuing wisdom led the Teacher to the brink of despair (Eccl. 1:17), a result that remains all too common in academic pursuits today. The Teacher concludes, "All is vanity and a chasing after wind" (Eccl. 2:17).

Wealth (Ecclesiastes 2:18–26)

Then the Teacher turns to wealth, which may be gained as a result of toil. What about the accumulation of wealth as the higher purpose behind work? This turns out to be worse than spending wealth to gain pleasure. Wealth brings the problem of inheritance. When you die, the wealth you accumulated will pass to someone else who may be completely undeserving. "Sometimes one who has toiled with wisdom and knowledge and skill must leave all to be enjoyed by another who did not toil for it. This also is vanity and a great evil" (Eccl. 2:21). This is so galling that the Teacher says, "I turned and gave my heart up to despair" (Eccl. 2:20).

At this point, we get our first glimpse of the character of God. God is a giver. "To the one who pleases him God gives wisdom and knowledge and joy" (Eccl. 2:26). This aspect of God's character is repeated several times in Ecclesiastes, and his gifts include food, drink, and joy (Eccl. 5:18, 8:15), wealth and possessions (Eccl. 5:19, 6:2), honor (Eccl. 6:2), integrity (Eccl. 7:29), the world we inhabit (Eccl. 11:5), and life itself (Eccl. 12:7).

Like the Teacher, many people today who accumulate great wealth find it extremely unsatisfying. While we are making our fortunes, no matter how much we have, it doesn't seem to be enough. When our fortunes are made and we begin to appreciate our mortality, giving away our wealth wisely seems to become a nearly intolerable burden. Andrew Carnegie noted the weight of this burden when he said, "I resolved to stop accumulating and begin the infinitely more serious and difficult task of wise distribution."[5] Yet if God is a giver, it is no surprise that the distribution of wealth, rather than its accumulation, might be more satisfying.

But the Teacher does not find satisfaction in giving wealth any more than in gaining it (Eccl. 2:18–21). The satisfaction that God in heaven finds in giving somehow escapes the Teacher under the sun. He does not seem to consider the possibility of investing wealth or giving it away for a higher purpose. Unless there is indeed a higher purpose beyond anything the Teacher discovers, the accumulation and distribution of wealth "also is vanity and a chasing after wind" (Eccl. 2:26).

Timing (Ecclesiastes 3:1–4:6)

If work has no single, unchanging purpose, perhaps it has a myriad of purposes, each meaningful in its own time. The Teacher explores this in the famous chapter beginning, "For everything there is a season, and a time for every matter under heaven" (Eccl. 3:1). The key is that every activity is governed by time. Work that is completely wrong at one time may be right and necessary at another. At one moment it is right to mourn and wrong to dance, and at another moment the opposite is true.

None of these activities or conditions is permanent. We are not angels in timeless bliss. We are creatures of this world going through the

---

[5] Andrew Carnegie, *Autobiography of Andrew Carnegie* (Boston: Houghton Mifflin, 1920), 255.

changes and seasons of time. This is another hard lesson. We deceive ourselves about the fundamental nature of life if we think our labors can bring about permanent peace, prosperity, or happiness. Someday, everything we have built will rightly be torn down (Eccl. 3:3). If our work has any eternal value, then the Teacher sees no sign of it "under the sun" (Eccl. 4:1). Our condition is doubly difficult in that we are creatures of the moment, but, unlike the animals, we have "a sense of past and future" in our minds (Eccl. 3:11). Thus the Teacher longs for that which has permanent value, even though he cannot find it.

Moreover, even the timely good that people try to do may be thwarted by oppression. "On the side of their oppressors there was power—with no one to comfort them" (Eccl. 4:1). Worst of all is oppression by the government. "I saw under the sun that in the place of justice, wickedness was there" (Eccl. 3:16). Yet the powerless are not necessarily any better. A common response to feeling powerless is envy. We envy those who have the power, wealth, status, relationships, possessions, or other things we lack. The Teacher recognizes that envy is as bad as oppression. "I saw that all toil and all skill in work come from one person's envy of another. This also is vanity and a chasing after wind" (Eccl. 4:4). The drive to gain achievement, pleasure, wisdom, or wealth either by oppression or by envy is an utter waste of time. Yet who has never fallen into both of these follies?

But the Teacher does not despair, for time is a gift from God himself. "He has made everything suitable for its time" (Eccl. 3:11a). It is right to cry at the funeral of a loved one, and it is good to rejoice at the birth of a child. And we should not refuse the legitimate pleasures our work may bring. "There is nothing better for them than to be happy and enjoy themselves as long as they live; moreover, it is God's gift that all should eat and drink and take pleasure in all their toil" (Eccl. 3:12–13).

These life lessons apply in particular to work. "So I saw that there is nothing better than that all should enjoy their work, for that is their lot" (Eccl. 3:22a). Work is *under* the curse, but work is not in itself a curse. Even the limited vision we have into the future is a kind of blessing, for it relieves us of the burden of trying to foresee all ends. "Who can bring them to see what will be after them?" (Eccl. 3:22b). If our work serves the times that we *can* foresee, then it is a gift from God.

At this point, we get two glimpses of God's character. First, God is awesome, eternal, omniscient, "so that all should stand in awe before him" (Eccl. 3:14). Although we are limited by the conditions of life under the sun, God is not. There is more to God than meets the eye. The transcendence of God—to give it a theological name—appears again in Ecclesiastes 7:13–14 and 8:12–13.

The second glimpse shows us that God is a God of justice. "God seeks out what has gone by" (Eccl. 3:15), and "God will judge the righteous and the wicked" (Eccl. 3:17). This idea is repeated later in Ecclesiastes 8:13, 11:9, and 12:14. We may not see God's justice in the apparent unfairness of life, but the Teacher assures us it will come to pass.

As we have noted, Ecclesiastes is a realistic exploration of life in the fallen world. Work is toilsome. Yet even amid the toil, our lot is to take pleasure in our toil and enjoy our work. This is not an answer to the conundrums of life, but a sign that God is in the world, even if we do not see clearly what that means for us. Despite this somewhat hopeful note, the exploration of timing ends with a double repetition of "a chasing after wind," once in Ecclesiastes 4:4 (as discussed above) and again in 4:6.

Friendship (Ecclesiastes 4:7–4:16)

Perhaps relationships offer real meaning in work. The Teacher extols the value of friendships at work. "Two are better than one, because they have a good reward for their *toil*" (Eccl. 4:9; emphasis added).

How many people find their closest friendships in the workplace? Even if we didn't need the pay, even if the work didn't interest us, we might find deep meaning in our work relationships. That's one reason that many people find retirement disappointing. We miss our workplace friends after we leave, and we find it difficult to form deep, new friendships without the common goals that brought us together with colleagues at work.

Building good relationships at work requires openness and a desire to learn from others. "Better is a poor but wise youth than an old but foolish king, who will no longer take advice" (Eccl. 4:13). Arrogance and power are often barriers to developing the relationships on which effective work depends (Eccl. 4:14–16), a truth explored in the Harvard

Business School article "How Strength Becomes a Weakness."[6] We become friends at work partly because it takes teamwork to do the work well. This is one reason many people are better at forming friendships at work than in social settings in which there is no shared goal.

The Teacher's exploration of friendship is more upbeat than his earlier explorations. Yet even so, work friendships are necessarily temporary. Job assignments change, teams are formed and dissolve, colleagues quit, retire, and get fired, and new workers join whom we may not like. The Teacher likens it to a new, young king whose subjects receive him gladly at first, but whose popularity drops as a new generation of youth comes to regard him as just another old king. In the end, neither career advancement nor fame offers satisfaction. "Surely this also is vanity and a chasing after wind" (Eccl. 4:16).

Joy (Ecclesiastes 5:1–6:9)

The Teacher's search for meaning in work ends with many short lessons that have direct application to work. First, listening is wiser than speaking, "therefore let your words be few" (Eccl. 5:2). Second, keep your promises, above all to God (Eccl. 5:4). Third, expect the government to be corrupt. This is not good, but it is universal, and it is better than anarchy (Eccl. 5:8–9). Fourth, obsession for wealth is an addiction, and like any other addiction, it consumes those it afflicts (Eccl. 5:10–12), yet it does not satisfy (Eccl. 6:7–8). Fifth, wealth is fleeting. It may disappear in this life, and it is sure to disappear at death. Don't build your life on it (Eccl. 5:13–17).

In the midst of this section, the Teacher explores again the gift of God in allowing us to enjoy our work and the wealth, possessions, and honor it may bring for a time. "It is fitting to eat and drink and find enjoyment in all the toil with which one toils under the sun the few days of the life God gives us" (Eccl. 5:18). Although the enjoyment is fleeting, it is real. "For they will scarcely brood over the days of their lives, because God keeps them occupied with the joy of their hearts" (Eccl. 5:20). This joy comes not from striving more successfully than others, but from re-

---

[6] Monci J. Williams, "How Strength Becomes a Weakness," *Harvard Management Update,* December 1996.

ceiving life and work as a gift from God. If joy in our work does not come as a gift from God, then it does not come at all (Eccl. 6:1–6).

As in the section on friendship, the Teacher's tone is relatively positive in this section. Yet the final result is still frustration. For we see plainly that all lives end in the grave, when the life lived wisely comes to nothing greater than the life lived foolishly. It is better to see this plainly than to try to live in a fairytale illusion. "Better is the sight of the eyes than the wandering of desire" (Eccl. 6:8a). But the end result of our lives remains "vanity and a chasing after wind" (Eccl. 6:9).

There Is No Way to Find Out What Is Good to Do (Ecclesiastes 6:10–8:17)

A life of toil amounts to a chasing after wind, for the results of work are not permanent in the world as the Teacher knows it. So he begins a search to find out what is best to do with the time he has. As seen earlier in the book, this block of material is divided into sections demarked by a phrase repeated at the end of each exploration. In frustration of the Teacher's hope, that phrase is "not find out," or its equivalent rhetorical question, "who can find out?"

The Ultimate Results of Our Actions (Ecclesiastes 7:1–14)

Our toil ends with our death. Ecclesiastes therefore recommends that we spend some serious time in the cemetery (Eccl. 7:1–6). Can we see any real advantage that one tomb has over another? Some people whistle past the graveyard, refusing to consider its lessons. Their laughter is like the crackling of burning thorns, as it is consumed in the flames (Eccl. 7:6).

Because our time is short, we cannot find out what impact we may have on the world. We cannot even find out why today is different from yesterday (Eccl. 7:10), let alone what tomorrow may bring. It makes sense to enjoy whatever good comes of our toil while we live, but we have no promise that the final end is good, for "God has made the one as well as the other, so that mortals may *not find* out anything that will come after them" (Eccl. 7:14; emphasis added).

One application we can draw from our ignorance of our legacy is that good ends are no justification for evil means. For we cannot see the ends of all the actions we take, and the power to mitigate the consequences of our means could come at any time. Politicians who appease public opinion now at the cost of public harm later, financial officers who hide a loss this quarter in the hope of making it up next quarter, graduates who lie on job applications with the hope of succeeding in jobs they are not qualified for—all of them are counting on futures they do not have the power to bring about. Meanwhile, they are doing harm now that can never truly be erased even if their hopes do come true.

Good and Evil (Ecclesiastes 7:15–28)

So we must try to act *now* according to the good. Yet we cannot really know whether any action we take is wholly good or wholly evil. When we imagine we are acting righteously, wickedness may creep in, and vice versa (Eccl. 7:16–18). For "surely there is no one on earth so righteous as to do good without ever sinning" (Eccl. 7:20). The truth of good and evil "is far off, and deep, very deep; *who can find* it out?" (Eccl. 7:24; emphasis added). As if to emphasize this difficulty, the characteristic phrase "not found" is repeated again twice in Ecclesiastes 7:28.

The best we can do is to fear God (Eccl. 7:18)—that is to say, to avoid arrogance and self-righteousness. A good self-diagnostic is to examine whether we have to resort to twisted logic and complicated rationalization to justify our actions. "God made human beings straightforward, but they have devised many schemes" (Eccl. 7:29). Work has many complexities, many factors that have to be taken into account, and moral certainty is usually impossible. But ethical pretzel logic is almost always a bad sign.

Power and Justice (Ecclesiastes 8:1–17)

The exercise of power is a fact of life, and we have a duty to obey those in authority over us (Eccl. 8:2–5). Yet we do not know whether they will use their authority justly. Quite possibly, they will use their power to harm others (Eccl. 8:9). Justice is perverted. The righteous are punished, and the wicked are rewarded (Eccl. 8:10–14).

In the midst of this uncertainty, the best we can do is to fear God (Eccl. 8:13) and enjoy the opportunities for happiness that he gives us. "I commend enjoyment, for there is nothing better for people under the sun than to eat, and drink, and enjoy themselves, for this will go with them in their toil through the days of life that God gives them under the sun" (Eccl. 8:15).

As in the previous section, the marker phrase "not find out" is repeated three times at the end of this topic. "*No one can find out* what is happening under the sun. However much they may toil in seeking, *they will not find it out*; even though those who are wise claim to know, *they cannot find it out*" (Eccl. 8:17; emphasis added). This brings to an end the Teacher's search to find out what is good to do with the limited time we have. Although he has discovered some good practices, the overall result is that he could not find out what is truly meaningful.

There Is No Way to Know What Comes Afterwards (Ecclesiastes 9:1–11:6)

Perhaps it would be possible to work out what is best to do in life if it were possible to know what comes afterwards. So the Teacher searches for knowledge about death (Eccl. 9:1–6), Sheol (Eccl. 9:7–10), the time of death (Eccl. 9:11–12), what comes after death (Eccl. 9:13–10:15), the evil that might come after death (Eccl. 10:16–11:2), and the good that might come (Eccl. 11:3–6). Again, a repeated marker phrase—in this case, "do not know" and its equivalent "no knowledge"—divides the material into sections.

The Teacher finds that it is simply not possible to know what lies ahead. "The dead know nothing" (Eccl. 9:5). "There is no work or thought or knowledge or wisdom in Sheol, to which you are going" (Eccl. 9:10). "Man does not know his time . . . the sons of men are ensnared at an evil time when it suddenly falls on them" (Eccl. 9:12 NASB; the NRSV gives an idiosyncratic translation that obscures the characteristic phrase). "No one knows what is to happen, and who can tell anyone what the future holds?" (Eccl. 10:14). "You do not know what disaster may happen on earth" (Eccl. 11:2). "You do not know which will prosper, this or that, or whether both alike will be good" (Eccl. 11: 6).

Despite our colossal ignorance about the future, the Teacher finds some things that are good to do while we have the chance. We will explore only those passages that are particularly relevant to work.

Throw Yourself into Your Work Wholeheartedly (Ecclesiastes 9:10)

"Whatever your hand finds to do, do with your might; for there is no work or thought or knowledge or wisdom in Sheol, to which you are going" (Eccl. 9:10). Although we cannot know the final result of our work, there is no point letting this paralyze us. Humans are created to work (Gen. 2:15), we need to work to survive, and so we might as well work with gusto. The same goes for enjoying the fruits of our work, whatever they may be. "Eat your bread with enjoyment, and drink your wine with a merry heart; for God has long ago approved what you do" (Eccl. 9:7).

Accept Success and Failure as a Part of Life (Ecclesiastes 9:11–12)

We should not fool ourselves into thinking either that our success is due to our own merits or that our failure is due to our own shortcomings. "I saw that under the sun the race is not to the swift, nor the battle to the strong, nor bread to the wise, nor riches to the intelligent, nor favor to the skillful; but time and chance happen to them all" (Eccl. 9:11). Success or failure may be due to dumb luck. This is not to say that hard work and ingenuity aren't important. They prepare us to make the most of the chances of life, and they may create opportunities that otherwise wouldn't exist. Yet one who succeeds at work may be no more deserving than another who fails. For example, Microsoft had a crack at success largely because of IBM's offhand decision to use the MS-DOS operating system for a backwater project called the personal computer. Bill Gates later reflected, "Our timing in setting up the first software company aimed at personal computers was essential to our success. The timing wasn't entirely luck, but without great luck it couldn't have happened." Asked why he had started a software company just at the time IBM was developing a personal computer, he replied, "I was born at the right place and time."[7]

---

[7]"Bill Gates Answers Most Frequently Asked Questions," http://download.microsoft.com/download/0/c/0/0c020894-1f95-408c-a571-1b5033c75bbc/billg_faq.doc.

Work Diligently and Invest Wisely (Ecclesiastes 10:18–11:6)

This passage contains the most direct financial advice to be found anywhere in the Bible. First, be diligent; otherwise your household economy will collapse like a leaky, rotten roof (Eccl. 10:18). Second, understand that in this life financial well-being does matter. "Money meets every need" (Eccl. 10:19) can be read in a cynical manner, but the text does not say that money is the only thing that matters. The point is simply that money is necessary for dealing with all kinds of issues. To put it in modern terms, if your car needs a new transmission, or your daughter needs college tuition, or you want to take your family on a vacation, it is going to take money. This is not greed or materialism; it is common sense.

Third, be careful about people in authority (Eccl. 10:20). If you belittle your boss or even a customer, you may live to regret it. Fourth, diversify your investments (Eccl. 11:1–2). "Send out your bread upon the waters" does not refer to charitable giving but to investments; in this case, the "waters" represent a venture in overseas trading. Thus giving portions to "seven" or "eight" refers to diverse investments, "for you do not know what disaster may happen on earth" (Eccl. 11:2). Fifth, don't be overly timid about investing (Eccl. 11:3–5). What will happen will happen, and you cannot control that (Eccl. 11:3). But this should not frighten us into putting money under a mattress where it yields nothing. Instead, we should find the courage to take reasonable risks. "Whoever observes the wind will not plant; whoever regards the clouds will not reap" (Eccl. 11:4). Sixth, understand that success is in God's hands. But you don't know what plans or purposes he has, so don't try to second-guess him (Eccl. 11:5). Seventh, be persistent (Eccl. 11:6). Don't work hard for a little while and then say, "I tried that, and it didn't work."

The Teacher's search for knowledge about the future ends at Ecclesiastes 11:5–6 with a triple repetition of the marker phrase "not know." This reminds us that although working wholeheartedly, accepting success and failure as part of life, and working diligently and investing wisely are good practices, they are merely adaptations to deal with our ignorance of the future. If we truly knew how our actions would play out, then we could plan confidently for success. If we knew which investments would turn out well, then we would not need to diversify as a hedge against systemic losses. It is hard to know whether to hang our heads in sorrow for the disasters that may befall us in this fallen world, or to praise God that it is still possible to muddle through, and maybe even to do well, in such a world. Or is the truth a bit of both?

A Poem on Youth and Old Age (Ecclesiastes 11:7–12:8)

The Teacher concludes with a poem exhorting the young to good cheer (Eccl. 11:7–12:1) and recounting the troubles of old age (Eccl. 12:2–8). It recapitulates the pattern found in the earlier sections of the book. There is much good to be found in our life and work, but ultimately it is all fleeting. The Teacher closes as he began: "Vanity of vanities, says the Teacher; all is vanity" (Eccl. 12:8).

Epilogue of Praise for the Teacher (Ecclesiastes 12:9–14)

There follows an epilogue about, rather than by, the Teacher. It praises his wisdom and repeats his admonition to fear God. It adds new elements not found earlier in the book—namely, the wisdom of following God's commandments in light of God's future judgment.

> Fear God, and keep his commandments; for that is the whole duty of everyone. For God will bring every deed into judgment, including every secret thing, whether good or evil. (Eccl. 12:13–14)

God's future judgment is seen as the key to sorting out the mix of good and evil that pervades work in the fallen world. The glimpses of God's character that we have seen in the book—God's generosity, justice, and transcendence beyond the confines of the world—depict an underlying goodness in the foundations of the world, if we could only live accordingly. This begins to hint that in God's time the tensions so vividly described by the Teacher will be brought into a harmony not visible in the Teacher's day under the sun. Is it possible that the epilogue envisions a day when the conditions of the Fall do not hold sway over our life and work?

Conclusions from Ecclesiastes

What are we to make of this mix of good and ill, meaning and vanity, action and ignorance, which the Teacher finds in life and work? Work is a "chasing after wind," as the Teacher continually reminds us. Like the wind, work is real and it has an impact while it lasts. It keeps us alive, and it offers opportunities for joy. Yet it is difficult to assess the full effect of our work, to foresee the unintended consequences for good and ill. And it is impossible to know what our work may lead to beyond the present moment. Does work amount to anything lasting, anything eternal, anything ultimately good? The Teacher says it is really not possible to know anything for certain under the sun.

But we may have a different perspective. Unlike the Teacher, followers of Christ today see a concrete hope beyond the fallen world. For we are witnesses to the life, death, and resurrection of a new Teacher, Jesus, whose power did not die with the end of his days under the sun (Luke 23:44). He announces that "the kingdom of God has come to you" (Matt. 12:28). The world we live in now is in the process of being brought under Christ's rule and redeemed by God. What the writer of Ecclesiastes did not know—could not know, as he was so keenly aware—is that God would send his Son not to condemn the world, but to restore the world to the way God intended it to be (John 3:17). The days of the fallen world under the sun are passing in favor of the kingdom of God on earth, where God's people "need no light of lamp or sun, for the Lord God will be their light" (Rev. 22:5). Because of this, the world in which we live is not only the remnant of the fallen world, but also the vanguard of the kingdom of Christ, "coming down out of heaven from God" (Rev. 21:2).

The work we do as followers of Christ therefore does—or at least could—have eternal value that could not have been visible to the

Teacher. We work not only in the world under the sun, but also in the kingdom of God. This is not to engage in a misguided attempt to correct Ecclesiastes with a dose of the New Testament. Rather, it is to appreciate Ecclesiastes as God's gift to us as it stands. For we too live daily life under much the same conditions the Teacher did. As Paul reminds us, "We know that the whole creation has been groaning in labor pains until now; and not only the creation, but we ourselves, who have the first fruits of the Spirit, groan inwardly while we wait for adoption, the redemption of our bodies" (Rom. 8:22–23). We groan under the same weight the Teacher did because we are still waiting for the fulfillment of God's kingdom on earth.

Ecclesiastes, then, offers two insights unmatched elsewhere in Scripture: an unvarnished account of work under the conditions of the Fall, and a witness of hope in the darkest circumstances of work.

An Unvarnished Account of Work under the Fall

If we know that work in Christ has a lasting value not visible to the Teacher, then how can his words still be helpful to us? To begin with, they affirm that the toil, oppression, failure, meaninglessness, sorrow, and pain we experience in work are real. Christ has come, but life for his followers has not yet become a walk in the garden. If your experience of work is hard and painful—despite God's promises of good—you are not crazy after all. God's promises are true, but they are not all fulfilled in the present moment. We are caught in the reality that God's kingdom has come to earth now (Matt. 12:28), but it is not yet brought to completion (Rev. 21:2). At the very least, it may be a comfort that Scripture dares to depict the harsh realities of life and work, while yet proclaiming that God is Lord.

If Ecclesiastes serves as a comfort to those working in harsh conditions, then it may also serve as a challenge to those blessed with good working conditions. Do not become complacent! Until work becomes a blessing to everyone, God's people are called to struggle for the benefit of all workers. We are indeed meant to eat, drink, and find enjoyment in all the toil we are blessed with. But we do this while we strive for and pray that God's kingdom come.

A Witness of Hope in the Darkest Circumstances of Work

Ecclesiastes also gives an example of how to maintain hope in the midst of the harsh realities of work in the fallen world. Despite the worst that he sees and experiences, the Teacher does not abandon hope in God's world. He finds the moments of joy, the sparks of wisdom, and the ways to cope with a world that is ephemeral, but not absurd. If God had abandoned humanity to the consequences of the Fall, then there would be no meaning, no good in work at all. Instead, the Teacher finds that there *are* meaning and goodness in work. His complaint is that they are always transitory, incomplete, uncertain, limited. Given the alternative—a world completely without God—these are actually signs of hope.

These signs of hope may be a comfort to us in our darkest experiences of life and work. Moreover, they give us an understanding of our co-workers who have not received the good news of Christ's kingdom. Their experience of work may be similar to the Teacher's. If we can imagine enduring the difficulties we experience, but without the promise of Christ's redemption, then we can gain a glimpse of the burden life and work may be to our co-workers. We should pray to God that this will at least give us more compassion. Perhaps it will also give us a more effective witness. For if we are to bear witness to Christ's good news, then we must start by entering the reality of those to whom we bear witness. Otherwise, our witness is meaningless, glib, self-serving, and vain.

The brilliance of Ecclesiastes may be precisely that it *is* so upsetting. Life is upsetting, and Ecclesiastes faces life honestly. We need to be upset when we become too accommodated to life "under the sun," too dependent on the comforts we may find in situations of prosperity and ease. We need to be upset in the opposite direction when we fall into cynicism and despair because of the hardships we face. Whenever we make an idol of the transitory achievements of our work and the arrogance it produces in us—and conversely whenever we fail to recognize the transcendent meaning of our work and the value of the people we work among—we need to be upset. Ecclesiastes may be uniquely capable of upsetting us to the glory of God.

Song of Songs and Work

Introduction to Song of Songs

The Song of Songs, also known as the Song of Solomon, is love poetry. Yet it is also a profound depiction of the meaning, value, and beauty of work. The Song sings of lovers who court, marry, and then work together in an ideal picture of life, family, and work. We will explore themes of hardship, beauty, diligence, pleasure, passion, family, and joy as they are depicted in the wide variety of work seen in the Song of Songs.

In the ancient world all poetry was sung, and the Song is, in fact, the lyrics to a song collection. It was performed by singers consisting of a male lead, a female lead, and a chorus. Song of Songs should probably be thought of as a concert piece created for an aristocratic audience in Solomon's court. It has strong analogies to the love music of ancient Egypt, which was also meant for such audiences and was composed in the centuries just prior to the age of Solomon.[1] The lyrics of Egyptian poetry, although in many ways similar to Song of Songs, are rather lighthearted and often focus on the ecstasy and afflictions of young lovers. The lyrics of Song of Songs, however, are not flippant or casual but profound and theological, and they provoke serious thought, including thought about work.

There are numerous interpretations of Song of Songs,[2] but we will approach it as a collection of songs that center on the love of a man and a woman. This is the plain sense of the text. It is the most fruitful way to explore meanings that actually arise from the text instead of being

---

[1] Michael V. Fox, *The Song of Songs and the Ancient Egyptian Love Songs* (Madison: University of Wisconsin Press, 1985).

[2] Other possible approaches are discussed in Duane A. Garrett and Paul A. House, *Song of Songs and Lamentations*, vol. 23b, *Word Biblical Commentary* (Nashville: Thomas Nelson, 2004), 59–81. None of these, however, are specifically applied to work.

imposed upon it. The love poetry celebrates the beauty of a wedding and the joy of love between man and woman.

Hardship and the Beauty of Work
(Song of Songs 1:1–8)

The Song begins with the woman speaking of her love for her man and, in the course of this, she speaks of how her skin has been darkened because her brothers made her work in the family vineyard (Song 1:6). Work arises only six verses into this song about love. In the ancient world, people tended to look down on dark skin not for racial reasons but for economic reasons: dark skin meant that you were in the peasant class and had to work in the sun. Fair skin meant that you were in the aristocracy, and therefore pale skin (not a tan!) was especially prized as a mark of beauty in women. But here, the woman's hard work has not really diminished her beauty (Song 1:5; "Dark am I, yet lovely," NIV[3]). Furthermore, her job has prepared her for the future, when she will tend her own vineyard (Song 8:12). A woman who works with her hands may not be an aristocrat, but she is beautiful and worthy of praise.

The loveliness of work, and working people, is often obscured by competing notions of beauty. The Greek world, whose influence is still deeply present in contemporary culture, regarded work as the enemy of beauty. But the biblical perspective is that work has an intrinsic beauty. Solomon builds himself a palanquin (a seat carried on poles), and the Song extols the beauty of the workmanship. It is literally a labor of love (Song 3:10). He puts its beauty to use in the service of love (transporting his beloved to their wedding; Song 3:11), yet the work was already beautiful in its own right. Work is not only a means to an end—transportation, harvest, or paycheck—but a source of aesthetic creativity. And believers are encouraged to see and praise the beauty in others' (including spouses') work.

---

[3] The NRSV translation, "I am black and beautiful," may give the erroneous impression that her dark complexion is due to ethnicity rather than exposure to the sun.

Diligence (Song of Songs 1:7–8)

The woman seeks her beloved, whom she regards as the finest of men. Her friends tell her that the obvious place to find him is at his work, where he is tending the sheep. Yet his work is arranged in a way that makes interaction with his beloved possible. There is no notion that work time belongs to the employer, while time off belongs to the family. Perhaps the reality of modern work makes family interaction at work impossible in many cases. Truckers shouldn't text their families while driving, and lawyers shouldn't receive a visit from their spouses during closing arguments. But perhaps it is not entirely a bad thing that the separation of work and family that arose with the factory system in the nineteenth century is beginning to fade in many industries.

When Work Is a Pleasure (Song of Songs 1:9–2:17)

In Song 1:9–2:7, the man and woman sing of their devotion to each other. He speaks of how beautiful she is, and she proclaims how happy she is in love. Then, in Song 2:8–17, they sing of the glories of the arrival of springtime, and he invites her to come away with him. This is in the context of the agricultural economy of ancient Israel, and a trip into the countryside in springtime is not just a picnic. It involves work. Specifically, pruning has to be done to ensure a good harvest (Song 2:12; "the time of singing" can also be translated "the time of pruning," as in the NASB). In addition, Song 2:15 says that foxes (animals that love to eat young grapes) have to be kept from the vineyards lest they spoil the harvest.

But the man and woman have light hearts. They turn this task into a game, chasing away the "little foxes." Their work is so amenable to games of love that it leads to the double entendre, "our vineyards are in blossom." This glorious picture of agricultural life in springtime hearkens back to the Garden of Eden, where tending the plants was meant to be a pleasure. Genesis 3:17–19 tells us that, because of sin, such labor has become drudgery. But this is not the original or proper meaning of work. This episode in the Song is a glimpse of how God desires life to be for us, almost as if sin had never happened. It is as if Isaiah 65:21 were already fulfilled: "They shall build houses and inhabit them; they shall

plant vineyards and eat their fruit." The kingdom of God brings not the
elimination of work, but the restoration of joy and delightful relationships in work. (For more on work in the ultimate kingdom of God, see
"Revelation and Work" in the *Theology of Work Bible Commentary*.)

Passion, Family, and Work (Song of Songs 3:1–8:5)

In a series of songs, the text describes the marriage of the man and
woman and their coming together. The woman yearns for the man (Song
3:1–5), and then she comes to him on a lovely palanquin (Song 3:6–11).[4]
The man, wearing a crown, receives her (Song 3:11). In an Israelite wedding, a bride arrived in a sedan surrounded by attendants (Song 3:7) and
she was received by her groom, who wore a crown. Song 3:11 confirms
that this text celebrates "the day of his wedding."[5]

The man then sings of his love for his bride (Song 4:1–15), and their
wedding night is described in vivid images and metaphors (Song 4:16–
5:8). The woman then sings of her love for her beloved (Song 5:9–6:3)
and another song on the woman's beauty follows (Song 6:4–9). The
couple then sings of their love for each other (Song 6:10–8:4). The text
is frankly sexual, and Christian preachers and writers have tended to
avoid the Song or to allegorize it out of concern that it is too racy for
polite religious society.

But the sex in the text is intentional. A song about the passion between two lovers on their wedding day would be missing something if
it failed to mention sex! And the sex is intimately connected to both the
household and the work in the Song. Upon their marriage, the lovers
create a household, the primary unit of economic activity in the ancient world. Without sex, it could not be populated with workers (that
is, children). Moreover, passion (including sex) between spouses is like
glue holding the household together through the prosperity, adversity,
joy, and stress that characterize a family's life and work. Today, many
couples report dissatisfaction with the amount of time they have for sex

---

[4]"Who is this?" (3:6)—translated misleadingly as "What is that?" in the
NRSV—is feminine in Hebrew, indicating that it refers to the woman.
[5]Garrett and House, 175–84.

and lovemaking. A major culprit is that one or both partners are too busy working.[6] The Song makes it clear that you should not let work push aside time for intimacy and sex with your spouse.

Throughout these verses, we see imagery drawn from the landscape of Israel and its agriculture and shepherding. The woman's body is a "garden" (Song 5:1). The man's "cheeks are like beds of spices" (Song 5:13). Enjoying his bride, he is like a man gathering lilies in a garden (Song 6:2). She is awesome like Jerusalem (Song 6:4). Her "hair is like a flock of goats moving down the slopes of Gilead" (Song 6:5). Her teeth are like a flock of ewes (Song 6:6). Her stature is like that of a palm tree (Song 7:7). They desire to go to the "vineyards" (Song 7:12). She rouses her beloved "under the apple tree" (Song 8:5). The joy of their love is intimately connected to the world of their work. They express their happiness with images drawn from what they see in their gardens and flocks.

This suggests that family and work belong together. In the Song, the whole of life is integrated. Before the Industrial Revolution, most people worked with family members in the households where they lived. This is still true in much of the world. The Song paints an idyllic view of this arrangement. The reality of household-based labor has been marred by poverty, grinding toil, humiliation, bonded service and slavery, and abusive relationships. Yet the Song expresses our desire—and God's design—that our work be woven into the tapestry of our relationships, beginning with family.

In developed economies, most paid work occurs outside the household. The Song of Songs does not offer specific means for integrating work with family and other relationships in today's societies. It should not be taken as a call for us all to move to farms and chase away the little foxes! But it does suggest that modern workplaces should not ignore their workers' family lives and needs. Many workplaces provide day care for workers' children, career development that respects parenting needs, time away for family care needs, and—in countries with private health care—medical insurance for workers' families. Yet these considerations are not available in all workplaces, and some have been cut by employers.

---

[6] International Planned Parenthood Federation, "FPAHK Survey on Marriage and Sex," http://www.ippf.org.

Most modern workplaces fall far short of the model of family care we see in the Song. The recent trend toward shifting work from offices to homes may or may not improve matters, depending on how costs, revenues, support services, and risks are distributed.

The Song could be an invitation to creativity as the twenty-first-century workplace takes shape. Families might start businesses in which family members can work together. Companies might employ spouses together or help one spouse to find work when relocating the other. Recent decades have seen much innovation and research in this area, both in secular and Christian—especially Catholic—circles.[7]

The Song should also increase our appreciation of unpaid work. In preindustrial households, there is little distinction between paid and unpaid work, since work occurs in an integrated unit. In industrial and post-industrial societies, much of the work occurs outside the household, earning wages to support the household. The unpaid work that remains to be done within the household often gets less respect than the paid work done outside. Money, rather than overall contribution to the household, becomes the measure of work's worth, and sometimes even of individuals' worth. Yet households could not function without the often unpaid work of maintaining the household, raising children, caring for aged and incapacitated family members, and sustaining social and community relationships. The Song depicts the value of work in terms of its overall benefit to the household, not its monetary contribution.

---

[7] The following are recommended for further exploration: Robert D. Austin and Lee Devin, "Knowledge Work, Craft Work and Calling," in *Global Neighbors: Christian Faith and Moral Obligation in Today's Economy*, ed. Douglas A. Hicks and Mark Valeri (Grand Rapids: Eerdmans, 2008); Pope John Paul II, *Laborem Exercens Encyclical Letter* (Homebush, NSW, Australia: St. Paul Publications, 1981); Pope John Paul II, *Sollicitudo Rei Socialis Encyclical Letter* (Homebush, NSW, Australia: St. Paul Publications, 1987); Pope John Paul II, *Centesimus Annus Encyclical Letter* (Boston: St. Paul Books, 1991); Wilder Robles, "Liberation Theology, Christian Base Communities, and Solidarity Movements: A Historical Reflection," in *Capital, Power, and Inequality in Latin America and the Caribbean*, ed. Richard L. Harris and Jorge Nef, new ed. (Lanham, MD: Rowman and Littlefield, 2008); Shirley J. Roels, "Christian Manufacturers at the Crossroads," in Hicks and Valeri, *Global Neighbors*; and Thomas W. Walker, "Who is My Neighbor? An Invitation to See the World with Different Eyes," in Hicks and Valeri, *Global Neighbors*.

The Song may pose a challenge to many churches and those who guide Christians, for it is uncommon for Christians to receive much help in arranging their work lives. Not enough churches are able to equip their members for making godly, wise, realistic choices about work in relationship to family and community. Undoubtedly, church leaders will rarely have the on-the-ground knowledge needed to help members land jobs or create workplaces that move toward the ideal depicted in the Song. If you want to know how to better integrate your work as a nurse, for example, with your family relationships, then you probably need to talk more with other nurses than with your pastor. But perhaps churches could do more to help their members recognize God's design for work and relationships, express their hopes and struggles, and join with similar workers to develop viable options.

Joy (Song of Songs 8:6–14)

Love is sacred and a thing to be protected. It cannot be bought (Song 8:7). The woman compares her love life with her husband to her tending of a vineyard (Song 8:12), asserting that although Solomon may have a great many vineyards to be tended by his workers (Song 8:11), her joy is in taking care of her own family. Happiness does not consist in wealth or in having others to do your work for you; it consists in working for the benefit of those you love. Love therefore does not consist only of expressing emotions but also in doing acts of love.

Conclusions from Song of Songs

The Song of Songs gives us an ideal picture of love and family, life and work. Joy in the shared work of the household is a central feature—almost as though sin had never happened. In the Song, work has a beauty that is integrated into a wholesome and joyful life. The Song shows us an ideal for which we should strive. Labor should be an act of love. Marriage and household relationships should support—and be supported by—work. Work is an essential element of married life, yet it must always serve—and never crowd out—the most fundamental element of all: love.

Introduction to the Prophets

Who Were the Prophets?

Called by God and filled with God's Spirit, a prophet spoke God's word to people who had in one way or another distanced themselves from God. In one sense, a prophet is a preacher. But in marketplace terms, a prophet is often a whistle-blower, particularly when an entire tribe or nation has turned away from God.

The prophets peopled the pages of Israel's history. Moses was God's prophet, used to rescue the Hebrew people from slavery in Egypt and then to lead them to the land God had promised them. Again and again, these people turned away from God. Moses was God's first mouthpiece to bring them back into a relationship with God. In the Old Testament history books (Joshua, Judges, 1 & 2 Samuel, 1 & 2 Kings, 1 & 2 Chronicles, Ezra, and Nehemiah), prophets such as Deborah, Samuel, Nathan, Elijah, Elisha, Huldah, and others came forward to speak God's word to a rebellious people.

Israel's religious worship was organized around the labor of priests, first in the tabernacle and later in the temple. The day-to-day job description of priests lay in slaughtering, butchering, and roasting the sacrificial animals brought by worshipers. But a priest's tasks went beyond the heavy physical work of dealing with thousands of animal sacrifices. A priest was also responsible to be a spiritual and moral guide to the people. While the priest was often seen primarily as the mediator between the people and God in the temple sacrifices, his larger duty was to teach God's law to the people (Lev. 10:11; Deut. 17:8–10; 33:10; Ezra 7:10).

In Israel's history, however, the priests themselves often became corrupt and turned away from God, leading the people in the worship of idols. Prophets arose when the priests failed to teach God's law to the people, and when kings and judges failed to govern the country justly.

In a sense, God called and spoke through prophets as whistle-blowers when the whole Israelite enterprise was on the brink of self-destruction.

One of the stunning tragedies of the people of God was their persistence in pursuing the worship of the many gods of their pagan neighbors. The common practices of this idolatrous worship included offering their children in the fires of Moloch and ritual prostitution with every imaginable lewd practice "on the high places, on the hills, and under every green tree" (2 Chr. 28:4). But an even greater evil in forsaking Yahweh came in forsaking God's structure for living in community as a distinct and holy people of God. Concern for the poor, the widow, the orphan, and the stranger in the land was replaced by oppression. Business practices overturned God's standard so that extortion, taking bribes, and dishonest gain became commonplace. Leaders used power to destroy lives, and religious leaders despised God's holy things. Far from enriching the nation, these ungodly practices led to the downfall of the nation. The prophets were often the last voices in the land, calling people back to God and to a just and healthy community.

In most cases, the prophets were not "professional" in the sense of earning a living from their prophetic activities. God tapped them for special duty while they were in the midst of other professions. Some prophets (e.g., Jeremiah and Ezekiel) were priests with the duties described above. Others were shepherds, including Moses and Amos. Deborah was a judge adjudicating issues for the Israelites. Huldah was probably a teacher in the scholarly sector of Jerusalem. The task of a prophet overlaid other jobs.

Situating the Prophets in Israel's History

The records of the earliest prophets are woven into the history of Israel in the books of Joshua through 2 Kings, rather than in a separate written record. Afterwards, the words and deeds of the prophets were preserved in separate collections corresponding to the final seventeen books of the Old Testament, Isaiah through Malachi, often called the "latter prophets," or sometimes the "literary prophets" because their words were written down as separate pieces of literature rather than being spread through books of history as the earlier prophets were.

When the unified kingdom split in two, the ten northern tribes (Israel) plunged immediately into idol worship. Elijah and Elisha, the last among the former prophets, were called by God to challenge these idolatrous Israelites to worship Yahweh alone. The first of the literary prophets, Amos and Hosea, were called to challenge the apostate northern kings of Israel from Jeroboam II through Hoshea. Because kings and people alike refused to return to Yahweh, in 722 BC God allowed the powerful empire of Assyria to overthrow the northern kingdom of Israel. The Assyrians, cruel and merciless, not only destroyed the cities and towns of the land, taking its wealth as booty, but they also took the people captive and dispersed them throughout the empire in an attempt to destroy forever all sense of nationhood (2 Kgs. 17:1–23).

As Israel neared its destruction, the small nation of Judah in the south flip-flopped between the worship of Yahweh and the worship of foreign gods. Good kings pulled the people back from idol worship and bad business practices, but bad kings reversed that. In the southern kingdom (Judah), the first literary prophets were Obadiah and Joel. They were whistle-blowers under kings Jehoram, Ahaziah, Joash, and Queen Athaliah.

Isaiah spoke for God in Judah under four kings—Uzziah, Jotham, Ahaz, and Hezekiah—with Micah also prophesying during that period. Hezekiah was followed on the throne by Manasseh, of whom Scripture records that he did more evil in the sight of the Lord than all his predecessors (2 Kgs. 21:2–16).

Manasseh was followed by good king Josiah who instituted a thorough cleansing of the temple, ridding it of much pagan worship. The people cleaning the temple found an ancient scroll that spelled judgment on the land, which led to the last revival of Yahweh worship in Judah. The prophets in Jerusalem at this time included Jeremiah and Zephaniah (though the high priest turned to a woman prophet, Huldah, to interpret the scroll for the king). Josiah was followed by kings whose disastrous political decisions eventually brought the Babylonian conqueror Nebuchadnezzar II against Jerusalem (2 Kgs. 23:31–24:17). In 605 BC,

Nebuchadnezzar took 10,000 Jews into exile in Babylon. The prophet Ezekiel was among those captives, while Habakkuk joined Jeremiah and Zephaniah, continuing their prophetic work in Jerusalem. When King Zedekiah allied himself with neighbor nations to fight off Babylon in 589, Nebuchadnezzar laid siege to Jerusalem that lasted more than two years (2 Kgs. 24:18–25:21; 2 Chr. 36). The city capitulated in 586, mainly because of famine, and was razed to the ground with its temple and palaces totally destroyed. Jeremiah remained in Jerusalem, continuing his prophetic work among the impoverished remnant in Judah, until he was carted off to Egypt. Meanwhile, Ezekiel continued to prophesy in Babylon to the exiled Jews living there.

Among the Jewish captives in the first deportation (605 BC) was the young man Daniel, whom God used in Babylon in the court of all the Babylonian emperors. When Babylon was overthrown by the Persians in 539 BC, the new Medo-Persian king Cyrus allowed the Jews to return to Judah and rebuild their city and its temple, first under Zerubbabel and then under Nehemiah. Daniel's prophecies span the Babylonian exile (Dan. 1:1) through Cyrus's decree ending the exile (Dan. 10:1).

Persian kings varied in their attitude toward the Jews. Under Cambyses (530–522) the rebuilding of Jerusalem was stopped (Ezra 4), but under Darius I (522–486) the second temple was completed (see Ezra 5–6). Here the post-exilic prophets Zechariah and Haggai challenged the Jews: "You live in paneled houses while God's house lies in ruins. Do something about it!" Darius was followed by Xerxes (486–464), whose reign is recorded in Esther 1–9. Following Xerxes came Artaxerxes (464–423), in whose reign Ezra returned to Jerusalem in 458 BC (Ezra 7–10), and Nehemiah followed in 445 BC (Neh. 1–2). It was in this period that the final post-exilic prophet Malachi wrote.

The book of Jonah does not take place in Israel, and the text gives no indication of its date. God gave Jonah a mission to Nineveh, the Assyrian capital, calling the Assyrian people to repentance. The Assyrians were enemies of Israel, but God's intent was to bless them nonetheless, consistent with God's promise that Abraham's people would be a blessing to all nations (Gen. 22:18).

Timeline of the Prophets

Period	Northern Kings (Israel)	Northern Prophets	Southern Kings (Judah)	Southern Prophets
United Kingdom Under Saul, David, and Solomon (c. 1030–931 BC)				
Divided Kingdom	Jeroboam (931–910 BC)		Rehoboam (931–913 BC)	
	Nadab (910–909 BC)	Elijah	Abijah (913 BC)	Obadiah
	Baasha (909–886 BC)	Elisha	Asa (911–870 BC)	Joel
	Elah (886 BC)	Amos	Jehoshaphat (873–848 BC)	Jonah
	Zimri (885 BC)	Hosea	Jehoram (853–841 BC)	Isaiah
	Omri (885–874 BC)		Queen Athaliah (841–835 BC)	Micah
	Ahab (874–853 BC)		Joash (835–796 BC)	Jeremiah
	Jehoram (852–841 BC)		Amaziah (796–767 BC)	Zephaniah
	Jehu (841–814 BC)		Uzziah (790–740 BC)	Habakkuk
	Jehoahaz (814–798 BC)		Jotham (750–731 BC)	
	Jehoash (798–782 BC)		Ahaz (735–715 BC)	
	Jeroboam II (793–753 BC)		Hezekiah (715–686 BC)	
	Zechariah (753–752 BC)		Manasseh (695–642 BC)	
	Shallum (752 BC)		Amon (642–640 BC)	
	Menahem (752–742 BC)		Josiah (640–609 BC)	
	Pekahiah (742–740 BC)		Jehoahaz (609 BC)	
	Pekah (752–732 BC)		Jehoiakim (609–597 BC)	
	Hoshea (732–722 BC)		Jehoiachin (597 BC)	
			Zedekiah (597–586 BC)	
Babylonian Exile				Ezekiel
				Daniel
Post-exilic Prophets			Zerubbabel, Governor	Haggai
			Nehemiah, Governor	Zechariah
				Malachi

Isaiah and Work

Introduction to Isaiah

The Prophet Isaiah received a vision of God—of his great power, his glorious majesty, and his purifying holiness. Glimpsing God's majesty led him to a humble view of himself and his society. "Woe is me! I am lost, for I am a man of unclean lips, and I live among a people of unclean lips" (Isa. 6:5). When we glimpse who God is in Scripture, it can cleanse away our inflated self-importance and the insufficiency of our lip service in worship. But it can also give us a clear picture of what is truly valuable in this life. It changes the way we live, the way we do business, and the way we worship. When we understand who God is and where we stand in relation to him, our values and our work ethic are transformed.

In particular, the book of Isaiah gives a clear, and at times a frightening, picture of God's expectations of leaders. In a sense, it is an extended—and mostly negative—performance review of the kings and other leaders of Israel and Judah. (In Isaiah, "Judah" refers to the southern kingdom of the divided nation of Israel, while "Israel" can refer either to the northern kingdom or—more frequently—to the Jewish people as a whole.) Modern workplaces differ significantly from those in ancient Israel. For example, the leaders seen in the book work in government, military, or religious occupations, but today's leaders also work in corporate, entrepreneurial, scientific, academic, and other spheres. Yet the writing of Isaiah can be applied to today's world if we understand what this book meant in its original setting, and we work out principles that can apply to the workplace today. Moreover, in Isaiah's view, the way we work today has value and meaning in the new creation that God promises for his people.

God's Assessment of Israel and Judah

The bulk of the book of Isaiah consists of the prophet Isaiah giving voice to God's assessment of Israel's failure to live up to the covenant between God and Israel. Isaiah is the first of the major Old Testament "literary prophets"—those whose prophecies are written in books titled with the name of the prophet. Some knowledge of the book of Deuteronomy is necessary in reading the writing prophets, because the failing grades God meted out to Israel's and Judah's leaders must be understood in light of the covenant embodied in the Law of Moses. Through Moses, God entered a covenant with his people. He promised them security, peace, and prosperity, secured by his presence among them. In return, they promised him worship and observance of the law he gave them. Isaiah, like the other writing prophets, proclaims the people's—and especially the leaders'—failure to obey God's law. It is not incidental that Jews of Jesus' day often summarized the Old Testament succinctly as "the Law and the Prophets." To be most clearly understood, the prophets should be read not only within their historical setting, but also against the background of God's covenant and law.

An Overview of the Book of Isaiah

According to Isaiah 1:1, the prophet Isaiah's career extended through the reigns of four kings in the southern kingdom of Judah: Uzziah, Jotham, Ahaz, and Hezekiah. He served as God's emissary to Judah for more than fifty years (from around 740 to 686 BC), roughly a hundred years before the other three major writing prophets—Jeremiah, Ezekiel, and Daniel. While the political scene in Judah was different from that in the northern kingdom of Israel, the sins of the people were distressingly similar: idol worship, the oppression and marginalization of the poor for personal gain, and business practices that fundamentally threatened God's law. Like his contemporary Amos (who delivered God's messages at the shrine in Bethel to the unrepentant people of Israel), Isaiah clearly saw that lip-service worship leads to self-serving social ethics.

Isaiah differs from Jeremiah and Ezekiel in that the character of his prophetic ministry blends foretelling (the seer seeing far into the future) in a greater measure with forth-telling[1] (preaching the truth to

---

[1]A prophet's job description includes both telling the truth and telling the future. Isaiah continually called the people back to just living by God's righteous

a sinful people). While the book of Isaiah provides several historical touch points that anchor the prophet in a particular period of Judah's history, the book ranges in its visions from Isaiah's own times through to the end of time when God creates "new heavens and a new earth" (Isa. 65:17). Some scholars have described the book of Isaiah as a vision of a mountain range in which the various peaks are visible, but the valleys stretching between the peaks (the time periods separating various prophetic insights) cannot be seen. For example, the prophecy to King Ahaz that God would give him the sign of a baby named Immanuel (Isa. 7:14) is picked up seven hundred years later by Matthew (Matt. 1:23) as a vision of the Messiah about to be born.[2]

The historical notes in the book anchoring the prophet Isaiah in the sixth century before Christ begin with his receiving a vision of God and a call to prophetic ministry "in the year that King Uzziah died," namely, 740 BC (Isa. 6:1). The text then passes over the sixteen-year reign of King Jotham (2 Kgs. 15:32–38) and picks up in Isaiah 7:1 with King Ahaz (2 Kgs. 16:1ff.), who faced the apparent imminent destruction of Jerusalem at the hand of the Syrians and their allies at the time, the northern kingdom of Israel. Later, in chapters 36–37, the prophet details King Hezekiah's dilemma when the Assyrian general Sennacherib laid siege to Jerusalem, threatening its total destruction (2 Kgs. 18:13–19:37).

Isaiah continues Hezekiah's story in chapters 38 through 39, a story of the king's deathly illness and God's willingness to extend his life for an additional fifteen years. In each of these historical touch points, the prophet Isaiah was directly involved with the kings in speaking God's words to them.

---

law (telling the truth), but he also saw far into the future and predicted events to come (telling the future). Most of the prophets were primarily preachers of righteousness, and their foretelling (predictive) work was less extensive into the future than was Isaiah's, Daniel's, or Micah's. While they warned sinful people of the impending disaster God would visit on them because of their sin, only a few prophets extended the range of their prophecies beyond the next punishment God would bring upon a sinful people.

[2] More precisely, this prophecy has a near-term fulfillment in the birth of a baby at the time of Ahaz, and an ultimate fulfillment in the virginal conception and birth of Jesus.

Isaiah's prophecy casts a vision for the people of God that ranges from impending national judgment to gracious restoration after the ensuing catastrophe, to the eschatological hope of something so different that it can be referred to only as new heavens and a new earth (Isa. 65:17). His work (predictive as well as exhortative) covers a range from the monarchy in Judah to the nation's exile in Babylon, to the restoration and return to Judah. He announces events from the coming of the Messiah to the coming of "new heavens and a new earth." Structurally, chapters 1–39 cover the period of Isaiah's active ministry, while the remaining chapters of the book (40–66) look deeply into the future for God's people. Thus the prophetic word of the Lord through Isaiah spans uncounted generations.

Isaiah's calling was to serve as God's emissary before the people of Judah and proclaim their sinful status in God's eyes. Later, the prophet insisted that his prophecies be recorded for future generations: "Go now, write it before them on a tablet . . . that it may be for the time to come as a witness forever. For they are a rebellious people, faithless children, children who will not hear the instruction of the LORD" (Isa. 30:8, 9). The people's sinfulness is defined by their disregard for God's law or God's covenant claims on them as his people. The prophecies against the sinful people are so strong that one could describe the situation as follows: God's desire for those whom he has called as *his* people is such that if they will not be *his* people, then they will be no people at all.

God's View of Our Work

Seven major themes touching our daily work emerge from Isaiah's writings: (1) there is an integral connection between our worship and our work life; (2) arrogant pride and self-sufficiency in our work will bring us down; (3) God despises wealth gained by exploiting poor and marginalized people; (4) God wills that as we trust in him, we may live in peace and prosperity; (5) our creator God is the source of everything; (6) in Isaiah, we see a powerful example of God's servant at work; and finally, (7) today's work finds its ultimate meaning in the new creation. These themes are discussed in the order of their first major appearance in the book of Isaiah.

Worship and Work (Isaiah 1)

Isaiah begins by insisting that religious rituals nauseate God when accompanied by sinful living:

> What to me is the multitude of your sacrifices? says the LORD; I have had enough of burnt offerings of rams and the fat of fed beasts; I do not delight in the blood of bulls, or of lambs, or of goats. . . . Trample my courts no more; bringing offerings is futile; incense is an abomination to me. . . . I will hide my eyes from you; even though you make many prayers, I will not listen; your hands are full of blood. Wash yourselves; make yourselves clean; remove the evil of your doings from before my eyes; cease to do evil, learn to do good; seek justice, rescue the oppressed, defend the orphan, plead for the widow. (Isa. 1:11–17)

Later, he repeats God's complaint: "These people draw near with their mouths and honor me with their lips, while their hearts are far from me, and their worship of me is a human commandment learned by rote" (Isa. 29:13). The catastrophe coming upon the nation is a direct result of its oppression of workers and lack of provision for those in economic need.

> Announce to my people their rebellion, to the house of Jacob their sins. Yet day after day they seek me and delight to know my ways, as if they were a nation that practiced righteousness and did not forsake the ordinance of their God; they ask of me righteous judgments, they delight to draw near to God. "Why do we fast, but you do not see? Why humble ourselves, but you do not notice?" Look, you serve your own interest on your fast day, and oppress all your workers. Look, you fast only to quarrel and to fight and to strike with a wicked fist. . . .
>
> Is not this the fast that I choose: to loose the bonds of injustice, to undo the thongs of the yoke, to let the oppressed go free, and to break every yoke? Is it not to share your bread with the hungry, and bring the homeless poor into your house; when you see the naked, to cover them, and not to hide yourself from your own kin? Then your light shall break forth like the dawn, and your healing shall spring up quickly; your vindicator shall go before you, the glory of the LORD shall be your rear guard. (Isa. 58:1b–4, 6–8)

In our world today, in which our daily work often seems disconnected from our weekend worship, God says, "If you know my law and
love me, you will not mistreat workers in the workplace." Isaiah knew
from personal experience that a genuine vision of God changes our lives,
including how we live as Christians in the workplace.

How does this occur? Again and again, Isaiah gives us a vision of
God, high and lifted up above all gods:

- "But the LORD of hosts, him you shall regard as holy; let him be
  your fear, and let him be your dread. He will become a sanctuary" (Isa. 8:13–14).

- God's unequaled power and might are tempered by his compassion for his people: "Why do you say, O Jacob, and speak, O
  Israel, 'My way is hidden from the LORD, and my right is disregarded by my God'? Have you not known? Have you not heard?
  The LORD is the everlasting God, the Creator of the ends of the
  earth. He does not faint or grow weary; his understanding is
  unsearchable. He gives power to the faint, and strengthens the
  powerless" (Isa. 40:27–29).

- "I am God, and also henceforth I am He; there is no one who can
  deliver from my hand; I work and who can hinder it?" (Isa. 43:13).

- "I am the first and I am the last; besides me there is no god. Who
  is like me? Let them proclaim it, let them declare and set it forth
  before me. Who has announced from of old the things to come?
  Let them tell us what is yet to be" (Isa. 44:6–7).

- "Listen to me, O Jacob . . . I am He; I am the first, and I am the
  last. My hand laid the foundation of the earth, and my right hand
  spread out the heavens" (Isa. 48:12–13).

We may tremble at God's power and might, but we are drawn into his
compassion for us. In response, we worship him, living our lives around
the clock in light of God's desire that we reflect his concern for justice
and righteousness. Our work and our worship are bound together by
our view of the Holy One. Our understanding of who God is will change

the way we work, the way we play, and the way we view and treat people who could benefit from our work.

The integral connection of our work with the practical application of our worship is also seen in the stories of the two kings the prophet used to highlight trusting God in the workplace. Both Ahaz and Hezekiah had leadership responsibilities in Judah as monarchs. Both faced terrifying enemies bent on the destruction of their nation and the city of Jerusalem. Both had the opportunity to believe God's word through the prophet Isaiah that God would not allow the nation to fall to the enemy. In fact, God's word to Ahaz was that what the terrified king most feared would not take place, but "if you do not stand firm in faith, you shall not stand at all" (Isa. 7:9). Ahaz refused to trust God for deliverance, turning instead to an imprudent alliance with Assyria.

A generation later, Hezekiah faced an even more formidable enemy, and Isaiah assured him that God would not allow the city to fall to Sennacherib's armies. Hezekiah chose to believe God, and "then the angel of the LORD set out and struck down one hundred eighty-five thousand in the camp of the Assyrians; when morning dawned, they were all dead bodies. Then King Sennacherib of Assyria left, went home, and lived at Nineveh" (Isa. 37:36–37).

In these two stories, Isaiah highlights for us the contrast between faith in God (the basis of our worship) and fear of those who threaten us. The workplace is one location where we face the choice between faith and fear. Where is our Lord when we are at work? He is Immanuel, "God with us" (Isa. 7:14), even in the workplace. What we believe about the character of God will determine whether we will "stand firm in faith" or if we will be overcome by fear of those who may have the power to do us harm.

Arrogant Pride and Self-Sufficiency (Isaiah 2)

In the writings of Isaiah, arrogant pride and self-sufficiency are particularly related to the denial of the authority and majesty of God in all spheres. We replace God's uniqueness with trust in human ingenuity or foreign gods. Isaiah addressed this issue head-on early in the book: "The haughty eyes of people shall be brought low, and the pride of everyone shall be humbled; and the Lord alone will be exalted on that day" (Isa. 2:11).

The nation's pride is exhibited in three things: its *wealth*, *military might*, and *idolatry*. The combination of these three factors creates a pernicious triad drawing the people away from a humble reliance on God. Instead, they rely on the work of their hands—idols as well as wealth and military might.

Isaiah describes their wealth in silver and gold: "There is no end to their treasures" (Isa. 2:7). He makes the same statement of their military prowess and the idols: there seemingly is no end to which the people do not go. The prophet ridicules the idols, crafted by their own hands and then worshiped as gods (Isa. 44:10–20). God abhors human pride and self-reliance. Accumulated wealth or the pursuit of wealth that presses the majesty of God to the margins of our daily lives is an offense to God: "Turn away from mortals, who have only breath in their nostrils, for of what account are they?" (Isa. 2:22). In chapter 39, King Hezekiah comes under God's judgment because he took it upon himself to show off the temple treasury to the emissaries from distant Babylon. Instead of trying to impress an adversary with the kingdom's wealth, the king should have humbled himself before God.

Exploitation and Marginalization (Isaiah 3)

A recurring charge throughout the book of Isaiah is that the leaders were unfaithful to God's covenant because they pursued wealth and status at the expense of the well-being of marginalized and poor people. In Isaiah 3:3–15, God pronounced judgment on the elders and the leaders of God's people for expanding their own wealth by plundering and grinding down the faces of the poor. Regarding the situation described in Isaiah 3:14, H. G. M. Williamson makes the following observation:

> This is generally associated with the development during this period of a class structure whereby the wealth, and hence power, came to be increasingly concentrated in the hands of a privileged minority at the expense of small-holders and the like. The need for loans, with the consequent perils of slavery . . . , foreclosure and ultimately debt slavery,

were the means whereby this could be pursued legally but, in the opinion of the prophets, unjustly.[3]

Similarly, in the Song of the Vineyard in Isaiah 5, the first of several "woes" pronounced against the people of Judah was precisely related to their exploitation of the poor for the accruing of their own wealth: "Ah, you who join house to house, who add field to field, until there is room for no one but you, and you are left to live alone in the midst of the land!" (Isa. 5:8).[4]

As the people of God, they were called to be different from the surrounding and competing cultures. The exploitation of the poor for the advancement of the social elite was a breach of God's covenant claims on his people to be *his* people. This pattern can be seen earlier in Israel's history in the reign of King Ahab through his foreign wife, Jezebel, who stole the vineyard of a farmer named Naboth after having him murdered. The prophet Elijah was incensed, stating, "The dogs shall eat Jezebel within the bounds of Jezreel!" (1 Kgs. 21:23). Isaiah saw the pattern of selfish ambition based on injustice against the poor and the marginalized continuing in Judah. He declared that the day was coming when God's Messiah would put a stop to it. "With righteousness he will judge the poor, and decide with equity for the meek of the earth" (Isa. 11:4).

While Isaiah zeroed in on the sins of God's people in Judah, he included God's judgment on the nations: "This is the plan that is planned concerning the whole earth; and this is the hand that is stretched out over all the nations" (Isa. 14:26). Babylon would be brought down (Isa. 13:9–11); within three years, Moab's glory would end (Isa. 15); Syria would go down (Isa. 17:7–8), as would Ethiopia (Isa. 18), Egypt (Isa. 19:11–13), and Tyre (Isa. 23:17). God would bring down Assyria's king for his arrogant heart and haughty looks (Isa. 10:12). "The earth lies polluted under its inhabitants; for they have transgressed laws. . . .

---

[3] H. G. M. Williamson, *Isaiah 1-5*, vol. 1, *A Critical and Exegetical Commentary on Isaiah 1–27* (London: T&T Clark, 2006), 271.

[4] Cf. Isa. 1:23; 3:9; 5:23; 10:1–2; 29:21. See also John Barton, "Ethics in the Book of Isaiah," in *Writing and Reading the Scroll of Isaiah: Studies of an Interpretive Tradition*, ed. Craig C. Broyles and Craig A. Evans, vol. 1 (Leiden: Brill, 1997), 89–70.

Therefore a curse devours the earth, and its inhabitants suffer for their guilt" (Isa. 24:5–6a).

God's concern for justice and righteousness leads him today to judge nations, governments, communities, corporations, institutions, organizations, and individuals who defraud and deceive others for personal gain. In our day, we see exploitation of entire nations by their own leaders, as in Myanmar; disaster brought on by the negligence of foreign corporations, as in the Bhopal disaster in India; and the defrauding of investors by individuals, such as Bernie Madoff. Just as significantly, we see—and engage in—seemingly minor injustices, such as unfair compensation, excessive workloads, oppressive contract terms and conditions, cheating on exams, and looking the other way when abuse occurs at home, at work, in church, and on the street. God will ultimately judge those who gain wealth or preserve their jobs or privileges by exploiting the poor and marginalized.

Peace and Prosperity (Isaiah 9)

In contrast to the arrogant pride and self-sufficiency that will bring us down or those who exploit the poor in order to gain wealth, a fourth theme in Isaiah says that as we put our trust in the one true God, we will live in peace and prosperity. The people of God will rejoice before God "as with joy at the harvest" (Isa. 9:3). By the power of God's spirit, people will dwell in peace and security and will enjoy their work (Isa. 32:15): "Happy will you be who sow beside every stream, who let the ox and the donkey range freely" (Isa. 32:20).

Similarly, one of the promises that followed Hezekiah's trust in God's deliverance from the Assyrian king Sennacherib was the people's enjoyment of the fruit of their own labors: "And this shall be the sign for you: This year eat what grows of itself, and in the second year what springs from that; then in the third year sow, reap, plant vineyards, and eat their fruit" (Isa. 37:30). Because of the stress of the impending invasion by Sennacherib, the land had lain dormant. God promised food from it even though it was not farmed. But for a people to enjoy the fruit of the vine, years of peace are required to carry out proper cultivation. Peaceful conditions are a blessing from God. Judah's successful labor in the field and vineyard served as a continuing sign of God's covenant love.

In the vision of the new Zion in Isaiah 62, one of God's promises related to the people's enjoyment of their own food and their own wine for which they had toiled (Isa. 62:8–9). Similarly, in the depiction of the new heavens and the new earth where the former things will be forgotten in the new creation, the people of God will no longer be oppressed but will build their own houses, drink their own wine, and eat their own food (Isa. 65:21–22).

In the Old Testament, since farming was the main occupation of the majority of the people, many examples in the Bible are drawn from agrarian life and expectations. But the larger principle is that God calls us, regardless of our vocation, to trust him in our work as well as in the more apparently religious aspects of our lives.

God enjoys the creative roles his people play as they endeavor to excel at what they do under God's covenant. "They shall plant vineyards and eat their fruit!" (Isa. 65:21). The problems arise when we try to overturn the Creator/creature distinction by replacing God's values and provision with our own values and unchecked ambition. This happens when we compartmentalize our work as a secular affair that seems disconnected from the kingdom of God. In a fallen world, of course, living faithfully does not always result in prosperity. But work done apart from faith can lead to even worse outcomes than material poverty. The early chapters of Isaiah's prophecy witness to Judah's discovery of exactly this.

Life, Knowledge, and Wisdom (Isaiah 28)

More than any other writing prophet, Isaiah takes us repeatedly to a vision of God that, once grasped, causes us to bow low in humble adoration. God is the source of all that we are, all that we have, and all that we know. Three hundred years earlier, Solomon had encapsulated this truth: "The fear of the LORD is the beginning of knowledge" (Prov. 1:7) and "The fear of the LORD is the beginning of wisdom" (Prov. 9:10). Now Isaiah shows us the God who is the source of that knowledge and wisdom, and why our understanding of who God is matters in our life and work.

God has given us our very being: "[You] have been borne by me from your birth, carried from the womb; even to your old age I am he, even when you turn gray I will carry you. I have made, and I will bear;

I will carry and will save" (Isa. 46:3–4). God has given us knowledge and understanding: "I am the LORD your God, who teaches you for your own good, who leads you in the way you should go" (Isa. 48:17). The God who made us and gave us understanding is the only source of such knowledge:

> Who has measured the waters in the hollow of his hand and marked off the heavens with a span, enclosed the dust of the earth in a measure, and weighed the mountains in scales and the hills in a balance? . . . See, he takes up the isles like fine dust. Lebanon would not provide fuel enough, nor are its animals enough for a burnt offering. All the nations are as nothing before him; they are accounted by him as less than nothing and emptiness. To whom then will you liken God, or what likeness compare with him? (Isa. 40:12–18)

Once we recognize God as the source of our life, our knowledge, and our wisdom, we have a new perspective on our work. The very fact that we have the knowledge or the skill to do the work we do takes us back to our source, God, who created us with the skill sets and interests that come together in our lives. Living in the "fear" (the awe-filled awareness) of the Lord is the starting point for knowledge and wisdom. Recognizing this also allows us to learn from others to whom God has given complementary knowledge or skill. Creative teamwork on the job is possible when we respect God's work in others as well as in ourselves.

When we experience God at work in us, our work becomes fruitful. "The farmer knows just what to do, for God has given him understanding" (Isa. 28:26, NLT). We could also say that "the artisan knows just what to do, for God has given him or her understanding." Or, "the entrepreneur knows just what to do, for God has given that person understanding." In mysterious ways, we become co-creators with God in our work as instruments in God's hand for purposes deeper than we even know.

Servant at Work (Isaiah 40)

Where "righteousness" in Isaiah 1–39 (often associated with justice, *mishpat*) is a term used to reveal Judah's shortcomings and infidelity, "righteousness" in Isaiah 40–55 is understood primarily as a gift from

God that he accomplishes on behalf of his people.[5] Isaiah himself serves as the prime example of the servant of God who brings this gift of God.

Justice or judgment is established in Isaiah 40–55 by the enigmatic "servant" embedded within this portion of Isaiah's witness. Isaiah 42:1–4, the first of the so-called Servant Songs, speaks of the servant as one who establishes justice in the earth. Here, in the figure of the servant, God answers Judah's cry for justice in Isaiah 40:27: "My way is hidden from the LORD, and my right [*mishpat*] is disregarded by my God." God's own divine initiative is now enacted to accomplish for his people what they could not accomplish for themselves. The means by which God will accomplish salvation both for Israel and for the nations is in this developing figure of God's servant. Righteousness and justice are accomplished by the servant.

The servant's narrative identity develops within these chapters from Israel per se in chapters 40–48 to an individual figure who takes on his own shoulders Israel's missional identity for both itself and for the nations in chapters 49–53. The reason for this shift from national Israel to a figure who is Israel incarnate (or an idealized Israel) is Israel's failure to fulfill its mission because of its sin.[6] What we observe in this servant figure is the unique means by which God communicates his gracious presence and restorative intentions to his wayward people. It is by the figure of the servant that righteousness (now understood as covenant fidelity to his people) is offered to them as a gift on the basis of God's own freedom and sovereign commitment to his promises. Righteousness is something to be received rather than attained.[7]

---

[5] For a fuller treatment of this issue as it relates to the final form of the book as a whole, see John N. Oswalt, "Righteousness in Isaiah: A Study of the Function of Chapters 56–66 in the Present Structure of the Book," in Broyles and Evans, 177–91.

[6] On the development of the servant in the literary presentation of Isaiah 40–55, see Christopher R. Seitz, " 'You are my Servant, You are the Israel in whom I will be glorified': The Servant Songs and the Effect of Literary Context in Isaiah," *Calvin Theological Journal* 39 (2004): 117–34.

[7] It was Gerhard von Rad who highlighted Isaiah 40–55's synonymous association of righteousness [*tsadeqah*] and salvation [*yeshua*]. Gerhard von Rad, *Old Testament Theology*, trans. D. M. G. Stalker, vol. 1 (San Francisco: HarperSanFrancisco, 1962), 372.

The two portraits of righteousness presented in Isaiah 1–39 and 40–55 are pursued to give us a nuanced understanding of righteousness in Isaiah 56–66. It is in this portion of Isaiah that some of the clearer portraits of a theology of work are offered. The righteousness offered as a gift in Isaiah 40–55 is now an obligation to be performed in chapters 56–66: "Thus says the LORD: 'Maintain justice, and do what is right, for soon my salvation will come, and my deliverance be revealed' " (Isa. 56:1).

The appeal in Isaiah 56–66 to maintain justice and do righteousness is a realized possibility now for the people of God because of God's prior gracious claim on them in the figure of the servant. The language of Isaiah 56:1 is linked to Isaiah 51:4–8, in which Judah is again called to pursue justice and righteousness. In this passage, the created possibility for the people of God to do righteousness is found in the last clauses of Isaiah 51:6, 8: God's righteousness and God's salvation will not fail but will last forever. As chapters 40–55 move in their literary shape, we see God's righteousness and salvation enacted in the person of the servant (Isa. 53) who suffers on behalf of and in the place of others. The appeals to "doing righteousness" in chapters 56–66 are made possible because of God's prior dealings with Israel's infidelity in the gracious and substitutionary action of the servant. In theological language, God's grace precedes law, as demonstrated by God's gracious initiative to redeem his people at all costs. This is the only means by which talk of human responsibility or righteous actions can occur. It is in the security of the forgiveness of God found in Jesus Christ that the impetus for good works materializes.[8]

The prophet turns the argument from the negative to the positive by presenting "the fast that I [God] choose" (Isa. 58:6). This fast includes loosing the chains of injustice, setting the oppressed free, sharing food with the hungry, providing the poor wanderer with shelter, clothing the

---

[8] Commenting on "righteousness" in Isa. 56–66, Oswalt states, "In short, there is a whole new motivation for doing righteousness. It is not now so much the fear of impending doom which compels righteousness, as it is the recognition that God is going to mercifully and righteously keep his covenant promises. We should be righteous, the writer says, because of the righteousness of God." "Righteousness in Isaiah," 188.

naked, and caring for one's family (Isa. 58:6–7).[9] Isaiah paints a picture of the values that must characterize the people of God, in stark contrast to those of most surrounding cultures. External religion or religious performance that can commingle with a work ethic characterized by a lack of concern for one's laborers (where laborers, employees, or subordinates are mere instruments for personal or business development), or by a leadership style that is given to strife, quarreling, backbiting, shortened fuses, and uncontrolled anger—these breach our loyalty to God. A claim is made on the people of God because of the prior forgiveness of our sins in the person and work of Jesus Christ. The promise following on the heels of the invective in chapter 58 is the breaking forth of all of God's promises in the midst of God's people: "Your light shall break forth . . . your vindicator shall go before you, . . . the glory of the LORD shall be your rear guard" (Isa. 58:8; cf. Isa. 52:12).

As we trace the development of "the servant" from national Israel to an idealized Israel, then to the servant of the Lord in chapters 52–53, then to the servants of that servant, we pause to reflect on the workplace implications of the model of servanthood we see in Jesus Christ. Isaiah carefully constructs his description of the servant to make it clear that he is a reflection of God himself.[10] Therefore, Christians have traditionally equated the servant with Jesus. Isaiah's picture of the servant's suffering in chapters 52–53 reminds us that as servants of God, we may be called to self-sacrifice in our work, as Jesus was.

> So marred was his appearance, beyond human semblance, and his form beyond that of mortals. . . . He was despised and rejected by others; a man of suffering and acquainted with infirmity; and as one from whom others hide their faces he was despised, and we held him of no account. . . . But he was wounded for our transgressions, crushed for our iniquities; upon

---

[9] Even if such a list has to do initially with the particular problems associated with the release from exilic bondage, the figural extension of these problems into other spheres of human conduct is not only legitimate but necessary. See Christopher R. Seitz, "The Book of Isaiah 40–66: Introduction, Commentary, and Reflections," in vol. 6, *The New Interpreter's Bible* (Nashville: Abingdon Press, 2001), 499.

[10] Richard J. Bauckham, *God Crucified: Monotheism and Christology in the New Testament* (Grand Rapids: Eerdmans, 1999), 50.

him was the punishment that made us whole, and by his bruises we are
healed. . . . Yet he did not open his mouth; like a lamb that is led to the
slaughter, and like a sheep that before its shearers is silent. (Isa. 52:14;
53:3, 5, 7)

An adequate vision of God will motivate us to make God's standard our
standard, so that we do not allow self-interest and self-aggrandizement
to pervert our work. Jesus, in his death and resurrection, met a need we
could not meet. God's standard calls us to meet the needs of justice and
righteousness through our work:

> Justice is turned back, and righteousness stands at a distance; for truth
> stumbles in the public square, and uprightness cannot enter. Truth is
> lacking, and whoever turns from evil is despoiled. The LORD saw it, and
> it displeased him that there was no justice. He saw that there was no
> one, and was appalled that there was no one to intervene; so his own arm
> brought him victory, and his righteousness upheld him. (Isa. 59:14–16)

As servants of the servant of the Lord, we are called to meet unmet
needs. In the workplace, this may have many faces: concern for a downtrodden employee or co-worker, alertness to the integrity of a product
being sold to consumers, eschewing process shortcuts that would deprive people of their input, even rejecting hoarding in times of scarcity.
As Paul wrote to the Galatians, "Bear one another's burdens, and in this
way you will fulfill the law of Christ" (Gal. 6:2).

As servants of the servant of the Lord, we may not receive the acclaim we desire. Rewards may be deferred. But we know that God is our
judge. Isaiah put it this way: "For thus says the high and lofty one who
inhabits eternity, whose name is Holy: I dwell in the high and holy place,
and also with those who are contrite and humble in spirit, to revive the
spirit of the humble, and to revive the heart of the contrite" (Isa. 57:15).

Work's Ultimate Meaning (Isaiah 60)

Throughout the book, Isaiah encourages Israel with the hope that
God will eventually put to right the wrongs the people are suffering in
the present. Work and the fruits of work are included in this hope. By

chapter 40, as the book moves from telling the truth about the present to telling the truth about the future, the sense of hope increases. The material about the suffering servant in chapters 40–59 can hardly be understood except as God's gift of hope in the future fulfillment of God's kingdom.

In chapters 60–66, this hope is finally expressed in full. God will gather his people together again (Isa. 60:4), vanquish the oppressors (Isa. 60:12–17), redeem the rebellious who repent (Isa. 64:5–65:10), and establish his just kingdom (Isa. 60:3–12). In place of Israel's faithless leaders, God himself will rule: "You shall know that I, the LORD, am your Savior and your Redeemer, the Mighty One of Jacob" (Isa. 60:16). The change is so radical that it amounts to a new creation, of parallel power and majesty to God's first creation of the world. "I am about to create new heavens and a new earth; the former things shall not be remembered or come to mind" (Isa. 65:17).

Chapters 60–66 are rich with vivid portraits of the perfect kingdom of God. In fact, a large fraction of New Testament imagery and theology are drawn from these chapters in Isaiah. The final chapters of the New Testament (Rev. 21–22) are, in essence, a recapitulation of Isaiah 65–66 in Christian terms.

It may be surprising to some how much of Isaiah 60–66 is related to work and the outcomes of work. The things people work for in life come to complete fruition at last, including:

- Markets and trading, including the movement of gold and silver (Isa. 60:6, 9), the bringing of firs, and the opening of gates for trade. "Your gates shall always be open; day and night they shall not be shut, so that nations shall bring you their wealth, with their kings led in procession." (Isa. 60:11)

- Agricultural and forest products including frankincense, flocks, rams (Isa. 60:6–7), cypress, and pine (Isa. 6:13)

- Transportation by land and sea (Isa. 60:6, 9), and even perhaps by air (Isa. 60:8)

- Justice and peace (Isa. 60:17–18; 61:8; 66:16)

- Social services (Isa. 61:1–4)

- Food and drink (Isa 65:13)

- Health and long life (Isa. 65:20)

- Construction and housing (Isa. 65:21)

- Prosperity and wealth (Isa. 66:12)

All these blessings have eluded Israel in their faithlessness to God. Indeed, the harder they tried to achieve them, the less they cared to worship God or follow his ways. The result was to lack them even more. But when the book of Isaiah presents Israel's future hope as the New Creation, all the preceding promises in the book come to the fore. The picture portrayed is that of a future eschatological or final day when the "righteous offspring of the servant" will enjoy all the blessings of the messianic age depicted earlier. Then people will actually receive the things they work for because "they shall not labor in vain" (Isa. 65:23). Israel's sorrow will be turned into joy, and one of the dominant motifs of this coming joy is the enjoyment of the work of their own hands.

Conclusions from Isaiah

As Christians living in the tension between the inauguration of God's kingdom and its coming fulfillment, our enjoyment of our work and the fruit of our labor to the praise of God's glory foreshadows the coming day when the tension will be removed. It might be said like this: When Christians enjoy their work and the fruit it produces to the praise of God's glory, they taste a bit of heaven on earth. When all is made right and the heavens and earth are as they were originally intended, work will not cease. It will continue and will be a great delight for those involved, for the sting of the Fall will have been irrevocably removed.

Work and enjoying the fruits of one's hard work are gifts of God to be enjoyed and shared with others. Through these gifts, we can contribute to human flourishing and to alleviating suffering. The prophecy of Isaiah presents a beautiful portrait of the fact that even in our work as we clock in Monday to Friday, we are to fulfill the law by loving God and loving our neighbor (cf. Matt. 22:33–40). In God's economy, we cannot love God and fail to love our neighbor. When our work is performed in this gracious context made possible by the forgiving, restorative work of Jesus Christ, our joy may be full. When labor and work become the twisted focus of our own self-aggrandizement at the expense of our subordinates' dignity and the oppression of the poor and marginalized, the invective prophetic word of Isaiah still comes to us with power: "This is not the fast I have chosen." When work and labor are enjoyed in the context of loving God and loving neighbor, a little bit of the new heavens and the new earth are tasted in the here and now.

Jeremiah & Lamentations and Work

Introduction to Jeremiah and Lamentations

The fundamental issue in the book of Jeremiah is whether the people will be faithful to God in the midst of a difficult environment. Dishonest ethical practices are condemned by God in the same breath as idolatry and religious hypocrisy, making it clear that this prophetic book is concerned not only with religious issues but with social and ethical issues as well. Jeremiah is concerned with faithfulness in religion, family, military, government, agriculture, and every sphere of life and work. We face a similar issue as workers today. We're called to be faithful to God in our work, but it's not easy to follow God's ways in many workplaces.

Jeremiah had to deal with the unfaithfulness to God of virtually all of the people. From kings and princes to priests and prophets, all were unfaithful to him. They still, on the whole, came to the temple, offered sacrifices, and called on the name of the Lord, but failed to acknowledge God in the way they lived the rest of their lives (Jer. 7:1–11). This is not unlike those today who attend church on Sunday and place their offerings in the collection plate, but live the rest of their lives as though God were not involved.

Within the framework of faithfulness to God, the book of Jeremiah offers a number of passages directly related to work and many others that deal with faithfulness to God in the wholeness of life, with clear implications for our work.

In his work-related oracles, Jeremiah did not introduce many new principles or commands. Instead, he accepted those revealed in earlier books of the Bible, especially in the Law of Moses. He then admonished God's people that they were not following God's law and warned that this would bring disaster upon them. When disaster came, he taught them how to live out God's law in their new—and bleak—situation. He encouraged them with God's promise that he would eventually restore their joy and prosperity if they would return to faithfulness.

Although Jeremiah lived about six hundred years before the Apostle Paul, what he said about work could easily be summed up in the words of Colossians 3:23: "Whatever your task, put yourselves into it, as done for the Lord and not for your masters."

Jeremiah and His Times

Most of us find our workplaces to be difficult, at least at times. One of the appeals of the book of Jeremiah is that the prophet's situation was extremely difficult. His workplace (among the governing elites of Judah) was corrupt and hostile to God's work. Jeremiah was constantly in danger, yet he could see God's presence in the most difficult situations. His perseverance reminds us that perhaps we can learn how to experience God's presence in the most difficult workplaces.

Jeremiah grew up in the small town of Anathoth, three miles northeast of Judah's capitol, Jerusalem. While close geographically, the two communities were far apart culturally and politically. Jeremiah was born into the priestly line of Abiathar but had little standing with the priests in Jerusalem. Centuries earlier, Solomon had removed Abiathar from authority (1 Kgs. 1:28–2:26) and replaced him with the priestly line of Zadok in Jerusalem.

When God called Jeremiah to be his prophet in Jerusalem, the prophet found himself in the midst of priests who did not accept his inherited priesthood. Jeremiah remained a suspicious and disliked outsider throughout his long career in Jerusalem. Those who face cultural, ethnic, racial, linguistic, religious, or other prejudices in today's workplaces can identify with what Jeremiah faced every day of his life.

The Reluctant Prophet's Call and Job Description

In the thirteenth year of King Josiah's reign (626 BC), in his early twenties, Jeremiah received God's call to be a prophet (Jer. 1:2). His job description was to carry God's messages "over nations and over kingdoms, to pluck up and to pull down, to destroy and to overthrow, to build and to plant" (Jer. 1:10). God's messages given through Jeremiah were not gentle and affirming, for the Jews were coming disastrously close to abandoning their faithfulness to God. God was making an attempt, through Jeremiah, to call them back before disaster struck. Like an outside consultant hired to shake up the status quo in a business, he was called to disrupt business as usual in the kingdom of Judah. Part of his assignment was to oppose the idolatry and evil practices that had become part of the worship in Judah.

His prophetic work began under the good king Josiah. It continued through Josiah's evil successors Jehoahaz, Jehoiakim, Jehoiachin, and Zedekiah, and through the total destruction of Jerusalem under the Babylonian ruler Nebuchadnezzar in 586 BC. During his four decades as God's prophet in Jerusalem, Jeremiah was constantly derided, a laughingstock to the citizens of the city. In fact, he narrowly escaped several plots against his life (Jer. 11:21; 18:18; 20:2; 26:8; 38).

Jeremiah did not apply for the position of prophet, and we do not read anywhere that he "accepted" God's call to be his mouthpiece. This is in contrast to Isaiah who, after his vision of God's holiness and majesty, heard God ask, "Whom shall I send and who will go for us?" Isaiah replied, "Here am I. Send me!" (Isa. 6:8). When God informed Jeremiah that he was to be his mouthpiece in Jerusalem, the prophet protested his youth and inexperience (Jer. 1:6–7). But God appears to have overridden that protest by immediately giving him prophetic messages for the people (Jer. 1:11–16). God then followed those messages with instructions, a warning, and a promise to the newly minted prophet:

> But you, gird up your loins; stand up and tell them everything that I command you. Do not break down before them, or I will break you before them. And I for my part have made you today a fortified city, an iron pillar, and a bronze wall, against the whole land—against the kings of Judah, its princes, its priests, and the people of the land. They will fight against you; but they shall not prevail against you, for I am with you, says the LORD, to deliver you. (Jer. 1:17–19)

Jeremiah knew from the beginning that his vocation as prophet was a tough one. His assignment would pit him against the whole nation of Judah from the king, princes, and priests down to the people in the streets of the city. Nonetheless, he felt a clear calling from God to do this difficult work, and he trusted God to lead him through it.

An Overview of the Book of Jeremiah

The book of Jeremiah reflects the ever-worsening situation that Jeremiah encountered. At various times, he had the unenviable tasks of challenging the religious hypocrisy, economic dishonesty, and oppressive practices of Judah's leaders and those who followed them. Jeremiah was the voice of warning, the watchman who brought attention to hard truths that others would rather ignore.

> Thus says the LORD concerning the house of the king of Judah . . . I will make you a desert, an uninhabited city. I will prepare destroyers against you. . . . And many nations will pass by this city, and all of them will say one to another, "Why has the LORD dealt in this way with that great city?" And they will answer, "Because they abandoned the covenant of the LORD their God." (Jer. 22:6–9)

He was the pessimist, who was in reality the realist. He was dismissed and ridiculed by false prophets who insisted that God would never let the city of Jerusalem fall to an invader.

Jeremiah's persistence in delivering his unwelcome message over four decades is remarkable. He simply would not quit what seemed like an impossible assignment. How many of us would have walked away from such a situation? Jeremiah's tenacious faithfulness in carrying out God's instructions is striking, given the unrelenting opposition and harsh criticism he faced. While he has often been called the "weeping prophet" because he mourned the sins of his people and grieved his own lack of success in turning them back to Yahweh, Jeremiah never flinched in his confidence that God, who placed him where he was, would vindicate the truth of his message. The prophet could be faithful to his unwanted call because God had promised to be faithful to him. "They will fight against you; but they shall not prevail against you, for I am with you, says the LORD, to deliver you" (Jer. 1:19).

In 605, Nebuchadnezzar of Babylon attacked Jerusalem and carried off ten thousand of the most able Jews (including Ezekiel and Daniel). At that point, Jeremiah's role was expanded to bring God's word to the Jews in exile (Jer. 29). Among the captured Jews were false prophets who assured the exiles that Babylon's days were numbered and God would never allow Jerusalem to be captured, while Jeremiah warned the exiles that they would be in Babylon for seventy years. Instead of acting on false hopes, the Jews there were to settle down in the land, build houses, plant gardens, marry off their children—and stop listening to the false prophets.

Meanwhile, the remaining inhabitants of Judah continued to refuse God's message. In 586 the Babylonians returned, sacked Jerusalem, pulled down its walls, destroyed its temple stone by stone, and carried off the remaining able-bodied people as captives. Once more, Jeremiah's role changed (Jer. 40–45). God kept him in the destroyed city, now governed briefly by Gedaliah, to encourage the new ruler and help the people understand what had happened and how they were to go forward amid the destruction. Yet once more, despite his plea that they would hear God's message, they put their faith in an unfortunate military alliance with Egypt that Babylon quickly defeated. Jeremiah was taken to Egypt, where he died. To the end, the prophet had to endure the rulers' stubborn refusal to heed God's messages and the ruinous outcomes that resulted. Prophets and workplace Christians alike may discover they do not have the ability to overcome every evil. Sometimes success means doing what you know is right even when everything turns out against you.

The final chapters (46–52) deal principally with the judgment God will bring upon all nations, not merely Judah. While God used Babylon against Judah, Babylon would not escape punishment either.

We cannot read Jeremiah without a vivid awareness of the disastrous results of the persistent faithlessness of Judah's leaders—the kings, the priests, and the prophets. Their shortsightedness and willingness to believe the lies they told one another led to the complete destruction of the nation and its capital, Jerusalem. The work God gives us to do is serious business. Failing to follow God's word in our work can inflict serious damage on ourselves and those around us. Leading the people of Israel was the job of the king, priests, and prophets. The national catastrophe that soon engulfed Israel was the direct result of their poor decisions and failure to perform their duties under the covenant.

Work-Related Themes in the Book of Jeremiah

The book of Jeremiah is not organized as a treatise on work. Because of this, work-related topics appear at scattered places in the book, sometimes separated by many chapters, other times overlapping within a single chapter or passage. We will take these topics and passages, as much as possible, in the order they appear in Jeremiah.

We have seen that Jeremiah's overwhelming concern is whether people are acting in faithfulness to God. As we read, we can ask ourselves whether we see our work as being a significant area where God wants us to be faithful to him. If it is, then we can expect to experience God's presence in our work. Therefore, our faithfulness to God and God's presence in our work are linked themes to which we will frequently return.

Calling to Work (Jeremiah 1)

As we have seen, God prepared Jeremiah from before his birth for the work of a prophet (Jer. 1:5) and, at the right time, appointed him to that work (Jer. 1:10). Jeremiah responded faithfully to God's call to work, and God gave him the knowledge he needed to accomplish it (Jer. 1:17).

Although Jeremiah's profession was prophet, there is no reason to believe that the pattern of God's call, followed by faithful human response, followed by God's equipping, is limited to prophets. God called and equipped Joseph (Gen. 39:1–6; 41:38–57), Bezalel and Oholiab (Exod. 36–39), and David (1 Sam. 16:1–13) for jobs as finance minister, construction chief, and king, respectively. In the New Testament, Paul says that God equips every faithful person for work according to God's purposes for the world (1 Cor. 12–14). We can see in Jeremiah a pattern for all those who follow God faithfully in their work. As William Tyndale stated long ago:

There is no work better than another to please God: to pour water, to wash dishes, to be a [cobbler], or an apostle, all are one; to wash dishes and to preach are all one, as touching the deed, to please God.[1]

God knows how we—like Jeremiah—are knit together according to God's design. God leads us to employ our abilities and talents in godly ways in the world. We likely will not have the same calling as Jeremiah. Nor will our call necessarily be as direct, specific, and unmistakable as Jeremiah's was. It would be an error to think that our calling to our work must resemble Jeremiah's. Perhaps God was extraordinarily direct with Jeremiah because Jeremiah was so deeply reluctant to accept God's call. In any case, we can be confident that God will equip us for our work, whatever it is, if we will be faithful to him in it.[2]

Goodness and Defilement of Work (Jeremiah 2)

Long before Jeremiah lived, God declared that work is good for people (Gen. 1–2). As we have noted elsewhere, Jeremiah's method was to accept what God had revealed earlier and call attention to how it is being lived out—or not lived out—in his day. In chapter 2, Jeremiah called out how the people were perverting the goodness of work. God said to his people, "I brought you into a fertile land to eat its fruit and its good things. But when you entered you defiled my land, and made my heritage an abomination" (Jer. 2:7). He added that the people "went after things that do not profit" (Jer. 2:8).

The Lord brought the people to a fertile land where their work would yield plentifully, but they rejected his presence by defiling his land. This is a standard expression of theological privilege in the ancient Near East: God created the land and owns it, but he has given the land to people who serve as his stewards of it. God gave his people the high privilege of working God's very own land, the place he had chosen as the location of his temple, the dwelling place of his presence. Although in Jeremiah's

---

[1] Quoted in Parker Society Vol. 42 (Cambridge: Cambridge University Press, 1841), 102.

[2] See "Calling" under "Key Topics" at www.theologyofwork.org.

time the people worked God's land with contempt, the work itself was created by God to be good. "You shall eat the fruit of the labor of your hands; you shall be happy, and it shall go well with you" (Ps. 128:2). Working the land is necessary and, when done in accordance with God's ways, brings enjoyment and a deep sense of God's presence and love. "There is nothing better for mortals than to eat and drink, and find enjoyment in their toil. This also, I saw, is from the hand of God" (Eccl. 2:24).

But work became defiled when people ceased to work in faithfulness. The people defiled the land because they stopped following God and "went after worthless things and became worthless themselves" (Jer. 2:5). When our work goes bad, it can be a diagnosis that our fellowship with God has dimmed. We may have ceased to spend time with God, perhaps because we are busy working so hard. Yet we are often tempted to try to fix the problem by spending more time at tasks "that do not profit" (Jer. 2:8), neglecting fellowship with God even further. Our tasks profit little not because we aren't working long enough hours, but because without God in our work, it has become fruitless and inefficient. What would happen if we went to the heart of the matter and spent more time in fellowship with God? Could we preview with God all the significant actions and decisions we anticipate making during the day ahead? Could we bring to mind and pray for all the people we expect to encounter? Could we review our work with God at the end of the day?

Acknowledgement of God's Provision (Jeremiah 5)

Jeremiah complained that "this people has a stubborn and rebellious heart; they have turned aside and gone away" (Jer. 5:23). It is God's land in which they are stewards, called to work it in the "fear" of the Lord. "Fear" (Hebrew *yare*) of God is often used in the Old Testament as a synonym for "living in response to God."[3] But Jeremiah pointed out that they had no awareness of God as the source of the rains and the assurance of the harvests. "They do not say in their hearts, 'Let us fear

---

[3] R. Laird Harris, Gleason L. Archer, Jr., and Bruce K. Waltke, eds., *Theological Wordbook of the Old Testament,* electronic ed. (Chicago: Moody Press, 1999), entry 907.

the LORD our God, who gives the rain in its season, the autumn rain and the spring rain, and keeps for us the weeks appointed for the harvest'" (Jer. 5:24). Thus they are unfaithful, imagining themselves to be the source of their own harvests (cf. Jer. 17:5–6). As a result, they no longer experienced good harvests. "Your iniquities have turned these away, and your sins have deprived you of good" (Jer. 5:25).

This section is one of the many places in chapters 1–25 that speak of the "pollution" of the land: "An appalling and horrible thing has happened in the land: the prophets prophesy falsely, and the priests rule as the prophets direct; my people love to have it so" (Jer. 5:30–31). In ancient times—when agriculture was the vast majority of the economy— the pollution of the land resulted in not only an aesthetic loss, but in the loss of productivity and plenty as well. It was also a rejection of the God who had given the land. Chris Wright notes that the land—like a sacrament or a visible sign—is a thermometer of our relationship with God.[4] The rape of the land (whether by corporations, armies, or individuals) denies God's ownership and purpose in making us stewards of the earth.

Material Success and Failure

Does God withhold material success from those who do evil in his sight? Jeremiah says what few modern Christians would dare to say: the *lack* of God's provision *might* be a sign that your work is not approved by God. God withheld the rains from Judah because of the sin of its inhabitants. "Your iniquities have turned these [the rains] away, and your sins have deprived you of good" (Jer. 5:25). The prophet did *not* say that *all* cases of lack of provision or success are signs of God's judgment. This is one of the open issues Jesus addressed almost six hundred years later when he said that the man born blind was not blind as a sign of God's judgment (John 9:2–3). Moreover, God even provides material good for those who are evil. According to Jesus, God "causes the sun to rise on the evil and on the good, and sends rain on the righteous and on the unrighteous" (Matt. 5:45). From the book of Jeremiah we can say only that material success depends on God's provision, and that God may—

---

[4]Christopher J. H. Wright, *Deuteronomy*, New International Biblical Commentary (Peabody, MA: Hendrickson Publishers, 1996).

at least at times—withhold material success from those who practice injustice and oppression.

We must, however, take caution. We must be careful not to make the short step of inferring an absolute cause-and-effect relationship between our sin and God's punishment in all situations of deprivation. Are the poor deprived because they are evil or lazy? Jeremiah would say that the poor are deprived because evil or lazy people oppress them.

Injustice, Greed, the Common Good, and Integrity (Jeremiah 5–8)

Injustice

In failing to acknowledge God as the source of good harvests, the people of Judah soon lost any sense of accountability to the Lord for how they worked. This led them to oppress and deceive the weak and defenseless:

> They know no limits in deeds of wickedness; they do not judge with justice the cause of the orphan, to make it prosper, and they do not defend the rights of the needy. (Jer. 5:28)

> They have held fast to deceit, they have refused to return. I have given heed and listened, but they do not speak honestly; no one repents of wickedness, saying "What have I done!" (Jer. 8:5–6)

What ought to have been done for the good of all in God's land was done solely for individuals' own profit and without fear of their God, for whom they were called to work. So God withheld rain, and they soon learned that they were not the source of their own success. There are parallels here in the economic crisis of 2008–2010 and its relationship to compensation, honesty in lending and borrowing, and the rush to make a quick profit at the cost of putting others at risk. It is important not to be simplistic, for today's major economic issues are too complex for generalized maxims drawn from Jeremiah. Yet there is a connection—complex though it is—between the economic well-being of people and nations and their spiritual lives and values. Economic well-being is a moral issue.

Greed

God calls people to a higher purpose than economic self-interest. Our highest end is our relationship with God, within which provision and material well-being are important, but limited, matters.

> I remember the devotion of your youth, your love as a bride, how you followed me in the wilderness, in a land not sown. Israel was holy to the LORD, the first fruits of his harvest. (Jer. 2:2–3)

Jeremiah looked around and found that greed—unbridled pursuit of economic gain—had displaced the love of God as the people's chief concern. "From the least to the greatest, everyone is greedy for unjust gain; from prophet to priest, everyone deals falsely" (Jer. 8:10). No one escaped Jeremiah's condemnation for their greed.[5] The prophet was not partial to the rich or the poor, the small or the great. We see him running "to and fro through the streets of Jerusalem" to find even "one person who acts justly and seeks the truth" (Jer. 5:1). First he asked the poor, but he found them hardened (Jer. 5:4). Then Jeremiah turned to the rich, "but they all alike had broken the yoke, they had burst the bonds" (Jer. 5:5).

As Walter Brueggemann states, "All persons, but especially the religious leaders, are indicted for their unprincipled economics. . . . This community has lost every norm by which to evaluate and assess its rapacious and exploitative greed."[6] The people's hearts were inclined toward getting rich rather than fearing God and loving others. Whether done by the rich (the king, Jer. 22:17) or the poor, such greed aroused divine wrath.

Working for the Benefit of All

God's intention is that we live and work for the benefit of others, not just ourselves. Jeremiah criticized the people of Judah for failing

---

[5] See, e.g., Jer. 2:30–32; 3:25; 7:21–24; 11:7–8; 22:21.

[6] Walter Brueggemann, *A Commentary on Jeremiah: Exile & Homecoming* (Grand Rapids: Eerdmans, 1998), 72–73.

to care for others who could not offer some economic benefit in return, including orphans and the needy (Jer. 5:28), aliens, widows, and innocents (Jer. 7:6). This is above and beyond the accusations he made against breaking specific elements of the law, such as stealing, murder, adultery, swearing falsely, and worshiping false gods (Jer. 7:9). Jeremiah made this charge against particular individuals ("scoundrels are found among my people," Jer. 5:26), against all individuals ("all you people of Judah," Jer. 7:2), against the leaders of business (the rich, Jer. 5:27) and government (judges, Jer. 5:28), against cities (Jer. 4:16–18; 11:12; 26:2; et al.) and against the nation as a whole ("This evil people," Jer. 13:10). Every element of society, individually and institutionally, had broken God's covenant.

Jeremiah's insistence that our work and its products serve the good of others is an important foundation for business ethics and personal motivation. Whether an action contributes to the good of other people is just as important as the whether the action is legal. It may be legal to conduct business in ways that harm customers, workers, or the community, but that does not make it legitimate in God's reckoning. For example, most companies are part of a supply chain leading from raw materials to parts to assemblies to finished goods to the distribution system to consumers. It may be possible for one player in the chain to gain power over the others, squeeze their margins, and capture all the profits. But even if this is done by legal means, is it good for the industry and the community? Is it even sustainable over the long term? It may also be legal for a union to preserve benefits for current workers by negotiating away benefits for new workers. But if the benefits are needed by *all* workers, is this really fulfilling the union's purpose?

These are complex issues, and there is no rigid answer to be found in Jeremiah. The relevance of Jeremiah is that the people of Judah, for the most part, thought they were living according to the law, including presumably its many economic/workplace regulations. For example, in contrast to some of the other prophets (e.g., Ezek. 45:9–12), Jeremiah does not suggest that the merchants he came in contact with were using unjust weights and measures, which would have broken the law as found in Leviticus 19:36. But God still found them unfaithful in their workplace and economic activity. They followed the regulations of the law but not its spirit. Jeremiah says that doing so ultimately prevented the whole people from enjoying the fruit of their labor in God's land.

Like the people of Judah, we all have chances either to hoard or to share the benefits we receive from our jobs. Some companies concentrate bonuses and stock options in the hands of senior executives. Others distribute them broadly among all workers. Some people try to take full credit for every accomplishment they had a hand in. Others give credit to co-workers as liberally as possible. Again, there are complex considerations involved, and we should avoid making snap judgments of others. But we could ask ourselves a simple question: Does the way I handle money, power, recognition, and the other rewards of my job benefit primarily me, or does it contribute to the good of my colleagues, my organization, and my society?

Likewise, organizations may lean toward either greed or the common good. If a business exploits monopoly power to extract high prices or uses deception to sell its products, then it is acting on greed for money. If a government exercises power to promote the interests of itself over its neighbors or of its leaders over its citizens, then it is acting on greed for power.

Jeremiah takes a broad understanding of the common good and its opposite, greed. Greed is not restricted to gains that violate some particular law. Instead, it includes any kind of gain that ignores the needs and circumstances of others. According to Jeremiah, no one in his day was free of such greed. Is it any different today?

Integrity

The word *integrity* means living life according to a single, consistent set of ethics. When we follow the same ethical precepts at home, at work, at church, and in the community, we have integrity. When we follow different ethical precepts in different spheres of life, we lack integrity.

Jeremiah complains about the lack of integrity he sees in the people of Judah. They seemed to believe that they could violate God's ethical norms in work and daily life, then come to the temple, act holy, and be saved from the consequences of their actions.

Will you steal, murder, commit adultery, swear falsely, make offerings to Baal, and go after other gods that you have not known, and then come and

stand before me in this house, which is called by my name, and say, "We
are safe!"—only to go on doing all these abominations? Has this house,
which is called by my name, become a den of robbers in your sight? You
know, I too am watching, says the LORD. (Jer. 7:9–11)

Jeremiah is calling them to lives of integrity. Otherwise their piety
means nothing to God. "I will cast you out of my sight," God says (Jer.
7:15). Our hearts are not right with God just because we go to the temple.
Our relationship with him is reflected in our actions, in what we do every
day, including what we do at work.

Faith in God's Provision (Jeremiah 8–16)

We saw in Jeremiah 5 that the people did not acknowledge God's
provision. If the people did not acknowledge God as the ultimate source
of the good things they already had, how much less would they have faith
to depend on God to provide for them in the future? John Cotton, the
Puritan theologian, says that faith needs to underlie everything we do in
life, including our work or vocation:

> A true believing Christian . . . lives in his vocation by his faith. Not only
> my spiritual life but even my civil life in this world, and all the life I live, is
> by the faith of the Son of God: He exempts no life from the agency of his
> faith.[7]

Here again lay the fundamental failure of the people of Judah in Jeremiah's day, their lack of faith. Sometimes Jeremiah expressed it as not
"knowing" the Lord, which is a term of fidelity.[8] At other times, he put it

[7] John Cotton, "Christian Calling," in *The Way of Life* (London, 1641),
436–51, quoted in Leland Ryken, *Worldly Saints: The Puritans as They Really
Were* (Grand Rapids: Zondervan, 1986), 26.

[8] E.g., Jer. 2:8; 4:22; 5:4–5; 8:7; 9:3-6; 22:16. "When Jeremiah talks . . .
about the knowledge of Yahweh, he is talking about compliance with covenantal
stipulations." Jack R. Lundbom, "Jeremiah, Book of," in *The Anchor Bible Dictionary*, ed. David Noel Freedman, vol. 3 (New York: Doubleday, 1992), 718b.
See Herbert B. Huffmon, "The Treaty Background of Hebrew *Yada'*," *Bulletin of
the American Schools of Oriental Research* 181 (February 1966): 31–37.

in the terms of failing to "hear"—that is, to listen, obey, even care about what God has said.[9] At still other times, he termed it a lack of "fear." But all of these are simply a lack of faith—a living, working faith in who God is and what he does or says. This lack bled into the people's view of work, leading to blatant violations of the law of God and the exploitation of others for their own gain.

The great irony is that by depending on their own actions in the place of faithfulness to the Lord in their work, the people ultimately failed to find enjoyment, fulfillment, and the good of life. God will eventually deal with their faithlessness, and "death shall be preferred to life by all the remnant that remains of this evil family" (Jer. 8:3). The laws of God are aimed at our own good and are given to keep us focused on our proper purpose.[10] When we set God's laws aside because they hinder us from taking care of ourselves in our own way, we depart from God's design for us to become our true selves. When we work dependent only on ourselves—and especially when we break God's laws in order to do so—work fails to achieve its proper end. We are in denial of God's presence in the world. We think we know better than God how to get the things we want. So we work according to our ways, not his. But our ways do not yield us the good things God intends to give us. As we experience this lack, we engage in increasingly desperate acts of self-interest. We cut corners, we oppress others, and we hoard what little we have. Now we are not only failing to receive what God wants to give us, we are also failing to produce anything of value for ourselves or others. If others in the community or nation act the same, we are soon fighting one another in pursuit of less and less satisfying products of our labor. We have become the opposite of who we are designed to be as the people of God. Now we "know and see that it is evil and bitter for you to forsake the LORD your God; the fear of me is not in you, says the Lord God of hosts" (Jer. 2:19).

---

[9] E.g., Jer. 7:23–28; 11:7–8; 32:23; 40:3; 43:4, 7; 44:23.

[10] Thomas Aquinas notes: "Now the extrinsic principle inclining to evil is the devil. . . .But the extrinsic principle moving to good is God, who both instructs us by means of His law, and assists us by His grace. . . . Now the first principle in practical matters . . . is the last end: and the last end of human life is bliss or happiness. . . . Consequently the law must regard principally the relationship to happiness." *Summa Theologica* Ia IIae, q.90, pro. and a.2.co.

The theme of the people abandoning God, losing faith in his provision, and oppressing one another in consequence is repeated at intervals throughout Jeremiah 8–16. "They refuse to know me, says the LORD" (Jer. 9:6). Therefore, their prosperity fades away, "the lowing of cattle is not heard; both the birds of the air and the animals have fled and are gone" (Jer. 9:10). As a consequence, they try to make up the loss by cheating one another. "They all deceive their neighbors and no one speaks the truth. . . . Oppression upon oppression, deceit upon deceit!" (Jer. 9:5–6).

Work within a Balanced Life (Jeremiah 17)

Jeremiah also turned his attention to the rhythm of work and rest. As always, the prophet began with God's earlier self-revelation; in this case, the Sabbath rest:

> On the seventh day God finished the work that he had done, and he rested on the seventh day from all the work that he had done. (Gen. 2:2)

> Remember the sabbath day, and keep it holy. Six days you shall labor and do all your work. But the seventh day is a sabbath to the LORD your God. (Exod. 20:8–10)

Jeremiah, however, encountered a people who refused to honor the Sabbath:

> Thus says the LORD: For the sake of your lives, take care that you do not bear a burden on the sabbath day or bring it in by the gates of Jerusalem. And do not carry a burden out of your houses on the sabbath or do any work, but keep the sabbath day holy, as I commanded your ancestors. Yet they did not listen or incline their ear; they stiffened their necks and would not hear or receive instruction. (Jer. 17:21–23)

Earlier in chapter 17, speaking through Jeremiah, God said:

> Cursed are those who trust in mere mortals and make mere flesh their strength, whose hearts turn away from the LORD. They shall be like a shrub in the desert, and shall not see when relief comes. They shall live in the parched places in the wilderness, in an uninhabited salt land. Blessed

are those who trust in the LORD, whose trust is the LORD. They shall be like a tree planted by water, sending out its roots by the stream. It shall not fear when heat comes, and its leaves shall stay green; in the year of drought it is not anxious, and it does not cease to bear fruit. (Jer. 17:5–8)

In essence, Jeremiah was repeating his point about faith in God's provision, which we discussed above in chapters 8–16, with the Sabbath as a case in point. By depending on ourselves instead of being faithful to God, we come to believe that we cannot afford to take time to rest. There is too much work to do if we are to succeed in our careers, in our households, and in our pastimes, so we break the Sabbath to get it done. But according to Jeremiah, if we trust in ourselves and make "mere flesh" our strength, then it will lead to "desert" as we push ourselves relentlessly 24/7 to achieve. We "shall not see when relief comes." In contrast, if we trust in the Lord, we will "not cease to bear fruit." Ignoring our need for balance between work and rest is ultimately counterproductive.

Blessing the Wider Society through Work (Jeremiah 29)

In Jeremiah 29, the prophet draws attention to God's intention that his people's work should bless and serve the communities around them, and not only the people of Israel.

Thus says the LORD of hosts, the God of Israel, to all the exiles whom I have sent into exile from Jerusalem to Babylon: Build houses and live in them; plant gardens and eat what they produce. Take wives and have sons and daughters . . . multiply there and do not decrease. But seek the welfare of the city where I have sent you into exile, and pray to the LORD on its behalf, for in its welfare, you will find your welfare. (Jer. 29:4–7)

This theme was already present in earlier chapters, as in God's command not to oppress the aliens living within Judah's borders (Jer. 7:6; 22:3). And it is a part of the covenant to which Jeremiah kept calling Judah. "Abraham shall become a great and mighty nation, and all the nations of the earth shall be blessed in him" (Gen. 18:18). Nonetheless, false prophets in exile assured the exiled Jews that God's favor would always rest on Israel, to the exclusion of its neighbors. Babylon would fall, Jerusalem would be saved, and the people would soon return home. Jeremiah attempted to counteract that false proclamation with God's true word to them: You will be in exile in Babylon for seventy years (Jer. 29:10).

Babylon would be this generation's only home. God called the people to work the land there diligently: "build houses . . . plant gardens and eat what they produce." The Jews were meant to flourish there as the people of God, even though it was a place of punishment and repentance for them. Moreover, the Jews' success in Babylon was tied to Babylon's success. "Pray to the LORD on its behalf, for in its welfare you will find your welfare" (Jer. 29:7). This call to civic responsibility twenty-six hundred years ago is valid today. We are called to work toward the prosperity of the entire community, not merely for our own limited interests. Like the Jews of Jeremiah's day, we are far from perfect. We may even be suffering for our faithlessness and corruption. Nonetheless, we are called and equipped to be a blessing to the communities in which we live and work.

God called his people to use their various job skills to serve the surrounding community. "Seek the welfare of the city where I have sent you into exile" (Jer. 29:7). It could be argued this passage doesn't prove that God has any real care for the Babylonians. He simply knows that as captives, the Israelites cannot prosper unless their captors do too. But as we have seen, caring for those beyond the people of God is an inherent element of the covenant, and it appears in the earlier teaching of Jeremiah. House builders, gardeners, farmers, and workers of all kinds were explicitly called to work for the good of the whole society in Jeremiah 29. God's provision is so great that even when his people's homes are destroyed, families deported, lands confiscated, rights violated, and peace shattered, they will have enough to prosper themselves and bless others. But only if they depend on God; hence the admonition to prayer in Jeremiah 29:7. In light of Jeremiah 29, it is difficult to read 1 Corinthians 12–14 and the other gifts passages in the New Testament as applying only to the church or to Christians. (See "1 Corinthians" in the *Theology of Work Bible Commentary* for a discussion of this point.) God calls and equips his people to serve the whole world.

God's Presence Everywhere

This should be no surprise, of course, because "the earth is the LORD's and all that is in it, the world, and those who live in it" (Ps. 24:1). God's presence is no longer to be found only in Jerusalem or Judah, but even in the enemy's capital city. We can be a blessing wherever we are because God is with us wherever we are. There in the heart of Babylon, God's people were called to work as in the presence of God. It is hard for us today to understand how shocking this would be to the exiles, who had thought up until then that God was fully present only in the temple in Jerusalem. Now they were told to live in God's presence without the temple and far from Jerusalem.

The feeling of exile is familiar to many working Christians. We are used to finding God's presence in church, among his followers. But in the workplace, working alongside both believers and nonbelievers, we may not expect to find God's presence. This doesn't mean that these institutions are necessarily unethical or hostile to Christians, but simply that they have agendas different from working in God's presence. Nonetheless, God is present, always looking to reveal himself to those who will recognize him there. Settle into the land: plant gardens and eat what they produce, work, and take home your pay. God is there with you.

Blessing for All Peoples

This brings us to an expanded notion of the common good. Pray for Babylon because Israel is intended to be a blessing for all humanity, not just for itself: "In you all the families of the earth shall be blessed" (Gen. 12:3). In the moment of utter defeat came the time they were called upon to bless even their enemies. This blessing included material prosperity, as Jeremiah 29:7 makes clear. How ironic that in chapters 1–25, God withheld his peace and prosperity from Judah because of their faithlessness; yet by chapter 29, God wanted to bless Babylon with peace and prosperity even though the Babylonians had no faith in the God of Judah. Why? Because Israel's proper end was to be a blessing for all nations.

This immediately calls into doubt any scheme designed for the special benefit of Christians. As part of our witness, Christians are called to compete effectively in the marketplace. We cannot run subpar businesses, expecting God to bless us while we underperform. Christians need to compete with excellence on a level playing field if we are to bless the world. Any trade organization, preferred supplier relationship, hiring preference, tax or regulatory advantage, or other system designed to benefit only Christians is not blessing the city. During the Irish famines in the mid-1800s, many Anglican churches provided food only to those who would convert from Roman Catholicism to Protestantism. The ill will this created still reverberates a hundred and fifty years later, and this was merely the self-dealing of one Christian sect against another. Imagine the much greater damage caused by Christians discriminating against non-Christians, which fills the pages of history from antiquity to this day.

The work of Christians in their faithfulness to God is intended for the good of everyone, beginning with those who are not God's people, and extending through them to God's people themselves. This is perhaps the most profound economic principle in Jeremiah: that working for the good of others is the only reliable way to work for your own good. Successful business leaders understand that product development, marketing, sales, and customer support are effective when they put the customer first. Here, surely, is a best practice that can be recognized by all working people, whether Christ-followers or not.

The Goodness of Work Restored (Jeremiah 30–33)

For twenty-three years, Jeremiah prophesied the coming destruction of Jerusalem (from God's case against Judah in chapters 2–28). Then in chapters 30–33, the prophet looked forward to the restoration of God's kingdom. He described it in terms of the joy of work without the defilement of sin:

> Again I will build you, and you shall be built, O virgin Israel! Again you
> shall take your tambourines, and go forth in the dance of the merry-
> makers. Again you shall plant vineyards on the mountains of Samaria;
> the planters shall plant, and shall enjoy the fruit. For there shall be a day
> when sentinels will call in the hill country of Ephraim: "Come, let us go up
> to Zion, to the LORD our God." (Jer. 31:4–6)

Houses and fields and vineyards shall again be bought in this land. (Jer. 32:15)

The overall frame of Jeremiah's prophecies is sin, then exile, then restoration, as we see here. Even the naming here ("virgin Israel") is a statement of renewal in comparison with Jeremiah 2:23–25, 33 and 3:1–5. While restoration in Judah was still far off, the prophet gave a reason for the hope promised to the exiles in 29:11. In the restored world, the people would still work; but while in the past their work led to futility, now they would enjoy the fruit. The restored people would have lives of work, enjoyment, feasting, and worship all tied into one. The picture of planting, harvesting, playing music, dancing, and enjoying the harvest depicts the pleasure of work in faithfulness to God. This remains the Christian vision of God's kingdom, fulfilled partially in the world today and completed in the new creation described in Revelation 21–22.

Faithfulness to God is not a side issue, but the heart of enjoying work and the things produced by work. The "new covenant" described in Jeremiah 31:31–34 and 32:37–41 repeated the importance of faithfulness.

> The days are surely coming, says the LORD, when I will make a new covenant with the house of Israel and the house of Judah. It will not be like the covenant that I made with their ancestors when I took them by the hand to bring them out of the land of Egypt—a covenant that they broke, though I was their husband, says the LORD. But this is the covenant that I will make with the house of Israel after those days, says the LORD: I will put my law within them, and I will write it on their hearts; and I will be their God, and they shall be my people. No longer shall they teach one another, or say to each other, "Know the LORD," for they shall all know me, from the least of them to the greatest. (Jer. 31:31–34)

In one stroke we see a restored world: work enjoyed by the people of God as it always ought to have been, with hearts faithful to the law of the Lord. The people will be restored to what they always ought to have been, working for the common good because of their experience of God's presence in every aspect of life. Robert Carroll remarks, "The rebuilt community is one in which work and worship are integrated."[11] While

---

[11] Robert P. Carroll, *Jeremiah: A Commentary*, Old Testament Library (London: SCM Press, 1986), 590.

we may not expect that this will be fully true for us now because we are still in a world of sin, we can gain glimpses of this reality now.

Slaves Set Free (Jeremiah 34)

One of the final new commands from God in Jeremiah is the renunciation of slavery (Jer. 34:9). The Law of Moses required Hebrew slaves to be set free after six years of service (Exod. 21:2–4; Deut. 15:12). Adults could sell themselves, and parents could sell their children, into servitude for six years. After that they must be released (Lev. 25:39–46). In theory, it was a more humane system than the serfdom or chattel slavery known in the modern era. But it was abused by masters who simply ignored the requirement to set slaves free at the end of the term, or who continually reenrolled slaves into a lifetime of consecutive six-year terms (Jer. 34:16–17).

Jeremiah 34:9 is remarkable because it called for an immediate release of all Hebrew slaves, without regard to how long they had been enrolled. And more dramatically, it provided that "no one should hold another Judean in slavery . . . so that they would not be enslaved again" (Jer. 34:9–10). In other words, it was the abolition of slavery, at least with respect to Jews having Jewish slaves. It is not clear whether this was meant to be a permanent abolition, or whether it was a response to the extreme circumstances of impending military defeat and exile. In any case, it was not enforced for long, and the masters soon re-enslaved their former slaves. But it is a breathtaking economic advance—or it would have been if it had become permanent.

From the beginning, God prohibited lifelong, involuntary slavery among Jews because "you were a slave in the land of Egypt, and the Lord your God redeemed you" (Deut. 15:15). If God stretched out his mighty arm to set a people free, how could he abide them being enslaved again, even by others of the same people? But in Jeremiah 34, God added a new factor: "granting a release to your neighbors and friends" (Jer. 34:17). That is, the humanity of the slaves—referred to by terming them "neighbors and friends"—demanded that they be released. They deserved freedom because they were—or should have been—beloved members of the community. This went beyond religious or racial classification, for people of different religions and races could be friends and neighbors with one another. It had nothing to do with being descendants of the particular nation, Israel, which God set free out of Egypt. Slaves should be set free simply because they were humans, just like their masters and the communities around them.

This underlying principle still applies. The millions of people still enslaved in the world urgently need to be released simply because of their humanity. Moreover *all* workers—not just those bound to their work in slavery—should be treated as "neighbors and friends." This principle applies as strongly against inhumane working conditions, violation of workers' civil rights, unjust discrimination, sexual harassment, and a host of lesser ills as much as it does against slavery per se. Anything we wouldn't subject our neighbors to, anything we wouldn't tolerate happening to our closest friends, we shouldn't tolerate in our companies, organizations, communities, or societies. To the degree that Christians shape the environment in our workplaces, we are under the same mandate as the people of Judah in Jeremiah's time.

Taking a Stand at Work (Jeremiah 38)

The bulk of the rest of Jeremiah describes Jeremiah's trials as a prophet (chapters 35–45), his oracles against the nations (chapters 46–51), and the narrated fall of Jerusalem (chapter 52). One passage stands out with relation to work, the story of Ebed-melech. The narrative is simple: Jeremiah preached to the people as Jerusalem was besieged by the Babylonian army. His message was that the city would fall and anyone who would go out and surrender to the Babylonians would live. The officials of Judah did not take this to be a properly motivational sermon. With the king's permission, they threw Jeremiah into a cistern where, presumably, he would either die of hunger during the siege or drown during the next rain (Jer. 38:1–6).

Then a surprising thing happened. An immigrant named Ebed-melech, a servant in the royal palace, heard that they had put Jeremiah into the cistern. While the king was sitting in the Benjamin Gate,

Ebed-melech went out of the palace and said to him, "My lord king, these men have acted wickedly in all they did to the prophet Jeremiah by throwing him into a cistern to die there of hunger, for there is no bread left in the city." Then the king commanded Ebed-melech, "Take three men with you from here and pull the prophet Jeremiah up from the cistern before he dies" (Jer. 38:7–10).

The turn of the king's decision most likely showed a simple apathy in the matter (though God can use a king's apathy as much as a king's activity). It is the nameless Gentile slave (Ebed-melech simply means "slave of the king") who stands out as faithful.[12] Although his immigration status and racial difference made him a vulnerable worker, his faithfulness to God led him to blow the whistle on injustice in his workplace. As a result, a life was saved. An anonymous cog in the wheel made a life-and-death difference.

Ebed-melech's action on the prophet's behalf illustrated Jeremiah's message that faithfulness to God outweighed all other workplace considerations. Ebed-Melech could not know in advance whether the king would act justly, or whether going outside the chain of command would be a career-limiting move (or a life-ending move, given what happened to Jeremiah). It appears that he trusted God to provide for him, however the king might respond. So Ebed-melech was praised by God. "I will surely save you . . . because you have trusted in me, says the LORD" (Jer. 39:18).

Jeremiah the Poet at Work: Lamentations

While we do not have proof within the Bible itself that the book of Lamentations was written by Jeremiah, rabbinic tradition, the parallel themes in Jeremiah and Lamentations, and the eyewitness character of the laments point to Jeremiah as the likely author of these five poems of lament.[13] Judah and its capital, Jerusalem, have been totally destroyed.

---

[12] "Ebed-melech is a rare man of character in a book filled with evil people and evil behavior. It is ironic that the one man whom we are told trusted God is not an Israelite, but an Ethiopian." Tom Parker, "Ebed-Melech as Exemplar," in *Uprooting and Planting: Essays on Jeremiah for Leslie Allen*, ed. John Goldingay (New York: T&T Clark, 2007), 258.

[13] The construction of these five poems of lament is intricate. Hebrew poetry structurally depends on meter and parallelism rather than on rhyme. Note

After a two-year siege, the Babylonians have captured the city, torn down its walls, looted and destroyed God's temple, and taken the able-bodied citizens into exile in Babylon.

Jeremiah is among the few survivors left in the land, living among those who had clung to life through the famine and watched starving children die, as false prophets continued to mislead the people about God's purposes. The book of Lamentations captures the desolation of the city and the despair of the people at the same time that it underscores the reason for this desolation.

Here we see the poet at work. In five tightly structured poems, he uses powerful images of the carnage in the city as God allows the punishment of his people for their vicious sins. But in spite of the emotional depth of his grief, the artist captures the devastation in a controlled poetic form. This is art in the service of emotional release. While a discussion of "work" doesn't often include the work of artists, these poems force us to acknowledge the power of art to encapsulate the highs and lows of human experience.

The artist embeds a note of hope in this despair, anchoring the future in the goodness of God:

> But this I call to mind, and therefore I have hope: the steadfast love of the LORD never ceases, his mercies never come to an end; they are new every morning; great is your faithfulness. "The LORD is my portion," says my soul, "therefore I will hope in him." The LORD is good to those who wait for him, to the soul that seeks him. (Lam. 3:21–25)

> For the Lord will not reject forever. Although he causes grief, he will have compassion according to the abundance of his steadfast love; for he does not willingly afflict or grieve anyone. (Lam. 3:31–33)

> Why should any who draw breath complain about the punishment of their sins? Let us test and examine our ways, and return to the LORD. Let us lift up our hearts as well as our hands to God in heaven. (Lam. 3:39–41)

---

that chapters 1, 2, 4, and 5 each have 22 verses and, except for chapter 5, they are acrostic: verses begin in order with the 22 letters of the Hebrew alphabet. Chapter 3 is a kind of triple-acrostic with 66 verses instead of 22 (so that vv. 1–3 begin with *aleph*, vv. 4–6 begin with *beth*, etc.).

In the destruction of Jerusalem, the innocent suffered alongside the guilty. Children starved and faithful prophets such as Jeremiah bore the same misery meted out to those whose sins brought an end to the city. This is the reality of life in a fallen world. When corporations collapse under the weight of bad decisions, gross negligence, or outright illegal practices, innocent people lose their jobs and pensions along with those who caused the debacle. At the same time, for the Christian in the workplace, the inequities in this life are not eternal. God reigns and his compassion never fails (Ps. 136). It's not easy to hang onto that divine reality in the midst of sinful systems and unprincipled leaders. But Lamentations tells us, "The Lord will not reject forever." We walk by faith in the living God whose faithfulness to us will not fail.

Ezekiel and Work

Introduction to Ezekiel

"If a man is righteous and does what is lawful and right . . . he shall surely live," says the Lord God. (Ezek. 18:5–9)

Living with God is not just a matter of worship and personal devotion. Living with God is also a matter of living life righteously, whether in the marketplace, at home, in church, or in society. This does not contradict the teaching that salvation comes only by grace through faith in Jesus Christ (Rom. 5:1); rather it points out that life with God begins with belief in Christ, but comes to completion in righteous living in every sphere of life.

The book of Ezekiel gives a compelling account of how the Jewish people suffer a severely diminished life of deprivation and oppression—and even death—as captives in the conquering empire of Babylon. When they question why God has allowed them to suffer this way, Ezekiel speaks God's answer: Because of their unjust ways of living (Ezek. 18:1–17). Israel's unrighteous ways encompassed every sphere of life: marriage and sexuality, worship and idolatry, commerce and government.

Our focus is on workplace practices, and Ezekiel has much to say about the workplace. His words touch on finance and debt, economic development, honesty, allocation of capital, workplace evaluations, fair return on investment, economic opportunism, success and failure, whistle-blowing, teamwork, executive compensation, and corporate governance. In addition, the dramatic call of Ezekiel to become a prophet gives us one example of how God calls someone to a particular kind of work.

Ezekiel's Call to Become a Prophet (Ezekiel 1–17)

Let us begin, as the book of Ezekiel does, with God's call to Ezekiel to become a prophet. When we meet Ezekiel, as a descendant of Jacob's son Levi, he is a priest by profession (Ezek. 1:2). As such, his day-to-day work had previously consisted of slaughtering, butchering, and roasting the sacrificial animals brought by worshipers to the temple in Jerusalem. As a priest, he also served as a moral and spiritual guide to the people, teaching them God's law and adjudicating disputes (Lev. 10:11; Deut. 17:8–10; 33:10).

But this priesthood was violently interrupted when he was taken as a captive to Babylon in the first deportation of Jews from Jerusalem in 605 BC. In Babylon, the Jewish community in exile was preoccupied with two questions: "Has God been unjust to us?" and "What did we do to deserve this?" Psalm 137:1–4 captures well the desolation of these exiled Jews:

> By the rivers of Babylon—there we sat down and there we wept when we remembered Zion. On the willows there we hung up our harps. For there our captors asked us for songs, and our tormentors asked for mirth, saying, "Sing us one of the songs of Zion!" How could we sing the LORD's song in a foreign land?

In exile in Babylon, Ezekiel receives a dramatic call from God. Like Isaiah's call (Isa. 6:1–8), Ezekiel's begins with a vision of God (Ezek. 1:4–2:8) and concludes with God's command to become a prophet. Direct calls to a particular kind of work are rare in the Bible, and Ezekiel's is one of the most dramatic. Although Ezekiel's original profession was the priesthood, God called him to a prophetic career that was as much political as religious. It is fitting that the vision in which he received his call includes political symbols such as chariot wheels (Ezek. 1:16), an army (Ezek. 1:24), a throne (Ezek. 1:26), and a sentinel (Ezek. 3:16), but no priestly symbols. Ezekiel's call should dispel any notion that calls from God are generally calls away from secular professions and into church ministry.[1] Or to put it more precisely, Ezekiel, like all of ancient Israel, doesn't regard *any* occupation as secular. Whatever work we do

---

[1] See "Calling" under "Key Topics" at www.theologyofwork.org.

is a reflection of our relationship with God. There is no need to change occupations to do God-serving work.

Ezekiel's prophetic career begins in Babylonian exile eleven years before the final destruction of Jerusalem. His first charge from God is to refute the empty promises of false prophets who were assuring the exiles that Babylon would be defeated and that they would soon go home. In the opening chapters of the book, Ezekiel is shown a series of visions depicting the horrors of the siege of Jerusalem and then the slaughter in the capture of the city.

Israel's Responsibility for Its Predicament (Ezekiel 18)

The exiled Jews' question "What did we do to deserve this?" comes out of the mistaken belief that they were being punished for their ancestors' actions rather than their own. We see this in the false proverb they quote: "The parents have eaten sour grapes, and the children's teeth are set on edge" (Ezek. 18:2). God rejects this accusation. The issue at stake is the exiles' refusal to take responsibility for their predicament, blaming it on the sins of previous generations.[2] God makes it clear, however, that each individual will be evaluated according to his own actions, whether righteous or wicked. The metaphor involving a righteous man (Ezek. 18:5–9), his sinful son (Ezek. 18:10–13), and his righteous grandson (Ezek. 18:14–17) illustrates that people are not held accountable for the morality of their ancestors. God holds each individual "soul" accountable.[3] Yet scholars are right to note that Ezekiel is still communal in focus.[4]

Righteousness is required individual by individual, but God's restoration will not occur until the entire nation of individuals adopts righteous living. In this way, God required righteous living and accountability from the exiles as a whole, independent of previous generations.

---

[2] Katheryn Pfisterer Darr, "Proverb Performance and Transgenerational Retribution in Ezekiel 18," in *Tiered Reality*, 209, nt. 63, 509–10.

[3] See *nephesh* in 18:4, 20, 27.

[4] Joel S. Kaminsky, *Corporate Responsibility in the Hebrew Bible* (Sheffield: Sheffield Academic Press, 1995), 177–78.

Ezekiel 18:5–9 notes a range of cultic and moral actions, both righteous and wicked. These actions become the principles by which a person is said to "live" or "die." Four of these actions are related to work: restoring a debtor's pledge, providing for the poor, not charging excessive interest, and working justly. Failure to uphold just and righteous standards—or even worse, shedding the blood of another person indiscriminately—will incur the "death penalty" (Ezek. 18:13).

The Righteous Man Does Not Oppress, But Restores to the Debtor His Pledge (Ezek. 18:5, 7)

This principle combines the general sin of oppression (Heb. *daka*) with the specific sin of not returning something taken in pledge (*ḥăbōl*) for a loan. To understand and apply this principle, we begin with the Israelite law regarding lending, summarized in *The Anchor Yale Bible Dictionary* this way:

> The necessity for loans is recognized openly in the Hebrew Bible, where an attempt is made to prevent the practice of requiring interest from debtors. Interest on loans in the ancient Near East could be exorbitant by modern standards (and might be required in advance, from the very principal of the loan). The attempt to convince creditors to forego potential profit was grounded in care for the community, which God had liberated from slavery. A brother might become poor and need a loan, but interest was not to be exacted, in the name of the same LORD "who brought you out of the land of Egypt" (Lev. 25:35–38). The desire for interest is seen as posing the danger that Israel might exchange one form of slavery for another—economic— form of oppression. It is notable that the whole of Leviticus 25 concerns precisely the issue of maintaining the integrity of what God had redeemed, in respect of the release which was to occur during sabbath and jubilee years (Lev. 25:1–34), in respect of loans (Lev. 25:35–38), and in respect of hired service (Lev. 25:39–55). The right of a creditor to receive a pledge against his loan is implicitly acknowledged within the pristine requirement not to expect interest, and abusive liberties with pledges received is forbidden (cf. Exod. 22:25–27; Deut. 24:10–13). But certain pledges, correctly handled, might yield their own profits, and foreigners in any case might be charged interest (cf. Deut. 23:19–20); even on a strict interpretation of the Torah, a creditor might make a living.[5]

---

[5] Bruce Chilton, "Debts," in *The Anchor Yale Bible Dictionary*, ed. David Noel Freedman, vol. 2 (New York: Doubleday, 1996), 114.

According to the Mosaic Law, it was generally not legal for a lender to take permanent possession of an item pledged in surety for a loan. Modern banking laws generally do permit lenders to retain (as in pawn shops) or repossess (as in auto loans and home mortgages) items given in surety. Whether the entire modern surety system is anti-biblical is beyond the scope of this chapter.[6]

Modern laws also place limits or regulate the process under which a lender can take possession of surety. It is generally illegal, for example, for a lender to occupy a mortgaged house and force the borrower out while the borrower is under court protection during bankruptcy proceedings. For a lender to do so anyway would be a form of oppression. It could occur only if the lender has the power and impunity to operate outside the law.

At the most basic level, in Ezekiel 18:7 God is saying, "Don't break the law in pursuit of what might seem rightfully yours, even if you have the power to get away with it." In real-life commercial practices, most lenders (loan sharks aside) don't forcibly repossess sureties outside the law. So perhaps Ezekiel 18:7 has nothing challenging for modern readers in legitimate enterprises.

But the application is broader than merely not breaking ancient Israel's lending laws. Underlying the whole Old Testament law on lending is the presumption that loans are made primarily for the good of the borrower, not the lender. The reason you lend people money on the surety of their cloak, even though you can keep the cloak only until sunset, is that you have extra money and the borrower is in need. As a lender, you have the right to an assurance that you will get your money back, but only if it has benefitted the borrower sufficiently so that he or she can pay you back. You shouldn't make a loan you know the borrower is unlikely to be able to repay, because you can't keep the collateral indefinitely.

This has obvious applications in the mortgage crisis of 2008–2009. Subprime lenders made home loans they knew millions of borrowers would likely fail to repay. To recoup their investment, the lenders relied on rising home prices, plus the ability to force a sale or repossess the

---

[6]This issue is addressed in "Financial Arrangements" in "Key Topics" at www.theologyofwork.org.

property in the likelihood of the borrower's default. The loans were made without regard to the borrower's benefit, so long as they benefitted the lenders. That at least was the intent. In reality, the sudden appearance of hundreds of thousands of foreclosed properties on the market depressed property values so low that lenders lost money even after repossessing the properties. God's declaration circa 580 BC that the oppressor's "blood shall be upon himself" (Ezek. 18:13) turned out to be true for the banking system circa AD 2000.

God's denunciation of arrangements that provide no benefit for buyers doesn't have to be limited to securitized debt obligations. Ezekiel 18:7 is about loans, but the same principle applies to products of all kinds. Withholding information about product flaws and risks, selling more expensive products than the buyer needs, mismatching the product's benefits to the buyer's needs—all of these practices are similar to the oppression depicted in Ezekiel 18:7. They can creep into even well-intentioned businesses, unless the seller makes the buyer's well-being an inviolable goal of the sales transaction. To care for the buyer is to "live," in the terminology of Ezekiel.

The Righteous Man Does Not Steal, But Instead Feeds the Hungry and Clothes the Naked (Ezekiel 18:7b)

This may seem like an odd pairing. Who could argue with the prohibition against robbery? But how is robbery connected with the obligation to give food to the hungry and provide clothing for the naked? As with Ezekiel 18:7a, the connection is the requirement to care about the economic well-being of the other. In this case, however, the "other" is not the counterparty to a commercial transaction, but simply another person encountered in the course of daily life. If you meet people with an item they need but you desire, you are not permitted to rob them of it. If you meet people who lack an item they need but you possess in excess, you are required to give it to them, or at least meet needs as basic as food and clothing.

Behind this somewhat jarring admonition lies God's economic law: we are stewards, not owners, of all that we have. We are to see wealth as *common*-wealth because all that we have is God's gift for the purpose that there not be any poor among us (Deut. 6:10–15; 15:1–18). This is clear in the laws requiring the canceling of debts every seven years and the redistribution of accumulated wealth in the Year of Jubilee (Lev. 25). Once every fifty years, God's people were to rebalance wealth in the land as a remedy to the evils that are endemic in human society. In the intervening years, they were to live as stewards of all they possessed:

> You shall not cheat one another, but you shall fear your God; for I am the Lord your God. You shall observe my statutes and faithfully keep my ordinances, so that you may live on the land securely. (Lev. 25:17–18)

> The land shall not be sold in perpetuity, for the land is mine; with me you are but aliens and tenants. (Lev. 25:23)

> If any of your kin fall into difficulty and become dependent on you, you shall support them; they shall live with you as though resident aliens. Do not take interest in advance or otherwise make a profit from them, but fear your God; let them live with you. You shall not lend them your money at interest taken in advance, or provide them food at a profit. I am the Lord your God, who brought you out of the land of Egypt, to give you the land of Canaan, to be your God. (Lev. 25:35–38)

Ezekiel's decree in Ezekiel 18:7b is not directly related to the theology of work because it has little to do with the actual production of things of value. Instead, it is a part of the theology of wealth, the stewardship and disposition of things of value. But there can be a connection. What if you were to work for the purpose of meeting someone else's needs rather than your own? While that precludes robbery, it would also motivate you to work in such a way that provided food, clothing, and other necessities for people in need. An example would be a pharmaceutical company that puts a compassionate-use policy into the planning of a new drug. So would a retail company that makes affordability a key element of its business model. Conversely, this principle seems to rule out a business that can succeed only by charging high prices for products that do not meet real needs, such as a pharmaceutical company that produces trivial reformulations in order to extend the terms of its patents.

The Righteous Man Does Not Take Advance or Accrued Interest (Ezekiel 18:8a)

Biblical scholars have given much time to researching and speculating about whether charging interest is absolutely forbidden by Old Testament law. The most natural translation of Ezekiel 18:8a may be the NASB: "He does not lend money on interest or take increase." Until well after the Reformation, Christians universally understood the Bible to prohibit charging interest on loans. Of course, this would severely hamper the productive deployment of capital, both in modern and ancient times, and contemporary interpreters seem disposed to soften the prohibition to excessive interest, as the NRSV does. To justify this further softening, some have argued that origination discounts (what we now call "zero-coupon bonds") were permitted in ancient Israel, and that only *additional* interest was forbidden, even if the loan was not repaid in a timely manner.[7] As with the topic of surety above, it is beyond the scope of this chapter to assess the legitimacy of the entire modern system of interest.[8] Instead, let us look at the outcome in either case.

If the stricter interpretation holds, then people with money will face the choice of whether or not to lend money at all. If they are not allowed to take interest, and not allowed to repossess surety, then they may prefer not to lend to anyone. But that answer is forbidden by God: "You should rather open your hand, willingly lending enough to meet the need, whatever it may be" (Deut. 15:8). In Luke 6:35, Jesus repeats and even expands this command: "Love your enemies, do good, and lend, expecting nothing in return." The loan is primarily for the benefit of the borrower, not the lender. The lender's fear that it may not be repaid must remain a minor concern. The potential lender has the capital, and the potential borrower needs it.

On the other hand, if we accept that the modern system of interest is legitimate, then this principle still applies. Capital must be invested productively; it cannot be hoarded because of fear. This is the literal mean-

---

[7] *Oriental and Biblical Studies: Collected Writings of E. A. Speiser*, ed. J. J. Finkelstein and Moshe Greenberg (Philadelphia: University of Pennsylvania Press, 1967), 131–33, 140–41.

[8] See "Financial Arrangements" in "Key Topics" at www.theologyofwork.org.

ing of Jesus' parable of the talents (Matt. 25:14–30). God has promised Israel, his treasured possession, that he will provide for their needs. If individuals find themselves with capital to spare, they owe it to the God of provision to employ it—whether by just investment or by donation—for the provision of those who are in need. Economic development is not forbidden—just the opposite: it is required. But it must be of productive benefit for those who need capital, and not merely for the self-interest of those who possess capital.

The Righteous Man Does No Wrong, But Judges Fairly Between Parties (Ezekiel 18:8b)

As he did earlier in the book, here Ezekiel presents his readers with a general rule (not doing wrong) connected to a specific rule (judging fairly between individuals). Once again, the unifying principle is that the person with more power must care about the need of the person with less power. In this case, the power involved is the power to judge between people. Every day most of us face moments when we have the power to judge between one person and another. It could be as small as deciding whose voice prevails in choosing where to have lunch. It could be as large as deciding whom to believe in an accusation of improper conduct. Seldom do we realize that each time we make a decision like this, we exercise the power to judge.

Many serious problems at work arise because people feel that they are consistently judged to be less important than others around them. That may stem from formal or official judgments, such as performance reviews, project decisions, employee awards, or promotions. Or it may stem from informal judgments, such as who pays attention to their ideas or how often they are the butt of jokes. In either case, God's people have an obligation to be aware of these kinds of judgments and to be fair in how they participate in them. It could be interesting to keep a record of how many judgments (large or small) we participate in during a single day, then ask how the righteous person in Ezekiel 18:8b would act in each one.

Ezekiel 18 is more than a set of rules for living in exile; it is an answer to the despair the exiles feel, expressed in the Ezekiel 18:2 proverb, "The parents have eaten sour grapes and the children's teeth are set on edge."[9] The argument of chapter 18 refutes the proverb, but not by eliminating transgenerational retribution altogether. Instead, the lesson of personal moral responsibility replies to exilic despair (see Ps. 137) and to questions of theodicy seen in the refrain, "The way of the Lord is unfair" (Ezek. 18:25, 29). In response to the exiles' questions— "If we are God's people, why are we in exile?" "Why are we suffering?" "Does God care?"—the Lord rebuts not with an answer, but with a call to live justly.

In the time between past transgression and future restoration, between promise and fulfillment, between question and answer, the exiles are to live justly.[10] It is here that meaning, purpose, and ultimate payoff can be found. God is not simply repeating laws of good and bad behavior for individuals to follow. Instead, he is calling for a national life of righteousness, when Israel will finally be "my people" (Ezek. 11:20; 14:11; 36:28; 37:23, 27).[11]

The marks of righteousness in Ezekiel 18 provide a representative sample of life in the new covenant when the community is characterized by "lawful" ethics (Ezek. 18:5, 19, 21, 27). The reader is challenged to live the new covenant life now as a means to secure hope for the future. In our day, Christians are members of the new covenant with the same call in Matthew 5:17–20 and 22:37–40. In this way, Ezekiel 18 is surprisingly instructional and transferable to our own lives in the workplace, no matter the venue.[12] Living out this personal righteousness in our professional pursuits adds life and meaning to our present

---

[9] One could argue that the problem was not with the proverb itself, but rather with the inappropriate application of it to the circumstances in exile. See Peter Enns, *Inspiration and Incarnation: Evangelicals and the Problem of the Old Testament* (Grand Rapids: Baker, 2005), 74.

[10] On this and the integration of theodicy and ethics, see Gordon H. Matties, *Ezekiel 18 and the Rhetoric of Moral Discourse*, Society of Biblical Literature Dissertation Series 126 (Atlanta: Scholars Press, 1990), 223–24.

[11] The false proverb of 18:2 is repeated in Jeremiah 31:29–31, where God explicitly contradicts it with the promise of "a new covenant" with Israel in the future. When Israel stops trying to shift the blame to its ancestors, then "the days are surely coming," says the Lord, "when I will make a new covenant with the house of Israel." This covenant will accomplish the fulfillment of God's promises and the forgiveness of Israel's sins (Jer. 31:34).

[12] Matties, 222; Darr, 223.

circumstances because it assumes a better tomorrow, ushers the future kingdom of God into the present, and provides a glimpse of what God anticipates from his people as a whole. God rewards such behavior, the type of which is possible only by means of new hearts and spirits (Ezek. 18:31–32; 2 Cor. 3:2–6).

Israel's Systemic Breakdown (Ezekiel 22)

If the exiled Jews in Babylon missed the positive example in chapter 18, then Ezekiel 22 gives them an explicit picture of where the nation went off the rails set by God. Jerusalem is the setting as the prophet looks at the political, economic, and religious factors that led to its ultimate destruction. According to Robert Linthicum, the purpose of the *political* system is to establish a politics of justice and obedience to God (Deut. 16:18–20; 17:8–18). The *economic* system is called to maintain an economics of stewardship and generosity (Deut. 6:10–15; 15:1–18). The *religious* system is primarily responsible to bring people into a relationship with God and to ground the political and economic systems in God (Deut. 10:12; 11:28). Religion provides the fences for the community and gives meaning to life. The political system provides the process, and the economic system supports the community. When the religious system gets out of order, everything else is up for grabs.[13] According to God's law, the disparity between rich and poor (wealth and poverty) is a direct indicator of a nation's or a community's distance from God.

In Ezekiel 22, the prophet now shows the exiled Jews why God's judgment on their nation must come: from the princes to the priests to the false prophets to all the people of the land, "you have all become dross" (Ezek. 22:19). God's patience has reached its end, and the wages of every form of "business" sin will bring death and destruction on the perpetrators. What is included in this catalog of sins? The use of power to shed blood (Ezek. 22:6); treating parents with contempt, oppressing the foreigner, and mistreating the fatherless and widows (Ezek. 22:7); slandering with a goal of shedding blood (Ezek. 22:9); sexual sins and

---

[13] Robert Linthicum, *City of God, City of Satan: A Biblical Theology for the Urban Church* (Grand Rapids: Zondervan, 1991).

harassment (Ezek. 22:11); charging interest and making a profit on the poor, extorting unjust gain (Ezek. 22:12); conspiring to ravage the people, taking treasures and many precious things, and making many widows in the process (Ezek. 22:25); doing violence to the law, profaning holy things, teaching error and shutting their eyes to God's Sabbaths (Ezek. 22:8, 26); officials like wolves tearing their prey for unjust gain (Ezek. 22:27); prophets whitewashing these deeds (cover-up) with false visions and lying divinations (Ezek. 22:28); and the people of the land practicing extortion, robbery, oppressing the poor and needy, mistreating foreigners, and denying them justice (Ezek. 22:29).

In the end, God looked for just one righteous person who would stand in the gap, but there was no one. It is this total disregard for righteous relationships that brings God's wrath and punishment. The chapter ends (Ezek. 22:31) with God removing his protective hand from the people as they self-destruct. How does God bring judgment? He lets the systems take their natural course without intervening. The downward spiral ends in destruction.

Ezekiel's words remain applicable to us today. There are still people who profit from illegal activities such as extortion, robbery, fraud, slander, and violence. More troubling, though, is the variety of ways people find to remain within the law while perpetrating injustice in the pursuit of gain. Targeting unsophisticated consumers for high-cost loans and financial instruments, unhealthful food and drink, and overpriced goods and services. Using lawsuits, imbalanced contract clauses, intimidating letters, and other tactics to prevent vulnerable people from exercising their legal rights. Engaging in deceptive advertising and sales practices. Cheating on taxes, hiding income, obtaining false qualifications for benefits. Failing to honor promises. If God were looking for even one righteous person today, would there be anyone who has always dealt uprightly in business and finance?

Where Does Success Come From? (Ezekiel 26–28)

The oracles against Tyre in Ezekiel 26–28 give a further example of unrighteous living. The Tyrians gloat over Jerusalem's destruction, anticipating profit in the absence of a trade competitor (Ezek. 26:2). God promises their punishment and humiliation (Ezek. 26:7–21) for failing to aid Judah in its time of need. "Tyre may be taken to represent the pursuit—through affluence, political prominence, even culture—of a security and autonomy that contradict the nature of created reality."[14] In reality, no person or nation can truly assure its own security and prosperity. Yet Tyre boasts of its commercial success, perfection, and abundance (Ezek. 27:2–4). This maritime powerhouse had become such by trading with (or taking advantage of) a plethora of peoples across the Mediterranean world (Ezek. 27:5–25), only to sink under the weight of its profuse cargo. Tyre's overconfidence and selfish dealings end with a shipwreck that draws the ridicule of the nations' merchants (Ezek. 27:26–36). God calls Tyre to account for her arrogance and material craving, climaxing with a poem against the king of Tyre in chapter 28. The king credits his own godlike status for having the ingenuity and wisdom to garner great prominence and material achievements.

Powerful figures today are also tempted to ascribe their success to divine favor or status. Goldman Sachs CEO Lloyd Blankfein noted the vital service that bankers provide by raising capital that helps companies grow, produce goods and services, and create jobs. But when the issue turned to record-breaking pay in the banking sector, his statement that "we are doing God's work" seemed to many to cross the line into self-idolization. Ezekiel's words still remind us that every sphere of work has the potential both for serving God's purposes and for rationalizing our own excesses.

The lessons from chapters 26 to 28 for working in the world are significant. God forbids us to imagine that we are the primary source of success at work. While our hard work, skill, perseverance, and other virtues contribute to success at work, they do not cause it. Underlying even the most successful self-made person is a universe of opportunities, fortuitous circumstances, others' labor, and the fact that our very existence comes from beyond ourselves.

Attributing success solely to ourselves leads to a hubris that breaks our relationship with God. Instead of thanking God for our success and

---

[14] Joseph Blenkinsopp, *Ezekiel*, Interpretation (Louisville: John Knox Press, 1990), 118.

trusting him to continue to provide for us, we think that we have succeeded on our own merits. But we don't have the power to control all circumstances, possibilities, people, and events on which our success depends. By attributing our success to ourselves, we force ourselves to try to control uncontrollable factors, creating severe pressure to stack the deck in our favor. While we may have succeeded in the past through honest, legitimate business dealings, we may now try to improve the odds by shading the truth in our favor, by rigging the bidding behind the scenes, by manipulating others into doing our will, or by currying favor with others with a few well-placed bribes. Even if we manage to stay on the right side of the law, we may become ruthless and "violent" (Ezek. 28:16) in our pursuit of trade.

The truly wise behave righteously, and in their thinking do not usurp the place of God while waiting for God to fulfill his promises. They remain true to their covenant with God, who will reward faithful living with the benefits appropriate to fulfilling the covenant (see the hope for Israel in Ezek. 28:22–26). God will ultimately separate the righteous and the wicked (Ezek. 34:17–22; cf. Matt. 25:31–46). This gives great hope to "exiles" who await the consummation of God's kingdom, whether they live in the ancient world or the modern world, especially when asking questions of justice and despair.[15]

The Call to Warn Others (Ezekiel 33)

Ezekiel 18 and 33 serve similar thematic and structural functions within the book as a whole.[16] The call to personal righteousness in order to "live" and the call to repent amid questions of God's justice first presented in chapter 18 are reviewed in chapter 33 in almost verbatim fashion.[17] However, chapter 33 introduces another idea not found in chapter 18: in Ezekiel 33:1–9, God reviews Ezekiel's call to be a watchman or

---

[15] See the same in Malachi 3:13–18.

[16] See Preston Sprinkle, "Law and Life: Leviticus 18.5 in the Literary Framework of Ezekiel," *Journal for the Study of the Old Testament* 31, no. 3 (March 2007): 275–93.

[17] Cf. esp., 18:21–22, cf. 33:14–16; 18:23, cf. 33:11; 18:24, cf. 33:12–13; 18:25–29, cf. 33:17–20.

sentinel for the nation as first established in chapter 3.[18] Like a watchman at the city gate, responsible for warning the city's inhabitants of enemy threat, Ezekiel is personally responsible for proclaiming God's impending judgment and encouraging repentance in order to relieve himself of blame:

> So you, mortal, I have made a sentinel for the house of Israel; whenever you hear a word from my mouth, you shall give them warning from me. If I say to the wicked, "O wicked ones, you shall surely die," and you do not speak to warn the wicked to turn from their ways, the wicked shall die in their iniquity, but their blood I will require at your hand. But if you warn the wicked to turn from their ways, and they do not turn from their ways, the wicked shall die in their iniquity, but you will have saved your life. (Ezek. 33:7–9)

This is an important addition to the call to righteousness introduced in Ezekiel 18 and recalled in chapter 33 on the eve of Jerusalem's destruction (Ezek. 33:21–22). God requires the sentinel to play an important role in the appeal to individual and corporate righteousness by taking personal responsibility and ownership of the exiles' repentance.

We are to identify not only with Ezekiel's audience (Ezek. 18) but also with Ezekiel himself. We accept the God-given task of calling others to live justly and return to a right relationship with God. In the Old Testament, a few individuals were called to be prophets with the mandate to bring God's word home to his people. But as members of the new covenant, all Christians are called to the prophet's job. The prophet Joel foresaw this when he spoke God's word thus, "I will pour out my Spirit on all flesh; your sons and your daughters shall prophesy, your old men shall dream dreams, and your young men shall see visions" (Joel 2:28). The Apostle Peter announced this as a present reality on the day of Pentecost (Acts 2:33).[19]

The prophetic responsibility of all Christians yields several lessons for a theology of work and bears on our witness in the workplace. God calls each of us to take personal responsibility for the fate of others. We

---

[18] Cf. esp., 3:17–19, cf. 33:7–9.

[19] For more on this, see R. Paul Stevens, *The Other Six Days* (Grand Rapids: Eerdmans, 2000), 169–73.

are to be sentinels in our own right as we hold ourselves accountable for the people around us. Not only are their lives at stake; ours are as well (Ezek. 33:9).

This does not come to us naturally in an age and culture that cherishes individualism. But God will indeed hold us accountable for the righteous living of others. As it was in Babylon, so it is now—the structures of society often tempt us to acquiesce in abusive or unfair practices. In terms of the workplace, this means that Christians bear personal responsibility to work for justice in their workplaces. This raises a few questions we may want to ask ourselves about this responsibility. For example:

- *Are we speaking God's words to people we work with?* Christians in every workplace observe—and feel pressure to participate in—things we know are not compatible with God's word. Do we put God's truth above the apparent comfort of fitting in? This is not a call to judgmentalism at work, but it may mean standing up for the person being scapegoated for the department's failure, or being the first to vote in favor of dropping a misleading advertising campaign. It could mean admitting your own role in perpetrating an office conflict or voicing confidence that writing an honest performance review will ultimately be worth the pain it seems to incur. These are ways of speaking God's words to others at work.

- *Are our lives illustrations of God's message?* We communicate not only in words but in actions as well. Throughout his ministry, Ezekiel was literally a walking, visual illustration of God's promises and judgments. A Silicon Valley CFO was asked by her CEO to "find" $2 million of additional profit to add to the quarterly report due in one week. The CFO knew it would require inaccurately categorizing certain expenses as investments, and certain investments as revenues. During the week she happened to have her monthly meeting with other Christian CFOs. They gave her the courage to stand up to her CEO. On the day the report was due, she told the CEO, "Here is the report with the additional $2 million of profit as you requested. It might even be legal, but it's not truly accurate. I can't sign it, so I know you will have to fire me." Her CEO's response? "If you won't sign it, then I won't either. I depend on you to know what you're doing. Bring me the original accurate report and we'll issue that and take our lumps for not meeting forecast profitability."[20] In both her words and actions, this CFO illustrated living according to God's word and that influenced the CEO to do the same.

Ezekiel 33 demonstrates that while each individual is called to personal righteousness, prophets are also responsible to warn fellow exiles to act rightly. The sentinel metaphor in Ezekiel 33 reflects God's expectation for our vested interest in the lives of others within our working world. This sets the stage for a similar idea in the next chapter, where the metaphor changes.

Israel's Failure of Leadership (Ezekiel 34)

Israel's leaders are indicted for their failure to care for the nation. Ezekiel 34 uses the metaphor of shepherding to illustrate how Israel's leaders (shepherds) oppressed the people (flock) within God's kingdom. The shepherds looked only to their own interests by clothing and feeding themselves at the expense of the needs of the flock (Ezek. 34:2–3, 8). Instead of strengthening and healing the sheep in their time of need, or pursuing them when lost, the shepherds fiercely dominated them (Ezek. 34:4). This left the sheep vulnerable to wild beasts (hostile nations) and scattered them throughout the world (Ezek. 34:5–6, 8). Thus God promises to save the sheep from the "mouths" of the shepherds (Israel's rulers), to search and care for his sheep, and to bring them back from where they were scattered (Ezek. 34:9–12). He will lead them back to their own land, feed them, and have them lie down in safety in good grazing ground (Ezek. 34:13–14). Ultimately, God will judge between the fat sheep (beneficiaries and participants in the oppression) and the lean sheep (the weak and oppressed, Ezek. 34:15–22). This deliverance climaxes with the future appointment of the ultimate shepherd, a second

---

[20] Reported to the executive editor of the Theology of Work Project on the condition of anonymity.

David, who will feed and care for God's flock as a prince should under God's kingship (Ezek. 34:23–24).[21] This will mark a time when God will make a covenant of peace with his sheep/people that will ensure God's blessings of protection, fruitfulness, and freedom in the land (Ezek. 34:25–31). By this all will know that God is with his people and is their true God (Ezek. 34:30–31).

The shepherding metaphor sends a message promising judgment on Israel's wicked rulers and hope for the downtrodden and disadvantaged of the nation. This message of leadership, drawn from shepherding, is applicable to other occupations. Good leaders seek the interest of others before "feeding" themselves. Leadership that imitates "the Good Shepherd" of John 10:11, 14 is fundamentally an office of servanthood that requires genuine care for the well-being of subordinates. Managing people is not about power trips or holding one's authority over others. Rather, godly supervisors seek to ensure that the people under their care are flourishing. This is consistent with best management practices taught at business schools and employed in many companies. But godly people do it out of faithfulness to God, not because it is accepted practice in their organizations.

Andrew Mein contends that most readers "pay too little attention to the way economic realities may inform any specific use of a metaphor, with the result that all of the biblical images of shepherding collapse into a rather monochrome picture of caring generosity."[22] While Ezekiel 34 reflects God's care for his sheep (like other shepherding passages, e.g., Jer. 23; Ps. 23; John 10), the chapter specifically reflects more about the economics of ancient sheepherding and thus applies more specifically to a leader's economic responsibilities. The shepherds have violated the economics of their obligations by "failing to produce the required return on an investment and misappropriation of the owner's property."[23] God holds them responsible while reclaiming his flock. It is too little merely

---

[21]The Davidic prince is certainly to be contrasted with the prince(s) of Israel denounced in Ezek. 19:1; 21:17, 30; 22:6.

[22]Andrew Mein, "Profitable and Unprofitable Shepherds: Economic and Theological Perspectives on Ezekiel 34," *Journal for the Study of the Old Testament* 31, no. 4 (June 2007): 496.

[23]Mein, 500.

to say that the shepherds of Israel have failed to look after the interest of the sheep. Rather, the shepherds have not worked for the interests of the sheep's owner who hired them and who expects a valuable return on his investment. This understanding could be applied today to questions of executive compensation and corporate governance. Ezekiel provides no general pronouncement on such issues, but provides criteria by which each corporation's practices could be assessed.

Thus Ezekiel 34 is a rich text for a theology of work. Leaders are to care for the needs and interests of those under their leadership (Phil. 2:3–4). Beyond that, they are responsible to accomplish the economic task they have been hired to do. We are to work for the profit and welfare of those who stand on rungs both above and below us on the corporate ladder (Eph. 6:5–9; Col. 3:22–24). Ultimately, all should work for the honor to which God is entitled.

In this light, profit or economic productivity is seen as a godly pursuit. Churches often seem to forget this, as if profit were a neutral or barely tolerable by-product of Christian work. But Ezekiel 34 implies that the worker who produces an economic loss or the manager who fails to get the team to accomplish the job is no better than those who mistreat co-workers or subordinates. Both the people and the job are important. When centuries later Paul writes, "Whatever your task, put yourselves into it, as done for the Lord and not for your masters" (Col. 3:23), he is standing in Ezekiel's shoes. Do the work you are paid to do (which includes making a profit as an inalienable component) as working for the Lord. If you work in a for-profit enterprise, then you are responsible to God for helping to make a profit.

But if profit is an obligation to God, then the Christian is obligated to pursue only godly profits. As followers of Jesus, we owe our company a good day's work—a properly executed sales plan, a sturdy framing job, or whatever our work product is. Employers should learn to expect that from us. Also, as followers of Jesus we can never provide our company with a false environmental statement, never mislead employees or take advantage of their ignorance, and never cover up a quality control problem. Employers should expect that from us as well. What makes us good and productive workers, loyal to our companies, also makes us honest and compassionate workers, committed to our Lord.

Israel's Covenantal Hope (Ezekiel 35–48)

Ezekiel's theology of work would be incomplete if not placed in the full context of the future restoration alluded to throughout the book. The covenant between God and Israel seems broken by Israel's failure to fulfill its obligations. But God will restore Israel and fulfill his promises when Israel returns to him. This fulfillment is climactically expressed in the restoration oracles and new temple section of the book (chapters 35–48). Here the reader sees a more thorough picture of the future that the faithful exile is to herald in the present through righteous living and corporate responsibility.

The promise of a Davidic shepherd in the future age of restoration is inherent to God's "covenant of peace" with Israel (Ezek. 34:25) and is called an "everlasting covenant" (Ezek. 37:24–26). Ezekiel looks forward to a day when this royal shepherd-king will usher in God's promised blessing for Israel and, more importantly, lead them into fulfilling their calling as "God's people."[24] Ezekiel is clear that God grants this by giving them an undivided heart and a new spirit to fulfill his laws as he commanded in Ezekiel 18:31 (see also Ezek. 11:19–20; 36:26–28; 39:29). God's people will be fully equipped for doing his will and will be sanctified by the presence of God in the new sanctuary in their midst (Ezek. 37:28). Ezekiel spends nine chapters mapping out this new temple for the day of restoration and the worship required (Ezek. 40–48). In light of the close parallels between Ezekiel 38–48 and Revelation 20–22, we may wonder if Ezekiel's vision anticipates a literal restoration of the temple, or whether this points to the greater reality of the New Jerusalem in which there is no temple "for its temple is the Lord God the Almighty and the Lamb" (Rev. 21:22).

As Christians, we place our trust in the ultimate shepherding of Christ. It is he who not only fulfilled individual righteousness, but also took full corporate responsibility for humanity by shedding his own blood on our behalf. By Jesus' death and resurrection, Ezekiel's day of covenant fulfillment has dawned for the Christian. But the day is not

---

[24] See Rolf Rendtorff, *The Covenant Formula: An Exegetical and Theological Investigation*, trans. Margaret Kohl (Edinburgh: T&T Clark, 1998).

done, and the covenant is not yet fully consummated. Ezekiel teaches us that when we are called to the workplace, we are called to righteous activity in exile as we embrace the challenges inherent in awaiting the consummation of God's kingdom. God requires a lifestyle of *individual righteousness and corporate responsibility indicative of the future fulfillment of the covenant.* By following in Jesus' footsteps, we can begin to live out God's future restoration in the workplace today.

Daniel and Work

Introduction to Daniel

How can you follow God and thrive in the secular world at the same time? Almost every workplace Christian faces this question daily, and many find the answer so difficult they are tempted to give up. Daniel, the central character of the book of Daniel, faces the question under extreme circumstances. Exiled from Jerusalem when God's people are conquered by the Babylonian empire, he must live out his life in an environment hostile to the Most High God. Yet circumstances bring him to a position of great opportunity in the service of the Babylonian king.

Should he withdraw from the corrupt and profane Babylonian government and seek a life pleasing to God in an enclave among other Jews? Should he relegate his faith to a private, personal sphere, perhaps praying to God in his closet, while living the life of Babylonian power and influence indistinguishably from those around him? Daniel chooses neither. Instead he embarks on a promising career while remaining publicly devoted to God. The story of how he navigates these treacherous waters is both guidebook and case study for today's workplace Christians.

The Big Picture of the Book of Daniel

The book of Daniel can be perplexing. It begins straightforwardly enough, with Daniel and his companions facing pressure to assimilate to the pleasures and vices of the Babylonian royal court. But the narrative becomes increasingly strange as dreams, visions, and prophecies come into the picture. At the halfway point (chapter 7), the book becomes unmistakably apocalyptic, portending the rise and fall of future kings and kingdoms, using imagery of bizarre events and creatures.[1] The apocalyptic genre is notoriously difficult to interpret, yet Daniel, like Revelation (the other book-length apocalypse in the Bible) provides much valuable material relevant to work, and it is worth trying to make sense of it for a theology of work.

This big picture of Daniel is that God is coming to overthrow the corrupt and arrogant pagan kingdoms where God's people are living in exile. Although his people are suffering now, their faithful suffering is one of the chief means by which God's power moves. This gives them a surprising ability to thrive now, a bright hope for the future, and a meaningful role to play in both present survival and future promise. We will explore the implications and applications that this big picture has for Christians in today's workplaces.

Introduction: In Exile at Babylon U. (Daniel 1)

The book of Daniel begins with the disaster that has finally ended the Jewish kingdom. Nebuchadnezzar (605–562 BC), the king of Babylon,

---

[1]The visions in chapters 7 through 12—suitably interpreted—closely match the actual unfolding of events in the succession of the Babylonian, Persian, Egyptian, and Greek empires over hundreds of years. This is especially true of Antiochus IV Epiphanes (11:31–39), and therefore many scholars date the writing of the book to his times, ca. 165 BC. Language, historical references, and genre are complicating factors. The dating of the book colors how the prophecies are interpreted. If it is dated ca. 165 BC, then the prophecies describe historical events under the guise of prophecy (i.e., after the fact). The chief problem with this viewpoint is it has the effect of undercutting the theology of the book itself. The ability of the prophet to foresee future events speaks to the key theological theme: God will bring about what the prophet has been given to foresee because of God's sovereign rule over the nations. For a thorough discussion of the late date theory, see John J. Collins, *Daniel*, Hermeneia (Minneapolis: Fortress, 1993) and John E. Goldingay, *Daniel*, vol. 30, *Word Biblical Commentary* (Nashville: Thomas Nelson, 1989). For the traditional conservative view, see Joyce G. Baldwin, *Daniel*, Tyndale Old Testament Commentaries (Downers Grove, IL: InterVarsity Press, 1978), Stephen R. Miller, *Daniel*, The New American Commentary (Nashville: Broadman & Holman, 1994), and Tremper Longman III, *Daniel*, The NIV Application Commentary (Grand Rapids: Zondervan, 1999). In any case, resolving this question is not directly necessary for understanding what the book says about work. In our discussion, we will accept the book's attribution of Daniel's words and visions to Daniel of the sixth century BC.

has conquered Jerusalem, deposed its king, and taken some of its royals and noble young men captive. As was typical in the ancient Near East, Nebuchadnezzar made sure to take vengeance on the gods (or, in this case, God) of the vanquished nation by plundering the temple and employing its former treasures to decorate the house of his own god (Dan. 1:1–3). By this we know that Nebuchadnezzar was an enemy not only to Israel, but also to Israel's God.

Among the youth taken captive were Daniel and his companions Hananiah, Mishael, and Azariah. They were enrolled in an indoctrination program designed to transform the exiles into loyal servants of their new king (Dan. 1:4–5). This presented both an opportunity and a challenge. The opportunity was to make good lives for themselves in a hostile land, and perhaps to bring God's power and justice to their new country. The prophet Jeremiah urged the Jewish exiles to do just that:

> Thus says the LORD of hosts, the God of Israel, to all the exiles whom I have sent into exile from Jerusalem to Babylon: Build houses and live in them; plant gardens and eat what they produce. Take wives and have sons and daughters; take wives for your sons, and give your daughters in marriage, that they may bear sons and daughters; multiply there, and do not decrease. But seek the welfare of the city where I have sent you into exile, and pray to the LORD on its behalf, for in its welfare you will find your welfare. (Jer. 29:4–7)

The challenge Daniel faced was assimilation at the expense of loyalty to his God and his people. The subjects Daniel would have studied probably included astrology, the study of animal entrails, rites of purification, sacrifice incantation, exorcism, and other forms of divination and magic.[2] These would have been odious to a devout Jew—far more at odds with Daniel's faith than most things at today's secular universities are for modern Christians. Moreover, he and his friends had to accept changes in their very names that previously proclaimed their allegiance to God (the "el" and "iah" elements). Nonetheless, Daniel embraced the challenge, secure in the belief that God would protect his faith and loyalty. He embraced Babylonian education, but he set limits to guard against actual assimilation into the pagan culture of his captors. He resisted the

---

[2] Goldingay, 16–17.

rich diet that was required for all trainees, refusing to "defile himself" (Dan. 1:8). The text doesn't make clear exactly what was objectionable about the diet.[3] Cultural traditions surrounding diet are strong, especially so to Jews, whose food laws distinguished them sharply from the surrounding nations (Lev. 11; Deut. 14). Perhaps keeping a separate diet gave Daniel a daily reminder of his allegiance to the Lord. Or perhaps it demonstrated that his physical prowess depended on God's favor rather than the king's dietary regimen. Perhaps the austerity of his diet kept him from developing a taste for luxury that would compromise his independence later.

In any case, the discussion of Daniel's diet highlights a much deeper point: God had a hand in the events in Daniel's life as well as in Nebuchadnezzar's, in Babylon and in every nation. Chapter 1 reflects this at the outset by stating, "The Lord let King Jehoiakim of Judah fall" (Dan. 1:2) and "God allowed Daniel to receive favor and compassion" (Dan. 1:9). Daniel and his friends exceeded the development of the other novitiates not because of their genius or their diet, but because "God gave knowledge and skill in every aspect of literature and wisdom" (Dan. 1:17). Daniel's wisdom came from a source other than the elite training provided by the king's professors, for "in every matter of wisdom and understanding concerning which the king inquired of them, he found them ten times better than all the magicians and enchanters in his whole kingdom" (Dan. 1:20). This set the pattern for the remainder of the book, as time and again events display the superiority of Daniel's wisdom—and more importantly, the power of his God—over the wisdom and power of the unbelieving nations and their kings (Dan. 5:14; 11:33–35; 12:3, 10).

Christians in today's workplaces experience many similarities to Daniel and his friends in exile at this Babylonian university. There is no way to escape the workplace other than withdrawing to insular com-

---

[3] The food laws in their technical detail may not have been the issue since wine was permitted by Jewish law, and since later we learn that Daniel did find suitable meat to eat in Babylon (Dan. 10:3). Nonetheless, there seems to be a hint of objection to the king's diet reminiscent of the Corinthians' qualms about eating meat sacrificed to idols (1 Cor. 8:1–13). The best explanation is Daniel's resistance to assimilation. For the assimilation view, see Goldingay, 19; Collins, 143; for refusal to commend the king's diet, see Longman, 53.

munities or choosing to work in Christian-only institutions, such as churches or Christian schools. The workplace offers many (but certainly not all) Christians a variety of opportunities for personal gain, such as good pay, job security, professional achievement and stature, comfortable working conditions, and interesting, creative work. In themselves, these are good things. But they tempt us with two serious evils: (1) the danger of becoming so enamored of the good material things that we become unwilling to risk their loss by standing up for what God requires of us; and (2) the spiritual danger of coming to believe that the good things come as a result of our own labor or genius, or as a result of our service to some power other than God.

Moreover, the workplace often demands accommodations that in themselves are not good things, such as deception, prejudice, mistreatment of the poor and powerless, pandering to unwholesome desires, taking advantage of others in their moments of need, and many more. In our times as much as in Daniel's, it is difficult to know which accommodations are good and which are ill. Was it good or acceptable for Daniel and his friends to study astrology? Could they learn to use knowledge of the skies without becoming ensnared by the superstitions in which it was couched? Is it good for Christians to study marketing? Can they learn to use knowledge of consumer behavior without becoming ensnared in the practice of deceptive advertising or exploitative promotions? The book of Daniel provides no specific guidelines, but it suggests some vital perspectives:

1. Christians should embrace education, even if it is conducted outside the bounds of Christian accountability.

2. Christians should embrace work in non-Christian and even hostile work environments.

3. Christians who work or study in non- or anti-Christian environments should take care to avoid uncritical assimilation into the surrounding culture. Christian practices include:

   Constant prayer and communion with God. Daniel prayed three times daily throughout his career (Dan. 6:10) and with special commitment during difficult times in his work (Dan. 9:3–4,

16–21). How many Christians actually pray for the specifics of their work lives? The book of Daniel constantly shows that God cares about the specific details of daily work.

Firm adherence to material markers of the faith, even if they are somewhat arbitrary. Daniel avoided eating the king's rich food and wine because it would have compromised his loyalty to God. We could argue whether this particular practice is universally required by God, but we cannot doubt that a living faith requires live markers of the boundaries of faithful behavior. Chick-fil-A draws the line at opening on Sunday. Many Catholic doctors will not prescribe artificial contraception. Other Christians find respectful ways to ask their colleagues for permission to pray for them. None of these can be taken as universal requirements, and indeed all of them could be argued by other Christians. But each of them helps their practitioners avoid a slow creep of assimilation by providing constant, public markers of their faith.

Active association and accountability with other Christians in the same kind of work. "Daniel made a request of the king, and he appointed Shadrach, Meshach, and Abednego over the affairs of the province of Babylon" (Dan. 2:49). Few Christians, however, have any forum where they can share concerns, questions, successes, and failures with others in their field. How are lawyers to learn how to apply the faith to law, except by regular, intentional discussions with other Christian lawyers? Likewise for engineers, artisans, farmers, teachers, parents, marketing managers, and every other vocation. Creating and nurturing these kinds of groups is one of the great unmet needs of workplace Christians.

Formation of good relationships with nonbelievers in your workplace. God caused the official overseeing Daniel's diet to show him favor and sympathy (Dan. 1:9), and Daniel cooperated with God by respecting the official and looking after his welfare (Dan. 1:10–14). Christians sometimes seem to go out of their way to antagonize and judge co-workers, but God commands, "If it is possible, so far as it depends on you, live peaceably with all" (Rom. 12:18). An excellent practice is to pray specifically for God's blessings for those among whom we work.

Adoption of a modest lifestyle, so that attachments to money, prestige, or power do not stand in the way of risking your job or career if you are pressured to do something contrary to God's commands, values, or virtues. Despite reaching the pinnacle of Babylonian education, position, and wealth, Daniel and his friends were constantly ready to lose everything in order to speak and act on God's word (Dan. 2:24; 3:12; 4:20; 5:17; 6:10, 21).

Although Daniel managed to walk the tightrope of partial cultural assimilation without religious and moral compromise, the stakes were high. Daniel's career and even his life were on the line, as was the life of the chief Babylonian official, Ashpenaz (Dan. 1:10). Yet by God's grace, Daniel remained composed and maintained his integrity. Even Daniel's enemies would later admit that "they could find no grounds for complaint or any corruption, because he was faithful, and no negligence or corruption was found in him" (Dan. 6:4).

God Will Overthrow Pagan Kingdoms and Replace Them with His Own Kingdom (Daniel 2)

Chapter 2 of Daniel introduces the vision that God will overthrow pagan kingdoms and replace them with his own kingdom.

Although Daniel was prospering and serving God in the midst of hostile territory, Nebuchadnezzar was becoming uneasy ruling his own land, even though his power was unchallenged. His dreams became troubled by his worries about the security of his empire. In one dream, Nebuchadnezzar saw a towering statue consisting of several elements made of different metals. The statue, enormous as it was, was smashed by a rock, and "became like chaff of the summer threshing floors" that "the wind carried . . . away, so that not a trace . . . could be found," but the rock "that struck the statue became a great mountain and filled the whole earth" (Dan. 2:35). Nebuchadnezzar's magicians, enchanters, and astrologers were of no use to him in interpreting this dream (Dan. 2:10–11), but by God's grace Daniel knew both the dream—without being told by the king what it was—and the interpretation (Dan. 2:27–28).

The episode contrasts Nebuchadnezzar's arrogance with Daniel's humility and dependence on God. Nebuchadnezzar and his Babylon were the paragon of pride. According to Daniel's interpretation, the statue's enormous metal components represented the kingdoms of Babylon and its successors (Dan. 2:31–45).[4] The astrologers' greeting to the king—"O king, live forever!" (Dan. 2:4)—emphasizes the king's pretense that he himself is the source of his power and majesty. But Daniel gives the king two shocking messages:

1. Your kingdom is not the result of your own doing. Rather, "God of heaven has given [you] the kingdom, the power, the might, and the glory" (Dan. 2:37). So all your pride is foolish and vain.

2. Your kingdom is doomed. "Just as you saw that a stone was cut from the mountain not by hands, and that it crushed the iron, the bronze, the clay, the silver, and the gold. The great God has informed the king what shall be hereafter. The dream is certain, and its interpretation trustworthy" (Dan. 2:45). Although this is not to happen in your time, it will bring all your supposedly mighty accomplishments to nothing.

In contrast, personal humility—and its conjoined twin, dependence on God's power—was Daniel's secret weapon for thriving. Humility allowed him to thrive, even in the exceptionally unpromising situation where he must forecast the kingdom's demise to the king himself. Daniel disclaimed any personal ability of his own. God alone has power and wisdom: "No wise men, enchanters, magicians, or astrologers can show to the king the mystery that the king is asking, but there is a God in heaven who reveals mysteries" (Dan. 2:27).

---

[4]The metals of the image in chapter 2 and the bestial kingdoms in chapter 7 are parallel references to the succession of these four earthly kingdoms: Babylon, Medo-Persia, Greece, and Rome; the alternative view that presupposes the work is second century contends for Babylon, Median, Persia, and Greece.

Amazingly, this humble attitude led the king to pardon—and even accept—Daniel's brazen message. He was ready to execute his astrologers en masse, but he "fell on his face, worshipped Daniel" (Dan. 2:46), and then "made him ruler over the entire whole of Babylon and chief prefect over all the wise men of Babylon" (Dan. 2:48). Nebuchadnezzar even came to some kind of belief in Yahweh. "The king said to Daniel, 'Truly, your God is God of gods and Lord of kings and a revealer of mysteries, for you have been able to reveal this mystery'" (Dan. 2:47).

For today's workplace Christians this offers two important points:

1. God will bring the arrogance, corruption, injustice, and violence of all workplaces to an end, although not necessarily during the time we work there. This is a source both of comfort and challenge. Comfort, because we are not responsible for correcting every evil in our workplaces, but only for acting faithfully in our spheres of influence, and also because the unfairness we may suffer at work is not the ultimate reality of our work. Challenge, because we *are* called to oppose the evil within our spheres of influence, costly to our careers as it may prove. Daniel was terrified by the severity of the message he had to deliver to Nebuchadnezzar: "Therefore, O king, may my counsel be acceptable to you: atone for your sins with righteousness, and your iniquities with mercy to the oppressed" (Dan. 4:27).

2. We must take our stands with humility rather than self-righteousness. We have seen how Daniel claimed no wisdom of his own. Likewise, in the first chapter, when Daniel was directed to eat from the king's table, he responded not in self-righteousness; rather, "he asked the palace master to allow him not to defile himself" (Dan. 1:8). Then he took time to understand the issue from the official's point of view. While remaining true to his principles, he found a compromise that would not back his boss into a corner: "Please test your servants for ten days" (Dan. 1:12). As believers in the workplace, we may confuse taking a stand for Christ with stubbornness or belligerence.

Taken together, these two points illustrate both the possibilities and the dangers of applying the book of Daniel to our work lives. At times we recognize that to be faithful to God, we must challenge people in power. But unlike Daniel, we lack the perfect reception of God's word. Just because we feel something strongly doesn't mean it is truly from God. Therefore, if even Daniel was humble in God's service, imagine how much humbler we should be. "God told me in a dream that I will be promoted above all of you," is a word we should probably keep to ourselves, no matter how strongly we believe it. Maybe it's best to assume that God will tell the people around us what he wants them to know, rather than direct us to tell it to them on his behalf.

Sufferings, Yet Rewards, for Faithful Witnesses to God in the Meantime (Daniel 3)

By God's grace, Daniel's humility enabled him to prosper in Nebuchadnezzar's court, even as God was preparing to cast down the king's empire. Even so, Daniel and his friends were about to suffer under a renewed fit of Nebuchadnezzar's arrogance. Unlike in the first and second chapters, in chapter 3 their faithfulness to God led to their suffering. Yet even in the midst of their suffering, God rewarded their faithfulness.

For a while, it appeared as though Nebuchadnezzar would renounce his arrogance, submit himself to God, and spare his empire the need to be overthrown by God's power. Regrettably, however, the very dream that led Nebuchadnezzar to recognize God's hand on Daniel may also be what incited the king to build a golden image that he required all his subjects to worship (Dan. 3:1, 5–6). The edifice signified the resurgent pride of the Babylonian king. Its gigantic structure (ninety feet high) was constructed on the level "plain of Dura," which would have exaggerated the commanding presence of the image (Dan. 3:1).

The king's disgraced astrologers saw a chance for revenge on Daniel. They played off of the king's resurgent pride and accused Daniel's friends of failing to worship the image (Dan. 3:8–12). The friends readily admitted their guilt and refused to bow down before the statue, despite the king's threat to throw them into a fiery furnace (Dan. 3:13–18). After years of successfully bridging the tension between the pagan environment of the Babylonian court and their fidelity to God, they faced a situation where no compromise was possible without violating their integrity. Previously, they served as models of how to thrive by following God in a hostile environment. Now they had to serve as models of how to suffer in the same environment.

> Shadrach, Meshach, and Abednego answered the king, "O Nebuchadnez-zar, we have no need to present a defense to you in this matter. If our God whom we serve is able to deliver us from the furnace of blazing fire and out of your hand, O king, let him deliver us. But if not, be it known to you, O king, that we will not serve your gods and we will not worship the golden statue that you have set up." (Dan. 3:16–18)

Today's workplace Christians seldom face such extreme hostility, at least in the Western world. But we could be ordered to do something that we cannot do in good conscience. Or, more likely, we might wake up one day and realize that we are already compromising God's desires for our work by the goals we pursue, the powers we exercise, the relationships we misuse, or the compromises we make. In any case, there may well come a day when we recognize that we must make a radical change, such as saying no, being fired, resigning, blowing the whistle, or standing up for someone else. We should expect to suffer for doing so. The fact that we may be doing God's will should not lead us to expect that God will prevent us from facing the consequences imposed by the powers that be. Working as a Christian is not another shortcut to success, but instead brings the constant danger of suffering.

This episode is especially poignant because it shows that Daniel and his friends lived in the same world we do. In our world, if you stand up to a boss over an issue of, say, sexual harassment or falsification of data, the most likely outcome is that you will be punished, marginalized, sullied, misunderstood, and maybe fired. Even if you succeed in ending the abuse and removing the offender from power, your own reputation may well suffer irreparable damage. It's so difficult to prove that you were right, and people are so reluctant to get involved, that the institution may protect itself by getting rid of you alongside the true offender. Shadrach, Meshach, and Abednego apparently expected no less for themselves, for they say outright that God may not intervene in their case. "If our God whom we serve is able to deliver us . . . let him deliver us. But if not, be it known to you, O king, that we will not serve your gods" (Dan. 3:17–18). Nonetheless, to them, being faithful to God was the right thing to do, whether or not it was path to success.

In this they are indeed models for us. We need to learn to speak the truth clearly, with humility, in our own workplaces. General Peter Pace, a former chairman of the U.S. military's Joint Chiefs of Staff, says, "What I have come to really admire is something I call intellectual courage. This is the ability to sit in a room full of very powerful people, and see a conversation going in one direction, and feeling in your gut that something is not right, and having the temerity to say, 'I see it differently, and here's why.'"[5] In practice, courage often results from being prepared. Daniel's friends knew the dangers inherent in their positions, and they were prepared to face the consequences of standing firm in their convictions. We should know where the ethical edges in our workplaces are and think through in advance what we would do if asked to do something contrary to God's word. "You need to know in advance what your 'walk-away' conditions are and practice your resignation speech for every job you take," was the advice of a longtime Harvard Business School professor. "Otherwise you can be lulled into doing almost anything, step-by-step."[6]

The Humbling of the Pagan King (Daniel 4)

Chapters 4 and 5 of the book of Daniel are to be read in concert. The topic of both is the humbling or overthrowing of the pagan kingdom. The magnificence of Babylon serves as the common setting for the humiliation of Nebuchadnezzar in chapter 4 and the demise of King Belshazzar in chapter 5.

In chapter 4, both Babylon's magnificence and the king's arrogance reached their zeniths. Yet once again, the king was troubled by his dreams. He saw an enormous tree whose "top reached to heaven" (Dan. 4:11), which provided fruit and shelter for all the animals. But at the

---

[5] Peter Pace, "General Peter Pace: The Truth as I Know It," interview by Al Erisman and David Gautschi, *Ethix* 61, September/October 2008, http://ethix.org/2008/10/01/the-truth-as-i-know-it.

[6] Memory recounted to the Theology of Work Project by an anonymous correspondent, April 2010.

command from a "holy watcher, coming down from heaven" (Dan. 4:13), the tree was cut down and the animals scattered. In the dream the stump became a man whose mind was changed into that of an animal and who was constrained to live among the animals and plants for an extended time (Dan. 4:13–16). The king commanded Daniel to interpret the dream, once again requiring Daniel to give unpleasant news to an emotionally unstable monarch (Dan. 4:18–19). The interpretation was that the tree represented Nebuchadnezzar himself, who would be punished for his arrogance by being driven insane and made to live like a wild animal until he would know "that the Most High has sovereignty over the kingdom of mortals and gives it to whom he will" (Dan. 4:25). Despite the stark warning, Nebuchadnezzar persisted in his pride, even boasting, "Is this not magnificent Babylon, which I have built as a royal capital by my mighty power and for my glorious majesty?" (Dan. 4:30). As a result, he was punished as the dream foretold (Dan. 4:33).

But perhaps Daniel's confrontational interpretation made a difference for, after a long time in the wilderness, the king repented and glorified God, and both his sanity and his kingdom were restored to him (Dan. 4:34–37). Daniel's stand did not persuade the king to renounce his arrogance before disaster struck, but it opened a door for the king's repentance and restoration after the fact.

At times our respectful, principled stands may lead to transformation in our workplaces, too. A consultant at an international management consulting firm—call him Vince—tells a story of confronting someone with a bit too much self-importance.[7] Vince was put in charge of a team of promising young employees at one of the firm's clients, a large industrial company. At the start of the project, a senior partner from the firm began to give a pep talk to the team. One of the client team members—call him Gary—interrupted him. Gary began to question the validity of the project. "Before we embark on this project," said Gary, "I think we should evaluate whether consulting firms like yours actually add value to their clients. I've been reading some articles that say this kind of study may not be as useful as it's cracked up to be." The senior

---

[7] Name withheld at request of source, telephone interview by William Messenger, January 17, 2010.

partner found a way to continue his pep talk, but afterwards he told Vince, "Get Gary off the team." Vince—mindful of Jesus' command to forgive a brother seventy-seven times (Matt. 18:22)—asked permission to see if he could get Gary to change his attitude. "It just doesn't seem right to damage his career over one mistake, big as it was," he said. "You have two weeks," the partner replied, "and you're putting yourself on the line, too." By God's grace—according to Vince—Gary did come to see the validity of the project and flung himself into the work wholeheartedly. The senior partner recognized the change and, at the end of the project, singled out Gary for special recognition at the closing banquet. Vince's stand made a difference for both Gary and his company.

The Overthrow of the Pagan Kingdom (Daniel 5)

Chapter 5 moves beyond the humbling of the pagan king to the out-right destruction of the Babylonian empire. Babylon's extravagance had few parallels in the ancient world.[8] It was an impregnable fortress built of two walls, an inner and outer wall, with the outer wall as long as eleven miles and as high as forty feet. A processional boulevard led to the spectacle of the Ishtar Gate, one of the city's eight gates, which displayed glittering blue-glazed brick. The city contained as many as fifty temples and numerous palaces. The famed "Hanging Gardens," known primarily from ancient historians, was one of the Seven Wonders of the World. Yet after the death of the strong-armed Nebuchadnezzar in 562 BC, the city's downfall took barely twenty years. The Persian king Cyrus (559–530 BC) took the city in 539 BC without significant resistance.

This momentous change in the political landscape is told from the perspective of what occurred in the palace of the new ruler, Belshazzar, on the night of the city's fall.[9] Belshazzar, at a sumptuous banquet, de-

---

[8] Evelyn Klengel-Brandt, "Babylon," in *The Oxford Encyclopedia of Archaeology in the Near East*, ed. Eric M. Meyers (Oxford: Oxford University Press, 1997), 251–56; Bill T. Arnold, *Who Were the Babylonians?* (Atlanta: Society of Biblical Literature, 2004), 96–99.

[9] Belshazzar was not a descendant of Nebuchadnezzar, but the son of and co-regent with King Nabonidus (556–539 BC), who had come to the throne in a military coup.

filed the sacred Jewish goblets stolen from the temple of Jerusalem and blasphemed the Lord as the meal degenerated into a drunken orgy (Dan. 5:1–4). Then, "immediately the fingers of a human hand appeared and began writing on the plaster of the wall" (Dan. 5:5). Belshazzar, proud ruler of the magnificent empire of Babylon, was so frightened by the handwriting on the wall that his face turned pale and his knees knocked together (Dan. 5:6). Neither he nor his enchanters, astrologers, and diviners were able to understand what it meant (Dan. 5:7–9). Only Daniel could perceive its message of doom: "The God in whose power is your very breath, and to whom belong all your ways, you have not honored. . . . You have been weighed on the scales and found wanting; . . . your kingdom is divided and given to the Medes and Persians" (Dan. 5:23, 27–28). And indeed, "That very night Belshazzar, the Chaldean king, was killed. And Darius the Mede received the kingdom" (Dan. 5:30–31).

In the end, God does bring the evil kingdom to an end. God's final victory, not our personal effectiveness, is the great hope of God's people. By all means, we should bloom where we are planted. If the opportunity arises, we can and should make a difference. Engagement, not withdrawal, is the model we see in every page of the book of Daniel. But our engagement with the world is not grounded on the expectation that we will achieve a certain degree of success, or that God will make us immune from the sufferings we see around us. It is grounded on the knowledge that everything good that happens in the midst of the fallen world is only a foretaste of the incomparable goodness that will come when God brings his own kingdom forth on earth. Ultimately, the question "Whose side are you on?" matters more than "What have you done for me lately?"

Sufferings, Yet Rewards, for Faithful Witnesses to God in the Meantime (Daniel 6)

Chapter 6 revisits a theme first introduced in chapter 3—that faithful witnesses to God experience both suffering and reward even while the pagan kingdom persists. Chapter 6 narrates a conspiratorial threat to Daniel's life, set in the reign of the Persian monarch Darius the Great

(522–486 BC). Daniel's competence merited his promotion to ruler over all the new empire, subservient only to the king himself (Dan. 6:3). But his rivals contrived a plan that exploited the only vulnerability the man had—Daniel's daily habit of prayer to his God. Darius was duped by the conspirators into decreeing a ban for thirty days on all religious expression except for prayer directed to the king. The penalty was death in the lions' den. To his great distress, Darius could not rescind the order since, according to tradition, "the law of the Medes and the Persians . . . cannot be revoked" (Dan. 6:8). Darius, although the most powerful man of his day, tied his own hands, making it impossible to rescue his favored administrator. The king conceded to Daniel, "May your God, whom you faithfully serve, deliver you!" (Dan. 6:16). And the Lord's angel performed what the king asked but could not perform. Daniel was thrown in the lions' den overnight but emerged in the morning unwounded (Dan. 6:17–23). This led the king to issue an edict of reverence for Daniel's God and to remove the threat of annihilation for the Jews as they continued to worship God (Dan. 6:26–27). Not even the implacable laws of the Medes and Persians could ensure the end of God's people. God's power overcame human deceit and royal dictate.

Nonetheless, Daniel did experience what most of us would call suffering along the way. Being the target of a government-sponsored character assassination attempt (Dan. 6:4–6) must have been a grueling experience, even if he was eventually cleared. Likewise, openly defying the king's edict for conscience' sake (Dan. 6:10–12) was a dangerous and courageous act. Daniel suffered immediate arrest and was thrown into a den of lions (Dan. 6:16–17). We should not let Daniel's eventual deliverance (Dan. 6:21–23) lead us to imagine that the experience wasn't painful and disturbing, to say the least. There are three lessons we can learn from Daniel's faithful witness to God:

1. Daniel did not limit himself to tasks he was certain he could accomplish on his own steam. There is no way to practice being thrown into a lion's den! Rather, he did his work on a daily basis in dependence on God. Daniel prayed three times a day (Dan. 6:10). He acknowledged God in every tough issue he faced. We, too, have to recognize we cannot fulfill our callings on our own.

2. Daniel epitomized the call Jesus would later give to be salt and light (Matt. 5:13–16) in our workplaces. Even Daniel's enemies had to admit, "We shall not find any ground for complaint against this Daniel unless we find it in connection with the law of his God" (Dan. 6:5). This meant that he was able to confront difficult situations with truth and actually bring about change. This happens several times when Daniel and his friends take a careful stand for the truth and it leads to a new decree by the king (Dan. 2:46–49; 3:28–30; 4:36–37; 5:29; 6:25–28).

3. Daniel's success in bringing about change demonstrates that God cares about the everyday issues of governance in a broken society. Just because God intends to replace the current regime eventually doesn't mean he doesn't care about making it more just, more fruitful, more livable now. Sometimes we don't engage with God in our work because we believe that our work doesn't seem important to God. But each decision is important to our God, and every worker needs to know this. The question that the theology of Daniel presents the worker is "Whose kingdom are you building?" Daniel excelled in his occupation laboring on behalf of the world's kingdoms, *and* he maintained his integrity as a citizen of God's kingdom. His service to the pagan kings *was* his service for the purposes of God. Christian workers must labor well in the present, knowing that the significance of our labor both resides in *and* transcends the here and now.

God Will Overthrow Pagan Kingdoms and Replace Them with His Own Kingdom (Daniel 7)

Chapter 7 brings us back to the first theme in the book of Daniel—that God will someday replace the corrupt kingdoms of this world with his own kingdom. Like Daniel and his companions, by God's grace we may find a way to get by—and perhaps even a way to thrive—as exiles here in the meantime. Yet the chief hope we have lies not in making the best of the present situation, but in anticipating the joy of coming kingdom of God.

Therefore, perseverance becomes a crucial virtue. We have to persevere until Christ returns to put things to right. Perseverance is a virtue praised in classical philosophy and in the Judeo-Christian tradition. Sometimes we encounter it in quotable packages, such as Einstein's admission, "It's not that I'm so smart, it's just that I stay with problems longer." The New Testament confirms the value of perseverance: "Blessed is anyone who endures temptation. Such a one has stood the test and will receive the crown of life that the Lord has promised to those who love him" (James 1:12). Perseverance in the life of the believer has its basis and source in the Lord God. It is not a matter of human integrity or honor. Christian endurance rests on the veracity of God's eternal covenant promises.

Beginning in chapter 7, the book of Daniel becomes frankly apocalyptic in genre. Apocalyptic literature, a special kind of prophetic oracle, describes the cataclysmic events of the last days. It was widespread in early Jewish and Christian literature. Among its traits are rich symbolism (chapter 7), description of the final universal battle between good and evil (Dan. 11:40–12:4), and a heavenly interpreter who explains the meaning of the vision to the prophet (Dan. 7:16, 23; 8:15; 9:21–23; 10:14). The prophet is exhorted to persevere faithfully until the vision is fulfilled (Dan. 7:25–27; 9:24; 10:18–19; 12:1–4, 13). This literary form accentuates the author's message about perseverance.

Chapters 7–12 recount how Daniel received haunting visions, which he reports in first-person testimony. The net result is a series of prophecies that envisages the tribulations of God's people at the hands of despotic leaders, but which ends in triumph secured by God's appointed deliverer. The book concludes with an exhortation of perseverance to Daniel: "Happy are those who persevere and attain the thousand three hundred thirty-five days. But you, go your way, and rest; you shall rise for your reward at the end of the days" (Dan. 12:12–13).

Oppression against God's people is a constant theme of these chapters (Dan. 7:21, 25; 9:26; 10:1). The oppressor—revealed by history to be Antiochus IV Epiphanes[10]—is described in disturbing surrealistic im-

---

[10] John Whitehorse, "Antiochus," in *The Anchor Bible Dictionary*, ed. David Noel Freedman, vol. 1 (New York: Doubleday, 1992), 269–70.

ages. He is the vicious "little horn" (the "abomination that desolates" in Dan. 11:31 and "contemptible person" in Dan. 11:21) who rejects the traditional gods of his ancestors, making himself to be the supreme deity.

The message of assurance from chapters 7–12 for workers is the assurance of a final reckoning that will justly reward the faithful work we do in life. In the here and now, good work is not always rewarded according to its honorable contributions to society. In many cases, its results are not even visible to us. Although Daniel and his friends turned the hearts of kings many times, it wasn't long before those kings reverted to their old selves. Likewise in our workplaces, our role as salt and light can hold back evil, but often will not lead to a permanent change. This doesn't diminish our responsibility in being salt and light, but the fruits of our labor will not be fully visible until the kingdom of God is fulfilled.

Conclusions from Daniel

The book of Daniel provides a hopeful picture of how God's people can survive and even thrive in a hostile environment by remaining faithful to God. God, according to the book of Daniel, cares deeply about the everyday lives of individuals and societies in a broken world. God intervenes directly in daily life, and also gives Daniel miraculous gifts that make it possible to thrive under an oppressive regime. Yet by no means does the book of Daniel promise worldly success as a reward for faithfulness. Rather, it promises both suffering and reward in mortal life, and thereby demonstrates that faithfulness and integrity are the keys to living well in this life as well as in the coming kingdom of God.

Daniel and his friends model many practical applications for workplace Christians: engaging with culture, adopting lifelong habits that build faithfulness and virtue, sharing in fellowship with Christian coworkers, adopting a modest life style, forming friendships with nonbelievers, showing genuine humility, taking a principled stand in workplace situations, embracing challenges we know we cannot meet without God's help, bringing salt and light to our workplaces, working with excellence and diligence in whatever our jobs are, anticipating suffering as a result of Christian faithfulness in the workplace, and persevering until God brings his kingdom—and our faithful labor—to fruition. We cannot know in advance whether our faithfulness to God's ways will result in worldly success or failure, any more than Daniel's friends could know whether they would be saved from the fiery furnace or burned up. But, like them, we can acknowledge that serving God in our work is what truly matters.

The Twelve Prophets and Work

Introduction to the Twelve Prophets

The books of the Twelve Prophets cover a range of conditions in the life of Israel, each of which brings its own challenges. The unifying theme of these prophets is that in God there is no split between the work of worship and the work of daily life, nor is there a split between individual well-being and the common good. The people of Israel are faithful or unfaithful, in varying degrees, to God's covenant with them, and the degree of their faithfulness is immediately apparent in their worship or their neglect to worship. The people's faithfulness, or lack of faithfulness, to God's covenant is reflected not only in the spiritual environment, but also in the social and physical environment, including the land itself. The people's degree of faithfulness is also visible in their ethics in life and work, which in turn determines the fruitfulness of their labor and their consequent prosperity or poverty. In the short term the wicked may prosper, but both God's discipline and the natural consequences of unjust work will eventually reduce the unjust to poverty and despair. Yet when people and societies work in faithfulness to God, he blesses them with an integrated spiritual-ethical-environmental health and prosperity.

These final twelve books of the Old Testament are usually referred to in the English-speaking Christian tradition as the Minor Prophets. In the Hebrew tradition these books are contained in a single scroll called "The Book of the Twelve." It forms a kind of anthology with a progression of thought and coherence of theme. The essential background of the collection is the covenant that God has made with his people, and the narrative told within the collection is the story of Israel's violation of the covenant, God's response in punishing or disciplining of Israel, and God's slowly unfolding restoration of the Israelite nation and society.[1]

---

[1] Paul R. House, *Old Testament Theology* (Downers Grove, IL: InterVarsity Press, 1998), 346–48.

That being the case, five of the first six books of the Twelve—Hosea, Joel, Amos, Obadiah, and Micah—reflect on the effect of the people's sin, both on the conduct of the covenant and on the events of the world. Then the next three—Nahum, Habakkuk, and Zephaniah—concern the punishment for sin, again with respect both to the covenant and to the world. The last three prophetic books—Haggai, Zechariah, and Malachi— concern the restoration of Israel, yet again with respect to a renewal of the covenant and partial restoration of Israel's standing in the world. Finally, Jonah is a special case. His prophecy does not concern Israel at all, but the non-Hebrew city-state of Nineveh. Both its setting and its composition are famously difficult to date reliably.

Historical Backdrop of the Twelve Prophets

There is much debate about the background and dating of the prophets of Israel and Judah. (See "Introduction to the Prophets" above for an overall discussion of the major issues and context of their writings.) With respect to the Twelve, let us give a brief outline. Within the first cluster, there is a broad consensus that Hosea, Amos, and Micah were situated in the eighth century BC. By that time, the United Kingdom of Israel ruled over by David and then Solomon had been split for some time into a northern kingdom, known as Israel, and a southern kingdom, known as Judah. Micah was a southerner speaking to the south; Amos was a southerner speaking to the north; and Hosea was a northerner speaking to the north.

As the eighth century opened, both the northern and southern kingdoms were enjoying a prosperity and security of borders unprecedented since the time of Solomon. But the clouds were gathering for those with eyes to see, such as our prophets. Internally, the economic and political situation became ever more precarious as dynastic struggles preoccupied the ruling class. Externally, the gradual reemergence of Assyria as a superpower in the region would become an ever-growing threat to both kingdoms. In fact, the northern kingdom was effectively eliminated by the Assyrian army circa 721 BC. It never reappeared again as a political entity, although traces of its existence remain to this day in Samaritan identity (2 Kgs. 17:1–18). The prophets lay the blame squarely on the people of Israel, and to a lesser extent Judah, for abandoning the worship of Yahweh in favor of idolatry and for violating the ethical requirements of the law. Despite these failings, the people lulled themselves into a false sense of security because of their covenant with Yahweh to be his people.

The south, under King Hezekiah, somehow survived the Assyrian threat (2 Kgs. 19), but faced an even greater challenge in the rise of the Babylonian empire (2 Kgs. 24). Unfortunately, Judah did not repent of its idolatry and ethical violations after its close escape from the Assyrians. Final defeat came at the hands of the Babylonians in 587 BC. This culminated in the destruction of Judah's societal infrastructure and the deportation of its leadership into exile in the Babylonian empire (2 Kgs. 24–25). The prophets regarded this defeat as evidence of God's punishment of the people. This is most sharply etched in the books of Nahum, Habakkuk, and Zephaniah among the prophets of the Twelve. They mirror the prophetic writings of Jeremiah and Ezekiel, who also date from this period. Separate books of the Bible record their prophetic careers (see "Jeremiah & Lamentations and Work" and "Ezekiel and Work"), and we will not discuss them here.

The great Persian king, Cyrus, defeated Babylon and took over its hegemony. In line with Persian policy, the empire permitted the Jewish people to return to their land and, perhaps more importantly, to reestablish their temple and other key institutions (Ezra 1). All this took place, it seems, at the pleasure of the Persian empire.[2] The prophets Haggai, Zechariah, and Malachi did their work during this phase of Israel's history.

In summary, the books of the Twelve Prophets span a wide range of background circumstances in the life of the people of God. Accordingly, it reflects several different paradigms within which faith at work needs to be expressed.

Faith and Work Before the Exile—Hosea, Amos, Obadiah, Joel, and Micah

Hosea, Amos, Obadiah, Joel, and Micah were active in the eighth century BC when the state was well developed but the economy was declining.

---

[2] Carol L. Meyers and Eric M. Meyers, *Haggai, Zechariah 1–8: A New Translation with Introduction and Commentary*, vol. 25B, *The Anchor Bible* (New York: Doubleday, 1987), xxxi–xxxii.

Power and wealth accumulated to the upper strata and left a growing disadvantaged class. There is some evidence that farmers began to concentrate on cash crops that could be sold to the growing urban population. This had the destabilizing effect of leaving farmers without a mix of crops and animals capable of weathering the loss of any particular or market.[3] Farming communities became vulnerable to annual variations in production, and the cities were correspondingly subject to vagaries in their food supply (Amos 4:6–9). As the prophets from this period begin to speak, the glory days of opulent building projects and territorial expansion are well past. Such circumstances provide the soil for corruption on the part of those desperate to hold on to their power and diminishing wealth, and a widening gap between the rich and the poor. As a result, God's prophets from this period have much to say to the world of work.

God Demands Change (Hosea 1:1–9; Micah 2:1–5)

God puts the blame for Israel's corruption on the people as a whole. They have abandoned God's covenant, which breaks both their connection with God and the just social structures of God's law, leading directly to corruption and economic decline. "Whoredom" is the term the prophets often use to describe Israel's breaking of the covenant (e.g., Jer. 3:2; Ezek. 23:7). To dramatize the situation, God takes the metaphor literally and commands the prophet Hosea to "take for yourself a wife of whoredom and have children of whoredom, for the land commits great whoredom by forsaking the LORD" (Hos. 1:2). Hosea obeys God's command, marries a woman named Gomer, who apparently fits the requirement, and has three children with her (Hos. 1:3). We are left to imagine what making a household and raising children with a "wife of whoredom" must have been like.

Although the prophets use the imagery of prostitution and adultery, God accuses Israel of economic and social corruption, not sexual immorality.

---

[3] See the analysis of Marvin L. Chaney, "Bitter Bounty: The Dynamics of Political Economy Critiqued by the Eighth-Century Prophets," in *The Bible and Liberation: Political and Social Hermeneutics,* ed. Norman K. Gottwald and Richard A. Horsley, rev. ed. (Maryknoll, NY: Orbis Books, 1993), 250–63.

Alas for those who devise wickedness and evil deeds on their beds! When the morning dawns, they perform it, because it is in their power. They covet fields, and seize them; houses, and take them away; they oppress householder and house, people and their inheritance. (Mic. 2:1–2)

This makes Hosea's family situation a dramatic example for those who work in corrupt or imperfect workplaces today. God deliberately put Hosea in a corrupt and difficult family situation. Could it be that God deliberately puts people in corrupt and difficult workplaces today? While we may seek a comfortable job with a reputable employer in a respectable profession, perhaps we can accomplish far more for God's kingdom by working in morally compromised places. If you abhor corruption, can you do more to fight it by working as a lawyer in a prestigious firm or as a building inspector in a mafia-dominated city? There are no easy answers, but God's call to Hosea suggests that making a difference in the world is more important to God than keeping our hands clean. As Dietrich Bonhoeffer in the midst of Nazi-controlled Germany wrote, "The ultimate question for a responsible man to ask, is not how to extricate himself heroically from the affair, but how the coming generation is to live."[4]

God Makes Change Possible (Hosea 14:1–9; Amos 9:11–15; Micah 4:1–5; Obadiah 21)

The same God who demands change also promises to make change possible. "A harvest is appointed when I would restore the fortunes of my people, when I would heal Israel" (Hos. 6:11–7:1). The Twelve Prophets carry a fundamental optimism that God is active in the world to change it for the better. Despite the apparent triumph of the wicked, God is ultimately in charge, and "the kingdom shall be the Lord's" (Obad. 21). Despite the calamity the people are bringing upon themselves, God is at work to restore the goodness of life and work intended from the beginning. "He is gracious and merciful, slow to anger, and abounding in steadfast love" (Joel 2:13). The closing oracles of Joel, Hosea, and Amos illustrate this in explicitly economic terms.

---

[4] Dietrich Bonhoeffer, *Letters and Papers from Prison*, ed. Eberhard Bethge, rev. ed. (New York: Touchstone, 1997), 7.

The threshing floors shall be full of grain, the vats shall overflow with wine and oil. . . . You shall eat in plenty and be satisfied, and praise the name of the LORD your God, who has dealt wondrously with you. And my people shall never again be put to shame. (Joel 2:24, 26)

[Israel] shall again live beneath my shadow, they shall flourish as a garden; they shall blossom like the vine, their fragrance shall be like the wine of Lebanon. (Hos. 14:7)

I will restore the fortunes of my people Israel, and they shall rebuild the ruined cities and inhabit them; they shall plant vineyards and drink their wine, and they shall make gardens and eat their fruit. (Amos 9:14)

God's word to his people in times of economic and social hardship is that his intent is to restore peace, justice, and prosperity, if the people will live by the precepts of his covenant. The means he will use is the work of his people.

Unjust Work (Micah 1:1–7; 3:1–2)

Despite God's intentions, work is subjected to human sin. The most egregious case is work that is inherently sinful. Micah mentions prostitution, probably in this case cult prostitution, and he promises that the wages from it would be burned (Mic. 1:7). A straightforward application of this would be to rule out prostitution as a legitimate occupation, even it if might be an understandable choice for those who have no other way to provide for themselves or their families. There are other jobs that also raise the question of whether or not this job should be done at all. We can all think of various examples, no doubt, and Christians would do well to seek work that benefits others and society as a whole.

But Micah is speaking to Israel as a whole, not only to individuals. He is critiquing a society in which social, economic, and religious conditions make prostitution viable. The question is not "Is it acceptable to earn a living as a prostitute?" but "How must society change to eliminate the need for anyone to do degrading or harmful work?" Micah calls to account not so much those who feel forced into doing bad work, but the leaders who fail to reform society. His words are scathing. "Listen, you heads of Jacob and rulers of the house of Israel! Should you not know justice?—you who hate the good and love the evil, who tear the skin off my people, and the flesh off their bones" (Mic. 3:1–2).

There are both similarities and differences between societies in Micah's and ours. The specific remedies God promises to ancient Israel are not necessarily what God intends today. Micah's prophetic words reflect the connection between ritual prostitution and idolatrous cults in his day. God promises to end the social abuses centered at the cultic shrines. "I will cut off your images and your pillars from among you, and you shall bow down no more to the work of your hands; and I will uproot your sacred poles from among you and destroy your towns" (Mic. 5:13–14). In our day, we need God's wisdom to find effective solutions to current social factors leading to sinful and oppressive work.

Working Unjustly (Hosea 4:1–10; Amos 5:10–15; 8:5–6; Joel 2:28–29)

When the prophets speak of prostitution, they are seldom concerned merely with that particular line of work. Typically, they are also using it as a metaphor of injustice, which by definition is unfaithfulness to God's covenant (Hos. 4:7–10). In a broad reminder that wages may be unjustly earned, Amos indicts the merchants who use inferior products, false weights, and other deceptions to reap a profit at the expense of vulnerable consumers. Amos makes several specific accusations against the Israelite's workplace practices. Work in Israel has become unjust and oppressive (Amos 5:7). Those who take a stand against corruption and exploitation— or even who simply tell the truth—are suppressed (Amos 5:10). Business owners use their power to exploit the poor and vulnerable (Amos 5:11). The law is no obstacle to their exploitation because there are plenty of officials ready to take a bribe and look the other way. In fact, government has abandoned its duty to care for the poor altogether (Amos 5:12). In all these cases, the problem is not that Israelites are in occupations that are inherently evil. The problem is that they are twisting occupations that God intends for good—business, real estate, law, and government—into means of oppression. They say to themselves, "We will make the ephah small and the shekel great [cheating on measurements], and practice deceit with false balances, buying the poor for silver and the needy for a pair of sandals, and selling the sweepings of the wheat" (Amos 8:5–6).

Many of today's legitimate ways of making a living may become unjust by the way they are performed. Should a photographer take pictures of anything a client asks, without regard for its effect on its subject and viewers? Should a surgeon perform any kind of elective surgery a patient might be willing to pay for? Is a mortgage broker responsible to ensure the ability of a borrower to repay the loan without undue hardship? Is it legitimate not to help failing co-workers because their failure makes us look better by comparison? If our work is a form of service under God, we cannot ignore such questions. We need to be careful not to imagine a hierarchy of work, however. The prophets' claim is not that some types of work are godlier than others, but that *all* types of work must be done as contributions to God's work in the world. "Even on the male and female slaves, in those days, I will pour out my spirit," God promises (Joel 2:29).

The Work of Individuals and Communities Are Interdependent (Amos 8:1–6; Micah 6:1–16)

Justice in work is not only an individual matter. People have a responsibility to make sure that everyone in society has access to the resources needed to make a living. Amos criticizes Israel for injustice in this respect, most vividly in an allusion to the law of gleaning. Gleaning is the process of picking up the stray heads of grain that remain in a field after the harvesters have passed through. According to God's covenant with Israel, farmers were not allowed to glean their own fields, but they were to allow poor people (literally "widows and orphans") to glean them as a way of supporting themselves (Deut. 24:19). This created a rudimentary form of social welfare, based on creating an opportunity for the poor to work (by gleaning the fields) rather than having to beg, steal, or starve. Gleaning is a way to participate in the dignity of work, even for those who are unable to participate in the labor market due to lack of resources, socioeconomic dislocation, discrimination, disability, or other factors. God not only wants everyone's needs to be met, but he also wants to offer everyone the dignity of working to meet their needs and the needs of others.

Amos complains that this provision is being violated. Farmers are not leaving the stray grain in their fields for the poor to glean (Mic. 7:1–2). Instead they offer to sell chaff—the waste left after threshing—to the poor at a ruinous price. "You trample on the needy, and bring ruin to the poor," Amos accuses them, ". . . selling the sweepings of the wheat" (Amos 8:4, 6). Amos accuses them of waiting restlessly for the end of Sabbath so they can carry on selling this cheap, adulterated food product to those who have no other option (Amos 8:5).

Moreover, they are cheating even those who can afford to buy pure grain, as is evident in rigged balances in the marketplace. "We will make the ephah [of wheat being sold] small and the shekel [selling price] great," they boast. Micah proclaims God's judgment against unjust commerce. "Can I tolerate wicked scales and a bag of dishonest weights?" says the Lord (Mic. 6:11). This tells us clearly that justice is not only a matter of criminal law and political expression but also of economic opportunity. The opportunity to work to meet individual and family needs is essential to the role of the individual within the covenant. Economic justice is a critical component of Micah's famous, ringing proclamation only three verses earlier: "What does the Lord require of you but to do justice, and to love kindness, and to walk humbly with your God?" (Mic. 6:8). God requires his people—as a daily matter of their walk with him—to love kindness and do justice individually and socially, in every aspect of work and economic life.

Work and Worship (Micah 6:6–8; Amos 5:21–24; Hosea 4–11)

Justice is not merely a secular issue, as the prophets see it. Micah's call for justice in 6:8 follows from an observation that justice is better than extravagant religious sacrifices (Mic. 6:6–7). Hosea and Amos expand this point. Through Amos, God objects to the disconnect between the religious observance and ethical action.

> I hate, I despise your festivals, and I take no delight in your solemn assemblies. Even though you offer me your burnt offerings and grain offerings, I will not accept them; and the offerings of well-being of your fatted animals I will not look upon. Take away from me the noise of your songs; I will not listen to the melody of your harps. But let justice roll down like waters, and righteousness like an ever-flowing stream. (Amos 5:21–24)

Hosea takes us deeper into the connection between being spiritually grounded and doing good work. Good work arises directly from faithfulness to God's covenant, and conversely, evil work takes us away from the presence of God.

> Hear the word of the LORD, O people of Israel; for the LORD has an indictment against the inhabitants of the land. There is no faithfulness or loyalty, and no knowledge of God in the land. Swearing, lying, and murder, and stealing and adultery break out; bloodshed follows bloodshed. Therefore the land mourns, and all who live in it languish; together with the wild animals and the birds of the air, even the fish of the sea are perishing. . . . My people are destroyed for lack of knowledge; because you have rejected knowledge, I reject you from being a priest to me. And since you have forgotten the law of your God, I also will forget your children. (Hos. 4:1–3, 6)

In fact, if we refuse to do just, ethical, good work, it calls into question our claim to be worshipers of God. If we devote one day a week to worshiping God, but then ignore his ways the other six, does the one day of worship represent our true selves? Hosea complains that that Israelites' ungodly ways of working put the lie to their claim to worship God. Their work is fraudulent, exemplified by moving boundary markers to cheat their neighbors out of land (Hos. 5:10). They practice deceit (Hos. 7:1), even while claiming to worship the Lord (Hos. 8:13–14), and they don't keep their promises (Hos. 10:4). To bolster their unjust ways, they enter political alliances with oppressive foreign powers (Hos. 11:5–12:1). They misuse the workplace skills God has given them (Hos. 13:2). They appear religious, but they disobey God (Hos. 11:7). Their corruption and injustice at work are actually signs that they have become devoted to false gods (Hos. 9:9–17).

This is a reminder that the world of work does not exist in a vacuum, separated from the rest of life. If we do not work according to the values and priorities of God's covenant, then our lives and work will be ethically and spiritually incoherent. The way we work during the week does not so much question whether we are obedient to the God we worship, but whether we truly worship God at all. If God is not the god of our lives every day, then he is probably not actually our god on Sunday either. If we do not please God in our work, we cannot please him in our worship.

Apathy Due to Wealth (Amos 3:9–15; 6:1–7)

The prophets criticize those whose wealth leads them to abandon working for the common good and who give up any sense of responsibility for their neighbors. Amos connects indolent wealth with oppression when he accuses the idle rich of wrongdoing, violence, and robbery (Amos 3:10). God will bring a swift end to the wealth of such people. God will "tear down the winter house as well as the summer house and the houses of ivory" (Amos 3:15). Amos levels an excoriating blast against the luxuries of "those who are at ease in Zion" (Amos 6:1). They are first in dissolution, he observes, as they "lounge on their couches" (Amos 6:4) and "sing idle songs to the sound of the harp" (Amos 6:5). When God punishes Israel, they will be "first to go into exile" (Amos 6:7).

Surprisingly similar complaints can be heard today against those who have wealth but do not employ it toward any good purpose. This applies to individuals and also to corporations, governments, and other institutions that use their wealth to exploit others' vulnerabilities, rather than to create anything useful in proportion to their wealth. Many Christians—perhaps the majority in the West—have some ability to change these things, at least in their immediate working environments. The prophets' words serve as a continual challenge and encouragement to care deeply about how work and wealth serve—or fail to serve—the people around us.

Faith and Work During the Exile— Nahum, Habakkuk, and Zephaniah

Nahum, Habakkuk, and Zephaniah were active during the period when the southern kingdom began rapidly declining. Internal incoherence and external pressure from the burgeoning Babylonian empire resulted in Judah becoming a vassal state to Babylon. Shortly afterwards, in 587 BC, an ill-advised rebellion brought down the wrath of the Babylonians, leading to the collapse of the state of Judah and the deportation of the elites to the center of the Babylonian empire (2 Kgs. 24–25). In exile, the people of Israel had to work out how to be faithful while separated from their key religious institutions, the temple, the priesthood, and even the land. If, as we have seen, the first six books are about the effect of the people's sin, these three—Nahum, Habakkuk, and Zephaniah—are about the resultant punishment during this period.

God's Punishing Hand at Work (Nahum 1:1–12; Habakkuk 3:1–19; Zephaniah 1:1–13)

Nahum's chief contribution is to make it clear that the political and economic disaster is God's punishment or disciplining of Israel. "I have afflicted you," God declares (Nah. 1:12). Habakkuk and Zephaniah declare that an essential part of God's punishment is that the people's ability to make an adequate living is diminished.

> The fig tree does not blossom, and no fruit is on the vines; though the produce of the olive fails and the fields yield no food; though the flock is cut off from the fold and there is no herd in the stalls. (Hab. 3:17)

> All the traders have perished; all who weigh out silver are cut off. (Zeph. 1:11)

This is seen not only in economic woes, but also in environmental problems (see below under "Work, Worship, and the Environment").

Are contemporary political, economic, and natural disasters punishments from God? There is no shortage of people willing to declare that particular disasters are signs of God's wrath. The 2011 earthquake and tsunami in Japan were attributed to divine punishment by both the Governor of Tokyo[5] and the host of an MSNBC television news show. But unless we have joined the ranks of the Twelve or the other prophets of Israel, we should be very reluctant to declare God's wrath in the events of the world. Did God himself reveal the reasons for the tsunami to these commentators, or did they draw conclusions on their own? Did he reveal his intent to a substantial number of people, well in advance, over many years, as he did with the prophets of Israel, or did it come to one or two people the day after? Were the modern-day declarers of God's punishment forged as prophets by years of suffering alongside those afflicted, as were Jeremiah, the Twelve, and the other prophets of ancient Israel?

---

[5] Brad Hirshfield, "Where Is God in Suffering?" *Washington Post*, March 16, 2011.

Idolatrous Work (Habakkuk 2:1–20; Zephaniah 1:14–18)

The punishment is of the people's own making. They have been working faithlessly, turning good materials of stone, wood, and metal into idols. But work that creates idols has no value, no matter how expensive the materials or well-crafted the results are.

> What use is an idol once its maker has shaped it—a cast image, a teacher of lies? For its maker trusts in what has been made, though the product is only an idol that cannot speak! (Hab. 2:18)

As Zephaniah puts it, "Neither their silver nor their gold will be able to save them" (Zeph. 1:18). Faithfulness is not a superficial matter of uttering praises to God while we work. It is the act of putting God's priorities first in our work. Habakkuk reminds us that "the LORD is in his holy temple; let all the earth keep silence before him!" (Hab. 2:20). This silence is not merely a religious observation, but a silencing of our own broken ambitions, fears, and motivations so that the priorities of God's covenant can become our priorities. Consider what awaits those who defraud others in banking and finance.

> "Alas for you who heap up what is not your own!" How long will you load yourselves with goods taken in pledge? Will not your own creditors suddenly rise, and those who make you tremble wake up? Then you will be booty for them. (Hab. 2:6–7)

Those who accumulate their ill-gotten gain in real estate—a phenomenon that seems constant throughout all the ages—are similarly traps for themselves.

> "Alas for you who get evil gain for your houses, setting your nest on high to be safe from the reach of harm!" You have devised shame for your house by cutting off many peoples; you have forfeited your life. The very stones will cry out from the wall, and the plaster will respond from the woodwork. (Hab. 2:9–11)

Those who exploit others' vulnerabilities also bring judgment on themselves.

> "Alas for you who make your neighbors drink, pouring out your wrath
> until they are drunk, in order to gaze on their nakedness!" You will be
> sated with contempt instead of glory. Drink, you yourself, and stagger!
> The cup in the Lord's right hand will come around to you, and shame will
> come upon your glory. (Hab. 2:15–16)

Work that oppresses or takes advantage of others ultimately brings about
its own downfall.

Today, we may not be literally crafting idols of precious materials
before which we bow down. But work also may be idolatrous if we imagine that we are capable of producing our own salvation. For the essence
of idolatry is that "its maker trusts in his own handiwork" (Hab. 2:18,
NASB, cf. NRSV above), rather than trusting in the God by whose guidance and power we are created to work. If we are ambitious for power
and influence because we think that without our wisdom, skill, and leadership, our work group, company, organization, or nation is doomed,
then our ambition is a form of idolatry. In contrast, if we are ambitious
for power and influence so that we can draw others into a network of
service in which everyone brings forth God's gifts for the world, then
our ambition is a form of faithfulness. If our response to success is self-congratulation, then we are practicing idolatry. If our response is thankfulness, then we are worshiping God. If our reaction to failure is despair,
then we are feeling the hollowness of a broken idol. But if our reaction is
the faith to try again, then we are experiencing the saving power of God.

Faithfulness in the Midst of Toil (Habakkuk 2:1; Zephaniah 2:1–4)

There is another dynamic at work in the exile. Notwithstanding the
emphasis of Nahum, Habakkuk, and Zephaniah on punishment, during
this period people also began to relearn how to work in faithful service
to God. This is fully explored in other chapters, such as "Jeremiah &
Lamentations and Work" and "Daniel and Work," but it is also hinted at
here in the books of the Twelve. The key point of this is that even in the
wretched circumstances of the exile, it is still possible to be faithful. As
Habakkuk watched the carnage around him, no doubt wishing he could
be somewhere else, he determined to stay at his post and listen for the
word of God there (Hab. 2:1). But more is possible than simply staying

at one's post, valuable as that may be. We may also find a way to be righteous and humble.

> Seek the LORD, all you humble of the land, who do his commands; seek righteousness, seek humility; perhaps you may be hidden on the day of the LORD's wrath. (Zeph. 2:3)

There are no ideal places of work. Some are deeply challenging to people of God, compromised in all sorts of ways, while others are flawed in more mundane ways. But even in difficult workplaces, we may still be faithful witnesses to God's purposes, both in the quality of our presence and in the quality of our work. Habakkuk reminds us that no matter how fruitless our work seems, God is present with us in our work, giving us a joy that even the worst conditions of labor cannot completely overcome.

> Though the fig tree does not blossom,
> and no fruit is on the vines;
> though the produce of the olive fails
> and the fields yield no food;
> though the flock is cut off from the fold
> and there is no herd in the stalls,
> yet I will rejoice in the LORD;
> I will exult in the God of my salvation.
> GOD, the Lord, is my strength;
> he makes my feet like the feet of a deer,
> and makes me tread upon the heights. (Hab. 3:17–19)

Or, as the paraphrase by Terry Barringer puts it,

> Though the contract finishes,
> And there is no work to be had;
> Though there is no demand for my skills,
> And no one publishes my work.
> Though the savings run out,
> And the pension is not enough to live on;
> Yet will I rejoice in the Lord,
> I will rejoice in God my Saviour.[6]

---

[6]Terry Barringer, cited in *The Bible and the Business of Life*, ed. Gordon Preece and Simon Carey Holt (Adelaide: ATF, 2004), 215.

As verse 19 suggests, good work is possible even in the midst of difficult circumstances, for the Lord is our strength. Faithfulness is not only a matter of enduring hardship, but also of making even the worst situation better in whatever ways we can.

Faith and Work After the Exile—Haggai, Zechariah, and Malachi

After the exile ended, Jewish civil society and religious life were restored in the land of God's promise. Jerusalem and its temple were rebuilt, along with the economic, social, and religious infrastructure of Jewish society. Accordingly, the books of the Twelve now shift to the challenges of work that follow sin and punishment.

The Need for Social Capital (Haggai 1:1–2:19)

One of the challenges we face in work is the temptation to put self and family ahead of society. The prophet Haggai paints a vivid picture of this challenge. He confronts people working hard to rebuild their own houses, while neglecting to put resources into the rebuilding of the temple, the center of the Jewish society. "Is it a time for you yourselves to live in your paneled houses, while this house lies in ruins?" (Hag. 1:4). He says that this failure to invest in social capital is actually diminishing their individual productivity.

> You have sown much, and harvested little; you eat, but you never have enough; you drink, but you never have your fill; you clothe yourselves, but no one is warm; and you that earn wages earn wages to put them into a bag with holes. (Hag. 1:6)

But as the Lord stirs up the spirit of the people and their leaders, they do begin to invest in rebuilding the temple and the fabric of society (Hag. 1:14–15).

Investing in social capital reminds us that there is no such thing as a "self-made person." Although individual effort may create great wealth, each of us relies on resources and social infrastructure that originate ultimately in God. "I will fill this house with splendor, says the LORD of hosts. The silver is mine, and the gold is mine, says the LORD of hosts" (Hag. 2:7–8). Prosperity is not a matter only—or even primarily—of personal effort, but of a community grounded in God's covenant. "In this place I will give prosperity, says the LORD of hosts" (Hag. 2:9).

We are foolish if we think we must provide for ourselves before we can afford to take time for God and the society of his people. The truth is that we cannot provide for ourselves except by the grace of God's generosity and the mutual work of his community. This is the same concept behind the tithe. It is not a sacrifice of 10 percent of the harvest, but a blessing of 100 percent of the amazing yield of God's creation.

In our own day, this reminds us of the importance of putting resources into the intangible aspects of life. Housing, food, automobiles, and other physical necessities are important. But God provides richly enough that we can also afford art, music, education, nature, recreation, and the myriad ways to feed the soul. Like the businessperson or carpenter, those who work in the arts, humanities, or leisure industries, or who put money toward the creation of parks, playgrounds, and theaters make every bit as much of a contribution to God's intended world.

This also suggests that investing in churches and church life is crucial to empowering Christians' work. Worship itself is intricately tied to doing good work, as we have seen, and perhaps we should engage in worship as formation for good work, rather than merely as private devotion or leisure. Moreover, the Christian community can be a powerful force for economic, civic, and social well-being if it can learn to bring the spiritual and ethical power of God's word to bear on matters of work in the economic, social, governmental, academic, and scientific fields.

Work, Worship, and the Environment (Haggai 1:1–2:19; Zechariah 7:8–14)

Haggai connects the economic and social well-being of the people with the state of the environment. By means of a play on words more obvious in Hebrew than in the English translation, Haggai links the desolation of the temple ("in ruins," Hebrew *hareb*, Hag. 1:9) with the desolation of land and its harvests ("drought," Hebrew *horeb*) and the consequent ruination of the general wellness of "human beings and animals, and on all their labors" (Hag. 1:11). The linchpin of this link is the health of the temple, which becomes a kind of cipher for the religious faithfulness or unfaithfulness of the people. So there is a three-way link among worship, socioeconomic health, environment, and worship. When there is disease in our physical environment, then there is disease in human society, and one of the marks of an unhealthy society is its contribution to the disease of the environment.

There is also a link between the way a community worships and cares for the land, and the economic and political condition of those who occupy the land. The prophets call us to relearn the lesson that a respect for the creator of the earth we occupy is a starting point for peace between the earth and its inhabitants. For Haggai, the drought of the land and the ruin of the temple are inseparable. True and wholehearted worship ushers in peace and blessing from the land.

> Since the day that the foundation of the Lord's temple was laid, consider: Is there any seed left in the barn? Do the vine, the fig tree, the pomegranate, and the olive tree still yield nothing? From this day on I will bless you. (Hag. 2:18–19)

Zechariah, too, draws a link between human sin and desolation of the land. Those in power "oppress the widow, the orphan, the alien or the poor" (Zech. 7:10). "They made their hearts adamant in order not to hear the law and the words that the Lord of hosts had sent" (Zech. 7:12). As a result, the environment became degraded, and thus "a pleasant land was made desolate" (Zech. 7:14). Joel, however, had observed the beginnings of this degradation long before the exile: "The vine withers, the fig tree droops. Pomegranate, palm, and apple—all the trees of the field are dried up; surely, joy withers away among the people" (Joel 1:12).

Given the importance of work and work practices to the well-being of the environment, if Christians were to do their work according to the vision of the Twelve Prophets, then we could have a profoundly beneficial impact on the planet and all those who inhabit it.[7] It is the urgent envi-

---

[7] For a further exploration of this link, see Tim Meadowcroft, *Haggai* (Sheffield: Sheffield Phoenix Press, 2006), 238–42.

ronmental responsibility of the faithful to learn in concrete ways how to ground their work in the worship of God.

Haggai's long oracle on purity (Hag. 2:10–19) also suggests a link between purity and the health of the land. God complains that because of the people's impurity, "with every work of their hands . . . what they offer there is unclean" (Hag. 2:14). This is part of the more general link between worship and the health of the environment. One possible application is that a pure environment means an environment being treated in sustainable ways by those to whom God has given responsibility for its well-being, namely, humanity. Thus purity entails a fundamental respect for the integrity of the whole created order, the health of its ecospheres, the viability and well-being of its species, and the renewability of its productivity. And so we return to the theme of Christians and responsible work practices.

Accordingly, if desolation is part of God's punishment for the sin of the people reported in the book of the Twelve, then productive land is part of their restoration. Indeed, in quite different circumstances, Zechariah has a similar vision to that of Amos during the time of Israelite prosperity: people experiencing well-being in the form of sitting under the fig trees that they planted. "On that day, says the LORD of hosts, you shall invite each other to come under your vine and fig tree" (Zech. 3:10). Peace with God includes care for the earth that God has made. Productive land, of course, has to be worked in order to yield its fruit. And so the world of work is intimately connected with the realization of abundant life.

Both Sin and Hope Remain Present in Work (Malachi 1:1–4:6)

Even in the time of restoration, human sin is never far away. Malachi, the third of the restoration prophets, complains that some of the people have begun to profit by exploiting the most vulnerable in Israelite society (the "lame or sick," Mal. 1:13), in particular by defrauding laborers of their wages (Mal. 3:5). God accuses them that when you defraud them, "you are robbing *me*!" (Mal. 3:8; emphasis added). Not surprisingly, such people also pollute the temple worship by stinting what they contribute in offerings (Mal. 1:8–19), and as a result the environment is also degraded (Mal. 3:11).

Yet the hope of the prophets remains, and work is at the center of it. It begins with a promise to restore the religious/social infrastructure of the temple.

See, I am sending my messenger to prepare the way before me, and the Lord whom you seek will suddenly come to his temple. The messenger of the covenant in whom you delight—indeed, he is coming, says the LORD of hosts. (Mal. 3:1)

It proceeds with the restoration of the environment. "I will rebuke the locust" (Mal. 3:11a), God promises, and then "you will be a land of delight" (Mal. 3:12). People go about their work ethically (Mal. 3:14, 18), and as a result the economy is restored, including "the produce of your soil" and "your vine in the field" (Mal. 3:11b).

Jonah and God's Blessing for All Nations

As noted in the introduction, the book of Jonah is an outlier among the Twelve Prophets because it does not take place in Israel, the text gives no indication of its date, it does not contain prophetic oracles, and the focus is not on the people to whom the prophet is sent but on his own personal experience.[8] Nonetheless, it shares the perspective of the other prophets that God is active in the world (Jonah 1:2, 17; 2:10), and that faithfulness to God (or lack of it) underlies a threefold link among worship, socioeconomic health, and the environment. When the sailors pray to the Lord and obey his word, the sea is calmed, and God provides for the well-being of the sailors and Jonah (Jonah 1:14–19). When Jonah returns to proper worship, the Lord returns the environment to its proper order: fish in the sea and people on dry land (Jonah 2:7–10). When Nineveh turns to the Lord, the animals and humans band together in harmony and the socioeconomic violations cease (Jonah 3:4–10). Although Jonah's setting is different from the rest of the Twelve Prophets, his theology is not. The unique contributions of the book of Jonah are (1) the focus on the prophet's call and response, and (2) the recognition

---

[8] Douglas Stuart, *Hosea–Jonah*, vol. 31, *Word Biblical Commentary* (Dallas: Word, 2002), 431.

that God is not working to bless Israel against the other nations, but to bless the other nations through Israel.[9]

Jonah's Call and Response (Jonah 1:1–17)

As is typical with Twelve Prophets, the book of Jonah begins with a call from God to the prophet (Jonah 1:1–2). Unlike the others, however, Jonah rejects God's call. Foolishly, he attempts to flee the presence of the Lord by taking a ship to foreign shores (Jonah 1:3). This imperils not only him but also his shipmates, for—as we have seen throughout the book of the Twelve—breaking covenant with God has tangible consequences, and the actions of individuals always affect the community.

God sends a storm. First, it ruins the mariners' commercial prospects, as they are forced to throw all the cargo into the sea to lighten the ship (Jonah 1:5). Eventually it threatens their very lives (Jonah 1:11). Only when Jonah offers to be thrown into the sea—which the sailors reluctantly accept—does the storm abate and the danger to the community subside (Jonah 1:12–15).

The purpose of a call from God is to serve other people, and Jonah's call is for the benefit of Nineveh. When he rejects God's guidance, not only do the people he was called to serve languish, but the people surrounding him suffer as well. If we accept that we are all called to serve God in our work—which is probably different from Jonah's work, but no less important to God (see the Theology of Work Project article "Vocation Overview" at www.theologyofwork.org)—then we recognize that failing to serve God in our work also diminishes our communities. The more powerful our gifts and talents, the greater the harm we are apt to do if we reject God's guidance in our work. Undoubtedly, we can all bring to mind people whose prodigious abilities enabled them to do great harm in the fields of business, government, society, science, religion, and all the rest. Imagine the good they could have done, the evil they could have avoided, if they had submitted their skills first to the worship and service of the Lord. Our gifts may seem puny in comparison, yet imagine the good we could do and the evil we could avert if we did our work in service to God over the course of a lifetime.

---

[9] Stuart, 434.

God's Blessing for All Nations (Jonah 1:16; 3:1–4:2)

Jonah disobeys God's call because he objects to God's intent to bless Israel's adversaries, the nation of Assyria and its capital city, Nineveh. When he ultimately relents and his mission is successful, he then resents God's mercy to them (Jonah 4:1–2). This is understandable, for in time Assyria would conquer the northern kingdom of Israel (2 Kgs. 17:6), and Jonah is being sent to bless people he despises. Nonetheless, this is God's will. Apparently, God's intent is to use the people of Israel to bless all nations, not just themselves. (See "Blessing for All Peoples," Jeremiah 29, in "Jeremiah & Lamentations and Work" above.)

Is it possible that we each try to place our own limitations on the reach of God's blessings through our work? We often assume we have to hoard the benefits of our work for ourselves, lest others gain an advantage over us. We may resort to secrecy and deception, cheating and cutting corners, exploitation and intimidation, in an effort to gain an advantage over rivals at work. We seem to accept as fact the unproven assumption that our success at work has to come at others' expense. Have we come to believe that success is a zero-sum game?

God's blessing is not a bucket with limited capacity, but an overflowing fountain. "Put me to the test, says the LORD of hosts; see if I will not open the windows of heaven for you and pour down for you an overflowing blessing" (Mal. 3:10). Despite the competition, resource constraints, and malevolence we often face at work, God's mission for us is nothing as puny as survival against all odds, but the magnificent transformation of our places of work to fulfill the creativity and productivity, the relationships and social harmony, and the environmental balance that God intended from the beginning.

Although Jonah initially refuses to participate in God's blessing for his adversaries, in the end his faithfulness to God overcomes his disobedience. Eventually he does warn Nineveh, and to his dismay they respond passionately to his message. The entire city, "everyone great and small" (Jonah 3:5b), from the king and his nobles to the people in the streets to the animals in their flocks, "turn from their evil ways and the violence that is in their hands" (Jonah 3:8). "The people of Nineveh believed God" (Jonah 3:5a), and "when God saw what they did, how they turned from their evil ways, God changed his mind about the calamity that he had said he would bring upon them; and he did not do it" (Jonah 3:10).

This is dismaying to Jonah because he continues to want to dictate the results of the work to which God called him. He wants punishment, not forgiveness, for Nineveh. He judges the results of his own work harshly (Jonah 4:5) and misses out on the joy of others. Do we do the same? When we lament the seeming lack of significance and success in our work, are we forgetting that only God can see the true value of our work?

Perhaps Jonah's hard-heartedness is driven by a concern for his reputation. He proclaimed God's word that "Nineveh shall be overthrown" (Jonah 3:4), but in the end it wasn't. Even though his own message is what led the people of Nineveh to repent and be spared destruction, is it possible that Jonah felt his credibility had been impaired? This seems to be the heart of his complaint in Jonah 4:2. He proclaimed what God led him to proclaim, but God changed his mind and that made Jonah look foolish. God is "ready to relent from punishing," but Jonah is not ready to look foolish, not even if that's what it takes to spare 128,000 people. Like Jonah, we might do well to ask whether our attitudes and actions at work have more to do with making ourselves look good than with bringing God's grace and love to the people around us.

Yet even Jonah's small, halting moments of obedience to God lead to blessings for those around him. On the ship, he acknowledges, "I worship the Lord, the God of heaven" (Jonah 1:9) and sacrifices himself for the sake of his shipmates. As a result, they are saved from the storm and, moreover, they become followers of the Lord. "The men feared the Lord even more, and they offered a sacrifice to the Lord and made vows" (Jonah 1:16).

If we recognize that our own work in God's service is hobbled by disobedience, resentment, laxity, fear, selfishness, or other ailments, then Jonah's experience may be an encouragement to us. Here we have a prophet who may be even more of a failure at faithful service than we are. Yet God accomplishes the fullness of his mission through Jonah's halting, flawed, intermittent service. By God's power, our poor service may accomplish everything that God intends.

God's Care for Those Who Respond to His Call
(Jonah 1:3, 12–14, 17; 2:10; 4:3–8)

In light of Jonah's experience, we might fear that God's calling will lead us into calamity and hardship. Wouldn't it be easier to hope God doesn't call us at all? It is true that responding to God's call may require great sacrifice and hardship.[10] Yet in Jonah's case, the hardship arises not from God's call, but from Jonah's disobedience to it. The shipwreck and the three-day burial at sea in the belly of the great fish arise directly from his attempt to flee God's presence. His later exposure to the sun and wind and his despair almost to the point of suicide (Jonah 4:3–8) are not hardships imposed by God. They come because Jonah refuses to accept the blessings of "a gracious God [who is] merciful, slow to anger, and abounding in steadfast love, and ready to relent from punishing" (Jonah 4:2).

The truth is that God is always working to care for and comfort Jonah. God moves people to compassion for Jonah, as when the sailors try to row the ship to land rather than accept Jonah's offer to be thrown overboard (Jonah 1:12–14). God sends a fish to save Jonah from drowning (Jonah 1:17) and then speaks to the fish to tell it to expel Jonah back onto dry land (Jonah 2:10). He grants Jonah favor among the enemy population of Nineveh, who treat him with esteem and heed his message. In Jonah's time of greatest need, God provides him with shade and shelter at Nineveh (Jonah 4:5–6).

If Jonah's case is any example, then God's call to serve others in our work need not come at the expense of our own well-being. To expect otherwise would be to remain trapped in the mind-set of the zero-sum game. Given the extraordinary measures God takes to provide for Jonah when he rejects God's call, imagine what blessings Jonah might have experienced if he had accepted the call from the beginning. The means to travel, friends ready to risk their lives for him, harmony with the world of nature, shade and shelter, the esteem of people among whom he works, and astounding success in his work—imagine how great a blessing these might have been if Jonah had accepted them as God intended. Even in

---

[10] A classic exploration of this topic is Dietrich Bonhoeffer's *The Cost of Discipleship* (New York: Macmillan, 1966), originally published in 1937.

the diminished form that Jonah forces upon himself, they show that God's call to service is also an invitation to blessing.

Conclusions from the Twelve Prophets

The books of the Twelve Prophets bring a unified perspective on work to a diversity of times and situations in the life of Israel. At all times they demonstrate that God is at work in the world, ready to bring about the best for his people, if they will only keep his covenant. Before the exile, the prophets challenge the elites of Israel about their use of power and their faithfulness in worship. Their constant theme is that no worship is acceptable to God unless it is accompanied by economic and political justice, for God does not recognize a split between the work of worship and the work of daily life. He does not accept that some may prosper while doing nothing for the common good and for the poorest and most vulnerable members of society.

Israel's failure to work/worship as God commands leads to the national catastrophe and exile in Babylon. During the exile, the prophets call the people to confront their failures, and in doing so discover that even in the worst of times they had the opportunity to be faithful. Again, their faithfulness is seen as much in their work as in their worship. Those who work only for selfish interest are no better off than those who worship idols. Indeed, by elevating work and the resultant wealth to ends in themselves, work in this fashion *is* idolatry. But those who work justly, according to God's covenant, will find that even in the worst circumstances God is present in their work, bringing joy and fruitfulness.

After the return from exile, the prophets challenge Israel to maintain godly priorities as they reestablish themselves in the land and rebuild it from a place of desolation. Once more, economic development, just commerce, government that provides for the common good, and work in the service of others form the basis of true worship. Everyone is called to work in cooperation with God and the community of faith toward the peace and well-being that God intends in his creation.

This is still our call today, as much as it was in ancient Israel. In the Hebrew ordering of the Old Testament, which Christians also observe, the books of the Twelve Prophets have the last word before the pages of the New Testament open. Therefore, they point toward Jesus, who came to fulfill the hopes of the prophets for abundant life in every sphere of human activity, including work, and in doing so brings into being the promise God made to Zechariah, "Thus says the LORD of hosts: My cities shall again overflow with prosperity" (Zech. 1:17).

Matthew and Work

Introduction to Matthew

Work is an essential component of God's kingdom. Matthew, the tax-collector-turned-apostle, recounts Jesus' actions and teachings to show us how God intends us to live and work in his new kingdom. As followers of Jesus Christ, we live in two worlds. We stand with one foot in the human world, where our work may be subject to unspoken expectations that may or may not be in accordance with God's ways. At the same time, as Christians, we are subjects of God's kingdom, committed to his values and expectations. In telling the story of Jesus, Matthew shows us how to navigate the human world using God's compass. In doing so, he constantly points us toward the world's true identity as the "kingdom of heaven." (Matthew uses "kingdom of heaven" and "kingdom of God" interchangeably; see Matt. 19:23–24). This kingdom "has come" to earth, even though it has not yet become completely realized here. Until it comes to completion, Jesus' followers are to live and work according to God's call as "resident aliens"[1] in this present world.

To guide us in this way of life and work, Jesus discusses workplace matters such as leadership and authority, power and influence, fair and unfair business practices, truth and deception, treatment of workers, conflict resolution, wealth and the necessities of life, workplace relationships, investing and saving, rest, and working in organizations with policies and practices that are at odds with biblical norms.

The Kingdom of Heaven Has Come Near

At the beginning of his earthly ministry, Jesus announces that "the kingdom of heaven has come near" (Matt. 4:17). When we read "kingdom

---

[1] Stanley Hauerwas and William Willimon, *Resident Aliens: Life in the Christian Colony* (Nashville: Abingdon Press, 1989).

of heaven," we may think of harps, clouds, and angel choirs, but Jesus is clear that the kingdom of heaven refers to God's rule on earth. The kingdom of heaven "*has come near.*" It has come *here* to *this* world.

The workplace consequences of living in God's kingdom are profound. Kingdoms are concerned with governance, economics, agriculture, production, justice, defense—issues we see in most workplaces. Jesus' teachings, as recorded by Matthew, speak directly to our life at work. In the Sermon on the Mount, he inducts his followers into the values, ethics, and practices of this new kingdom. In the Lord's Prayer, he instructs them to pray, "Your kingdom come. Your will be done, *on earth* as it is in heaven" (Matt. 6:9–10). The Gospel of Matthew concludes as Jesus commissions his followers to go to work throughout the world, because he has received "all authority in heaven and *on earth*" and will be present with them in their work on earth (Matt. 28:18–20). Matthew is clear that this kingdom is not fully realized on earth as we know it, but will reach completion when we see "the Son of Man coming on the clouds of heaven with power and great glory" (Matt. 24:30). Meanwhile, we turn our backs on the old ways of work, so that the new way of the kingdom of heaven is made visible in us as we live. Even now, we work according to its values and practices.

Working as Citizens of God's Kingdom (Matthew 1–4)

We live in what theologians call "the already, but not yet." The kingdom of heaven has already been inaugurated by Jesus in his earthly ministry, but has not yet been fully realized—not until Christ returns in person as King. Meanwhile, our lives—including our work, our leisure, our worship, our joy, and our sorrow—are framed by the reality of living in a world still subjected to the old, corrupt ways of the Fall (Gen. 3), yet claimed by its true Lord, Christ. As Christians, we put ourselves wholly under Jesus as Lord. Our habits on earth are now to reflect the coming kingdom of heaven. This is not to boast that we are more godly than others, but to accept the challenge of growing into God's ways. God calls his people to many different roles and occupations on earth. In all these roles and occupations, we are to live out the true reality: the reign of God that is coming from heaven to earth.

At the same time, we cannot escape the ills of the world brought on by the Fall, including death (1 Cor. 15:15–26), sin (John 1:29), and Satan (Rev. 12:9). Jesus himself experienced terrible, though temporary, suffering at the hands of sinful men, and so may we. In our work, we may suffer greatly through forced labor, permanent unemployment, or even work-related death. Or we may suffer in smaller ways as we deal with challenging co-workers, unpleasant working conditions, promotions deserved but not received, or a thousand other setbacks. Sometimes we suffer from the consequences of our own sin at work. Others may suffer much more than we, but all of us can learn from the Gospel of Matthew how to live as Christ-followers in a fallen world.

Why Should We Listen to Jesus? (Matthew 1–2)

The opening chapters of Matthew's Gospel narrate in rapid-fire succession stories demonstrating that Jesus is the Lord whose coming inaugurates the kingdom of heaven on earth. They explain who Jesus is in terms of Scripture fulfilled (the Messiah) and show that his entrance into the world is the epicenter of all of God's dealings with humanity. The Gospel of Matthew begins with a description of Jesus' ancestry and birth: the baby in a Bethlehem manger is in the line of Israel's great king, David, and is a true Hebrew, going back to Abraham (Matt. 1:1–2:23). With each story, Matthew's references to the Old Testament Scriptures show how Jesus' coming reflects a particular ancient text.[2] We listen to Jesus because he is God's anointed, the promised Messiah, God entering the world in human flesh (John 1:14).

Jesus Calling (Matthew 3–4)

Nearly thirty years have elapsed between chapters 2 and 3. John the Baptist reveals Jesus' true identity as the Son of God to the crowds

---

[2] For example, Matthew 1:18–25 refers to Isaiah 7:14; Matthew 2:1–6 to Micah 5:1–3, 2 Samuel 5:3, and 1 Chronicles 11:2; and Matthew 2:13–15 to Hosea 11:1.

at the Jordan River (Matt. 3:17). Then Jesus, following his baptism by John, successfully withstands the temptations of the devil in the wilderness (Matt. 4:1–11), in contrast to Adam or the Israelites who had failed. (For more about the temptations of Jesus, see "Luke 4:1–13" below in "Luke and Work.") In this, we preview the ancient roots of the coming kingdom: it is "Israel" as God originally intended it. And we see its revolutionary aspects; it brings victory over the prince of the fallen world.

Work is an essential element of God's intent for the world. When God created Adam, he immediately gave him work to do (Gen. 2:15); throughout the Old Testament, God's people were also given work to do (Exod. 20:9). It should not surprise us that Jesus, too, was a laborer (Matt. 13:55). Jesus' baptism, his wilderness temptations, and his prior work experience as a carpenter prepared him for the public work he would now begin (Matt. 4:12).

Here we encounter the first passage speaking directly to the question of calling. Soon after Jesus begins to preach the coming of the kingdom of heaven, he calls the first four of his disciples to follow him (Matt. 4:18–21). Others later respond to his call, making up the Twelve—the band of those called apart by Jesus to serve as his intimate students and the first servant-leaders for the renewed people of God (cf. Matt. 10:1–4; 19:28; Eph. 2:19–21). Each of the Twelve is required to leave his former occupation, income, and relationships in order to travel with Jesus throughout Galilee. (The personal, family, and social sacrifices this required are discussed under "Mark 1:16–20" in "Mark and Work.") To these and other followers, Jesus holds out no hope of security or family ties. When Jesus later calls the tax collector Matthew, the implication is that Matthew will give up his work of tax collecting (Matt. 9:9).[3]

Does a call from Jesus mean that we have to stop working at our current job and become a preacher, pastor, or missionary? Is this passage

---

[3] We see the same call to a radical life change in Jesus' injunction to a potential disciple: "Let the dead bury their own dead" (Matt. 8:18–22). As R. T. France put it, "The kingdom of heaven apparently involves a degree of fanaticism which is willing to disrupt the normal rhythms of social life." R. T. France, *The Gospel of Matthew*, New International Commentary on the New Testament (Grand Rapids: Eerdmans, 2007), 331.

teaching us that discipleship means abandoning nets and boats, saws and chisels, payrolls and profits?

The answer is no. This passage *describes* what happened to four men by the Sea of Galilee that day. But it does not *prescribe* the same thing for every follower of Jesus Christ. For the Twelve, following Jesus did mean leaving their professions and their families in order to itinerate with their roving master. Both then and now, there are professions that require similar sacrifices, including military service, sea trade, or diplomacy, among many others. At the same time, we know that even during Jesus' earthly ministry not all true believers in him quit their day jobs to follow him. He had many followers who remained in their homes and occupations. Often he made use of their ability to provide meals, lodging, and financial support for him and his companions (e.g., Simon the Leper in Mark 14:3, or Mary, Martha, and Lazarus in Luke 10:38, John 12:1–2). Often, they gave him entry to their local communities, which is something his traveling companions could not have done. Interestingly, Zacchaeus was also a tax collector (Luke 19:1–10), and although his life as a tax collector was transformed by Jesus, we see no evidence that he was called to leave the profession.

But this passage also leads us to a deeper truth about our work and following Christ. We may not have to give up our jobs, but we have to give up allegiance to ourselves, or to anyone or any system contrary to God's purposes. In a sense, we become double agents for God's kingdom. We may remain in our workplace. We may perform the same tasks. But now we employ our work to serve the new kingdom and our new master. We still work to bring home a paycheck, but at a deeper level we also work to serve people, as our master did. When you serve people because of your allegiance to Christ, "you serve the Lord Christ," as Paul puts it (Col. 3:24).

This is more radical than it may first appear. We are challenged in the work we do. To the extent possible, we should seek to do those things that bring human flourishing, either through our part in carrying on the creation mandate, or our part in carrying out the redemption mandate. In short, we do those things that support people's dreams and bring healing to the brokenness around us.

So we see that although a call from Jesus may not change *what* we do for a living, it always changes *why* we work. As followers of Jesus, we work above all to serve him. In turn, this leads to a change in *how* we work, and especially how we treat other people. The ways of the new King include compassion, justice, truth, and mercy; the ways of the old prince of this world are devastation, apathy, oppression, deceit, and vindictiveness. The latter can no longer have any role in our work. This is more challenging than it may appear, and we could never hope to do so on our own. The practices required to live and work in these new ways can arise only from God's power or blessing in our work, as will emerge in chapters 5 through 7.

The Kingdom of Heaven at Work in Us (Matthew 5–7)

Chapters 5 through 7 in Matthew's Gospel give us the most complete version of Jesus' Sermon on the Mount. While this very long passage (111 verses) is often treated as a series of discrete segments (thought by some to have been compiled from different teaching occasions), there is a cohesion and a flow of thought in the sermon that deepens our understanding of how the kingdom of heaven is at work in us, in our work, and in our family and community life.

The Beatitudes (Matthew 5:1–12)

The Sermon on the Mount opens with the beatitudes—eight statements beginning with the word *blessed*.[4] This word affirms a state of blessing that already exists. Each beatitude declares that a group of people usually regarded as afflicted is actually blessed. Those blessed do not have to do anything to attain this blessing. Jesus simply declares that they have already been blessed. Thus the beatitudes are first of all declarations of God's grace. They are not conditions of salvation or road maps to earn entry to God's kingdom.

---

[4] The word *blessed* translates the Greek word *makarios*. It doesn't pray for a blessing but affirms an existing state of blessedness. There is another Greek word, *eulogia*, which is also translated into English as "blessed." It is the word used to pray that God will bless or bring something good to a person or a community. It does not appear in the beatitudes.

Those who belong to each blessed group experience God's grace because the kingdom of heaven has come near. Consider the second beatitude, "Blessed are those who mourn" (Matt. 5:4). People do not normally think of mourning as a blessing. It is a sorrow. But with the coming of the kingdom of heaven, mourning becomes a blessing because the mourners "will be comforted." The implication is that God himself will do the comforting. The affliction of mourning becomes the blessing of profound relationship with God. That is a blessing indeed!

Although the primary purpose of the beatitudes is to declare the blessings given by God's kingdom, most scholars also regard them as painting a picture of the character of that kingdom.[5] As we step into God's kingdom, we hope to become more like those named as blessed—more meek, more merciful, more hungry for righteousness, more apt to make peace, and so on. This gives the beatitudes a moral imperative. Later, when Jesus says, "Make disciples of all nations" (Matt. 28:19), the beatitudes describe the character these disciples are meant to take on.

The beatitudes describe the character of God's kingdom, but they are not *conditions* of salvation. Jesus does not say, for example, "Only the pure in heart may enter the kingdom of heaven." This is good news because the beatitudes are impossibly hard to fulfill. Given that Jesus says, "Everyone who looks at a woman with lust has already committed adultery with her in his heart" (Matt. 5:28), who could truly be "pure in heart" (Matt. 5:8)? If it were not for God's grace, no one would actually be blessed. The beatitudes are not a judgment against all who fail to measure up. Instead, they are a blessing for any who consent to join themselves to God's kingdom as it "comes near."

A further grace of the beatitudes is that they bless God's community, not just God's individuals. By following Jesus, we become blessed members of the kingdom community, even though our character is not yet formed in God's likeness. Individually, we fail to fulfill the characteristics of some or all of the blessings. But we are blessed nonetheless by

---

[5] Donald A. Hagner, *Matthew 1–13*, vol. 33A, *Word Biblical Commentary* (Nashville: Thomas Nelson, 1993), 97. This view, though widely held, is not universal. For a brief outline of various alternatives, see W. F. Albright and C. S. Mann, *Matthew*, vol. 26 of *The Anchor Bible* (New York: Doubleday, 1971), 50–53.

the character of the entire community around us. Citizenship in God's kingdom begins now. The character of the kingdom community is perfected when Jesus returns, "coming on the clouds of heaven with power and great glory" (Matt. 24:30).

With this understanding, we are ready to examine the specific character of each of the beatitudes and explore how it applies to work. We cannot attempt to discuss each beatitude exhaustively, but we hope we can lay the groundwork for receiving the blessings and living out the beatitudes in our daily work.[6]

"Blessed Are the Poor in Spirit, for Theirs Is the Kingdom of Heaven" (Matthew 5:3)

The "poor in spirit" are those who cast themselves on God's grace.[7] We personally acknowledge our spiritual bankruptcy before God. It is the tax collector in the temple, beating his breast and saying, "God, be merciful to me, a sinner" (Luke 18:9–14). It is an honest confession that we are sinful and utterly without the moral virtues needed to please God. It is the opposite of arrogance. In its deepest form, it acknowledges our desperate need for God. Jesus is declaring that it is a blessing to recognize our need to be filled by God's grace.

Thus, at the very beginning of the Sermon on the Mount, we learn that we don't have the spiritual resources in ourselves to put Jesus' teachings into practice. We can't fulfill God's call by ourselves. Blessed

---

[6] For a deeper exploration in the same vein, see David Gill, *Becoming Good: Building Moral Character* (Downers Grove: InterVarsity Press, 2000).

[7] Luke renders this as "blessed are you who are poor" (Luke 6:20). Scholars have debated which of the two accounts is primary. Jesus opens his ministry in Luke 4:16–18 by reading from Isaiah 61:1, saying that he has come "to bring good news to the poor." When John the Baptist questions whether Jesus is the Messiah, Jesus replies, "the poor have good news brought to them" (Matt. 11:5). But other scholars point out that "the poor" are the humble and devout who seek God, which suggests that "poor in spirit" is the primary sense. This accords with Isaiah 66:2, "But this is the one to whom I will look, to the humble and contrite in spirit, who trembles at my word." Jesus references "the poor" fifteen times in the Gospels. Three times he refers to those who have nothing to eat, but eleven times he refers to the humble and pious who seek God. Perhaps the best resolution is that the biblical concept of the "poor" refers both to socioeconomic poverty and spiritual bankruptcy, and the consequent need to depend on God.

are those who realize they are spiritually bankrupt, for this realization turns them to God, without whom they cannot fulfill what they are created to do and be. Much of the rest of the sermon rips away from us the self-delusion that we are capable of acquiring a state of blessedness on our own. It aims to produce in us a genuine poverty of spirit.

What is the practical result of this blessing? If we are poor in spirit, we are able to bring an honest appraisal of ourselves to our work. We don't inflate our résumé or boast about our position. We know how difficult it is to work with people who cannot learn, grow, or accept correction because they are trying to maintain an inflated picture of themselves. So we commit ourselves to honesty about ourselves. We remember that even Jesus, when he started working with wood, must have needed guidance and instruction. At the same time, we acknowledge that only with God at work within us can we put Jesus' teachings into practice on the job. We seek God's presence and strength in our lives each day as we live as Christians where we work.

In the fallen world, poverty of spirit may seem to be a hindrance to success and advancement. Often this is an illusion. Who is likely to be more successful in the long run? A leader who says, "Fear not, I can handle anything, just do as I say," or a leader who says, "Together, we can do it, but everyone will have to perform better than ever before"? If there was ever a time when an arrogant, self-promoting leader was considered greater than a humble, empowering leader, that time is passing, at least within the best organizations. For example, a humble leader is the first characteristic mark of companies that achieve sustained greatness, according to Jim Collins's well-known research.[8] Of course, many workplaces remain stuck in the old kingdom of self-promotion and inflated self-appraisal. In some situations, the best practical advice may be to find another workplace if at all possible. In other cases, leaving the job may not be possible, or it may not be desirable, because by staying a Christian could be an important force for good. In these situations, the poor in spirit are all the more a blessing to those around them.

---

[8] Jim Collins, *Good to Great: Why Some Companies Make the Leap . . . And Others Don't* (New York: HarperBusiness, 2001), 20.

"Blessed Are Those Who Mourn, for They Will Be Comforted" (Matthew 5:4)

The second beatitude builds on our mental recognition of our poverty of spirit by adding an emotional response of sorrow. When we face the evil in our own lives, it saddens us; when we face the evil in the world—which includes possible evil in our workplace—that, too, touches our emotions with grief. The evil may come from ourselves, from others, or from sources unknown. In any case, when we honestly mourn evil words, evil deeds, or evil policies on the job, God sees our sorrow and comforts us with the knowledge that it will not always be this way.

Those blessed with mourning about their own failings can receive comfort at work by admitting their errors. If we make a mistake with a colleague, student, customer, employee, or other person, we admit it and ask their pardon. This takes courage! Without the emotional blessing of sadness over our actions, we would probably never muster the guts to admit our mistakes. But if we do, we may be surprised how often people are ready to forgive us. And if, on occasion, others take advantage of our admission of fault, we can fall back on the blessing of nonarrogance that flows from the first beatitudes.

Some businesses have found expressing sorrow to be an effective way to operate. Toro, the manufacturer of tractors and lawn equipment, adopted a practice of showing concern to people injured while using their products. As soon as the company learns of an injury, it contacts the injured person to express sorrow and offer help. It also asks for suggestions to improve the product. Surprising as it may sound, this approach has reduced the number of customer lawsuits over a period of many years.[9] Virginia Mason Hospital found similar results from acknowledging their role in patient deaths.[10]

"Blessed Are the Meek, for They Will Inherit the Earth" (Matthew 5:5)

The third beatitude puzzles many people in the workplace, in part because they don't understand what it means to be meek. Many assume the

---

[9] "Kendrick B. Melrose: Caring about People: Employees and Customers," *Ethix* 55 (Sept. 2007), http://ethix.org/2007/10/01/caring-about-people-employees-and-customers.

[10] "Dr. Gary Kaplan: Determined Steps to Transformation," *Ethix* 73 (Jan. 2001), http://ethix.org/2011/01/11/dr-gary-s-kaplan-determined-steps-to-transformation.

term means *weak, tame,* or *deficient in courage.* But the biblical understanding of meekness is power under control. In the Old Testament, Moses was described as the meekest man on earth (Num. 12:3, KJV). Jesus described himself as "meek and lowly" (Matt. 11:28–29, KJV), which was consistent with his vigorous action in cleansing the temple (Matt. 21:12–13).

Power under God's control means two things: (1) refusal to inflate our own self-estimation; and (2) reticence to assert ourselves *for* ourselves. Paul captures the first aspect perfectly in Romans 12:3: "For by the grace given to me I say to everyone among you not to think of yourself more highly than you ought to think, but to think with sober judgment, each according to the measure of faith that God has assigned." Meek people see themselves as servants of God, not thinking more highly of themselves than they ought to think. To be meek is to accept our strengths and limitations for what they truly are, instead of constantly trying to portray ourselves in the best possible light. But it does not mean that we should deny our strengths and abilities. When asked if he was the Messiah, Jesus replied, "The blind receive their sight, the lame walk, the lepers are cleansed, the deaf hear, the dead are raised, and the poor have good news brought to them. And blessed is anyone who takes no offense at me" (Matt. 11:4–6). He had neither an inflated self-image nor an inferiority complex, but a servant's heart based on what Paul would later call "sober judgment" (Rom. 12:3).

A servant's heart is the crux of the second aspect of meekness: reticence to assert ourselves *for* ourselves. We exercise power, but for the benefit of all people, not just ourselves. The second aspect is captured by Psalm 37:1–11a, which begins with, "Do not fret because of the wicked," and ends with "the meek shall inherit the land." It means we curb our urge to avenge the wrongs done against us, and instead use whatever power we have to serve others. It flows from the sorrow for our own weaknesses that comprises the second beatitude. If we feel sorrow for our own sins, can we really feel vengeful over the sins of others?

It can be very challenging to put our power at work under God's control. In the fallen world, it seems to be the aggressive and the self-promoting who get ahead. "You don't get what you deserve, you get what you negotiate."[11] In the workplace, the arrogant and powerful seem to

---

[11] Chester L. Karass, *In Business and in Life: You Don't Get What You Deserve, You Get What You Negotiate* (n.p.: Stanford Street Press, 1996).

win, but in the end they lose. They don't win in personal relationships. No one wants an arrogant, self-seeking friend. Men and women who are hungry for power are often lonely people. Nor do they win in financial security. They think they possess the world, but the world possesses them. The more money they have, the less financially secure they feel.

In contrast, Jesus said that the meek "will inherit the earth." As we have seen, the earth has become the location of the kingdom of heaven. We tend to think of the kingdom of heaven as *heaven*, a place completely different (golden streets, gates of pearl, a mansion over the hilltop) from anything we know here. But God's promise of the kingdom is a new heaven and a new *earth* (Rev. 21:1).

Those who submit their power to God will inherit the perfect kingdom coming to earth. In this kingdom, we receive by God's grace the good things the arrogant fruitlessly strive for in the present earth, and more. And this is not a future reality only. Even in a broken world, those who recognize their true strengths and weaknesses can find peace by living realistically. Those who exercise power for the benefit of *others* are often admired. The meek engage others in decision making and experience better results and deeper relationships.

"Blessed Are Those Who Hunger and Thirst for Righteousness, for They Will Be Filled" (Matthew 5:6)

Understanding the fourth beatitude turns on understanding what Jesus meant by *righteousness*. In ancient Judaism, to act righteously meant "to acquit, vindicate, restore to a right relationship."[12] The righteous are those who maintain right relationships—with God and with the people around them. On the basis of right relationships, those who commit infractions are acquitted of guilt.

Have you received the blessing of being filled with right relationships? It flows from meekness (the third beatitude) because we can only form right relationships with others when we cease making all our actions revolve around ourselves. Do you hunger and thirst for right relationships—with God, with your co-workers, with your family, and your

---

[12] David Noel Freedman, *The Anchor Yale Bible Dictionary* (New York: Doubleday, 1996), 5:737.

community? Hunger is a sign of life. We are genuinely hungry for good relationships if we yearn for others for their own sake, not just as snack food for meeting our own needs. If we see that we have God's grace for this, we will hunger and thirst for right relationships, not only with God, but with the people with whom we work or live.

Jesus says that those who have this hunger will find their appetites filled. It is easy to see the wrongs in our workplaces and to want to do battle to fix them. If we do this, we are hungering and thirsting for righteousness, desiring to see wrongs righted. The Christian faith has been the source of many of the greatest reforms in the work world, perhaps most notably the abolition of slavery in Great Britain and the United States, and the genesis of the Civil Rights movement. But again, the flow of the beatitudes is important. We don't take on these battles in our own strength, but only in recognition of our own emptiness, mourning our own unrighteousness, submitting our power to God.

"Blessed Are the Merciful, for They will Receive Mercy" (Matthew 5:7)

If you are blessed with sorrow for your own failings (the second beatitude) and with right relationships (the fourth beatitude), you will not find it difficult to show mercy to others on the job or anywhere else. Mercy consists of treating people better than they deserve from us. Forgiveness is a type of mercy. So is aiding someone whom we have no obligation to help, or forbearing to exploit someone's vulnerability. Mercy, in all these senses, is the driving force of Christ's incarnation, death, and resurrection. Through him, our sins are forgiven and we ourselves receive aid by the gift of God's spirit (1 Cor. 12). The Spirit's reason for showing us this mercy is simply that God loves us (John 3:16).

At work, mercy has a highly practical effect. We are to aid others to attain their best outcomes, regardless of how we feel about them. When you assist a co-worker, whom you may not like and who may have even wronged you in the past, you are showing mercy. When you are the first contestant in an audition and you warn the later contestants that the judge is in a foul mood, you are showing mercy, though it may give them an advantage over you. When a competitor's child is sick, and you agree to reschedule your presentation to the client so your competitor won't have to choose between caring for the child and competing for the business, you are showing mercy.

These kinds of mercy may cost you an advantage you could otherwise have taken. Yet they benefit the work outcome, as well as the other person. Assisting someone you don't like helps your work unit achieve its goals, even if it doesn't benefit *you* personally. Or—as in the case of the competitor with a sick child—if it doesn't benefit *your* organization, it benefits the client you aim to serve. The underlying reality of mercy is that mercy benefits someone beyond yourself.

An environment of forgiveness in an organization offers another surprising result. It improves the organization's performance. If someone makes a mistake in an organization where mercy is not shown, they are likely not to say anything about it, hoping it will not be noticed and they will not be blamed.

This diminishes performance in two ways. The first is that an error covered up may be much more difficult to deal with later. Imagine a construction job where a worker makes a mistake with a foundation fitting. It is easy to fix if it is brought to light and repaired right away. But it will be very expensive to fix after the structure is built and the foundation buried. The second is that the best learning experiences come out of learning from errors. As Soichiro Honda said, "Success can only be achieved through repeated failure and introspection. In fact, success represents the 1 percent of your work that only comes from the 99 percent that is called failure."[13] Organizations don't have the opportunity to learn if mistakes are not brought forward.

"Blessed Are the Pure in Heart, for They Will See God" (Matthew 5:8)

The sixth beatitude echoes Psalm 24:3–5:

Who shall ascend the hill of the LORD?
    And who shall stand in his holy place?
Those who have clean hands and pure hearts,
    who do not lift up their souls to what is false,
    and do not swear deceitfully.
They will receive blessing from the LORD,
    and vindication from the God of their salvation.

---

[13] Tom Peters, *Thriving on Chaos* (New York: Knopf, 1987), 259–66.

"Clean hands and pure hearts" denote integrity, singleness of devotion, undivided loyalty. Integrity goes well beyond avoiding deceit and bad behavior. The root of integrity is wholeness, meaning that our actions are not choices we put on or take off as may seem convenient, but stem from the whole of our being. Notice that Jesus pronounces the blessing of being pure in heart not right after the blessing of hungering for righteousness, but after the blessing of showing mercy. Purity of heart arises not from perfection of our will, but from reception of God's grace.

We can determine how much of this blessing we have received by asking ourselves: How much commitment do I have to integrity, when I might be able to get away with skillful deception? Do I refuse to let my opinion of someone be shaped by gossip and innuendo, no matter how juicy? To what extent are my actions and words accurate reflections of what is in my heart?

It is hard to argue against personal integrity in the workplace, yet in a fallen world it is often the butt of jokes. Like mercy and meekness, it can be seen as weakness. But it is the person of integrity who will "see God." While the Bible is clear that God is invisible and "dwells in unapproachable light" (1 Tim. 1:17; 6:16), the pure in heart can perceive and sense God's reality in this life. In fact, without integrity, the deceits we propagate against others eventually make us unable to perceive the truth. We inevitably begin to believe our own fabrications. And this leads to ruin in the workplace, because work based on unreality soon becomes ineffective. The impure have no desire to see God, but those who are part of Christ's kingdom are blessed because they see reality as it truly is, including the reality of God.

"Blessed Are the Peacemakers, for They Will Be Called Children of God" (Matthew 5:9)

The seventh beatitude takes every Christian worker into the task of conflict resolution. Conflicts arise whenever people have differences of opinion. In a fallen world, the tendency is to ignore conflict or suppress it by using force, threat, or intimidation. But all of those are violations of the integrity (the sixth beatitude) of the people in conflict. In God's kingdom, it is a blessing to bring people together who are in conflict. Only then is it possible to resolve the conflict and restore the relationships.

(Later in this article, we will explore Jesus' method for conflict resolution in Matt. 18:17–19).

The result of conflict resolution is peace, and peacemakers will be called "children of God." They will reflect the divine character in their actions. God is the God of peace (1 Thess. 5:16) and we show ourselves to be his children when we seek to make peace in the workplace, in the community, in our homes, and in the whole world.

"Blessed Are Those Who Are Persecuted for Righteousness' Sake" (Matthew 5:10)

The eighth and final beatitude may strike us as negative. Up to this point, the beatitudes have focused on humility, meekness, right relationships, mercy, purity of heart, and peacemaking—all positive qualities. But Jesus includes the possibility of "persecution for righteousness' sake." This arises from the previous seven, because the forces that oppose God's ways still hold great power in the world.

Note that persecution arising from *unrighteous* behavior is not blessed. If we fail through our own fault, we should expect to suffer negative consequences. Jesus is talking about the blessing of being persecuted for doing right. But why would we be persecuted for righteousness? The reality in a fallen world is that if we demonstrate genuine righteousness, many will reject us. Jesus elaborates by pointing out that the prophets, who like him announced God's kingdom, were persecuted: "Blessed are you when people revile you and persecute you and utter all kinds of evil against you falsely on my account. Rejoice and be glad, for your reward is great in heaven, for in the same way they persecuted the prophets who were before you" (Matt. 5:11–12). Righteous people in the workplace may be subjected to active, even severe persecution by people who benefit—or believe they benefit—from injustice there.

For example, if you speak up for—or merely befriend—people who are victims of gossip or discrimination in your workplace, expect persecution. If you are the president of a trade association, and you speak out against an unfair subsidy your members are receiving, don't expect them to re-elect you. The blessing is that active persecution for the right reasons indicates that the powers of darkness believe you are succeeding in furthering God's kingdom.

Even the best organizations and most admirable people are still tainted by the Fall. None are perfect. The eighth beatitude serves as a reminder to us that working in a fallen world requires courage.

Salt and Light in the World of Work (Matthew 5:13–16)

Following the beatitudes in the Sermon on the Mount, Jesus tells his followers that people who receive these blessings *matter*:

> "You are the salt of the earth; but if salt has lost its taste, how can its saltiness be restored? It is no longer good for anything, but is thrown out and trampled under foot. You are the light of the world. A city built on a hill cannot be hid. No one after lighting a lamp puts it under the bushel basket, but on the lampstand, and it gives light to all in the house. In the same way, let your light shine before others, so that they may see your good works and give glory to your Father in heaven." (Matt. 5:13–16)

If you are a follower of Jesus living the beatitudes, you matter. You have an important role to play because you are the salt of the earth. Salt preserves and Christians help preserve what is good in the culture. In the ancient world, salt was very valuable: the Greeks thought it contained something almost divine, and the Romans sometimes paid their soldiers with salt. A soldier who didn't carry out his duties "was not worth his salt." You are a seasoning agent. In a sense, you can bring the distinctive flavor of God's values to all of life. You can make life palatable.

Note that salt, to be effective, must be in contact with the meat or fish it is to preserve. To be effective, we must be involved where we work and where we live. This puts us in a tension because the dominant culture doesn't necessarily like us. The majority of the time, living according to the beatitudes may make us more successful in work. But we need to be prepared for the times it doesn't. What will we do if showing mercy, making peace, or working for justice jeopardizes our position at work? Withdrawing from the world is no answer for Christians. But it is difficult to live in the world, ready to challenge its ways at any time. In Matthew 5:10–12, Jesus acknowledged the reality of persecution. But in our contacts with the culture, we must retain our "saltiness," our distinctiveness. It's a balancing act we're called upon to maintain.

"You are the light of the world." The job description of a Christian is not only to maintain personal holiness, but also to touch the lives of everyone around us. At work, we touch many people who do not encounter Christ in church. It may be our most effective place to witness to Christ. But we have to be careful about how we witness for Christ at work. We are being paid to do our work, and it would be dishonest to stint our employers by using work time for evangelism. Moreover, it would be dishonorable to create divisions at work or a hostile environment for nonbelievers. We must avoid any possible taint of seeking self-promotion by proselytizing. And we always run the risk that our failings at work may bring shame on the name of Christ, especially if we seem to be enthusiastic about evangelism but shoddy in actual work.

With all these dangers, how can we be salt and light at work? Jesus said our light is not necessarily in the witness of our words, but in the witness of our deeds—our "good works." "Let your light so shine before men that they may see your good deeds and glorify your Father who is in heaven." The beatitudes have spelled out some of those good works. In humility and submission to God, we work for right relations, for merciful actions, and for peace. When we live as people of blessing, we are salt and light—in the workplace, in our homes, and in our nation.

Living Out the "Righteousness" of the Kingdom of Heaven (Matthew 5:17–48)

Jesus makes a startling statement in Matthew 5:20: "I tell you, unless your righteousness exceeds that of the scribes and Pharisees, you will never enter the kingdom of heaven." Ordinary people in his day revered the apparent righteousness of the religious leaders and could not imagine ever matching them in their piety. Jesus shocks them by stating that entrance into God's kingdom was available only to those whose righteousness exceeded that of the scribes and Pharisees. Who, then, could be saved? The problem lay in equating righteousness with external piety, a common understanding of the word both then and now. But the word *righteousness* throughout the Bible (as noted above in the fourth beatitude) always denotes right relationships—with God and with people around us. This includes those in the workplace.

This becomes plain in the illustrations that follow. In Matthew 5:21–26, it is not enough not to murder someone; we must guard against harboring anger that leads to insults and broken relationships. We may feel anger, but the right way to handle anger is try to resolve conflict (Matt. 18:15–19), not to push the person away with insults or slander. Jesus is clear that a right relationship between you and your brother or sister is so vital that you should forego religious practices until you have cleared the matter between the two of you.

In the workplace, anger may be used to manipulate others. Or anger may overwhelm you because you feel unfairly treated. Deal with the issue: take the first step toward reconciliation, even though it may put you in a position of humility. Engaging in fair, open conflict resolution is the way of the new kingdom. Again, blessed are the peacemakers.

Wealth and Provision (Matthew 6)

Jesus speaks about wealth frequently. Wealth and provision are not in themselves work, but they are often the result of work, our own or someone else's. A central tenet of economics is that the purpose of work is to increase wealth, making this a work-related topic. Here are Jesus' teachings on wealth and daily provision as they appear in the Sermon on the Mount.

"Give Us This Day Our Daily Bread" (Matthew 6:11)

Immediately before this request for daily bread in the Lord's Prayer, we read, "Your kingdom come. Your will be done, on earth as it is in heaven" (Matt. 6:10). In God's kingdom, receiving our daily bread is a certainty, but in our world marred by sin, daily sustenance is questionable. Although God has given humanity everything we need to produce enough food to feed everyone on earth, we have not ended hunger. Thus Jesus' first word about wealth or daily provision is this petition: "Give us this day our daily bread." We turn to God for the bread we need.

But note that the petition is plural: Give *us* this day *our* daily bread. We don't pray only for our own bread, but for bread for those who have none. As people longing to maintain right relationships with others, we take others' need of bread into consideration: we share what we have with those who have need. If every person, business, institution, and government worked according to the purposes and principles of God's kingdom, no one would be hungry.

Store Your Treasure in Heaven, Not on Earth (Matthew 6:19–34)

Not only are we to ask God for our daily provision, but we also are warned against stockpiling material wealth and other treasures on earth:

> "Do not store up for yourselves treasures on earth, where moth and rust consume and where thieves break in and steal; but store up for yourselves treasures in heaven, where neither moth nor rust consumes and where thieves do not break in and steal. For where your treasure is, there your heart will be also." (Matt. 6:19–21)

"Treasures in heaven" is not a vaporous reference to kindly thoughts in God's heart or some such platitude. God's kingdom will ultimately rule on earth. "Treasures in heaven" are things of worth in God's coming kingdom, such as justice, opportunity for everyone to be productive, provision for everyone's needs, and respect for the dignity of every person. The implication is that we would do better to invest our money in activities that transform the world, than in securities that protect our accumulated surplus.

Is it wrong, then, to have a retirement portfolio or even to care about the material things of this world for ourselves or for others? The answer is again both no and yes. The *no* comes from the fact that this passage is not the only one in the Bible speaking to questions of wealth and provision for those who are dependent on us. Other passages counsel prudence and forethought, such as, "Those who gather little by little will increase [wealth]" (Prov. 13:11b), and, "The good leave an inheritance to their children's children" (Prov. 13:22). God guides Joseph to store up food for seven years in advance of a famine (Gen. 41:25–36), and Jesus speaks favorably in the parable of the talents (Matt. 25:14–30, which will be discussed later) of investing money. In light of the rest of Scripture, Matthew 6:19–34 cannot be a blanket prohibition.

But the *yes* part of the answer is a warning, summed up beautifully in verse 21: "Where your treasure is, there will your heart be also."

We might expect this sentence to run the other way: "Where your heart is, there your treasure will be also." But Jesus' actual words are more profound. Money changes the heart more than the heart decides how to handle money. Jesus' point is not "You tend to put your money into things that matter to you," but, "The possessions you own will change you so that you care more about them than about other things." Choose carefully what you own, for you will inevitably begin to value and protect it, to the potential detriment of everything else.

We may call this the "Treasure Principle," namely, that *treasure transforms*. Those who invest their deepest treasure in the things of this world will find they are no longer serving God but money (Matt. 6:24). That can lead to anxiety coming from the uncertainties of money (Matt. 6:25–34). Will it be eroded by inflation? Will the stock market crash? Will the bonds default? Will the bank fail? Can I be sure that what I've saved will be enough to handle anything that could possibly happen?

The antidote is to invest in ways that meet people's genuine needs. A company that provides clean water or well-made clothes may be investing in the kingdom of God, whereas an investment that depends on politically motivated subsidies, overheated housing markets, or material shortages may not. This passage in Matthew 6 is not a rule for portfolio management, but it does tell us that our commitment to the ways and means of God's kingdom extends to how we manage such wealth as we have.

The question, then, is what kind of attention you should pay to material needs and the accumulation of resources. If you pay *anxious* attention, you are foolish. If you let them *displace your trust in God*, you are becoming unfaithful. If you pay *excessive* attention to them, you will become greedy. If you acquire them *at the expense of other people,* you are becoming the kind of oppressor against whom God's kingdom is pitched.

How are we to discern the line between appropriate and inappropriate attention to wealth? Jesus answers, "Strive first for the kingdom of God and his righteousness, and all these things will be given to you" (Matt. 6:33). First things first. Despite our large capacity for self-deception, this question can help us observe carefully where our treasure has put us. That will tell us something about our hearts.

Moral Guidance (Matthew 7)

"Do Not Judge, So That You May Not Be Judged" (Matthew 7:1–5)

Jesus calls us to realism about ourselves that will keep us from picking at or judging someone else:

> "Do not judge, so that you may not be judged. For with the judgment you make you will be judged, and the measure you give will be the measure you get. Why do you see the speck in your neighbor's eye, but do not notice the log in your own eye? Or how can you say to your neighbor, 'Let me take the speck out of your eye,' while the log is in your own eye? You hypocrite, first take the log out of your own eye, and then you will see clearly to take the speck out of your neighbor's eye." (Matt. 7:1–5)

This may seem to pose a problem in the workplace. Successful work often depends on making assessments of other people's character and work. Bosses must assess their subordinates, and in some organizations, vice versa. We must often decide whom to trust, whom to choose as partners, whom to employ, which organization to join. But verse 5, with the word *hypocrite* and the admonition, "First take the log out of your own eye," shows that Jesus is speaking against false or unnecessary judgment, not against honest assessment. The problem is that we are constantly making judgments unaware. The mental pictures we make of others in our workplaces are composed more of our biased perceptions than of reality. Partly, this is because we see in others whatever serves to make us feel better about ourselves. Partly, it is to justify our own actions when we do not act as servants to others. Partly, it is because we lack the time or inclination to collect true information, which is much harder to do than storing up random impressions.

It may be impossible to overcome this false judgmentalism on our own. This is why consistent, fact-based assessment systems are so important in workplaces. A good performance appraisal system requires managers to gather real evidence of performance, to discuss differing perceptions with employees, and to recognize common biases. On a personal level, between those who are not one another's bosses, we can accomplish some of the same impartiality by asking ourselves "What role do I have in that?" when we notice ourselves forming a judgment against someone else. "What evidence leads me to that conclusion? How does this judgment benefit me? What would that person say in response to this judgment?" Perhaps the surest way to remove the log in our own eye is to take our judgment directly to the other person and ask them to respond to our perception. (See the section on conflict resolution in Matthew 18:15–17.)

The Golden Rule (Matthew 7:12)

"In everything do to others as you would have them do to you; for this is the law and the prophets" (Matt. 7:12). This brings us back to true righteousness, the mending and sustaining of right relationships on the job as well as elsewhere. If we have time for only one question before making a decision-taking action, the best one may be, "Is this how I would want it to be done to me?"

Lord, Have Mercy (Matthew 8–9)

In chapters 5 through 7, we heard Jesus teaching about the kingdom of heaven coming to earth. In chapters 8 through 9, we see him enacting that kingdom through deeds of compassion and mercy. He heals an ostracized leper (Matt. 8:1–4), he has compassion on an officer of the Roman occupying forces (Matt. 8:5–20), and he delivers demoniacs sitting in the midst of a perfect storm of misery (Matt. 8:28–9:1). In all these cases, Jesus' compassion leads him to act to reclaim God's creation. The compassion of his followers can be expressed in equally practical ways.

As Jesus demonstrates the coming of the kingdom, he calls those who follow him "laborers" (Matt. 9:37–38). Some of us are led to work in physical and emotional healing, similar to Jesus' work in these chapters. Others are led to work in occupations that provide food, water, shelter, transportation, education, health care, justice, safety, or good government, similar to Jesus' work providing wooden goods until he was about thirty. Given the time Jesus spent healing people, it is surprising that most people think of him as a preacher rather than as a doctor. Still others are led to express their creativity in art, entrepreneurism, design, fashion, research and development, made as we are in the image of a creative God (Gen. 1). The point is that for Jesus there is no separation between the secular and the sacred, between the spiritual and physical aspects of announcing the kingdom of God.

Laborers Deserve Their Food (Matthew 10)

In chapter 10, Jesus sends out his disciples to proclaim the coming kingdom and to demonstrate it through powerful deeds of mercy and compassion. He instructs them to make no provision for their needs (Matt. 10:9–10), but instead to depend on the generosity of others. He is clear that the gospel is not to become a matter of commerce: "You received without payment; give without payment" (Matt. 10:8).

The lesson here for us is that earning money and thinking about finances are not bad; indeed, it is through our labor that God provides for us, for "the laborers deserve their food" (Matt. 10:10). But the warning is against allowing our earnings to become our primary focus at work. As workers under the Lord of the new kingdom, our primary focus is on the value of the work, not on the paycheck. Jesus' instructions here are meant to keep God in the forefront of our hearts (cf. James 4:13–16). Whatever the signature at the bottom of our paycheck, God is ultimately underwriting it all.

Tales of Two Kingdoms (Matthew 11–17)

As we walk through Matthew's Gospel, we see that opposition to Jesus—his message and his actions—is increasing. It culminates in Matthew 12:14 with the religious leaders' decision to stop him, even if it means killing him. This foreshadows and sets in motion the end to which the whole narrative is pointing: Jesus' crucifixion in Jerusalem. Knowing what lies ahead of him, Jesus nevertheless tells his followers,

"Come to me, all you that are weary and are carrying heavy burdens, and I will give you rest. Take my yoke upon you, and learn from me; for I am gentle and humble in heart, and you will find rest for your souls. For my yoke is easy, and my burden is light." (Matt. 11:28–30)

If we do our work in yoke with him, we will find fulfillment and experience good relationships with God and people.[14] When God gave work to Adam in the Garden of Eden, the work was easy and the burden light under God's authority. When the human pair rebelled against their Maker, the character of work changed to hard labor against thorns and thistles (Gen. 3). Jesus invites us to work in yoke with him with the promise of rest for our souls. (For more on working in yoke with Christ, see "2 Corinthians 6:14–18" in "2 Corinthians and Work.")

Working on the Sabbath (Matthew 12:1–8)

One of the chief areas of conflict between Jesus and his opponents was in keeping the Sabbath. In this passage, Jesus is criticized by religious leaders for allowing his followers to pluck and eat grain on the Sabbath. The Pharisees regarded this as work, which was forbidden on the Sabbath. Jesus dismisses both their interpretation and their motivation. He argues that plucking just enough grain to satisfy immediate hunger does not break the Sabbath, because both King David and the temple priests did so without incurring God's rebuke (Matt. 12:3–5). Moreover, true adherence to the Law of Moses should be motivated by compassion and mercy (Matt. 12:6). God's love of mercy (allowing hungry people to pick grain to eat) is higher than God's desire for sacrifice (following Sabbath regulations), as had already been revealed in Micah 6:6–8. The gift of a day of rest each week is a promise from God that we do not have to work incessantly just to make ends meet. It is not a judgment against relieving someone's hunger or need on the Sabbath.

The connection between the Jewish Sabbath and the Christian worship on Sunday, and the application of Jewish Sabbath law to the Christian life are discussed in greater depth in the sections on "Mark 1:21–45"

---

[14] Frederick Dale Bruner, *The Christbook, Matthew 1–12*, vol. 1, *Matthew: A Commentary* (Grand Rapids: Wm. B. Eerdmans, 2007), 537–40.

and "Mark 2:23–3:6" in "Mark and Work," and the sections on "Luke 6:1–11; 3:10–17" in "Luke and Work."

Parables of the Kingdom (Matthew 13)

Beginning in chapter 13, in the face of opposition, Jesus' teaching style changes. Instead of proclaiming the kingdom clearly, he begins to speak in parables that are meaningful to believers but incomprehensible to unbelievers. Most of these brief stories are about workers: a sower planting a field (Matt. 13:3–9); a woman kneading yeast into bread (Matt. 13:33); a treasure hunter (Matt. 13:44); a pearl merchant (Matt. 13:45–46); some fishermen (Matt. 13:47–50); and a householder (Matt. 13:52). For the most part, these stories are not about the work they depict. Jesus does not tell us how to properly sow a field, how to bake bread, or how to invest in commodities. Instead, Jesus uses material objects and human labor as elements of stories that give us insight into God's kingdom. Our work is capable of bearing meaning, even of illustrating eternal realities. This reminds us that we and the world around us spring from God's creation and remain parts of God's kingdom.

Paying Taxes (Matthew 17:24–27 and 22:15–22)

In Jesus' day, Jews paid taxes both locally to the Jewish temple and to the pagan government in Rome. Matthew records two separate instances depicting Jesus' view on paying these taxes. The first incident is recorded in Matthew 17:24–27, where the collectors of the temple tax ask Peter whether Jesus pays that tax. Jesus, knowing of this conversation, asks Peter, "What do you think, Simon? From whom do kings of the earth take toll or tribute? From their children or from others?" Peter answers, "From others." Jesus responds, "Then the children are free. However, so that we do not give offense to them, go to the sea and cast a hook; take the first fish that comes up; and when you open its mouth, you will find a coin; take that and give it to them for you and me."

The second incident, concerning the Roman tax, is found in Matthew 22:15–22. Here the Pharisees and Herodians want to entrap Jesus with the question, "Is it lawful to pay taxes to the emperor, or not?" Jesus knows the malice in their hearts and responds with a cutting question:

"Why are you putting me to the test, you hypocrites? Show me the coin used for the tax." When they hand him a denarius, he asks, "Whose head is this, and whose title?" They respond, "The emperor's." Jesus ends the conversation with the words, "Give therefore to the emperor the things that are the emperor's, and to God the things that are God's."

Our true citizenship is in God's kingdom, and we devote our resources to God's purposes. But we give to earthly powers what is due. Paying taxes is one of the bedrock obligations we as citizens or residents undertake for the services we enjoy in any civilized society. Those services include the work of first responders (police, firefighters, medical people, and so on), as well as the social nets in place to assure justice or aid for the poor, the aged, and others in need. The Roman Empire was not governed primarily for the benefit of the common people, yet even so it provided roads, water, policing, and sometimes relief for the poor. We may not always agree on the type or extent of services our governments should provide, but we know that our taxes are essential in providing for our personal protection and for the help of those who cannot help themselves.

Even though not all of government activity serves God's purposes, Jesus does not call us to flout the tax requirements of the nations where we reside (Rom. 13:1–10; 1 Thess. 4:11–12). Jesus is saying in essence that we do not necessarily have to resist paying taxes as a matter of principle. When possible, we should "live peaceably with all" (Rom. 12:18; Heb. 12:14; cf. 1 Pet. 2:12), while also living as lights shining in the darkness (Matt. 5:13–16; Phil. 2:15). To work at our jobs and to refuse to pay our taxes in a way that brings dishonor to God's kingdom would be neither peaceable nor winsome.

This has direct applications to work. Workplaces are subject to governmental laws and powers, in addition to taxes. Some governments have laws and practices that may violate Christian purposes and ethics, as was true of Rome in the first century. Governments or their employees may demand bribes, impose unethical rules and regulations, subject people to suffering and injustice, and use the taxes for purposes contrary to God's will. As with taxes, Jesus does not demand that we resist every one of these abuses. We are like spies or guerrillas in enemy territory. We can't get bogged down in fighting the enemy kingdom at every stronghold. Instead, we must act strategically, always asking what will most further the establishment of God's kingdom on earth. Of course, we must never *engage* in abusive practices for our own benefit. (This topic is also discussed under "Luke 19:1–10; 20:20–26" in "Luke and Work.")

Living in the New Kingdom (Matthew 18–25)

In chapters 18 through 25 of Matthew's Gospel, Jesus gives concrete images of what life in God's kingdom is like. In many cases, these pictures apply particularly to work.

Conflict Resolution (Matthew 18:15–35)

All workplaces experience conflict. In this passage, Jesus gives us a template for dealing with someone who has wronged us. He does not say, "Get even!" or "Strike back!" Instead, he lays out a process that begins with seeking one-on-one to be reconciled. The beatitude of meekness means putting aside your self-justification long enough to express yourself respectfully and factually to the one who has hurt you, and to open yourself to their perspective (Matt. 18:15). This does not mean submitting to further abuse, but opening yourself to the possibility that your perception is not universal. But suppose that doesn't resolve the conflict? The fallback second step is to ask people who know you both to go with you as you take up the issue again with the person who caused pain or injury. If the conflict still is not resolved, then bring the matter to the leadership (the church, in Matthew 18:16, which is addressing church conflict specifically) for an impartial judgment. If that judgment doesn't resolve the issue, the offender who fails to abide by the judgment is removed from the community (Matt. 18:17).

Although Jesus was speaking about conflict with "another member of the church" (Matt. 18:15), his method is a remarkable precursor to what is now recognized as best practice in the workplace. Even in the finest workplaces, conflicts arise. When they do, the only effective resolution is for those in conflict to engage each other directly, not to complain to others. Rather than play out a personal conflict in front of an audience, get with the person privately. In the age of electronic communication, Jesus' approach is more important than ever. All it takes is a name or two in the "cc:" line or one press of the "reply all" button to turn a simple disagreement into an office feud. Even though two people could keep an e-mail chain to themselves, the possibilities for misunderstanding are multiplied when an impersonal medium such as e-mail is used. It might be best to take Jesus' advice literally: "Go and point out the fault when the two of you are alone" (Matt. 18:15).

Pointing out the fault is a two-way street. We need to be open to hearing faults pointed out to us as well. Listening—Jesus mentions listening *three times* in these three verses—is the crucial element. Contemporary conflict resolution models usually focus on getting the parties to listen to each other, even while preserving the option to disagree. Often, attentive listening leads to the discovery of a mutually acceptable resolution. If it doesn't, then others with the appropriate skills and authority are asked to get involved.

The Rich Young Man (Matthew 19:16–30)

The issue of money, discussed earlier in Matthew 6, raises its head again with the story of the rich young man who was drawn to Jesus. The young man asks Jesus, "What good deed must I do to have eternal life?" Jesus tells him to keep the commandments, and he responds that he has done that from his youth. A distinctive element in Matthew's narrative is that the young man then asks Jesus, "What do I still lack?" He shows great insight in asking this question. We can do everything that appears right but still know that something is not right on the inside. Jesus responds, "Sell your possessions and give the money to the poor, and you will have treasure in heaven; then come, follow me" (Matt. 19:21).

We know from the four Gospels that Jesus did not call all of his hearers to give away all their possessions. Not all people are as burdened by their possessions as this young man was. In his case, the challenge was radical because of his strong attachment to wealth (Matt. 19:22). God knows precisely what is in our hearts and what is needed as we serve him.

Is our treasure in our work, our jobs, our performance and skills, our retirement funds? These are good things (gifts from God) in their place. But they are secondary to seeking first the kingdom of God (Matt. 6:33) and a right (righteous) relationship with God and with others. We hold our wealth and our work on an open palm lest, like the rich young man, we end up turning away sorrowfully from God. (This story is discussed in greater depth in the entries for "Mark 10:17–31" and "Luke 18:18–30.")

The Laborers in the Vineyard (Matthew 20:1–16)

This parable is unique to Matthew's Gospel. The owner of a vineyard hires day laborers at various times throughout the day. The ones hired at six o'clock in the morning put in a full day's work. Those hired at five o'clock in the afternoon put in only one hour of work. But the owner pays everyone a full day's wage (a denarius). He goes out of his way to make sure that everyone knows that all are paid the same in spite of the different number of hours worked. Not surprisingly, those hired first complain that they worked longer but earned no more money than those who started late in the day.

> "But [the owner] replied to one of them, 'Friend, I am doing you no wrong; did you not agree with me for the usual daily wage? . . . Am I not allowed to do what I choose with what belongs to me? Or are you envious because I am generous?' So the last will be first, and the first will be last." (Matt. 20:13, 15–16)

Unlike the parable of the sower (Matt. 13:3–9; 18–23), Jesus does not give us an explicit interpretation. As a result, scholars have offered many interpretations. Because the people in the story are laborers and managers, some assume it is about work. In that case, it seems to say, "Don't compare your pay to others" or "Don't be dissatisfied if others get paid more or work less than you do in a similar job." It could be argued that these are good practices for workers. If you earn a decent wage, why make yourself miserable because others have it even better? But this interpretation of the parable can also be used to justify unfair or abusive labor practices. Some workers may receive lower wages for unfair reasons, such as race or sex or immigrant status. Does Jesus mean that we should be content when we or other workers are treated unfairly?

Moreover, paying people the same regardless of how much work they do is a questionable business practice. Wouldn't it give a strong incentive to all workers to show up at five o'clock in the afternoon the next day? And what about making everyone's pay public? It does reduce the scope for intrigue. But is it a good idea to force those working longer hours to watch while those who worked only one hour are paid an identical wage? It seems calculated to cause labor strife. Pay for nonperformance, to take the parable literally, doesn't seem to be a recipe for business success. Can it really be that Jesus advocates this pay practice?

Perhaps the parable is not really about work. The context is that Jesus is giving surprising examples of those who belong to God's kingdom: for example, children (Matt. 19:14) who legally don't even own themselves. He is clear that the kingdom does not belong to the rich, or at least not to very many of them (Matt. 19:23–26). It belongs to those who follow him, in particular if they suffer loss. "Many who are first will be last, and the last will be first" (Matt. 19:30). The present parable is followed immediately by another ending with the same words: "the first will be last, and the last will be first" (Matt. 20:16). This suggests that the story is a continuation of the discussion about those to whom the kingdom belongs. Entry into God's kingdom is not gained by our work or action, but by the generosity of God.

Once we understand the parable to be about God's generosity in the kingdom of heaven, we may still ask how it applies to work. If you are being paid fairly, the advice about being content with your wage may stand. If another worker receives an unexpected benefit, wouldn't it be graceful to rejoice, rather than grumble?

But there is also a broader application. The owner in the parable pays all the workers enough to support their families.[15] The social situation in Jesus' day was that many small farmers were being forced off their land because of debt they incurred to pay Roman taxes. This violated the God of Israel's command that land could not be taken away from the people who work it (Lev. 25:8–13), but of course this was of no concern to the Romans. Consequently, large pools of unemployed men gathered each morning, hoping to be hired for the day. They are the displaced,

---

[15] A denarius was the standard one-day wage in first-century Palestine.

unemployed, and underemployed workers of their day. Those still waiting at five o'clock have little chance of earning enough to buy food for their families that day. Yet the vineyard owner pays even them a full day's wage.

If the vineyard owner represents God, this is a powerful message that in God's kingdom, displaced and unemployed workers find work that meets their needs and the needs of those who depend on them. We have already seen Jesus saying that "laborers deserve their food" (Matt. 10:10). This does not necessarily mean that earthly employers have a responsibility for meeting all the needs of their employees. Earthly employers are not God. Rather, the parable is a message of hope to everyone struggling to find adequate employment. In God's kingdom, we will all find work that meets our needs. The parable is also a challenge to those who have a hand in shaping the structures of work in today's society. Can Christians do anything to advance this aspect of God's kingdom right now?

Servant Leadership (Matthew 20:20–28)

Despite this parable of God's grace and generosity, despite hearing Jesus remark twice that the first shall be last and the last first, Jesus' disciples are still missing the point. The mother of James and John asks Jesus to grant her two sons the most prominent places in his coming kingdom. The two men are standing there and Jesus turns to them and asks, "Are you able to drink the cup that I am about to drink?" They respond, "We are able." When the other ten disciples hear about this, they are angry. Jesus takes this opportunity to challenge their notions about prominence.

> "You know that the rulers of the Gentiles lord it over them, and their great ones are tyrants over them. It will not be so among you; but whoever wishes to be great among you must be your servant, and whoever wishes to be first among you must be your slave; just as the Son of Man came not to be served but to serve, and to give his life a ransom for many." (Matt. 20:25–28)

True leadership is found in serving others. What this looks like will vary according to the workplace and situation. This doesn't mean that a CEO must take a monthly turn sweeping the floors or cleaning the toilets, nor that any worker can cite helping someone else as an excuse for not doing their own work well. It does mean that we do all our work with the aim of serving our customers, co-workers, shareholders, and others whom our work affects. Max De Pree was a long time CEO of Herman Miller and member of the *Fortune* Hall of Fame. He wrote in his book *Leadership Is an Art,* "The first responsibility of a leader is to define reality. The last is to say thank you. In between the two, the leader must become a servant and a debtor. That sums up the progress of an artful leader."[16]

The servant is the person who knows his or her spiritual poverty (Matt. 5:3) and exercises power under God's control (Matt. 5:5) to maintain right relationships. The servant leader apologizes for mistakes (Matt. 5:4), shows mercy when others fail (Matt. 5:7), makes peace when possible (Matt. 5:9), and endures unmerited criticism when attempting to serve God (Matt. 5:10) with integrity (Matt. 5:8). Jesus set the pattern in his own actions on our behalf (Matt. 20:28). We show ourselves to be Christ-followers by following his example.

Words and Deeds (Matthew 21:28–41)

The parable of the two sons (Matt. 21:28–32) is about two brothers whose father tells them to go work in his vineyard. One tells his father that he will but doesn't do it. The other tells his father that he won't go but ends up working all day among the vines. Jesus then asks the question: "Which of the two did the will of his father?" The answer is clear: the one who actually worked, though initially refusing to do so. This parable continues earlier stories in Matthew about the people who actually are part of God's kingdom. Jesus tells the religious leaders in his audience that "tax collectors and prostitutes are going into the kingdom of God ahead of you" (Matt. 21:31).[17] The folks who look the least religious will enter God's kingdom ahead of religious leaders, because in the end they do God's will.

---

[16] Max De Pree, *Leadership Is an Art* (New York: Doubleday, 1989), 9.

[17] Jesus illustrates this in 21:32: The religious leaders had listened to John the Baptist but scorned him; tax collectors listened to him, believed, repented, and were baptized. But the religious leaders refused to hear the prophet's message or to repent, excluding themselves from God's kingdom.

In work, this reminds us that actions speak louder than words. Many organizations have mission statements declaring that their top aims are customer service, product quality, civic integrity, putting their people first, and the like. Yet many such organizations have poor service, quality, integrity, and employee relations. Individuals may do the same thing, extolling their plans, yet failing to implement them. Organizations and individuals falling into this trap may have good intentions, and they may not recognize they are failing to live up to their rhetoric. Workplaces need both effective systems for implementing their mission and goals, and impartial monitoring systems to give unvarnished feedback.

The parable immediately following the parable of the wicked tenants (Matt. 21:33–41) takes place in a workplace, namely, a vineyard. However, Jesus makes it clear that he is not talking about running a vineyard, but about his own rejection and coming murder at the instigation of the Jewish religious authorities of his day (Matt. 21:45). The key to applying it to today's workplace is verse 43: "The kingdom of God will be taken away from you and given to a people that produces the fruits of the kingdom." We all have been given responsibilities in our work. If we refuse to do them in obedience to God, we are working at odds with God's kingdom. In every job, our ultimate performance appraisal comes from God.

Serving Upward and Downward (Matthew 24:45–51)

This parable is about a slave who has been put in charge of the entire household. This includes the responsibility to give other slaves their allowance of food at the proper time. Jesus says, "Blessed is that slave whom his master will find at work when he arrives" (Matt. 24:46). That slave will be promoted to additional responsibility. On the other hand, Jesus observes,

> "But if that wicked slave says to himself, 'My master is delayed,' and he begins to beat his fellow slaves, and eats and drinks with drunkards, the master of that slave will come on a day when he does not expect him and at an hour that he does not know. He will cut him in pieces and put him with the hypocrites, where there will be weeping and gnashing of teeth." (Matt. 24:48–51)

In a modern workplace context, the slave would be equivalent to a manager with a duty to the owners while managing other workers. The owner's interests are met only when the workers' needs are met. The manager has responsibilities to both those above and below him in authority. Jesus says that it is the servant-leader's duty to look to the needs of those under him as well as those above him. He cannot excuse himself for mistreating those under his authority by claiming it is somehow for the benefit of his superiors. He depicts this reality dramatically in the punishment meted out to the worker who cares only for his own interests (Matt. 24:48–51).

The Parable of the Talents (Matthew 25:14–30)

One of Jesus' most significant parables regarding work is set in the context of investments (Matt. 25:14–30). A rich man delegates the management of his wealth to his servants, much as investors in today's markets do. He gives five talents (a large unit of money)[18] to the first servant, two talents to the second, and one talent to the third. Two of the servants earn 100 percent returns by trading with the funds, but the third servant hides the money in the ground and earns nothing. The rich man returns, rewards the two who made money, but severely punishes the servant who did nothing.

The meaning of the parable extends far beyond financial investments. God has given each person a wide variety of gifts, and he expects us to employ those gifts in his service. It is not acceptable merely to put those gifts on a closet shelf and ignore them. Like the three servants, we do not have gifts of the same degree. The return God expects of us is commensurate with the gifts we have been given. The servant who received

---

[18] According to NRSV footnote *f*, "a talent was worth more than 15 years' wages of a laborer," in other words, about $US 1 million in today's currency. The Greek word *talanton* was first used for a unit of weight (probably about 30–40 kg.), then later for a unit of money equivalent to the same weight of gold, silver (probably what is meant here), or copper (Donald A. Hagner, *Matthew 14–18*, vol. 33b, *Word Biblical Commentary* [Nashville: Thomas Nelson, 1995]). The present-day use of the English word *talent* to indicate an ability or gift is derived from this parable (Walter C. Kaiser Jr. and Duane Garrett, eds., *Archaeological Study Bible* [Grand Rapids: Zondervan, 2006], 1608.)

one talent was not condemned for failing to reach the five-talent goal; he was condemned because he did nothing with what he was given. The gifts we receive from God include skills, abilities, family connections, social positions, education, experiences, and more. The point of the parable is that we are to use whatever we have been given for God's purposes. The severe consequences to the unproductive servant, far beyond anything triggered by mere business mediocrity, tell us that we are to invest our lives, not waste them.

Yet the particular talent invested in the parable is *money*, on the order of a million U.S. dollars in today's world. In modern English, this fact is obscured because the word *talent* has come to refer mainly to skills or abilities. But this parable concerns money. It depicts investing, not hoarding, as a godly thing to do if it accomplishes godly purposes in a godly manner. In the end, the master praises the two trustworthy servants with the words, "Well done, good and trustworthy slave" (Matt. 25:23). In these words, we see that the master cares about the results ("well done"), the methods ("good"), and the motivation ("trustworthy").

More pointedly for the workplace, it commends putting capital at risk in pursuit of earning a return. Sometimes Christians speak as if growth, productivity, and return on investment were unholy to God. But this parable overturns that notion. We should invest our skills and abilities, but also our wealth and the resources made available to us at work, all for the affairs of God's kingdom. This includes the production of needed goods and services. The volunteer who teaches Sunday school is fulfilling this parable. So are the entrepreneur who starts a new business and gives jobs to others, the health service administrator who initiates an AIDS-awareness campaign, and the machine operator who develops a process innovation.

God does not endow people with identical or necessarily equal gifts. If you do as well as you can with the gifts given to you by God, you will hear his "Well done." Not only the gifts, but also the people have equal worth. At the same time, the parable ends with the talent taken from the third servant being given to the one with ten talents. Equal worth does not necessarily mean equal compensation. Some positions require more skill or ability and thus are compensated accordingly. The two servants who did well are rewarded in different amounts. But they are both praised identically. The implication of the parable is that we are to use whatever talents we've been given to the best of our ability for God's glory, and when we have done that, we are on an equal playing field with other faithful, trustworthy servants of God. (For a discussion of the highly similar parable of the ten minas see "Luke 19:11–27" in "Luke and Work.")

Sheep and Goats (Matthew 25:31–46)

Jesus' final teaching in this section examines how we treat those in need. In this account, when Jesus returns in his glory, he will sit on his throne and separate people "as a shepherd separates the sheep from the goats" (Matt. 25:32). The separation depends on how we treat people in need. To the sheep he says,

> "Come, you that are blessed by my Father, inherit the kingdom prepared for you from the foundation of the world; for I was hungry and you gave me food, I was thirsty and you gave me something to drink, I was a stranger and you welcomed me, I was naked and you gave me clothing, I was sick and you took care of me, I was in prison and you visited me." (Matt. 25:34–36)

These are all people in need, whom the sheep served, for Jesus says, "Just as you did it to one of the least of these who are members of my family, you did it to me" (Matt. 25:40). To the goats, he says,

> "Depart from me . . . for I was hungry and you gave me no food, I was thirsty and you gave me nothing to drink, I was a stranger and you did not welcome me, naked and you did not give me clothing, sick and in prison and you did not visit me. . . . Just as you did not do it to one of the least of these, you did not do it to me." (Matt. 25:41–43, 45)

Individually and corporately, we are called to help those in need. We are "bound in the bundle of the living under the care of the LORD your God" (1 Sam. 25:29), and we cannot ignore the plight of human beings suffering hunger, thirst, nakedness, homelessness, sickness, or imprisonment. We work in order to meet our own needs and the needs of those dependent on us; but we also work in order to have something to give to those in need (Heb. 13:1–3). We join with others to find ways to come alongside those who lack the basic necessities of life that we may take for granted. If Jesus' words in this passage are taken seriously, more may hang on our charity than we realize.

Jesus does not say exactly *how* the sheep served people in need. It may have been through gifts and charitable work. But perhaps some of it was through the ordinary work of growing and preparing food and drink; helping new co-workers come up to speed on the job; designing, manufacturing, and selling clothing. All legitimate work serves people who need the products and services of the work, and in so doing, serves Jesus.

The Body of Christ (Matthew 26)

The plot to kill Jesus moves forward as Judas (one of the Twelve) goes to the religious leaders with an offer to turn him over to the temple soldiers. With events moving quickly toward crucifixion, Jesus shares a final meal with his disciples. In that meal, Jesus chooses the manufactured items of bread and wine to represent himself and his coming sacrifice. Holding up a loaf of bread, he says, "This is my body" (Matt. 26:26); then holding up the skin of wine, he says, "This is my blood" (Matt. 26:28). The Son of God is the product of no one's work, not even the Father's. In the words of the Nicene Creed, he is "begotten, not made." But he chooses common, tangible things like bread and wine, made by people, to illustrate his sacrifice. As Alan Richardson puts it:

> Without the toil and skill of the farmer, without the labor of the bakers, the transport workers, the banks and offices, the shops and distributors— without, in fact, the toil of mines and shipyards and steel-works and so on—*this* loaf would not have been here to lay upon the altar this morning. In truth, the whole world of human work is involved in the manufacture of the bread and wine which we offer. . . . Here is the strange unbreakable link that exists between the bread that is won in the sweat of man's face and the bread of life that is bought without money or without price.[19]

The entire community participates.

---

[19] Alan Richardson, *The Biblical Doctrine of Work*, Ecumenical Bible Studies No. 1 (London: SCM Press for the Study Department of the World Council of Churches, 1952; repr. 1954), 70.

We cannot pretend to know why Jesus chose tangible products of human labor to represent himself rather than natural articles or abstract ideas or images of his own design. But the fact is that he *did* dignify these products of work as the representation of his own infinite dignity. When we remember that in his resurrection he also bears a physical body (Matt. 28:9, 13), there can be no room to imagine the kingdom of God as a spiritual realm divorced from the physical reality of God's creation. After creating us (Gen. 2:7; John 1), he chose articles of our handiwork to represent himself. This is a grace almost beyond comprehension.

Jesus' Death, Resurrection, and Commissioning of His Followers (Matthew 27–28)

More than any other Gospel writer, Matthew emphasizes the earth-shattering implications of the death and resurrection of Jesus Christ, and brings us back to the central motif of the kingdoms of heaven and earth. The darkening of the heavens, the shaking of the earth, and the resurrection of the dead (Matt. 27:45–54) would have been clear signs to the Jews that the present age was ending and the age to come had begun. Yet life and work seem to go on as they always had; it was business as usual. Did anything really change at that cross on Golgotha's hill?

The Gospel according to Matthew answers with a resounding yes. Jesus' crucifixion was the deathblow for a world system founded on pretensions of human power and wisdom. His resurrection marks the definitive intrusion of God's ways into the world. The reign of God's kingdom has not yet taken in the entire earth, but Christ governs all those who will follow him.

Jesus' earthly ministry was ending. Matthew 28:16–20 narrates his commissioning of those who followed him:

> Now the eleven disciples went to Galilee, to the mountain to which Jesus had directed them. When they saw him, they worshiped him; but some doubted. And Jesus came and said to them, "All authority in heaven and on earth has been given to me. Go, therefore, and make disciples of all na-tions, baptizing them in the name of the Father and of the Son and of the Holy Spirit, and teaching them to obey everything that I have commanded you. And remember, I am with you always, to the end of the age."

This passage is often referred to as the Great Commission, and Christians tend to focus on its evangelistic aspect. But the commission is actually to "make disciples," not merely to "win converts." As we have seen throughout this article, work is an essential element of being a disciple. Understanding our work in the context of the Lordship of Christ is part of fulfilling the Great Commission.

We have our marching orders. We are to take the good news to all nations, baptizing those who believe the good news, and teaching them "to obey everything that I have commanded you" (Matt. 26:20). As we look back over these twenty-eight chapters of Matthew, we see many commands that touch us in the workplace. These teachings are for us and for those who come after us.

Conclusion to Matthew

God cares about our work, and the Scriptures have much to say about this. As noted at the beginning, the Gospel according to Matthew addresses the theology and practice of work on many fronts: leadership and authority, power and influence, business practices, truth and deception, treatment of workers, conflict resolution, wealth and the necessities of life, workplace relationships, investing and saving, rest, and living in God's kingdom while working in secular places.

Christians often assume that our lives are to be split into two realms, the secular and the sacred. Our work can become merely a way of earning a living, a secular activity with no godly significance. Going to church and personal devotion are assumed to be the only sacred elements of life. A misreading of Matthew could support this split. The kingdom of the earth could represent the material, secular parts of life; and the kingdom of heaven, the sacred, ethereal parts. But a true reading of Matthew is that both kingdoms include all of life. The kingdom of God has both material and spiritual aspects, and so does the kingdom of the fallen earth. The Christian way is to put our entire life, including our work life, at the service of God's kingdom, which Christ is bringing to earth even now.

Jesus calls his followers to live and work in the midst of the fallen world, while holding fast to God's purposes, virtues, and principles. For individual Christians, the sacred and the secular cannot be separated: "No one can serve two masters" (Matt. 6:24). In this universe created and sustained by God, there is no "secular" space, immune to his influence, out of his control, or over which he does not claim sovereignty.

But while the kingdom of darkness remains, the kingdom of God is also at hand. The world's people and systems often do not reflect the ways of God. Those called by Christ have to learn how to serve God's kingdom faithfully, while learning to exist amid the very real powers that oppose God's way. The Christian worldview cannot be one of escape or disregard for this world. Above all people, Christians should rightly be engaged in creating structures that reflect the kingdom of God in all realms of life, the workplace included. We are to model the practices of God's kingdom in our workplaces, especially practices in which we turn over our power and wealth to God and depend on his power and provision. This is what it means to live (not just speak) the paradigmatic prayer of the Lord: "Thy kingdom come. Thy will be done, on earth as it is in heaven."

Mark and Work

Introduction to Mark

The Gospel of Mark, like the other Gospels, is about the work of Jesus. His work is to teach, to heal, to perform signs of God's power, and most of all to die and be raised to life for the benefit of humanity. Christ's work is absolutely unique. Yet it is also a seamless part of the work of all God's people, which is to cooperate with God in restoring the world to the way God intended it from the beginning. Our work is not Christ's work, but our work has the same end as his. Therefore the Gospel of Mark is not *about* our work, but it *informs* our work and *defines* the ultimate goal of our work.

By studying Mark, we discover God's call to work in the service of his kingdom. We discern the rhythms of work, rest, and worship God intends for our lives. We see the opportunities and dangers inherent in earning a living, accumulating wealth, gaining status, paying taxes, and working in a society that does not necessarily aim toward God's purposes. We meet fishermen, laborers, mothers and fathers (parenting is a type of work!), tax collectors, people with disabilities that affect their work, leaders, farmers, lawyers, priests, builders, philanthropists (mostly women), a very rich man, merchants, bankers, soldiers, and governors. We recognize the same bewildering range of personalities we encounter in life and work today. We encounter people not as isolated individuals, but as members of families, communities, and nations. Work and workers are everywhere in the Gospel of Mark.

Mark is the briefest Gospel. It contains less of Jesus' teaching material than Matthew and Luke. Our task, then, must be to pay close attention to the details in Mark to see how his Gospel applies to non-church work. The primary work-related passages in Mark fall into three categories: (1) call narratives, as Jesus calls disciples to work on behalf of God's kingdom; (2) Sabbath controversies concerning the rhythm of work and rest; and (3) economic issues concerning wealth and its accumulation, and taxation. We will discuss the call narratives under the heading "Kingdom and Discipleship," the Sabbath controversies under the heading "Rhythms of Work, Rest, and Worship," and the episodes related to taxation and wealth under "Economic Issues." In each of these categories, Mark is primarily concerned with how those who would follow Jesus must be transformed at a deep level.

As with the other Gospels, Mark is set against a background of turbulent economic times. During the Roman era, Galilee was undergoing major social upheaval, with land increasingly owned by a wealthy few—often foreigners—and with a general movement away from small-scale farming to larger-scale, estate-based agriculture. Those who had once been tenant farmers or even landowners were forced to become day laborers, often as a result of having lost their own property through the foreclosure of loans taken to pay Roman taxes.[1] Set against such a background, it is small wonder that economic and fiscal themes emerge in Mark's narrative and in the teaching of Jesus, and an awareness of this social context allows us to appreciate undercurrents in these that we might otherwise have overlooked.

Kingdom and Discipleship (Mark 1–4; 6; 8)

The Beginning of the Gospel (Mark 1:1–13)

The accounts of John's preaching and of Jesus' baptism and temptation say nothing directly about work. Nevertheless, as the narrative gateway to the Gospel, they provide the basic thematic context for all that follows and cannot be bypassed as we move to passages more obviously applicable to our concerns. An interesting point is that Mark's title (Mark 1:1) describes the book as "the *beginning* of the good news about Jesus Christ." From a narrative point of view, drawing attention to the beginning is striking, because the Gospel seems to lack an ending. The earliest manuscripts suggest that the Gospel ends suddenly with Mark 16:8: "So they went out and fled from the tomb, for terror and amazement had seized them; and they said nothing to anyone, for they were afraid." The

---

[1] Sean Freyne, *Jesus: A Jewish Galilean* (London: T&T Clark, 2004), 45–46.

text ends so abruptly that scribes added the material now found in Mark 16:9–20, which is composed from passages found elsewhere in the New Testament. But perhaps Mark intended his Gospel to have no ending. It is only "the beginning of the good news of Jesus Christ," and we who read it are participants in the continuing Gospel. If this is so, then our lives are a direct continuation of the events in Mark, and we have every reason to expect concrete applications to our work.[2]

We will see in greater detail that Mark always portrays human followers of Jesus as beginners who fall far short of perfection. This is true even of the twelve apostles. Mark, more than any of the other Gospels, presents the apostles as unperceptive, ignorant, and repeatedly failing Jesus. This is highly encouraging, for many Christians who try to follow Christ in their work feel inadequate in doing so. Take heart, Mark exhorts, for in this we are like the apostles themselves!

John the Baptist (Mark 1:2–11) is presented as the messenger of Malachi 3:1 and Isaiah 40:3. He announces the coming of "the Lord." Combined with the designation of Jesus as "Christ, the Son of God" (Mark 1:1), this language makes clear to the reader that Mark's central theme is "the kingdom of God," even though he waits until Mark 1:15 to use that phrase and to connect it to the gospel ("good news"). "The kingdom of God" is not a geographical concept in Mark. It is the reign of the Lord observed as people and peoples come under God's rule, through the transforming work of the Spirit. That work is highlighted by Mark's brief description of the baptism and temptation of Jesus (Mark 1:9–13), which by its brevity emphasizes the descent of the Spirit onto Jesus and his role in driving him into (and presumably through) the temptation by Satan.

This passage cuts across two opposite, yet popular, conceptions of the kingdom of God. On the one hand is the idea that the kingdom of God does not yet exist, and will not until Christ returns to rule the world in person. Under this view, the workplace, like the rest of the world, is enemy territory. The Christian's duty is to survive in the enemy territory of this world long enough to evangelize, and profitably enough to meet personal needs and give money to the church. The other is the idea that the kingdom of God is an inner, spiritual domain, having nothing to do with the world around us.

---

[2] J. David Hester, "Dramatic Inconclusion: Irony and the Narrative Rhetoric of the Ending of Mark," *Journal for the Study of the New Testament* 17 (1995): 61–86.

Under this view, what the Christian does at work, or anywhere else aside from church and individual prayer time, is of no concern to God at all.

Against both of these ideas, Mark makes it clear that Jesus' coming inaugurates the kingdom of God as a present reality on earth. Jesus says plainly, "The time is fulfilled, and the kingdom of God has come near; repent, and believe in the good news" (Mark 1:15). The kingdom is not fulfilled at present, of course. It does not yet govern the earth, and will not do so until Christ returns. But it is here now, and it is real.

Therefore, to submit to the reign of God and to proclaim his kingdom has very real consequences in the world around us. It may well bring us into social disrepute, conflict, and, indeed, suffering. Mark 1:14, like Matthew 4:12, draws attention to John's imprisonment and links this to the commencement of Jesus' own proclamation that "the kingdom has come near" (Mark 1:15). The kingdom is thus set over against the powers of the world, and as readers we are forcefully shown that to serve the gospel and to honor God will not necessarily bring success in this life. Yet at the same time, by the Spirit's power, Christians are called to serve God for the benefit of those around them, as the healings Jesus performs demonstrate (Mark 1:23–34, 40–45).

The radical significance of the Holy Spirit's coming into the world is made clearer later in the Gospel through the Beelzebul controversy (Mark 3:20–30). This is a difficult section, and we have to be quite careful in how we deal with it, but it is certainly not unimportant to the theology of the kingdom that undergirds our theology of work. The logic of the passage seems to be that by casting out demons, Jesus is effectively liberating the world from Satan, depicted as a strong man now bound. Like their Lord, Christians are meant to employ the Spirit's power to transform the world, not to escape the world or to accommodate to it.

The Calling of the First Disciples (Mark 1:16–20)

This section needs to be treated cautiously: while the disciples are paradigms of the Christian life, they also occupy a unique position in the story of salvation. Their summons to a distinctive kind of service, and to the forsaking of their current employment, does not establish a universal pattern for Christian life and vocation. Many, indeed most, of those who follow Jesus do not quit their jobs to do so. Nevertheless, the way in which the demands of the kingdom cut across and override the usual principles of society is transferable and enlightening to our work. The opening clause of Mark 1:16 presents Jesus as itinerant ("as he passed along"), and he calls these fishermen to follow him on the road. This is more than just a challenge to leave behind income and stability or, as we might put it, to get out of our "comfort zone." Mark's account of this incident records a detail lacking in the other accounts, namely, that James and John leave their father Zebedee "with the hired men" (Mark 1:20). They themselves were not hired men or day laborers, but rather were a part of what was probably a relatively successful family business. As Suzanne Watts Henderson notes in relation to the response of the disciples, the "piling up of particulars underscores the full weight of the verb [to leave]: not just nets are left behind, but a named father, a boat and indeed an entire enterprise."[3] For these disciples to follow Jesus, they have to demonstrate a willingness to allow their identity, status, and worth to be determined primarily in relation to him.

Fishing was a major industry in Galilee, with a connected sub-industry of fish salting.[4] At a time of social turbulence in Galilee, these two related industries supported each other and remained steady. The willingness of the disciples to forsake such stability is quite remarkable. Economic stability is no longer their chief purpose for working. Yet even here we must be cautious. Jesus does not reject the earthly vocation of these men but reorients it. Jesus calls Simon and Andrew to be "fishers of people" (Mark 1:17), thereby affirming their former work as an image of the new role to which he is calling them. Although most Christians are not called to leave their jobs and become wandering preachers, we are called to ground our identity in Christ. Whether we leave our jobs or not, a disciple's identity is no longer "fisherman," "tax collector," or anything else except "follower of Jesus." This challenges us to resist the temptation to make our work the defining element of our sense of who we are.

---

[3] Suzanne Watts Henderson, *Christology and Discipleship in the Gospel of Mark* (Cambridge: Cambridge University Press, 2006), 63.

[4] Freyne, 48–53. For the place of fishing in the taxation structures, see Bruce Malina and Richard Rohrbaugh, *A Social-Scientific Commentary on the Synoptic Gospels* (Minneapolis: Fortress Press, 1992), 44–45.

The Paralytic Man (Mark 2:1–12)

The story of Jesus healing the paralytic man raises the question of what the theology of work means for those who do not have the ability to work. The paralytic man, prior to this healing, is incapable of self-supporting work. As such, he is dependent on the grace and compassion of those around him for his daily survival. Jesus is impressed by the faith of the man's friends. Their faith is active, showing care, compassion, and friendship to someone who was excluded from both the financial and relational rewards of work. In their faith, there is no separation between being and doing.

Jesus sees their effort as an act of collective faith. "When Jesus saw *their* faith, he said to the paralytic, 'Son, your sins are forgiven'" (Mark 2:5). Regrettably, the *community* of faith plays a vanishingly small role in most Christians' work lives in the modern West. Even if we receive help and encouragement for the workplace from our church, it is almost certain to be *individual* help and encouragement. In earlier times, most Christians worked alongside the same people they went to church with, so churches could easily apply the Scriptures to the shared occupations of laborers, farmers, and householders. In contrast, Western Christians today seldom work in the same locations as others in the same church. Nonetheless, today's Christians often work in the same *types* of jobs as others in their faith communities. So there could be an opportunity to share their work challenges and opportunities with other believers in similar occupations. Yet this seldom happens. Unless we find a way for *groups* of Christian workers to support one another, grow together, and develop some kind of work-related Christian community, we miss out on the communal nature of faith that is so essential in Mark 2:3–12.

In this brief episode, then, we observe three things: (1) Work is intended to benefit those who can't support themselves through work, as well as those who can; (2) faith and work are not separated as being and doing, but are integrated into action empowered by God; and (3) work done in faith cries out for a community of faith to support it.

The Calling of Levi (Mark 2:13–17)

The calling of Levi is another incident that occurs as Jesus is moving (Mark 2:13–14). The passage stresses the public nature of this summons.

Jesus calls Levi while teaching a crowd (Mark 2:14), and Levi is initially seen "sitting at the tax booth." His employment would make him a figure of contempt for many of his Galilean contemporaries. There is a measure of debate over just how heavily Roman and Herodian taxation was felt in Galilee, but most think that the issue was rather sore. The actual collection of taxes was contracted out to private tax collectors. A tax collector paid the tax for his entire territory upfront, and collected the individual taxes from the populace later. To make this profitable, he had to charge the populace more than the actual tax rate and the tax collector pocketed the mark-up. The Roman authorities thereby delegated the politically sensitive work of tax collection to members of the local community, but it led to a high rate of effective tax, and it opened the doors to all sorts of corruption.[5] It is likely that this was one of the factors contributing to land loss in Galilee, as landowners took loans to pay monetary taxes and then, if their harvests were poor, lost their properties as collateral. The fact that we initially encounter Levi in his tax booth means that he is, in effect, a living symbol of Roman occupation and a reminder of the fact that some Jews were willing collaborators with the Romans. The link made in Mark 2:16 between tax collectors and "sinners" reinforces the negative associations.[6]

Where Luke stresses that Levi leaves everything to answer Jesus' call (Luke 5:28), Mark simply recounts that Levi follows him. The tax collector then throws a banquet, opening his house to Jesus, his disciples, and a mixed group including other tax collectors and "sinners." While the image is suggestive of a man seeking to share the gospel with his business colleagues, the reality is probably a little more subtle. Levi's "community" comprises his colleagues and others who, as "sinners," are shunned by leading figures in the community. In other words, their work made them part of a sub-community that had high-quality social relationships internally, but low-quality relationships with the communities around them. This is true for many kinds of work today. Our co-workers may be much more open to us than our neighbors are. Being a member of a work community may help us facilitate an encounter with the reality of the gospel for our co-workers.

---

[5] Malina and Rohrbaugh, 189–90.

[6] The Mishnaic text *m. Toharot* 7:6 states that if a tax collector enters a house, then it becomes unclean.

Interestingly, the hospitality of communal eating is a major part of Jesus' ministry and suggests a concrete way by which such encounters might be hosted. The hospitality of lunch with colleagues, a jog or workout at the gym, or a shared beverage after work can build deeper relationships with our co-workers. These friendships have lasting value themselves, and through them the Holy Spirit may open the door to a kind of friendship evangelism.

This raises a question. If Christians today were to host a meal with colleagues from work, friends from their neighborhood, and friends from their church, what would they talk about? The Christian faith has much to say about how to be a good worker and how to be a good neighbor. But do Christians know how to speak about them in a common language understandable to their colleagues and neighbors? If the conversation turned to workplace or civic topics such as a job search, customer service, property taxes, or zoning, would we be able to speak meaningfully to nonbelievers about how Christian concepts apply to such issues? Do our churches equip us for these conversations? It appears that Levi—or Jesus—was able to speak meaningfully about how Jesus' message applied to the lives of the people gathered there. (The question of taxation will recur later in the Gospel and we defer until then some of our questions about Jesus' attitude toward it.)

The Twelve (Mark 3:13–19)

In addition to the accounts of the calling of specific disciples, there is also the account of the appointing of the apostles. There is an important point to be noted in Mark 3:13–14, namely, that the Twelve constitute a special group within the broader community of disciples. The uniqueness of their apostolic office is important. They are called to a distinctive form of service, one that may depart significantly from the experience most of us will have. If we are to draw lessons from the experience and roles of the disciples, then it must be through recognition of how their actions and convictions relate to the kingdom, not merely the fact that they left their jobs to follow Jesus.

The qualifications listed for Simon, James, John, and Judas in Mark 3:16–19 are relevant here. Simon's name is, of course, supplemented with the new name given to him by Jesus, "Peter," which closely resembles the Greek word for "rock" (*petros*). One cannot help but wonder if there is both a certain irony and a certain promise in the name. Simon, as fickle and unstable as he will prove to be, is named The Rock, and one day he will live up to that name. Like him, our service to God in our workplaces, just as elsewhere in our lives, will not be a matter of instantaneous perfection, but rather one of failure and growth. This is a helpful thought at times when we feel we have failed and brought the kingdom into disrepute in the process.

Just as Simon is given a new name, so too are the sons of Zebedee, referred to as the "Sons of Thunder" (Mark 3:17). It is a quirky nickname, and seems humorous, but it also quite likely picks up on the character or personality of these two men.[7] It is an interesting point that personality and personality types are not effaced by inclusion in the kingdom. This cuts both ways. On one hand, our personalities continue to be part of our identity in the kingdom, and our embodiment of the kingdom in our place of work continues to be mediated through that personality. The temptation to find our identity in some stereotype, even a Christian one, is challenged by this. Yet, at the same time, our personalities may be marked by elements that themselves ought to be challenged by the gospel. There is a hint of this in the title given to Zebedee's sons, since it suggests a short temper or a tendency toward conflict and, even though the name is given with fondness, it may not be a nickname to be proud of.

The issue of personality makes a significant contribution to our understanding of applying the Christian faith to our work. Most of us would probably say that our experiences of work, both good and bad, have been greatly affected by the personalities of those around us. Often the very character qualities that make someone an inspiring and energizing colleague can make that person a difficult one. A motivated and excited worker might be easily distracted by new projects, or might be prone to quickly formed (and quickly expressed) opinions. Our own personality plays a huge role too. We may find others easy to work with or difficult, based as much on our personalities as theirs. Likewise, others may find *us* easy or difficult to work with.

But it is more than a matter of getting along with others easily. Our distinctive personalities shape our abilities to contribute to our organization's work—and through it to the work of God's kingdom—for better or worse. Personality gives us both strengths and weaknesses. To a certain degree, following Christ means allowing him to curb the

---

[7] Robert. A. Guelich, *Mark 1–8:26*, vol. 34A, *Word Biblical Commentary* (Nashville: Thomas Nelson, 1989), 162.

excesses of our personality, as when he rebuked the Sons of Thunder for their misguided ambition to sit at his right and left hands (Mark 10:35–45). At the same time, Christians often err by setting up particular personality traits as a universal model. Some Christian communities have privileged traits such as extraversion, mildness, reticence to use power, or—more darkly—abusiveness, intolerance, and gullibility. Some Christians find that the traits that make them good at their jobs—decisiveness, skepticism about dogma, or ambition, for example—make them feel guilty or marginalized in church. Trying to be something we are not, in the sense of trying to fit a stereotype of what a Christian in the workplace ought to be like, can be highly problematic and can leave others feeling that we are inauthentic. We may be called to imitate Christ (Phil. 2:5) and our leaders (Heb. 13:7), but this is a matter of emulating virtue, not personality. Jesus, in any case, chose people with a variety of personalities as his friends and workers. Many tools are available to help individuals and organizations make better use of the variety of personality characteristics with respect to decision making, career choice, group performance, conflict resolution, leadership, relationships at work, and other factors.

While on one level this needs to be related to a theology of wealth or property, on another level it needs to be related to the point at which the theologies of church and work meet. It is always tempting, and in fact can seem like an obligation, to maintain a network of Christians within the working environment and to seek to support one another. While laudable, there needs to be a certain reality injected into this. Some of those who present themselves as followers of Jesus may, in fact, have misplaced hearts, and this may affect the opinions they advocate. At such times, our responsibility as Christians is to be prepared to challenge one another in love, to hold one another to account as to whether we are truly operating according to the standards of the kingdom.

Discipleship in Process (Mark 4:35–41; 6:45–52; 8:14–21)

The Gospel of Mark, more than the other Gospels, highlights the ignorance, weakness, and selfishness of the disciples. This comes despite the many good things Mark has to say about them, including their response to Jesus' initial call (Mark 1:16–20) and to his commissioning of them (Mark 6:7–13).[8]

Certain incidents and narrative devices develop this portrait. One is the repetition of boat scenes (Mark 4:35–41; 6:45–52; 8:14–21), which parallel one another in emphasizing the disciples' inability to truly comprehend Jesus' power and authority. The last boat scene is closely followed by the unusual two-stage healing of a blind man (Mark 8:22–26), which may function as a kind of narrative metaphor for the only partial vision of the disciples regarding Jesus.[9] Then follows Peter's confession of Christ (Mark 8:27–33), with his dramatic moment of insight followed immediately by Satanic blindness on the apostle's part. The disciples' limited grasp of Jesus' identity is matched by their limited grasp of his message. They continue to desire power and status (Mark 9:33–37; 10:13–16; 10:35–45). Jesus challenges them several times for their failure to recognize that following him requires a fundamental attitude of self-sacrifice. Most obviously, of course, the disciples desert Jesus at the time of his arrest and trial (Mark 14:50–51). The juxtaposition of Peter's threefold denial (Mark 14:66–72) with the death of Jesus throws the cowardice and courage of the two men, respectively, into sharper relief.

Yet Peter and the others will go on to lead the church effectively. The angel who speaks to the women following the resurrection (Mark 16:6–7) gives them a message to the disciples (and Peter is singled out!), promising a further encounter with the resurrected Jesus. The disciples will be very different following this encounter, a fact that Mark does not explore but that is well developed in Acts, so that the resurrection is the key event in effecting such change.

What relevance does this have to work? Simply and obviously, that as disciples of Jesus with our own work to do, we are imperfect and in process. There will be a good deal that we will be required to repent of, attitudes that will be wrong and will need to change. Significantly, we must recognize that, like the disciples, we may well be wrong in much of what we believe and think, even about gospel matters. On a daily level, then, we must prayerfully reflect on how we are embodying the reign of God and prepare to

---

[8] Henderson, *in toto.*

[9] Guelich, 426.

show repentance over our deficiencies in this regard. We may feel tempted to portray ourselves as righteous, wise, and skilled in our workplaces, as a witness to Jesus' righteousness, wisdom, and excellence. But it would be a more honest and more powerful witness to portray ourselves as we really are—fallible and somewhat self-centered works-in-process, evidence of Jesus' mercy more than demonstrators of his character. Our witness is then to invite our co-workers to grow along with us in the ways of God, rather than to become like us. Of course, we need to exercise ourselves rigorously to growth in Christ. God's mercy is not an excuse to be complacent in our sin.

Rhythms of Work, Rest, and Worship (Mark 1–4; 6; 13)

The First Days of the Movement (Mark 1:21–45)

A major block of material (Mark 1:21–34) takes place on the Sabbath, the day of rest. Within this block, some of the action is located in the synagogue (Mark 1:21–28). It is significant that the weekly routine of work, rest, and worship is integrated into Jesus' own life and is neither ignored nor discarded. In our own age, where such a practice has been greatly diminished, it is important to remind ourselves that this weekly rhythm was endorsed by Jesus. Of course, it is also significant that Jesus does his work of both truth and healing on this day. This will later bring him into conflict with the Pharisees. It also highlights that the Sabbath is not just a day of rest from work, but also a day of active love and mercy.[10]

As well as the weekly rhythm, there is also a daily rhythm. Following the Sabbath, Jesus rises while it is still "very dark" to pray (Mark 1:35). His first priority of the day is to connect with God. The emphasis on the solitude of Jesus in this time of prayer is important, stressing that this prayer is not a public performance, but a matter of personal communion.

Daily prayer seems to be an extremely difficult practice for many workplace Christians. Between early morning family responsibili-

---

[10] David Shepherd, *Seeking Sabbath: A Personal Journey* (Oxford: Bible Reading Fellowship, 2007) is a helpful and thought-provoking reflection on the significance of the Sabbath for the contemporary world and highly recommended for further reading.

ties, long commutes, early working hours, a desire to get ahead of the day's responsibilities, and late nights needed to accomplish the day's work (or entertainment), it seems almost impossible to establish a consistent routine of morning prayer. And later in the day is harder still. Nowhere does Mark depict judgment against those who do not or cannot pray daily about the work that lies ahead of them. But he does depict Jesus—busier than anyone around him—praying about the work and the people God sets before him every day. Amid the pressures of working life, daily prayer may seem to be a personal luxury we can't afford to indulge. Jesus, however, couldn't imagine going to his work without prayer, much as most of us couldn't imagine going to work without shoes.

Regular time set apart for prayer is a good thing, but it is not the only way to pray. We can also pray in the midst of our work. One practice many have found helpful is to pray very briefly at multiple times during the day. "Daily Devotions for Individuals and Families," found in the Book of Common Prayer (pages 136–143), provides brief structures for prayer in the morning, at noon, in the later afternoon and at night, taking account of the rhythms of life and work during the day. Even briefer examples include a one- or two-sentence prayer when moving from one task to another, praying with eyes open, offering thanks silently or out loud before meals, keeping an object or verse of Scripture in a pocket as a reminder to pray and many others. Among the many books that help establish a daily prayer rhythm are *Finding God in the Fast Lane* by Joyce Huggett[11] and *The Spirit of the Disciplines* by Dallas Willard.[12]

The Lord of the Sabbath (Mark 2:23–3:6)

We have noticed already, in our discussion of Mark 1:21–34, that the Sabbath is integrated into the weekly rhythm of Jesus' life. The clash that takes place between Jesus and the Pharisees is not over whether to observe the Sabbath but over *how* to observe it. For the Pharisees, the Sabbath was primarily defined in negative terms. What,

---

[11] Joyce Huggett, *Finding God in the Fast Lane* (Suffolk, UK: Kevin Mayhew, 2004).

[12] Dallas Willard, *The Spirit of the Disciplines: Understanding How God Changes Lives* (San Francisco: Harper and Row, 1988).

they would ask, is prohibited by the commandment to do no work (Exod. 20:8–11; Deut. 5:12–15)?[13] To them, even the casual action of the disciples in picking ears of grain constitutes a kind of work and thus ignores the prohibition. It is interesting that they describe this action as "not lawful" (Mark 2:24), even though such a specific application of the fourth commandment is lacking in the Torah. They regard their own interpretation of the law as authoritative and binding, and do not consider the possibility that they might be wrong. Even more objectionable for them is Jesus' act of healing (Mark 3:1–6), which is depicted as the key event leading the Pharisees to plot against Jesus.

In contrast to the Pharisees, Jesus regards the Sabbath positively. The day of freedom from work is a gift for humanity's good: "The sabbath was made for humankind, not humankind for the sabbath" (Mark 2:27). Moreover, the Sabbath affords opportunities to exercise compassion and love. Such a view of the Sabbath has good prophetic antecedent. Isaiah 58 links the Sabbath with compassion and social justice in the service of God, culminating with a description of God's blessing on those who will "call the sabbath a delight" (Isa. 58:13–14). The juxtaposition of compassion, justice, and Sabbath suggests that the Sabbath is most fully used as a day of worship by the demonstration of compassion and justice. After all, the Sabbath itself is a remembrance of God's justice and compassion in delivering Israel from slavery in Egypt (Deut. 5:15).

The first Sabbath account (Mark 2:23–28) is triggered by the disciples' action of picking ears of grain.[14] While Matthew adds that the disciples were hungry, and Luke describes their action of rubbing the ears of grain between their hands before eating them, Mark simply describes them as picking the grain, which conveys the casual nature of the action. The disciples were probably absently picking at the seeds and nibbling them. The defense that Jesus offers when challenged by the Pharisees seems a little strange at first, because it is a story about the temple, not the Sabbath.

---

[13] Rabbinic traditions on this point are widespread. Most obviously, see *m. Sabb.* 7:2 and *m. Besah* 5:2.

[14] Lutz Doering, "Sabbath Laws in the New Testament Gospels," in *The New Testament and Rabbinic Literature*, ed. F. García Martínez and P. J. Tomson (Leiden: Brill, 2009), 208–20.

"Have you never read what David did when he and his companions were hungry and in need of food? He entered the house of God, when Abiathar was high priest, and ate the bread of the Presence, which it is not lawful for any but the priests to eat, and he gave some to his companions." (Mark 2:25–26)

Scholars are divided over how—or even whether—Jesus' argument works according to principles of Jewish exegesis and argumentation.[15] The key is to recognize the concept of "holiness." Both the Sabbath and the temple (with its contents) are described as "holy" in Scripture.[16] Sabbath is sacred time, the temple is sacred space, but lessons that may be derived from the holiness of one may be transferred to the other.

Jesus' point is that the holiness of the temple does not preclude its participation in acts of compassion and justice. The sacred spaces of earth are not refuges of holiness *against* the world, but places of God's presence *for* the world, for his sustenance and restoration of the world. A place set apart for God fundamentally *is* a place of justice and compassion. "The sabbath [and by implication, the temple] was made for humankind, and not humankind for the sabbath" (Mark 2:27). Matthew's version of this account includes the detail, "I desire mercy and not sacrifice," from Hosea 6:6 (Matt. 12:7). This makes explicit the point that we see with more reserve in Mark.

The same point emerges in the second Sabbath controversy, when Jesus heals a man in a synagogue on the Sabbath (Mark 3:1–6). The key question that Jesus asks is, "Is it lawful to do good or to do harm on the Sabbath, to save life or to kill?" The silence of the Pharisees in the face of this question serves as a confirmation that the Sabbath is honored by doing good, by saving life.

How does this apply to our work today? The Sabbath principle is that we must consecrate a portion of our time and keep it free from the demands of work, allowing it to take on a distinctive character of worship. This is not

---

[15] Guelich, 121–30.

[16] The Sabbath is referred to as holy in Exodus 31:14–15, picking up on the command in the Decalogue to "keep it holy" (Exod. 20:8), recognizing that God himself has "consecrated" it (Exod. 20:11). This notion of holiness links the Sabbath to the temple, which is characteristically understood as "holy" (see, for example, Ps. 5:7 or Ps. 11:4) and, of course, has at its heart the "Holy of Holies."

to say that the Sabbath is the only time of worship, nor that work cannot be a form of worship itself. But the Sabbath principle allows us time to focus on God in a different way than the working week allows, and to enjoy his blessing in a distinctive way. Crucially, too, it gives us space to allow our worship of God to manifest itself in social compassion, care, and love. Our worship on the Sabbath flavors our work during the week.

Recognizing that there is no single Christian perspective about the Sabbath, the Theology of Work Project explores a somewhat different point of view in the section on "Sabbath and Work" in the chapter "Luke and Work."

Jesus the Builder (Mark 6:1–6)

An incident in Jesus' hometown gives a rare insight into his work prior to becoming a traveling preacher. The context is that Jesus' hometown friends and acquaintances can't believe that this familiar local boy has become a great teacher and prophet. In the course of their complaints, they say, "What deeds of power are being done by his hands! Is not this the carpenter, the son of Mary and brother of James and Joses and Judas and Simon, and are not his sisters here with us?" (Mark 6:2–3). This is the only passage in the Bible to directly state Jesus' trade. (In Matthew 13:55, Jesus is called "the carpenter's son," and Luke and John do not mention his profession.) The underlying Greek (*tekton*) refers to a builder or craftsman in any kind of material,[17] which in Palestine would generally be stone or brick. The English rendering "carpenter" may reflect the fact that in London wood was the more common building material at the time the first English translations were made.

In any case, a number of Jesus' parables take place at construction sites. How much of Jesus' personal experience might be reflected in these parables? Did he help construct a fence, dig a wine press, or build a tower in a vineyard, and observe the strained relations between the landowner and the tenants (Mark 12:1–12)? Did one of his customers run out of money halfway through building a tower and leave an unpaid

---

[17] Ken M. Campbell, "What was Jesus' Occupation?" *Journal of the Evangelical Theological Society* 48, no. 3 (September 2005): 501–19.

debt to Jesus (Luke 14:28–30)? Did he remember Joseph teaching him how to dig a foundation all the way to solid rock, so that the building can withstand wind and flood (Matt. 7:24–27)? Did he ever hire assistants and have to face grumbling about pay (Matt. 20:1–16) and pecking order (Mark 9:33–37)? Was he ever supervised by a manager who asked him to join in a scheme to defraud the owner (Luke 16:1–16)? In short, how much of the wisdom in Jesus' parables was developed through his experience as a tradesman in the first-century economy? If nothing else, remembering Jesus' experience as a builder can help us see the parables in a more concrete light.

Parables at Work (Mark 4:26–29 and 13:32–37)

Mark contains only two parables that are not also found in the other Gospels. Both of them concern work, and both are very short.

The first of these parables, in Mark 4:26–29, compares the kingdom of God to growing grain from seed. It has similarities to the more familiar parable of the mustard seed, which follows immediately afterwards, and to the parable of the sower (Mark 4:1–8). Although the parable is set in the workplace of agriculture, the role of the farmer is deliberately minimized. "He does not know how" the grain grows (Mark 4:27). Instead, the emphasis is on how the kingdom's growth is brought about by the inexplicable power of God. Nonetheless, the farmer must "rise night and day" to cultivate the crop (Mark 4:26) and go in with his sickle (Mark 4:28) to reap the harvest. God's miracle is given among those who do their assigned work.

The second uniquely Marcan parable, in Mark 13:32–37, illustrates the need for Jesus' disciples to watch for his second coming. Intriguingly, Jesus says, "It is like a man going on a journey, when he leaves home and puts his slaves in charge, each with his work, and commands the doorkeeper to be on the watch" (Mark 13:34). While he is away, each servant is charged to keep doing his work. The kingdom is not like a master who goes to a far country and promises to eventually call his servants to join him there. No, the master will be coming back, and he gives his servants the work of growing and maintaining his household for his eventual return.

Both parables take it as a given that Jesus' disciples are diligent workers, whatever their occupation. We will not discuss the other parables here, but refer instead to the extensive explorations in "Matthew and Work" and "Luke and Work."

Economic Issues (Mark 10–12)

The Rich Young Man and Attitudes to Wealth and Status (Mark 10:17–31)

Wealth (Mark 10:17–22)

Jesus' encounter with a rich man who asks "What must I do to inherit eternal life?" constitutes one of the few passages in Mark that speaks directly to economic activity. The man's question leads Jesus to list (Mark 10:18) the six most socially oriented commandments in the Decalogue. Interestingly, "Do not covet" (Exod. 20:17; Deut. 5:21) is presented with a definite commercial twist as "Do not defraud." The rich man says that he has "kept all of these since my youth" (Mark 10:20). But Jesus states that the one thing he lacks is treasure in heaven, obtained by sacrificing his earthly wealth and following the vagrant from Galilee. This presents an obstacle that the rich man cannot pass. It seems that he loves the comforts and security afforded by his possessions too much. Mark 10:22 emphasizes the affective dimension of the situation: "When he heard this, he was shocked and went away grieving." The young man is emotionally disturbed by Jesus' teaching, indicating an openness to its truth, but he is not able to follow through. His emotional attachment to his wealth and status overrules his willingness to heed the words of Jesus.

Applying this to work today requires real sensitivity and honesty with regard to our own instincts and values. Wealth is sometimes a *result* of work—ours or someone else's—but *work itself* can also be an emotional obstacle to following Jesus. If we have privileged positions—as the rich man did—managing our careers may become more important than serving others, doing good work, or even making time for family, civic, and spiritual life. It may hinder us from opening ourselves to an unexpected calling from God. Our wealth and privilege may make us arrogant or insensitive to the people around us. These difficulties are not unique to people of wealth and privilege, of course. Yes, Jesus' encounter with the rich man highlights that it is hard to motivate yourself to change the world if you are already on top of the heap. Before those of us of modest means and status in the Western world let ourselves off the hook, let us ask whether, by world standards, we also have become complacent because of our (relative) wealth and status.

Before we leave this episode, one crucial aspect remains. "Jesus, looking at him, loved him" (Mark 10:21). Jesus' purpose is not to shame or browbeat the young man, but to love him. He calls him to leave his possessions first of all for his *own* benefit, saying, "You will have treasure in heaven; then come, follow me." *We* are the ones who suffer when we let wealth or work cut us off from other people and remove us from relationship with God. The solution is not to try harder to be good, but to accept God's love; that is, to follow Christ. If we do this, we learn that we can trust God for the things we really need in life, and we don't need to hold on to our possessions and positions for security. (This parable is further discussed under "Luke 18:18–30" in "Luke and Work.")

Status (Mark 10:13–16, 22)

A distinctive aspect to Mark's rendering of the story is its juxtaposition with the account of the little children being brought to Jesus, and the subsequent statement that the kingdom is to be received like such infants (Mark 10:13–16). What links the two passages is probably not the issue of security, of relying on financial resources rather than on God. Rather, the point of contact is the issue of status. In ancient Mediterranean society, children were without status, or at least were of a low status.[18] They possessed none of the properties by which status was judged. Crucially, they owned nothing. The rich young man, by contrast, has an abundance of status symbols (Mark 10:22) and he owns much. (In Luke's account, he is explicitly called a "ruler," Luke 18:18.) The rich

---

[18] Malina and Rohrbaugh, 238. "Children had little status within the community or family. A minor child was on a par with a slave and only after reaching maturity was he/she a free person who could inherit the family estate. The term 'child/children' could also be used as a serious insult (see Matthew 11:16–17)."

young man may miss entering the kingdom of God as much because of his slavery to status as because of his slavery to wealth per se.

In today's workplaces, status and wealth may or may not go hand in hand. For those who grow in both wealth and status through their work, this is a double caution. Even if we manage to use wealth in a godly manner, it may prove much harder to escape the trap of slavery to status. Recently a group of billionaires received much publicity for pledging to give away at least half of their wealth.[19] Their generosity is astounding, and in no way do we wish to criticize any of the pledgers. Yet we might wonder, with the value of giving so recognized, why not give away much more than half? Half a billion dollars still exceeds by far any amount needed for a very comfortable life. Is it possible that the status of remaining a billionaire (or at least a half-billionaire) is an impediment to devoting an entire fortune to the purposes that are so clearly important to a donor? Is it any different for workers of more modest means? Does regard for status keep us from devoting more of our time, talent, and treasure to the things we recognize as truly important?

The same question can be asked of people whose status does not correlate with wealth. Academics, politicians, pastors, artists, and many others may gain great status through their work without necessarily making a lot of money. Status may arise from working, say, at a particular university or remaining the toast of a certain circle. Can that status become a form of slavery that keeps us from jeopardizing our position by taking an unpopular stance or moving on to more fruitful work elsewhere?

How painful might it be to put our work-related status at risk—even a little bit—in order to serve another person, diminish an injustice, maintain your moral integrity, or see yourself in God's eyes? Jesus had all this status and even more. Perhaps that's why he worked so hard to set aside his status through daily prayer to his Father and by putting himself constantly in disreputable company.

The Grace of God (Mark 10:23–31)

The subsequent words of Jesus (Mark 10:23–25) elaborate the significance of the encounter, as Jesus stresses the difficulty faced by the wealthy in entering the kingdom. The young man's reaction illustrates

---

[19] Stephanie Strom, "Pledge to Give Away Half Gains Billionaire Adherents," *New York Times*, August 4, 2010.

the attachment the rich have to their wealth and to the status that goes with it; significantly, the disciples themselves are "perplexed" by Jesus' statements about the wealthy. It is perhaps noteworthy that when he repeats his statement in Mark 10:24, he addresses the disciples as "children," declaring them unburdened by status. They have already been unburdened by wealth as a result of following him.

Jesus' analogy of the camel and the eye of the needle (Mark 10:25) probably has nothing to do with a small gate in Jerusalem,[20] but could be a pun on the similarity of the Greek word for a camel (*kamelos*) and that for a heavy rope (*kamilos*). The deliberately absurd image simply emphasizes the impossibility of the rich being saved without divine help. This applies to the poor as well, for otherwise "who can be saved?" (Mark 10:26). The promise of such divine help is spelled out in Mark 10:27: "For mortals it is impossible, but not for God; for God all things are possible." This keeps the passage (and hopefully us, as readers) from descending into a simple cynicism toward the rich.

This leads Peter to defend the disciples' attitudes and history of self-denial. They have "left everything" to follow Jesus. Jesus' reply affirms the heavenly reward that awaits all those who make such sacrifices. Again, the things left by such people ("house or brothers or sisters or mother or father or children or fields") potentially have connotations of status and not merely material abundance. In fact, Mark 10:31 pulls the whole account together with a forceful emphasis on status: "Many who are first will be last, and the last will be first." Up until this point, the account could reflect either a love for things in and of themselves, or for the status that those things provide. This last statement, though, places the emphasis firmly upon the issue of status. Soon after, Jesus declares this in explicit workplace terms: "Whoever wishes to become great among you must be your servant, and whoever wishes to be first among you must be slave of all" (Mark 10:44). A slave, after all, is simply a worker with no status, not even the status of owning their own ability to work. The proper status

---

[20] This is simply a myth that has circulated in popular Christian circles. William Barclay popularized it in his Daily Study Bible Commentary; see William Barclay, *The Gospel of Matthew* (Louisville, KY: Westminster John Knox Press, 2001), 253. It is unclear what the origins of this myth are, but no such gate has ever been found, in Jerusalem or elsewhere.

of Jesus' followers is that of a child or slave—no status at all. Even if we hold high positions or bear authority, we are to regard the position and authority as belonging to God, not ourselves. We are simply God's slaves, representing him but not assuming the status that belongs to him alone.

The Temple Incident (Mark 11:15–18)

The incident where Jesus drives out the vendors and moneychangers from the temple has mercantile overtones. There is a debate over the precise significance of this action, both in terms of the individual Gospel accounts and in terms of the Historical Jesus tradition.[21] Certainly, Jesus aggressively drives out those who are engaging in trade in the temple courts, whether selling clean animals and birds for sacrifice or exchanging appropriate coinage for temple offerings. It has been suggested that this is a protest over the extortionate rates being charged by those involved in the trade, and thus the abuse of the poor as they come to make offerings.[22] Alternatively, it has been seen as a rejection of the annual half-shekel temple tax.[23] Finally, it has been interpreted as a prophetic sign act, disrupting the processes of the temple as a foreshadowing of its coming destruction.[24]

Assuming we equate the temple to the church in today's environment, the incident is mostly outside our scope, which is non-church-related work. We can note, though, that the incident does cast a dim light on those who would attempt to use the church to secure workplace advantages for themselves. To join or use a church in order to gain a favored business position is both commercially damaging for the community and

---

[21] N.T. Wright, *Jesus and the Victory of God* (London: SPCK, 1996), 413–28; and more recently, J. Klawans, *Purity, Sacrifice, and the Temple: Symbolism and Supersessionism in the Study of Ancient Judaism* (New York: Oxford University Press, 2005), 213–45.

[22] Craig A. Evans, "Jesus' Action in the Temple," in *Jesus in Context: Temple, Purity, and Restoration*, ed. C. A. Evans and B. Chilton (Leiden: Brill, 1997), 395–440, esp. 419–28. Evans surveys various strands of evidence that the priests were widely regarded as greedy and corrupt. His argument is set in opposition to E. P. Sanders, *Jesus and Judaism* (Philadelphia: Fortress, 1985), 61–76. Evans's arguments are, in turn, challenged by Klawans, *Purity, Sacrifice, and the Temple*, 225–29.

[23] R. J. Bauckham, "Jesus' Demonstration in the Temple," in *Law and Religion: Essays on the Place of the Law in Israel and Early Christianity*, ed. B. Lindars (Cambridge: James Clarke, 1988), 72–89, esp. 73–74.

[24] Wright, 413–28; Sanders, 61–76.

spiritually damaging for the individual. By no means do we mean that churches and their members should avoid helping each other become better workers. But if the church becomes a commercial tool, its integrity is damaged and its witness clouded.

Taxes and Caesar (Mark 12:13–17)

The issue of taxation has arisen obliquely already, in the discussion of the call narrative of Levi (Mark 2:13–17, see above). This section treats the matter a little more directly, although the meaning of the passage is still debatable in terms of its logic. It is interesting that the whole incident described here essentially represents a trap. If Jesus affirms Roman taxation, he will offend his followers. If he rejects it, he will face charges of treason. Because the incident hinges on such particular circumstances, we should be cautious about applying the passage to dissimilar contemporary situations.

The response of Jesus to the trap revolves around the concepts of image and ownership. Examining the common denarius coin (essentially a day's wage), Jesus asks whose "image" (or even "icon") is upon the coin. The point of the question is probably to allude deliberately to Genesis 1:26–27 (humans made in the image of God) in order to create a contrast. Coins bear the image of the emperor, but humans bear the image of God. Give to the emperor what is his (money), but give to God what is his (our very lives). The core element, that humans bear the *imago Dei*, is unstated, but it is surely implied by the parallelism built into the logic of the argument.

In using such argumentation, Jesus subordinates the taxation issue to the greater demand of God upon our lives, but he does not thereby deny the validity of taxation, even that of the potentially abusive Roman system. Nor does he deny that money belongs to God. If money belongs to Caesar, it belongs even more to God because Caesar himself is under God's authority (Rom. 13:1–17; 1 Pet. 2:13–14). This passage is no warrant for the often expressed fallacy that business is business and religion is religion. As we have seen, God recognizes no sacred-secular divide. You cannot pretend to follow Christ by acting as if he cares nothing about your work. Jesus is not proclaiming license to do as you please at work, but peace about the things you cannot control. You can control whether you defraud others in your work (Mark 10:18), so don't do it. You cannot control whether you have to pay taxes (Mark 12:17), so pay them. In this passage, Jesus doesn't say what your obligation might be if you can control (or influence) your taxes, for example, if you are a Roman senator or a voter in a twenty-first-century democracy. (This incident is discussed in greater depth under "Luke 20:20–26" in "Luke and Work.")

The Cross and Resurrection (Mark 14:32–16:8)

The topics of status and grace return to the fore as Jesus faces his trial and crucifixion. "The Son of Man came not to be served but to serve, and to give his life a ransom for many" (Mark 10:45). Even for him the path of service requires renouncing all status:

> "The Son of Man will be handed over to the chief priests and the scribes, and they will condemn him to death; then they will hand him over to the Gentiles; they will mock him, and spit upon him, and flog him, and kill him; and after three days he will rise again." (Mark 10:33–34)

The people—correctly—proclaim Jesus as Messiah and King (Mark 11:8–11). But he sets aside this status and submits to false accusations by the Jewish council (Mark 14:53–65), an inept trial by the Roman government (Mark 15:1–15), and death at the hands of the humanity he came to save (Mark 15:21–41). His own disciples betray (Mark 14:43–49), deny (Mark 14:66–72), and desert him (Mark 14:50–51), except for a number of the women who had supported his work all along. He takes the absolute lowest place, forsaken by God and men and women, in order to grant us eternal life. At the bitter end, he feels abandoned by God himself (Mark 15:34). Mark, alone among the Gospels, records him crying the words of Psalm 22:1, "My God, my God, why have you forsaken me?" (Mark 15:34). On the cross, Jesus' final work is to absorb all of the world's forsakenness. Perhaps being misunderstood, mocked, and deserted was as hard on him as was being put to death. He was aware that his death would be overcome in a few days, yet the misunderstanding, mockery, and desertion continue to this day.

Many today also feel abandoned by friends, family, society, even God. The sense of abandonment at work can feel very strong. We can be marginalized by co-workers, crushed by labor and danger, anxious about our performance, frightened by the prospect of layoffs, and made desperate by inadequate pay and meager benefits, as was so memorably described in Studs Terkel's book, *Working*. The words of Sharon Atkins, a receptionist in Terkel's book, speak for many people: "I'd cry in the morning. I didn't want to get up. I'd dread Fridays because Monday was always looming over me. Another five days ahead of me. There never seemed to be any end to it. Why am I doing this?"[25]

But God's grace overcomes even the most crushing blows of work and life for those who will accept it. God's grace touches people from the immediate moment of Jesus' submission, when the centurion recognizes, "Truly this man was God's Son!" (Mark 15:39). Grace triumphs over death itself when Jesus is restored to life. The women receive word from God that "he has been raised" (Mark 16:6). In the section on Mark 1:1–13, we noted the abruptness of the ending. This is not a pretty story for religious pageants but God's gut-wrenching intervention in the grit and grime of our ragged lives and work. The busted tomb of the crucified criminal is more proof than most of us can stand that "many who are first will be last, and the last will be first" (Mark 10:31). Yet this amazing grace is the one way our work can yield "a hundredfold now in this age" and our lives lead into "the age to come, eternal life" (Mark 10:30). No wonder that "terror and amazement had seized them; and they said nothing to anyone, for they were afraid" (Mark 16:8).

Conclusion to Mark

The Gospel of Mark is not organized as an instruction manual for human work, but work is visible on every page. We have drawn out some of the most significant threads in this tapestry of life and labor, and applied them to issues of twenty-first-century work. There are many kinds of work, and many contexts in which people work. The unifying theme is that all of us are called to the work of growing, restoring, and governing God's creation, even while we await the final accomplishment of God's intent for the world when Christ returns.

---

[25] Studs Terkel, *Working* (New York: The New Press, 1972), 31.

Within this grand outline, it is striking that much of Mark's narrative revolves around identity themes. Mark shows that entering the kingdom of God requires transformation in our personal identity and communal relationships. Issues of status and identity were wrapped up with wealth and employment in the ancient world in a much more formal way than is the case today. But the underlying dynamics have not changed radically. Issues of status still influence our choices, decisions, and goals as workers. Roles, labels, affiliations, and relationships all factor into our employment and can cause us to make decisions for better or worse. We can all be vulnerable to the desire to assert our place in society by means of our property, wealth, or potential influence, and this, in turn, can affect our vocational decisions. All of these elements factor into our sense of identity, of who we are. Jesus' challenge to be ready to relinquish the claims of earthly status is, therefore, of fundamental significance. Relatively few may be called to the particular choices made by the twelve disciples, to leave their employment entirely, but the challenge to subordinate worldly identity to the demands of the kingdom is universal. Self-denial is the essence of following Jesus. Such an attitude involves the refusal to allow our identity to be determined by our status in a fallen world.

Such a radical self-denial is impossible without grace. God's grace is the miracle that transforms life and work, so that we are capable of living and serving in God's kingdom while we dwell in a fallen world. Yet God's grace seldom comes through instantaneous transformation. The narrative of the disciples is one of failure and restoration, of eventual, not immediate, change. Like them, our service in the kingdom of God remains marred by sin and failure. Like them, we find it necessary to repent of much along the way. Perhaps, though, we will also be like them in leaving a lasting legacy in the world, a kingdom whose borders have been expanded by our activity, and whose life has been enriched by our citizenship. As hard as it is to give up the things that inhibit us from following Christ to the full in our work, we find that serving him in our work is far more rewarding (Mark 10:29–32) than serving ourselves and our follies.

Luke and Work

Introduction to Luke

The Gospel of Luke proclaims Jesus as the king who is coming into the world. Appointed by God, his rule will put right everything that has gone wrong following the rebellion and fall of humanity that began with Adam and Eve. At present, much of the world is governed by rebels against God's authority. Yet this world is God's kingdom nonetheless, and the stuff of daily life—including work—is the stuff of God's kingdom. God cares very deeply about the governance, productivity, justice, and culture of his world.

Jesus is both the king and model for all those who hold lesser authority. Although Christians are familiar with referring to Jesus as "king," somehow for many of us this title has come to seem primarily religious, rather than referring to an actual kingdom. We say that Jesus is the king, but we often mean that he is the king of the priests. We think of him as the founder of a religion, but Luke demonstrates that he is the re-founder of a realm—the kingdom of God on earth. When Jesus is personally present, even Satan and his minions acknowledge his rule (e.g., Luke 8:32) and his power is unchallengeable. After he returns, temporarily, to heaven, his model shows the citizens of his kingdom how to exercise authority and power in his stead.

Jesus' leadership extends to every aspect of life, including work. It is no surprise, then, that Luke's Gospel has wide application to work. Luke pays deep attention to work-related topics such as wealth and power, economics, government, conflict, leadership, productivity and provision, and investment, as we will discuss. We will proceed roughly in the order of Luke's text, occasionally taking passages out of order so we can consider them in a unit with other passages sharing the same theme. We will not attempt to discuss the passages that contribute little to an understanding of work, workers, and workplaces. It may prove surprising how much of Luke's Gospel turns out to be related to work.

The Kingdom of God Shows Up at Work (Luke 1–5)

God at Work (Luke 1–2; 4)

Zechariah's Surprising Day at Work (Luke 1:8–25)

Luke's Gospel begins in a workplace. This continues Yahweh's long history of appearing in workplaces (e.g., Gen. 2:19–20; Exod. 3:1–5). Zechariah is visited by the angel Gabriel on the most important workday of his life—the day he was chosen to minister in the holy place of the Jerusalem temple (Luke 1:8). While we may not be accustomed to thinking of the temple as a place of labor, the priests and Levites there were engaged in butchery (the sacrificial animals did not kill themselves), cooking, janitorial work, accounting, and a wide variety of other activities. The temple was not simply a religious center, but the center of Jewish economic and social life. Zechariah is impacted deeply by his encounter with the Lord—he is unable to speak until he has given witness to the truth of God's word.

The Good Shepherd Appears among the Shepherds (Luke 2:8–20)

The next workplace encounter takes place a few miles down the road from the temple. A group of shepherds watching their flocks by night are visited by an angelic host announcing the birth of Jesus (Luke 2:9). Shepherds were generally regarded as disreputable, and others looked down on them. But God looks down on them with favor. Like Zechariah the priest, the shepherds have their workday interrupted by God in a surprising way. Luke describes a reality in which an encounter with the Lord is not reserved for Sundays, retreats, or mission trips. Instead, each moment appears as a moment of potential in which God can reveal himself. The daily grind may serve to dull our spiritual senses, like the people of Lot's generation whose routines of "eating and drinking, buying and selling, planting and building" blinded them to the coming judgment on their city (Luke 17:28–30).[1] But God is able to break into the midst of everyday life with his goodness and glory.

---

[1] Note also the men in the parable who refuse the invitation to the wedding banquet because they need to look at their recently purchased field (Luke 14:18) and oxen (Luke 14:19). Rather than being open to find God in their work, they use work as a means to avoid God.

Jesus' Job Description: King (Luke 1:26–56; 4:14–22)

If it seems strange for God to announce his plan to save the world in the midst of two workplaces, it might seem even stranger that he introduces Jesus with a job description. But he does, when the angel Gabriel tells Mary she is to give birth to a son: "He will be great, and will be called the Son of the Most High and the Lord God will give to him the throne of his ancestor David. He will reign over the house of Jacob forever, and of his kingdom there will be no end" (Luke 1:32–33).

While we may be unaccustomed to thinking of "king of Israel" as Jesus' job, it is definitely his work according to Luke's Gospel. Details of his work as king are given: performing mighty deeds, scattering the proud, bringing down rulers from their thrones, lifting up the humble, filling the empty with good things, sending the rich away empty, helping Israel, and showing mercy to Abraham's descendants (Luke 1:51–55). These famous verses, often called the Magnificat, portray Jesus as a king exercising economic, political, and perhaps even military power. Unlike the corrupt kings of the fallen world, he employs his power to benefit his most vulnerable subjects. He does not curry favor with the powerful and well-connected in order to shore up his dynasty. He does not oppress his people or tax them to support luxurious habits. He establishes a properly governed realm where the land yields good things for all people, safety for God's people, and mercy to those who repent of evil. He is the king that Israel never had.

Later, Jesus confirms this job description when he applies Isaiah 61:1–2 to himself: "The Spirit of the Lord is upon me, because he has anointed me to bring good news to the poor. He has sent me to proclaim release to the captives and recovery of sight to the blind, to let the oppressed go free, to proclaim the year of the Lord's favor" (Luke 4:18–19). These are political and governmental tasks. Thus, in Luke at least, Jesus' occupation is more closely related to present-day political work than it is to today's pastoral or religious professions.[2] Jesus is

---

[2] Even those books that call Christ the "head of the church"—that is, Ephesians (4:15, 5:23) and Colossians (1:18)—also speak of him as the "head over everything" (Eph. 1:22, NIV) and the "head over every ruler and authority" (Col. 2:10). Christ is the chief of state, the head of all things—or will be, when the redemption of the world is complete—of which the church is a special subset.

highly respectful of the priests and their special role in God's order, but he does not primarily identify himself as one of them (Luke 5:14; 17:14).

The tasks Jesus claims for himself benefit people in need. Unlike the rulers of the fallen world, he rules on behalf of the poor, the prisoners, the blind, the oppressed, and those who have fallen into debt (whose lands are returned to them during the year of the Lord's favor; see Lev. 25:8–13). His concern is not only for people in desperate need. He cares for people in every station and condition, as we will see. But his concern for the poor, the suffering, and the powerless distinguishes him starkly from the rulers he has come to displace.

Jesus Calls People at Work (Luke 5:1–11, 27–32)

Twice Jesus goes to people's workplaces to call them to follow him. The first is when Jesus gets some fishermen to interrupt their work and let him use their boat as a podium. Then he gives them some excellent fishing tips and suddenly calls them to become his first disciples (Luke 5:1–11). The second is when he calls Levi, who is at his work of collecting taxes (Luke 5:27–32). These people are called to follow Jesus by leaving their professions. We tend to think of them as full-time church workers, but full-time "ambassadors" (2 Cor. 5:20) would be a more accurate description. Although these individuals are called to a particular kind of work in Jesus' kingdom, Luke isn't saying that some callings (e.g., preaching) are higher than others (e.g., fishing). Some of Jesus' followers—like Peter, John, and Levi—follow Jesus by leaving their current employment (Luke 5:11). We will soon meet others—such as Mary and Martha (Luke 10:38–41), another tax collector named Zacchaeus (Luke 19:1–10), and a Roman military officer (Luke 1–10)—who follow Jesus by living transformed lives in their present occupations. In one case (Luke 8:26–39), Jesus commands a person *not* to leave his home and travel around with him.

Those who travel with Jesus apparently cease wage-earning work and depend on donations for provision (Luke 9:1–6; 10:1–24). But this is not a sign that the highest form of discipleship is to leave our jobs. It is a specific call to these individuals and a reminder that all our provision is from God, even if he typically provides for us through conventional employ-

ment. There are many models for following Christ in our various occupations. (For more about Jesus' calling of the disciples, see "Mark 1:16–20"
in "Mark and Work" and "Matthew 3–4" in "Matthew and Work.")

Besides appearing in workplaces, Jesus also sets many of his parables in workplaces, including the parables of the new patches/wine-
skins (Luke 5:36–39), the wise and foolish builders (Luke 6:46–49), the
sower (Luke 8:4–15), the watchful servants (Luke 12:35–41), the wicked
servant (Luke 12:42–47), the mustard seed (Luke 13:18–19), the yeast
(Luke 13:20–21), the lost sheep (Luke 15:1–7), the lost coin (Luke 15:8–
10), the prodigal son (Luke 15:11–32), and the wicked tenants (Luke
20:9–19). Workplaces are where Jesus turns when he wants to say, "The
kingdom of God is like . . ." These passages are not generally meant to
teach about the workplaces in which they are set, although sometimes
they do provide a bit of workplace guidance. Rather, Jesus uses familiar
aspects of workplaces primarily to make points about God's kingdom
that transcend the parables' particular settings. This suggests that ordinary work has great significance and value in Jesus' eyes. Otherwise
it would make no sense to illustrate God's kingdom in workplace terms.

John the Baptist Teaches Workplace Ethics (Luke 3:8–14)

Much of Luke consists of Jesus' teaching. As it happens, the first
teaching in Luke is directly about work, although it comes from John
the Baptist rather than Jesus. John exhorts his audience to "bear fruits
worthy of repentance" (Luke 3:8) lest they face judgment. When they
ask specifically, "What should we do?" (Luke 3:10, 12, 14), John gives
economic, not religious, responses. First, he tells those who have an
abundance of possessions (two tunics or ample food) to share with those
who have nothing (Luke 3:10). He then gives instructions to tax collectors and soldiers, relating directly to their work. Tax collectors should
collect only what they are required to, rather than padding the tax bill
and pocketing the difference. Soldiers should not use their power to
extort money and accuse people falsely. They should be content with
their pay (Luke 3:13–14).

When John tells the tax collectors, "Collect no more than the amount
prescribed for you" (Luke 3:13), he was speaking radical words to a pro-

fession marked by entrenched, systemic injustice. Taxes throughout Palestine were gathered through a system of "tax farming" in which governors and other high-level officials outsourced the right to collect taxes in their jurisdictions.[3] In order to win a contract, a prospective tax collector would have to agree to give the official a certain amount over and above the actual Roman tax. Likewise, the tax collectors' own profits were the amounts they charged over and above what they passed up to the governmental officials. Since the people had no way to know what the actual Roman tax was, they had to pay whatever the tax collector assessed them. It would have been hard to resist the temptation for self-enrichment, and almost impossible to win bids without offering fat profits to the governmental officials.

Notice that John does not offer them the option to stop being tax collectors. The situation is similar for those Luke calls "soldiers." These are probably not disciplined Roman soldiers but employees of Herod, who at that time ruled Galilee as a client king for Rome. Herod's soldiers could (and did) use their authority to intimidate, extort, and secure self-gain. John's instruction to these workers is to bring justice to a system deeply marked by injustice. We should not underestimate how difficult that would have been. Holding citizenship in God's kingdom while living under the rule of kings of the fallen world can be dangerous and difficult.

Jesus Is Tempted to Abandon Serving God (Luke 4:1–13)

Just before Jesus begins his work as king, Satan tempts him to abandon his allegiance to God. Jesus goes to the wilderness, where he fasts for forty days (Luke 4:2). Then he faces the same temptations the people of

---

[3] John Nolland, *Luke 1–9:20*, vol. 35a, *Word Biblical Commentary* (Nashville: Thomas Nelson, 1989), 150: "Tax collectors had to work in a social context whose very structures were defined by graft and corruption. The honest tax collector would face problems akin to those faced today by a businessman seeking to operate without graft in relation to the bureaucracies of certain countries." Robert H. Stein, *Luke* (Nashville: Broadman, 1992), 134: "The soldiers probably were not Romans but Jews whom Herod Antipas employed (cf. Josephus, *Antiquities* 18.5.1 [18.113]) perhaps to assist tax collectors in their duties. Soldiers were . . . not required to resign [by Jesus] but to avoid the sins of their professions, i.e., violent intimidation ('extort'), robbing by false accusation, and dissatisfaction with wages (or perhaps 'rations')."

Israel faced in the wilderness of Sinai. (The answers Jesus gives to Satan are all quotes from Deuteronomy 6–8, which tells the story of Israel in the wilderness.) First, he is tempted to trust in his own power to satisfy his needs, rather than trusting in God's provision (Luke 4:1–3; Deut. 8:3, 17–20): "If you are the Son of God, command this stone to become a loaf of bread" (Luke 4:3). Second, he is tempted to switch his allegiance to someone (Satan) who flatters him with shortcuts to power and glory (Luke 4:5–8; Deut. 6:13; 7:1–26): "If you, then, will worship me, it will all be yours." Third, he is tempted to question whether God really is with him, and therefore to try forcing God's hand in desperation (Luke 4:9–12; Deut. 6:16–25): "If you are the Son of God, throw yourself down from here" (the temple). Unlike Israel, Jesus resists these temptations by relying on God's word. He is the man that the people of Israel—like Adam and Eve before them—were meant to be, but never were.

As parallels to the temptations of Israel in Deuteronomy 6–8, these temptations are not unique to Jesus. He experiences them much as we all do. "For we do not have a high priest who is unable to sympathize with our weaknesses, but we have one who in every respect has been tested as we are, yet without sin" (Heb. 4:15). Like Israel, and like Jesus, we can expect to be tempted as well, in work as in all of life.

The temptation to work solely to meet our own needs is very high at work. Work *is* intended to meet our needs (2 Thess. 3:10), but not *only* to meet our needs. Our work is meant to serve others also. Unlike Jesus, we do not have the option of self-service by means of miracles. But we can be tempted to work just enough for the paycheck, to quit when things get difficult, to shirk our share of the load, or to ignore the burden our poor work habits force others to carry. The temptation to take shortcuts is also high at work.

The temptation to question God's presence and power in our work may be the greatest of these temptations. Jesus was tempted to test God by forcing his hand. We do the same thing when we become lazy or foolish and expect God to take care of us. Occasionally this happens when someone decides God has called him or her to some profession or position, and then sits around waiting for God to make it happen. But we are probably more likely to be tempted by giving up on God's presence and power in our work. We may think our work means nothing to God, or that God only cares about our church life, or that we cannot pray for God's help for the day-to-day activities of work. Jesus expected God to participate in his work every day, but he did not demand that God do the work for him.

The entire episode begins with God's Spirit leading Jesus into the wilderness to fast for forty days. Then, as now, fasting and going on a retreat was a way to draw close to God before embarking on a major life change. Jesus was about to begin his work as king, and he wanted to receive God's power, wisdom, and presence before he started. This was successful. When Satan tempted Jesus, he had spent forty days in God's spirit. He was fully prepared to resist. Yet his fast also made the temptation more visceral: "He was famished" (Luke 4:2). Temptation often comes upon us far sooner than we expect, even at the beginning of our working lives. We may be tempted to enroll in a get-rich-quick scheme, instead of starting at the bottom of the ladder in a genuinely productive profession. We may come to face to face with our own weaknesses for the first time, and be tempted to compensate by cheating or bullying or deception. We may think we can't get the job we want with the skills we have, so we are tempted to misrepresent ourselves or fabricate qualifications. We may take a lucrative but unfulfilling position "just for a few years, until I'm settled," in the fantasy that we will later do something more in line with our calling.

Preparation is the key to victory over temptation. Temptations usually come without warning. You may be ordered to submit a false report. You may be offered confidential information today that will be public knowledge tomorrow. An unlocked door may offer a sudden opportunity to take something that isn't yours. The pressure to join in gossiping about a co-worker may arise suddenly during lunch break. The best preparation is to imagine possible scenarios in advance and, in prayer, plan how to respond to them, perhaps even write them down along with the responses you commit to God. Another protection is to have a group of people who know you intimately, whom you can call on short notice to discuss your temptation. If you can let them know before you act, they may help you through the temptation. Jesus, being in communion with his Father in the power of the Holy Spirit, faced his temptations with the support of his peer community—if we may so describe the Trinity.

Our temptations are not identical to Jesus', even if they have broad similarities. We all have our own temptations, large and small, depending on who we are, our circumstances, and the nature of our work. None of us is the Son of God, yet how we respond to temptation has life-changing consequences. Imagine the consequences if Jesus had turned aside from his calling as God's king and had spent his life creating luxuries for himself, or doing the bidding of the master of evil, or lying around waiting for the Father to do his work for him.

Healing in Luke

In Jesus' day, as now, the work of healing and health was essential. Jesus heals people in thirteen episodes in the Gospel of Luke: 4:31–37; 4:38–44; 5:12–16; 5:17–26; 7:1–10; 7:11–17; 7:21; 8:26–39; 8:40–56; 9:37–45; 13:10–17; 17:11–19; and 18:35–43. By doing so, he brings wellness to suffering people, as he announced he would do when he took on the mantle of king. In addition, the healings are actualizations of the coming kingdom of God, in which there will be no sickness (Rev. 21:4). God not only *commands* people to work for others' benefit, he *empowers* people to do so. God's power is not restricted to Jesus himself, for in two passages Jesus empowers his followers to heal people (Luke 9:1–6, 10:9). Yet all the healings depend on God's power. Theologian Jürgen Moltmann sums this up beautifully: "Jesus' healings are not supernatural miracles in a natural world. They are the only truly 'natural' thing in a world that is unnatural, demonized, and wounded."[4] They are a tangible sign that God is putting the world back to right.

The healings reported in the Gospels are generally miraculous. But Christians' nonmiraculous efforts to restore human bodies can also be seen as extensions of Jesus' life-giving ministry. It would be a mistake not to notice how important healing is to the redemptive work of God's kingdom. This work is performed daily by doctors, nurses, technologists, claims processors, hospital parking lot attendants, and countless others whose work makes healing possible. Luke himself was a physician

---

[4] Jürgen Moltmann, *The Way of Jesus Christ* (Minneapolis: Fortress Press, 1995), 69.

(Col. 4:14), and we can imagine his particular interest in healing. However, it would be a mistake to infer that the healing professions are inherently higher callings than other professions.

Sabbath and Work (Luke 6:1–11; 13:10–17)

The Sabbath is an essential part of the biblical understanding of work, and Jesus teaches about the Sabbath in the Gospel of Luke. Work and rest are not opposing forces, but elements of a rhythm that make good work and true recreation possible. Ideally, that rhythm meets people's needs for provision and health, but in a fallen world, there are times when it does not.

Lord of the Sabbath (Luke 6:1–11)

In Luke 6:1–5, it is the Sabbath, and Jesus and his disciples are hungry. They pluck heads of grain in a field, rub them in their hands, and eat the kernels. Some Pharisees complain that this constitutes threshing and is therefore working on the Sabbath. Jesus responds that David and his companions also broke the sacred rules when they were hungry, entering the house of God and eating the consecrated bread that only priests were allowed to eat. We might imagine that the connection between these two episodes is hunger. When you are hungry it is permissible to work to feed yourself, even if it means working on the Sabbath. But Jesus draws a somewhat different conclusion: "The Son of Man is Lord of the sabbath" (Luke 6:5). This suggests that keeping the Sabbath is grounded in understanding God's heart, rather than developing increasingly detailed rules and exceptions.

Set Free on the Sabbath (Luke 13:10–17)

Other healings Jesus performs on the Sabbath are described in Luke 6:9 and 14:5. Nonetheless, it would be hard to piece together a theology of the Sabbath from only the events in Luke. But we can observe that Jesus anchors his understanding of the Sabbath in the needs of people. Human needs come before keeping the Sabbath, even though keeping the Sabbath is one of the Ten Commandments. Yet by meeting human needs on the Sabbath, the commandment is fulfilled, not abolished. The healing of the crippled woman on the Sabbath provides a particularly rich example of this. "There are six days on which work ought to be done," the indignant synagogue ruler chides the crowd. "Come on those days and be cured, and not on the sabbath day" (Luke 13:14). Jesus' reply begins with the law. If people water their animals on the Sabbath, as was lawful, "ought not this woman, a daughter of Abraham whom Satan bound for eighteen long years, be set free from this bondage on the sabbath day?" (Luke 13:16). (Additional discussions of the Sabbath—in some cases with a differing perspective—can be found under "Mark 1:21–45" and "Mark 2:23–3:6" in "Mark and Work.")

The Ethics of Conflict (Luke 6:27–36; 17:3–4)

Do Good to Those Who Hate You (Luke 6:27–36)

All workplaces experience conflict. In Luke 6:27–36, Jesus addresses situations of conflict. "Love your enemies, do good to those who hate you, bless those who curse you, pray for those who abuse you" (Luke 6:27–28). Luke leaves no doubt that this is a teaching for the economic world, for he specifically relates it to lending money: "Lend [to your enemies], expecting nothing in return" (Luke 6:35). This doesn't seem like a viable commercial lending strategy, but perhaps we can understand it at a more abstract level. Christians must not use their power to crush people with whom they are in conflict. Instead, they must actively work for their good. This can apply to the workplace at two levels.

At the individual level, it means that we must work for the good of those with whom we are in conflict. This does not mean avoiding conflict or withdrawing from competition. But it does mean, for example, that if you are competing with a co-worker for promotion, you must help your co-worker/opponent do their work as well as they can, while trying to do yours even better.

At the corporate level, it means not crushing your competition, suppliers, or customers, especially with unfair or unproductive actions such as frivolous lawsuits, monopolization, false rumors, stock manipulation, and the like. Every occupation has its own circumstances, and it would be foolish to draw a one-size-fits-all application from this passage in Luke. Competing hard in business via intentional fraud might be different from competing hard in basketball via an intentional foul. Therefore, an essential element of believers' participation in an occupation is to try to work out what the proper modes of conflict and competition are in light of Jesus' teaching.

Rebuke, Repent, Forgive (Luke 17:3–4)

Later, Jesus again addresses interpersonal conflict: "If your brother or sister sins against you, rebuke them; and if they repent, forgive them" (Luke 17:3, NIV). We shouldn't take this as family therapy only, because Jesus applies the term "brother" to all those who follow him (Mark 3:35). It is good organizational behavior to confront people directly and to restore good relationships when the conflict is resolved. But the next verse breaks the bounds of common sense. "If the same person sins against you seven times a day, and turns back to you seven times and says, 'I repent,' you must forgive" (Luke 17:4). In fact, Jesus not only commands forgiveness, but the absence of judgment in the first place. "Do not judge, and you will not be judged; do not condemn, and you will not be condemned" (Luke 6:37). "Why do you see the speck of sawdust in your neighbor's eye, but do not notice the log in your own eye?" (Luke 6:41).

Would it be wise to be so nonjudgmental at work? Isn't sound judgment a requirement for good organizational governance and performance? Perhaps Jesus is talking about giving up not good judgment but judgmentalism and condemnation—the hypocritical attitude that the problems around us are entirely someone else's fault. Perhaps Jesus doesn't so much mean, "Ignore repeated moral lapses or incompetence," so much as, "Ask yourself how your actions may have contributed to the problem." Perhaps he doesn't mean, "Don't assess others' performance," so much as, "Figure out what you can do to help those around you succeed." Perhaps Jesus' point is not leniency but mercy: "Do to others as you would have them do to you" (Luke 6:31).

God's Provision (Luke 9:10–17; 12:4–7, 22–31)

Throughout Luke, Jesus teaches that living in God's kingdom means looking to God, rather than human effort, as the ultimate source of the things we need for life. Our labor is not optional, but neither is it absolute. Our labor is always a participation in the grace of God's provision.

Jesus Feeds Five Thousand (Luke 9:10–17)

Jesus demonstrates this in actions before he teaches it in words. In the feeding of the five thousand (Luke 9:10–17), God, in the person of Jesus, takes responsibility for meeting the crowd's need for food. He does it because they are hungry. Exactly how Jesus works this miracle is not stated. He makes use of ordinary food—the five loaves of bread and two fish—and by God's power, a little bit of food becomes enough to feed so many people. Some of Jesus' disciples (the fishermen) were in the food service profession and others (e.g., Levi the tax collector) were in civil service. He employs their accustomed labor, as they organize the crowd and serve the bread and fish. Jesus incorporates, rather than replaces, the ordinary human means of providing food, and the results are miraculously successful. Human work is capable of doing good or doing harm. When we do as Jesus directs, our work is good. As we so often see in the Gospel of Luke, God brings miraculous results out of ordinary work—in this case, the work of providing the necessities of life.

Jesus Teaches about God's Provision (Luke 12:4–7, 22–31)

Later, Jesus teaches about God's provision: "I tell you, do not worry about your life, what you will eat, or about your body, what you will wear. . . . Can any of you by worrying add a single hour to your span of life? If then you are not able to do so small a thing as that, why do you worry about the rest?" (Luke 12:22, 25–26). Jesus offers this as plain common sense. Since worrying cannot add so much as an hour to your life, why worry? Jesus doesn't say not to work, only not to worry about whether your work will provide enough to meet your needs.

In an economy of plenty, this is excellent advice. Many of us are driven by worry to labor in jobs we don't like, keeping hours that detract from our enjoyment of life, neglecting the needs of others around us. To us, the goal doesn't seem like "more" money but rather "enough" money, enough to feel secure. Yet seldom do we actually feel secure, no matter how much more money we make. In fact, it's often true that the more successful we are at bringing in more money, the less secure we feel because we now have more to lose. It's almost as if we would be better off if we had something genuine to worry about, as do the poor ("Blessed are you who are hungry now, for you will be filled," Luke 6:21). To break out of this rut, Jesus says to "strive for [God's] kingdom, and these things will be given to you as well" (Luke 12:31). Why? Because if your ultimate goal is God's kingdom, then you have the assurance that your ultimate goal will be met. And feeling that assurance, you can recognize that the money you make actually is enough, that God is providing for your needs. To earn a million dollars and be afraid you may lose it is like being a million dollars in debt. To earn a thousand dollars and to know that you will ultimately be fine is like getting a thousand-dollar gift.

But what if you don't have a thousand dollars? About a third of the world's population subsists on less than a thousand dollars a year.[5] These people may have enough to live on today, but face the threat of hunger or worse at any moment, whether or not they are believers. It is difficult to reconcile the hard fact of poverty and starvation with God's promise of provision. Jesus is not ignorant of this situation. "Sell your possessions and give to the poor," he says (Luke 12:33, NIV), for he knows that some people are desperately poor. That's why we must give to them. Perhaps if all Jesus' followers used our work and wealth to alleviate and prevent poverty, we would become the means of God's provision for the desperately poor. But since Christians have not done so, we will not pretend to speak here on behalf of people who are so poor that their provision is doubtful. Instead, let us ask whether our own provision is presently in doubt. Is our worry in proportion to any genuine danger of lacking what we really need? Are the things we worry about genuine needs? Are the things we worry about for ourselves remotely comparable to the things the desperately poor need that we do nothing to provide for them? If not, then anything but Jesus' advice not to worry about the necessities of life would be foolhardy.

---

[5] Peter Greer and Phil Smith, *The Poor Will Be Glad* (Grand Rapids: Zondervan, 2009), 29.

The Shrewd Manager and the Prodigal Son (Luke 16:1–13; 15:11–32)

The Parable of the Shrewd Manager (Luke 16:1–13)

The key to security about the things we need is not anxious earning and saving, but trustworthy service and spending. If God can trust us to spend our money to meet the needs of others, then the money we ourselves need will also be provided. This is the point of the parable of the dishonest manager. In it, a manager squanders his master's property and, as a result, is notified he will be fired. He uses his last days on the job to defraud his master further, but there is a strange twist to how he does it. He does not try to steal from his master. Perhaps he knows it will be impossible to take anything with him when he leaves the estate. Instead, he fraudulently reduces the debts of his masters' debtors, hoping that they will reciprocate the favor and provide for him when he is unemployed.

Like the dishonest manager, we cannot take anything with us when we depart this life. Even during this life our savings can be destroyed by hyperinflation, market crashes, theft, confiscation, lawsuits, war, and natural disaster. Therefore, building up large savings offers no real security. Instead, we should spend our wealth to provide for other people, and depend on them to do the same for us when the need arises. "Make friends for yourselves by means of dishonest wealth so that when it is gone, they may welcome you into the eternal homes" (Luke 16:9). By providing for his master's debtors, the dishonest steward is creating friendships. Mutual fraud is probably not the best way to build relationships. But apparently it is better than not building relationships at all. Building relationships is far more effective for gaining security than building wealth is. The word *eternal* signifies that good relationships help us in times of trouble in this life, and they will also endure into eternal life.

An extreme example of this principle occurs whenever war, terror, or disaster destroys the economic fabric of society. In a refugee camp, a prison, or a hyperinflated economy, the wealth you formerly may have had cannot procure even a crust of bread. But if you have provided for others, you may find them providing for you in your most difficult hour. Note that the people the dishonest manager helps are not wealthy people.

They are debtors. The dishonest manager is not depending on their riches but on the relationship of mutual dependence he has built with them.

Yet Jesus is *not* saying to depend on the fickle sentiments of people you may have helped over the years. The story turns quickly from the debtors to the master in the story (Luke 16:8), and Jesus endorses the master's maxim, "Whoever is faithful in a very little is faithful also in much" (Luke 16:10). This points to God as the guarantor that using money for relationships will lead to lasting security. When you build good relationships with other people, you come to have a good relationship with God. Jesus does not say which matters more to God, the generosity to the poor or the good relationships with people. Perhaps it is both: "If then you have not been faithful with the dishonest wealth, who will entrust to you the true riches?" (Luke 16:11). True riches are good relationships with people founded on our mutual adoption as God's children, and a good relationship with God is realized in generosity to the poor. Good relationships produce good fruit, which gives us greater ability to build good relationships and be generous to others. If God can trust you to be generous with a little bit of money and use it to build good relationships, he will be able to entrust you with greater resources.

This suggests that if you do not have enough savings to feel secure, the answer is not trying to save more. Instead, spend the little you have on generosity or hospitality. Other people's responses to your generosity and hospitality may bring you more security than saving more money would. Needless to say, this should be done wisely, in ways that truly benefit others, and not merely to assuage your conscience or flatter people targeted as future benefactors. In any case, your ultimate security is in God's generosity and hospitality.

Echoes of the Prodigal Son (Luke 15:11–32)

This may be surprising financial advice: Don't save, but spend what you have to draw closer to other people. Notice, however, that it comes immediately after the story of the prodigal son (Luke 15:11–32). In that story, the younger son wastes his entire fortune, while the older son saves his money so frugally that he can't even entertain his closest friends (Luke 15:29). The younger son's profligacy leads to ruin. Yet his squandering of the wealth leads him to turn to his father in utter

dependence. The father's joy at having him back washes away any negative feelings he has about the son costing him half a fortune. By contrast,
the older son's firm grasp on what's left of the family's wealth turns him
away from a close relationship with his father.

In the stories of both the dishonest manager and the prodigal son,
Jesus does not say that wealth is inherently bad. Rather, he says that the
proper use of wealth is to spend it, preferably on God's purposes—but if
not that, then on things that will increase our dependence on God.

Wealth in Luke

The last two passages move from the topic of provision to the topic
of wealth. Although Jesus has nothing against wealth, he views wealth
with suspicion. Market economies are predicated upon the generation,
exchange, and accumulation of privately owned wealth. This reality is
so deeply embedded in many societies that the pursuit and accumulation of personal wealth has become, for many, an end in itself. But,
as we have seen, Jesus does not see the accumulation of wealth as a
proper end in itself. Just as one's work (modeled upon the life of Jesus)
must exhibit a profound concern for others and an unwillingness to
use work-related power or authority only for self-gain, so also wealth
must be used with a deep concern for neighbors. While Luke's second
volume, Acts (see "Acts and Work"), has more wealth-related material,
his Gospel also poses significant challenges to dominant assumptions
about wealth.

Concern for the Wealthy (Luke 6:25; 12:13–21; 18:18–30)

Jesus' first problem with wealth is that it tends to displace God in
the lives of wealthy people. "For where your treasure is, there your heart
will be also" (Luke 12:34). Jesus wants people to recognize that their
lives are defined not by what they have, but by God's love for them and
his call upon their lives. Luke expects us—and the work we do—to be
fundamentally transformed by our encounters with Jesus.

But having wealth seems to make us stubbornly resistant to any
transformation of life. It affords us the means to maintain the status

quo, to become independent, to do things our own way. True, or eternal, life is a life of relationship with God (and other people), and wealth that displaces God leads ultimately to eternal death. As Jesus said, "What does it profit them if they gain the whole world, but lose or forfeit themselves?" (Luke 9:25). The wealthy may be lured away from life with God by their own wealth, a fate that the poor escape. "Blessed are you who are poor, for yours is the kingdom of God," says Jesus (Luke 6:20). This is not a promise of future reward, but a statement of present reality. The poor have no wealth to stand in the way of loving God. But "woe to you who are full now, for you will be hungry" (Luke 6:25). "Be hungry" seems a bit of an understatement for "miss eternal life by putting God outside your sphere of interest," but that is clearly the implication. Yet perhaps there is hope even for the wretchedly rich.

The Parable of the Rich Fool (Luke 12:13–21)

The parable of the rich fool (Luke 12:13–21) takes up this theme dramatically. "The land of a rich man produced abundantly," too much to fit in the man's barns. "What should I do?" he worries, and he decides to tear down his barns and build bigger ones. He is among those who believe that having more wealth will lead to less worry about money. But before he discovers how empty his worrisome wealth is, he meets an even starker fate—death. As he prepares to die, God's mocking question is a double-edged sword, "The things you have prepared, whose will they be?" (Luke 12:20). One edge is the answer, "not yours," for the wealth he counted upon to satisfy him for many years will pass instantly to someone else. The other edge cuts even deeper, and it is the answer, "yours." You—the rich fool—will indeed get what you have prepared for yourself, a life after death without God, true death indeed. His wealth has prevented him from the need to develop a relationship with God, exhibited by his failure to even think of using his bumper crop to provide for those in need. "So it is with those who store up treasures for themselves but are not rich toward God" (Luke 12:21).

Friendship with God is seen here in economic terms. God's friends who are rich provide for God's friends who are poor. The rich fool's problem is that he hoards things *for himself, not producing jobs or prosperity for others*. This means both that he loves wealth instead of God, and that he is not generous toward the poor. We can imagine a rich person who truly loves God and holds wealth lightly, one who gives liberally to the needy, or better yet, invests money in producing genuine goods and services, employs a growing workforce, and treats people with justice and fairness in their work. In fact, we can find many such people in the Bible (for example, Joseph of Arimathea, Luke 23:50) and in the world around us. Such people are blessed both in life and afterwards. Yet we do not want to remove the sting of the parable: if it is possible to grow (economically and otherwise) with grace, it is also possible to grow only with greed; the final accounting is with God.

The Rich Ruler (Luke 18:18–30)

Jesus' encounter with the rich ruler (Luke 18:18–30) points to the possibility of redemption from the grip of wealth. This man has not let his riches entirely displace his desire for God. He begins by asking Jesus, "Good Teacher, what must I do to inherit eternal life?" In response, Jesus summarizes the Ten Commandments. "I have kept all these since my youth," replies the ruler (Luke 18:21), and Jesus accepts him at his word. Yet even so, Jesus sees the corrupting influence that wealth is working on the man. So he offers him a way to end wealth's pernicious influence. "Sell all that you own and distribute the money to the poor, and you will have treasure in heaven; then come, follow me" (Luke 18:22). Anyone whose deepest desire is for God would surely leap at the invitation to daily, personal intimacy with God's Son. But it is too late for the rich ruler—his love of wealth already exceeds his love for God. "He became sad; for he was very rich" (Luke 18:23). Jesus recognizes the symptoms and says, "How hard it is for those who have wealth to enter the kingdom of God! Indeed, it is easier for a camel to go through the eye of a needle than for someone who is rich to enter the kingdom of God" (Luke 18:24–25).

By contrast, the poor often show amazing generosity. The poor widow is able to give away everything she has for the love of God (Luke 21:1–4). This is no summary judgment by God against wealthy people, but an observation of the heavy grip of wealth's seductive power. The people standing near Jesus and the ruler also recognize the problem and despair over whether anyone can resist the lure of wealth, though they themselves have given away everything to follow Jesus (Luke 18:28). Jesus, however, does not despair, for "what is impossible for mortals is possible for God" (Luke 18:27). God himself is the source of strength for our desire to love God more than wealth.

Perhaps wealth's most insidious effect is that it can prevent us from desiring a better future. If you are wealthy, things are good as they are now. Change becomes a threat rather than an opportunity. In the case of the rich ruler, this blinds him to the possibility that life with Jesus could be incomparably wonderful. Jesus offers the rich ruler a new sense of identity and security. If he could only have imagined how that would more than make up for the loss of his wealth, perhaps he could have accepted Jesus' invitation. The punch line comes when the disciples speak of all they've given up, and Jesus promises them the overflowing riches of belonging to the kingdom of God. Even in this age, Jesus says, they will receive "very much more" in both resources and relationships, and in the coming age, eternal life (Luke 18:29–30). This is what the rich ruler is tragically missing out on. He can see only what he will lose, not what he will gain. (The story of the rich ruler is further discussed under "Mark 10:17–31" in "Mark and Work.")

Concern for the Poor (Luke 6:17–26; 16:19–31)

The well-being of the rich is not Jesus' only concern with regard to wealth. He also cares about the well-being of the poor. "Sell your possessions," he says, "and give alms [to the poor]. Make purses for yourselves that do not wear out, an unfailing treasure in heaven, where no thief comes near and no moth destroys" (Luke 12:33). If the hoarding of wealth is harming the rich, how much more is it harming the poor?

God's persistent concern for the poor and powerless is inherent in the Magnificat (Luke 1:46–56), the Sermon on the Plain (Luke 6:17–26), and indeed throughout Luke's Gospel. But Jesus brings it to a point in the parable of Lazarus and the rich man (Luke 16:19–31). This rich man dresses in grand clothes and lives in luxury, while he does nothing to help relieve Lazarus, who is dying of hunger and disease. Lazarus dies, but so, of course, does the rich man, which reminds us that wealth has no great power after all. The angels carry Lazarus to heaven, apparently for no reason other than his poverty (Luke 16:22), unless perhaps for a love of God that was never displaced by wealth. The rich man goes to Hades, apparently for no reason other than his wealth (Luke 16:23), unless perhaps for a love of wealth that drove out any room for God or other people. The implication is strong that the rich man's duty was to care for Lazarus' needs when he was able (Luke 16:25). Perhaps by so doing, he could have found room again in himself for a right relationship with God and avoided his miserable end. Further, like many of the rich, he cared for his family, wanting to warn them of the judgment to come, but his care for God's wider family as revealed in the law and prophets was sadly lacking, and not even one returning from the dead could remedy that.

Generosity: The Secret to Breaking Wealth's Grip (Luke 10:38–42; 14:12–14; 24:13–35)

This suggests that God's secret weapon is generosity. If by God's power you can be generous, wealth begins to lose its grip on you. We have already seen how deeply generosity worked in the heart of the poor widow. It is much harder for the rich to be generous, but Jesus teaches how generosity might be possible for them too. One crucial path to generosity is to give to people who are too poor to pay you back.

> [Jesus] said also to the one who had invited him, "When you give a luncheon or dinner, do not invite your friends or your brothers or relatives or your rich neighbors, in case they may invite you in return, and you would be repaid. But when you give a banquet, invite the poor, the crippled, the lame, and the blind. And you will be blessed, because they cannot repay you, for you will be repaid at the resurrection of the righteous." (Luke 14:12–14)

Generosity that earns favors in return is not generosity but favor-buying. Real generosity is giving when no payback is possible, and this is what is rewarded in eternity. Of course, the reward in heaven could be taken as a kind of delayed gratification rather than true generosity: you give because you expect to be paid back at the resurrection, rather than during earthly life. This seems like a wiser sort of favor-buying, but favor-buying nonetheless. Jesus' words do not rule out interpreting generosity as eternal favor-buying, but there is a deeper, more satisfying interpretation. True generosity—the kind that doesn't expect to be paid back in this life or the next—breaks wealth's God-displacing grip. When you give away money, money releases its grip on you, but only if you put the money permanently beyond your reach. This is a psychological reality, as well as a material and spiritual one. Generosity allows room for God to be your God again, and this leads to the true reward of the resurrection—eternal life with God.

Mary and Martha (Luke 10:38–42)

The story of Martha and Mary (Luke 10:38–42) also puts generosity in the context of love for God. Martha works to prepare dinner, while Mary sits and listens to Jesus. Martha asks Jesus to rebuke her sister for not helping, but instead Jesus commends Mary. Regrettably, this story has often suffered from dubious interpretations, with Martha becoming the poster child for all that is wrong with the life of busyness and distraction, or what the medieval church called the active or working life, which was permitted but inferior to the perfect life of contemplation or monasticism. But the story must be read against the backdrop of Luke's Gospel as a whole, where the work of hospitality (a vital form of generosity in the ancient Near East) is one of the chief signs of the in-breaking of God's kingdom.[6]

Mary and Martha are not enemies but sisters. Two sisters squabbling about household duties cannot reasonably be construed as a battle between incompatible modes of life. Martha's generous service is not minimized by Jesus, but her worries show that her service needs to be grounded in Mary's kind of love for him. Together, the sisters embody the truth that generosity and love of God are intertwined realities. Martha performs the kind of generosity Jesus commends in Luke 14:12–14, for he is someone who cannot pay her back in kind. By sitting at Jesus' feet, Mary shows that all our service ought to be grounded in a lively personal relationship with him. Following Christ means becoming like Martha and Mary. Be generous and love God. These are mutually reinforcing, as is the two sisters' relationship with each other.

---

[6] See Brendan Byrne, *The Hospitality of God: A Reading of Luke's Gospel* (Collegeville, MN: Liturgical Press, 2000).

The Road to Emmaus (Luke 24:13–35)

The episode on the road to Emmaus is a fitting example of generosity for all Jesus' followers. At first it seems to take Jesus' death almost too lightly, or are we wrong to see something humorous in the two disciples instructing Jesus in the latest news? "Are you the only stranger in Jerusalem who does not know the things that have taken place there in these days?" they ask (Luke 24:18). One can almost imagine Cleopas adding, "Where have you been?" Jesus takes it in stride and lets them talk, but then turns the tide and makes them listen. Gradually, the light begins to dawn on them that perhaps the women's story of the Messiah's miraculous resurrection is not as crazy as they initially thought.

If this were all there was to the story, we might learn nothing more than that we are often "foolish . . . and . . . slow of heart to believe" (Luke 24:25) all that God has written. But the disciples do one thing right in this story—something so apparently insignificant it would be easy to miss. They offer hospitality to Jesus: "Stay with us, because it is almost evening and the day is now nearly over" (Luke 24:29). Jesus blesses this small act of generosity with the revelation of his presence. In the breaking of the bread they at last recognize him (Luke 24:32). When we offer hospitality, God uses it not only as a means of serving those in need of refreshment, but also as an invitation for us to experience Jesus' presence ourselves.

Investing in Jesus' Work (Luke 8:3; 10:7)

The parable of the shrewd manager (Luke 16:1–13) teaches the importance of using money wisely. Luke provides examples in the persons of those who invest their money in Jesus' work: Mary Magdalene, Joanna, and Susanna are named alongside the twelve disciples because of their financial support for Jesus' work. It is surprising how prominently women figure in this list, because few women in the ancient world possessed wealth. Yet "these women were helping to support them out of their own means" (Luke 8:3, NIV). Later, when Jesus sends out evangelists, he tells them to depend on the generosity of the people among whom they serve, "for the laborer deserves to be paid" (Luke 10:7).

What may seem surprising is that these two somewhat off-hand comments are all that Luke says about giving to what we would now recognize as the church. Compared to the unceasing concern Jesus shows for giving to the poor, he doesn't make much of giving to the church. Nowhere, for instance, does he interpret the Old Testament tithe as belonging to the church. This is not to say that Jesus sets generosity to the poor against generosity to the church. Instead, it is a matter of emphasis. We should note that giving money is not the only means of generosity. People also participate in God's redemptive work by creatively employing their skills, passions, relationships, and prayers.

Power and Leadership in Luke

As king, Jesus is the leader of God's realm. He employs his power in many ways recorded in the Gospel of Luke. Yet Christians are often reluctant to exercise leadership or power, as if the two were inherently evil. Jesus teaches otherwise. Christians are called to lead and to exercise power, but unlike the powers of the fallen world, they are to use it for God's purposes rather than for their own self-interest.

Persistence: The Parable of the Persistent Widow (Luke 18:1–8)

In the parable of the persistent widow (Luke 18:1–8), a poor, power-less person (the widow) persists in nagging a corrupt, powerful person (the judge) to do justice for her. The parable *assumes* John the Baptist's teaching that holding a position of power and leadership obligates you to work justly, especially on behalf of the poor and weak. But Jesus focuses the parable on a different point, that we are "to pray always and to not lose heart" (Luke 18:1). He identifies the hearers—us—with the woman, and the prayed-to person—God—with the corrupt judge, a strange com-bination. Assuming that Jesus doesn't mean that God is corrupt, the point must be that if persistence pays off with a corrupt human of limited power, how much more will it pay off with a just God of infinite power.

The purpose of the parable is to encourage Christians to persevere in their faith against all odds. But it also has two applications for those who work in positions of leadership. First, the juxtaposition of a corrupt judge with a just God implies that God's will is at work even in a corrupt world. The judge's job is to do justice, and by God, he *will* do justice by the time the widow is finished with him. Elsewhere, the Bible teaches that the civil authorities serve by God's authorization, whether they acknowledge it or not (John 19:11; Rom. 13:1; 1 Pet. 2:13). So there is hope that even in the midst of systemic injustice, justice may be done. A Christian leader's job is to work toward that hope at all times. We cannot right every wrong in the world in our lifetimes. But we must never give up hope, and never stop working for the greater good[7] in the midst of the imperfect systems where our work occurs. Legislators, for example, seldom have a choice of voting for a good bill versus a bad bill. Usually the best they can do is to vote for bills that do more good than bad. But they must continually look for opportunities to bring bills to a vote that do even less harm and even more good.

The second point is that only God can bring about justice in a corrupt world. That is why we must pray and not give up in our work. God can bring miraculous justice in a corrupt world, just as God can bring miraculous healing in a sick world. Suddenly, the Berlin wall opens, the apartheid regime crumbles, peace breaks out. In the parable of the persistent widow, God does not intervene. The widow's persistence alone leads the judge to act justly. But Jesus indicates that God is the unseen actor: "Will not God grant justice to his chosen ones who cry to him day and night?" (Luke 18:7).

Risk: The Parable of the Ten Minas (Luke 19:11–27)

The parable of the ten minas ("pounds" in the NRSV translation) is set in the workplace of high finance. A rich—and soon to be powerful— nobleman goes on an extended trip to be crowned king. Most of his people hate him and send word ahead that they oppose this coronation (Luke 19:14). In his absence, he assigns three of his servants to invest his money. Two of them take the risk of investing their master's money. They earn handsome returns. A third servant is afraid to take the risk, so he puts the money in a safe place. It earns no return. When the master returns,

---

[7] The use of the term "greater good" implies that the consequences of our actions are important in Christian ethics. This mode of ethical thinking, called "consequentialism," may be unfamiliar to those who are used to thinking of the Bible only in terms of ethical rules. However, the Bible makes use of all three modes of ethical reasoning that have been identified over the centuries: rules, consequences, and virtues. By no means does this make the Bible "relativistic" or "utilitarian," to name two ethical systems that truly are foreign to biblical thinking.

he has become king of the whole territory. He rewards the two servants who made money for him, promoting them to high positions of their own. He punishes the servant who kept the money safe but unproductive. Then he commands that all who opposed him be killed in his presence.

Jesus tells this parable immediately before going to Jerusalem, where he is to be crowned king ("Blessed is the king who comes in the name of the Lord," Luke 19:38) but is soon rejected by his people. This identifies Jesus with the nobleman in the parable, and the crowd shouting "Crucify him!" (Luke 23:21) with the people in the parable who oppose the nobleman's coronation. By this we know that the people have profoundly misjudged their soon-to-be king, except for the two servants who work diligently in his absence. The parable, in this context, warns us that we must decide if Jesus is indeed God's appointed king and be prepared to abide the consequences of our decision either to serve him or oppose him.[8]

This parable makes explicit that citizens of God's kingdom are responsible to work toward God's goals and purposes. In this parable, the king tells his servants directly what he expects them to do, namely, to invest his money. This specific calling or command makes it clear that preaching, healing, and evangelism (the apostles' callings) are not the only things God calls people to do. Of course, not everyone in God's kingdom is called to be an investor, either. In this parable, only three of the country's residents are called to be investors. The point is that acknowledging Jesus as king requires working toward his purposes in whatever field of work you do.

Seen in this light, the parable suggests that if we choose to accept Jesus as king, we must expect to lead risky lives. The servants who invested the master's money faced the risk of being attacked by those around them who rejected the master's authority. And they faced the risk of disappointing their master by making investments that might lose money. Even their success exposes them to risk. Now that they have tasted success and been promoted, they risk becoming greedy or power-mad. They face the risk that their next investments—which will involve much greater sums—will fail and expose them to much more severe

---

[8] Darrell L. Bock, *Luke 9:51–24:53*, Baker Exegetical Commentary on the New Testament (Grand Rapids: Baker Books, 1996), 1525–45.

consequences. In Anglo-American business (and sports) practice, CEOs (and head coaches) are routinely fired for mediocre results, whereas those in lower-level positions are fired only for exceptionally poor performance. Neither failure nor success is safe in this parable, or in today's workplace. It is tempting to duck for cover and search for a safe way of accommodating to the system while waiting for things to get better. But ducking for cover is the one action Jesus condemns in the parable. The servant who tries to avoid risk is singled out as unfaithful. We are not told what would have happened if the other two servants had lost money on their investments, but the implication is that all investments made in faithful service to God are pleasing to him, whether or not they achieve their intended payoff. (For a discussion of the highly similar parable of the talents, see "Matthew 25:14–30" in "Matthew and Work.")

Humble Service (Luke 9:46–50; 14:7–11; 22:24–30)

Jesus declares that leadership requires humble service to others, as we see in three additional passages. In the first (Luke 9:46–50), Jesus' disciples begin arguing who will be the greatest. Jesus replies that the greatest is the one who welcomes a child in his name. "The least among all of you is the greatest." Notice that the model is not the child, but the person who welcomes a child. Serving those whom everyone else considers not worth their time is what makes a leader great.

The second passage (Luke 14:7–11) is Jesus' response to the social posturing he sees at a banquet. Not only is it a waste of time, Jesus says, it's actually counterproductive. "All who exalt themselves will be humbled, and those who humble themselves will be exalted." As applied to leadership, this means that if you try to take credit for everything, people will want to stop following you, or get distracted from their work by trying to make you look bad. But if you give credit to others, people will want to follow you and that will lead to true recognition.

The third passage (Luke 22:24–30) returns to the question of who is the greatest among the disciples. This time Jesus makes himself the model of leadership through service. "I am among you as one who serves." In all three stories, the concepts of service and humility are tied together. Effective leadership requires—or *is*—service. Service requires acting as if you are less important than you think you are.

Taxing Issues (Luke 19:1–10; 20:20–26)

All along, Luke has identified Jesus as the one who is bringing God's rule to earth. In chapter 19, the people of Jerusalem finally recognize him as a king. As he rides into town on a colt, crowds line the road and sing his praises: "Blessed is the king who comes in the name of the Lord! Peace in heaven, and glory in the highest heaven!" (Luke 19:38). As we know, God's kingdom encompasses all of life, and the issues Jesus chooses to discuss immediately before and after his entry into Jerusalem touch on taxes and investments.

Zacchaeus, the Tax Collector (Luke 19:1–10)

As he passes through Jericho on his way to Jerusalem, Jesus comes upon a tax collector named Zacchaeus, who is sitting in a tree to get a better view of Jesus. "Zacchaeus, hurry and come down; for I must stay at your house today," Jesus says (Luke 19:5). The encounter with Jesus profoundly changes the way Zacchaeus works. Like all tax collectors in Roman client states, Zacchaeus made his money from overcharging people on their taxes. Although this was what we might now call "industry standard practice," it depended on deceit, intimidation, and corruption. Once Zacchaeus comes into the kingdom of God, he can no longer work this way. "Zacchaeus stood there and said to the Lord, 'Look, half of my possessions, Lord, I will give to the poor; and if I have defrauded anyone of anything, I will pay back four times as much'" (Luke 19:8). Exactly how—or whether—he will continue to make a living, he doesn't say, for it is beside the point. As a citizen of God's kingdom, he cannot engage in business practices contrary to God's ways.

Render unto God What Is God's (Luke 20:20–26)

After Jesus is welcomed as king in Jerusalem, there is a passage in Luke that has often been used wrongly to separate the world of work from the kingdom of God: Jesus' saying about taxes. The teachers of the law and the chief priests try to "trap him by what he said, so as to hand him over to the jurisdiction and authority of the governor" (Luke 20:20). They ask him whether it is lawful to pay taxes to Caesar. In response, he asks them to show him a coin, and immediately they produce a denarius. He asks whose portrait is on it and they reply, "Caesar's." Jesus says, "Then give back to Caesar what is Caesar's, and to God what is God's" (Luke 20:25, NIV).

This reply has sometimes been interpreted as separating the material from the spiritual, the political from the religious, and the earthly and from the heavenly realms. In church (God's realm), we must be honest and generous, and look after the good of our brothers and sisters. At work (Caesar's realm), we must shade the truth, be driven by worry about money, and look out for ourselves above all. But this misunderstands the sharp irony in Jesus' reply. When he says, "Give back to Caesar what is Caesar's," he is not sanctioning a separation of the material from the spiritual. The premise that Caesar's world and God's world do not overlap makes no sense in light of what Jesus has been saying throughout the Gospel of Luke. What is God's? Everything! Jesus' coming into the world as king is God's claim that the entire world is God's. Whatever may belong to Caesar also belongs to God. The world of taxes, government, production, distribution, and every other kind of work is the world that God's kingdom is breaking into. Christians are called to engage that world, not to drop out of it. This passage is the opposite of a justification of separating the work world from the Christian world. Give to Caesar what is Caesar's (taxes) and to God what is God's (everything, taxes included). (For a more thorough discussion of this incident, see the section on "Matthew 17:24–27 and 22:15–22" in "Matthew and Work.")

The Passion (Luke 22:47–24:53)

Jesus' work climaxes in his willing self-sacrifice on the cross, as with his last gasp he breathes out trust in God: "Father, into your hands I commend my spirit" (Luke 23:46). By Jesus' self-sacrifice and by the Father's mighty deed of resurrection, Jesus passes fully into the position of eternal king foretold at his birth. "The Lord God will give to him the throne of his ancestor David. He will reign over the house of Jacob *forever*" (Luke 1:32–33). This is truly God's beloved Son, faithful unto death as he works on behalf of all who have fallen into the poverty of sin and death, in need of a redemption we cannot provide ourselves. In this light, we see that Jesus' care for the poor and powerless is both an end in itself and a sign of his love for everyone who will follow him. We are *all* poor and powerless in the face of our sin and the world's brokenness. In his resurrection we find ourselves transformed in every aspect of life, as we are caught up in this extravagant love of God.

Conclusion to Luke

The Gospel of Luke is the story of the emergence of the kingdom of God on earth in the person of Jesus Christ. As the true king of the world, Christ is both the ruler to whom we owe our allegiance and the model for how we are to exercise whatever authority we are given in life.

As our ruler, he gives us one great commandment in two parts: "You shall love the Lord your God with all your heart, and with all your soul, and with all your strength, and with all your mind; and your neighbor as yourself. . . . Do this, and you will live" (Luke 10:27–28). In one sense, this commandment is nothing new. It is simply a summary of the Law of Moses. What is new is that the kingdom based on this law has been inaugurated by God's incarnation in the person of Jesus. It was God's intent from the beginning that humanity should live in this kingdom. But from the time of Adam and Eve's sin onwards, people have lived instead in the kingdom of darkness and evil. Jesus has come to reclaim the earth as God's kingdom and to create a community of God's people who live under his rule, even while the kingdom of darkness retains much of its sway. The essential response of those who come to citizenship in Christ's kingdom is that they live *all* of their lives—including work—in pursuit of the purposes and according to the ways of his kingdom.

As our model, Jesus teaches us these purposes and ways. He calls us to work at tasks such as healing, proclamation, justice, power, leadership, productivity and provision, investment, government, generosity, and hospitality. He sends God's spirit to give us everything we need to fulfill our specific callings. He promises to provide for us. He commands us to provide for others, and thereby suggests that his provision for us will generally come in the form of other people working on our behalf. He warns us of the trap of seeking self-sufficiency through wealth, and he teaches us that the best way to avoid the trap is to use our wealth in furtherance of relationships with God and with other people. When conflicts arise in our relationships, he teaches us how to resolve them so they lead to justice and reconciliation. Above all, he teaches that citizenship in God's kingdom means working as a servant of God and of people. His self-sacrifice on the cross serves as the ultimate model of servant leadership. His resurrection to the throne of God's kingdom confirms and establishes forever the active love of our neighbor as *the* way of eternal life.

John and Work

Introduction to John

Work pervades the Gospel of John. It starts with the work of the Messiah, who is God's agent of the creation of the world. Christ's work of creation predates the Fall, predates his incarnation in the form of Jesus of Nazareth, and predates his work of redemption. He is sent by God to be the redeemer of the world precisely because he is already the co-creator of the world. His work of redemption is not a novel course of action, but a restoration of the world to the path it was always intended to take. It is a fulfillment of the creation's promise.

Human labor is an integral part of the fulfillment of creation (Gen. 2:5). But the work humans do has become corrupted, so the redemption of *work* is an integral part of the Messiah's redemption of the world. During his earthly ministry, we will see that the work Jesus does for the Father is an integral aspect of Father and Son's love for each other. "The words that I say to you I do not speak on my own; but the Father who dwells in me does his works" (John 14:10). This provides the model for redeemed human labor, which is likewise meant to nurture our love for one another as we work together in God's good world. In addition to modeling good work, Jesus teaches about workplace topics such as calling, relationships, creativity and productivity, ethics, truth and deception, leadership, service, sacrifice and suffering, and the dignity of labor.

One of John's chief interests is to remind people that a casual glance at Jesus will never do. Those who remain with him find his simple images opening up into an entirely new way of looking at the world. This is as true of work as it is of anything else. The Greek word for "work" (*ergon*) appears over twenty-five times in the Gospel, while the more general term for "doing" (*poieō*) occurs over one hundred times. In most cases, the words refer to Jesus' work for the Father; but even this, it turns out, will hold promise for ordinary human employment. The key to making sense of this material is that it takes work to work out what the Gospel of John means. The meaning often lies deeper than a casual reading can uncover. Therefore, we will delve into a limited number of passages with particular meaning for work, workers, and workplaces. We will pass over passages that do not contribute essentially to our topic.

The Word's Work in the World (John 1:1–18)

"In the beginning was the Word, and the Word was with God, and the Word was God. He was in the beginning with God. All things came into being through him, without him not one thing came into being." The majestic opening of John's Gospel shows us the limitless scope of the Word's work. He is the definitive self-expression of God, the one through whom God created *all things* in the beginning. He stretches out the cosmos as the canvas for the expression of God's glory.

The Word is working; and because his work began in the beginning, all subsequent human labor is derived from his initial labor. *Derived* is not too strong a word, because everything people work with was created by him. The work God did in Genesis 1 and 2 was performed *by* the Word. This may seem too fine a point to press, but many Christians continue to labor under the delusion that the Messiah only began working once things had gone irredeemably wrong, and that his work is restricted to saving (invisible) souls to bring them to (immaterial) heaven. Once we recognize that the Messiah was working materially with God from the beginning, we can reject every creation-denying (and thus work-denigrating) theology.

Therefore we need to correct a common misunderstanding. John's Gospel is *not* grounded in a dichotomy of the spiritual versus the material, or the sacred versus the profane, or any other dualism. It does not portray salvation as the liberation of the human spirit from the shackles of the material body. Dualistic philosophies such as these are regrettably common among Christians. Their proponents have often turned to the language of the Gospel of John to support their views. It is true that John frequently records Jesus' use of contrasts such as light/darkness (John 1:5; 3:19; 8:12; 11:9–10; 12:35–36), belief/unbelief (John 3:12–18; 4:46–54; 5:46–47; 10:25–30; 12:37–43; 14:10–11; 20:24–31) and spirit/

flesh (John 3:6–7). These contrasts highlight the conflict between God's ways and the ways of evil. But they do not constitute a division of the universe into dual sub-universes. They certainly do not call Jesus' followers to abandon some sort of "secular" world in order to enter a "spiritual" one. Instead, Jesus employs the contrasts to call his followers to receive and use the power of God's spirit in the present world. Jesus states this directly in John 3:17: "God did not send the Son into the world to condemn the world, but in order that the world might be saved through him." Jesus came to restore the world to the way God intended it to be, not to lead an exodus out of the world.

If further evidence for God's ongoing commitment to the creation is needed, we may turn to John 1:14: "The Word became flesh and lived among us." The incarnation is not the triumph of the spirit over the flesh, but the fulfillment of what the flesh was created for in the beginning. And the flesh is not a temporary base of operations, but the Word's permanent abode. After his resurrection, Jesus invites Thomas and the others to touch his flesh (John 20:24–31) and later has a breakfast of fish with them (John 21:1–14). At the end of the Gospel, Jesus tells his disciples to wait "until I return" (John 21:22–23, NIV), not "until I get us all out of here." A God hostile to, or uninterested in, the material realm would hardly be inclined to take up permanent residence within it. If the world in general is of such immense concern to God, it stands to reason that the work done within that world matters to him as well.

Calling Disciples/Friends (John 1:35–51)

We will return to the conventional term "disciples" momentarily, but the term "friends" captures the essence of John's depiction of the disciples. "I have called you friends," says Jesus (John 15:15). The relational element is critical: they are Jesus' friends who first and foremost remain in his presence (John 1:35–39; 11:54; 15:4–11). John appears to go out of his way to crowd as many people as possible onstage with Jesus in chapter 1. John the Baptist points Jesus out to Andrew and another disciple. Andrew gets his brother Simon. Philip, who is from the same town as Andrew and Simon, finds Nathanael. It is not simply that Jesus will advance his mission *through* a web of interpersonal relationships. Weaving a web of relationships *is the point* of the whole enterprise.

But the disciples are not just buddies basking in the radiance of Jesus' friendship. They are also his workers. They are not working in an obvious way yet in chapter 1 (though even the fetching of siblings and neighbors is a type of evangelistic labor), but work they will. Indeed, as we will see, it is precisely this connection between friendship and labor that holds the key to John's theology of work. Work produces results while it also builds relationships, and this is another echo of Genesis 2:18–22.

The Wedding Planner (John 2:1–11)

Jesus' "first sign" (John 2:11), changing water into wine, lays the foundation for understanding the subsequent signs. This is no parlor trick done to attract attention to himself. He does it reluctantly, and the miracle is hidden even from the master of the banquet. Jesus does it only in the face of pressing human need and to honor his mother's request. (Running out of wine at the wedding would have brought great shame on the bride, the groom, and their families, and that shame would have lingered long in the village culture of Cana.) Far from being an unmoved mover (as some Greeks regarded God), Jesus shows himself to be the loving, responsive Son of the loving, eternal Father and the beloved human mother.

The fact that he turns the water to wine shows that he is like the Father not only in love, but also in his power over the creation. Attentive readers of John should not be surprised that the Word who made all things, now made flesh himself, is able to bring material blessings to his people. To deny that Jesus can work miracles would be to deny that Christ was with God in the beginning. What is most surprising, perhaps, is that this apparently unplanned miracle ends up pointing unmistakably to Jesus' ultimate purpose. He has come to draw people to God's consummate wedding feast, where they will joyfully dine with him together. Jesus' mighty works, done with the stuff of the present world order, are amazing blessings in the here and now; and they also point to still greater blessings in the world to come.

Jesus' Hand in All Things (John 3:1–36)

Jesus' discussions with Nicodemus and his disciples hold innumerable treasures. We will begin with a verse that has profound implications for human labor: "The Father loves the Son and has placed all things in his hands" (John 3:35). While the immediate context emphasizes the fact that the Son speaks the Father's words, the remainder of the Gospel makes it clear that "all things" really does mean "all things." God has authorized his Messiah to create all things, God sustains all things through him, and God will bring all things to their appointed goal through him.

This passage reiterates what we learned in the prologue: the Father involves the Son in the founding and sustaining of the world. What is new is the revelation of *why* the Father chose to include the Son, rather than simply creating by himself. It was an act of love. The Father shows his love for the Son by placing all things in his hands, beginning with the act of creation. The world is a "labor of love" in the fullest sense of the word. Work must be something more wonderful than we usually give it credit for if *adding* to someone's workload is an act of love. We will develop this all-important idea further as we see Jesus in action throughout the remainder of the Gospel.

But chapter 3 does more than reiterate how the Word took on human flesh. It also illustrates the inverse process, how human flesh can become filled with God's Spirit. "Very truly, I tell you, no one can enter the kingdom of God without being born of water and Spirit" (John 3:5). We receive God's Spirit ("enter his kingdom") through a form of *birth*. Birth is a process that occurs in the flesh. When we become truly spiritual, we do not slough off the flesh and enter some immaterial state. Instead, we are more perfectly born—born "from above" (John 3:3)—into a state of union of Spirit and flesh, like Jesus himself.

During his discussion with Nicodemus, Jesus says that those born from above will "come to the light, so that it may be clearly seen that their deeds have been done in God" (John 3:21). Later he uses the metaphor of *walking* in the light to illustrate the same idea (John 8:12; 11:9–10; 12:35–36). This has important ethical implications for work. If we are conducting all our work openly, we have a powerful tool for remaining faithful to the ethics of God's kingdom. But if we find ourselves hiding

or obscuring our work, it is often a strong indication that we are following an unethical path. This is not an unbending rule, for Jesus himself
acted in secret at times (John 7:10), as did his followers, such as Joseph
of Arimathea (John 19:38). But at the least we might ask, "Who is my
secrecy truly protecting?"

For example, consider a man heading a business in mission in Africa that builds boats for use on Lake Victoria. He says he is frequently
approached by local officials who want him to pay a bribe. The request
is always made in secret. It is not a documented, open payment, as is
a tip or an expediting fee for faster service. There are no receipts and
the transaction is not recorded anywhere. He has used John 3:20–21 as
an inspiration to draw these requests into the light. He will say to the
official requesting the bribe, "I don't know much about these kinds of
payments. I would like to bring in the ambassador, or the management,
to get this documented." He has found this to be a helpful strategy for
dealing with bribery.

It is important to understand that the metaphor of walking in the
light is not a one-size-fits-all rule. Confidentiality and secrecy can have
a proper place in work, as in personnel matters, online privacy, or trade
secrets. But even if we deal with information that should not be made
public, we seldom need to act in complete darkness. If we are hiding our
actions from others in our departments or from people with a legitimate
interest, or if we would be ashamed to see them reported in the news,
then we may have a good indication that we are acting unethically.

Water Works (John 4)

The story of the woman at the well (John 4:1–40) has as much direct
discussion of human labor as any story in John; but one has to draw
deeply to taste it all. Many Christians are familiar with the woman's
inability to move from the everyday work of drawing water to Jesus'
pronouncements on the life-giving power of his word. This motif permeates the Gospel: the crowds repeatedly show an inability to transcend
everyday concerns and address the spiritual aspects of life. They do not
see how Jesus can offer them his body as bread (John 6:51–61). They
think they know where he is from (Nazareth, John 1:45–46), but they fail

to see where he is really from (heaven); and they are equally ignorant as to where he is going (John 14:1–6).

All of this is certainly relevant for thinking about work. Whatever we think of the intrinsic good of a steady water supply (and every drink we take confirms that it is indeed a good thing!), this story surely tells us that physical water alone cannot confer on us eternal life. In addition, it is easy for modern Westerners to miss the drudgery of the woman's daily water chores, and ascribe her reluctance to fetch the water to sheer laziness. But the curse on labor (Gen. 3:14–19) bites hard, and she can be forgiven for wanting a more efficient delivery system.

We should not conclude, however, that Jesus comes to free us from work in the grimy material world so that we can bathe in the sublime waters of spiritual serenity. We must first, as always, remember the comprehensive nature of Christ's work as depicted in John 1: the Messiah made the water in the well, and he made it good. If he then uses that water to illustrate the dynamics of the Spirit's work in the hearts of would-be worshippers, that could be seen as an *ennoblement* of the water rather than a downgrading of it. The fact that we reckon first with the Creator, then with the creation, is no slight on the creation, especially since one function of creation is to point us toward the Creator.

We see something similar in the aftermath of the story, where Jesus uses reaping as a metaphor to help the disciples understand their mission in the world:

> "Do you not say, 'Four months more, then comes the harvest'? But I tell you, look around you, and see how the fields are ripe for harvesting. The reaper is already receiving wages and is gathering fruit for eternal life, so that sower and reaper may rejoice together." (John 4:35–36)

In addition to providing the palpable blessing of the daily bread for which we are instructed to pray, agricultural work can *also* serve as a way of understanding the advance of God's kingdom.

More than that, Jesus directly dignifies labor in this passage. We first have the statement, "My food is to do the will of him who sent me and to complete his work [Gk. *ergon*]" (John 4:34). It is worth noting that the first appearance of the Greek word *ergon* in the Bible[1] shows

---

[1] That is, in the Septuagint, the ancient Greek translation of the Hebrew Bible.

up in Genesis 2:2: "On the seventh day God finished the work [Gk. "his works," *erga*] that he had done, and he rested on the seventh day from all the work that he had done [again, "his works," *erga* in Gk.]." While we cannot be certain that Jesus is alluding to this verse in Genesis, it makes sense in light of the rest of the Gospel to take "God's work" in John 4:34 to mean the comprehensive restoration or completion of the work God had done in the beginning.

There is something more subtle at work here as well. In John 4:38, Jesus makes the somewhat cryptic statement, "I sent you to reap that for which you did not labor. Others have labored, and you have entered into their labor." He is referring to the fact that the disciples have a field of Samaritans ripe for the kingdom, if they will only open their eyes to the opportunity. But who are the "others" who have done the "labor"? Part of the answer seems to be, surprisingly, the woman at the well, who is remembered more for her spiritual slowness than for her subsequent effective testimony for Jesus: "Many Samaritans from that city believed in him because of the woman's testimony, 'He told me everything I have ever done'" (John 4:39). The disciples will simply be reaping where the woman has sown. Yet there is still another worker here: Christ himself. Back at the beginning of the story, we read that Jesus was "tired" from his journey. A more literal translation would be that Jesus was "labored" from his journey. The word translated "tired" is *kekopiakōs*, literally "labored." This is the same root that appears in John 4:38 (and nowhere else in John's Gospel): ". . . you did not labor [*kekopiakate*] . . . others have labored [*kekopiakasin*] . . . you have entered into their labor [*kopon*] . . ." In truth, Jesus was labored from his journey in Samaria. The field of Samaria is ripe for harvest in part because Christ has labored there. Whatever work we do as Christ's followers is filled with the glory of God, because Christ has already worked the same fields to prepare them for us.

As we have seen, the redemptive work of Christ after the Fall is of a kind with his creative/productive work from the beginning of time. Likewise, the redemptive work of his followers is in the same sphere as the creative/productive work typified by homemakers drawing water and farmers reaping crops.

Evangelism is one of the many forms of human work, neither higher nor lower than homemaking or farming. It is a distinctive form of work, and nothing else can substitute for it. The same may be said of drawing water and harvesting grain. Evangelism does not displace creative/productive work to become the only truly worthy human activity, particularly since any work well done by Christians is a testimony to the renewing power of the Creator.

Who Works When, and Why? (John 5)

The healing of the man at the pool of Bethsaida brings to the surface a controversy familiar from Matthew, Mark, and Luke: Jesus' penchant for healing on the Sabbath. If the controversy is familiar, however, Jesus' self-defense takes a slightly different angle in John's Gospel. His lengthy argument is crisply summarized in John 5:17: "My Father is still working, and I also am working." The principle is clear. God keeps the creation going even on the Sabbath, and therefore Jesus, who shares the divine identity, is permitted to do the same. Jesus was almost certainly not alone in arguing that God was at work on the Sabbath, but his deduction justifying his own work is unique.

As a result, we cannot use this story to deduce the propriety or impropriety of *our* working on the Sabbath. We may be doing God's work, but we do not share the divine identity as Christ does. Human work having life-or-death consequences—military self-defense (1 Macc. 2:41) or pulling an animal from a ditch—was already accepted as legitimate on the Sabbath. The healing itself is not questioned in this episode, even though the man would have suffered no harm had Jesus waited until Sunday to heal him. Instead, Jesus is criticized for permitting him to carry a mat—a form of work, according to the Jewish Law—on the Sabbath. Does this imply that Jesus permits us to drive to vacation on the Sabbath? Fly on Sunday to a business meeting that begins on Monday morning? Operate a continuous casting plant 24/7/365? There is no hint here that Jesus is merely widening the list of activities permitted on the Sabbath. Instead, let us apply the theme we see running through John—work that maintains and redeems the creation (material or spiritual), and contributes to closer relationships with God and people, is appropriate for the Sabbath. Whether any particular work fulfills this description must be discerned by the person(s) involved. (For more on this topic, see "Matthew 12:1–8" in "Matthew and Work," "Mark 1:21–45" and "Mark 2:23–3:6" in "Mark and Work," and "Luke 6:1–11; 13:10–17" in "Luke and Work.")

A clearer, and more important, lesson for us from this narrative is that God is still at work to maintain the present creation, and Jesus furthers that work in his healing ministry. Jesus' signs are at one level the in-breaking of the new world. They demonstrate "the powers of the age to come" (Heb. 6:5). At the same time, they are also the up-keeping of the present world. It seems perfectly appropriate to see this as a paradigm for our own myriad jobs. As we act in faith to restore what has been broken (as doctors, nurses, auto mechanics, and so forth), we call people to remember the goodness of the creator God. As we act in faith to develop the capacities of the creation (as programmers, teachers, artists, and so on), we call people to reflect on the goodness of humanity's God-given dominion over the world. The work of redemption and the work of creation/production, done in faith, both shout out our trust in the God who is, and who was, and who is to come. God created all things through Christ, is restoring them to his original intent through Christ, and will bring them to their appointed goal through Christ.

Bread of Life (John 6)

John's telling of the feeding of the five thousand (John 6:1–15) echoes many of the themes we saw in the wedding feast at Cana and the healing of the paralytic man. Again, Jesus works to sustain life in the present world, even as the sign points toward the ultimate life he alone can offer. John 6:27–29, however, poses a particular challenge for the theology of work:

> "Do not work for the food that perishes, but for the food that endures for eternal life, which the Son of Man will give you. For it is on him that God the Father has set his seal." Then they said to him, "What must we do to perform the works of God?" Jesus answered them, "This is the work of God, that you believe in him whom he has sent."

A quick reading reveals at least two major issues: first, Jesus appears to issue a direct command not to work; and second, he appears to reduce even work for God to belief.

The first issue is fairly easy to address. All Scripture, like all communication, must be seen in context. The issue in John 6 is that people want to keep Jesus around to serve as a Magical Baker King, who will keep the loaves coming. Thus when Jesus says, "You are looking for me, not because you saw signs, but because you ate your fill of the loaves" (John 6:26), he is rebuking their spiritual shortsightedness. They ate the bread, but they were unable to see what this sign signified. It is the same lesson we learned in chapter 4. Eternal life comes not from an unending supply of food, but from the living Word who proceeds from the mouth of God. Jesus ceases the preliminary work (serving loaves) when it no longer results in the desired end product (relationship with God). Any competent worker would do the same. If adding more salt ceases to make the soup taste better, a decent cook stops adding salt. Jesus doesn't mean "stop working," but stop working for more stuff (food) when more stuff isn't what you need. This may sound too obvious to need the Word of God to tell us, but who among us doesn't need to hear that truth again this very day? The apparent prohibition against working for temporal gain is a hyperbolic expression designed to focus on mending the crowd's relationship to God.

As for the issue of work being reduced simply to belief, this must be seen against the backdrop of the rest of the Gospel and the theology of John's letters. John delights in pushing things to extremes. On the one hand, his high view of God's sovereignty and creative power leads him to exalt a humble dependence on God, as we see in this chapter. God's work on our behalf is infinite—we need only to believe him and accept the work of God in Christ. On the other hand, Jesus is equally capable of laying the emphasis on our active obedience: "Whoever says, 'I abide in him,' ought to walk just as he walked" (1 John 2:6), and again, "The love of God is this, that we *obey* his commandments" (1 John 5:3). We might join these two extremes with the Pauline expression, "the obedience of faith" (Rom. 1:5), or James 2:18, "I by my works will show you my faith."

Seeing and Believing (John 9)

Jesus and his disciples see a man born blind (chapter 9). The disciples look on him as a lesson or case study on the sources of sin. Jesus looks on him with compassion and works to remedy his condition. Christ's unusual method of healing and the subsequent actions of the no-longer-blind man again show that the world of flesh and blood—and mud—is the place of God's kingdom. Jesus' method—mixing spit with dirt and putting it on the man's eyes—is not madness, but a calculated echo of the creation of mankind (Gen. 2:7). In both biblical and Greek tradition, mud (*pēlos*) is used to describe what people are made of. Note, for example, Job 10:9, where Job says to God, "Remember that you fashioned me like clay; and will you turn me to dust again?"[2]

Life, and Looming Death (John 10–12)

As Jesus draws near to Jerusalem for the last time, he does his greatest sign—the raising of Lazarus at Bethany (John 11:1–44). Jesus' opponents, who have already tried to stone him (John 8:59; 10:31), decide that both Jesus and Lazarus must go. With his death looming, Jesus speaks about the cross in a paradoxical way. He uses what appears to be the language of exaltation, saying that he will be "lifted up" and draw all people to himself (John 12:32). Yet John makes clear in the follow-up note that this refers to the "lifting up" of the cross. Is this mere wordplay? Not at all. As Richard Bauckham points out, it is in the work of supreme self-sacrifice on the cross that Jesus fully reveals that he is indeed the exalted Son of God. "Because God is who God is in his gracious self-giving, God's identity, we can say, is not simply revealed but enacted in the event of salvation for the world which the service and self-humiliation of his Son accomplishes."[3]

---

[2] This verse is especially interesting because the "clay" is in synonymous parallelism with dust, using the same Hebrew word for dust as in the creation of Adam in Genesis 2:7. For other associations of humanity and mud in the Bible, see, e.g., Isaiah 29:16; 45:9; Jeremiah 18:6; Sirach 33:13; Romans 9:21; cf. also Job 33:6; outside the Bible, see, e.g., Aristophanes, *Birds* 686; Herodas, *Mimes* 2.29.

[3] Richard J. Bauckham, *God Crucified: Monotheism and Christology in the New Testament* (Grand Rapids: Eerdmans, 1999), 68.

Jesus' coming self-sacrifice would extract many forms of cost. It would cost him his death, of course, but also excruciating pain and thirst (John 19:28). It cost him the heartbreak of seeing his disciples (except John) desert him and his mother bereft of him (John 19:26–27). It cost him the shame of being misunderstood and wrongly blamed (John 18:19–24). These costs were unavoidable if he was to do the work God set before him. The world could not come into being without the work of Christ in the beginning. The world could not be restored to God's intention without the work of Christ on the cross.

Our work may also call for costs that are not fair to us, but which cannot be avoided if we are to complete our work. Jesus worked to bring true life to others. To the extent that we use our work as an arena for self-glorification, we depart from the pattern set for us by the Lord Jesus. Is Jesus acknowledging that work performed for others has an unavoidable cost? Perhaps so. Doctors earn a good salary from healing people (at least in the modern West) yet suffer an unavoidable burden of pain from witnessing their patients' suffering. Plumbers get an enviable hourly rate, but also get covered with excrement from time to time. Elected officials work for justice and prosperity for their citizens, but like Jesus, bear the sorrow of knowing, "you always have the poor with you" (John 12:8). In each of these professions, there might be ways to avoid suffering alongside others—minimizing interaction with unsedated patients; plumbing only in new, unsoiled houses; or hardening our hearts to the most vulnerable people in society. Would doing so be following the pattern of Jesus? Although we often speak of work as how you make your living, any compassionate worker also experiences work as how you break your heart. In this way, we work like Jesus.

Servant Leadership (John 13)

Up to this point in John, we have seen Jesus doing work that no one else had ever done before—making water into wine, giving sight to the blind, raising the dead. Now he does what almost anyone can do, but what few want to. He washes feet. The king does the work of a slave.

In doing so, Jesus brings to a head the question that has been following us through the entire course of John's Gospel—to what extent is

Jesus' work an example for our own work? It would be easy to answer, "Not at all." None of us are the Lord. None of us die for the sins of the world. But when he washes the disciples' feet, Jesus explicitly tells them—and by extension us—that we *are* to follow his example. "So if I, your Lord and Teacher, have washed your feet, you also ought to wash one another's feet. For I have set you an example" (John 13:14–15). Jesus *is* an example we are meant to follow, so far as we are able.

This attitude of humble service should accompany all we do. If the CEO walks the production floor, it should be as if coming to wash the assembly workers' feet. So, too, the gas station attendant should clean the bathroom floors as if being there to wash the motorists' feet. This is not so much a matter of action as attitude. Both the CEO and the gas station attendant can probably serve people better through other activities than washing feet, even if their employees or customers were willing. But they should see themselves as performing humble service. Jesus, the Spirit-filled teacher who reigns over the entire cosmos, deliberately performs a concrete act of lowly service to demonstrate what ought to be the habitual attitude of his people. By doing so, he both dignifies and demands from his followers humble acts of service. Why? Because doing so brings us tangibly face to face with the reality that godly work is performed for the benefit of others, not merely for our own fulfillment.

The concept of servant leadership has received widespread attention in business and government in recent years. It arises not only in the Gospel of John but also in many parts of the Bible.[4]

Farewell Words (John 14–17)

Chapters 14 through 17, often called the Upper Room Discourse, contain so much profound theology that we can only touch on a few salient points. But it is important to recognize that Jesus' words are not a dispassionate lecture. He is in anguish for the disciples whom he loves

---

[4] Other resources include *Servant Leadership* by Robert Greenleaf (Mahwah, NJ: Paulist Press, 1977), and *Leadership Is an Art* by Max De Pree (New York: Doubleday, 1992).

and whom he must soon leave, and his words are designed above all to comfort them in their distress.

Work and Relationships (John 14–17)

An emphasis on personal relationships suffuses the theology of these chapters. Jesus tells the disciples, "I do not call you servants any longer . . . but I have called you friends" (John 15:15). They work for him, but in a spirit of friendship and collegiality. It is in the fullest sense of the term a family business. The work and the relationships intertwine, for Jesus is not working on his own. "The words that I say to you I do not speak on my own; but the Father who dwells in me does his works. Believe me that I am in the Father and the Father is in me" (John 14:10–11). Neither will the disciples be left as orphans to muddle through the world as best they can (John 14:18). Through the Spirit, Jesus will be with them, and they will do the same things he has been doing (John 14:12).

This is deeper than it may appear. It does not mean merely that after Jesus dies, his disciple/friends can still experience him in prayer. It means that they are active participants in the world-creation/restoration that fuels the loving relationship between the Father and the Son. They do the work of the Son and Father, and they join the intimacy of the Son and Father (and the Spirit, as we shall see in a moment). The Father shows his love for the Son by allowing him to share in the glory of world formation and re-creation.[5] The Son shows his love for the Father by ever and only doing his will, making and remaking the world for the Father's glory according to the Father's wishes in the power of the Spirit. The disciple/friends enter into this ever-flowing love of the Father, Son, and Spirit, not only by mystical reflection but also by embracing the Son's mission and working as he did. The call to share in the love is inextricable from the call to share in the labor. The Son's prayer, "I in them and you in me, that they may become completely one" (John 17:23),

---

[5] Cf. John 3:35, 5:19–20. The statement in John 17:5, "So now, Father, glorify me in your own presence with the glory that I had in your presence before the world existed," may well refer specifically to the glory of sharing in world formation. This would form a fitting bookend to the inclusion of Christ in the primal creation in John 1:1–3.

is matched by, "As you have sent me into the world, so I have sent them into the world" (John 17:18), and it issues forth in "Do you love me? . . . Feed my sheep" (John 21:17).

An essential aspect of human labor is the opportunity it provides for fellowship through common projects. For many people, the workplace provides the most significant context outside family for personal relationships. Even those who work alone—inside or outside their own homes—are typically enmeshed in a web of relationships involving suppliers, customers, and so on.[6] We have seen that Jesus calls his disciples not only as co-laborers but also as a community of friends. The relational aspect of work is not an accidental by-product of an essentially utilitarian enterprise of labor. Rather, it is an absolutely critical component of work itself, going back to the time when Adam and Eve worked together in the garden. "Then the LORD God said, 'It is not good that the man should be alone; I will make him a helper as his partner'" (Gen. 2:18). The creation becomes the means of interpersonal connection as humans work alongside one another, and in so doing enter into God's labor to bring creation to its fulfillment.

This can be a tremendous encouragement to project-oriented people who are sometimes made to feel unspiritual because of their reluctance to spend an abundance of time talking about their feelings. Talking with other people is a necessary activity for developing relationships, but we should not neglect the importance of doing work as a means for nurturing relationships. Working together can build relationships in and of itself. It is no accident that we spend a great deal of time working with and for other people. Modeled on God's own work within the Trinity, we are able to find *relationship in work*. Work toward a common goal is one of the chief ways God brings us together and makes us truly human.

Work and Productivity (John 14–17)

The metaphor of vine and branches begins with the blessing of relationship with Jesus and through him with the Father (John 15:1). "As

---

[6] Expressed beautifully, for example, in Robert Frost's "The Tuft of Flowers" with the memorable lines, "'Men work together,' I told him from the heart, 'Whether they work together or apart.'" Robert Frost, *A Boy's Will* (New York: Henry Holt, 1915), 49.

the Father has loved me, so I have loved you; abide in my love" (John 15:9). Yet the outcome of this love is not passive bliss but productive labor, metaphorically expressed as bearing fruit. "Those who abide in me and I in them bear much fruit" (John 15:5). The God who produced the universe wants his people to be productive too. "My Father is glorified by this, that you bear much fruit" (John 15:8). Our ability to do work that makes a lasting difference in the world is a great gift from God. "I appointed you to go and bear fruit, fruit that will last, so that the Father will give you whatever you ask him in my name" (John 15:16). The promise of effectiveness echoes Jesus' earlier promise that "the one who believes in me will also do the works that I do and, in fact, will do greater works than these" (John 14:12).

The fruit borne by Jesus' followers is sometimes taken to refer to converts to Christianity. "Greater works than these" would then mean "more converts than I myself made." For those called to evangelism, this is certainly true. If Jesus is speaking in this passage only to the apostles—appointed as they were to preach the good news—then perhaps fruit refers only to converts. But if he is speaking to believers in general, then fruit must refer to the whole range of work to which believers are called. Since the entire world was created through him, "the works that I do" include every imaginable kind of good work. For us to do "greater works" than heretofore seen could mean designing better software, feeding more people, educating wiser students, improving the effectiveness of organizations, increasing customer satisfaction, employing capital more productively, and governing nations more justly. The value of bearing fruit does not lie in whether we work in business, government, health care, education, religion, or any other field. The value lies in whether our work serves people's needs. "I am giving you these commands so that you may love one another" (John 15:17). Service is the active form of love.

Stranger in a Strange Land (John 18–20)

Rather than risk reducing John's passion narrative to a proof-text for work issues, we will address a single verse that is as important for what it does not say as for what it says: "Jesus answered [Pilate], 'My kingdom is not from this world. If my kingdom were from this world, my followers would be fighting to keep me from being handed over to the Jews. But as it is, my kingdom is not from here'" (John 18:36). On the positive side, we find here a marvelous summary of the Passion. Jesus is proclaiming that he is indeed a king, but not the sort of king who is liable to be recognized by a wily politico like Pilate. If Jesus must sacrifice himself for the life of the world, he will do so. And he must indeed sacrifice himself, because his kingship, which is both absolute and absolutely self-giving, will inevitably draw a death sentence from the powers that be.

But it is equally important to recognize what Jesus is not proclaiming. He is not saying that his kingdom is an ephemeral, internal religious experience that does not impinge on economic, political, or social issues in the real world. As the NRSV, the NIV, and other translations indicate, his kingdom is instead *from* another realm (John 18:36). His rule—like he himself—originates *from* heaven. But he has come *to* earth, and his kingdom is a real kingdom on this earth, more real than even Rome could ever be. His kingdom come to earth has a different set of operating principles. It is powerfully at work *within* the world, but it does not receive its marching orders *from the present rulers* of the world. Jesus doesn't explain at the time what it means for his kingdom to be *from* another world yet *in* the world he himself constructed. But he reveals it in vivid terms later, in the vision reported in Revelation 21 and 22, when the New Jerusalem comes down out of heaven. Jesus' kingdom descends to take its rightful place as the capital of this world, where all his disciples find their eternal home. Whenever Jesus speaks of eternal life or the kingdom of God, he is referring to the earth we inhabit now, transformed and perfected by the Word and the power of God.

Beloved Disciples (John 21)

The final chapter of John provides an opportunity to reflect not so much on work itself, but on the identity of the worker. The disciples are fishing when they meet Jesus. This is sometimes seen as a bad thing, as if they are fishing when they ought to be preaching the kingdom of God. But there is nothing in the text that suggests disapproval. Rather, Jesus blesses their labor with a miraculous catch. Afterwards, they return to their appointed work as preachers, yet even this reflects only their specific calling and is no slight on fishing as such.

However we take the setting, the impetus of the chapter is the restoration of Peter and the contrast of his future with that of the "disciple whom Jesus loved" (John 21:20). Peter's threefold affirmation of his love for Jesus restores his relationship with Jesus after his earlier threefold denial. Looking to the future, Peter will endure martyrdom, while it is cryptically hinted that the Beloved Disciple will enjoy a longer life. We will focus our attention on the latter figure, since his self-designation speaks directly to the question of human identity.

It is a curious thing that the identity of the Beloved Disciple is never revealed in the Fourth Gospel. Most scholars deduce that he is the Apostle John (though there are some dissenters[7]), but the real question is why he shrouds his name in such secrecy. One answer would be that he wishes to distinguish himself from other disciples. He is specially loved by Jesus. But this would be a strange motive in a Gospel permeated with Christ's model of humility and self-sacrifice.

A far better explanation is that he terms himself the "disciple whom Jesus loved" as a way of representing what is true of *all* disciples. We are all to find our identity first and foremost in the fact that Jesus loves us. When you ask John who he is, he does not answer by giving his name, his family connections, or his occupation. He responds, "I am someone Jesus loves." In John's words, the Beloved Disciple finds himself "leaning on Jesus' bosom" (John 13:23, KJV), and likewise, the Messiah finds his identity "in the bosom of the Father" (John 1:18, KJV).[8] In the same way, we are to find out who we are, not in what we have done, or in who we know, or in what we have, but in Jesus' love for us.

Yet if Jesus' love for us—or, we may say, the Father's love for us through Jesus—is the source of our identity and motivation of our lives, we work out this love in our activity in God's creation. One crucial aspect

---

[7] D. A. Carson, *The Gospel According to John*, The Pillar New Testament Commentary (Grand Rapids: Eerdmans, 1991), 68–81.

[8] These are the only two occurrences of "bosom," Gk. *kolpos*, in John's Gospel. We have used the King James Version because most modern translations (NASB excepted) miss this parallelism.

of that activity is our daily work. Through God's grace, work can become an arena where we live out our relationship with God and others through loving service. Our everyday labor, however humble or exalted it may be in others' estimation, becomes the place where *God's* glory is displayed. By God's grace, as we work, we become living parables of the love and glory of God.

Acts and Work

Introduction to Acts

The Acts of the Apostles depicts the early church working hard to grow itself and serve others in the face of opposition, shortages of people and money, government bureaucracy (church bureaucracy came later), internal strife, and even the forces of nature. Their work shows similarities to what Christians face in non-church-related workplaces today. A small group of people put all their heart into work that brings Christ's love to people in every sphere of life, and they find the amazing power of the Holy Spirit at work in them as they do it. If this is not what we experience in our daily work, perhaps God wants to guide, gift, and empower our work as much as he did theirs.

Work takes center stage, as you might expect in a book about the "acts" of the leaders of the early church. The narrative is abuzz with people walking, speaking, healing, giving generously, making decisions, governing, serving food, managing money, fighting, manufacturing clothes, tents, and other goods, baptizing (or washing), debating, arguing, making judgments, reading and writing, singing, defending themselves in court, gathering wood, building fires, escaping hostile crowds, embracing and kissing, holding councils, apologizing, sailing, abandoning ship, swimming, rescuing people, and through it all, praising God. The men and women in the book of Acts are ready to do whatever it might take to accomplish their mission. No work is too menial for the highest among them, and no work too daunting for the lowliest.

Yet the depth of the book of Acts stems not so much from what the people of the early church do, but why and how they engage in this amazing burst of activity. The *why* is service. Serving God, serving colleagues, serving society, serving strangers—service is the motivation behind the work Christians do throughout the book. This should come as no surprise because Acts is in fact the second volume of the story that began in the Gospel of Luke, and service is also the driving motivation of Jesus and his followers in Luke. (See "Luke and Work" for essential background information on Luke and his audience.)

If the *why* is service, then the *how* is to constantly challenge the structures of Roman society, which was based not on service but exploitation. Luke continually contrasts the ways of God's kingdom with the ways of the Roman Empire. He pays attention to Jesus' and his followers' many interactions with the officials of the empire. He is well aware of the systems of power—and the socioeconomic factors that support them—operative in the Roman Empire. From the emperor to nobles, to officials, to landowners, to freemen, to servants and slaves, each layer of society existed by wielding power over the layer below. God's way, as seen in the Gospel of Luke and the book of Acts, is just the opposite. God's society exists for service, and especially for service to those in weaker, poorer, or more vulnerable positions.

Ultimately, then, Acts is not a model of the kinds of activities we should engage in as Christ's followers, but a model of the commitment to service that should form the foundation of our activities. Our activities are different from the apostles', but our commitment to service is the same.

The Beginning of God's New World (Acts 1–4)

A Community with a Mission (Acts 1:6)

In the book of Acts, Jesus' mission to restore the world as God intended it to be is transformed into the mission of the community of Jesus' followers. Acts traces the life of the community of Jesus' followers as the Spirit forms them into a group of people who work and use work-related power and wealth differently from the world around them. The work begins with the creation of the unique community called the church. Luke begins with the community "when they had come together" and continues with the mission to "restore the kingdom to Israel" (Acts 1:6). To accomplish this work, the community must first be oriented to its vocation for the kingdom of God, and then to its identity as the kingdom of God's witnesses in daily life.

An Orienting Vocation for the Kingdom of God (Acts 1:8)

The book of Acts begins with a post-resurrection interaction between Jesus and his disciples. Jesus teaches his disciples about "the kingdom of God" (Acts 1:3). They respond with a question about establishing a sociopolitical kingdom: "Lord, is this the time when you will restore the kingdom to Israel?" (Acts 1:6).[1] Jesus' response relates closely to our lives as workers.

> "It is not for you to know the times or periods that the Father has set by his own authority. But you will receive power when the Holy Spirit has come upon you; and you will be my witnesses in Jerusalem, in all Judea and Samaria, and to the ends of the earth." (Acts 1:7–8)

First, Jesus closes down the disciples' curiosity about the timeline of God's plan. "It is not for you to know the times or periods that the Father has set by his own authority" (Acts 1:7). We are to live in anticipation of the fullness of God's kingdom, but not in a way that wonders about the precise timing of God's return in Christ. Second, Jesus does not deny that God will establish a sociopolitical kingdom, that is, "restore the kingdom to Israel," as the disciples' question put it.

Jesus' disciples were all well versed in the Scriptures of Israel. They knew that the kingdom described by the prophets was no other-worldly reality, but that it was a real kingdom of peace and justice in a world renewed by the power of God. Jesus does not deny the reality of this coming kingdom, but he expands the boundaries of the disciples' expectation by including all creation in the hoped-for kingdom. This is not merely a new kingdom for the territory of Israel, but "in Jerusalem, and in all Judea and Samaria, and to the ends of the earth" (Acts 1:8). The fulfillment of this kingdom is not yet ("at this time") but it is here, in this world.

---

[1] *Apokathistēmi*, the restoration verb used by Luke, is used by the Septuagint and Josephus to describe Israel's hope for national restoration (see Exod. 4:7; Hos. 11:11; Josephus, *Antiquities of the Jews* 11.2, 14, *inter alia*). See also David L. Tiede, "The Exaltation of Jesus and the Restoration of Israel in Acts 1," *Harvard Theological Review* 79, no. 1 (1986): 278–86; and James D. G. Dunn, *Acts of the Apostles*, Epworth Commentaries (Peterborough, UK: Epworth Press, 1996), 4.

> I saw the holy city, the new Jerusalem, coming down out of heaven from God. . . . And I heard a loud voice from the throne saying, "See, the home of God is among mortals." (Rev. 21:2–3)

The kingdom of heaven comes to earth, and God dwells here, in the redeemed world. Why is it not here yet? Jesus' teaching suggests that part of the answer is because his disciples have work to do. Human work was needed to complete God's creation even in the Garden of Eden (Gen. 2:5), but our work was crippled by the Fall. In Acts 1 and 2, God sends his Spirit to empower human work: "You will receive power when the Holy Spirit has come upon you; and you will be my witnesses" (Acts 1:8a). Jesus is giving his followers a vocation—witnessing, in the sense of bearing witness to the Spirit's power in every sphere of human activity—that is essential to the coming of the kingdom. God's gift of the Holy Spirit fills the gap between the essential role that God assigned to human work and our ability to fulfill that role. For the first time since the Fall, our work has the power to contribute to fulfilling God's kingdom at the return of Christ. Scholars, by and large, view Acts 1:8 as the programmatic statement for this second of Luke's two volumes.

Indeed, the entire book of Acts can be taken as a (sometimes faltering) expression of the Christian vocation to bear witness to the risen Jesus. But bearing witness means far more than evangelizing. We must not fall into the mistake of thinking Jesus is talking only about the work of the individual sharing the gospel with an unbeliever through his or her words. Instead, bearing witness to the coming kingdom primarily means living now according to the principles and practices of God's kingdom. We will come to see that the most effective form of Christian witness is often—even primarily—the shared life of the community as it goes about its work.

The shared Christian vocation of witness is possible only through the power of the Holy Spirit. The Spirit transforms individuals and communities in ways that result in the sharing of the fruits of human labor—especially power, resources, and influence—with the community and the surrounding culture. The community witnesses when the strong aid the weak. The community witnesses when its members use their resources to benefit the wider culture. The community witnesses when those around them see that working in the ways of justice, goodness, and beauty leads to fuller life.

The locations mentioned by Jesus reveal that the witness of the disciples puts them in social danger. Jesus' group of Jewish disciples is commanded to speak for a man who has only recently been crucified as an enemy of the Roman Empire and a blasphemer of the God of Israel. They are called to take up this vocation in the city in which their teacher was killed, among the Samaritans—historic, ethnic enemies of the Jews—and in the broad reaches of the Roman Empire.[2]

In summary, Acts begins with an orienting vocation that calls Jesus' followers to the primary task of witness. Witness means, above all, living in accordance with the ways of God's coming kingdom. As we will see momentarily, the most important element of this life is that we work primarily for the good of others. This vocation is made possible by the power of the Holy Spirit and is to be exercised with little regard for social barriers. This orienting vocation does not denigrate the value of human work or the working lives of Jesus' disciples in favor of proclaiming Jesus by word alone—quite the opposite. Acts will argue forcefully that all human work can be a fundamental expression of God's kingdom.

An Orienting Identity as God's Kingdom Witnesses in Daily Life (Acts 2:1–41)

There is no question that the story of Pentecost is central to the life of the early Christian community. This is the event that initiates the vocation of witness described in Acts 1:8. This section of Acts makes claims on all workers in two ways. First, the Pentecost account identifies its Christian hearers within a new community that brings to life the re-creation of the world—that is, the kingdom of God—promised by God through the prophets. Peter explains the phenomenon at Pentecost by referring to the prophet Joel.

---

[2] For references to antipathy between Samaritans and Jews, see Josephus, *Antiquities of the Jews* 18:30; *Jewish War* 2:32ff. For the reference to the "ends of the earth" implying the full extent of peoples and places in the Roman Empire, see David W. Pao, *Acts and the Isaianic New Exodus* (Grand Rapids: Baker Academic, 2002), 91–96.

"These [men] are not drunk, as you suppose, for it is only nine o'clock
in the morning. No, this is what was spoken through the prophet Joel:
'In the last days it will be, God declares, that I will pour out my Spirit
upon all flesh, and your sons and your daughters shall prophesy, and
your young men shall see visions, and your old men shall dream dreams.
Even upon my slaves, both men and women, in those days I will pour
out my Spirit; and they shall prophesy. And I will show portents in the
heaven above and signs on the earth below, blood, and fire, and smoky
mist. The sun shall be turned to darkness and the moon to blood, before
the coming of the Lord's great and glorious day. Then everyone who
calls on the name of the Lord shall be saved.'" (Acts 2:15–21)

Peter refers to a section of Joel that describes the restoration of God's
exiled people. Peter uses this section to claim that God has initiated his
once-and-for-all deliverance of his people.[3] In the book of Joel, the return of God's people to the land both fulfills God's covenantal promises
and initiates the re-creation of the world. Joel describes this re-creation
with breathtaking imagery. As God's people return to the land, the desert
comes to life as a sort of new Eden. Dirt, animals, and people all rejoice
at the victory of God and the deliverance of God's people (see Joel 2).
Among the rich images in this section of Joel, we hear that the restoration of God's people will lead to immediate economic impact: "The LORD
said: 'I am sending you grain, wine, and oil, and you will be satisfied; and
I will no more make you a mockery among the nations'" (Joel 2:19). The
climax of this act of deliverance for Joel is the outpouring of the Spirit
upon the people of God. Peter understands the coming of the Spirit to
mean that the early Jesus-followers are—in some real, even if profoundly
mysterious, manner—participants in God's new world.

A second important and closely related point is that Peter describes
salvation as rescue from a "corrupt generation" (Acts 2:40). Two things
need clarification. First, Luke does not describe salvation as escape from

---

[3] The Christian modification of Israelite expectations about the end of the
age is called "inaugurated eschatology" and is often organized under the rubric
of a kingdom that is simultaneously *already* present and *not yet* consummated.
Israel expected the day of the Lord to come in one climactic stage. Early Christians
discovered that the day of the Lord was initiated at Jesus' resurrection and with
the outpouring of the Spirit, but that the kingdom would not come in full until
the return of Jesus.

this world into a heavenly existence. Instead, salvation begins right in the midst of this present world. Second, Luke expects that salvation has a present-tense component. It begins now as a different way of living, contrary to the patterns of this "corrupt generation." Because work and its economic and social consequences are so central to human identity, it should come as no surprise that one of the first patterns of human life to be reconstituted is the manner in which Christians manage their power and possessions. The flow, then, of this early section of Acts moves like this: (1) Jesus suggests that all human life should bear witness to Christ; (2) the coming of the Spirit marks the initiation of the long-promised "day of the Lord" and initiates people into God's new world; and (3) expectations of the "day of the Lord" include profound economic transformations. Luke's next move is to point to a new people, empowered by the Spirit, living according to a kingdom economy.

An Orienting Community That Practices the Ways of God's Kingdom (Acts 2:42–47; 4:32–37)

After Peter announces the Spirit's creation of a new kind of community, Acts traces the rapid growth of such communities in a variety of places. The community summaries in Acts 2:42–47 and 4:32–37 are the most concentrated descriptions. Indeed, the texts themselves are remarkable in describing the scope of commitment and shared life of the early believers.[4] Because the summaries have many similarities, we will discuss them in tandem.

---

[4] Much has been written about the parallels between the community summaries and groups within Luke's historical context. Essene/Qumran parallels: Brian J. Capper, "The Interpretation of Acts 5.4," *Journal for the Study of the New Testament* 6, no. 19 (1983): 117–31; Brian J. Capper, "The Palestinian Cultural Context of Earliest Christian Community of Goods," in *The Book of Acts in Its Palestinian Setting*, ed. Richard J. Bauckham (Grand Rapids: Eerdmans, 1995), 323–56; Greco-Roman friendship parallels: Alan C. Mitchell, "The Social Function of Friendship in Acts 2.44–47 and 4.32–37," *Journal of Biblical Literature* 111, no. 2 (1992): 255–72; Greco-Roman utopian parallels: Gregory E. Sterling, "'Athletes of Virtue': An Analysis of the Summaries in Acts (2.41–47; 4.32–35; 5.12–16)," *Journal of Biblical Literature* 113, no. 4 (1994): 679–96; parallels with Greco-Roman associations: Philip A. Harland, *Associations, Synagogues, and Congregations: Creating a Place in Ancient Mediterranean Society* (Min-

Acts 2:42–47 *They devoted themselves to the apostles' teaching and fellowship, to the breaking of bread and the prayers. Awe came upon everyone, because many wonders and signs were being done by the apostles. All who believed were together and had all things in common; they would sell their possessions and goods and distribute the proceeds to all, as any had need. Day by day, as they spent much time together in the temple, they broke bread at home and ate their food with glad and generous hearts, praising God and having the goodwill of all the people. And day by day the Lord added to their number those who were being saved.*

Acts 4:32–37 *Now the whole group of those who believed were of one heart and soul, and no one claimed private ownership of any possessions, but everything they owned was held in common. With great power the apostles gave their testimony to the resurrection of the Lord Jesus, and great grace was upon them all. There was not a needy person among them, for as many as owned lands or houses sold them and brought the proceeds of what was sold. They laid it at the apostles' feet, and it was distributed to each as any had need. There was a Levite, a native of Cyprus, Joseph, to whom the apostles gave the name Barnabas (which means "son of encouragement"). He sold a field that belonged to him, then brought the money, and laid it at the apostles' feet.*

While these texts do not describe work directly, they are keenly concerned with the deployment of power and possessions, two realities that are often an outcome of human labor. The first thing to note, in contrast to the surrounding society, is that Christian communities cultivate a very different set of practices with regard to the use of power and possessions. It is clear that the early Christians understood that the power and possessions of the individual were not to be saved for the comfort of the individual, but were to be expended or wisely invested for the good of the Christian community. Stated succinctly, goods are for the good of another. More than anything else, life in the kingdom of God means working for the good of others.

Two things should be stated here. First, these texts ask us to understand our identity primarily as members of the Christian community.

neapolis: Augsburg Fortress, 2003); John S. Kloppenborg, "Collegia and *Thiasoi*: Issues in Function, Taxonomy and Membership," in *Voluntary Associations in the Graeco-Roman World*, ed. John S. Kloppenborg and S. G. Wilson (London: Routledge, 1996), 16–30.

The good of the community is the good of each individual member. Second, this is a radical departure from the patronage economy that marked the Roman Empire. In a patronage system, gifts from the rich to the poor create a structure of systematic obligation. Every gift from a benefactor implies a social debt now owed by the beneficiary. This system created a sort of pseudo-generosity in which generous patrons often gave out of self-interest, seeking to accrue honor connected to patronage.[5] In essence, the Roman economy viewed "generosity" as a means to social power and status. These notions of systematic reciprocal obligation are completely absent in the descriptions in Acts 2 and 4. In the Christian community, giving is to be motivated by a genuine concern for the flourishing of the beneficiary, not for the honor of the benefactor. Giving has little to do with the giver and everything to do with the receiver.

This is a completely different socioeconomic system. Like Luke's Gospel, Acts regularly demonstrates that Christian conversion results in a reoriented approach to possessions and power. Moreover, this insistence that goods are to be used for the sake of the neighbor is patterned explicitly on Jesus' life, mission, and—primarily—his self-giving death.

The Economics of Radical Generosity (Acts 2:45; 4:34–35)

There is continuing debate about whether or not these community summaries advocate a certain economic system, with some commentators describing the practice of the community as "proto-communism" and others seeing a mandatory divestiture of goods. The text, however, does not suggest an attempt to change the structures beyond the Christian community. Indeed, it would be difficult to think of a small, marginalized, socially powerless group having designs on changing the imperial economic system. It is clear that the community did not fully opt out of the economic systems of the empire. Likely, fishermen remained members of fishing cartels and artisans continued to do business in the market.[6] Paul, after all, continued making tents to support his missionary travels (Acts 18:3).

---

[5] It is not difficult to notice that giving within the Christian community can still function in this way.

[6] See Harland; also Kloppenborg.

Rather, the text suggests something far more demanding. In the earliest church, people of means and power liquidated their goods for the sake of the less powerful "from time to time" (Acts 4:34, NIV) as anyone "had need" (Acts 2:45; 4:35). This describes a kind of radical availability as the normal status of each person's possessions. That is, the resources—material, political, social, or practical—of any member were put at the constant disposal of the Christian community, even while individual members continued to oversee their particular resources. Rather than systematically prescribing the distribution of wealth in such a way as to ensure flat equality, the earliest church accepted the reality of economic disequalibrium, but practiced a radical generosity whereby goods properly existed for the benefit of the whole, not the individual. This form of generosity is, in many ways, more challenging than a rigid system of rules. It calls for ongoing responsiveness, mutual involvement in the lives of community members, and a continual willingness to hold possessions loosely, valuing the relationships within the community more than the (false) security of possessions.[7]

It is highly likely that this system within a system was inspired by the economic ideals expressed in Israel's law, climaxing with the practice of Jubilee—the once-in-fifty-years redistribution of land and wealth within Israel (Lev. 25:1–55). Jubilee was designed by God to ensure that all people had access to the means of making a living, an ideal that appears never to have been widely practiced by God's people. Jesus, however, introduces his ministry with a set of texts from Isaiah 61 and 58 that produce a great many Jubilee themes:

> "The Spirit of the Lord is upon me, because he has anointed me to bring good news to the poor. He has sent me to proclaim release to the captives and recovery of sight to the blind, to let the oppressed go free, to proclaim the year of the Lord's favor." (Luke 4:18–19)

Jubilee ethic is further alluded to in Acts 4:34, where Luke tells us that "there were no needy persons among them." This appears to be a

---

[7] Christopher M. Hays, *Luke's Wealth Ethics: A Study in Their Coherence and Character*, Wissenschaftliche Untersuchungen zum Neuen Testament 2.275 (Tubingen: Mohr-Siebeck, 2010), explores the ethics of wealth in Luke and Acts in depth.

direct echo of Deuteronomy 15:4, where the practice of the Sabbath year (a mini-Jubilee occurring once every seven years) is designed to ensure that "there will be no one in need among you."

It is fitting that the Christian community would see this as a model for their economic life. But whereas in ancient Israel the Sabbath year and the Jubilee were to be practiced only every seven and fifty years, respectively, radical availability marked the resources of the early Christian community. We can imagine it in terms similar to the Sermon on the Mount. "You have heard that it was said of old, 'Give back your land to those who are landless once every fifty years,' but I say to you, 'Make your power and resources available any time you see the need.'" Radical generosity based on the needs of others becomes the basis of economic practice in the Christian community. We will explore this in depth through the incidents in the book of Acts.

The practices of the early churches challenge contemporary Christians to think imaginatively about models for radical generosity today. How could radical availability stand as a witness to the kingdom of God and form a plausible alternative way of structuring human life in a culture marked by the tenacious pursuit of personal wealth and security?

The Holy Spirit Empowers Radical Generosity with Every Kind of Resource (Acts 2:42–47; 4:32–37)

Two final points are important to note with regard to the use of resources in the early Christian community. First is the necessity of the Holy Spirit to the practice of radical generosity. The descriptions of the community in Acts 2:42–47 and 4:32–37 follow immediately from the first two major manifestations of the Holy Spirit. Luke could not be clearer in forging a link between the Spirit's presence and power and the ability of the community to live with Christ-like generosity. We must understand that one of the fundamental works of the Spirit in the life of the early Christians was the cultivation of a community that took a radically different stance toward the deployment of resources. So, while we often get caught up in looking for the more spectacular manifestations of the Spirit (visions, tongues, and so on), we need to reckon with the fact that the simple act of sharing or consistent hospitality might be one of the most magnificent gifts of the Holy Spirit.

Second, lest we begin to think that this word is only for those with financial resources, we see Peter and John demonstrate that all resources are to be used for the sake of others. In Acts 3:1–10, Peter and John encounter a beggar at the gate of the temple. The beggar is looking for money, though Peter and John have none. They do, however, have a witness to the coming of the kingdom through the life, death, and resurrection of Jesus. Hence, Peter replies, "Silver or gold I do not have, but what I have I give you. In the name of Jesus Christ of Nazareth, walk" (Acts 3:6). Here is an example of resource-sharing that is not connected to monetary wealth. The use of power and position to build community will occur on several further occasions in Acts.

Perhaps the most moving expression occurs when Barnabas—who, in Acts 4:32–37, is an example of radical generosity of financial resources—also puts his social resources at Paul's disposal, helping welcome him into the reluctant fellowship of the apostles in Jerusalem (see Acts 9:26–27). Another example is Lydia, who employs her high social standing in the textile industry in Thyatira as a means of entry for Paul into the city (Acts 16:11–15). Social capital is to be deployed, like any other capital, for the good of the kingdom as understood by the Christian community.

A Just Community Is a Witness to the World (Acts 2:47; 6:7)

When resources are properly deployed in the life of the Christian community—as they are after the selection of the table servers in Acts 6—the community becomes a magnet. The community's life of justice—marked primarily by the other-centered use of power and possessions—draws people to it and to its head, Jesus. When the community uses its possessions and privileges to give life to those in need, when the resources of the individual are fully committed to benefit others in the community, people flock to join. We have seen already that "the Lord added to their number daily those who were being saved" (Acts 2:47). It is evident in the aftermath of the Spirit-empowered service in Acts 6 as well. The community-forming, justice-promoting work of the seven deacons results in life for many: "The word of God continued to spread; the number of the disciples increased greatly in Jerusalem, and a great many of the priests became obedient to the faith" (Acts 6:7).

A Clash of Kingdoms: Community and Power (Acts 5–7)

Acts takes place in the earthy reality of a genuine community, and it does not gloss over the threat that the effects of sin pose to communities. The first two major threats to the Christian community that Luke presents are resource-related issues. As we will see, Ananias and Sapphira, as well as the Hebrew/Aramaic speaking sector of the community, fall into sin in relation to their stewardship of resources and power. For Luke, this defect threatens the very life of the community.

Ananias and Sapphira: A Case of Malicious Identity (Acts 5:1–11)

The deaths of Ananias and Sapphira (Acts 5:1–11) are nothing if not frightful and puzzling. The two, a married couple, sell a piece of property and publicly give the proceeds to the community. However, they secretly hold back a portion of the money for themselves. Peter detects the deception and confronts the two separately. Merely hearing Peter's accusation causes each of them to fall dead on the spot. To our ears, their fate seems out of proportion to their infraction. Peter acknowledges that they were under no obligation to donate the money. "While it remained unsold, did it not remain your own?" he says. "And after it was sold, were not the proceeds at your disposal?" (Acts 5:4). Private property has not been abolished, and even those in the community of love-for-neighbor may legitimately choose to hold the resources God has entrusted to them. So why does lying about the money bring instant death?

Many attempts have been made to describe the reason for their deaths and even simply to name the sin they committed.[8] It appears, fundamentally, that Ananias and Sapphira's transgression is that they are counterfeit community members. As the scholar Scott Bartchy puts it, "By lying in order to achieve an honor they had not earned, Ananias and Sapphira not only dishonored and shamed themselves as patrons

---

[8] See options for interpretation in Joseph A. Fitzmyer, *The Acts of the Apostles*, *The Anchor Bible* (New York: Doubleday, 1998), 318–19.

but also revealed themselves to be outsiders, non-kin."[9] They are not so much misers as imposters.[10]

Their deceit demonstrates that they are still functioning as members of the Roman patronage system, while they pretend to have become members of the Christian love-of-neighbor system. They attempt to look like Barnabas in his other-centered approach to stewarding resources (Acts 4:36–37). But their motivation is actually to gain honor for themselves on the cheap. In so doing, they actually function as part of the Roman patronage economy. They look generous, but they are giving for the sake of status, not love. Moreover, their lie about their stewardship of resources is interpreted by Peter as a lie to the Holy Spirit and to God (Acts 5:3–4). How striking that a lie to the community is equated with a lie to the Spirit of God! And a lie about resources is as serious as a lie about "religious" matters. We have seen already that one of the primary roles of the Holy Spirit is to form God's people into a community that uses resources in accordance with a deep concern for others. It is not surprising, then, that Ananias and Sapphira's faked act of generosity is depicted as falsifying the work of the Spirit. Their false generosity and their attempt to deceive the Holy Spirit are a threat to the identity of the Christian community. This is a sober reminder of the serious stakes connected to the Christian community and to our own participation within it.

Ananias and Sapphira's deceit occurs in the realm of money. What if it occurred in the realm of work itself? What if they had falsely pretended to serve their masters as though serving God (Col. 3:22–24), or to treat subordinates justly (Col. 3:25), or to engage in conflict honestly (Matt. 18:15–17)? Would deceiving the Christian community about such things have caused a similarly unacceptable threat to the community?

---

[9] S. Scott Bartchy, "Community of Goods in Acts: Idealization or Social Reality?" in *The Future of Early Christianity: Essays in Honor of Helmut Koester*, ed. Birger A. Pearson, A. Thomas Krabel, George W. E. Nickelsburg, and Norman R. Petersen (Minneapolis: Fortress Press, 1991), 316.

[10] For a full treatment of this narrative with respect to economic and communal implications, see Aaron J. Kuecker, "The Spirit and the 'Other,' Satan and the 'Self': Economic Ethics as a Consequence of Identity Transformation in Luke-Acts," in *Engaging Economics: New Testament Scenarios and Early Christian Reception*, ed. Bruce W. Longenecker and Kelly D. Liebengood (Grand Rapids: Eerdmans, 2009), 81–103.

Luke doesn't report any such cases in Acts, yet the same principle applies. Genuinely belonging to the Christian community carries with it a fundamental change in our orientation. We now act in all ways—including work—to love our neighbors as ourselves, not to increase our social status, wealth, and power.

The Spirit and the Worker (Acts 6:1–7)

Themes from the account of Ananias and Sapphira are present in Acts 6:1–7, which marks the first intra-group dispute in the Christian community. The Hellenists are probably Greek-speaking Jews who have returned to Jerusalem from one of the many Diaspora communities in the Roman Empire. The Hebrews are probably Jews who are from the historic land of Israel (Palestine) and who primarily speak Aramaic and/ or Hebrew. It takes very little social imagination to see what is happening in this situation. In a community that sees itself as the fulfillment of Israel's covenant with God, members who are more prototypically Israelite are receiving more of the group's resources than the others. This sort of situation happens regularly in our world. Those who are most similar to the leaders of a movement on the basis of background, culture, status, and so on often benefit from their identity in ways unavailable to those who are in some way different.

Serving the Word and Serving Tables Are Equally Valuable (Acts 6:2–4)

One of the greatest contributions that Acts makes to a theology of work emerges from the apostles' response to the intra-community injustice of Acts 6:1–7. The work of administering justice—in this case, by overseeing food distribution—is just as important as the work of preaching the word. This may not be clear at first because of a misleading translation in the NRSV and the NIV:

> The twelve called together the whole community of the disciples and said, "It is not right that we should neglect the word of God in order to wait on tables." (Acts 6:2, NRSV)

> "It would not be right for us to neglect the ministry of the word of God in order to wait on tables." (Acts 6:2, NIV)

It is hard not to read some condescension in the voices of the apostles in these English translations. In the minds of some, working with the word of God is "ministry" (as the NIV puts it), while the work of "waiting" at tables is somehow menial. One line of interpretation has followed this sense, suggesting that waiting on tables was "trivial,"[11] a "humble task"[12] or one of the "lower tasks"[13] in the community. This line of interpretation sees Stephen's subsequent preaching as the "real" purpose behind the Spirit's influence in 6:3.[14] There would be no need for the Holy Spirit to get involved in the menial task of managing the allocation of resources.

But this line of argument depends on dubious translations. The Greek verb translated as "wait" in the NRSV and NIV is *diakoneō*, which carries the sense of service or ministry. The King James Version and the NASB put it more accurately as "serve."

> "It is not reason [i.e., right] that we should leave the word of God, and serve tables." (Acts 6:2, KJV)

> "It is not desirable for us to neglect the word of God in order to serve tables." (Acts 6:2, NASB)

Moreover, just a few words later, in Acts 6:3–4, even the NRSV and the NIV translate the same word as "serving" and "ministry," respectively.

> "We, for our part, will devote ourselves to prayer and to serving the word." (Acts 6:3–4, NRSV)

> "[We] will give our attention to prayer and the ministry of the word." (Acts 6:4, NIV)

In other words, the Greek word for the work of the word is exactly the same (in verb form) as the word for the work of distributing resources,

[11] Fitzmyer, 344.

[12] John Michael Penney, "The Missionary Emphasis of Lukan Pneumatology," *Journal of Pentecostal Theology* (Sheffield, UK: Sheffield Academic Press, 1997), 65n11.

[13] Joseph T. Lienhard, "Acts 6.1–6: A Redactional View," *Catholic Biblical Quarterly* 37 (1975): 232.

[14] Youngmo Cho, *Spirit and Kingdom in the Writings of Luke and Paul* (Waynesborough, GA; Paternoster, 2005), 132.

diakonia, "serving." The NRSV and NIV translators rightly regard the work of preaching as "serving" and "ministry." Yet they condescend to a more demeaning word when referring to the work of food distribution, "waiting" tables. In contrast, the KJV and NASB translators do not read such condescension into the text. Whether working with the word or with food on tables, both groups "serve" in these translations.

The Greek text gives the important sense that the work of serving those in need is on par with the apostolic work of prayer and preaching. The apostles serve the word, and the deacons (as they have come to be called) serve those in need. Their service is qualitatively the same, although the specific tasks and skills are different. Both are essential in the formation of God's people and for the witness of God's people in the world. The life of the community depends upon these forms of service, and Luke does not give us the sense that one is more powerful or more spiritual than the other.

Despite all this, could it be argued that the condescension is not just a matter of translation but is really present in the disciples' own words? Could the apostles themselves have imagined that they were chosen to serve the word because they were more gifted than those who were chosen to serve tables? If so, they would be falling back into something similar to the Roman patronage system, setting themselves up with a status too high to sully by serving tables. They would be substituting a new source of status (gifts of the Holy Spirit) for the old Roman one (patronage). The gospel of Christ goes deeper than this! In the Christian community there is no source of status.

Ironically, one of the table-servers, Stephen, turns out to be even more gifted as a preacher than most of the apostles (Acts 6:8–7:60). Yet despite his preaching gift, he is set aside for the service of resource distribution. At that moment, at least, it was more important to God's purposes for him to work as a table-server than as a word-server. For him, at least, no lingering hunger for status stands in the way of accepting this call to serve tables.

The Work of Community Leadership Is a Work of the Holy Spirit (Acts 6:3)

The workers best suited to heal the ethnic divide in the Acts 6 community are qualified because they are known to be "full of the Spirit and of wisdom." Like those qualified for prayer and preaching, the table-servers' ability is the result of spiritual power. Nothing less than the power of the Spirit makes possible meaningful, community-building, peace-making work among Christians. This passage helps us to see that all work that builds the community or, more broadly, that promotes justice, goodness, and beauty, is—in a deep sense—service (or ministry) to the world.

In our churches, do we recognize the equal ministry of the pastor who preaches the word, the mother and father who provide a loving home for their children, and the accountant who gives a just and honest statement of her employer's expenditures? Do we understand that they are all reliant upon the Spirit to do their work for the good of the community? Every manner of good work has the capacity—by the power of the Spirit—to be a means of participation in God's renewal of the world.

Work and Identity (Acts 8–12)

The next section of Acts moves the Christian community, by the power of the Spirit, across cultural barriers as the gospel of Jesus Christ is extended to foreigners (Samaritans), social outcasts (the Ethiopian eunuch), enemies (Saul), and all ethnicities (Gentiles). This section tends to introduce figures by giving their occupation (roughly rendered). In this section we meet:

- Simon, a sorcerer (Acts 8:9–24)

- An Ethiopian eunuch, who is an important economic official for the queen of Ethiopia (Acts 8:27)

- Saul, the Pharisee and persecutor of Christians (Acts 9:1)

- Tabitha, a garment maker (Acts 9:36–43)

- Cornelius, a Roman centurion (Acts 10:1)

- Simon, a tanner (Acts 10:5)

- Herod, a king (Acts 12)

Issues of work are not Luke's main concern in this section, so we must be careful not to make too much of the naming of occupations. Luke's point is that the way these people exercise their vocation marks them as heading either toward the kingdom or away from it.

Those headed into the kingdom use the fruits of their labor to serve others as witnesses of God's kingdom. Those headed away from the kingdom use the fruits of their labor solely for personal gain. This is evident from a short summary of some of these characters. Several of them seek only personal gain from their work and its accompanying power and resources:

- Simon offers money to the apostles so that he can have power to bestow the Holy Spirit (Acts 8:18–19)—a clear effort to maintain his social status as a "man [who] is the power of God that is called Great" (Acts 8:10).

- Saul uses his network of relationships to persecute followers of Jesus (Acts 9:1–2), in order to protect the social status he enjoyed as a zealous Jew (Acts 22:3) and Pharisee (Acts 26:5).

- Herod uses his power as Rome's client-king to bolster his popularity by killing James the apostle (Acts 12:1–2). Herod later allows himself to be acclaimed as a god, the ultimate patronage status claimed by the Roman emperors (Acts 12:20–23).

The consequences of these acts are dire. Simon is strongly rebuked by Peter (Acts 8:20–23). Saul is confronted by the risen Jesus, who identifies himself with the very community Paul is persecuting (Acts 9:3–9). Herod is struck dead by an angel of the Lord and eaten by worms (Acts 12:23). Standing in counterpoint to them are several people who use their position, power, or resources to bless and bring life:

- Tabitha, a garment-maker, makes clothes to share with widows in her community (Acts 9:39).

- Simon, a leather-worker, opens his home to Peter (Acts 10:5).

- Cornelius, a Roman centurion already known for generosity (Acts 10:4), uses his connections to invite a great number of friends and family to hear the preaching of Peter (Acts 10:24).

Though he was introduced prior to this section, Barnabas—who we know from Acts 4:37 is a Levite—uses his position within the community to graft Saul into the apostolic fellowship, even when the apostles resist (Acts 9:26–27), and to validate the conversions of Gentiles in Antioch (Acts 11:22–24). We should note that Acts 11:24 shares the secret of Barnabas's ability to use his resources and position in such a way as to build the community of Christians. There we learn explicitly that Barnabas was "full of the Holy Spirit."

The message in all these examples is consistent. The power, prestige, position, and resources that arise from work are meant to be used for the sake of others—and not only for one's own benefit. This, again, is modeled on no less a figure than Jesus, who in Luke's Gospel uses his authority for the benefit of the world and not only for his own sake.

Acts 11:27–30 gives a community example of the use of resources for the good of others in need. In response to a Spirit-inspired prophecy of a worldwide famine, "The disciples determined that according to their ability, each would send relief to the believers living in Judea" (Acts 11:29). Here we see the use of the fruit of human labor for the benefit of others. And here we see that this sort of generosity was not merely spontaneous and episodic but planned, organized, and deeply intentional. (The collection for the church in Jerusalem is discussed further in the section on 1 Corinthians 16:1–3 in "1 Corinthians and Work.")

Acts 11:1–26 begins an account of how the Christian community resolved a deep dispute about whether a Gentile must convert to Judaism before becoming a follower of Jesus. This dispute is discussed in an article on chapter 15 below.

A Clash of Kingdoms: Community and Power Brokers (Acts 13–19)

We will explore this section according to four main themes relevant to the theology of work that emerges from Acts. First, we will examine one further passage relating to vocation as witness. Second, we will discuss how the Christian community exercises the power of leadership and decision-making itself. Third, we will look at how the Spirit-led community engages the powers that be in the wider culture. Fourth, we will examine whether following Christ rules out certain forms of vocation and civic engagement. Finally, we will explore Paul's own practice of continuing to work as a tentmaker on his missionary journeys.

Vocation in the Context of Community (Acts 13:1–3)

Acts 13:1–3 introduces us to a set of practices in the church at Antioch. This community is remarkable both for its ethnic diversity and its commitment to practical witness of the kingdom of God.[15] We have seen already how Luke shows that work—especially the use of power and resources—functions as a form of witness.[16] We have seen in Acts 6:1–7 that this applies equally to vocations we naturally associate with ministry (such as being a missionary) and those we are more likely to call "work" (such as hospitality). All vocations have the potential to serve and witness the kingdom, especially when employed in the pursuit of justice and righteousness.

Acts 13:1–3 shows the Christian community trying to discern how the Spirit is leading them to witness. Paul and Barnabas are singled out to work as traveling evangelists and healers. What is remarkable is that this discernment is accomplished communally. The Christian community, rather than the individual, is best able to discern the vocations of its individual members. This could mean that today's Christian communities should participate alongside families and young people as they seek answers for questions such as, "What do you want to do when you grow up?" "What will you do after graduation?" or "To what is God calling you?" This would require Christian communities to develop a much greater expertise in vocational discernment than is presently common. It would also require them to take a much more serious interest in work that serves the world beyond the structures of the church. Merely asserting authority over young people's work lives is not enough. Young people

---

[15] Ben Witherington III, *The Acts of the Apostles: A Socio-Rhetorical Commentary* (Grand Rapids: Eerdmans, 1998), 392.

[16] It is worth noting, once again, that the proper function of the community—marked particularly by generosity, economic justice, and God-and-other-centered love—regularly results in the growth of the kingdom (Acts 2:47; 6:7; 9:31; etc.).

will pay attention only if the Christian community can help them do a fuller job of discernment than they can do by other means.

Doing this well would be a double form of witness. First, young people from all religious traditions—and those who have no tradition—struggle deeply with the burden of choosing or finding work. Imagine if the Christian community could genuinely help reduce their burden and improve the outcomes. Second, the great majority of Christians work outside the structures of the church. Imagine if all of us engaged in our work as a means of Christian service to the world, improving the lives of the billions of people we work alongside and on behalf of. How much more visible would that make Christ in the world?

Community discernment of vocation continues throughout Acts, with Paul taking many missionary partners from the community—Barnabas, Timothy, Silas, and Priscilla, to name but a few. Second, testifying again to Luke's realism, we see that this shared vocation to witness does not eliminate the relational tension brought about by human sinfulness. Paul and Barnabas have such a serious dispute over the inclusion of John Mark (who had deserted the team on a previous engagement) that they go their separate ways (Acts 15:36–40).

Leadership and Decision-Making in the Christian Community (Acts 15)

An example of the radical reorienting of social interactions in the Christian community arises during a deep dispute about whether Gentile Christians must adopt Jewish laws and customs. In hierarchical Roman society, the patron of a social organization would dictate such a decision to his followers, perhaps after listening to various opinions. But in the Christian community, important decisions are made by the group as whole, relying on their equal access to the guidance of the Holy Spirit.

The dispute actually begins in chapter 11. Peter experiences a surprising revelation that God is offering "the repentance that leads to life" (Acts 11:18) to Gentiles without requiring them to become Jews first. But when he travels to Jerusalem in the company of some uncircumcised (Gentile) men, some of the Christians there complain that he is violating Jewish law (Acts 11:1–2). When challenged in this way, Peter does not become angry, does not attempt to lord it over the men by reminding them of his leading position among Jesus' disciples, does not denigrate their opinions, and does not impugn their motives. Instead, he tells the story of what happened to lead him to this conclusion and how he sees God's hand in it: "If then God gave them the same gift that he gave us when we believed in the Lord Jesus Christ, who was I that I could hinder God?" (Acts 11:17). Notice that he portrays himself not as wise, nor morally superior, but as one who was on the verge of making a serious mistake until corrected by God.

Then he leaves it to his challengers to respond. Having heard Peter's experience, they do not react defensively, do not challenge Peter's authority in the name of James (the Lord's brother and the leader of the Jerusalem church), and do not accuse Peter of exceeding his authority. Instead, they too look for God's hand at work and reach the same conclusion as Peter. What began as a confrontation ends with fellowship and praise. "When they heard this, they were silenced. And they praised God" (Acts 11:18). We can't expect every dispute to be resolved so amicably, but we can see that when people acknowledge and explore the grace of God in one another's lives, there is every reason to hope for a mutually upbuilding outcome.

Peter departs Jerusalem in concord with his former antagonists, but there remain others in Judea who are teaching that Gentiles must first convert to Judaism. "Unless you are circumcised according to the custom of Moses," they say, "you cannot be saved" (Acts 15:1). Paul and Barnabas are in Antioch at the time, and they, like Peter, have experienced God's grace to the Gentiles without any need for conversion to Judaism. The text tells us that the division was serious, but a mutual decision was made to seek the wisdom of the Christian community as a whole. "After Paul and Barnabas had no small dissension and debate with them, Paul and Barnabas and some of the others were appointed to go up to Jerusalem to discuss this question with the apostles and the elders" (Acts 15:2).

They arrive in Jerusalem and are greeted warmly by the apostles and elders (Acts 15:4). Those who hold the opposite opinion—that Gentiles must first convert to Judaism—are also present (Acts 15:5). They all decide to meet to consider the matter and engage in a lively debate

(Acts 15:6). Then Peter, who is of course among the apostles in Jerusalem, repeats the story of how God revealed to him his grace for the Gentiles without the need to convert to Judaism (Acts 15:7). Paul and Barnabas report their similar experiences, also focusing on what God is doing rather than claiming any superior wisdom or authority (Acts 15:12). All the speakers receive a respectful hearing. Then the group considers what each has said in the light of Scripture (Acts 15:15–17). James, functioning as the head of the church in Jerusalem, proposes a resolution. "I have reached the decision that we should not trouble those Gentiles who are turning to God, but we should write to them to abstain only from things polluted by idols and from fornication and from whatever has been strangled and from blood" (Acts 15:19–20).

If James were exercising authority like a Roman patron, that would be the end of the matter. His status alone would decide the issue. But this is not how the decision unfolds in the Christian community. The community does accept his decision, but as a matter of agreement, not command. Not only James, but all the leaders—in fact, the entire church—have a say in the decision. "The apostles and the elders, with the consent of the whole church, decided . . ." (Acts 15:22). And when they send word to the Gentile churches of their decision "to impose on you no further burden" (Acts 15:28b), they do so in the name of the whole body, not the name of James as patron. "We have decided unanimously to choose representatives and send them to you" (Acts 15:25). Moreover, they claim no personal authority, but only that they have tried to be obedient to the Holy Spirit. "For it has seemed good to the Holy Spirit and to us . . . ," they report (Acts 15:28a). The word *seem* indicates a humility about their decision, underscoring that they have renounced the Roman patronage system with its claims of power, prestige, and status.

Before we leave this episode, let us notice one more element of it. The leaders in Jerusalem show remarkable deference to the experience of workers in the field—Peter, Paul, and Barnabas—working on their own far from headquarters, each facing a particular situation that required a practical decision. The leaders in Jerusalem highly respect their experience and judgment. They communicate carefully about the principles that should guide decisions (Acts 15:19–21), but they delegate decision-making to those closest to the action, and they confirm the decisions made by Peter, Paul, and Barnabas in the field. Again, this is a radical departure from the Roman patronage system, which concentrated power and authority in the hands of the patron.

The beneficial effects of the practice of uniform education about mission, principles, and values combined with localized delegation of decision-making and action are well known because of their widespread adoption by business, military, educational, nonprofit, and government institutions in the second half of the twentieth century. The management of virtually every type of organization has been radically transformed by it. The resulting unleashing of human creativity, productivity, and service would be no surprise to the leaders of the early church, who experienced the same explosion in the rapid expansion of the church in the apostolic age.

However, it is not clear that churches today have fully adopted this lesson with respect to economic activity. For example, Christians working in developing countries often complain that they are hampered by the rigid stances of churches far away in the developed world. Well-meaning boycotts, fair-trade rules, and other pressure tactics may have the opposite consequences of what was intended. For example, an economic development missionary in Bangladesh reported about negative results of the imposition of child labor restrictions by his sponsoring organization in the United States. A company he was helping develop was required to stop buying materials that were produced using workers under sixteen years old. One of their suppliers was a company consisting of two teenaged brothers. Because of the new restrictions, the company had to stop buying parts from the brothers, which left their family without any source of income. So their mother had to return to prostitution, which made things much worse for the mother, the brothers, and the rest of the family. "What we need from the church in the U.S. is fellowship that is not oppressive," the missionary later said. "Having to comply with well-intentioned Western Christian dictates means we have to hurt people in our country."[17]

---

[17] Name of source withheld at his request due to security concerns. Notes taken by William Messenger at the Theology of Work Project Conference, Hong Kong, July 29, 2010.

The Community of the Spirit Confronts the Brokers of Power (Acts 16; 19)

In the latter half of Acts, Paul, his companions, and various Christian communities come into conflict with those who wield local economic and civic power. The first incident occurs in Pisidian Antioch, where "the devout women of high standing and the leading men of the city" (Acts 13:50) are incited against Paul and Barnabas and expel them from the city. Then, in Iconium, Paul and Barnabas are maltreated by "both Gentiles and Jews, with their rulers" (Acts 14:5). In Philippi, Paul and Silas are imprisoned for "disturbing" the city (Acts 16:19–24). Paul has run-ins with the city officials of Thessalonica (Acts 17:6–9) and the proconsul of Achaia (Acts 18:12). Later, he comes into conflict with the silversmiths' guild of Ephesus (Acts 19:23–41). The conflicts culminate with Paul's trial for disturbing the peace in Jerusalem, which occupies the final eight chapters of Acts.

These confrontations with local powers should not be surprising given the coming of God's Spirit announced by Peter in Acts 2. There we saw that the coming of the Spirit was—in some mysterious way—the initiation of God's new world. This was bound to threaten the powers of the old world. We have seen that the Spirit worked in the community to form a gift-based economy very different from the Roman economy based on patronage. Christian communities formed a system-within-a-system, where believers still participated in the Roman economy but had a different manner of using resources. Conflict with local leaders was precisely due to the fact that these leaders had the greatest stake in maintaining Rome's patronage economy.

The confrontations in Acts 16:16–24 and Acts 19:23–41 both merit deeper discussion. In them, the shape of the kingdom clashes deeply with economic practices of the Roman world.

Confrontation over the Liberation of a Slave Girl in Philippi (Acts 16:16–24)

The first of the two confrontations occurs in Philippi, where Paul and Silas encounter a girl with a spirit of divination.[18] In the Greco-Roman

---

[18] See John R. Levison, *Filled with the Spirit* (Grand Rapids: Eerdmans, 2009), 318–20, for a description of this type of spirit in Greco-Roman perceptions.

context, this type of spirit was associated with fortune-telling—a connection that "brought her owners a great deal of money" (Acts 16:16). This seems to be an example of the grossest form of economic exploitation. It is puzzling that Paul and Silas do not act more quickly (Acts 16:18). Perhaps the reason is that Paul wants to make a connection with her or her owners before correcting them. When Paul does act, however, the result is spiritual liberation for the girl and financial loss for her owners. The owners respond by dragging Paul and Silas before the authorities on charges of disturbing the peace.

This incident demonstrates powerfully that the ministry of liberation Jesus proclaimed in Luke 4 can run counter to at least one common business practice, the exploitation of slaves. Businesses that produce economic profit at the expense of human exploitation are in conflict with the Christian gospel. (Governments that exploit humans are just as bad. We discussed earlier how Herod's violence against his people and even his own soldiers led to his death at the hands of an angel of the Lord). Paul and Silas were not on a mission to reform the corrupt economic and political practices of the Roman world, but the power of Jesus to liberate people from sin and death cannot help but break the bonds of exploitation. There can be no spiritual liberation without economic consequences. Paul and Silas were willing to expose themselves to ridicule, beating, and prison in order to bring economic liberation to someone whose sex, economic status, and age made her vulnerable to abuse.

If we look ahead two thousand years, is it possible that Christians have accommodated to, or even profited from, products, companies, industries, and governments that violate Christian ethical and social principles? It is easy to rail against illegal industries such as narcotics and prostitution, but what about the many legal industries that harm workers, consumers, or the public at large? What about the legal loopholes, subsidies, and unfair government regulations that benefit some citizens at the expense of others? Do we even recognize how we may benefit from the exploitation of others? In a global economy, it can be difficult to trace the conditions and consequences of economic activity. Well-informed discernment is needed, and the Christian community has not always been rigorous in its critiques. In fact, the book of Acts does not give principles for gauging economic activity. But it does demonstrate that economic matters are gospel matters. In the persons of Paul and Silas, two of the greatest missionaries and heroes of the faith, we have all the proof we need that Christians are called to confront the economic abuses of the world.

Chapters 17 and 18 contains much of interest with regard to work, but for the sake of continuing the discussion of confrontations arising from the gospel's challenge to the systems of the world, this article is followed by the account of the confrontation in Acts 19:21–41, returning then to chapters 17, 18, and the other parts of chapter 19.

Confrontation over the Disruption of Trade in Ephesus (Acts 19:21–41)

The following discussion falls a little out of order (skipping over Acts 19:17–20 for the moment) so that we can cover the second incident of confrontation. It occurs in Ephesus, home to the Temple of Artemis. The Artemis cult in Ephesus was a powerful economic force in Asia Minor. Pilgrims streamed to the temple (a structure so grand that it was considered one of the Seven Wonders of the Ancient World) in hopes of receiving from Artemis enhanced success in the hunt, in the field, or in the family. In this context, as with other tourism centers, many of the local industries were tied to the ongoing relevance of the attraction.[19]

> A man named Demetrius, a silversmith who made silver shrines of Artemis, brought no little business to the artisans. These he gathered together, with the workers of the same trade, and said: "Men, you know that we get our wealth from this business. You also see and hear that not only in Ephesus but in almost the whole of Asia this Paul has persuaded and drawn away a considerable number of people by saying that gods made with hands are not gods. And there is danger not only that this trade of ours may come into disrepute but also that the temple of the great goddess Artemis will be scorned, and she will be deprived of her majesty that brought all Asia and the world to worship her." When they heard this, they were enraged and shouted: "Great is Artemis of the Ephesians!" The city was filled with the confusion; and people rushed together to the theater, dragging with them Gaius and Aristarchus, Macedonians who were Paul's travel companions. (Acts 19:24–29)

---

[19] See Witherington, 592–93.

As Demetrius recognizes, when people become followers of Jesus, they can be expected to change the way they use their money. Ceasing to buy items related to idol worship is merely the most obvious change. Christians might also be expected to spend less on luxury items for themselves and more on necessities for the benefit of others. Perhaps they will consume less and donate or invest more in general. There is nothing prohibiting Christians from buying silver items in general. But Demetrius is right to see that patterns of consumption will change if many people start believing in Jesus. This will always be threatening to those profiting most from the way things were before.

This prompts us to wonder which aspects of economic life in our own context might be incommensurate with the Christian gospel. For example, is it possible that, contrary to Demetrius's fears, Christians have continued to buy goods and services incompatible with following Jesus? Have we become Christians, yet continued to buy the equivalent of silver shrines to Artemis? Certain "aspirational" branded items come to mind, which appeal to buyers' desires to associate themselves with the social status, wealth, power, intelligence, beauty, or other attributes implied by the items' "brand promise." If Christians claim that their standing comes solely from the unconditional love of God in Christ, does self-association with brands function as a kind of idolatry? Is buying a prestigious brand essentially similar to buying a silver shrine to Artemis? This incident in Ephesus warns us that following Jesus has economic consequences that may make us uncomfortable at times, to say the least.

Engaging the Culture with Respect (Acts 17:16–34)

Despite the need to confront the power brokers in the wider culture, confrontation is not always the best way for the Christian community to engage the world. Often, the culture is misguided, struggling, or ignorant of God's grace, but not actually oppressive. In these cases, the best way to proclaim the gospel may be to cooperate with the culture and engage it with respect.

In Acts 17, Paul provides a model for engaging the culture respectfully. It begins with observation. Paul strolls the streets of Athens and observes the temples of the various gods he finds there. He reports that he "looked carefully" at the "objects of . . . worship" he found there (Acts 17:22), which he notes were "formed by the art and imagination" of the people (Acts 17:29). He read their literature, knew it well enough to quote, and treated it respectfully enough to incorporate it into his preaching about Christ. In fact, it even contains some of God's truth, Paul says, for he quotes it as saying, "As even some of your own poets have said, 'For we too are his offspring'" (Acts 17:28). A commitment to the radical transformation of society does not mean that Christians have to oppose everything about society. Society is not so much totally godless—"for in him we live and move and have our being"—as God-unaware.

In a similar way, we need to be observant in our workplaces. We can find many good practices in our schools, our businesses, in government, or other workplaces, even though they do not arise within the Christian community. If we are truly observant, we see that even those unaware or scornful of Christ are nonetheless made in the image of God. Like Paul, we should cooperate with them, rather than try to discredit them. We can work with nonbelievers to improve labor/management relationships, customer service, research and development, corporate and civic governance, public education, and other fields. We should make use of the skills and insights developed in universities, corporations, nonprofits, and other places. Our role is not to condemn their work, but to deepen it and show that it proves that "he is not far from each one of us" (Acts 17:27). Imagine the difference between saying, "Because you don't know Christ, all your work is wrong," and "Because I know Christ, I think I can appreciate your work even more than you do."

Yet at the same time, we need to be observant about the brokenness and sin evident in our workplaces. Our purpose is not to judge but to heal, or at least to limit the damage. Paul is particularly observant of the sin and distortion of idolatry. "He was deeply distressed to see that the city was full of idols" (Acts 17:16). The idols of modern workplaces, like the idols of ancient Athens, are many and varied. A Christian leader in New York City says,

> When I'm working with educators, whose idol is that all the world's problems will be solved by education, my heart connects to their heart about wanting to solve the world's problems, but I would point out to them that

they can only go so far with education, but the real solution comes from Christ. The same is true for many other professions.[20]

Our careful observations, like Paul's, make us more astute witnesses of Christ's unique power to set the world to rights.

> "While God has overlooked the times of human ignorance, now he commands all people everywhere to repent, because he has fixed a day on which he will have the world judged in righteousness by a man whom he has appointed, and of this he has given assurance to all by raising him from the dead." (Acts 17:30–31)

Tent-Making and Christian Life (Acts 18:1–4)

The passage most often connected to work in the book of Acts is Paul's tent-making in Acts 18:1–4. Although this passage is familiar, it is often understood too narrowly. In the familiar reading, Paul earns money by making tents, in order to support himself in his real ministry of witnessing to Christ. This view is too narrow, because it doesn't see that the tent-making itself is a real ministry of witnessing to Christ. Paul is a witness when he preaches and when he makes tents and uses his earnings to benefit the broader community.

This fits directly into Luke's view that the Spirit empowers Christians to use their resources for the sake of the whole community, which in turn witnesses to the gospel. Remember that Luke's orienting idea for Christian life is that of witness, and the entirety of one's life has the potential to bear witness. It is striking, then, that Paul is an exemplar of this Spirit-formed practice.

It is certainly true that Paul wants to support himself. Yet his impulse was not only to support himself in his preaching ministry, but also to provide financial support to the entire community. When Paul describes his economic impact among the Ephesians, he says:

> I coveted no one's silver or gold or apparel. You yourselves know that these hands ministered to my necessities, *and to those who were with*

---

[20] Telephone interview with Katherine Leary Alsdorf, Executive Director, Center for Faith and Work, Redeemer Presbyterian Church, New York, December 15, 2012.

me. In all things *I have shown you that by so toiling one must help the weak,* remembering the words of the Lord Jesus, how he said, *"It is more blessed to give than to receive."* (Acts 20:33–35, emphasis added, RSV)

Paul's money-earning work was an effort to build up the community economically.[21] Paul employs his skills and possessions for the sake of the community, and he explicitly says that this is an example others should follow. He does not say that everyone should follow his example of preaching. But he does say everyone should follow his example of toiling to help the weak and being generous in giving, as Jesus himself taught. Ben Witherington argues convincingly that Paul is not claiming any higher status arising from his apostolic position, but rather is "stepping down the social ladder for the sake of Christ."[22]

In other words, it is not the case that Paul engages in tent-making as a necessity so that he can do his "real job" of preaching. Instead, Paul's varieties of work in the sewing shop, marketplace, synagogue, lecture hall, and prison are all forms of witness. In any of these contexts, Paul participates in God's restorative project. In any of these contexts, Paul lives out his new identity in Christ for the sake of God's glory and out of love for his neighbors—even his former enemies. Even as he is being transported across the sea as a prisoner, he employs his gifts of leadership and encouragement to guide the soldiers and sailors holding him captive to safety during a severe storm (Acts 27:21–38). If he had not had the gift of being a preacher and apostle, he would still have been a witness to Christ simply by the way he engaged in making tents, toiling for the sake of the community, and working for the good of others in all situations.

"Tent-making" has become a common metaphor for Christians who engage in a money-earning profession as a means to support what is often called "professional ministry." The term "bi-vocational" is often used to indicate that two separate professions are involved, the money-earning one and the ministry one. But Paul's example shows that all aspects of human life should be a seamless witness. There is little room to draw

---

[21] This ethic is also expressed by Paul in 1 Thessalonians 1:9 and 1 Corinthians 9:1–15.

[22] Witherington, 547.

distinctions between "professional ministry" and other forms of witness. According to Acts, Christians actually have only one vocation—witnessing to the gospel. We have many forms of service, including preaching and pastoral care, making tents, building furniture, giving money, and caring for the weak. A Christian who engages in a money-earning profession such as making tents, in order to support a non-money-earning profession such as teaching about Jesus, would be more accurately described as "dual-service" rather than "bi-vocational"—one calling, two forms of service. The same would be true of any Christian who serves in more than one line of work.

The Gospel and Limits to Vocation and Engagement (Acts 19:17–20)

Acts 19:13–16 presents an odd story that leads to the repentance of "a number of those who had practiced magic" (Acts 19:19). They collected their magic books and burned them publicly, and Luke tells us that the value of the scrolls burned by these converts was 50,000 drachmas. This has been estimated as the equivalent to 137 years of continuous wages for a day laborer or enough bread to feed 100 families for 500 days.[23] Incorporation into the community of God's kingdom has massive economic and vocational impact.

While we cannot be certain whether those who repented of their engagement in magic were repenting of a means of earning a living, such a costly collection of books was unlikely to have been a mere hobby. Here we see that the change in life precipitated by faith in Jesus is immediately reflected in a vocational decision—a result familiar from Luke's Gospel. In this case, the believers found it necessary to abandon their former occupation entirely.

In many other cases, it is possible to remain in a vocation but necessary to practice it in a different way. For example, imagine that a salesperson has built a business selling unnecessary insurance to senior citizens. He or she would have to cease that practice, but could continue in the profession of selling insurance sales by switching to a product line that is beneficial for those who buy it. The commissions might be less (or

---

[23] Darrell L. Bock, *Acts*, Baker Exegetical Commentary on the New Testament (Grand Rapids: Baker, 2007), 605.

not), but the profession has plenty of room for legitimate success and lots of ethical participants.

A much more difficult situation occurs in professions that could be done legitimately, but in which illicit practices are so thoroughly entrenched that it is difficult to compete without violating biblical principles. Many civil servants in high-corruption nations face this dilemma. It might be possible to be an honest building inspector, but very difficult to do if your official pay is $10 a week and your supervisor demands a $100 a month fee to let you keep your job. A Christian in that situation faces a difficult choice. If all the honest people leave the profession, so much the worse for the public. But if it is difficult or impossible to make a living honestly in the profession, how can a Christian remain there? This is something Luke discusses in Luke 3:9, when John the Baptist counsels soldiers and tax collectors to remain in their jobs but to cease the extortion and fraud practiced by most of their profession. (See the section on Luke 3:1–14 in "Luke and Work" for more on this passage.)

Leadership as Witness (Acts 20–28)

The last eight chapters of Acts present an action-packed account of an attempt on Paul's life, followed by his imprisonment at the hands of two Roman governors and his harrowing shipboard journey to trial in Rome. In many ways, Paul's experience recapitulates the culmination of Jesus' ministry, and Acts 20–28 could be thought of as a kind of Passion of Paul. The aspect of these chapters most relevant to work is the depiction of Paul's leadership. We will focus on what we see of his courage, his suffering, his respect for others, and his concern for the well-being of others.

Paul's Courage

After the conflicts in Philippi and Ephesus, Paul receives threats of imprisonment (Acts 20:23; 21:11) and death (Acts 20:3; 23:12–14). These threats are not idle, for indeed two attempts are actually made on his life (Acts 21:31; 23:21). Paul is taken into custody by the Roman government (Acts 23:10) and a suit is brought against him (Acts 24:1–9), which, though false, ultimately leads to his execution. Given the episodes of conflict we have already explored, it is no surprise that following the ways of God's kingdom leads to conflict with the oppressive ways of the world.

Yet through it all, Paul maintains an extraordinary courage. He continues his work (preaching) despite the threats, and even dares to preach to his captors, both Jewish (Acts 23:1–10) and Roman (Acts 24:21–26; 26:32; 28:30–31). In the end, his courage proves decisive, not only for his work of preaching, but for saving the lives of hundreds of people in the midst of a shipwreck (Acts 27:22–23). His own words sum up his attitude of courage as those around him shrink back in fear. "What are you doing, weeping and breaking my heart? For I am ready not only to be bound but even to die in Jerusalem for the name of the Lord Jesus" (Acts 21:13).

The point, however, is not that Paul is a man of extraordinary courage, but that the Holy Spirit gives each of us the courage we need to do our work. Paul credits the Holy Spirit for keeping him going in the face of such adversity (Acts 20:22; 21:4; 23:11). This is an encouragement to us today, because we also can depend on the Holy Spirit to give us the courage we may lack. The danger is not so much that courage may fail us in the moment of greatest terror, but that general worry will deter us from taking even the first step into following the ways of God's kingdom in our work. How often do we fail to defend a colleague, serve a customer, challenge a boss, or speak up about an issue, not because we are under actual pressure, but because we are afraid that if we do we might offend someone in authority? What if we adopted a position that before we will act contrary to God's ways at work, we at least have to receive an actual order to do so? Could we begin by counting on the Holy Spirit to sustain us at least that far?

Paul's Suffering

Paul needs every ounce of courage because of the heavy sufferings he knows his work will bring. "The Holy Spirit testifies to me in every city that imprisonment and persecutions are waiting for me" (Acts 20:23), he says. He is kidnapped (Acts 21:27), beaten (Acts 21:30–31; 23:3), threatened (Acts 22:22; 27:42), arrested many times (Acts 21:33; 22:24, 31; 23:35; 28:16), accused in lawsuits (Acts 21:34; 22:30; 24:1–2; 25:2, 7; 28:4), interrogated (Acts 25:24–27), ridiculed (Acts 26:24), ignored (Acts 27:11), shipwrecked (Acts 27:41) and bitten by a viper (Acts 28:3). Tradition says that Paul is eventually put to death for his work, although this is not recounted anywhere in the Bible.

Leadership in a broken world entails suffering. Anyone who will not accept suffering as an essential element of leadership cannot be a leader, at least not a leader in the way God intends. In this, we see another radical refutation of the Roman patronage system. The Roman system is structured to insulate the patron from suffering. Patrons alone, for example, had the right to escape corporal punishment, as we see when Paul's status as a citizen (a patron, albeit of a household of one) is the only thing that protects him from an arbitrary flogging (Acts 22:29). Paul nonetheless embraces bodily suffering, along with many other forms, as the necessity of a leader in Jesus' way. Today, we may seek to become leaders for the same reason men in ancient Rome sought to exercise patronage—to avoid suffering. We might succeed in gaining power and perhaps even insulating ourselves from the hurts of the world. But our leadership cannot benefit others if we will not accept hurt to ourselves to a greater or lesser degree. And if our leadership does not benefit others, it is not God's kind of leadership.

Paul's Respect

Despite Paul's utter conviction that he is in the right about both his beliefs and his conduct, he shows respect for everyone he encounters. This is so disarming, especially to those who are his enemies and captors, that it gives him an unimpeachable opportunity as a witness of God's kingdom. When he arrives in Jerusalem, he respects the Jewish Christian leaders there and complies with their odd request to demonstrate his continued faithfulness to the Jewish law (Acts 21:17–26). He speaks respectfully to a crowd that has just beaten him (Acts 21:30–22:21), to a soldier who is about to flog him (Acts 22:25–29), to the Jewish council that accuses him in a Roman court of law—even to the point of apologizing for inadvertently insulting the high priest—(Acts 23:1–10), to the Roman governor Felix and his wife Drusilla (Acts 24:10–26), to Felix's successor Festus (Acts 25:8–11; 26:24–26), and to King Agrippa and his wife Bernice (Acts 26:2–29) who imprison him. On his journey there, he treats with respect the centurion Julius (Acts 27:3), the governor of Malta (Acts 28:7–10), and the leaders of the Jewish community in Rome (Acts 28:17–28).

We should not confuse the respect Paul shows with timidity about his message. Paul never shrinks from boldly proclaiming the truth, wherever the chips may fall. After being beaten by a Jewish crowd in Jerusalem who falsely suspect him of bringing a Gentile into the temple, he preaches a sermon to them that concludes with the Lord Jesus commissioning him to preach salvation to the Gentiles (Acts 22:17–21). He tells the Jewish council in Acts 23:1–8, "I am on trial concerning the hope of the resurrection of the dead" (Acts 23:6). He proclaims the gospel to Felix (Acts 24:14–16) and proclaims to Festus, Agrippa, and Bernice, "I stand here on trial on account of my hope in the promise made by God to our ancestors" (Acts 26:6). He warns the soldiers and sailors on the boat to Rome that "the voyage will be with danger and much heavy loss, not only of the cargo and the ship, but also of our lives" (Acts 27:10). The book of Acts ends with Paul "proclaiming the kingdom of God and teaching about the Lord Jesus Christ with all boldness and without hindrance" (Acts 28:30–31).

Paul's respect for others often wins him a hearing and even turns enemies into friends, notwithstanding the boldness of his words. The centurion about to flog him intervenes with the Roman tribune, who orders him released (Acts 22:26–29). The Pharisees conclude, "We find nothing wrong with this man. What if a spirit or an angel has spoken to him?" (Acts 23:9). Felix determines that Paul "was charged with nothing deserving death or imprisonment" (Acts 23:29) and becomes an avid listener who "used to send for him very often and converse with him" (Acts 24:26). Agrippa, Bernice, and Festus come to see that Paul is innocent, and Agrippa begins to be persuaded by Paul's preaching. "Are you so quickly persuading me to become a Christian?" he asks (Acts 26:28). By the end of the voyage to Rome, Paul has become the de facto leader of the ship, issuing orders that the captain and centurion are happy to obey (Acts 27:42–44). On Malta, the governor welcomes and entertains Paul and his companions, and later provisions their ship and sends them away with honor (Acts 28:10).

Not everyone returns Paul's respect with respect, of course. Some vilify, reject, threaten, and abuse him. But, in general, he receives far more respect from people than do the masters of the Roman patronage system among whom he operates. The exercise of power may command the appearance of respect, but the exercise of true respect is much more likely to earn a response of true respect.

Paul's Concern for Others

Most of all, Paul's leadership is marked by his concern for others. He accepts the burden of leadership not to make his life better, but to make others' lives better. His very willingness to travel to hostile places to preach a better way of life is proof enough of this. Yet we also see his concern for others in concrete, personal ways. He heals a boy who is severely injured by a fall from an upper-floor window (Acts 20:9–12). He prepares the churches he has planted to carry on after his death, and encourages them when they are overcome with "much weeping" (Acts 20:37). He attempts to preach the good news even to those who are trying to kill him (Acts 22:1–21). He heals all the sick on the island of Malta (Acts 28:8–10).

A striking example of his concern for others occurs during the shipwreck. Although his warning not to make the voyage had been ignored, Paul pitches in to help and encourage the crew and passengers when the storm strikes.

> Since they had been without food for a long time, Paul then stood up among them and said, "Men, you should have listened to me and not have set sail from Crete and thereby avoided this damage and loss. I urge you now to keep up your courage, for there will be no loss of life among you, but only of the ship. For last night there stood by me an angel of the God to whom I belong and whom I worship, and he said, 'Do not be afraid, Paul; you must stand before the emperor; and indeed, God has granted safety to all those who are sailing with you.' So keep up your courage, men, for I have faith in God that it will be exactly as I have been told." (Acts 27:21–25)

His concern does not end with words of encouragement but proceeds with practical acts. He makes sure everyone eats to keep up their strength (Acts 27:34–36). He devises a plan that will save everyone's life, including those who can't swim (Acts 27:26, 38, 41, 44). He directs preparations for running the ship aground (Acts 27:43b), and prevents the sailors from abandoning the soldiers and passengers (Acts 27:30–32). As a result of his concerns and actions, not a single life is lost in the wreck (Acts 27:44).

Paul's leadership encompasses far more than the four factors of courage, suffering, respect, and concern for others, and it is visible far beyond Acts 20–28. Yet these factors as presented in these chapters form one of the most stirring demonstrations of leadership in the Bible and remain as much of an example today as they were in Luke's day.

Conclusion to Acts

Investigating work and work-related issues in Acts presents a coherent treatment of vocation in God's world. In Acts, a Christian view of work is not relegated simply to the realm of ethics. Rather, work is an active form of witness in God's redemption of the world. The logic of Acts moves in this direction:

1. The coming of the Spirit initiates Christ's kingdom—God's new world—in a new way. The Roman patronage system that seeks status for the self is replaced with a spirit of love that seeks the good of others. This follows the example of Jesus who spends himself for the sake of others—evident above all in the cross.

2. The Christian vocation is characterized by Spirit-empowered witness to Christ's kingdom, not only by proclamation but also by acting in accord with God's spirit of love in everyday life.

3. The Christian vocation is given to the entire community of believers, not merely to individuals. The believers' practice is not perfect—sometimes very far from perfect—but it is a real participation in the new world, nonetheless.

4. The community bears witness to Christ's kingdom by working and using work-related resources—power, wealth, and status—for the sake of others and the community as a whole. Membership in the community goes hand in hand with a transformed way of life, leading to love and service. An exemplary result is the practice of radical generosity with every kind of resource.

5. When work is performed in this way, every profession can be an act of witness by practicing the structures of justice, righteousness, and beauty brought forth by God's kingdom.

6. The Christian community thus produces a way of working that challenges the structures of the fallen world, and sometimes brings it into conflict with the world's power-holders. Nonetheless, the intent of the community is not to clash with the world but to transform it.

7. Leadership is a prominent arena in which the new spirit of love and service for others is enacted. Authority is shared and leadership is encouraged at every level of the community. Leaders accept the burden of acting for the good of others, and they respect the wisdom and authority of those they lead. Leadership attributes—including courage, suffering, respect, and concern for others—come to the fore in the example of the Apostle Paul.

Acts helps us to see that all of human life—including our work and the fruit that emerges from our work—can be a means of participating through the power of the Spirit already emerging in God's kingdom coming to earth. In this way work is not only dignified but also essential to the human vocation of witness. As it was from the beginning, work is central to what it means to be fully human. Workers today are called to be cultivators and transformers of earth, culture, family, business, education, justice, and every other sphere—all for the sake of God's kingdom.

Romans and Work

Introduction to Romans

Paul's letter to the Romans is best known for its vision of God's gracious actions toward humanity through the cross and resurrection of Christ. "It is the power of God for salvation to everyone who has faith" (Rom. 1:16). There is something deeply wrong with us individually, and with the world as a whole, from which we need to be saved, and Romans tells us how God is saving us from it.

Romans is deeply theological, but it is not abstract. God's salvation is not a concept for analytical discourse in Romans, but a call to action (Rom. 6:22). Paul tells how God's salvation affects our wisdom, our honesty, our relationships, our judgment, our ability to endure setbacks, our character, and our ethical reasoning, all of which are essential to our work. Here, in the nitty-gritty of human relationships and the desire to do good work, is where God's salvation takes hold in our world.

Written sometime during the reign of the Roman Emperor Nero (AD 54–68), the letter to the Romans hints of darkness and danger surrounding the Roman house churches, which comprised both Jewish and Gentile converts to Christ. Some of the Jewish members of the congregations had been exiled by an edict of Emperor Claudius in 49 and had only recently returned, probably having lost their property and financial stability in the meantime (Acts 18:2). Anti-Jewish sentiment in the wider Roman culture surely exerted pressures upon the Christian churches. Paul's extended reflection on God's faithfulness to both Jew and Gentile in this letter was not an abstract pondering of the ways of God, but a skillful theological reflection on these historical events and their consequences. The result is a set of practical tools for making moral decisions leading to a new quality of life in every place where people live and work.

The letter to the Romans has been exceptionally important in the development of Christian theology. To give just two examples, Martin

Luther broke with Pope Leo X largely because of his disagreement with what he perceived to be the Roman Catholic understanding of Romans. And Karl Barth's *Epistle to the Romans* was arguably the most influential theological work of the twentieth century.[1] In the past twenty-five or thirty years, a major theological debate concerning the relationship between salvation and good works has arisen about Romans and the rest of Paul's letters, often called the New Perspective on Paul. The general commentaries on Romans explore these issues at length. We will focus specifically on what the letter contributes to the theology of work. Of course, we need to have a basic understanding of Paul's general points before applying them to work, so we will do a certain amount of general theological exploration as needed.

The Gospel of Salvation—Paul's Vocation (Romans 1:1–17)

The opening verse of Romans announces Paul's own vocation, the work that God has called him to do: proclaiming the gospel of God in word and deed. So what is the gospel of God? Paul says that it is "the power of God for salvation to everyone who has faith, to the Jew first and also to the Greek. For in it the righteousness of God is revealed through faith for faith; as it is written, 'The one who is righteous will live by faith'" (Rom. 1:16–17, NRSV). For Paul, the gospel is more than words—it is the power of God for salvation. He emphasizes that this salvation is not for one group of people only but is intended to help anyone on earth to be among the people of God, by faith. Romans, then, is above all about God's salvation.

What is salvation? Salvation is the work of God that sets human beings in right relationship with God and with one another. As we will see momentarily, what we are being saved from are broken relationships—with God and with other people—that unleash the evil forces of sin and death in the world. Therefore, salvation is first of all the healing of broken relationships, beginning with the healing that reconciles the

---

[1] See, for example, Ian A. McFarland, *Creation and Humanity: The Sources of Christian Theology* (Louisville: Westminster John Knox Press, 2009), 138.

Creator and the created, God and us. Our reconciliation with God leads to freedom from sin and a newness of life that is not limited by death.

Christians have sometimes reduced Paul's gospel of salvation to something like, "Believe in Jesus so that you personally can go to heaven when you die." This is true, as far as it goes, but grossly inadequate. To begin with, a statement like that says nothing about relationships other than between the individual and God, yet Paul never ceases talking about relationships among people and between people and the rest of God's creation. And Paul has much more to say about faith, about life in Jesus, about God's kingdom, and about the quality of life both before and after death than could ever be encapsulated in a single slogan.

Likewise salvation cannot be reduced to a single moment in time. Paul says both that we "were saved" (Rom. 8:24) and that we "will be saved" (e.g., Rom. 5:9). Salvation is an ongoing process rather than a one-time event. God interacts with each person in a dance of divine grace and human faithfulness over time. There are decisive moments in the process of being saved, of course. The central moments are Christ's death on the cross and resurrection from the dead. "We were reconciled to God through the death of his Son," Paul tells us (Rom. 5:10), and "He who raised Christ from the dead will give life to your mortal bodies also" (Rom. 8:11).

Each of us might also regard the first time we said we believe in Christ as a decisive moment in our salvation. Romans, however, never speaks of a moment of personal salvation, as if salvation happened to us in the past and is now in storage until Christ comes again. Paul uses the past tense of salvation only to speak of Christ's death and resurrection, the moment when Christ brought salvation to the world. When it comes to each believer, Paul speaks of an ongoing process of salvation, always in the present or future tenses. "One believes with the heart and so is justified, and one confesses with the mouth and so is saved" (Rom. 10:10). Not "believed" and "confessed," past tense, but "believes" and "confesses," present tense. This leads directly to, "Everyone who calls on the name of the Lord shall be saved," future tense (Rom. 10:13). Salvation is not something that was given to us. It is always being given to us.

We take the trouble to emphasize the ongoing action of salvation because work is one of the preeminent places where we act in life. If salvation were something that happened to us only in the past, then what we do at work (or anywhere in life) would be irrelevant. But if salvation is something going on in our lives, then it bears fruit in our work. To be more precise, since salvation is the reconciliation of broken relationships, then our relationships with God, with other people, and with the created world at work (as everywhere in life) will be getting better as the process of salvation takes hold. Just to give a few examples, our salvation is evident when we take courage to speak an unpopular truth, listen to others' views with compassion, help colleagues attain their goals, and produce work products that help other people thrive.

Does this mean that we must work—and keep working—to be saved? Absolutely not! Salvation comes solely through "the grace of God and the free gift in the grace of one man, Jesus Christ" (Rom. 5:15). It "depends on faith" (Rom 4:16) and nothing else. As N. T. Wright puts it, "Whatever language or terminology we use to talk about the great gift that the one true God has given to his people in and through Jesus Christ, it remains precisely a gift. It never is something we can earn. We can never put God into our debt; we always remain in his."[2] We do not work to be saved. But because we are being saved we do work that bears fruit for God (Rom. 7:4). We will return to the question of how salvation is given to us in "Judgment, Justice, and Faith" below in Romans 3.

In sum, salvation is the ultimate work of Christ in the world, the goal toward which believers always "press on," as Paul puts it (Phil. 3:12). Salvation underlies everything Paul and everything believers do in work and life.

Our Need for Salvation in Life and Work (Romans 1:18–1:32)

We saw in Romans 1:1–17 that salvation begins with reconciliation to God. People have become estranged from God because of their "godlessness and wickedness" (Rom. 1:18). "Although they knew God, they neither glorified him as God nor gave thanks to him" (Rom. 1:21). We were created to walk in intimacy with God among the creatures of the

---

[2] N. T. Wright, *After You Believe: Why Christian Character Matters* (New York: HarperOne, 2010), 69.

Garden of Eden (Gen. 1–2), but our relationship with God has become so broken that we no longer recognize God. Paul calls this state a "debased mind" (Rom. 1:28).

Lacking the presence of mind to remain in the presence of the real God, we try to make our own gods. We have "exchanged the glory of the immortal God for images made to look like mortal man and birds and four-footed animals or reptiles" (Rom. 1:23). Our relationship with God is so thoroughly damaged that we cannot tell the difference between walking with God and carving an idol. When our real relationship with the true God is broken, we create fake relationships with false gods. Idolatry, then, is not merely one sin among others, but the essence of a broken relationship with God. (For more on idolatry, see "You Shall Not Make for Yourself an Idol," Exodus 20:4, at www.theologyofwork.org.)

When our relationship with God is broken, our relationships with other people also break down. Paul lists some of the broken aspects of human relationships that ensue.

> They were filled with every kind of wickedness, evil, covetousness, malice. Full of envy, murder, strife, deceit, craftiness, they are gossips, slanderers, God-haters, insolent, haughty, boastful, inventors of evil, rebellious toward parents, foolish, faithless, heartless, ruthless. (Rom. 1:29–31)

We experience nearly all these forms of broken relationships at work. Covetousness, strife, and envy over others' positions or paychecks, malice and rebellion toward those in authority, gossip and slander of co-workers and competitors, deceit and faithlessness in communications and commitments, insolence, haughtiness, and boastfulness of those who experience success, foolishness in decisions, heartlessness and ruthlessness by those in power. Not all the time of course. Some workplaces are better and some worse. But every workplace knows the consequences of broken relationships. All of us suffer from them. All of us contribute to causing them.

We may even compound the problem by making an idol of work itself, devoting ourselves to work in the vain hope that it alone will bring us meaning, purpose, security, or happiness. Perhaps this seems to work for a time, until we are passed over for promotion or are fired or laid off or retire. Then we discover that work comes to an end, and meanwhile we have become strangers to our family and friends. Like "mortal men and birds and four-footed animals and reptiles," work was created by God (Gen. 2:15) and is inherently good, yet it becomes evil when elevated to the place of God.

All Have Sinned (Romans 2–3)

Sadly, this brokenness extends even to Paul's own workplace, the Christian church, and in particular the Christians in Rome. Despite being God's own people (Rom. 9:25), "called to be saints" (Rom. 1:7), the Christians in Rome are experiencing a breakdown in their relationships with one another. Specifically, Jewish Christians are judging Gentile Christians for not conforming to their own peculiar expectations, and vice versa. "You say, 'We know that God's judgment on those who do such things is in accordance with the truth,'" Paul notes (Rom. 2:2). Each side claims that they know God's judgments and speak for God. Claiming to speak for God makes their own words into idols, illustrating in miniature how idolatry (breaking relationship with God) leads to judgment (breaking relationship with other people).

Both sides are wrong. The truth is that both Gentiles and Jews have strayed from God. Gentiles, who should have recognized the sovereignty of God in the creation itself, have given themselves over to the worship of idols and to all the destructive behavior that follows from this basic mistake (Rom. 1:18–32). Jews, on the other hand, have become judgmental, hypocritical, and boastful that they are the people of the Torah. Paul summarizes both situations by saying, "All who have sinned apart from the law will also perish apart from the law, and all who have sinned under the law will be judged by the law" (Rom. 2:12).

But the crux of the problem is not that each side misunderstands God's expectations. It is that each side judges the other, destroying the relationships that God had brought into being. It is crucial to recognize the role of judgment in Paul's argument. Judgment causes broken relationships. The specific sins noted in Romans 1:29–31 are not the causes of our broken relationships, but the results. The causes of our broken relationships are idolatry (toward God) and judgment (toward people). In fact, idolatry can be understood as a form of judgment, the judgment that God is not adequate and that we can create better gods on our own. Therefore, Paul's overarching concern in chapters 2 and 3 is our judgment of others.

> You have no excuse, whoever you are, when you judge others; for in passing judgment on another you condemn yourself, because you, the judge, are doing the very same things. You say, "We know that God's judgment on those who do such things is in accordance with truth." Do you imagine, whoever you are, that when you judge those who do such things and yet do them yourself, you will escape the judgment of God? (Rom. 2:1–3)

If we wonder what we have done that puts us in need of salvation, the answer above all is judgment and idolatry, according to Paul. We judge others, though we have no right to do so, and thus we bring God's judgment on ourselves as he works to restore true justice. To use a modern metaphor, it is like the Supreme Court overturning a corrupt judge in a lower court who didn't even have jurisdiction in the first place.

Does this mean that Christians are never to assess people's actions or to oppose people at work? No. Because we work as God's agents, we have a duty to assess whether the things happening in our workplaces serve or hinder God's purposes and to act accordingly (see Rom. 12:9–13:7 for some examples from Paul). A supervisor may need to discipline or fire an employee who is not doing his or her job satisfactorily. A worker may need to go over a supervisor's head to report an ethical or policy violation. A teacher may need to give a low grade. A voter or politician may need to oppose a candidate. An activist may need to protest a corporate or government injustice. A student may need to report cheating by another student. A victim of abuse or discrimination may need to cut off contact with the abuser.

Because we are responsible to God for the outcomes of our work and the integrity of our workplaces, we do need to assess people's actions and intentions and to take action to prevent injustice and do good work. But this does not mean that we judge others' worthiness as human beings or set ourselves up as morally superior. Even when we oppose others' actions, we do not judge them.

It can be difficult to tell the difference sometimes, but Paul gives us some surprisingly practical guidance. Respect the other person's conscience. God has created all people in such a way that "what the law requires is written on their hearts, to which their own conscience also bears witness" (Rom. 2:15). If others are genuinely following their own conscience, then it is not your job to judge them. But if you are setting up yourself as morally superior, condemning others for following their own moral compass, you are probably passing judgment in a way for which "you have no excuse" (Rom. 2:1).

Judgment, Justice, and Faith (Romans 3)

Judgment, the Source of Broken Relationships (Romans 3:1–20)

What can be done with a world of people separated from God by idolatry and from one another by judgment? God's true justice is the answer. In Romans 3, as Paul describes what happens in salvation, he puts it in terms of God's justice. "Our injustice serves to confirm the justice of God" (Rom. 3:5).

Before proceeding, we need to say a bit about the terminology of justice and righteousness. Paul uses the Greek word for justice, *dikaiosynē* and its various forms, thirty-six times in Romans. It is translated as "righteousness" most often and as "justice" (or "justification") less frequently. But the two are the same in Paul's language. The primary use of *dikaiosynē* is in courts of law, where people are seeking justice to restore a situation that is not right. Therefore, salvation means being made right with God (righteousness) and with other people and all of creation (justice). A full exploration of the relationship between the words *salvation*, *justification*, and *righteousness* is beyond the scope of this chapter but will be addressed in any general commentary on Romans.[3]

If this seems abstract, ask yourself whether you can see concrete implications at work. Is it the case that the (false) judgments people make about one another are the root of broken relationships and injustice where you work? For example, if a manager and employee disagree over the employee's performance review, which of these causes greater

---

[3] See, for example, N. T. Wright, *"The Letter to the Romans,"* vol. 10, *The New Interpreter's Bible* (Nashville: Abingdon Press, 1994).

damage—the performance gap itself or the hostility arising from their judgment? Or if someone gossips about another person at work, which causes greater damage—embarrassment over the item that was gossiped about or resentment over the judgment revealed by the gossiper's tone and the listeners' snickers?

If our false judgment is the root of our broken relationships with God, other people, and the creation, how can we possibly find salvation? The thing we need—justice/righteousness—is the one thing we are most incapable of. Even if we want to be put back into right relationships, our inability to judge rightly means that the harder we try, the worse we make the problem. "Who will rescue me?" Paul cries (Rom. 7:24).

We cannot hope to be rescued by anyone else, for they are in the same boat we're in. "Everyone is a liar," Paul tell us (Rom. 3:4). "There is no one who is righteous, not even one; there is no one who seeks God. All have turned aside, together they have become worthless; there is no one who shows kindness, there is not even one" (Rom. 3:10–12). "All have sinned and fall short of the glory of God" (Rom 3:23).

Yet there is hope—not in humanity, but in God's faithfulness. "Will their unfaithfulness nullify the faithfulness of God?" Paul asks. "By no means!" he replies (Rom 3:3–4). On the contrary, "injustice serves to confirm the justice of God." This means our workplaces are settings for grace just as much as our churches or families. If we feel that our workplace is too secular, too unethical, too hostile to faith, too full of greedy, soulless people, then it is exactly the place where the cross of Christ is effective! God's grace can bring reconciliation and justice in a factory, office block, or petrol station just as fully as in a cathedral, abbey, or church. Paul's gospel is not only for the church, but for the whole world.

God's Justice, the Solution to Our False Judgments (Romans 3:21–26)

Given that our judgment is false and hypocritical, how can we ever find righteousness and justice? This is the question that leads into the dramatic crux of Romans 3. God's response is the cross of Christ. God gives his justice/righteousness to us because we are unable to bring justice/righteousness ourselves. God accomplishes this through the cross of Jesus, in which he demonstrates that "he himself is righteous and that he justifies the one who has faith in Jesus" (Rom. 3:26).

God's means of accomplishing this is through the death and resurrection of Jesus. "God proves his love for us in that while we still were sinners Christ died for us" (Rom. 5:8). God freely chose to accept the cross of Christ as though it were a holy sacrifice of atonement in the Jewish temple (Rom. 3:25). As on the Day of Atonement, God chose to pass over people's wrongdoing in order to establish a kind of new beginning for all who believe. And although Jesus was a Jew, God regards the cross as an offer of salvation to all people. Through the cross, everyone can be restored to a right relationship with God.

Although we lack righteousness/justice, God has both in infinite supply. Through the cross of Jesus, God gives us the righteousness/justice that restores our broken relationships with God, other people, and all creation. When God gives us salvation, he gives us righteousness/justice.

> The *righteousness* of God has been disclosed, and is attested by the law and the prophets, the *righteousness* of God through faith in Jesus Christ for all who believe. For there is no distinction, since all have sinned and fall short of the glory of God; they are now *justified* by his grace as a gift, through the redemption that is in Christ Jesus, whom God put forward as a sacrifice of atonement by his blood, effective through faith. He did this to show his *righteousness*, because in his divine forbearance he had passed over the sins previously committed; it was to prove at the present time that he himself is *righteous* and that he *justifies* the one who has faith in Jesus. (Rom. 3:21–26; emphasis added)

The cross is God's surprising justice—surprising because although God is not the sinner, God makes the sacrifice. Does this mean anything in today's secular workplaces? It could be a very hopeful note. In situations where the problems in our workplaces are caused by our own errors or injustice, we can count on God's righteousness/justice to overcome our failings. Even though we can't make ourselves right, God can work his righteousness/justice in us and through us. In situations where others' errors and injustice cause the problems, we may be able to set things right by sacrificing something of ourselves—in imitation of our Savior—even though we did not cause the problem.

For example, consider a work group that operates in a culture of blame. Rather than working together to fix problems, people spend all their time trying to blame others whenever problems arise. If your workplace is a culture of blame, it may not be your fault. Perhaps your boss is the blamer-in-chief. Even so, could a sacrifice by you bring reconciliation and justice? The next time the boss starts to blame someone, imagine if you stood up and said, "I remember that I supported this idea the last time we talked about it, so you'd better blame me too." What if the time after that, two or three other people did the same thing along with you? Would that begin to make the blame game fall apart? You might end up sacrificing your reputation, your friendship with the boss, even your future job prospects. But is it possible that it could also break the hold of blame and judgment in your work group? Could you expect God's grace to take an active role through your sacrifice?

Faith/Faithfulness, the Entry to God's Justice (Romans 3:27–31)

In the previous section we looked at Romans 3:22–26 and highlighted the righteousness/justice that God gives us in salvation. Now let us look again at the passage to highlight the role of faith.

> The righteousness of God has been disclosed, and is attested by the law and the prophets, the righteousness of God through *faith* in Jesus Christ for all who *believe*. For there is no distinction, since all have sinned and fall short of the glory of God; they are now justified by his grace as a gift, through the redemption that is in Christ Jesus, whom God put forward as a sacrifice of atonement by his blood, effective through *faith*. He did this to show his righteousness, because in his divine forbearance he had passed over the sins previously committed; it was to prove at the present time that he himself is righteous and that he justifies the one who has *faith* in Jesus. (Rom. 3:21–26; emphasis added)

Clearly, God's gift of righteousness/justice is intimately tied up in faith and belief. This brings us to one of the most famous themes in Romans, the role of faith in salvation. In many ways, the Protestant Reformation was founded on paying attention to this and similar passages in Romans, and their importance remains central to Christians of virtually every kind today. While there are many ways of describing it, the central idea is that people are restored to a right relationship with God by faith.

The Greek root-word *pistis* is translated as "faith" (or sometimes "believe," as in one instance above), but also as "faithfulness" as in Romans 3:3. The English language distinguishes between faith (mental assent, trust, or commitment) and faithfulness (actions consistent with one's faith). But in Greek there is only the single word *pistis* for both faith and faithfulness. There is no separating what a person believes from the evidence of that belief in the person's actions. If you have faith, you will act in faithfulness. Given that in most workplaces our faithfulness (what we do) will be more directly evident than our faith (what we believe), the relationship between these two aspects of *pistis* takes on a particular significance for work.

Paul speaks of "the *pistis* of Jesus" twice here, in Romans 3:22 and 3:26. If translated literally, the Greek says "*pistis* of Jesus," not "*pistis* in Jesus." The literal wording of Romans 3:22 is thus that we are saved by Jesus' faithfulness to God (the *pistis* of Jesus). In other passages, *pistis* clearly refers to *our* faith in Jesus, such as Romans 10:9, "If you confess with your lips that Jesus is Lord and believe in your heart that God raised him from the dead, you will be saved." In truth, our faith in Jesus cannot be separated from Jesus' faithfulness to God. Our faith in Jesus comes about because of Jesus' faithfulness to God on the cross, and we respond by living faithfully to him and placing our trust in him. Remembering that our salvation flows from Jesus' faithfulness, not merely our state of belief, keeps us from turning the possession of faith into a new form of works-righteousness, as if our act of saying "I believe in Jesus" is what brings us salvation.

The full meaning of faith/faithfulness in Paul's writing has two important implications for work. First of all, it puts to rest any fear that by taking our work seriously we might waver in recognizing that salvation comes solely by God's gift of faith. When we remember that Christ's faithfulness on the cross has already accomplished the work of salvation, and that our faith in Christ comes solely by God's grace, then we recognize that our faithfulness to God in our work is simply a response to God's grace. We are faithful in our work because God has given us faith as a free gift.

Second, the faithfulness of Christ impels us to become more and more faithful ourselves. Again, this is not because we think that our faithful actions earn us salvation, but because having been given faith in Christ, we earnestly desire to become more like him. Paul speaks of this as the "obedience of faith" (Rom. 1:5, 26). Without faith, it is impossible to be obedient to God. But if God gives us faith, then we can respond in obedience. In fact, much of the latter half of Romans is devoted to showing us how to be more obedient to God as a result of the grace God has given us through faith.

An Exemplary Faith: Abraham Trusted God's Promises (Romans 4)

As we have seen in Romans 1–3, the cross of Christ brings salvation to all people—Jews and Gentiles alike. In Christ, God puts all people back into right relationship with God and one another without regard to the provisions of the Jewish law. For this reason, Paul's principal focus throughout Romans is helping the divided and quarreling Christians in Rome to reconcile their broken relationships in order to live faithfully into what God has accomplished in Christ.

This interpretation of Christ's death raises a problem for Paul, however, since he is writing not only to uncircumcised Gentiles but also to circumcised Jews, for whom the law still matters. Further, Paul's interpretation seems to ignore the story of Abraham, understood to be "father" of the Jews, who was in fact circumcised as a sign of his covenant with God (Gen. 17:11). Doesn't the story of Abraham suggest that entering the covenant of God requires male circumcision for all peoples, whether Jewish or Gentile?

"No," argues Paul in Romans 4. Interpreting the story of Abraham from Genesis 12:1–3, 15:6, and 17:1–14, Paul concludes that Abraham had faith that God would honor his word and make the childless Abraham the father of many nations through his barren wife Sarah. Consequently, God reckoned Abraham's faith as righteousness (Rom. 4:3, 9, 22). Paul reminds his readers that God's acknowledgment of Abraham's righteousness took place long *before* Abraham was circumcised, which came *later* as a *sign* of his already-existing faith in God (Rom. 4:10–11).

In other words, at the time God reckoned Abraham's faith as putting him in right relationship with God, Abraham shared the same status as an uncircumcised Gentile in Paul's world. Thus, concludes Paul, Abraham became the father of both Jews and Gentiles through the righteousness of faith rather than righteousness under the Jewish law (Rom. 4:11–15).

The example of Abraham in Romans 4 provides Christians with great hope for our work and workplaces. Abraham's example of trusting God's promises—despite adverse circumstances and seemingly impossible odds—emboldens us not to waver in trust when we face challenges at work or when God does not seem to be present (see Rom. 4:19). God did not immediately fulfill the promise to Abraham, which further encourages us to be patient in waiting for God to renew or redeem our circumstances in life.

Grace Reigns for Eternal Life through Jesus Christ (Romans 5)

In Romans 5 Paul links this divine gift of righteousness to the obedience of Christ and the grace that now flows into the world through him. Several important features of this chapter illuminate our experiences of work.

Grace Transforms Suffering in Our Life in Christ (Romans 5:1–11)

In Romans 5:1–11 Paul offers more encouragement by reminding the Romans that *through* Christ we have *already* "gained access" to God's "grace in which we stand" (Rom. 5:2). Grace signifies God's life-giving power that raised Jesus from the dead. Grace continues to bring new and more abundant life into the world to and through Christ's followers. By living *Christ's* obedient life of faith and faithfulness in our own circumstances, we experience God's life-giving grace that can bring us joy and peace at work, at home, and in every context of life.

Nevertheless, trusting the grace of God often calls for steadfast patience in the face of many challenges. Just as Christ suffered in the course of his obedience to God, we too may experience suffering when we embody Christ's life of faith and faithfulness. Paul even says he "boasts" in his suffering (Rom. 5:3), knowing that his suffering is a participation in the suffering Jesus experienced in his mission to reconcile the world to God (Rom. 8:17–18). Moreover, suffering often brings growth.

Suffering produces endurance, and endurance produces character, and character produces hope, and hope does not disappoint us, because God's love has been poured into our hearts. (Rom. 5:3–5)

Therefore God does not promise that life and work will be happy for believers all the time. Many people suffer at work. Work can be boring, degrading, humiliating, exhausting, and heartless. We can be underpaid, endangered, and discriminated against. We can be pressured to violate our consciences and God's principles. We can be fired, laid off, made redundant, downsized, terminated, unemployed or underemployed for long periods. We can bring suffering on ourselves by our own arrogance, carelessness, incompetence, greed, or malice against others. We can suffer even in good jobs. We should never be content with abuse or mistreatment at work, but when we have to endure suffering at work, all is not lost. God's grace is poured out on us when we suffer, and it makes us stronger if we remain faithful.

To give an example, preparing the soil and caring for crops cannot guarantee that the grain will grow tall or the vegetables will ripen. Poor weather, drought, insects, and blight can ruin the harvest. Yet, through grace, farmers may come to accept all these aspects of nature, while trusting God's care. This in turn shapes the patient, faithful character of farmers who come to care deeply for all of God's creation. A deep appreciation of nature, in turn, can be a great asset for the work of farming.

Similarly, grace empowers us to remain faithful and hopeful even when the employer for whom we work closes their doors during hard economic times. So, too, God's life-giving power sustains many highly educated young adults who still have trouble finding meaningful employment. Grace also inspires a team to persevere in developing a new product, even after repeated failures, knowing that what they learn by failing is what makes the product better.

God's love sustains us through all kinds of suffering in life and work. "Hope does not disappoint us, because God's love has been poured into our hearts." Even when suffering threatens to harden our hearts, God's love makes us agents of his reconciliation, which we have received in Christ (Rom. 10–11).

Grace and Righteousness Lead to Eternal Life through Christ (Romans 5:12–21)

Romans 5:12–21 reflects a dense and complex theological argument involving a number of different contrasts between the disobedient Adam and the obedient Christ, through whom we are made righteous and promised eternal life. The passage gives us assurance that Christ's obedient act of self-giving for others puts all who come to him into right relationship with God and one another. As participants in Christ's faith and faithfulness, we receive a share of the divine gifts of righteousness and eternal life promised by God through Christ. Therefore, we no longer participate in Adam's disobedience but find eternal life by participating in Christ's obedience to God.

Paul speaks of God's grace operating in both the present time and eternity. Reconciliation has already been given through Christ (Rom. 5:11), so that we are already able to live God-honoring lives. Yet God's reconciliation is not yet complete and is still in the process of "*leading* to eternal life" (Rom. 12:21). If we have received Christ's reconciliation, then our work now is an opportunity to contribute to the better future where Christ is leading. Innovators gain new possibilities to create, design, and build products that improve the common good. Service workers have new opportunities to make other lives better. Artists or musicians can create aesthetic beauty that enhances human life for God's glory. None of these are means to eternal life. But every time we work to make the world more as God intends it to be, we receive a foretaste of eternal life. When we remain obedient to Christ's pattern of faith and faithfulness in our workplace settings, no matter what the circumstances, we can trust that our life is eternally secure in the hands of our faithful God.

Walking in Newness of Life (Romans 6)

Although God's grace has come into the world to bring reconciliation and justice, there are still evil spiritual powers at work opposing the life-giving power of God's grace (Rom. 6:14). Paul often personifies these evil spiritual forces, calling them such names as "sin" (Rom. 6:2), "flesh" (Rom. 7:5), "death" (Rom. 6:9), or "this world" (Rom. 12:2). Human beings must choose whether, through their actions in daily life, to partner with God through Christ or with these evil forces. Paul calls choosing to partner with God "walking in newness of life" (Rom. 6:4). He compares walking in newness of life to Christ's new life after being raised from the dead. "Just as Christ was raised from the dead by the glory of the father, so we too might walk in newness of life" (Rom. 6:4). In our lives here and now, we can begin to live—or "walk"—in reconciliation and justice just as Christ now lives.

To walk in newness of life requires us to abandon our judgmentalism and to do God's justice rather than continuing in our self-serving habits (Rom. 6:12–13). As instruments of God's justice, believers act in ways *through which* the life-giving power of God's grace builds up people and communities in Christ. This is far more active than merely refraining from bad behavior. Our calling is to become instruments of justice and reconciliation, working to root out the effects of sin in a troubled world.

For example, workers may have fallen into a habit of judging management as evil or unfair, and vice versa. This may have become a convenient pretext for workers to cheat the company, use paid time for personal activities, or fail to do excellent work. Conversely, it may be a convenient excuse for managers to discriminate against workers they don't personally like, or to evade safety or workplace fairness regulations, or to withhold information from workers. Merely following the regulations or refraining from cheating would not be walking in newness of life. Instead, walking in newness of life would require us first of all to give up our judgments of the other side. Once we no longer regard them as unworthy of our respect, then we can begin to discern specific ways to restore good relationships, reestablish just and fair dealings with one another, and build up one another and our organizations.

Making this kind of change in our life and work is exceedingly difficult. Paul says that sin continually seeks to "exercise dominion in your mortal bodies, to make you obey their passions." However good our intentions, we soon fall back into our broken ways. Only God's grace, made real in Christ's death, has the power to pry us free from our habits of judgment (Rom. 6:6).

Therefore God's grace does not cast us "free" to wander aimlessly back into our old ills. Instead he offers to strap us into new life in Christ. The bindings will chafe whenever we begin to wander off course, and Paul admits that walking in newness of life will feel a lot like slavery at first. Our choice, then, is *which kind* of slavery to accept—slavery to newness of life or slavery to our old sins. "You are slaves of the one you obey, either of sin, which leads to death, or of obedience, which leads to righteousness [justice]" (Rom. 6:25). "But now that you have been freed from sin and enslaved to God, the advantage you get is sanctification [newness of life]. The end is eternal life" (Rom. 6:22). The advantage of walking in newness of life is not that it feels freer than slavery to sin, but that it results in justice and life, rather than shame and death.

Walking in Newness of Life in the Workplace (Romans 6)

What does it mean to be a "slave" of God's grace in our places of work? It means that we do not make decisions at work based on how things affect us, but about how they affect our master, God. We make decisions as God's stewards or agents. This is actually a familiar concept in both Christian faith and the secular workplace. In the Christian faith, Christ himself is the model steward, who gave up his own life in order to fulfill God's purposes. Similarly, many people in the workplace have a duty to serve the interests of others, rather than their own. Among them are attorneys, corporate officers, agents, trustees and boards of directors, judges, and many others. Not many workplace stewards or agents are as committed as Jesus was—willing to give their lives to fulfill their duties—but the concept of agency is an everyday reality in the workplace.

The difference for Christians is that our duty ultimately is to God, not the state or shareholders or anyone else. Our overarching mission must be God's justice and reconciliation, not merely obeying the law, making a profit, or satisfying human expectations. Unlike Albert Carr's claim that business is just a game in which normal rules of ethics don't apply,[4]

---

[4] Albert Z. Carr, "Is Business Bluffing Ethical?" *Harvard Business Review* 46 (January/February 1968).

walking in newness of life means integrating justice and reconciliation into our lives at work.

For instance, walking in newness of life for a high school teacher might mean repeatedly forgiving a rebellious and troublesome student, while also seeking new ways to reach that student in the classroom. For a politician, walking in newness of life might mean drafting new legislation that includes input from a number of different ideological perspectives. For a manager, it might mean asking the forgiveness of an employee in front of everyone who is aware of the manager's transgression against the employee.

Walking in newness of life requires us to look deeply into our patterns of work. Bakers or chefs might easily see how their work helps feed hungry people, which in itself is a form of justice. The same bakers and chefs might also need to look more deeply at their personal interactions in the kitchen. Do they treat people with dignity, help others succeed, bring glory to God? Walking in newness of life affects both the ends we try to accomplish and the means we use to do so.

The Invasive Power of "Sin" (Romans 7)

In chapter 7, Paul continues to emphasize that newness of life in Christ frees us from being "captive" to the "old written code" of the law (Rom. 7:6). Nonetheless, the law itself is not the problem with human existence, for "the law is holy, and the commandment is holy and just and good" (Rom. 7:12). Instead, concludes Paul, the problem is the God-opposing power he calls "sin" taking up residence in human beings (Rom. 7:13). Sin has taken advantage of the law's commandments by using them as tools to deceive people (Rom. 7:11), thus preventing each person from being able to obey the law as God intended (Rom. 7:14, 17, 23).

Sin's power is not merely making bad choices or doing things we know we shouldn't. It is as if an evil power has invaded the territory of each person's spirit and taken control, "sold into slavery under sin," as Paul puts it (Rom. 7:14). Under this slavery to sin, we are unable to do the good called for in the commandments and known in our hearts (Rom. 7:15–20). This occurs despite our good intentions to do what God desires (Rom. 7:15–16, 22).

In other words, knowledge of what is good is not enough to overcome the power of sin that has invaded us! "For I do not do the good I want, but the evil I do not want is what I do" (Rom. 7:19). We can be rescued from this plight only by the intervention of another, more powerful spiritual force—the Holy Spirit who becomes the focus in Romans 8.

We are well aware that knowing what God wants is not enough to keep us on the right track in workplace situations. For instance, even when we know in our minds that God wants us to treat everyone with respect, we sometimes fall prey to the false perception that we could get ahead by speaking poorly about a co-worker. Likewise, in the work of parenting, mothers and fathers know that shouting in anger at a young child is not good. But sometimes the power of sin overtakes them and they do so anyway. A lawyer who charges clients for services by the hour knows he should keep scrupulous time records, but may nevertheless be overpowered by sin to pad his hours to increase his income.

Alone, we are especially vulnerable to the power of sin within us. Wherever we work, we would do well to seek out others (Rom. 12:5) and help one another resist this power that tries to overcome our will to do what is right and good. For example, a small but growing number of Christians are joining small peer groups of people who work in similar situations. Peer groups meet anywhere from an hour once a week, often at work locations, to half a day once a month. Members commit to telling each other the details of situations they face at work and to discussing them from a faith perspective, developing options and committing to action plans. A member might describe a conflict with a co-worker, an ethical lapse, a feeling of meaninglessness, a company policy that seems unfair. After gaining the others' insights, the member would commit to a course of action in response and report to the group about results at future meetings. (For more on this, see "Equipping Churches Connect Daily Work to Worship" at www.theologyofwork.org.)

Living According to the Spirit (Romans 8)

Living According to the Spirit Leads to a New Quality of Life (Romans 8:1–14)

Believers are free from the law, but walking in newness of life is based on a firm moral structure (hence, "the *law* of the Spirit," Rom. 8:2). Paul calls this moral structure "living according to the Spirit" or "setting our minds on the Spirit" (Rom. 8:5). Both terms refer to the process of moral reasoning that guides us as we walk in newness of life.

This kind of moral compass does not work by listing specific acts that are right or wrong. Instead it consists of following the "law of the Spirit of life in Christ Jesus" that has freed believers "from the law of sin and death" (Rom. 8:1–2). The words *life* and *death* are the keys. As discussed earlier in Romans 6, Paul understands "sin," "death," and the "flesh" as spiritual forces in the world that lead people to act in ways that are contrary to God's will and produce chaos, despair, conflict, and destruction in their lives and in their communities. By contrast, living according to the Spirit means doing whatever brings life instead of death. "To set the mind on the flesh [our old patterns of judgment] is death but to set the mind on the Spirit is life and peace" (Rom. 8:6). Setting the mind on the Spirit means looking for whatever will bring more life to each situation.

For example, the Jewish law taught that "you shall not murder" (Exod. 20:13). But living according to the Spirit goes far beyond not literally murdering anyone. It actively seeks opportunities to bring better life to people. It can mean cleaning a hotel room so that guests remain healthy. It can mean clearing the ice from a neighbor's sidewalk (or pavement) so pedestrians can walk safely. It can mean studying for years to earn a Ph.D. in order to develop new treatments for cancer.

Another way to put it is that living according to the Spirit means living a *new quality of life* in Christ. This comes from setting aside our judgments of what another person deserves and seeking instead what would bring them a better quality of life, deserved or not. When making assignments, a manager could assign a task that stretches subordinates' abilities, rather than limiting them to what they are already capable of, then inviting them to check in every day for guidance. When asked to lend a replacement tool, a skilled tradesperson could instead show a junior worker a new technique that will prevent breaking the tool the next time around. When asked "Why did our dog die?" a parent could ask a child "Are you afraid someone you love might die?" instead of only explaining the pet's immediate cause of death. In each of these situations, the moral goal is to bring a better quality of life to the other person, rather than to fulfill a demand of the law.

Bringing life, rather than fulfilling the law, is the moral compass of those who are being saved by God's grace. We are free to live according to the Spirit rather than to enslave ourselves to the law because "there is now no condemnation for those who are in Christ Jesus" (Rom. 8:1).

Paul's inclusion of "peace" as an aspect of setting our minds on the Spirit (Rom. 13:6, as above) points out the social aspects of living according to the Spirit because peace is a social phenomenon.[5] When we follow Christ, we try to bring a new quality of life to our society, not just to ourselves. This means paying attention to the social conditions that diminish life at work and elsewhere. We do what we can to make life better for people we work among. At the same time, we work to bring justice/righteousness to the social systems that shape the conditions of work and workers.

Christians can be a positive force for improvement—even survival—if we can help our organizations set their minds on the need for a new quality of life. We probably can't change our organizations much on our own. But if we can build relationships with others, earn people's trust, listen to the people nobody else listens to, we may help the organization break out of its ruts. Plus, we bring the secret ingredient—our faith that God's grace can use us to bring life to even the deadest situation.

Conversely, if we do not set our minds on the Spirit at work, we can be arrogant and destructive, whether in our relationships with fellow workers, competitors, clients, or others. Setting our minds on the Spirit requires constantly evaluating the *consequences* or *fruit* of our work, always asking whether our work enhances the quality of life for other people. If we are honest in our assessments, no doubt it also requires daily repentance and the grace to change.

---

[5] Robert Jewett, *Romans: A Commentary* (Minneapolis: Fortress Press, 2007), 487.

Suffering with Christ in Order to Be Glorified with Christ (Romans 8:15–17)

Paul contrasts life in the Spirit with life under the Jewish law. Paul says believers have received a "spirit of adoption" as children of God, rather than "a spirit of slavery to fall back into fear" (Rom. 8:15). Everyone who "belongs to" Christ (Rom. 8:9–10) is now an adopted child of God. In contrast, those under the law live in slavery to the power of sin and also in fear—presumably fear of the law's threats of punishment for disobedience. Believers are free of this fear, since there is now "no condemnation for those who are in Christ Jesus" (Rom. 8:1). When we live faithfully in Christ, we do not face the law's threats of punishment, even when we get things wrong in our daily life and work. Hardships and failures may still mar our work, but God's response is not condemnation but redemption. God will bring something worthwhile out of our faithful work, no matter how bad it seems at present.

At least two aspects of these verses inform our approach to work or life in our workplaces. First, as adopted children of God, we are never alone in our work. No matter what our dissatisfaction or frustrations with the people we work among, or the work, or even a lack of support for the work from our families, the Spirit of God in Christ abides with us. God is always looking for an opportunity to redeem our suffering and turn it into something good and satisfying in our lives. As we observed earlier in connection with Romans 5, faithfully enduring hardship and suffering in our work can lead to the formation of our character and ground our hope for the future. (See "Grace Transforms Suffering in Our Life in Christ," above in Romans 5:1–11.)

Second, at one time or another, most people encounter failures, frustrations, and hardships in their work. Our work places obligations on us that we wouldn't otherwise have, even obligations as simple as showing up on time every day. Faithfully engaging these challenges can actually make the work more rewarding and satisfying. Over time these experiences give us greater confidence in God's redeeming presence and greater experience of his motivating and energizing Spirit.

In some situations you may be welcomed and promoted for bringing reconciliation and justice to your place of work. In other situations you may be resisted, threatened, punished, or terminated. For example, bad relationships are an unfortunate feature of many workplaces. One department may habitually sabotage another department's accomplishments. Strife between managers and workers may have become institutionalized. People may be terrorized by an office bully, an academic clique, a shop floor gang, a racial dividing line, or an abusive boss. If you bring reconciliation in situations like these, productivity may increase, turnover may be reduced, morale may soar, customer service may rebound, and you may be praised or promoted. On the other hand, the bullies, cliques, gangs, racial divides, and abusive bosses are almost certain to oppose you.

Eagerly Awaiting Bodily Redemption for Ourselves and God's Creation (Romans 8:18–30)

Being "glorified" with Christ (Rom. 8:17) is our hope for the future. But according to Paul that hope is part of a *process* already underway. We are to engage patiently in it, with the expectation that at some point it will be completed (Rom. 8:18–25). The gift of the Holy Spirit already received as "first fruits" of this process (Rom. 8:23) signifies our adoption as children of God (Rom. 8:14–17, 23). This constitutes proof that the process is underway.

This process culminates in "the redemption of our bodies" (Rom. 8:23). This is not a rescue of our souls out of our physical bodies, but the transformation of our bodies along with the entire creation (Rom. 8:21). This process has already begun, and we experience its "first fruits" (Rom. 8:24) in our life and work today. But far more and better is yet to come, and at present the "whole creation" groans in "labor pains" as it eagerly anticipates being set free from its own "bondage to decay" (Rom. 8:19–23). Paul is clearly drawing on imagery from Genesis 2–3, where not only Adam but also creation itself was subjected to decay and death, no longer able to live into what God created them to be. This reminds us to consider the impact of our work on all of God's creation, not only on people. (For more on this topic, see "Dominion" in Genesis 1:26 and 2:5 at www.theologyofwork.org.)

The process is slow and sometimes painful. We "groan" while we wait for it to be accomplished, Paul says, and not only us individually but "the whole creation has been groaning in labor pains" (Rom. 8:22–23). This echoes the groaning of Israel while enslaved in Egypt (Exod. 6:5) and reminds us that nearly 30 million people are still enslaved in the world today.[6] We can never be content with merely our own release from the evil forces in the world, but we must serve God faithfully until he completes his salvation in every part of the world.

Nonetheless, the salvation of the world is sure, for "all things work together for good for those who love God and are called according to his purpose" (Rom. 8:28). God is at work in us now, and the time is coming when God's salvation will be complete in the world. God's original verdict "It is very good" (Gen. 1:31) is vindicated by the transformation at work in us now, to be fulfilled in God's time.

Because the transformation is not yet complete, we have to be prepared for difficulties along the way. Sometimes we do good work, only to see it wasted or destroyed by the evil that is presently in the world. Even if we do good work, our work may be vandalized. Our recommendations may be watered down. We may run out of capital, lose the election to a scoundrel, drown in red tape, fail to engage a student's interest. Or we may succeed for a time, and then find our results undone by later events. Health workers, for example, have been on the verge of eradicating polio on several occasions, only to face new outbreaks due to political opposition, ignorance, vaccine-related transmission, and the swift pace of modern travel.[7]

Nothing Can Come Between Us and the Love of God (Romans 8:31–39)

God is for us, says Paul, having given his own Son for "all of us" (Rom. 8:31–32). Nothing is able to come between us and the love of God in Christ Jesus our Lord (Rom. 8:35–39). "Neither death, nor life, nor angels, nor rulers, nor things present, nor things to come, nor powers, nor height, nor depth, nor anything else in all creation, will be able

---

[6] "Inaugural Global Slavery Index Reveals More Than 29 Million People Living in Slavery," *Global Slavery Index 2013*, October 4, 2013, http://www .globalslaveryindex.org/category/press-release.

[7] "Poliomyelitis Eradication," in *Wikipedia*, http://en.wikipedia.org/wiki/ Poliomyelitis_eradication.

to separate us from the love of God in Christ Jesus our Lord" (Rom. 8:38–39). Many of these things seem to threaten us in the sphere of work. We face menacing or incompetent bosses (rulers). We get stuck in dead-end jobs (things present). We make sacrifices now—working long hours, taking classes after work, serving in low-paid internships, moving to another country looking for work—that we hope will pay off later but may never pan out (things to come). We lose our jobs because of economic cycles or regulations or unscrupulous actions by power-ful people we never even see (powers). We are forced by circumstance, folly, or the crimes of others into degrading or dangerous work. All these things can do us real hurt. But they cannot triumph over us.

Christ's faithfulness—and ours, by God's grace—overcomes the worst that life and work can do to us. If career progress, income, or prestige is our highest goal at work, we may end up disappointed. But if salvation—that is, reconciliation with God and people, faithfulness, and justice—is our chief hope, then we will find it amid both the good and bad in work. Paul's affirmations mean that no matter what the difficulties we encounter with our work, or the complexities and challenges we face with co-workers or superiors in our workplaces, the love of God in Christ always abides with us. The love of God in Christ is the steadying force in the midst of adversity now, as well as our hope for bodily redemption in the future.

God's Character Is to Have Mercy on Everyone (Romans 9–11)

In Romans 9–11, Paul returns to the immediate problem the letter is meant to address—the conflict between Jewish and Gentile Christians. Since this is not our primary concern in the theology of work, we will summarize quickly.

Paul discusses God's history with Israel, with special attention to God's mercy (Rom. 9:14–18). He explains how God's salvation comes also to the Gentiles. Jews experienced God's salvation first, beginning with Abraham (Rom. 9:4–7). But many have fallen away, and at present it seems as if the Gentiles are more faithful (Rom. 9:30–33). But the

Gentiles should not become judgmental, for their salvation is interwoven with the Jews (Rom. 11:11–16). God has preserved a "remnant" of his people (Rom. 9:27, 11:5) whose faithfulness—by the grace of God—leads to the reconciliation of the world.

For Jews and Gentiles alike, then, salvation is an act of God's mercy, not a reward for human obedience (Rom. 9:6–13). With this in mind, Paul takes on a number of arguments on both sides, always concluding that "God has mercy on whomever he chooses" (Rom. 9:18). Neither Jews nor Gentiles are saved by their own actions, but by God's mercy.

Salvation from God, says Paul, comes by confessing Jesus as Lord and believing that God raised him from the dead (Rom. 10:9–10). In other words, salvation comes to everyone who trusts in the life-giving power of God that enriches the lives of both Jews and Gentiles who follow Jesus as Lord (see Rom. 10:12–13). Disobedience—whether of Gentiles or Jews—provides God with the opportunity to show the world the mercy of God toward everyone (Rom. 11:33). Paul's concern in this letter is to *reconcile* broken relationships between Jewish and Gentile followers of Jesus.

Romans 9–11 offers hope to all of us in our work and in our workplaces. First, Paul emphasizes God's desire to have mercy on the disobedient. All of us, at one point or another in our working lives, have failed to embody Christ's faith and faithfulness in some aspect of our work. If God has mercy on us (Rom. 11:30), we are called to have mercy on others in our work. This does not mean ignoring poor performance or keeping quiet in the face of harassment or discrimination. Mercy is not the enablement of oppression. Instead, it means not letting a person's failures lead us to condemn the person in their entirety. When someone we work with makes a mistake, we are not to judge them as incompetent but to assist them in recovering from the error and learning how not to repeat it. When someone violates our trust, we are to hold that person accountable, while at the same time offering forgiveness that, if met with repentance, creates a path for reestablishing trust.

Second, this section of the letter reminds us of our responsibility to persevere as faithful Christians so that we might be the faithful "remnant" (Rom. 11:5) on behalf of those who have temporarily stumbled in their obedience of faith. When we see those around us fail, our task is not to judge them but to stand in for them. Perhaps our faithfulness can mitigate the damage done to others and even deliver those who caused it from harsh punishment. If we see a colleague mistreat a customer or a subordinate, for example, perhaps we can intervene to correct the situation before it becomes a firing offense. When we remember how close we have come to stumbling or how many times we have failed, our response to others' failings is mercy, as was Christ's. This does not mean we allow people to abuse others. It does mean we put ourselves at risk, as did Christ, for the redemption of people who have erred under the power of sin.

Third, these chapters remind us to demonstrate for the rest of our colleagues what the obedience of faith looks like in daily life and work. If we actually walk in newness of life (see "Walking in Newness of Life" in Romans 6) and set our minds on how our actions can bring a new quality of life to those around us (see "Living According to the Spirit Leads a New Quality of Life" in Romans 8), won't others be attracted to do the same? Our actions at work may be the loudest praise we can ever offer to God and the most attractive witness our co-workers ever see. God's desire is for everyone in the world to be reconciled to God and to one another. So every aspect of our work and life becomes an opportunity to bear witness for Christ—to be one of God's reconciling agents in the world.

Fourth, we need to remain humble. When we, like the factions to whom Paul was writing, judge our own position as superior to those around us, we imagine that we have the inside track to God. Paul speaks directly against this arrogance. We don't know everything about how God is at work in others. As General Peter Pace, retired chairman of the joint chiefs of staff of the U.S. Armed Forces, puts it, "You should always tell the truth as you know it, and you should understand that there is a whole lot that you don't know."[8]

The specific ways we embody this ministry of reconciliation in the world are as diverse as our work and workplaces. Thus we turn to Romans 12 for further direction from Paul on how to discern ways to carry out God's reconciling love in our work.

---

[8] Peter Pace, "General Peter Pace: The Truth as I Know It," *Ethix* 61 (September/October 2008), http://ethix.org/2008/10/10/the-truth-as-i-know-it.

The Community of Grace at Work (Romans 12)

Romans 12 highlights the social and community aspects of salvation. Paul was not writing to an individual but to the community of Christians in Rome, and his constant concern is their life together—with a special emphasis on their work. As we saw in Romans 1–3, salvation in Christ comprises reconciliation, righteousness and justice, and faith and faithfulness. Each of these has a communal aspect—reconciliation *with others*, justice *among people*, faithfulness *to others*.

Be Transformed by the Renewing of Your Minds (Romans 12:1–3)

To bring the communal aspect of salvation to life means a reorientation of our minds and wills from self-serving to community-serving.

> Do not be conformed to this world, but be transformed by the renewing of your minds, so that you may discern what is the will of God—what is good and acceptable and perfect. For by the grace given to me I say to everyone among you not to think of yourself more highly than you ought to think, but to think with sober judgment, each according to the measure of faith that God has assigned. (Rom. 12:2–3)

Let's begin with the second half of this passage, where Paul makes the communal aspect explicit. "I say to everyone among you not to think of yourself more highly than you ought to think." In other words, think less about yourself and more about others, more about the community. Later in chapter 12 Paul amplifies this by adding, "Love one another with mutual affection" (Rom. 12:10), "Contribute to the needs of the saints," "Extend hospitality to strangers" (Rom. 12:13), "Live in harmony with one another" (Rom. 12:17), and "Live peaceably with all" (Rom. 12:18).

The first part of this passage reminds us that we are unable to put others first without God's saving grace. As Paul points out in Romans 1, people are enslaved to a "debased mind" (Rom. 1:28), "futile in their thinking," darkened by "senseless minds" (Rom. 1:21), which results in doing every kind of evil to one another (Rom. 1:22–32). Salvation is liberation from this slavery of the mind, "so that you may discern what is the will of God—what is good and acceptable and perfect." Only if our minds are transformed from self-centeredness to other-centeredness—

imitating Christ, who sacrificed himself for others—can we put reconciliation, justice, and faithfulness ahead of self-serving aims.

With transformed minds, our purpose shifts from justifying our self-centered actions to bringing new life to others. For example, imagine that you are a shift supervisor at a restaurant and you become a candidate for promotion to manager. If your mind is not transformed, your chief goal will be to beat the other candidates. It will not seem hard to justify (to yourself) actions such as withholding information from the other candidates about supplier problems, ignoring sanitation issues that will become visible only in the others' shifts, spreading dissent among their workers, or avoiding collaboration on improving customer service. This will harm not only the other candidates but also their shift workers, the restaurant as a whole, and its customers. On the other hand, if your mind is transformed to care first about others, then you will help the other candidates perform well, not only for their sake but also for the benefit of the restaurant and its workers and customers.

Sacrificing for the Sake of the Community (Romans 12:1–3)

Needless to say, putting others ahead of ourselves requires sacrifice. "Present your bodies as a living sacrifice," Paul exhorts (Rom. 12:1). The words *bodies* and *living* emphasize that Paul means practical actions in the world of daily life and work. All believers become living sacrifices by offering their time, talent, and energy in work that benefits other people and/or God's entire creation.

We can offer a living sacrifice to God every waking moment of our lives. We do it when we forgive someone who transgresses against us in our workplace or when we take the risk to help heal a dispute between others. We offer a living sacrifice when we forego unsustainable use of the earth's resources in pursuit of our own comfort. We offer a living sacrifice when we take on less-than-satisfying work because supporting our family matters more to us than finding the perfect job. We become a living sacrifice when we leave a rewarding position so our spouse can accept a dream job in another city. We become a living sacrifice when, as a boss, we take the blame for a mistake a subordinate makes in his or her work.

Involving the Community in Your Decisions (Romans 12:1–3)

The transformation of the mind "so that you may discern what is the will of God" (Rom. 12:2) comes hand in hand with involving the community of faith in our decisions. As those in the process of being saved, we bring others into our decision-making processes. The word Paul uses for "discern" is literally "to test" or "to approve" in Greek (*dokimazein*). Our decisions must be tested and approved by other believers before we can have confidence that we have discerned the will of God. Paul's warning "not to think of yourself more highly than you ought to think" (Rom. 12:3) applies to our decision-making capability. Don't think you have the wisdom, the moral stature, the breadth of knowledge, or anything else needed to discern God's will by yourself. "Do not claim to be wiser than you are" (Rom. 12:6). Only by involving other members of the faithful community, with its diversity of gifts and wisdom (Rom. 12:4–8) living in harmony with one another (Rom. 12:16), can we develop, test, and approve reliable decisions.

This is more challenging than we might like to admit. We may gather to receive moral teaching as a community, but how often do we actually talk to one another when making moral decisions? Often decisions are made by the person in charge deliberating individually, perhaps after receiving input from a few advisors. We tend to operate this way because moral discussions are uncomfortable, or "hot" as Ronald Heifetz puts it. People don't like to have heated conversations because "most people want to maintain the status quo, avoiding the tough issues."[9] In addition, we often feel that community decision making is a threat to whatever power we possess. But making decisions on our own usually just means following preconceived biases, in other words, being "conformed to this world" (Rom. 12:2).

This raises a difficulty in the sphere of work. What if we don't work in a community of faith, but in a secular company, government, academic institution, or other setting? We could assess our actions communally with our co-workers, but they may not be attuned to the will of God. We could assess our actions communally with our small group

---

[9] Martin Linsky and Ronald A. Heifetz, *Leadership on the Line: Staying Alive Through the Dangers of Leading* (Boston: Harvard Business Review Press, 2002), 114.

or others from our church, but they probably will not understand our work very well. Either—or both—of these practices is better than nothing. But better still would be to gather a group of believers from our own workplace—or at least believers who work in similar situations—and reflect on our actions with them. If we want to assess how well our actions as programmers, fire fighters, civil servants, or school teachers (for example) implement reconciliation, justice, and faithfulness, who better to reflect with than other Christian programmers, fire fighters, civil servants, or school teachers? (See "Equipping Churches Encourage Everyone to Take Responsibility" in *The Equipping Church* at www .theologyofwork.org for more on this topic.)

Work as Members of One Another (Romans 12:4–8)

One essential practical application of walking in newness of life is to recognize how much we all depend on one another's work. "For as in the body we have many members, and not all of the members have the same function, so we, who are many, are one body in Christ, and individually we are members one of another" (Rom. 12:4–5). This interdependence is not a weakness, but a gift from God. As we are being saved by God, we become more integrated with one another.

Paul applies this to the work that each of us does in our particular role. "We have gifts that differ" (Rom. 12:6a) he notes, and when he names a few of them, we see that they are forms of work: prophecy, ministry, teaching, exhortation, generosity, leadership, and compassion. Each of them is a "grace given to us" (Rom. 12:6b) that enables us to work for the good of the community.

Paul develops this process in the context of a specific community—the church. This is fitting because the entire letter revolves around a problem in the church—the conflict between Jewish and Gentile believers. But the list is not particularly "churchy." All of them are equally applicable to work outside the church. Prophecy—"to proclaim a divinely imparted message" or "to bring light to something that is hidden"[10]—is the ability to apply God's word to dark situations, something desperately needed

---

[10] Gerhard Kittel, Gerhard Friedrich, and Geoffrey William Bromiley, eds., *Theological Dictionary of the New Testament* (Grand Rapids: Eerdmans, 1985), 960.

in every workplace. Ministry—with its cognate "administration"—is the ability to organize work so that it does in fact serve those it's supposed to serve, e.g., customers, citizens, or students. Another term for it is "management." Teaching, exhortation (or "encouragement"), and leadership are obviously as applicable to secular settings as to church. So is generosity, when we remember that giving our time, our skills, our patience, or our expertise to assist others at work are all forms of generosity.

Compassion is a vastly underrated element of work. While we might be tempted to view compassion as a hindrance in the competitive world of work, it is actually essential for doing our work well. The value of our work comes not merely from putting in hours, but from caring about how our goods or services serve others—in other words, by compassion. Autoworkers who do not *care* whether their parts are put on properly are of no use to the company, customers, or co-workers, and will sooner or later be candidates for dismissal. Or if the auto *company* doesn't care whether its workers care about its customers, the customers will soon enough switch to another brand. The exceptions to this are products and services that intentionally profit from customers' weaknesses—addictive substances, pornography, products that play on fears about body image and the like. To make money in cases like this, it may be necessary *not* to have compassion for customers. The very fact that it's possible to make money from harming customers in these fields suggests that Christians should try to avoid those workplaces in which compassion is not essential to success. Legitimate occupations make money from meeting people's true needs, not from exploiting their weaknesses.

With all these gifts, the life-giving power of God is experienced in particular *acts* and ways of *doing* things. In other words, the power of God that enriches people's lives comes through concrete *actions* taken by the followers of Jesus. God's grace produces action in God's people for the good of others.

Specific Behavioral Principles to Guide Moral Discernment (Romans 12:9–21)

Paul identifies specific guiding principles to help us serve as conduits to others for God's life-giving power. He introduces this section with his overarching concern to let love be genuine—or, literally, "unhypocritical" (Rom. 12:9). The rest of Romans 12:9–13 elaborates on genuine love, including honor, patience in suffering, perseverance in prayer, generosity to those in need, and hospitality to everyone.

Of particular note is Romans 12:16–18, where Paul encourages the Romans to "live in harmony with one another." Specifically, he says, this means associating with the least powerful in the community, resisting the urge to repay evil for evil, and, whenever possible, living peaceably with everyone.

If we have genuine love, then we care about the people we work for and among. By definition, when we work, we do so at least partly as a means to an end. But we can never treat the people we work among as a means to an end. Each is inherently valuable in his or her own right, so much so that Christ died for each one. This is genuine love, to treat each person as one for whom Christ died and rose again to bring new life.

We show genuine love when we honor the people with whom we work, calling everyone by name regardless of their status, and respecting their families, cultures, languages, aspirations, and the work they do. We show genuine love when we are patient with a subordinate who makes a mistake, a student who learns slowly, a co-worker whose disability makes us uncomfortable. We show genuine love through hospitality to the new employee, the late-night arrival, the disoriented patient, the stranded passenger, the just-promoted boss. Every day we face the possibility someone will do us some evil, small or great. But our protection is not to do evil to others in self-defense, nor to be worn down into despair, but to "overcome evil with good" (Rom. 12:21). We cannot do this by our own power, but only by living in the Spirit of Christ.

Living under the Power of God (Romans 13)

"Let every person be subject to the governing authorities," says Paul. "Those authorities that exist have been instituted by God" (Rom. 13:1). Knowing that the systems of Rome's rule were not in line with God's justice, this counsel must have been hard for some in the Roman churches to hear. How could obeying the idolatrous, ruthless Roman emperor be a way of living in the Spirit? Paul's answer is that God is sovereign over every earthly authority and that God will deal with the authorities at the right time. Even Rome, powerful though it might have been, was ultimately subject to the power of God.

In the workplace, it is often true that "rulers are not a terror to good conduct, but to bad" (Rom. 13:3). Bosses often organize work effectively and create a fair environment for ironing out disputes. Courts regularly settle cases involving patents, land title, labor relations, and contracts equitably. Regulators often serve to protect the environment, prevent fraud, enforce workplace safety, and ensure equal access to housing opportunities. Police generally apprehend criminals and assist the innocent. The fact that even nonbelieving authorities so often get things right is a mark of God's grace in the world.

But authorities in business, government, and every workplace can get things devastatingly wrong and sometimes abuse power for selfish ends. When this happens, it helps to distinguish between human-generated powers (even if they are significant) and the power of God that lies over, behind, and through all of creation. Often the human powers are so much closer to us that they can tend to block out our sense of God's movement in our lives. This passage serves as an encouragement to discern where God is active and to join our lives to those activities of God that will foster true fullness of life for us and for all.

People who worked at Tyco International when Dennis Kozlowski was CEO must have wondered why he was allowed to get away with raiding the company's coffers to pay for his outrageous personal lifestyle. We can imagine that those who tried to work with integrity may have felt afraid for their jobs. Some otherwise ethical people may have succumbed to the pressure to participate in Kozlowski's schemes. But eventually Kozlowski was found out, charged, and convicted of grand larceny, conspiracy, and fraud.[11] Those who trusted that justice would eventually be restored ended up on the right side of the story.

Paul offers practical advice to the Roman Christians, who were living in the center of the most powerful human authorities the Western world had ever known. Obey the law, pay your taxes and commercial

---

[11] Michael J. De La Merced, "Released from Prison," *New York Times,* December 4, 2013, B6.

fees, give respect and honor to those in positions of authority (Rom. 12:7). Perhaps some had thought that, as Christians, they should rebel against Roman injustice. But Paul seems to see self-centeredness in their attitude, rather than God-centeredness. Self-serving rebelliousness will not prepare them for God's "day" (Rom. 13:12) that is coming.

For example, in some countries tax evasion is so commonplace that needed services cannot be provided, bribery (to enable the evasion) corrupts officials at every level, and the tax burden is unfairly distributed. The government loses legitimacy in the eyes of both the taxpayers and the tax evaders. Civil instability slows economic growth and human development. No doubt, much of the money that is collected is used for purposes inconsistent with Christian values, and many Christians may respond by evading taxes along with everyone else. But what would happen if Christians committed, in an organized fashion, to pay their taxes *and* to monitor the government's use of funds? It could take decades to reform government in this manner, but would it eventually work? Paul's argument in Romans 12 suggests it would.

Many Christians live in democracies today, which gives the additional responsibility to vote for wise laws that express God's justice as best we can. Once the votes are counted, we have a responsibility to obey the laws and the authorities, even if we disagree with them. Paul's words imply that we are to obey the legitimate authorities, even while we may be working to change unjust ones through democratic means.

In every sphere of life, we have an ongoing responsibility to resist and to transform all unjust systems, always putting the common good above self-interest. Even so, we are to show respect to the authorities, whether at work, school, church, government, or civic life. We believe that change will occur not because we express outrage, but because God is sovereign over all.

Paul completes chapter 13 noting that by loving other people, we fulfill the commandments. Living in the Spirit inherently fulfills the Jewish law, even by those who don't know it. He reiterates that this comes not by human striving, but by the power of Christ in us. "Put on the Lord Jesus Christ," he concludes (Rom. 13:14).

Welcoming—Living Peacefully with Different Values and Opinions (Romans 14–15)

At this point in the letter, Paul has finished developing his method of moral reasoning. Now he pauses to give some implications arising from it in the unique context of the Roman churches, namely, in the disputes among believers.

The chief implication for the Roman churches is welcome. The Roman Christians are to welcome one another. It's not hard to see how Paul derives this implication. The goal of moral reasoning, according to Romans 6, is to "walk in newness of life," meaning to bring a *new quality of life* to those around us. If you are in a broken relationship with someone, welcome is inherently a new quality of life. Welcome is reconciliation in practice. Quarrels seek to exclude others, but welcome seeks to include them, even when it means respecting areas of disagreement.

Welcoming Overcomes Quarrels over Differing Opinions (Romans 14:1–23)

"Welcome those who are weak in faith, but not for the purpose of quarreling over opinions," begins Paul (Rom. 14:1). The "weak in faith" may be those who lack confidence in their own convictions on disputed issues (see Rom. 14:23) and rely on strict rules to govern their actions. Specifically, some of the Jewish Christians kept the strictures of Jewish dietary laws and were offended by other Christians consuming non-kosher meat and drink. Apparently they refused even to eat with those who did not keep kosher.[12] Although they regarded their strictness as a strength, Paul says it becomes a weakness when it causes them to judge those who do not share their conviction. Paul says that those who keep kosher "must not pass judgment on those who eat [non-kosher meat]."

Nonetheless, Paul's response to their weakness is not to argue with them, nor to ignore their beliefs, but to do whatever will make them feel welcome. He tells those who do not keep kosher not to flaunt their freedom to eat anything, because doing so would require the kosher-keepers

---

[12] Wright, "The Letter to the *Romans*," 735.

either to break fellowship with them or to violate their consciences. If there is no kosher meat to be found, then the non-kosher should join with the kosher and eat only vegetables, rather than demanding that the kosher-keepers violate their consciences. "It is wrong for you to make others fall by what you eat," Paul says (Rom. 14:20).

Both groups feel strongly that their views are morally important. The strong believe that for Gentiles to keep kosher is a refusal of God's grace in Christ Jesus. The weak believe that not keeping kosher—and the merely eating with people who don't keep kosher—is an affront to God and a violation of the Jewish law. The argument is heated because freedom in Christ and obedience to God's covenants are truly important moral and religious issues. But relationships in the community are even more important. Living in Christ is not about being right or wrong on any particular issue. It is about being in right relationship with God and with one another, about "peace and joy in the Holy Spirit" (Rom. 14:17).

Moral disagreements can be even more difficult at work, where there is less common ground. An interesting aspect in this regard is Paul's special concern for the weak. Although he tells both groups not to judge each other, he places a greater practical burden on the strong. "We who are strong ought to put up with the failings of the weak, and not to please ourselves" (Rom. 15:1). Our model for this is Jesus, "who did not please himself" (Rom. 15:3). This means that those who are in the right, or in the majority, or who otherwise have the most power are called to voluntarily refrain from violating the consciences of others. In most workplaces, the opposite occurs. The weak must accommodate themselves to the dictates of the strong, even if doing so violates their conscience.

Imagine, for example, that someone in your workplace has religious or moral convictions that require a particular modesty of dress, say covering the hair or the shoulders or legs. These convictions could be a form of weakness, to use Paul's terminology, if they make that person uncomfortable around others who do not conform to their idea of modest dress. Probably you would not object to the person wearing such modest dress themselves. But Paul's argument implies that *you* and all your co-workers should also dress modestly according to the other person's standards, at least if you want to make your workplace a place of welcome and reconciliation. The strong (those not hampered by legalism about dress codes) are to welcome the weak (those offended by others' dress) by accommodating to their weakness.

Remember that Paul does not want us to demand that others accommodate to our compunctions. That would turn us into the weak, whereas Paul wants us to become strong in faith. We should not be the ones tsk-tsk-ing about others' dress, language, or taste in music on the job. Imagine instead that Christians had a reputation for making everyone feel welcome, rather than for judging others' tastes and habits. Would that help or hinder Christ's mission in the world of work?

Welcoming Builds up the Community (Romans 14:19–15:33)

Another aspect of welcoming is that it strengthens the community. "Each of us must please the neighbor for the good purpose of building up the neighbor" (Rom. 15:3) in much the same way that a welcoming host makes sure that a visit strengthens the guest. The "neighbor" here is another member of the community. "Let us then pursue what makes for peace and *mutual* upbuilding," Paul says (Rom. 14:19). Mutual upbuilding means working together in community.

From chapters 14 and 15, we see that welcoming is a powerful practice. Paul is not talking about simply saying hello with smiles on our faces. He is talking about engaging in deep moral discernment as a community, yet remaining in warm relationship with those who come to different moral conclusions, even on important matters. As far as Paul is concerned, the continuing relationships in the community are more important than the particular moral conclusions. Relationships bring a quality of life to the community that far exceeds any possible satisfaction from being right about an issue or judging another to be wrong. It also is a more attractive witness to the world around us. "Welcome one another, therefore, just as Christ has welcomed you, *for the glory of God*" (Rom. 15:7). When we welcome one another, the final result by God's mercy (Rom. 15:9) is that "all the peoples praise him" (Rom. 15:12).

A Community of Leaders (Romans 16)

Chapter 16 of Romans belies many people's common assumptions about the nature of Paul's work—namely, that he was a solitary, heroic figure, enduring hardships to carry out his lonely and exalted calling to spread the gospel among the Gentiles. In Romans 16, however, Paul makes it clear that his work was a community effort. Paul mentions twenty-nine co-workers by name, plus many more by terms such as "the church in their house" and "the brothers and sisters who are with them." Paul's list sets equal value upon the work of both women and men, without distinct roles for either, and seems to include people of various social stations. Several are clearly wealthy, and some of those may be freedmen and freedwomen. Others may well be slaves. Paul praises the particular work of many, such as those who "risked their necks" (Rom. 16:3), "worked very hard" (Rom. 16:6), "were in prison with me" (Rom. 16:7), "worked hard in the Lord" (Rom. 16:12), or acted "as a mother to me" (Rom. 16:13). He mentions the work of Tertius "the writer [scribe] of this letter" (Rom. 16:22) and Erastus "the city treasurer" (Rom. 16:23).

Observing Paul within such a wide circle of co-workers undercuts the modern Western emphasis on individuality, especially in the work-place. Like everyone he names, Paul worked *in* community *for the good of* community. This final section of the letter lets us know that the gospel is *everyone's* work. Not all are apostles. We are not all called to leave our jobs and travel around preaching. Paul's list of the varied gifts of service in Romans 12:6–8 makes that clear. No matter what kind of work occupies our time, we are called to act as servants of the good news of God's salvation for all people. (See "Work as Members of One Another," in Romans 12:4–8.)

These greetings also remind us that church leaders are workers. It is sometimes tempting to see Paul's work as somehow distinct from other kinds of work. But Paul's repeated reference to the *work* of those he names reminds us that what is true of Paul's ministry is true of all work-places. Here, where we spend much of our time each week, is where we will either learn to walk in newness of life (Rom. 6:4)—or remain mired in the power of death. In our workplace relationships we are invited to seek the good of the other, according to the model of Christ. In the often

mundane work of our minds and hearts and hands is where we are offered the chance to become channels of God's grace for others.

In the final verses of Romans, it is apparent that no one's work stands
in isolation; it is interwoven with the work of others. Paul recognizes
those who have gone before him, passing on their faith to him, those who
have worked beside him, and those who have risked their lives for him
and for their common work. This point of view calls each of us to look
at the whole fabric of community that constitutes our places of work, to
consider all the lives intertwined with ours, supporting and enhancing
what we are able to do, all who give up something that they might want
for themselves in order to benefit us and to benefit the work that goes
beyond us into God's world.

Conclusion to Romans

Paul's dominant concern in Romans is salvation—God's reconciliation of the world through the cross of Jesus Christ. In Christ, God is
working to reconcile all people to himself, to reconcile people to one
another, and to redeem the created order from the evil forces of sin,
death, and decay. Paul's concern is not abstract but practical. His aim is
to heal the divisions among Christians in Rome and to enable them to
work together to accomplish God's will for their lives and work.

In this setting, Paul shows how salvation comes to us as a free gift
bought by God's faithfulness in the cross of Christ and by God's grace
in bringing us to faith in Christ. In no way does this free gift imply that
God does not care about the work we do and the way we work. Instead,
Paul shows how receiving God's grace transforms both the work we do
and the way we do it. Although we don't work to earn salvation, as God
is saving us, he gives us the amazing diversity of gifts needed to serve
one another and build up our communities. As a result, we walk in a new
way of life, bringing life in Christ to those around us and, in God's time,
to the fullness of creation.

1 Corinthians and Work

Introduction to 1 Corinthians

No other letter in the New Testament gives us a more practical picture of applying the Christian faith to the day-to-day issues of life and work than 1 Corinthians. Topics such as career and calling, the lasting value of work, overcoming individual limitations, leadership and service, the development of skills and abilities (or "gifts"), fair wages, environmental stewardship, and the use of money and possessions are prominent in the letter. The unifying perspective on all these topics is love. Love is the purpose, means, motivation, gift, and glory behind all work done in Christ.

The City of Corinth (1 Corinthians)

The Apostle Paul's first letter to the church in Corinth, which he founded on his second missionary journey (AD 48–51), is a treasure trove of practical theology for Christians facing everyday challenges. It provides Paul's instruction to Christians grappling with real-life issues, including conflicts of loyalty, class differences, conflicts between personal freedom and the common good, and the difficulty of leading a diverse group of people to accomplish a shared mission.

In Paul's time, Corinth was the most important city in Greece. Sitting astride the isthmus that joins the Peloponnesian Peninsula to mainland Greece, Corinth controlled both the Saronic Gulf to the east and the Gulf of Corinth to the north. Merchants wanted to avoid the difficult, dangerous sea journey around the fingers of the Peloponnese, so a great deal of the goods flowing between Rome and the western empire and the rich ports of the eastern Mediterranean were hauled across this isthmus. Almost all of it passed through Corinth, making it one of the empire's great commercial centers. Strabo, an older contemporary of Paul, noted that

"Corinth is called 'wealthy' because of its commerce, since it is situated on the Isthmus and is master of two harbors, of which the one leads straight to Asia, and the other to Italy; and it makes easy the exchange of merchandise from both countries that are so far distant from each other."[1]

The city had something of a boomtown atmosphere during the middle of the first century as freed slaves, veterans, merchants, and tradesmen streamed into the city. Though what we might now call "upward mobility" was elusive in the ancient world, Corinth was one place where it might be possible, with a little luck and a lot of hard work, to establish oneself and enjoy a reasonably good life.[2] This contributed to the unique ethos of Corinth, which viewed itself as prosperous and self-sufficient, a city whose core value was "entrepreneurial pragmatism in the pursuit of success."[3] Many cities in today's world aspire to this very ethos.

The Church in Corinth and Paul's Letters (1 Corinthians)

Paul arrived in Corinth in the winter of AD 49/50[4] and lived there for a year and a half. While there he supported himself by working in tentmaking—or perhaps leatherworking[5] (Acts 18:2), the trade he had learned as a boy—in the workshop of Aquila and Priscilla (see 1 Cor. 4:12). He lays out his reasons for following this course in 1 Corinthians 9 (see below), even though he could have taken advantage of full-time support as a missionary from the start, as indeed he later does (Acts 18:4 and 2 Cor. 11:9).

In any case, his Sabbath-day preaching in the synagogue soon bore fruit, and the church in Corinth was born. The church seems to have been made up of not more than a hundred people when Paul wrote 1 Corinthians. Some were Jews, while most were Gentiles. They met in

---

[1] Strabo, *Geographica* 8.6.20.

[2] Donald Engels, *Roman Corinth: An Alternative Model for the Classical City* (Chicago: University of Chicago Press, 1990), 49.

[3] Anthony C. Thiselton, *The First Epistle to the Corinthians: A Commentary on the Greek Text, New International Greek Testament Commentary* (Grand Rapids: Eerdmans, 2000), 4.

[4] Gordon Fee, *The First Epistle to the Corinthians* (Grand Rapids: Eerdmans, 1987), 5.

[5] Ronald F. Hock, *The Social Context of Paul's Ministry: Tentmaking and Apostleship* (Philadelphia: Fortress Press, 1980), 21–22.

the houses of two or three wealthier members, but most belonged to the large underclass that populated all urban centers.[6]

Paul continued to be keenly interested in the development of the church even after he left Corinth. Paul had written the congregation at least one letter prior to 1 Corinthians (1 Cor. 5:9) in order to address a problem that had come up after his departure. Members of the house of Chloe, who may have had business interests to attend to in Ephesus, visited Paul there and reported that the church in Corinth was in danger of coming apart at the seams over various divisions of opinion (1:11). In entrepreneurial Corinthian style, competing groups were creating parties around their favorite apostles in order to gain status for themselves (chs. 1–4). Many were up in arms due to serious differences over the sexual behavior and business ethics of some of their members (chs. 5–6). Then another group of representatives from the church arrived with a letter in hand (7:1, 16:17) querying Paul on a number of important issues, such as sex and marriage (ch. 7), the propriety of eating meat that had been previously offered to idols (chs. 8–10) and worship (chs. 11–14). Finally, Paul had also learned from one of these sources, or perhaps Apollos (see 16:12), that some in the Corinthian church were denying the future resurrection of believers (ch. 15).

These questions hardly grew out of academic discussions. The Corinthians wanted to know how as followers of Christ they should act in matters of daily life and work. Paul gives answers throughout 1 Corinthians, making it one of the most practical books of the New Testament.

All Are Called (1 Corinthians 1:1–3)

In the opening paragraph of 1 Corinthians, Paul lays out themes that he will address in more detail in the body of his letter. It is no coincidence that the concept of calling is front and center in the introduction. Paul states in the very first verse that he was "called to be an apostle of Christ Jesus by the will of God" (1:1). A strong conviction that he was called directly by God pervades Paul's letters (see e.g. Gal. 1:1) and is

---

[6] Wayne A. Meeks, *The First Urban Christians: The Social World of the Apostle Paul,* 2nd ed. (New Haven: Yale University Press, 2003), 51–73.

fundamental to his mission (see Acts 9:14–15). It lent him remarkable fortitude in the face of enormous challenges. Likewise, the Corinthian believers are "called" along with "all those who in every place call on the name of our Lord Jesus Christ" (1 Cor. 1:2). We will soon see that the basis of our calling is not individual satisfaction but community development. Although Paul doesn't develop this point until later in the letter (see 7:17–24), even at this juncture it is clear he thinks all believers are meant to pursue the calling designed for them by God.

Spiritual Resources Available
(1 Corinthians 1:4–9)

According to the conventions of ancient letter writing, a greeting was followed by a section in which the author praised the recipient.[7] In most of his letters, Paul modifies this literary form by offering thanksgiving rather than praise and by using a standard phrase much like we have here: "I give thanks to my God always for you . . ." (see 1:4, as well as Rom. 1:8; Phil. 1:3; Col. 1:3; 1 Thess. 1:2; and 2 Thess. 1:3). In this case, Paul expresses his thanks that the Corinthian believers have experienced the grace of God in Christ. This is more than some vague piety. Rather, Paul has something quite specific in mind. The believers in Corinth have been "enriched in [Christ]" (1 Cor. 1:5) so that they "are not lacking in any spiritual gift as you wait for the revealing of our Lord Jesus Christ" (1:7). Paul specifically names two gifts, speech and knowledge, that the Corinthian church enjoyed in abundance.

For our purposes, it is especially important to note that Paul is convinced that the believers in Corinth have received the spiritual resources they need to fulfill their calling. God has called them, and he has given them gifts that will enable them to be "blameless on the day of our Lord Jesus Christ" (1:8). Although the day of perfection has not arrived yet, whether at work or anywhere else, Christians already have access to the gifts that will come to complete fruition on that day.

---

[7] Peter T. O'Brien, *Introductory Thanksgivings in the Letters of Paul*, in vol. 49 of *Novum Testamentum* (Leiden: Brill, 1977), 11.

It is hard to imagine that all Corinthian Christians felt as if their work was a special occupation designed individually for them by God. Most of them were slaves or common laborers, as we will see. What Paul must mean is that whether or not each person's occupation seems special, God gives the gifts needed to make everyone's work contribute to God's plan for the world. No matter how insignificant our work seems, no matter how much we long to have a different job, the work we do now is important to God.

The Need for a Common Vision (1 Corinthians 1:10–17)

Paul states in thesis-like fashion what he is trying to accomplish by writing 1 Corinthians.[8] "I appeal to you, brothers and sisters, by the name of our Lord Jesus Christ, that all of you be in agreement and that there be no divisions among you, but that you be united in the same mind and the same purpose" (1 Cor. 1:10). The verb he uses in this final phrase is a metaphor that connotes mending of human relationships. Thus Paul is urging the Corinthians to overcome the factionalism that has damaged the unity of the church.

Modern Western culture highly values diversity, so we are in danger of construing Paul's injunctions negatively. He is not arguing for conformity of thought (as other passages make clear), but he understands quite clearly that a sense of common purpose and vision is essential. If there is continual strife and disagreement about basic values and convictions and no cohesion among its members, any organization is doomed to failure. Although Paul is writing to a church, we know he also thought Christians should contribute to the workings of society at large. "Be subject to rulers and authorities, to be obedient, to *be ready for every good work*" (Titus 3:1; emphasis added). Therefore, we should seek common purpose not only in church but also in the places we work. Our role as Christians is to do good work in unity and harmony with both believers and nonbelievers. This does not mean we acquiesce to immorality

---

[8] Margaret M. Mitchell, *Paul and the Rhetoric of Reconciliation* (Louisville: Westminster John Knox Press, 1993).

or injustice. It does mean that we develop good relationships, support co-workers, and care to do our work excellently. If we cannot in good conscience do our work wholeheartedly, we need to find someplace else to work, rather than grumble or shirk.

Friends in Low Places (1 Corinthians 1:18–31)

Paul reminds the congregation in Corinth that most of them do not come from the ranks of the privileged classes. "Not many of you were wise by human standards, not many were powerful, not many were of noble birth" (1 Cor. 1:26). But the effectiveness of the church did not depend on having people with all the connections, educations, or fortunes. God accomplishes his purposes with ordinary people. We have already seen that the value of our work is based on God's gifts, not on our credentials. But Paul draws a further point. Because we are nobody special by nature, we can never treat other people as insignificant.

> God chose what is foolish in the world to shame the wise; God chose what is weak in the world to shame the strong; God chose what is low and despised in the world, things that are not, to reduce to nothing things that are, *so that no one might boast in the presence of God.* (1 Cor. 1:27–29; emphasis added)

Since Paul's day, many Christians have attained positions of power, wealth, and status. His words remind us that we insult God if we allow these things to make us arrogant, disrespectful, or abusive toward people in lower-status positions. Many workplaces still accord special privileges to higher-ranking workers, bearing no relevance to the actual work at hand. Aside from pay differences, high-status workers may enjoy fancier offices, first-class travel, executive dining rooms, reserved parking, better benefits packages, company-paid club memberships, residences, drivers, personal services, and other perquisites. They may receive special deference—for example, being called "Mr." or "Ms." or "Professor"—when others in the organization are called by first names only. In some cases, special treatment may be appropriate, based on the nature of the work performed and organizational responsibilities. But in other cases, such privileges may create unwarranted gradations of human worth and dignity. Paul's point is that such distinctions have no place among the people of God. If we enjoy—or suffer—such distinctions at work, we might ask ourselves whether they contradict the equal dignity of persons in the presence of God and, if so, what we might do to remedy them.

It Takes All Sorts (1 Corinthians 3:1–9)

We noted above that the main problem in the Corinthian church was that of factionalism. Cliques were forming under the banner of Paul's name versus the name of Apollos, another missionary to the Corinthian church. Paul will have none of this. He and Apollos are simply servants. Although they have different roles, neither of them is more valuable than the other. The planter (Paul) and the irrigator (Apollos)—to use an agricultural metaphor—are equally vital to the success of the harvest, and neither is responsible for the growth of the crop. That is entirely God's doing. The various workers have a common goal in mind (a bounteous harvest), but they have different tasks in line with their abilities and calling. All are necessary and no one can do every necessary task.

Paul, in other words, is aware of the importance of diversification and specialization. In his famous 1958 essay, "I, Pencil," economist Leonard Read followed the course of the manufacture of a common pencil, making the point that no single person knows how to make one. It is actually the product of several sophisticated processes, only one of which a given individual can master. By the grace of God, different people are able to play different roles in the world's workplaces. But specialization at times leads to interpersonal or interdepartmental factionalism, poor lines of communication, and even personal vilification. If Christians believe what Paul says about the God-given nature of different roles, perhaps we can take the lead in bridging dysfunctional divides in our organizations. If we are able simply to treat others with respect and value the work of people different from ourselves, we may be making significant contributions to our workplaces.

An important application of this is the value of investing in worker development, whether our own or that of people around us. In Paul's letters, including 1 Corinthians, it sometimes seems that Paul never does anything himself (see, for example, 14–15) but instructs others how to do it. This is not arrogance or laziness, but mentoring. He would far rather invest in training effective workers and leaders than in calling all the shots himself. As we mature in serving Christ in our places of work, perhaps we will find ourselves doing more to equip others and less to make ourselves look good.

Do Good Work (1 Corinthians 3:10–17)

Paul introduces the metaphor of a building under construction in order to make a new point—do good work. This point is so important to understanding the value of work that it is worth including the passage in its entirety here.

> According to the grace of God given to me, like a skilled master builder I laid a foundation, and someone else is building on it. Each builder must choose with care how to build on it. For no one can lay any foundation other than the one that has been laid; that foundation is Jesus Christ. Now if anyone builds on the foundation with gold, silver, precious stones, wood, hay, straw—the work of each builder will become visible, for the Day will disclose it, because it will be revealed with fire, and the fire will test what sort of work each has done. If what has been built on the foundation survives, the builder will receive a reward. If the work is burned up, the builder will suffer loss; the builder will be saved, but only as through fire. (1 Cor. 3:10–15)

This may be the most direct statement of the eternal value of earthly work in all of Scripture. The work we do on earth—to the extent we do it according to the ways of Christ—survives into eternity. Paul is speaking specifically of the work done by the community of the church, which he likens to a temple. Paul compares himself to a "skilled master builder" who has laid the foundation, which is, of course, Christ himself. Others build on top of this foundation, and each one is responsible for his own work. Paul likens good work to gold, silver, and precious stones, and shabby work to wood, hay, and straw. Though some have tried to assign specific meanings to each of these materials, it is more likely that the difference is simply that some materials have the ability to withstand testing by fire while others do not.

Paul is not making any judgment about any individual's salvation, for even if anyone's work fails the test, "the builder will be saved." This passage is not about the relationship between a believer's "good works" and his heavenly reward, though it has often been read in that way. Instead, Paul is concerned with the church as a whole and how its leaders work within the church. If they contribute to the unity of the church, they will be commended. If, however, their ministry results in strife and factionalism, they are actually provoking God's wrath, because he passionately protects his living temple from those who would destroy it (vv. 16–17).

Although Paul is writing about the work of building a Christian community, his words apply to all kinds of work. As we have seen, Paul regards Christian work to include the work believers do under secular authority as well as in the church. Whatever our work, it will be evaluated impartially by God. The final assize will be better than any performance review, since God judges with perfect justice—unlike human bosses, however just or unjust they may be—and he is able to factor in our intent, our limitations, our motives, our compassion, and his mercy. God has called all believers to work in whatever circumstances they find themselves, and he has given us specific gifts to fulfill that calling. He expects us to use them responsibly for his purposes, and he will inspect our work. And to the degree that our work is done in excellence, by his gifts and grace, it will become part of God's eternal kingdom. That should motivate us—even more than our employer's approval or our paycheck— to do as good a job as we possibly can.

Leadership as Service (1 Corinthians 4:1–4)

In this passage, Paul offers a definitive statement of what it means to be a leader: "Think of us in this way, as servants of Christ and stewards of God's mysteries" (1 Cor. 4:1). "Us" refers to the apostolic leaders through whom the Corinthians had come to faith and to whom the various factions in the church claimed allegiance (1 Cor. 4:6). Paul uses two words in this verse to elaborate what he means. The first, *hypēretēs* ("servants"), denotes an attendant, a servant who waits on or assists someone. In this sense, leaders attend personally to the needs of the people they lead. Leaders are not exalted, but humbled, by accepting leadership. The job requires patience, personal engagement, and individual attention to the needs of followers. The second is *oikonomos* ("stewards"), which describes a servant or slave who manages the affairs of a household or estate. The chief distinction in this position is trust. The steward is trusted to manage the affairs of the household for the benefit of the owner. Likewise, the leader is trusted to manage the group for the benefit of all its members, rather than the leader's personal benefit. This quality is explicitly ascribed to Timothy (2 Cor. 4:17), Tychicus (Eph. 6:21; Col. 4:7), Paul (1 Tim. 1:12), Antipas (Rev. 2:13), and, above all, Christ (2 Tim. 2:13; Heb. 2:17). These are the kinds of people God relies on to carry out his plan for his kingdom.

Modern workplaces often set up systems to reward leaders for using their teams to accomplish the organization's objectives. This is probably a wise practice, unless it encourages leaders to attain such rewards at the expense of the people they lead. Leaders are indeed responsible to accomplish—or better yet, exceed—the work their teams are assigned to do. But it is not legitimate to sacrifice the needs of the group in order to obtain the leader's personal rewards. Instead, leaders are called to accomplish the group's goals *by meeting the needs* of the group.

Working with Nonbelievers (1 Corinthians 5:9–10)

In chapter 5, Paul introduces the question of working with nonbelievers, a question he will explore more fully in chapter 10 and ultimately in 2 Corinthians 6 (see "Working with Nonbelievers" in 2 Corinthians). At this point, he says simply that Christians are not called to withdraw from the world because of fears about ethics. "I wrote to you in my letter not to associate with sexually immoral persons—not at all meaning the immoral of this world, or the greedy and robbers, or idolaters, since you would then need to go out of the world" (1 Cor. 5:9–10). By mentioning the greedy, robbers, and idolaters, he explicitly indicates he is including the work world in his instructions. Although we are to avoid immorality ourselves, and we are not to associate with immoral *Christians*, Paul expects us to work with nonbelievers, even those who do not observe God's ethical principles. Needless to say, this is a difficult proposition, although he defers getting into specifics until chapter 10. The point he makes here is simply that Christians are forbidden from trying to create some kind of Christian-only economy and leaving the world to fend for itself. Instead, we are called to take our place in the work of the world alongside the people of the world.

Bloom Where You Are Planted
(1 Corinthians 7:20–24)

In the middle of a chapter that deals primarily with issues relating to marriage and singleness, Paul makes an important statement about calling and work. Other things being equal, believers should remain in the life situation in which they found themselves when they were converted (7:20). The specific question that Paul is dealing with does not directly impinge upon most people in the Western world, though it is critical in many parts of the globe today. What should believers who are slaves do if they have the chance to gain freedom?

Slavery in the ancient world was a complex phenomenon that is by no means identical to its modern manifestations, neither that of the pre-Civil War American South, nor debt bondage in contemporary South Asia, nor sex trafficking in virtually every country on earth. Certainly, it was equally heinous in many cases, but some slaves, particularly the household slaves Paul probably has in mind here, were better off, at least economically, than many free people. Many educated people, including doctors and accountants, actually chose slavery for precisely that reason. Thus, for Paul, it was a genuinely open question whether slavery or freedom would be the better lot in any given situation. Modern forms of slavery, on the other hand, always severely diminish the lives of those enslaved.

The question then is not whether slavery should be abolished, but whether slaves should seek to become free. It is difficult to determine the precise nature of Paul's instruction here because the Greek of 1 Corinthians 7:21 is ambiguous, so much so that it is open to two divergent

interpretations. As the NRSV and a number of commentators understand it, it should be rendered as follows: "Were you a slave when called?
Do not be concerned about it. Even if you can gain your freedom, make
use of your present condition now more than ever." Equally possible
(and more likely, in our opinion), however, is the sense given in the NIV,
NASB, and KJV, which is, "Were you a slave when you were called? Don't
let it trouble you—although if you can gain your freedom, do so" (NIV).
Whatever Paul's advice, his underlying belief is that, compared to the
difference between in Christ and not in Christ, the difference between
being a slave and a free person is relatively minor. "For whoever was
called in the Lord as a slave is a freed person belonging to the Lord, just
as whoever was free when called is a slave of Christ" (7:22). Thus, if there
are no compelling reasons to change your status, it is probably best to
remain in the situation in which you were called.

Paul's teaching here has important application for the workplace.
While we may feel that getting the right job is the most important factor
in serving God or experiencing the life he intends for us, God is much
more concerned that we make the most of every job we have over the
course of our lives. In a given instance, there may be good reasons to
change jobs or even professions. Fine, go ahead and do so. Yet any morally legitimate job can fulfill God's calling, so don't make finding your
life's work *into* your life's work. There is no hierarchy of more godly and
less godly professions. Certainly this cautions us against believing that
God calls the most serious Christians into church jobs.

Maintain the Proper Perspective
(1 Corinthians 7:29–31)

Paul addresses the question of whether the promised return of the
Lord implies that Christians should abandon ordinary daily life, including work.

> I mean, brothers and sisters, the appointed time has grown short; from
> now on . . . let those who buy [be] as though they had no possessions, and
> those who deal with the world as though they had no dealings with it. For
> the present form of this world is passing away. (1 Cor. 7:29–31)

Apparently some believers neglected family duties and ceased working, in the same way you might neglect to sweep the floor before moving to a new house. Paul had previously dealt with this situation in the church in Thessalonica and given unambiguous instructions.

> Anyone unwilling to work should not eat. For we hear that some of you are living in idleness, mere busybodies, not doing any work. Now such persons we command and exhort in the Lord Jesus Christ to do their work quietly and to earn their own living. (2 Thess. 3:10–12)

Paul's logic will be easier to understand if we recognize that verse 29 does not indicate merely that "the time is short" in the sense that Jesus' second coming is almost here. Paul uses a verb here that describes how an object is pushed together (*synestalmenos*), so that it becomes shorter or smaller as a whole. "Time has been compressed" might be a better translation, as suggested by the NASB rendering, or "Time has been shortened." What Paul apparently means is that since Christ has come, the end of the vast expanse of time has at last become visible. "The future outcome of this world has become crystal clear," writes scholar David E. Garland.[9] Verse 31 explains that "the present form of this world is passing away." The "present form" has the sense of "the way things are" in our fallen world of damaged social and economic relationships. Paul wants his readers to understand that Christ's coming has already effected a change in the very fabric of life. The values and aspirations that are simply taken for granted in the present way of doing things are no longer operative for believers.

The proper response to the compression of time is not to cease working but to work differently. The old attitudes toward everyday life and its affairs must be replaced. This brings us back to the paradoxical statements in 1 Corinthians 7:29–31. We should buy, yet be as though we have no possessions. We should deal with the world as though not dealing with the world as we know it. That is, we may make use of the things this world has to offer, but we shouldn't accept the world's values and principles when they get in the way of God's kingdom. The things we buy, we should

---

[9] David E. Garland, *1 Corinthians*, Baker Exegetical Commentary on the New Testament (Grand Rapids: Baker, 2003), 329.

employ for the good of others instead of holding tightly to them. When we bargain in the market, we should seek the good of the person from whom we buy, not just our own interests. In other words, Paul is calling believers to "a radically new understanding of their relationship to the world."[10]

Our old attitude is that we work to make life more comfortable and satisfying for ourselves and those close to us. We seek to gather things into our possession that we think will bring us status, security, and advantage over others. We compartmentalize worship of our gods first, then attention to our marriage second, then work third, and then civic engagement fourth, if we have any time and energy left. The new attitude is that we work to benefit ourselves, those close to us, *and all those for whom Jesus worked and died.* We seek to release the things in our possession for use where they will make the world more as God desires it. We integrate our lives of worship, family, work, and society and seek to invest in—rather than shuffle around—physical, intellectual, cultural, moral, and spiritual capital. In this we emulate the forefather of the people of God, Abraham, to whom God said, "I will bless you, and make your name great, so that you will be a blessing" (Gen. 12:2).

Everyone Gets Their Fair Share (1 Corinthians 9:7–10)

In chapter 9, Paul explains why he initially chose not to accept direct financial support from the Corinthian church even though he had a right to it. He begins by asserting the right of workers, including apostles, to receive wages for their work. We serve the Lord in our work, and the Lord intends that we draw sustenance from it in return. Paul gives three examples from daily life that illustrate this point. Soldiers, vintners, and shepherds all derive economic benefit for their labors. Paul, however, rarely appeals to convention alone to make his case, so he quotes Deuteronomy 25:4 ("You shall not muzzle an ox while it is treading out the grain") in support of his argument. If even animals deserve a share of the fruits of their labor, then surely any person who participates in bringing about some benefit should share in that benefit.

---

[10] Fee, 336.

This text has clear implications for the workplace, especially for employers. Workers deserve a fair wage. In fact, the Bible threatens employers with dire consequences if they deny their employees just compensation (Lev. 19:13; Deut. 24:14; James 5:7). Paul knows that a variety of factors affect the determination of a fair wage, and he does not try to prescribe a figure or formula. Likewise, the complexities of supply and demand, regulation and unionization, wages and benefits, and power and flexibility in today's labor markets are beyond the scope of this chapter. But the principle is not. Those who employ human labor cannot neglect the needs of those whose work they employ.

Nonetheless, Paul chooses not to make use of his right to receive wages for his work as an apostle. Why? Because in his case, given the sensitivities in the church in Corinth, to do so might "put an obstacle in the way of the gospel of Christ." As it happens, God has made it possible for him to earn a living there by introducing him to fellow tentmakers (or leatherworkers), Priscilla and Aquila, who live in Corinth (Acts 18:1–3; Rom. 16:3). Paul doesn't expect that God will arrange things so that all church workers can afford to work for free. But in this case, God did, and Paul accepts God's provision with thanks. The point is that only the worker has the right to offer to work without fair remuneration. The employer has no right to demand it.

God's Glory Is the Ultimate Goal (1 Corinthians 10)

In the course of an extended argument beginning in chapter 8 on an issue of critical importance to believers in Corinth—the propriety of eating meat that had previously been offered to idols—Paul articulates a broad principle concerning the use of the earth's resources. He says, quoting Psalm 24:1, "The earth and its fullness are the Lord's" (1 Cor. 10:26). That is, because everything comes from God, any food may be eaten irrespective of its previous use for pagan cultic purposes. (In a Roman city, much of the meat sold in the market would have been offered to idols in the course of its preparation.[11]) There are two aspects of this principle that apply to work.

---

[11] Hans Conzelman, *1 Corinthians*, trans. James W. Leitch (Philadelphia: Fortress Press, 1975), 176, incl. nn. 11–13.

First, we may extend Paul's logic to conclude that believers may use all that the earth produces, including food, clothing, manufactured goods, and energy. However, Paul sets a sharp limit to this use. If our use harms another person, then we should refrain. If the context of a dinner party at which meat offered to idols is the issue, then another person's conscience may be the reason we need to refrain from eating it. If the context is worker safety, resource scarcity, or environmental degradation, then the well-being of today's workers, the access to resources by today's poor, and the living conditions of tomorrow's population may be the reasons we refrain from consuming certain items. Since God is the owner of the earth and its fullness, the use we make of the earth must be in line with his purposes.

Second, we are expected to engage in commerce with nonbelievers, as we have already seen from 1 Corinthians 5:9–10. If Christians were buying meat only from Christian butchers, or even from Jews, then of course there would have been no reason to worry whether it had been offered to idols. But Paul asserts that believers are to engage in commerce with society at large. (The concerns in chapter 8 also assume that Christians will engage in social relationships with nonbelievers, although that is not our topic here.) Christians are not called to withdraw from society but to engage society, including society's places of work. As noted earlier, Paul discusses the limits to this engagement in 2 Corinthians 6:14–18 (see "Working with Nonbelievers" in 2 Corinthians).

"Therefore, whatever you eat or drink, or whatever you do, do everything for the glory of God," says Paul (1 Cor. 10:31). This verse by no means legitimates every conceivable activity. It should not be construed to mean that absolutely anything could be done in a way that brings glory to God. Paul's point is that we have to discern whether our actions—including work—are consistent with God's purposes in the world. The criterion is not whether we associate with nonbelievers, whether we use materials that could be used for ill by others, whether we deal with people who are not friends with God, but whether the work we do contributes to God's purposes. If so, then whatever we do will indeed be done for the glory of God.

The upshot is that all vocations that add genuine value to God's created world in a way that benefits humanity are true callings that bring

God glory. The farmer and grocery clerk, the manufacturer and the emissions regulator, the parent and the teacher, the voter and the governor can enjoy the satisfaction of serving in God's plan for his creation.

Gifted Communities (1 Corinthians 12:1–14:40)

The use of what have come to be called "spiritual gifts" (12:1) seems to have caused much contention in the church of Corinth. It seems that the gift of tongues (i.e., Spirit-led ecstatic utterances) in particular was being used to accentuate status differences in the church, with those who practiced this gift claiming to be more spiritual than those who didn't (see 12:1–3, 13:1, 14:1–25).[12] In countering, Paul articulates a broad understanding of the gifts of God's Spirit that has major applications to work.

The first thing to observe is that the term "spiritual gifts" is too narrow to describe what Paul is talking about. They are "spiritual" in the broad sense of originating from God's Spirit, not in the narrow sense of being disembodied or paranormal. And "gift" is only one of a number of terms Paul uses for the phenomenon he has in mind. In chapter 12 alone, he calls the various gifts "services" (12:5), "activities" (12:6), manifestations" (12:7), "deeds," "forms," and "kinds" (12:28). The exclusive use of the term "spiritual gift" to refer to what Paul also calls "manifestation of God's spirit for the common good" or "kind of service" tends to skew our thinking.[13] It suggests that God's Spirit supersedes or ignores the "natural" skills and abilities God has given us. It implies that the recipient of the "gift" is its intended beneficiary. It makes us think that worship, rather than service, is the primary purpose of the Spirit's working. All of these are false assumptions, according to 1 Corinthians. The Holy Spirit does not dispense with our bodily abilities, but honors and employs them (12:14–26). The community or organization, not merely the individual, benefits (12:7). The purpose is to build up the community (14:3–5) and

---

[12] See Dale B. Martin, *The Corinthian Body* (New Haven: Yale University Press, 1995), 87–92.

[13] For a scholarly discussion of the problems involving the term "spiritual gifts," see Kenneth Berding, "Confusing Word and Concept in 'Spiritual Gifts': Have We Forgotten James Barr's Exhortations?" *Journal of the Evangelical Theological Society* 43 (2000): 37–51.

serve outsiders (14:23–25), not merely to improve the quality of worship. "Giftings" might be a better term to use, since it carries these important connotations better.

Second, Paul seems to be providing a number of examples rather than an exhaustive list. Paul also lists gifts of God in Romans 12:6–8, Ephesians 4:11, and 1 Peter 4:10–11, and the differences among the lists suggest they are illustrative rather than exhaustive. Among them there is no standard list or even a standard way of referring to the various ways the gifts are given. Contrary to much popular literature on the subject, then, it is impossible to compile a definitive list of *the* spiritual gifts. They exhibit a striking variety. Some are what we would call supernatural (speaking in unknown languages), while others seem to be natural abilities (leadership) or even personality traits (mercy). As we have seen, Paul tells us to "do everything for the glory of God" (1 Cor. 10:31), and here he lists a few of the amazing things God will give us the ability to do.

Paul has the church in mind here (14:4, 12), and some Christians suppose this passage to mean that the Spirit gives gifts *only* for use inside the church. However, Paul gives no reason to suppose that these gifts are limited to the confines of the church. God's kingdom encompasses the whole world, not just the institutions of the church. Believers can and should exercise their giftings in every setting, including the workplace. Many of the giftings named here—such as leadership, service, and discernment—will be of immediate benefit in the workplace. Others will no doubt be given to us as needed to serve God's purposes in whatever work we do. We should by all means develop the giftings we have been given and use them for the common good in every sphere of life.

In fact, the most important question is not who, where, what, or how we exercise the giftings of God's Spirit. The most important question is why we employ the gifts. And the answer is, "For love." Gifts, talents, and abilities—coming as they do from God—are sources of excellence in our work. But as he begins to discuss the importance of love, Paul says, "I will show you a still more excellent way" (12:31), "for the greatest of these is love" (13:13). If I exercise every wondrous gifting of God's Spirit "but do not have love," says Paul, "I am nothing" (13:2). Chapter 13 is often read at weddings, but it is actually a perfect manifesto for the workplace.

Love is patient; love is kind; love is not envious or boastful or arrogant or rude. It does not insist on its own way; it is not irritable or resentful; it does not rejoice in wrongdoing, but rejoices in the truth. It bears all things, believes all things, hopes all things, endures all things. (13:4–7)

If Christians would exhibit these kinds of love in our places of work, how much more productive and enriching would work be for everyone? How much glory would it bring our Lord? How much closer would we come to God's fulfillment of our prayer, "Thy kingdom come on earth"?

Our Work Is Not in Vain (1 Corinthians 15:58)

In chapter 15, Paul conducts a lengthy discussion of the resurrection, and he applies his conclusions directly to work. "[Excel] in the work in the Lord because you know that in the Lord your labor is not in vain" (1 Cor. 15:58). How does a correct understanding of the resurrection—that believers will be raised bodily—ground the conclusion that our labor for the Lord is of lasting significance ("not in vain")?

First of all, we must recognize that if life in the fallen world around us were all there were to life, our labor would be in vain (1 Cor. 15:14–19). Paul's use of the word *vain* brings to mind Ecclesiastes' extended meditation on the vanity of work under the conditions of the Fall. (See Ecclesiastes and Work at www.theologyofwork.org.) Even if there is life beyond the fallen state of the present world, our work would be in vain if the new world were completely disconnected from the present one. At most, it would launch us (and perhaps others) into the new world. But we have already seen that work done according to God's ways survives into eternity (1 Cor. 3:10–15). In the second half of chapter 15, Paul develops this matter further by stressing a fundamental continuity between pre- and post-resurrection bodily existence, in spite of vast differences in their respective substances. "This perishable body must put on imperishability, and this mortal body must put on immortality" (1 Cor. 15:53). Our soul does not change out of the old body into a new body—as if donning a new suit of clothes—but our present body "puts on immortality." The old continues into the new, though radically transformed. It is precisely this continuity that lends meaning to our present existence and guarantees that our labor for God is of lasting value.[14]

We Share Our Resources with Those in Hardship (1 Corinthians 16:1–3)

One ongoing project that Paul pursued throughout his missionary journeys was that of collecting money for congregations in Judea suffering economic hardship.[15] He mentions this collection not only here but also in Galatians 2:10, and he explains the theological rationale for it more thoroughly in Romans 15:25–31 and 2 Corinthians 8–9. For our purposes, it is important to note that, according to Paul, part of what a believer earns should be given for the benefit of those who cannot provide adequately for themselves. For Paul, one of the essential functions of the church is to take care of its worldwide members' needs. The Old Testament prescribed both fixed tithes and free-will offerings,[16] which together supported the operations of the temple, the maintenance of the state, and the relief of the poor. But this system had ceased with the demise of the Jewish kingdoms. Paul's collection for the poor in Judea essentially assumes for the church the relief aspect once provided by the Old Testament tithes and offerings.

The New Testament nowhere affirms certain fixed percentages, but Paul encourages generosity (see 2 Cor. 8–9), which would hardly mean less than Old Testament levels. Over the next several centuries, as the church grew, its role as a social service provider became an essential element of society, outlasting even the Roman Empire.[17] Whatever the amount given, believers are expected to determine it ahead of time as

---

[14] N. T. Wright, *The Resurrection of the Son of God*, vol. 3 of Christian Origins and the Question of God (Minneapolis: Fortress Press 2003), 359–60.

[15] For an overview, see Scot McKnight, "Collection for the Saints" in *Dictionary of Paul and His Letters*, ed. Gerald F. Hawthorne et al. (Downers Grove, IL: InterVarsity Press, 1993), 143–47.

[16] See E. P. Sanders, *Judaism: Practice and Belief, 63 BCE-66 CE (London: SCM Press,* 1992).

[17] Jeannine E. Olson, *Calvin and Social Welfare* (Selinsgrove, PA: Susquehanna University Press, 1989), 18.

a part of their budget and bring their offerings regularly to the weekly gatherings of the congregation. In other words, it takes a sustained lifestyle change to reach this level of generosity. We are not talking about pocket change.

These principles demand renewed consideration in our time. Governments have displaced the church as the prime providers of social welfare, but are there some forms of service that God equips Christians to do uniquely well? Could Christians' work, investment, and other economic activity be a means of serving those facing economic hardship? In Paul's day, there was limited scope for Christians to start businesses, engage in trade, or provide training and education, but today those could be means of creating jobs or providing for economically disadvantaged people. Is the purpose of giving merely to bind the church more closely together around the world (certainly one of Paul's objectives), or also to care for our neighbors? Could it be that today God calls believers to give money *and* to conduct business, government, education, and every other form of work as a means of taking care of people in hardship? (These questions are explored in depth in "Provision and Wealth" at www.theologyofwork.org.)

Conclusion to 1 Corinthians

First Corinthians has much to contribute to a biblical understanding of work. Above all, it establishes a healthy sense of calling to every legitimate kind of work. In his opening words, Paul stresses that God has called both him and the Corinthian believers to follow Christ. God provides every believer with spiritual resources and concrete giftings for the service of others. Our effectiveness does not depend on our own merits, but on God's power. Depending on his power, we can and must seek to do good work. God leads us to a common vision and purpose in our work, which requires a diverse array of people working in a wide variety of jobs. Leaders are needed to bring this diversity and variety into effective focus.

Leaders in God's kingdom are servants of those they lead, responsible for accomplishing their groups' tasks while at the same time meeting their needs. Whatever our position, it is more important to work each day according to God's purposes than to spend all our time and energy looking for the perfect job. Because we know Christ will return to fulfill God's restoration of the world to his original intent, we have the confidence to work diligently toward Christ's coming kingdom. When we work according to our abilities, God rewards our work with a fair share of the fruits of our labor. Christians are called to standards of fair wages and fair work.

Our ultimate goal is God's kingdom and his glory. This gives us freedom to use the resources of the world, but we must steward them for the benefit of all people, including future generations. In fact, we should not even think in terms of balancing the needs of one individual versus another, but in terms of building up communities of mutual support and service. Love is the mainspring of God's kingdom, and when we work out of love for the people for whom Christ worked and died, our work is not in vain. It has eternal significance and survives along with us into the new world of God's kingdom fulfilled. In the meantime, we take extra care to use the resources at our disposal to care for those in need.

2 Corinthians and Work

Introduction to 2 Corinthians

If 1 Corinthians gives us unparalleled insight into the everyday life of a New Testament church, 2 Corinthians offers us a unique glimpse into the heart and soul of the apostle whose work founded and built that church. We see Paul at work, teaching and exemplifying transparency, joy, good relationships, sincerity, reputation, service, humility, leadership, performance and accountability, reconciliation, working with nonbelievers, encouragement, generosity, timely fulfillment of obligations, and the proper use of wealth.

These workplace topics arose because of the daily struggles and opportunities Paul encountered in his own work as an apostle. During the period leading up to the composition of 2 Corinthians, Paul faced any number of "disputes without and fears within," as he describes them (2 Cor. 7:5). These clearly left their mark on him, and the result is a letter like no other in the New Testament—intensely personal, exhibiting a full range of emotions from anguish and agitation to exuberance and confidence. As a result of this adversity, Paul became a more effective leader and worker. All those who want to learn how to be more effective in their work—and who are willing to trust God for the ability to do so—will find a practical model in Paul and his teachings in 2 Corinthians.

Paul's Interactions with the Church in Corinth (2 Corinthians)

In the introduction to 1 Corinthians we noted that Paul established the church of Corinth during his first sojourn there (winter 49/50 through summer 51). Later he wrote one letter to the Corinthian church that no longer exists (it is mentioned in 1 Cor. 5:9) and one letter that does—our 1 Corinthians. He also visited the church three times (2 Cor. 12:14; 13:1). We know from Romans 16:1 that Paul wrote his epistle to the Romans during one of his stays in Corinth.

Nonetheless, Paul's relationship with the church in Corinth was strained. At one point he wrote them what has come to be known as the "severe letter"[1]—that apparently was quite harsh (see 2 Cor. 2:4). He sent it off to the Corinthians with Titus in the hope it would bring about a change of heart among his antagonists in Corinth. The unresolved conflict with the church in Corinth made Paul restless as he waited to hear back from them (2 Cor. 1:12–13). When Titus finally arrived in the autumn of 55 he brought good news from Corinth. Paul's severe letter had, in fact, proven to be remarkably beneficial. The believers in Corinth who had been the cause of so much sorrow were truly grieved about the rupture in their relationship with Paul, and their sorrow had led to repentance (2 Cor. 7:8–16).

In response to that news, Paul wrote 2 Corinthians, or more precisely the first seven chapters, to express his joy and gratitude both to God and to the Corinthians for the restored relationship between them. In these chapters he models the kind of transparency, joy, attention to relationships, integrity, reputation, service, dependence on God, ethical conduct, character, and encouragement that God calls all Christians to embody. Following this, in chapters 8 and 9, he turns to the topics of generosity and timely fulfillment of obligations as he exhorts the Corinthians to contribute to the relief of Christians in Jerusalem, which they had promised to do. In this section Paul highlights how our needs are met by God's generosity, not only so we lack nothing we need but also so we have plenty to share with others. In chapters 10 through 13 he describes the marks of godly leadership, apparently in response to disturbing news he received about so-called "super-apostles" who were leading some of the Corinthian church astray. Although we are not concerned here with church leadership per se, Paul's words in this section are directly applicable to all workplaces.

Thank God for Relationships (2 Corinthians 1:1–11)

Second Corinthians begins with Paul's sincere thanks for the deep relationship he has with the Corinthians. They are so closely knit together

---

[1] See Charles H. Talbert, *Reading Corinthians: A Literary and Theological Commentary on 1 and 2 Corinthians* (New York: Crossroad, 1987), xviii–xxi.

that whatever happens to one, it is as if it happens to all. He writes, "If we are being afflicted, it is for your consolation and salvation" (2 Cor. 1:6). "As you share in our sufferings, so you also share in our consolation" (2 Cor. 1:7). Paul's description of the relationship sounds almost like a marriage. Given the strained relationship between Paul and the church that comes into view during the letter, this intimacy may be surprising. How could people with huge disagreements, disappointments, and even anger at each other say things such as, "Our hope for you is unshaken" (2 Cor. 1:7)?

The answer is that good relationships do not arise from mutual agreement but mutual respect in the pursuit of a common goal. This is a crucial point for our lives at work. We generally do not choose our co-workers, just as the Corinthians did not choose Paul to be their apostle and Paul did not choose those God would lead to faith. Our relationships at work are not based on mutual attraction but on the need to work to-gether to accomplish our common tasks. This is true whether our work is to plant churches, manufacture auto parts, process insurance or gov-ernment forms, teach at a university, or any other vocation. The more difficult things are, the more important good relationships become.

How do we build good relationships at work? In a sense, the rest of 2 Corinthians is an exploration of various means of building good work-ing relationships—transparency, integrity, accountability, generosity, and so on. We will discuss all of them in this context. But Paul makes it clear that we cannot achieve good relationships through skills and meth-ods alone. What we need above all is God's help. For this reason, praying for each other is the cornerstone of good relationships. "Join in helping us by prayers," Paul asks and then speaks of "the blessing granted to us through the prayers of many" (2 Cor. 1:11).

How deeply do we invest in relationships with the people we work among? The answer might be measured by the extent to which we pray for them. Do we care enough about them to pray for them? Do we pray for their specific needs and concerns? Do we bother to learn enough about their lives so that we *can* pray for them in concrete ways? Do we open our own lives enough so that others can pray for us? Do we ever ask the people in our workplaces whether we can pray for them or them for us? They may not share our faith, but people almost always appreciate an authentic offer to pray for them or a request to pray (or hope) for us.

Transparency (2 Corinthians 1:12–23)

As Paul moves into the body of his second letter to the Corinthians, he addresses the complaint that he had not been open and honest with them. Although he promised to visit Corinth again, Paul had backed out twice. Was Paul being insincere or speaking out of both sides of his mouth? Was he maneuvering behind the scenes to get his way behind others' backs? Paul addresses these questions in 2 Corinthians 1:12–14. He is proud that his behavior among the Corinthians has been transparent at all times. His actions were not the machinations of what he calls "fleshly wisdom" (2 Cor. 1:12). He cancelled his visits, not to gain an advantage for himself or save face, but because he did not want to shame or rebuke the Corinthians again. Therefore, he delayed coming back to Corinth in the hope that, when he did come, he could bring joy rather than recrimination and reproof (2 Cor. 1:23–24).

Though Paul's integrity had been questioned, he knew that because of his history of transparency with them, they would continue to trust him. "We have behaved in the world with frankness and godly sincerity," he reminds them (2 Cor. 1:12). Because they have seen him in action, they know he says what he means without vacillating (2 Cor. 1:17–20). This makes him sure they "will understand until the end" (2 Cor. 1:1–13), once they know all the factors he has had to consider. His proof of their trust is that even without knowing everything, Paul tells them, "You have already understood us in part" (2 Cor. 1:13).

In our work today, are we transparent enough so that people have a reason to trust us? On a daily basis, every person, company, and organization faces temptations to hide the truth. Are we obscuring our motivations in order to falsely gain trust from a customer or a rival? Are we making decisions in secret as a way of avoiding accountability or hiding factors others would object to? Are we pretending to support co-workers in their presence, but speaking derisively behind their backs? Paul's example shows us that these actions are wrong. Moreover, whatever brief advantage we might gain from them is more than lost in the long term because our co-workers learn not to trust us. And if our co-workers cannot trust us, can God?

This doesn't mean, of course, that we always reveal all the information we have. There are confidences, personal and organizational, that cannot be broken. Not everyone needs to be privy to all information. At times the honest answer may be, "I can't answer that question because I have a duty of privacy to someone else." But we shouldn't use confidentiality as an excuse to prevaricate, to gain an edge on others, or to portray ourselves in a falsely positive light. If and when questions surface about our motives, a solid track record of openness and reliability will be the best antidote for misplaced doubts.

Transparency is so important to Paul's work with the Corinthians that he returns to the theme throughout the letter. "We refuse to practice cunning or to falsify Gods word; but by the open statement of the truth we commend ourselves" (2 Cor. 4:2). "We have spoken frankly to you Corinthians; our heart is wide open to you" (2 Cor. 6:11).

Working for the Joy of Others (2 Corinthians 1:24)

Joy is the next means of building relationships that Paul discusses. "I do not mean to imply that we lord it over your faith; rather we are workers with you for your joy, because you stand firm in the faith" (2 Cor. 1:24). Even though he was an apostle with God-given authority, Paul brought joy to others by the way he led them—not lording it over them but working alongside them. This explains why he was such an effective leader and why the people associated with him became strong and reliable co-workers. Paul's words echo what Jesus said to his disciples when they were arguing about who among them was the greatest:

> The kings of the Gentiles lord it over them; and those in authority over them are called benefactors. But not so with you; rather the greatest among you must become like the youngest, and the leader like one who serves. (Luke 22:25–26)

The essence of Christian work, Paul maintains, is nothing less than working alongside others to help them attain greater joy.

What would our workplaces look like if we tried to bring others joy through the way we treat them?[2] This does not mean trying to make

---

[2] Dennis W. Bakke, *Joy at Work: A Revolutionary Approach to Fun on the Job* (Seattle: PVG, 2005), and Raymond Bakke, William Hendricks, and Brad

everyone happy all the time, but treating co-workers as people of value and dignity, as Paul did. When we pay attention to others' needs at work, including the need to be respected and the need to be entrusted with meaningful work, we follow Paul's own example.

The Priority of Relationships
(2 Corinthians 2:12–16)

Another means to healthy interactions at work is simply taking the time and effort to develop and invest in relationships. Having left Ephesus, Paul went to Troas, a port city in the northwest corner of Asia Minor, where he expected Titus to arrive from his visit to Corinth (see the introduction above for details). While Paul was there he went about his missionary work with his usual vigor, and God blessed his efforts. But in spite of a promising beginning in a city of great strategic importance,[3] Paul cut short his work in Troas because, as he puts it, "my mind could not rest because I did not find my brother Titus there" (2 Cor. 2:13). He simply could not attend to his work, his very passion, because of the anguish he felt over his strained relationship with the Corinthian believers. So he left for Macedonia in the hope of finding Titus there.

Two things are striking about this passage. First, Paul places significant value on his relationships with other believers. He cannot remain aloof and unburdened when these relationships are in disrepair. We cannot say with absolute certainty that he was familiar with Jesus' teaching about leaving one's gift at the altar and being reconciled to one's brother (Matt. 5:23–24), but he clearly understood the principle. Paul is eager to see things patched up, and he invests a great deal of energy and prayer in pursuing that end. Second, Paul places a high priority on bringing about reconciliation, even if it causes significant delay in his work schedule. He does not try to convince himself that he has a great opportunity for ministry that will not come around again, and that therefore he can't be

---

Smith, *Joy at Work Bible Study Companion* (Lake Mary, FL: Charisma House, 2005) explore this question in detail.

[3] See Jerome Murphy-O'Connor, *Paul: A Critical Life* (Oxford: Clarendon, 1996), 300.

bothered with the Corinthians and their momentary needs. Repairing the rupture in his relationship with them takes precedence.

The lesson for us is obvious. Relationships matter. Clearly, we cannot always drop what we're doing at a moment's notice and attend to strained relationships. But no matter what our task, relationships *are* our business. Tasks are important. Relationships are important. So, in the spirit of Matthew 5:23–24, when we learn—or even suspect—that a relationship has been strained or broken in the course of our work, we do well to ask ourselves which is more pressing at the moment, the completion of the task or the restoration of a relationship. The answer may vary, depending on circumstances. If the task is big enough, or the strain in relationship serious enough, we do well not only to ask which is more pressing but also to seek counsel from a respected brother or sister.

Sincerity (2 Corinthians 2:17)

As in 2 Corinthians 1:12, Paul again addresses lingering questions about his delay in visiting Corinth. The Corinthians seem offended because he did not initially accept financial support from the church in Corinth. His response is that supporting himself was a matter of sincerity. Could people trust that he really believed what he was preaching, or was he doing it just to make money like the "peddlers of God's word" (2 Cor. 2:17) who could be found in any Roman city? It appears he did not want to be lumped together with the philosophers and rhetoricians of his day who charged hefty fees for their speeches.[4] Instead he and his co-workers were "persons of sincerity." They were quite clearly not going from place to place preaching the gospel in order to get rich, but they understood themselves as individuals who were sent by God and answered to God.

This reminds us that motivation is not just a private matter, especially when it comes to money. The way we handle money shines like a laser pointer on the question of our sincerity as Christians. People want to see whether we handle money in accordance with our high principles or ditch our principles when there's money to be made. Are we lax with

---

[4] See Murray J. Harris, *The Second Epistle to the Corinthians: A Commentary on the Greek Text* (Grand Rapids: Eerdmans, 2005), 253–54.

our expense accounts? Do we hide income under the table? Do we engage in dubious tax shelters? Do we push for raises, commissions, and bonuses at the expense of others? Do we take financial advantage of people in difficult circumstances? Do we twist contracts to gain a disproportionate financial gain? The question is not only whether we can justify ourselves, but also whether those around us can recognize that our actions are consistent with Christian beliefs. If not, we bring dishonor to ourselves and to the name of Christ.

A Genuine Reputation (2 Corinthians 3)

Paul begins this section of 2 Corinthians with two rhetorical questions, both of which expect a negative answer.[5] "Are we beginning to commend ourselves again? Surely we do not need, as some do, letters of recommendation to you or from you, do we?" (2 Cor. 3:1). Paul—their old friend—wryly asks whether he needs the letters of introduction or commendation that others who had presented themselves to the church apparently possessed. Such letters were common in the ancient world, and generally it was necessary to take them with a grain of salt. The Roman statesman Cicero wrote scores of them, for instance, making lavish use of the stereotypical language of praise the genre demanded. Recipients became so jaded, however, that sometimes he felt it necessary to write a second letter so that the recipients would know whether to take the first letter seriously.[6] Letters of commendation, in other words, were often not worth the papyrus they were written on.

Paul had no need of them in any case. The Corinthian believers knew him intimately. The only letter of recommendation he required was already written on their hearts (2 Cor. 3:3). Their very existence as a church, as well as their individual conversions in response to Paul's preaching, was all the commendation Paul needed or wanted concern-

---

[5] Harris, 258.

[6] See Cicero, *Epistulae ad Familiares (The Letters to His Friends)*, 13.6a. For a thorough discussion see Peter Marshall, *Enmity in Corinth: Social Conventions in Paul's Relations with the Corinthians*, Wissenschaftliche Untersuchungen zum Neuen Testament 2.23 (Tübingen: Mohr Siebeck, 1987), 91–129, esp. 93–95.

ing his apostleship. They could see the fruit of Paul's labor, which left no doubt that he was an apostle sent by God. Further, Paul insists, he is not claiming competence in his own strength. "Our competence is from God" (2 Cor. 3:5), he writes. The question is not whether Paul has piled up credentials and recommendations, but whether his work is a contribution to the kingdom of God.

How do we build our reputations today? In the United States, many young people choose their activities based not on how they can best contribute to their communities, or even on what they actually enjoy, but upon how the activities will look on a university or graduate school application. This can continue during our working lives, with every job assignment, professional affiliation, dinner party, and social event calculated to associate us with prestigious people and institutions. Paul chose his activities based on how he could best serve the people he loved. Following his lead, we should work so as to leave solid evidence of jobs well done, of lasting results, and of people whose lives have been impacted for the better.

Leading and Serving (2 Corinthians 4)

Second Corinthians 4 brings together themes that are closely related in Paul's work—transparency, humility, weakness, leadership, and service. Because we are seeing Paul at work in a real-life situation, the themes are entangled as Paul tells the story. But we will try to discuss the themes one at a time in order to explore each one as clearly as possible.

Transparency and Humility (2 Corinthians 4)

In chapter 4 Paul returns to the theme of transparency, as we noted in our discussion of 2 Corinthians 1:12–23. This time he emphasizes the importance of humility for maintaining transparency. If we are going to let everyone see the reality of our life and work, we had better be prepared to be humbled.

Naturally, it would be much easier to be transparent with people if we had nothing to hide. Paul himself says, "We have renounced the shameful things that one hides" (2 Cor. 4:2). But transparency requires that we remain open, even if we have engaged in conduct that is not commendable.

For the truth is, we are all susceptible to errors of intention and execution. "We have this treasure in clay jars," Paul reminds us (2 Cor. 4:7), alluding to the typical household vessels of his day that were made of common clay and easily breakable. Anyone who visits the remains of the Ancient Near East can testify to the shards of these vessels lying scattered everywhere. Paul reinforces this idea later by recounting that God gave him a "thorn in the flesh" in order to restrain his pride (2 Cor. 12:7).

Maintaining transparency when we know our own weaknesses requires humility and especially the willingness to offer a genuine apology. Many apologies by public figures sound more like thinly veiled justifications than actual apologies. This may be because, if we depend on ourselves as the source of our confidence, to apologize would be to risk our ability to carry on. Yet Paul's confidence is not in his own rightness or ability, but in his dependence on the power of God. "We have this treasure in clay jars, so that it may be made clear that this extraordinary power belongs to God and does not come from us" (2 Cor. 4:7). If we too acknowledged that the good things we accomplish are not a reflection on us but on our Lord, then maybe we could have the courage to admit our mistakes and look to God to put us back on track again. At the very least, we could stop feeling that we have to maintain our image at all costs, including the cost of deceiving others.

Weakness as the Source of Strength (2 Corinthians 4)

Our weakness, however, is not just a challenge to our transparency. It is actually the source of our true abilities. Enduring suffering is not an unfortunate side effect experienced in some circumstances; it is the actual means of bringing about genuine accomplishment. Just as the power of Jesus' resurrection came about *because* of his crucifixion,[7] so the apostles' fortitude in the midst of adversity testifies to the fact that the same power is at work in them.

In our culture, no less than in Corinth, we project strength and invincibility because we feel they are necessary to climb the ladder of success. We try to convince people that we are stronger, smarter, and more competent than we really are. Therefore, Paul's message of vulnerability

---

[7] Harris, 349.

may sound challenging to us. Is it apparent in the way you go about your work that the strength and vitality you project is not your own, but rather God's strength on display in your weakness? When you receive a compliment, do you allow it to add to your aura of brilliance? Or do you recount the ways God—perhaps working through other people—made it possible for you to exceed your native potential? We usually want people to perceive us as ultra-competent. But aren't the people we admire most the ones who help *other* people bring their gifts to bear?

If we hold up under difficult circumstances without trying to conceal them, it will become apparent that we have a source of power outside of ourselves, the very power that effected Jesus' resurrection from the dead.

Serving Others by Leading (2 Corinthians 4)

Humility and weakness would be unbearable if our purpose in life were to make something great of ourselves. But service, not greatness, is the Christian's purpose. "We do not proclaim ourselves; we proclaim Jesus Christ as Lord and ourselves as your slaves for Jesus' sake" (2 Cor. 4:5). This verse is one of the classic biblical statements of the concept that has come to be known as "servant leadership." Paul, the foremost leader of the Christian movement beyond the confines of Palestine, calls himself "your slave for Jesus' sake" (2 Cor. 4:5).

Again, Paul seems to be reflecting on Jesus' own teaching here (see 2 Cor. 1:24 above). As leaders, Jesus and his followers served others. This fundamentally Christian insight should inform our attitude in any leadership position. This does not mean that we refrain from exercising legitimate authority or that we lead timidly. Rather, it implies that we use our position and our power to further others' well-being and not only our own. In fact, Paul's words "your slaves for Jesus' sake" are stricter than they may at first appear. Leaders are called to seek other people's well-being *ahead* of their own, as slaves are compelled to do. A slave, as Jesus pointed out, works all day in the fields, then comes in and serves dinner to the household, and only afterwards may eat and drink (Luke 17:7–10).

Leading others by serving will inevitably lead to suffering. The world is too broken for us to imagine there is a chance we may escape suffering while serving. Paul suffered affliction, perplexity, and persecution nearly to the point of death (2 Cor. 4:8–12). As Christians, we should not accept leadership positions unless we intend to sacrifice the privilege of taking care of ourselves before taking care of others.

Performance and Accountability
(2 Corinthians 5:1–15)

In 2 Corinthians 5 Paul, who constantly faced situations that could result in his death, reminds the Corinthians that at the final judgment each person will be "recompensed according to what he has done in the body, whether good or evil" (2 Cor. 5:10) These are unusual words for Paul (though not as unusual as one might expect; see Rom. 2:6–10), whom we normally associate with the doctrine of grace, meaning that our salvation is entirely unmerited and not the result of our own works (Eph. 2:8–9). It is, however, important that we allow our picture of Paul to be formed by what he actually says, rather than by some caricature. When we analyze Paul's teaching in its entirety, we find it is in harmony with that of Jesus, James, and even the Old Testament. For all of them, faith that does not express itself in good works is no faith at all. Indeed, faith and obedience are so closely intertwined that even Paul can, as he does here, refer to the latter rather than the former when he actually has both in mind. What we do in the body cannot help but reflect what God's grace has done for us. What pleases the Lord can be described either as faith or, as here, as works of righteousness made possible by God's grace.

In any case, Paul's message is clear enough: How we live our lives matters to God. In workplace terms, our performance matters. Moreover, we will have to give an account to the Lord Jesus for all that we have done and left undone. In workplace terms, this is accountability. Performance and accountability are profoundly important to the Christian life, and we cannot dismiss them as secular concerns of no importance to God. God cares whether we are slacking off, neglecting our duties, not showing up for work, or going through the motions without genuine attention to our work.

This does not mean that God always agrees with what our work-places expect from us. God's idea of good performance may be different from that of our manager or supervisor. In particular, if meeting our employer's performance expectations requires unethical activities or harming others, then God's review of our performance will be different from our employer's. If your boss expects you to mislead customers or denigrate co-workers, for God's sake aim for a poor performance review from your boss and a good review from God.

God holds us to a high standard of conduct. One day we will answer for the way we have treated our co-workers, bosses, employees, and customers, not to mention our family and friends. This does not negate the doctrine of grace, but instead shows us how God intends his grace to transform our lives.

Reconciling the Whole World
(2 Corinthians 5:16–21)

If it sounds as if Paul is calling us to grit our teeth and try harder to be good, then we are missing the point of 2 Corinthians. Paul intends for us to see the world in a completely new way, so that our actions stem from this new understanding, not from trying harder.

> If anyone is in Christ, there is a new creation: everything old has passed away; see, everything has become new! All this is from God, who reconciled us to himself through Christ, and has given us the ministry of reconciliation; that is, in Christ God was reconciling the world to himself, not counting their trespasses against them, and entrusting the message of reconciliation to us. (2 Cor. 5:17–19)

Paul wants us to become so thoroughly transformed that we become members of a "new creation." The mention of "creation" immediately takes us back to Genesis 1–2, the story of God's creation of the world. From the beginning God intended that men and women work together (Gen. 1:27; 2:18), in concert with God (Gen. 2:19), to "till the ground" (Gen. 2:15), "give names" to the creatures of the earth, and exercise "dominion" (Gen. 1:26) over the earth as God's stewards. God's intent for creation, in other words, includes work as a central reality of existence. When humans disobeyed God and marred the creation, work became cursed (Gen. 3:17–18), and humans no longer worked alongside God.

Thus when Paul says, "Everything has become new," *everything* includes the world of work as a core element.

God brings the new creation into existence by sending his Son into the old creation to transform or "reconcile" it. "In Christ, God was reconciling *the world* to himself." Not just one aspect of the world, but the whole world. And those who follow Christ, who are reconciled to God by Christ, are appointed to carry on Christ's work of reconciliation (2 Cor. 5:18). We are agents to bring reconciliation to all spheres of the world. Every day as we go out to do our work we are to be ministers of this reconciliation. This includes reconciliation between people and God (evangelism and discipleship), between people and people (conflict resolution), and between people and their work (goods and services that meet genuine needs and improve the quality of life and care for God's creation).

There are three essential elements of the work of reconciliation. First, we must understand accurately what has gone wrong among people, God, and the creation. If we do not truly understand the ills of the world, then we cannot bring genuine reconciliation any more than an ambassador can effectively represent one country to another without knowing what's going on in both. Second, we must love other people and work to benefit them rather than to judge them. "We regard no one from a human point of view," Paul tells us (2 Cor. 5:16)—that is, as an object to be exploited, eliminated, or adulated, but as a person for whom "Christ died and was raised" (2 Cor. 5:15). If we condemn the people in our workplaces or withdraw from the daily places of life and work, we are regarding people and work from a human point of view. If we love the people we work among and try to improve our workplaces, products, and services, then we become agents of Christ's reconciliation. Finally, being seeds of God's creation, of course, requires that we remain in constant fellowship with Christ. If we do these things, we will be in a position to bring Christ's power to reconcile the people, organizations, places, and things of the world so that they too can become members of God's new creation.

Transparency Revisited (2 Corinthians 6:11)

As we noted earlier (in 2 Cor. 1:12–23), transparency is a recurring theme in this letter. It crops up again here when Paul writes, "We have spoken frankly to you Corinthians; our heart is wide open to you" (2 Cor. 6:11). We might say that his life was an open book before them. Though he adds nothing new to what he has said previously, it becomes more and more apparent how important the topic of transparency is for him. When questions arise about his ministry, he can appeal to his earlier dealings with the Corinthians with absolute certainty that he has always been honest with them about himself. Can we say the same of ourselves?

Working with Nonbelievers (2 Corinthians 6:14–18)

In 2 Corinthians 6:14–18 Paul takes up the question of close relationships with non-Christians. Up to this point, Paul has vividly portrayed the importance of good relationships with the people with whom we work. Paul says in 1 Corinthians 5:9–10 that we should work with non-Christians, and he discusses how to do so in 1 Corinthians 10:25–33 (see 1 Corinthians 10).

But perhaps there are limits to the intimacy of Christians' working relationships with non-Christians. Paul tells the Corinthians, "Do not be mismatched with unbelievers," as the NRSV puts it, or to translate the Greek term (*heterozygountes*) more literally, "Do not be unequally yoked with unbelievers." His words are reminiscent of Leviticus 19:19, which prohibits mating different kinds of animals together, and Deuteronomy 22:10, which prohibits yoking an ox and donkey together while plowing. These two Old Testament precedents refer to mating and to work, respectively. We are concerned here with work.

What, then, are the limits in working with nonbelievers? Perhaps the key is the term "yoked." When two animals are yoked together, they must move in lockstep. If one turns left, the other also turns left, whether or not it consents. This is different from, say, animals grazing in a herd, which cooperate but still have the freedom to move separately and even to depart from the herd if they choose. If two animals—or, metaphorically, two people—are yoked, each is bound by whatever the other chooses to do. Two people are yoked if one person's choices compel the other person to follow the same choices, even without their consent. A yoking is when either person is bound by the unilateral decisions and actions of the other.

Paul does not want us to be *un*equally yoked. So what would it mean to be *equally* yoked? Jesus has already given us the answer to that question. "Take my yoke upon you," he calls to those who follow him (Matt. 11:29a). Paul tells us not to be unequally yoked with nonbelievers because we are already yoked to Jesus. One part of his yoke is around us, and the other is on Jesus' shoulders. Jesus, like the lead ox in a team, determines the bearing, the pace, and the path of the team, and we submit to his leadership. Through his yoke, we feel his pull, his guidance, his direction. By his yoke, he trains us to work effectively in his team. His yoke is what leads us, sensitizes us, and binds us to Jesus. Being yoked to Jesus makes us partners with him in restoring God's creation in every sphere of life, as we explored in 2 Corinthians 5:16–21. No other yoke that would pull us away from the yoke of Jesus could ever be equal to that! "My yoke is easy, and my burden is light," Jesus tells us (Matt. 11:29b), yet the work we are doing with him is no less than the transformation of the entire cosmos.

When Paul tells us not to be unequally yoked in working relationships, he is warning us not to get entangled in work situations that prevent us from doing the work Jesus wants us to do or that prevent us from working in Jesus' ways. This has a strong ethical element. "What partnership is there between righteousness and lawlessness?" Paul asks (2 Cor. 6:14). If the dictates of a work situation lead us to harm customers, deceive constituents, mislead employees, abuse co-workers, pollute the environment, or such, then we would be yoked into a violation of our duties as stewards of God's kingdom. Yet ethics is not the only element. Besides *preventing* us from doing anything unethical, being yoked with Jesus also *leads* us to work to reconcile or restore the world to God's vision for it. At the very least, this suggests that we pay careful attention to the motivations, values, integrity, working methods, and similar factors when deciding where and with whom we work.

To be unequally yoked with unbelievers, then, is to be in a situation or relationship that binds you to the decisions and actions of people who have values and purposes incompatible with Jesus' values and purposes.

A few examples may help. A business partnership—joint, unlimited ownership of a business—would generally seem to be a form of yoking.

If one partner signs a contract, spends money, buys or sells property—or even violates the law—the other partner is bound by that action or decision. To form a business partnership in this sense would very likely be a form of unequal yoking. Even if the believer trusts that the nonbelieving partner(s) would not do anything unethical, is it possible that the nonbelieving partner(s) would want to run the business for the purposes of transforming the world to be more as God intends it to be? Even if the partnership does not force the believer to do evil, would it hinder him or her from doing all the good Christ desires? Joining an army, making a pledge of office, raising money for a nonprofit organization, or buying property jointly might have similar consequences.

In contrast, a single commercial transaction—buying or selling an item between two parties—would generally not seem to be a form of yoking. The parties agree in advance on a single item of business and then perform what they agreed to. (The Christian, of course, should only agree to do the transaction if it is in accordance with God's values and purposes.) Neither party is bound by anything the other party might do after the transaction. Teaching a class, writing or being interviewed for a newspaper article, volunteering in a civic event, and babysitting a child are other examples similarly limited in scope and duration.

Buying stock is probably somewhere in between. As part owners in the corporation, stock owners are morally—though probably not legally— bound by the decisions of the directors, executives, and other employees, but only for as long as they own the stock. Likewise, getting a job, joining a faculty, raising money for a nonprofit organization or political campaign, and signing a contract all commit us to living with the consequences of others' choices, but not forever.

As these examples show, there is no hard-and-fast rule for what it means to be unequally yoked. In practice, it may be difficult to say whether a particular working relationship is a form of yoking. Getting a job in a secular organization is probably not a form of yoking. But going so far into debt that you can't afford to quit your job probably turns any employee relationship into a de facto yoking. You have lost the freedom to resign if the organization engages in ungodly activities. One rising lawyer was offered a partnership in a prestigious law firm, but declined when he observed how many of those who became partners got divorced soon after.[8] It seemed to him that accepting a partnership would yoke him to values and practices incompatible with the commitment he made to put his wife first among the people in his life.

Finally, we must be careful to not turn Paul's words into an us-versus-them mentality against nonbelievers. Paul knew as well as anyone that believers fall far short of the values and purposes of God. We should be careful not to be unequally yoked, even with Christians whose conduct would pull us away from the yoke of Christ. Even more, we need to receive Christ's grace every day so that being yoked with us doesn't cause someone else to be pulled away from working according to Christ's ways and purposes. Nor can we judge or condemn nonbelievers as inherently unethical, since Paul himself refused to do so. "For what have I to do with judging those outside? Is it not those who are inside that you are to judge? God will judge those outside" (1 Cor. 5:12–13). We are called not to judge but to discern whether our working relationships are leading us to work for the purposes and according to the ways of Christ.

Perhaps the best guidance is to ask ourselves the question Paul asks, "What does a believer share with an unbeliever?" (2 Cor. 6:15). If the answer is that we share similar values and goals with respect to the work we may undertake together, then it may serve God's will to work closely with nonbelievers. You can assess the opportunities and risks by exploring in advance all the commitments entailed in any work relationship. Consider how your individual capabilities and limitations might reduce or exacerbate the risk of being pulled away from working as God intends. This means that the decision whether to participate may be different for each person. Considering our differing strengths and weaknesses, a free association for one person could be a binding yoke for another. A recent graduate, for example, might find it relatively easy to quit a job, compared to a CEO with a large investment and reputation at stake. In other words, the larger our role in a working relationship, the more important it is to make sure we're not yoking ourselves into a situation we won't be able to handle in a godly way. In any case, all Christians would

---

[8] An incident reported confidentially to a member of the Theology of Work Project Steering Committee. Recorded August 24, 2011 at the Theology of Work Project 2011 summer conference in Los Angeles.

do well to consider carefully the entanglements that can arise in every workplace relationship, job, partnership, and transaction.

The Encouragement of Praise (2 Corinthians 7)

Immediately after admonishing the Corinthians, Paul praises them. "I often boast about you; I have great pride in you" (2 Cor. 7:4). It may come as a surprise for some to find Paul boasting so unapologetically about the church in Corinth. Many of us have been brought up to believe that pride is a sin (which is, of course, quite true) and even that pride in someone else's accomplishments is questionable. Further, we might wonder whether Paul's pride in the Corinthians is misplaced. This was a congregation beset with many difficulties, and there are some stinging rebukes in his letters to them. He wears no rose-colored glasses when it comes to the Corinthians. But Paul is entirely unabashed by such concerns. He does not shy away from giving praise where praise is due, and it seems that he is genuinely proud of the progress the believers in Corinth have made in spite of his tense relations with them. He notes his pride in them is well deserved, not a cheap trick of flattery (2 Cor. 7:11–13). He repeats in 2 Corinthians 7:14 the point that praise must be genuine when he says, "Everything we said to you was true, so our boasting to Titus has proved true as well."

This reminds us of the importance of specific, accurate, and timely praise for co-workers, employees, and others with whom we interact at work. Inflated or generalized praise is hollow and may seem insincere or manipulative. And unrelenting criticism destroys rather than builds up. But words of genuine appreciation and gratitude for work well done are always appropriate. They are evidence of mutual respect, the foundation of true community, and they motivate everyone to continue their good work. We all look forward to hearing the Lord say, "Well done, good and faithful servant" (Matt. 25:21, NIV), and we do well to give similar praise whenever it's warranted.

Generosity Is Not Optional (2 Corinthians 8:1–9)

As we noted in the introduction, 2 Corinthians 8 and 9 form a separate section of Paul's letter in which he addresses the topic of the collection for the churches in Judea. This project was a passion of the apostle's, and he promoted it vigorously in his churches (1 Cor. 16:1–3). Paul begins this section by pointing to the exemplary generosity of the churches in Macedonia and implying that he expects no less from the Corinthians. Just as the believers in Corinth have displayed an abundance of faith, ability to proclaim the truth,[9] knowledge, enthusiasm, and love, so they should also strive to abound in the "gift" (Gk. *charis*) of generosity. The term "gift" has a double meaning here. It has the sense of "spiritual gift," referring to God's gift to them of the virtue of generosity, and it has the sense of "donation," referring to their gifts of money to the collection. This makes the point doubly clear that generosity is not an option for Christians, but part of the Spirit's work in our lives.

In the workplace, a generous spirit is the oil that makes things run smoothly on a number of levels. Employees who sense that their employers are generous will be more willing to make sacrifices for their organizations when they become necessary. Workers who are generous with their co-workers will create a ready source of help for themselves and a more joyful and satisfying experience for everyone.

Generosity is not always a matter of money. To name only a few examples, employers can be generous by taking time to mentor workers, providing a workplace of beauty, offering opportunities for training and development, genuinely listening to someone with a problem or complaint, or visiting an employee's family member in the hospital. Co-workers can offer generosity by helping others do their work better, making sure no one is left out socially, standing up for those who suffer misuse, offering true friendship, sharing praise, apologizing for offenses, and simply learning the names of workers who might otherwise be invisible to us. Steve Harrison tells of two surgical residents at the University of Washington who competed to see who could learn the names of more nurse's aides, custodians, transport, and dietary staff and then greet them by name whenever they saw them.[10]

---

[9] Literally, "in speech." See Harris, 574.

[10] Steve Harrison, *The Manager's Book of Decencies* (New York: McGraw-Hill, 2007), 67.

Timely Fulfillment of Obligations (2 Corinthians 8:10–12)

Paul reminds the believers in Corinth that they had already signaled their intentions to participate in the collection for the churches in Judea during the previous year. They seem, however, to have become sidetracked. Perhaps lingering doubts about Paul's ministry and the tensions that surfaced during his previous visit play a role here. In any case, their effort is flagging, and at the time of Paul's writing they have not yet gathered all the contributions from individual members, as he had previously instructed them to do (1 Cor. 16:1–3).

Paul's advice is straightforward. "Finish doing it, so that your eagerness may be matched by completing it according to your means" (2 Cor. 8:11). Paul's advice is as relevant now as it was then, especially in our work. What we start we should finish. Obviously, there are many situations in which circumstances change or other priorities take precedence so that we have to adjust our commitments. This is why Paul adds, "according to your means." But often, as in the Corinthians' situation, the problem is merely one of dragging our feet. Paul reminds us of the need to carry through on our commitments. Other people are counting on us.

This advice may seem too simple to need mentioning in the word of God. Yet Christians underestimate how important this is as a matter of witness, in addition to productivity. If we do not fulfill ordinary commitments at work, how can our words or actions possibly convince people that our Lord will fulfill his promise of eternal life? Better to deliver a report, a part, or a raise on time than to deliver a lunchtime argument for the divinity of Christ.

Sharing the Wealth (2 Corinthians 8:13–15)

Paul reminds the Corinthians of the underlying principle behind the collection. "It is a question of a fair balance between your present abundance and their need" (2 Cor. 8:14). It is not that the Judean churches should experience relief to the detriment of the Gentile churches, but rather that there should be an appropriate balance between them. The

Judean believers were in need, and the Corinthian church was experiencing a measure of prosperity. The time might come when the tables would
be turned, and then aid would flow in the other direction, "so that their
abundance may be for your need" (2 Cor. 8:14).

Paul invokes two images to explain what he means. The first one, balance, is abstract, but in the ancient world, as now, it appeals to our sense
that in the natural world and in society equilibrium leads to stability
and health.[11] The recipient benefits because the gift alleviates an abnor-
mal lack. The giver benefits because the gift prevents acclimation to an
unsustainable abundance. The second image is concrete and historical.
Paul reminds the Corinthians of the ancient days when God gave the
people of Israel manna to sustain themselves (Exod. 16:11–18). Though
some gathered much and others comparatively little, when the daily ra-
tion was distributed, no one had either too little or too much.

The principle that the richer should give their wealth to the poorer
to the degree that everyone's resources are in "balance" is challenging
to modern notions of individual self-reliance. Apparently, when Paul
calls Christians "slaves for Jesus' sake" (2 Cor. 5:4), he means that 100
percent of our wages and our wealth belong directly to God, and that God
might want us to distribute them to others to the point that the income
we keep for our personal use is in equal balance with theirs.

We must be careful, however, not to make simplistic applications to
the structures of today's world. A full discussion of this principle among
Christians has become difficult because it gets caught up in the political
debates about socialism and capitalism. The question in those debates
is whether the state has the right—or duty—to compel the balance of
wealth by taking from the richer and distributing to the poorer. This is
a different matter from Paul's situation, in which a group of churches
asked their members to voluntarily give money for distribution by another church for the benefit of its poor members. In fact, Paul does not
say anything at all about the state in this regard. As for himself, Paul
says he has no plans to compel anyone. "I do not say this as a command"
(2 Cor. 8:8), he tells us, nor is collection to be made "reluctantly or under
compulsion" (2 Cor. 9:7).

---

[11] Harris, 590.

Paul's purpose is not to create a particular social system but to ask those who have money whether they are truly ready to put it at God's service on behalf of the poor. "Show them the proof of your love and of our reason for boasting about you," he implores (2 Cor. 8:24). Christians should engage in plenty of discussion about the best ways to alleviate poverty. Is it through giving alone, or investment, or something else, or some mix? What role do the structures of the church, business, government, and nonprofit organizations have? Which aspects of legal systems, infrastructure, education, culture, personal responsibility, stewardship, hard work, and other factors must be reformed or developed? Christians need to be on the forefront of developing not only generous but effective means of bringing poverty to an end.[12]

But there can be no question about the pressing urgency of poverty and no reluctance to balance our use of money with the needs of others around the world. Paul's forceful words show that those who enjoy superabundance cannot be complacent when so many people in the world suffer extreme poverty.

You Can't Out-Give God (2 Corinthians 9)

In urging the Corinthian believers to give generously, Paul is aware that he must address a very human concern in a world of limited resources. Some of his hearers must have been thinking, "If I give as altruistically as Paul is urging me to give, there may not be enough to meet my own needs." Making use of an extended agricultural metaphor, Paul assures them that in God's economy things work differently. He has already alluded to a principle from the book of Proverbs, noting that the "one who sows sparingly will also reap sparingly, and the one who sows bountifully will also reap bountifully" (compare 2 Cor. 9:6 with Prov. 11:24–25). He followed this up by quoting an aphorism from the Greek version of Proverbs 22:8, that "God loves a cheerful giver" (2 Cor. 9:7).

---

[12] John Stott, *The Grace of Giving: 10 Principles of Christian Giving,* Lausanne Didasko Files (Peabody, MA: Hendrickson Publishers, 2012), discusses giving in depth, based on his reading of 2 Corinthians 8–9.

From this he infers a promise that for the one who gives generously, God can and will cause all sorts of blessings[13] to abound.

Paul, therefore, assures the Corinthians that their generosity does not come at the risk of future poverty. On the contrary, generosity is the route to *prevent* future deprivation. "God is able to provide you with every blessing in abundance, *so that* by always having enough of every-thing, you may share abundantly in every good work" (2 Cor. 9:8). In the next two verses he assures those who sow (or "scatter") generously to the poor that God will provide them with enough seed for that sowing *and* for bread for their own needs. He underscores this when he says, "You will be enriched in every way for your great generosity, which will produce thanksgiving to God through us" (2 Cor. 9:11), a promise that encompasses and goes beyond material blessings.

Although Paul is clearly speaking of material generosity and blessing, we must be careful not to turn an assurance of God's provision into an expectation of getting rich. God is no pyramid scheme! The "abundance" Paul speaks of means "having *enough* of everything," not getting rich. The so-called "prosperity gospel" profoundly misunderstands passages like this. Following Christ is not a money-making scheme, as Paul has been at pains to say throughout the letter.

This has obvious applications in giving away the fruits of our labor, that is, in donating money and other resources. But it applies equally well in giving of ourselves *during* our labor. We need not fear that by helping others succeed at work we will compromise our own well-being. God has promised to give us all that we need. We can help others look good at work without fearing it will make us look lackluster by com-parison. We can compete fairly in the marketplace without worrying that it takes a few dirty tricks to make a living in a competitive business. We can pray for, encourage, support, and even assist our rivals because we know that God, not our competitive advantage, is the source of our provision. We must be careful not to distort this promise into the false

---

[13] The term for "every" or "all" (*pan*) here has the connotation of "every kind of" rather than "every possible" blessing. Cf. Gerhard Kittel, Gerhard Friedrich, and Geoffrey William Bromiley, eds., *Theological Dictionary of the New Testament* (Grand Rapids: Eerdmans, 1985), 631c.

gospel of health and wealth, as many have done. God does not promise true believers a big house and an expensive car. But he does assure us that if we look to the needs of others, he will make sure that our needs will be met in the process.

Assessing Performance (2 Corinthians 10–13)

As we noted in the introduction, 2 Corinthians 10 through 13 constitute the third section of the letter. The most relevant parts for work come in chapters 10 and 11, which expand the discussion of on-the-job performance that began in chapter 5. Here Paul is defending himself in the face of attacks by a few people he facetiously calls "super-apostles" (2 Cor. 11:5). In doing so, he offers specific insights directly applicable to performance assessment.

The false super-apostles had been criticizing Paul for not measuring up to them in terms of eloquence, personal charisma, and evidence of signs and wonders. Naturally, the "standards" they chose were nothing more than self-descriptions of themselves and their ministries. Paul points out what an absurd game they were playing. People who judge by comparing others to themselves will always be self-satisfied. Paul refuses to go along with such a self-serving scheme. As far as he is concerned, as he had already explained in 1 Corinthians 4:1–5, the only judgment—and therefore the only commendation—that is worth its salt is the judgment of the Lord Jesus.

Paul's perspective has direct relevance to our workplaces. Our performance on the job will likely be assessed in quarterly or annual reviews, and there is certainly nothing wrong with that. Problems arise when the standards by which we measure ourselves or others are biased and self-serving. In some organizations—typically those only loosely accountable to their owners and customers—a small circle of intimates may gain the ability to judge the performance of others primarily based on whether it falls in line with the insiders' self-interests. Those outside the inner circle are then evaluated primarily in terms being "with us" or "against us." This is a difficult spot to find ourselves in, yet because Christians measure success by God's assessment rather than promotion, pay, or even continued employment, we may be the very people who can bring redemption to such corrupt organizations. If we should find ourselves as beneficiaries of corrupt, self-dealing systems, what better witness to Christ could we find than to stand up for the benefit of others who have been harmed or marginalized, even at the expense of our own comfort and security?

Conclusion to 2 Corinthians

The unique circumstances that led Paul to write 2 Corinthians resulted in a letter with many important lessons for work, workers, and workplaces. Paul repeatedly stresses the importance of transparency and integrity. He urges his readers to invest in good and joyful relationships at work and to pursue reconciliation when relationships are broken. He measures godly work in terms of service, leadership, humility, generosity, and the reputations we earn through our actions. He argues that performance, accountability, and the timely fulfillment of obligations are essential duties of Christians at work. He gives standards for unbiased performance evaluation. He explores the opportunities and challenges of working with nonbelievers. He implores us to use the wealth we gain from work for the good of the community, even to the point of making equal use of it to benefit others as we do to benefit ourselves. He assures us that in doing so we increase, rather than decrease, our own financial security because we come to depend on God's power rather than our own weakness.

Paul's words are extremely challenging because he says that serving others, even to the point of suffering, is the way to be effective in God's economy, just as Jesus himself effected our salvation by his suffering on the cross. Paul, while falling far short of Jesus' divine perfection, is willing to live his life as an open book, an example of how God's strength overcomes human frailty. Because of his openness, Paul is credible when he claims that working according to God's ways, purposes, and values is truly the way to a fuller life. He passes on to us the words of the Lord Jesus himself, "My grace is sufficient for you, for power is made perfect in weakness" (2 Cor. 12:9). This admonition is just as important to our work today as it was to the Corinthians when Paul wrote this fascinating letter.

Galatians, Ephesians, Philippians, and Work

Galatians, Ephesians and Philippians are three short but rich books among the letters of Paul in the New Testament. Because of their brevity, their contribution to the theology of work is combined here into a single chapter. However, the three letters have their own distinctive themes, and we will explore each letter on its own.

Galatians and Work

> For you were called to freedom, brothers and sisters; only do not use your freedom as an opportunity for self-indulgence, but through love become slaves to one another. (Gal. 5:13)

Introduction to Galatians

How do we live as believers in Jesus Christ? If the Christian life begins when we put our faith in Christ as Savior and Lord, how do we express this faith in our daily lives, including our work?

For many of us, the answer to these questions lies in ordering our behavior according to certain basic rules. Thus, for example, when it comes to the workplace, we might adopt the following to-do list: (1) Show respect to colleagues; (2) don't use inappropriate language; (3) don't gossip; (4) be guided by biblical values when making decisions; and (5) speak of faith in Christ if possible. Although this list could easily be much longer, it contains valuable guidance that reflects biblical priorities.

But there is a danger for Christians in such a list, whether in the workplace or elsewhere. It's the danger of legalism, of turning the Christian life into a set of rules rather than our free response to God's grace in Christ and a network of relationships centered in Christ. Moreover, those who approach the Christian life legalistically often tend to put on their to-do list items that are inessential or perhaps even incorrect.

Paul and the Galatians

This is exactly what happened with the believers in Galatia in the mid-first century. In response to the preaching of the Apostle Paul, they had put their faith in Christ and began living as Christians. But, before long, they started shaping their lives according to a list of do's and don'ts. In this effort, the Galatians were influenced by outsiders who claimed to be Christians and who insisted that the Christian life required keeping the Law of Moses as understood by certain contemporary schools of thought. In particular, these "Judaizers" were persuading the Galatians to live like Jews in matters of circumcision (Gal. 5:2–12) and the ceremonial law (Gal. 4:10).

Paul wrote the letter we call "Galatians" in order to get the Christians in Galatia back on the right track. Though he did not address workplace issues directly, his basic instructions on the nature of the Christian life speak incisively to our interests in faith and work. Moreover, Galatians contains work-related imagery, especially drawn from the first-century practice of slavery. Christians, according to Paul, are to live in freedom, not in slavery to the Law of Moses and other earthly powers (Gal. 4:1–11). Yet, ironically, those who exercise their freedom in Christ should choose to "become slaves to one another" through love (Gal. 5:13).

Biblical scholars almost unanimously agree that Galatians was written by the Apostle Paul to a group of churches in the Roman province of Galatia, in what is now central Turkey, sometime between AD 49 and 58.[1] Paul was writing to churches he had founded through the preaching of the good news of Jesus Christ. These churches existed in a culturally and religiously diverse environment and had recently been influenced by Judaizers (Jewish Christians who argued that all Christians must keep the whole law if they want to experience the full Christian life).

---

[1] See Richard N. Longenecker, *Galatians*, vol. 41 of the *Word Biblical Commentary* (Waco, TX: Word, 1990), lxxiii–lxxxvii.

Paul underscores the freedom we have in Christ in his response to the Galatians and the Judaizers who were corrupting them. Applied to the workplace, Galatians helps us understand and engage in our work with a freedom that is essential to the gospel of Jesus Christ.

After introducing himself, Paul greets the Galatians, referring to Christ as one "who gave himself for our sins to set us free from the present evil age" (Gal. 1:3). Thus he introduces the theme of freedom, which is central to the letter to the Galatians and to living as a believer in Jesus.

Understanding Life in Christ (Galatians 1:6–4:31)

Paul begins by identifying the problem among the Galatians. They "are turning to a different gospel" (Gal. 1:6). This "gospel" requires Gentiles "to live like Jews" (Gal. 2:14). In order to show that this "gospel" is really not a gospel—that is, good news—at all, Paul presents a variety of arguments, including his autobiography (Gal. 1:10–2:21), the receiving of the Spirit through faith (Gal. 3:1–5), the offspring of Abraham through faith (Gal. 3:6–29), the analogy of slaves and children (Gal. 4:1–11), a personal, emotional appeal (Gal. 4:12–20), and the allegory of the slave woman and the free woman (Gal. 4:21–31).

At several points in chapters 1–4 in his explication of the Christian life, Paul uses the language and imagery of slavery to fortify his understanding of life in Christ. Slavery, which in Galatians signifies primarily the absence of freedom, is that from which the Galatians had been delivered by their faith in Christ. "You are no longer a slave but a child" (Gal. 4:7). Their desire to follow the Law of Moses rather than to rely on their faith is, in effect, a senseless return to the bondage of slavery (Gal. 4:8–10). Even the Law of Moses, when understood properly, commends freedom rather than slavery to the law itself (Gal. 4:21–31).

So we see that Paul uses workplace imagery (slavery) to illustrate a spiritual point about religious legalism. Yet the point does apply directly to the workplace itself. A legalistic workplace—in which bosses try to control every motion, every word, every thought that employees have—is contrary to freedom in Christ. Workers of all types owe obedience to their legitimate superiors. And organizations of all types owe freedom to their workers to the full extent compatible with the true needs of the work.

Living in Christ (Gal. 5–6)

Galatians 5:1 completes the crescendo of the first four chapters with a roaring call to freedom. "For freedom Christ has set us free. Stand firm, therefore, and do not submit again to a yoke of slavery." Yet this does not mean that Christians should do whatever they please, gratifying their own sinful desires and neglecting those around them. On the contrary, Paul explains, "For you were called to freedom, brothers and sisters; only do not use your freedom as an opportunity for self-indulgence, but through love become slaves to one another" (Gal. 5:13). Christians are free in Christ from slavery to this world and its power, including the Law of Moses. Yet in this freedom, they should choose out of love to serve one another with humility. Such "slavery" is not bondage, but an ironic exercise of true freedom in Christ.

Living in the Spirit (Galatians 5:13–23)

The Spirit of God, given to Christians when they believe the good news of Christ (Gal. 3:2–5), helps us to live out our faith each day (Gal. 5:16). Those who "live by the Spirit" will reject and be safe from the "works of the flesh," which include "fornication, impurity, licentiousness, idolatry, sorcery, enmities, strife, jealousy, anger, quarrels, dissensions, factions, envy, drunkenness, carousing, and things like these" (Gal. 5:19–21). Parts of this list sound all too similar to life in many workplaces—strife, jealousy, anger, quarrels, dissensions, factions and envy. Even seemingly religious practices such as idolatry and sorcery have real manifestations in the workplace. If we are called to live in the Spirit at all, then we are called to live in the Spirit at work.

Paul specifically warns us against "self-indulgence" in the name of freedom (Gal. 5:13). Instead, we should choose to "become slaves [or servants] to one another." At work, this means we are to assist our co-workers even when we are in competition or at odds with them. We are to confront fairly and resolve our jealousies, angers, quarrels, dissensions, factions, and envy (see Matt. 18:15–17), rather than nurture resentment. We are to create products and services that exceed our customers' legitimate expectations, because a true servant seeks what is best for the person served, not merely what is adequate.

The Spirit of God is not, however, simply a divine naysayer who keeps us out of trouble. Rather, the Spirit at work in believers produces new attitudes and actions. In agriculture, fruit is a delicious result of long-term growth and cultivation. The metaphor "fruit of the Spirit" signals that God cares about the kind of people we are becoming, rather than only what we are doing today. We are to cultivate "love, joy, peace, patience, kindness, generosity, faithfulness, gentleness, and self-control" (Gal. 5:22–23) over the course of a lifetime. We have no reason to believe that this fruit is meant only for relationships among Christians in our churches and families. On the contrary, just as we are to be guided by the Spirit in every facet of life, so we are to demonstrate the fruit of the Spirit wherever we are, including the places in which we work. Patience in the workplace, for example, does not refer to indecisiveness or failure to act urgently in business matters. Instead, it means a freedom from the anxiety that would tempt us to act before the time is ripe, such as firing a subordinate in a fit of anger, berating a colleague before hearing an explanation, demanding a response before a student has time to consider, or cutting a customer's hair before being completely sure what kind of style the customer wants. If the fruit of the Spirit seems to have little to do with work, perhaps we have narrowed our imagination of what spiritual fruit really is.

Working for the Good of Others (Galatians 6:1–10)

The first part of Galatians 6 employs a variety of work-related words to instruct Christians in how to care for others in tangible ways. Christians are to be generous to others as we "bear one another's burdens" (Gal. 6:2). Yet, lest we be overtaken by pride and imagine that our work on behalf of others excuses poor work of our own, believers must "test their own work" and "carry their own loads" (Gal. 6:4–5).

The analogy of sowing and reaping allows Paul to encourage the Galatians to focus on the life of the Spirit rather than the flesh (Gal. 6:7–8). Sowing in the Spirit involves purposeful effort: "Let us *work* for the good of all, and especially for those of the family of faith" (Gal. 6:10). Christians are to labor for the common good, in addition to caring for their fellow believers. Surely, if we are to *work* for the good of others, one place we should do it is in the workplace.

The Center of the Gospel (Galatians 6:11–18)

In his closing remarks, Paul reminds the Galatians of the center of the gospel, which is the cross of Christ: "May I never boast of anything except the cross of our Lord Jesus Christ, by which the world has been crucified to me, and I to the world" (Gal. 6:14).

Conclusion to Galatians

In his concluding use of crucifixion language (Gal. 6:14), Paul echoes what he had said earlier in the letter: "I have been crucified with Christ; and it is no longer I who live, but it is Christ who lives in me. And the life I now live in the flesh I live by faith in the Son of God, who loved me and gave himself for me" (Gal. 2:19b-20). Faith in Christ is not only believing certain facts about his life, death, and resurrection, but also dying with Christ so that he might live in us. This "Christ in us" reality does not disappear when we enter our offices, warehouses, shops, and boardrooms. Rather, it urges and empowers us to live for Christ, in the power of the Spirit, every moment, in every place.

The Christian life is based upon faith. But faith is not passive assent to the truth of the gospel. Rather, in the daily experience of the Christian, faith becomes alive and active. According to Paul, faith can even be said to be "*working* through love" (Gal. 5:6). Thus faith at work in our lives energizes loving actions, even as the Spirit of God helps us to be more loving both in heart and in action (Gal. 5:22). We reject the slavery of trying to justify ourselves by our work. However, when we embrace our freedom in Christ through faith, our work leads to love, joy, peace, patience, kindness, generosity, faithfulness, gentleness, and self-control. We see our work as a primary context in which to exercise our freedom in Christ so as to love others and "work for the good of all" (Gal. 6:10). If we do not see the fruit of faith in our places of work, then we are cutting off a major part of our life from Christ's mastery.

Ephesians and Work

I therefore, the prisoner in the Lord, beg you to lead a life worthy of the calling to which you have been called. (Eph. 4:1)

Introduction to Ephesians

What is the place of our work in the grand scheme of things? Is work just an activity we need to get by in life? Or is it also a place where we find meaning, healing, and personal integration?[2] Does our work have a place in the cosmos of God's creation? Does it mean anything alongside Christ's work of redeeming the world?

The letter to the Ephesians tells the story of God's cosmic work, beginning before the creation of the world, continuing in Christ's work of redemption, and leading up to the present moment and beyond. It draws us into this work both as awestruck observers of the drama and as active participants in God's work.

Thus Ephesians gives a new perspective, not only about God but also about ourselves. Our lives, our actions, and indeed our work take on fresh meaning. We live differently, we worship differently, and we work differently because of what God has done and is doing in Christ. We do what we do with our lives, including our professional lives, in response to God's saving activity and in fulfillment of the assignment he has given us to cooperate with him. Each one of us has been called by God to participate in God's work in the world (Eph. 4:1).

The letter we know as "Ephesians" is both similar to and different from other New Testament letters attributed to the Apostle Paul. It is similar most of all to Colossians, with which it shares common themes, structures, and even sentences (Eph. 6:21–22; Col. 4:7–8).[3] Ephesians is different from the other Pauline letters in its exalted style, distinctive vocabulary, and in some of its theological perspectives. Moreover, it is much

---

[2] See, for example, Dan P. McAdams, *The Redemptive Self: Stories Americans Live By* (New York: Oxford University Press, 2005); Donald E. Polkinghorne, *Narrative Knowing and the Human Sciences* (Albany: State University of New York, 1988).

[3] See "Colossians & Philemon and Work."

less oriented to a particular situation in the life of a particular church than Paul's other letters.[4] In this commentary, authorship by Paul is assumed.

Rather than focusing on the needs of one particular congregation, the letter to the Ephesians presents an expansive theological perspective on the work of God in the universe and the central role of the church of Jesus Christ within that work. Each individual believer contributes to this ecclesial effort as one who has been "created in Jesus Christ for good works" (Eph. 2:10) and who is essential to the growth and ministry of the church (Eph. 4:15–16).

God's Grand Plan: A Theological Vision (Ephesians 1:1–3:21)

The first half of Ephesians unfolds the grand narrative of God's salvation of the whole cosmos. Even before the "foundation of the world," God graciously chose us in Christ for relationship with him and to live out his purpose in the world (Eph. 1:4–6). At the core of this purpose, God will "gather up all things in Christ, things in heaven and things on earth" (Eph. 1:10). To put it differently, God will restore the whole cosmos, once broken by sin, under the authority of Christ. The fact that God will renovate his creation reminds us that this world—including farms, schools, and corporations—matters to God and has not been abandoned by him.

God's restoring work, centered in Christ, involves human beings, both as recipients of God's grace and as participants in his ongoing work of gracious restoration. We are saved by grace because of faith, not because of our works (Eph. 2:8–9). But our works are vital to God, "for we are what he has made us, created in Christ Jesus for good works, which God prepared beforehand to be our way of life" (Eph. 2:10). Thus we are not saved by works but for works. These works, which include all that we do, are a part of God's renewal of creation. Therefore, our activity in the workplace is one crucial element of that which God has prepared for us to do in fulfillment of his purpose for us.

---

[4] For discussion of these issues and their implications, see Andrew T. Lincoln, *Ephesians*, vol. 42 of the *Word Biblical Commentary* (Nashville: Thomas Nelson, 1990), xlvii–lxxiv; "Ephesians, Letter to the" in *Dictionary of Paul and His Letters*, eds. Gerald F. Hawthorne, Ralph P. Martin, and Daniel G. Reid (Downers Grove, IL: InterVarsity Press, 1993).

The church features prominently in God's plan for putting the world back together in Christ. His death on the cross not only made possible our personal salvation (Eph. 2:4–7), but also mended the breach between Jews and Gentiles (Eph. 2:13–18). This unity between former enemies epitomizes the unifying work of God. Thus the church serves as a demonstration to the whole universe of the nature and ultimate success of God's cosmic plan (Eph. 3:9–10). But the church is not merely a unit of people who gather once a week to do religious activities together. Rather, the church is the community of all believers, doing everything they do in all the places of life, whether working together or separately. In every sphere of life, we have "the power at work within us [which] is able to accomplish abundantly far more than all we can ask or imagine" (Eph. 3:20). Notice that Paul uses the civic term "citizens" (Eph. 2:19) to describe Christians, rather than the religious term "worshippers." In fact, Ephesians gives virtually no instructions about what the church should do when it gathers, but several instructions about how its members should work, as we will see momentarily.

God's Grand Plan: A Practical Guide (Ephesians 4:1–6:24)

The second half of Ephesians begins with an exhortation to live out the vision of the first half of the letter. "I therefore, the prisoner in the Lord, beg you to lead a life worthy of the calling to which you have been called" (Eph. 4:1). Every Christian shares in this calling. Thus our truest and deepest *vocation* (from the Latin word for "calling") is to do our part to advance the multifaceted mission of God in the world. This calling shapes everything else we do in life, including our work—or what we sometimes refer to as our "vocation." Of course, God may call us to specific jobs for expressing our fundamental calling to live for the praise of God's glory (Eph. 1:12). Thus as doctors and lawyers, clerks and waiters, actors and musicians, and parents and grandparents, we lead a life worthy of our calling to Christ and his activity in the world.

Working Hard for Good and for Giving (Ephesians 4:28)

Among the practical exhortations in Ephesians 4–6, two passages deal specifically with work-related concerns. The first has to do with the purpose of work. "Thieves must give up stealing; rather let them labor and work honestly with their own hands, so as to have something to share with the needy" (Eph. 4:28). Though pointed immediately at those who steal, Paul's advice is relevant to all Christians. The Greek translated in the NRSV as "honestly" (*to agathon*) literally means "to the good." God is always leading Christians to the good. The workplace is a crucial setting for us to do many of the good works that God has prepared for us (Eph. 2:10).

Through our work, we also earn sufficient resources to share with the needy, whether directly through the church or by other means. Although a theology of work is not quite the same as a theology of charity, this verse explicitly links the two. The overall message is that the purpose of work is to do good both by what our work accomplishes directly and by what our work enables us to give to others outside of work.

Mutuality in Working for the Lord (Ephesians 5:21–6:9)

The second practical consideration is relationships. Our calling as Christians impacts our basic relationships, especially those in the family and the workplace. (Prior to the industrial age, households were equally places of family life and places of work.) Ephesians 5:21–6:9 underscores this point by including specific instructions for relationships within the household (wives/husbands, children/fathers, slaves/masters). Lists of this sort were common in the moral discourse of the Greco-Roman world and are represented in the New Testament (see, for example, Col. 3:18–4:1 and 1 Pet. 2:13–3:12).[5]

We are particularly interested in Ephesians 6:5–9, a passage that addresses the relationship between slaves and masters. Paul addresses Christians who are masters, Christians who are slaves under Christian masters, and Christians who are slaves under nonbelieving masters. This text is similar to a parallel passage in Colossians (Col. 3:22–4:1). (See "Colossians" in "Colossians & Philemon and Work" for the historical background on slavery in the first-century Roman Empire, which is helpful for understanding this section of Ephesians.) To summarize briefly,

---

[5] See David Noel Freedman, "Haustafeln" and "Household Codes" in *The Anchor Bible Dictionary* (New York: Doubleday, 1992).

Roman slavery has both similarities to and differences from paid work in the twenty-first century. The chief similarity is that both ancient slaves and contemporary workers serve under the authority of masters or supervisors. With regard to the work itself, both groups have a duty to meet the expectations of those in authority over their work. The chief difference is that ancient slaves (and those in modern times as well) owe not only their work but also their lives to their masters. Slaves cannot quit, they have limited legal rights and remedies for mistreatment, they do not receive pay or compensation for their work, and they do not negotiate working conditions. In short, the scope for abuse of power by masters over slaves is far greater than that for supervisors over workers.

We will begin by exploring this section of Ephesians as it applies to actual slaves. Then we will consider applications to the form of paid labor that dominates developed economies today.

Christian Slaves (Ephesians 6:6–8)

The letter to the Ephesians encourages slaves to see themselves as "slaves of Christ" who "render service with enthusiasm" for the Lord rather than their human masters (Eph. 6:6–7). The fact that their work is for Christ will encourage them to work hard and well. Paul's words are therefore a comfort when masters order slaves to do good work. In that case, God will reward the slave (Eph. 6:8) even if the master doesn't, as is typically the case with slaves (Luke 17:8).

But why would slaving away for an earthly master necessarily be "doing the will of God" (Eph. 6:6)? Surely a master could order a slave to do work that is far from the will of God—abusing another slave, cheating a customer, or encroaching on someone else's fields. Paul clarifies, "Slaves, obey your earthly masters with fear and trembling, in singleness of heart, *as you obey Christ*" (Eph. 6:5). Slaves can only do for their masters what could be done *for Christ*. If a master orders slaves to do evil work, then Paul's words are dreadfully challenging, for the slave would have to refuse the master's orders. This could lead to unpleasant consequences, to say the least. Nonetheless, Paul's command is inescapable. "Render service . . . as to the Lord, and not to men and women" (Eph. 6:7). The Lord's commands supersede the commands of any master. Indeed, what else could "singleness of heart" mean, if not to set aside every order that conflicts with duty to Christ? "No one can serve two masters," said Jesus (Matt. 6:24). The punishment for disobeying an earthly master may be fearsome, but it may be necessary to suffer it in order to work "as to the Lord."

Christian Masters (Ephesians 6:5–11)

It is cruel for a master to force a slave to choose between obedience to the master and obedience to Christ. Therefore, Paul tells masters to "stop threatening" their slaves (Eph. 6:9). If masters order slaves to do good work, then threats should not be necessary. If masters order slaves to do evil work, then their threats are like threats against Christ. As in the letter to the Colossians, Ephesians agrees that masters should re-member that they have a Master in heaven. But Ephesians underscores the fact that both slaves and masters "have the *same* Master" (Eph. 6:9). For this reason, Ephesians says that masters are to "do the same for your slaves" (Eph. 6:9)—that is, to give orders to slaves as though they were giving the orders to (or for) Christ. With this in mind, no Chris-tian master could order a slave to do evil work, or even excessive work. Though the earthly distinction of master and slave remains intact, their relationship has been altered with an unprecedented call to mutuality. Both parties are subject to Christ alone "in singleness of heart" (Eph. 6:5). Neither can lord it over the other, since only Christ is Lord (Eph. 6:7). Neither can shirk the duty of love to the other. This passage ac-cepts the economic and cultural reality of slavery, but it contains fertile seeds of abolitionism. In Christ's kingdom, "there is no longer slave or free" (Gal. 3:28).

Slavery continues to flourish in our world today, much to our shame, though it's often called human trafficking or forced labor. The inner logic of Ephesians 6:5–9, as well as the broader story of Ephesians, motivates us to work for the end of slavery. Most of us, however, will not experience slavery in a personal way, either as slaves or as masters. Yet we do find ourselves in workplace relationships where someone has authority over another person. By analogy, Ephesians 6:5–9 teaches both employers and employees to order, perform, and reward only work that could be done by or for Christ. When we are ordered to do good work, the issue is simple, though not always easy. We do it to the best of our ability, regardless of the compensation or appreciation we receive from our bosses, customers, regulators, or anyone else in authority over us.

When we are ordered to do evil work, the situation is more complicated. On the one hand, Paul tells us to "obey your earthly masters . . . as you obey Christ." We cannot lightly disobey those in earthly authority over us, any more than we can lightly disobey Christ. This has even caused some to question whether whistleblowing, work stoppages, and complaints to regulatory authorities are legitimate for Christian employees. At the very least, a difference of opinion or judgment is not by itself good enough cause to disobey a valid order at work. It is important not to confuse "I don't want to do this work, and I don't think it's fair for my boss to tell me to do it" with "It is against God's will for me to do this work." Paul's instruction to "obey your earthly masters with fear and trembling" suggests that we obey the orders of those in authority over us unless we have strong reason to believe doing so would be wrong.

Yet Paul adds that we obey earthly masters as a way of "doing the will of God from the heart." Surely, if we are ordered to do something clearly against God's will—for example, a violation of biblical commands or values—then our duty to our higher master (Christ) is to resist the ungodly order from a human boss. The crucial distinction often requires finding out whose interests would be served by disobeying the order. If disobeying would protect the interests of another person or the larger community then there is a strong case for disobeying the order. If disobeying the order would protect only our personal interests, the case is weaker. In some cases, protecting others could even jeopardize our careers or cost us our livelihoods. No wonder Paul says, "Be strong in the Lord" and "Put on the whole armor of God" (Eph. 6:10, 11).

Yet surely we express compassion for those—including maybe ourselves at times—who face the choice of obeying a genuinely ungodly order or suffering personal loss such as getting fired. This is especially true in the case of workers near the bottom of the economic ladder, who may have few alternatives and no financial cushion. Workers are routinely ordered to perform a variety of petty evils, such as lying ("Tell her I'm not in the office"), cheating ("Put an extra bottle of wine on table 16's tab—they're too drunk to even notice"), and idolatry ("I expect you to act like this job is the most important thing in the world to you"). Do we have to resign over every one of them? Other times, workers may be ordered to do serious evils. "Threaten to drag her name through the mud if she won't agree to our terms." "Find an excuse to fire him before he uncovers any more falsified quality control records." "Dump it in the river tonight when no one is around." Yet the alternative of losing a job and seeing our family slide into poverty may be—or seem—even worse than following the ungodly order. Often it's not clear which alternatives are more in accord with biblical values and which are less. We must acknowledge that the decisions can be complex. When we are pressured to do something wrong, we need to depend on God's power to stand firmer against evil than we ever believed we could. Yet we also need to bear Christ's word of compassion and forgiveness when we find that Christians cannot overcome all the evils of the world's workplaces.

When we are the ones in authority, then, we should order only work that Christ would order. We do not order subordinates to harm themselves or others in order to benefit ourselves. We do not order others to do what in good conscience we will not do. We do not threaten those who refuse our orders out of conscience or justice. Though we are bosses, we have bosses of our own, and Christians in authority still have a heightened duty to serve God by the way we command others. We are Christ's slaves, and we have no authority to order or obey anyone else in opposition to Christ. For each of us, no matter our position in the workplace, our work is a way of serving—or failing to serve—God.

Conclusion to Ephesians

Only a few verses of Ephesians deal precisely with the workplace and even these are directed at thieves, slaves, and masters. But when we glimpse how God is restoring all of creation through Christ, and when we discover that our work plays an essential role in that plan, then our workplace becomes a primary context for us to do the good works that God has prepared for us. Ephesians does not tell us specifically what good works God has prepared for each of us in our work. We must look to other sources to discern that. But it does tell us that God calls us to do all of our work for the good. Relationships and attitudes in the workplace are transformed as we see ourselves and our co-workers mainly in terms of our relationship with Jesus Christ, the one true Lord.

Ephesians encourages us to take a new perspective on our lives, one in which our work is an outgrowth of God's own work of creating the world and redeeming it from sin. We work in response to God's call to follow Jesus in every aspect of our lives (Eph. 4:1). At work, we discover the opportunity to do many of the good works that God intends for us to do. Thus in our offices, factories, schools, households, stores, and every other place of work, we have the opportunity to "render service with enthusiasm" to the Lord (Eph. 6:7).

Philippians and Work

> Work out your own salvation with fear and trembling; for it is God who is at work in you, enabling you both to will and to work for his good pleasure. (Phil. 2:11b-12)

Introduction to Philippians

Work requires effort. Whether we do business or drive trucks, raise children or write articles, sell shoes or care for the disabled and aged, our work requires personal effort. If we don't get up in the morning and get going, our work won't get done. What motivates us to get out of bed each morning? What keeps us going throughout the day? What energizes us so that we can do our work with faithfulness and even excellence?

There are a wide variety of answers to these questions. Some might point to economic necessity. "I get up and go to work because I need the money." Other answers might refer to our interest in our work. "I work because I love my job." Still other answers might be less inspiring. "What gets me up and keeps me going all day? Caffeine!"

Paul's letter to the Christians in Philippi provides a different sort of answer to the question of where we find strength to do our work. Paul says that our work is not the result of *our own* effort, but that *God's* work in us is what gives us our energy. What we do in life, including on the job, is an expression of God's saving work in Christ. Moreover, we find the strength for this effort by the power of God within us. Christ's work is to serve people (Mark 10:35), and God empowers us to serve alongside him.

Almost all scholars agree that the Apostle Paul wrote the letter we know as Philippians sometime between AD 54 and 62.[6] There is no unanimity about the place from which Paul wrote, though we know it was written during one of his several imprisonments (Phil. 1:7).[7] It is clear that Paul wrote this personal letter to the church in Philippi, a community he planted during an earlier visit there (Phil. 1:5; Acts 16:11–40). He wrote in order to strengthen his relationship with the Philippian church, to update them on his personal situation, to thank them for their support of his ministry, to equip them to confront threats to their faith, to help them get along better, and, in general, to assist them in living out their faith.

Philippians uses the word *work* (*ergon* and cognates) several times (Phil. 1:6; 2:12–13, 30; 4:3). Paul uses it to describe God's work of salvation and the human tasks that flow from God's saving work. He doesn't directly address issues in the secular workplace, but what he says about work has important applications there.

God's Work in Us (Philippians 1:1–26)

In the context of his opening prayer for the Philippians (Phil. 1:3–11), Paul shares his conviction of God's work in and among the Philippian believers. "I am confident of this, that the one who began a good work among you will bring it to completion by the day of Jesus Christ" (Phil. 1:6). The "work" Paul refers to is the work of new birth in Christ, which leads to salvation. Paul himself had a hand in that work by preaching the gospel to them. He continues that work as their teacher and apostle, and he says it is "fruitful *labor* for me" (Phil. 1:22). Yet the underlying worker is not Paul but God, for God is "the one who began a good work among you" (Phil. 1:6). "This is God's doing" (Phil. 1:28).

---

[6] Gerald F. Hawthorne, *Philippians*, rev. and exp. by Ralph P. Martin, in vol. 43 of the *Word Biblical Commentary* (Nashville: Thomas Nelson, 2004), xxvii–xxix, xxxix–l.

[7] See Gerald F. Hawthorne, Ralph P. Martin, and Daniel G. Reid, eds., "4.3. Place and Date" of "Philippians, Letter to the," in *Dictionary of Paul and His Letters* (Downers Grove, IL: InterVarsity Press, 1993).

The NRSV speaks of God's work "among you," while most English translations speak of God's work "in you." Both are apropos, and the Greek phrase *en humin* can be rendered either way. God's good work begins *in* individual lives. Yet it is to be lived out *among* believers in their fellowship together. The main point of verse 6 is not to restrict God's work either to individuals or the community as a whole, but rather to underscore the fact that all of their work is God's work. Moreover, this work isn't completed when individuals "get saved" or when churches are planted. God continues working in and among us until his work is complete, which happens "by the day of Jesus Christ." Only when Christ returns will God's work be finished.

Paul's job is evangelist and apostle, and there are marks of success and ambition in his profession, as in any other. How many converts you win, how much funding you raise, how many people praise you as their spiritual mentor, how your numbers compare to other evangelists—these can be points of pride and ambition. Paul admits that these motivations exist in his profession, but he insists that the only proper motivation is love (Phil. 1:15–16). The implication is that this is true in every other profession as well. We are all tempted to work for the marks of success—including recognition, security, and money—which can lead to "selfish ambition" (*eritieias*, perhaps more precisely translated as "unfair self-promotion").[8] They are not entirely bad, for they often come as we accomplish the legitimate purposes of our jobs (Phil. 1:18). Getting the work done is important, even if our motivation is not perfect. Yet in the long run (Phil. 3:7–14), motivation is even more important and the only Christ-like motivation is love.

Do Your Work in a Worthy Manner (Philippians 1:27–2:11)

Since our work is actually God's work in us, our work should be worthy, as God's work is. But apparently we have the ability to hinder God's work in us, for Paul exhorts, "Live your life in a manner worthy of the gospel of Christ" (Phil. 1:27). His topic is life in general, and there

---

[8] James Strong, *Enhanced Strong's Lexicon* (Ontario: Woodside Bible Fellowship, 1995), G2052.

is no reason to believe he means to exclude work from this exhortation. He gives three particular commands:

1. "Be of the same mind" (Phil. 2:2).

2. "Do nothing from selfish ambition or conceit, but in humility regard others as better than yourselves" (Phil. 2:3).

3. "Look not to your own interests, but the interests of others" (Phil. 2:4).

Again, we can work according to these commands only because our work is actually God's work in us, but this time he says it in a beautiful passage often called the "Hymn of Christ" (Phil. 2:6–11). Jesus, he says, "did not regard equality with God as something to be exploited, but emptied himself taking the form of a slave, and being born in human likeness. And being found in human form, he humbled himself and became obedient to the point of death—even death on a cross" (Phil. 2:8–9). Therefore God's work in us—specifically Christ's work in us—is always done humbly with others, for the benefit of others, even if it requires sacrifice.

"Be of the Same Mind" (Philippians 2:2)

The first of the three commands, "Be of the same mind," is given to Christians as a body. We shouldn't expect it to apply in the secular workplace. In fact, we don't always want to have the same mind as everyone around us at work (Rom. 12:2). But in many workplaces, there is more than one Christian. We should strive to have the same mind as other Christians where we work. Sadly, this can be very difficult. In church, we segregate ourselves into communities in which we generally agree about biblical, theological, moral, spiritual, and even cultural matters. At work we don't have that luxury. We may share the workplace with other Christians with whom we disagree about such matters. It may even be hard to recognize others who claim to be Christians as Christians, according to our judgments.

This is a scandalous impediment to both our witness as Christians and our effectiveness as co-workers. What do our non-Christian colleagues think of our Lord—and us—if we get along worse with each other than with nonbelievers? At the very least, we ought to try to identify other Christians in our workplaces and learn about their beliefs and practices. We may not agree, even about matters of great importance, yet it is a far better witness to show mutual respect than to treat others who call themselves Christians with contempt or bickering. If nothing else, we should set aside our differences enough to do excellent work together, if we really believe that our work truly matters to God.

Having the same mind as Christ means "having the same love" as Christ (Phil. 2:2). Christ loved us to the point of death (Phil. 2:8), and we are to have the same love he had (Phil. 2:5). This gives us something in common not only with other believers but also with nonbelievers in our workplaces: we love them! Everyone at work can agree with us that we should do work that benefits them. If a Christian says, "My job is to serve you," who would disagree with that?

"Do Nothing from Selfish Ambition or Conceit" (Philippians 2:3)

Regarding others as better than ourselves is the mind-set of those who have the mind of Christ (Phil. 2:3). Our humility is meant to be offered to all the people around us, and not just to Christians. For Jesus' death on the cross—the ultimate act of humility—was for sinners and not for the righteous (Luke 5:32; Rom. 5:8; 1 Tim. 1:15).

Workplaces offer unlimited opportunities for humble service. You can be generous in giving credit to others for success and stingy in passing out blame for failure. You can listen to what someone else is saying instead of thinking ahead to your reply. You can try another person's idea instead of insisting on your own way. You can give up your envy at another person's success or promotion or higher salary, or, failing that, you can take your envy to God in prayer instead of to your buddies at lunch.

Conversely, workplaces offer unlimited opportunities for selfish ambition. As we have seen, ambition—even competition—is not necessarily bad (Rom. 15:20; 1 Cor. 9:24; 1 Tim. 2:5), but unfairly advancing your own agenda is. It forces you to adopt an inaccurate, inflated assessment of yourself ("conceit"), which puts you into an ever more remote fantasyland where you can be effective neither in work nor in faith. There are two antidotes. First, make sure your success depends on and contributes to others' success. This generally means operating in genuine teamwork with others in your workplace. Second, continually seek accurate feedback about yourself and your performance. You may find that your performance is actually excellent, but if you learn that from accurate sources, it is not conceit. The simple act of accepting feedback from others is a form of humility, since you subordinate your self-image to their image of you. Needless to say, this is helpful only if you find accurate sources of feedback. Submitting your self-image to people who would abuse or delude you is not true humility. Even as he submitted his body to abuse on the cross, Jesus maintained an accurate assessment of himself (Luke 23:43).

"Look Not to Your Own Interests, But to the Interests of Others" (Philippians 2:4)

Of the three commands, this may be the hardest to reconcile with our roles in the workplace. We go to work—at least in part—in order to meet our needs. How then can it make sense to avoid looking to our own interests? Paul does not say. But we should remember that he is speaking to a community of people, to whom he says, "Let each of you look not to your own interests, but to the interests of others" (Phil. 2:4). Perhaps he expects that if everyone looks not to their individual needs, but to the needs of the whole community, then everyone's needs will be met. This is consistent with the body analogy Paul uses in 1 Corinthians 12 and elsewhere. The eye does not meet its need for transportation but relies on the foot for that. So each organ acts for the good of the body, yet finds its own needs met.

Under ideal circumstances, this might work for a close-knit group, perhaps a church of equally highly committed members. But is it meant to apply to the nonchurch workplace? Does Paul mean to tell us to look to the interests of our co-workers, customers, bosses, subordinates, suppliers, and myriad others around us, instead of our own interests? Again, we must turn to Philippians 2:8, where Paul depicts Jesus on the cross as our model, looking to the interests of sinners instead of his own. He lived out this principle in the world at large, not the church, and so must we. And Paul is clear that the consequences for us include suffering and loss, maybe even death. "Whatever gains I had, these I have come to regard as loss because of Christ." There is no natural reading of Philippians 2 that lets us off the hook of looking to the interests of others at work instead to our own.

Following Christ as Ordinary Christians (Philippians 2:19–3:21)

In fact, Philippians gives us three examples—Paul, Epaphroditus, and Timothy—to show us how all Christians are meant to follow Christ's model. "Join in imitating me, and observe those who live according to the example you have in us," Paul tells us (Phil. 3:17). He depicts each of these examples in a framework based on the "Hymn of Jesus" in chapter 2.

Person	Sent to a difficult place	In obedience/slavery	Taking grave risks	For the benefit of others
Jesus	Found in human form (2:7)	Taking the form of a slave (2:7)	Obedient to the point of death (2:8)	Emptied himself (2:7)
Paul	Live in the flesh (1:22)	Servant of Jesus Christ (1:1)	Imprisonment (1:7) Becoming like Christ in death (3:10)	For your progress and joy (1:25)
Timothy	Send Timothy to you soon (2:19)	Like a son with a father (2:22)	(Not specified in Philippians, but see Rom. 6:21)	Will be genuinely concerned for your welfare (2:20)
Epaphroditus	Send you Epaphroditus (2:25)	Your messenger (2:25)	Came close to death (2:30)	To minister to my need (2:25)

The message is clear. We are called to do as Jesus did. We cannot hide behind the excuse that Jesus is the only Son of God, who serves others so we won't have to. Nor are Paul, Epaphroditus, and Timothy supermen whose exploits we can't hope to duplicate. Instead, as we go to work we are to put ourselves into the same framework of sending, obedience, risk, and service to others:

Person	Sent to a difficult place	In obedience/ slavery	Taking grave risks	For the benefit of others
Workplace Christians	Go to non-Christian workplaces	Work under the authority of others	Risk career limitation for our motivation to love as Christ loves	Are called by God to put others' interests ahead of our own

Are we allowed to temper the command to serve others *instead of* ourselves with a little common sense? Could we, say, look first to the interests of others whom we can trust? Could we look to the interests of others *in addition* to our own interests? Is it okay to work for the common good in situations where we can expect to benefit proportionally, but look out for ourselves when the system is stacked against us? Paul doesn't say.

What should we do if we find ourselves unable or unwilling to live quite so daringly? Paul says only this, "Do not worry about anything, but in everything by prayer and supplication with thanksgiving let your requests be made known to God" (Phil. 4:6). Only by constant prayer, supplication, and thanksgiving to God can we get through the difficult decisions and demanding actions required to look to the interests of others instead of our own. This is not meant as abstract theology but as practical advice for daily life and work.

Everyday Applications (Philippians 4:1–23)

Paul describes three everyday situations that have direct relevance for the workplace.

Resolving Conflict (Philippians 4:2–9)

Paul asks the Philippians to help two women among them, Euodia and Syntyche, come to peace with each other (Phil. 4:2–9). Although our instinctive reflex is to suppress and deny conflict, Paul lovingly brings it into the open where it can be resolved. The women's conflict is not specified, but they are both believers who Paul says "have struggled beside me in the work of the gospel" (Phil. 4:3). Conflict occurs even between the most faithful Christians, as we all know. Stop nurturing resentment, he tells them, and think about what is honorable, just, pure, pleasing, commendable, excellent, and praiseworthy in the other person (Phil. 4:8). "The peace of God, which surpasses all understanding" (Phil. 4:7) seems to begin with appreciating the good points of those around us, even (or especially) when we are in conflict with them. After all, they are people for whom Christ died. We should also look carefully at ourselves and find God's reserves of gentleness, prayer, supplication, thanksgiving, and letting go of worry (Phil. 4:6) inside ourselves.

The application to today's workplace is clear, though seldom easy. When our urge is to ignore and hide conflict with others at work, we must instead acknowledge and talk (not gossip) about it. When we would rather keep it to ourselves, we should ask people of wisdom for help—in humility, not in hopes of gaining an upper hand. When we would rather build a case *against* our rivals, we should instead build a case *for* them, at least doing them the justice of acknowledging whatever their good points are. And when we think we don't have the energy to engage the other person, but would rather just write off the relationship, we must let God's power and patience substitute for our own. In this we seek to imitate our Lord, who "emptied himself" (Phil. 2:7) of personal agendas and so received the power of God (Phil. 2:9) to live out God's will in the world. If we do these things, then our conflict can be resolved in terms of what the true issues are, rather than our projections, fears, and resentments. Usually this leads to a restored working relationship and a kind of mutual respect, if not friendship. Even in the unusual cases where no reconciliation is possible, we can expect a surprising "peace of God, which surpasses all understanding" (Phil. 4:7). It is God's sign that even a broken relationship is not beyond the hope of God's goodness.

Supporting Each Other in Work (Philippians 4:10–11, 15–16)

Paul thanks the Philippians for their support for him, both personal (Phil. 1:30) and financial (Phil. 4:10–11, 15–16). Throughout the New Testament, we see Paul always striving to work in partnership with other Christians, including Barnabas (Acts 13:2), Silas (Acts 15:40), Lydia (Acts

16:14–15), and Priscilla and Aquila (Rom. 16:3). His letters typically end with greetings to people with whom he has worked closely, and are often from Paul and a co-worker, as Philippians is from Paul and Timothy (Phil. 1:1). In this he is following his own advice of imitating Jesus, who did almost everything in partnership with his disciples and others.

As we noted in Philippians 2, Christians in the secular workplace don't always have the luxury of working alongside believers. But that doesn't mean we can't support one another. We could gather with others in our professions or institutions to share mutual support in the specific challenges and opportunities we face in our jobs. The "Mom-to-Mom" program[9] is a practical example of mutual support in the workplace. Mothers gather weekly to learn, share ideas, and support each other in the job of parenting young children. Ideally, all Christians would have that kind of support for their work. In the absence of a formal program, we could talk about our work in our usual Christian communities, including worship and sermons, Bible studies, small groups, church retreats, classes, and the rest. But how often do we? Paul went to great lengths to build community with the others in his calling, even employing messengers to make long sea voyages (Phil. 2:19, 25) to share ideas, news, fellowship, and resources.

Handling Poverty and Plenty (Philippians 4:12–13, 18)

Finally, Paul discusses how to handle both poverty and plenty. This has direct workplace relevance because work makes the difference between poverty and plenty for us, or at least for those of us who are paid for our work. Again, Paul's advice is simple, yet hard to follow. Don't idolize your work in expectation that it will always provide plenty for you. Instead, do your work because of the benefit it brings to others, and learn to be content with however much or little it provides for you. Tough advice indeed. Some professions—teachers, health workers, customer service people, and parents, to name a few—may be used to working overtime without extra pay to help people in need. Others expect to be amply rewarded for the service they perform. Imagine a senior executive or investment banker working without a contract or bonus target say-

---

[9] See www.momtomom.org.

ing, "I take care of the customers, employees, and shareholders, and am happy to receive whatever they choose to give me at the end of the year." It's not common, but a few people do it. Paul says simply this:

> I know what it is to have little, and I know what it is to have plenty. In any and all circumstances I have learned the secret of being well-fed and of going hungry, or having plenty and of being in need. I can do all things through him who strengthens me. . . . I have been paid in full and have more than enough; I am fully satisfied. (Phil. 4:12–13, 18)

The point is not how much or how little we are paid—within reason—but whether we are motivated by the benefit our work does for others or only for our self-interest. Yet that motivation itself should move us to resist institutions, practices, and systems that result in extremes of either too much plenty or too much poverty.

Conclusion to Philippians

Though Paul does not address the workplace distinctly in Philippians, his vision of God's work in us lays a foundation for our considerations of faith and work. Our jobs provide a major context in which we are to live out the good work God has begun in us. We are to seek the same mind as other Christians in our places of life and work. We are to act as though others are better than ourselves. We are to look to the interests of others instead of our own. Without directly addressing work, Paul seems to demand the impossible from us in the workplace! But what we do in the workplace is not just our effort—it is God's work in and through us. Because God's power is unlimited, Paul can say boldly, "I can do all things through him who strengthens me" (Phil. 4:13).

Colossians & Philemon and Work

Introduction to Colossians and Philemon

Whatever you do, in word or deed, do everything in the name of the Lord Jesus, giving thanks to God the Father through him. Whatever your task, put yourselves into it, as done for the Lord and not for your masters, since you know that from the Lord you will receive the inheritance as your reward; you serve the Lord Christ. (Col. 3:17, 23–24)

Why would the Apostle Paul[1] insist that the Christians at Colossae live their daily lives under such a comprehensive mandate of controlling every word and deed? In these two brief but rich letters Paul explores in detail both the theological rationale behind these two overlapping commands and the implications of this lifestyle in all of the primary relationships of life—with our spouses and families, and with our colleagues, employees, or bosses in the workplace.

Background on Colossae and the Colossians

The City of Colossae

Cities grow as they develop commercial centers that provide jobs for their residents. The ancient city of Colossae was built on a major trade route through the Lycus River Valley in the Roman province of Asia

---

[1] The authorship of the letter to the Colossians has been questioned by a number of scholars, but because it is not the purpose of this commentary to address authorship, the letter's self-attribution to Paul will be accepted here. This debate has a negligible effect on understanding the letter's application to the workplace.

Minor (in the southwest corner of modern-day Turkey). There the Colossians manufactured a beautiful dark red wool cloth (*colossinum*) for
which the city became famous. But Colossae's importance as a business
center diminished significantly around 100 BC, when the neighboring
city of Laodicea was founded as an active and commercially aggressive
competitor. The two towns, along with neighboring Hierapolis, were
destroyed by earthquakes in AD 17 (in the reign of Tiberius) and again in
60 (in the reign of Nero). Rebuilt after each earthquake, Colossae never
regained its early prominence, and by 400 the city no longer existed.

The Colossian Church

The Apostle Paul had spent two years planting a church in Ephesus, and in Acts 19:10 we learn that, radiating from that center, "all the
residents of Asia, both Jews and Greeks, heard the word of the Lord."
Whether Paul himself fanned out in missionary activity throughout the
province or whether some of his converts did so, a church was planted
in Colossae. It is likely that Epaphras founded the Colossian church (Col.
1:7), and from 1:21 we assume that the church was composed mainly
of Gentiles.

Philemon was a citizen of Colossae and an upright leader in that
church. He also was a slaveholder whose slave Onesimus had escaped,
had later encountered the Apostle Paul, and had responded to the gospel
message about Jesus. In the letter to the Colossians, Paul addresses how
our relationship to God through Jesus Christ affects us in the workplace.
Specifically, he writes about how slaves are to do their work for their
masters and how masters are to treat their slaves. The short personal
letter to Philemon extends our understanding of Paul's command in
Colossians 4:1.

The Purpose of the Letter

The letters to the Colossians and to Philemon are believed to have
been written by Paul from prison sometime circa 60 to 62. At that time,
Nero was the cruel and insane emperor of the Roman Empire who could
ignore the claims of Paul's Roman citizenship.

From prison, Paul had heard that the Colossian Christians, who had at one time been strong in their faith, were now vulnerable to deception about the faith (2:4, 8, 16, 18, 21–23). He wrote to refute each of the theological errors the Colossians were tempted to embrace. The letters, however, take readers far beyond these issues of deception. Paul cared deeply that all of his readers (today as well as the Colossians two thousand years ago) understood the context of their lives within God's story, and what that looks like in their relationships on the job.

God at Work, Jesus at Work (Colossians 1:15–20)

The first half of Paul's letter to the Colossians can be summarized in nine words:

Jesus made it all.
Then Jesus paid it all.

Jesus Made It All

The Colossian letter assumes that the reader is familiar with the opening lines of the first book of the Bible, "In the beginning when God created the heavens and the earth" (Gen. 1:1). The second chapter of Genesis then states that "on the seventh day God finished the work that he had done, and he rested on the seventh day from all the work that he had done" (Gen. 2:2). The creation of all that exists was *work*, even for God. Paul tells us that Christ was present at the creation and that God's work in creation is Christ's work:

He is the image of the invisible God, the firstborn of all creation; for in him all things in heaven and on earth were created, things visible and invisible, whether thrones or dominions or rulers or powers—all things have been created through him and for him. He himself is before all things, and in him all things hold together. (Col. 1:15–17)

In other words, Paul attributes all of creation to Jesus, a theme also developed in the Gospel of John (1:1–4).

Jesus Paid It All

Paul then goes on to make clear to his readers that Jesus was not only the agent who created all that exists, but he is also the agent of our salvation:

> For in him all the fullness of God was pleased to dwell, and through him God was pleased to reconcile to himself all things, whether on earth or in heaven, by making peace through the blood of his cross. (Col. 1:19–20)

Paul puts Christ's work in creation side by side with his work in redemption, with themes of creation dominating the first part of the passage (Col. 1:15–17) and themes of redemption dominating the second half (Col. 1:18–20). The parallelism is especially striking between 1:16, "in him all things in heaven and on earth were created," and 1:20, "to reconcile to himself all things." The pattern is easy to see: God created all things through Christ, and he is reconciling those same things to himself through Christ. James Dunn writes,

> What is being claimed is quite simply and profoundly that the divine purpose in the act of reconciliation and peacemaking was to restore the harmony of the original creation . . . resolving the disharmonies of nature and the inhumanities of humankind, that the character of God's creation and God's concern for the universe in its fullest expression could be so caught and encapsulated for them in the cross of Christ.[2]

In sum, Jesus made it all and then Jesus paid it all so that we can have a relationship with the living God.

God Worked in Creation, Making Humans Workers in His Image (Colossians 1:1–14)

In Colossians 1:6, by allusion Paul takes us back to Genesis 1:26–28.

> Then God said, "Let us make humankind in our image, according to our likeness; and let them have dominion over the fish of the sea, and over the

---

[2] James D. G. Dunn, *The Epistles to the Colossians and to Philemon: A Commentary on the Greek Text*, The New International Greek Testament Commentary (Grand Rapids: Eerdmans, 1996), 104.

birds of the air, and over the cattle, and over all the wild animals of the earth, and over every creeping thing that creeps upon the earth." So God created humankind in his image, in the image of God he created them; male and female he created them. God blessed them, and God said to them, "Be fruitful and multiply, and fill the earth and subdue it; and have dominion over the fish of the sea and over the birds of the air and over every living thing that moves upon the earth."

Here is God the creator at work, and the apex of his activity is the creation of humanity in the divine image and likeness. To the newly minted man and woman, he gives two tasks (the tasks are given to both the male and the female): they are to be fruitful and multiply, filling the earth they are then to subdue or govern. Paul picks up the language of Genesis 1 in Colossians 1:6, giving thanks to God that the gospel is progressing in their midst, "bearing fruit and growing" as it goes out into the entire world. He then repeats this in 1:10—the Colossians are to bear fruit and grow in their understanding of God and in their work on his behalf. Whether the tasks are the work of parenting, the multifaceted work of subduing the earth and governing it, or the work of ministry, in our work they and we are image-bearers of God who works. We were created as workers in the beginning, and Christ redeems us as workers.

Jesus, the Image of the Invisible God (Colossians 1:15–29)

What difference does it make that we are bearers of the divine image in our work? One implication of this is that in our work we will reflect God's work patterns and values. But how do we know God so that we know what those patterns and values are? In Colossians 1:15, Paul reminds us that Jesus Christ is "the image of the invisible God." Again, "For in him the whole fullness of deity dwells bodily" (Col. 2:9). It is "in the face of Jesus Christ" that we can know God (2 Cor. 4:6). During Jesus' earthly ministry, Philip asked him, "Lord, show us the Father, and we will be satisfied." Jesus responded, "Have I been with you all this time, Philip, and you still do not know me? Whoever has seen me has seen the Father. How can you say, 'Show us the Father'?" (John 14:8–9).

Jesus reveals God to us. He shows us how we as God's image-bearers are to carry out our work. If we need help in grasping this, Paul spells it out: first, he describes Jesus' infinite power in creation (Col. 1:15–17), and then he immediately ties that to Jesus' willingness to set that power aside, to incarnate God on earth in word and deed, and then to die for our sins. (Paul says this directly in Philippians 2:5–9.) We look at Jesus. We listen to Jesus to understand how we are called to image God in our work.

How, then, can God's patterns and values apply in our work? We start by looking specifically at Jesus' work as our example.

Forgiveness

First, we see that God "has rescued us from the power of darkness and transferred us into the kingdom of his beloved Son" (Col. 1:13). Because Jesus has done that, Paul can appeal to us to "bear with one another and, if anyone has a complaint against another, forgive each other; just as the Lord has forgiven you, so you also must forgive" (Col. 3:13). It was on this basis that Paul could ask Philemon, the slave master, to forgive and receive Onesimus as a brother, no longer as a slave. We are doing our work in the name of the Lord Jesus when we bring that attitude to our relationships in the workplace: we make allowances for others' faults and we forgive those who offend us.

Self-sacrifice for the Benefit of Others

Second, we see Jesus with infinite power creating all that is, "things visible and invisible, whether thrones or dominions or rulers or powers" (Col. 1:16). Yet we also see him setting aside that power for our sake, "making peace through the blood of his cross" (Col. 1:20), so that we might have a relationship with God. There are times when we may be called on to set aside the authority or power we have in the workplace to benefit someone who may be undeserving. If Philemon is willing to set aside his slave-owner authority over Onesimus (who does not deserve his mercy) and take him back in a new relationship, then in this way Philemon images the invisible God in his workplace.

Freedom from Cultural Accommodation

Third, we see Jesus living a new reality that he offers to us: "If you have been raised with Christ, seek the things that are above, where Christ is, seated at the right hand of God. Set your minds on things that are above, not on things that are on earth, for you have died, and your life is hidden with Christ in God" (Col. 3:1–3). We are no longer bound by cultural mores that stand in contrast to the life of God within us. We are in the world, but we are not of the world. We can march to a different drumbeat. The culture of the workplace can work against our life in Christ, but Jesus calls us to set our hearts and our minds on what God desires for us and in us. This calls for a major reorientation of our attitudes and values.

Paul called Philemon to this reorientation. First-century Roman culture gave slaveholders complete power over the bodies and lives of their slaves. Everything in the culture gave Philemon full permission to treat Onesimus harshly, even to have him killed. But Paul was clear: As a follower of Jesus Christ, Philemon had died and his new life was now in Christ (Col. 3:3). That meant rethinking his responsibility not only to Onesimus but also to Paul, to the Colossian church, and to God his judge.

"I'm Doing Alright by Myself" (Colossians 2:1–23)

Paul warns the Colossians against falling back into the old orientation toward self-help. "See to it that no one takes you captive through philosophy and empty deceit, according to human tradition, according to the elemental spirits of the universe, and not according to Christ" (Col. 2:8). In "A Good Man is Hard to Find," Flannery O'Connor ironically put those words—"I'm doing alright by myself"—in the mouth of a serial killer proclaiming that he doesn't need Jesus.[3] This is an apt summary of the ethos of the false teachers plaguing the saints at Colossae. In their "self-imposed piety" (Col. 2:23), spiritual progress could be attained by

---

[3] Flannery O'Connor, "A Good Man Is Hard to Find," in *Collected Works* (New York: Library of America, 1988).

rough treatment of the body, mystical visions (Col. 2:18), and observing special days and food laws (Col. 2:16, likely derived from the Old Testament). These teachers believed that by marshaling the resources at their disposal, they could overcome sin on their own.

This important point forms the foundation for Paul's exhortations to workers later in the letter. Genuine progress in the faith—including progress in the way we glorify God in our workplace—can spring only out of our trust in God's work in us through Christ.

Heavenly Living for Earthly Good: The Shape of our Reorientation (Colossians 3:1–16)

This call to reorientation means that we reshape our lives to think and do according to Jesus' ethics in situations he never encountered. We cannot relive Jesus' life. We must live our own lives for Jesus. We have to respond to questions in life for which Jesus does not give specific answers. For example, when Paul writes, "Set your minds on things above, not on the things that are on earth" (Col. 3:2), does this mean that prayer is preferable to painting a house? Does Christian progress consist of thinking less and less about our work and more and more about harps and angels and clouds?

Paul does not abandon us to raw speculation about these things. In Colossians 3:1–17, he makes it clear that "to set your minds on things that are above" (Col. 3:2) means expressing the priorities of God's kingdom *precisely in the midst of everyday earthly activities*. In contrast, to set your mind on earthly things is to live by the values of the world system that sets itself up in opposition to God and his ways.

What does this putting to death "whatever belongs to your earthly nature" (Col. 3:5) look like in concrete daily life? It does not mean wearing a hair shirt or taking ice-cold baths for spiritual discipline. Paul has just said that "severe treatment of the body" does no good in stopping sin (Col. 2:23).

First, it does mean putting to death "fornication, impurity, passion, evil desire, and greed (which is idolatry)" (Col. 3:5). We are called to turn aside from sexual immorality (as if degraded sex could bring you an upgraded life) and greed (as if more stuff could bring more life). The assumption, of course, is that there is in fact a proper place for gratification of sexual desire (marriage between a man and a woman) and a proper degree for the gratification of material desire (that which results from trust in God, diligent labor, generosity toward neighbors, and thankfulness for God's provision).

Second, Paul states, "You must get rid of all such things—anger, wrath, malice, slander, and abusive language from your mouth. Do not lie to one another, seeing that you have stripped off the old self with its practices and have clothed yourselves with the new self, which is being renewed in knowledge according to the image of its creator" (Col. 3:8–10). The words "to one another" indicate that Paul is speaking to the church, that is, to those who are believers in Christ. Does this mean it is permissible to continue to lie to others outside the church? No, for Paul is not talking about a change in behavior alone but a change in heart and mind. It is difficult to imagine that having taken on a "new self," you could somehow put back on the old self when dealing with nonbelievers. Once you "get rid of all such things," they are not meant to be brought back.

Of these vices, three are particularly relevant to the workplace: greed, anger, and lying. These three vices can appear within what would otherwise be legitimate business pursuits.

- *Greed* is the unbridled pursuit of wealth. It is proper and necessary for a business to make a profit or for a nonprofit organization to create added value. But if the desire for profit becomes boundless, compulsive, excessive, and narrowed to the quest for personal gain, then sin has taken hold.

- *Anger* can appear in conflict. It is necessary for conflict to be expressed, explored, and resolved in any workplace. But if conflict is not dealt with openly and fairly, it degenerates into unresolved anger, rage, and malicious intent, and sin has taken hold.

- *Lying* can result from promoting the company's prospects or the product's benefits inaccurately. It is proper for every enterprise to have a vision for its products, services, and its organization that goes beyond what is presently in place. A sales brochure ought to describe the product in its highest, best use, along with warnings about the product's limitations. A stock prospectus ought to describe what the company hopes to accomplish if it is successful, and also the risks the company may encounter along the way. If the desire to portray a product, service, company, or person in a visionary light crosses the line into deception (an unbalanced portrayal of risks vs. rewards, misdirection, or plain fabrication and lies), then sin once again reigns.

Paul does not attempt to give universal criteria to diagnose when the proper virtues have degenerated into vices, but he makes it clear that Christians must learn to do so in their particular situations.

When Christians "put to death" (Col. 3:5) the person they used to be, they are then to put on the person God wants them to be, the person God is recreating in the image of Christ (Col. 3:10). This does not consist in hiding one's self away for constant prayer and worship (though we are all called to pray and worship, and some may be called to do that as a full-time vocation). Rather, it means reflecting God's own virtues of "compassion, kindness, humility, meekness and patience" (Col. 3:12) in whatever we do.

An encouraging word comes from Paul's exhortation to "put up with one another" (Col. 3:13, as it may be translated). Most translations read "bear with one another," but this does not fully capture Paul's point. He seems to be saying that there are all kinds of people in the church (and we can readily apply this to the workplace as well) with whom we won't naturally get along. Our interests and personalities are so different there can be no instinctive bonding. But we put up with them anyway. We seek their good, we forgive their sins, and we endure their irritating idiosyncrasies. Many of the character traits Paul extols in his letters can be summarized in the phrase "He/she works well with others." Paul himself mentions co-workers Tychicus, Onesimus, Aristarchus, Mark, Justus, Epaphras, Luke, Demas, Nympha, and Archippus (Col. 4: 7–17). Being a "team player" is not simply a résumé-enhancing cliché. It is a foundational Christian virtue. Both putting to death the old and putting on the new are immensely relevant to daily work. Christians are meant to show the new life of Christ in the midst of a dying world, and the workplace is perhaps the main forum where that type of display can take place.

- Christians may be tempted, for example, to fit in at work by participating in the gossip and the complaining that permeates many workplaces. It is likely that every workplace has people whose on- and off-hours actions make for juicy stories. It is not lying, is it, to repeat the stories?

- It is likely that every workplace has unfair policies, bad bosses, nonfunctional processes, and poor channels of communication. It is not slander, is it, to complain about those grievances?

Paul's exhortation is to live differently even in fallen workplaces. Putting to death the earthly nature and putting on Christ means directly confronting people who have wronged us, instead of gossiping about them behind their backs (Matt. 18:15–17). It means working to correct inequities in the workplace and forgiving those that do occur.

Someone may ask, "Don't Christians run the risk of being rejected as cheerless, 'holier-than-thou' types if they don't speak the way others do?" This could be the case if such Christians disengage from others in an effort to show that they are better than other people. Co-workers will sniff that out in a second. But if, instead, Christians are genuinely clothing themselves with Christ, the vast majority of people will be happy to have them around. Some may even secretly or openly appreciate the fact that someone they know is at least trying to live a life of "compassion, kindness, humility and patience" (Col. 3:12). In the same way, Christian workers who refuse to employ deception (whether by rejecting misleading advertising copy or balking at glorified Ponzi schemes) may find themselves making some enemies as the price of their honesty. But it also is possible that some co-workers will develop a new openness to Jesus' way when the Securities and Exchange Commission knocks on the office door.

Doing Our Work as for the Lord (Colossians 3:17, 23)

So what does it mean to do our work "in the name of the Lord Jesus" (Col. 3:17)? How do we do our work wholeheartedly, "as done for the Lord and not for your masters" (Col. 3:23)? To do our work in the name of the Lord Jesus carries at least two ideas:

- We recognize that we represent Jesus in the workplace. If we are Christ-followers, how we treat others and how diligently and faithfully we do our work reflects on our Lord. How well do our actions fit with who he is?

- Working in "Jesus' name" also implies that we live recognizing that he is our master, our boss, the one to whom we are ultimately accountable. This leads into Paul's reminder that we work for the Lord and not for human masters. Yes, we most likely have horizontal accountability on the job, but the diligence we bring to our work comes from our recognition that, in the end, God is our judge.

When Paul writes, "Whatever you do, in word or deed, do everything in the name of the Lord Jesus, giving thanks to God the Father through him" (Col. 3:17), we can understand this verse in two ways: a shallow way and a deeper way. The shallow way is to incorporate some Christian signs and gestures into our workplace, like a Bible verse posted on our cubicle or a Christian bumper sticker on our truck. Gestures like this can be meaningful, but in and of themselves they do not constitute a Christ-centered work-life. A deeper way to understand Paul's challenge is to pray specifically for the work we are in the midst of doing: "God, please show me how to respect both the plaintiff and the defendant in the language I use in this brief."

An even deeper way would be to begin the day by imagining what our daily goals would be if God were the owner of our workplace. With this understanding of Paul's injunction, we would do all the day's work in pursuit of goals that honor God. The apostle's point is that in God's kingdom, our work and prayer are integrated activities. We tend to see them as two separate activities that need to be balanced. But they are two aspects of the same activity—namely, working to accomplish what God wants accomplished in fellowship with other people and with God.

Of Slaves and Masters, Ancient and Contemporary (Colossians 3:18–4:1)

At this point, Colossians moves on to what is called a "household code," a set of specific instructions to wives and husbands, children and parents, slaves and masters. These codes were common in the ancient world. In the New Testament, they occur in one form or another six times—in Galatians 3:28; Ephesians 5:15–6:9; Colossians 3:15–4:1; 1 Timothy 5:1–22; 6:1–2; Titus 2:1–15; and 1 Peter 2:11–3:9. For our purposes here, we will explore only the section in Colossians having to do with the workplace (slaves and masters in 3:18–4:1).

If we are to appreciate fully the value of Paul's words here for contemporary workers, we need to understand a bit about slavery in the ancient world. Western readers often equate slavery in the ancient world with the chattel system of the pre-Civil War South in the United States, a system notorious for its brutality and degradation. At the risk of over-simplification, we might say that the slave system of the ancient world was both similar to and different from the former U.S. system. On the one hand, in ancient times, foreign captives of war laboring in mines were arguably far worse off than slaves in the American South. At the other extreme, however, some slaves were well-educated, valued members of the household, serving as physicians, teachers, and estate managers. But all were considered to be their master's property, so that even a household slave could be subject to horrific treatment with no necessary legal recourse.[4]

What relevance does Colossians 3:18–4:1 have for workers today? Much as working for wages or a salary is the dominant form of labor in developed countries today, slavery was the dominant form of labor

---

[4] For a fuller description of first-century slavery, see S. Scott Bartchy, *MALLON CHRESAI: First Century Slavery and the Interpretation of 1 Corinthians 7:21*, Society of Biblical Literature Dissertation Series No. 11 (Missoula: Scholars Press, University of Montana, 1973; reprinted by Wipf & Stock, 2003).

in the Roman Empire. Many slaves worked in jobs we would recognize today as occupations, receiving food, shelter, and often a modicum of comforts in return. Slaveholders' power over their slaves was similar in some respects to, but much more extreme than, the power that employers or managers have over workers today The general principles Paul puts forward concerning slaves and masters in this letter can be applied to modern managers and employers, provided we adjust for the significant differences between our situation now and theirs then.

What are these general principles? First, and perhaps most important, Paul reminds slaves that their work is to be done in integrity in the presence of God, who is their real master. More than anything else, Paul wants to recalibrate the scales of both slaves and masters so that they weigh things with the recognition of God's presence in their lives. Slaves are to work "fearing the Lord" (Col. 3:22) because "you serve the Lord Christ" (Col. 3:24). In sum, "Whatever your task, put yourselves into it [literally, "work from the soul"] as done for the Lord and not for your masters" (Col. 3:23). In the same way, masters [literally, "lords"] are to recognize that their authority is not absolute—they "have a Master in heaven" (Col. 4:1). Christ's authority is not bounded by church walls. He is Lord of the workplace for both workers and bosses.

This has several practical consequences. Because God is watching workers, there is no point in being a mere "people pleaser" who gives "eye service" (literal translations of the Greek terms in Col. 3:22). In today's world, many people try to curry favor with their bosses when they are around, and then slack off the moment they are out the door. Apparently it was no different in the ancient world. Paul reminds us that the Ultimate Boss is always watching and that reality leads us to work in "sincerity of heart," not putting on a show for management, but genuinely working at the tasks set before us. (Some earthly bosses tend to figure out over time who is playacting, though in a fallen world slackers can sometimes get away with their act.)

The danger of being caught for dishonesty or poor work is reinforced in Colossians 3:25. "For the wrongdoer will be paid back for whatever wrong has been done, and there is no partiality." Because the previous verse refers to a reward from God for faithful service, we may presume that God is also in view as the punisher of the wicked. However, it is noteworthy here that the fear of punishment is not the prime motivation. We do not do our jobs well simply to avoid a bad performance review. Paul wants good work to spring out of a good heart. He wants people to work well because it is the right thing to do. Implicit here is an affirmation of the value of labor in God's sight. Because God created us to exercise dominion over his creation, he is pleased when we fulfill that by pursuing excellence in our jobs. In this sense, the words "Whatever your task, put yourselves into it!" (Col. 3:23) are as much a promise as a command. By the spiritual renewal offered us in Christ by God's grace, we can do our jobs with zest.

Colossians 3:22–4:1 makes it clear that God takes all labor seriously, even if it is done under imperfect or degrading conditions. The cataracts removed by a well-paid ocular surgeon matter to God. So, too, does the cotton picked by a sharecropper or even by a plantation slave. This does not mean that exploitation of workers is ever acceptable before God. It does mean that even an abusive system cannot rob workers of the dignity of their work, because that dignity is conferred by God himself.

One of the noteworthy things about the New Testament household codes is the persistence of the theme of *mutuality*. Rather than simply telling subordinates to obey those over them, Paul teaches that we live in a web of interdependent relationships. Wives and husbands, children and parents, slaves and masters all have obligations to one another in Christ's body. Thus hard on the heels of the commands to slaves comes a directive to masters: "Masters, treat your slaves justly and fairly, for you know that you also have a Master in heaven" (Col. 4:1). Whatever leeway the Roman legal system might have given to slaveholders, they must ultimately answer in God's courtroom where justice for all is upheld. Of course, justice and fairness must be interpreted afresh in each new situation. Consider the concept of the "just wage," for example. A just wage on a Chinese farm may have a different cash value from a just wage in a Chicago bank. But there is mutual obligation under God for employers and employees to treat each other justly and fairly.

Philemon

A workplace application of the theme of mutuality is alluded to in Colossians and discussed in Paul's letter to Philemon, the shortest book of the Bible. In Colossians, Paul mentions "the faithful and beloved brother," Onesimus (Col. 4:9). The letter to Philemon tells us that Onesimus was the slave of a Christian named Philemon (Philem. 16). Onesimus apparently escaped, became a Christian himself, and then became an assistant to Paul (Philem. 10–11, 15). Under Roman law, Philemon had the right to punish Onesimus severely. On the other hand, Paul—as an apostle of the Lord—had the right to command Philemon to release Onesimus (Philem. 17–20). But instead of resorting to a hierarchy of rights, Paul applies the principle of mutuality. He requests that Philemon forgive Onesimus and forego any punishment, while at the same time requesting that Onesimus return voluntarily to Philemon. He asks both men to treat each other as brothers, rather than as slave and master (Philem. 12–16). We see a three-way application of the principle of mutuality among Paul, Philemon, and Onesimus. Each of them owes something to the others. Each of them has a claim over the others. Paul seeks to have all the debts and claims relinquished in favor of a mutual respect and service. Here we see how Paul applies the virtues of compassion, kindness, humility, gentleness, patience, and putting up with each other's faults (Col. 3:12–13) in a real workplace situation.

Paul's use of persuasion, rather than command (Philem. 14), is a further application of the mutuality principle. Rather than dictating a solution to Philemon, Paul approaches him with respect, lays out a persuasive argument, and leaves the decision in Philemon's hands. Philemon could not have failed to notice Paul's clear desire and his statement that he would be following up with him (Philem. 21). But Paul manages the communication in an artful way that provides a model for resolving issues in the workplace.

Conclusion to Colossians and Philemon

Colossians gives us a picture of God's standard for work. As employees, we serve our employers with integrity, giving a full measure of work for the wages we are paid (Col. 3:23). As supervisors, we treat those under us as God treats us—with compassion, kindness, humility, gentleness, and patience (Col. 3:12). God intends that our work be done in reciprocal relationships, in which each party contributes to, and benefits from, the overall work. But even if the other parties fail in their reciprocal duty, Christians fulfill their obligations (Col. 3:22–4:1). Following Jesus' example, we offer forgiveness in the face of conflict (Col. 1:13) and we lay aside our power when necessary for the good of others (Col. 1:20). This does not mean we lack rigorous standards or accountability, or that Christians in business and other workplaces cannot compete vigorously and successfully. It does mean that we offer forgiveness. It does mean that Christians cannot always go along with what their workplace culture deems acceptable (Col. 3:1–3), particularly if it would lead to unfair or unjust treatment of a co-worker or employee (Col. 4:1). We see this illustrated in the case of Onesimus and Philemon. Whatever our work, we strive for excellence, for we do it in the name of the Lord Jesus, not merely for human masters, knowing that we will receive an inheritance from the Lord as a reward (Col. 3:23–24).

1 & 2 Thessalonians and Work

Introduction to 1 & 2 Thessalonians

"We work hard, so you don't have to." That's the advertising line for a modern bathroom cleaner,[1] but—with a little adjustment—it might have fit well as a slogan for some Christians in the ancient city of Thessalonica. "Jesus worked hard so I don't have to." Many believed the new way of living offered by Jesus was cause to abandon the old way of living that involved hard work, and so they became idle. As we will see, it is difficult to know exactly why some Thessalonians were not working. Perhaps they mistakenly thought that the promise of eternal life meant that this life no longer mattered. But these idlers were living off the largesse of the more responsible members of the church. They were consuming the resources intended to meet the needs of those genuinely unable to support themselves. And they were becoming troublesome and argumentative.

In his letters to the Thessalonians, Paul would have none of this. He made it clear that Christians need to keep at their labors, for the way of Christ is not idleness but service and excellence in work.

Thessalonica and Its Church

The capital of the Roman province of Macedonia and a major Mediterranean seaport, Thessalonica had a population of over 100,000.[2] Not only did it have a natural harbor, it was also located on key north-south trade routes and on the busy east-west Ignatian Way, the road that linked

---

[1] From a U.S. television commercial for a bathroom cleaning product with "Scrubbing Bubbles."

[2] Rainer Riesner, *Die Frühzeit des Apostels Paulus: Stüdien zur Chronologie, Missionsstrategie, und Theologie,* in Wissenschaftliche Untersuchungen zum Neuen Testament (Tübingen: Mohr, 1994), 301.

Italy to the eastern provinces. People were drawn from nearby villages to this great city, which was a bustling center of trade and philosophy. Thessalonica's natural resources included timber, grain, continental fruits, and gold and silver (although it is questionable if the gold and silver mines were operational in the first century AD). Thessalonica was also notably pro-Roman and self-governing, and it enjoyed the status of a free city. As its citizens were Roman citizens, it was exempt from paying tribute to Rome.[3]

The church at Thessalonica was founded by Paul and his co-workers Timothy and Silas during the so-called Second Missionary Journey in AD 50. God worked mightily through the missionaries and many became Christians. While some Jews believed (Acts 17:4), the majority of the church was Gentile (1 Thess. 1:9–10). Although it did have some relatively wealthy members—such as Jason, Aristarchus, and a number of "the leading women" (Acts 17:4, 6–7; 20:4)—it seems to have consisted largely of manual laborers (1 Thess. 4:11) and presumably some slaves. In 2 Corinthians, Paul states that the "churches of Macedonia" were marked by "extreme poverty" (2 Cor. 8:2), and the Thessalonian church would have been included in their ranks.

The precise situations that prompted Paul to write these two letters[4] have been much debated. For our purposes, it is sufficient to say that Paul wanted to encourage believers who were trying to live faithful Christian lives in a hostile pagan environment. In addition to the typical struggles against things such as idolatry and sexual immorality, they were also confused about the end times, the role of everyday work, and the life of faith.

---

[3] For further information on Thessalonica, see Gene L. Green, *The Letters to the Thessalonians* (Grand Rapids: Eerdmans, 2002), 1–47.

[4] Paul's authorship of 2 Thessalonians is taken at face value here (2 Thess. 1:1; 3:17), although the question of authorship has been debated at length, as is discussed in the general-purpose commentaries. (By comparison, Paul's authorship of 1 Thessalonians is not significantly disputed.) In any case, the question of authorship has little or no bearing on the contribution of either letter to understanding work in the Christian perspective.

Working Faith, Finishing Up, and Keeping the Faith (1 Thessalonians 1:1–4:8; 4:13–5:28; 2 Thessalonians 1:1–2:17)

Working Faith (1 Thessalonians 1:1–4:8)

In light of the problems with work that will emerge later in the epistles, it is interesting that Paul begins by remembering the Thessalonians' "work of faith, and labor of love, and perseverance of hope in our Lord Jesus Christ" (1 Thess. 1:3). Paul writes his letters carefully and, if nothing else, this opening serves to introduce the vocabulary of labor into his discussion. The verse reminds us that faith is not simply mental assent to the propositions of the gospel. It takes work. It is the total life response to the commands and promises of the God who renews us and empowers us through his Spirit. The Thessalonians are apparently responding well in their daily lives of faith, though they need encouragement to keep living lives of moral purity (1 Thess. 4:1–8).

The question of work emerges directly again in chapter 2, when Paul reminds the Thessalonians that he and his friends worked night and day so that they would not be a burden to them (1 Thess. 2:9). Paul says this so that the Thessalonians will be certain how much Paul cares for them, despite his physical absence from them. But it may also serve as a rebuke to members of the congregation who might have been sponging off of the generosity of fellow believers. If anyone had a right to receive from the Thessalonians, it was Paul, whose hard work had mediated the new life of Christ to them in the first place. But Paul took no money from the Thessalonians in compensation. Instead, he labored hard as a tradesman as an expression of his concern for them.

Finishing Up (1 Thessalonians 4:13–5:28)

Paul goes on to console the Thessalonians about those in their community who have died. They are not dead but only sleeping, because Jesus will awaken them on the last day (1 Thess. 4:13–18). They don't need to worry about when that day will come, because that is in the Lord's hands. Their only concern should be to keep walking in the light, remaining faithful and hopeful in the midst of a dark world (1 Thess. 5:11). Among other things, this means that they are to respect those who work (1 Thess. 5:12–13; the reference may be to the "work" of instructing people in the faith, but it could equally be workers in general, in distinction from the idlers) and to rebuke the slackers among them (1 Thess. 5:14). The promise of eternal life is more reason—not less—for working hard in this life. This is so because the good we do lasts forever, because "we belong to the day" of Christ's redemption, rather than to the night of oblivion (1 Thess. 5:4–8). Each day gives us an opportunity to "do good to one another and to all" (1 Thess. 5:15).

Keeping the Faith (2 Thessalonians 1:1–2:17)

As 2 Thessalonians opens, we learn that Paul is still happy that the Thessalonians are maintaining their faith in a difficult environment, and he encourages them that Jesus will return to set all things right (2 Thess. 1:1–12). But some of them are worried that the Day of the Lord has already come and that they have missed it. Paul lets them know that the day has not come, and in fact it will not come until Satan makes one last grand attempt to deceive the world through "the lawless one" (presumably the figure we commonly call "the Antichrist"; 2 Thess. 2:8). They should take heart: God will judge Satan and his minions, but bring eternal blessing to his beloved children (2 Thess. 2:9–17).

Faithful Work (1 Thessalonians 4:9–12 and 2 Thessalonians 3:6–16)

First Thessalonians 4:9–12 and 2 Thessalonians 3:6–16 address work directly.[5] Scholars continue to debate precisely what led to the

---

[5] On the relationship between the instructions about sexual purity in 1 Thessalonians 4:3–7 and the instructions in 4:9–12, see Traugott Holtz, *Der erste Brief an die Thessalonicher* in Evangelisch-katholischer Kommentar zum Neuen Testament (Zürich: Benziger, 1986), 161–62; Karl P. Donfried, "The Cults of Thessalonica and the Thessalonian Correspondence," *New Testament Studies* 31, no. 3 (1985): 341–42; and Earl J. Richard, *First and Second Thessalonians, Sacra Pagina* (Collegeville: Michael Glazier, 1995), 194, 202.

problem of idleness at Thessalonica. While we are most concerned to hear how Paul wants the problem solved, it will be helpful to make some suggestions as to how the problem might have arisen in the first place.

- Many believe that some of the Thessalonians had stopped working because the end times were at hand.[6] They might have felt that they were already living in God's kingdom, and there was no need to work; or they might have felt that Jesus was coming at any minute, and thus there was no point to work. The Thessalonian letters do speak quite a bit about misunderstandings about the end times, and it is interesting that the passages about idleness in 1 Thessalonians 4:9–12 and 2 Thessalonians 3:6–16 both come in the context of teaching on the end times. On the other hand, Paul does not make an explicit connection between idleness and eschatology.

- Others have suggested a "nobler" reason for the idleness: people had given up their day jobs in order to preach the gospel. (One could see how such a move would be eased if they had the sort of eschatological fervor noted in the first view.)[7] Such would-be evangelists stand in sharp contrast to Paul, the foremost evangelist, who nonetheless works with his own hands lest he become a burden to the church. The churches in Macedonia were known

---

[6] See, e.g., G. Agrell, *Work, Toil and Sustenance: An Examination of the View of Work in the New Testament, Taking into Consideration Views Found in Old Testament, Intertestamental and Early Rabbinic Writings*, trans. S. Westerholm and G. Agrell (Lund: Ohlssons, 1976), 122–23; John A. Bailey, "Who Wrote II Thessalonians?" *New Testament Studies* 25, no. 02 (1979): 137; Peter Müller, *Anfänge der Paulusschule: Dargestellt am zweiten Thessalonicherbrief und am Kolosserbrief, in Abhandlungen zur Theologie des Alten und Neuen Testaments* (Zürich: Theologischer, 1988), 162–67; K. Romanuik, "Les Thessaloniciens étaient-ils des parassuex?" *Ephemerides Theologicae Lovanienses* 69 (1993): 142–45; and A. M. Okorie, "The Pauline Work Ethic in 1 and 2 Thessalonians," *Deltio Biblikon Meleton* 14 (1995): 63–64.

[7] See, e.g., John Barclay, "Conflict in Thessalonica," *Catholic Biblical Quarterly* 55 (1993), 512–30; Trevor J. Burke, *Family Matters: A Socio-Historical Study of Kinship Metaphors in 1 Thessalonians* (London: T&T Clark, 2003), 213ff.

for their evangelistic zeal, yet it remains unclear whether the idle in Thessalonica were necessarily using their free time for evangelistic labors.

- A third view sees the problem as more sociological than theological.[8] Some manual laborers were unemployed (whether through laziness, persecution, or general economic malaise) and had become dependent on the charity of others in the church. They discovered that life as the client of a rich patron was significantly easier than life as a laborer slogging out a day's work. The injunction for Christians to care for one another formed a ready pretext for them to continue in this parasitic lifestyle.

It is difficult to choose between these different reconstructions. They all have something in the letters to support them, and it is not hard to see modern analogies in the modern church. Many people today undervalue everyday work because "Jesus is coming soon, and everything is going to burn up anyway." Plenty of Christian workers justify substandard performance because their "real" purpose in the workplace is to evangelize their co-workers. And questions of unhelpful dependence on the charity of others arise both in the local context (e.g., pastors who are asked to give money to a man whose mother died . . . for the third time this year) and the global context (e.g., the question of whether some foreign aid does more harm than good).

We can, however, move forward even in the absence of complete certainty about what was going on to cause the problem of idleness in Thessalonica. First, we may note that the views above share a common, but false, supposition—namely, *Christ's coming into the world has radically diminished the value of everyday labor.* People were using

---

[8] See, with various points of emphasis, D. E. Aune, "Trouble in Thessalonica: An Exegetical Study of 1 Thess. 4:9–12, 5:12–14 and II Thess. 6:6–15 in Light of First-Century Social Conditions," ThM thesis (Regent College, 1989); Colin R. Nicholl, *From Hope to Despair: Situating 1 & 2 Thessalonians*, Society for New Testament Studies Monograph Series (Cambridge: Cambridge University Press, 2004), 157ff; Ben Witherington, *1 and 2 Thessalonians: A Socio-Rhetorical Commentary* (Grand Rapids, Eerdmans, 2006), 43–44.

some aspect of Christ's teaching—whether it was his second coming, or his commission to evangelize the world, or his command for radical sharing in the community—to justify their idleness. Paul will have none of it. Responsible Christian living embraces work, even the hard work of a first-century manual laborer. It is equally clear that Paul is disturbed when people take advantage of the generosity of others in the church. If people can work, they should work. Finally, the idleness of Christians appears to have given the church a bad name in the pagan community.

Christians Are Expected to Work (1 Thessalonians 4:9–12; 5:14)

Christians are Expected to Work, to the Degree They are Able

Paul highlights that God expects every Christian who can work to do so (1 Thess. 4:11–12). He exhorts the Thessalonians "to work with [their] hands" (1 Thess. 4:11) and to "have need of no one" (1 Thess. 4:12). Rather than evading work, the Thessalonian Christians are to be industrious, laboring so as to earn their own living and thereby avoid putting undue burdens on others. Being a manual laborer in a Greco-Roman city was a hard life by modern and ancient standards, and the thought that it might not be necessary must have been appealing. However, abandoning work in favor of living off the work of others is unacceptable. It is striking that Paul's treatment of the issue in 1 Thessalonians is framed in terms of "brotherly love" (1 Thess. 4:9). The idea is plainly that love and respect are essential in Christian relationships, and that living off the charity of others unnecessarily is unloving and disrespectful to the charitable brother(s) or sister(s) concerned.

It is important to remember that work does not always mean paid work. Many forms of work—cooking, cleaning, repairing, beautifying, raising children, coaching youth, and thousands of others—meet the needs of family or community but do not receive remuneration. Others—the arts come to mind—may be offered free of charge or at prices too low to support those who do them. Nonetheless, they are all work.

Christians are not necessarily expected to earn money, but to work to support themselves, their families, and the church and community.

The Creation Mandate Remains in Effect

The mandate in Genesis 2:15 ("The Lord God took the man and put him in the Garden of Eden to work it and keep it") is still in effect. The work of Christ has not eliminated or supplanted humanity's original work, but it has made it more fruitful and ultimately valuable. Paul may have the Genesis 2:15 text in view when he refers to the idlers with the Greek adjective, adverb, and verb derived from the root *atakt-* ("disorder") in 1 Thessalonians 5:14, 2 Thessalonians 3:6 and 11, and 1 Thessalonians 5:7, respectively. These words all portray the idlers' behavior as disorderly, betraying an "irresponsible attitude to the obligation to work."[9] The order being violated may well be the work mandate in Genesis 2.

Paul's insistence on the ongoing validity of work is not a concession to a bourgeois agenda, but rather reflects a balanced perspective on the already/not yet of God's kingdom. Already, God's kingdom has come to earth in the person of Jesus, but it has not yet been brought to completion (1 Thess. 4:9–10). When Christians work with diligence and excellence, they demonstrate that God's kingdom is not an escapist fantasy, but a fulfillment of the world's deepest reality.

Christians are to Work with Excellence

Given the importance of work, Christians are to be the best workers they can be. Failure to work with excellence may bring the church into disrepute. Many Cynics in the Greco-Roman world abandoned their jobs, and this behavior was widely regarded as disgraceful.[10] Paul is aware that

---

[9] Gerhard Kittel, Gerhard Friedrich, and Geoffrey William Bromiley, eds., *Theological Dictionary of the New Testament* (Grand Rapids: Eerdmans, 1985), 8:48. For a helpful study, see Ceslas Spicq, "Les Thessalonicien 'inquiets' etaient-ils des parrassuex?" *Studia theologica* 10 (1956): 1–13.

[10] See Abraham J. Malherbe, *The Letters to the Thessalonians*, Anchor Bible (New York: Doubleday, 2000), 258–29; idem, *Paul and the Thessalonians: The Philosophic Tradition of Pastoral Care* (Philadelphia: Fortress, 1987), 99–107.

when Christians evade their responsibility to work, the standing of the church as a whole is undermined. In 1 Thessalonians 4:11–12, Paul is evidently concerned that society is getting a wrong view of the church. In the context of the Greco-Roman world his concern makes a lot of sense, for what was happening in the Thessalonian church not only fell below society's standards for decency, but it also made the charitable Christians look gullible and foolish. Paul does not want Christians to fall below society's standards in regard to work, but rather to exceed them. Moreover, by failing to fulfill their proper role within society, these Christians are in danger of stirring up more anti-Christian rumors and resentment. Paul is eager that those who persecute the church should have no legitimate grounds for their hostility. With respect to work, Christians should be model citizens. By placing the idlers under discipline, the church would effectively be distancing itself from their defective behavior.

Mature Christians are to set an example for young Christians by modeling a good work ethos. Although Paul knew it was the right of the minister of the gospel to be financially supported (1 Tim. 5:17–18), he himself refused to take advantage of this (1 Thess. 2:9; 2 Thess. 3:8). He saw the need to set new converts an example of what the Christian life looked like, and that meant joining them in manual labor. Itinerant philosophers in the Greco-Roman world were often quick to burden their converts financially, but Paul did not care about having an easy life or projecting an image of superiority over his spiritual charges. Christian leadership is servant leadership, even in the arena of work.

Manual Labor and Hard Work Are Honorable

The positive view of hard work that Paul was promoting was countercultural. The Greco-Roman world had a very negative view of manual labor.[11] To some extent, this is understandable in view of how unpleasant urban workhouses were. If the idle in Thessalonica were in fact

---

[11] So, e.g., Gustav Wohlenberg, *Der erste und zweite Thessalonicherbrief,* Kommentar zum Neuen Testament (Leipzig: Deichert, 1903), 93; I. Howard Marshall, *1 and 2 Thessalonians,* New Century Bible Commentary (London: Marshall, Morgan, and Scott, 1983), 223; Ernest Best, *The First and Second Epistles to the Thessalonians,* 2nd ed., British New Testament Conference (London: A & C Black, 1986), 338.

unemployed manual laborers, it is not difficult to appreciate how easy it would have been to rationalize this exploitation of the charity of their brothers and sisters over against returning to their workhouses. After all, weren't all Christians equal in Christ? However, Paul has no time for any rationalizations. He approaches the matter from an understanding strongly rooted in the Old Testament, where God is portrayed as creating Adam to work, and Adam's manual labor is not divorced from worship, but rather is to be a form of worship. In Paul's assessment, manual labor is not beneath Christians, and Paul himself had done what he demands that these idle brothers do. The apostle plainly regards work as one way believers may honor God, show love to their fellow-Christians, and display the transforming power of the gospel to outsiders. He wants the idle brothers to embrace his perspective and to set an impressive, not disgraceful, example for their unbelieving contemporaries.

Those Truly Unable to Work Should Receive Assistance (1 Thessalonians 4:9–10)

Paul is an advocate of social welfare and charitable giving, but only for those who are genuinely in need. Paul clearly regards the early manifestations of generous provision for the unemployed Thessalonian Christians as appropriate expressions of Christian love (1 Thess. 4:9–10). Moreover, even after the expression of love on the part of some was selfishly exploited by others, he still calls for the church to continue to do good by giving to those in genuine need (2 Thess. 3:13). It would have been easy for the benefactors to become disillusioned with charitable giving in general and to shy away from it in the future.

The key factor in determining whether someone unemployed was worthy of charity or welfare was a willingness to work (2 Thess. 3:10). Some who are perfectly capable of working do not, simply because they do not want to—they do not merit financial or material assistance. On the other hand, some cannot work due to some incapacity or mitigating circumstance—they are clearly deserving of financial and material assistance. Verse 13 assumes that there are legitimate charitable cases in the Thessalonian church.

In practice, of course, it is difficult to determine who is slacking versus who is willing yet genuinely unable to work or find a job. If the close-knit members of the Thessalonian church had a hard time discerning who among them was worthy to receive financial support, imagine how much more difficult it is for a far-flung modern city, province, or nation. This reality has led to deep divisions among Christians with respect to social policy, as practiced by both the church and the state. Some prefer to err on the side of mercy, providing relatively easy access and generous, sometimes long-term, benefits to people in apparent financial hardship. Others prefer to err on the side of industriousness, requiring relatively stringent proof that the hardship is due to factors beyond the recipient's control, and providing benefits limited in amount and duration. A particularly thorny question has been support of single mothers with small children and of all persons unemployed for long periods during economic recessions. Does such support provide care to the most vulnerable members of society, particularly children in vulnerable families? Or does it subsidize a culture of removal from working society, to the detriment of both the individual and the community? These are difficult, challenging issues. Biblical passages such as those in the Thessalonian letters should figure deeply in Christians' social and political understanding. Our conclusions may put us in opposition with other Christians, but this is not necessarily a cause to withdraw from political and social participation. Yet we should engage politics and social discourse with respect, kindness, a healthy humility that our views are not infallible, and an awareness that the same passages may lead other believers to contrary conclusions. The Thessalonian letters reveal God's values and insights applied to the ancient Thessalonian context. But they do not constitute an indisputable social or party program as applied in today's very different contexts.

It is clear that Paul has in mind both that all the Thessalonian Christians should work to the degree they are able and that the church should take care of those in genuine need. He wants the finances of the benefactors in the church to be used strategically rather than frittered away idly. Indeed, if the idle get back to work, they too will be in a position to be givers rather than recipients, and the church's capacity to spread the gospel and minister to the poor and needy within and without the church will be increased. The biblical insistence that Christians should work so as to be self-supporting wherever possible ultimately has in view the extension of the kingdom of God on the earth.

Idleness (2 Thessalonians 3:6–15)

Idleness Is a Matter for the Christian Community, Not Just the Individual

The words of 2 Thessalonians 3:10 are critical. "If anyone is not willing to work, neither should he eat." God regards shirking work as a grave offense, so grave that the church is called to correct its idle members. Paul exhorts the church to "warn" those dodging their obligation to work (1 Thess. 5:14) and issues a "command in the name of our Lord Jesus Christ" in 2 Thessalonians 3:6–15 that the church impose disciplinary measures on the offending brothers. The discipline is relatively harsh, which underscores that idleness was no minor foible in Paul's assessment. The church is called upon to "disassociate from" those who shirk their responsibility to work, presumably meaning that they are to avoid including them when they gather together in Christian fellowship. The intention was, of course, to induce a short, sharp shock in the offending brothers by alienating them, and thereby bring them back into line.

Idleness Leads to Mischief

The negative consequences of shirking work go beyond the burden placed on others. Those who evade work often end up spending their time on unwholesome pursuits. Paul's exhortation of the Thessalonian manual laborers "to aspire to lead a quiet life" and "to attend to [their] own business" (1 Thess. 4:11) hints at what 2 Thessalonians 3:11 states explicitly, "We hear that some among you are living in a disorderly manner, not doing their own work but being busybodies." The Greek word *periergazomai* ("busybodies") refers to meddling in other people's affairs.[12] A similar

---

[12] Johannes P. Louw and Eugene A. Nida, *Greek-English Lexicon of the New Testament Based on Semantic Domains,* 2 vols. (New York: UBS, 1988),

thought is expressed by Paul in 1 Timothy 5:13, where Paul says of younger widows being supported by the church that "they are not only lazy, but also gossips and busybodies, talking about things they should not." It seems that the Thessalonian idlers were interfering in other people's business and being argumentative. Idleness breeds trouble.

Conclusion to 1 & 2 Thessalonians

Workplace themes are woven into the fabric of the Thessalonian letters. They are most visible in several explicit passages, and especially in 2 Thessalonians. Underlying both letters is the principle that Christians are called to work to the degree they are able. Work is required to put food on the table, so eaters should be workers. Moreover work is honorable, reflecting God's intent for humanity in creation. Not everyone has equal capacity to work, so the measure of work is not the quantity of achievement, but the attitude of service and commitment to excellence. Therefore, those who work as hard and as well as they are able have a full share in the community's bounty. In contrast, those who shirk their duty to work should be confronted by the church. If they continue to be idle, they should not be supported by others' means. As a last resort, they should even be removed from the community, for idleness leads to not only consuming the fruit of others' labor, but also to active disruption of the community by meddling, gossip, and obstruction.

---

§88.243; Horst Balz and Gerhard Schneider, *Exegetical Dictionary of the New Testament,* 3 vols., trans. J. W. Medendorp and Douglas W. Scott (Grand Rapids: Eerdmans, 1990–93), 3:73.

The Pastoral Epistles
and Work

Introduction to the Pastoral Epistles

The Pastoral Epistles were written to leaders in the early church. Yet much of what they say applies to Christians in other workplaces as well. In applying them to nonchurch work, the critical task will be to reflect on the similarities and differences between churches and other workplace organizations. Both types are voluntary organizations (generally) with structures and goals. Both are ultimately governed by the same Lord. Both are composed of human beings made in God's image. Both face major challenges at times, yet are designed to endure and adapt in future generations. These similarities suggest that many of the same biblical principles will apply to each, as will be discussed in depth.

From ancient times, the letters 1 Timothy, 2 Timothy, and Titus have been grouped together as the "Pastoral Epistles." These letters outline the qualification, development, and promotion of leaders; organizational structures for the care, compensation, and discipline of members; and the setting and execution of individual and organizational goals. They are concerned with the good governance, effectiveness, and growth of an organization—in particular, the church. In 1 Timothy 3:14–15 Paul expresses the major theme of all three letters: "I am writing these instructions to you so that, if I am delayed, you may know how one ought to behave in the household of God, which is the church of the living God, the pillar and bulwark of the truth."

But there are differences as well. The church has as its mission the calling and equipping of people to commit their lives to Christ, to serve his kingdom, and to worship God. It was instituted by God as the body of Christ, and he has promised it will remain a going concern until Christ's return. Other organizations have different missions, such as creating economic value (businesses), protecting members (labor unions), educating children and adults (schools and universities), and administering defense, justice, and other civic needs (governments). They are instituted as bodies (corporations or states) by charters and constitutions, and may come in and out of existence. These differences do not mean that other organizations are inferior to the church, but rather that each kind must be respected for its particular mission. Nonetheless, the Pastoral Epistles provide fertile material for reflecting on how relationships within nonchurch workplaces ought to be created and maintained, while highlighting the special role of the church community. Although the Pastoral Epistles are concerned primarily with organizations, they do not necessarily exclude those who work in families, sole proprietorships, and other such workplaces. For brevity, from here forward, the term "workplace" will be used to mean the nonchurch workplace only.

1 Timothy: Working for Order in God's Household

Each of the three Pastoral Epistles takes the form of a letter from the Apostle Paul giving counsel to one of his co-workers.[1] In 1 Timothy, Paul gives instructions his younger colleague Timothy about how to minister within the church and how to deal with false teachers. Yet the last words of the letter—"Grace be with you [plural]" (1 Tim. 6:21)—indicate that the letter is meant to be overheard by the whole church in Ephesus so that all may benefit from Paul's counsel to Timothy.

Because the letters share some common themes, we will combine our discussion of related passages among the letters. The themes will be explored according to the order they first arise in the Pastoral Epistles.

---

[1]This discussion will assume Pauline authorship of the Pastoral Epistles, although this is not critical for applying the letters to the workplace. For a thorough discussion of this perspective on authorship, see William D. Mounce, *Pastoral Epistles*, vol. 4, *Word Biblical Commentary* (Nashville: Thomas Nelson, 2000), lxxxiii–cxxix.

True Belief Leads to a Sound Organization
(1 Timothy 1:1–11, 18–20; 3:14–16)

One of the repeated and stressed themes in 1 Timothy is the tight connection between belief and behavior, or teaching and practice. Sound, or "healthy," teaching leads to godliness while false teaching is unproductive at best and damning at worst. From the onset of the letter, Paul charges Timothy to "instruct certain people not to teach any different doctrine" (1 Tim. 1:3) because this different doctrine, along with myths and genealogies, does not promote "the divine training that is known by faith" (1 Tim. 1:4).

Paul is speaking of the importance of sound doctrine in the church, but his words apply just as well to the workplace. W. Edwards Deming, one of the founders of continuous quality improvement, called his methods a "system of profound knowledge." He said, "Once the individual understands the system of profound knowledge, he will apply its principles in every kind of relationship with other people. He will have a basis for judgment of his own decisions and for transformation of the organizations that he belongs to."[2] Knowledge of the deepest truth is essential in any organization.

Luke Timothy Johnson has translated 1 Timothy 1:4 more transparently as "God's way of ordering reality as it is apprehended by faith."[3] The church is—or should be—ordered according to God's way. Few would dispute that. But should other organizations also be ordered according to God's way? The first-century Greco-Roman world believed that society should be ordered according to "nature." Thus if nature is the creation of God, then God's way of ordering creation should be reflected in the way society is ordered as well. As Johnson observes, "There is no radical discontinuity between the will of God and the structures of society. The structures of the *oikos* (household) and the

---

[2] W. Edwards Deming, *The New Economics for Industry, Government, Education,* 2nd ed. (Cambridge, MA: MIT Press, 2000), 92.

[3] Luke Timothy Johnson, *The First and Second Letters to Timothy: A New Translation with Introduction and Commentary, The Anchor Yale Bible Commentaries* (New York: Doubleday, 2001), 149.

ekklēsia (church) are not only continuous with each other, but both are parts of the dispensation [administration] of God in the world."[4] Workplaces, households, and churches all reflect the one and only ordering of creation.

A true understanding of God's ways is essential in all workplaces. For example, a prominent theme in Creation is that human beings were created good. Later we fell into sin, and a central Christian truth is that Jesus came to redeem sinners. Workers are therefore human beings who sin, yet who may experience redemption and become good as God always intended. The truth about goodness, sin, and redemption needs to be factored into organizational practices. Neither churches nor workplaces can function properly if they assume that people are good only and not sinners. Accounts need to be audited and harassment needs to be stopped. Customer service needs to be rewarded. Priests and pastors, employees and executives need to be supervised. Similarly, neither churches nor workplaces can assume that people who err or sin should be discarded automatically. The offer of redemption—and practical help to make the transformation—needs to be made. In churches, the focus is on spiritual and eternal redemption. Nonchurch workplaces are focused on a more limited redemption related to the mission of the organization. Probation, performance improvement plans, retraining, reassignment to a different position, mentoring, and employee assistance programs—as opposed to immediate firing—are examples of redemptive practices in certain workplaces, especially in the West. The particulars of what is actually redemptive will vary considerably of course depending on the type of organization, its mission, the surrounding cultural, legal, and economic environment, and other factors.

If Christians in the marketplace are to understand how God would have them and those around them act (cf. 1 Tim. 3:15), they must understand God's revelation in the Bible and believe in it. Truth leads to love (1 Tim. 1:5), while false doctrine promotes "speculations" (1 Tim. 1:4), "controversy" (1 Tim. 6:4), and spiritual destruction (1 Tim. 1:19). Knowledge of God's ways as revealed in his word cannot be the domain of Bible scholars alone, nor is biblical understanding relevant

---

[4] Johnson, *The First and Second Letters to Timothy,* 149.

only within the church. Christian workers must also be biblically informed so that they can operate in the world according to God's will and for his glory.

All Christians have a leadership role, regardless of their place in the organization. Executives usually have the greatest opportunity to shape the strategy and structure of an organization. All workers have continual opportunities to develop good relationships, produce excellent products and services, act with integrity, help others develop their abilities, and shape the culture of their immediate work groups. Everyone has a sphere of influence at work. Paul advised Timothy not to let his perceived lack of status prevent him from trying to make a difference. "Let no one despise your youth, but set the believers an example in speech and conduct, in love, in faith, in purity" (1 Tim. 4:12).

It is interesting to note that some of this reality is already perceived in contemporary workplaces. Many organizations have "mission statements" and "core values." These words mean roughly the same thing to secular organizations as "beliefs" or "doctrine" mean to churches. Organizations, like churches, pay close attention to culture. This is further evidence that what workers believe or what an organization teaches affects how people behave. Christians in the workplace should be at the forefront of shaping the values, mission, and culture of the organizations in which we participate, to the degree we are able.

Prayer, Peace, and Order are Needed at Work as in Church (1 Timothy 2:1–15)

Paul begins this chapter by urging that "supplications, prayers, intercessions, and thanksgivings be made for everyone, for kings and all who are in high positions" (1 Tim. 2:1–2). The aim of this prayer is that Christians "may lead a quiet and peaceable life in all godliness and dignity" (1 Tim. 2:2). Presumably, these first-century rulers had the power to make life difficult and disruptive for Christians. So Paul urges Christians to pray for their civic rulers. Prayer, peace, and order are Christians' first instruments of engagement with the secular world.

Again we see that Paul's instructions are grounded in the oneness of God, the singularity of Christ as mediator, Christ's universal ransom, and God's universal desire for all to be saved (1 Tim. 2: 3–7). Christ is the Lord of creation and the Savior of the world. His realm includes every workplace. Christians should be praying for all of those who are in their particular workplace, especially those who have supervisory roles "in high positions." Christians should strive to do their jobs without disrupting the work of others, without calling undue attention to themselves, and without constantly challenging authority—in other words, working "in all godliness and dignity" (1 Tim. 2:2). For Christians, this kind of peaceable and submissive behavior is not motivated by fear, people-pleasing, or social conformity, but by a healthy appreciation for the order God has established and by a desire for others to "come to the knowledge of the truth" (1 Tim. 2:4). As Paul says elsewhere, "God is a God not of disorder but of peace" (1 Cor. 14:33).

Does this conflict with the duty to be at the forefront of shaping the mission and core values of our workplaces? Some Christians try to shape missions and values through confrontation around controversial issues, such as same-sex partner benefits, health insurance exclusion for abortion and/or contraceptives, union organizing, display of religious symbols and the like. If successful, this approach may help shape the mission and value of the organization. But it often disrupts others' work, breaks the peace, and disrespects supervisors' authority.

What is needed instead is a more personal, deeper, and more respectful engagement of organizational culture. Rather than clashing over health benefits, could Christians invest in friendships with co-workers and become a source of counseling or wisdom for those facing major life decisions? Instead of pushing the boundary between freedom of speech and harassment, could Christians do their assigned work with such excellence that co-workers ask *them* to explain the source of their strength? Instead of arguing about peripheral issues such as holiday decorations, could Christians help improve the core activities of their workplaces, such as job performance, customer service, and product design, and so earn the respect of those around them? In answering such questions, we can remember that Paul's advice to Timothy is balanced, not self-contradictory. Live in peace and cooperation with those around us. Seek to influence others by serving them, not trying to lord it over them. Isn't that what the King of kings did?

Integrity and Relational Ability are Key Leadership Qualities (1 Timothy 3:1–13; Titus 1:5–9)

First Timothy 3:1–13 is well known and finds a parallel in Titus 1:5–9. Both 1 Timothy 3:1–7 and Titus 1:5–9 lay out qualifications for elders and overseers,[5] whereas 1 Timothy 3:8–13 describes qualifications for deacons including, possibly, women deacons. A variety of qualifications is given, but the common thread seems to be moral integrity and ability to relate well to people. Competence to teach, though mentioned as a qualification for elders (1 Tim. 3:2; Titus 1:9), doesn't receive the same emphasis overall. In these lists, we again observe the connection between the household and the church: managing one's family well is viewed as requisite experience for managing God's household (1 Tim. 3:4–5, 12; Titus 3:6; cf. 1 Tim. 3:15). We will reflect on this connection more in a subsequent section.

As noted earlier, different organizations have different missions. Therefore, the qualifications for leadership are different. It would be a misapplication of this passage to use it as a general qualifications list for workplaces. "Serious" may not be the right qualification for a tour guide, for example. But what about the priority given to moral integrity and relational ability? Moral qualities such as "above reproach," "clear conscience," "faithful [or trustworthy] in all things," and relational qualities such as "hospitable," "not quarrelsome," and "temperate" are much more prominent than specific skills and experience.

If this is true for church leadership, does it also apply for workplace leadership? The well-publicized moral and relational failings of a few prominent business and government leaders in recent years have made integrity, character, and relationships more important than ever in most workplaces. It is no less important to properly develop and select leaders in workplaces than it is in churches. But as we prepare for jobs and careers, do we put a fraction of as much effort into developing ethical character and relational abilities as into developing specialized skills and accumulating credentials?

---

[5] See Philip H. Towner, *The Letters to Timothy and Titus*, New International Commentary on the New Testament (Grand Rapids: Eerdmans, 2006), 246–47, for a brief discussion of the terms "elder" (Greek *presbyteros*) and "overseer" (*episkopos*).

Interestingly, many of the early church leaders were also workplace leaders. Lydia was a dealer in the valuable commodity of purple dye (Acts 16:14, 40). Dorcas was a garment maker (Acts 9:26–41). Aquila and Priscilla were tentmakers (or leatherworkers) who became business partners with Paul (Acts 18:2–3). These leaders were effective in the church after having already proven effective in the workplace and gaining the respect of the wider community. Perhaps the basic qualifications of leadership in church, work, and civic spheres have much in common.

God's Creation Is Good (1 Timothy 4:1–5)

First Timothy affirms "God's way of ordering reality" and that this divine ordering has implications for how Christians should behave in their households, churches, and—by an extension of the text's logic—in their workplaces. The clearest affirmation of God's creation order comes in 1 Timothy 4:1–5. In 1 Timothy 4:4 Paul plainly declares, "Everything created by God is good." This is a clear echo of Genesis 1:31, "God saw everything that he had made, and indeed, it was very good." Within the context of the letter, this sweepingly positive appraisal of creation is used to combat false teachers who are forbidding marriage and certain foods (1 Tim. 4:3). Paul counters their teaching by asserting that these things ought to be received with thanksgiving (1 Tim. 4:3, 4). Food, and anything else in God's creation, is "sanctified" by God's word and by prayer (1 Tim. 4:5). This does not mean that God's word and prayer *make* God's creation good when it isn't good already. Rather, in thankfully acknowledging God as the creator and provider of all things, a Christian sets apart created things such as food for a holy and God-honoring purpose. As a Christian, it is possible even to eat and drink to the glory of God (1 Cor. 10:31).

This affirmation of creation means there is no created material that is inherently evil to work with, and no job engaged with creation that is unacceptable for Christians to do if it doesn't violate God's will. In other words, a Christian can dig wells, design computer chips, scrub toilets, walk on the moon, fix cell phones, plant crops, or harvest trees to the glory of God. None of these jobs or materials is inherently evil. Indeed, each job can please God. This may seem intuitive to those in the modern

Western world who don't struggle much with asceticism, as the ancient Greek and Roman world did. But 1 Timothy 4:4 reminds even us not to view the material realm as something neutral in moral value or to view something such as technology, for example, as inherently evil. The goodness of all of God's creation allows us to live and work in joyful freedom, receiving all things as from God's hands.

Good Relationships Arise from Genuine Respect (1 Timothy 5:1–6:2; Titus 2:1–10)

First Timothy 4:6–16 is full of specific directives Paul gives to Timothy. It would be helpful for Christian workers to remember that training in godliness is a crucial component of professional development (cf. 1 Tim. 4:8). We quickly move from this section, however, to the next, which runs from 1 Timothy 5:1–6:2. Again, this section is similar to a section of Titus 2:1–10. Being a member of the church should not lead us to exploit others within the church (cf. 1 Tim. 5:16; 6:2), but rather should lead us to work harder to bless them. This applies also at work.

In particular, these two passages describe how men and women, old and young, masters and slaves, ought to behave within the family of God. The first two verses of this section in 1 Timothy are important ones. "Do not speak harshly to an older man, but speak to him as to a father, to younger men as brothers, to older women as mothers, to younger women as sisters—with absolute purity." This command does not flatten any distinction between families and the church (as 1 Tim. 5:4, 8 makes clear), but it does suggest that the kindness, compassion, loyalty, and purity that should characterize our most intimate family relationships should also characterize our relationships with those in God's family, the church.

Paul's exhortation to "absolute purity" reminds us that violations of sexual boundaries do occur in families and churches, as well as in workplaces. Sexual harassment can go unchallenged—even unnoticed by those not being harassed—in workplaces. We can bring a blessing to every kind of workplace by paying deeper attention to how men and women are treated, and by raising a challenge to inappropriate and abusive words and actions.

Is it right to think of a workplace as a family? No and yes. No, it is not truly a family, for the reasons portrayed so amusingly in the television series *The Office*. Membership in a workplace is conditional on fulfilling a role adequately. Unlike family members, employees who no longer meet the approval of management are subject to dismissal. Employment is not permanent, not "something you somehow haven't to deserve."[6] It would be naive—possibly even abusive—to pretend that a workplace is a family.

Yet in certain senses, a workplace can be *like* a family, if that term is used to describe the respect, commitment, open communication, and care that family members should show toward one another. If Christians were known for treating co-workers likewise, it could be a great point of the church's redemptive service to the world. Mentoring, for example, is an extremely valuable service that experienced workers can offer to newer colleagues. It resembles the investment that parents make in their children. And just as we protect family members from abuse and exploitation, Christ's love impels us to do the same for people in our workplaces. Certainly we should never engage in abuse or exploitation of others at work, because we imagine we owe them less respect or care than we do to family (or church) members. Rather, we should strive to love all our neighbors, including those in the workplace, as our family and as ourselves.

Godliness with Contentment Is Great Gain (1 Timothy 6:3–10, 17–19)

The last section of 1 Timothy is packed with powerful exhortations and warnings for rich Christians. (We will skip over Paul's charges to Timothy in verses 11–16 and 20, which are directed to Timothy in his particular situation.) First Timothy 6:3–10 and 17–19 have direct workplace applications. In reading and applying these passages, however, we must avoid two common mistakes.

First, this passage does not teach that there is no "gain" to be had by being godly. When Paul writes that those who are "depraved in mind and

---

[6] Robert Frost, "The Death of the Hired Man," line 125, in *North of Boston* (New York: Henry Holt, 1915).

bereft of the truth" imagine that "godliness is a means of gain" (1 Tim. 6:5), what he is denouncing is the mind-set that godliness necessarily leads to financial gain in this life or that godliness should be pursued for the sake of immediate, financial gain. The folly of this thinking is threefold:

1. God often calls his saints to suffer material want in this life and, therefore, God's people should not set their hope on the "uncertainty of riches" (1 Tim. 6:17).

2. Even if someone were to gain great riches in this life, the gain is short-lived because, as John Piper puts it, "There are no U-Hauls behind hearses" (1 Tim. 6:7).[7]

3. Craving wealth leads to evil, apostasy, ruin, and destruction (1 Tim. 6:9–10).

Note carefully, however, that Paul encourages his readers to know that there is *great gain* in godliness when it is combined with contentment in the basic necessities of life (1 Tim. 6:6, 8). Our God is a God "who richly provides us with everything for our enjoyment" (1 Tim. 6:17). Paul commands the righteous rich "to do good, to be rich in good works, generous, and ready to share" (1 Tim. 6:18)—not to sell everything they have and become poor. They are to be rich in good works *so that* they might store up for themselves "the treasure of a good foundation for the future, so that they may take hold of the life that really is life" (1 Tim. 6:19). In other words, godliness *is* a means of gain as long as that gain is understood as life and blessings in the presence of God and not only more money now. Paul's exhortation in 1 Timothy 6:18–19 is similar to Jesus' teaching, "Store up for yourselves treasures in heaven, where neither moth nor rust consumes and where thieves do not break in and steal" (Matt. 6:20; cf. Matt. 19:21; Luke 12:33).

The second mistake to avoid is thinking that this passage and its condemnation of a love for money means that no Christian worker should

---

[7] John Piper, *Desiring God: Meditations of a Christian Hedonist*, rev. and exp. ed. (Colorado Springs: Multnomah, 2003), 188.

ever seek a raise or promotion or that no Christian business should try to make a profit. There are many reasons why someone could want more money; some of them could be bad but others could be good. If someone wanted more money for the status, luxury, or ego boost it would provide, then this would indeed fall under the rebuke of this section of Scripture. But if someone wanted to earn more money in order to provide adequately for dependents, to give more to Christ-honoring causes, or to invest in creating goods and services that allow the community to thrive, then it would not be evil to want more money.[8] To reject the love of money is not to oppose every desire to be successful or profitable in the workplace.

2 Timothy: Encouragement for a Faithful Worker

The letter of 2 Timothy, like 1 Timothy, is addressed from the Apostle Paul to his younger co-worker and is perhaps the last written letter we have from Paul. Unlike 1 Timothy, however, 2 Timothy appears to be more of a personal letter in which Paul encourages Timothy and gives him a solemn charge to remain faithful even after Paul has departed. The very fact that 2 Timothy has been preserved and included in the Christian canon of Scripture indicates, however, that this personal letter has significance beyond its original, particular context.

Cultures Can Persist for Generations (2 Timothy 1:1–2:13; 3:10–17)

One of the striking features of 2 Timothy is the theme of generational faithfulness. Toward the beginning of the letter Paul reminds Timothy of the faith that lived in his grandmother, his mother, and then in Timothy himself (2 Tim. 1:5). This progression suggests that the faithful witness and example of Timothy's grandmother and his mother were among the means God used to bring Timothy to faith. This understanding is confirmed later in the letter when Paul encourages Timothy to "continue

---

[8] See Wayne Grudem's important book, *Business for the Glory of God: The Bible's Teaching on the Moral Goodness of Business* (Wheaton, IL: Crossway, 2003), for a more detailed account of this assertion.

in what you have learned and firmly believed, knowing from whom you learned it, and how from childhood you have known the sacred writings" (2 Tim. 3:14–15a). Paul too, as a member of an older generation, is a model for Timothy to follow. Paul writes, "Join with me in suffering for the gospel" (2 Tim. 1:8), "Hold to the standard of sound teaching that you have heard from me" (2 Tim. 1:13), and "You have observed my teaching, my conduct, my aim in life, my faith, my patience, my love, my steadfastness, my persecutions" (2 Tim. 3:10–11a).

Not only has Timothy received teaching from previous generations, but Paul intends for him to pass on what he has learned to succeeding generations as well: "What you have heard from me through many witnesses entrust to faithful people who will be able to teach others as well" (2 Tim. 2:2). This theme challenges Christian workers to consider what kind of legacy they want to leave behind at their places of employment and in their industry. The first step toward leaving a positive legacy is to do your job faithfully and to the best of your ability. A further step would be to train your successor, so that whoever is going to replace you one day is prepared to do your job well. A Christian worker should be humble enough to learn from others and compassionate enough to teach patiently. Yet in the end, Christian workers must ask themselves whether they left a legacy of redemption in words and deeds.

The generational aspect of 2 Timothy applies not just to individuals, but to all kinds of corporations, both for-profit and not-for-profit. The corporate form was created so that organizations could outlive the individuals who comprise them, without the need to reform the entity at each transition. One of the basic principles of financial audits is that the corporation must be a "going concern," meaning that it must be operating in a sustainable manner.[9] When an organization's pay practices, debt burden, risk management, financial control, quality control, or any other factor become seriously detrimental to its sustainability, its leaders have a duty to call for change.

---

[9] *AG ISA (NZ) 570 The Auditor-General's Statement On Going Concern*, The Auditor-General's Auditing Standards, Controller and Auditor-General, http://www.oag.govt.nz.

This does not mean that corporations should never merge, disband, or otherwise go out of existence. Sometimes an organization's mission has been fulfilled, its purpose becomes obsolete, or it ceases to provide significant value. Then its existence may need to end. But even so, its leaders have a responsibility for the legacy the corporation will leave in society after it is dissolved. For example, a number of companies expose their retirees to the risk of poverty because they have not adequately funded their pension liabilities. Municipal and state governments are even more prone to this failing. Organizations have a duty—from both a biblical and a civic perspective—to ask whether their operations are shifting liabilities to future generations.

Likewise, 2 Timothy suggests organizations must operate in an environmentally and socially sustainable way. To depend for success on unsustainable resource extraction or environmental pollution is a violation of the generational principle. To deplete the community's "social capital"—meaning the educational, cultural, legal, and other social investments that provide the educated workforce, means of transactions, peaceable society, and other factors that workplace organizations depend on—would also be unsustainable. To a certain degree, workplaces invest in environmental and social capital by paying taxes to support governments' environmental and social programs. But perhaps they would have more reliable access to environmental and social capital if they did more to create sustainable systems on their own initiative.

Guard the Tongue (2 Timothy 2:14–26)

In the next section, Paul counsels Timothy with a number of exhortations that could directly apply to the workplace. Paul repeatedly warns Timothy to avoid "wrangling over words" (2 Tim. 2:14), "profane chatter" (2 Tim. 2:16), and "stupid and senseless controversies" (2 Tim. 2:23). This is a good reminder for Christian workers that not all talk at the water cooler is profitable, even if it is not downright evil. Are the conversations we engage in and the ways we speak helpful to those around us? Do our words serve as ambassadors of reconciliation and redemption (2 Cor. 5:20)? Unhelpful conversations can spread like gangrene

(2 Tim. 2:17), lead to ruin and impiety (2 Tim. 2:14, 16), and breed quarrels (2 Tim. 2:23). One thinks of similar warnings in James (cf. James
3:2–12) about the destructive potential of words.

In fact, the most important form of witness to Jesus is the way Christians talk with co-workers when we're not talking about Jesus. Three
words of gossip may destroy three thousand words of praise and piety.
But Christians who consistently encourage, appreciate, respect, and demonstrate care by their words are a powerful witness for Jesus, even if their
words are seldom directly about him. Humility and strictly avoiding judgmentalism are the surest ways to avoid stupid and senseless controversies.

Paul also urges Timothy to "shun youthful passions and pursue righteousness" (2 Tim. 2:22). This may remind us that employees bring their
personal difficulties with them to work. Alcohol and drug abuse affect
virtually every workplace, and "fully one quarter of employees who use the
Internet visit porn sites during the workday . . . and hits are highest during office hours than at any other time of day."[10] Another exhortation that
can be applied to Christian workers is that "the Lord's servant must not
be quarrelsome but kindly to everyone, an apt teacher, patient, correcting
opponents with gentleness" (2 Tim. 2:24–25a). Indeed, much of the portrait Paul sketches of Timothy in this letter could be held up as something
for Christian workers to strive toward. Paul, writing a letter to Timothy,
becomes a support network for him. We might ask what kinds of support
networks today's organizations would do well to provide for workers.

The Time of Difficulty Is Now (2 Timothy 3:1–9)

The fourth and final chapter of 2 Timothy consists mainly of Paul's
charge to Timothy, Paul's reflections on his life, and specific instructions
and greetings. There is no doubt that some of this material could apply
indirectly to work. However, we will examine just one more paragraph
in the letter—2 Timothy 3:1–9.

The first verse gives the main point of the paragraph. "In the last
days distressing times will come" (2 Tim. 3:1). What the description that

---

[10] Anna Kuchment, "The Tangled Web of Porn in the Office," *Newsweek*
(December 8, 2008), http://www.newsweek.com/2008/11/28/the-tangled-web
-of-porn-in-the-office.

follows makes clear, however, is that Timothy is living in these last days already (cf. 2 Tim. 3:2, 5). That the "last days" are already upon all of us is the clear and consistent witness of the New Testament (see Acts 2:17; Heb. 1:2; James 5:3; 2 Pet. 3:3). Christians need to be prepared for the hardship and suffering associated with these last days. Paul later warns, "Indeed, all who want to live a godly life in Christ Jesus will be persecuted" (2 Tim. 3:12).

This is a sobering reminder to those Christians who work in environments that may be difficult but are far less threatening than the social realities of the first century or of many places in the world today. As Christians, we should expect mistreatment at work, injustice, prejudice, opposition, and mockery. If we experience few of these things, we have cause for rejoicing, but we should not allow our present benevolent working conditions to lull us to sleep. The days may be coming when being faithful to Christ at work results in more than strange looks and jokes behind our backs. Indeed, workers at any time might find themselves pressured to act unethically or contrary to God's word. At that time it will be seen more clearly whether we have more than a mere "outward form of godliness" (2 Tim. 3:5). If we do, we know that God will stand by us and give us strength (2 Tim. 4:17).

Titus: Working for Good Deeds

Paul's letter to Titus is the final Pastoral Epistle and has many similarities to 1 and 2 Timothy. (For Titus 1:5–9, see 1 Timothy 3:1–13 above. For Titus 2:1–10, see 1 Timothy 5:1–6:2 above.) In this letter, Paul reminds Titus that he had left him in Crete to "put in *order* what remained to be done" (Titus 1:5). Like Timothy, Titus needed to combat false teaching, install proper leadership, and ensure that the people were devoted to good works (Titus 3:8, 14).

Be Zealous for Good Works (Titus 2:11–3:11)

We have already considered the leadership qualifications described in Titus 1:5–9 and the church family relationships described in Titus

2:1–10 in previous sections of this chapter. Much of the rest of this letter can be summarized by Paul's vision of God's people being zealous for good works. This vision certainly applies to Christian workers—they should be devoted to good works at their place of employment. Good works, of course, means work done in such a way as to please God, more than self or anyone else. Good works carry out the purposes of God seen in his creation of the world. They make the world a better place. They help redeem the brokenness of the world and reconcile people to one another and to God. Devotion to this kind of work drives Christian workers more than a passion to do their jobs well for the sake of money or performance reviews. Yet for Christians to have this godly passion for good works, we must understand what makes these good works possible and why we are doing them. The letter to Titus addresses both of these issues.

First, it is critical for Christians to remember that God "saved us, not because of any works of righteousness that we had done, but according to his mercy" (Titus 3:5). Our conduct in the workplace, at home, or anywhere else does not establish our relationship with God. We cannot "earn" his mercy. Nevertheless, the letter to Titus teaches unambiguously that God's grace not only forgives our sins but also trains us to "renounce impiety and worldly passions, and in the present age to live lives that are self-controlled, upright, and godly" (Titus 2:12). Jesus gave himself so that he might both "redeem us from all iniquity" and "purify for himself a people of his own who are zealous for good deeds" (Titus 2:14). The wonderful section of Titus 3:3–7 describes God's mercy in conversion and justification as the foundation of the command for believers "to be subject to rulers and authorities, to be obedient, to be ready for every good work, to speak evil of no one, to avoid quarreling, to be gentle, and to show every courtesy to everyone" (Titus 3:1–2). The grace that God grants in salvation results in a godly (though imperfect) life of obedience and good works. Would reminding ourselves of this reality throughout the day's activities lead us to become more effective servants of Christ and stewards of creation?

Second, this section in Titus reminds us of the purposes of good works. Good works are intended to meet the needs of others and to make our corner of God's creation productive (Titus 3:14). This hearkens back to the mandate to till the ground and make it fruitful (Gen. 2:5, 15). Good works serve God and people, but they are not done primarily to earn favor from God and people. The production of good works is not the opposite of faith but the essential consequence of faith. It is the response we give to God after our "rebirth and renewal by the Holy Spirit" (Titus 3:5). "Having been justified by his grace, we might become heirs according to the hope of eternal life" (Titus 3:7), and as a result we devote ourselves "to good works; these things are excellent and profitable to everyone" (Titus 3:8). Paul is not talking about giving speeches, passing out tracts, or telling people about Jesus. He is talking about good works in the ordinary sense of doing things that others recognize will meet people's needs. In workplace terms, we could say he means something such as helping new co-workers come up to speed on the job, more so than inviting them to join a Bible study.

Moreover, godly behavior is encouraged "so that the word of God may not be discredited" (Titus 2:5) and so that opponents will have nothing evil to say (Titus 2:8). Positively stated, godly behavior is encouraged for Christians, "so that in everything they may be an ornament to the doctrine of God our Savior" (Titus 2:10). Right doctrine leads to good works, and good works make the truth of God attractive to others. That is the aim behind Christian workers' devotion to good works at their jobs—to live out by their actions the truth they proclaim with their lips. This may prove a powerful witness both to defuse antipathy toward Christians and to appeal to nonbelievers to follow Christ themselves.

Throughout the letter Paul gives practical instructions for doing good works. Most of them can be applied to the workplace. We take our cue on this from the letter itself. Nothing about the instructions to older women, for example (be reverent, don't slander, don't become slaves to drink, teach what is good), suggests that *only* older women should follow them, just as nothing about Timothy's instructions suggests they can be applied at church. (On the question of whether instructions to slaves can be applied to modern employees, see Colossians 3:18–4:1 in "Colossians & Philemon and Work.")

Almost any workplace looking for a statement of organizational values and good practices could begin well simply by cutting and pasting from Titus. Paul's advice includes the following:

Respect

- Show respect to everyone (Titus 3:1).

- Be hospitable (Titus 1:8).

- Be kind (Titus 2:5).

- Don't engage in conflict about inconsequential matters (Titus 3:9).

- Don't be arrogant, quick tempered, or obstinate (Titus 1:7, 8).

- Don't use violence as a means of supervision (Titus 1:7). Use gentleness instead (Titus 3:1).

Self-control

- Be self-controlled (Titus 1:8; 2:6).

- Don't be greedy for gain (Titus 1:7).

- Don't become addicted to alcohol (Titus 1:7; 2:3).

- Avoid envy and ill will (Titus 3:3).

Integrity

- Act with integrity (Titus 1:8).

- Love goodness (Titus 1:8).

- Submit to those in authority over you in the workplace (Titus 2:9). Obey the civil authorities (Titus 3:1).

- Respect others' property (Titus 2:10) and manage it faithfully on their behalf if you have a fiduciary duty (Titus 2:5).

Authority and Duty

- Exercise the authority you have been given (Titus 2:15).

- Be prudent (Titus 1:8).

- Silence rebellious people, idle talkers, deceivers, slanderers, and those who intentionally cause personal divisions (Titus 1:10; 2:3; 3:10). Rebuke them sharply (Titus 1:13).

- Train others under your leadership in these same virtues (Titus 2:2–10).

We must be careful not to turn such applications into a simplistic dogma. "Be prudent," therefore, need not mean there is never an appropriate time to take educated risks. "Use gentleness" need not mean never to exercise power. These are applications to modern workplaces from an ancient letter for the church. These items from Titus serve as an excellent source of principles and values well suited to good leadership, both in the church and in the workplace.

Conclusion to the Pastoral Epistles

The Pastoral Epistles focus on organization, relationships, and leadership within the household of God. The household of God begins with the family, extends to the church, and often applies to the workplace. The God who called into being the family and the church is also the God who created work. He established an order for the church that brings peace, prosperity, and stability. The same—or a highly similar—order can bring the same blessings to other workplaces.

The first order of business for any organization is to understand the true nature of God and his creation. Every workplace needs to be founded on the "pillar and bulwark of the truth" (1 Tim. 3:15), if it is to be effective. We begin by recognizing the truth of God's good creation, the fall of humanity, the persistence of God's grace in the world, the mission of Christ and the church to redeem the world and its people, and the promise of the restoration of God's perfect order. We acknowledge that redemption arises solely as God's free gift, resulting in our desire and ability to perform all sorts of good works. We thereby make the world productive and serve the needs of people.

The Pastoral Epistles lay out the implications of this truth for organizing the church, with special concern for leadership and good relationships. The considerations also apply to nonchurch workplaces, as long as the differences between the church and other organizations are respected. Workplace applications of the Pastoral Epistles are not always direct nor obvious, but the truth found in these letters, when prayerfully applied to the workplace, can manifest God's way of ordering reality and thereby bring glory to the one "whom no one has ever seen or can see" (1 Tim. 6:16).

Hebrews and Work

Introduction to Hebrews

The book of Hebrews offers a deep foundation for understanding the value of work in the world. It offers practical help for overcoming evil at work, developing a rhythm of work and rest, serving the people we work among, enduring hardship, bringing peace to our workplaces, persevering over long periods, offering hospitality, cultivating a life-giving attitude toward money, and finding faithfulness and joy in workplaces where Christ's love often seems in short supply.

The book is founded on one essential message: Listen to Jesus! Some believers were feeling pressure to give up on the Messiah and turn back toward the old covenant. Hebrews reminds them that Jesus the King, through whom the world was created, is also the consummate High Priest in the heavenly places, who has initiated a new and better covenant with concrete consequences on earth. He is the ultimate sacrifice for sin, and he is the ultimate intercessor for us in our daily lives. We should look nowhere else for salvation but entrust ourselves to Christ, living in obedience to him until he brings us into the transformed and renewed city of God. There we will find an eternal Sabbath rest, which is not the cessation of work, but the perfection of the cycle of work and rest intended by God in the seven days of creation.

Christ Created and Sustains the World (Hebrews 1:1–2:8)

Critical to the theology in Hebrews is that Christ created and sustains the world. He is the Son "through whom [God] also created the worlds" (Heb. 1:2). Therefore, Hebrews is a book about Christ, the creator, at work in his workplace, the creation. This may be surprising to some who are used to thinking of the Father alone as creator. But Hebrews is consistent with the rest of the New Testament (e.g., John 1:3; Col. 1:15–17) in naming Christ as the Father's agent in creation.[1] Because Christ is fully God, "the reflection of God's glory and the exact imprint of God's very being" (Heb. 1:3), the writer of Hebrews can refer interchangeably to Christ or the Father as the Creator.

How then does Hebrews portray Christ at work in the creation? He is a builder, founding the earth and constructing the heavens. "In the beginning, Lord, you founded the earth, and the heavens are the work of your hands" (Heb. 1:10). Moreover, he sustains the present creation, bearing "all things by his powerful word" (Heb. 1:3). "All things," of course, includes us as well: "For every house is built by someone, but the builder of all things is God . . . and *we* are his house if we hold firm" (Heb. 3:4, 6). All of creation is built by God through his Son. This strongly affirms the creation as the primary place of God's presence and salvation.

The imagery of God as worker continues throughout Hebrews. He put together or pitched the heavenly tent (Heb. 8:2; by implication, Heb. 9:24), constructed a model or a blueprint for Moses' tabernacle (Heb. 8:5), and designed and built a city (Heb. 11:10, 16; 12:22; 13:14). He is a judge in a court as well as the executioner (Heb. 4:12–13; 9:28; 10:27–31; 12:23). He is a military leader (Heb. 1:13), a parent (Heb. 1:5; 5:8; 8:9; 12:4–11), a master who arranges his household (Heb. 10:5), a farmer (Heb. 6:7–8), a scribe (Heb. 8:10), a paymaster (Heb. 10:35; 11:6), and a physician (Heb. 12:13).[2]

It is true that Hebrews 1:10–12, quoting Psalm 102, does point out a contrast between the Creator and the creation:

> In the beginning, Lord, you founded the earth, and the heavens are the work of your hands; they will perish, but you remain; they will all wear out like clothing; like a cloak you will roll them up, and like clothing they will be changed. But you are the same, and your years will never end.

---

[1] See Sean M. McDonough, *Christ as Creator: Origins of a New Testament Doctrine* (Oxford: Oxford University Press, 2010).

[2] See Robert Banks, *God the Worker: Journeys into the Mind, Heart and Imagination of God* (Sutherland, NSW: Albatross Books, 1992), and R. Paul Stevens, *The Other Six Days* (Grand Rapids: Eerdmans, 2000), 118–23, for a discussion of God's work.

This is very much in keeping with the emphasis on the transitory nature of life in this world, and the need to seek the enduring city of the new heavens and the new earth. Nonetheless, the emphasis of Hebrews 1:10–12 is on the might of the Lord and his deliverance, rather than the fragility of the cosmos.[3] The Lord is at work in the creation.

Human beings are not only *products* of God's creation, we are also sub-creators (or co-creators, if you prefer) with him. Like his Son, we are called to the work of ordering the world. "What are human beings that you are mindful of them, or mortals, that you care for them? You have made them for a little while lower than the angels; you have crowned them with glory and honor, *subjecting all things under their feet*" (Heb. 2:6–8, quoting Ps. 8).[4] If it sounds a bit vain to regard mere humans as participants in the work of creation, Hebrews reminds us, "Jesus is not ashamed to call them brothers and sisters" (Heb. 2:11).

Therefore, our work is meant to resemble God's work. It has undying value. When we make computers, airplanes, and shirts, sell shoes, underwrite loans, harvest coffee, raise children, govern cities, provinces, and nations, or do any kind of creative work, we are working alongside God in his work of creation.

The point is that Jesus is the one supremely in charge of the creation, and only by working in him are we restored to fellowship with God. This alone makes us capable to take our place again as vice-regents of God on earth. Humanity's created destiny is being achieved in Jesus, in whom we find the pattern (Heb. 2:10; 12:1–3), provision (Heb. 2:10–18), end, and hope for all our work. Yet we do so during a time marked by frustration and the menace of death, which threatens our very existence with meaninglessness (Heb. 2:14–15). Hebrews acknowledges that "we do not yet see everything in subjection" to the ways of his kingdom (Heb. 2:8). Evil plays a strong hand at present.

---

[3] Moreover, the citation of Psalm 102 fits in a stream of passages that feature the cosmos as that which was created through the Son and is in the process of being cleansed.

[4] Old Testament quotations in Hebrews are always from the Septuagint, the ancient Greek-language translation of the Hebrew Scriptures. For this reason, they do not always correspond closely to modern translations, which are based on the Hebrew Masoretic text rather than the Septuagint.

All of this is crucial for understanding what Hebrews will later say about heaven and "the coming world" (Heb. 2:5). Hebrews is not contrasting two different worlds—a bad material world with a good spiritual world. Rather, it is acknowledging that God's *good* creation has become subject to evil and is therefore in need of radical restoration in order to become fully good again. *All* of creation—not just human souls—is in the process of being redeemed by Christ. "In subjecting *all things* to them [human beings], God left nothing outside their control" (Heb. 2:8).

The Creation Has Become Subject to Evil (Hebrews 2:14–3:6)

Although Christ created the world entirely good, it has become tainted and subject to "the one who has the power of death, that is, the devil" (Heb. 2:14). The writer of Hebrews says little about how this happened, but he speaks at length about how God is working to "free those who all their lives were held in slavery by the fear of death," namely, "the descendants of Abraham" (Heb. 2:16); this means Abraham's descendants, both through Isaac (the Jews) and Ishmael (the gentiles)—that is to say, everyone. The question asked by Hebrews is, how will God free humanity from evil, death, and the devil? The answer is, through Jesus Christ, the great high priest.

We will explore Jesus' priesthood in greater depth when we turn to the central chapters of the book (Heb. 5–10). For now we simply note that the opening chapters of the book stress that Jesus' creative work and his priestly work are not isolated from one another. Hebrews brings together both: "Lord, you founded the earth, and the heavens are the work of your hands" (Heb. 1:10), and "So that through death he might destroy the one who has the power of death, that is, the devil" (Heb. 2:14). This tells us that Christ is God's agent of both the original creation and the work of *redemption*. Christ's work of creation leads him, after the Fall, to "free those who all their lives were held in slavery" (Heb. 2:5) and to "make a sacrifice of atonement for the sins of the people" (Heb. 2:17).

We know very well how far our workplaces have fallen from God's original intent. Some workplaces exist primarily because we need to restrain the evil that now infests the world. We need police to restrain criminals, diplomats to restore peace, medical professionals to heal disease, evangelists to call people back to God, auto body shops to repair accidents, investigative journalists to uncover corruption, and engineers to rebuild decaying bridges. And every workplace suffers greatly from the Fall. Mismanagement, labor-management disputes, gossip, harassment, discrimination, laziness, greed, insincerity, and a host of other problems large and small, impede our work and our relationships at every turn. God's solution is not to abandon his creation, or to evacuate human beings from it, but to utterly transform it, to re-create it in its essential goodness. To accomplish this, he sends his Son to become incarnate *in* the world, just as he was the creator *of* the world. In our workplaces, we become Christ's "holy partners in a heavenly calling" (Heb. 3:1) to both sustain and restore his creation. This does not replace the creative work that began in the Garden of Eden, but instead tempers it and adds to it. Creative and redemptive works occur side by side and are intertwined until Christ's return and the abolition of evil.

Life in the Wilderness: Journey to the New World (Hebrews 3:7–4:16)

As much as the creation is therefore the good work of God in Christ, there is still a stark contrast between the present broken world and the glorious world to come. In Hebrews 2:5, the author describes his main topic as "the coming world, about which we are speaking." This suggests that the primary focus throughout the book is on creation perfected by God at the consummation of all things. This is borne out by the lengthy discussion of "Sabbath rest" that dominates chapters 3 and 4.

Throughout the book, Hebrews often takes an Old Testament text as its point of departure. In this case, it draws upon the Exodus story to illuminate the idea of Sabbath rest. Like Israel in the Exodus, the people of God are on a pilgrimage toward the promised place of salvation. In Israel's case, it was Canaan. In our case, it is the perfected creation. The Sabbath rest in Hebrews 4:9–10 is not simply a cessation of activity

(Heb. 4:10) but also a Sabbath *celebration* (Heb. 12:22).[5] Continuing with the Old Testament story, Hebrews takes the conquest of the land under Joshua as a further sign pointing toward our ultimate rest in the world to come. Joshua's rest is incomplete and needs fulfillment that comes only through Christ. "For if Joshua had given them rest, God would not speak later about another day" (Heb. 4:8).

At least two crucial things flow from this. First, life in the present world is going to involve difficult work. This is implied by the idea of the *journey*, which is essential to the Exodus story. All who have ever traveled know that any journey involves an immense amount of labor. Hebrews uses the Sabbath motif to depict not only rest but also the work that surrounds it. You work for six days, and then you rest. Likewise, you work hard in Christ during your life journey, and then you rest in Christ when God's kingdom is fulfilled. Of course, Hebrews is not implying you do nothing *but* work—as we will see shortly, there are also times of rest. Nor is it saying that activity ends when Christ's kingdom comes to completion. The point is that Christians have work to do in the here and now. We are not supposed to plop down in the wilderness, put our feet up, and wait for God to show up and make our lives perfect. God is working through Christ to bring this broken world back to what he intended for it in the beginning. We are privileged to be invited to participate in this grand work.

The second point concerns weekly Sabbath rest and worship. It is important to note that the author of Hebrews does not address the question of the weekly Sabbath, either to affirm it or to condemn it. It is likely that he assumed his readers would observe the Sabbath in some way, but we cannot be sure. In Hebrews the value of weekly rest is governed by its consequences for the coming kingdom. Does resting now connect us more deeply to God's promise of future rest? Does it sustain us on the journey of life? Is keeping Sabbath now an act of faith in which we celebrate the joy we know will be fulfilled in eternity? It certainly seems that some sort of Sabbath rest (however that might be worked out in any

---

[5] J. Laansma, *I Will Give You Rest: The Rest Motif in the New Testament with Special Reference to Mt 11 and Heb 3–4*, vol. 98, Wissenschalftliche Untersuchungen zum Neuen Testament (Tübingen: Mohr Siebeck, 1997).

given community) would be an ideal way to remind us that our labor is not an endless cycle of drudgery leading nowhere, but rather purposeful activity punctuated by worship and rest.

Seen in this light, our weekly work routines—the six days, as much as the one—can become exercises in spiritual awareness. When we feel the bite of the curse on work (Gen. 3:16–19) through economic breakdowns, poor management, gossipy co-workers, unappreciative family members, inadequate pay, and the like, we remind ourselves that God's house has been badly damaged by his human tenants, and we long for its complete restoration. When our work goes well, we remind ourselves that God's creation, and our work in it, is a good thing, and that in some measure our good work is furthering his purposes for the world. And on our Sabbath, we take time for worship and rest.

Our Great High Priest (Hebrews 5:1–10:18)

The central section of Hebrews is dominated by the theme of Jesus as our great high priest. Taking Psalm 110 as his guide, the author of Hebrews argues that the Messiah was destined to be "a priest according to the order of Melchizedek" (Heb. 5:6), and that this priesthood is superior to the Levitical priesthood that supervised the religious life of Israel. According to Hebrews, the old priesthood, under the old covenant, could not genuinely take away sins but could only remind the people of their sins by the endless sacrifices offered by imperfect and mortal priests. Jesus' priesthood offers one definitive sacrifice for all time and offers us a mediator who always lives to intercede for us. We will highlight here the implications of these two themes of *sacrifice* and *intercession* on how we go about our work.

Christ's Sacrifice Makes Possible Our Service (Hebrews 5:1–7:28)

Jesus, through his self-sacrifice, succeeded in taking away human sin forever. "When Christ had offered for all time a single sacrifice for sins, 'he sat down at the right hand of God.' . . . For by a single offering he has perfected for all time those who are sanctified" (Heb. 10:12, 14). "Unlike the other high priests, he has no need to offer sacrifices day after day, first for his own sins, and then for those of the people; this he did once for all when he offered himself" (Heb. 7:27). This complete atonement for sin is often referred to as "the work of Christ."

It may seem that the forgiveness of sins is a purely church or spiritual matter with no implications for our work, but this is far from true. On the contrary, the definitive sacrifice of Jesus promises to liberate Christians to live lives of passionate service to God in every sphere of life. The text highlights the ethical—that is, practical—consequences of forgiveness in Hebrews 10:16, "I will put my laws in their hearts, and I will write them on their minds." In other words, we who are forgiven will desire to do God's will (in our hearts) and will receive the wisdom, vision, and ability to do so (in our minds).

How is this so? Many people regard church activities in roughly the same way as some Israelites regarded the rituals of the old covenant. If we are to get on God's good side, such people reckon, we need to do some religious things, since that seems to be the sort of thing God is interested in. Going to church is a nice, easy way to meet the requirement, although the downside is that we have to keep doing it every week so that the "magic" doesn't wear off. The supposed good news is that once we meet our religious obligations, we are then free to go about our business without too much concern about God. We won't do anything heinous, of course, but we are basically on our own until we refill our buckets with God's favor by attending church again next week.

The book of Hebrews lays waste to such a view of God. While the Levitical system was a part of God's good purposes for his people, it was always meant to point beyond itself to the future, definitive sacrifice of Christ. It was not a magical favor dispensary but a canteen for the journey. Now that Christ has come and offered himself on our behalf, we can experience the genuine forgiveness of sins through God's grace directly. There is no further point in making perpetual ritual cleansings. We have no buckets that need to be—or can be—filled with God's favor by doing religious activities. Trusting in Christ and his sacrifice, we are in the right with God. Hebrews 10:5 puts it as clearly as can be: "When Christ came into the world, he said, 'Sacrifices and offerings you have not desired, but a body you have prepared for me'" (Heb. 10:5).

None of this, of course, means that Christians shouldn't go to church or that rituals have no place in Christian worship. What is crucial, though, is that the consummate sacrifice of Christ means that our worship is not a self-contained religious exercise sealed off from the rest of our lives. Instead, it is a "sacrifice of praise" (Heb. 13:15) that refreshes our connection with our Lord, cleanses our conscience, sanctifies our will, and thus frees us to serve God each day, wherever we are.

We are sanctified for service. "See, God, I have come to do your will, O God," says Christ (Heb. 10:7). Service is the inevitable outcome of forgiveness by God. "How much more will the blood of Christ, who through the eternal Spirit offered himself unblemished to God, cleanse our consciences from acts that lead to death, so that we may serve the living God!" (Heb. 9:14, NIV).[6]

Ironically, then, a focus on Christ's priestly, heavenly work should lead us to be of tremendous practical, earthly service. The sacrifice Christ offered, which leads ultimately to a renewal of heaven as well as earth (Heb. 12:26; see also Rev. 21:1), was enacted here on earth. Likewise, our own service is performed here in the rough and tumble of everyday life. But we walk and work in this world in the confidence that Jesus has gone before us and completed the same journey we are on. This gives us confidence that our labor for him in every area of life will not be in vain.

Christ's Intercession Empowers Our Life and Work (Hebrews 7:1–10:18)

Priests in ancient Israel not only offered sacrifices for the people, but they also offered prayers of intercession. Thus Jesus prays for us before the throne of God (Heb. 7:25). "[Jesus] is able for all time to save those who approach God through him, since he always lives to make intercession for them" (Heb. 7:25). "He entered into heaven itself, now

---

[6]We have used the NIV here because of a quirk in the NRSV translation, which reads "worship" instead of "serve." "Worship" is indeed a possible translation of the Greek *latreuein*, which like the Hebrew *abad* can mean either "worship" or "serve." But in this context, the NRSV is alone among the major translations in translating it as "worship." The NIV, TNIV, NASB, KJV, and others render it here as "serve."

to appear in the presence of God on our behalf" (Heb. 9:24). We need Jesus to be "always" interceding in the presence of God on our behalf because we continue to sin, fall short, and stray away. Our actions speak ill of us before God, but Jesus' words about us are words of love before the throne of God.

To put it in workplace terms, imagine the fear a young engineer might feel when he is called to meet the chief of the state highway department. What will he possibly say to the chief? Recognizing that the project he is working on is running late and over budget makes him more afraid. But then he learns that his supervisor, a beloved mentor, will also be at the meeting. And it turns out his supervisor is great friends with the chief of the highway department from their days back at university. "Don't worry," the mentor assures the engineer, "I'll take care of things." Won't the young engineer have much greater confidence to approach the chief in the presence of the chief's friend?

Hebrews emphasizes that Jesus not only is a high priest but also a high priest in solidarity with us. "For we do not have a high priest who is unable to sympathize with our weaknesses, but we have one who in every respect has been tested as we are, yet without sin" (Heb. 4:15). To return to a verse we discussed earlier, Jesus speaks to God of the "body you have prepared for me" (Heb. 10:5). Christ came in a genuine human body, and he really did embrace life as one of us.

In order to be a faithful high priest, the author reasons, Jesus has to be able to sympathize with the people. He cannot do this if he has not experienced the same things they have experienced. And so he states quite carefully that Jesus *learned* obedience. "Although he was a Son, he learned obedience through what he suffered" (Heb. 5:8). This does not mean, of course, that Jesus had to learn to obey in the way we do—by ceasing to disobey God. It means that he needed to *experience suffering and temptation firsthand* to qualify as a high priest. Other verses make the same point in equally expressive language, that Jesus' sufferings "perfected" him (Heb. 2:10; 5:9; 7:28). The full meaning of "perfect" is not only "flawless" but also "complete." Jesus was already flawless—but *to be qualified as our high priest*, he needed those sufferings to complete him for the job. How else could he genuinely relate to us as we struggle in this world day by day?

What is most encouraging here is that this suffering and learning took place in the setting of Jesus' *work*. He does not come as a kind of a theological anthropologist who "learns" about the world in a detached, clinical way, or as a tourist popping by for a visit. Instead he weaves himself into the fabric of real human life, including real human labor. When we face struggles at work, we can then turn to our sympathetic high priest with the full assurance that he knows firsthand what we are going through.

Realizing the Faith (Hebrews 10–11)

Following Jesus is hard work, and only faith in the eventual fulfillment of his promises can keep us going. "Now faith is the assurance of things hoped for, the conviction of things not seen" (Heb. 11:1). We need faith that the promises God made are true, however unlikely that might seem in the present circumstances. A more precise translation of this verse helps us see the practical importance of faith. "Now faith is the *realization* of things hoped for, the *proving* of things not seen."[7] "Realization" is particularly appropriate here, because the double sense it has in English perfectly captures the nuances of the examples of faith given in Hebrews 11. When we at last see things clearly, that is one form of realization. We finally understand. But the second form of realization is seeing things made real, when what we hoped for has finally come true. The heroes of faith in Hebrews 11 realize things in both ways. Taking up the second half of the verse, they are so convinced of what God has said that they prove it by what they do.

Hebrews gives us the practical examples of Noah, Abraham, Moses, and others from the Old Testament. They were all looking forward to the fulfillment of God's promise for something better than their present experience. Noah had faith in the righteous world beyond the flood, and he

---

[7]W. Bauer, W. F. Arndt, F. W. Gingrich, and F. W. Danker, *Greek-English Lexicon of the New Testament and Other Early Christian Literature*, 3rd ed. (Chicago: University of Chicago Press, 2001), under *pistos*. The King James Version is closer to the Greek than some of the modern translations: "Now faith is the substance of things hoped for, the evidence of things not seen."

realized that faith meant building an ark to save his household (Heb. 11:7). Abraham had faith in the coming kingdom (or "city") of God (Heb. 11:10), and he realized that faith meant setting out on a journey to the land God promised him, even though he did not know where he was going (Heb. 11:8–12). Moses had faith in a life in Christ far surpassing the pleasures he could have claimed as a son of Pharaoh's daughter, and he realized that faith meant "choosing rather to share ill-treatment with the people of God than to enjoy the fleeting pleasures of sin" (Heb. 11:25–26). These hopes and promises were not completely fulfilled in their lifetimes, yet they lived every day as if already experiencing God's power to fulfill them.

Faith like this is not wishful thinking. It is taking seriously God's self-revelation in Scripture (Heb. 8:10–11), combined with a "repentance from dead works" (Heb. 6:1), perseverance in "love and good deeds" (Heb. 10:24), and an ability to see the hand of God at work in the world (Heb. 11:3), despite the evil and brokenness around us. Ultimately, faith is a gift from the Holy Spirit (Heb. 2:4), for we could never hold on to such faith by our own force of will.

This was a crucial message for the audience of Hebrews, who were tempted to throw away their hope in Christ in exchange for a more comfortable life in the here and now. Their eyes were fixed not on future glory, but on present deprivation. The book's word of exhortation is that the promises of God are more enduring, more glorious, and indeed more real than fleeting pleasures in the here and now.

If we are to realize the faith God has given us, we have to work in the midst of the tension between God's promise for the future and the realities of today. On the one hand, we should fully recognize the provisional, finite nature of all that we do. We will not be surprised when things don't work out as we had hoped. "All these, though they were commended for their faith, did not receive what was promised" (Heb. 11:39). Situations arise in which our best efforts to do good work are thwarted not only by circumstance, but also by the deliberate misdeeds of human beings. This may cause us grief, but it will not lead us to despair, because we have our eyes fixed on God's city to come.

Sometimes our work is thwarted by our own weakness. We fall short of the mark. Consider the list of names in Hebrews 11:32. When we read their stories we see clearly their own failures, sometimes significant failures. If we read about Barak's timidity as a general (Judg. 4:8–9) through human eyes, we likely would see no faith at all. Yet God sees their faith through God's eyes and credits their work by his grace, not their accomplishment. We can take heart in this when we also have stumbled. We may have spoken harshly to a co-worker, been impatient with a student, ignored our responsibility to our family, and done our work poorly. But we have faith that God is able to bring about his intent for the world even in the midst of our weakness and failure.

On the other hand, *precisely because* we have our eyes on God's city to come, we seek to live according to the ways of that city to the greatest possible extent in every aspect of daily life and work. The heroes of the faith in Hebrews realized their faith in all kinds of workplaces. They were people "who through faith conquered kingdoms, administered justice, obtained promises, shut the mouths of lions, quenched raging fire, escaped the edge of the sword, won strength out of weakness, became mighty in war, put foreign armies to flight" (Heb. 11:33–34).

Imagine a building contractor, which is a fitting illustration for a book concerned with God's cosmic house building. The contractor has a clear vision of life in God's coming kingdom. He knows it will be characterized by justice, harmonious relationships, and enduring beauty. As a person of faith, he seeks to *realize* this vision in the present. He stewards the earth's raw materials in the construction of the home, creating a home of beauty but not wasteful opulence. He treats his workers with the concern and respect that will be characteristic of God's future city. He shows heavenly love to his clients by listening to their hopes for their earthly homes, trying to realize those hopes within the constraints of money and materials. He perseveres through troubles, when the antique radiator is two inches too long for the bathroom, or when a carpenter cuts an expensive joist two inches too short. He accepts that an earthquake or hurricane could destroy all his labors in minutes, yet he puts his whole self into his work. Amid both the joys and the frustrations, he wants to live out the values of God's city by showing consistent love to others in the quality of his personal relationships and in the quality of the houses he builds. And he trusts that every building, frail and imperfect as it is, is a witness day by day to the great city to come, "whose architect and builder is God" (Heb. 11:10).

Enduring Hardship, Pursuing Peace (Hebrews 12:1–16)

Hebrews moves from providing examples of faithful saints to providing challenges for the people of its own day. Like the rest of the New Testament, Hebrews describes the Christian life as full of hardships. We are to endure these hardships as measures of God's fatherly discipline. Through them, we come to share in Christ's holiness and righteousness. Just as the Son came under discipline and so was perfected (Heb. 5:7–10), God's sons and daughters undergo the same process.

It is the most common thing in the world for us to interpret our hardships as divine punishment. Those who oppose us may even view it as such, hurling our very real sins and faults in our faces. But Hebrews reminds us there is no punishment for those who have been forgiven through the all-sufficient, once-for-all sacrifice of Christ. "Where these have been forgiven, there is no longer any sacrifice for sin" (Heb. 10:18). Our loving Father will discipline us (Heb. 12:4–11), but discipline is not punishment (1 Cor. 11:32). Discipline is hard training, but it is a form of love, "For the Lord disciplines those whom he loves" (Heb. 12:6). Let no one pretend to interpret our hardships as God's punishment. "He disciplines us for our good, in order that we may share his holiness" (Heb. 12:10).

But this discipline is not only for our personal benefit. Hebrews goes on to exhort Jesus' followers to "pursue peace with everyone, and the holiness without which no one will see the Lord." The "peace" of which Hebrews 12:14 speaks is the full notion of the Hebrew *shalom*, which conveys an ultimate state of justice and prosperity, shared among the whole community. It is the final goal of salvation. It is captured in another way later in the chapter with the imagery of the holy, heavenly city of Zion (Heb. 12:22–24).

We know how hard it is to endure hardship and pursue peace in our work. Having received the promises of God, we naturally hope they will immediately make our work more pleasant. We want to be fruitful, multiply our wealth, and gain authority—all good things in God's eyes (Gen. 1:28)—and to enjoy friendships (Gen. 2:18) in and through our work. If instead we encounter hardship, money troubles, lack of power, and hostility from co-workers, endurance may be the last thing on our minds. It may seem much easier to give up, quit, or change jobs—if we have the choice—or to disengage, slack off, or pursue a rough justice of our own making. Or we may grow weary and lose heart, remaining at our work but losing interest in doing it as a service to God. May God give us the grace to endure difficult workplace situations! The hardships we face in our work may be God's means of discipline for us, to grow us into more faithful and useful people. If we cannot maintain integrity, serve others, and pursue reconciliation in the midst of difficult jobs or hostile work environments, how can we become like Jesus, "who endured such hostility against himself from sinners" (Heb. 12:3)?

Shaking Things Up (Hebrews 12:18–29)

One of the widespread misunderstandings of Hebrews is that it pits the heavenly (uncreated) world against the earthly (created) one, that it anticipates an annihilation of the cosmos while heaven remains as God's unshakable kingdom. Such a misunderstanding might seem to find support in texts such as Hebrews 12:26–27.

> At that time his voice shook the earth; but now he has promised, "Yet once more I will shake not only the earth but also the heaven." This phrase, "Yet once more," indicates the removal of what is shaken—that is, created things—so that what cannot be shaken may remain.

But upon closer examination, we see that heaven and earth are not very different from each other. The heavens will be shaken as well as the earth (Heb. 12:26). Hebrews describes the heavenly world as a "creation" just as much as the cosmos (Heb. 8:2; 11:10). It speaks of resurrection (Heb. 6:2, 11:35), which is a reclamation, not an annihilation, of creation. It understands the cosmos (Heb. 1:2–6, 11:3) to be the inheritance of the Son. It proclaims that the offering of Christ was a bodily, in-this-world event of flesh and blood (Heb. 12:24; 13:2; 13:20). Ultimately, "shaking" is the removal of whatever is imperfect or sinful from both heaven and earth, not the destruction of the earth in favor of heaven.

The language here is a reference to Haggai 2, where "shaking" refers to the overthrow of foreign occupiers, so that Israel and its temple can be reconstructed. This reference, and the argument of Hebrews as a whole, indicates that the ultimate result of this shaking will be the filling of God's temple—on earth—with glory. The entire cosmos becomes God's temple, cleansed and reclaimed. In Haggai 2, the shaking of heaven and earth leads to the *realization* of the peace on earth we are exhorted to pursue earlier in Hebrews 12. "'In *this place* I will give prosperity [*shalom*],' says the Lord of Hosts" (Hag. 2:9).

What is transient, then, is not the created world but the imperfection, evil, and strife that infect the world. Pouring our lives into God's kingdom means working through the *creation* and *redemption* that belong to the advancing rule of Christ (Heb. 7:2). No matter whether we are fry cooks, educators, athletes, managers, homemakers, ecologists, senators, firefighters, pastors, or anyone else, the way to participate in Christ's kingdom is not to abandon "worldly" work in favor of "spiritual" work. It is to persevere—with thanksgiving to God (Heb. 12:28)—in all kinds of work under the discipline of Christ.

Hospitality (Hebrews 13:1–3)

Amid the various concluding exhortations in Hebrews 13, two have a special relevance for work. Let us begin with Hebrews 13:2 where it says, "Do not neglect to show hospitality to strangers, for by doing that some have entertained angels without knowing it" (Heb. 13:1–2). The verse alludes to Abraham and Sarah entertaining visitors (Gen. 18:1–15) who turn out to be angels (Gen. 19:1), the very bearers of the promise of a son to Abraham and Sarah (Gen. 18:10), which figures so prominently in this book (Heb. 6:13–15; 11:8–20). These verses also remind us of the many acts of hospitality by Jesus (e.g., Matt. 14:13–21; Mark 6:30–44; Luke 9:10–17; John 2:1–11; 6:1–14; 21:12–13) and those who followed him (e.g., Mark 1:31; Luke 5:9), and parables such as the wedding banquet (Matt. 22:1–4; Luke 14:15–24).

Hospitality may be one of the most underrated forms of work in the world—at least, in the modern Western world. Many people work hard to practice hospitality, even though for most people it is unpaid work. Yet few, if asked what their occupation is, would say, "I offer hospitality." We are more likely to see it as a diversion or a private interest, rather than a service to God. Yet hospitality is a great act of faith—that God's provision will bear the expense of giving away food, drink, entertainment, and shelter; that the risk of damage or theft of property will be bearable; that time spent with strangers will not diminish time with family and friends; and, most of all, that strange people are worth caring about. Even if we have to go out of our way to give it—to prison, for example (Heb. 13:3)—hospitality is one of the most significant acts of work or service that human beings can do (Matt. 25:31–40).

In addition, almost all workers have the opportunity to practice an ethos of hospitality in the course of their jobs. Many people work in hospitality industries. Do we recognize that we are fulfilling Hebrews 13:1–3 when we provide a clean, well-maintained hotel room, or a healthful, delicious dinner, or cater a party or reception? No matter the industry or occupation, every interaction with a co-worker, customer, supplier, client, or stranger in the workplace is a chance to make others feel welcomed and valued. Imagine the witness to God's love if Christians had a reputation for hospitality in the course of ordinary business.

Money Matters (Hebrews 13:5–6)

The second work-related exhortation in chapter 13 concerns the love of money: "Keep your lives free from the love of money, and be content with what you have; for he has said, 'I will never leave you or forsake you'" (Heb. 13:4–5). This command to be free of the love of money suggests that financial pressures were among the special problems faced by the original readers of this book. This was already indicated in Hebrews 10:32–36 and indirectly by Hebrews 11:25–26. Perhaps the emphasis on the future "city" (Heb. 11:10; 12:22; 13:14) was stimulated in part by their experience of economic and social alienation from their present city.

We have full confidence of protection and provision by our God, but in no respect does this guarantee that we will enjoy lives of material prosperity. Jesus never promised us an easy life, and our hard work may not be rewarded in this life with wealth or luxury. The point of Hebrews 13:5–6 is that the Lord will provide all that we need *for a life founded on faith*. Of course, plenty of faithful believers have experienced severe financial hardship, and many have even died from exposure, thirst, hunger, disease, and worse. They died that way *through* faith, not for a *lack* of it. The author of Hebrews is perfectly aware of this, having recounted Christians who suffered torture, mocking, flogging, imprisonment, stoning, being sawn in two, death by the sword, destitution, persecution, torment, and wandering across mountains, deserts, in caves and holes in the ground (Heb. 11:35–38)! Ultimately God's promises and our prayers are fulfilled just as they were for his Son—through resurrection from the dead (Heb. 5:7–10). This book operates with a transformed economic vision, that our needs are met in the advance of God's kingdom, rather than in our personal prosperity. Therefore, if we have nothing, we do not despair; if we have enough, we are content; and if we have much, we sacrifice it for the sake of others.

The warning against the love of money does not stem from a discovery that God's kingdom in creation, the material world, is somehow less spiritual than God's kingdom in heaven. It stems, rather, from the startling awareness that in a fallen world, the love of money creates an attachment to the present order that stands in the way of our working toward the transformation of the world. If money is the chief reason we take a job, start a company, run for office, join a church, choose our friends, invest our resources, spend our time, or find a mate, then we are not living by faith.

Working Outside the Camp (Hebrews 13:11–25)

The third work-related exhortation in chapter 13 is to "go to [Jesus] outside the camp and bear the abuse he endured" (Heb. 13:13). According to Hebrews 13:11–13, "The bodies of those animals whose blood is brought into the sanctuary by the high priest as a sacrifice for sin are burned outside the camp," outside the realm of the holy, in the place of the unclean. "Jesus also suffered outside the city gate," outside the camp, in the realm of the unholy, "to sanctify the people by his own blood."

Hebrews thus draws the lesson that we should also journey outside the camp and join Jesus there.

Many Christians work in places "outside the camp" of holiness, that is, in workplaces where hostility, ethical challenges, and suffering are regular occurrences. Sometimes we feel that to follow Christ well, we need to find holier workplaces. But this passage from Hebrews shows us that the opposite is true. To follow Christ fully is to follow him to the places where his saving help is desperately needed, but not necessarily welcomed. Doing the work of Jesus' kingdom entails suffering along with Jesus. The phrase "bearing his disgrace" echoes the faith of Moses, who chose the "disgrace of Christ" over the honor and treasures of Egypt (Heb. 11:24–26). This "disgrace" was the loss of honor and possessions mentioned earlier in the book. Sometimes, sacrificing our possessions, privileges, and status may be the only way we can help others. Yet helping others is precisely why God sends us to work "outside the camp" in the first place. "Do not neglect to do good and to share what you have, for such sacrifices are pleasing to God" (Heb. 13:16).

Conclusion to Hebrews

Hebrews summons us into the world of God's promise to Abraham— a promise to bring all humanity into the sacred space of his kingdom. It announces the fulfillment of God's will to incorporate all the cosmos into the sphere of his own holiness. As a people on a pilgrimage into God's kingdom, we are called to invest our lives, including our work lives, in the cosmos whose architect and builder is God. The book of Hebrews exhorts us to be content with what God provides and to work for peace (*shalom*) and holiness for all. We are to gladly suffer the loss of honor and possessions for the joy that lies ahead of us. In this journey, we are supplied, emboldened, and encouraged by God's Son, the true priest whose self-sacrifice opens a way for the world to be purified and restored to what God intended from the beginning. Even in the midst of our suffering, thanksgiving is our basic attitude and wellspring of perseverance. Christ calls us to make the values of his kingdom known within the economic, social, and political structures of a fallen world.

This requires escaping the trap of living for money. What we do, and what we refrain from doing, are both predicated on these values. We have one work, whatever our occupation, and one ambition—to "do his will, working among us that which is pleasing in his sight, through Jesus Christ, to whom be glory forever and ever" (Heb. 13:21).

The General Epistles and Work

Introduction to the General Epistles

The seven letters of James, 1 and 2 Peter, 1, 2, and 3 John, and Jude are often called the General (or Catholic) Epistles because they seem to speak to the Christian church in general, rather than to individual churches. They are also united by their interest in practical matters such as organizational leadership, hard work, fairness, good relationships, and effective communication.

The General Epistles reflect the essential challenge Christians faced in the Roman Empire—how to follow Jesus in a tough environment. Early Christians faced problems such as slavery, favoritism, and abuse by the rich and powerful. They dealt with harsh words and conflicts. They dealt with the real tensions between ambition and dependence on God, and the fear that doing things God's way would put them in conflict with those in authority. In general, they felt a sense of alienation living and working in a world that seemed incompatible with following Jesus.

Many of today's Christians experience similar tensions at work. On the one hand, many Christians have more opportunity to serve God in their work than in any other sphere of life. Business, government, educational, nonprofit, and at-home workplaces accomplish a tremendous amount of good in society. On the other hand, most workplaces are generally not dedicated toward God's purposes, such as serving the common good, working for the benefit of others, deepening relationships among people, spreading justice, and developing character. Because workplaces' ultimate aims—generally maximizing profit—are different from Christians' ultimate aims, we should expect to experience tension in our dual roles as followers of Christ and workers in the nonchurch workplace. Although most workplaces are not intentionally evil—just as many parts of the Roman Empire were not actively hostile to Jesus' followers—it can still be challenging for Christians to serve God in their work. Because the General Epistles were written to guide Christians experiencing tensions in the world around them, they can be helpful to workplace Christians today.

These General Epistles address such practical concerns head on. Two major principles underlie the variety of items treated in these letters:

1. We can trust God to provide for us.

2. We must work for the benefit of others in need.

From these two principles, the General Epistles derive instructions that have surprisingly practical applications in the twenty-first-century workplace. But perhaps we should not be surprised. God chose the Roman Empire as the place where God would enter human life in the form of Jesus Christ. God is also choosing today's workplace as a point of his presence.

James: Faith and Work

James brings an action-oriented perspective to the principles that we can trust God to provide for us and that we must work for the benefit of others in need. If faith is real—if we truly trust God—then our faith will lead to all kinds of practical actions for the benefit of others in need. This perspective makes James an eminently practical book.

Perseverance, Wisdom, and Spiritual Growth (James 1:1–3)

James begins by emphasizing the deep connection between daily life and spiritual growth. Specifically, God uses the difficulties and challenges of daily life and work to increase our faith. "My brothers and sisters, whenever you face trials of any kind, consider it nothing but joy, because you know that the testing of your faith produces endurance, and let endurance have its full effect, so that you may be mature and complete, lacking in nothing" (James 1:2–4). "Any kind" of trial can be an impetus for growth—including troubles at work—but James is particularly interested in challenges so intense that they result in "the testing of [our] faith."

What kinds of challenges do we face at work that might test our faith in—or faithfulness to—Christ? One kind might be religious hostility. Depending on our situation, faith in Christ could expose us to anything from minor prejudice to limited job opportunities to dismissal or even bodily harm or death in the workplace. Even if others don't put pressure on us, we may tempt ourselves to abandon our faith if we think that being identified as a Christian is holding back our careers.

Another kind of trial could be ethical. We can be tempted to abandon faith—or faithfulness—by committing theft, fraud, dishonesty, unfair dealings, or taking advantage of others in order to enrich ourselves or advance our careers. Another kind of trial arises from failure at work. Some failures can be so traumatic that they shake our faith. For example, getting laid off (made redundant) or dismissed from a job may be so devastating that we question everything we previously relied on, including faith in Christ. Or we may believe that God called us to our work, promised us greatness, or owes us success because we have been faithful to him. Failure at work then seems to mean that God cannot be trusted or does not even exist. Or we may be so gripped by fear that we doubt God will continue to provide for our needs. All of these work-related challenges can test our faith.

What should we do if our faith is tested at work? Endure (James 1:3–4). James tells us that if we can find a way not to give into the temptation to abandon the faith, to act unethically, or to despair, then we will find God with us the whole time. If we don't know how to resist these temptations, James invites us to ask for the wisdom we need to do so (James 1:5). As the crisis passes, we find that our maturity has grown. Instead feeling the lack of whatever we were afraid of losing, we feel the joy of finding God's help.

Depending on God (James 1:5–18)

In speaking about wisdom, James begins to develop the principle that we can trust God to provide for us. "If any of you is lacking in wisdom, ask God, who gives to all generously and ungrudgingly, and it will be given you" (James 1:5). It may seem surprising that we can ask God for wisdom about the tasks of ordinary work—making decisions, assessing opportunities, trusting colleagues or customers, investing resources, and so on—but James tells us to "ask in faith, never doubting" that God will give us the wisdom we need. Our problem is not that we expect too much help from God at work, but that we expect too little (James 1:8).

It is absolutely essential to grasp this. If we doubt that God is the source of all we need, then we are what James calls "double-minded." We have not yet made up our mind whether to follow Christ or not. This makes us "unstable in every way," and we will not be able to accomplish much for the benefit of anyone, or able even to "receive anything from the Lord" on our own behalf (James 1:7). James is under no illusions about how hard it can be to trust God. He knows all too well the trials his audience is already beginning to experience throughout the breadth of the Roman Empire (James 1:1–2). Yet he insists that the Christian life must begin with trusting God to provide.

He immediately applies this to the economic sphere in James 1:9–11. Rich people must not delude themselves that this is due to their own effort. If we depend on our own abilities, we will "wither away" even while we go about our business. Conversely, poor people should not think this is due to God's disfavor. Instead, they should expect to be "raised up" by God. Success or failure comes from many factors beyond ourselves. Those who have ever lost their livelihood due to recession, corporate sale, office relocation, crop failure, discrimination, hurricane damage, or a thousand other factors can testify to that. God does not promise us economic success at work, nor does he doom us to failure, but he uses both success and failure to develop the perseverance needed to overcome evil. If James 2:1–8 invites us to call on God in times of trouble, then verses 9–11 remind us to call on him in times of success as well.

Notice that although James contrasts the goodness of God with the evil of the world, he does not allow us to imagine that we are on the side of angels and those around us on the side of devils. Instead, the divide between good and evil runs down the middle of every Christian's heart. "One is tempted by one's own desire, being lured and enticed by it" (James 1:14). He is speaking to church members. This should make us slow to identify church as good and workplace as bad. There is evil in both spheres—as church scandals and business frauds alike remind us—yet by God's grace we may bring goodness to both.

In fact, the Christian community is one of the means God uses to raise up the poor. God's promise to provide for the poor is fulfilled—in part—by the generosity of his people, and their generosity is a direct result of God's generosity to them. "Every generous act of giving, with every perfect gift, is from above, coming down from the Father of lights" (James 1:17). This affirms both that God is the ultimate source of provision and that believers are responsible to do all they can to bring God's provision to those in need.

Listening, Taking Action, and Avoiding Anger (James 1:19–21)

James continues his practical guidance with words about listening. Christians need to listen well both to people (James 1:19) and to God (James 1:22–25). "Be quick to listen, slow to speak, slow to anger" (James 1:19). We listen, not as a technique to influence anyone else, but as a way to let God's word "rid [*ourselves*] of all sordidness and rank growth of wickedness" (James 1:21). Interestingly, James suggests that listening to others—and not just listening to God's word—is a means of ridding ourselves of wickedness. He does not say that other people speak God's word to us. Instead, he says that listening to others removes the anger and arrogance that keep us from doing God's word spoken in Scripture. "Your anger does not produce God's righteousness. . . . Welcome with meekness the implanted word that has the power to save your souls" (James 1:20–21). When others speak words that we do not welcome—words of disagreement, criticism, dismissal—it is easy to respond in anger, especially in high-pressure situations at work. But doing so usually makes our position worse, and always discredits our witness as Christ's servants. How much better to trust God to defend our position, rather than defending ourselves by angry, hasty speech.

This advice applies to all kinds of work and workplaces. Listening is well established in business literature as a crucial leadership skill.[1]

---

[1]To give one example, the first result on the Harvard Business School Publications website www.harvardbusiness.org on Sept. 18, 2009, browsing under the topic "Interpersonal Skills," is "Listening to People."

Businesses must listen carefully to their customers, employees, investors, communities, and other stakeholders. In order to meet people's true needs, organizations need to listen to the people whose needs they hope to meet. This reminds us that the workplace can be fertile soil for God's work, just as the Roman Empire was, hardship and persecution notwithstanding.

Working for the Benefit of Others in Need (James 1:22–28)

This brings us to the second principle of faithful work—working for the benefit of others in need. "Be doers of the word, and not merely hearers who deceive themselves" (James 1:22). This principle follows naturally from the principle of trusting God to provide for our needs. If we trust God to provide for our needs, then it frees us to work for the benefit of others. On the other hand, if our trust in God does not lead us to act for the benefit of others in need, then James suggests that we don't really trust God. As James puts it, "Religion that is pure and undefiled before God the Father is this: to care for orphans and widows in their distress" (James 1:27). Belief means trust, and trust leads to action.

The source of James's insight seems to be Jesus himself, especially his teachings about the poor and the practical care he showed to a variety of marginalized people. This can be seen, for example, in James's allusions to Jesus' teachings regarding the special place of the poor in God's kingdom (James 2:5; Luke 6:20), along with Jesus' warnings about rotting treasures "on the earth" (James 5: 1–5; Matt. 6:19).

This has direct application to work because meeting needs is the number one mark of a successful workplace, whether in business, education, health care, government work, the professions, nonprofits, or others. A successful organization meets the needs of its customers, employees, investors, citizens, students, clients, and other stakeholders. This is not James's primary focus—he is focused particularly on the needs of people who are poor or powerless—but it nonetheless applies. Whenever an organization meets people's true needs, it is doing God's work.

This application is not limited to serving customers in established businesses. It requires even greater creativity—and demonstrates God's provision even more—when Christians meet the needs of people who are too poor to be customers of established businesses. For example, a group of Christians started a furniture factory in Vietnam to provide jobs for people at the lowest level of the socioeconomic spectrum there. Through the factory, God provides for the needs of both overseas customers needing furniture and local workers who were previously unemployed.[2] Similarly, TriLink Global, an investment firm led by Gloria Nelund, helps start businesses in the developing world as a means to meeting the needs of poor and marginalized people.[3]

Christians' duty does not end with serving the poor and needy through individual workplaces. Social structures and political-economic systems strongly affect whether the needs of the poor are met. To the degree that Christians can influence these structures and systems, we have a responsibility to ensure that they meet the needs of poor and needy people, as well as the needs of rich and powerful people.

Discriminating Against the Poor and Currying Favor with the Rich (James 2:1–13)

James applies both of his underlying principles as a warning against favoritism toward the rich and powerful. He begins with the second principle—working for the benefit of others in need. "You do well if you really fulfill the royal law according to the scripture, 'You shall love your neighbor as yourself.' But if you show partiality, you commit sin" (James 2:8–9). The sin is that when we favor the rich and powerful, we are serving ourselves rather than others. This is because the rich and powerful have the potential to bestow a bit of their riches and power on us. The poor can do nothing for us. But they are the people in need. James illustrates the point by depicting the special treatment that a wealthy, well-dressed person might be given in church, while a poor, shabby person is treated with contempt. Even in something as simple as coming to church, the poor are in need of a word of welcome. The rich—being welcomed everywhere—are not in need.

---

[2] Interview by William Messenger on July 29, 2010, in Hong Kong. Name of source withheld by request.

[3] Al Erisman, "Gloria Nelund: Defining Success in the Financial World," *Ethix* 80 (March/April 2012), available at http://ethix.org/category/archives/issue-80.

James draws on Leviticus 19:18—"Love your neighbor as yourself"—to indicate that showing favoritism toward the rich and excluding or slighting the poor is no less an offense against God's law than murder or adultery (James 2:8–12). Doing this means that either we are not treating our neighbors as ourselves, or we are failing even to recognize that a poor person is our neighbor.

Although James is talking about church gatherings, there are workplace applications. At work, we can pay attention to people who can help us or to people who need our help. In a healthy workplace, this might be merely a matter of emphasis. In a dysfunctional workplace—where people are pitted against each other in a struggle for power—it takes courage to stand on the side of the powerless. Refusing to play favorites is especially dangerous when we are faced with socially entrenched favoritism such as ethnic discrimination, gender stereotyping, or religious bigotry.

Although James couches his argument in terms of working to benefit others in need, this application implicitly raises the principle of trusting in God. If we truly trusted God for our provision, then we wouldn't be tempted to favor the rich and powerful so much. We wouldn't be afraid to associate ourselves with the unpopular crowd at work or school. James is not exhorting us to do good works *despite* lacking faith in Christ and trusting God's provision. James is demonstrating how good works *are made possible* by faith in Christ. Ironically, the poor themselves already live this truth on a daily basis. "Has not God chosen the poor in the world to be rich in faith and to be heirs of the kingdom that he has promised to those who love him?" (James 2:5). This is likely an allusion to Jesus' words in the Sermon on the Mount or Plain (Matt. 5:3; Luke 6:20). The poor are not inheriting the kingdom because they are better people than the rich, but because they put their trust in God. Lacking the means to depend on themselves, or to curry favor with the rich, they have learned to depend on God.

Faith and Work(s) (James 2:14–26)

James takes up the topic of work in detail in the second part of chapter 2. When discussing work, he invariably uses the plural "works" (Greek *erga*) rather than the singular "work" (Greek *ergon*). This leads some to suppose that James uses "works" to mean something different from "work." However, *erga* and *ergon* are simply plural and singular forms of the same word.[4] James is describing any kind of work, from works of kindness, such as giving food to someone who is hungry, to on-the-job work, such as increasing the sustainable yield of rice paddies. His use of the plural shows that he expects Christians' work to be continual.

James's focus on work has led to deep controversy about the letter. Luther famously disliked James because he read James 2:24 ("You see that a person is justified by works and not by faith alone") to be a con-tradiction of Galatians 2:16 ("A person is justified not by the works of the law but through faith in Jesus Christ"). Other leaders of the Protestant Reformation did not share this view, but Luther's objection came to dominate the Protestant reading of James.[5] Although we cannot go into the long debate about Luther and the book of James here, we can inquire briefly whether James's emphasis on work is at odds with the Protestant rejection of "justification by works."

What does James himself say? James 2:14 is arguably the center-piece of his argument, so we will consider this section before moving on to James 2:1–13: "What good is it, my brothers and sisters, if you say you have faith but do not have works?" James bluntly answers his own question by stating, "So faith by itself, if it has no works, is dead" (James 2:17)—as dead (as he notes in a carefully chosen example) as someone in desperate need of food who receives only empty words of well-wishing from his neighbor (James 2:15–16). James takes it for granted that be-lieving in Christ (trusting in God) will move you to feel compassion for— and act to help—someone in need.

We have opportunities every day to meet the needs of people we work for and among. It can be as simple as making sure a confused customer finds the right item for their need or noticing that a new co-worker needs help but is afraid to ask. James urges us to take special concern for those who are vulnerable or marginalized, and we may need to practice notic-ing who these people are at our places of work.

---

[4]See Gk. #2041 in James Strong, *Enhanced Strong's Lexicon* (Ontario: Woodside Bible Fellowship, 1995), and #2240 in Gerhard Kittel, Gerhard Fried-rich, and Geoffrey William Bromiley, eds., *Theological Dictionary of the New Testament* (Grand Rapids: Eerdmans, 1985), 6:635.

[5]Luke Timothy Johnson, "The Letter of James," vol. 12, *The New Inter-preter's Bible* (Nashville: Abingdon Press, 1998), 177.

This is the heart of the book of James. James does not imagine that work is at odds with faith. There can be no "justification by works" because there can be no good works unless there is already faith (trust) in God. James doesn't mean that faith can exist without works yet be insufficient for salvation. He means that any "faith" that doesn't lead to works is dead; in other words, it is no faith at all. "As the body without the spirit is dead, so faith without works is also dead" (James 2:26). James doesn't command Christians to work for the benefit of others in need *instead of* placing faith in Christ, or even *in addition* to placing faith in Christ. He expects that Christians will work for the benefit of others in need *as a result of* placing faith in Christ.[6]

The insight that Christian faith always leads to practical action is in itself a lesson for the workplace. We cannot divide the world into spiritual and practical, for the spiritual *is* the practical. "You see that [Abraham's] faith was active along with his works," James says (James 2:22). Therefore we can never say, "I believe in Jesus and I go to church, but I keep my personal faith out of my work." That kind of faith is dead. James's words "You see that a person is justified by works and not by faith alone" (James 2:24) challenge us to work out our commitment to Christ in our daily activities.

The rest of the letter gives practical applications of the two underlying principles of trust in God and working to benefit others in need. Given our assessment of James 2:14–26, we will proceed with the perspective that these applications are outworkings of faith in Christ, valid in James's day and instructive in ours.

Taming the Tongue (James 3:1–12)

James follows up his practical guidance about listening (see James 1:19–21) with similar advice about speaking. Here he employs some of the fiercest language in the book. "The tongue is a fire. The tongue is placed among our members as a world of iniquity; it stains the whole body, sets on fire the cycle of nature, and is itself set on fire by hell. . . . It

---

[6] For a discussion of how this understanding of faith squares with that of Paul, see Douglas Moo, *The Letter of James* (Grand Rapids: Eerdmans, 2000), 37–43, 118–44.

is a restless evil, full of deadly poison" (James 3:6, 8). James is no doubt well aware of the Old Testament proverbs that speak about the life-giving power of the tongue (e.g., Prov. 12:18, "Rash words are like sword thrusts, but the tongue of the wise brings healing"), but he is also aware of the tongue's death-dealing powers. Many Christians rightly take care not to harm others through harsh speech at church. Shouldn't we be just as careful at work not to "curse those who are made in the likeness of God"? (James 3:9, referring to Gen. 1:26–27). Water-cooler gossip, slander, harassment, disparagement of competitors—who has never been injured by harsh words in the workplace, and who has never injured others?

Selfish Ambition and Investing in Others (James 3:13–4:12)

James 3:14–4:12 also employs the paired principles of dependence on God and service to others in need. As usual, James puts them in reverse order, discussing service first and trust later. In this case, James starts with an admonition against selfish ambition, followed by an exhortation to submit to God.

Selfish Ambition (James 3:13–4:12)

Selfish ambition is the opposite serving the needs of others. Not only does it place our needs *before* others', it actually pits our needs *against* theirs. In the grip of selfish ambition we actively work to undermine other people. This breaks the peace and prevents us from serving anyone but ourselves.

Selfish Ambition Is the Impediment to Peacemaking (James 3:16–4:11)

Selfish ambition causes us to advance ourselves at the expense of others. This turns everyone else into an enemy, which inherently disrupts the peace, order and wellness of the organization. The passage is aptly summarized by James 3:16: "For where there is envy and selfish ambition, there will also be disorder and wickedness of every kind." As a remedy, James highlights a particular practice that overcomes selfish ambition: peacemaking.[7] "A harvest of righteousness is sown in peace for those who make peace" (James 3:18). In typical fashion, he alludes to a workplace—

---

[7] Again echoing the Sermon on the Mount (Matt. 5:9).

grain harvesting in this case—to make his point. He names several elements of peacemaking: grieving for the harm we do others (James 4:9), humbling ourselves (James 4:10), refraining from slander, accusation, and judgment (James 4:11), and mercy and sincerity (James 3:17). All of these can and should be employed by Christians in the workplace.

Selfish Ambition Is Overcome by Submission to God (James 4:2–5)

Selfish ambition causes quarrels and fights within the Christian community, and James says the underlying cause is their failure to depend on God. "You covet something and cannot obtain it; so you engage in disputes and conflicts. You do not have, because you do not ask. You ask and do not receive, because you ask wrongly, in order to spend what you get on your pleasures" (James 4:2–3). We fail to depend on God when we don't even ask him for what we need. Interestingly, the reason we don't depend on God is because we want to serve our own pleasures rather than serving others. This wraps the two principles into an integral unit. James states this metaphorically as an adulterous love affair with the world, by which he means the wealth and pleasure we are tempted to believe we can find in the world without God (James 4:4–5).[8]

Investing in Others (James 4:1–12)

Although James uses the metaphor of adultery, he is talking about selfish ambition in general. In the workplace, one temptation is to use others as stepping stones to our own success. When we steal the credit for a subordinate's or co-worker's work, when we withhold information from a rival for promotion, when we shift the blame to someone not present to defend themselves, when we take advantage of someone in a difficult situation, we are guilty of selfish ambition. James is right that this is a chief source of quarrels. Ironically, selfish ambition may impede success rather than promote it. The higher our position in an organization, the more we depend on others for success. It can be as simple as delegating work to subordinates, or as complex as coordinating an international project team. But if we have a reputation for stepping on

---

[8] James borrows the metaphor of adultery from the Old Testament prophets, who frequently used it to depict the pursuit of wealth and pleasure as substitutes for God.

other people to get ahead, how can we expect others to trust and follow our leadership?

The remedy lies in submitting to God, who created all people in his image (Gen. 1:27) and who sent his Son to die for all (2 Cor. 5:14). We submit to God whenever we put our ambition in the service of others ahead of ourselves. Do we want to rise to a position of authority and excellence? Good, then we should begin by helping *other* workers increase their authority and excellence. Does success motivate us? Good, then we should invest in the success of those around us. Ironically, investing in others' success may also turn out to be the best thing we can do for ourselves. According to economists Elizabeth Dunn of the University of British Columbia and Michael Norton of Harvard Business School, investing in other people makes us happier than spending money on ourselves.[9]

Business Forecasting (James 4:13–17)

James moves to a new application in giving a warning specifically about business forecasting.[10] Somewhat unusually, he focuses first on the principle of trusting God. He opens with sobering words: "Come now, you who say, 'Today or tomorrow we will go to such and such a town and spend a year there, doing business and making money.' Yet you do not even know what tomorrow will bring. What is your life? For you are a mist that appears for a little while and then vanishes" (James 4:13–14). It might seem that James is condemning even short-term business planning. Planning ahead, however, is not his concern. Imagining that we are in control of what happens is the problem.

The following verse helps us see James's real point: "Instead, you ought to say, 'If the Lord wishes, we will live and do this or that'" (James 4:15). The problem is not planning; it is planning as if the future lies in our hands. We are responsible to use wisely the resources, abilities,

---

[9] Elizabeth Dunn and Michael Norton, *Happy Money: The Science of Smarter Spending* (New York: Simon & Schuster, 2013).

[10] These warnings seem to echo both Jesus' teaching and the Old Testament prophets. See, for example, Ezekiel 34:3; Amos 2:6–7; 5:12; Micah 2:2; 6:12–16; Matthew 6:19; Luke 6:24–25; 12:13–21; 32–34; 16:19–31; 18:18–30. Note also that James 1:1–18 focuses on understanding past and present success and failure, while this section focuses on forecasting the future.

connections, and time that God gives us. But we are not in control of the outcomes. Most businesses are well aware how unpredictable outcomes are, despite the best planning and execution that money can buy. The annual report of any publicly traded corporation will feature a detailed section on risks the company faces, often running ten or twenty pages. Statements such as "Our stock price may fluctuate based on factors beyond our control" make it clear that secular corporations are highly attuned to the unpredictability James is talking about.

Why then does James have to remind believers of what ordinary businesses know so well? Perhaps believers sometimes delude themselves that following Christ will make them immune to the unpredictability of life and work. This is a mistake. Instead, James's words should make Christians more aware of the need to continually reassess, adapt, and adjust. Our plans should be flexible and our execution responsive to changing conditions. In one sense, this is simply good business practice. Yet in a deeper sense, it is a spiritual matter, for we need to respond not only to market conditions but also to God's leading in our work. This brings us back to James's exhortation to listen with deep attention. Christian leadership consists not in forcing others to comply with our plans and actions, but in adapting ourselves to God's word and God's unfolding guidance in our lives.

Oppression of Workers (James 5:1–6)

James returns to the principle that work must serve the needs of others. His words in the beginning of chapter 5 are scathing. He warns "the rich" to "weep and wail for the miseries that are coming to you" (James 5:1). While the gold in their vaults and the robes in their closets may look as shiny as ever, James is so certain of their coming judgment that he can speak as if their riches were already decomposing: "Your riches have rotted, and your clothes are moth-eaten. Your gold and silver have rusted" (James 5:2–3). Their self-indulgence has succeeded only in "fattening" them "for the day of slaughter" (James 5:5). The day of slaughter seems to be a reference to the day in which God judges those whom he called to lead and care for his people, but who preyed on them instead (Zech. 11:4–7).

These rich people are doomed both for how they acquired their wealth and for what they did (or didn't do) with it once they had it.

James echoes the Old Testament as he excoriates them for their unjust business practices: "Listen! The wages of the laborers who mowed your fields, which you kept back by fraud, cry out, and the cries of the harvesters have reached the ears of the Lord of hosts" (James 5:4; cf. Lev. 19:13).[11] Money that should be in the hands of laborers sits instead in the treasuries of the landowners. And there it stays—they hoard their wealth and ignore the needy around them (James 5:3).

Business leaders must be especially diligent about paying their workers fairly. An analysis of what constitutes fair pay is beyond the scope of this discussion,[12] but James's words "the wages you have kept back by fraud" (James 5:4) are an accusation of abuse of power on the part of these particular wealthy landowners. The workers were owed wages, but the rich and powerful found a way out of paying them without incurring punishment by the legal system. The rich and powerful often have means to subvert the judiciary, and it's astonishingly easy to exercise unfair power without even recognizing it. Abuses of power include misclassifying employees as independent contractors, inaccurately registering workers in a lower skill code, paying women or minorities less for doing the same job as others, and using children for jobs so dangerous that adults refuse to do them. Misuse of power can never be excused just because it is a so-called standard practice.

James also condemns those who "have lived on the earth in luxury and in pleasure" (James 5:5). The question of what constitutes living in luxury and in pleasure is also complex, but it confronts many Christians in one way or another. James's chief concern in this passage is the well-being of the poor, so the most relevant question may be, "Does the way I live enhance or diminish the lives of poor people? Does what I do with money help lift people out of poverty or does it help keep people impoverished?"

Waiting for the Harvest (James 5:7–20)

James concludes his letter with a variety of exhortations on patience, truthfulness, prayer, confession, and healing. As always, these appeal

---

[11] Leviticus 19 is one of James's favorite Old Testament passages; see Luke Timothy Johnson, *Brother of Jesus, Friend of God* (Grand Rapids: Eerdmans, 2004), 123ff.

[12] See, however, "Pay" at www.theologyofwork.org.

either to the principle that faithful works must benefit others or that it must be done in dependence on God, or both. And as usual, James makes direct applications to the workplace.

Patience

James begins with a workplace example to illustrate the looming return of Christ: "Be patient, therefore, beloved, until the coming of the Lord. The farmer waits for the precious crop from the earth, being patient with it until it receives the early and the late rains. You also must be patient. Strengthen your hearts, for the coming of the Lord is near" (James 5:7–8). He then echoes these words as he draws to a close: "Elijah was a human being like us, and he prayed fervently that it might not rain, and for three years and six months it did not rain on the earth. Then he prayed again, and the heaven gave rain and the earth yielded its harvest" (James 5:17–18).

Patience at work is a form of dependence on God. But patience is hard in the workplace. Work is done to obtain a result—otherwise it wouldn't be work—and there is always the temptation to grasp for the result without actually doing the work. If we're investing to make money, wouldn't we like to get rich quick rather than slow? That mentality leads to insider trading, Ponzi schemes, and gambling away the grocery money at the slot machines. If we're working to get promoted, shouldn't we position ourselves better in our supervisor's eyes by any means available? That leads to backstabbing, stealing credit, gossip, and team disintegration. If we're working to meet a quota, couldn't we meet it faster by doing lower-quality work and passing off the problems to the next person in the production chain? And these are not only problems of personal morality. A production system that rewards poor quality is as bad or worse than the worker who takes advantage of it.

Truthfulness

"Above all, my beloved, do not swear, either by heaven or by earth or by any other oath, but let your 'Yes' be yes and your 'No' be no, so that you may not fall under condemnation" (James 5:12). Imagine a workplace in which people always told the truth—not simply avoiding lying but always saying whatever would give the hearer the most accurate understanding of the way things really are. There would be no need for oaths and swearing, no retroactive clarifications, no need for contract provisions defining who gets what in the case of misstatements or fraud. Imagine if sellers always provided maximally informative data about their products, contracts were always clear to all parties, and bosses always gave accurate credit to their subordinates. Imagine if *we* always gave answers that communicated as accurate a picture as possible, rather than subtly concealing unflattering information about our work. Could we succeed in our present jobs or careers? Could we succeed if everyone became maximally truthful? Do we need to change our definition of success?[13]

Prayer

James returns to the principle of dependence on God in his discussion of prayer. "Are any among you suffering? They should pray" (James 5:13). "If any of you is lacking in wisdom, ask God" (James 1:5). James is inviting us to get specific with God. "God, I don't know how to handle this production failure, and I need your help before I go talk to my boss." God is able to accomplish what we need, though he does not guarantee to answer every prayer exactly as we expect. Many Christians seem strangely reluctant to pray about the specific issues, situations, persons, needs, fears, and questions we encounter every day at work. We forget James's exhortation to ask for specific guidance and even particular outcomes. Have faith, says James, and God will answer us in the real situations of life. "Ask God, who gives to all generously and ungrudgingly, and it will be given you" (James 1:5).

Confession and Healing

James exhorts us to confess our sins to one another, so that we may be healed (James 5:16). The most interesting words for the workplace are "to one another." The assumption is that people sin against each other, not just against God, and at work that is certainly the case. We face daily pressure to produce and perform, and we have limited time

---

[13] For more on this topic, see "Truth and Deception" at www.theologyof work.org.

to act, so we often act without listening, marginalize those who disagree, compete unfairly, hog resources, leave a mess for the next person to clean up, and take out our frustrations on co-workers. We wound and get wounded. The only way to be healed is to confess our sins *to one another*. If someone just shot down a co-worker's promotion by inaccurately criticizing that person's performance, the wrongdoer needs to confess it to the one wronged at work, not just to God in private prayer time. The wrongdoer may have to confess it to the rest of the department too, if he or she is really going to heal the damage.

What is our motivation for confession and healing? So that we may serve the needs of others. "Whoever brings back a sinner from wandering will *save the sinner's soul from death*" (James 5:20; emphasis added). Saving someone from death is serving a very deep need! And perhaps—since we are all sinners—someone else will save us from death by turning us from the error of our ways.

1 Peter: Serving the World as Resident Alien Priests

Writing to a group of Christians who are being slandered, falsely accused, and perhaps even physically abused because of their allegiance to Jesus (1 Pet. 2:12, 18–20; 3:13–17; 4:4, 14, 19), Peter explains how Christians are called to transform their suffering into service to the world. Christ has called us to follow him in a world that does not recognize him. We are resident aliens in this strange land, which is not yet our true home. Therefore, we are bound to experience "various trials" (1 Pet. 1:6). Yet we are not victims of the world, but servants to the world—"a holy priesthood" as Peter puts it (1 Pet. 2:5)—bringing God's blessings to the world. The job of the Christian, then, is to live in this alien land, blessing it until Christ returns and restores the territory to his kingdom.

Resident Aliens and Priests (1 Peter 1:1–2:12)

In the opening line of his letter, Peter addresses his readers as "exiles . . . who have been chosen" (1 Pet. 1:1), a phrase that foreshadows Peter's entire message. This phrase has two parts, "exiles" and "chosen."

If you are a citizen of Christ's kingdom, you are an exile, because at present the world around you is not under Christ's rule. You are living under foreign rule. While you await Christ's return, your true citizenship in his kingdom is "kept in heaven for you" (1 Pet. 1:4). Like exiles in any country, you do not necessarily enjoy the favor of the rulers of the land where you live. Christ came to this land himself but was "rejected by mortals" (1 Pet. 2:4), and all citizens of his kingdom should expect the same treatment. Nonetheless, God has called us to stay here, to reside in this alien land while conducting the work of Christ (1 Pet. 1:15–17).

Although couched in a political metaphor, Peter's discussion rings with workplace terminology: "deeds" (1 Pet. 1:17), "silver or gold" (1 Pet. 1:18), "tested by fire" (1 Pet. 1:7), "purified" (1 Pet. 1:22), and "built into a . . . house" (1 Pet. 2:5). Peter's workplace terms remind us that we live in a world of work, and we have to find a way of following Christ in the midst of the working world around us.

Having described what it means to be "exiles," Peter takes up the other term from 1 Peter 1:1—"chosen." If you're a Christian, you have been chosen by God. For what purpose? To be one of God's priests in the foreign country you inhabit. "Like living stones, let yourselves be built into a spiritual house, to be a holy priesthood, to offer spiritual sacrifices acceptable to God through Jesus Christ" (1 Pet. 2:5). The title of priest, or "royal priesthood," is repeated in 1 Peter 2:9.

Priests in Ancient Israel Offer Sacrifices and Blessings for Israel

Before continuing, we must understand what it meant to be a priest in ancient Israel. Priests performed two chief functions: offering sacrifices in the Temple in Jerusalem, and pronouncing the priestly blessing.[14] In order to perform their duty of offering sacrifices, priests had to be able to enter the inner portions of the temple and—once a year, in the case of the high priest—to stand in the Holy of Holies before the divine presence. In order to say the priestly blessing, priests had to speak for God

---

[14] The priestly blessing was commanded by God to be offered by priests in Numbers 6:23–24 and consists of the words in Numbers 6:24–26, "The Lord bless you and keep you; the Lord make his face shine upon you and be gracious to you; the Lord lift up his countenance upon you and give you peace."

himself. Both of these duties required priests to enter God's presence. This in turn required exceptional purity or holiness, since God's presence cannot abide anything impure or polluted.[15] Yet priests served part time according to a rotation system (Luke 1:8) and had ordinary jobs as their chief means of livelihood. They could not sequester themselves from daily life but had to maintain purity despite the dirt and corruption of the world.

Christians as Priests Offer Self-Sacrifice and Blessings for Others in Need

So for Peter to call Christians "a holy priesthood" (1 Pet. 2:5) and "a royal priesthood" (1 Pet. 2:9) does *not* mean that all Christians should think of themselves as professional pastors. It does not mean that becoming an evangelist or missionary is the highest way of fulfilling God's call to be chosen people. It means that Christians are to live lives of exceptional purity in the midst of whatever our livelihoods are. Only so can we offer sacrifices to God and blessings from God on behalf of the people around us.

Peter states this directly: "Beloved, I urge you as aliens and exiles to abstain from the desires of the flesh that wage war against the soul. Conduct yourselves honorably among the Gentiles, so that, though they malign you as evildoers, they may see your honorable deeds and glorify God when he comes to judge" (1 Pet. 2:11–12). (Notice the concern to glorify God's presence "when he comes to judge.")

Of course, Christians do not perform the same sacrifice as Jewish priests (we do not slaughter animals). Instead, we perform the kind of sacrifice our Lord did: self-sacrifice for the benefit of others in need. "To this you have been called," Peter says, "because Christ also suffered for you, leaving you an example, so that you should follow in his steps" (1 Pet. 2:21). This is not to be taken over-literally as death on a cross, but is to be understood as "spiritual sacrifices" (1 Pet. 2:5)—

---

[15] For God's holiness and the consequent need for human holiness in his presence, see Leviticus 11:44–45. For the extensive cleansing and consecration process of the high priest on the Day of Atonement, see Leviticus 11:44–45. For the extensive cleansing and consecration process of the high priest on the Day of Atonement, see Leviticus 16.

meaning acts performed at the expense of self for the benefit of others in need (1 Pet. 4:10). Our workplaces offer daily opportunities for self-sacrifices—small or large.

This brief survey of 1 Peter 1:3–2:10 fills out the picture Peter paints when he calls his readers "exiles . . . who have been chosen." The term "exiles" means that we live out this vocation as resident aliens in a land that is yet to be our home—a place currently characterized by systemic injustice and corruption. The term "chosen" affirms that followers of Jesus—a "royal priesthood"—have the priest's vocation to be a blessing to the world, especially through self-sacrifice.

Suffering under the World's Authorities (1 Peter 2:13–4:19)

What might it look like for Christians to exercise our calling as resident aliens and priests in the work environment? Peter addresses this directly in instructions to his readers as foreigners and slaves. As foreigners, we are to honor and submit to the civil rule of whatever country we find ourselves in (1 Pet. 2:13–14), even though our citizenship in God's kingdom entitles us to live as "free people" (1 Pet. 2:16). As slaves—which apparently constituted a large segment of Peter's readers, since he does not address any other class of workers—we should submit ourselves to our masters, whether they treat us justly or unjustly (1 Pet. 2:18–19). In fact, unjust treatment is to be expected (1 Pet. 4:12), and it offers us an opportunity to follow in Christ's footsteps by suffering without retaliating (1 Pet. 2:21). Notice that Peter is talking about suffering unjustly, not suffering from the consequences of your own incompetence, arrogance, or ignorance. Of course, you need to suffer obediently when receiving just punishment.

In practical terms, you are not free to disobey those in authority even in order to get what you think is rightfully yours. You will surely find yourself in situations where you don't get what you deserve—a promotion, a raise, an office with a window, a decent health care plan. You may even find your employer actively cheating you, forcing you to work off the clock, punishing you for your boss's errors. It might seem ethical to cheat your employer just enough to make up what you were cheated out of—calling in sick when you're not, charging personal items to the company, stealing office supplies or goofing off on company time. But no, "It is better to suffer for doing good, if suffering should be God's will, than to suffer for doing evil" (1 Pet. 3:17). God does not give you the option to take back what was wrongfully taken from you. The fact that you lied to or cheated someone to make up for how they lied to or cheated you does not make your action less evil. Your call is to do right, even in a hostile work environment (1 Pet. 2:20). "Do not repay evil with evil or insult with insult" (1 Pet. 3:9). Instead, Christians should treat those in authority—even harsh and unjust masters—with respect and honor.

Why? Because our vocation as priests is to bless people, and we can't do that while defending ourselves, just as Christ could not die for the salvation of the world while defending himself (1 Pet. 2:21–25). Christ, of course, was not afraid to exercise power and challenge authority in certain circumstances, and Peter is not claiming to recapitulate the entire gospel here. Other parts of the Bible—especially the Prophets—emphasize God's call to resist oppressive and illegitimate authority. And submission doesn't always mean obedience. We can submit to authority by disobeying openly and accepting the consequences, as Jesus himself did. Here and throughout the epistle, Peter draws us almost exclusively to the self-sacrifice of Christ as a model.

Instructions for Leaders and Followers (1 Peter 5)

Peter now gives instructions for church leaders, termed "elders" ("presbyters" and "bishops" in the Anglicized Greek derivations used in many churches today). The advice is good for workplace leaders, too. It focuses on serving others. "Tend the flock of God . . . willingly [and] eagerly" (1 Pet. 5:2). Don't be greedy for money (1 Pet. 5:2). Don't lord it over others, but be an example for others to emulate (1 Pet. 5:3). Peter advises humility to the young—in fact, to everyone—when he quotes Proverbs 3:34, "God opposes the proud, but gives grace to the humble" (1 Pet. 5:5). These are not unique to 1 Peter, and we will not expand on them here. It is enough to remember that the concept of servant-leadership, circulating widely in today's workplace, is well known to Peter. How could it be otherwise, since Jesus is the servant-leader par excellence (1 Pet. 4:1–2, 6)?

2 Peter: Work and New Creation

Second Peter reinforces many of the themes we saw in James and 1 Peter concerning the need for holy living and endurance in suffering. We will not repeat these, but instead discuss only chapter 3, which raises a profound challenge to a theology of work. If "the present heavens and earth have been reserved for fire, being kept until the day of judgment and destruction of the godless" (2 Pet. 3:7), what is the value of our work in the present day? To borrow the title of Darrell Cosden's important book, what is the heavenly good of earthly work?[16]

The End of the World and the End of Work? (2 Peter 3:1–18)

Does our earthly work matter to God? Darrell Cosden has given a resounding "yes" to that question. Central to his argument is the bodily resurrection of Jesus, which (1) affirms the goodness of the material world, (2) demonstrates that there is continuity between the present world and new creation,[17] and (3) is a sign that new creation, while not fully realized, has been initiated. Our work is ultimately valuable because the fruits of our labor, having been redeemed and transformed, will have a home in heaven. But chapter 3 seems to call into question two integral aspects of Cosden's theology of work: (1) the inherent goodness of created matter, and (2) the continuity between this present world and the world to come, the new creation.

Peter is responding here to lawless scoffers who claimed that God would not intervene in history to judge evil (2 Pet. 3:3–4). He appears to describe a future that lacks all continuity with the present world; instead, it looks like the annihilation of the cosmos:

---

[16] Darrell Cosden, *The Heavenly Good of Earthly Work* (Peabody, MA: Hendrickson Publishers, 2006).

[17] "Jesus' nail-scarred hands and feet are the prototype for the coming new creation. What we find true in his body, we also find true in this vision. What we have done—although it is ambivalent at best on its own—once redeemed and transformed, does find a home in the new creation." Cosden, 76.

1. "The present heavens and earth have been reserved for fire, being kept until the day of judgment and destruction of the godless." (2 Pet. 3:7)

2. "The heavens will pass away with a loud noise, and the elements will be dissolved with fire, and the earth and everything that is done on it will be disclosed." (2 Pet. 3:10)

3. "All these things are to be dissolved." (2 Pet. 3:11)

4. "The heavens will be set ablaze and dissolved, and the elements will melt with fire." (2 Pet. 3:12)

5. But we should not be too quick to assume that annihilation is really in view here.[18] Peter is using the end-times imagery commonly found in Old Testament prophetic oracles to assure his readers of God's impending judgment. The Old Testament prophets and Second Temple Jewish literature regularly employed fire imagery metaphorically to refer to both the purging of the righteous and the destruction of all evil.[19]

A reading of 2 Peter 2:7, 10 and 2 Peter 3:12 in keeping with the conventions of apocalyptic literature, would understand the fire and melting imagery as a metaphor for the process in which God separates good from evil.[20] This is how Peter uses fire imagery in his first letter,

---

[18] See Richard J. Bauckham, *Jude, 2 Peter,* ed. Bruce M. Metzger, David A. Hubbard, and Glenn W, Barker, vol. 50, *Word Biblical Commentary* (Dallas: Word, 1983); and John Dennis, "Cosmology in the Petrine Literature and Jude," in *Cosmology and New Testament Theology,* ed. Jonathan Pennington and Sean McDonough (London: Continuum, 2008), 157–77, for thorough discussions of this complex passage.

[19] See, for example, Isaiah 30:30; 66:15–16; Nahum 1:6; Zephaniah 1:18; 3:8; Zechariah 13:7–9; Malachi 3:2–3; 4:1–2; Sirach 2; Wisdom of Solomon 3. The New Testament uses fire imagery this way as well: 1 Corinthians 3:10–15; 1 Peter 1:5–7; 4:12–13, etc.

[20] Douglas Moo, "Nature in the New Creation: New Testament Eschatology and the Environment," *Journal of the Evangelical Theological Society* 49, no. 3 (2006), 468. See also Al Wolters, who argues that the fire imagery refers to the

reminding his readers that, like gold, they too will be tested through fire; those who make it through the fire will be praised and honored by God (1 Pet. 1:5–7). These passages stress not that the heavens and the earth will be literally annihilated, but rather that all evil will be utterly consumed. Likewise, Peter carefully describes the world in terms of transformation and testing: "dissolved," "melt with fire," "judgment," "reserved for fire." Douglas Moo points out that the word Peter uses for "dissolved" in 2 Peter 3:10–12, *luō*, does not connote annihilation, but instead speaks to radical transformation. He suggests that an alternate translation might be "undone."[21]

Peter's reference to the flood of Noah's time (2 Pet. 3:5–6) should caution us against reading "deluged" to mean total annihilation. The world did not cease to exist, but was purified of all humanity's wickedness. Humanity's goodness—limited to Noah, his family, their possessions, and their work of tending the animals on board—was preserved, and life resumed on the physical earth.

Finally, Peter's positive vision of the ultimate future describes a renewal of the material order: "But, in accordance with his promise, we wait for new heavens and a new earth, where righteousness is at home" (2 Pet. 3:13). This is no thin, disembodied netherworld, but a new cosmos that contains both a "heaven" and an "earth." In 2 Peter 3:10 we read that "the earth and everything that is done on it will be disclosed." Disclosed, not destroyed. Thus even after the burning, "works" will remain.

This is not to say that 2 Peter is the chief source for the theology of the eternal value of present work, but only that 2 Peter is consistent with such a theology. While we may not receive as much detail as we would want, clearly for Peter there is some sort of continuity between what we do on earth now and what we will experience in the future. All evil will be utterly consumed, but all that is righteous will find a permanent home in the new creation. Fire not only consumes, it purges. The dissolution does not signal the end of work. Rather, work done for God finds its true end in the new heavens and new earth.

---

process of God refining the world. Al Wolters, "Worldview and Textual Criticism in 2 Peter 3:10," *Westminster Theological Journal* 49 (1987), 405–13.

[21] Moo, "Nature in the New Creation," 468–69.

1 John: Walking in the Light

Although written under greatly different circumstances than James,[22] 1 John also challenges the notion that faith can live without "works," that is, acts of obedience toward God. In chapter 2, John states that genuine knowledge of God is manifested by transformed character and behavior, epitomized in obedience to God:

> Now by this we may be sure that we know him, if we obey his commandments. Whoever says, "I have come to know him," but does not obey his commandments, is a liar, and in such a person the truth does not exist; but whoever obeys his word, truly in this person the love of God has reached perfection. By this we may be sure that we are in him: whoever says, "I abide in him," ought to walk just as he walked. (1 John 2:3–6)

Again in keeping with James, 1 John regards caring for those in need as one expression of genuine knowledge of God. "How does God's love abide in anyone who has the world's goods and sees a brother or sister in need and yet refuses help?" (1 John 3:17). First John takes us one step further in understanding the relationship between faith and works or, to use John's terms, between knowledge of God and obedience.

Using a variety of images, John explains that our obedience to God indicates, and is the result of, a prior reality variously described as passing from darkness to light (1 John 2:8–11), being loved by God (1 John 3:16; 4:7–10, 16, 19–20), being born of God or made children of God (1 John 2:29; 3:1–2, 8–9), or passing from death to life (1 John 3:14). According to John, right living is first and foremost a result and response to God's love toward us:

> Everyone who loves is born of God and knows God. Whoever does not love does not know God, for God is love. God's love was revealed among us in this way: God sent his only Son into the world so that we might live through him. In this is love, not that we loved God but that he loved us and sent his Son to be the atoning sacrifice for our sins. (1 John 4:7–10)

---

[22] Colin G. Kruse, *The Letters of John* (Grand Rapids: Eerdmans, 2000), 14–28.

John describes the result of this process as the ability to "walk in the light as he himself is in the light" (1 John 1:7). God's love through Jesus' atoning sacrifice brings us into a qualitatively different kind of existence, whereby we are able to see and walk in keeping with God's will for our lives. We don't merely turn on the light once in a while. We walk in the light continually, as a new way of life.

This has immediate significance to workplace ethics. In recent years, there has been increasing attention to "virtue ethics" after a long history of neglect in Protestant thought and practice.[23] Virtue ethics focuses on the long-term formation of moral character, rather than on formulating rules and calculating consequences of immediate decisions. Not that rules or commands are irrelevant—"For the love of God is this, that we obey his commandments" (1 John 5:3)—but that long-term moral formation underlies obedience to the rules. A full discussion is beyond the scope of this discussion,[24] but John's concept of walking in the light as a way of life certainly commends the virtue approach. What we do (our "works") springs inevitably from who we are becoming (our virtues). "We love because he first loved us" (1 John 4:19), and we are becoming like him (1 John 3:2).

One specific application of the light metaphor is that we should be open and transparent in our workplace actions. We should welcome scrutiny of our actions, rather than trying to hide our actions from the light of day. We could never defraud investors, falsify quality records, gossip about co-workers, or extort bribes while walking in the light. In this sense, 1 John 1:7 echoes the Gospel of John 3:20–21, "All who do evil hate the light and do not come to the light, so that their deeds may not be exposed. But those who do what is true come to the light, so that it may be clearly seen that their deeds have been done in God."[25]

For example, Rob Smith heads a business-in-mission organization in Africa that builds boats for use on Lake Victoria. He says he is

---

[23] See the introduction to Stanley Hauerwas, *Character and the Christian Life* (Notre Dame: University of Notre Dame Press, 2001).

[24] See Alistair Mackenzie and Wayne Kirkland, "Ethics," at www.theology ofwork.org./key-topics/ethics.

[25] For a fuller discussion, see "John and Work" in *The Theology of Work Bible Commentary*, vol. 4 or at www.theologyofwork.org.

frequently approached by local officials who want him to pay a bribe. The request is always made in secret. It is not a documented, open payment, as is a tip or an expediting fee for faster service. There are no receipts and the transaction is not recorded anywhere. He has used John 3:20–21 as an inspiration to draw these requests into the light. He will say to the official requesting the bribe, "I don't know much about these kinds of payments. I would like to bring in the ambassador, or the management, to get this documented." He has found this to be a helpful strategy to dealing with bribery. Although it is widely believed that bribery is an effective—albeit unethical—means of increasing market share and profit, research by George Serafeim at Harvard Business School indicates that paying bribes actually decreases a company's financial performance in the long term.[26]

In a related manner, 1 John underscores that we don't need full-time jobs in ministry to do meaningful work in God's kingdom. While most Christians don't have jobs in which they get paid to do the so-called "spiritual" tasks of preaching and evangelism, all Christians can walk in the light by obeying God in their actions (1 John 3:18–19, 24). All such actions come from God's prior love, and therefore are deeply spiritual and meaningful. Thus nonchurch work has value, not only because it is a place where you may get a chance to evangelize, or because the wages you earn can go toward funding missions, but because it is a place where you can embody fellowship with Christ by serving others around you. Work is a highly practical way of loving your neighbor, because work is where you create products and services that meet the needs of people nearby and far away. Work is a spiritual calling.

In this sense, 1 John brings us full circle back to James. Both stress that acts of obedience are integral to the Christian life, and indicate how this factors into a theology of work. We are able to obey God, at work and elsewhere, because we are becoming like Christ, who laid down his life for the benefit of others in need.

---

[26] George Serafeim, "The Real Cost of Bribery," *Harvard Business School Working Knowledge,* November 4, 2013, http://hbswk.hbs.edu/item/7325.html.

2 John and Work

The Second Letter of John fits into the overall framework of the General Epistles, while offering its own insights about life and work in Christ. It is short, but full of practical instruction.

Truthfulness (2 John 1–11)

Truth and Love at Work (2 John 1–6)

Each of John's letters is notable for bringing the concepts "truth" and "love" together into a single idea (1 John 3:18; 2 John 1, 3; 3 John 3). Here in 2 John, we find the most extended development of this idea.

> Grace, mercy, and peace will be with us from God the Father and from Jesus Christ, the Father's Son, in truth and love. I was overjoyed to find some of your children walking in the truth, just as we have been commanded by the Father. But now, dear lady, I ask you, not as though I were writing you a new commandment, but one we have had from the beginning, let us love one another. (2 John 3–5)

According to John, love plus truth equals an environment in which "grace, mercy and peace will be with us."

Regrettably, we often act as though grace, mercy, and peace depend on love *minus* truth. We may hide or shade uncomfortable truths in our communications with others at work in the misguided belief that telling the truth would not be loving. Or we may fear that telling the truth will lead to conflict or ill will, rather than grace or peace. Thinking we are being merciful, we fail to tell the truth.

But love must always begin with the truth. Love comes to us through Christ, and Christ is the perfect embodiment of the truth of God. That is to say, God knows the way things really are, and he wraps his knowledge in love and brings it to us through his Son. So if we are ever to love as God loves, we must begin with the truth, not with falsity, evasion, or fairytales. It is true that telling the truth may lead to conflict or upset feelings—ours or others'. But genuine grace, mercy, and peace come from facing reality and working through difficulties to genuine resolutions.

Jack Welch, a former CEO of General Electric (USA), was a controversial figure due in part to his practice of giving truthful, candid performance reviews. He let employees know on a monthly basis how well they were meeting expectations. Once a year he told them whether they were top performers, middle performers who needed to improve in specific areas, or bottom performers who were in danger of losing their jobs.[27] Some may regard this as harsh, but Welch regarded it as loving:

> I've come to learn that the worst kind of manager is the one who practices false kindness. I tell people, You think you're a nice manager, that you're a kind manager? Well, guess what? You won't be there someday. You'll be promoted. Or you'll retire. And a new manager will come in and look at the employee and say, "Hey, you're not that good." And all of a sudden, this employee is now fifty-three or fifty-five, with many fewer options in life. And now you're gonna tell him, "Go home"? How is that kind? You're the cruelest kind of manager.[28]

The Cost of Truthfulness (2 John 7–11)

"Many deceivers have gone out into the world," John reminds us (2 John 7), and telling the truth can bring us into conflict with those who benefit from deception. Do we choose to tell the truth despite opposition, or do we participate in the deception? If we choose deception, we had better at least admit that we are no longer honest people. (See "You Shall Not Bear False Witness Against Your Neighbor" in Deuteronomy 5:20; Exodus 20:16 at www.theologyofwork.org for more on this topic.)

Ed Moy, later to become the head of the U.S. Mint, tells the story of his first job out of college. When he started the job, he had to fill out an expense report for his use of the company car, identifying his personal use of the car and separating this from his company use. The practice in the office had been had been to list personal use only for the travel from

---

[27]"Should I Rank My Employees?" *Wall Street Journal*, April 7, 2009, http://guides.wsj.com/management/recruiting-hiring-and-firing/should-i-rank-my-employees.

[28]Jack Welch, in "What I've Learned: Jack Welch" *Esquire*, December 31, 2006, http://www.esquire.com/news-politics/interviews/a2380/wil0104jack welch/#ixzz2nkRA41TP.

home to work, claiming the rest as company use even if the purpose of the trip was personal. When Ed honestly broke out his personal use, his boss almost fired him, explaining, "We are underpaid, and this is our way to gain more income. Your report will make the rest of us look bad." Ed respectfully said, "You can fire me if that is what you need to do. But would you really want someone working for you who would lie over such a small thing? How could you trust that person when the stakes were higher?" Ed kept his job, though the transition was a bit difficult![29]

What are we to do about relationships with deceitful people and false teachers? Ed's example suggests that breaking off contact is not necessarily the best solution. We may be able to do more for the cause of truth and love by remaining engaged and telling the truth in the midst of deception than by leaving the scene. Besides, if we broke contact with everyone who ever practiced deception, would anyone be left, even ourselves?

The Value of In-Person Communications (2 John 12–13)

John ends the letter by saying that he wants to continue the conversation in person. "Although I have much to write to you, I would rather not use paper and ink; instead I hope to come to you and talk with you face to face" (2 John 12). Perhaps he realizes that whatever else he has to communicate could be misunderstood if presented in the impersonal medium of writing a letter. This gives us a valuable insight about sensitive communications—some things are better said in person, even if distance makes it difficult to see one another face to face.

In twenty-first-century workplaces we find even more complex challenges to personal communication. Remote communication choices today include video conferencing, telephone, texting, letter, e-mail, social media, and many other variations. But effective communication still requires matching the medium to the nature of the message. E-mail might be the most effective medium for placing an order, for example, but probably not for communicating a performance review. The more

---

[29] Ed Moy, "Faith and Work: Spiritual Insights from a Career in Business & Public Service," at *Kiros*, Seattle, October 11, 2013. Audio recording available at http://kiros.btexpo.ws/media.

complicated or emotionally challenging the message, the more immediate and personal the medium needs to be. Pat Gelsinger, former senior vice president at Intel Corporation, says,

> I have a personal rule. If I go back and forth with somebody in email more than four or five times on the same topic, I stop. No more. We get on the phone, or we get together face to face. I have learned that if you don't resolve something quickly, by the time you get together one of you is mad at the other person. You think they are incompetent since they could not understand the most straightforward thing that you were describing. But it is because of the medium, and it is important to account for this.[30]

The wrong medium for a particular communication can easily lead to misunderstanding, which is failure to transmit the truth. And the wrong medium can also get in the way of showing love. So choosing the right medium for communication is an essential aspect of communicating truth and showing love to people with whom we work. We need to communicate with respect and compassion, even in difficult conversations, and especially when we communicate with people we don't like very much. Sometimes this means meeting face to face, even if it is inconvenient or uncomfortable.

3 John and Work

Like 2 John, 3 John is so short that is not divided into chapters. Nonetheless, it contains two passages applicable to work.

Gossip (3 John 1–12)

John addresses the letter to a "co-worker" (2 John 8) named Gaius. John demonstrates a personal touch when he says, "I pray that all may go well with you, and that you may be in good health, just as it is well with your soul" (3 John 2). He pays attention to his co-worker's body (health)

---

[30] Pat Gelsinger, "Faster Chips, More Opportunity?" interview in *Ethix* 57 (January/February 2008), http://ethix.org/2008/02/01/faster-chips-more -opportunity.

and soul. By itself, this is an important lesson for the workplace—not to see colleagues merely as workers but as whole people.

John then offers himself as an example of someone who is not being treated well in his work. A member of the congregation named Diotrephes has been trying to undermine "our authority," John says, by "spreading false charges against us" (3 John 10). In all three of his letters, John's primary concern has been bringing together truth and love (3 John 1). Diotrephes is doing the complete opposite—speaking falsely in hate. You can almost feel John's pain as he says—to use the more dramatic translation of the New International Version—"I will call attention to what he is doing, gossiping maliciously about us" (3 John 10, NIV).

It is doubly painful that Diotrephes is a believer. This reminds us that being a Christian does not by itself make us perfect. No doubt Diotrephes thinks of himself in the right. What we recognize as false gossip, he may well consider simply warning others so they can protect themselves.

When we give our opinion of others in our places of work, do we ever make unfavorable impressions about ourselves or others? One simple test would help us see ourselves as others see us. Would we talk about people the same way if they were in the room? If not, we are very likely giving a false impression of those we're speaking about, as well as giving a bad impression about ourselves. John, while he has a complaint about Diotrephes, is not gossiping. He knows that his letter will be read aloud in the church, so his complaint will be in the open for Diotrephes to hear and respond to.

Giving his opponent an opportunity to respond to his complaint is an essential element of John's combining of truth and love. He believes that his complaint against Diotrephes is true, yet he recognizes that his opponent deserves an opportunity to explain or defend himself. How different from the kind of trial-by-press campaigns conducted by many public figures today, in which insinuations are spread through the mass media, where there is no opportunity to respond on the same scale.

This principle applies not only to how we speak of individuals but also groups. To collectively denigrate others is as bad as, if not worse than, gossiping or slandering an individual. Virtually every kind of unjust treatment of people at work begins by casting them as members of an inferior or dangerous group. Whenever we hear this happening, it signals our opportunity to speak out against prejudice and guilt by association and in favor of finding the truth of the specific situation.

John's commendation of Demetrius, the brother carrying the letter, is also interesting. John uses his influence as a leader in the church to raise up Demetrius to Gaius and his church. John commends Demetrius for both his life of truth and the respect given him by fellow believers. Leaders in the workplace can use their power and influence effectively toward the end of truth, justice, love, and mercy, even when the gospel is not outwardly acknowledged.

Greet People by Name (3 John 13–15)

The letter ends with the same thought that concludes 2 John. John has things to communicate that would be better said face to face than in pen and ink (3 John 13–14). But there is a twist in 3 John that offers another insight for our daily work. At the very end, John adds, "Greet the friends there, each by name." Speaking a person's name adds further to the personal touch that John recognizes is needed in communication.

Many of us come face to face with hundreds of people in the course of our work. To some degree, we need to communicate with each of them, even if only to avoid knocking into each other in the hallway. How many of them do we know well enough to greet by name? Do you know your boss's boss's boss's name? Probably. Do you know the name of the person who empties the trash in your workplace? Do you greet people by name when you are in conflict with them? Do you learn the names of newcomers to the organization who may need your help at some point? The names you bother to learn and those you don't can reveal a lot about your level of respect and compassion for people. John cares enough to greet "each" person by name.

Jude

The brief letter of Jude paints a startling picture of one very dysfunctional workplace—a church blighted by ungodly leaders. Some of the problems are unique to churches, such as denying Jesus Christ (Jude 4) and heresy ("Korah's rebellion," Jude 8). Others could occur in a secular workplace: rejection of authority, slander (Jude 8), violence ("the way of Cain"), and greed ("Balaam's error," Jude 8).[31] The worst abuses are perpetrated by leaders who gorge themselves at the expense of their flocks. "They feast with you without fear. They are shepherds who care only for themselves" (Jude 12, NRSV alt. reading). Jude's words apply equally to church leaders misappropriating church funds for their own pleasures, executives plundering a corporate pension fund to prop up reported profits (and thus their bonuses), or employees surfing the web on company time.

In the face of this malfeasance, Jude gives a command as surprising in the workplace as in the church: Have mercy. "Have mercy on some who are wavering; save others by snatching them out of the fire; and have mercy on still others with fear, hating even the tunic defiled by their bodies" (Jude 22–23). Jude is not afraid to take strong action against evil. His mercy is not soft or weak, as his images of fire, fear, and defiled bodies indicate. Jude's mercy is severe. But it is mercy nonetheless, for its hope is not merely to punish the offenders but to save them.

This severe mercy may be what some workplace situations require. Someone who commits fraud, harasses other workers, or lies to customers cannot be let off lightly. That leads only to greater evil. But discipline cannot turn into mere revenge. In Christ's eyes, no person is beyond hope. The godly leader treats each person with respect and tries to discern what kind of discipline might lead them back into the fold.

Conclusion to the General Epistles

The General Epistles begin with the twin principles that following Christ makes us able to trust God for our provision, and that trusting God for our provision leads us to work for the benefit of others in need. These principles underlie a variety of practical instructions for life at work (especially in James) and theological insights for understanding the place of work in the life of faith. This raises two questions for us:

---

[31] Bauckham, *Jude, 2 Peter*.

(1) Do we believe these principles? and (2) Are we in fact applying them in our work lives?

Do We Believe the Two Principles?

We see countless situations in our workplaces. Some cast doubt on whether God can be trusted for our provision. Others affirm it. We all know people who seemed to trust God but didn't get what they needed. People lose jobs, houses, retirement savings, even life itself. On the other hand, we receive good things we could never have expected and never have caused to happen ourselves. A new opportunity arises, a small thing we did leads to a big success, an investment works out well, a stranger provides for our needs. Is it true that we can trust God to provide what we truly need? The General Epistles call us to wrestle with this deep question until we have a firm answer. This could mean wrestling with it for a lifetime. Yet that would be better than ignoring it.

The principle that we should work primarily for the benefit of others in need is likewise questionable. It is at odds with the basic assumption of economics—that all workers act primarily to increase their own wealth. It clashes with society's prevailing attitude about work—"Look out for Number One." We demand proof (if we have the power to do so) that we are being paid adequately. Do we equally demand proof that our work benefits others adequately?

Are We Applying the Two Principles in Our Work?

We can assess our level of trust in God's provision by examining the things we do to provide for ourselves. Do we hoard knowledge to make ourselves indispensable? Do we require employment contracts or golden parachutes to feel secure in our future? Do we come to work in fear of being laid off? Do we obsess over work and neglect our families and communities? Do we hold on to an ill-fitting job, despite humiliation, anger, poor performance, and even health problems, because we are afraid there may be nothing else for us? There are no rigid rules, and some or all of these actions may be wise and appropriate in certain situations (obsession excepted). But what does the pattern of what we do at work say about our degree of trust in God for our provision?

The most powerful measure of our trust in God, however, is not what we do for ourselves but what we do for others. Do we help others around us to do well at work, even thought they might get ahead of us? Do we risk our positions to stand up for our co-workers, customers, suppliers, and others who are powerless or in need? Do we choose—within whatever scope of choice we may have—to work in ways that benefit others in need, as much as ways that benefit ourselves?

We need to hold ourselves and others highly accountable for applying these principles to work every day, as the letter of Jude reminds us. Obeying God's word is not a matter of religious sensibilities but of flesh-and-bone consequences for ourselves and those affected by our work. Yet accountability leads us not toward judgmentalism but toward a merciful heart.

The General Epistles challenge us to re-conceptualize our notion not only of work but of who it is we're working for. If we trust God to provide for our needs, then we can work for him and not for ourselves. When we work for God, we serve others. When we serve others, we bring God's blessing into a world in which we live as members of society, yet citizens of another kingdom. God's blessings brought into the world through our work become God's next steps in transforming the world to become our true home. Therefore, as we work "in accordance with his promise, we wait for new heavens and a new earth, where righteousness is at home" (2 Pet. 3:13).

Revelation and Work

Introduction to Revelation

The book of Revelation provides some of the keenest insights in Scripture concerning the "big picture" of work. Yet it is a tough nut to crack, not only because of its intrinsic difficulty but because of the myriad interpretations that have grown up around the book. We cannot hope to solve these problems here, but we may (perhaps) find enough common ground to glean insights from the final book of the Bible.

Perhaps the greatest gap in interpretation is between those who see the book as primarily future, addressing the absolute end of history from chapter 6 on, and those who see most of the book as relating to events around the time John wrote (generally seen as the late first century AD). The good news is that responsible interpreters who hold the "futurist" view acknowledge that the events in the future are modeled on God's work in the past, most notably in Creation and the Exodus from Egypt. Likewise, even those who interpret the book primarily from the standpoint of the first century acknowledge that it does talk about the ultimate future (e.g., the New Jerusalem). For this reason, no one should object to finding *enduring spiritual truths* in the images of the book, nor in seeing a significant future orientation in the promises contained within it.

The Time of God's Kingdom (Revelation 1)

Before the book of Revelation is even a few verses old, John says something that might seem to undercut a robust theology of work: "The time is near!" Some take this to mean that John thought Jesus was coming right away in his lifetime and that he got it wrong; others believe it means that once the end-time events start happening, they will move quickly. Neither of these fit well with the rest of the New Testament, since it is clear that, in some sense, the "end times" begin with the death and resurrection of Jesus (see Heb. 1:1; 1 Cor. 10:11; Acts 2:17). So it is best to take "The time is near" to mean "God's kingdom is in your face!" with the implicit question, "How then are you going to live?" The apparent certainties of everyday life must be seen against the kingdom of God, which is already breaking into the world.

This has profound consequences for our view of work. While there is much in Scripture to commend work, nothing in the present state of affairs should be viewed as absolute. As we will see, work done faithfully for God's glory has enduring value, but God must always be allowed the first and final word. Living in light of his values is critical; there can be no compromise with the world system and its idolatrous ways.

Messages to the Churches (Revelation 2 and 3)

The messages to the seven churches emphasize the importance of works in the Christian life, and thus indirectly contribute to a proper understanding of work in general. The messages to several churches begin, "I know your works . . ." Ephesus is rebuked for not doing the works they did at first (Rev. 2:5), and Sardis likewise has not completed the work it ought to have done for Jesus (Rev. 3:2).

It bears repeating that "works" are not a bad thing in the Bible. They are rather the concrete expression of our love for God. The myth that God only cares about our heart and our feelings is a major reason work in general has been given short shrift in some Protestant circles.

There is evidence that the notorious worldliness of the Laodicean church was evident in its outlook on work and economics. When Jesus counsels these believers to buy from him gold refined in the fire, white garments to hide their nakedness, and salve to heal their eyes, he is likely playing off three of the major industries in Laodicea: banking, wool, and ophthalmology. It seems likely that the Laodiceans assumed that the resources available to them from their culture were all they needed in life. Churches, especially in prosperous countries, must recognize that material abundance can often mask spiritual poverty. Success in our work should never lead us to a sense of self-sufficiency.

The Throne Room of God (Revelation 4 and 5)

John's vision in chapters 4 and 5 is at the heart of Revelation. It is in essence a visualization of the Lord's Prayer: "Thy kingdom come, thy will be done, on earth as it is in heaven." Through Jesus' faithful witness and sacrificial death, God's kingdom will come.

We may highlight from chapter 4 that God is praised precisely as Creator of all things (esp. Rev. 4:11; cf. Rev. 14:7, where the essence of the "good news" is to worship "the one who made heaven and earth, the sea and the springs of water"). The visible world is not an afterthought, or a mere prelude to heaven, but an expression of God's glory and the basis upon which his creatures may praise him. This again is foundational for a proper understanding of work. If the world is simply an illusion separating us from the real life of heaven, work in the world will necessarily be seen as more or less a complete waste of time. If, by contrast, the world is the good creation of God, the prospects for meaningful work become more hopeful. While we must remember the world is always contingent upon God, and that the present world order is subject to considerable shaking up, it is equally important to remember that the world as God's creation stands meaningfully in his presence and is designed for his praise. In chapter 5, it is worth noting in this regard that the redemption secured by Christ, which permits God's kingdom to move forward, is precipitated by Christ's work in the visible creation. As Jacques Ellul notes, Jesus' reception of the kingdom is based on his work on earth: "The terrestrial event provokes the celestial event. . . . What happens in the divine world is defined, determined, provoked by the venture of Jesus upon the earth."[1]

The Strange Way Forward (Revelation 6–16)

God's plan to advance his kingdom, however, takes a surprising turn: before deliverance comes disaster. Yet it is perhaps not so surprising as all that. Chapters 6–16 are most reminiscent of the paradigmatic episode

---

[1]Jacques Ellul, *Apocalypse*, trans. G. W. Schreiner (New York: Seabury, 1977), 47–48.

of God's deliverance of his people, the Exodus from Egypt. Water turning to blood, locust plagues, darkening of the heavenly bodies—all these mark out that God is bringing about the end-times exodus of his people from the latter-day Pharaohs who oppress them. Again, whether we imagine this as largely in John's day or at some point in the future does not take away the basic point. God's ways are consistent from age to age; the patterns of history repeat as God works his way toward the new heavens and new earth.[2]

The importance of this for the workplace is profound. Let us take the well-known four horsemen of the Apocalypse (Rev. 6). It is generally agreed that they represent War and its devastating consequences of death, famine, and plague.[3] Especially of interest for us is the notice in 6:6, "I heard what seemed to be a voice in the midst of the four living creatures saying, 'A quart of wheat for a day's pay, and three quarts of barley for a day's pay, but do not damage the olive oil and the wine!'" While the notice about the oil and wine is obscure (it may signify that the judgment is only partial[4]), the prices of the wheat and barley are clearly inflated (Aune says it is eight times the normal price of wheat and five and one-thirds times the normal price of barley).[5]

While this could be referring to some future devastation, the cycle is all too familiar to every generation—humanity's inability to get along peaceably leads to horrific economic consequences. Since Christians are caught up in these sufferings (see the fifth seal, Rev. 6:9–11), we must

---

[2] If we take Revelation as primarily focused on John's day, the "exodus" theme might refer in the first instance to the fact that those who maintain their faithful witness will "go out" to God's presence upon their death. A futurist view would lay emphasis on the literal overthrow of the wicked kingdoms and the entry of God's people in the millennial kingdom (which may or may not be conceived of as centered in Israel). In any case, in both scenarios, the ultimate fulfillment of the exodus motif is the entry of God's people into the New Jerusalem (see below).

[3] See, e.g., Ben Witherington, *Revelation* (Cambridge: Cambridge University Press, 2003), 132–34; Grant R. Osborne, *Revelation*, vol. 27, *Baker Exegetical Commentary on the New Testament* (Grand Rapids: Baker Academic, 2002), 274; G. K. Beale, *Revelation* (Grand Rapids: Eerdmans, 1999), 370–71.

[4] For authors favoring this view, see the discussion in Osborne, 281.

[5] See the extensive discussion in David E. Aune, "Rev. 6–16," vol. 52b, *Word Biblical Commentary* (Dallas: Word, 1998), 397–400.

face the fact that our work and workplaces are often subjected to forces beyond our control. As awful as these forces may be, however, another message of Revelation 6 is that they are under God's control. To the extent that we are able, we must strive to create workplaces where justice is upheld and where people can experience the blessing of developing the gifts God has given them. But we must also recognize that God's providence permits catastrophes to enter our lives as well. Revelation encourages us to look to the ultimate destination of the New Jerusalem in the midst of an often bumpy road.

There is also perhaps an implicit challenge in 6:6 to avoid exploiting the vulnerable in the time of need. Economic realities may require price hikes in a crisis, but that is no excuse for making a tidy profit from the misery of others.

The bowl judgments in chapters 8 and 9 teach a similar lesson, though here the emphasis is on environmental disaster. Since the precise mechanics are not mentioned, the ecological devastation could perhaps involve human pollution as well as more overtly supernatural phenomena. The key is that God strikes the world in its capacity as the nurturer of idolatrous humanity. This is done not only to punish but also to wake people up to the fact that the earth is as much God's as heaven is. We cannot engineer our way out of God's presence. We cannot manipulate the environment to serve as a shelter from him.

As Revelation moves on, the emphasis shifts from God's judgments on the world to the faithful witness of his people under the reign of the Beast (who may be a single idolatrous ruler at the very end of history, or the archetype of all such idolatrous rulers). It is (deliberately) ironic that the faithful "conquerors" (Rev. 2–3) are at one level "conquered" by the Beast (Rev. 13:7), though they are ultimately vindicated by God (Rev. 11:11). The suffering of the saints includes economic suffering: those who refuse the notorious "mark of the Beast" are not allowed to "buy or sell" (Rev. 13:17). The analogies with the "mark" of Ezekiel 9 suggest that the mark of the Beast is a symbol for adherence to the idolatrous (Roman?) system ("666" can render "Nero Caesar," the consummate bad emperor). But even if one takes a more literal and futurist view, the spiritual lesson is clear: the refusal to follow the world's system of false worship can sometimes lead to negative economic consequences for the faithful. This can happen in a greater or lesser way in any soci-ety.[6] John is not denying that following God's ways can lead to positive economic consequences (as is clearly taught in Proverbs, for example). But in keeping with the rest of Revelation, he is saying that the forces of evil—though ultimately under God's control—can twist things such that what should lead to blessing instead leads to suffering. Christians must always set their mind to do what is right and honoring to God, realizing that this could lead to exclusion from economic opportunity. Judgment on idolaters is certain, and no amount of financial gain is worth throwing one's lot in with those who oppose God. This is why the Beast-followers of chapter 13 are immediately contrasted with the 144,000 of chapter 14, "in whose mouths no lie was found" (Rev. 14:5). They maintain their faithful and true witness to God no matter what.

A Tale of Two Cities (Revelation 17–22)

The most important insights into the big picture of work, however, come in the concluding chapters, where the worldly city Babylon is set against God's city, the New Jerusalem. The introductions of the cities in 17:1 and 21:9 are set in clear parallel:

> "Come, I will show you the judgment of the great whore who is seated on many waters."

> "Come, I will show you the bride, the wife of the lamb."

Babylon represents the dead-end street of humanity's attempt to build their culture apart from God. It has every appearance of being the paradise for which humanity has always longed. It is no coincidence that its gold and jewels recall those of the New Jerusalem (Rev. 17:4). Like the New Jerusalem, Babylon exercises authority over the nations and receives their wealth (note the references to "the merchants of the earth" in Rev. 18:3 and the lament of the sea traders in Rev. 18:15–19).

But it is in fact a counterfeit, doomed to be exposed by God in the final judgment. Especially instructive is the cargo list in Revelation 18:11–13

---

[6] See the judicious comments of Osborne, 518.

(see Bauckham, "Economic Critique,"[7] which describes the luxury goods flowing into Babylon). The list is modeled on Ezekiel 27:12–22 and the fall of Tyre, but it has been updated to include the luxury goods popular in Rome in John's day.

> And the merchants of the earth weep and mourn for her, since no one buys their cargo anymore—cargo of gold, silver, jewels and pearls, fine linen, purple, silk and scarlet, all kinds of scented wood, all articles of ivory, all articles of costly wood, bronze, iron, and marble, cinnamon, spice, incense, myrrh, frankincense, wine, olive oil, choice flour and wheat, cattle and sheep, horses and chariots, slaves—and human lives.

The final note about "human lives" likely relates to the slave trade, and it is the final nail in the coffin of Babylon's exploitative empire: she will stop at nothing, not even trafficking in human flesh, in pursuit of sensual self-indulgence.

The lesson that God would judge a city for its economic practices is a sobering thought. Economics is clearly a moral issue in the book of Revelation. The fact that much of the condemnation appears to stem from its self-indulgence should hit with particular force at modern consumer culture, where the constant search for more and better can lead to a myopic focus on satisfying real or imagined material needs. But the most worrisome thing of all is that Babylon looks *so close* to the New Jerusalem. God did create a good world; we are meant to enjoy life; God does delight in the beautiful things of earth. If the world system were a self-evident cesspool, the temptation for Christians to fall to its allures would be small. It is precisely the genuine benefits of technological advance and extensive trading networks that constitute the danger. Babylon promises all the glories of Eden, without the intrusive presence of God. It slowly but inexorably twists the good gifts of God—economic interchange, agricultural abundance, diligent craftsmanship—into the service of false gods.

At this point, one might feel that any participation in the world economy—or even any local economy—must be so fraught with idolatry that the only solution is to withdraw completely and live alone in the

---

[7] Richard Bauckham, "The Economic Critique of Rome in Revelation 18," in *The Climax of Prophecy: Studies in the Book of Revelation* (Edinburgh: T&T Clark, 1993), 338–83.

wilderness. But Revelation offers an alternative vision of life together: the New Jerusalem. This is "the city that comes down from heaven," and as such it is the consummate representation of God's grace. It stands in stark contrast to the self-made monstrosity that is Babylon.[8]

At one level, the New Jerusalem is a return to Eden—there is a river flowing through its midst, with the tree of life standing by with fruit-laden branches and leaves for the healing of the nations (Rev. 22:2). Humanity can once again walk in peace with God. Indeed, it outstrips Eden, since the glory of the Lord itself provides the illumination for the city (Rev. 22:5).

But the New Jerusalem is not simply a new and better garden: it is a garden-*city*, the urban ideal that forms the counterweight to Babylon. There is, for instance, still meaningful human participation in the life of the celestial city come to earth. Central to this, of course, is the worship people bring to God and the Lamb. But there seems to be more than this in the note that "people will bring into [the New Jerusalem] the glory and honor of the nations" (Rev. 21:24–26). In the ancient world, it was desirable to build a temple with the best materials from all over the world; this is what Solomon did for the temple in Jerusalem. More than that, people would bring gifts from far and wide to adorn the temple after its completion. It is probable that the image of kings bringing their gifts to the New Jerusalem flows from this background. It does not seem too much of a stretch to imagine that these gifts are the products of human culture, devoted now to the glory of God.[9]

We must also consider the implications of Old Testament visions of the future, which see it in meaningful continuity with present-day life. Isaiah 65, for example, is a critical background text for Revelation

---

[8] Richard Bauckham, *The Theology of the Book of Revelation* (Cambridge: Cambridge University Press, 1993), 126–43.

[9] Cf. G. B. Caird, *The Revelation of Saint John* (Peabody, MA: Hendrickson, 1993), 279: "Nothing from the old order which has value in the sight of God is debarred from entry into the new. John's heaven is no world-denying Nirvana, into which men may escape from the incurable ills of sublunary existence, but the seal of affirmation on the goodness of God's creation. The treasure that men find laid up in heaven turns out to be *the treasures and wealth of the nations,* the best they have known and loved on earth redeemed of all imperfections and transfigured by the radiance of God." See also Darrell T. Cosden, *The Heavenly Good* (Peabody, MA: Hendrickson Publishers, 2006), 72–77.

21–22 and provides its foundational teaching, "I am about to create new heavens and a new earth; the former things shall not be remembered or come to mind" (cf. Rev. 21:1). Yet this same chapter says of the future blessings of God's people, "They shall build houses and inhabit them; they shall plant vineyards and eat their fruit. They shall not build and another inhabit; they shall not plant and another eat; for like the days of a tree shall the days of my people be, and my chosen shall long enjoy the work of their hands" (Isa. 65:21–22). We can certainly argue that Isaiah is pointing, in ways suitable to his times, to something much greater than mere agricultural abundance—but he can hardly be pointing to less. Yet *less* is precisely what is typically offered in a vision of "heaven" consisting of nothing more than clouds, harps, and white robes.

Parsing out precisely how this works is not easy. Will there still be farming in the new heavens and new earth? Will a godly computer programmer's 1.0 software be consigned to the flames while version 2.0 enters the heavenly city? The Bible does not answer these types of questions directly, but we may once more look at the big picture. God created humans to exercise dominion over the earth, which entails creativity. Would it be sensible for such a God to then turn and regard work done in faith as useless and cast it aside? On balance, it seems far more likely that he would raise it up and perfect all that is done for his glory. Likewise, the prophetic vision of the future envisions people engaged in meaningful activity in the creation. Since God does not go into detail as to how this transfer of products from the now-world to the new-world works, or what exact things we might be doing in the future state, we can only guess at what this means concretely. But it does mean that we can be "always excelling in the work of the Lord, because [we] know that in the Lord [our] labor is not in vain" (1 Cor. 15:58).[10]

Conclusion to Revelation

What does this all mean for everyday life in the workplace? Revelation does not provide detailed instructions for best workplace practices,

---

[10] See Cosden, passim, and Miroslav Volf, *Work in the Spirit* (Oxford: Oxford University Press, 1991), esp. 88–122.

but it does provide some important guidelines, especially with respect to big picture issues. It is not enough to burrow our heads down and do our jobs and mind our business. We have to have some sense of where things are going, and why we are doing what we are doing.

The greater one's position of authority, the greater one's responsibility is to see that organization is directed toward ends that will glorify God, and that it is practiced in a way that expresses love for neighbor. In contrast to the exploitative nature of Babylon, Christian business should strive for mutual benefit: a fair exchange of goods and services, just treatment of workers, and a view toward the long-term good of the people and societies partnering in the enterprise.

While most workplaces today are not formally or informally affiliated with pagan gods (as they often were in the ancient world), subtler forms of idolatry can creep in unawares. One contemporary analogue to biblical Babylon would be a company that sees its own profit and continuity as the ultimate goals of its existence (with perhaps the CEO on the cosmic throne!). We must always remember that all of life is open to God and subject to his approval or disapproval. The annihilation of Babylon serves as a grim reminder that God is not mocked, and that this goes for our workplace dealings as much as religious concerns.

Ultimately, these loyalties reveal themselves in deeds. Those who commit themselves to the way of Jesus must strive to be above reproach in their ethics. The saints stand in abiding need of the forgiveness available through Jesus' blood, and they are called to imitate his fateful witness in their everyday lives.

But it is appropriate to conclude with the positive vision of the New Jerusalem. While there is necessarily a radical break between the now-world and the new-world, there is also a strong sense of continuity between the two. After all, the New Jerusalem is still the New *Jerusalem*. It shares things in common with the earthly city; indeed, it can be seen at one level as the consummation of all that the earthly Jerusalem aspired to be. In the same way, our future is ultimately a gift of God. Yet in the mysteries of his creative goodness, our deeds follow after us (Rev. 14:13)—certainly our deeds of kindness and our worship to God and the works of our hands as well.

Bibliography

Agrell, G. *Work, Toil and Sustenance: An Examination of the View of Work in the New Testament, Taking into Consideration Views Found in Old Testament, Intertestamental and Early Rabbinic Writings.* Translated by S. Westerholm and G. Agrell. Lund: Ohlssons, 1976.

Albright, W. F., and C. S. Mann. *Matthew.* Vol. 26, *The Anchor Bible.* New York: Doubleday, 1971.

Amnesty International. "Conflict Diamonds." http://www.amnestyusa.org /our-work/issues/business-and-human-rights/oil-gas-and-mining -industries/conflict-diamonds.

Arnold, Bill T. "Jesus' Demonstration in the Temple." In *Law and Religion: Essays on the Place of the Law in Israel and Early Christianity.* Edited by B. Lindars, 72–89. Cambridge: James Clarke, 1988.

———. *Who Were the Babylonians?* Atlanta: Society of Biblical Literature, 2004.

Aune, David E. "Rev. 6–16." Vol. 52b, *Word Biblical Commentary.* Dallas: Word, 1998.

———. "Trouble in Thessalonica: An Exegetical Study of 1 Thess. 4.9–12, 5.12–14 and II Thess. 6.6–15 in Light of First-Century Social Conditions." ThM thesis, Regent College, 1989.

Bailey, John A. "Who Wrote II Thessalonians?" *New Testament Studies* 25, no. 2 (1979): 137.

Bakke, Dennis W. *Joy at Work: A Revolutionary Approach to Fun on the Job.* Seattle: PVG, 2005.

Bakke, Raymond, William Hendricks, and Brad Smith. *Joy at Work Bible Study Companion.* Lake Mary, FL: Charisma House, 2005.

Baldwin, Joyce G. *Daniel.* Tyndale Old Testament Commentaries. Downers Grove, IL: InterVarsity Press, 1978.

Balz, Horst R., and Gerhard Schneider. *Exegetical Dictionary of the New Testament.* Translated by J. W. Medendorp and Douglas W. Scott. Grand Rapids: Eerdmans, 1990–93.

Banks, Robert. *God the Worker: Journeys into the Mind, Heart, and Imagination of God*. Eugene, OR: Wipf & Stock, 2008.

———. "The Role of the Bible in Bureaucratic Decision-Making." *Private Values and Public Policy: The Ethics of Decision-Making in Government Administration*. Sydney: Lancer Books, 1983.

Barclay, John. "Conflict in Thessalonica." *Catholic Biblical Quarterly* 55 (1993): 512–30.

Barclay, William. *The Gospel of Matthew*. Louisville, KY: Westminster John Knox Press, 2001.

Barker, Kenneth, ed. *The NIV Study Bible*. Grand Rapids: Zondervan, 1999.

Barringer, Terry. Quoted in *The Bible and the Business of Life*. Edited by Gordon Preece and Simon Carey Holt. Adelaide: ATF, 2004.

Bartchy, S. Scott. "Community of Goods in Acts: Idealization or Social Reality?" In *The Future of Early Christianity: Essays in Honor of Helmut Koester*. Edited by Birger A. Pearson, A. Thomas Krabel, George W. E. Nickelsburg, and Norman R. Petersen. Minneapolis: Fortress Press, 1991.

———. *MALLON CHRESAI: First Century Slavery and the Interpretation of 1 Corinthians 7:21*. Society of Biblical Literature Dissertation Series No. 11. Missoula: Scholars Press, University of Montana, 1973. Reprinted by Wipf & Stock, 2003.

Barton, John. "Ethics in the Book of Isaiah." Vol. 1, *Writing and Reading the Scroll of Isaiah: Studies of an Interpretive Tradition*. Edited by Craig C. Broyles and Craig A. Evans. Leiden: Brill, 1997.

Bauckham, Richard J. *God Crucified: Monotheism and Christology in the New Testament*. Grand Rapids: Eerdmans, 1999.

———. *Jude, 2 Peter*. Edited by Bruce M. Metzger, David A. Hubbard, and Glenn W. Barker. Vol. 50, *Word Biblical Commentary*. Dallas: Word Books, 1983.

———. "The Economic Critique of Rome in Revelation 18." *The Climax of Prophecy: Studies in the Book of Revelation*. Edinburgh: T&T Clark, 1993.

———. *The Theology of the Book of Revelation*. Cambridge: Cambridge University Press, 1993.

Bauer, W., W. F. Arndt, F. W. Gingrich, and F. W. Danker. *Greek-English Lexicon of the New Testament and Other Early Christian Literature*. 3rd ed. Chicago: University of Chicago Press, 2001.

Beale, G. K. *Revelation*. Grand Rapids: Eerdmans, 1999.

Berding, Kenneth. "Confusing Word and Concept in 'Spiritual Gifts': Have We Forgotten James Barr's Exhortations?" *Journal of the Evangelical Theological Society* 43 (2000): 37–51.

Best, Ernest. *The First and Second Epistles to the Thessalonians*. 2nd ed. British New Testament Conference. London: A & C Black, 1986.

"Bill Gates Answers Most Frequently Asked Questions," http://download .microsoft.com/download/0/c/0/0c020894-1f95-408c-a571-1b5 033c75bbc/billg_faq.d oc.

Blenkinsopp, Joseph. *Ezekiel*. Interpretation. Louisville: John Knox Press, 1990.

Block, Daniel I. *Judges, Ruth*. Vol. 6, The New American Commentary. Nashville: Broadman & Holman, 1999.

———. "Unspeakable Crimes: The Abuse of Women in the Book of Judges." *The Southern Baptist Theological Journal* 2 (1998): 46–55.

Block, D. I., and J. Clinton McCann. *Judges*. Interpretation. Louisville: Westminster John Knox Press, 1989.

Bock, Darrell L. *Acts. Baker Exegetical Commentary on the New Testament*. Grand Rapids: Baker, 2007.

———. *Luke 9:51–24:53. Baker Exegetical Commentary on the New Testament*. Grand Rapids: Baker Books, 1996.

Boling, Robert G. "Gideon (Person)." *The Anchor Bible Dictionary*. Edited by David Noel Freedman. New York: Doubleday, 1992.

Bonhoeffer, Dietrich. *The Cost of Discipleship*. New York: Macmillan, 1966.

———. *Letters and Papers from Prison*. Edited by Eberhard Bethge. Rev. ed. New York: Touchstone, 1997.

Brueggemann, Walter. "The Book of Exodus." Vol. 1, *The New Interpreter's Bible: Genesis to Leviticus*. Nashville: Abingdon Press, 1994.

———. *A Commentary on Jeremiah: Exile & Homecoming*. Grand Rapids: Eerdmans, 1998.

———. *Reverberations of Faith: A Theological Handbook of Old Testament Themes*. Louisville: Westminster John Knox Press, 2002. See esp. "Sabbath."

Bruner, Frederick Dale. *The Christbook, Matthew 1–12*. Vol. 1, *Matthew: A Commentary*. Grand Rapids: Wm. B. Eerdmans, 2007.

Budd, Phillip J. *Numbers.* Vol. 5, *Word Biblical Commentary.* Dallas: Word, 1998.

Burke, Trevor J. *Family Matters: A Socio-Historical Study of Kinship Metaphors in 1 Thessalonians.* London: T&T Clark, 2003.

Bush, Frederic W. *Ruth–Esther.* Vol. 9, *Word Biblical Commentary.* Dallas: Word, 1998.

Byrne, Brendan. *The Hospitality of God: A Reading of Luke's Gospel.* Collegeville, MN: Liturgical Press, 2000.

Caird, G. B. *The Revelation of Saint John.* Peabody, MA: Hendrickson, 1993.

Campbell, Ken M. "What was Jesus' Occupation?" *Journal of the Evangelical Theological Society* 48, no. 3 (September 2005): 501–19.

Capper, Brian J. "The Interpretation of Acts 5.4." *Journal for the Study of the New Testament* 6, no. 19 (1983): 117–31.

———. "The Palestinian Cultural Context of Earliest Christian Community of Goods." In *The Book of Acts in Its Palestinian Setting.* Edited by Richard J. Bauckham, 323–56. Grand Rapids: Eerdmans, 1995.

Carnegie, Andrew. *Autobiography of Andrew Carnegie.* Boston: Houghton Mifflin, 1920.

Carr, Albert Z. "Is Business Bluffing Ethical?" *Harvard Business Review* 46 (January/February 1968).

Carroll, Robert P. *Jeremiah: A Commentary.* Old Testament Library. London: SCM Press, 1986.

Carson, D. A. *The Gospel According to John. The Pillar New Testament Commentary.* Grand Rapids: Eerdmans, 1991.

Cassuto, Umberto Moshe David. *A Commentary on the Book of Exodus.* Skokie, IL: Varda Books, 2005.

Chamorro-Premuzic, Tomas. "Less-Confident People Are More Successful." *Harvard Business Review.* July 6, 2012. http://blogs.hbr.org/2012/07/less-confident-people-are-more-su/.

Chaney, Marvin L. "Bitter Bounty: The Dynamics of Political Economy Critiqued by the Eighth-Century Prophets." In *The Bible and Liberation: Political and Social Hermeneutics.* Edited by Norman K. Gottwald and Richard A. Horsley. Rev. ed. Maryknoll, NY: Orbis Books, 1993.

Chen, Pauline. "When Doctors Admit Their Mistakes." *New York Times*. August 19, 2010.

Childs, Brevard S. *Memory and Tradition in Israel*. London: SCM Press, 1962.

Chilton, Bruce. "Debts." Vol. 2, *The Anchor Yale Bible Dictionary*. Edited by David Noel Freedman. New York: Doubleday, 1996.

Chisholm, Robert B., Jr. *From Exegesis to Exposition: A Practical Guide to Using Biblical Hebrew*. Grand Rapids: Baker, 1998.

Chivers, C. J. "Putin Is Approved as Prime Minister." *New York Times*. May 9, 2008. http://www.nytimes.com/2008/05/09/world/europe/09russia.html?_r=0.

Cho, Youngmo. *Spirit and Kingdom in the Writings of Luke and Paul*. Waynesborough, GA: Paternoster, 2005.

Cicero. *Epistulae ad Familiares (The Letters to His Friends)*. Translated by W. Glynn Williams. 3 vols. Loeb Classical Library. Cambridge, MA: Harvard University Press, 1929.

Clifford, Richard J. "Introduction to Wisdom Literature." Vol. 5, *The New Interpreter's Bible*. Nashville: Abingdon Press, 1997.

Clines, David J. A. *Theme of the Pentateuch*. 2nd ed. London: T&T Clark, 1997.

Collins, Jim. *Good to Great: Why Some Companies Make the Leap . . . And Others Don't*. New York: HarperBusiness, 2001.

Collins, John J. *Daniel*. Hermeneia. Minneapolis: Fortress, 1993.

Conzelman, Hans. *1 Corinthians*. Translated by James W. Leitch. Philadelphia: Fortress Press, 1975.

Cosden, Darrell T. *The Heavenly Good of Earthly Work*. Peabody, MA: Hendrickson, 2006.

Cotton, John. "Christian Calling." In *The Way of Life*. London, 1641. Quoted in Leland Ryken. *Worldly Saints: The Puritans as They Really Were*. Grand Rapids: Zondervan, 1986.

Cowles, C. S., Eugene H. Merrill, Daniel L. Gard, and Tremper Longman III. *Show Them No Mercy: 4 Views on God and Canaanite Genocide*. Grand Rapids: Zondervan, 2003.

Craigie, Peter C. *Psalms 1–50*. 2nd ed. Vol. 19, *Word Biblical Commentary*. Nashville: Nelson Reference & Electronic, 2004.

Darr, Katheryn Pfisterer. "Proverb Performance and Transgenerational Retribution in Ezekiel 18." *Ezekiel's Hierarchical World: Wrestling with a Tiered Reality*. Edited by Stephen L. Cook and Corrine L. Patton. Atlanta: Society of Biblical Literature, 2004.

De La Merced, Michael. "Released from Prison." *New York Times*. December 4, 2013.

De Maistre, Joseph-Marie. Letter 76. *Lettres et Opuscules*. August 27, 1811. Quoted in Edward Latham. *Famous Sayings and Their Authors*. London: Swan Sonnenschein, 1906.

De Pree, Max. *Leadership Is an Art*. New York: Doubleday, 1989.

Deming, Edwards W. *The New Economics for Industry, Government, Education*. 2nd ed. Cambridge, MA: MIT Press, 2000.

Dennis, John. "Cosmology in the Petrine Literature and Jude." *Cosmology and New Testament Theology*. Edited by Jonathan Pennington and Sean McDonough. London: Continuum, 2008.

Dillard, Raymond B. *2 Chronicles*. Vol. 15, *Word Biblical Commentary*. Dallas: Word, 1998.

Doering, Lutz. "Sabbath Laws in the New Testament Gospels." In *The New Testament and Rabbinic Literature*. Edited by F. García Martínez and P. J. Tomson, 208–20. Leiden: Brill, 2009.

Donfried, Karl P. "The Cults of Thessalonica and the Thessalonian Correspondence." *New Testament Studies* 31, no. 3 (1985): 341–42.

Dostoevsky, Fyodor. *The Brothers Karamazov*. Translated by Richard Pevear and Larissa Volokhonsky. San Francisco: North Point Press, 1990.

Douglas, Mary. *Purity and Danger: An Analysis of the Concepts of Pollution and Taboo*. London: Routledge, 1966.

"Dr. Gary Kaplan: Determined Steps to Transformation." *Ethix* 73 (Jan. 2001). http://ethix.org/2011/01/11/dr-gary-s-kaplan-determined-steps-to-transformation.

Duckworth, Angela L., and Martin E. P. Seligman. "Self-Discipline Outdoes IQ in Predicting Academic Performance of Adolescents." *Psychological Science* 16, no.12 (2005): 939–44.

Dunn, Elizabeth, and Michael Norton. *Happy Money: The Science of Smarter Spending*. New York: Simon & Schuster, 2013.

Dunn, James D. G. *Acts of the Apostles. Epworth Commentaries*. Peterborough, UK: Epworth Press, 1996.

———. *The Epistles to the Colossians and to Philemon: A Commentary on the Greek Text*. The New International Greek Testament Commentary. Grand Rapids: Eerdmans, 1996.

Ellul, Jacques. *Apocalypse*. Translated by G. W. Schreiner. New York: Seabury, 1977.

———. *The Politics of God & the Politics of Man*. Grand Rapids: Eerdmans, 1972.

Engels, Donald. *Roman Corinth: An Alternative Model for the Classical City*. Chicago: University of Chicago Press, 1990.

Enns, Peter. *Inspiration and Incarnation: Evangelicals and the Problem of the Old Testament*. Grand Rapids: Baker, 2005.

———. "Law of God." Vol. 4, *New International Dictionary of Old Testament Theology and Exegesis*. Edited by Willem A. VanGemeren. Grand Rapids: Zondervan, 1997.

Erisman, Al. "Gloria Nelund: Defining Success in the Financial World," interview in *Ethix* 80 (March/April 2012). http://ethix.org/category /archives/issue-80.

Evans, Craig A. "Jesus' Action in the Temple." In *Jesus in Context: Temple, Purity, and Restoration*. Edited by Craig A. Evans and B. Chilton, 395–44. Leiden: Brill, 1997.

"Ezra-Nehemiah, Books of." *The Anchor Bible Dictionary*. Edited by David Noel Freedman. New York: Doubleday, 1992.

Fee, Gordon D. *The First Epistle to the Corinthians*. Grand Rapids: Eerdmans, 1987.

Fitzmyer, Joseph A. *The Acts of the Apostles. The Anchor Bible*. New York: Doubleday, 1998.

Fox, Michael V. *The Song of Songs and the Ancient Egyptian Love Songs*. Madison: University of Wisconsin Press, 1985.

France, R. T. *The Gospel of Matthew. New International Commentary on the New Testament*. Grand Rapids: Eerdmans, 2007.

Freedman, David Noel. "Haustafeln" and "Household Codes." *The Anchor Bible Dictionary*. 6 vols. New York: Doubleday, 1992.

Freedman, David Noel, ed. *The Anchor Yale Bible Dictionary*. Vol. 5. New York: Doubleday, 1996.

Fretheim, Terence E. *Exodus: Interpretation: A Bible Commentary for Teaching and Preaching*. Louisville: Westminster John Knox Press, 1991.

Freyne, Sean. *Jesus: A Jewish Galilean*. London: T&T Clark, 2004.

Friedman, Milton. "The Social Responsibility of Business Is to Increase Its Profits." *New York Times*. September 13, 1970.

Friesen, Garry, and J. Robin Maxson. *Decision Making and the Will of God: A Biblical Alternative to the Traditional View*. Portland, OR: Multnomah Books, 2004.

Frost, Robert. "The Death of the Hired Man." *North of Boston*. New York: Henry Holt, 1915.

———. "The Tuft of Flowers." In *A Boy's Will*. New York: Henry Holt, 1915.

Garland, David E. *1 Corinthians*. Baker Exegetical Commentary on the New Testament. Grand Rapids: Baker, 2003.

Garrett, Duane A., and Paul A. House. *Song of Songs and Lamentations*. Vol. 23b, *Word Biblical Commentary*. Nashville: Thomas Nelson, 2004.

Gayne, Roy. *The NIV Application Commentary: Leviticus, Numbers*. Grand Rapids: Zondervan, 2004.

Gelsinger, Pat. "Faster Chips, More Opportunity?" interview in *Ethix* 57 (January/February 2008). http://ethix.org/2008/02/01/faster-chips-more-opportunity.

Gill, David W. *Becoming Good: Building Moral Character*. Downers Grove, IL: InterVarsity Press, 2000.

———. *Doing Right: Practicing Ethical Principles*. Downers Grove, IL: InterVarsity Press, 2004.

Goldingay, John E. *Daniel*. Vol. 30, *Word Biblical Commentary*. Nashville: Thomas Nelson, 1989.

Gray, John. *Joshua, Judges, and Ruth*. The New Century Bible Commentary. London: Nelson, 1967.

Green, Gene L. *The Letters to the Thessalonians*. Grand Rapids: Eerdmans, 2002.

Greenleaf, Robert. *Servant Leadership*. Mahwah, NJ: Paulist Press, 1977.

Greer, Peter, and Phil Smith. *The Poor Will Be Glad*. Grand Rapids: Zondervan, 2009.

Grudem, Wayne. *Business of the Glory of God: The Bible's Teaching on the Moral Goodness of Business*. Wheaton, IL: Crossway, 2003.

Guelich, Robert A. *Mark 1–8:26*. Vol. 34A, *Word Biblical Commentary*. Nashville: Thomas Nelson, 1989.

Hagner, Donald A. *Matthew 1–13*. Vol. 33A, *Word Biblical Commentary*. Nashville: Thomas Nelson, 1993.

———. *Matthew 14–18*. Vol. 33B, *Word Biblical Commentary*. Nashville: Thomas Nelson, 1995.

Harland, Philip A. *Associations, Synagogues, and Congregations: Creating a Place in Ancient Mediterranean Society*. Minneapolis: Augsburg Fortress, 2003.

Harris, Murray J. *The Second Epistle to the Corinthians: A Commentary on the Greek Text*. Grand Rapids: Eerdmans, 2005.

Harris, R. Laird, Gleason L. Archer, Jr., and Bruce K. Waltke. *Theological Wordbook of the Old Testament*. Chicago: Moody Press, 1999.

Harrison, Roland K. "Baker." Vol. 1, *The International Standard Bible Encyclopedia*. Edited by Geoffrey W. Bromiley. Grand Rapids: Eerdmans, 1979.

Harrison, Steve. *The Manager's Book of Decencies*. New York: McGraw-Hill, 2007.

Hart, Ian. "Genesis 1:1–2:3 as a Prologue to the Book of Genesis." *TynBul* 46, no. 2 (1995): 315–37.

Hauerwas, Stanley. *Character and the Christian Life*. Notre Dame: University of Notre Dame Press, 2001.

Hauerwas, Stanley, and William Willimon. *Resident Aliens: Life in the Christian Colony*. Nashville: Abingdon Press, 1989.

Hawthorne, Gerald F. *Philippians*. Revised and expanded by Ralph P. Martin. Vol. 43, *Word Biblical Commentary*. Nashville: Thomas Nelson, 2004.

Hawthorne, Gerald F., Ralph P. Martin, and Daniel G. Reid, eds. "Ephesians, Letter to the." *Dictionary of Paul and His Letters*. Downers Grove, IL: InterVarsity Press, 1993.

Hawthorne, Gerald F., Ralph P. Martin, and Daniel G. Reid, eds. "Philippians, Letter to the." *Dictionary of Paul and His Letters*. Downers Grove, IL: InterVarsity Press, 1993.

Hays, Christopher M. *Luke's Wealth Ethics: A Study in Their Coherence and Character*. Wissenschaftliche Untersuchungen zum Neuen Testament 2.275. Tubingen: Mohr-Siebeck, 2010.

Heifetz, Ronald A. *Leadership without Easy Answers*. Cambridge, MA: Harvard University Press, 1994.

Heifetz, Ronald A., and Martin Linsky. *Leadership on the Line: Staying Alive through the Dangers of Leading*. Boston: Harvard Business Review Press, 2002.

Henderson, Suzanne Watts. *Christology and Discipleship in the Gospel of Mark*. Cambridge: Cambridge University Press, 2006.

Hester, J. David. "Dramatic Inconclusion: Irony and the Narrative Rhetoric of the Ending of Mark." *Journal for the Study of the New Testament* 17 (1995): 61–86.

Hill, Alexander. *Just Business: Christian Ethics for the Marketplace*. 2nd ed. Downers Grove, IL: IVP Academic, 2008.

Hirshfield, Brad. "Where is God in Suffering?" *Washington Post*, March 16, 2011.

Hock, Ronald F. *The Social Context of Paul's Ministry: Tentmaking and Apostleship*. Philadelphia: Fortress Press, 1980.

Holmes, Arthur. *All Truth is God's Truth*. Downers Grove, IL: Inter Varsity Press, 1983.

Holtz, Traugott. *Der erste Brief an die Thessalonicher*. Evangelisch-katholischer Kommentar zum Neuen Testament. Zürich: Benziger, 1986.

House, Paul R. *Old Testament Theology*. Downers Grove, IL: InterVarsity Press, 1998.

Houston, Walter J. *Purity and Monotheism: Clean and Unclean Animals in Biblical Law*. London: Bloomsbury, 2009.

Howard, David M., Jr. *Joshua*. Vol. 5, The New American Commentary. Nashville: Broadman & Holman, 1998.

Huffmon, Herbert B. "The Treaty Background of Hebrew *Yada.*'" *Bulletin of the American Schools of Oriental Research* 181 (February 1966): 31–37.

Huggett, Joyce. *Finding God in the Fast Lane*. Suffolk, UK: Kevin Mayhew, 2004.

Hunter, John E. "The Man Who Looked Four Ways." *Finding the Living Christ in the Psalms*. Grand Rapids: Zondervan, 1972.

Hurowitz, Victor. "The Priestly Account of Building the Tabernacle." *Journal of the American Oriental Society* 105 (1985): 21–30.

"Inaugural Global Slavery Index Reveals More than 29 Million People Living in Slavery." *Global Slavery Index 2013*. October 4, 2013. http://www.globalslaveryindex.org/category/press-release.

International Planned Parenthood Federation. "FPAHK Survey on Marriage and Sex." http://www.ippf.org.

Jewett, Robert. *Romans: A Commentary*. Minneapolis: Fortress Press, 2007.

Johnson, Luke Timothy. *Brother of Jesus, Friend of God*. Grand Rapids: Eerdmans, 2004.

———. *The First and Second Letters to Timothy: A New Translation with Introduction and Commentary*. *The Anchor Yale Bible Commentaries*. New York: Doubleday, 2001.

———. "The Letter of James." Vol. 12, *The New Interpreter's Bible*. Nashville: Abingdon Press, 1998.

Kaiser, Jr., Walter C., and Duane Garrett, editors. *Archaeological Study Bible*. Grand Rapids: Zondervan, 2006.

Kaminsky, Joel S. *Corporate Responsibility in the Hebrew Bible*. Sheffield: Sheffield Academic Press, 1995.

Kan, Man Yee, Oriel Sullivan, and Jonathan Gershuny. "Gender Convergence in Domestic Work: Discerning the Effects of Interactional and Institutional Barriers from Large-scale Data." *Sociology* 45, no. 2 (2011): 234–51.

Karass, Chester L. *In Business and in Life: You Don't Get What You Deserve, You Get What You Negotiate*. N.p.: Stanford Street Press, 1996.

Keller, Timothy. *Counterfeit Gods: The Empty Promises of Money, Sex, and Power, and the Only Hope That Matters*. New York: Dutton Adult, 2009.

———. "If I Perish, I Perish." Sermon. New York: Redeemer Presbyterian Church, April 22, 2007. MP3 and compact disk. http://www.gospel inlife.com/if-i-perish-i-perish-5680.html.

————. "Keller on Rules of the Bible: Do Christians Apply Them Inconsistently?" The Gospel Coalition. http://thegospelcoalition.org/blogs/tgc/2012/07/09/making-sense-of-scriptures-inconsistency/.

"Kendrick B. Melrose: Caring about People: Employees and Customers." *Ethix* 55 (Sept. 2007). http://ethix.org/2007/10/01/caring-about-people-employees-and-customers.

Kitchen, Kenneth A. "Cupbearer." *New Bible Dictionary.* 3rd ed. Edited by I. Howard Marshall, A. R. Millard, J. I. Packer, and D. J. Wiseman. Downers Grove, IL: InterVarsity Press, 1996.

Kittel, Gerhard, Gerhard Friedrich, and Geoffrey William Bromiley, eds. *Theological Dictionary of the New Testament.* Grand Rapids: Eerdmans, 1985.

Klawans, J. *Purity, Sacrifice, and the Temple: Symbolism and Supersessionism in the Study of Ancient Judaism.* New York: Oxford University Press, 2005.

Klengel-Brandt, Evelyn. "Babylon." In *The Oxford Encyclopedia of Archaeology in the Near East.* Edited by Eric M. Meyers, 251–56. Oxford: Oxford University Press, 1997.

Kline, Meredith. *Kingdom Prologue: Genesis Foundations for a Covenantal Worldview.* Eugene, OR: Wipf & Stock, 2006.

Kloppenborg, John S. "Collegia and *Thiasoi*: Issues in Function, Taxonomy and Membership." In *Voluntary Associations in the Graeco-Roman World.* Edited by John S. Kloppenborg and S. G. Wilson, 16–30. London: Routledge, 1996.

Kraman, Steve S., and Ginny Hamm. "Risk Management: Extreme Honesty May Be the Best Policy." *Annals of Internal Medicine* 131 (December 1999): 963–67.

Kruse, Colin G. *The Letters of John.* Grand Rapids: Eerdmans, 2000.

Kuchment, Anna. "The Tangled Web of Porn in the Office." *Newsweek.* December 8, 2008. http://www.newsweek.com/2008/11/28/the-tangled-web-of-porn-in-the-office.

Kuecker, Aaron J. "The Spirit and the 'Other,' Satan and the 'Self': Economic Ethics as a Consequence of Identity Transformation in Luke-Acts." In *Engaging Economics: New Testament Scenarios and Early Christian Reception.* Edited by Bruce W. Longenecker and Kelly D. Liebengood, 81–103. Grand Rapids: Eerdmans, 2009.

Küng, Hans. *Global Responsibility: In Search of a New World Ethic.* New York: Continuum, 1993.

Laansma, J. *I Will Give You Rest: The Rest Motif in the New Testament with Special Reference to Mt 11 and Heb 3–4.* Vol. 98, Wissenschalftliche Untersuchungen zum Neuen Testament. Tübingen: Mohr Siebeck, 1997.

Levison, John R. *Filled with the Spirit.* Grand Rapids: Eerdmans, 2009.

Lienhard, Joseph T. "Acts 6.1–6: A Redactional View." *Catholic Biblical Quarterly* 37 (1975): 232.

Lincoln, Andrew T. *Ephesians.* Vol. 42, *Word Biblical Commentary.* Nashville: Thomas Nelson, 1990.

Linthicum, Robert. *City of God, City of Satan: A Biblical Theology for the Urban Church.* Grand Rapids: Zondervan, 1991.

Longenecker, Richard N. *Galatians.* Vol. 41, *Word Biblical Commentary.* Waco, TX: Word, 1990.

Longman, Tremper, III. *Daniel.* The NIV Application Commentary. Grand Rapids: Zondervan, 1999.

Louw, Johannes P., and Eugene A. Nida. *Greek-English Lexicon of the New Testament Based on Semantic Domains.* 2 vols. New York: UBS, 1988.

Lundbom, Jack R. "Jeremiah, Book of." Vol. 3, *The Anchor Bible Dictionary.* Edited by David Noel Freedman. New York: Doubleday, 1992.

Mackenzie, Alistair, and Wayne Kirkland. "Ethics." Theology of Work Project. December 1, 2010. http://theologyofwork.org/key-topics/ethics.

Mafico, Temba L. J. "Judge, Judging." *The Anchor Bible Dictionary.* Edited by David Noel Freedman. New York: Doubleday, 1992.

Malherbe, Abraham J. *Paul and the Thessalonians: The Philosophic Tradition of Pastoral Care.* Philadelphia: Fortress, 1987.

———. *The Letters to the Thessalonians. The Anchor Bible.* New York: Doubleday, 2000.

Malina, Bruce, and Richard Rohrbaugh. *A Social-Scientific Commentary on the Synoptic Gospels.* Minneapolis: Fortress, 1992.

Marshall, I. Howard. *1 and 2 Thessalonians.* New Century Bible Commentary. London: Marshall, Morgan and Scott, 1983.

Marshall, Peter. *Enmity in Corinth: Social Conventions in Paul's Relations with the Corinthians.* Wissenschaftliche Untersuchungen zum Neuen Testament 2.23. Tübingen: Mohr Siebeck, 1987.

Martens, Elmer. *God's Design: A Focus on Old Testament Theology*. 3rd ed. Grand Rapids: Baker, 1994.

Martin, Dale B. *The Corinthian Body*. New Haven: Yale University Press, 1995.

Matthews, Victor H. "Hospitality and Hostility in Judges 4." *Biblical Theology Bulletin* 21, no. 1 (1991): 13–21.

———. "Nomadism, Pastoralism." *Eerdmans Dictionary of the Bible*. Edited by David Noel Freedman, Allen C. Myers, and Astrid B. Beck. Grand Rapids: Eerdmans, 2000.

Matties, Gordon H. *Ezekiel 18 and the Rhetoric of Moral Discourse*. Society of Biblical Literature Dissertation Series 126. Atlanta: Scholars Press, 1990.

McAdams, Dan P. *The Redemptive Self: Stories Americans Live By*. New York: Oxford University Press, 2005.

McConville, J. Gordon, and Stephen N. Williams. *Joshua*. Two Horizons Old Testament Commentary. Grand Rapids: Eerdmans, 2010.

McDonough, Sean M. *Christ as Creator: Origins of a New Testament Doctrine*. Oxford: Oxford University Press, 2010.

McFarland, Ian A. *Creation and Humanity: The Sources of Christian Theology*. Louisville: Westminster John Knox Press, 2009.

McKnight, Scot. "Collection for the Saints." *Dictionary of Paul and His Letters*. Edited by Gerald F. Hawthorne et al. Downers Grove, IL: InterVarsity Press, 1993.

Meadowcroft, Tim. *Haggai*. Sheffield: Sheffield Phoenix Press, 2006.

Meeks, Wayne A. *The First Urban Christians: The Social World of the Apostle Paul*. 2nd ed. New Haven: Yale University Press, 2003.

Mein, Andrew. "Profitable and Unprofitable Shepherds: Economic and Theological Perspectives on Ezekiel 34." *Journal for the Study of the Old Testament* 31, no. 4 (June 2007): 493–504.

Melrose, Ken. Correspondence to the Theology of Work Project. July 30, 2013.

Meyers, Carol L., and Eric M. Meyers. *Haggai, Zechariah 1–8: A New Translation with Introduction and Commentary*. Vol. 25B, *The Anchor Bible*. New York: Doubleday, 1987.

Milgrom, Jacob. "Excursus 74: The Levitical Town: An Exercise in Realistic Planning." *Numbers*. JPS Torah Commentary. Philadelphia: Jewish Publication Society, 1990.

———. *Leviticus 1–16*. New Haven: Yale University Press, 1998.

———. *Leviticus: A Book of Ritual and Ethics, A Continental Commentary*. Minneapolis: Fortress Press, 2004.

Miller, Stephen R. *Daniel*. The New American Commentary. Nashville: Broadman & Holman, 1994.

Mitchell, Alan C. "The Social Function of Friendship in Acts 2.44–47 and 4.32–37." *Journal of Biblical Literature* 111, no. 2 (1992).

Mitchell, Margaret M. *Paul and the Rhetoric of Reconciliation*. Louisville: Westminster John Knox Press, 1993.

Mitchell, T. C. "Nomads." *New Bible Dictionary*. 3rd ed. Edited by I. Howard Marshall. Downers Grove, IL: InterVarsity Press, 1996.

Moll, Rob. "Christian Microfinance Stays on a Mission." *Christianity Today*. May 27, 2011. http://www.christianitytoday.com/ct/2011/may/stayingonmission.html.

Moltmann, Jürgen. *The Way of Jesus Christ*. Minneapolis: Fortress Press, 1995.

Moo, Douglas. "Nature in the New Creation: New Testament Eschatology and the Environment." *Journal of the Evangelical Theological Society* 49, no. 3 (2006): 468–69.

———. *The Letter of James*. Grand Rapids: Eerdmans, 2000.

Motyer, J. A. *The Message of Exodus: The Days of Our Pilgrimage*. Downers Grove, IL: IVP Academic, 2005.

Mounce, William D. *Pastoral Epistles*. Vol. 4, *Word Biblical Commentary*. Nashville: Thomas Nelson, 2000.

Moy, Ed. "Faith and Work: Spiritual Insights from a Career in Business & Public Service." At *Kiros*, Seattle, October 11, 2013. http://kiros.btexpo.ws/media.

Müller, Peter. *Anfänge der Paulusschule: Dargestellt am zweiten Thessalonicherbrief und am Kolosserbrief*. Abhandlungen zur Theologie des Alten und Neuen Testaments. Zürich: Theologischer, 1988.

Murphy, Roland. *Ecclesiastes*. Vol. 23a, *Word Biblical Commentary*. Dallas: Word, 2002.

———. *Proverbs*. Vol. 22, *Word Biblical Commentary*. Nashville: Thomas Nelson, 1998.

Murphy-O'Connor, Jerome. *Paul: A Critical Life*. Oxford: Clarendon, 1996.

Nash, Laura. *Believers in Business*. Nashville: Thomas Nelson, 1994.

"Nehemiah (person)." *The Anchor Bible Dictionary*. Edited by David Noel Freedman. New York: Doubleday, 1992.

Nicholl, Colin R. *From Hope to Despair in Thessalonica: Situating 1 & 2 Thessalonians*. Society for New Testament Studies Monograph Series. Cambridge: Cambridge University Press, 2004.

Nolland, John. *Luke 1–9:20*. Vol. 35A, *Word Biblical Commentary*. Nashville: Thomas Nelson, 1989.

O'Brien, Peter T. *Introductory Thanksgivings in the Letters of Paul*. Vol. 49, *Novum Testamentum*. Leiden: Brill, 1977.

O'Connor, Flannery. "A Good Man Is Hard to Find." *Collected Works*. New York: Library of America, 1988.

Okorie, A. M. "The Pauline Work Ethic in 1 and 2 Thessalonians." *Deltio Biblikon Meleton* 14 (1994): 63–64.

Olson, Jeannine E. *Calvin and Social Welfare*. Selinsgrove, PA: Susquehanna University Press, 1989.

Osborne, Grant R. *Revelation*. Vol. 27, *Baker Exegetical Commentary on the New Testament*. Grand Rapids: Baker Academic, 2002.

Oswalt, John N. "Righteousness in Isaiah: A Study of the Function of Chapters 56–66 in the Present Structure of the Book." Vol. 1, *Writing and Reading the Scroll of Isaiah: Studies of an Interpretive Tradition*. Edited by Craig C. Broyles and Craig A. Evans. Leiden: Brill, 1997.

Pace, Peter. "General Peter Pace: The Truth as I Know It." Interviewed by Al Erisman and David Gautschi. *Ethix* 61 (September/October 2008). http://ethix.org/2008/10/01/the-truth-as-i-know-it.

Pao, David W. *Acts and the Isaianic New Exodus*. Grand Rapids: Baker Academic, 2002.

Parker, Tom. "Ebed-Melech as Exemplar." *Uprooting and Planting: Essays on Jeremiah for Leslie Allen*. Edited by John Goldingay. New York: T&T Clark, 2007.

Peck, M. Scott. *People of the Lie: The Hope for Healing Human Evil*. 2nd ed. New York: Touchstone, 1998.

Penney, John Michael. "The Missionary Emphasis of Lukan Pneumatology." *Journal of Pentecostal Theology*. Sheffield, UK: Sheffield Academic Press, 1997.

Peters, Tom. *Thriving on Chaos*. New York: Knopf, 1987.

Piper, John. *Desiring God: Meditations of a Christian Hedonist*. Colorado Springs: Multnomah, 2003.

Pitt-Rivers, Julian. "The Stranger, the Guest, and the Hostile Host: Introduction to the Study of the Laws of Hospitality." *Contributions to Mediterranean Sociology*. Edited by John G. Peristiany. Paris: Mouton, 1968.

"Poliomyelitis Eradication." *Wikipedia*. http://en.wikipedia.org/wiki/Poliomyelitis_eradication.

Polkinghorne, Donald E. *Narrative Knowing and the Human Sciences*. Albany: State University of New York, 1988.

Rendtorff, Rolf. *The Covenant Formula: An Exegetical and Theological Investigation*. Translated by Margaret Kohl. Edinburgh: T&T Clark, 1998.

Richard, Earl J. *First and Second Thessalonians*. Sacra Pagina. Collegeville: Michael Glazier, 1995.

Richardson, Alan. *The Biblical Doctrine of Work. Ecumenical Bible Studies no. 1*. London: SCM Press for the Study Department of the World Council of Churches, 1952. Reprinted 1954.

Riesner, Rainer. *Die Frühzeit des Apostels Paulus: Stüdien zur Chronologie, Missionstrategie, und Theologie*. Tübingen: Mohr, 1994.

Rigsby, Richard O. "First Fruits." *The Anchor Yale Bible Dictionary*. Edited by David Noel Freedman. New York: Doubleday, 1992.

Roberts, Mark D. *Ezra, Nehemiah, Esther*. Vol. 11, The Preacher's Commentary. Nashville: Thomas Nelson, 2002.

Robinson, Haddon W. *Decision-Making by the Book: How to Choose Wisely in an Age of Options*. Wheaton, IL: Victor Books, 1991.

Romanuik, K. "Les Thessaloniciens étaitent-ils des parasseuz?" *Ephemerides Theologicae Lovanienses* 69 (1993): 142–45.

"Russia's Putin set to return as president in 2012." *BBC News Europe*. September 24, 2011. http://www.bbc.com/news/world-europe-15045816.

Sanders, E. P. *Jesus and Judaism*. Philadelphia: Fortress Press, 1985.

———. *Judaism: Practice and Belief, 63 BCE-66 CE*. London: SCM Press, 1992.

Schaeffer, Francis A. *Genesis in Space and Time*. Downers Grove, IL: InterVarsity Press, 1972.

Scott, Jack B. "82 הָפִיא." In *Theological Wordbook of the Old Testament*. Edited by R. Laird Harris, Gleason L. Archer, Jr., and Bruce K. Waltke. Chicago: Moody Press, 1999.

Seitz, Christopher R. "The Book of Isaiah 40–66: Introduction, Commentary, and Reflections." Vol. 6, *The New Interpreter's Bible*. Nashville: Abingdon Press, 2001.

———. " 'You are my Servant, You are the Israel in whom I will be glorified': The Servant Songs and the Effect of Literary Context in Isaiah." *Calvin Theological Journal* 39 (2004): 117–34.

Serafeim, George. "The Real Cost of Bribery." *Harvard Business School Working Knowledge*. November 4, 2013. http://hbswk.hbs.edu/item/7325.html.

Shepherd, David. *Seeking Sabbath: A Personal Journey*. Oxford: Bible Reading Fellowship, 2007.

"Should I Rank My Employees?" *Wall Street Journal*. April 7, 2009. http://guides.wsj.com/management/recruiting-hiring-and-firing/should-i-rank-my-employees.

Speiser, E. A. *Oriental and Biblical Studies: Collected Writings of E. A. Speiser*. Edited by J. J. Finkelstein and Moshe Greenberg. Philadelphia: University of Pennsylvania Press, 1967.

Spicq, Ceslas. "Les Thessalonicien 'inquiets' etaient-ils des parrassuex?" *Studia theologica* 10 (1956): 1–13.

Sprinkle, Preston. "Law and Life: Leviticus 18.5 in the Literary Framework of Ezekiel." *Journal for the Study of the Old Testament* 31, no. 3 (March 2007): 275–93.

Stein, Robert H. *Luke*. Nashville: Broadman, 1992.

Sterling, Gregory E. " 'Athletes of Virtue': An Analysis of the Summaries in Acts (2.41–47; 4.32–35; 5.12–16)." *Journal of Biblical Literature* 113, no. 4 (1994).

Stevens, R. Paul. *The Other Six Days*. Grand Rapids: Eerdmans, 2000.

Stevens, R. Paul, and Alvin Ung. *Taking Your Soul to Work*. Grand Rapids: Eerdmans, 2010.

Stott, John. *The Grace of Giving: 10 Principles of Christian Giving*. Lausanne Didasko Files. Peabody, MA: Hendrickson Publishers, 2012.

Strabo. *Geographica.* Translated and edited by Horace Leonard Jones. 8 vols. Loeb Classical Library. Cambridge, MA: Harvard University Press, 1930–1965.

Strom, Stephanie. "Pledge to Give Away Half Gains Billionaire Adherents." *New York Times,* August 4, 2010.

Strong, James. *Enhanced Strong's Lexicon.* Ontario: Woodside Bible Fellowship, 1995.

Stuart, Douglas. *Hosea–Jonah.* Vol. 31, *Word Biblical Commentary.* Dallas: Word, 2002.

Sullivan, Missy. "Lost Inheritance." *Wall Street Journal Money.* March 8, 2012. http://online.wsj.com.

Tabor, James, and Randall Buth. *Living Biblical Hebrew for Everyone.* Pasadena, CA: Internet Language Corp., 2003.

Talbert, Charles H. *Reading Corinthians: A Literary and Theological Commentary on 1 and 2 Corinthians.* New York: Crossroad, 1987.

Terkel, Studs. *Working.* New York: The New Press, 1972.

Thiselton, Anthony C. *The First Epistle to the Corinthians: A Commentary on the Greek Text.* New International Greek Testament Commentary. Grand Rapids: Eerdmans, 2000.

Tidball, Derek. *The Message of Leviticus.* Downers Grove, IL: InterVarsity Press, 2005.

Tiede, David L. "The Exaltation of Jesus and the Restoration of Israel in Acts 1." *Harvard Theological Review* 79, no. 1 (1986).

Towner, Philip H. *The Letters to Timothy and Titus.* New International Commentary on the New Testament. Grand Rapids: Eerdmans, 2006.

United Nations Development Programme. *Issue Brief: Rule of Law and Development.* New York: United Nations, 2013).

United States Department of Labor. "Fact Sheet: Workplace Shootings 2010." *Bureau of Labor Statistics.* http://www.bls.gov/iif/oshwc/cfoi/osar0014.htm.

Volf, Miroslav. *Work in the Spirit.* Oxford: Oxford University Press, 1991.

Von Rad, Gerhard. *Old Testament Theology.* Vol. 1. Translated by D. M. G. Stalker. San Francisco: HarperSanFrancisco, 1962.

Wakely, Robin. "#5967 NSHK." Vol. 3, *New International Dictionary of Old Testament Theology and Exegesis*. Edited by Willem A. Van-Gemeren. Grand Rapids: Zondervan, 1997.

"Wall Street and the Financial Crisis: Majority and Minority Staff Report." Washington DC: United States Senate, Permanent Subcommittee on Investigations. http://hsgac.senate.gov/public/file...isisReport.pdf.

Waltke, Bruce K. *The Book of Proverbs: Chapters 1–15*. Grand Rapids: Wm. B. Eerdmans, 2004.

———. *Genesis: A Commentary*. Grand Rapids: Zondervan, 2001.

Waltke, Bruce, and Alice Mathews. *Proverbs and Work*. Theology of Work Project. See esp. "The Valiant Woman." http://www.theology ofwork.org/old-testament/proverbs/.

Waltke, Bruce K., and Charles Yu. *An Old Testament Theology: An Exegetical, Canonical, and Thematic Approach*. Grand Rapids: Zondervan, 2007.

Walton, John H. *Genesis*. The NIV Application Commentary. Grand Rapids: Zondervan, 2001.

Walton, John H., Victor H. Matthews, and Mark W. Chavalas. *The IVP Bible Background Commentary: Old Testament*. Downers Grove, IL: IVP Academic, 2000.

Welch, Jack. "What I've Learned: Jack Welch." *Esquire*. December 31, 2006. http://www.esquire.com/features/what-ive-learned/wil0104 jackwelch#ixzz2nkRA41TP.

Wenham, Gordon J. *Exploring the Old Testament: A Guide to the Pentateuch*. Vol. 1. Downers Grove, IL: IVP Academic, 2008.

———. *Genesis 1–15*. Vol. 1, *Word Biblical Commentary*. Dallas: Word, 1998.

Wesley, John. *Covenant Renewal Service*. 2nd ed. London, 1781. *Wesley Center Online*. http://wesley.nnu.edu/john-wesley/covenant-service -directions-for-renewing-our-covenant-with-god/.

Whitehorse, John. "Antiochus." Vol. 1, *The Anchor Bible Dictionary*. Edited by David Noel Freedman. New York: Doubleday, 1992.

Wiersbe, Warren W. *Joshua–Esther*. The Bible Exposition Commentary: Old Testament. Colorado Springs: Victor, 2004.

Willard, Dallas. *The Spirit of the Disciplines: Understanding How God Changes Lives*. San Francisco: Harper and Row, 1988.

Williams, Monci J. "How Strength Becomes a Weakness." *Harvard Management Update* (December 1996).

Williamson, H. G. M. *Ezra, Nehemiah*. Vol. 16, *Word Biblical Commentary*. Waco, TX: Word Books, 1985.

———. *Isaiah 1–5*. Vol. 1, *A Critical and Exegetical Commentary on Isaiah 1–27*. London: T&T Clark, 2006.

Witherington III, Ben. *The Acts of the Apostles: A Socio-Rhetorical Commentary*. Grand Rapids: Eerdmans, 1998.

———. *1 and 2 Thessalonians: A Socio-Rhetorical Commentary*. Grand Rapids: Eerdmans, 2006.

———. *Revelation*. Cambridge: Cambridge University Press, 2003.

Wohlenberg, Gustav. *Der erste und zweite Thessalonicherbrief*. Kommentar zum Neuen Testament. Leipzig: Deichert, 1903.

Wolters, Al. "Proverbs XXXI 10–31 as Heroic Hymn: A Form-Critical Analysis." *Vetus Testamentum* 38 (October 1988): 446–57.

———. "Worldview and Textual Criticism in 2 Peter 3:10." *Westminster Theological Journal* 49 (1987), 405–13.

Wright, Addison G. "The Riddle of the Sphinx: The Structure of the Book of Qoheleth." *Catholic Biblical Quarterly* 30 (1968): 313–34.

Wright, Christopher J. H. *Deuteronomy*. New International Biblical Commentary. Peabody, MA: Hendrickson Publishers, 1996.

———. *The Mission of God: Unlocking the Bible's Grand Narrative*. Downers Grove, IL: IVP Academic, 2006.

———. *Old Testament Ethics for the People of God*. Downers Grove, IL: InterVarsity Press, 2004.

Wright, David P. "The Disposal of Impurity: Elimination Rites in the Bible and in Hittite and Mesopotamian Literature." *Society of Biblical Literature Dissertation Studies* 101 (1987): 34–36.

Wright, N. T. *After You Believe: Why Christian Character Matters*. New York: HarperOne, 2010.

———. *Jesus and the Victory of God*. London: SPCK, 1996.

———. "The Letter to the Romans." Vol. 10, *The New Interpreter's Bible*. Nashville: Abingdon Press, 1994.

———. *The Resurrection of the Son of God*. Vol. 3, Christian Origins and the Question of God. Minneapolis: Fortress Press, 2003.

Contributors

John Alsdorf resides in New York City and is a member of the Theology of Work Project's steering committee.

Katherine Leary Alsdorf is founder and director emeritus of the Center for Faith and Work at Redeemer Presbyterian Church in New York City. She is a member of the Theology of Work Project's steering committee.

Patricia Anders is editorial director of Hendrickson Publishers in Peabody, Massachusetts. She serves as editorial director for the commentary.

Jill L. Baker is an independent researcher of ancient Near Eastern archaeology and faculty fellow at Florida International University, Honors College, in Miami, Florida. She contributed to the commentary on 1 & 2 Samuel, 1 & 2 Kings, and 1 & 2 Chronicles.

Cara Beed is retired lecturer in sociology in the Department of Social Science, retired graduate advisor for the Faculty of Education, and retired honorary fellow at the Australian Catholic University in Melbourne, Victoria, Australia. She is a writer and researcher with works published in many international journals. She is a member of the Theology of Work Project's steering committee.

Daniel Block is the Gunther H. Knoedler Professor of Old Testament at Wheaton College in Wheaton, Illinois. He contributed to the commentary on Ruth.

Daniel T. Byrd is special assistant to the provost at the University of La Verne in La Verne, California. He served as a member of the Theology of Work Project's steering committee from 2007 to 2009.

Alice Camille is a nationally known Roman Catholic author, religious educator, and retreat leader. She resides in Desert Hot Springs, California. She contributed to the commentary on Joshua and Judges.

Darrell Cosden is professor of theological studies at Judson University in Elgin, Illinois. He served as a member of the Theology of Work Project's steering committee from 2007 to 2010.

Al Erisman is executive in residence at Seattle Pacific University in Seattle, Washington, and former director of technology at the Boeing Company. He serves as co-chair of the Theology of Work Project's steering committee. He contributed to the commentary on 2 John and 3 John.

Nancy S. Erisman volunteers as a board member of KIROS and on the leadership team at Westminster Chapel Women in the Workplace in Bellevue, Washington. She served as a contributing editor to the commentary.

Jarrett Fontenot resides in Baton Rouge, Louisiana. He served as a contributing editor to the commentary.

Larry Fowler resides in Gig Harbor, Washington. He served as a contributing editor to the commentary.

Russell Fuller is professor of Old Testament at Southern Baptist Theological Seminary in Louisville, Kentucky. He contributed to the commentary on Psalms.

Duane A. Garrett is the John R. Sampey Professor of Old Testament Interpretation at Southern Baptist Theological Seminary in Louisville, Kentucky. He contributed to the commentary on Deuteronomy, Ecclesiastes, and Song of Songs, and served as editor for the poetical books.

Mark S. Gignilliat is associate professor of divinity at Beeson Divinity School, Samford University in Birmingham, Alabama. He contributed to the commentary on Isaiah and served as editor for the prophetic books.

Michaiah Healy is youth pastor at the Vineyard Christian Fellowship of Greater Boston in Cambridge, Massachusetts. She served as a contributing editor to the commentary.

Bill Heatley is the former executive director of Dallas Willard Ministries in Oak Park, California, and served as a member of the Theology of Work Project's steering committee. He contributed to the commentary on Colossians and Philemon.

Bill Hendricks is president of the Giftedness Center in Dallas, Texas. He is a member of the Theology of Work Project's steering committee.

Brian Housman is executive pastor at the Vineyard Christian Fellowship of Greater Boston in Cambridge, Massachusetts. He contributed to the commentary on 1 & 2 Samuel, 1 & 2 Kings, and 1 & 2 Chronicles.

L. T. Jeyachandran is former chief engineer (civil) at the Department of Telecommunications for the government of India in Calcutta, India, and former executive director of Ravi Zacharias International Ministries (Asia-Pacific) in Singapore. He is a member of the Theology of Work Project's steering committee.

Timothy Johnson is assistant professor of Old Testament and Hebrew at Nashotah House Theological Seminary in Nashotah, Wisconsin. He contributed to the commentary on Job.

Randy Kilgore is senior writer and workplace chaplain at Desired Haven Ministries/Made to Matter in North Beverly, Massachusetts. He is a member of the Theology of Work Project's steering committee.

Alexander N. Kirk resides in Wilmington, Delaware, and contributed to the commentary on 1 & 2 Timothy and Titus.

Aaron Kuecker is associate professor of theology and director of the Honors College at LeTourneau University in Longview, Texas. He contributed to the commentary on Luke and Acts.

Jon C. Laansma is associate professor of classical languages and New Testament at Wheaton College and Wheaton Graduate School in Wheaton, Illinois. He contributed to the commentary on Hebrews.

Clint Le Bruyns is director and senior lecturer at the Theology and Development Programme at the University of KwaZulu-Natal in Pietermaritzburg, KwaZulu-Natal, South Africa. He is a member of the Theology of Work Project's steering committee.

John G. Lewis is director of Saint Benedict's Workshop and Missioner for Christian Formation at the Episcopal Diocese of West Texas in San Antonio, Texas. He consulted on the commentary on Romans.

Kelly Liebengood is associate professor of biblical studies at LeTourneau University in Longview, Texas. He contributed to the commentary on James, 1 & 2 Peter, 1 John, and Jude.

Kerry E. Luddy is director of community relations and discipleship at Brighton Presbyterian Church in Rochester, New York. She served as a contributing editor to the commentary.

Grant Macaskill is senior lecturer in New Testament studies at the University of Saint Andrews in St. Andrews, Fife, Scotland, United Kingdom. He contributed to the commentary on Mark.

Alistair Mackenzie is a Teaching Fellow at Laidlaw College in Christchurch, New Zealand. He is a member of the Theology of Work Project's steering committee.

Ryan P. Marshall is minister to students at Redeemer Community Church in Needham, Massachusetts. He served as a contributing editor to the commentary.

Steven D. Mason is associate provost and dean of faculty at LeTourneau University in Longview, Texas. He contributed to the commentary on Ezekiel.

Alice Mathews is the Lois W. Bennett Distinguished Professor Emerita at Gordon-Conwell Theological Seminary in South Hamilton, Massachusetts. She is a member of the Theology of Work Project's steering committee. She contributed to the commentary on Genesis 1–11, Proverbs, 1 & 2 Samuel, 1 & 2 Kings, 1 & 2 Chronicles, Introduction to the Prophets, Isaiah, Jeremiah, Lamentations, and Matthew. She also served as a consulting editor for the commentary.

Kenneth Mathews is professor of divinity at Beeson Divinity School, Samford University, in Birmingham, Alabama. He contributed to the commentary on Daniel.

Sean McDonough is professor of New Testament at Gordon-Conwell Theological Seminary in South Hamilton, Massachusetts. He is a member of the Theology of Work Project's steering committee. He contributed to the commentary on Joshua, Judges, John, and Revelation, and served as editor for biblical studies and the Epistles.

Tim Meadowcroft is senior lecturer in biblical studies at Laidlaw College in Auckland, New Zealand. He contributed to the commentary on Hosea, Joel, Amos, Obadiah, Micah, Nahum, Habakkuk, Zephaniah, Haggai, Zechariah, and Malachi.

William Messenger is executive editor of the Theology of Work Project in Boston, Massachusetts, and adjunct faculty member of Laidlaw-Carey Graduate School in Auckland, New Zealand. He also serves on the board of directors of ArQule, Inc. He is a member of the Theology of Work Project's steering committee. He contributed to the commentary on Jonah and served as general editor.

Andy Mills is Executive Chairman and President of Archegos Capital Management LP, and Co-Chairman of the Grace & Mercy Foundation. He was formerly president and CEO at Thomson Financial and Professional Publishing Group in Boston, Massachusetts. He serves as co-chair of the Theology of Work Project's steering committee.

Joshua Moon resides in Minneapolis, Minnesota. He contributed to the commentary on Jeremiah and Lamentations.

Colin R. Nicholl is an independent researcher and author in Northern Ireland, United Kingdom. He contributed to the commentary on 1 & 2 Thessalonians.

Valerie O'Connell is an independent consultant in Burlington, Massachusetts. She served as a contributing editor to the commentary.

Jane Lancaster Patterson is assistant professor of New Testament at Seminary of the Southwest in Austin, Texas. She consulted on the commentary on Romans.

Jonathan T. Pennington is associate professor of New Testament and director of Ph.D. studies at Southern Baptist Theological Seminary in Louisville, Kentucky. He contributed to the commentary on Matthew and served as editor for the Gospels and Acts.

Gordon Preece is director of Ethos: the Evangelical Alliance Centre for Christianity and Society in Melbourne, Victoria, Australia. He is a member of the Theology of Work Project's steering committee.

Mark D. Roberts is the executive director for the Max De Pree Center for Leadership at Fuller Theological Seminary. He is a member of the Theology of Work Project's steering committee. He contributed to the commentary on Ezra, Nehemiah, Esther, Galatians, Ephesians, and Philippians.

Haddon Robinson is the Harold John Ockenga Distinguished Professor of Preaching, senior director of the Doctor of Ministry program, and former interim president of Gordon-Conwell Theological Seminary in South Hamilton, Massachusetts. He is president and chair emeritus of the Theology of Work Project.

Justin Schell is on the global leadership and support team with The Lausanne Movement. He served as a contributing editor to the commentary.

Andrew J. Schmutzer is professor of biblical studies at Moody Bible Institute in Chicago, Illinois. He contributed to the commentary on Genesis 1–11.

Bob Stallman is professor of Bible and Hebrew at Northwest University in Kirkland, Washington. He contributed to the commentary on Genesis 12–50, Exodus, Leviticus, and Numbers.

Christine S. Tan is director of marketing and social media at the Theology of Work Project in Boston, Massachusetts. She served as a contributing editor to the commentary.

Hanno van der Bijl resides in Mobile, Alabama. He is web editor at the Theology of Work Project and served as a contributing editor to the commentary.

Bruce Waltke is professor emeritus of biblical studies at Regent College in Vancouver, British Columbia, Canada. He has also held teaching positions at Westminster Theological Seminary in Glenside, Pennsylvania, and Knox Theological Seminary in Fort Lauderdale, Florida, where he is a distinguished professor of Old Testament. He contributed to the commentary on Proverbs and served as editor for the Pentateuch.

Joel White is lecturer in New Testament at Giessen School of Theology in Giessen, Germany. He contributed to the commentary on 1 & 2 Corinthians.

Andy Williams is program manager at HOPE International in Kigali, Rwanda. He served as a contributing editor to the commentary.

David Williamson is director emeritus of Laity Lodge in Kerrville, Texas. He is a member of the Theology of Work Project's steering committee.

Lindsay Wilson is academic dean and senior lecturer in Old Testament at Ridley Melbourne Mission and Ministry College in Melbourne, Victoria, Australia. He contributed to the commentary on Psalms.

Index of Names and Subjects

Note: page numbers in *italics* indicate most significant occurrences.

629, *631–32, 671–74*, 676, *681–82*,
734, 764–65, 785–86, 789–91, 897
gifts, 61–62, 64, 84, *87–88, 115, 215–*
16, 537, 577–79, 634, *673–74*, 679,
734, 748–49, *761–63, 785–86. See
also* skills
gleaning, *126–28*, 192–93, *232–35,
524*
globalization, 689
God's work, *5–6*, 24, *80–84, 85–86,
114–15, 205–6, 216–17, 224–25,
279–82*, 288, *315–17*, 329, *337–40,
345–47*, 348, *439–40*, 600–601,
608, *639*, 644, *647, 649–50, 651,
704–6, 711–13*, 716, *718, 801, 808–
9, 821*, 823, *873–76, 879–80, 933*
gossip, *104–5, 183–84*, 361, *378*, 707,
848–49, *864–65*, 903, *924–26*
governance, 242–45, *256*, 425, 513
government, *63*, 101, *145, 158–60*,
192, 206–7, *231–34*, 242–43,
248–49, *261–63*, 267–68, *284,
334–35, 375–76*, 404, 425, *511–13*,
523, 613, *615, 635*, 638–39,
737–38, 765, 864, 899
government (official), *61–65*, 83,
209–10, *212–13*, 262, 284, 2110–
247, *375–76*
grace, 52–53, 111, 148–49, 156, 169,
335–36, 548–49, 573, *609*, 706,
716–18, 719–20
greed, 217–18, 313, *381–82, 459, 461*,
487, *563, 615–16*, 627–28, 629,
707, *827*
grief. *See* sorrow
growth. *See* productivity
guilt, *122–23*

healing, 83, *268–69*, 588, *619–20*,
651, 652, 654, 910
healthcare, *125*, 147–48, 619–20
Henderson, Suzanne Watts, *588*
hiring practices, *111*, 128, *129–30*,
234–35, 365
holiness, *118–20*, 125, *126*

Holy Spirit, 92, 114–15, *587, 666,
667–69*, 673, 679–80, *697, 761*
homemakers, 347, *420, 568*, 650, *857*
honesty, *49–50*, 96, *128–29, 134–35*,
208–9, *326–27*, 329, *358–64*, 557,
647–48, 770–71, 775–76, 908,
909–20, 919, *921–23*
hospitality, 42–43, *45–48, 592*, 626,
633, 673, 741, 888–89
hostility, 286, 328, *335, 506–8,
511–13, 558*, 588, 710–11, *740–41,
866*, 895, *910. See also* sacrifice,
serving God (consequences of),
suffering
Huggett, Joyce, *596*
human flourishing, *16–17, 33–34*,
65, 121, *126–28*, 132, *133, 136*,
138–40, 146, *159–60, 164, 192–93,
232–35*, 267–68, *288*, 325–26,
345, *358–59, 459–61, 465–68,
480–81*, 522–23, *524*, 527, *532–33,
547, 563*, 574, *579–80, 623, 625,
627, 630, 631, 635, 658, 666, 667,
670, 672, 674, 681*, 689, *723, 724,
732, 734, 742*, 754, *757–58, 760,
761–63*, 765, *787–89*, 797, 802,
814, 864, *898, 899, 907, 940*
humbleness, *30–31*, 61, 64, *152*, 154,
196, *269*, 301, *307–8*, 311, 314, 316,
318–19, 329, *380–81, 439–40,
505*, 506, *550–51, 553*, 605, *637,
656, 686, 690, 698–99*, 730, 740,
775–76, 809, 813, 903

identity, 94–95, 119, *589, 593*, 605,
660–61, 664, 667–69, *675–76*, 691
idolatry, *94–96, 102–3, 154–55*, 170–
74, 185, *210–12*, 214–18, 263–64,
293–94, 324, 331, *381–82*, 404,
424–25, 436, *529–30, 691, 692,
707, 708, 826–27, 937–38*
immigration, *44, 126–28, 134,
193–94*, 230, 235–36, 261–62
inadequacy (feelings of), *214–15*, 260,
335, 587, 594, 776